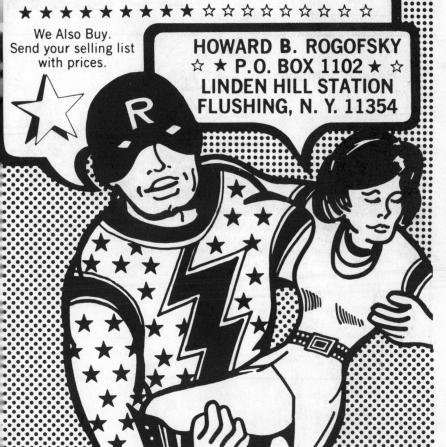

With women becoming more and more recognized for their contributions to modern society, we offer this reflective view of their role in the comics.

ACKNOWLEDGEMENTS

Larry Bigman (Frazetta-Williamson data); Glenn Bray (Kurtzman data); Gary Carter (D. C. data); J. B. Clifford Jr. (E. C. data); Wilt Conine (Fawcett data); Dr. S. M. Davidson (Cupples & Leon data); Al Dellinges (Kubert data); Kim Weston (Disney and Barks data); Kevin Hancer (Tarzan data); Charles Heffelfinger and Jim Ivey (March of Comics listing); Grant Irwin (Quality data); Fred Nardelli (Frazetta data); Mike Nolan (MLJ, Timely, Nedor data); George Olshevsky (Timely data); Richard Kravitz (Kelly data); Frank Scigliano (Little Lulu data); Gene Seger (Buck Rogers data); Rick Sloane (Archie data); David R. Smith, Archivist, Walt Disney Productions (Disney data); Don and Maggie Thompson (Four Color listing); Mike Tiefenbacher, Jerry Sinkovec, and Richard Yudkin (Atlas and National data); Tom Bocci (Classic Comics data and pricing); Raymond True (Classic Comics data); Greg Robertson (National data); Jim Vadeboncoeur Jr. (Williamson and Atlas data); Andrew Zerbe and Gary Behymer (M. E. data).

My appreciation must also be extended to Jim Bertin, Dan Hering, Bruce Hamilton, Mitchell Mehdy, Rev Winfree, Gary Carter, David Caffey, and Danny Knowles who loaned material for photographing and especially to Hugh O'Kennon who spent a weekend helping me photograph his stock. Special acknowledgement is also given to Lee Boyett, Stan Gold, Greg Eide, Bruce Hamilton, John Fishel, Michael Rosen, and Dave Noah for submitting an unusual amount of corrective data; to Dr. Richard Olson for rewriting grading definitions; to Charles Heffelfinger for rewriting "Understanding the Classics"; to Bill Sarill for his article on preservation; to Gary Coddington, John Snyder, Mike Sawyer, and Ron Prager (pricing); to Tom Inge for his "Chronology of the American Comic Book"; to Art Amsie, Carl Macek and Trina Robbins for their exclusive article, "Women in Comics"; to Jayson Disbrow for his beautifully illustrated article; to Bill Ward for his outstanding cover, article and photos just for this edition; to Sol Harrison (DC Comics), Thurman Scott (Sheena) and Will Eisner for permission to use their characters; to Mike Gold (DC Comics) for data; to Bill Spicer and Zetta DeVoe (Western Publishing Co.) for their contribution of data, and especially to Bill for his kind permission to reprint portions of his and Jerry Bails' America's Four Color Pastime; to Robert Crestohl for his statistical compilation; and to Walter Presswood and Dave Noah for their help in editing this volume.

I will always be indebted to Jerry Bails, Landon Chesney, and Larry Bigman whose advice and concern have helped in making The Price Guide a reality; to my wife, Martha, for her encouragement and help in putting this reference work together; and to everyone who placed ads in this edition.

Acknowledgement is also due to the following people who have so generously contributed much needed data for this edition:

Ronald J. Ard
Bob Barrett
Bob Beerbohm
John Benson
Gary Berman
Ben Blake
Walter Bonnett
Glenn Bray
Scott Brizel
Dr. Barry M. Brooks
Dr. Bruce C. Brumfield
James Carper
James R. Carper, Jr.
Edy Chandler
Larry Charet
Bruce Chartier
Darrah Chavey
Victor Chin
L. A. Cianfaglione
Bill Click
John T. Clifford
William D. Coble, Jr.
Dale Lee Coovert
John Corneille
Gregory Costello
Charles Cuny
Robert A. Dane
Howard Leroy Davis
Joe Desris
Jay Disbrow
Paul Dilella
Mike Dragoo
Robert Drennen
Lloyd Eells
Greg Eide
George A. Evans
Sam Falin
Richard Feinberg
Willard Fong
Fred Fragassi
Al Freize
Jim Friedman
Ray Funk
Frank Gabbard
John Garbarino
Doug Gay
Jeff Genega
Steve Geppi
Ian Gerber
Don Gleason
Don Glut
Stan Gold
Max Gottfried
Derald Gregg
Lowell Guddall
Sam Gurley
Gary Hall
Kyle Hall
Richard Hall
Rick Hall
Kevin Hancer
Terry Harms
Dave Harper
Don Harper
Jon Hart

Jim Haynes
Bruce Helford
Bob Hencey
Peter Herstedt
Tim Hessee
Steve S. Hill
John Hitchcock
Thomas Hof
Horse, Thief
Dan Horton
Dr. Jerry F. Howell
C. Richard Hunt
James Hurst
John Iavarone
Billy Ingram
Ron Ives
Steven R. Johnson
William Joppeck
Lou Jurena
Kingsley Kelley
Jeffrey A. Kilian
Mike Kirby
David L. Klees
Jeff Kmiec
Wilfried Kohl
Jim Kovacs
Timothy Kupin
Jeff Langstaff
Mike Larson
James Lawson
Daniel Levitt
Peter Lind
Rick Lowell
David Luebke
Rory M. MacAuley
Greg Manos
John Manson
Jack Marble
Douglas Marsh
David Marston
Robert Mathis
Tom Mattevi
Raymond May
Fred McFadden
Paul McKlveen
Jon Merrill
John Meyer
W. T. Michaelson
Mark Miller
Johnny G. Miner
Ken Mitchell
J. & D. Moak
Roger Moe
Paul Moino
Stan Molson
Bill Mullins
R. A. Murray
Kevin Nickel
Richard O'Brien
George Olshevsky
Keith Omelusik
Sylvan, Israel Oppenheimer
Buddy Paige
Frank Passic
Alan K. Patterson

Jeff L. Patton
Scott Pell
Dennis Petilli
Donald Puff
Robert Rector
Chuck Redding
Michael Redman
Bob Reed
Robert Ripin
Robert Rivard
Dan Rodas
Doug Ropp
Troy Rose
Michael Sagert
Joe Sarno
Michael Sawyer
Steven C. Schaffer
William Schoch
Horst Schroder
Randy Scott
Hendrik Sharples
Jim Silva
R. H. Silva, Jr.
Calvin Slobodian
David J. Smith
A. Souza
Nick & Lee Spassky
Mark Steiner
Mark Stevens
Steve Strom
Tom Struck
Klaus Strzyz
William Sumlin III
David Edward Taeusch
Brett Taylor
Matt Thomas
Jim Thompson
Lang Thompson
Sue Thompson
Iver Torikian
Raymond Vaskas
Ronald C. Verville
Waldo Vieira
Jim Walsh
V. L. Walsh
Tom Ward, Jr.
Bill Webster
Robin A. Webster
Dennis Weedman
Robert E. Weintz
Stephen Weisenbach
David Welch
Michael J. Weng
Kim Weston
Steve Willins
Rev Winfree
Larry Wingate
Mark Worthen
David Yaruss
Brew Yates
Ronald J. Young
Richard Yudkin
Nick Yutko
Randall Zbiciak
Raymond M. Zbiciak

The
Comic Book
PRICE GUIDE
1978-1979

BOOKS FROM 1900—PRESENT INCLUDED

CATALOGUE & EVALUATION GUIDE—ILLUSTRATED

By

ROBERT M. OVERSTREET

SPECIAL CONTRIBUTORS TO THIS EDITION
Art Amsie, Carl Macek,
Jayson Disbrow and Bill Ward

SPECIAL ADVISORS TO THIS EDITION
● Larry Bigman ● Tom Bocci ● L.C. Chesney ● Bruce Hamilton
● Tannar Miles ● Hugh O'Kennon ● Robert Selvig ● Terry Stroud

PREFACE

Comic book values listed in this reference work were recorded from convention sales, dealers' lists, adzines, and by special contact with dealers and collectors from coast to coast. Prices paid for rare comics vary considerably from one locale to another. We have attempted to list a realistic average between the lowest and highest range observed. The reader should keep in mind that the prices listed only reflect the market just prior to publication. Any new trends that have developed since the preparation of this book would not be shown.

The values listed are reports, not estimates. Each new edition of the guide is actually an average report of sales that occurred during the year; not an estimate of what we feel the books will be bringing next year. Even though many prices listed will remain current throughout the year, the wise user of this book would keep abreast of current market trends to get the fullest potential out of his invested dollar.

Everyone connected with the publication of this book advocates the collecting of comic books for fun and pleasure, as well as for nostalgia, art, and cultural values. Second to this is investment, which, if wisely-placed in the best quality books (condition and contents considered), will yield dividends over the long term.

Some comic book titles listed are incomplete, especially in regard to first and last issues, but this will be remedied in future editions as the information becomes available. All titles are listed as if they were one word, ignoring spaces, hyphens and apostrophes. Page counts listed will always include covers.

The Guide will be listing only American comic books. Canadian, English and other foreign comics will not be listed due to space limitation (See Canadian Comics). Some variations of the regular comic book format will be listed. These basically include those pre-1933 comic strip reprint books with varying size--usually with cardboard covers, but sometimes with hardback. As forerunners of the modern comic book format, they deserve to be listed despite their obvious differences in presentation. Other books that will be listed are giveaway comics--but only those that contain known characters or work by known artists.

Many books of the late 1940s had pages cut out of them before distribution to help the paper drives. In recent years many of the Gold Key books are also published by Whitman and are generally considered to be worth less than the originals.

By the same token, books in the very rare class are seldom offered for sale. This makes it difficult to arrive at a realistic market value. Arbitrary values are placed on these, although even this varies considerably. Among the issues in this category are: Action No. 1, Detective Nos. 27 and 28, Whiz No. 2 (No. 1), Superman No. 1, Marvel Mystery No. 1, Batman No. 1, Jumbo No. 1, More Fun Nos. 52 and 53, Captain America No. 1, Walt Disney Nos. 1 and 2, Color No. 4, Silver Streak No. 6, Wow No. 1, Black and White Nos. 16 and 20, Shock Illustrated No. 3 and Motion Picture Funnies Weekly No. 1.

This book is the most comprehensive listing of comic books ever attempted. Comic book titles, dates of first and last issues, publishing companies, origin and special issues are listed when known. Many of the better artists are pointed out also. When more than one artist worked on a story, their names are separated by a (/). The first name did the pencil drawings and the second did the inks. When two or more artists work on a story, only the most prominent will be noted. There has been some confusion in past editions as to which artist to list and which to leave out. We wish all good artists could be listed, but due to space limitation, only the very best can. The following list of artists are considered to be either the best in the comic field or are historically significant and should be pointed out. Artists designated with an (*) indicate that only their most noted work will be listed. The rest will eventually have all their work shown as the information becomes available. This list could change from year to year as new artists come into prominence. It should also be noted that there are several artists who are as prolific as they are talented and whose works cannot be listed simply because of space limitations. Among these are John Severin and Russ Heath.

Adams, Neal	Fine, Lou	Orlando, Joe
*Baker, Matt	Foster, Harold	Raboy, Mac
Barks, Carl	Frazetta, Frank	Raymond, Alex
Beck, C. C.	Gottfredson, Floyd	Siegel & Shuster
Brunner, Frank	Ingels, Ghastly	Simon & Kirby (S & K)
*Buscema, John	Jones, Jeff	Smith, Barry
Cole, Jack	Kamen, Jack	Stanley, John
Craig, Johnny	Kelly, Walt	*Starlin, Jim
Crandall, Reed	Kirby, Jack	Steranko, Jim
Davis, Jack	Krenkel, Roy	Torres, Angelo
*Ditko, Steve	Krigstein, Bernie	Toth, Alex
Eisner, Will	*Kubert, Joe	Ward, Bill
*Elder, Bill	Kurtzman, Harvey	Williamson, Al
Evans, George	Manning, Russ	Wolverton, Basil
Everett, Bill	*Meskin, Mort	Wood, Wallace
Feldstein, Al		Wrightson, Berni

The following abbreviations are used with the cover reproductions throughout the book for copyright credit purposes. The companies they represent are listed here:

(ACE) Ace Periodicals
(ACG) American Comics Group
(AJAX) Ajax-Farrell
(AP) Archie Publications
(ATLAS) Atlas Comics (see below)
(AVON) Avon Periodicals
(BP) Better Publications
(C & L) Cupples & Leon
(CC) Charlton Comics
(CEN) Centaur Publications
(CCG) Columbia Comics Group
(CG) Catechetical Guild
(CHES) Harry 'A' Chesler
(DC) DC Comics, Inc.
(DELL) Dell Publishing Co.
(DMP) David McKay Publishing
(DS) D. S. Publishing Co.
(EAS) Eastern Color Printing Co.
(EC) E. C. Comics
(ENWIL) Enwil Associates
(EP) Elliott Publications
(ERB) Edgar Rice Burroughs
(FAW) Fawcett Publications
(FF) Famous Funnies
(FH) Fiction House Magazines
(FOX) Fox Features Syndicate
(GIL) Gilberton
(GK) Gold Key
(GP) Great Publications
(HARV) Harvey Publications
(HILL) Hillman Periodicals
(HOKE) Holyoke Publishing Co.

(KING) King Features Syndicate
(LEV) Lev Gleason Publications
(MCG) Marvel Comics Group
(ME) Magazine Enterprises
(MLJ) MLJ Magazines
(NOVP) Novelty Press
(PG) Premier Group
(PINE) Pines
(PMI) Parents' Magazine Institute
(PRIZE) Prize Publications
(QUA) Quality Comics Group
(REAL) Realistic Comics
(RH) Rural Home
(S & S) Street and Smith Publishers
(SKY) Skywald Publications
(STAR) Star Publications
(STD) Standard Comics
(STJ) St. John Publishing Co.
(SUPR) Superior Comics
(TC) Tower Comics
(TM) Trojan Magazines
(TOBY) Toby Press
(UFS) United Features Syndicate
(VITL) Vital Publications
(WDP) Walt Disney Publications
(WEST) Western Publishing Co.
(WHIT) Whitman Publishing Co.
(WHW) William H. Wise
(WMG) William M. Gaines (E. C.)
(WP) Warren Publishing Co.
(YM) Youthful Magazines
(Z-D) Ziff-Davis Publishing Co.

ATLAS COMICS. The following list of publishers all printed ATLAS comics and are coded throughout the book. The ATLAS GLOBE insignia first appeared in November 1951 and lasted until September 1957 after which Marvel took over.

ATLAS Publisher's Abbreviation Codes:
ACI: Animirth Comics, Inc.
AMI: Atlas Magazines, Inc.
ANC: Atlas News Co., Inc.
BPC: Bard Publishing Corp.
BFP: Broadcast Features Pubs.
CSI: Classics Syndicate
CCC: Comic Combine Corp.
CDS: Current Detective Stories
CFI: Crime Files, Inc.

CPC: Chipiden Publishing Corp.
CnPC: Cornell Publishing Corp.
CPI: Crime Publications, Inc.
CmPI: Comedy Publications, Inc.
CPS: Canam Publishing Sales Corp.
CmPS: Complete Photo Story
SSI: Classics Syndicate, Inc.
EPI: Emgee Publications, Inc.
FPI: Foto Parade, Inc.
GPI: Gem Publishing, Inc.

HPC: Hercules Publishing Corp.
IPS: Interstate Publishing Corp.
JPI: Jaygee Publications, Inc.
LMC: Leading Magazine Corp.
MALE: Male Publishing Corp.
MAP: Miss America Publishing Corp.
MCI: Marvel Comics, Inc.
MMC: Mutual Magazine Corp.
MjMC: Marjean Magazine Corp.
MPC: Medalion Publishing Corp.
MgPC: Margood Publishing Corp.
MPI: Manvis Publications, Inc.
NPI: Newsstand Publications, Inc.
NPP: Non-Pareil Publishing Corp.
OCI: Official Comics, Inc.
OMC: Official Magazine Corp.

OPI: Olympia Publications, Inc.
PPI: Postal Publications, Inc.
PrPI: Prime Publications, Inc.
RCM: Red Circle Magazines, Inc.
SAI: Sports Actions, Inc.
SnPC: Snap Publishing Co.
SPC: Select Publishing Co.
SPI: Sphere Publications, Inc.
TCI: Timely Comics, Inc.
20 CC: 20th Century Comics Corp.
USA: U. S. A. Publications, Inc.
VPI: Vista Publications, Inc.
WFP: Western Fiction Publishing
WPI: Warwick Publications, Inc.
ZPC: Zenith Publishing Co., Inc.

TERMINOLOGY. The following terms are used occasionally in this edition and are explained here: "B & W"—Black and White art; "Bondage cover"—usually denotes a female in bondage; "cameo"—when a character appears briefly in one or two panels; "debut, first app., intro"—mean the same thing, i. e., the first time that a character appears anywhere; "flashback"—when a previous story is being recalled; "G. A."—Golden Age (1930s - 1950s); "origin"—when the story of the character's creation is given; "extremely rare"—1 to 20 copies known to exist; "very rare"—20 to 50 copies; "rare"— 50 to 100 copies; "scarce"—100 to 1,000 copies (the quantities given will change as new information is compiled; "S & K"—Simon & Kirby (artists); "X-over"—when one character crosses over into another's strip.

A SPECIAL PLEA. Please notify us of any omissions, corrections, or deletions of data in this volume so that we may include it in the next edition.

IMPORTANT. This book is not a "for sale" list of comic books. The publisher of this reference work is a collector, and has no comic books for sale. Therefore, the prices are for your information only.

DEALERS' POSITION. Prices listed herein are an indication of what collectors (not dealers) would probably pay. For one reason or another, these collectors might want certain books badly, or else need specific issues to complete their runs. Dealers are not in a position to pay the full prices listed, but work on a percentage depending largely on the amount of investment required and the quality of material offered. Usually they will pay from 20 to 70 per cent of the list price depending on how long it will take them to sell the collection after making the investment; the higher the demand and better the condition, the more the percentage. Most dealers are faced with expenses such as advertising, travel, telephone and mailing plus convention costs: entrance, table fee, hotel, etc. These costs all go in before the books are sold. The high demand books usually sell right away but there are many other titles that are difficult to sell due to low demand. Sometimes a dealer will have cost tied up in this type of material for several years before finally moving it. Remember, his position is that of handling, demand and overhead. Most dealers are victims of these economics. Good Luck and Happy Hunting.

Robert M. Overstreet

Advertise in the Guide

s book reaches more serious comic collectors than any other publication and has proven
esults due to its world-wide circulation and use. Your ad will pull all year long until the
edition comes out.

lay Ad space is sold in full, half, fourth, and eighth page sizes. Ad rates are set in the early
prior to each edition's release. Write at that time for rates (between Oct.—Dec.).

PRINTED SIZES

FULL PAGE—8" long x 5" wide. HALF PAGE—4" long x 5" wide.
FOURTH PAGE—4" long x 2½" wide. EIGHTH PAGE—2" long x 2½" wide.
CLASSIFIED ADS will be retyped and reduced about one-half. No
artwork permitted. Rate is based on your 4" typed line. DISPLAY
CLASSIFIED ADS: The use of borders or bold face type or cuts or other
decorations change your classified ad to display—rates same as regular
display.

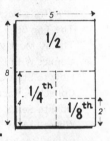

NOTE: Submit your ad on white paper in a proportionate version
of the actual printed size. All full and half page advertisers will
receive a complimentary copy of the Guide. The NEW Guide will
be professionally done throughout...so to reflect a consistently high
quality from cover to cover, we must ask that all ads be neatly and
professionally done. Full payment must be sent with all ads. All
but classified ads will be run as is.

Ad deadline next edition—Jan. 15

BOB OVERSTREET
Hunt Cliff Dr. N.W.
Cleveland, Tennessee 37311

The PRICE GUIDE has become the STANDARD REFERENCE WORK in the field and is
distributed to thousands of comic collectors throughout the world. Don't miss this opportunity
to advertise in the Guide.

NOTICE: All advertisements are accepted and placed in the Price Guide in good faith. However,
we cannot be held responsible for any losses incurred in your dealings with the advertisers.
If, after receiving legitimate complaints, and there is sufficient evidence to warrant such action,
these advertisers will be dropped from future editions.

SPECIAL NOTICE

If copyrighted characters are planned for your ad, the following must be done: Send a copy of
your ad layout (including characters) to the company(s) or copyright owner(s) involved request-
ing permission for their use. A copy of this permission must be sent to us with your ad. DC
Comics and Marvel Comics have indicated that you will have no problem getting permission,
so if you must use their characters...write for the permission. For DC, write: Public Relations,
DC Comics, Inc., 75 Rockefeller Plaza, N. Y., N. Y. 10019. For Marvel, write: Marvel Comics,
c/o Sol Brodsky, 575 Madison Ave., N. Y., N. Y. 10022. Other companies such as Disney could
be more of a problem. At any rate, we cannot accept any ads with copyrighted characters
without a copy of the permission.

TABLE OF CONTENTS

Atlas Publisher's Abbreviation Codes A-3
Dealers' Position A-4
Terms Used in This Edition A-4
Advertising Information A-5
Grading of Comic Books A-7
Grading Definitions A-7
Storage and Deacidification of Comic Books, by Bill Sarill A-8
1977 Market Report A-10
Why People Collect Comic Books A-11
Scarcity of Comic Books A-11
The Top 100 Titles (Compiled by Robert Crestohl) A-12
Investor's Data A-13
The Top 50 Titles—Rate of Increase A-14
The 50 Most Valuable Books A-14
Comics With Little If Any Value A-15
How to Start Collecting Comic Books A-15
Collecting Back Issues A-16
How to Sell Your Comics A-16
Where to Buy and Sell Comic Books A-17
Comic Book Mail Order Services A-17
How to Select Fanzines A-18
Fan Publications of Interest A-18
Collecting Strips A-19
Collecting Foreign Comics A-19
Canadian Reprints, by J. B. Clifford and Ronald J. Ard A-20
Collecting Original Art A-21
The History of Comics Fandom A-21
Comic Book Conventions, by Larry Bigman A-23
Comic Book Conventions for 1978 . . . . A-24
"A Chronology of the Development of The American Comic Book,"
by Tom Inge A-25
"Confessions of a Former Comic Book Artist," by Jayson Disbrow . A-31
"The Man Behind Torchy," by Bill Ward A-39
"Women in Comics," by Carl Macek and Art Amsie A-54
"Tarpe' Mills...An Appreciation," by Trina Robbins A-76
"Understanding the Classics," by Charles Heffelfinger . See Classic Comics

Before a comic book's true value can be assessed, its condition or state of preservation must be determined. In most comic books, especially in the rarer issues, the better the condition, the more desirable the book. The scarcer first and/or origin issues in PRISTINE MINT condition will bring several times the price of the same book in POOR condition. The grading of a comic book is done by simply looking at the book and describing its condition, which may range from absolutely perfect newsstand condition (PRISTINE MINT) to extremely worn, dirty, and torn (POOR). Numerous variables influence the evaluation of a comic's condition and **all** must be considered in the final evaluation. More important characteristics include tears, missing pieces, wrinkles, stains, yellowing, brittleness, tape repairs, water marks, spine roll, writing, and cover lustre. The significance of each of these will be described more fully in the grading scale definitions. As grading is the most subjective aspect of determining a comic's value, it is very important that the grader must be careful and not allow wishful thinking to influence what the eyes see. It is also very important to realize that older comics in above MINT condition are extremely scarce and are rarely advertised for sale; most of the nicer comics advertised range from NEAR MINT to MINT. To the novice, grading will appear difficult at first, but as experience is gained, accuracy will improve. Whenever in doubt, consult with a reputable dealer or experienced collector in your area. The following grading guide is given to aid the hobbyist:

GRADING DEFINITIONS

The hardest part of evaluating a comic is being honest and objective with yourself, and knowing what characteristics to look for in making your decision. The following characteristics should be checked in evaluating books, especially those in higher grades: degree of cover lustre, degree of color fading, staples, staple areas, spine condition, top and bottom of spine, edges of cover, centering, brittleness, browning/yellowing, flatness, tightness, interior damage, tape, tears, folds, water marks, color flaking, and general cleanliness. After examining these characteristics a comic may be assigned to one of the following grades:

PRISTINE MINT (PM): File copies; perfect; absolutely perfect in every way, regardless of age. The cover has full lustre, is crisp, and shows no imperfections of any sort. The cover and all pages are white, the spine is tight, flat, and clean; not even the slightest blemish can be detected around staples, along spine, at corners or edges. Arrival dates pencilled on the cover are not acceptable. As comics must be truly perfect to be graded PM, they are obviously extremely scarce even on the newsstand. Books in this grade bring 10 to 20 per cent more.

MINT (M): Almost perfect, as above but with slight loss of lustre, or a slight off-centered cover, or a minor printing error. Could have pencilled arrival dates, slight color fading, and near white to white cover and pages. No physical defects are acceptable of any sort; e.g., a tiny color flake missing from spine or side of cover would make an otherwise MINT comic grade NEAR MINT.

NEAR MINT (NM): Almost perfect; tight spine, flat and clean; just enough minor defects of wear noticeable with close inspection to keep it out of the MINT category; i. e, a small flake of color missing at a staple, corner or edge or slight discoloration on inside cover or pages; near perfect cover gloss retained.

VERY FINE (VF): Slight wear beginning to show; possibly a small wrinkle or crease at staples or where cover has been opened a few times; still clean and flat with most of cover gloss retained.

FINE (FN): Tight cover with some wear, but still relatively flat, clean and shiny. Stress lines around staples and along spine beginning to show; minor color flaking possible at spine, staples, edges or corners.

VERY GOOD (VG): Obviously a read copy with original printing lustre and gloss almost gone; some discoloration, but not soiled; some signs of wear and minor markings, but none that deface the cover; usually needs slight repair around staples and along spine which could be rolled; cover could have a minor tear or crease where a corner was folded under or a loose centerfold; no chunks missing, tape or brown pages.

GOOD (G): An average used copy complete with both covers and no panels missing; slightly soiled or marked with possible creases, minor tears or splits, rolled spine and small color flaking, but perfectly sound and legible. A well-read copy, but perfectly acceptable with no chunks missing, tape or brown pages.

FAIR (F): Very heavily read and soiled, but complete with possibly a small chunk out of cover; tears needing repairs and multiple folds and wrinkles likely; damaged by the elements, but completely sound and legible.

POOR (P): Damaged; heavily weathered; soiled; or otherwise unsuited for collection purposes.

IMPORTANT: Books with defects such as pages or panels missing, coupons cut, torn or taped covers and pages, brown or brittle pages, restapled, taped spines, pages or covers, water-marked, printing defects, rusted staples, stained, holed, or other imperfections that distract from the original beauty, are worth less than if free of these defects. Coverless comics in nice condition will bring about one-fifth to one-half Good price (retail) depending on the title, and more on the key books.

Many of the early reprint comics were printed in hardback with dust jackets. Books with dust jackets are worth more. The value can increase from 20 to 50 per cent depending on the rarity of book. Usually, the earlier the book, the greater the percentage. The condition of the dust jacket should be graded independently of the book itself.

CAUTION: Tape should not be used under any circumstances for comic repair. Most tapes contain harmful chemicals that will eventually destroy the paper which they touch. Today, many collectors find it objectionable and resist collecting books repaired in this way, as it destroys the natural beauty of the comic. Comic repair should be left to those who know how.

STORAGE AND DEACIDIFICATION OF COMIC BOOKS
by Bill Sarill

The enemies of comic books are heat, light, mold, moisture, air pollution and acidity. Books should be stored upright (not flat) in a dark unheated or air-conditioned room, with an ideal relative humidity (RH) of 50%. Higher RH will promote mold growth and rusted staples, whereas at lower RH paper will tend to lose its flexibility. Serious collectors should invest in a sling psychrometer, an inexpensive device for measuring RH which is available through laboratory suppliers. RH itself can be controlled by use of household humidifiers and dehumidifiers. Sunlight and ultraviolet light (from fluorescent fixtures) are harmful to paper; incandescent lamps should be used when illumination is needed, the books stored in darkness at all other times.

Tests by the Barrow Research Laboratory show that the lifetime of book paper is multiplied by a factor of 4.5 with every drop in temperature of 27 degrees Fahrenheit. Conversely, higher temperatures lead to a rapid aging of paper with subsequent browning and embrittlement. Air conditioning at the lowest comfortable temperature is therefore recommended. Air filters and purifiers should also be used to reduce dust and pollutants.

Collectors often seal their books in polyethylene bags. Although inexpensive, such bags offer only limited protection. Polyethylene film is relatively permeable to moisture; in addition it may contain volatile plasticizers which penetrate and discolor books in as little as one year. Vinyl and vinyl-related products (such as Saran Wrap) are even more destructive to paper, and should never be used for wrapping books. The preferred material is Mylar type S, a clear polyester film which is the least permeable and most inert of all the plastics. Mylar envelopes for book storage can be made from sheet Mylar sealed with 3M double coated tape No. 415. (This tape has been tested and found safe for archival use.)

Books, whether bagged or not, should never be stored in ordinary cardboard boxes. Most cardboard is dangerously acidic and this acid can penetrate through polyethylene bags. File boxes (sold by stationers and some dealers) are not suitable for permanent storage unless constructed of acid-free board.

It is our conviction that binding books is not a suitable method of preservation. Binding of itself will not protect books from environmental deterioration, and the mutilation caused by sewing and trimming is of course irreversible. For those who desire the appearance of a library of bound volumes, an alternative is to have a competent bookbinder construct cases of acid-free millboard in which comic books may be stored. These cases can be made to resemble books, and their cost is generally no more than the cost of binding.

Acidity remains the chief culprit in the aging of paper. In addition to acid migration from cardboard, sources of acidity include air pollution, alum-rosin size, residual bleaches from the papermaking process, and lignin, a complex organic acid found in most pulpwood papers. As described in the 1977 edition of The Guide, acidity may be neutralized by a variety of processes of which the least expensive is vapor phase deacidivication (VPD). The use of cyclohexylamine carbonate in the form of VPD paper continues to remain the most popular VPD method. In this process sheets of VPD paper are interleaved among pages of a stack of books, and the books sealed within an airtight bag for one week; at the end of this time, the sheets may be discarded and the treatment is complete. NOTE: It has reached our attention that some collectors have been leaving

VPD sheets within books for as long as six months. VPD paper should NEVER be kept within books for extended periods, as the sheets may eventually fuse to the comic book pages.

One difficulty in deacidifying comic books has been the presence of lignin, which tends to evolve gradually in comic book paper and which necessitates continuing deacidification of books at intervals of 10 to 15 years.

THE 1977 MARKET REPORT

1977 ushered in one of the coldest winters on record. In Florida, Larry Bigman saw snow for his first time, while in Buffalo, Claude Held was hoping he would never see it again. In spite of the hard winter and the long dry summer, the comic market saw growth and renewed interest as the year progressed. Due to the triple spread of prices, comics in very good condition began and continued to sell well all year long which is a good indication of a vibrant and healthy market. Naturally as in the past, mint condition books again set new sales records. 1976 was a big year for huge collections turning up and 1977 was no exception. It seems that the peak of yet-to-be-found collections hasn't been reached. This means that there will be a good supply of rare book finds yet to come—and this will feed an even larger comic book collector's market in the future. Beginning in 1975, several mint runs of Dell and Gold Key comics have and continue to be offered for sale in the Eastern marketplace. Those in the know refer to these as "Poughkeepsie" books. Due to their unusually nice condition, these books have always brought record prices. Evidently, they are coming from a warehouse and at this date no one knows how many more Dell runs will be coming out. Western Publishing Co. indexed and filed their Color and Four-Color comics simply as Four Color. Therefore, The Guide is dropping the term "Color Comics" and will be listing these books under Four Color, following WPC's example.

Barks' paintings continued to command high prices during 1977. Carl is currently doing a "King" series which bring prices in the $1,500 to $2,000 range when auctioned. A Money Bin painting sold for $6,000 and the Bi-centennial painting for $12,500 while offers upwards of $10,000 were made for some of his other nicer paintings.

Everett Raymond Kinstler received worldwide publicity for painting President Ford's official portrait.

More unlisted books turned up this year such as a no-number Feature Book, a Frazetta, Western Hearts No. 2, a no number Jungle Jo and many others. During the year several copies of Wild Bill Hickok No. 4 were sold for high prices believed to have a Frazetta cover; unfortunately, Frazetta denies it and experts agree.

Our hearts go out to Al Williamson for the loss of his wife and to the family and friends of Roy Crane who passed away on July 8.

The Fourth Motion Picture Funnies Weekly sold at the San Diego con and a Very Good to Fine copy of Marvel No. 1 was sold out of Canada for $7,500 and another in Fine to Very Fine for the same price.

Comic characters are getting greater exposure with the Spiderman, Conan and Howard the Duck newspaper strips and the

Spiderman, Wonder Woman and Hulk TV shows. A Sheena movie is in the works also.

In our travels around the country this year, many changes in the market have been noted and are reflected throughout the pages of this book. The following groups seemed to be generally in the highest demand: Avon, Disney, E. C., Walt Kelly, Silver Age D. C. & Marvel, heroine and good girl art comics.

WHY PEOPLE COLLECT COMICS

Collecting is one of the most universal avocations of man. There is no end to the list of things people collect. Every artifact of man and nature—from matchbook covers to great works of art—is, at one time or another, the object of some collector's frantic search. To the non-collector this mania must seem incomprehensible; but to the collector himself, it is a fascinating and continuously rewarding pastime.

Many people would be surprised to learn that along with coins, stamps, and books, one of the most prized collectors' items throughout the world is panel art—i. e., comic magazines, newspaper comic strips, and related material. People of all ages, from all walks of life collect "comics." Scientists, engineers, teachers, actors, artists, writers, businessmen, laborers, students, and people from every possible background spend many delightful hours with this hobby.

People collect panel art for a variety of reasons. Some collectors are amateur comic artists and writers, or even professionals in the field, who collect outstanding examples of cartoons and strips as inspiration for their own work. Others collect and study the comics as examples of popular art, interesting in their own right, or because they reflect the culture of the period in which they are produced. However, the vast majority of panelologists (i. e., comic collectors) want only to enhance their own enjoyment of this popular medium or recapture "the sense of wonder" that the comics provided in their youth. In addition to true collectors, there are also those who speculate in comics—i. e., merely buy comics to resell at a profit. There is a little bit of the speculator in all collectors.

SCARCITY OF COMIC BOOKS

Most all comic books prior to 1942 are very hard to find and rarely turn up. The paper drives of World War II and beyond consumed untold millions of comic books, not to mention the hundreds of thousands sent overseas to the armed services. This, associated with the American tradition of burning what few comics and magazines were left, has produced today an extremely rare collector's item—the comic book.

Because of the publicity given comic collecting by the news media, plus the ever-growing ranks of serious collectors, unknown numbers of people were influenced to save their comics. Comic books of the 1960s-70s were searched out and bought up in the thousands by (I) dealers, to supply the growing numbers of comic collectors, and (2) others speculating that they, like the golden age books, would someday become valuable. Due to this, books from 1964 to present are for the most part in plentiful supply, while books prior to this time are scarce and their rarity increases with age. Sometimes local distributing problems can produce temporary scarcity in certain issues, but usually this is only a localized condition.

Most collectors pay the highest prices for first issues, origin issues, or books with special covers, stories, and artists. This "higher demand" produces a scarcity on these particular books, forcing the price up. Unless collecting habits change dramatically in the near future, this trend should continue.

TOP HUNDRED TITLES

The following statistical table, compiled by Robert Crestohl, lists the top (most valuable) 100 titles in mint condition. The place in rank is given for each title by year, with its corresponding value. These tables can be very useful in forecasting trends in the market place. For instance, the investor might want to know which title is yielding the best dividend from one year to the next, or you might just be interested in seeing how the popularity of titles change from year to year.

Marvel Mystery Comics is still ahead of Action Comics although the latter increased by 36% last year. Big gains have also been noted by the following titles: Animal Comics (up 35%); Classic Comics (up 48%); Crime SuspenStories (up 34%); Dick Tracy (up 60%); Fantastic Four (up 32%); Green Lantern (up 41%); Red Raven (up 71%); Amazing Spiderman (up 40%); Showcase (up 51%); and Uncle Scrooge (up 58%).

Motion Picture Funnies Weekly jumped from 42nd to 18th place while several other titles came from nowhere to 80th place (Red Raven); 83rd (Show Case), 85th (The Amazing Spiderman), 89th (Uncle Scrooge), and 92nd (Crime SuspenStories).

As the tables indicate, Silver Age titles are still on the go and continue to be a good investment.

TOP HUNDRED TITLES 1974 - 1977 WITH TOTAL VALUE OF MINT RUN
(Figures Listed Denote Rank and Total Value of Mint Run For Each Year)

TITLE	1977 RANK	& VALUE	1976 RANK	& VALUE	1975 RANK	& VALUE	1974 RANK	& VALUE
MARVEL MYSTERY COMICS	1	$21130	1	$16660	2	$10528	3	$ 7820
ACTION COMICS	2	19972	2	14706	1	12241	1	10996
DETECTIVE COMICS	3	15682	3	13588	3	10486	2	8305
WHIZ COMICS	4	12874	4	11708	4	9654	4	7590
MORE FUN COMICS	5	12183	6	8712	6	7174	7	5474
WALT DISNEY'S COMICS & STORIES	6	11327	5	9527	5	8033	5	6314
ADVENTURE COMICS	7	9527	7	7564	7	6434	6	5838
CAPTAIN AMERICA	8	8974	8	7452	8	5173	9	4199
DONALD DUCK	9	7892	10	6044	10	4890	15	3169
SUPERMAN	10	7788	9	6287	9	5047	8	4282
ALL STAR COMICS	11	5934	11	5440	11	4506	10	3630
BATMAN	12	5765	12	5241	13	4317	11	3604
CAPT. MARVEL ADVENTURES	13	5552	14	4678	12	4373	12	3410
FLASH COMICS	14	5320	16	4091	17	3370	18	2765
MASTER COMICS	15	5272	13	4824	14	3950	16	3042
ALL AMERICAN COMICS	16	4748	15	4250	15	3752	14	3194
FAMOUS FUNNIES	17	4732	18	3834	16	3703	13	3396
MOTION PICTURE FUNNIES WEEKLY	18	4500	42	2000	----	----	----	----
POLICE COMICS	19	4278	17	3926	19	2916	20	2198
DICK TRACY	20	3966	27	2472	26	2094	26	1804
HUMAN TORCH	21	3767	19	3105	23	2195	36	1431
MICKEY MOUSE MAGAZINE	22	3452	34	2220	25	2140	24	1837
WORLD'S FAIR & FINEST	23	3448	21	2852	22	2267	29	1706
KING COMICS	24	3304	20	3054	18	3054	17	3004
SUBMARINER	25	3266	23	2700	34	1819	40	1348
JUMBO COMICS	26	3255	22	2713	20	2626	19	2356
PEP COMICS	27	3197	28	2370	30	1948	33	1608
STAR SPANGLED COMICS	28	2974	24	2605	21	2303	22	1904
SILVER STREAK COMICS	29	2855	25	2488	31	1943	39	1369
PLANET COMICS	30	2806	35	2207	40	1698	41	1330
DAREDEVIL	31	2702	26	2479	24	2166	31	1646
NATIONAL COMICS	32	2628	29	2346	38	1735	42	1296
WOW COMICS	33	2581	39	2043	45	1579	46	1180
SENSATION COMICS	34	2572	33	2268	29	1977	34	1568
CLASSIC COMICS	35	2489	52	1682	48	1489	50	1114
SMASH COMICS	36	2462	31	2330	35	1813	38	1414
HIT COMICS	37	2459	30	2332	42	1614	44	1207
MILITARY COMICS	38	2432	32	2281	33	1829	37	1420
ALL WINNERS COMICS	39	2395	46	1870	56	1270	51	1100
CRACK COMICS	40	2392	36	2119	41	1657	48	1155
DARING MYSTERY COMICS	41	2385	43	1995	50	1420	70	890
MYSTIC COMICS	42	2360	48	1815	55	1280	74	850
POPULAR COMICS	43	2289	38	2075	28	2075	21	2010
USA COMICS	44	2265	44	1950	51	1370	61	985
FEATURE COMICS	45	2224	41	2014	36	1747	30	1665
WONDER WOMAN	46	2208	40	2038	44	1592	45	1196
GREEN LANTERN	47	2173	56	1540	53	1325	55	1080
SUPER COMICS	48	2169	37	2078	27	2078	23	1865
LOONEY TUNES	49	2076	45	1891	43	1613	56	1076
TIP TOP COMICS	50	2072	47	1847	32	1843	27	1787

TITLE	1977 RANK	1977 VALUE	1976 RANK	1976 VALUE	1975 RANK	1975 VALUE	1974 RANK	1974 VALUE
JUNGLE COMICS	51	1985	53	1657	47	1533	35	1498
CAPTAIN MARVEL JR.	52	1976	51	1739	46	1544	47	1160
OUR GANG	53	1931	58	1470	70	1042	93	754
ACE COMICS	54	1910	49	1768	39	1732	28	1721
THE FUNNIES	55	1839	50	1755	37	1736	32	1625
TARGET COMICS	56	1735	55	1573	49	1460	43	1284
MICKEY MOUSE	57	1713	59	1464	61	1157	75	837
LITTLE LULU	58	1664	60	1451	71	1036	84	793
TOP NOTCH COMICS	59	1642	54	1595	52	1360	49	1154
SHADOW COMICS	60	1638	61	1335	54	1300	52	1088
BLACKHAWK	61	1601	67	1264	86	905	76	832
ANIMAL COMICS	62	1525	74	1130	98	765	----	530
ZIP COMICS	63	1514	57	1499	59	1182	67	913
FANTASTIC FOUR	64	1462	77	1108	----	612	----	434
TARZAN	65	1448	62	1317	60	1181	54	1081
AIRFIGHTERS & AIRBOY	66	1436	65	1282	58	1216	65	936
BLUE BOLT	67	1430	75	1128	69	1046	64	946
BOY COMICS	68	1402	64	1291	63	1141	60	1002
NEW FUNNIES	69	1385	63	1298	87	895	86	791
PLASTIC MAN	70	1380	68	1207	81	948	89	769
WEIRD FANTASY	71	1323	80	1090	91	878	82	805
EXCITING COMICS	72	1311	70	1192	66	1090	63	948
WINGS COMICS	73	1293	71	1169	64	1136	69	909
WEIRD SCIENCE	74	1290	83	1070	88	888	81	810
YOUNG ALLIES	75	1288	73	1140	82	935	95	731
COMIC CAVALCADE	76	1276	72	1164	75	970	71	881
SPARKLER COMICS	77	1272	69	1199	62	1143	53	1082
SUPERBOY	78	1222	84	1060	83	925	91	766
MYSTERY MEN	79	1203	81	1088	73	1010	85	792
RED RAVEN	80	1200	----	700	----	500	----	280
COMICS ON PARADE	81	1191	78	1101	65	1103	66	924
BLUE RIBBON COMICS	82	1189	86	1040	74	1005	68	910
SHOWCASE	83	1188	----	785	----	569	----	443
RED RYDER	84	1183	76	1126	93	844	92	756
AMAZING SPIDERMAN	85	1177	----	838	----	387	----	271
MAD COMICS & MAGAZINES	86	1175	87	1023	72	1017	96	730
VAULT OF HORROR	87	1167	96	905	97	771	98	677
ALL FLASH COMICS	88	1149	79	1091	90	882	87	784
UNCLE SCROOGE	89	1144	----	723	----	566	----	404
HAUNT OF FEAR	90	1139	93	939	----	717	----	662
SPEED COMICS	91	1108	92	952	80	952	90	768
CRIME SUSPENSTORIES	92	1107	----	828	----	665	----	634
CRACKAJACK FUNNIES	93	1102	82	1073	68	1073	58	1042
THRILLING COMICS	94	1101	89	1008	78	960	80	816
BIG SHOT COMICS	95	1086	90	1007	67	1066	57	1045
AMAZING MYSTERY FUNNIES	96	1080	88	1010	79	956	62	955
WONDERWORLD	97	1078	66	1270	57	1220	59	1040
BLUE BEETLE	98	1069	91	1005	77	965	72	857
MARVEL FAMILY	99	1057	100	868	94	838	----	592
JOURNEY INTO MYSTERY & THOR.	100	1055	97	900	----	667	----	472

INVESTOR'S DATA

The following table denotes the rate of appreciation of the top 50 titles over the past seven years (1971-1977) since the first Price Guide was published. The retail value for a complete mint run of each title in 1977 is compared to its corresponding value in 1971. By dividing the 1977 value by the 1971 value, it is easy to calculate the exact rate of appreciation of each title in terms of percentage points.

For example: a complete mint run of ACTION COMICS retailed at $19,972 in 1977 and $2,354 in 1971. From these figures it is calculated that every $100 investment in this title in 1971 would be worth exactly $848.43 in 1977. Whether the run be in mint, fine or good condition, this figure would remain relatively constant.

The following table is meant as a guide to the investor and it is hopeful that it may aid him in his decision in what titles to invest. However, it should be pointed out that trends may change at any time and that some titles can develop into real comers from a presently dormant state. In the long run, however, if the investor sticks to the titles that are appreciating steadily every year, he can't go very far wrong.

It is interesting to note that even the titles that are appreciating the slowest are still increasing much faster than economic inflationary values during the same time period.

TITLE	1977 RANK & VALUE		1971 RANK & VALUE		1977 VALUE FOR EACH $100 in 1971
MARVEL MYSTERY COMICS	.1	$21130	4	$2584	$817.72
ACTION COMICS	.2	19972	6	2354	848.43
DETECTIVE COMICS	.3	15682	3	2747	570.88
WHIZ COMICS	.4	12874	13	1357	948.71
MORE FUN COMICS	.5	12183	2	2816	432.63
WALT DISNEY'S COMICS & STORIES	.6	11327	11	1487	761.74
ADVENTURE COMICS	.7	9527	1	3066	310.73
CAPTAIN AMERICA	.8	8974	17	1303	688.72
DONALD DUCK	.9	7892	49	604	1306.63
SUPERMAN	10	7788	12	1460	533.42
ALL STAR COMICS	11	5934	9	1657	358.12
BATMAN	12	5765	19	1246	462.68
CAPT. MARVEL ADVENTURES	13	5552	26	1009	550.25
FLASH COMICS	14	5320	14	1344	395.83
MASTER COMICS	15	5272	25	1021	516.36
ALL AMERICAN COMICS	16	4748	23	1189	399.33
FAMOUS FUNNIES	17	4732	7	2343	201.96
MOTION PICTURE FUNNIES WEEKLY	18	4500	----	N/A	N/A
POLICE COMICS	19	4278	27	903	473.75
DICK TRACY	20	3966	24	1116	355.38
HUMAN TORCH	21	3767	42	632	596.04
MICKEY MOUSE MAGAZINE	22	3452	18	1252	275.72
WORLD'S FAIR & FINEST	23	3448	30	841	409.99
KING COMICS	24	3304	5	2490	132.69
SUBMARINER	25	3266	50	601	543.43
JUMBO COMICS	26	3255	16	1320	246.59
PEP COMICS	27	3197	28	880	363.30
STAR SPANGLED COMICS	28	2974	32	830	358.31
SILVER STREAK COMICS	29	2855	82	394	724.62
PLANET COMICS	30	2806	48	613	457.75
DAREDEVIL	31	2702	41	639	422.85
NATIONAL COMICS	32	2628	39	676	388.76
WOW COMICS	33	2581	53	574	449.65
SENSATION COMICS	34	2572	38	681	377.68
CLASSIC COMICS	35	2489	----	N/A	N/A
SMASH COMICS	36	2462	31	833	295.56
HIT COMICS	37	2459	64	523	470.17
MILITARY COMICS	38	2432	65	520	467.69
ALL WINNERS COMICS	39	2395	57	545	439.45
CRACK COMICS	40	2392	48	613	390.21
DARING MYSTERY COMICS	41	2385	----	220	1084.09
MYSTIC COMICS	42	2360	95	340	694.12
POPULAR COMICS	43	2289	10	1598	143.24
USA COMICS	44	2265	87	365	620.55
FEATURE COMICS	45	2224	20	1214	183.20
WONDER WOMAN	46	2208	62	537	411.17
GREEN LANTERN	47	2173	83	390	557.18
SUPER COMICS	48	2169	15	1321	164.19
LOONEY TUNES	49	2076	54	558	372.04
TIP TOP COMICS	50	2072	8	2088	99.23

The following table shows the rate of increase of the 50 most valuable single books over the past seven years. Comparisons would be the same as the previous table of the Top 50 titles. Ranking in most cases is relative since so many books fall under the same value. These books are listed alphabetically.

50 MOST VALUABLE BOOKS

TITLE	1977 RANK	VALUE	1976 VALUE
MARVEL COMICS No. 1	.1	$7500	$5000
ACTION No. 1	.2	5250	4200
MOTION PICTURE FUNNIES WEEKLY No. 1	.3	4500	2000
WHIZ No. 1	.4	3750	3500
DETECTIVE No. 27	.5	3600	3500
SUPERMAN No. 1	.6	2400	2000
BATMAN No. 1	.7	1800	1600
CAPTAIN AMERICA No. 1	.8	1800	1500
WALT DISNEY'S COMICS & STORIES Vol. 1 No. 1	.9	1800	1200
ACTION No. 2	10	1500	1200
CAPTAIN MARVEL No. 1	11	1500	1000
DONALD DUCK TELLS ABOUT THE KITES (SCE)	12	1500	1000
MARVEL MYSTERY No. 5	13	1500	1200
MORE FUN No. 52	14	1500	1000
DONALD DUCK MARCH OF COMICS No. 4	15	1350	1000
MARVEL MYSTERY No. 2	16	1350	1200
ACTION No. 3	17	1200	800
ACTION No. 5	18	1200	500
DETECTIVE No. 28	19	1200	1000
DONALD DUCK COLOR No. 4	20	1200	1000

TITLE	1977 RANK	VALUE	1976 VALUE
DONALD DUCK B&W No. 20	21	1200	800
DONALD DUCK FOUR COLOR No. 9	22	1200	1000
DONALD DUCK TELLS ABOUT THE KITES (PG&E)	23	1200	900
RED RAVEN No. 1	24	1200	700
WOW No. 1	25	1200	700
WHIZ No. 2	26	1125	1000
MARVEL MYSTERY No. 3	27	1050	900
MICKEY MOUSE COLOR No. 16	28	975	800
BOY EXPLORERS No. 2	29	900	500
DONALD DUCK B&W No. 16	30	900	600
DONALD DUCK FOUR COLOR No. 29	31	900	700
DONALD DUCK MARCH OF COMICS No. 20	32	900	700
MORE FUN No. 53	33	900	600
WALT DISNEY'S COMICS & STORIES Vol. 1 No. 2	34	900	600
HUMAN TORCH No. 1	35	855	700
ACTION No. 4	36	750	600
ALL AMERICAN No. 16	37	750	600
CAPTAIN AMERICA No. 2	38	750	600
DARING MYSTERY No. 1	39	750	500
DETECTIVE No. 33	40	750	600
MARVEL MYSTERY No. 4	41	750	700
SILVER STREAK No. 6	42	750	600
SPECIAL EDITION No. 1	43	750	700
SUPERMAN No. 2	44	750	500
WHIZ No. 3	45	750	700
ACTION No. 7	46	675	450
ACTION No. 10	47	675	450
MARVEL MYSTERY No. 8	48	675	600
MARVEL MYSTERY No. 9	49	675	600
DICK TRACY FEATURE BOOK No no.	50	645	500

COMICS WITH LITTLE IF ANY VALUE

There exists in the comic book market, as in all other collector's markets, items, usually of recent origin, that have relatively little if any value. Why even mention it? We wouldn't, except for one thing—this is where you could probably take your worst beating, investment-wise. Since these books are listed by dealers in such profusion, at prices which will vary up to 500 per cent from one dealer's price list to another, determining a realistic "market" value is almost impossible. And since the same books are listed repeatedly, list after list, month after month, it is difficult to determine whether or not these books are selling. In some cases, it is doubtful that they are even being collected. Most dealers must get a minimum price for their books; otherwise, it would not be profitable to handle. This will sometimes force a value on an otherwise valueless item. On the other hand, you might buy a vastly over-priced golden-age comic and still expect to recover your loss after a reasonable passage of time. This, unfortunately, is not true of so many titles that we are put in a rather awkward position of listing.

THE PRICE GUIDE'S POSITION: We don't want to leave a title out just because it is presently valueless. And at the same time, we don't want to presume to "establish" what is collectible and what isn't. The passage of time and a change in collectors' interests can make almost any comic potentially valuable. Some books, by virtue of their age, will someday obtain a value as a cultural or historical curiosity. Therefore, we feel that all books, regardless of the demand for them, should be listed.

Since speculation in the comic book market began around 1964, most all titles since that time have been saved and are in plentiful supply. These books have been included for your information and can be found listed throughout The Guide with arbitrary values assigned (under 50 cents). The collector would be well advised to compare prices between several dealers' lists before ordering this type of material.

HOW TO START COLLECTING

Most collectors of comic books begin by buying new issues in mint condition directly off the newsstand. (Subscription copies are, as a rule, folded and, hence, unsuited for collecting purposes.) Each week new comics appear on the stands that are destined to become true collectors items. The trick is to locate a store that carries a complete line of comics. In several localities this may be difficult. Most panelologists frequent several magazine stands in order not to miss something they want. Even then, it pays to keep in close contact with collectors in other areas. Sooner or later, nearly every collector has to rely upon a friend in Fandom to obtain for him an item that is unavailable locally.

Once you have located a good source of new comics, find out on what days the books are delivered. Plan to drop by regularly as soon after the comics are checked in as possible. This way you may avoid missing an issue, and you will also stand a better chance of getting mint copies. You will find that comics rapidly become damaged on the stands, especially when they are displayed in certain kinds of racks.

Before you buy any comic to add to your collection, you should carefully inspect its condition. Unlike stamps and coins, defective comics are generally not highly prized. The cover should be properly cut and printed. Remember that every blemish or sign of wear depreciates the beauty and value of your comics.

The serious panelologist usually purchases extra copies of popular titles. He may trade these multiples for items unavailable locally (for example, foreign comics), or he may store the multiples for resale at some future date. Such speculation is, of course, a gamble, but unless collecting trends change radically in the future, the value of certain comics in mint condition should appreciate greatly, as new generations of readers become interested in collecting.

COLLECTING BACK ISSUES

In addition to current issues, most panelologists want to locate back issues. Some energetic collectors have had great success in running down large hoards of rare comics in their home towns. Occasionally, rare items can be located through agencies that collect old papers and magazines, such as the Salvation Army. The lucky collector can often buy these items for much less than their current market value. Placing advertisements in trade journals, newspapers, etc., can also produce good results. However, don't be discouraged if you are neither energetic nor lucky. Most panelologists build their collections slowly but systematically by placing mail orders with dealers and other collectors.

Comics of early vintage are extremely expensive if they are purchased through a regular dealer or collector, and unless you have unlimited funds to invest in your hobby, you will find it necessary to restrict your collecting in certain ways. Every enthusiast defines his collection in a different manner. Some collect only runs of certain titles. Others collect only selected issues, which carry special stories or work by a favorite artist. Many collect only incomplete runs of their favorite titles, concentrating on certain periods. However you define your collection, you should be careful to set your goals well within your means.

HOW TO SELL YOUR COMICS

If you have a collection of comics for sale, large or small, the following steps should be taken. (l) Make a detailed list of the books for sale, being careful to grade them accurately, showing any noticeable defects; i. e., torn or missing pages, centerfolds, etc. (2) Decide whether to sell wholesale to a dealer all in one lump or to go through the long laborious process of advertising and selling piece by piece to collectors. Both have their advantages and disadvantages.

In selling to dealers, you will get the best price by letting everything go at once—the good with the bad—all for one price. Simply select names either from ads in this book or from some of the adzines mentioned below. Send them your list and ask for bids. The bids received will vary depending on rarity and condition of the books you have. The rarer and better the condition, the higher the bids will be.

On the other hand, you could become a dealer and sell the books yourself. Order a copy of one or more of the adzines. Take note how most dealers lay out their ads. Type up your ad copy, carefully pricing each book (using the Guide as a reference). Send finished ad copy with payment to adzine editor to be run. You will find that certain books will sell at once while others will not sell at all. The ad will probably have to be retyped, remaining books repriced, and run again. Price books according to how fast you want them to move. If you try to get top dollar, expect a much longer period of time. Otherwise, the better deal you give the collector, the faster they will move. Remember, in being your own dealer, you will have overhead expenses in postage, mailing supplies and advertising cost. Some books might even be returned for refund due to misgrading, etc.

In selling all at once to a dealer, you get instant cash, immediate profit, and eliminate the long process of running several ads to dispose of the books; but if you have patience, and a small amount of business sense, you could realize more profit selling them directly to collectors yourself.

WHERE TO BUY AND SELL
Throughout this book you will find the advertisements of many reputable dealers who sell back-issue comics magazines. If you are an inexperienced collector, be sure to compare prices before you buy. Never send large sums of money through the mail. Send money orders or checks for your personal protection. Beware of bargains, as the items advertised sometimes do not exist, but are only a fraud to get your money.

The Price Guide is indebted to everyone who placed ads in this volume, whose support has helped in curbing printing costs. Your mentioning this book when dealing with the advertisers would be greatly appreciated.

Attend a comic convention this year. There you will find an abundance of comic material for sale, as well as a chance to meet others who share your interest. Check the following publications for announcements of cons to be held in your area:

The Buyers Guide
Dynapubs, 15800 Rt. 84 North
East Moline, Ill. 61244

Collector's Dream Magazine
P. O. Box 127, Station T.
Toronto, Ont. M6B 3Z9 Canada

The RBCC
1014 Salzedo, Apt. 10
Coral Gables, Fla. 33134

The Price Guide highly recommends the above adzines, which are full of ads buying and selling comics, pulps, radio tapes, premiums, toys and other related items. You can also place ads to buy or sell your comics in the above publications.

COMIC BOOK MAIL ORDER SERVICES
The following offer a mail order service on new comic books. Write for rates and details:

DAVID & NEAL BRAUNSTEIN, Eldorado Comics, Dept. R, P. O. Box 153, Pennsauken, N. J. 08110

BILL COLE, P. O. Box 60, Wollaston, Mass. 02170

DELTA - T COMICS, 11407 55 Avenue, Edmonton, Alberta, Canada T6H 0X3

THE FANTASY MAIL CO., P. O. Box 7476, Rochester, N. Y. 14615

FOUR COLOR DREAMS COMIC SERVICE, 9 St. Catherine Drive, St. Peters, Mo.   63376

RELIABLE COMICS BY MAIL, 8525 Colesville Road, Silver Spring, Md. 20910
Telephone: 301-565-9255

SEA GATE DIST., INC., P. O. Box 177, Coney Island Station, Brooklyn, N. Y. 11224

STYX COMIC SERVICE, P. O. Box 3791, Winnipeg, Manitoba, Canada R2W 3R6

HOW TO SELECT FANZINES

In the early 1960s, only a few comic fanzines were being published. A fan could easily afford to subscribe to them all. Today, the situation has radically changed, and it has become something of a problem to decide which fanzines to order.

Fanzines are not all of equal quality or general interest. Even different issues of the same fanzine may vary signficantly. To locate issues that will be of interest to you, learn to look for the names of outstanding amateur artists, writers, and editors, and consult fanzine review columns. Although you may not always agree with the judgements of the reviewers you will find these reviews to be a valuable source of information about the content and quality of the current fanzines.

When ordering a fanzine, remember that print runs are small and the issue you may want may be out of print (OP). Ordinarily in this case, you will receive the next issue. Because of irregular publishing schedules that nearly all fanzines must, of necessity, observe, allow up to 90 days or more for your copy to reach you. It is common courtesy when addressing an inquiry to an ama-publisher to enclose a self-addressed, stamped envelope.

FAN PUBLICATIONS OF INTEREST

BATMANIA—Richard H. Morrissey, 55 Claudette Circle, Framingham, Mass. 01701—for Batman fans.

BULL DOG—Steve Kristiansen, 6216 185th Pl. SW, Lynwood, Wash. 98036 (For Comic Strip Collectors).

CAPTAIN GEORGE'S WHIZZBANG—"Captain George" Henderson, 594 Markham St., Toronto, Ontario, Canada.

CARTOON—The Cartoon Museum—Jim Ivey, 561 Obispo Ave., Orlando, Fla. 32807.

CHRONICLE—George Breo, 5600 Milwaukee Ave., Chicago Ill. 60646.

CLASSICS COLLECTORS CLUB NEWSLETTER—Raymond True, 1930 W. Warwick Lane, Roselle, Ill. 60172.

THE CLASSICS READER—W.J. Briggs, M.A.C.I., 720 Midland Ave., Scarborough, Ontario Canada M1K4C9

COMIC DETECTIVE—Bart Bush, 713 Sugar Maple, Ponco City, Okla. 74601.

COMIC FAN VENTURE—632 Gibbon St., Williams Lake, B. C., Canada

COMIC MEDIA—Richard Burton, 22 Woodhaw, Egham, Surrey TW20, 9AP, England.

THE COMIC PRESS—Russell Condello, 34 Burt Street, Rochester, New York 14609, Articles about Silver Age Comics, 90 cents.

THE COMIC READER—Street Enterprises, P. O. Box 255, Menomonee Falls, Wisc. 53051. (Gives advance information on all new comics being published).

COMIX WORLD—Clay Geerdes, 915 Indian Rock Road, Berkeley, Calif. 94707-zine on underground comics.

DENIS GIFFORD'S BRITISH COMIC CATALOGUE—1874-1974; $30, 224 p., clothbound with 1700 titles listed. Write: ISBS Inc., 10300 S. W. Allen Blvd., Beaverton, Oregon 97005.

ERBANIA—D. Peter Ogden, 8001 Fernview Lane, Tampa, Fla.33615—ERB Zine.

ERB-dom—Camille Cazedussus Jr., Rt. 2, Box 119, Clinton, La. 70722.

FAN INFORMER—Arvell M. Jones, 5729 Cadillac, Detroit, Mich. 48213.

FANDOM MEDIA—Paul Hugli, 9440 Nichols, Bellflower, Calif., 90706.

FANTASY UNLIMITED—Alan Austin, 47 Hesperus Crescent, Millwall, London, E14 9A8, England.

GRAPHIC STORY MAGAZINE—Bill Spicer, 329 North Ave. 66, Los Angeles, California 90042.

GRAPHIC STORY QUARTERLY & WONDERWORLD—Richard Kyle, P. O. Box 16168, Long Beach, Calif. 90806.

THE HEROINES SHOWCASE—The Comics Heroines Fan Club—Steven R. Johnson, P. O. Box 1329, Campbell, California 95008.

INFINITY—Gary Berman, 19750 F. Peck Ave., Flushing, N. Y. 11365.

MEDIASCENE—Supergraphics, Box 445, Wyomissing, Pa. 19610 (Subscriptions: 6/$4, Articles on current comics media).

THE MENOMONEE FALLS GAZETTE—A weekly newspaper featuring the best daily adventure strips. Write: P. O. Box 255, Menomonee Falls, Wisc. 53051.

NIMBUS—Frank Lovece, editor—Write Sam de la Rosa, 328 Canavan, San Antonio, Texas 78221.

OLDE TIME COMICS—64 page tabloid reprinting early newspaper strips. Published quarterly by Tower Press, Inc., Folly Mill Road, Seabrook, N. H. 03874.

PHANTASMAGORIA —Kenneth Smith, Box 20020-A, L. S. U. Station, Baton Rouge, La. 70803. Articles on fine art & science fiction.

PITTSBURGH FAN FORUM—Benjamin Pondexter, 827 Anaheim St., Pittsburgh, Pa. 15219—A monthly newsletter & fanzine.

SCIENCE FICTION REVIEW—Richard E. Geis, P. O. Box 11408, Portland, Oregon 97211.

SQUA TRONT—John Benson, editor. For back and recent issues write: Jerry Weist, c/o The Million Year Picnic, 36 Boylston St., Cambridge, Mass. 02138.

TREK—The Phantom Empire, 5600 N. Freeway No. 341, Houston Texas 77022—A full tabloid zine for Star Trek fans.

COLLECTING STRIPS

Collecting newspaper comic strips is somewhat different than collecting magazines, although it can be equally satisfying.

Obviously, most strip collectors begin by clipping strips from their local paper, but many soon branch out to strips carried in out-of-town papers. Naturally this can become more expensive and it is often frustrating, because it is easy to miss editions of out-of-town papers. Consequently, most strip collectors work out trade agreements with collectors in other cities in order to get an uninterrupted supply of the strips they want. This usually necessitates saving local strips to be used for trade purposes only.

Back issues of strips dating back several decades are also available from time to time from dealers. The prices per panel vary greatly depending on the age, condition, and demand for the strip. When the original strips are unavailable, it is sometimes possible to get photostatic copies from collectors, libraries, or newspaper morgues.

COLLECTING FOREIGN COMICS

One extremely interesting source of comics of early vintage—one which does not necessarily have to be expensive—is the foreign market. Many American strips, from both papers and magazines, are reprinted abroad (both in English and in other languages) months and even years after they appear in the states. By working out trade agreements with foreign collectors, one can obtain, for practically the cover price, substantial runs of a number of newspaper strips and reprints of American comics books dating back five, ten, or occasionally even twenty or more years. These reprints are often in black and white, and sometimes the reproduction is poor, but this is not always the case. In any event, this is a source of material that every serious collector should look into.

Once the collector discovers comics published in foreign lands, he often becomes fascinated with the original strips produced in these countries. Many are excellent, and have a broader range of appeal than those of American comic books. They are published in magazines of every conceivable size and description. Any comics collection is enhanced by the addition of foreign comics. It is possible to build substantial collections of these magazines through the generous assistance of fans in countries like Australia, England, South Africa, Ireland, Scotland and Canada. Look for their ads in the adzines listed under "Where to Buy and Sell" or check with dealers, some of which stock foreign comics.

CANADIAN REPRINTS
EC's: by J. B. Clifford
Several EC titles were published in Canada by Superior Comics from 1949 to at least 1953. Canadian editions of the following EC titles are known: (Pre-Trend) Saddle Romances, Moon Girl, A Moon A Girl. . .Romance, Modern Love, Saddle Justice; (New-Trend) Crypt of Terror-Tales From the Crypt, Haunt of Fear, Vault of Horror, Weird Science, Weird Fantasy, Two-Fisted Tales, Frontline Combat, and Mad. Crime SuspenStories was also published in Canada under the title Weird SuspenStories. No reprints of Shock SuspenStories by Superior are known, nor have any "New Direction" reprints ever been reported. No reprints later than January 1954 are known. Canadian reprints sometimes exchanged cover and contents with adjacent numbers (e. g., a Frontline Combat 12 with a FC No. 11 cover). They are distinguished both in cover and contents. As the interior pages are always reprinted poorly, these comics are of less value (about ½) than the U. S. Editions; also, they were printed later than the U. S. editions from rubber plates made from the original plates. On some reprints, the Superior seal replaces the EC seal. Superior publishers took over Dynamic in 1947.

Dells: by Ronald J. Ard
Canadian editions of Dell comics, and presumably other lines, began in March-April, 1948 and lasted until February-March, 1951. They were a response to the great Canadian collar crisis of 1947. Intensive development of the post-war Canadian economy was financed almost entirely by American capital. This massive import of money reached such a level that Canada was in danger of having a grossly disproportionate balance of payments which could drive it into technical bankruptcy in the midst of the biggest boom in its history. The Canadian government responded by banning a long list of imports. Almost 500 separate items were involved. Alas, the consumers of approximately 499 of them were politically more formidable than the consumers of comic books.

Dell responded by publishing its titles in Canada, through an arrangement with Wilson Publishing Company of Toronto. This concern has not existed for a number of years and it is reasonable to assume that its sole business was the production and distribution of Dell titles in Canada. There is no doubt that they had a captive market. If you check the publication data on the U. S. editions of the period you will see the sentence "Not for sale in Canada." Canada was thus the only area of the Free World in those days technically beyond the reach of the American comic book industry.

We do not know whether French editions existed of the Dell titles put out by Wilson. The English editions were available nationwide. They were priced at 10 cents and were all 36 pages in length, at a time when their American parents were 52 pages. The covers were made of coarser paper, similar to that used in the Dell Four Color series in 1946 and 1947 and were abandoned as the more glossy cover paper became more economical. There was also a time lag of from six to eight weeks between, say, the date an American comic appeared on a Seattle comics rack and the date that the Canadian edition appeared on its Vancouver counterpart.

Many Dell covers had seasonal themes and by the time the Canadian edition came out (two months later) the season was over. Wilson solved this problem by switching covers around so that the appropriate season would be reflected when the books hit the stands. Most Dell titles were published in Canada during this period including the popular Atom Bomb giveaway, Walt Disney Comics and Stories and the Donald Duck and Mickey Mouse Four Color one-shots. The quality of the Duck one-shots is equal to that of their American counterparts and generally bring about 30% less.

By 1951 the Korean War had so stimulated Canadian exports that the restrictions on comic book importation, which in any case were an offense against free trade principle, could be lifted without danger of economic collapse. Since this time Dell, as well as other companies, have been shipping direct into Canada.

COLLECTING ORIGINAL ART
In addition to magazines and strips, some enthusiasts also collect the original art for the comics. These black and white, inked drawings are usually done on illustration paper at about 30 per cent up (i. e., 30 per cent larger than the original printed panels). Because original art is a one-of-a-kind article, it is highly prized and often difficult to obtain.

Interest in original comic art has increased tremendously in the past several years. Many companies now return the originals to the artists who have in turn offered them for sale, usually at cons but sometimes through agents and dealers. As the collection grows, extra or less pleasing items are often used as swapping material with other collectors. Cartoons have now become generally accepted as an art form by academics; museums are purchasing comic art for their permanent collections. As with any other area of collecting, rarity and demand governs value. Although the masters' works bring fine art prices, most art is available at moderate prices. Comic strips are the most popular facet with collectors, followed by comic book art. Once scarce, current and older comic book art has surfaced within the last few years. In 1974 several original painted covers of vintage comic books and coloring books turned up from Dell, Gold Key, Whitman, and Classic Comics. Gag, sports, political, and other type cartoons are sought by relatively few.

THE HISTORY OF COMICS FANDOM
At this time it is possible to discern two distinct and largely unrelated movements in the history of Comics Fandom. The first of these movements began about 1953 as a response to the then-popular, trend-setting EC line of comics. The first true comics fanzines of this movement were short-lived. Bhob Stewart's EC FAN BULLETIN was a hectographed newsletter that ran two issues about six months apart; and Jimmy Taurasi's FANTASY COMICS, a newsletter devoted to all science-fiction comics of the period, was a monthly that ran for about six months. These were followed by other newsletters, such as Mike May's EC FAN JOURNAL, and George Jennings' EC WORLD PRESS. EC fanzines of a wider and more critical scope appeared somewhat later. Two of the finest were POTRZEBIE, the product of a number of fans, and Ron Parker's HOOHAH. Gauging from the response that POTRZEBIE received from a plug in an EC letter column, Ted White estimated the average age of EC fans to lie in the range of 9 to 13, while many EC fans were in their mid-teens. This fact was taken as discouraging to many of the faneds, who

had hoped to reach an older audience. Consequently, many of them gave up their efforts in behalf of Comics Fandom, especially with the demise of the EC groups, and turned their attention to science-fiction fandom with its longer tradition and older membership. While the flourish of fan activity in response to the EC comics was certainly noteworthy, it is fair to say that it never developed into a full-fledged, independent, and self-sustaining movement.

The second comics fan movement began in 1960. It was largely a response to (though it later became a stimulus for) the Second Heroic Age of Comics. Most fan historians date the Second Heroic Age from the appearance of the new FLASH comics magazine (numbered 105 and dated February 1959). The letter departments of Julius Schwartz (editor at National Periodicals), and later those of Stan Lee (Marvel Group) and Bill Harris (Gold Key) were most influential in bringing comics readers into Fandom. Beyond question, it was the reappearance of the costumed hero that sparked the comics fan movement of the sixties. Sparks were lit among some science-fiction fans first, when experienced fan writers, who were part of an established tradition, produced the first in a series of articles on the comics of the forties—ALL IN COLOR FOR A DIME. The series was introduced in XERO No. 1 (September 1960), a general fanzine for science-fiction fandom edited and published by Dick Lupoff.

Meanwhile, outside science-fiction fandom, Jerry Bails and Roy Thomas, two strictly comics fans of long-standing, conceived the first true comics fanzine in response to the Second Heroic Age. The fanzine, ALTER EGO, appeared in March 1961. The first several issues were widely circulated among comics fans, and were to influence profoundly the comics fan movement to follow. Unlike the earlier EC fan movement, this new movement attracted many fans in their twenties and thirties. A number of these older fans had been active collectors for years but had been largely unknown to each other. Joined by scores of new, younger fans, this group formed the nucleus of a new movement that is still growing and shows every indication of being self-sustaining. Although it has borrowed a few of the more appropriate terms coined by science-fiction fans, Comics Fandom of the Sixties was an independent if fledging movement, without, in most cases, the advantages and disadvantages of a longer tradition. What Comics Fandom did derive from science-fiction fandom it does so thanks largely to the fanzines produced by so-called double fans. The most notable of this type is COMIC ART, edited and published by Don and Maggie Thompson.

Listed below are some of the major events in the Comics Fan Movement of the early 1960s.

1960
Sept.   XERO No. 1 (Dick Lupoff) with "AICFAD" on First Heroic Age.

1961
Feb.   locs in BRAVE & BOLD No. 35 initiate wide-scale fan contacts.
Mar.   ALTER EGO No. 1 (Jerry Bails and Roy Thomas).
Apr.   COMIC ART No. 1 (Don Thompson).
Sept.   THE COMICOLLECTOR No. 1 (Jerry Bails).
Oct.   ON THE DRAWING BOARD (J. Bails); later THE COMIC READER.
Dec.   THE ROCKET'S BLAST No. 1 (G. B. Love).

1962
June   First ALLEY AWARDS POLL.
July   KOMIX ILLUSTRATED No. 1 (Bill White).
Sept.   THE KOMIX NO. 1 (John Wright, South Africa)
    MASQUERADER No. 1 (Mike Vosburg).
    SUPER HERO No. 1 (Mike Tuohey).
Dec.   THE COMIC WORLD No. 1 (Robert Jennings).

1963
Apr.   FIGHTING HERO COMICS NO. 1 (G. B. Love).
June   STAR-STUDDED COMICS NO. 1 (The Texas Trio).
Aug.   DATELINE: COMICDOM NO. 1 (Ronn Foss).
Oct.   Ratification of the ACADEMY CHARTER.

1964

Feb.	FANTASY ILLUSTRATED NO. 1 (Bill Spicer).
Mar.	ALLEY TALLY, first weekend fan party.
Apr.	WHO'S WHO IN COMICS FANDOM (L. Lattanzi).
May	First Detroit fan-meet.
	First Chicago fan-meet.
	Fanclave at the home of Russ Manning.
June	SLAM-BANG NO. 1 (Rick Weingroff).
July	BATMANIA NO. 1 (Bill White).
Oct.	VOICE OF COMICDOM NO. 2 (first issue) (Golden Gate Publishers).
	CAPA-alpha No. 1 (first comics-oriented APA).
	FORUM NO. 1 (Paul Gambaccini).
	reprints of first BUCK ROGERS strips (Edwin Aprill).
Dec.	DOWN UNDER NO. 1 (John Ryan, Australia).

1965

Mar., Apr.	Widespread publicity about Comicdom in magazines and newspapers throughout the world.
July	THE GUIDEBOOK OF COMICS FANDOM (Bill Spicer).

COMIC BOOK CONVENTIONS

As is the case with most other aspects of comic collecting, comic book conventions, or cons as they are referred to, were originally conceived as the comic-book counterpart to science-fiction fandom conventions. There were many attempts to form successful national cons prior to the time of the first one that materialized, but they were all stillborn. It is interesting that after only three relatively organized years of existence, the first comic con was held. Of course, its magnitude was nowhere near as large as most established cons held today.

What is a comic con? As might be expected, there are comic books to be found at these gatherings. Dealers, collectors, fans, whatever they call themselves can be found trading, selling, and buying the adventures of their favorite characters for hours on end. Additionally if at all possible, cons have guests of honor, usually professionals in the field of comic art, either writers, artists, or editors. The New York cons virtually ooze pros out of every nook and cranny, because most of them do live in New York. The committees put together panels for the con attendees where the assembled pros talk about certain areas of comics, most of the time fielding questions from the assembled audience. At cons one can usually find displays of various and sundry things, usually original art. There might be radio listening rooms; there is most certainly a daily showing of different movies, usually science-fiction or horror type. Of course there is always the chance to get together with friends at cons and just talk about comics; one also has a good opportunity to make new friends who have similar interests and with whom one can correspond after the con.

It is difficult to describe accurately what goes on at a con. The best way to find out is to go to one or more if you can.

WHERE TO GO TO SEE WHAT YOU WANT TO SEE

If you are seriously into the many varied aspects of comic fandom, then the opportunity to attend a comic convention will be difficult to pass up. Any of the large cons has its own distinguishing features which guarantee its enjoyability. As is obvious, though, each con is different; each has activities that may not appeal to everyone. Therefore, if you can only afford to visit one convention, your choice is important in relation to your interests. This section is to guide one's decision as to which convention should be attended.

If you want to see professionals, there is no question that any of the New York cons are best, as well as the San Diego convention. Of course, because of the dearth of pros in the other areas of the country, the other cons sometimes get guests to attend who are not usually seen at cons. So don't discount the other cons outside New York and San Diego. For example, Orlando Con '75 specialized in the many fine artists and writers in the comic strip field.

If it's comics and more comics that you want, once again the New York cons would probably be best because of the heavy dealer attendance. Of course, the increasing scarcity and prices of the older comics makes it difficult to find and to buy them at almost any con. So the solution to this is to go to all the cons. Actually, though, the New York cons (those being the N. Y. Comic Art Convention and Creation) are best, with the other national cons trailing not too very far behind. Many people, though, dislike the New York cons due to their immensity and impersonality. For these persons, the other national cons are the only ones worth attending. The decision is yours.

If you are looking for cinematic thrills, conventions all have varied film lineups. The Texas and Oklahoma cons have the con circuit cornered in the genres of serials and B-westerns. As would be expected, though, most conventions concentrate on science fiction and horror movies, with minimal straying from this format. Again, if the movie schedule is your deciding factor, take a look at the convention advertisements in the various adzines. The committees usually have firmed up the lineups early enough for a potential attendee to decide whether he wishes to make the trip.

The addresses below are those currently available for conventions upcoming in 1977-78. Unfortunately, addresses for certain major conventions are unavailable as this list is being compiled. Once again, the best way to keep abreast of conventions is through the various adzines. Please remember when writing for convention information to include a self-addressed, stamped envelope for reply. Most conventions are non-profit, so they appreciate the help. Here is the list:

COMIC BOOK CONVENTIONS FOR 1978

THE ALL-AMERICAN COMIC-CON—c/o Old Weird Herald's, 6804 N.E. Broadway, Portland, Oregon 97213 Phone (503) 254-4942—July 14, 15, 16.

ATLANTA COMICS & FANTASY FAIR '78—Gary Cook, 7015 Knollwood Dr., Morrow, Georgia 30260

BAYCON 4—Salvador Dichiera, P.O. Box 3931, San Francisco, Ca. 94119—July 21-23

CHICAGO COMICON—Larry Charet, 1219-A West Devon Ave., Chicago, Ill. 60660—August, 1978

CREATION CON—Box 6547, Flushing, N. Y. 11365—May 19-21 & Thanksgiving 1978.

DELAWARE VALLEY COMIC ART CONVENTION—Howard Leroy Davis, 38 Simpson Avenue, Pitman, N. J. 08071—Nov. 17-19.

HOLLYWOOD COMIC BOOK & SCIENCE FICTION CONVENTION—Bruce Schwartz, 921 N. Gardner Apt. 9, L.A., Calif. 90046

HOUSTON CON '78—P.O. Box 12613, Houston, Tx . 77087—June 22-25, Sheraton Hotel.

ITHACON III—Bill Turner, 1043 Auburn Rd., Grotton, N. Y. 13073. Phone (607) 533-7623—April 15 & 16.

NEW YORK COMIC ART CONVENTION '78—Phil Seuling, P. O. Box 177, Coney Island Station, Brooklyn, N. Y. 11224.

NEWCON '78—Don Phelps, P. O. Box 85, Cohasset, Mass. 02025.

SAN DIEGO COMIC-CON—Box 17066, San Diego, Calif. 92117. July 26-30

A Chronology of the Development of
THE AMERICAN COMIC BOOK

By
M. Thomas Inge*

Precursors: The facsimile newspaper strip reprint collections constitute the earliest "comic books." The first of these was a collection of Richard Outcault's **Yellow Kid** from the Hearst **New York American** in March 1897. Commerical and promotional reprint collections, usually in cardboard covers, appeared through the 1920s and featured such newspaper strips as **Mutt and Jeff**, **Foxy Grandpa**, **Buster Brown**, and **Barney Google**. During 1922 a reprint magazine, **Comic Monthly**, appeared with each issue devoted to a separate strip, and in 1929 George Delacorte published 13 issues of **The Funnies** in tabloid format with original comic pages in color, becoming the first four-color comic newsstand publication.

1933: The Ledger syndicate published a small broadside of their Sunday comics on 7" by 9" plates. Employees of Eastern Color Printing Company in New York, sales manager Harry I. Wildenberg and salesman Max C. Gaines, saw it and figured that two such plates would fit a tabloid page, which would produce a book about 7½" x 10" when folded. Thus 10,000 copies of **Funnies on Parade**, containing 32 pages of Sunday newspaper reprints, was published for Proctor and Gamble to be given away as premiums. Some of the strips included were: **Joe Palooka**, **Mutt and Jeff**, **Hairbreadth Harry**, and **Reg'lar Fellas**. M. C. Gaines was very impressed with this book and convinced Eastern Color that he could sell a lot of them to such big advertisers as Milk-O-Malt, Wheatena, Kinney Shoe Stores, and others to be used as premiums and radio give-aways. So, Eastern Color printed **Famous Funnies: A Carnival of Comics**, and then **Century of Comics**, both as before, containing Sunday newspaper reprints. Mr. Gaines sold these books in quantities of 100,000 to 250,000.

1934: The give-away comics were so successful that Mr. Gaines believed that youngsters would buy comic books for ten cents like the "Big Little Books" coming out at that time. So, early in 1934, Eastern Color ran off 35,000 copies of **Famous Funnies, Series 1**, 64 pages of reprints for Dell Publishing Company to be sold for ten cents in chain stores. Selling out promptly on the stands, Eastern Color, in May 1934, issued **Famous Funnies** No. 1 (dated July 1934) which became, with issue No. 2 in July, the first monthly comic magazine. The title continued for over 20 years through 218 issues, reaching a circulation peak of nearly one million copies. At the same time, Mr. Gaines went to the sponsors of Percy Crosby's **Skippy**, who was on the radio, and convinced them to put out a Skippy book, advertise it on the air, and give away a free copy to anyone who bought a tube of Phillip's toothpaste. Thus 500,000 copies of

With the invaluable assistance of Bill Blackbeard and helpful suggestions and comments by William M. Gaines, Bob Overstreet, Hames Ware, Don and Maggie Thompson, Jerry Bails, and Ron Goulart, to all of whom the compiler is grateful.

Skippy's Own Book of Comics was run off and distributed through drug stores everywhere. This was the first four-color comic book of reprints devoted to a single character.

1935: Major Malcolm Wheeler-Nicholson's National Periodical Publications issued in February a tabloid-sized comic publication called **New Fun,** which became **More Fun** after the first issue and converted to the normal comic-book size after issue six. **More Fun** was the first comic book of a standard size to publish original material and continued publication until 1949. **Mickey Mouse Magazine** began in the summer, to become **Walt Disney's Comics and Stories** in 1940, and combined original material with reprinted newspaper strips in most issues.

1936: In the wake of the success of **Famous Funnies**, other publishers, in conjunction with the major newspaper strip syndicates, inaugurated more reprint comic books: **Popular Comics** (News-Tribune, February), **Tip Top Comics** (United Features, April), **King Comics** (King Features, April), and **The Funnies** (new series, NEA, October). Four issues of **Wow Comics**, from David McKay and Henle Publications, appeared, edited by S. M. Iger and including early art by Will Eisner, Bob Kane, and Lou Fine.

1937: The first non-reprint comic book devoted to a single theme (although single-theme pulp magazines had included comic strips earlier) was **Detective Comics**, an offshoot of **More Fun**, which began in March to continue to the present. The book's initials, "D.C.," have long served to refer to National Periodical Publications, which was purchased from Major Nicholson by Harry Donenfeld late this year.

1938: "D.C." copped a lion's share of the comic book market with the publication of **Action Comics** No. 1 in June which contained the first appearance of Superman by writer Jerry Siegel and artist Joe Shuster, a discovery of Max C. Gaines. The "man of steel" inaugurated the "Golden Era" in comic book history. Fiction House, a pulp publisher, entered the comic book field in September with **Jumbo Comics**, featuring Sheena, Queen of the Jungle, and appearing in over-sized format for the first eight issues.

1939: The continued success of "D.C." was assured in May with the publication of **Detective Comics** No. 27 containing the first episode of Batman by artist Bob Kane and writer Bill Finger. **Superman Comics** appeared in the summer. Also, during the summer, a black and white premium comic titled **Motion Picture Funnies Weekly** was published to be given away at motion picture theatres. The plan was to issue it weekly and to have continued stories so that the kids would come back week after week not to miss an episode. Four issues were planned but only one came out. This book contains the first appearance and origin of the Sub-Mariner by Bill Everett (8 pages) which was later reprinted in **Marvel Comics**. In November, the first issue of **Marvel Comics** came out, featuring the Human Torch by Carl Burgos and the Sub-Mariner reprint with color added.

1940: The April issue of **Detective Comics** No. 38 introduced Robin the Boy Wonder as a sidekick to Batman, thus establishing the "Dynamic Duo" and a major precedent for later costume heroes who would also have boy companions. **Batman Comics** began in the spring. Over 60 different comic book titles were being issued, including **Whiz Comics** begun in February by Fawcett Publications. A creation of writer Bill Parker and artist C. C. Beck, **Whiz's** Captain Marvel was the only superhero ever to surpass Superman in comic book sales. Drawing on their own popular pulp magazine heroes, Street and Smith Publications introduced **Shadow Comics** in March and **Doc Savage Comics** in May. A second trend was established with the summer appearance of the first issue of **All-Star Comics**, which brought several superheroes together in one story and in its third issue that winter would announce the establishment of the Justice Society of America.

1941: Wonder Woman was introduced in the spring issue of **All-Star Comics** No. 8, the creation of psychologist William Moulton Marston and artist Harry Peter. **Captain Marvel Adventures** began this year. By the end of 1941, over 160 titles were being published, including **Captain America** by Jack Kirby and Joe Simon, **Police Comics** with Jack Cole's Plastic Man and later Will Eisner's Spirit, **Military Comics** with Blackhawk by Eisner and Charles Cuidera, **Daredevil Comics** with the original character by Charles Biro, **Air Fighters** with Airboy also by Biro, and **Looney Tunes & Merrie Melodies** with Porky Pig, Bugs Bunny, and Elmer Fudd, reportedly created by Bob Clampett for the Leon Schlesinger Productions animated films and drawn for the comics by Chase Craig. Also, Albert Kanter's Gilberton Company initiated the **Classics Illustrated** series with **The Three Musketeers**.

1942: **Crime Does Not Pay** by editor Charles Biro and publisher Lev Gleason, devoted to factual accounts of criminals' lives, began a different trend in realistic crime stories. **Wonder Woman** appeared in the summer. John Goldwater's character Archie, drawn by Bob Montana, first published in **Pep Comics**, was given his own magazine **Archie Comics**, which has remained popular over 35 years. The first issue of **Animal Comics** contained Walt Kelly's "Albert Takes the Cake," featuring the new character of Pogo. In mid-1942, the undated Dell Four Color title, No. 9, **Donald Duck Finds Pirate Gold**, appeared with art by Carl Barks and Jack Hannah. Barks, also featured in **Walt Disney's Comics and Stories**, remained the most popular delineator of Donald Duck and later introduced his greatest creation, Uncle Scrooge, in **Christmas on Bear Mountain** (Dell Four Color No. 178).

1945: The first issue of **Real Screen Comics** introduced the Fox and the Crow by James F. Davis, and John Stanley began drawing the **Little Lulu** comic book based on a popular feature in the **Saturday Evening Post** by Marjorie Henderson Buell from 1935 to 1944.

1950: The son of Max C. Gaines, William M. Gaines, who earlier had inherited his father's firm Educational Comics (later Entertaining Comics), began publication of a series of well-written and masterfully drawn titles which would establish a "New Trend" in comics magazines: **Crypt of Terror** (later **Tales from the Crypt**, April), **The Vault of Horror** (April), **The Haunt of Fear** (May), **Weird Science** (May), **Weird Fantasy** (May), **Crime SuspenStories** (October), and **Two-Fisted Tales** (November), the latter stunningly edited by Harvey Kurtzman.

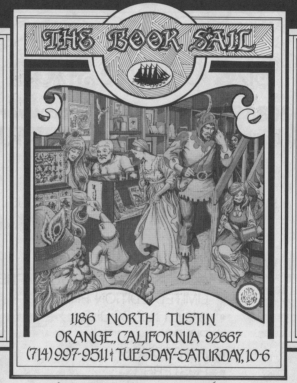

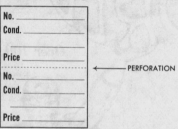

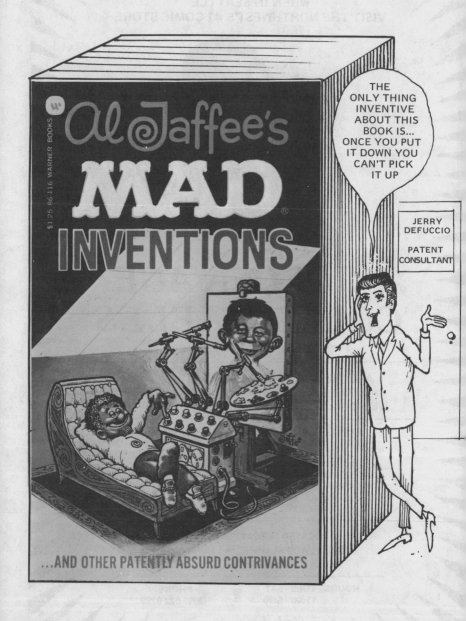

Hey, Look!

ACTION NO.1
BATMAN NO.1
WALT DISNEY COMICS & STORIES NO.1
1ST DONALD DUCK!
FANTASTIC FOUR NO.1
THE WORLD'S FIRST COMIC BOOK!
1ST MICKEY MOUSE!
SPIDERMAN NO. 1
SUPERMAN NO.1
UNCLE SCROOGE NO.1

#1

© WDP

Sleuthing done dirt cheap!

Can't find that number one (or origin issue)? Then why not try me?

Yes, I have **all** of the **No. 1** issues shown above & other **hard-to-find** comics especially those much sought after **early Marvels** (there are always available in stock a near complete set of all Marvel titles).

And besides this I also have the following:

(A) **WALT DISNEY** comics - all titles: Mickey Mouse, Donald Duck, Uncle Scrooge, Firestone & other Giveaways & Disney Collectibles: pop-ups, figures, games, Disney posters etc., etc.,

(B) **DC COMICS** (Golden Age, Silver Age up to the present- the **old** Flash, Green Lantern, Superman, Batman, as well as newer super-heroes of the 70's).

(C) **GOLDEN AGE & SILVER AGE** comics- these include Quality, Timely, Fox, Avon, Fiction House, Fawcetts, Motion Picture Comics, Dell, Westerns, Funny Animal Comics, Classics, etc.

(D) **MAD** comics - Panic, Humbug, Trump, Help & Horror, Crime & **EC** comics.

(E) Hundreds of **BIG LITTLE BOOKS**- all titles at **LESS** than catalog prices. Also available- the **original** Cupples & Leon comic "books".

(F) Rare **PULPS**- Doc Savage (1930's & 1940's); science fiction & pulp hero titles; **ARKHAM HOUSE** books

(G) **ORIGINAL ART**- including **Carl Barks** (Uncle Scrooge artist); Winsor McCay (**Little Nemo** artist); George Herriman (**Krazy Kat** artist) & other fine classic as well as modern artists.

(H) 50,000 **SUNDAY COMIC PAGES** . Just about every major & minor comic strip character from the early 1900's to the 1960's. Strips include: **Little Nemo, Krazy Kat, Mickey Mouse, Donald Duck, Popeye, Tarzan, Flash Gordon, Prince Valiant, Terry & The Pirates, Dick Tracy, Superman. Pogo** & many, many more too numerous to list here.

I also **BUY & TRADE**, so let me know what you have. For my latest **giant** 30 page 1978 catalog- "Number One Plus", write to the address below enclosing $1.00 in cash (or stamps). Hurry now or you could miss out on getting that issue you've been looking for!

write: **HAL VERB**
P.O. BOX 1815
SAN FRANCISCO, CA. 94101

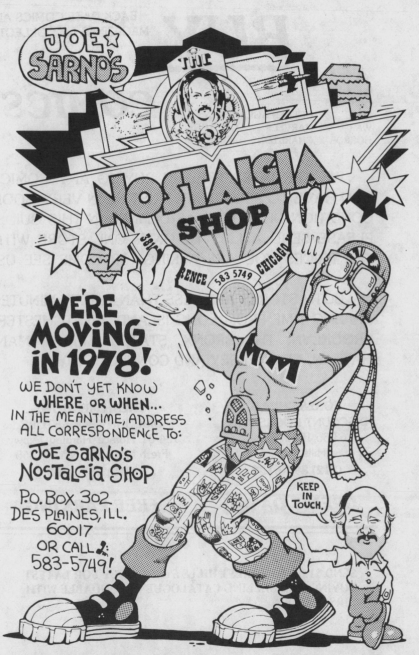

G.FREEMAN '78

Specialist in Everything !!

OVER 250,000 COMICS IN
STOCK, SEND 25¢ FOR MY
HUGE CATALOGUE WITH
THE **LOW, LOW** PRICES
AND SEE WHY I HAVE
OVER 10,000 PEOPLE ON
MY MAILING LIST.

MARVEL, D.C., HARVEY, DELL,
CLASSICS ILLUSTRATED,
GOLD KEY, ARCHIE,
DISNEY'S, CHARLTON,
ESOTERIC COMICS,
WARREN MAGAZINES,
BLB'S, COMIC DIGESTS,
ARKHAM HOUSE HARDCOVERS
STARWARS / TREK ITEMS,
R.E.H., ETC., ETC.
WE ALSO BUY / TRADE.

DOUG SULIPA'S
COMIC WORLD

116~388 Donald St.
Winnipeg, Manitoba Canada R3B·2J4
PHONE: (204) 943·1968 or 269·1783

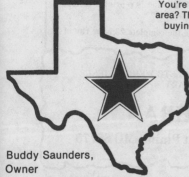

The Collector's Treasure...

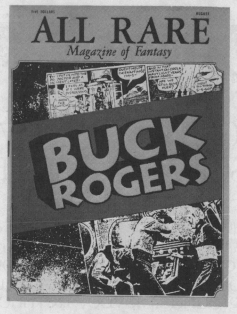

Price: $5.00

This issue includes:

★ Phil Nowlan's "Armageddon—2419"—
(the origin of BUCK ROGERS) reprinted from
Amazing Stories, August 1928!

★ Pictorial review of the 1939 movie serial
adaptation of BUCK ROGERS!

★ Illustrated history of BUCK ROGERS in the
Big Little Books, toys, and radio premiums
of the 1930s!

★ Full-color BUCK ROGERS comics section
from 1934 with Calkins/Keaton art!

Order Your Copy Today—
Send Check or Money Order to:

Comicade Enterprises
P. O. Box 12
Ellicott Square Station
Buffalo, N. Y. 14205

BIGMAN COMICS

GREAT EXPECTATIONS

All of fandom knows how rare "Great Expectations" by Gilberton Publications is, but there are some great expectations which are even rarer. The great expectations fandom has in a comic dealer. I try to live up to these expectations and I offer these guarantees as proof that I will:

1. All comics sold through the mail can be returned within 7 days for any good reason for a complete refund. (as long as they are returned in the same condition I sent them out in).

2. All comics sold personally can be returned within 7 days for a complete refund if they are defective in any way.

3. If any order is delayed for more than two weeks through the incompetance of myself or any of my workers, the order will be sent out and the money will be refunded. (So you will be getting the comics for free). I do not expect to have to send out any free orders.

Any collectors in Toronto or visiting Toronto call me at 633-5157 or 633-6015 (area code 416) then come on over. Send your want list or send 25¢ for my complete list. I also buy comics send me what you have for sale. Howie Goldfarb 99 Cocksfield Ave. Downview, Ontario Canada M3H 3T3

What Is The GREAT ESCAPE

The Great Escape Is

— The Mid-South's most complete fun and fantasy shop where collectors and readers from Nashville and surrounding areas buy, trade and sell regularly. Our stock includes

*COMIC BOOKS
New Issues weeks before they hit local news-stands
Back Issues more than 50,000 to choose from, including many rare collectors' items

*RECORDS
Thousands of used records of all kinds for collectors and fans.

*AND LOTS MORE, including
Baseball Cards
Prints and Posters
Playboys
Movie Memorabilia
Fanzines
SiFi and Fantasy Stuff
Monster Mags
Pulp Magazines

NEED EXTRA CASH? We're always in the market for any of the above. Bring 'em by the store, or send us a list of what you have for sale, listing issue numbers and conditions if possible. We also trade.

The Great Escape Is

an organization of dedicated professionals that offers a wide range of services to collectors everywhere

*Mail Order Service
We are working hard to give you the best and fastest service available anywhere. Send us your want lists and we'll try to find the issues your heart desires. Let us know your general interests (Marvels, DCs, Disneys or whatever) and we'll put you on our mailing list to get periodic special sale information and price lists. Please include self-addressed stamped envelope to help with costs. We always give cash refunds for items sold out — never credit slips. Satisfaction is always guaranteed. We belong to the National Central Bureau, an organization dedicated to reliability and absolute honesty. Give us a try — we want the opportunity to prove we're the best place to depend on for the items you want.

*Service to Louisville Area Customers
Our man in Louisville is Mark Steiner, 1240 Bicknell, (Zip Code 40215). Write him or call him at 366-4805. Get your new issues long before the newstands, or let him find that back issue you need.

The Great Escape

HOURS: Mon-Sat 10-6
Sun   Closed

NATIONAL CENTRAL BUREAU WSA NO. 678

CENTRALLY LOCATED in the university and Music Row area, just off I-40.

The Great Escape
Gary Walker, Paul Howley and Cliff Furline
1919 Division Street
Nashville, Tennessee 37203
Phone (Area Code 615) 327-0646

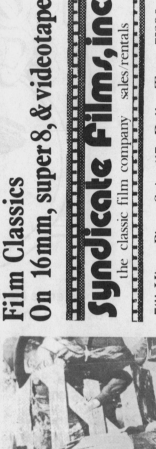

HUGH O'KENNON

2204 HAVILAND DRIVE

RICHMOND, VA. 23229

Tel. (804) 270-2465

Buying - Selling - Collector's Comic Books

I Offer The Following To ALL Customers:

- ACCURATE GRADING
- SATISFACTION GUARANTEED
- PROMPT DEPENDABLE SERVICE
- REASONABLE PRICING
- EXPERIENCE

Selling - A list of all Comics for sale is available. Please forward 50 cents for a copy (refundable with first order).

Buying - Write for MY offer before you sell your comic books.

FANTASY CASTLE T.M.

ILLUSTRATED CATALOG

• COMIC BOOK PRICE LIST •

1978

THIS CATALOG CONTAINS A COMPLETE AND COMPREHENSIVE LISTING OF ALL SILVER AGE COMIC BOOKS (1960 TO DATE) DIVIDED INTO **MARVEL, D.C.** AND **MISCELLANEOUS COMICS** SECTIONS. IT IS FULLY ILLUSTRATED AND HAS NOTATIONS ON ALL KEY ISSUES (ORIGINS, FIRST APPEARANCES, ARTIST ISSUES, ETC.) THE PRICES QUOTED IN THIS BOOK ARE IN FINE CONDITION AND ARE SUBJECT TO CHANGE WITHOUT PRIOR NOTICE.

$1.00

• POSTERS •

THERE ARE OVER 250 FANTASY POSTERS LISTED IN THIS CATALOG, FEATURING WORK BY SUCH ARTISTS AS **FRANK FRAZETTA, KEN KELLY, BORIS VALLEJO** AND MANY MORE. IN ADDITION TO THIS, THERE IS A FULL ASSORTMENT OF POSTERS ON **COMIC BOOK HEROES, STAR TREK, SCIENCE FICTION, MOVIE RELATED** AND **ROCK AND ROLL.**

• PAPERBACK BOOKS •

THE **FANTASY CASTLE** HAS A COMPLETE ASSORTMENT OF **SCIENCE FICTION & FANTASY PAPERBACK BOOKS.** WE HAVE JUST ABOUT EVERY TITLE THAT IS IN PRINT FROM ALL OF THE MAJOR PUBLISHING COMPANIES AND MOST OF THE MINOR ONES.

• T-SHIRTS •

THERE ARE OVER FIFTY DESIGNS TO CHOOSE FROM IN THE **FANTASY CASTLE'S** T-SHIRT DEPARTMENT - ALL **SCIENCE FICTION & FANTASY** ORIENTED. WE SELL THE TRANSFERS ALONE OR APPLY THEM TO ONE OF OUR MANY SHIRTS IN STOCK (YOUR CHOICE OF SIZE AND COLOR).

• MISCELLANEOUS ITEMS •

THE **FANTASY CASTLE** 1978 CATALOG ALSO CONTAINS AN ASSORTMENT OF MANY DIFFERENT FANTASY ITEMS. AMONG THEM ARE **FANTASY GAMES** (INCLUDING DUNGEONS AND DRAGONS), **ART BOOKS** AND **FANZINES, STAR WARS RELATED ITEMS,** ETC.

ORDERING INSTRUCTIONS

THE 1978 **FANTASY CASTLE ILLUSTRATED CATALOG** WILL BE AVAILABLE IN MARCH FOR THE PRICE OF ONE DOLLAR PER COPY. SEND $1.00 NOW AND RECEIVE A CATALOG CRAMMED FULL OF JUST ABOUT EVERYTHING AVAILABLE IN THE COMIC BOOK, SCIENCE FICTION AND FANTASY FIELDS.

ORDER NOW ONLY $1.00
(Free with "Knights of the Castle Membership")

KNIGHTS OF THE CASTLE

JOIN THE **KNIGHTS OF THE CASTLE** DISCOUNT CLUB AND RECEIVE: 1. A 10% DISCOUNT ON ALL ITEMS PURCHASED FROM THE **FANTASY CASTLE.** 2. ALL STORE NEWSLETTERS AND BULLETINS OF SPECIAL DISCOUNTS. 3. ALL CATALOGS OF THE **FANTASY CASTLE** (BEGINNING WITH THE ONE SHOWN ABOVE) FREE OF CHARGE.

JOIN NOW FOR ONLY $3.50 PER YEAR

20940 VENTURA BOULEVARD • WOODLAND HILLS, CA 91364 • (213) 888-5660

WOMEN IN COMICS

Women have played an important role in comics right from the beginning. The following pages will show the various ways in which women have been portrayed.

WOMEN AS NON-PRINCIPALS: This category includes women in subordinate roles to some male character.

Blondie No. 23, 1950. © King

Daredevil No. 3, 1941. © Lev

Popeye 4-Color 168, 1947. © King

Superman No. 27, 1944. © DC

WOMEN AS PRINCIPALS (General): Includes women about whom the central theme or story revolved.

Brenda Starr V2 No. 5, 1948. © Supr

Dale Evans No. 11, 1950. © DC

Tillie The Toiler 4-Color No. 213, 1948. © King

WOMEN AS PRINCIPALS (cont'd.) — The Little Ones......

Nancy & Sluggo
No. 102, 1954.
© UFS

Little Orphan Annie
4-Color No. 18, 1942.
© News Synd.

Little Lulu 4-Color
No. 110, 1946.
© West

Alice In Wonderland
4-Color No. 331,
1951.   © WDP

WOMEN AS DECORATION: This category refers to women that served no useful function, except as decoration — sex being the main selling point. Quite often the women were shown in bondage.

Blue Beetle No. 54, 1948
© Fox

Bruce Gentry No. 1, 1948
© Supr. Jack Kamen
cover art

Crime Reporter No. 1,
1948. © STJ
Matt Baker cover art

Exciting No. 59, 1946
© BP
Schomburg cover art

Hickory No. 3, 1950
© Qua

Jo—Jo No. 17, 1948
© Fox.   Jack Kamen
bondage cover art

Jungle No. 46, 1943
© FH

Junior No. 13, 1948
© Fox
Al Feldstein cover art

The Saint No. 1, 1947. © Avon
Jack Kamen cover art

Startling No. 46, 1947. © BP
Graham Ingels cover art

Strange Worlds No. 5, 1951. © Avon
Wallace Wood cover art

Wings No. 90, 1948. © FH

WOMEN AS PRINCIPALS (Sexy): This category includes the adventure Heroines, the jungle girls, and the pin-up beauties.

Adventure......

Canteen Kate No. 2, 1952, © STJ Matt Baker cover art

Claire Voyant No. 2, 1946. © The Newspaper PM Jack Kamen cover art

Crimes By Women No. 3, 1948. © Fox

Firehair No. 1, 1948. © FH

Molly O'Day No. 1, 1945. © Avon

Planet No. 46, 1947 (Mysta of the Moon) © FH

Katy Keene No. 57,
1961. © AP

Meet Corliss Archer
No. 2, 1948. © Fox
Al Feldstein cover art

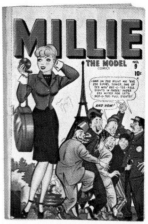

Millie No. 9, 1947
© MCG

Mitzi No. 1, 1948
© MCG

Mopsy No. 1, 1948
© STJ

Rusty No. 14, 1947
© MCG

Suzie No. 62, 1948
© AP

Tessie No. 7, 1946
© MCG

Torchy No. 1, 1949
© DC (Qua)
Bill Ward cover art

More Pin-ups......

Sunny No. 11, 1947. © Fox
Al Feldstein cover art

Torchy No. 5, 1950. © DC(Qua)
Bill Ward cover art

Jungle Girls......

Sheena No. 4, 1948. © FH

Zoot No. 11, 1947. © Fox
Jack Kamen bondage cover art

More Jungle Girls......

All Top No. 16, 1949
(Rulah) © Fox

Exciting No. 61, 1948
(Judy Of The Jungle)
© BP. Schomburg
air brush cover

Fight No. 64, 1949
(Tiger Girl) © FH

Jumbo No. 111, 1948
(Sheena) © FH

Nyoka No. 43, 1950
© Faw

Rima No. 1, 1974
© DC

Thrilling No. 62, 1947
(Princess Pantha)
© BP

White Princess of the Jungle
No. 1, 1951. © Avon
E.R. Kinstler cover art

Zegra No. 3, 1948
© Fox

WOMEN AS PRINCIPALS — Love Comics: These books portrayed women in the traditional role of falling in love and getting married. Many good artists worked on these books before their demise in the late 1950's.

Forbidden Love No. 1, 1950
© Qua

Hollywood Secrets No. 1, 1949. © Qua
Bill Ward cover art

Range Romances No. 3, 1950
© Qua

Teen-Age Romances No. 42, 1955
© STJ. Matt Baker cover art

Phantom Lady No. 17, 1948. © DC (Fox). This classic bondage cover by Matt Baker represents the high point in this genre.

America's Best No. 30, 1949
(Miss Masque) © BP
Schomburg cover art

Black Cat No. 1, 1946
© Harv

Blonde Phantom No. 14, 1947
© MCG

Bulletman No. 3, 1942
(Bulletgirl) © Faw
Mac Raboy cover art

Hawkman No. 3, 1964
(Hawkgirl) © DC

The Human Torch No. 27,
1947 (Asbestos Lady)
© MCG

Lady Luck No. 88, 1950
© Will Eisner

Marvel Mystery No. 82, 1947
(Origin & 1st app. Namora) © MCG

Mary Marvel No. 1, 1945
© Faw

Miss America No. 1, 1944
© MCG

Miss Fury No. 2, 1942
© Tarpe Mills

Moon Girl No. 3, 1948
© WMG

Ms. Marvel No. 1, 1976
© MCG

Red Sonja No. 1, 1976
© MCG

Sensation No. 12, 1942
(Wonder Woman) © DC

Sun Girl No. 1, 1948
© MCG

Supergirl No. 3, 1973
© DC

Venus No. 15, 1951
© MCG

Wonder Woman No. 41,
1950,   © DC

Comic Cavalcade No. 1, 1942. © DC. This cover sums up the progression of the woman in comics from an accessory of a man to his equal or even his better.

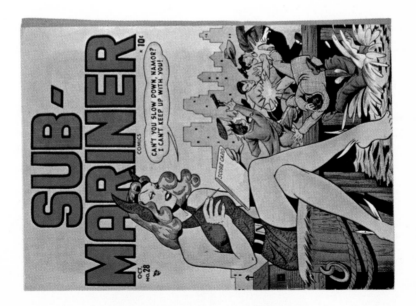

Sub-Mariner No. 28, 1948 (Namora). © MCG

1952: In October "E.C." published the first number of **Mad** under Kurtzman's creative editorship.

1953: All Fawcett titles featuring Captain Marvel were ceased after many years of litigation in the courts during which National Periodical Publications claimed that the super-hero was an infringement on the copyrighted Superman.

1954: The appearance of Fredric Wertham's book **Seduction of the Innocent** in the spring was the culmination of a continuing war against comic books fought by those who believed they corrupted youth and debased culture. The U. S. Senate Subcommittee on Juvenile Delinquency investigated comic books and in response the major publishers banded together in October to create the Comics Code Authority and adopted, in their own words, "the most stringent code in existence for any communications media."

1955: In an effort to avoid the Code, "E. C." launched a "New Direction" series of titles, such as **Impact, Valor, Aces High, Extra, M.D.,** and **Psychoanalysis,** none of which lasted beyond the year. **Mad** was changed into a larger magazine format with issue No. 24 in July to escape the Comics Code entirely.

1956: Beginning with the Flash in **Showcase** No. 4, Julius Schwartz began a popular revival of "D.C." superheroes which would lead to the "Silver Age" in comic book history.

1960: After several efforts at new satire magazines (**Trump** and **Humbug**), Harvey Kurtzman, no longer with Gaines, issued in August the first number of another abortive effort, **Help!**, where the early work of underground cartoonists Jay Lynch, Skip Williamson, Gilbert Shelton, and Robert Crumb appeared.

1961: Stan Lee edited in November the first **Fantastic Four,** featuring Mr. Fantastic, the Human Torch, the Thing, and the Invisible Girl, and inaugurated an enormously popular line of titles from Marvel Comics featuring a more contemporary style of superhero.

1962: Lee introduced **The Amazing Spider Man** in August, with art by Steve Ditko, **The Hulk** in May and **Thor** in August, the last two produced by Dick Ayers and Jack Kirby.

1965: James Warren issued **Creepy,** a larger black and white comic book, outside Comics Code's control, which emulated the "E.C." horror comic line. Warren's **Eerie** began in September and **Vampirella** in September 1969.

1968: Robert Crumb's **Zap** No. 1 appeared, the first popular underground comic book.

1970: Editor Roy Thomas at Marvel begins **Conan the Barbarian** based on fiction by Robert E. Howard with art by Barry Smith.

1972: **The Swamp Thing** by Berni Wrightson begins in November from "D.C."

1973: In February, "D.C." revived the original Captain Marvel with new art by C. C. Beck and reprints in the first issue of **Shazam** and in October **The Shadow** with scripts by Denny O'Neil and art by Mike Kaluta.

1974: "D.C." began publication in the spring of a series of over-sized facsimile reprints of the most valued comic books of the past under the general title of "Famous First Editions," beginning with a reprint of **Action** No. 1 and including afterwards **Detective Comics** No. 27, **Sensation Comics** No. 1, **Whiz Comics** No. 2, **Batman** No. 1, **Wonder Woman** No. 1, **All-Star Comics** No. 3, and **Flash Comics** No. 1.

1975: In the first collaborative effort between the two major comic book publishers of the previous decade, Marvel and "D.C." produced together an over-sized comic-book version of **MGM's Marvelous Wizard of Oz** in the fall, and then the following year in an unprecedented cross-over produced **Superman vs. the Amazing Spider-Man**, written by Gerry Conway, drawn by Ross Andru, and inked by Dick Giordano.

1976: Frank Brunner's Howard the Duck, who had appeared earlier in Marvel's **Fear** and **Man-Thing**, was given his own book in January, which because of distribution problems became an over-night collector's item. After decades of litigation, Jerry Siegel and Joe Shuster were given financial recompense and recognition by National Periodical Publications for their creation of Superman, after several friends of the team made a public issue of the case.

1977: Stan Lee's **Spiderman** was given a second birth, fifteen years after his first, through a highly successful newspaper comic strip, which began syndication on January 3 with art by John Romita. This invasion of the comic strip by comic book characters continued with the appearance on June 6 of Marvel's **Howard the Duck**, with story by Steve Gerber and visuals by Gene Colan. In an unusually successful collaborative effort, Marvel began publication of the comic book adaption of the George Lucas film **Star Wars**, with script by Roy Thomas and art by Howard Chaykin, at least three months before the film was released nationally on May 25. The demand was so great that all six issues of **Star Wars** were reprinted at least seven times, and the installments were reprinted in two volumes of an over-sized Marvel Special Edition and a single paperback volume for the book trade.

✦Confessions of a Former Comic Book Artist✦

by Jay Disbrow

Considering the vast horde of comic book characters Disbrow created back in the early 1950's, we shudder to contemplate the sheer volume of work they represented.

I herewith confess that I entered the comic book field with full knowledge of the consequences. If this was to mean that I would be shunned by the world's intelligentsia, so be it. Let me further add that I did not "settle" for the comics in lieu of some loftier profession; I deliberately chose them as my career. In the eyes of some this may cast me in the role of an eccentric, but if so I gladly embrace the stigma.

To me the comics were not merely a profession, they were almost a way of life. They represented an inner compulsion that demanded expression. Adventure comic story plots were bred within the very fiber of my being, and they struggled incessantly to get out of my psyche and into print. I could no more restrain that driving force than I could swim the Amazon River at its widest point.

This mania for adventure comic expression began in early childhood. As a small boy living in Asbury Park, New Jersey, I was totally beguiled by the artistic genius of Alex Raymond. I lived from week to week in anticipation of each installment of Flash Gordon. By the time I was ten years of age, the Raymond mystique had so enmeshed my fancy that I took a solemn oath in simulated blood by the full moon, swearing that I would one day become an adventure comic artist.

"But wait," cries a reader, "your work looks nothing like Alex Raymond's! There is no resemblance at all!"

To which I reply, "Thank goodness for that!" I accepted Raymond's inspiration but nothing more. I strove for my own artistic style and my own method of story telling.

That art style has been described in a number of ways, some flattering, some not so flattering. But in all cases the basic assumption is the same, namely that Disbrow's art is a product of his own development and bears little resemblance to the techniques of other adventure comic artists.

From the time I was fourteen years of age I was drawing adventure comic stories at a furious pace. I made up the plots as I went along, filling in the narration and the dialog panel by panel. I did the lettering with a fountain pen and I inked in the pages with Esterbrook pen points and crow quills. I remember how surprised I was years later to discover that the pros inked their pages with a red sable brush.

The D. C. line of comics was my favorite in those days, and since all their leading stories were exactly thirteen pages in length, I decided that my stories would also be thirteen pages long. I began to write comic book SCRIPTS, and unbeknownst to me at the time, I was doing it just like the pros, except my ˜scripts were hand-printed instead of typed.

While thus concentrating on the literary aspects of my craft, I did not neglect the artistic. I strove manfully to develop my illustrating skills. I faithfully studied the funamentals of artistic construction, particularly the human figure in action. The mysteries of perspective were formidable but eventually solved. Jungle and desert backgrounds, rock barriers, and exotic locales were my favorite settings. (I shuddered at the necessity of drawing city buildings at various angles, but I made the effort nevertheless.)

As a teenager I sent my comic pages to Alex Raymond, Hal Foster and Burne Hogarth for criticism. These titans of the syndicate world who were my heroes graciously took their time to encourage me in the pursuit of my chosen career. The progress was slow and grim. The struggle was all uphill. There were moments of sheer exaltation at the accomplishments attained, and the periods of deep frustration at setbacks encountered.

Finally in the fall of 1946, with high school behind me, I decided the time had come to sally forth to conquer my world in the realm of the comics. Ah, the brash confidence of youth.

I went to D. C. Publications on New York's Lexington Avenue and presented them with a comic book feature that was surely the finest piece of illustrated narrative ever conceived in the mind of man. The D. C. editor unceremoniously rejected it.

Realizing that D. C. could not appreciate such high quality work, I took my feature to the other New York comic book publishers, and they too rejected it. This situation called for rigid self-examination. What was wrong? Where did the problem lie? Why couldn't those stupid editors see how foolish they were to reject such quality work? When I finally saw the truth it was a traumatic experience.

I finally realized that my only hope for continued existence was to go to work for a living, which I did. However, I did not abandon my dream of a career in comics. I continued to write story plots and draw comics at nights and on weekends. I assiduously studied the books of Andrew Loomis and George Bridgman. I struggled for long hours to purge the stiffness from my figures. I practiced drawing facial expressions under various light and shadow conditions. I wrestled with the problem of capturing all kinds of human emotions in my various characters.

I went to the comic book editors again and again. I was rejected by them time again and again! When this condition continued for more than three years, I felt like a rubber ball being bounced from one editor to another. The urge to give up the struggle was often strong. But the will to succeed was even stronger, so I stuck it out with grim determination.

I formed many friendships and made many acquaintances among the people in the comic book field during those bleak years. But the one who stands out the sharpest in my memory is the late Wendell Crowley, editor of the Captain Marvel group at Fawcett Publications. From 1946 thru 1949 I visited Wendell's New York office dozens of times, submitting my constantly updated comic samples.

Wendell Crowley was the kind of editor who could be sympathetic toward a novice artist without coddling him. My work was not yet good enough for Fawcett, but he would no sooner suggest that I give up the struggle than to stop breathing. One day in January 1950, he suggested that I try to obtain a staff job at the S. M. Iger studios, and he supplied me with their new address which I discovered to be on New York's West 53rd Street.*

*The Iger establishment was one of three major New York shops that supplied comic art to various publishers (the other two being Chesler studios and the Binder agency). Iger's chief client was Fiction House Publications. At least half of Fiction House's output was done at the Iger studios.

I hurried over to 53rd Street and quickly located the correct building. It looked like a two-story apartment house (it had been) situated beside an enormous row of brownstone apartments. It had a brilliant red door that fronted on the street level. As I opened the door to go inside, I expected to find an interior straight out of a Sax Romer novel. Instead I found a well furnished modern office. And there, seated behind an enormous desk, was a man who had become a living legend even in that day: Jerry Iger, grand monarch of the Iger Empire.

Jerry must have seen in my samples a definite artistic potential, for he immediately hired me as an inker. At first I was stunned by this unbelievable good news! After more than three years of frustration and bitter disappointment, I had at last arrived! I was now on the inside! I had at last become a professional!

For about three weeks I lived in a dream world. I did not deplore the necessity of rising at 5:15 in the morning and walking three miles in bitter cold weather to the railroad station. Nor did I object to the two-hour train ride twice each day. Since I had entered the magic world I had sought since childhood, a few inconveniences would not disturb me.

From the moment I began working at the Iger studios I determined to apply myself rigorously so I could learn all the professional touches as quickly as possible. However, for the first two and a half months I did nothing but ink in pages that were pencilled by other artists.

Eventually my area of responsibility broadened and soon I was doing pencil breakdowns from scripts provided by Fiction House and other publishers. I pencilled stories of Sheena, Kaanga, Firehair, Long Bow, and a host of other Fiction House features. Once I started pencilling stories I rarely had an opportunity to ink any of them. The Iger studios were like a production line factory where quantity was more important than the application of individual talent.

After I had been with the Iger

This is Sheeah, Disbrow's favorite leading lady of the jungle, with Kigah her pet saber-tooth tiger, from the story "The Curse of Sheeah," Terrors of the Jungle No. 7.

studios for more than a year, I decided the time had come to launch out into that vast ocean of free lance opportunity. I felt that I had now garnered enough professional skills to take the plunge.

During some free time at the Iger studios I visited a few publishers' offices, this time carrying my PUBLISHED samples. I picked up a few insignificant assignments in various places, but nothing important developed until I visited the office of Star Publications (then on New York's East 32nd Street). There I met the famed L. B. Cole, editor of Star.

Leonard B. Cole (who was written up most favorable in last year's *Price Guide*) was an artist of surpassing talent. The comic book covers he rendered for Star and other publishers are now part of the historical memorabilia of comic book fandom. He excelled not only in comics but in the realm of fine arts as well.

Leonard Cole looked over my samples and liked them. He gave me a script based on a teenage comedy story. I pencilled this story at nights and one weekend and brought it back to Cole one evening after work at the Iger studio. He liked the pencilling and told me to proceed with the inks and lettering.

When I returned the completed comic pages to him, Leonard was so pleased he indicated he would probably have enough work to keep me occupied on a regular basis. On the strength of this promise, I tendered my resignation at the Iger studios. Jerry and I shook hands, wished each other well, and I turned and walked out of his door for the last time.

I illustrated two more scripts for Leonard Cole, then I heard nothing from him for three weeks. It was now the spring of 1951. I went into his office one day and presented him with a special recommendation that I had been saving for some time.

"Why not let me write my own scripts?" I asked him. "After all, I've had plenty of experience at it."

The "experience" I referred to were the comic stories I had written as a teenager, but I didn't tell him that.

Leonard agreed to let me try. He told me he had the nucleus of an idea for a story which he did not have time to develop. "I'm going to give you a shot at it," he said.

The basic concept concerned a man who fell into an opening in the earth and plunged straight downward for miles. He hit bottom and was unconscious for weeks. The unknown chemistry of this subterranean world intermingled with the molecular structure of his body and caused him to turn into an enormous hairy monster.

I went home and began working on the story. I took the basic skeleton of Cole's idea, filled it out, pieced it into narrative form, and typed it into a finished script. I took this back to the Star office and presented it to Leonard. He read it and was pleased. I then pencilled, lettered, and inked the story. It appeared in *Blue Bolt Weird* No. 112 under the title "The Beast From Below."

This essentially was the beginning of my short but stimulating career at Star Publications. For the next three and one half years I wrote and illustrated more than one hundred comic book stories and fillers for Star. It is recognized as being rare for a comic artist to

Action was the name of the game in the adventure comic book stories.
This meant a super-abundance of fight scenes. Whenever possible Disbrow
included as much of this fast-paced fisticuff action as space would permit.

write his own material. Usually the ability to formulate story plots and to compose narration and dialogue is the special purview of those who specialize in writing only. I thought very little of this at the time, for I had conditioned myself in this direction as a teenager. To me the only important thing about my dual role of artist-writer was the thrill of creating comic stories.

For Star's three mystery magazines—*Blue Bolt Weird, Startling Terror Tales, Shocking Mystery Cases*—Leonard Cole had a definite preference for ghost stories, and he wanted me to write and illustrate them. I thought ghost stories were silly; I preferred to do monster tales. (I had an entire pantheon of monsters I was holding in reserve.) This difference of opinion sometimes led to conflict. But we usually resolved the matter amicably by producing ghost stories.

However I was able to turn out quite a number of monster tales, some of them dealing with creatures from distant planets. My

favorite monster character was a female being named Nogramog who appeared in the story "Love From A Gorgon" (*Startling Terror Tales* No. 13). This creature presented me with the greatest challenge of my comic career. The idea was to create a terribly grotesque hairy monstrosity, which at the same time generated sympathy. It turned out that despite her horrendous appearance, she was an object of pity.

In addition to my work at Star, I also wrote and illustrated several stories for Trojan Publications and American Comics Group. My last comic book story was completed in January 1955. This was a western, which was very symbolic for me, for just as the frontier marshal of the Old West hung up his badge and guns at retirement and rode off into the sunset, so I hung up the symbols of my comic book career and rode off into the world of commercial art where I have been ever since.

This was not an easy transition for me to make because my heart remained with the comics for a long time to come, but with the passing of years I managed to adjust.

Now my off-duty time is devoted to free lance writing and lecturing. For many years I have had the good fortune of writing and illustrating feature articles for various newspapers and magazines. I have also been asked to lecture before groups (professional, educational, religious, social, military, and philanthropic) on a wide variety of topics.

LET THEM GO, OR I'LL TEAR YOU APART WITH MY BARE HANDS!

JAYSON

The comic book heroes of the 1930's, '40's and '50's were all men of high resolve and purpose. A passion for justice and a sense of destiny characterized each one.

Whenever possible I paint pictures. Goache is my favorite medium, and science fiction my favorite subject (with a liberal sprinkling of dinosaurs thrown in). But of all the creative pursuits I have engaged in, the adventure comics remain my favorite medium of expression. There will always be a special place in my heart for the comics, for they were the sweet infatuation of my childhood, my youth, and my young manhood. I will forever cherish the memory of those golden years of achievement.

At this point someone is certain to exclaim, "If you loved the comics so much, why on earth did you leave them?"

I have an excellent answer. I left the comics for the same reason a man leaves his home when it is enveloped in flame, or a crew of seamen abandon ship when their vessel is sinking in a heavy sea. It was purely a matter of survival.

My comic book career flourished during the latter half of the Golden Age of comic books. The end of an age is always characterized by upheaval. Whether it be a historical, industrial, or social era, the ending is usually chaotic. The comic book world was no exception. With the close of the Golden Age, many artists, writers, and editors suffered severe dislocation. Many publishers were forced out of business. I held on as long as I could, but I could see the end coming early in 1954. Star folded within a year of the time I left them. (During their final year they subsisted on reprints only.) From where I stood it looked like the end of the comic book industry.

I like to think of this situation as having a precedent in classical history. The great law giver of ancient Rome, Marcus Tullius Cicero, lived at a time when the Republic of Rome was coming to a shattering end. To Cicero, it seemed that the destruction of the Roman nation was at hand. What he could not see was the fact that the Republic of Rome was being replaced by the Roman Empire, and that great empire would endure for five additional centuries.

What I could not see in 1954 was the coming of the Silver Age of comic books, and the incredible movement of comic fandom that has swept the nation in the past decade. The enormous comic book conventions held nation-wide each year are enough to boggle the mind of any former comic book practitioner.

Now, twenty-three years after my exit from the comic book scene, I am happy to observe that the comics are alive and well and living in the hearts of thousands in comic fandom. Many of the young artists and writers in the field today are superb craftsmen who could carry the comic book medium to heights of grandeur never before attained.

I personally would like to see comic books retain the pristine splendor that was theirs during the Golden Age, when subjects such as adultery, sexual promiscuity, and other social taboos were never so much as hinted at. A passion for justice was the primary motivation of all comic book heroes in those days. Was this corny and naive? You bet it was. But it also was the prime element that created comic fandom, for it was those naive vintage comic books of the forties and fifties that were traditionally sought after by the fans since the inception of comic fandom.

Here's hoping that in the years ahead the creative people in the comic book industry will cover themselves with an even greater glory than in the past. And as they do, this is one former comic book artist-writer who will be standing on the sidelines cheering them on.

THIS YEAR RIDGEWOOD LOST THEIR SHIRTS
BEFORE THE SEASON EVEN STARTED!

Some early Ward art for a high school
newspaper.

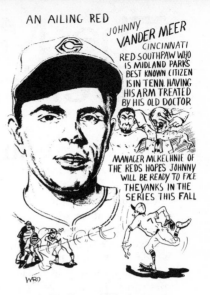

AN AILING RED

JOHNNY
VANDER MEER
CINCINNATI
RED SOUTHPAW WHO
IS MIDLAND PARKS
BEST KNOWN CITIZEN
IS IN TENN. HAVING
HIS ARM TREATED
BY HIS OLD DOCTOR

MANAGER McKECHNIE OF
THE REDS HOPES JOHNNY
WILL BE READY TO FACE
THE YANKS IN THE
SERIES THIS FALL

Ward's first published artwork.

Bill polishing up final details on this
year's cover.

Bill at his studio bar. This plus the
serving table seen at left was made
by Bill from a castle dining room
piece.

The Man Behind Torchy

By
BILL WARD

The first indication I had that drawing might be something more than a hobby-interest for me was at the age of seventeen when I spent a week at Ocean City, Maryland, many moons ago. Beer jackets—the over-forty group will remember them—were in vogue then. For the uneducated, a beer jacket was a white denim jacket that kids drank beer in. Most people decorated them with sayings like, "Oh you kid", "Take me I'm yours", etc.

I decorated mine with girls and mermaids. Kids on the beach started asking me if I would do theirs. I charged one dollar each and did hundreds, which enabled me to keep myself at that delightful spot for the entire summer season. The thing about this that impressed me wasn't that I had been able to support myself in art with absolutely no training (I hadn't even taken art in high school), but what a fantastic way it had been for me to meet girls. Right then and there I decided to become an artist. Anyway my last name spelled backwards is "draw," so I guess it just had to be.

On my first day at Pratt Institute in Brooklyn, our instructor said, "I suggest that at the beginning you students draw what you're interest in most. You who like animals,

draw them; those interested in landscapes, paint them." I knew what I had to do. . .I drew girls. . .and I've been doing it to this day. Incidentally, Bob Kuhn, America's foremost animal painter, was in my class. He went in another direction.

Brooklyn's Pratt Institute, a giant complex today, was a converted canning factory when I went there. Although it was, and still is, the finest commercial art school in the country, it did me little good. A sure war was approaching, and I was bound to go in at the age of nineteen. I paid little attention to my studies, concentrating on girls and fraternity life. Consequently, I wasn't much of an artist when I graduated in 1941.

Pratt had a placement bureau, and they got me a job with a high class art service in Manhattan at $18 a week. To my dismay it was not as an illustrator but to sweep floors, run errands, sweep floors, stir up the tempera bottles, and sweep floors. . . .I mean how many times a day can you sweep floors? We were still mired in a depression and jobs were hard to find, so I had to stay there at all costs.

It seemed as though I was always frantically looking for something to do. This then, the lack of enough work to keep me busy and to justify the job, was the worst and most difficult part of my career; and it was quite a come-down from my glamorous life at Ocean City, Maryland. If the chicks could have seen me then, frustrated, broom in hand. . . .

It's funny how things happen—sometimes an infinitesimal thing can change the course of your life and send you in a completely new direction. For example:

The art service finally let me get into the art picture in a small way. They had the Ford automobile account, and I was at the board pasting up a brochure. I had to make a cut with a matt knife and to my horror, when I lifted up the paper I discovered that beneath it I had cut a full color painting of a Ford car in half. I was fired on the spot.

A few days later back in the fraternity house (I roomed there after graduating) I was completely deflated and reading a three-day-old newspaper in a brother's room when I noticed the word "Ward" written at the top of one of the pages. "Oh jeeze, I forgot to tell you, Pratt phoned the other day. . .they had a job for you!" he told me when I pointed it out to him.

It has occurred to me many times that if I hadn't sliced through that *&$%+@ painting and if I hadn't gone into my fraternity brother's room for a beer and found my name written on an old newspaper, I no doubt never could have been a comic book artist; and Ken Bald, creator of the syndicated strip "Dr. Kildare," John Spranger, artist of the syndicated strip "The Saint," Kurt Schaffenburger, one of "Superman's" top artists to this day, Vic Dowd, Bob Boyagin, Ray

Hartford, Bob Butts, and about twenty-five other Pratt graduates probably wouldn't have either. Through these strange series of circumstances, I was due to meet the man who was to have the greatest impact on my career.

Jack Binder worked out of his apartment in the Bronx along with an assistant, Pete Riss, a fabulous Russian who unfortunately passed away a few years ago. The thing that pleased me the most when I phoned Jack was that he was moving to Englewood, N. J., a stone's throw away from Ridgewood, a town where I had spent most of my life (and have to this day, I might add). Strangely, Jack Binder wasn't that great an artist, but as a teacher he was a genius. Pratt had the finest teachers in the land, but to me none could have held a candle to this self-taught comic artist.

When I arrived at his apartment in the Bronx, Jack greeted me brusquely: "Sit down at that table and draw me a bridge. I want to see what kind of an eye for detail you have."

An eye for detail, like perfect pitch in music, is something you have or you don't have. Teaching won't help you much more than train you to be more observant. Memory, the ability to retain images, wasn't one of my fortes. Fortunately I had driven across the George Washington Bridge so many times I was able to do a fairly respectable job. "Good enough," he grunted, "I'll start you on backgrounds."

So Jack Binder, Pete Riss, and I moved into the upstairs of a huge barn in Englewood, N. J. Jack's wife and seven kids resided in the old clapboard farmhouse nearby. Jack layed out, Pete pencilled and inked the figures, and I pencilled and inked the backgrounds.

Jack had a good contact with Fawcett and we did stories mainly for them, such as "Mr. Scarlet," "Bullet Man," and "Ibis." Others that I remember were "Captain Battle," "Doc Savage," "Ajax," "Black Owl," "Saga," "The Shadow," and "Fury."

Fortunately for me, Jack spent a great deal of time training me. He taught me how to "feather" with a brush. "I want you to gain control of the brush to the point where you can feather on the head of a pin," said he. "Feathering" is a series of lines close together, curling, swirling, all equal distance apart. This is the way you create the shading that forms the muscles on figures and renders the hair. He had me practice this in my spare time until I mastered the art. Consequently control of the brush is one of my best assets today. Note Torchy's hair on the cover as an example. He also taught me to ink around the figure with the inside of the brush, the part that's against the flesh, so that if you put solid black behind the fingers, for example, their shape would be right.

Jack was being forced to spend more and more time selling and less time laying out since we were now turning out much more work. It was my great luck that he decided to teach me how to lay out stories. He impressed on me how important it was not to think of each story as ordinary comic book art, but as though it were "Prince Valiant," "Flash Gordon," or something else terribly important; to get keyed up, excited about it. He told me to think of myself as director of a play

acting out the parts of each actor in my mind, then sketching them out on paper. To my amazement, layout and storytelling came easily to me under his tutorage, the only thing in art that ever had.

Jack now needed a background man to do the work I had been doing, so one day in July of 1941 he asked me if I knew of anyone who could do backgrounds.

"Know of anyone. . .I know twenty-five or more."

"Seriously?"

"Seriously."

"Get them."

"All twenty-five?"

"Yes."

Comic books were mushrooming—after all it was their "Golden Era." Unable to find enough trained artists, the publishers were turning more and more to shops. I phoned the fraternity house. A wealth of raw talent lay there, ready to be gulped down by the artist-hungry comic book boom. Recently graduated a mere year after me, they lay ready and waiting.

For Jack Binder the timing was excellent. It was less than a month after they had graduated and Pratt hadn't had a chance yet to place them with their employment service. I was overwhelmed and a bit apprehensive at their response. Almost all were coming, all my brothers. Most importantly of all, better artists than I were coming; could they reduce me to a minor role?

Of course they could. One of the unusual things about artists is that they can't be unionized. It has been tried many times, but seniority means nothing. A talented kid, just out of art school, can do a better job than the little talented man who has worked twenty-five years in the field.

A group of ten or more showed up first, headed by Ken Bald, destined to be the most successful amongst us, destined eventually to be Jack's art director of a shop of over forty men. Comic books in those days were, to say the least, frowned on by art students at Pratt. They were thought of as the lowest rung on the ladder for a graduate— we all wanted to be illustrators. However, remember that we were still in the depths of the Depression—jobs were few and far between. All ten were absorbed; more and more trickled in as they gave up and accepted their fate.

The room in the barn was at least 55' x 30', enough room for forty men at least. Had I made a mistake? Would I be driven back to become a background man, the bottom of the ladder? As it turned out I had just enough training by Jack to maintain my lofty position as the sole layout man for the Binder shop. The scripts poured in, most written by Jack's brother Otto, a prolific science fiction writer and Fawcett's foremost writer. The shop grew to twenty, then thirty men.

Perhaps it might be of interest to mention the system that Jack developed as time went on. On the back of each page was a box with eight categories listed: layout, pencilling main figures, pencilling secondary figures, pencilling backgrounds, inking main figures, inking secondary figures, inking backgrounds, and lettering.

As each man did his individual bit, he signed the back of the page. Pay was simple: he was allotted a dollar for each item signed. Hence, Jack Binder was getting complete lettered pages for $8 each.

It always intrugied me that with eight men working on the same page a shop-style developed. However, there were over thirty men working altogether, not just eight. True, I did all the layouts, but there were three or four persons each in the other categories, mixed together with each succeeding job, resulting in no true shop style. Yet somehow it was recognizable, and it is to me to this day. I can always spot it in the books of the "Golden Era."

Wendell Crowley had been a life-long friend, my closest as I look back on it. He had just finished his freshman year at the University of Oklahoma and was home for summer vacation. Jack needed an all-purpose man: someone to erase pages, to deliver pages, and to go out for coffee. So Wendell Crowley entered our happy group. He was destined to be the foremost comic book editor of all time.

In no time Wendell's class showed through and he graduated from clean-up and delivery man to editor of Binder's whole shebang. We both lived in Ridgewood and the war was on now. Gas was rationed to five gallons a week. I had a 1936 Ford and so did he. We alternated driving together to Englewood. We made that five gallons last, coasting down every little hill with the clutch in, as we all may have to do again soon.

If I were on my deathbed, thinking back on the happiest days of my working life, I think I would select those days in 1941-42 in the Binder shop. We were mostly all kids, twenty years or younger, developing our talents, making good money in the depression, and most of all, enjoying ourselves.

The Englewood High School baseball field was just down the road. At noontimes we went there to toss a ball around. Then we started playing softball. Finally two teams were formed: pencillers and inkers, natural antagonists. Each day, rain or shine, we played a seven-inning game on into the winner. Jack was going mad, production was lagging, and we were taking two hours for lunch. He knew better than to try to stop us, not at $8 a page. We had other fun besides the games. One day I was taking a break, standing by the rickety old barn window staring out at the rain. As I turned to go back to my board, I happened to glance down and couldn't believe what I saw on the top of the guy's head who sat inking. He was one of the few older men in the shop and had a bald spot, but only close inspection could tell you so. This inker, who shall be nameless even after 35 years, had inked in his bald spot with black India ink. Probably with the aid of a mirror, he had done it beautifully: fine brush feathering, flowing along exactly in the direction he had combed the thinning surrounding hairs.

"Wendell," I whispered a few moments later, "go over to the window and look down at the top of -----'s head."

Wendell, all six feet nine of him, ambled over to the window, stretched, and glanced down. A look of disbelief came over his face.

"Jeeze," he grunted when he came back to me, "he never inked anything that good for us." Good old Wendell—dead now seven years—always the company man.

It was at this point that an event happened that to this day I have a hard job accepting, not to mention

understanding.

Although I had been the sole layout man for a long time at Jack's, I was still the fastest man in the shop on backgrounds due to my training in the early days at the shop. Towards the close one day, Jack came to me and asked if I could do him a special favor: he needed six backgrounds pencilled and inked by the following morning on a story that was late. . .could I do them?

I realized about three in the morning that I should have turned him down. I had layed out all day, a strain in itself on the eyes, and now I could scarcely see the page.

I managed to finish the job but the quality of the work was poor, as you might expect—"hacked out" as we used to say. I went home to sleep just before the shop opened. When I returned in the afternoon, Ken Bald, the art director called me over to his desk.

"Sorry Bill, but Jack is furious over the quality of your backgrounds. He's asked me to lay you off."

I couldn't blame Ken; he was just doing his job, but it did hurt to leave a shop filled with fellows whose jobs I had obtained for them—good jobs in a terrible depression. Of course Jack in his anger momentarily forgot that my real contribution to his shop was layout, not backgrounds.

A week later Wendell, who had taken it worse than I had, phoned, a note of glee in his voice.

"Jack wants you back," he said, "production has been cut in half. We don't have anyone good at layout." Brother did I strut triumphantly back into that shop!

Draughtsmanship had always been my main problem: the ability to draw the figure in any position, at any angle. This was the fruits of my inattention at Pratt. Now however, under Jack's guidance my draughtsmanship was improving. After hundreds and hundreds of layouts, I felt I was now able to do a strip on my own.

My chance came when Jack was offered a complete book of *Captain Marvel* (to this day I don't know, but it may have been No. 1), a great feather in his cap. I had layed out a few *Whiz* Captain Marvels for C. C. Beck. Jack knew that the shop style wouldn't do, so when he took me off layout for the time being to do the book, it was my greatest break. Bob Butts did all the backgrounds and I did all of the figures.

I was no Beck, but Fawcett liked the job and I felt I was on my way. After over a year of layout, inking, pencilling, and backgrounds, I finally got to do a story, and not only that, an entire book on CAPTAIN MARVEL!

One day on the trip home from Binder's, as we coasted down the hills, I told Wendell I felt I was now able to handle a strip. . .who would he suggest I go to?

All artists have idols in their fields. Most of us at Binder's admired the work of Beck and Mac Raboy at Fawcett; Simon and Kirby of Captain America; and most of all the group at Quality Comics, Will Eisner of the Spirit, Jack Cole of Plastic Man, Lou Fine, and my personal favorite, Reed Crandall of Blackhawk fame.

Wendell said, "Shoot for the top; try Quality. If you're rejected there, go right down the line."

I had incredible good luck. My timing was perfect. When I walked into George Brenner's office, the top editor at "Quality," he welcomed me with open arms. Reed Crandall, you see, had just been drafted.

My head was whirling. I had been hoping for some little secondary story in a book, something I could do on weekends. They offered me the moon instead; Blackhawk in its entirety, covers and all. And I had to replace who was in my mind the greatest comic book artist of them all—impossible!

When I left Binder's, I didn't realize at the time but the happiest portion of my life came to an end. Gone were the daily baseball games, the close association with all my friends, the camaraderie. I became a free lance artist, destined to work at home (with the exception of four years in the army) for the next thirty-five years.

I never regretted leaving however for Binder's shop didn't last long. . .the draft took care of that. Working at home, by the way, has its benefits. You're your own boss and you can regulate your time. If it rains on the weekend-you can

Military Comics No. 29, ©DC(Qua) Ward cover art.

work right on through, then take sunny days off the following week. I have a waterfront beach house in the sand dunes at Montauk Point, on the tip of Long Island. When the weather man predicts a spell of good weather, I head out there and work and fish on my own beach. However, I'd still swap it all for those days in the shop.

Insecurity is the main problem in freelancing. The only way you can protect yourself is by having lots of accounts so that if one goes wrong you have the others to fall back on. Also, you might get two or three jobs to do at once from two different publishers. You can't say, "Oh I'm sorry, I'm working on something for someone else." All you can do is burn a little midnight oil.

I took naturally to Blackhawk. My training by Jack in layout stood me in good stead. All of that practice in inking paid off. They especially liked my covers. I'm especially proud of *Military* No. 30, a shot of that silly Blackhawk plane coming at you, cannons firing, Blackhawk piloting, Chop-Chop waving his meat cleaver

menacingly over his shoulder.

I drew that idiotic plane (from the early *Military Comics*) for years before it was changed to a jet. I used to wonder what nut designed the damn thing. Of course it could never fly—ridiculous to think so.

A few years ago I was leafing through a copy of a 1942 "Aerosphere" that I had acquired. Imagine my astonishment. . .there it was, an actual photograph of that same silly plane! Reading on I found it was an experimental model, the Grumman "Sky Rocket," that the army had rejected. Can you blame them?. . .but it must have at least flown!

I was doing great in the fall of 1942. My training was behind me and I had my own strip. Somehow I still wasn't satisfied. Now that my ability to draw girls had improved, the girls on the old beer jacket looked amateurish to me now. I felt that the world should have a chance to see my girls.

I worked up some cartoon ideas and went to see Ken Brown, who edited "Army Laughs." He liked them and shortly I was selling cartoons to "Army Laughs" and

Grumman "Sky Rocket" XF5F-1. An experimental aircraft with an astonishing resemblance to the Blackhawk plane.

"Buddies." "Film Fun" came next, and soon I had quite a few accounts. I was getting, unknown to me of course, closer and closer to "Torchy."

Suddenly, when I was at the top of the world, as had happened to multitudes of others, I found myself on a train heading for Fort Dix, N. J. Yes, I had been drafted. It was December 7, 1942, one year after Pearl Harbor. Whenever anyone asks me when I went into the service, I say, "December 7th." Well it was, wasn't it?

After basic training I was put into the Eastern Defense Command. I went to an Automatic Weapons outfit at Quonset Point Naval Air Base, R. I., still active today. Yes, I said Naval. For some unexplained reason the Army manned the anti-aircraft guns at the Naval Air Base. I was put into communications, which I didn't know at the time would turn out to be a bonanza for me. Night after night I sat in the air field tower, with earphones on connected to the searchlights and anti-aircraft guns that surrounded the field.

I received a letter from Wendell with the great news that he had left Binder's to become editor of *Captain Marvel* at Fawcett. He went on to say that he needed someone to lay out stories for his artists. Me, why not me? I had all the time in the world in the tower. A week later I sat in the tower with earphones on, a drawing board in my lap, laying out stories for Wendell.

The Navy guys in the tower stood in awe of the soldier who sat hour after hour, day after day, week after week, drawing pictures. What perseverance, what dedication, what a nut! Of course they didn't know that during the day I would sneak over to the base post office and mail the stuff to Wendell, and that I probably was making more money than the Admiral on the base.

One night while working away in the tower, a naval officer approached me, "Say, son, rather than doing all this silly practicing, how would you like to do a real comic strip for the "Quonset Point Scout". . .actually get something into print?"

I was desperate. If I said "Yes," it was going to cost me money and I would have less time for layout. If I said "No," they would smell a rat, and once they found out I was making money, forget it, jealousy would take over. Ex-service men know what I mean.

Would you believe that this was the beginning of Torchy? I was actually forced into it. True she was a brunette and her name was Ack-Ack-Amy, but she had the same fabulous shape and she was a nit-wit who always won out in the end. Right away the strip took off. After all she was more interesting than how to disassemble your M-1 rifle or how to replace the back-plate group: the type of thing that the paper had been featuring.

In those days every soldier had a M.O.S. number, describing his occupation. When a chicken-plucker or a plumber was needed, they just checked the M.O.S. numbers and picked him out. I was picked out and sent to Fort Hamilton right on the edge of New York City to do training aids for the War Department. I didn't complain; after all New York had more lonesome chicks than any

Ack-Ack Amy strip by Pvt. Bill Ward.

other place in the country. Almost immediately a major approached me and suggested I do a similar strip for the Fort Hamilton paper. I sighed and agreed, my fame (tiny as it was) had preceeded me. Anyway, anything was better than getting shot at.

So Torchy was born. I dyed Ack-Ack-Amy's hair blonde, changed her name and Voila, there she was. Shortly the strip was appearing in Army papers all over the world. And I was making out with the lonesome dolls in Manhattan like mad. I felt like I was back at Ocean City once again, minus the beer jacket, of course.

The Training Aid hut that I worked in was next to the post theater. It was the Army's policy to send small groups of soldiers who had been entertainers in civilian life, overseas to entertain troops in the front lines, in places that the USO couldn't reach. They rehearsed their acts outside of the theater while waiting for a boat. Bobby Breen and other well-known stars moved through, all privates but looking like generals in their tailor-made uniforms. Then Mickey Rooney, the top-salaried star in Hollywood, came in. No tailor-made uniform for him, and

what a great guy he was. I'm afraid I used to envy him his success. He used to drop into the hut for a cup of coffee to get out of the cold, and I got to know him pretty well. He was so excited, just like a little kid, for he had just married Miss Alabama. "This is it," he told me. How was he to know then there were five more to come.

One winter's day in the hut I said to him, "Boy, you're a lucky guy, a big success, a millionaire before you're twenty."

Very seriously he replied, "Look. . .at the age of five I played Mickey McGuire, and I've had to work my butt off from then on. While you were chasing chicks and going to football games I was going to work at 6 a. m., seven days a week, returning late at night. I never had any youth." I envied him no longer, but to me he was real class.

There was a full colonel on the post who had a serious stutter. He arrived at the hut one day, a panic-stricken expression on his face. He stuttered to me that he was being sent across country on a lecture tour. He hoped that I would be able to make it easier for him by drawing large illustrations that would show in picture form whatever he was speaking about,

FIGHTING TANK OF THE WEEK

M2595 Japanese Light Tank

At present there are fifteen or more known models of tanks in the Japanese Army. Basic types are few and new designations are given to the slightest modifications. For convenience, the tanks are classified according to weight as tankettes, light, medium and heavy tanks.

LIGHTLY ARMED AND ARMORED

The M2595 is a light tank which has been used in New Guinea and Burma. Though it is only lightly armed and armored, it fits the purposes of jungle warfare. The M2595 has a cramped fighting compartment, seems to have fine workmanship, and has a combined welded and riveted hull. It carries a crew of three; has an average speed of about 25 m.p.h.

Data prepared by A.A-2 Section,
Headquarters Antiaircraft Artillery Command, E.D.C.

Learn
These Characteristics

HEIGHT   : 7 feet (approx.)
LENGTH   : 14½ feet (approx.)
WIDTH   : Nearly 7 feet.
WEIGHT   : About 8 tons.
SUSPENSION: Two pair of bogie wheels on each side.
ARMAMENT : One 37mm in the turret; and two 7.7mm MGs.
ARMOR   : Light.

The above two illustrations were done by Bill while in the Service - early 1940's.

plus lettering, to eliminate the need for a lot of words from him.

I jumped at it: I saw a three-day pass in the offing. The problem was he wanted me to deliver the finished drawings to his plane the following day. I stayed up all night and finished the job just in time to make the plane! I received a commendation from the colonel the following week and promptly forgot about it. A short while after being discharged from the Army three years later, I was astonished to receive the Medal of Merit in the mail. A letter stated that the Army had decided to issue it to every GI who had received a commendation from a full colonel, or higher.

A day later a female writer on the local paper phoned me. "Oh, we feel so honored, Mr. Ward, you are the only one in this area to receive the Medal of Merit. We'd like to do a story on how you got it."

I was horrified. I couldn't say that I received the medal simply for drawing pictures, so I replied, "Please. . .my war experiences. . .You know. . .well, I just can't speak about them."

I was nervous when I returned to Quality after the war. Going there to get work when at least half of their great artists had been drafted was one thing. Returning along with all of them was another kettle of fish. I figured I'd be lucky to get some secondary strips.

However, things worked out great. Reed Crandall was given *Military,* changed now to *Modern Comics,* and I was given the *Blackhawk* book. Unfortunately there was one difference for us: we were just to do pencilling—inkers were to take over from there.

A few words about "inkers." I've always contended, perhaps unfairly,

that an inker was an artist that couldn't handle a strip on his own, that all he had to do was go over the pencil lines with a brush. I was very disappointed with the way my Blackhawks turned out. They weren't nearly as good as the complete jobs I'd done before the war.

If it affected me, it affected Reed Crandall far more. Never again was he to create the classic Blackhawks that he did in 1941-42. His bold yet simple inking style was lost as the inkers butchered his pencilling. He and I were destined to go on doing Blackhawk this way for seven years.

Drawing Blackhawk was probably as difficult a job as there was in the comics. There were seven main characters and they had to be shown constantly, really overcrowding the panels. I envied the writers—they could type out "Show all seven Blackhawks in a mele with the thugs" in probably ten seconds. Imagine how long it took me to draw it.

One of the most difficult things I found about drawing the Blackhawk characters was their military hats. A hat has to look just right, if it doesn't it looks silly. There's no in-between. Agitated about pencilling and the length of time it took me, I developed a way of solving the hat problem. I had them all knocked off in their first fight, which usually occurred by the second page. Then for the rest of the story they would be bare headed.

I got away with it for about six months, then, not some astute editor, but some damn smart alecky kid wrote George Brenner, "Why don't the Blackhawks get a new hatter? They don't seem to fit very well. They all get knocked off at the beginning of each story."

They really ripped into me over this. So in the next story the Blackhawks all had to swim underwater out to a submarine. You're right, I drew them swimming underwater with their hats on. "All right, Ward, let's not overdo it," George Brenner screamed into the phone.

I think it was around 1946 that Busy Arnold, Quality's publisher, asked me if I could do another story for *Modern* and did I have any ideas? I mentioned the fact that I had drawn a strip about a daffy blonde in the Army called "Torchy." He went for the idea, and I convinced him to let me ink it. At long last Torchy was in the comics.

The strip was very popular, running in both *Modern* and *Doll Man* for about three years. They were getting so much mail on it that Busy decided to do a *Torchy* book. I was ecstatic; my creation, that daffy blonde chick, was going to have a book of her own.

Then disaster struck, the greatest disappointment of my career. I had finished the cover and the lead story for issue No. 1, when George Brenner phoned and told me they were taking me off *Torchy*! Romance comics had come on the scene at the same time and they were instantly best-sellers. None of the other artists, due to the fact they had had no experience doing women, could handle it—it had to be me. They planned on a bunch of books, and I was to do the covers and lead stories. It meant lots more money for me, but I was furious!

I phoned Busy and pleaded with him that *Torchy* was my baby. I just wouldn't turn her over to another artist. We ended up with a compromise. If I could find the time, he would let me do as many of the covers as I could manage, plus the same with the lead stories.

Gil Fox did most of *Torchy* from then on, although I was able to do half of the covers and several lead stories. Gil, a great guy and a good friend, took over and did a remarkable job following my style. As a matter of fact it was more than a bit disconcerting to me that he could. I worked day and night to turn the romance pencilling out so that I could do *Torchy*. However, romance was selling like mad, so more titles were added.

Love Confessions No. 1, 1949, © Qua, Ward cover art.

The demise of *Torchy?* I shall never forget it. There was a psychiatrist by the name of Dr. Wertham who milked publicity from criticizing comic books and the negative effect they were supposedly having on kids.

I used to deliver my finished jobs to Quality's office in Manhattan. One day I was walking along Madison Avenue when I spotted Dick Arnold, Busy's son and an editor now, ambling along on the other side of the street. "There goes our worst offender!" he screeched to a friend, pointing at me.

I ran across the street to find out what the hell he meant and he threw a bombshell. "Dr. Wertham has come out with an 'unfit' list, and *Torchy* is on the list! I couldn't believe it. Torchy, that innocent little blonde, the stories equally innocent. Can you imagine that happening today?

Torchy No. 6, 1950, ©DC(Qua), Ward cover art.

As it turned out, comics, for me anyway, didn't last long after that. Television was the culprit. Bit by bit it took the audience away. Pay started going down along with sales. Suddenly, Quality threw in the towel and went out of business.

It was then that I discovered that it wasn't all a bed of roses to be a freelance artist. I didn't bother to look for more comic book work because all the outfits were laying off artists as sales plummeted. The person who saved me was Abe Goodman of "Humorama," the largest buyer of cartoons in the

world at that time. He remains a close friend to this day.

Anxious to continue the small success that I'd had selling cartoons before the war, in the fall of 1946 I had dropped into Abe Goodman's office with some of my stuff and he started buying my girls right away. For over twenty years Abe bought thirty cartoons a month from me. Whenever times were rough, and they were occasionally, I could count on that bread and butter income. A great demand for my girls started to come in from foreign countries, and he paid me a royalty on each sale. None of the other publishers ever paid me for foreign sales although they made plenty.

Around 1954 Bob Sproul started "Cracked" magazine. I was in the first issue, and I have been to this day. I've been very lucky with most of the publishers that I've worked for over the years: Jack Binder, Busy Arnold, Abe Goodman, and Bob Sproul—men of fine character who treated me fairly at all times. What more could one ask?

From a 1965 calendar by Ward

I'll close with a couple of comic book horror stories, but not the type you may think I mean. At Quality there was a supply room where they kept all the original art, the covers and the current books. It was expected that the artists would go in there as they left and help themselves. The original artwork was always destroyed eventually, so it didn't matter to them. When I think now how I could have had Will Eisner's *Spirit* covers from 1943 on, Jack Cole's *Plastic Man* covers, Reed Crandall's *Doll Man, Blackhawk, Buccaneer* covers too, not to mention their stories! All that I wanted! I did take four Crandall covers to hang in my son's room, and they gave me a thirteen-page 1942 Blackhawk story to follow his style when I took over from him, most of which I gave to my friends' kids for their rooms, after the war before I had kids of my own.

However, on each trip I made to the city, I always loaded up with Quality's current magazines, placing them in a large closet at my mother's house where I had a studio. I had no interest in comic books of other publishers, but I did buy *Captain America* Nos. 1-13, until I went into the service. I liked the unique way Simon and Kirby had their figures fairly explode out of the panels at you, the tremendous foreshortening. Check the value of *Captain America* in this *Price Guide*. I'm afraid to or I might shoot myself! Along with this then, over the years from 1941 to 1953 I filled that enormous closet at my mother's to the ceiling, mostly with comic books I had barely looked at.

When my mother passed away, unfortunately just before the comic book collector's craze came along, I lived with my wife and family in another part of Ridgewood, and I had to get rid of the things in her home. When I came to the closet, bursting with at least 5,000 Golden Era comics, it seemed too big a job to move it over to my house, so I burned the lot, the first 13 *Captain America*'s included.

Impossible to top that?. . .don't you believe it. There was an older man trying to establish himself as a background man in the Binder shop around 1942. His name: Windsor McCay Jr. His name ring a bell? It didn't to any of us twenty-year-olds. One day he brought about forty daily strips with him to work. He went up and down the aisle, saying, "My father created the first comic strip,'Little Nemo.' Wouldn't you fellows like to have some? I don't particularly want them." Before you start calling the young artists at the Binder shop morons, you have to remember that these were the days before all the publicity about comics and their origins came out. Windsor McCay's weird figures were just badly drawn figures to us. Not one of us took one. I'm sure if I'd asked he'd have given me the whole batch.

Thirty-four years later, last year, I was reading a comic fan newsletter and noted a feature on comics and what they were worth. I almost had a heart attack when I read that "Little Nemo" headed the list at $3,000 to $4,000 a strip. What's that they say. . .hindsight is better than foresight? oh well, back to the old drawing board.

WOMEN IN COMICS

by
Carl Macek
in collaboration with
Art Amsie

The significance of women in comics has never been quite fully realized. It is as complex and difficult to discuss as the nature of art itself. There are many psychological as well as cultural, social and aesthetic concerns which combine to make the subject of women in comics an important facet in the study of popular American culture. Obviously one can appreciate the characters and comic books on the level of pure fandom, yet there is a valid basis for the varied forms in which women appear in comics. To get a proper perspective on the role of women in comics, it is necessary not only to see and read comics from the past forty-odd years but also to try and understand them in an accurate structural context.

Sure, there have been numerous essays by fans and professional writers on the subject of super-heroines; the term "good girl art" has been coined to help explain an aspect of women in comics which goes beyond the boundaries of archtype and iconography; the relationship between sex and violence found in comics has been dealt with in works like Gershon Legman's *Love and Death* and Wertham's notorious *Seduction of the Innocent*; even advocates of Women's Liberation have turned to characters like Wonder Woman to serve as models and cultural signposts in regard to the role of women in society. To date the most comprehensive treatment of this subject is *L'Enfer des Bulles* by Jacques Sadoul. Even with all this the overall impact of women in comics has not been given the full treatment. There are many crucial questions unanswered or, what is worse, never asked. One must talk about the good as well as the bad; the flamboyant along with the plain; the one-shots and the mainstays; the heroines and the villainesses—only in this way can an overview to the subject of women in comics begin to take shape.

Long-time comic fan and historian Art Amsie has done exactly that. The subject of women in comics has always held a fascination for Art, and over the years he has managed to chronicle their development. As he became more involved in his study, Art began to realize that the subject of women in comics was so complex that a number of categories should be designated to give structure to his project. Art selected four major areas of interest: women as non-principal characters; women as principal characters (general); women as principal characters (sexy); and women as costumed heroines. These divisions should help us arrive at a more detailed picture of women in comics.

Probably one of the most over-looked and seemingly unnecessary categories is women as non-principal characters. This grouping, in effect, tends to examine women as background objects, elements within the context of comics which can serve as catalysts or dramatic tools. What then is so important about someone who functions as a stooge or a sidekick? The important word to deal with is character. The rationale behind this almost too obvious case of over-classification is a structural device central to the topic of women in comics. Nowhere can comic books be better seen as a truly narrative form than when dealing with characters in non-principal roles. It is here that countless girl Fridays, reporters, nurses, secretaries, maids, girl friends, waitresses, sweethearts, molls, neighbors, relatives and cheap pick-ups serve as living backdrops in creating dramatic situations. As secondary characters all these myriad women were easily thrown into comics which demanded conventional plot

development or resolution. Without trying to compromise the liberated attitudes of most contemporary women, these non-principal characters fall into two distinct classes: the background females used simply to create the proper mood or ambiance, and the unique, distinguishable and everpresent companion or foil.

It is in this latter attitude that women as non-principal characters are given a chance to shine. Their presence can be seen throughout the history of comics. The crazy antics of Olive Oyl in regard to that lovable swab Popeye; Tess Trueheart's devotion to Dick Tracy; Daisy Mae's constant search for a husband in Al Capp's "Li'l Abner;" Lana Lang, Lori Lemaris and Lois Lane's involvement with Clark Kent/Superman; Gwen Stacey and Spiderman; even Beverly and Howard the Duck's complex relationship—if nothing else, these characters, as well as countless others, provide contrast and

Howard the Duck and Beverly from Howard the Duck No. 2, 1976, ©MCG

Death of Gwen Stacy from Spider-Man No. 121, 1973. ©MCG

motivation for much of what is considered plot in many comic strips and comic books. This involvement with secondary characters goes beyond the proverbial notion of "boy meets girl" by stressing the ability of comics to create drama. The point of view that must be used in dealing with this particular categorization is one which has its roots in the theatre—there are no small parts, only small actors. This motto can be applied to the medium of comics as well. Comic book characters are ultimately actors drawn on paper which express particular values and sensibilities. They may be totally unmemorable or conversely the most interesting aspect of the strip. (Chic Young exemplified this in his comic "Blondie," where the main action revolves around Dagwood Bumstead while the strip is named after the family's most fully realized member, his wife Blondie.) The only real difference between women as non-principals and the rest of Art Amsie's groupings is that, in this case, women are represented as a type or gender rather than on an individual basis. It is true that a number of personalities managed to transcend their back-seat status and stand out as unique characters, yet the majority of women as non-principals exist to form a crust on the pie of humanity found populating the comic book universe.

On the subject of women serving merely as decoration, Art Amsie has this to say: "In this category, sex rears its sensuous head—or at least peeks around the corner. The women in this category generally served no useful function, except as decoration or sexy adjuncts to the hero. They provided a pretty face (sometimes with matching body) to look at; that was all. In fact, they were more of a hindrance than help. . .most often they were superfluous or even hazardous on dangerous missions. They made no technical contribution, took up valuable cargo space, distracted the hero, and were constantly in need of protection or rescue. All of this made for a very exciting, if quite implausible, story line." These women didn't always help the hero inside the book, but when put on the covers, they did help to sell a lot of comics. The classic early examples of this group were Dale Arden (Flash Gordon); Wilma Deering (Buck Rogers); Narda (Mandrake); Burma (Terry and the Pirates).

For many artists, drawing women was not only a job, it was a pleasure. A large number of female characters were created during the 1940s which served as little more than excuses to exploit, in a loving manner, the fascination found in a

Buck Rogers and Wilma Deering from Famous Funnies No. 209, 1953
© John S. Dille. Art by Frank Frazetta.

shapely woman. This phase of comic book history, along with the pin-ups and sexy adventure and costumed heroines which will be covered later, has been termed the good girl art period. It is here that sexuality was surreptitiously brought forth in the comics. Cleavage reached a new "low" in comics like *Slave Girl* and *Dagar*. The covers and inside pages of books like *Blue Beetle, Hickory,*

Blue Beetle No. 49, 1947, © Fox, Jack Kamen cover art.

Wonder Comics No. 14, 1947, © BP, Schomburg cover art (Bondage).

AND GOLLY... THOSE PEOPLE! WHY, THEY'RE BODIES! DEAD BODIES THAT HAVE BEEN STUFFED! OHHHH...

Lingerie scene from Blue Beetle No. 51, 1947, © Fox

Wonder, Bruce Gentry, Jo-Jo and *The Saint*, to name a few, were loaded with every cheesecake pose you can think of.

It is only logical to follow up these non-principal players with the general category of women as principal characters. To some purists these are the only two valid categories that exist when dealing with the subject. Either a woman is the star of a particular comic, or she remains delegated to function on the sideline. This criterion does not work in discussing women in comics. The differentiations are more complicated. There are so many different characters involved in so many varied activities that Art Amsie felt this category should be drawn thusly. The concept of women as principal characters (general) deals with domestic realities. Women featured in these comics serve functional roles as indicators of society. No heroics, no bondage, no real perils—rather the dramatic structure when dealing with these women is concerned with the problems of coping with life. Art points out that these stories were mostly non-physical,

non-hazardous and revolved around themes of either a social, emotional or economic nature.

There are several significant sub-divisions in this particular classification of women in comics. The most obvious is the working girl. The rest can be broken down into categories of juveniles, classy debutantes and wise matrons.

Starting in the 1940s there was a dramatic rise in the number of working girl comics published. This trend might be seen as a reaction to the maleless conditions brought about by the Second World War as well as a reintroduction of comic strip characters popular in the 1920s and 1930s. Whatever the reason for her appearance on the scene, the new career woman found a perfect home in the comics. The beautiful but dumb concept was rejected in favor of an image of the complete woman. Characters like Jane Arden, Tillie the Toiler, Winnie Winkle, Brenda Starr, Dixie Dugan sans Joe Palooka, Rosie the Riviter, Ella Cinders, Susie Q. Smith, Linda Carter—Student Nurse, Judy Canova and even Lucille Ball (in *I Love Lucy*

From cover of Pictorial Romances No. 11, 1952, ©STJ. Art by Matt Baker.

Comics) presented a vision of women, both real and fictional, that projected independence and completeness. Whether dramatic or humorous, the emphasis was generally on characterization. Aspects of sensuality were played down, with values like providing for a family or trying to make ends meet becoming more significant. These female characters were shown to function with a large degree of self-control. The career girl and personality comics were not especially well drawn nor were they masterpieces of the form. Rather they serve to present a vision of women emerging from their cocoons of repression endowed with the qualities of determination and drive. The war years gave rise to women like Gale Gordon and her All Girl Squadron, Jane Martin—War Nurse, Ranger Girl and her Rangers of Freedom

and Sky Girl who related directly to the war scene.

The younger principal characters such as Little Dot, Little Orphan Annie, Little Lotta, Little Iodine, Little Audrey and the irrepressible Little Lulu form a totally different impression of growing up female. In these comics life was viewed as a wild, roller-coaster ride of fun and mischief. Whatever truths learned in regard to growing up were usually presented in a light and unpedantic manner. John Stanley's Little Lulu was a magnificent example of the ability of comics to deal with profound concepts in a completely entertaining way. Adapted from the one-panel gag cartoons developed by Marge for the Saturday Evening Post, Little Lulu was a perfect everygirl. She was exposed to nearly every emotional trap and was able to survive without much damage. Stanley could blend

From cover of Little Audrey No. 18, 1951, ©Paramount Pictures.

fantasy and reality in the Lulu stories while maintaining a consistent and totally uncomplicated style. The anxieties faced by Lulu and her peers were really no problem at all. Most of these youngsters managed to overcome them by a strong dose of common sense.

The matron, so well defined by Mary Worth, also utilized common sense to solve problems. These older characters functioned as a stabilizing factor in the organic composition of women in comics. Even debutantes like Fritzi Ritz, Mopsy, Hedy Devine, Miss Beverly Hills of Hollywood and Mitzi were never seriously compromised. Many of these characters, however, were not popular enough to have their own books. The majority of them can be found as back-up features in the 1940s and '50s comics. When seen as a group there is a unique feeling which exists in relation to women as principal characters.

The one fairly consistent theme which links women to one another is the fact that they were able to maintain a sense of control over the elements of their environment. Granted, comic book life is ideal, and the problems found therein are merely tools of the storytellers and creators. Nevertheless, from Little Lulu to Mary Worth the ability of women to solve problems was everpresent. In this way the categorization of women as principals (general) does point to the acceptance and eventual social parity that women were beginning to experience not only in the comic medium but also in the real world.

The next category, women as principal characters (sexy), covers a wide variety of types: pin-ups, jungle girls, adventure heroines, villainesses and women in love comics. During the war years of the 1940s, many female comic book characters were created not only for entertaining readers at home but for the armed forces abroad as well. America was fascinated with the female anatomy to such a degree that the pin-up became a regular household item found on calendars, serving trays and even beer cans. Comic books were no exception.

Cut-outs from Katy Keene No. 17, 1954,
© AP

There are many characters which stand out in this category. One of the most obvious was Katy Keene—America's Pin-Up Queen. Her comics resembled a huge collection of pin-ups and paper doll cut-outs. In this way it was hoped that Katy Keene would be able to satisfy the needs of both young boys and girls. Katy was a refugee from the Archie series, and she brought to her strip a raw-edged innocence which seemed to make everything look like sunshine and roses. Besides Katy Keene, the 1940s produced the epitome of pin-up girl comics in Bill Ward's Torchy.

In 1943, while a private at Fort Hamilton in New York, Bill Ward created a beguiling creature he named Torchy, the Blonde Bombshell. The idea met with such a favorable response from the servicemen that after the war Bill Ward went to peddle his beautiful, shapely and sweet creation to the comic book market. Torchy was picked by Quality as a supporting feature in *Modern Comics* as well as in *Dollman*. Eventually she was given her own bok. This lasted for only six issues. The question of whether or not the public was ready for a return to the beautiful but not very wise principal character was never fully resolved. Torchy remains, however, a symbol of the ideal American woman in the good girl art period. She was a classic example of what Philip Wylie was talking about in his non-fiction book *A Generation of Vipers*. There was a certain fixation on breasts and female accessories that was overt in this period. Many people believe this stems from an underlying feeling of guilt and apprehension in regard to competition from women at this time. In these comics cheesecake was something you looked at. The main examples of this type of role for women in comics was a fetishist's dream. Negligee and unmentionables were as common as word balloons.

Another version of the pin-ups

Lingerie scene from Blue Beetle No. 48, 1947, © Fox

were the bobby-sox comics. In books like *Betty & Veronica, Patsy Walker, Ginger, A Date With Judy* and *Sunny* among others, sexuality worms its way onto nearly every page. Often the covers of the books themselves present a crazy double entendre making a game out of the courting ritual. The "cheesecake" cover on *Patsy Walker* #71 and Al Feldstein's work for Fox *Meet Corliss Archer, Junior* can serve as prime examples. Many more times, stories were concerned with the proper development of relationships with the opposite sex. These comics attempted to define the role of the teenager in society. They were produced with the idea of encouraging readers to form a peer group identity. Some of these comics contained fashion hints and techniques for applying make-up. The effect of this adolescent

Patsy Walker No. 71, 1957, ©MCG,
Cheesecake cover.

Willie No. 15, 1948, ©MCG

coaching was seemingly designed to give young women a chance to experience social norms second-hand.

The development of the heroine in comic books can be traced back to Fiction House. Primarily a publishing concern involved with the production of pulp magazines, Fiction House turned its attention to the comic book field in the key year 1938. This was a transitional year which saw the birth of super-hero comics when Superman appeared as the lead story of *Action Comics* No. 1. This year also signaled the rise in popularity that the comic medium would be exposed to in the next decade.

With the explosion of super-hero type comics in the 1940s, Fiction House was able to ride the crest of the wave and transfer many of its pulp titles and characters into comics such as *Fight, Planet, Wings* and *Jungle*. Their initial 1938 effort, *Jumbo*

Comics, interestingly enough, had nothing whatsoever to do with their previous pulp titles. Rather, this comic was an anthology-format, black & white illustrated, oversized magazine—literally a jumbo comic—which featured a jungle heroine named Sheena. The credit

Jumbo No. 94, 1946, ©FH.
Classic Sheena cover.

or this initial female hero goes to Fiction House's art director, Jerry Iger, and a talented artist named Will Eisner. At that time they were not sure of the reaction that Sheena, Queen of the Jungle, would receive. The strip was to last through 1953 in *Jumbo Comics* with Sheena getting her own quarterly comic in 1942.

Sheena was the first of a huge number of jungle heroines who would find their way onto the pages of comics in the 1940s and 1950s. Exotic personalities like Camilla, Tiger Girl, South Sea Girl, Zegra, Princess Pantha, Tegra, Rulah, Jann of the Jungle, Cave Girl, Kara, Judy of the Jungle, White Princess, Saari the Jungle Goddess, Lorna, Jungle Lil and Nyoka the Jungle Girl created enough activity in and around the jungle to make people wonder about the term "monkey business." Not all these jungle women were found swinging under the Fiction House banner, yet even as an Avon or Fox character these jungle girls still responded to the same stimuli, had basic rules of conduct and used similar settings in which to perform their feats of heroism. Images of long flowing hair, flashing blades, exotic environments and delicately skimpy costumes epitomized the jungle girl comics. Most of the plots were the same. They all seemed to revolve around the ritual of protection rather than an active interest in solving crimes. The jungle heroine was not an avenger or crime-fighter. Rather, she attempted to protect the elements of her environment from contaminating outside influences and self-generated perils. The growth of women as major heroines did not stop with the jungle girl.

By the early 1940s, the Second World War was in full swing. Fiction House, as well as a number of other comic book publishers, was able to capitalize on this

Tiger Girl from cover of Fight Comics No. 59, 1948, © FH

South Sea Girl from Seven Seas No. 1, 1946, © Universal Phoenix. Art by Matt Baker.

From the cover of White Princess of the Jungle No. 2, 1951, © Avon

unfortunate situation in their various books. In this period most comics were given a patriotic sensibility. Not only would soldiers be reading comic books as a main source of entertainment on the front, but people at home were able to experience the brutalities of war on a vicarious level.

It was in this emotionally charged atmosphere that a number of adventure heroines cropped up. Aside from the obvious superheroines to be discussed later in this essay, female stars such as Canteen Kate, Futura, Senorita Rio, Jane Arden of the Space Patrol, Firehair, and Mysta of the Moon dealt with patriotic themes while maintaining the consistent integrity of their strips. There was a great deal of national pride put into the creation of these heroines. They were to serve their publishers on a number of levels. Initially they were used as divertisement for the soldiers—the pin-up style of Matt Baker, Fran Hopper, Bob Powell and Lily Renee was well received

Senorita Rio from a mid-forties Fight Comics, © FH

and well appreciated by the service man. These characters were also responsible for changing the attitudes of comic readers in regard to the role of women in comics.

But as the role of women became more active, the anti-heroine began to appear on the scene. This development draws from a number of the above mentioned groups only, in this case, the woman was seen as a villain rather than a hero. There are literally hundreds of these villainesses that emerged in the comics of the period. As early as 1936 in *New Comics,* H. Rider Haggard's classic fatale woman, She, was given comic book life. It was always more interesting to be threatened by a woman. For one thing it pointed to the weakness ound in all men. It also showed that the truly virtuous hero could withstand almost any temptation. Milton Caniff refined the image of the villainess in *Terry and the Pirates* with his remarkable Dragon Lady—an exotic, mysterious and utterly captivating personality. The Human Torch has as a nemesis at one time a creation dubbed the Asbestos Lady. There were a host of Mata Hari-like spies who tried their best to undermind the solid foundations of patriotism exhibited in American comics during the war. Names like Illyria—Queen of All Spies, The Spider Queen, Madam Satan all point to a kind of imagery which sets these women up as vamps or evil personified.

The most abundant use of the femme fatale was found in Eisner's *The Spirit*. With characters like Sand Saref, Throne Strand, P'Gell, Silk Satin, Castenet, Agent Cosmek, The Black Queen, Powder Pouf, Flaxen Weaver and a score of others, Eisner was able to extend

Silk Satin from The Spirit No. 18, 1949, © **Will Eisner**

the limits of the fatale woman. His vivid characters were designed to work off the personality profile of Denny Colt, the Spirit. They were aggressive, vicious, beautiful to look at and ultimately ruthless. Eisner himself when commenting on the Black Queen realized the difference between the heroine and the arch villainess: "Exotic female villains were not new. I had grown up on Caniff's Dragon Lady and those that often inhabited the more way-out pulps. This was an effort, the first in many, to produce an interesting (and sexy) female villain. The Black Queen was compounded of all the fantasies that I thought would stir my readers. . . .I had Sheena, Queen of the Jungle, which I had created for the Fiction House line a few years earlier, do a lot of manhandling. This was the same in reverse."

Going beyond the creation of classy villainesses, many comics of the period were happy to deal generically with the concept of female villains. Comics like *Women*

Dragon Lady from cover of Terry & The Pirates No. 3, 1947, © **News Synd.**

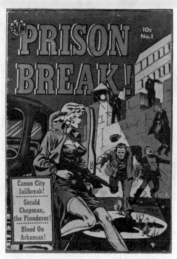

Prison Break! No. 1, 1951, © Avon. Wallace Wood cover art.

Outlaws, Crimes By Women, Gangsters and Gun Molls, Reform School Girl and scores of various crime comics with women depicted boldly on the cover reinforced this association. Sex and violence was not new to the American scene. It had been around for a number of years in pulps, on film and in much of the contemporary literature of the Twentieth Century. The concepts of bondage, torture, dominance, girl-fights, the use of the knife and gun, the femme fatale and the embrace of love and death—all Freudian elements—combines to give comic books an image of perverse sexuality. The role of women in these comics, generally found in the post-war period, is as murderess or totally evil. A classic example of this type of role can be seen in "The Widow of Death" in *Underworld True Crime Stories* No. 3. In this grotesque story a woman murders nearly a person per page (sometimes more). If this action itself were not enough, the artist

decided to show the murders in th most graphic way (axes chunkin into bodies, etc.). The point to b made from all this is not that thes comics are a bad influence o youth or that they form a distorte picture of reality. That is a questio which can never be answere adequately enough. Rather, thes comics point to a vision o American society whose corruptio knew no bounds. No one was saf from the influence of violence an decay lying below the surface of relatively calm environment.

Broadway Romances No. 1, 1950, © Qua Bill Ward cover art.

One way to escape from the realities presented in these crime comics was with love and romance strips. Here again the image of women is protracted to totally idealized limits. This is a major area in which women were used as the major character. Their thoughts and emotions were supposedly laid bare in the pages of these confession and true romance books. A large percentage of these love comics were banal. They merely served their purpose of providing material

Campus Loves No. 1, 1950, © Qua
Bill Ward cover art.

Teen-Age Romances No. 18, 1951, © STJ
Matt Baker cover art.

for an audience willing to suspend their disbelief and escape into the dreams and wish-fulfillments accomplished by the romance books.

However there is enough input by talented artists such as Kubert *(Hollywood Confessions)*, Crandall *(Range Romance)*, Frazetta *(Personal Love)*, Kirby *(Young Romance)*, Ward *(Heart Throbs)*, Matt Baker *(Teen-Age Temptations)*, Wallace Wood *(My Secret Romance)* and Al Feldstein *(Modern Love)* that the subject should be covered. It is strange that at the time of this writing there are no romance books published by any comic book line since at one time they formed an integral part of the comic book field. Many of the pre-trend E. C. comics had a romance origin. Books like *A Moon, A Girl. . .Romance, Modern Love* and *Saddle Romances* segue into titles like *Weird Fantasy* and *Weird Science*. Artists such as Matt Baker found a perfect outlet for their aesthetic abilities in romance comics. The effect is stunning when

seen in perspective.

Overall, romance and love books prove to be dull. Yet taken on an individual basis they provide an interesting direction for women in comics. The temperament, personality, fashion styles, pent-up desires and frustrations of American women can be found in these comics. They are as vital a category as women as heroines, only in the case of romance books the action takes place between the panels, not in them.

Art Amsie's last category, women as costumed heroines, is both an obvious and intensely complex group to deal with. It is almost like dipping into Pandora's Box of complications when trying to unravel the threads that hold the subject of women in comics together. A major emphasis on the problem-solving capability of women is a natural lead-in to the subject of heroines. This perspective forms the core of this classification. In looking to popular American culture, it is easy to see a tradition of heroism which explodes from the pages of books and magazines throughout American fiction. The sheer number of adventurers, pioneers, soldiers, explorers, leaders and rascals that make up this body of heroes managed to give America a fabricated, yet functional mythology. By the time comic books were producing original material to satisfy the large number of depression-age patrons, it was only natural that a new army of heroes would be created to fill the void. The situation was not male dominated, with numerous real and fictional female characters being canonized in the pages of comic after comic.

At this point there is a distinction that should be made between the heroine and the super-heroine. Where can the line be drawn between these two vital forces? Are they really two separate entities? The problem lies in the means rather than the ends. Both characters accomplish feats of bravery, both serve as champions. One may have a secret identity. One may wear a flashy costume. Various powers may be used in supernatural ways. Even though the issue might remain floundering in a sea of controversy, it is important to point out some critical differences between the plain heroine and the superheroine.

Throwing redundancy to the wind, one can define superheroines as characters possessing, by some supernatural power, a unique quality or ability. The goals of these superheroines can be met as part of their birthright (Supergirl), by rigorous training (as in the case of Wonder Woman), or through the use of distinguishable costumes, the assumption of an alter ego, or the manipulation of a talisman or magical phrase. The superheroine serves as an avenger solving crimes and fighting evil wherever it can be found. The difference with the plain heroine rests in the fact that she deals with problems faced in her own environment. She does not transcend the ability of her mortality to combat her foes. The plain heroine's exploits are not precipitated from a need to overcome crime but rather to protect and defend her own existence. The superheroine is an active crimefighter. The plain heroine, for the most part, is most passive. Indeed, there are numerous crossovers in regard to these simplistic standards. The point that must be stressed is that, regardless of the means used in justifying their particular adventures, both the heroine and the superheroine perform the same function.

One costumed heroine comic that actually stood out in relation to the more conventional female heroes of the time was Fox's

Phantom Lady from P.L. No. 15, 1947, ©DC(Fox)

Sandra Knight (Phantom Lady) from
P.L. No. 15, 1947, © DC(Fox)

outrageous Phantom Lady series.
The strip was started in 1947 by
Matt Baker. Initially the comic
lasted for ten issues. Baker's
artwork is a classic example of good
girl art. Phantom Lady's female
form is given a flawless
representation throughout the
series. Many of the covers for the
strip were outstanding, depicting
Phantom Lady prominently in the
foreground menaced, tortured or
bound and threatened. The action
in the comic was swift and the
layout of the panels was anything
but conventional.

This visual flamboyance was
characteristic of Matt Baker's style.
He went to work for the Iger
studios in the mid-Forties
producing a number of classic
heroine strips. He died ten years
later, at the age of 36, of a
rheumatic heart condition. In the
few years that he produced comics,
he was a prolific and exquisite
craftsman. Not only did he work on
Phantom Lady, but he was
responsible for the beautiful South
Sea Girl for *Seven Seas Comics*,
Tiger Girl, Sky Girl, Mitzi in *Movie
Comics* and numerous romance
comics. He even had time to do the
Classics Illustrated version of *Lorna
Doone* complete with magnificently
drawn women and men. His women
were the ultimate comic book
heroines—stylish, effervescent and
proud.

Another artist distinguished in
the field of superheroine comics
was Tarpe Mills. Her contribution
to the genre was the totally unique
and fascinating M i s s F u r y.
Originally a comic strip created in
the early 1940s, the drama of Miss
Fury was chronicled in a series of
eight reprint comics published by
Timely Comics from 1942 to 1946.
Miss Fury was actually a Brazilian
heiress who inherited a costume of
black panther skin endowned with
supernatural powers. The use of the
powerful panther skin is ironic, for
with every good deed it also
b r o u g h t t w o misfortunes.
Regardless of this melodramatic
situation, Tarpe Mills created an
incredible cast of characters to
revolve around the adventures of

Miss Fury from cover of M.F. No. 7,
1946, © Tarpe' Mills

Miss Fury. The major part of the comic saw Miss Fury in and out of her street clothes as Marla Drake. The villainess of the strip was the beautiful and ruthless adventuress Erica Von Kampf. A totally absorbing personality, Erica was a striking image with her blonde bangs cut in a triangular shape to conceal the swastika branded on her forehead.

the Brazilian bombshell guerilla. It was this type of sensibility coupled with the creative drive of a highly independent woman artist that made Miss Fury a unique entity in the comics.

The subject of superheroines is equally as large. The majority of them functioned during the war years rather than after them. The credit for the first truly popular

Miss Fury receives her skin, from M.F. No. 3, 1944, © **Tarpe' Mills**

Miss Fury was a curious blend of heroine and superheroine comics. The entire ambiance of the strip was dreamlike in its simplicity, the dialogue was straightforward and quite mature. Reading Miss Fury was almost like watching a movie. Part of this is due, certainly, to Tarpe Mills' (pronounced Tarp/a) contributions as both writer and artist. Originally a high fashion model, the beautiful Tarpe Mills suddenly switched gears and became a comic strip artist. Miss Fury was not her only contribution to the world of comics. During the 1940s she also produced an adventure strip entitled "The Purple Zombie" as well as the exotic "Mann of India." Neither of these matched the quality and sophistication of storytelling found in Miss Fury. In order to give a bit more panache to the comics, Tarpe Mills included paper dolls of Marla Drake, Erika Von Kampf and Era,

superheroine must go to psychologist William Moulton Marston and artist Harry G. Peters. In 1941 they collaborated to create a race of Amazons epitomized by Wonder Woman. Her first appearance was in *All-Star Comics* No. 8. Wonder Woman then appeared in *Sensation Comics* No. 1 in January 1942, followed by her

Introduction of Wonder Woman from All-Star No. 8, 1941, © **DC**

Lynda Carter, TV Wonder Woman.

Wonder Woman as a ravashing beauty bursting with sexual vitality, there was a strange attitude of perverse sexuality which surfaced in the characterizations of Wonder Woman's various foes ("Eet ees always best to keep a strong man under lock and key"–*Sensation Comics* No. 40). Wonder Woman as a character remained ambivalent to sexual advances. The real sexual aberration was found in the concepts of dominance and bondage used by her adversaries.

Times changed and Wonder Woman changed along with them. This is reflected in the visual style of the strip. From Peters' almost primitive style to the clean Milton Caniff-inspired work of Ross Andru and Mike Esposito, the character of Wonder Woman remained virtually the same. Then during the consciousness-raising period of the Woman's Liberation media influx, Wonder Woman became a jump-suited secret agent. This phase of her career lasted for nearly twenty issues. She later returned as the familiar costumed superheroine, only by this time television had picked up Wonder Woman as a property. The setting had eventually been returned to the period of the Second World War and Wonder Woman was turned full circle to begin again where she started thirty-odd years earlier. At this time the comic artists working on the strip gave Wonder Woman the physical attributes of her television counterpart, Lynda Carter. After several decades and changes the Amazon Princess was finally given a womanly figure. She had hips and filled out her bodice with an intensity which harkened back to the period of good girl art.

Very few superheroines could be affected by society for as long a

own magazine in the summer of that same year. Beyond this historical significance, Wonder Woman can be seen as one of the few comic book characters, super-hero of otherwise, which managed to survive the strains of the publishing world continuously for the past 35 years.

Wonder Woman came into being as a response on the part of the dedicated publishers to give their girl readers the same articulator of wish fulfillment that boys were finding in various male superheroes. As Peters saw her, Wonder Woman was an ageless personality, not an idealized female like Sheena but rather gifted with a mature appearance. Although the strip was not designed to showcase

period as Wonder Woman was. Most were ephemeral, granted a short-lived career in which to leave their mark on comic book history. Druing the war all sorts of super women were summoned to fight America's enemies. Characters like Liberty Belle, Commandette, Miss

Liberty Belle from Star Spangled No. 28, 1944, ©DC

Victory, Yankee Girl, Miss Masque, USA—the Spirit of Old Glory, Pat Parker and the Girl Commandos, Miss America and others were constantly on the hunt for foreign spies as well as attempting to spoil

Miss Masque from America's Best No. 26, 1948, ©BP

the plot of the Axis forces. What was left of the superheroines after the war is still interesting.

It is a fact of comic book life that many superheroines were created to serve as supporting characters for already well-established superheroes

Kitten from Cat-Man No. 8, 1942, ©Hoke

Catman had Kitten. Dollman shared the spotlight with Dollgirl. Rocket Man was always rescuing Rocket Girl. The same pattern seemed to take shape with Bulletman and Bulletgirl. Hawkman was actually

Namora from Namora No. 1, 1948, ©MCG. Art by Bill Everett.

Bulletgirl from Bulletman No. 2, 1941, ©DC(Faw)

married to Hawkgirl. A small percentage of these supporting superheroines were able to graduate into their own books (Mary Marvel and Namora).

The costumed heroines who had their own strips, either in their own books or as back-up features, were prominent mostly in the post-war period. It was here that the likes of Sun Girl, Moon Girl, Black Cat, Black Canary, Blonde Phantom, Lady Luck, Venus, and Pat Patriot could be found. Although a prolific part of the heroine scene, these characters never really caught on in the popular sense of Wonder Woman or Sheena. These heroines had adventures that were interesting but lacked the abundance of action that characterized the male superhero comics.

A brief look at the contemporary use of women in comics can serve as a good example of the changing attitudes of American culture. Disregarding Kurtzman and Elder's Little Annie Fanny, in the past few years a number of new female

Black Cat from Black Cat No. 5, 1947, ©Harv

Lady Luck from Lady Luck No. 86, 1949, ©Will Eisner

Pat Patriot from Daredevil No. 4, 1941, © Lev

Blonde Phantom from All Winners No. 1, 1948, © MCG

superheroines and barbarians have been entered into the canon of comic book characters. There was an attempt to bring back Sheena as Shanna by Marvel Comics in 1972. This was followed by another creature known as The Cat, drawn by Wally Wood. DC worked up a beautiful creation called The Black Orchid which flew through the pages of Adventure comics so fast that many readers missed the entire three issue series. Even an attempt to adapt Hudson's classic *Green Mansions* as *Rima, The Jungle Girl* never truly got off the ground. More recently there has been an

The Cat No. 1, 1972, © MCG

Shanna No. 2, 1972, © MCG

Adventure No. 428, 1973, © DC (Black Orchid)

Starfire No. 7, 1977, © DC

avalanche of women in comics. Marvel has come out with Ms. Marvel and Red Sonja. DC has countered with Isis and Starfire. Supergirl, whose initial ten issue series failed a few years ago, is making a comeback as Powergirl. And in a moment of crazed inspiration Marvel is bringing out Spiderwoman. It certainly appears that women are experiencing a renaissance in terms of comic book exposure. Even Charlton tried their hand at producing a Bionic Woman comic. The odd thing about all this is that only one of these comics is written by a woman (*Red Sonja,* and that is only co-written by Clara Noto with Roy Thomas). Most of the people who buy these comics are not women. They just like to stare at the pretty pictures.

It is obvious that there is enough material to go on indefinitely on the subject of women in comics. It is an area that

has been given only a select scrutiny. In looking at these comics an attempt has been made to focus on a few outstanding characters, either in terms of artistic rendering or cultural significance. The whole story has not been told. There are still many avenues to explore in relation to the field of women in comics. It is hoped that this article will provide a starting point in order to fully explore the subject. The interrelationships between pulp characters like The Domino Lady and Margaret Brudage's erotic *Weird Tales* covers haven't even been discussed. Nell Brinkley's pert tabloid flappers and the pinup art of Zoe Mozert, Petty and Varga are still another influence. There is much to appreciate in regard to women in comics. All it takes is a point of view and the ability to find relevance in the simplest of characters and situations.

Tarpe' Mills.....An Appreciation

by Trina Robbins

Even as a kid I knew quality when I saw it—knew that the Sunday Spirit section was the best thing going in my local paper, and ate up every comic with a female protagonist, from Invisible Scarlet O'Neil to Moon Girl. So it's a wonder I missed Miss Fury. There must have been no New York papers that carried her.

I have since made up for the lost time. Several summers ago at a New York comic art convention, someone told me that if I liked superheroines I'd LOVE Miss Fury, and the search began. First I acquired some Sunday quarter pages, just enough to whet my appetite, and soon I had the comic books—numbers one through seven. When I finally bought a run of Sunday pages that brought me from 1945 through 1947, I stayed up all night reading them.

Tarpe Mills spins a yarn unequalled by anyone in comics but Eisner. She combines the drama and suspense of an excellent World War II movie with intriguing characterization and a chic, dashing style that is feminine without being weak or "cutesy," an unfortunately common fault with many women cartoonists.

If I were casting Mills' characters (a hobby of mine—for instance, Eisner's Sand Sareef is definitely Lauren Bacall while Silk Satin is Ingrid Bergman), I'd give Marlene Dietrich the role of Baroness Erica Von Kampf, probably the most outstanding character in the Miss Fury epic. As usual, the bad girls are much more interesting that the good ones, and Miss Fury herself—Marla Drake—pales beside the platinum-haired adventuress, her pointed bangs concealing a swastika branded on her forehead.

For the one-armed German General Bruno, with whom Erica has a love-hate relationship, Mills seems to have presaged Yul Brynner, although he could easily have been based on Eric Von Stroheim. It's disturbing to find oneself liking this ruthless Prussian, until we remember Rommel, and the fact that the German military had no love for Hitler; indeed, that a bunch of Generals tried to assassinate him. True to form, when Bruno foresees the war as already lost, he is prepared to break with Hitler and make a separate peace in order to save what is left of his country.

Mills has a female view of male characters and creates some that I, as a woman, find irresistable. Probably her most interesting good guy is Albino Jo, the college-educated albino Brazilian Indian.

No appreciation of Tarpe Mills could fail to include her great feel for fashion. It is possible to document what the most stylish women were wearing in the Forties just by studying Miss Fury. And it's refreshing to find in Mills a cartoonist and a woman, fascinated by tales of adventure and espionage, yet who never gave up her girlhood love of paper dolls.

Men may find in Miss Fury lots of action and good girl art. I find in her a long lost sister.

The correct title listing for each comic book can be determined by consulting the indicia (publication data) on the beginning interior pages of the comic. The official title is determined by those words of the title in capital letters only, and not by what is on the cover.

Titles are listed in this book as if they were one word, ignoring spaces, hyphens, and apostrophes, to make finding titles easier.

A-1 (See A-One)

ABBIE AN' SLATS (--With Becky #1-4) (See Fight for Love, Treasury of Comics, & United 1940 - 1948 (Reprints)   Comics) United Features Syndicate

	Good	Fine	Mint
Single Series #25,28('40)	8.00	16.00	24.00
#1(1947)	3.00	6.00	9.00
2-4: #3 reprints from Sparkler #68-72			
	2.00	4.00	6.00

ABBOTT AND COSTELLO (--Comics)
1948 - 56 (Mort Drucker art in most issues)
St. John Publishing Co.

#1	4.00	8.00	12.00
2-9	2.50	5.00	7.50
10-Kubert art	3.00	6.00	9.00
11-20	1.35	2.75	4.00
21-30	1.00	2.00	3.00
31-40	.65	1.35	2.00
3-D #1 (11/53)	4.00	8.00	12.00

ABBOTT AND COSTELLO (TV)
Feb, 1968 - #22, Aug, 1971 (Hanna-Barbera)
Charlton Comics

#1	.25	.50	.75
2-10	.15	.35	.50
11-22		.20	.35

ABC (See America's Best TV Comics)

ABRAHAM LINCOLN LIFE STORY
1958 (25¢)
Dell Publishing Co.

#1	2.00	4.00	6.00

ABSENT-MINDED PROFESSOR, THE (See 4-Color Comics #1199)

ACE COMICS
April, 1937 - #151, Oct-Nov, 1949
David McKay Publications

#1-Jungle Jim by Alex Raymond, Krazy Kat			
begin	55.00	110.00	165.00
2	20.00	40.00	60.00
3-5	15.00	30.00	45.00
6-10	10.00	20.00	30.00

	Good	Fine	Mint
11-The Phantom begins	10.00	20.00	30.00
12-25	8.00	16.00	24.00
26-Origin Prince Valiant-30.00	60.00	90.00
27-30	6.00	12.00	18.00
31-40: #37-Krazy Kat ends-5.00	10.00	15.00
41-50	4.00	8.00	12.00
51-60	3.00	6.00	9.00
61-90	2.75	5.50	8.25
91-100	2.00	4.00	6.00
101-127	1.75	3.50	5.25
128-Brick Bradford begins	1.50	3.00	4.50
129-133	1.50	3.00	4.50
134-Last Prince Valiant	1.50	3.00	4.50
135-The Lone Ranger begins-1.50	3.00	4.50
136-151	1.50	3.00	4.50

ACE KELLY (See Tops Comics)

ACES HIGH
Mar-Apr, 1955 - #5, Nov-Dec, 1955
E.C. Comics

#1	8.00	16.00	24.00
2-5	5.00	10.00	15.00

NOTE: *All have stories by Davis, Evans, Krigstein, & Wood; Evans covers #1-5.*

ACTION ADVENTURE (War)
June, 1955 - #4, Oct, 1955
Gillmore Magazines

V1#2-4	.50	1.00	1.50

ACTION COMICS
June, 1938 - Present
National Per. Publ./Detective Comics

#1-Origin & 1st app. Superman by Siegel & Shuster, Marco Polo, Tex Thompson, Pep Morgan, Chuck Dawson & Scoop Scanlon; intro. Zatara; reprinted in Famous 1st Edition. Superman story is missing 4 pgs. which was included when reprinted in Superman #1.   1875.00 4687.50 7500.00
          (Prices vary widely on this book)
#1(1976)Soft cover, 16pgs. in color; reprints complete Superman story from #1('38)
(Giveaway)	1.00	2.00	3.00
2	600.00	1200.00	1800.00
3 (Scarce)	450.00	900.00	1350.00
4	300.00	600.00	900.00
5 (Rare)	450.00	900.00	1350.00

6-1st app. Jimmy Olsen (called office boy)
	250.00	500.00	750.00
7,10-Superman covers	250.00	500.00	750.00
8,9	225.00	450.00	675.00

11,12,14:#14-Clip Carson begins, ends #41

Single Series #25. © UFS

Abbott & Costello =25. © STJ

Ace Comics =13. © DMP

1

Action Comics #1, © DC

Action Comics #18, © DC

Action Comics #48, © DC

(Action Comics cont'd)	Good	Fine	Mint
	110.00	220.00	330.00
13-Superman cover; last Scoop Scanlon			
	150.00	300.00	450.00
15-Superman cover	125.00	250.00	375.00
16	80.00	160.00	240.00
17-Superman cover; last Marco Polo			
	80.00	160.00	240.00
18-Origin 3 Aces	60.00	120.00	180.00
19,20-Superman covers	70.00	140.00	210.00
21,22,24,25	40.00	80.00	120.00
23-1st app. Luthor & Black Pirate by Moldoff			
	50.00	100.00	150.00
26-30	25.00	50.00	75.00
31,32	20.00	40.00	60.00
33-Origin Mr. America	25.00	50.00	75.00
34-40: #37-Origin Congo Bill. #40-Last Black			
Pirate	20.00	40.00	60.00
41	20.00	40.00	60.00
42-Origin Vigilante; Bob Daley becomes Fatman; Black Pirate ends	22.50	45.00	67.50
43-50: Intro. Stuff #45	15.00	30.00	45.00
51	12.00	24.00	36.00
52-Fatman & Mr. America become the Americommandos; origin Vigilante retold			
	15.00	30.00	45.00
53-60: #56-Last Fatman. #58-Kubert Vigilante begins, ends #70	12.00	24.00	36.00
61-70: #63-Last 3 Aces	10.00	20.00	30.00
71-80: #74-Last Mr. America. #80-2nd app. Mr. Mxyztplk	8.00	16.00	24.00
81-90	7.00	14.00	21.00
91-100	6.50	13.00	19.50
101-120	6.00	12.00	18.00
121-130: #127-Vigilante by Kubert; Tommy Tomorrow begins	5.00	10.00	15.00
131-160: #135,136,138-Zatara by Kubert			
	4.00	8.00	12.00
161-180	3.00	6.00	9.00
181-200: #191-Intro. Janu in Congo Bill. #198-Last Vigilante	2.50	5.00	7.50
201-230: #224-1st Golden Gorilla story			
	2.00	4.00	6.00
231-251: #242-Origin & 1st app. Brainiac(7/58). #248-Congo Bill becomes Congorilla. #251-Last Tommy Tomorrow	1.50	3.00	4.50
252-Origin & 1st app. Supergirl and Metallo			
	10.00	20.00	30.00
253,255-260	1.35	2.75	4.00
254-2nd app. Bizarro, 1st Bizarro World story			
	2.00	4.00	6.00
261-270: #261-Last Congorilla; origin Streaky the Super Cat	1.00	2.00	3.00
271-290: #276-1st app. Brainiac 5. #280-Congorilla app.	.80	1.60	2.40
291-300: #292-1st Superhorse. #293-Origin Comet	.65	1.35	2.00
301-320	.50	1.00	1.50

	Good	Fine	Mint
321-340: #334-Giant G-20 (Origin Supergirl)			
	.40	.80	1.20
(80 pg. Giant G-20)	.65	1.35	2.00
341-360: #347-Giant Supergirl G-33; #360-Giant Supergirl G-45	.35	.70	1.05
(80 pg. Giant G-33, G-45)	.50	1.00	1.50
361-380: #373-Giant Supergirl G-57; #376-Last Supergirl in Action. #377-Legion begins			
	.30	.60	.90
(80 pg. Giant G-57)	.40	.80	1.20
381-402: #392-Last Legion in Action. #393-402-All Superman issues	.20	.40	.60
403-420: #403-1st app 52pg. ish; last #413. #411-Origin Eclipso(reprt.). #413-Last 25¢ ish; Metamorpho begins; ends #418. #419-Intro. Human Target	.20	.40	.60
421-424: #422&423-Origin Human Target; Green Arrow app. #421,424	.15	.30	.45
425-Adams art; Atom begins	.50	1.00	1.50
426-436,438-442,444-448,450	.15	.30	.45
437,443-100pg. Giants	.35	.70	1.05
449-68pg. ish	.30	.60	.90
451-460: #455-Last Green Arrow			
	.15	.30	.45
461-470: #467-Last Atom	.15	.30	
471-480	.15	.30	
U.S. Navy Giveaway #1 (1944)-Regular comic format	20.00	40.00	60.00
--Special Edition #2(1944)-U.S. Navy Giveaway (68 pgs.) Regular comic format			
	20.00	40.00	60.00

NOTE: *Supergirl's origin in #262,280,285,291, 305,309. Adams covers-#356,358,359,361-64, 366,367,370-74,377-79 (inks), 398-400,402, 404-06,419,466,468,473. Infantino covers- #396,397; stories-#419,437. Bob Kane's Clip Carson-#14-41. Meskin art-#42-121 (most). Toth stories-#406,407,413.*

ACTION MINIATURE
1946
National Periodical Publications

No#-Vigilante story based on movie serial			
	5.00	10.00	15.00

ACTUAL CONFESSIONS (Formerly Love Adventures)
#13, October, 1952
Atlas Comics (MPI)

#13	.35	.70	1.05

ACTUAL ROMANCES
Oct, 1949 - #2, 1949 (52 pgs.)
Marvel Comics (IPS)

#1	1.00	2.00	3.00
2	.50	1.00	1.50

ADAM AND EVE
1975
Spire Christian Comics (Fleming H. Revell Co.)

	Good	Fine	Mint
By Al Hartley	.15	.30	.45

ADAM-12 (TV)
Dec, 1973 - #10, Feb, 1976
Gold Key

#1	.20	.40	.60
2-10		.20	.30

ADDAMS FAMILY (TV)
Oct, 1974 - #3, Apr, 1975 (Hanna-Barbera)
Gold Key

#1-3	.20	.40	.60

ADLAI STEVENSON
Dec, 1966
Dell Publishing Co.

#12-007-612-Life story	1.50	3.00	4.50

ADULT TALES OF TERROR ILL. (See Terror Ill.)

ADVENTURE BOUND (See 4-Color Comics #239)

ADVENTURE COMICS (Formerly New Adventure)
#31, Oct, 1938 - Present
National Periodical Publications

	Good	Fine	Mint
#31	15.00	30.00	45.00

32-39: #32-Anchors Aweigh (ends #52), Barry
   O'Neil (ends #60, not in #33), Captain
   Desmo (ends #47), Dale Daring (ends #57),
   Federal Men (ends #70), The Golden Dragon
   (ends #36), Rusty & His Pals (ends #52)
   by Bob Kane, Todd Hunter (ends #38) and
   Tom Brent (ends #39) begin; #39-Jack Wood
   begins, ends #42.   12.00 24.00 36.00
40-Intro. & 1st app. The Sandman. Socko
   Strong begins, ends #54
                               125.00 250.00 375.00

41	35.00	70.00	105.00

42-47: #47-Steve Conrad Adventurer begins,
   ends #76   25.00 50.00 75.00
48-Origin & 1st app. The Hourman by Bernard
   Baily   125.00 250.00 375.00

49,50	27.50	55.00	82.50

51-60: #53-Intro. Jimmy "Minuteman" Martin
   & the Minutemen of America in Hourman;
   ends #78. #58-Paul Kirk Manhunter begins,
   ends #72   27.50 55.00 82.50
61-Intro. & 1st app. Starman by Jack Burnley
                               90.00 180.00 270.00

62-65	30.00	60.00	90.00

	Good	Fine	Mint
66-Origin Shining Knight	35.00	70.00	105.00
67-Origin Mist	30.00	60.00	90.00
68	27.50	55.00	82.50

69-Intro. Sandy the Golden Boy (Sandman's
   sidekick); Sandman dons new costume
                               30.00 60.00 90.00

70-Last Federal Men	25.00	50.00	75.00

71-Jimmy Martin becomes costume aide to the
   Hourman   27.50 55.00 82.50
72-1st Simon & Kirby Sandman
                               85.00 170.00 255.00
73-Origin Manhunter by Simon & Kirby; begin
   new series   90.00 180.00 270.00
74-Thorndyke replaces Jimmy, Hourman's
   Assistant   40.00 80.00 120.00

75,76	40.00	80.00	120.00

77-Origin Genius Jones; Mist story
                               40.00 80.00 120.00
78-80-Last Simon & Kirby Manhunter & Burnley
   Starman   40.00 80.00 120.00
81-90: #83-Last Hourman. #84-Mike Gibbs begins, ends #102   22.50 45.00 67.50
91,92-Last Manhunter & Simon & Kirby Sandman
                               20.00 40.00 60.00
93-102-Last Starman, Sandman, & Genius Jones.
   Most-S&K covers   10.00 20.00 30.00
103-Aquaman, Green Arrow, Johnny Quick, Superboy begin   15.00 30.00 45.00

104-110	10.00	20.00	30.00
111-120	7.00	14.00	21.00
121-130	5.00	10.00	15.00

131-140: #132-Shining Knight 1st return to
   King Arthur time; origin aide Sir Butch
                               4.00   8.00 12.00

141-149	3.00	6.00	9.00

150,151,153,155,157,159,161,163-All have 6pg.
   Shining Knight stories by Frank Frazetta
                               12.00 24.00 36.00
152,154,156,158,160,162,164-166-Last Shining
   Knight   3.00   6.00   9.00

167-200	2.50	5.00	7.50
201-220	2.25	4.50	6.75

221-246,248-250: #207-Last Johnny Quick (not
   in #205). #210-1st Krypto app.
                               2.00   4.00   6.00
247-1st Legion of Super Heroes app.
                               12.00 24.00 36.00
251-255: All Kirby Green Arrow. #255-Intro.
   Red Kryptonite in Superboy 2.00   4.00   6.00
256-Origin Green Arrow by Kirby
                               3.00   6.00   9.00

257-259	1.50	3.00	4.50
260-Origin Aquaman	2.00	4.00	6.00

261-270: #262-Origin Speedy in Green Arrow.
   #269-Intro. Aqualad; last Green Arrow (not
   in #206). #270-Congorilla begins, ends

Adventure Comics #39, © DC

Adventure Comics #46, © DC

Adventure Comics #72, © DC

Adventure Comics # 74, © DC   Adventure Into Mystery #5, © MCG   Adventures For Boys #1, © Bailey Ent.

	Good	Fine	Mint
(Adventure Comics cont'd)			
#281,283.	1.25	2.50	3.75
271-280: #275-Origin Superman-Batman team.			
#279-Intro. White Kryptonite in Superboy			
	1.00	2.00	3.00
281-290: #281-Last Congorilla. #282-Intro.			

Star Boy of Legion. #283-Intro. The Phantom Zone. #284-Last Aquaman in Adv. #285-1st Bizarro World story (ends #299) in Adv.-see Action #260. #288,289-Intro. Devin, the Knave from Krypton.

	.80	1.60	2.40
291-299: #294-1st Legion of Super Pets. #299-Last Bizarro World story.	.60	1.20	1.80
300-Legion series begins	1.35	2.75	4.00
301-310: #304-Death of Lightning Lad in Legion. #307-Intro. Element Lad in Legion. #308-Intro. Lightning Lass of Legion	.60	1.20	1.80

311-320: #312-Lightning Lad back in Legion. #315-Last new Superboy story. #317-Intro. Dream Girl in Legion; Lightning Lass becomes Light Lass; Hall of Fame series begins

	.60	1.20	1.80
321-330: #327-Intro. Lone Wolf in Legion	.60	1.20	1.80

331-350: #345-Last Hall of Fame; returns in #356,371. #346-1st app. Karate Kid, Princess Projectra, Ferro Lad, & Nemesis

	.50	1.00	1.50
351-380: #353-Death of Ferro Lad in Legion. #380-Last Legion in Adv.	.35	.70	1.05

381-400: #381-Supergirl begins. #390-Giant Supergirl G-69. #399-Unpubbed G.A. Black Canary story

	.30	.60	.90
(80 pg. Giant G-69)	.50	1.00	1.50
401-410: #403-Giant Legion ish G-81; #409-52pg. ish begins; ends #420	.25	.50	.75
(68pg. Giant G-81)	.50	1.00	1.50

411-416: #412-Animal Man origin reprt/Str. Adv. #180. #413-Hawkman by Kubert; G.A. Robotman reprt/Det. #178. #416-100pg. Giant Supergirl DC-10

	.20	.40	.60
(Giant DC-10)	.40	.80	1.20
417-Morrow Vigilante; Frazetta Shining Knight reprt/Adv. #161.	.35	.70	1.05
418-Black Canary by Toth; unpubbed G.A. Dr. Mid-Nite story	.20	.40	.60
419-Black Canary by Toth & Zatanna story	.20	.40	.60

420-430: #424-Last Supergirl in Adv. #425-New look, content change to adventure; Toth art; origin Capt. Fear. #428-Black Orchid begins, ends #430; Dr. 13 app.

	.20	.40	.60
431-Spectre revived, ends #440; Toth art	.15	.30	.45

	Good	Fine	Mint
432-440: #435-Aquaman begins. #438-Unpubbed 7 Soldiers of Victory begins, ends #443	.15	.30	.45
441-452: #446-The Creeper begins. #452-Aquaman ends	.15	.30	
453-458: #453-Superboy begins	.15	.30	
459 ($1.00 size)	.35	.70	1.05

NOTE: _Legion_ app.-#267,282,290,293. _Vigilante_ app.-#420,426,427. _Adams_ covers-#365-69, 371-73,375-79,381-83. _Infantino_ art-#399, 411,416. _Kaluta_ cover-#425. _Kirby_ art-#250-256. _Kubert_ art-#413. _Meskin_ story-#81. _Morrow_ stories-#413-18,422. _Nino_ art-#432-33. _Orlando_ pencils-#457,458. _Simon/Kirby_ covers-#72-102. _Staton_ story-#456. _Toth_ story-#425.

ADVENTURE COMICS
No date (Early 1940's) Soft cover, 32 pgs.
IGA

Two different issues; Super-Mystery reprints from 1941   10.00   20.00   30.00

ADVENTURE INTO FEAR
1951
Superior Publ. Ltd.

#1	1.35	2.75	4.00

ADVENTURE INTO MYSTERY
May, 1956 - #8, July, 1957
Atlas Comics (OPI #1-7/BFP #8)

#1-Everett cover	1.50	3.00	4.50
2,3,6,8	.65	1.35	2.00
4-Williamson story, 4pgs.	2.50	5.00	7.50
5-Everett cover/story + Orlando story			
	1.00	2.00	3.00
7-Torres story	1.25	2.50	3.75

ADVENTURE IS MY CAREER
1945, 36 pgs.
U.S. Coast Guard Academy/Street & Smith

No #-Simon art	3.00	6.00	9.00

ADVENTURES FOR BOYS
Dec, 1954
Bailey Enterprises

Comics, text, & photos	1.35	2.75	4.00

ADVENTURES IN DISNEYLAND (Giveaway)
1955, 12 pgs. (Dist. by Richfield Oil)
Walt Disney Productions

	2.50	5.00	7.50

4

ADVENTURES IN PARADISE (See 4-Color #1301)

ADVENTURES IN ROMANCE
Nov, 1949   (Slightly large size)
St. John Publishing Co.

	Good	Fine	Mint
#1-Two Leonard Starr stories; Frank Bolle, Warren King art	2.00	4.00	6.00

ADVENTURES IN SCIENCE (See Classics Special)

ADVENTURES IN 3-D
Nov, 1953 - #2, Jan, 1954
Harvey Publications

	Good	Fine	Mint
#1-Nostrand + Powell art, #2-Powell art	4.00	8.00	12.00

ADVENTURES INTO DARKNESS
#5, 1952 - #14, 1954
Better-Standard Publications/Visual Editions

	Good	Fine	Mint
#5-Toth art ?	1.00	2.00	3.00
6,7,10-14	.50	1.00	1.50
8,9-Toth art ?	1.00	2.00	3.00

ADVENTURES INTO TERROR (Formerly Joker)
#43, Nov, 1950 - #31, May, 1954
Marvel/Atlas Comics(CDS/ACI)

#43,44	2.00	4.00	6.00
#3-5	1.25	2.50	3.75
6,8	1.00	2.00	3.00
7-Wolverton art, 6pgs.	7.00	14.00	21.00
9,10,12-Krigstein stys.	1.50	3.00	4.50
11,13-20	.80	1.60	2.40
21-31	.65	1.35	2.00

NOTE: *Everett cover-#13. G.Kane story-#7.
Wolverton cover panel-#5. Wolvertonesque art
by Matt Fox-#25.*

ADVENTURES INTO THE UNKNOWN
Fall, 1948 - #174, Aug, 1967 (#1-33, 52pgs.)
American Comics Group

#1	7.00	14.00	21.00
2,4,5	3.50	7.00	10.50
3-Feldstein story, 9pgs.	7.00	14.00	21.00
6-10	2.00	4.00	6.00
11-20	1.50	3.00	4.50
21-26,28-30	1.35	2.75	4.00
27-Williamson/Krenkle story, 8pgs.			
	7.00	14.00	21.00
31-50	1.00	2.00	3.00
51-59 (3-D effect)	1.20	2.40	3.60
60,61-Last pre-code ish	.65	1.35	2.00
62-90	.50	1.00	1.50
91,95,96(#95 on inside),107,116-All contain			

	Good	Fine	Mint
Williamson stories	1.75	3.35	5.00
92-94,97-106,108-115,117-127			
	.35	.70	1.05
128-Williamson story reprinted from Forbidden Worlds #63	.80	1.60	2.40
129-150	.25	.50	.75
151-153: #153-Magic Agent app.			
	.20	.40	.60
154-Nemesis series begins (origin), ends #170			
	.35	.70	1.05
155-167,169-174: #157-Magic Agent app.			
	.20	.40	.60
168-Ditko story	.40	.80	1.20

NOTE: *"Spirit of Frankenstein" series in #5,
6,8-10,12,16. Buscema story-#100,106,109,
110,158. Craig story-#160. Whitney story-
Most ish. #15,23,26,27,56-141; covers-most
#12-20,57-150.*

ADVENTURES INTO WEIRD WORLDS
Jan, 1951 - #30, June, 1954
Marvel/Atlas Comics(ACI)

#1-Heath story	2.50	5.00	7.50
2	1.50	3.00	4.50
3-9	1.00	2.00	3.00
10-Krigstein story	1.50	3.00	4.50
11-30	.80	1.60	2.40

NOTE: *Everett story-#10; covers-#10,12,13,20.
Robinson story-#13.*

ADVENTURES IN WONDERLAND
Apr, 1955 - #5, Feb, 1956 (Jr. Readers Guild)
Lev Gleason Publications

#1-Maurer art	1.50	3.00	4.50
2-4	1.00	2.00	3.00
5-X-Mas issue	1.50	3.00	4.50

ADVENTURES OF ALAN LADD, THE
Oct-Nov, 1949 - #9, Feb-Mar, 1951
National Periodical Publications

#1	4.00	8.00	12.00
2-9	2.50	5.00	7.50

NOTE: *Toth art in some issues.*

ADVENTURES OF ALICE (Also see Alice in Wonderland & -- at Monkey Island)
1945
Pentagon Publishing Co./Civil Service

#1	2.50	5.00	7.50
2-Through the Magic Looking Glass			
	2.00	4.00	6.00

Adventures Into Terror #5, © MCG

Adventures Into The Unknown #41, © ACG

Adventures Into Weird Worlds #1, © MCG

Adventures of D.M. & J.L. #8, © DC   Adventures of Ozzie & Harriet #4, © DC   Adventures of The Big Boy #1, © MCG

ADVENTURES OF BOB HOPE, THE
Feb-Mar, 1950 - #109, Feb-Mar, 1968
National Periodical Publications

	Good	Fine	Mint
#1	5.00	10.00	15.00
2	2.50	5.00	7.50
3-10	1.50	3.00	4.50
11-20	1.00	2.00	3.00
21-50	.85	1.75	2.50
51-93,95-105: #103-Infantino art			
	.40	.80	1.20
94-Aquaman cameo	.50	1.00	1.50
106-109-Adams cvrs/stories	1.00	2.00	3.00

ADVENTURES OF DEAN MARTIN & JERRY LEWIS, THE
(Jerry Lewis #41 on)
July-Aug, 1952 - #40, Oct, 1957
National Periodical Publications

#1	4.00	8.00	12.00
2	2.00	4.00	6.00
3-10	1.35	2.75	4.00
11-30	.80	1.60	2.40
31-40	.50	1.00	1.50

ADVENTURES OF G.I. JOE
1969   (3¼"x7")
Giveaways

#1-Danger of the Depths. 2-Flying Space Adventure. 3-Secret Mission to Spy Island. 4-White Tiger Hunt. 5-Fantastic Free Fall. 6-Eight Ropes of Danger. 7-Capture of the Pygmy Gorilla. 8-Hidden Missle Discovery. 9-Space Walk Mystery. 10-Fight for Survival. 11-The Sharks' Surprise. 12-Secret of the Mummy's Tomb. each....	.20	.40	.60

ADVENTURES OF HOMER COBB, THE
Sept, 1947
Say/Bart Prod. (Canadian)

#1-Feldstein art	5.00	10.00	15.00

ADVENTURES OF HOMER GHOST
June, 1957 - #2, August, 1957
Atlas Comics

V1#1, V1#2	.35	.70	1.05

ADVENTURES OF JERRY LEWIS, THE (Dean Martin & Jerry Lewis #1-40)(See Super DC Giant)
#41, Nov, 1957 - #124, May-June, 1971
National Periodical Publications

#41-60	.50	1.00	1.50
61-80	.35	.70	1.05

	Good	Fine	Mint
81-91,93-96,98-100	.25	.50	.75
92-Superman cameo	.35	.70	1.05
97-Batman/Robin x-over	.35	.70	1.05
101-104-Adams cvrs/stys.	1.00	2.00	3.00
105-Superman x-over	.35	.70	1.05
106-111,113-116	.25	.50	.75
112-Flash x-over	.35	.70	1.05
117-Wonder Woman x-over	.35	.70	1.05
118-124	.25	.50	.75

ADVENTURES OF MANUEL PACIFICO, TUNA FISHERMAN, THE
1951   (Giveaway)(16pgs. in color)
Breast O' Chicken Giveaway (Frieda-Bart Hind)

#1-4	1.50	3.00	4.50

ADVENTURES OF MIGHTY MOUSE (Mighty Mouse Adventures #1)
#2, Jan, 1952 - #16, Jan, 1955
St. John Publishing Co.

#2-5	1.50	3.00	4.50
6-16	1.00	2.00	3.00

ADVENTURES OF MIGHTY MOUSE (2nd Series)
(Two #144's; Formerly Paul Terry's Comics; #128-137 have no #'s)(Becomes Mighty Mouse #161 on)
#126, Aug, 1955 - #160, Oct, 1963
St. John/Pines/Dell/Gold Key

#126(8/55), 127(10/55)-St. John			
	.80	1.60	2.40
No#(#128, 4/56)-#144(8/59)Pines			
	.80	1.60	2.40
#144(10-12/59)-#155(7-9/62)Dell			
	.65	1.35	2.00
#156(10/62)-#160(10/63)Gold Key			
	.65	1.35	2.00

NOTE: *Early issues titled "Paul Terry's Adventures of --".*

ADVENTURES OF MR. FROG & MISS MOUSE (See Dell Jr. Treasury #4)

ADVENTURES OF OZZIE AND HARRIET, THE
Oct-Nov, 1949 - #5, June-July, 1950 (Radio)
National Periodical Publications

#1	2.50	5.00	7.50
2-5	1.50	3.00	4.50

ADVENTURES OF PATORUZU
Aug, 1946 - Winter, 1946
Green Publishing Co.

No #'s-Contains Animal Crackers reprints			
	1.00	2.00	3.00

ADVENTURES OF PINKY LEE, THE (TV)
July, 1955 - #5, Nov, 1955
Atlas Comics

	Good	Fine	Mint
#1	1.50	3.00	4.50
2-5	1.00	2.00	3.00

ADVENTURES OF QUAKE & QUISP, THE
(See Quaker Oats "Plenty of Glutton")

ADVENTURES OF REX THE WONDER DOG, THE
Jan-Feb, 1952 - #46, Nov-Dec, 1959
National Periodical Publications

	Good	Fine	Mint
#1(Scarce)	7.00	14.00	21.00
2-10: #3-Toth art	1.50	3.00	4.50
11-20	1.20	2.40	3.60
21-46	.80	1.60	2.40

NOTE: *Infantino, Gil Kane art in most issues.*

ADVENTURES OF ROBIN HOOD, THE (Formerly
Robin Hood)
#8, Nov, 1957 (Based on Richard Green TV Show)
Magazine Enterprises (Sussex Publ. Co.)

	Good	Fine	Mint
#8	1.00	2.00	3.00

ADVENTURES OF ROBIN HOOD, THE
March, 1974 - #7, Jan, 1975 (Disney Cartoon)
Gold Key

	Good	Fine	Mint
#1(90291-403)-Partial reprints of $1.50 editions	.20	.40	.60
2-7		.20	.35

ADVENTURES OF THE BIG BOY (Eastern & Western
editions of early issues)
1956 - Present   (Giveaway)
Timely Comics/Webs Adv. Corp./Illus. Features

	Good	Fine	Mint
#1-Everett art	20.00	40.00	60.00
2-5,7,8-Everett art	5.00	10.00	15.00
6,9-50	1.00	2.00	3.00
51-100	.35	.70	1.05
101-150	.20	.40	.60
151-240		.20	.30
#1-10('77)		.10	.15
Summer, '59 ish, lg.size	1.50	3.00	4.50

ADVENTURES OF THE DETECTIVE
No date(1930's) 36pgs.;9½x12" B&W(Soft cover)
Humor Publ. Co.

Not reprints; Ace King by Martin Nodle

	Good	Fine	Mint
	6.00	12.00	18.00

ADVENTURES OF THE JAGUAR, THE
Sept, 1961 - #15, 1963

Archie Publications (Radio Comics)

	Good	Fine	Mint
#1-Origin Jaguar	2.00	4.00	6.00
2,3	1.00	2.00	3.00
4,5-Catgirl app.	.65	1.35	2.00
6-10: #6-Catgirl app.	.60	1.20	1.80
11-15: #13,14-Catgirl, Black Hood app. in both	.50	1.00	1.50

ADVENTURES OF TINKER BELL (See 4-Color #982)

ADVENTURES OF TOM SAWYER (See Dell Jr.
Treasury #10)

ADVENTURES OF YOUNG DR. MASTERS, THE
Aug, 1964 - #2, Nov, 1964
Archie Comics (Radio Comics)

	Good	Fine	Mint
#1,2	.50	1.00	1.50

ADVENTURES ON THE PLANET OF THE APES
Oct, 1975 - #11, Dec, 1976
Marvel Comics Group

	Good	Fine	Mint
#1-Reprints from Planet of the Apes in color; Starlin cover	.35	.70	1.05
2-5	.20	.40	.60
6-11	.15	.30	.45

NOTE: *Alcala* reprints-#10,11. *Starlin*
cover-#6.

AFRICA
1955
Magazine Enterprises

	Good	Fine	Mint
#1(A-1 #137)-Cave Girl & Thun'da; Powell cover + 4 stories	4.00	8.00	12.00

AFRICAN LION (See 4-Color #665)

AFTER DARK
May, 1955 - #8, Sept, 1955
Sterling Comics

	Good	Fine	Mint
#6-8-Sekowsky art in all	1.00	2.00	3.00

AGGIE MACK
Jan, 1948 - #8, July, 1949
Superior Comics Ltd.

	Good	Fine	Mint
#1-Feldstein "Johnny Prep"	3.35	6.75	10.00
2,3-Kamen covers	1.75	3.35	5.00
4-Feldstein "Johnny Prep"; Kamen cover	2.50	5.00	7.50
5-8-Kamen cvrs/stys.	2.50	5.00	7.50

AGGIE MACK (See 4-Color #1335)

Adventures of The Jaguar #14, © AP

Aggie Mack #1, © SUPR

Air Ace V3#5, © S & S

Airboy Comics V3#8, © S & S   Air War Stories #1, © Dell   Alarming Adventures #3, © Harv

AIN'T IT A GRAND & GLORIOUS FEELING?
1922 (28pgs.)(Full color; 9x9½";cardboard
Whitman Publishing Co.   cover)

	Good	Fine	Mint
Sunday strip reprints; Briggs art			
	12.00	24.00	36.00

AIR ACE (Bill Barnes #1-12)
V2#1, Jan, 1944 - V5#8, Feb-Mar, 1947
Street & Smith Publications

	Good	Fine	Mint
V2#1-12	1.75	3.35	5.00
V3#1-8	1.25	2.50	3.75
V4#1-8	1.00	2.00	3.00
V5#1-8: #8-Powell art	.65	1.35	2.00

AIRBOY COMICS (Airfighters #1-22)
V2#11, Dec, 1945 - V10#4, May, 1953(No V3#3)
Hillman Periodicals

	Good	Fine	Mint
V2#11,12-Valkyrie in #12	5.00	10.00	15.00
V3#1,2(no #3)	3.00	6.00	9.00
4-The Heap app. in Skywolf			
	3.00	6.00	9.00
5-8: Valkyrie in #6	3.00	6.00	9.00
9-Origin The Heap	3.00	6.00	9.00
10,11	3.00	6.00	9.00
12-Skywolf & Airboy x-over; Valkyrie app.			
	4.00	8.00	12.00
V4#1-Iron Lady app.	2.50	5.00	7.50
2-Rackman begins	2.00	4.00	6.00
3,10,12	2.00	4.00	6.00
4-Simon & Kirby cover	3.00	6.00	9.00
5-9,11-S&K stories	4.00	8.00	12.00
V5#1-9: #4-Infantino Heap	2.00	4.00	6.00
10-Origin The Heap	2.00	4.00	6.00
11,12	2.00	4.00	6.00
V6#1-5,7	2.00	4.00	6.00
6,8-Origin The Heap	2.00	4.00	6.00
9-12	2.00	4.00	6.00
V7#1-7,9,11,12	2.00	4.00	6.00
8,10-Origin The Heap	2.00	4.00	6.00
V8#1-12	1.50	3.00	4.50
V9#1-12: #2-Valkyrie app.	1.50	3.00	4.50
V10#1-4	1.50	3.00	4.50

NOTE: *Krigstein story-V5#12(pencils), V8#4.*
McWilliams art-V3#7. Powell story-V8#1,6.
Starr story-V5#1.

AIR FIGHTERS COMICS (Airboy #23, V2#11 on)
Nov, 1941 - V2#10, Fall, 1945
Hillman Periodicals

	Good	Fine	Mint
V1#1-Black Commander only app.			
	40.00	80.00	120.00
2-Origin Airboy & Iron Ace; Black Angel, Flying Dutchman & Skywolf begin; 1st Valkyrie app.; Fuji art			

	Good	Fine	Mint
	70.00	140.00	210.00
3-Origin The Heap & Skywolf			
	30.00	60.00	90.00
4	23.50	46.75	70.00
5,6	16.50	33.25	50.00
7-12	12.00	24.00	36.00
V2#1-9: #2-Intro. Valkyrie. #7-Valkyrie app.			
	10.00	20.00	30.00
10-Origin The Heap & Skywolf			
	10.00	20.00	30.00

AIR FORCES (See American Air Forces)

AIR WAR STORIES
Sept-Nov, 1964 - #8, Aug, 1966
Dell Publishing Co.

	Good	Fine	Mint
#1-Glanzman cvr/art begins	.50	1.00	1.50
2-8	.25	.50	.75

ALADDIN (See Dell Jr. Treasury #2)

ALAN LADD (See Adventures of --)

ALARMING ADVENTURES
Oct, 1962 - #3, Feb, 1963
Harvey Publications

	Good	Fine	Mint
#1-3-Williamson + Crandall art in all			
	1.50	3.00	4.50

ALARMING TALES
Sept, 1957 - #6, July, 1958
Harvey Publications (Western Tales)

	Good	Fine	Mint
#1(1st Series)-Kirby cover & 4 stories			
	2.50	5.00	7.50
2-Four Kirby stories	2.00	4.00	6.00
3,4-Kirby stories	1.50	3.00	4.50
5-Kirby/Williamson story	1.50	3.00	4.50
6-Williamson/Torres sty.	1.50	3.00	4.50

ALBERT THE ALLIGATOR & POGO POSSUM
(See 4-Color Comics #105,148)

ALBUM OF CRIME
1959 (132 pgs.)
Fox Features Syndicate

No#-See Fox Giants. Contents can vary and
    determines price.

ALBUM OF LOVE
1949 (132 pgs.)
Hero Books (Fox)

No#-See Fox Giants. Contents can vary and
    determine price.

AL CAPP'S DOGPATCH (Also see Mammy Yokum)
#71, June, 1949 - #4, Dec, 1949
Toby Press

	Good	Fine	Mint
#71(#1)-Reprints from Tip Top #112-114	2.00	4.00	6.00
#2-4: #4-Reprints from Little Abner #73	1.75	3.35	5.00

AL CAPP'S SHMOO (See Oxydol-Dreft)
July, 1949 - 1950 (None by Al Capp)
Toby Press/Harvey Publications

#1	4.00	8.00	12.00
2-5	2.50	5.00	7.50

AL CAPP'S WOLF GAL
1952
Harvey Publications/Toby Press, #2

#1,2-Edited reprint from Li'l Abner #63,64	3.50	5.00	10.50

ALEXANDER THE GREAT (See 4-Color #688)

ALGIE
Dec, 1953 - #3, 1954
Timor Publ. Co.

#1	.50	1.00	1.50
2,3	.35	.70	1.05
Super Reprint #15	.35	.70	1.05

ALICE (New Advs. in Wonderland)
1952
Ziff-Davis Publ. Co.

#2-Davy Berg art	1.00	2.00	3.00
3-9	.80	1.60	2.40
10,11-Davy Berg art	.80	1.60	2.40

ALICE AT MONKEY ISLAND (See The Advs.of Alice)
#3, 1946
Pentagon Publ. Co. (Civil Service)

#3	2.00	4.00	6.00

ALICE IN WONDERLAND (See Advs. of Alice,
4-Color #331,341, Dell Jr. Treasury #1, Movie
Comics, Single Series #24, Walt Disney Showcase #22, & World's Greatest Stories)

ALICE IN WONDERLAND
1965
Western Printing Company

--Meets Santa Claus('50's), no date, 16 pgs.	2.00	4.00	6.00

	Good	Fine	Mint
Rexall Giveaway(1965, 16pgs., 5x7¼") Western Printing(TV-Hanna-Barbera)	1.50	3.00	4.50
Wonder Bakery Giveaway(16pgs. color, no #, no date)(Continental Baking Co.)	1.50	3.00	4.50

ALIENS, THE
Dec, 1967; 1972
Gold Key

#1-Reprints from Magnus #1,3,4,6-10, all by Russ Manning	.65	1.35	2.00
#1-2nd printing ('72)	.35	.70	1.05

ALL-AMERICAN COMICS (-- Western #103-126,
-- Men of War #127 on)
April, 1939 - #102, Oct, 1948
National Periodical Publ./All-American

#1-Hop Harrigan, Scribbly, Toonerville Folks, Ben Webster, Spot Savage, Mutt & Jeff, Red White & Blue, Adv. in the Unknown, Tippie, Reg'lar Fellars, Skippy, Bobby Thatcher, Mystery Men of Mars, Daiseybelle, & Wiley of West Point begin	70.00	140.00	210.00
2-Ripley's Believe It or Not begins, ends #24	35.00	70.00	105.00
3-5: #5-The American Way begins, ends #10	20.00	40.00	60.00
6,7: #6-Last Spot Savage. #7-Last Bobby Thatcher	16.50	33.25	50.00
8-The Ultra Man begins	25.00	50.00	75.00
9,10	20.00	40.00	60.00
11-15: #12-Last Toonerville Folks. #13-Popsicle Pete begins, ends #26,28. #15-Last Tippie & Reg'lar Fellars	15.00	30.00	45.00
16-Origin & 1st app. Green Lantern (Rare)	300.00	600.00	900.00
(Prices vary widely on this book)			
17	65.00	130.00	195.00
18	55.00	110.00	165.00
19-Origin & 1st app. The Atom; Last Ultra Man	65.00	130.00	195.00
20-Atom dons costume; Hunkle becomes the Red Tornado; Rescue on Mars begins, ends #25	40.00	80.00	120.00
21-23: #21-Last Wiley of West Point & Skippy. #23-Last Daiseybelle; 3 Idiots begin, end #82	30.00	60.00	90.00
24-Sisty & Dinky become the Cyclone Kids; Ben Webster ends	30.00	60.00	90.00
25-Origin & 1st app. Dr. Mid-Nite; Hop Harrigan becomes Guardian Angel; last Adventure in the Unknown	50.00	100.00	150.00

Al Capp's Shmoo #1. © UFS

All-American Comics #30. © DC

All-American Comics #85. © DC

All-American Men of War #42, © DC   All-American Western #108, © DC   All-Famous Police Cases #14, © Star

(All-American cont'd)	Good	Fine	Mint
26-Origin & 1st app. Sargon, the Sorcerer	35.00	70.00	105.00
27-Intro. Doiby Dickles, Green Lantern's sidekick	35.00	70.00	105.00
28-(#28 on cvr, #27 on inside) Hop Harrigan gives up costumed identity	20.00	40.00	60.00
29,30	20.00	40.00	60.00
31-40: #35-Doiby learns Green Lantern's I.D.	15.00	30.00	45.00
41-50: #50-Sargon ends	12.00	24.00	36.00
51-60	10.00	20.00	30.00
61-Origin Solomon Grundy	20.00	40.00	60.00
62-70: #70-Kubert Sargon	8.00	16.00	24.00
71-Last Red White & Blue	7.00	14.00	21.00
72-Black Pirate begins (not in #74-82); last Atom	7.00	14.00	21.00
73-80: #73-Winky, Blinky & Noddy begins, ends #82	7.00	14.00	21.00
81-90: #89-Origin Harlequin. #90-Origin Icicle	6.00	12.00	18.00
91-99-Last Hop Harrigan	6.00	12.00	18.00
100-1st app. Johnny Thunder by Alex Toth	12.00	24.00	36.00
101-Last Mutt & Jeff	8.00	16.00	24.00
102-Last Green Lantern, Black Pirate & Dr. Mid-Nite	8.00	16.00	24.00

NOTE: *No Atom in #47,62-69. Moldoff covers-#16-23. Toth stories-#88,92,96,98-102; covers-#92,96-102.*

ALL-AMERICAN MEN OF WAR (Previously All-American Western)
#127, Aug-Sept, 1952 - #117, Sept-Oct, 1966
National Periodical Publications

#127,128 (1952)	4.00	8.00	12.00
#2(12-1/'52-53)-#5	2.50	5.00	7.50
6-20	2.00	4.00	6.00
21-28	1.35	2.75	4.00
29,30,32-Wood stories	2.50	5.00	7.50
31,33-50	1.00	2.00	3.00
51-70: #67-1st Gunner & Sarge by Andru	.65	1.35	2.00
71-80	.60	1.20	1.80
81-100: #82-Johnny Cloud begins, ends #111, 114,115	.40	.80	1.20
101-117: #112-Balloon Buster series begins, ends #113. #115-Johnny Cloud app.	.25	.50	.75

NOTE: *Drucker story-#74. Grandenetti story-#9,128. Infantino story-#8. Krigstein story-#128('52),2,3,5. Kubert story-#36,38,41,43, 47,49,50,52,53,55,56,60,63,65,69,71-73,103; cover-#41. Tank Killer in #69,71,76 by Kubert.*

ALL-AMERICAN SPORTS
October, 1967
Charlton Comics

	Good	Fine	Mint
#1	.15	.30	.45

ALL-AMERICAN WESTERN (Previously All-American Comics; Becomes All-American Men of War)
Nov, 1948 - #126, June-July, 1952
National Periodical Publications

#103-110-Johnny Thunder continues by Toth	4.00	8.00	12.00
111-126-All Toth art	2.50	5.00	7.50

NOTE: *Kubert art-#103-105,107,111,112(1 pg.), 113-115,121. Kurtzman 1 pg.-#112(Pot-Shot Pete).*

ALL COMICS
1945
Chicago Nite Life News

#1	2.50	5.00	7.50

ALLEY OOP (See 4-Color #3 & Super Book #9)

ALLEY OOP
1947 - 1949
Standard Comics

#1	6.00	12.00	18.00
2-5	4.00	8.00	12.00
6-18	3.00	6.00	9.00

ALLEY OOP
1955 - #3, 1956 (Newspaper reprints)
Argo Publ.

#1	3.35	6.75	10.00
2,3	2.75	5.50	8.00

ALLEY OOP
1963; 1965
Dell Publishing Co.

#1,2('63)	1.50	3.00	4.50
#1,2('65)	1.00	2.00	3.00

ALL-FAMOUS CRIME
1949 - #10, Nov, 1951
Star Publications

#1	1.75	3.35	5.00
2-8,10	.75	1.50	2.25
9-Used in Seduction of the Innocent, pgs. 6 and 18	4.00	8.00	12.00

ALL FAMOUS CRIME STORIES
1949   (132 pgs.)
Fox Features Syndicate

No#-See Fox Giants. Contents can vary and
   determines price.

ALL-FAMOUS POLICE CASES
Oct, 1951 - #16, Sept, 1954
Star Publications

	Good	Fine	Mint
#1	1.00	2.00	3.00
2-6	.65	1.35	2.00
7-Kubert art	1.75	3.35	5.00
8,10-16	.65	1.35	2.00
9-L.B. Cole art; used in Seduction of the
Innocent	4.00	8.00	12.00

ALL-FLASH
Summer, 1941 - #32, Dec-Jan, 1948-49
National Periodical Publ./All-American

#1-Origin The Flash retold by E. E. Hibbard
	80.00	160.00	240.00
2	30.00	60.00	90.00
3,4	25.00	50.00	75.00
5-Winky, Blinky & Noddy begins, ends #32
	20.00	40.00	60.00
6-10	15.00	30.00	45.00
11-13: #12-Origin The Thinker. #13-The King
app.	12.00	24.00	36.00
14-Green Lantern cameo	13.50	26.75	40.00
15-20: #18-Mutt & Jeff begins, ends #22
	9.00	18.00	27.00
21-31	7.00	14.00	21.00
32-Origin The Fiddler	8.00	16.00	24.00

NOTE: *Book length stories #2-13,15,16.*

ALL FOR LOVE
Apr-May, 1957 - V3#2, Jun-Jul, 1959
Prize Publications

V1#1	.65	1.35	2.00
2-6	.30	.65	1.00
V2#1-5	.25	.50	.75
V3#1,2: #2-Powell art	.20	.40	.60

ALL FUNNY COMICS
Winter, 1943-44 - #23, May-June, 1948
National Periodical Publ. (Detective)

#1-Genius Jones begins	3.00	6.00	9.00
2	1.75	3.35	5.00
3-12,16-Last Genius Jones
	1.35	2.75	4.00
13-15,17-23	.80	1.60	2.40

ALL GOOD (-- Comics)

1944 (132 pgs.); Spring, 1946 (36 pgs.)
R. W. Boigt Publ.(1944)/Fox Features Synd.

	Good	Fine	Mint
#1(1944)-The Bouncer, Purple Tigress, Puppe-
teer, & The Green Mask	5.00	10.00	15.00
1946-Joy Family, Dick Transom, Rick Evans,
One Round Hogan	4.00	8.00	12.00

ALL GOOD
1949   (260 pgs.) (50¢)
St. John Publishing Co.

(8 funny animal comics bound together)
                         2.75   5.50   8.00

ALL GREAT
1944; 1945 (132 pgs.) 1946 (36 pgs.)
Fox Features Syndicate

1944-Capt. Jack Terry, Rick Evans, Jaguar
Man	5.00	10.00	15.00
1945-Green Mask, Bouncer, Puppeteer, Rick
Evans, Rocket Kelly	5.00	10.00	15.00
#1(1946)-Crazy Horse, Bertie Benson, Gussie
the Cub	2.00	4.00	6.00

ALL GREAT   (Dagar, Desert Hawk #14 on)
#14, Oct, 1947 - #13, Dec, 1947
Fox Features Syndicate

#14-Brenda Starr reprints	8.00	16.00	24.00
13-Origin Dagar, Desert Hawk; Brenda Starr
(all reprts.); Kamen cover
	8.00	16.00	24.00

ALL-GREAT CONFESSIONS
1949   (132 pgs.)
Fox Features Syndicate

No#-See Fox Giants. Contents vary and
   determines price.

ALL GREAT CRIME STORIES
1949   (132 pgs.)
Fox Features Syndicate

No#-See Fox Giants. Contents vary and
   determines price.

ALL GREAT JUNGLE ADVENTURES
1949   (132 pgs.)
Fox Features Syndicate

No#-See Fox Giants. Contents vary and
   determines price.

ALL HERO COMICS
March, 1943   (100 pgs.)
Fawcett Publications

All Flash # 10. © DC

All Great #13. © Fox

All Love Romances #26. © Ace

All-Negro Comics #1, © All-Negro Comics   All-New Comics #2, © Harv   All Select #7, © MCG

(All Hero Comics cont'd)   Good   Fine   Mint
#1-Captain Marvel Jr., Capt. Midnight, Golden
   Arrow, Ibis the Invincible, Spy Smasher,
   & Lance O'Casey   50.00 100.00 150.00

ALL HUMOR COMICS
Spring, 1946 - #17, December, 1949
Quality Comics Group

#1   2.00   4.00   6.00
 2-9   1.00   2.00   3.00
10-17   .65   1.35   2.00

ALL LOVE (-- Romances #26)(Formerly Ernie)
#26, May, 1949 - #32, May, 1950
Ace Periodicals (Current Books)

#26(#1)-Ernie app.   1.00   2.00   3.00
 27-L.B. Cole story   1.00   2.00   3.00
 28-32   .50   1.00   1.50

ALL-NEGRO COMICS
June, 1947   (15¢)
All-Negro Comics

#1 (Rare)   50.00 100.00 150.00

ALL-NEW COLLECTORS' EDITION (Formerly Limited
Collectors' Edition)
January, 1978 - Present
DC Comics, Inc.

#C-53-Rudolph the Red-Nosed Reindeer
                              .35   .70   1.05
 C-54-Superman Vs. Wonder Woman
                              .40   .80   1.20
 C-55-Superboy & the Legion of Super-Heroes
                              .40   .80   1.20
 C-56-Superman Vs. Muhamad Ali
                              .40   .80   1.20
 C-57-Welcome Back Kotter .35   .70   1.05
 C-58-Superman Vs. Shazam! .40   .80   1.20

ALL-NEW COMICS (-- Short Stories #1-3)
Jan, 1943 - #14, Nov, 1946; #15, Mar-Apr, 1947
Harvey Publications

#1-Steve Case, Crime Rover, Johnny Rebel,
   Kayo Kane, The Echo, Night Hawk, Ray
   O'Light, Detective Shane begin; Red Blazer
   on cover only   25.00   50.00   75.00
 2-Origin Scarlet Phantom
                           15.00   30.00   45.00
 3   10.00   20.00   30.00
 4   9.00   18.00   27.00
 5   9.00   18.00   27.00
 6-The Boy Heroes & Red Blazer (text story)
   begin; Black Cat app.; Intro Sparky in

                                   Good   Fine   Mint
   Red Blazer   9.00   18.00   27.00
 7-Kubert & Powell art; Black Cat & Zebra
   app.   10.00   20.00   30.00
 8-Shock Gibson app.; Kubert & Powell art
                           10.00   20.00   30.00
 9-Black Cat app.; Kubert art
                           10.00   20.00   30.00
10-The Zebra app.; Kubert art (3 stories)
                           10.00   20.00   30.00
11-Girl Commandos app.   8.00   16.00   24.00
12-Kubert art   8.00   16.00   24.00
13-Stuntman by Simon & Kirby; Green Hornet,
   Joe Palooka, Flying Fool app.
                           10.00   20.00   30.00
14-The Green Hornet & The Man in Black Called
   Fate by Powell, Joe Palooka app.
                            7.00   14.00   21.00
15-(Extremely Rare)-Small size (5½x8½"-Black
   & White, 32pgs.) Distributed to mail subscribers only. Black Cat and Joe Palooka
   app.   (Sold in San Francisco
                    in 1976 for $500.00)
(Also see Boy Explorers #2, Flash Gordon #5,
and Stuntman #3.)

ALL PICTURE ADVENTURE COMICS
1952
St. John Publishing Co.

#1,2   1.00   2.00   3.00

ALL PICTURE ALL TRUE LOVE STORY
October, 1952   (100 pgs.)
St. John Publishing Co.

#1-Canteen Kate; Matt Baker art
                             5.00   10.00   15.00

ALL-PICTURE COMEDY CARNIVAL
October, 1952   (100 pgs.)
St. John Publishing Co.

#1   2.00   4.00   6.00

ALL REAL CONFESSION MAGAZINE
#3, Mar, 1949 - #4, Apr, 1949   (132 pgs.)
Hero Books (Fox)

#3,4-See Fox Giants. Contents can vary and
   determines price.

ALL ROMANCES (Mr. Risk #7 on)
Aug, 1949 - #6, June, 1950
A. A. Wyn (Ace Periodicals)

#1   1.00   2.00   3.00
 2-6   .65   1.35   2.00

ALL-SELECT COMICS (Blonde Phantom #12 on)
Fall, 1943 - #11, Fall, 1946
Timely Comics (Daring Comics)

	Good	Fine	Mint
#1-Capt. America, Human Torch, Sub-Mariner begin; Black Widow app.	100.00	200.00	300.00
2-Red Skull app.	40.00	80.00	120.00
3-The Whizzer begins	30.00	60.00	90.00
4,5-Last Sub-Mariner	20.00	40.00	60.00
6-The Destroyer app.	16.50	33.25	50.00
7-9: #8-No Whizzer	16.50	33.25	50.00
10-The Destroyer & Sub-Mariner app.; last Capt. America & Human Torch issue	15.00	30.00	45.00
11-1st app. Blonde Phantom; Miss America app.	20.00	40.00	60.00

ALL SPORTS COMICS
Oct-Nov, 1948 - #4, Apr-May, 1949 (52 pgs.)
Hillman Periodicals

#1	1.20	2.40	3.60
2-4: #2-Krigstein pencils	.70	1.40	2.10

ALL STAR COMICS (-- Western #58 on)
Summer/40 - #57, 2-3/51; #58, 1-2/76 - Present
National Periodical Publ./All-American Publ.

#1-The Flash(#1 by Harry Lampert), Hawkman (by Shelly), Hourman, The Sandman, The Spectre, Hop Harrigan, Red White & Blue begin; Ultra Man's only app.	200.00	400.00	600.00
2-Green Lantern, Johnny Thunder begin	100.00	200.00	300.00
3-Origin Justice Society of America; Dr. Fate & The Atom begin, Red Tornado cameo; last Red White & Blue; reprinted in Famous First Edition	250.00	500.00	750.00
4	90.00	180.00	270.00
5-Intro. & 1st app. Shiera Sanders as Hawkgirl	80.00	160.00	240.00
6-Johnny Thunder joins JSA	65.00	130.00	195.00
7-Batman, Superman, Flash cameo; last Hourman; Doiby Dickles app.	65.00	130.00	195.00
8-Origin & 1st app. Wonder Woman; Dr. Fate dons new helmet; Dr. Mid-Nite & Starman begin; Shiera app.; Hop Harrigan JSA guest	100.00	200.00	300.00
9-Shiera app.	60.00	120.00	180.00
10-Flash, Green Lantern cameo, Sandman new costume	60.00	120.00	180.00
11-Wonder Woman begins; Spectre cameo; Shiera app.	50.00	100.00	150.00
12-Wonder Woman becomes Secretary of JSA	50.00	100.00	150.00

	Good	Fine	Mint
13-15: Sandman w/Sandy in #14&15; #15-Origin Brain Wave; Shiera app.	45.00	90.00	135.00
16-19: #17-Last Hop Harrigan. #19-Sandman w/Sandy	40.00	80.00	120.00
20-Dr. Fate & Sandman cameo	35.00	70.00	110.00
21-Spectre & Atom cameo; Dr. Fate by Kubert; Dr. Fate, Sandman end	30.00	60.00	90.00
22,23: #23-Origin Psycho Pirate; last Spectre & Starman	30.00	60.00	90.00
24-Flash & Green Lantern cameo; Mr. Terrific only app.; Wildcat, JSA guest; Kubert Hawkman begins	30.00	60.00	90.00
25-27: #25-The Flash & Green Lantern start again. #27-Wildcat, JSA guest	27.50	55.00	82.50
28-30	25.00	50.00	75.00
31,32	22.50	45.00	67.50
33-Solomon Grundy, Hawkman, Doiby Dickles app.	40.00	80.00	120.00
34,35-Johnny Thunder cameo in both	22.50	45.00	67.50
36-Batman & Superman JSA guests	40.00	80.00	120.00
37-Johnny Thunder cameo; origin Injustice Society; last Kubert Hawkman	20.00	40.00	60.00
38-Black Canary begins; JSA Death issue	25.00	50.00	75.00
39,40: 39-Last Johnny Thunder	20.00	40.00	60.00
41-Black Canary joins JSA; Injustice Society app.	17.50	35.00	52.50
42-Atom & the Hawkman don new costume	17.50	35.00	52.50
43-49	17.50	35.00	52.50
50-Frazetta art, 3 pgs.	20.00	40.00	60.00
51-56	17.50	35.00	52.50
57-Kubert story, 6 pgs. (Scarce)	20.00	40.00	60.00
58('76)-Flash, Hawkman, Dr. Mid-Nite, Wildcat, Dr. Fate, Green Lantern, Star Spangled Kid, Robin & Power Girl app.	.40	.80	1.20
59-70	.20	.40	.60

NOTE: *No Atom-#27,36; no Dr. Fate-#9,13; no Flash-#8,9,11-23; no Green Lantern-#9; no Johnny Thunder-#5,36; no Wonder Woman-#9,10, 23. Burnley Starman-#8-13. Kubert Hawkman-#24-30,33-37. Simon & Kirby Sandman-#14-17, 19. Staton stories-inks #66-70. Wood story-#58-65; covers-#63,64.*

ALL STAR WESTERN (All Star #1-57)
Apr-May, 1951 - #120, Aug-Sept, 1961
National Periodical Publications

All Star Comics #18, © DC

All Star Comics #29, © DC

All Star Western #81, © DC

13

(All Star Western cont'd)

	Good	Fine	Mint
#58-Trigger Twins begin, end #116			
	4.00	8.00	12.00
59-66	2.00	4.00	6.00
67-Johnny Thunder begins; Gil Kane art			
	3.00	6.00	9.00
68-80	1.75	3.35	5.00
81-98	1.35	2.75	4.00
99-Frazetta reprinted from Jimmy Wakely #4			
	4.00	8.00	12.00
100-107,109-116,118-120	1.35	2.75	4.00
108-Origin Johnny Thunder	2.00	4.00	6.00
117-Origin Super Chief	2.00	4.00	6.00

NOTE: _Infantino art in most issues. Madame app.-#117-119._

ALL STAR WESTERN (Weird Western Tales #12 on)
Aug-Sept, 1970 - #11, Apr-May, 1972
National Periodical Publications

	Good	Fine	Mint
#1-Reprints; Infantino art	.35	.70	1.05
2-Outlaw begins; El Diablo by Morrow begins	.25	.50	.75
3-8: #3-Origin El Diablo. #5-Last Outlaw ish. #6-Billy the Kid begins, ends #8			
	.25	.50	.75
9-3pg. Frazetta reprint	.50	1.00	1.50
10-Jonah Hex begins, #11	.15	.30	.45

NOTE: _Adams covers-#1-5; #7-11, 52 pgs.; Morrow stories-#2-4,10,11._

ALL SURPRISE
Fall, 1943 - #12, Winter, 1946-47
Timely/Marvel(CPC)

	Good	Fine	Mint
#1-Super Rabbit & Gandy & Sourpuss			
	1.35	2.75	4.00
2-10,12	1.00	2.00	3.00
11-Kurtzman "Pigtales" story			
	2.00	4.00	6.00

ALL TEEN (Formerly All Winners; Teen #21 on)
#20, January, 1947
Marvel Comics (WFP)

	Good	Fine	Mint
#20	1.35	2.75	4.00

ALL-TIME ROMANCE
1955
Ajax/Farrell Publications

	Good	Fine	Mint
#22	.40	.80	1.20

ALL TIME SPORTS COMICS
Oct-Nov, 1948 - #7, Oct-Nov, 1949
Hillman Periodicals

	Good	Fine	Mint
#1	1.00	2.00	3.00
2-7	.65	1.35	2.00

ALL TOP
1944 (132 pgs.)
William H. Wise Co.

Capt. V, Merciless the Sorceress, Red Robbins, One Round Hogan, Mike the M.P., Snooky, Pussy Katnip app. 4.00 8.00 12.00

ALL TOP COMICS (My Experience #19 on)
1945 - #18, July, 1949; 1957 - 1959
Fox Features Synd./Green Publ./Norlen Mag.

	Good	Fine	Mint
#1-Cosmo Cat & Flash Rabbit begin			
	2.00	4.00	6.00
2-7	1.35	2.75	4.00
8-Blue Beetle, Phantom Lady, & Rulah, Jungle Goddess begin (11/47)			
	25.00	50.00	75.00
9-Kamen cover	15.00	30.00	45.00
10-Kamen bondage cover	16.50	33.25	50.00
11-17: #15-No Blue Beetle			
	15.00	30.00	45.00
18-Dagar, Jo-Jo, Rulah app. only; No Phantom Lady, Blue Beetle	8.00	16.00	24.00
#6(1957-Green Publ.)-Patoruzu the Indian; Cosmo Cat on cover only	.75	1.50	2.25
#6(1958-Literary Ent.)-Muggy Doo; Cosmo Cat on cover only	.75	1.50	2.25
#6(1959-Norlen)-Atomic Mouse; Cosmo Cat on cover only	.75	1.50	2.25
#6(1959)-Little Eva	.75	1.50	2.25
#6(Cornell)-Supermouse on cover			
	.75	1.50	2.25
#6(Cornell)	.75	1.50	2.25

NOTE: _Jo-Jo by Kamen-#12,18._

ALL TRUE ALL PICTURE POLICE CASES
Oct, 1952 - #2, Nov, 1952 (100 pgs.)
St. John Publishing Co.

	Good	Fine	Mint
#1-Rebound Son of Sinbad; art by Kubert + others	4.00	8.00	12.00
2-Comics rebound	3.00	6.00	9.00

ALL-TRUE CRIME (--Cases #1,26-35; Formerly Official True Crime Cases)
#26, Feb, 1948 - #52, Sept, 1952
Marvel/Atlas Comics(LMC/OCI #27/CFI #28,29)

	Good	Fine	Mint
#1 (100 pgs.)	3.00	6.00	9.00
26(#1)	1.50	3.00	4.50
27(4/48)	1.00	2.00	3.00
28-41,43-48,50-52	.65	1.35	2.00
42,49-Krigstein art	1.50	3.00	4.50

All Top #10. © Fox

All True Crime #36. © MCG

All True Romance #1. © Ajax

14

All Winners #16, © MCG

All Winners #1('48), © MCG

Amazing Adult Fantasy #10, © MCG

ALL-TRUE DETECTIVE CASES (Kit Carson #5 on)
Feb-Mar, 1954 - #4, Aug-Sept, 1954
Avon Periodicals

	Good	Fine	Mint
#1	2.00	4.00	6.00
2,3	1.35	2.75	4.00
4-Wood, Kamen stories	3.00	6.00	9.00
No# (100 pgs.)-7 pg. Kubert story, Kinstler back cover	3.00	6.00	9.00

ALL TRUE ROMANCE (-- Illustrated #3)
Mar, 1951 - #34, Mar, 1958; #4, Nov, 1957
Artful Publ. #1-3/Harwell(Comic Media)/Ajax-
Farrell(Excellent Publ.)/Four Star Comic Corp.

#1(3/51)	1.00	2.00	3.00
2,3(12/51)	.65	1.35	2.00
4-34	.50	1.00	1.50
#4(Farrell, '57)	.35	.70	1.05

ALL WESTERN WINNERS (Formerly All Winners; becomes Western Winners with #5)
#2, Winter, 1948-49 - #4, April, 1949
Marvel Comics(CDS)

#2-Origin Black Rider, Kid Colt & Two-Gun Kid	5.00	10.00	15.00
3,4	2.50	5.00	7.50

ALL WINNERS COMICS (All Teen #20; Official True Crime Cases #22 on; #1 advertised as All Aces)
Summer, 1941 - #19, Summer, 1946; #21, Win-
ter, 1946-47 (no #20) (#21 continued from
Young Allies #20)
Timely/Marvel Comics (USA, Young Allies, Inc.)

#1-The Angel & Black Marvel only app.; Capt. America by Simon & Kirby, Human Torch & Sub-Mariner begin	200.00	400.00	600.00
2-The Destroyer & The Whizzer begin; Simon & Kirby Capt. America	90.00	180.00	270.00
3	65.00	130.00	195.00
4,5	50.00	100.00	150.00
6-The Black Avenger only app.; no Whizzer story	45.00	90.00	135.00
7-10	35.00	70.00	105.00
11-18: #12-Last Destroyer; no Whizzer story; no Human Torch #14-16	25.00	50.00	75.00
19,21-All Winners Squad, Miss America only app.	40.00	80.00	120.00

NOTE: *Everett Sub-Mariner-#1,3,4; Burgos Torch-#1,3,4.*

(2nd Series-Aug, 1948)
(Becomes All Western Winners with #2)

	Good	Fine	Mint
#1-The Blonde Phantom, Capt. America, Human Torch, & Sub-Mariner app.	25.00	50.00	75.00

ALL YOUR COMICS
1944 (132 pgs.); 1946 (36 pgs.)
Fox Features Syndicate (R. W. Voight)

#1-(1944)-The Puppeteer, Red Robbins, & Merciless app.	4.00	8.00	12.00
#1-(1946)-Red Robbins, Merciless the Sorcerer app.	3.00	6.00	9.00

ALMANAC OF CRIME
1948   (148 pgs.)
Fox Features Syndicate

No#-See Fox Giants. Contents can vary and
determines price.

ALONG THE FIRING LINE WITH ROGER BEAN
1916 (Hardcover, B&W)(6x17")(66 pgs.)
Chas. B. Jackson

#3-by Chic Jackson(1915 daily strips)	7.00	14.00	21.00

AL OF FBI   (See Little Al of the FBI)

ALPHONSE & GASTON & LEON
1903 (15"x10" Sunday strip reprints in color)
Hearst's New York American & Journal

by Fred Opper	15.00	37.50	60.00

ALVIN   (TV) (See 4-Color #1042)
Oct-Dec, 1962 - #28, Oct, 1973
Dell Publishing Co.

#12-021-212	.35	.70	1.05
2-28	.20	.40	.60
Alvin For President(10/64)	.15	.30	.45
-- & His Pals in Merry Christmas With Clyde Crashcup & Leonardo #1(02-120-402)12-2/64, reprinted in 1966	.35	.70	1.05

AMAZING ADULT FANTASY (Amazing Adventures #1-6; Amazing Fantasy #15)
#7, Dec, 1961 - #14, July, 1962
Marvel Comics Group (AMI)

#7	3.00	6.00	9.00
8-14: All Ditko stories	2.50	5.00	7.50

AMAZING ADVENTURE FUNNIES (Fantoman #2 on)
June, 1940 - #2, Sept, 1940
Centaur Publications

(Amazing Adventure Funnies cont'd)

	Good	Fine	Mint
#1-The Fantom of the Fair by Gustavson, The Arrow, Skyrocket Steele From the Year X by Everett - All reprints from Amazing Mystery Funnies & Funny Pages; Burgos art	40.00	80.00	120.00
2-Reprints. This issue came out after Fantoman #2	20.00	40.00	60.00

AMAZING ADVENTURES
1950 - #6, Fall, 1952
Ziff-Davis Publ. Co.

#1-Wood, Schomburg, Anderson, Whitney stories	7.00	14.00	21.00
2-5-Anderson art	2.50	5.00	7.50
6-Krigstein story	3.00	6.00	9.00

AMAZING ADVENTURES (Amaz. Adult Fantasy #7)
June, 1961 - #6, Nov, 1961
Marvel Comics Group (AMI)

#1-Origin Dr. Droom by Kirby; Ditko & Kirby art in all; Kirby covers #1-6	7.00	14.00	21.00
2	3.35	6.75	10.00
3-6: Last Dr. Droom	2.50	5.00	7.50

AMAZING ADVENTURES
Aug, 1970 - #39, Nov, 1976
Marvel Comics Group

#1-Inhumans by Kirby & Black Widow begin	.75	1.50	2.25
2-4-Last Kirby Inhumans	.50	1.00	1.50
5-8-Adams art; #8-Last Black Widow	.65	1.35	2.00
9,10: #10-Last Inhumans(origin reprint by Kirby)	.40	.80	1.20
11-Beast begins, ends #17	.25	.50	.75
12-17	.25	.50	.75
18-War of the Worlds begins; 1st app. Kill-raven; Adams art	.65	1.35	2.00
19-39: #34-Death of Hawk	.25	.50	.75

NOTE: *Adams* covers-#6-8, *pencils* part-#18; *Chaykin* story-#19; *Everett* inks-#3-5,9; *Kirby* art-#1-4; *Ploog* inks-#12. *Craig Russell* art-#27-39.

AMAZING ADVENTURES OF CAPTAIN CARVEL AND
HIS CARVEL CRUSADERS, THE (See Carvel Comics)

AMAZING CHAN & THE CHAN CLAN, THE (TV)
May, 1973 - #4, Feb, 1974 (Hanna-Barbera)
Gold Key

#1-4		.15	.30

AMAZING COMICS (Complete #2)
Fall, 1944
Timely Comics

	Good	Fine	Mint
#1-The Destroyer, The Whizzer, The Young Allies, Sergeant Dix	40.00	80.00	120.00

AMAZING DETECTIVE CASES
#3, Nov, 1950 - #14, Sept, 1952
Marvel/Atlas Comics(CCC)

#3	1.00	2.00	3.00
4-10	.65	1.35	2.00
11,13,14: #13-Everett story, 4 pgs.	.65	1.35	2.00
12-Krigstein art	1.50	3.00	4.50

AMAZING FANTASY (--Adult Fantasy #7-14;
Amazing Adventures #1-6)
#15, Aug, 1962
Marvel Comics Group(AMI)

#15-Origin & 1st app. of Spider-Man by Ditko; Kirby/Ditko cover	120.00	240.00	360.00

AMAZING GHOST STORIES (Formerly Nightmare)
#14, Oct, 1954 - #16, Feb, 1955
St. John Publishing Co.

#14-Kinstler art	1.75	3.35	5.00
15-Reprints Weird Thrillers #5	1.00	2.00	3.00
16-Kubert reprints of Weird Thrillers #4	1.50	3.00	4.50

AMAZING-MAN COMICS
#5, Sept, 1939 - #27, Feb, 1942
Centaur Publications

#5(#1)-Origin A-Man the Amazing Man by Bill Everett; The Cat-Man by Tarpe Mills (also #8), Mighty Man, Minimidget & Sidekick Ritty, & The Iron Skull begin	60.00	120.00	180.00
6-Origin The Amazing Man retold; The Shark begins	30.00	60.00	90.00
7-Magician From Mars begins	20.00	40.00	60.00
8-11: #11-Zardi, the Eternal Man begins; Amazing Man dons costume; last Everett issue	16.50	33.25	50.00
12,13	12.00	24.00	36.00
14-Dr. Hypno begins (called Dr. Psycho #14)	10.00	20.00	30.00
15-20	10.00	20.00	30.00
21-TNT Todd app.	8.00	16.00	24.00
22-Dash Darnell, The Human Meteor & The Voice app.	8.00	16.00	24.00

Amazing Adventures #4, © MCG

Amazing Fantasy #15, © MCG

Amazing-Man Comics #19, © Cen

Amaz. Mystery Funnies V2#6, © Cen

Amazing Spider-Man #1, © MCG

Amazing Spider-Man #9, © MCG

	Good	Fine	Mint
(Amazing-Man Comics cont'd)			
23-Intro. Tommy the Amazing Kid; The Marks-			
man only app.	8.00	16.00	24.00
24,27	8.00	16.00	24.00
25,26-Meteor Martin by Wolverton in both			
	20.00	40.00	60.00

AMAZING MYSTERIES
#32, May, 1949 - #35, Jan, 1950
Marvel Comics (CCC)

#32-35	1.00	2.00	3.00

AMAZING MYSTERY FUNNIES
Aug, 1938 - V3#8, Sept, 1940 (#24)
Centaur Publications

V1#1-Everett cover; Dick Kent Adv. story;			
Skyrocket Steele in the Year X on cover			
only	50.00	100.00	150.00
2-Everett & Eisner art			
	25.00	50.00	75.00
3-Everett & Eisner art; Everett cover			
	15.00	30.00	45.00
3(#4,12/38)-No# on cover, #3 on inside			
	12.00	24.00	36.00
V2#1-3: #1-Everett art	10.00	20.00	30.00
4-Dan Hastings begins; ends #5			
	10.00	20.00	30.00
5,6	10.00	20.00	30.00
7-Intro. The Fantom of the Fair; Everett,			
Gustavson, Burgos art			
	30.00	60.00	90.00
8-Origin & 1st app. Speed Centaur			
	16.50	33.25	50.00
9-11	12.00	24.00	36.00
12-Wolverton art	17.50	35.00	52.50
V3#1(#17)-Intro. Bullet	10.00	20.00	30.00
18,20	10.00	20.00	30.00
19,21-24-All have Space Patrol by			
Wolverton	20.00	40.00	60.00

AMAZING SAINTS
1974   (39¢)
Logos International

True story of Phil Saint	.15	.30

AMAZING SPIDER-MAN, THE (See Amazing Fant-
asy, Aurora, Book & Record--, Giant Comics
To Color, Marvel Treasury Ed., Spectacular
--, & Spidey Super Stories)

AMAZING SPIDER-MAN, THE
March, 1963 - Present
Marvel Comics Group

#1-Retells origin by Steve Ditko; F.F. x-

	Good	Fine	Mint
over; Kirby cover	100.00	200.00	300.00
1-Reprint from the Golden Record Comic set			
	1.35	2.75	4.00
with record....	2.00	4.00	6.00
2	30.00	60.00	90.00
3-Human Torch cameo; intro. Doc Ock			
	20.00	40.00	60.00
4-6: #5-Dr. Doom app.	15.00	30.00	45.00
7-10: #8-Fant.-4 app.	9.00	18.00	27.00
11-15: #14-Intro. Green Goblin; Hulk x-over			
	6.00	12.00	18.00
16-20: #17-Fant.-4 app.	3.35	6.75	10.00
21-30	2.00	4.00	6.00
31-38-Last Ditko ish.	1.35	2.75	4.00
39-60	1.00	2.00	3.00
61-80	.75	1.50	2.25
81-89	.60	1.20	1.80
90-Death of Capt. Stacy	1.00	2.00	3.00
91-93,95,99,100	.50	1.00	1.50
94-Origin retold	.65	1.35	2.00
96-98-Drug books not approved by CCA			
	1.00	2.00	3.00
101-Intro. Morbius	.75	1.50	2.25
102-Origin Morbius	.75	1.50	2.25
103-120	.40	.80	1.20
121-Death of Gwen Stacy	2.00	4.00	6.00
122-Death Green Goblin	2.00	4.00	6.00
123-140: #124-Intro. Man Wolf, origin-#125.			
#129-1st app. The Punisher			
	.25	.50	.75
141-150	.20	.40	.60
151-170	.15	.30	.45
171-178		.15	.30
Annual #1(1964)	5.00	10.00	15.00
Annual #2	3.00	6.00	9.00
Special #3,4	1.75	3.35	5.00
Special #5-8	1.00	2.00	3.00
King Size #9 ('73)	.65	1.35	2.00
Annual #10(6/76)-1st app. Human Fly			
	.50	1.00	1.50
Annual #11 (9/77)	.25	.50	.75
Giant-Size #1 (7/74)	.65	1.35	2.00
Giant-Size #2	.50	1.00	1.50
Giant-Size #3-6(9/75): #4-The Punisher app.			
	.40	.80	1.20
Giveaway-Esquire & Eye Magazines(2/69)-Minia-			
ture)-Still attached	2.00	4.00	6.00
-- vs. the Prodigy Giveaway, 16pgs. in color			
('76)-5x6½"-Sex education; distr. thru			
Planned Parenthood	.65	1.35	2.00

NOTE: *Ditko art-#1-38, Annuals #1,2. Kirby
story-#8. Starlin art-#113,114.*

AMAZING WILLIE MAYS, THE
No Date (Aug, 1954?)
Famous Funnies Publ.

No #	2.00	4.00	6.00

AMBUSH (See 4-Color Comics #314)

	Good	Fine	Mint
Mason	4.00	8.00	12.00

AMERICA IN ACTION
1942; 1945 (36 pgs.)
Dell(Imp. Publ. Co.)/Mayflower House Publ.

	Good	Fine	Mint
1942-Dell-(68pgs.)	2.50	5.00	7.50

#1(1945)-Has 3 adaptations from American history; Kiefer, Schrotter & Webb art

	2.50	5.00	7.50

AMERICAN COMICS
1940's
Theatre Giveaways (Liberty Theatre, Grand Rapids, Mich. known)

Many possible combinations. "Golden Age" superhero comics with new cover added and given away at theatres. Following known: Superman #59, Capt. Marvel #20, Capt. Marvel Jr. #5, Action #33, Whiz #39. Value would vary with book and should at least be equal to the original.

AMERICAN AIR FORCES (See A-1 Comics)
1944 - 1945; 1951 - 1954
William H. Wise(Flying Cadet Publ. Co./Hasan (#1))/Life's Romances/Magazine Ent. #5 on

#1-Article by Zack Mosley, creator of Smilin'			
Jack	3.00	6.00	9.00
2-4	1.75	3.35	5.00

NOTE: *All part comic, part magazine. Art by Whitney, Chas. Quinlan, H.C. Kiefer, and Tony Dipreta.*

#5(A-1#45),6(A-1#54),7(A-1#58),8(A-1#65),
9(A-1#67),10(A-1#74),11(A-1#79),12(A-1#91)

	1.35	2.75	4.00

NOTE: *Powell art-#5,6,8,9,11,12.*

AMERICAN GRAPHICS
1954 (25¢)
Henry Stewart

#1-The Maid of the Mist, The Last of the			
Eeries(Indian Legends of Niagara)(Sold at Niagara Falls)	2.00	4.00	6.00
2-Victory at Niagara & Laura Secord (Heroine of the War of 1812)	2.00	4.00	6.00

AMERICAN INDIAN, THE (See Picture Progress)

AMERICAN LIBRARY
1944 (68pgs.)(15¢)
David McKay Publications

#3-6: #4-Case of the Crooked Candle-Perry

AMERICA'S BEST COMICS
Feb, 1942 - #31, July, 1949
Nedor/Better/Standard Publications

#1-The Woman in Red, Black Terror, Captain Future, Doc Strange, The Liberator, & Don Davis, Secret Ace begin

	40.00	80.00	120.00
2-Origin The American Eagle; The Woman in Red ends	20.00	40.00	60.00
3-Pyroman begins	15.00	30.00	45.00
4	13.50	26.75	40.00
5-Last Captain Future-not in #4; Lone Eagle app.	12.00	24.00	36.00
6,7-American Crusader app. in #6	9.00	18.00	27.00
8-Last Liberator	8.00	16.00	24.00
9-The Fighting Yank begins; The Ghost app.	8.00	16.00	24.00
10-13,15-20	6.00	12.00	18.00
14-Last American Eagle	6.00	12.00	18.00
21,24	4.00	8.00	12.00
22-Capt. Future app.	4.00	8.00	12.00
23-Miss Masque begins; last Doc Strange	6.00	12.00	18.00
25-Last Fighting Yank; Sea Eagle app.	5.00	10.00	15.00
26-The Phantom Detective & The Silver Knight app.	5.00	10.00	15.00
27,28-Commando Cubs app.; Doc Strange in #27	5.00	10.00	15.00
29-Last Pyroman	5.00	10.00	15.00
30,31	5.00	10.00	15.00

NOTE: *American Eagle not in #3,8,9,13. Fighting Yank not in #10,12,14. Liberator not in #2,6,7. Pyroman not in #9,11,14-16, 23,25-27. Schomburg (Xela) covers-#25,27,29.*

AMERICA'S BEST TV COMICS
1967 (Produced by Marvel Comics)
American Broadcasting Company

#1-Spider-Man, Fantastic Four, Casper, King Kong, George of the Jungle, Journey to the Center of the Earth app. (Promotes new TV cartoon show) 1.00 2.00 3.00

AMERICA'S BIGGEST COMICS BOOK
1944 (196 pgs.) (One Shot)
Better Publications

#1-The Grim Reaper, The Silver Knight, Zudo, the Jungle Boy, Commando Cubs, Thunderhoof app. 7.00 14.00 21.00

The American Air Forces #1. © WHW

America's Best #8. © STD

America's Best #27. © STD

18

America's Funniest #1, © WHW | America's Greatest #1, © Faw | Andy Hardy (Bendix Giveaway), © Dell

AMERICA'S FUNNIEST COMICS
1941 (80 pgs.) (15¢)
William H. Wise

	Good	Fine	Mint
No#(#1), 2	2.00	4.00	6.00

AMERICA'S GREATEST COMICS
1941 - #8, Summer, 1943 (100 pgs.)
Fawcett Publications

#1-Bulletman, Spy Smasher, Capt.Marvel, Minute Man & Mr. Scarlet begin	85.00	170.00	255.00
2	40.00	80.00	120.00
3	25.00	50.00	75.00
4-Commando Yank begins; Golden Arrow & Ibis the Invincible & Spy Smasher cameo in Captain Marvel	20.00	40.00	60.00
5	20.00	40.00	60.00
6	15.00	30.00	45.00
7-Balbo, the Boy Magician app.; Captain Marvel, Bulletman cameo in Mr. Scarlet	15.00	30.00	45.00
8-Capt. Marvel Jr. & Golden Arrow app.; Spy Smasher x-over in Capt. Midnight; no Minute Man or Commando Yank	15.00	30.00	45.00

AMERICA'S SWEETHEART SUNNY (See Sunny)

ANARCHO DICTATOR OF DEATH (See Comics Novel)

ANCHORS ANDREWS (The Saltwater Daffy)
1/53 - #4, 7/53 (Anchors the Saltwater-- #4)
St. John Publishing Co.

#1	1.00	2.00	3.00
2-4	.65	1.35	2.00

ANDY & WOODY (See March of Comics #40,55,76)

ANDY BURNETT (See 4-Color Comics #865)

ANDY COMICS
June, 1948
Current Publications

#20-Archie-type comic	.65	1.35	2.00

ANDY DEVINE WESTERN
Dec, 1950 - 1952
Fawcett Publications

#1	5.00	10.00	15.00
2-10	2.50	5.00	7.50
11-21	1.75	3.35	5.00

ANDY GRIFFITH (See 4-Color #1252,1341)

ANDY HARDY COMICS (See Movie Comics #3, Fiction House)
1952 - #6, 9-11/54
Dell Publishing Co.

	Good	Fine	Mint
4-Color #389,447,480,515	.80	1.60	2.40
#5,6	.50	1.00	1.50
-- & the New Automatic Gas Clothes Dryer('52, 16pgs.,5x7¼")-Bendix Giveaway	1.00	2.00	3.00

ANDY PANDA
1943 - Nov-Jan, 1962 (Walter Lantz)
Dell Publishing Co.

4-Color #25('43)	20.00	40.00	60.00
4-Color #54('44)	12.00	24.00	36.00
4-Color #85('45)	6.00	12.00	18.00
4-Color #130('46),154,198	3.00	6.00	9.00
4-Color #216,240,258,280,297	1.75	3.35	5.00
4-Color #326,345,358	1.20	2.40	3.60
4-Color #383,409	1.00	2.00	3.00
#16-30	.65	1.35	2.00
31-56	.50	1.00	1.50
(See March of Comics #5,22,79 & Super Book #4,15,27.)			

ANDY PANDA
Aug, 1973 - Present (Walter Lantz)
Gold Key

#1-Reprints	.20	.40	.60
2-10-All reprints		.15	.30
11-22-All new stories		.15	.30

ANGEL
Aug, 1954 - #16, Nov-Jan, 1958-59
Dell Publishing Co.

4-Color #576(8/54)	.50	1.00	1.50
#2(5-7/55) - #16	.35	.70	1.05

ANGEL AND THE APE (Meet Angel #4-7)
11-12/68 - #6, 9-10/69 (See Showcase #77)
National Periodical Publications

#1-6: Wood art in all	.40	.80	1.20

ANGELIC ANGELINA
1909 (11½x17"; 30pgs.; 2 colors)
Cupples & Leon Company

By Munson Paddock	10.00	20.00	30.00

ANIMAL ADVENTURES
Dec, 1953 - #3, 1954
Accepted Publications

#1-3	.65	1.35	2.00

ANIMAL ANTICS (Movie Town -- #20 on)
Mar-Apr, 1946 - #19, Mar-Apr, 1949
National Periodical Publications

	Good	Fine	Mint
#1-Raccoon Kids begin	2.50	5.00	7.50
2-19: #14-Post art	1.00	2.00	3.00

ANIMAL COMICS
1942 - #30, Dec-Jan, 1947-48
Dell Publishing Co.

#1-1st Pogo app. by Walt Kelly (Dan Noonan art in most issues)	135.00	270.00	405.00
2-Uncle Wiggily begins	55.00	110.00	165.00
3,5	40.00	80.00	120.00
4,6,7-No Pogo	20.00	40.00	60.00
8-10	23.50	46.75	70.00
11-15	16.50	33.25	50.00
16-20	10.00	20.00	30.00
21-30: #25-30-"Jigger" by John Stanley	7.00	14.00	21.00

NOTE: #18-30-Dan Noonan art. Gollub art in
most later issues.

ANIMAL CRACKERS (Also see Advs. of Patoruzu)
1946 - #31, July, 1950; 1959
Green Publ. Co./Norlen/Fox Feat.(Hero Books)

#1-Super Cat begins	1.00	2.00	3.00
2-31	.35	.70	1.05
#31(Fox)-Formerly My Love Secret	.65	1.35	2.00
9(1959-Norlen)	.35	.70	1.05
No#, no date, no publ.	.35	.70	1.05

ANIMAL FABLES
July-Aug, 1946 - #7, Nov-Dec, 1947
E.C. Comics

#1	12.00	24.00	36.00
2-6	8.00	16.00	24.00
7-Origin Moon Girl	20.00	40.00	60.00

ANIMAL FAIR (Fawcett's --)
March, 1946 - #11, Feb, 1947
Fawcett Publications

#1	2.00	4.00	6.00
2-6	1.00	2.00	3.00
7-11	.65	1.35	2.00

ANIMAL FUN
1953
Premier Magazines

#1-(3-D)	4.00	8.00	12.00

ANIMAL WORLD, THE (See 4-Color Comics #713)

ANIMATED COMICS
No date given (Summer, 1947?)
E.C. Comics

	Good	Fine	Mint
#1 (Scarce)	35.00	70.00	105.00

ANIMATED FUNNY COMIC TUNES (See Funny Tunes)

ANIMATED MOVIE-TUNES (Also see Movie Tunes)
Fall, 1945
Margood Publishing Co. (Timely)

#1-Super Rabbit	1.00	2.00	3.00

ANNETTE (See 4-Color Comics #905)

ANNETTE'S LIFE STORY (See 4-Color #1100)

ANNIE OAKLEY
Spr, 1948 - #4, 11/48; #5, 6/55 - #11, 6/56
Marvel/Atlas Comics(MPI #1-4/CDS #5 on)

#1 (1st Series)(1948)	3.00	6.00	9.00
2-Kurtzman art	3.00	6.00	9.00
3,4	1.75	3.35	5.00
5 (2nd Series)(1955)	1.35	2.75	4.00
6-8: #8-Woodbridge art	1.35	2.75	4.00
9-Williamson story, 4pgs.	2.00	4.00	6.00
10,11	1.00	2.00	3.00

ANNIE OAKLEY AND TAGG
1953 - 1965
Dell Publishing Co./Gold Key

4-Color #438	1.75	3.35	5.00
4-Color #481,575	1.35	2.75	4.00
#4(7-9/55)-#10	1.00	2.00	3.00
11-18(1-3/59)	.65	1.35	2.00
#1(7/65-G.K.)	.35	.70	1.05

ANOTHER WORLD (See Strange Stories From --)

ANTHRO (See Showcase)
July-Aug, 1968 - #6, July-Aug, 1969
National Periodical Publications

#1-Howie Post art in all	.40	.80	1.20
2-5	.20	.40	.60
6-Wood inks	.20	.40	.60

ANTONY & CLEOPATRA (See Ideal, A Classical
Comic)

A-1 COMICS (A-1 appears on covers #1-18 only)
See individual title listings. 1st two issues not numbered.
1944 - #139, Sept-Oct, 1955
Life's Romances Publ.-#1/Compix/Magazine Ent.

Animal Comics #10. © Dell

Animal Fair #1. © Faw

Annie Oakley #1. © MCG

A-1 Comics #3, © ME

A-1 Comics #11, © ME

A-1 Comics #37, © ME

	Good	Fine	Mint
(A-1 Comics cont'd)			

#1-Dotty Dripple(1 pg.), Mr. Ex, Bush Berry, Rocky, Lew Loyal(20pgs.)
| | 1.00 | 2.00 | 3.00 |
| 2-Dotty Dripple | 1.00 | 2.00 | 3.00 |

3-8,10-Texas Slim & Dirty Dalton, The Corsair, Teddy Rich, Inca Dinca, Tommy Tinker, Little Mexico & Tugboat Tim, The Masquerader & others
	1.00	2.00	3.00
9-Texas Slim (all)	1.50	3.00	4.50
11,12-Teena	1.00	2.00	3.00

13-Guns of Fact & Fiction (1948). Ingels & J. Craig art
| | 3.00 | 6.00 | 9.00 |

14-Tim Holt Western Adventures #1 (1948)
	12.00	24.00	36.00
15-Teena	1.00	2.00	3.00
16-Vacation Comics	.65	1.35	2.00
17-Tim Holt #2	6.00	12.00	18.00

18-Jimmy Durante. Last issue to carry A-1 on cover
	4.00	8.00	12.00
19-Tim Holt #3	6.00	12.00	18.00
20-Jimmy Durante	3.00	6.00	9.00

21-Joan of Arc(1949)-Ogden Whitney art
	3.00	6.00	9.00
22-Dick Powell(1949)	1.00	2.00	3.00
23-Cowboys 'N' Indians #6	1.00	2.00	3.00

24-Trail Colt #1-Frazetta, reprinted in Manhunt #13. Ingels cvr. 10.00 20.00 30.00

25-Fibber McGee & Molly(1949)
| | 1.00 | 2.00 | 3.00 |

26-Trail Colt #2-Ingels cover
| | 8.00 | 16.00 | 24.00 |

27-Ghost Rider #1(1950)-Origin Ghost Rider
| | 17.50 | 35.00 | 52.50 |

28-Christmas-(Koko & Kola #6)(5/47)
| | 1.00 | 2.00 | 3.00 |

29-Ghost Rider #2-Frazetta cover (1950)
| | 15.00 | 30.00 | 45.00 |
| 30-Jet #1-Powell art | 5.00 | 10.00 | 15.00 |

31-Ghost Rider #3-Frazetta cover & origin (1951)
	15.00	30.00	45.00
32-Jet Powers #2	3.00	6.00	9.00
33-Muggsy Mouse #1('51)	.50	1.00	1.50

34-Ghost Rider #4-Frazetta cover (1951)
| | 15.00 | 30.00 | 45.00 |

35-Jet Powers #3-Williamson & Evans story
| | 7.00 | 14.00 | 21.00 |
| 36-Muggsy Mouse #2 | .50 | 1.00 | 1.50 |

37-Ghost Rider #5-Frazetta cover (1951)
| | 15.00 | 30.00 | 45.00 |

38-Jet Powers #4-Williamson & Wood story
	8.00	16.00	24.00
39-Muggsy Mouse #3	.50	1.00	1.50
40-Dogface Dooley #1('51)	1.00	2.00	3.00
41-Cowboys 'N' Indians #7	1.00	2.00	3.00
42-Best of the West #1	6.00	12.00	18.00
43-Dogface Dooley #2	1.00	2.00	3.00
44-Ghost Rider #6	4.00	8.00	12.00

	Good	Fine	Mint
45-American Air Forces #5	1.35	2.75	4.00
46-Best of the West #2	3.00	6.00	9.00

47-Thun'da, King of the Congo #1-Frazetta cover & stories('52) 120.00 240.00 360.00
| 48-Cowboys 'N' Indians #8 | 1.00 | 2.00 | 3.00 |
| 49-Dogface Dooley #3 | 1.00 | 2.00 | 3.00 |

50-Danger Is Their Business #11 (1952)
	2.00	4.00	6.00
51-Ghost Rider #7 ('52)	4.00	8.00	12.00
52-Best of the West #3	3.00	6.00	9.00
53-Dogface Dooley #4	1.00	2.00	3.00

54-American Air Forces #6 (8/52)
| | 1.35 | 2.75 | 4.00 |

55-U.S. Marines #5-Powell art
	1.35	2.75	4.00
56-Thun'da #2	8.00	16.00	24.00
57-Ghost Rider #8	4.00	8.00	12.00
58-American Air Forces #7	1.35	2.75	4.00
59-Best of the West #4	3.00	6.00	9.00
60-The U.S. Marines #6	1.35	2.75	4.00

61-Space Ace #5(1953)-Guardineer art
| | 4.00 | 8.00 | 12.00 |

62-Starr Flagg, Undercover Girl #5
| | 8.00 | 16.00 | 24.00 |

63-Manhunt #13-Frazetta reprinted from A-1 #24
	8.00	16.00	24.00
64-Dogface Dooley #5	1.00	2.00	3.00
65-American Air Forces #8	1.35	2.75	4.00
66-Best of the West #5	3.00	6.00	9.00
67-American Air Forces #9	1.35	2.75	4.00
68-U.S. Marines #7	1.35	2.75	4.00
69-Ghost Rider #9(10/52)	4.00	8.00	12.00
70-Best of the West #6	2.50	5.00	7.50
71-Ghost Rider #10(12/52)	4.00	8.00	12.00
72-U.S. Marines #8	1.35	2.75	4.00
73-Thun'da #3	7.00	14.00	21.00

74-American Air Forces #10
	1.35	2.75	4.00
75-Ghost Rider #11(3/52)	3.35	6.75	10.00
76-Best of the West #7	2.00	4.00	6.00

77-Manhunt #14 (classic cover)
	2.35	4.75	7.00
78-Thun'da #4	6.00	12.00	18.00
79-American Air Forces #11	.85	1.70	2.50
80-Ghost Rider #12(6/52)	3.35	6.75	10.00
81-Best of the West #8	2.00	4.00	6.00

82-Cave Girl #11(1953)-Powell art (Origin)
	7.00	14.00	21.00
83-Thun'da #5	6.00	12.00	18.00
84-Ghost Rider #13(8/53)	3.35	6.75	10.00
85-Best of the West #9	2.00	4.00	6.00
86-Thun'da #6	6.00	12.00	18.00
87-Best of the West #10	2.00	4.00	6.00

88-Bobby Benson's B-Bar-B Riders #20
| | 1.50 | 3.00 | 4.50 |
| 89-Home Run #3 | .60 | 1.20 | 1.80 |

90-Red Hawk #11(1953)-Powell art
| | 2.00 | 4.00 | 6.00 |

(A-1 Comics cont'd)	Good	Fine	Mint
91-American Air Forces #12	.85	1.70	2.50
92-Dream Book of Romance #5			
	1.00	2.00	3.00
93-Great Western #8('54)-Origin The Ghost Rider	3.00	6.00	9.00
94-White Indian #11-Frazetta reprints			
	20.00	40.00	60.00
95-Muggsy Mouse #4	.50	1.00	1.50
96-Cave Girl #12, with Thun'da; Powell art			
	6.00	12.00	18.00
97-Best of the West #11	2.50	5.00	7.50
98-Undercover Girl #6	6.00	12.00	18.00
99-White Indian #12-Frazetta reprints			
	20.00	40.00	60.00
100-Badmen of the West #1-Meskin art(?)			
	5.00	10.00	15.00
101-Dream Book of Romance #6			
	1.35	2.75	4.00
102-			
103-Best of the West #12	2.50	5.00	7.50
104-White Indian #13-Frazetta reprints (1954)			
	20.00	40.00	60.00
105-Great Western #9-Ghost Rider app.; Powell art, 6pgs.; Bolle cvr.	2.00	4.00	6.00
106-Dream Book of Love #1-Powell & Bolle art			
	1.35	2.75	4.00
107-Hot Dog #1	.65	1.35	2.00
108-Red Fox #15 (1954)	2.50	5.00	7.50
109-Dream Book of Romance #7 (7-8/54)			
	1.35	2.75	4.00
110-Hot Dog #2	.65	1.35	2.00
111-I'm A Cop #1('54)	1.75	3.35	5.00
112-Ghost Rider #14('54)	4.00	8.00	12.00
113-Great Western #10	2.00	4.00	6.00
114-Dream Book of Love #2-Guardineer, Bolle art			
	1.35	2.75	4.00
115-Hot Dog #3	.65	1.35	2.00
116-Cave Girl #13	6.00	12.00	18.00
117-White Indian #14	6.00	12.00	18.00
118-Undercover Girl #7	6.00	12.00	18.00
119-Straight Arrow's Fury #1			
	2.50	5.00	7.50
120-Badmen of the West #2	2.50	5.00	7.50
121-Mysteries of Scotland Yard #1; reprints from Manhunt	2.50	5.00	7.50
122-Black Phantom #1(11/54)	6.00	12.00	18.00
123-Dream Book of Love #3(10-11/54)			
	1.35	2.75	4.00
124-Dream Book of Romance #8(10-11/54)			
	1.35	2.75	4.00
125-Cave Girl #14	6.00	12.00	18.00
126-I'm A Cop #2-Powell art	1.00	2.00	3.00
127-Great Western #11('54)	2.00	4.00	6.00
128-I'm A Cop #3	1.00	2.00	3.00
129-The Avenger #1('55)	7.00	14.00	21.00
130-Strongman #1	4.00	8.00	12.00
131-The Avenger #2('55)	3.00	6.00	9.00

	Good	Fine	Mint
132-Strongman #2	3.00	6.00	9.00
133-The Avenger #3	3.00	6.00	9.00
134-Strongman #3	3.00	6.00	9.00
135-White Indian #15	6.00	12.00	18.00
136-Hot Dog #4	.65	1.35	2.00
137-Africa #1	4.00	8.00	12.00
138-The Avenger #4	3.00	6.00	9.00
139-Strongman #4-Powell art			
	3.00	6.00	9.00

APACHE
1951
Fiction House Magazines

	Good	Fine	Mint
#1	2.00	4.00	6.00
I.W. Reprint #1	.65	1.35	2.00

APACHE KID (Formerly Reno Browne; Western
Gunfighters #20 on)(Also see Two-Gun Western)
#53, 12/50 - #10, 1/52; #11, 12/54 - #19,4/56
Marvel/Atlas Comics(MPC #53-10/CPS #11 on)

#53(#1)	2.50	5.00	7.50
2-5	1.50	3.00	4.50
6-10 (1951-52)	1.35	2.75	4.00
11-19 (1954-56)	1.00	2.00	3.00

APACHE MASSACRE (See Chief Victorio's --)

APACHE TRAIL
Sept, 1957 - #4, June, 1958
Steinway/America's Best

#1	.75	1.50	2.25
2-4	.40	.80	1.20

APPROVED COMICS
March, 1954
Approved Comics

#1-The Hawk; same as The Hawk #5			
	1.00	2.00	3.00

AQUAMAN (See Showcase, Brave & the Bold,
Super DC Giant, Adventure, DC Super-Stars
#7, Detective, and World's Finest)

AQUAMAN
1-2/62 - #56, 3-4/71; #57, 8-9/77 - Present
National Periodical Publications/DC Comics

#1-Intro. Quisp	4.00	8.00	12.00
2,3	2.00	4.00	6.00
4-10	1.00	2.00	3.00
11-20: #11-Intro. Mera. #18-Aquaman weds Mera	.65	1.35	2.00
21-30: #23-Birth of Aquababy. #29-Intro.			

A-I Comics #90, © ME

Apache Kid #6, © MCG

Aquaman #12, © DC

(Aquaman cont'd)	Good	Fine	Mint
Ocean Master, Aquaman's step-brother			
	.60	1.20	1.80
31,32,34-40	.40	.80	1.20
33-Intro. Aqua-Girl	.50	1.00	1.50
41-47,49	.35	.70	1.05
48-Origin reprinted	.40	.80	1.20
50-52-Adams Deadman	1.50	3.00	4.50
53-56('71)	.25	.50	.75
57('77),59,60	.15	.30	.45
58-Origin retold	.15	.30	.45

NOTE: *Aparo* story-#40. *Newton* story-#60.

AQUANAUTS (See 4-Color Comics #1197)

ARCHIE AND ME
Oct, 1964 - Present
Archie Publications

#1	2.00	4.00	6.00
2-5	1.00	2.00	3.00
6-10	.65	1.35	2.00
11-30	.35	.70	1.05
31-42	.25	.50	.75
43-63-(All Giants)	.20	.40	.60
64-97-(Reg. Size)		.15	.30

ARCHIE...ARCHIE ANDREWS, WHERE ARE YOU?
Feb, 1977 - Present   (Digest size, 160 pgs.)
Archie Publications

#1	.35	.70	1.05
2,3	.25	.50	.75

ARCHIE AS PUREHEART THE POWERFUL
Sept, 1966 - #6, Nov, 1967
Archie Publications (Radio Comics)

#1	.75	1.50	2.25
2-6	.40	.80	1.20

NOTE: *Evilheart cameos in all. Title: -- As Capt. Purehear the Powerful-#4,6; -- As Capt. Pureheart-#5.*

ARCHIE AT RIVERDALE HIGH
Aug, 1972 - Present
Archie Publications

#1	.50	1.00	1.50
2-10	.35	.70	1.05
11-30	.20	.40	.60
31-50		.15	.30

ARCHIE COMICS (See Pep & Oxydol-Dreft)
Winter, 1942-43 - Present
MLJ Magazines/Archie Publications #20 on

#1-Intro. Veronica	45.00	90.00	135.00

	Good	Fine	Mint
2	20.00	40.00	60.00
3-5	10.00	20.00	30.00
6-10	7.00	14.00	21.00
11-20	5.00	10.00	15.00
21-30	3.00	6.00	9.00
31-50	2.00	4.00	6.00
51-70: #69-Katy Keene sty.	1.50	3.00	4.50
71-100	1.00	2.00	3.00
101-130	.65	1.35	2.00
131-190	.35	.70	1.05
191-220	.25	.50	.75
221-240	.15	.30	.45
241-270		.15	.30
Annual #1(1949)	9.00	18.00	27.00
Annual #2(1951)	4.00	8.00	12.00
Annual #3-6(1952-55)	3.00	6.00	9.00
Annual #7-15(1956-65)	1.50	3.00	4.50
Annual #16-26(1966-75)	.65	1.35	2.00

Annual Digest #27('75)-#31('77): #29-196pgs., rest are 160 pgs.   .50 1.00 1.50

--All-Star Specials(Wint.'75)-$1.25; 6 remaindered Archie comics rebound in each; titles: "The World of Giant Comics", "Giant Grab Bag of Comics","Triple Giant Comics", & "Giant Spec. Comics"
                        .65 1.35 2.00

Mini-Comics (1970-Fairmont Potato Chips Giveaway-Miniature)(8 issues-No#'s, 8pgs. each)   .35 .70 1.05

ARCHIE SHOE-STORE GIVEAWAY
1944-45; 12-15 pgs. of games, puzzles, stories like Superman-Tim books. No #'s - came out monthly.
Archie Publications

                        5.00 10.00 15.00

ARCHIE COMICS DIGEST
Aug, 1973 - Present   (Small size, 160 pgs.)
Archie Publications

#1	.50	1.00	1.50
2-10	.25	.50	.75
11-27	.20	.40	.60

ARCHIE GIANT SERIES MAGAZINE (--'s Christmas Stocking #1-6)(No #36-135, No #252-451)
1959 - Present
Archie Publications

#7-Katy Keene Holiday Fun 4.00 8.00 12.00
 8-Betty & Veronica Summer Fun('60)
 9-The World of Jughead(12/60)
10-Archie's Christmas Stocking(1/61)
11-Betty & Veronica Spectacular(6/61)
12-Katy Keene Holiday Fun(9/61)

Archie and Me #1, © AP   Archie Comics #1, © AP   Archie Annual #5, © AP

	Good	Fine	Mint
13-Betty & Veronica Summer Fun(10/61)			
14-The World of Jughead(12/61)			
each....	1.75	3.35	5.00
15-Archie's Christmas Stocking(1/62)			
16-Betty & Veronica Spectacular(6/62)			
17-Archie's Jokes(9/62)			
18-Betty & Veronica Summer Fun(10/62)			
19-The World of Jughead(12/62)			
20-Archie's Christmas Stocking(1/63)			
each....	1.35	2.75	4.00
21-Betty & Veronica Spectacular(6/63)			
22-Archie's Jokes(9/63)			
23-Betty & Veronica Summer Fun(10/63)			
24-The World of Jughead(12/63)			
25-Archie's Christmas Stocking(1/64)			
26-Betty & Veronica Spectacular(6/64)			
27-Archie's Jokes(8/64)			
28-Betty & Veronica Summer Fun(9/64)			
29-Around the World With Archie(10/64)			
30-The World of Jughead(12/64)			
31-Archie's Christmas Stocking(1/65)			
32-Betty & Veronica Spectacular(6/65)			
33-Archie's Jokes			
34-Betty & Veronica Summer Fun(9/65)			
35-Around the World With Archie(10/65)			
each....	.80	1.60	2.40
136-The World of Jughead(12/65)			
137-Archie's Christmas Stocking(1/66)			
138-Betty & Veronica Spectacular(6/66)			
139-Archie's Jokes(6/66)			
140-Betty & Veronica Summer Fun(8/66)			
141-Around the World With Archie(9/66)			
each....	.65	1.35	2.00
142-Archie's Super-Hero Special - Origin Capt.			
Pureheart, Capt. Hero, & Evilheart			
	1.00	2.00	3.00
143-The World of Jughead(12/66)			
144-Archie's Christmas Stocking(1/67)			
145-Betty & Veronica Spectacular(6/67)			
146-Archie's Jokes(6/67)			
147-Betty & Veronica Summer Fun(8/67)			
148-World of Archie(9/67)			
149-World of Jughead(10/67)			
150-Archie's Christmas Stocking(1/68)			
151-World of Archie(2/68)			
152-World of Jughead(2/68)			
153-Betty & Veronica Spectacular(6/68)			
154-Archie Jokes(6/68)			
155-Betty & Veronica Summer Fun(8/68)			
156-World of Archie(10/68)			
157-World of Jughead(12/68)			
158-Archie's Christmas Stocking(1/69)			
159-Betty & Veronica Christmas Spect.(1/69)			
160-World of Archie(2/69)			
each....	.65	1.35	2.00
161-World of Jughead(2/69)			
162-Betty & Veronica Spectacular(6/69)			
163-Archie's Jokes(8/69)			
164-Betty & Veronica Summer Fun(9/69)			
165-World of Archie(9/69)			
166-World of Jughead(9/69)			
167-Archie's Christmas Stocking(1/70)			
168-Betty & Veronica Christmas Spect.(1/70)			
169-Archie's Christmas Love-In(1/70)			
170-Jughead's Eat-Out Comic Book Mag.(12/69)			
171-World of Archie(2/70)			
172-World of Jughead(2/70)			
173-Betty & Veronica Spectacular(6/70)			
174-Archie's Jokes(8/70)			
175-Betty & Veronica Summer Fun(9/70)			
176-Li'l Jinx Giant Laugh-Out(8/70)			
177-World of Archie(9/70)			
178-World of Jughead(9/70)			
179-Archie's Christmas Stocking(1/71)			

	Good	Fine	Mint
180-Betty & Veronica Christmas Spect.(1/71)			
181-Archie's Christmas Love-In(1/71)			
182-World of Archie(2/71)			
183-World of Jughead(2/71)			
184-Betty & Veronica Spectacular(6/71)			
185-Li'l Jinx Giant Laugh-Out(6/71)			
186-Archie's Jokes(8/71)			
187-Betty & Veronica Summer Fun(9/71)			
188-World of Archie(9/71)			
189-World of Jughead(9/71)			
190-Archie's Christmas Stocking(12/71)			
191-Betty & Veronica Christmas Spect.(2/72)			
192-Archie's Christmas Love-In(1/72)			
193-World of Archie(3/72)			
194-World of Jughead(4/72)			
195-Li'l Jinx Christmas Bag(1/72)			
196-Sabrina's Christmas Magic(1/72)			
197-Betty & Veronica Spectacular(6/72)			
198-Archie's Jokes(8/72)			
199-Betty & Veronica Summer Fun			
200-World of Archie(10/72)			
each....	.25	.50	.75
201-Betty & Veronica Spectacular(10/72)			
202-World of Jughead(11/72)			
203-Archie's Christmas Stocking(12/72)			
204-Betty & Veronica Christmas Spect.(2/73)			
205-Archie's Christmas Love-In(1/73)			
206-Li'l Jinx Christmas Bag(12/72)			
207-Sabrina's Christmas Magic(12/72)			
208-World of Archie(3/73)			
209-World of Jughead(4/73)			
210-Betty & Veronica Spectacular(6/73)			
211-Archie's Jokes(8/73)			
212-Betty & Veronica Summer Fun(9/73)			
213-World of Archie(10/73)			
214-Betty & Veronica Spectacular			
215-World of Jughead			
216-Archie's Christmas Stocking(12/73)			
217-Betty & Veronica Christmas Spect.(2/74)			
218-Archie's Christmas Love-In(1/74)			
219-Li'l Jinx Christmas Bag(12/73)			
220-Sabrina's Christmas Magic(12/73)			
221-Betty & Veronica Spectacular(Advertised			
as World of Archie)(6/74)			
222-Archie's Jokes(Advertised as World of			
Jughead)(8/74)			
223-Li'l Jinx(8/74)			
224-Betty & Veronica Summer Fun(9/74)			
225-World of Archie(9/74)			
226-Betty & Veronica Spectacular(10/74)			
227-World of Jughead(10/74)			
228-Archie's Christmas Stocking(12/74)			
229-Betty & Veronica Christmas Spect.(12/74)			
230-Archie's Christmas Love-In(11/74)			
231-Sabrina's Christmas Magic(1/75)			
232-World of Archie(3/75)			
233-World of Jughead(4/75)			
234-Betty & Veronica Spectacular(6/75)			
235-Archie's Jokes(8/75)			
236-Betty & Veronica Summer Fun(9/75)			
237-World of Archie(9/75)			
238-Betty & Veronica Spectacular(10/75)			
239-World of Jughead(10/75)			
240-Archie's Christmas Stocking(12/75)			
241-Betty & Veronica Christmas Spect.(12/75)			
242-Archie's Christmas Love-In(1/76)			
243-Sabrina's Christmas Magic(1/76)			
244-World of Archie(3/76)			
245-World of Jughead(4/76)			
246-Betty & Veronica Spectacular(6/76)			
247-Archie's Jokes(8/76)			
248-Betty & Veronica Summer Fun(9/76)			
249-World of Archie(9/76)			
250-Betty & Veronica Spectacular(10/76)			
251-World of Jughead(10/76)			
each....	.15	.30	.45

(Archie Giant Series Mag. cont'd)

	Good	Fine	Mint
452-Archie's Christmas Stocking(12/76)			
453-Betty & Veronica Christmas Spect.(12/76)			
454-Archie's Christmas Love-In(1/77)			
455-Sabrina's Christmas Magic(1/77)			
456-World of Archie(3/77)			
457-World of Jughead(4/77)			
458-Betty & Veronica Spectacular(6/77)			
459-Archie's Jokes(8/77)-Shows 8/76 in error			
460-Betty & Veronica Summer Fun(9/77)			
461-World of Archie(9/77)			
462-Betty & Veronica Spectacular(10/77)			
463-World of Jughead(10/77)			
each....	.15	.30	.45

ARCHIE'S CHRISTMAS LOVE-IN (See Archie Giant
Series Mag. #169,181,192,205,218,230,242,454)

ARCHIE'S CHRISTMAS STOCKING (Archie Giant Ser-
1954 - #7, 1959 (Annual)(25¢) ies Mag. #7 on)
Archie Publications

#1	4.00	8.00	12.00
2-7	2.00	4.00	6.00

*(See Archie Giant Ser. Mag. #10,15,20,25,31,
137,144,150,158,167,179,190,203,216,228,240,
452.)*

ARCHIE'S CLEAN SLATE
1973   (35¢)
Spire Christian Comics (Fleming H. Revell Co.)

#1	.20	.40	.60

ARCHIE'S GIRLS, BETTY AND VERONICA
1950 - Present
Archie Publications

#1	10.00	20.00	30.00
2	5.00	10.00	15.00
3-5	3.35	6.75	10.00
6-10	2.50	5.00	7.50
11-20: #14-Katy Keene app.	2.00	4.00	6.00
21-30	1.50	3.00	4.50
31-60	1.00	2.00	3.00
61-100	.50	1.00	1.50
101-140: #118-Origin Superteen. #119-Last			
Superteen story	.25	.50	.75
141-180	.20	.40	.60
181-220	.15	.30	.45
221-264		.15	.30
Annual #1(1953)	4.00	8.00	12.00
Annual #2-5(1958)	2.00	4.00	6.00
Annual #6-8(1960)	1.50	3.00	4.50

ARCHIE'S JOKE BOOK MAGAZINE (See Joke Book--)

1953 - #3, Summer, 1954; #15, 1954 - Present
Archie Publications

	Good	Fine	Mint
1953-One Shot (Rare)	7.00	14.00	21.00
#1	4.00	8.00	12.00
2,3 (No #4-14)	2.50	5.00	7.50
15-30: #16,17-Katy Keene app. (#15 formerly			
Archie's Rival Reggie)	1.35	2.75	4.00
31-40,42,43	1.00	2.00	3.00
41-1st comic work by Neal Adams('59), 1 pg.			
	3.00	6.00	9.00
44-48-Adams art in all, 1-2 pgs.			
	1.75	3.35	5.00
49-60	.50	1.00	1.50
61-100	.30	.60	.90
101-140	.20	.40	.60
141-200	.15	.30	.45
201-240		.15	.30
Drug Store Giveaway(#39 with new cover)			
	1.35	2.75	4.00

ARCHIE'S JOKES (See Archie Giant Series Mag.
#17,22,27,33,139,146,154,163,174,186,198,
211,222,235,247,459)

ARCHIE'S LOVE SCENE
1973   (35¢)
Spire Christian Comics (Fleming H. Revell Co.)

#1	.35	.70	1.05

ARCHIE'S MADHOUSE (Madhouse Ma-ad #67 on)
Sept, 1959 - #66, Feb, 1969
Archie Publications

#1	4.00	8.00	12.00
2	2.50	5.00	7.50
3-5	2.00	4.00	6.00
6-10	1.35	2.75	4.00
11-20	.65	1.35	2.00
21,23-40	.35	.70	1.05
22-1st app. Sabrina, the Teen-age Witch(9/62)			
	.35	.70	1.05
41,42,44-66	.20	.40	.60
43-Mighty Crusaders cameo	.25	.50	.75
Annual #1(1962-63)	1.00	2.00	3.00
Annual #2-6('64-69)(Becomes Madhouse Ma-ad			
Annual #7 on)	.25	.50	.75

NOTE: *Cover title #61-65 is "Madhouse" and
#66 is "Madhouse Ma-ad Jokes."*

ARCHIE'S MECHANICS
Sept, 1954 - 1955
Archie Publications

#1(15¢)-52pgs. (Rare)	7.00	14.00	21.00
2,3(10¢) (Scarce)	5.00	10.00	15.00

Archie's Girls--#80. © AP

Archie's Joke Book #73. © AP

Archie's Madhouse #18. © AP

Archie's Mechanics #1, © AP

Archie's Rival Reggie #6, © AP

Army & Navy #1, © S & S

ARCHIE'S ONE WAY (Religious)
1972   (35¢)
Spire Christian Comics(Fleming H. Revell Co.)

	Good	Fine	Mint
#1	.20	.40	.60

ARCHIE'S PAL, JUGHEAD (Jughead #127 on)
1949 - #126, Nov, 1965
Archie Publications

	Good	Fine	Mint
#1	15.00	30.00	45.00
2	8.00	16.00	24.00
3-5: #5-Intro. Moose & Midge			
	6.00	12.00	18.00
6-10	4.00	8.00	12.00
11-20	2.50	5.00	7.50
21-40	1.75	3.35	5.00
41-80	1.35	2.75	4.00
81-100	.85	1.75	2.50
101-126	.50	1.00	1.50
Annual #1(1953)	4.00	8.00	12.00
Annual #2-5(1954-56)	2.00	4.00	6.00
Annual #6-8(1957-60)	1.50	3.00	4.50

ARCHIE'S PALS 'N' GALS
1951 - #6, 1957-58; #7, 1958 - Present
Archie Publications

	Good	Fine	Mint
#1(116 pgs.)	6.00	12.00	18.00
2(Annual)(1957)	3.00	6.00	9.00
3-7(Annual, '57-58)	2.00	4.00	6.00
8(1958)-#20	1.00	2.00	3.00
21-40	.65	1.35	2.00
41-60	.35	.70	1.05
61-90	.20	.40	.60
91-120	.15	.30	.45

ARCHIE'S PARABLES
1975
Spire Christian Comics(Fleming H. Revell Co.)

By Al Hartley	.35	.70	1.05

ARCHIE'S RIVAL REGGIE (See Reggie)

ARCHIE'S RIVAL REGGIE (Archie's Joke Book Mag.
1950 - #14, Aug, 1954   & Reggie #15 on)
Archie Publications

#1	8.00	16.00	24.00
2	4.00	8.00	12.00
3-5	2.50	5.00	7.50
6-14	1.50	3.00	4.50

ARCHIE'S SONSHINE
1974
Spire Christian Comics(Fleming H. Revell Co.)

	Good	Fine	Mint
No #	.25	.50	.75

ARCHIE'S SUPER HERO SPECIAL (See Archie
Giant Series Mag. #142)

ARCHIE'S TV LAUGH-OUT
1969 - Present
Archie Publications

#1	.60	1.20	1.80
2-10	.20	.40	.60
11-20	.15	.30	.45
21-54		.15	.30

ARCHIE WHERE ARE YOU DIGEST
1977
Archie Publications

#3(8/77), #4(11/77)	.25	.50	.75

ARISTOCATS (See Movie Comics & Walt Disney
Showcase #16)

ARISTOKITTENS, THE (--Meet Jiminy Cricket #1
Oct, 1971 - #9, 2/74 (#6-52pgs.) (Disney)
Gold Key

#1	.15	.30	.45
2-9		.15	.30

ARIZONA KID, THE
March, 1951 - #6, Jan, 1952
Marvel/Atlas Comics(CSI)

#1	3.00	6.00	9.00
2-4	1.75	3.35	5.00
5,6	1.35	2.75	4.00

ARMY AND NAVY (Supersnipe #6 on)
May, 1942 - #5
Street & Smith Publications

#1-Cap Fury & Nick Carter			
	10.00	20.00	30.00
2- " " " " "	4.00	8.00	12.00
3,4	3.00	6.00	9.00
5-Intro. & 1st app. Supersnipe			
	8.00	16.00	24.00

ARMY AT WAR (See Our Army at War)

ARMY ATTACK (Formerly U.S. Air Force #1-37)
July, 1965 - #47, Feb, 1967
Charlton Comics

V1#1	.25	.50	.75
2-5	.20	.40	.60

26

(Army Attack cont'd)

	Good	Fine	Mint
V2#38(7/65)-#47	.15	.30	.45

NOTE: *Glanzman* art-#1-3. *Montes/Bache* art-#44.

ARMY WAR HEROES
Dec, 1963 - #38, June, 1970
Charlton Comics

	Good	Fine	Mint
#1	.40	.80	1.20
2-20	.20	.40	.60
21-38: #23-Origin & 1st app. Iron Corporal			
series by Glanzman. #24-Intro. Archer &			
Corp. Jack series	.15	.30	.45

NOTE: *Montes/Bache* art-#1,16,17,21,23-25,27-30.

AROUND THE BLOCK WITH DUNC & LOO (See Dunc & Loo)

AROUND THE WORLD IN 80 DAYS (See 4-Color Comics #784 & A Golden Picture Classic)

AROUND THE WORLD UNDER THE SEA (See Movie Classics)

AROUND THE WORLD WITH ARCHIE (See Archie Giant Series Mag. #29,35,141)

AROUND THE WORLD WITH HUCKLEBERRY & HIS FRIENDS (See Dell Giant #44)

ARRGH! (Satire)
Dec, 1974 - #5, Sept, 1975
Marvel Comics Group

	Good	Fine	Mint
#1-Everett reprint	.25	.50	.75
2-5	.15	.30	.45

NOTE: *Alcala* art in #2; cover-#3. *Everett* reprint-#2. *Grandenetti* story-#4.

ARROW, THE
Oct, 1940 - #3, Oct, 1941
Centaur Publications

	Good	Fine	Mint
#1-The Arrow begins	30.00	60.00	90.00
2	16.00	32.00	48.00
3-Origin Dash Darwell, the Human Meteor;			
origin The Rainbow	16.00	32.00	48.00

NOTE: *Gustavson* art-#1,2.

ARROWHEAD
April, 1954 - #4, Nov, 1954
Atlas Comics (CPS)

	Good	Fine	Mint
#1-Sinnott art in all	1.75	3.35	5.00
2-4	1.00	2.00	3.00

ASTONISHING (Marvel Boy #1,2)
#3, April, 1951 - #63, Aug, 1957

Marvel/Atlas Comics(20CC)

	Good	Fine	Mint
#3-Marvel Boy cont'd.	7.00	14.00	21.00
4-6-Last Marvel Boy; #4-Stan Lee app.			
	6.00	12.00	18.00
7-20	1.00	2.00	3.00
21-24	.65	1.35	2.00
25-Crandall story	1.35	2.75	4.00
26-36-Last pre-code ish(1/54)			
	.65	1.35	2.00
37-53,56,58,59	.65	1.35	2.00
54-Torres art	1.00	2.00	3.00
55-Crandall & Torres art	1.25	2.50	3.75
57-Williamson/Krenkel story, 4 pgs.			
	2.00	4.00	6.00
60-Williamson/Mayo Story, 4 pgs.			
	2.00	4.00	6.00
61,63	.65	1.35	2.00
62-Torres + Powell story	1.00	2.00	3.00

NOTE: *Ditko* story-#50,53. *Drucker* story-#41. *Everett* story-#3-6,12,37,47,58; covers-#4,5, 15,18,29,47,51,53,55,59,60,62. *Kirby* story-#56. *Krigstein* story-#13,14,16,19,45,47. *Morrow* story-#52,61. *Orlando* story-#47,58. *Woodbridge* story-#62,63. Canadian reprints exist.

ASTONISHING TALES (See Ka-Zar)
8/70 - #36, 7/76; #37, 1977 - Present
Marvel Comics Group

	Good	Fine	Mint
#1-Ka-Zar by Kirby(pencils)& Dr. Doom by			
Wood begin	1.00	2.00	3.00
2-Kirby & Wood art	.60	1.20	1.80
3-6: Smith art; Wood art-#3,4; Everett			
inks-#6	.65	1.35	2.00
7-9: #8-Last Dr. Doom	.35	.70	1.05
10-Smith/Buscema art	.65	1.35	2.00
11,14-20: #11-Origin Ka-Zar; #20-Last Ka-Zar			
	.25	.50	.75
12-Man Thing by Adams	.65	1.35	2.00
13-Man Thing app.	.25	.50	.75
21-24: #21-It! the Living Colossus begins,			
ends #24	.20	.40	.60
25-Deathlok the Demolisher begins			
	.40	.80	1.20
26-30: #29-Guardians of the Galaxy app.			
	.20	.40	.60
31-Wrightson cover inks	.20	.40	.60
32-38	.15	.30	.45

NOTE: *Buscema* art-#9,10.

ASTRO BOY (TV)(Also see March of Comics#285)
August, 1965
Gold Key

	Good	Fine	Mint
#1(10151-508)	.35	.70	1.05

Army War Heroes #1. © CC

The Arrow #1. © Cen

Astonishing #6, © MCG

The Atom & Hawkman #40, © DC

Atoman #1, © Spark Publ.

Atomic Comics #1, © Green Publ. Co.

ASTRO COMICS
1969, 1970 (Giveaway)
American Airlines (Harvey)

	Good	Fine	Mint
No#-Has Harvey's Casper, Spooky, Hot Stuff, & Stumbo the Giant	.65	1.35	2.00

ATLANTIS, THE LOST CONTINENT (See 4-Color Comics #1188)

ATOM, THE (See Action, All-American, Brave & the Bold, Detective, Showcase, & World's Finest)

ATOM, THE (-- & Hawkman #39 on)
Jun-Jul, 1962 - #38, Aug-Sept, 1968
National Periodical Publications

#1	5.00	10.00	15.00
2	2.50	5.00	7.50
3-1st Time Pool story; origin Chronos	2.00	4.00	6.00
4,5: #4-Snapper Carr x-over	1.75	3.35	5.00
6-10: #7-Hawkman x-over. #8-Justice League	1.00	2.00	3.00
11-20: #18-Zatanna x-over	.65	1.35	2.00
21-30: #29-Golden Age Atom x-over	.40	.80	1.20
31-38: #31-Hawkman x-over. #36-G.A. Atom x-over. #37-Intro. Major Mynah; Hawkman cameo	.35	.70	1.05

NOTE: *Anderson* art-#39,43,44; inks-#1-11,13, 40,41; cover inks-#1-25,31-35,37. *Gil Kane* art-#1-37; covers-#1-37. *Pool* stories also in #6,9,12,17,21,27,35.

ATOM AGE (See Classics Special)

ATOM-AGE COMBAT
June, 1952 - #5, April, 1953
St. John Publishing Co.

#1	2.00	4.00	6.00
2-5: #3-Mayo art, 6pgs.	1.35	2.75	4.00
1(2/58-St. John)	1.75	3.35	5.00

ATOM-AGE COMBAT
Nov, 1958 - #3, March, 1959
Fago Magazines

#1	1.50	3.00	4.50
2,3	1.00	2.00	3.00

ATOMAN
Feb, 1946 - #2, April, 1946
Spark Publications

	Good	Fine	Mint
#1-Origin Atoman; Jerry Robinson & Mort Meskin art; Kidcrusaders, Wild Bill Hickok, Marvin the Great app.	8.00	16.00	24.00
2	5.00	10.00	15.00

ATOM AND THE HAWKMAN, THE (Formerly The Atom)
#39, 10-11/68 - #45, 10-11/69
National Periodical Publications

#39,42-45	.35	.70	1.05
40,41-Hawkman by Kubert; covers-#39-45	.50	1.00	1.50

ATOM ANT (TV)
January, 1966 (Hanna-Barbera)
Gold Key

#1(10170-601)	.25	.50	.75

ATOMIC ATTACK
1952 - #8, Oct, 1953
Youthful Magazines

#1	2.00	4.00	6.00
2-8	1.25	2.50	3.75

ATOMIC BOMB
1942
Jay Burtis Publications

#1-Airmale & Stampy	3.00	6.00	9.00

ATOMIC BUNNY
1958 - #19, Dec, 1959
Charlton Comics

#12-19	.40	.80	1.20

ATOMIC COMICS
1946 (Reprints)
Daniels Publications (Canadian)

#1-Rocketman, Yankee Boy, Master Key	3.00	6.00	9.00
2-4	2.00	4.00	6.00

ATOMIC COMICS
Jan, 1946 - #4, July-Aug, 1946
Green Publishing Co.

#1-Radio Squad by Siegel & Shuster; Barry O'Neal app.	3.35	6.75	10.00
2-4: #2-Lucky Wings, Congo King, Kid Kane, Prop Powers, & Inspector Dayton begin. #3-Zero Ghost Detective app.; no Prop Powers	2.00	4.00	6.00

ATOMIC MOUSE (See Blue Bird)
March, 1953 - #54, June, 1963
Capitol Stories/Charlton Comics

	Good	Fine	Mint
#1-Origin	1.75	3.35	5.00
2-10	.65	1.35	2.00
11-25,27-54	.40	.80	1.20
26(68pgs.)	.80	1.60	2.40

ATOMIC RABBIT
August, 1955 - #11, March, 1958
Charlton Comics

#1-Origin; Al Fago art	1.75	3.35	5.00
2-10-Fago art in most	.65	1.35	2.00
11-(68pgs.)	.80	1.60	2.40

ATOMIC SPY CASES
Mar-Apr, 1950
Avon Periodicals

#1	3.00	6.00	9.00

ATOMIC THUNDERBOLT, THE
Feb, 1946 - #2, April, 1946
Regor Company

#1-Intro. Atomic Thunderbolt & Mr. Murdo,			
2	4.00	8.00	12.00

ATOMIC WAR!
Nov, 1952 - #8, 1953
Ace Periodicals (Junior Books)

#1	3.35	6.75	10.00
2-8	2.00	4.00	6.00

ATOM THE CAT
Aug, 1955 - #16, May, 1959
Charlton Comics

#1	.50	1.00	1.50
2-10,12-16	.35	.70	1.00
11-(64pgs.)	.40	.80	1.20

ATTACK
May, 1952 - #60, Nov, 1959
Youthful Mag./Trojan/Charlton #54 on

#1	1.00	2.00	3.00
2-10	.65	1.35	2.00
11-60: #54-100pgs.	.25	.50	.75

ATTACK! (Attack At Sea V4#5)(Also see
Special War Series #2)
1962 - #4, Oct, 1967: 9/71 - #15, 3/75
Charlton Comics

	Good	Fine	Mint
No#(#1)-('62) Special Edition			
	.35	.70	1.05
2('63), 3(Fall, '64)	.20	.40	.60
V4#2(10/65),3(10/66),4(10/67)			
	.15	.30	.45
#1(9/71)	.20	.40	.60
2-15(3/75): #4-American Eagle app.			
	.15	.30	.45

ATTACK AT SEA (Formerly Attack!, '67)
October, 1968
Charlton Comics

V4#5	.15	.30	.45

ATTACK ON PLANET MARS
1951
Avon Periodicals

No#-Infantino, Kubert & Wood art; adaptation			
of Tarrano the Conqueror by Ray Cummings			
	12.00	24.00	36.00

AUGIE DOGGIE (TV) (See Whitman Comic Books)
Oct, 1963 (Hanna-Barbera)
Gold Key

#1	.25	.50	.75

AURORA COMIC SCENES INSTRUCTION BOOKLET
1974 (Slick paper, 8pgs.)(6-1/4x9-3/4")
(Included with superhero model kits)
Aurora Plastics Co. (in full color)

#181-140-Tarzan; Adams art	.65	1.35	2.00
#182-140-Spider-Man; #183-140-Tonto(Gil Kane			
art); #184-140-Hulk; #185-140-Superman;			
#186-140-Superboy; #187-140-Batman; #188-140-			
The Lone Ranger(1974); #192-140-Captain			
America(1975); #193-140-Robin			
each....	.35	.70	1.05

AUTHENTIC POLICE CASES
Feb, 1948 - #37, Jan, 1955
St. John Publishing Co.

#1-Hale the Magician by Tuska begins			
	1.75	3.35	5.00
2-Lady Satan app.	1.35	2.75	4.00
3-Veiled Avenger app.	1.00	2.00	3.00
4-7: #5-Late 30's Jack Cole reprint. #7-			
Masked Black Jack app.	.90	1.80	2.70
8-14-Vic Flint in all; Matt Baker art be-			
gins-#8	1.50	3.00	4.50
15-Drug story; Vic Flint app.			
	2.00	4.00	6.00
16,18-24	1.00	2.00	3.00
17-Matt Baker cover	1.50	3.00	4.50

Atomic War! #1, © Ace

Attack On Planet Mars, © Avon

Authentic Police Cases #3, © STJ

The Avenger #1(A-1 #129), © ME   The Avengers #1, © MCG   The Avengers #4, © MCG

(Authentic Police Cases cont'd)

	Good	Fine	Mint
25-28 (All 100 pgs.)	2.00	4.00	6.00
29-33,35,37	1.00	2.00	3.00
34-Drug cover/story	2.00	4.00	6.00
36-Vic Flint strip reprts.	1.00	2.00	3.00

NOTE: *Matt Baker covers on many issues from #8 up.*

AVENGER, THE (See A-1 Comics)
1955 - #4, Aug-Sept, 1955
Magazine Enterprises

	Good	Fine	Mint
#1(A-1#129)-Origin	7.00	14.00	21.00
2(A-1#131),3(A-1#133),4(A-1#138)	3.00	6.00	9.00
IW Reprint #9('64)-Reprints #1(new cover) ('60-61)	1.35	2.75	4.00

NOTE: *Powell stories-#3-5; covers-#1-3.*

AVENGERS, THE
Sept, 1963 - Present
Marvel Comics Group

	Good	Fine	Mint
#1-Origin The Avengers (Thor, Iron Man, Hulk, Ant-Man, Wasp)	40.00	80.00	120.00
2	20.00	40.00	60.00
3	10.00	20.00	30.00
4-Revival of Captain America who joins the Avengers	10.00	20.00	30.00
4-Reprint from the Golden Record Comic set	.80	1.60	2.40
With Record....	1.50	3.00	4.50
5	5.00	10.00	15.00
6-10: #9-Intro. Wonder Man-joins Avengers & dies in same story	3.35	6.75	10.00
11-19: #15-Death of Zemo. #16-New Avengers line-up(Hawkeye, Quicksilver, Scarlet Witch join; Thor, Iron Man, Giant-Man & Wasp leave). #19-Intro. Swordsman; origin Hawkeye	1.75	3.35	5.00
20-22: Wood inks	1.35	2.75	4.00
23-30: #28-Giant-Man becomes Goliath	1.00	2.00	3.00
31-40	.65	1.35	2.00
41-50: #48-Origin new Black Knight	.50	1.00	1.50
51-56,59,60: #59-Intro. Yellowjacket. #60-Wasp & Yellowjacket wed.	.50	1.00	1.50
57-Intro. The Vision	.80	1.60	2.40
58-Origin The Vision	.80	1.60	2.40
61-65,68-70: #63-Goliath becomes Yellowjacket; Hawkeye becomes the new Goliath	.40	.80	1.20
66,67-Smith stys/cvr #66	1.00	2.00	3.00
71-80: #80-Intro. Red Wolf	.40	.80	1.20
81-92: #83-Intro. The Liberators (Wasp, Valkyrie, Scarlet Witch, Medusa & the Black			

	Good	Fine	Mint
Widow). #87-Origin the Black Panther. #92-Adams cover	.40	.80	1.20
93-Adams cover/story	2.50	5.00	7.50
94-96-Adams cover/stories	1.25	2.50	3.75
97-G.A. Capt. America, Sub-Mariner, H.Torch, Patriot, Vision, Blazing Skull, Fin, Angel, & New Capt. Marvel x-over	.50	1.00	1.50
98-Goliath becomes Hawkeye; Smith cover/stories w/Buscema	.80	1.60	2.40
99-Smith art/cover	.80	1.60	2.40
100-Smith art/covers; featuring everyone who was an Avenger minus Wonderman	1.25	2.50	3.75
101-106,108-110	.35	.70	1.05
107-Starlin art	.50	1.00	1.50
111-120: #114-1st app. Mantis	.30	.60	.90
121-130	.25	.50	.75
131-140: #134-35-True origin The Vision	.20	.40	.60
141-149: #144-Origin & 1st app. Hellcat	.20	.40	.60
150-Kirby art; reprints	.15	.30	.45
151-160	.15	.30	.45
161-167		.15	.30
Annual #7(11/77)-Starlin cover/story	.40	.80	1.20
Special #1(9/67)	2.00	4.00	6.00
" #2(9/68)	1.00	2.00	3.00
" #3(9/69)	.80	1.60	2.40
" #4(1/71),#5(1/72)	.65	1.35	2.00
" #6(11/76)	.40	.80	1.20
Giant Size #1(8/74)	.65	1.35	2.00
" " #2,3	.40	.80	1.20
" " #4(6/75),#5(12/75)	.40	.80	1.20

NOTE: *Buscema stories-#41(1st at Marvel),98, 152,153. Kane/Everett cover-#97. Kirby art-#1-8,16; covers-#1-30,155,158; layouts-#14,15.*

AVENGERS, THE (TV)
11/68 ("John Steed & Emma Peel" cover title)
Gold Key

	Good	Fine	Mint
#1	.65	1.35	2.00

NOTE: *The Avengers is official title on inside.*

AVIATION ADVENTURES & MODEL BUILDING
12/46 - #17, 2/47 (True Aviation Adv.--#15)
Parents' Magazine Institute

	Good	Fine	Mint
#16,17-Half comics and half pictures	.80	1.60	2.40

AVIATION CADETS
1943
Street & Smith Publications

(Aviation Cadets cont'd)	Good	Fine	Mint
	2.00	4.00	6.00

AWFUL OSCAR (Formerly Oscar)
#12, Aug, 1949 - #13, Oct, 1949
Marvel Comics Group

#12,13	1.00	2.00	3.00

BABE (--, Darling of the Hills, later issues)
6-7/48 - 1950 (Also see Big Shot, Sparky Watts)
Prize/Headline/Feature

#1-Boody Rogers art	4.00	8.00	12.00
2-11-All by Boody Rogers	2.50	5.00	7.50

BABE AMAZON OF OZARKS
#5, 1948
Standard Comics

#5	2.00	4.00	6.00

BABE RUTH SPORTS COMICS
April, 1949 - #11, Feb, 1951
Harvey Publications

#1-Powell art	1.50	3.00	4.50
2-11: #8-Powell art	.80	1.60	2.40

BABES IN TOYLAND (See 4-Color #1282 and
Golden Pix Story Book ST-3)

BABY HUEY AND PAPA (See Paramount Animated--)
May, 1962 - #33, Jan, 1968
Harvey Publications

#1	1.00	2.00	3.00
2-10	.40	.80	1.20
11-20	.15	.30	.45
21-33		.10	.20

BABY HUEY IN DUCKLAND
Nov, 1962 - #14, Sept, 1966 (25¢ Giant)
Harvey Publications

#1	.65	1.35	2.00
2-5	.35	.70	1.05
6-14	.15	.30	.45

BABY HUEY, THE BABY GIANT (Also see Casper,
& Harvey Hits #22)
Sept, 1956 - #97, Oct, 1971; #98, Oct, 1972
Harvey Publications

#1	3.00	6.00	9.00
2	1.50	3.00	4.50
3-5	1.00	2.00	3.00
6-10	.65	1.35	2.00

	Good	Fine	Mint
11-30	.30	.65	1.00
31-60	.15	.30	.45
61-98		.10	.20

BABY SNOOTS (Also see March of Comics #359,
Aug, 1970 - #22, Nov, 1975   371,396,401)
Gold Key

#1	.25	.50	.75
2-22: #22-Titled Snoots, the Forgetful Ele-			
fink		.15	.30

BACHELOR FATHER (TV)
1962
Dell Publishing Co.

4-Color #1332(#1)	.65	1.35	2.00
#2-Written by Stanley	.80	1.60	2.40

BACHELOR'S DIARY
1949
Avon Periodicals

#1	2.00	4.00	6.00

BADGE OF JUSTICE
#22, 1/55 - #23, 3/53; 4/55 - #4, 10/55
Charlton Comics

#22(1/55),#23(3/55)	.60	1.20	1.80
#1	.60	1.20	1.80
2-4	.35	.70	1.05

BADMEN OF THE WEST
1951   (Giant - 132 pgs.)
Avon Periodicals

#1-Contains rebound copies of Jesse James,			
King of the Bad Men of Deadwood, Badmen			
of Tombstone; other combinations possible.			
Issues with Kubert stories......			
	5.00	10.00	15.00

BADMEN OF THE WEST! (See A-1 Comics)
1953 - #2, 1954
Magazine Enterprises

#1(A-1#100)-Meskin art?	5.00	10.00	15.00
2(A-1#120)	2.50	5.00	7.50

BADMEN OF TOMBSTONE
1950
Avon Periodicals

No#	2.00	4.00	6.00

Babe Ruth Sports #10. © Harv

Baby Huey #1. © Harv

Badmen of the West Giant #1. © Avon

Baffling Mysteries #26, © Ace   Bambi 4-Color #30, © WDP   Barney Baxter 4-Color #20, © King

BAFFLING MYSTERIES (Formerly Indian Braves
#1-4; Heroes of the Wild Frontier #26-28)
1951 - #26(10/55),29,30, 1955
Periodical House (Ace Magazines)

	Good	Fine	Mint
#5-26,29,30: #10-E.C. Crypt Keeper copy on			
cover	1.00	2.00	3.00

NOTE: *Cameron stories-#16,20.*

BALBO (See Mighty Midget Comics)

BALOO & LITTLE BRITCHES
April, 1968 (Walt Disney)
Gold Key

#1-From the Jungle Book	.40	.80	1.20

BALTIMORE COLTS
1950
American Visuals Corp.

	1.75	3.35	5.00

BAMBI (See 4-Color #12,30,186, Movie Comics,
Movie Classics, and Walt Disney Showcase #31)

BAMBI (Disney)
1941, 1942
K. K. Publications (Giveaway)

1941-Horlick's Malted Milk & various toy			
stores-text & pictures; most copies mailed			
out with store stickers on cover			
	12.00	24.00	36.00
1942-Same as 4-Color #12, but no price			
(Scarce)	25.00	50.00	75.00

BAMM BAMM & PEBBLES FLINTSTONE
Oct, 1964 (Hanna-Barbera)
Gold Key

#1	.25	.50	.75

BANANA OIL
1924 (52 pgs. - Black & White)
MS Publ. Co.

Milt Gross art; not reprints			
	8.00	16.00	24.00

BANANA SPLITS, THE (TV)(See March of Comics
2/69 - #8, 10/71 (Hanna-Barbera) #364)
Gold Key

#1	.20	.40	.60
2-8	.15	.30	.45

BAND WAGON (See Hanna-Barbera --)

BANG-UP COMICS
Dec, 1941 - #3, June, 1942
Progressive Publications

	Good	Fine	Mint
#1-Cosmo Mann & Lady Fairplay begin; Buzz			
Balmer by Rick Yager in all			
	25.00	50.00	75.00
2,3	15.00	30.00	45.00

BANNER COMICS (Captain Courageous #6)
#3, May, 1941 - #5, Jan, 1942
Ace Magazines

#3-Captain Courageous & Lone Warrior & Side-			
kick Dicky begin	30.00	60.00	90.00
4,5	25.00	50.00	75.00

BARBARIANS, THE
June, 1975
Atlas Comics/Seaboard Periodicals

#1-Origin, only app. Andrax; Iron Jaw app.			
	.35	.70	1.05

BARBIE & KEN
May-July, 1962 - #5, Nov-Jan, 1963-64
Dell Publishing Co.

#01-053-207(#1)	.65	1.35	2.00
2-5	.40	.80	1.20

BARKER, THE
Autumn, 1946 - 1949
Quality Comics Group/Comic Magazine

#1	2.50	5.00	7.50
2	1.50	3.00	4.50
3-10	1.25	2.50	3.75
11-14	.60	1.20	1.80
15-Jack Cole pencils	1.00	2.00	3.00

NOTE: *Jack Cole art in some issues.*

BARNEY AND BETTY RUBBLE (Flintstone's Neighbors)
Jan, 1973 - #23, Dec, 1976 (Hanna-Barbera)
Charlton Comics

#1	.25	.50	.75
2-23		.15	.30

BARNEY BAXTER
1938 - 1956
David McKay/Dell Publishing Co.

Feature Book #15(McKay-'38)			
	12.00	24.00	36.00
4-Color #20('42)	12.00	24.00	36.00
#4,5	8.00	16.00	24.00
1,2(1956-Argo)	1.50	3.00	4.50

BARNEY GOOGLE (See Comic Monthly)
1923 - 1928(Daily strip reprints;B&W)(52pgs.)
Cupples & Leon Co.

	Good	Fine	Mint
#1	12.00	24.00	36.00
2-6	8.00	16.00	24.00

NOTE: *Started in 1918 as newspaper strip;*
Spark Plug began 1922, 1923.

BARNEY GOOGLE & SNUFFY SMITH
1942 - April, 1964
Dell Publishing Co./Gold Key

4-Color #19('42)	15.00	30.00	45.00
4-Color #40('43)	6.00	12.00	18.00
Large Feature Comic #11(1943)			
	10.00	20.00	30.00
#1(1950-Dell)	2.50	5.00	7.50
2,3	1.75	3.35	5.00
#1(10113-404)Gold Key, 4/64			
	1.00	2.00	3.00

BARNEY GOOGLE & SNUFFY SMITH
May, 1951 - #4, Feb, 1952   (Reprints)
Toby Press

#1	2.50	5.00	7.50
2,3	1.50	3.00	4.50
4-Kurtzman story "Pot Shot Pete", 5pgs.;			
reprints John Wayne #5-2.00	4.00	6.00	

BARNEY GOOGLE AND SNUFFY SMITH
March, 1970 - #6, Jan, 1971
Charlton Comics

#1	.40	.80	1.20
2-6	.20	.40	.60

BARNYARD
1944 - 1950; 1957
Nedor/Polo Mag./Standard(Animated Cartoons)

#1	1.75	3.35	5.00
2-12,16	.65	1.35	2.00
13-15,17,20,21,23,27-All contain Frazetta			
text illos	2.00	4.00	6.00
18,19,22,24,25-All contain Frazetta stories			
& text illos	5.00	10.00	15.00
26,28-31	.50	1.00	1.50
10(1957)	.25	.50	.75

BARRY M. GOLDWATER
March, 1965   (Complete Life Story)
Dell Publishing Co.

No#	1.75	3.35	5.00

BASEBALL AS THE STARS PLAY IT

1954 (3½x4")(8 diff.)(16pgs. in color)
Wilson Certified Franks giveaway

	Good	Fine	Mint

#1-Pointers on Pitching. 2-Batting & Field-
ing Secrets. 3-Playing the Infield. 4-How to
Catch. 5-Circus Cut-Out & Fun Book. 6-Western
Cut-Out & Fun Book. 7-Dress-Up & Fun Book.
8-Travel Cut-Out & Fun Book.

each....	.25	.50	.75

BASEBALL COMICS
Spring, 1949
Will Eisner Productions

#1-Will Eisner cvr/stys.	10.00	20.00	30.00

BASEBALL HEROES
1952   (One Shot)
Fawcett Publications

No #	2.00	4.00	6.00

BASEBALL THRILLS
1951 - #10, Summer, 1952
Ziff-Davis Publ. Co.

#1	1.00	2.00	3.00
2-10	.50	1.00	1.50

BASIL (-- the Royal Cat)
Jan, 1953 - #4, Sept, 1953
St. John Publishing Co.

#1-4	.35	.70	1.05

BAT LASH (See Showcase #76)
Oct-Nov, 1968 - #7, Oct-Nov, 1969
National Periodical Publications

#1	.40	.80	1.20
2-7	.25	.50	.75

BATMAN (See Aurora, Book & Record Set, Detec-
tive, 80-Pg. Giants, Giant Comics to Color,
Limited Coll. Ed., 100-Pg. Super Spec., 3-D
Batman, & World's Finest)

BATMAN
Spring, 1940 - Present
National Per. Publ./Detective Comics/DC Comics

#1-Origin the Batman retold by Bob Kane; see
   Detective #33 for 1st origin; 1st app.
   Joker & Catwoman; has Batman story without Robin originally planned for Detective #38; reprinted in Famous 1st Editions

550.00	1375.00	2200.00

(Prices vary widely on this book)

Barney Google #1, © Toby

Baseball Heroes, © Faw

Baseball Thrills #2, © Z-D

33

Batman #1, © DC

Batman #4, © DC

Batman #15, © DC

(Batman cont'd)	Good	Fine	Mint
2	200.00	400.00	600.00
3-1st Catwoman in costume			
	100.00	200.00	300.00
4	90.00	180.00	270.00
5	60.00	120.00	180.00
6-10	40.00	80.00	120.00

11-15: #13-Jerry Siegel, creator of Superman
appears in a Batman story

	30.00	60.00	90.00
16-Intro. Alfred	35.00	70.00	105.00
17-20	18.00	36.00	54.00

21-30: #24-Last app. of Tweedledum & Tweedledee. #25-Only Joker-Penguin team-up

	15.00	30.00	45.00
31-40: #32-Origin Robin retold			
	10.00	20.00	30.00
41-46	8.00	16.00	24.00
47-Origin The Batman retold			
	20.00	40.00	60.00

48-50: #49-1st Vicki Vale. #50-Two-Face app.

	7.00	14.00	21.00
51-60: #57-Centerfold is a 1950 calendar			
	6.00	12.00	18.00
61-70: #68-Two-Face app.	5.00	10.00	15.00
71-80	4.00	8.00	12.00
81-90: #81-Two-Face app.	3.50	7.00	10.50
91-100	3.00	6.00	9.00
101-120	2.50	5.00	7.50
121-130	1.75	3.35	5.00

131-140: #131-Intro. 2nd Batman & Robin series. #139-Intro. old Batgirl

	1.35	2.75	4.00
141-150	1.00	2.00	3.00

151-170: #164-New look & Mystery Analysts
series begins

	.80	1.60	2.40
171-180: #176-Giant G-17	.60	1.20	1.80
(80 pg. Giant G-17)	.80	1.60	2.40

181-190: #181-Contains poster of Batman &
Robin. #182-Giant G-24. #185-Giant G-27.
#187-Giant G-30

	.35	.70	1.05
(80 pg. Gaint G-24,27,30)	.60	1.20	1.80

191-200: #193-Giant G-37. #197-New Batgirl
app. #198-Giant G-43, reprints origin.
#200-Retells origin of Batman & Robin

	.35	.70	1.05
(80 pg. Giant G-37,43)	.40	.80	1.20

201-210: #203-Giant G-49, #208-Giant G-55-New
art by Gil Kane

	.25	.50	.75
(80 pg. Giant G-49,55)	.35	.70	1.05

211-218: #213-Giant G-61-origin Alfred; new
origin of Robin. #214-Alfred given a last
name-"Pennyworth". #218-Giant G-67

	.20	.40	.60
(80 pg. Giant G-61,67)	.35	.70	1.05
219-Adams story	1.35	2.75	4.00
220	.20	.40	.60

221,223-231: #223-Giant G-73. #228-Giant G-79

	Good	Fine	Mint
	.20	.40	.60
(80 pg. Giant G-73,79)	.35	.70	1.05
222-Beatles app.	1.00	2.00	3.00

232,234,237: Adams stories. #234-52pg. ish begin, end #242.

	1.35	2.75	4.00

233,235,236,238-242: #233-Giant G-85. #238-
DC-8 100pg. Super Spec.; unpubbed G.A. Atom
story; Doom Patrol origin reprint

	.20	.40	.60
(80 pg. Giant G-85)	.35	.70	1.05
(100 pg. DC-8)	.65	1.35	2.00
243-245-Adams stories	1.00	2.00	3.00
246-250	.20	.40	.60
251-Adams story; Joke app.	1.00	2.00	3.00
252,253: #253-Shadow app.	.20	.40	.60
254-100pg. editions begin	.35	.70	1.05
255-Adams story	1.00	2.00	3.00
256-261-Last 100pg. issue	.35	.70	1.05
262-68pgs.	.20	.40	.60
263-280	.15	.30	.45
281-299		.15	.30
300(52pgs.)	.20	.40	.60
Annual #1(8-10/61) Curt Swan cover			
	4.00	8.00	12.00
" #2,3(Summer, '62)	2.50	5.00	7.50
" #4-7(7/64)	1.50	3.00	4.50
Pizza Hut giveaway(12/77)-exact reprints of			
#122 & #123	.20	.40	.60
Prell Shampoo giveaway('66)-16pgs."The Joker's			
Practical Jokes"-6-7/8x3-3/8"			
	.50	1.00	1.50

NOTE: _Adams_ covers-#200,203,210,217,219,220-
222,224-27,229,230,232,234,236-41,243-45,
251,255. _Burnley_ stories-#10,12-18,20,25,27;
cover-#28. _Infantino_ stories-#234,235,255;
covers-#164-75,177-81,183,184,188-92,194-99.
Kaluta covers-#242,248,253. _Bob Kane_ stor-
ies-#1,2; covers-#1-5,7. _Robinson/Roussos_
stories-#13,15-17,20,22,24,25,27,28,31,33,
37. _Robinson_ stories-#12,14,18; covers-#6,
8-10,12-15,18,21,26,27,30,37,39. _Wrightson_
inks-#265.

BATMAN (Kellogg's Poptarts comics)
1966 (Set of 6) (16 pgs.)
National Periodical Publications

"The Man in the Iron Mask", "The Penguin's
Fowl Play", "The Joker's Happy Victims", "The
Catwoman's Catnapping Caper", "The Mad Hatt-
er's Hat Crimes", "The Case of Batman II"

each....	.50	1.00	1.50

NOTE: _Infantino_ art on Catwoman and Joker
issues.

BATMAN FAMILY, THE
Sept-Oct, 1975 - Present (68 pgs.-#1-4)
National Periodical Publications/DC Comics

(Batman Family cont'd)	Good	Fine	Mint

#1-Origin Bat Girl-Robin team-up(The Dynamite
Duo); reprints + one new story begins;

	Good	Fine	Mint
Adams reprint.	.35	.70	1.05
2-5	.25	.50	.75
6-12,14-16	.20	.40	.60
13-Newton story	.25	.50	.75
17-($1.00 size)	.35	.70	1.05

BATMAN MINIATURE (See Batman Kellogg's)

BATMAN RECORD COMIC
1966   (One Shot)
National Periodical Publications

#1	.65	1.35	2.00

BAT MASTERSON (TV)
8-10/59; 12-1/59-60 - #9, 11-1/61-62
Dell Publishing Co.

4-Color #1013 (8-10/59)	.65	1.35	2.00
#2-9	.35	.70	1.05

BATS (See Tales Calculated to Drive You --)

BATTLE
March, 1951 - #70, June, 1960
Marvel/Atlas Comics(FPI #1-62/Male #63 on)

	Good	Fine	Mint
#1	1.50	3.00	4.50
2-10: #4-1st Buck Pvt. O'Tool			
	.65	1.35	2.00
11-20	.60	1.20	1.80
21,23-Krigstein story	1.35	2.75	4.00
22,24-36,38-40	.50	1.00	1.50
37-Kubert story	1.50	3.00	4.50
41-Kubert/Moskowitz story	1.50	3.00	4.50
42-48	.50	1.00	1.50
49-Davis story	1.75	3.35	5.00
50-54,56-58	.40	.80	1.20
55-Williamson story, 5pgs.	2.00	4.00	6.00
59-Torres story	1.00	2.00	3.00
60-62: Combat Kelly app.-#60,62; Combat Casey			
app.-#61	.40	.80	1.20
63-66: #63-Ditko story. #64-66-Kirby stories			
+ Davis-#66	1.00	2.00	3.00
67-Williamson/Crandall story, 4 pgs. + Kirby			
story + Davis	2.00	4.00	6.00
68-Williamson w/Kirby pencils, 4 pgs. +			
Kirby/Ditko story	2.00	4.00	6.00
69-Kirby story	.65	1.35	2.00
70-Kirby/Ditko story	.65	1.35	2.00

NOTE: *Berg stories-#8,62. Everett story-#36,
50,70; cover-#56,57. Kirby cover-#64-69. Orlando story-#47. Powell story-#53,55. Robinson story-#39. Severin art-many issues. Woodbridge story-#52,55.*

BATTLE ACTION
Feb, 1952 - #12, 5/53; #13, 10/54 - #31, 8/57
Atlas Comics(NPI)

	Good	Fine	Mint
#1	1.00	2.00	3.00
2-7,9,10: #6-Robinson cover/story			
	.65	1.35	2.00
8-Krigstein story	1.35	2.75	4.00
11-26,28,29,31	.50	1.00	1.50
27,30-Torres stories	1.00	2.00	3.00

NOTE: *Battle Brady app. #5,6,10-12. Woodbridge
stories-#28,30.*

BATTLE ATTACK
Oct, 1952 - #8, Dec, 1955
Stanmor Publications

#1	1.00	2.00	3.00
2-8	.40	.80	1.20

BATTLE BRADY (Men in Action #1-9)
#10, Jan, 1953 - #14, June, 1953
Atlas Comics (IPC)

#10-14	.65	1.35	2.00

BATTLE CRY
1952 - #20, Sept, 1955
Stanmor Publications

#1	1.00	2.00	3.00
2-10: #8-1st Pvt. Ike app.(also in #10-12,17)			
	.40	.80	1.20
11-20	.30	.60	.90

BATTLEFIELD (War Adventures on the --)
April, 1952 - #11, May, 1953
Atlas Comics (ACI)

#1	1.00	2.00	3.00
2-5	.65	1.35	2.00
6-11	.50	1.00	1.50

BATTLEFIELD ACTION
#16, Dec, 1957 - #62, Feb-Mar, 1966
Charlton Comics

#16	.25	.50	.75
17-30: #19-Check story	.15	.30	.45
31-62		.15	.30

NOTE: *Montes/Bache art-#43,55,62.*

BATTLE FIRE
April, 1955 - #7, 1955
Aragon Magazine/Stanmor Publications

#1	.80	1.60	2.40
2-7	.40	.80	1.20

Battle #19, © MCG

Battle Attack #1, © Stanmor

Battle Fire #1, © Stanmor

35

Battlefront #5, © MCG   Battle Squadron #3, © Stanmor   Beanbags #1, © Z-D

BATTLEFRONT
June, 1952 - #48, Aug, 1957
Atlas Comics (FPI)

	Good	Fine	Mint
#1	1.35	2.75	4.00
2,5	.65	1.35	2.00
3,4-Robinson book-length story in each			
	1.00	2.00	3.00
6-10: Combat Kelly in all	.60	1.20	1.80
11-21,23-30: Battle Brady in #14,16			
	.50	1.00	1.50
22-Kubert story	1.35	2.75	4.00
31-39	.35	.70	1.05
40,42-Williamson story	2.00	4.00	6.00
41,43-47	.35	.70	1.05
48-Crandall art	.80	1.60	2.40

NOTE: *Check story-#43. Drucker story-#28. Everett story-#44. Morrow story-#41. Orlando story-#47. Powell story-#21,25,47. Robinson story-#1,2,4,5; cover-#4. Woodbridge story-#45,46.*

BATTLEFRONT
#5, 1952
Standard Comics

	Good	Fine	Mint
#5-Toth art	1.35	2.75	4.00

BATTLE GROUND
Sept, 1954 - #20, 1957
Atlas Comics (OMC)

	Good	Fine	Mint
#1	1.00	2.00	3.00
2-10	.50	1.00	1.50
11,13,18-Williamson story in each(4pgs. #11)			
	2.00	4.00	6.00
12,15-17,19,20	.35	.70	1.05
14-Kirby story	1.00	2.00	3.00

NOTE: *Drucker story-#7,12,13. Krigstein story-#9. Orlando story-#17.*

BATTLE HEROES
Sept, 1966 - #2, Nov, 1966 (25¢)
Stanley Publications

	Good	Fine	Mint
#1,2	.20	.40	.60

BATTLE OF THE BULGE (See Movie Classics)

BATTLE REPORT
Aug, 1952 - #6, June, 1953
Ajax/Farrell Publications

	Good	Fine	Mint
#1	1.00	2.00	3.00
2-6	.40	.80	1.20

BATTLE SQUADRON
April, 1955 - #5, Dec, 1955
Stanmore Publications

	Good	Fine	Mint
#1	1.00	2.00	3.00
2-5	.40	.80	1.20

BATTLE STORIES
1952 - #11, 1953
Fawcett Publications

	Good	Fine	Mint
#1-Evans story	1.50	3.00	4.50
2-11	.65	1.35	2.00

BATTLE STORIES
1963 - 1964
Super Comics

	Good	Fine	Mint
Reprints #10-12,15-18; Jet Powers in #15 by Powell	.40	.80	1.20

BEACH BLANKET BINGO (See Movie Classics)

BEAGLE BOYS, THE (Walt Disney)
Nov, 1964 - Present
Gold Key

	Good	Fine	Mint
#1	.50	1.00	1.50
2-5	.35	.70	1.05
6-10	.25	.50	.75
11-20	.20	.40	.60
21-40		.15	.30

BEANBAGS
Winter, 1951 - #2, Spring, 1952
Ziff-Davis Publ. Co. (Approved Comics)

	Good	Fine	Mint
#1,2	.80	1.60	2.40

BEANIE THE MEANIE
1958 - #3, May, 1959
Fago Publications

	Good	Fine	Mint
#1-3	.35	.70	1.05

BEANY AND CECIL (TV) (Bob Clampett's --)
Jan, 1952 - 1955; 7-9/62 - #5, 7-9/63
Dell Publishing Co.

	Good	Fine	Mint
4-Color #368	1.50	3.00	4.50
4-Color #414,448,477,530,570,635			
	.80	1.60	2.40
#01-057-209	.65	1.35	2.00
2-5	.40	.80	1.20

BEAR COUNTRY (Disney) (See 4-Color #758)

BEATLES, THE (See Strange Tales #130, My Little Margie #54, Jimmy Olsen #79, Summer Love)

BEATLES, LIFE STORY, THE
Sept-Nov, 1964   (35¢)
Dell Publishing Co.

	Good	Fine	Mint
#1-Stories with color photo pin-ups	7.00	14.00	21.00

BEATLES YELLOW SUBMARINE (See Movie Comics
under <u>Yellow</u> --)

BEAVER VALLEY (See 4-Color #625)

BEDKNOBS & BROOMSTICKS (See Walt Disney
Showcase #6)

BEE 29, THE BOMBARDIER
February, 1945
Neal Publications

#1-(Funny Animal)	1.35	2.75	4.00

BEEP BEEP, THE ROAD RUNNER (TV)
July, 1958 - #14, 8-10/62; 10/66 - Present
Dell Publishing Co./Gold Key

4-Color #918,1008,1046	.80	1.60	2.40
#4-14(Dell)	.40	.80	1.20
#1	.50	1.00	1.50
2-5	.35	.70	1.05
6-18	.25	.50	.75
19-with pull-out poster	.25	.50	.75
20-40	.20	.40	.60
41-68-(Gold Key)	.15	.30	.45
Florida Power & Light Giveaway ('67)			
	.20	.40	.60

(See March of Comics #351,353,375,387,397)

BEETLE BAILEY
#469, 5/53 - #38, 5-7/62; #39, 11/62 - #53,
5/66; #54, 8/66 - #66, 1968; #67, 2/69 -
#119, 11/76
Dell Publishing Co./Gold Key #39-53/King #54-
66/Charlton #67 on

4-Color #469,521,552,622	.80	1.60	2.40
#5-10	.40	.80	1.20
11-50	.25	.50	.75
51-119	.15	.30	.45
Bold Detergent Giveaway(1969)-same as regular			
ish (#67) minus price	.15	.30	.45
Cerebral Palsy Assn. Giveaway V2#71(1969)-			
V2#73(1/70)	.15	.30	.45
R-02(1973) Premium, 36pgs. in color; Blondie,			
Popeye app.	.15	.30	

BEHIND PRISON BARS
1952
Realistic Comics (Avon)

	Good	Fine	Mint
#1	3.00	6.00	9.00

BEHOLD THE HANDMAID
1954   (Religious giveaway)
George Pflaum

	2.00	4.00	6.00

BELIEVE IT OR NOT (See Ripley's)

BEN AND ME (See 4-Color Comics #539)

BEN BOWIE & HIS MOUNTAIN MEN
1952 - #19, May-July, 1959
Dell Publishing Co.

4-Color #443	1.35	2.75	4.00
4-Color #513,557,599,626,657			
	1.00	2.00	3.00
#7-10	.65	1.35	2.00
11-Intro. & origin Yellow Hair			
	.65	1.35	2.00
12-19	.40	.80	1.20

BEN CASEY (TV)
June-July, 1962 - #10, June-Aug, 1965
Dell Publishing Co.

#12-063-207	.65	1.35	2.00
#2(10/62)-#10	.40	.80	1.20

BEN CASEY FILM STORY
November, 1962
Gold Key

#30009-211-All photos	1.50	3.00	4.50

BENEATH THE PLANET OF THE APES (See Movie
Comics)

BEN FRANKLIN KITE FUN BOOK
1975   (5x7")(16 pgs.)
Southern Calif. Edison Co.

	.20	.40	.60

BEN HUR (See 4-Color Comics #1052)

BEN ISRAEL
1974   (39¢)
Logos International

	.25	.50	.75

BEOWULF
Apr-May, 1975 - #6, Feb-Mar, 1976
National Periodical Publications

Beep Beep--#5, © Dell   Beetle Bailey #39, © King   Beowulf #1, © DC

The Berrys #1, © Argo   Best Love #33, © MCG   Best of The West #8(A-1 #81), © ME

(Beowulf cont'd)	Good	Fine	Mint
#1	.35	.70	1.05
2-6	.25	.50	.75

BERRYS, THE
May, 1956
Argo Publ.

#1-Reprints daily & Sunday strips & daily
   Animal Antics by Ed Nofziger.

	1.00	2.00	3.00

BEST COMICS
Nov, 1939 - 1940
Better Publications

#1-Red Mask begins	13.50	26.75	40.00
2-4	8.00	16.00	24.00

BEST FROM BOY'S LIFE, THE
Oct, 1957 - #5, Oct, 1958   (35¢)
Gilberton Company

#1-Space Conquerors & Kam of the Ancient

Ones app.; also #3	.65	1.35	2.00
2-5	.50	1.00	1.50

BEST LOVE   (Formerly Sub-Mariner)
#33, Aug, 1949 - #36, April, 1950
Marvel Comics (MPI)

#33,34	.50	1.00	1.50
35,36-Everett stories?	1.00	2.00	3.00

BEST OF BUGS BUNNY, THE
Oct, 1966 - #2, 1968
Gold Key

#1,2	.35	.70	1.05

BEST OF DENNIS THE MENACE, THE
Summer, 1959 - #5, Spring, 1961 (100 pgs.)
Hallden/Fawcett Publications

#1	1.50	3.00	4.50
2-5	1.25	2.50	3.75

BEST OF DONALD DUCK, THE
Nov, 1965   (36pgs.)
Gold Key

#1-Reprints 4-Color #223 by Carl Barks

	6.00	12.00	18.00

BEST OF DONALD DUCK & UNCLE SCROOGE, THE
Nov, 1964 - #2, Sept, 1967   (25¢)
Gold Key

#1(#30022-411)('64)-Reprints 4-Color #189 &

408 by Carl Barks	10.00	20.00	30.00

2(#30022-709)('67)-Reprints 4-Color #256 &
"7 Cities of Cibola" by Barks

	8.00	16.00	24.00

BEST OF MARMADUKE, THE

1960 (A Dog)	Good	Fine	Mint
Charlton Comics			

#1-Brad Anderson's strip reprints

	.35	.70	1.05

BEST OF THE WEST   (See A-1 Comics)
1951 - #12, April-June, 1954
Magazine Enterprises

#1(A-1#42)-Ghost Rider, Durango Kid, Straight
  Arrow, Tim Holt begin 6.00   12.00   18.00
2(A-1#46),3(A-1#52),4(A-1#59),5(A-1#66)

	3.00	6.00	9.00

6(A-1#70),7(A-1#76),8(A-1#81),9(A-1#85),
  10(A-1#87),11(A-1#97),12(A-1#103)

	2.50	5.00	7.50

BEST OF UNCLE SCROOGE & DONALD DUCK, THE
November, 1966   (25¢)
Gold Key

#1(#30030-611)-Reprints part 4-Color #159 &
  456 & Uncle Scrooge #6 by Carl Barks

	8.00	16.00	24.00

BEST OF WALT DISNEY COMICS, THE
1974 (In Color)(Walt Disney)($1.50)(52 pgs.)
8½x11" cardboard covers; 32,000 printed of ea.
Western Publishing Co.

#96170-Reprints 1st story less 1 pg. from
  4-Color #62   1.00   2.00   3.00
  96171-Reprints Mickey Mouse and the Bat
  Bandit of Inferno Gulch from 1934 (strips)
  by Gottfredson   1.00   2.00   3.00
  96172-Reprints Uncle Scrooge #386 & 2 other
  stories   1.00   2.00   3.00
  96173-Reprints "Ghost of the Grotto" (from
  4-Color #159) & "Christmas on Bear Mtn."
  (from 4-Color #178)   1.00   2.00   3.00

BEST ROMANCE
#5, Feb-Mar, 1952 - #6, May, 1952
Standard Comics (Visual Editions)

#5-Toth art	1.50	3.00	4.50
6	.65	1.35	2.00

BEST SELLER COMICS   (See Tailspin Tommy)

BEST WESTERN (Western Outlaws & Sheriffs
#58, 6/49 - #59, 8/49   #60 on)
Marvel Comics (IPC)

	Good	Fine	Mint
#58,59-Black Rider	1.50	3.00	4.50

BETTY AND HER STEADY
1950
Avon Periodicals

#1	1.50	3.00	4.50
2	1.00	2.00	3.00

BETTY AND ME
Aug, 1965 - Present   (Giants #36 on)
Archie Publications

#1	1.50	3.00	4.50
2-5: #3-Origin Superteen; in new costume			
#4-7; dons new helmet #5, ends #8			
	.65	1.35	2.00
6-10	.50	1.00	1.50
11-35	.35	.70	1.05
36-55(52pgs.)	.20	.40	.60
56-89		.15	.30

BETTY & VERONICA (See Archie's Girls --)

BETTY & VERONICA CHRISTMAS SPECTACULAR (See
Archie Giant Series Mag. #159,168,180,191,
204,217,229,241,433)

BETTY & VERONICA SPECTACULAR (See Archie
Giant Series Mag. #11,16,21,26,32,138,145,153,
162,173,184,197,201,210,214,221,226,234,238,
246,250,458,462)

BETTY & VERONICA SUMMER FUN (See Archie
Giant Series Mag. #8,13,18,23,28,34,140,147,
155,164,175,187,199,212,224,236,248,460)

BEVERLY HILLBILLIES (TV)
Apr-Jun, 1963 - #21, Oct, 1971
Dell Publishing Co.

#1	.50	1.00	1.50
2-10	.25	.50	.75
11-21	.15	.30	.45

BEWARE (Formerly Fantastic; Chilling Tales
#10, 6/52 - #12, 10/52   #13 on)
Youthful Magazines

#10-12	1.00	2.00	3.00

BEWARE
Jan, 1953 - #15, May, 1955
Trojan Magazines/Merit Publ.

	Good	Fine	Mint
#13(#1)	1.35	2.75	4.00
14-16(#2-4)	.70	1.40	2.10
5-9,11,12: Check art #8-10			
	.70	1.40	2.10
10-Frazetta/Check cover; Disbrow art			
	10.00	20.00	30.00
13,15	.60	1.20	1.80
14-Krenkel/Harrison cvr.	1.25	2.50	3.75

BEWARE! (Tomb of Darkness #9 on)
March, 1973 - #8, May, 1974
Marvel Comics Group

#1	.20	.40	.60
2,6,8	.15	.30	.45
7-Torres reprt./Mystical Tales #7			
	.20	.40	.60

BEWARE TERROR TALES
May, 1952 - 1953
Fawcett Publications

#1-Powell art	1.50	3.00	4.50
2-11: #8-Powell art	1.00	2.00	3.00

BEWARE THE CREEPER (See 1st Issue Special &
5-6/68 - #6, 3-4/69   Showcase)
National Periodical Publications

#1-Ditko art	1.00	2.00	3.00
2-6-Ditko art	.50	1.00	1.50

BEWITCHED (TV)
April-June, 1965 - #14, Oct, 1969
Dell Publishing Co.

#1	.25	.50	.75
2-14	.20	.40	.60

BEYOND, THE
Nov, 1950 - #33, 1955
Ace Magazines

#1	1.50	3.00	4.50
2-10	.65	1.35	2.00
11-20	.50	1.00	1.50
21-33	.40	.80	1.20

NOTE: *Cameron story-#20,21,24-26,30. #1 was
to appear as Challenge of the Unknown #7.*

BEYOND THE GRAVE
July, 1975 - #6, June, 1976
Charlton Comics

#1	.15	.30	.45
2-6		.15	.30

NOTE: *Ditko stories-#1-3,5; covers-#2,3.*

Best Western #59. © MCG

Beware the Creeper #1. © DC

The Beyond #7. © Ace

Big All-American #1, © DC

The Big Book of Fun Comics #1, © DC

Big Shot Comics #79, © CCG

BIBLE TALES FOR YOUNG FOLK
Aug, 1953 - #5, March, 1954
Atlas Comics (OMC)

	Good	Fine	Mint
#1	2.50	5.00	7.50
2-Everett, Krigstein sty.	1.75	3.35	5.00
3-5	1.25	2.50	3.75

BIG ALL-AMERICAN COMIC BOOK, THE
1944   (One Shot)   (132 pgs.)
All-American/National Periodical Publ.

#1-Wonder Woman, Green Lantern, Flash, The
   Atom, Wildcat, Scribbly, The Whip, Ghost
   Patrol, Hawkman by Kubert (1st on Hawkman),
   Hop Harrigan, Johnny Thunder, Little Boy
   Blue, Mr. Terrific, Mutt & Jeff app.; Sar-
   gon on cover only   100.00 200.00 300.00

BIG BOOK OF FUN COMICS
Spring, 1936   (52 pgs.)
National Periodical Publications

#1 (Rare) - Large size; reprints New Fun
   #1-5(1st DC Annual)   50.00 100.00 150.00

BIG BOOK ROMANCES
February, 1950   (148 pgs.)
Fawcett Publications

#1-Contains remaindered Fawcett romance com-
   ics - several combinations possible
                          2.50   5.00   7.50

BIG BOY (See Adventures of the --)

BIG CHIEF WAHOO
1942
Eastern Color Print./George Dougherty

#1-Newspaper reprints	7.00	14.00	21.00
2-Steve Roper app.	4.00	8.00	12.00
3-5	3.00	6.00	9.00
6-10	2.00	4.00	6.00
11-23	1.50	3.00	4.50

NOTE: *Kerry Drake* *in some issues.*

BIG CIRCUS, THE (See 4-Color #1036)

BIG COUNTRY, THE (See 4-Color #946)

BIG DADDY ROTH
Oct-Nov, 1964 - #4, Apr-May, 1965 (Mag. 35¢)
Millar Publications

#1-Toth art	2.50	5.00	7.50
2-4-Toth art	1.50	3.00	4.50

BIG HERO ADVENTURES (See Jigsaw)

BIG JIM'S P.A.C.K.
No date   (16 pgs.)
Mattel, Inc. (Marvel Comics)

	Good	Fine	Mint
Giveaway with Big Jim doll		.15	.30

BIG JOHN AND SPARKIE
1952   (Formerly Sparkie, Radio Pixie)
Ziff-Davis Publ. Co.

#4	1.35	2.75	4.00

BIG LAND, THE (See 4-Color #812)

BIG RED (See Movie Comics)

BIG SHOT COMICS
May, 1940 - #104, Aug, 1947
Columbia Comics Group

#1-Intro. Skyman; The Face (Tony Trent), The
   Cloak (Spy Master), Marvelo, Monarch of
   Magicians, Joe Palooka begin
                          50.00 100.00 150.00

2-Origin Skyman	25.00	50.00	75.00
3-The Cloak called Spy Chief			
	15.00	30.00	45.00
4,5	10.00	20.00	30.00
6-10	7.00	14.00	21.00
11-13	6.00	12.00	18.00
14-Origin Sparky Watts	7.00	14.00	21.00
15-Origin The Cloak	8.00	16.00	24.00
16-20	6.00	12.00	18.00

21-30: #29-Intro. Capt. Yank. #30-Bo (a dog)
   newspaper strip reprints by Frank Beck
   begins, ends #104   4.00   8.00   12.00
31-40: #32-Vic Jordan newspaper strip reprint
   begin, end #50   3.00   6.00   9.00
41-50: #42-No Skyman. #50-Origin The Face
   retold   2.50   5.00   7.50
51-60   2.00   4.00   6.00
61-70: #63 on- Tony Trent, the Face
                        1.50   3.00   4.50
71-80: #73-The Face cameo. #74,80-The Face
   app. in Tony Trent. #78-Last Charlie Chan
   strip reprints   1.25   2.50   3.75
81-90: #85-Tony Trent marries Babs Walsh
                        1.25   2.50   3.75
91-104   1.00   2.00   3.00
        (Skyman in Outer Space #70-94)
NOTE: *Mart Bailey* art on "The Face"-#1-104.
Sparky Watts by Boody Rogers-#14-42,77-104,
(by others #43-76). Others than *Tony Trent*
wear "The Face" mask in #46-63,93. *Skyman by
Ogden Whitney*-#1,2,4,12-37,49,70-101. *Skyman*
covers-#1,6,10,11,14,16,20,27,89,100.

BIG TEX
June, 1953
Toby Press

	Good	Fine	Mint
#1	1.00	2.00	3.00

BIG-3
Autumn, 1940 - #7, January, 1942
Fox Features Syndicate

#1-Blue Beetle, The Flame, & Samson begin			
	35.00	70.00	105.00
2	16.50	33.25	50.00
3-5	12.00	24.00	36.00
6-Last Samson	10.00	20.00	30.00
7-V-Man app.	10.00	20.00	30.00

BIG THRILL BOOKLET (See Tom Mix & Chewing Gum)
1934 (3x2¼")(8pgs., cover & centerfold in color)(24 books in set)(4 sets)
Goudey Chewing Gum (Giveaway)

Buck Jones #1-6	1.00	2.00	3.00
Buck Rogers #1-6	2.00	4.00	6.00
Dick Tracy #1-6	1.50	3.00	4.50
Tailspin Tommy #1-6	1.00	2.00	3.00

NOTE: *Prices are per book. There are 24 different books under each title or 96 in all.*

BIG TOP COMICS, THE
1951   (No month)
Toby Press

#1,2	.65	1.35	2.00

BIG TOWN (Radio/TV)
Jan, 1951 - #50, Mar-Apr, 1958
National Periodical Publications

#1	3.00	6.00	9.00
2	1.50	3.00	4.50
3-10	1.35	2.75	4.00
11-50	.65	1.35	2.00

BIG VALLEY, THE (TV)
June, 1966 - #6, Oct, 1969
Dell Publishing Co.

#1-6	.25	.50	.75

BILL BARNES COMICS (Air Ace V2#1 on)
Oct, 1940 - #12, 1942
Street & Smith Publications

#1	12.00	24.00	36.00
2-Barnes as The Phantom Flyer app.			
	7.00	14.00	21.00
3-5	5.00	10.00	15.00

	Good	Fine	Mint
6-12	3.00	6.00	9.00

BILL BATTLE, THE ONE MAN ARMY
Oct, 1952 - 1953
Fawcett Publications

#1	1.00	2.00	3.00
2-6	.65	1.35	2.00

BILL BOYD WESTERN
Jan, 1950 - #23, June, 1952
Fawcett Publications

#1	5.00	10.00	15.00
2-10	2.50	5.00	7.50
11-23	1.50	3.00	4.50

BILL BUMLIN (See Treasury of Comics #3)

BILL STERN'S SPORTS BOOK
Spring-Summer, 1951 - V2#2, Winter, 1952
Ziff-Davis Publ. Co.

V1#10(1951)	.65	1.35	2.00
V2#2(1952)-Krigstein art	1.50	3.00	4.50

BILLY AND BUGGY BEAR
1958; 1964
I.W. Enterprises/Super

I.W. Reprint #1(Early Timely Funny Animal),

7(1958)	.40	.80	1.20
Super Reprint #10(1964)	.40	.80	1.20

BILLY BUCKSKIN WESTERN (Two-Gun Western #4)
Nov, 1955 - #3, March, 1956
Atlas Comics (IMC #1/MgPC #2,3)

#1-Mort Drucker art	1.50	3.00	4.50
2- " " "	.75	1.50	2.25
3-Williamson story + Drucker art			
	2.00	4.00	6.00

BILLY BUNNY (Black Cobra #6 on)
Feb-Mar, 1954 - #5, Oct-Nov, 1954
Excellent Publications

#1-5	.35	.70	1.05

BILLY BUNNY'S CHRISTMAS FROLICS
1952   (100 pgs.)
Farrell Publications

#1	1.00	2.00	3.00

BILLY MAKE BELIEVE (See Single Series #14)

Big Town #29, © DC

Bill Boyd Western #2, © FAW

Billy Buckskin Western #3, © MCG

Billy West #1, © STD   Black & White #7, © The Lone Ranger, Inc.   Black & White #15, © N.Y. News Synd.

BILLY THE KID
#7, 1957 - #121, 12/76; #122, 9/77 - #123,
Charlton Publishing Co.   10/77

	Good	Fine	Mint
#7-14,17-19: #11-68pgs.	.50	1.00	2.00
15-Origin	.80	1.60	2.40
16-Two pgs. Williamson	1.35	2.75	4.00
20-22-Three Severin stys.	1.00	2.00	3.00
23-40	.35	.70	1.05
41-60	.20	.40	.60

61-80: #66-Bounty Hunter series begins. Not
in #79,82,84-86   .15   .30   .45
81-121: #87-Last Bounty Hunter. #11-Origin
& 1st app. The Ghost Train; Sutton art.
#117-Gunsmith & Co., The Cheyenne Kid app.,
122,123('77)   .15   .30

BILLY THE KID ADVENTURE MAGAZINE
Oct, 1950 - #30, 1955
Toby Press

#1-Williamson/Frazetta, 2 pgs.
                    6.00   12.00   18.00
2,4-8,10   1.35   2.75   4.00
3-Williamson/Frazetta "The Claws of Death",
4pgs. + Williamson sty.9.00 18.00 27.00
9-Kurtzman Pot-Shot Pete 3.00 6.00   9.00
11,12,15-20   1.00   2.00   3.00
13-Kurtzman reprint/John Wayne #12 (Genius)
                    1.50   3.00   4.50
14-Williamson/Frazetta; reprint of #1, 2pgs.
                    2.50   5.00   7.50
21,23-30   .80   1.60   2.40
22-One pg. Williamson/Frazetta reprint/#1
                    1.35   2.75   4.00

BILLY THE KID AND OSCAR
Winter, 1945 - #3, Summer, 1946 (Funny Animal)
Fawcett Publications

#1	1.00	2.00	3.00
2,3	.50	1.00	1.50

BILLY WEST
1949 - 1950
Standard Comics (Visual Editions)

#1	1.75	3.35	5.00
2-10: #7,8-Schomburg cvr.	1.00	2.00	3.00

NOTE: *Celardo* art-#1,3,4,9; cover-#3.
Moreira story-#3.

BING CROSBY (See Feature Films)

BINGO (-- Comics) (H. C. Blackerby)
1945   (Reprints National material)
Howard Publ.

	Good	Fine	Mint
#1-L. B. Cole cover	1.35	2.75	4.00

BINGO, THE MONKEY DOODLE BOY
Aug, 1951; Oct, 1953
St. John Publishing Co.

#1(8/51)	1.50	3.00	4.50
1(10/53)	1.00	2.00	3.00

BINKY (Formerly Leave It To --)
#72, 6-7/70 - #81, 10-11/71; #82, Sum/77 -
National Per. Publ./DC Comics   Present

#72-81		.20	.40
82('77)		.15	.30

BINKY'S BUDDIES
Jan-Feb, 1969 - #12, Nov-Dec, 1970
National Periodical Publications

#1	.20	.40	.60
2-12		.15	.30

BIONIC WOMAN, THE (TV)
October, 1977
Charlton Publications

#1		.15	.30

BLACK AND WHITE (Large Feature Comics #25 on)
1939 - 1941   (All strip reprints)
Dell Publishing Co.

#1-Dick Tracy Meets the Blank
                80.00 160.00 240.00
2-Terry & the Pirates 50.00 100.00 150.00
3-Heigh-Ho Silver! The Lone Ranger (text &
illo)(76pgs.)   25.00   50.00   75.00
4-Dick Tracy Gets His Man
                    40.00   80.00 120.00
5-Tarzan by Harold Foster (origin); reprints
1st dailies from '29-100.00 200.00 300.00
6-Terry & the Pirates & The Dragon Lady; reprints dailies from 1936
                    35.00   70.00 105.00
7-(Scarce)-The Lone Ranger-Hi-Yo Silver the
L.R. to the Rescue 40.00   80.00 120.00
8-Dick Tracy Racket Buster
                    40.00   80.00 120.00
9-King of the Royal Mtd.15.00 30.00 45.00
10-(Scarce)-Gangbusters (# appears on inside
front cover)   20.00   40.00   60.00
11-Dick Tracy Meets Doc Hump
                    40.00   80.00 120.00
12-Smilin' Jack   15.00   30.00   45.00
13-Dick Tracy & Scotty 40.00 80.00 120.00

42

(Black & White cont'd)

	Good	Fine	Mint
14-Smilin' Jack	15.00	30.00	45.00
15-Dick Tracy & the Kidnapped Princess			
	40.00	80.00	120.00
16-Donald Duck-1st app. on back			
cover(6/41-Disney)	400.00	800.00	1200.00

(Prices vary widely on this book)

	Good	Fine	Mint
17-Gangbusters(1941)	12.00	24.00	36.00
18-Phantasmo	15.00	30.00	45.00
19-Dumbo Comic Paint Book (Disney)			
	75.00	150.00	225.00
20-Donald Duck Comic Paint Book (Rarer than			
#16) (Disney)	500.00	1000.00	1500.00

(Prices vary widely on this book)

	Good	Fine	Mint
21-Private Buck	5.00	10.00	15.00
22-Nuts & Jolts	6.00	12.00	18.00
23-The Nebbs	6.00	12.00	18.00
24-Popeye (Thimble Theatre) 1/2 by Segar			
	30.00	60.00	90.00

NOTE: *Covers to #10-24 are made of unstable paper stock and are rarely found in fine - mint condition.*

BLACKBEARD'S GHOST   (See Movie Comics)

BLACK BEAUTY   (See 4-Color Comics #440)

BLACK CAT COMICS   (-- Western #16-19;
-- Mystery #29 on)
June-July, 1946 - #28, April, 1951
Harvey Publications (Home Comics)

	Good	Fine	Mint
#1-Kubert art	20.00	40.00	60.00
2-Kubert art	10.00	20.00	30.00
3	8.00	16.00	24.00
4-The Red Demons begin (The Demon #4 & 5)			
	8.00	16.00	24.00
5,6-The Scarlet Arrow app.; S&K art in both;			
Powell story #6	8.00	16.00	24.00
7-Vagabond Prince by S&K + 1 more story			
	9.00	18.00	27.00
8-S&K art	7.00	14.00	21.00
9-Origin Stuntman by S&K (reprint/Stuntman			
#1); Kerry Drake begins, ends #12			
	15.00	30.00	45.00
10-20: #13-Kerry Drake app. #17-Mary Worth			
app.	5.00	10.00	15.00
21-28	4.00	8.00	12.00

BLACK CAT MYSTERY   (Formerly Black Cat; --
Western Mystery #54; --Western #55,56; --Mys-
tery #57; --Mystic #58-62; Black Cat #63-65)
#29, June, 1951 - #65, April, 1963
Harvey Publications

	Good	Fine	Mint
#29-35,37,38,40	2.00	4.00	6.00
36,39-Used in Seduction of the Innocent			
	4.00	8.00	12.00

	Good	Fine	Mint
41-44,46-53	2.00	4.00	6.00
45-Colorama (classic) by Bob Powell			
	4.00	8.00	12.00
54-Two Black Cat stories	4.00	8.00	12.00
55,56-Black Cat app.	3.00	6.00	9.00
57-Kirby cover	2.50	5.00	7.50
58-60-Four Kirby stys.	4.00	8.00	12.00
61-Nostrand story & classic "Colorama" re-			
printed from #45	2.50	5.00	7.50
62	1.50	3.00	4.50
63-65-All Giants(25¢)-Black Cat app.			
	2.00	4.00	6.00

NOTE: *Kirby cover-#57. Meskin story-#51. Nostrand art-#44-49,61. Powell story-#44,51,52,
57.*

BLACK COBRA   (Formerly Billy Bunny)
#1, 10-11/54; #6(#2),12-1/54-55; #3,2-3/55
Ajax/Farrell Publications

	Good	Fine	Mint
#1	3.00	6.00	9.00
6(#2)-Formerly B.Bunny	2.00	4.00	6.00
3	2.00	4.00	6.00

BLACK DIAMOND WESTERN   (Desperado #1-8)
#9, 1949 - #60, 1956
Lev Gleason Publications

	Good	Fine	Mint
#9-Origin; Wolverton art	3.35	6.75	10.00
10-15	1.75	3.35	5.00
16-28-Wolverton's Bing Bang Buster			
	2.50	5.00	7.50
29,30,32-60	.65	1.35	2.00
31-One pg. Frazetta	1.35	2.75	4.00

BLACK FURY   (Wild West #58)(See Blue Bird)
May, 1955 - #57, 3-4/66 (Horse stories)
Charlton Comics Group

	Good	Fine	Mint
#1	.65	1.35	2.00
2-15	.40	.80	1.20
16-18-Ditko art	1.00	2.00	3.00
19-57	.20	.40	.60

BLACK GOLIATH
Feb, 1976 - #5, Nov, 1976
Marvel Comics Group

	Good	Fine	Mint
#1	.35	.70	1.05
2-5	.20	.40	.60

BLACKHAWK   (Formerly Uncle Sam #1-8)
#9, Winter, 1944 - #243, Oct-Nov, 1968;
#244, 1-2/76 - #250, 11-12/76
Comic Magazines(Quality)#9-107; National Per.
Publ., #108(1/57) on

Black Cat Western #54, © Harv

Black Diamond Western #14, © Lev

Blackhawk #29 © DC

Blackhawk #81, © DC   The Black Knight #4, © MCG   Black Magic V8#3, © Prize

(Blackhawk cont'd)	Good	Fine	Mint
#9(1944)	50.00	100.00	150.00
10(1946)	25.00	50.00	75.00
11-15	17.50	35.00	52.50
16-20	12.00	24.00	36.00
21-30	7.00	14.00	21.00
31-40	6.00	12.00	18.00
41-60: #50-1st Killer Shark; origin in text			
	4.00	8.00	12.00
61-80: #70-Return of Killer Shark. #71-Origin retold. #75-Intro. Blackie the Hawk			
	3.00	6.00	9.00
81-107	2.50	5.00	7.50
108-Re-intro. Blackie, the Hawk, their mascot; not in #115			
	3.00	6.00	9.00
109-117	1.35	2.75	4.00
118-Frazetta reprint/Jimmy Wakely #4, 3 pgs.			
	6.00	12.00	18.00
119-130	1.00	2.00	3.00
131-142,144-160: #133-Intro. Lady Blackhawk.			
	.65	1.35	2.00
143-Kurtzman reprt/Jimmy Wakely #4			
	1.00	2.00	3.00
161-163,165-190	.40	.80	1.20
164-Origin retold	.65	1.35	2.00
191-197,199-202,204-210: Combat Diary series begins. #197-New look for Blackhawks			
	.40	.60	1.20
198-Origin retold	.50	1.00	1.50
203-Origin Chop Chop	.50	1.00	1.50
211-243(1968): #228-Batman, Green Lantern, Superman, The Flash cameos. #230-Blackhawks become superheroes. #242-Return to old costumes	.25	.50	.75
244,245('76)-Kubert covers; Evans story in ea.	.20	.40	.60
246-250: #250-Check dies; Evans stories in all	.20	.40	.60

NOTE: _Crandall_ stories-#10,11,16,18-20,22-26, 30-33,39-44,46-50,52-58,60,63,64,66,67; covers-#18-20,22. _Kubert_ cover-#245. _Ward_ stories-#16-27(Chop Chop, 8pgs. ea.); pencilled stories-#17-63(approx.).

BLACKHAWK INDIAN TOMAHAWK WAR, THE
1951
Avon Periodicals

No#-Kinstler cover; Kit West story			
	2.00	4.00	6.00

BLACK HOOD COMICS (Formerly Hangman #2-8; Laugh Comics #20 on)
#9, Winter, 1944 - #19, Summer, 1946
MLJ Magazines

#9-The Hangman & The Boy Buddies cont'd.			
	10.00	20.00	30.00

	Good	Fine	Mint
10-The Hangman & Dusty, the Boy Detective app.	5.00	10.00	15.00
11-Dusty app.; no Hangman	4.00	8.00	12.00
12-18	4.00	8.00	12.00
19-I.D. exposed	4.00	8.00	12.00

BLACK JACK (Rocky Lane's --)
#20, Nov, 1957 - #30, Nov, 1959
Charlton Comics

#20-22,25,27,29,30	.50	1.00	1.50
23-Williamson art	1.75	3.35	5.00
24,26,28-Ditko art	.80	1.60	2.40

BLACK KNIGHT, THE
1952 - 1953
Toby Press

#1(1952)	3.00	6.00	9.00
1(5/53)(Toby)	2.00	4.00	6.00
Super Reprint #11(1963)	1.00	2.00	3.00

BLACK KNIGHT, THE
May, 1955 - #5, April, 1956
Atlas Comics (MgPC)

#1	9.00	18.00	27.00
2-5	6.00	12.00	18.00

BLACK LIGHTNING
April, 1977 - Present
National Periodical Publ./DC Comics

#1	.25	.50	.75
2-6	.15	.30	.45

BLACK MAGIC (--Magazine)(Becomes Cool Cat)
10-11/50 - V7#3, 7-8/60; V7#4,9-10/60 - V8#5, 11-12/61
Crestwood Publ. to V4#5/Headline to V7#2/
Crestwood (Prize)

V1#1-S&K story, 10pgs.	8.00	16.00	24.00
2-S&K cvr/sty.,17pgs.	5.00	10.00	15.00
3(2-3/51)-S&K story	4.00	8.00	12.00
4-S&K cvr/sty.,9pgs.	4.00	8.00	12.00
5-S&K story	3.00	6.00	9.00
6-S&K cvr/sty, 3pgs.	3.00	6.00	9.00
V2#1(10-11/51),4,5,7(6/52,#13 on cover)-S&K art	2.50	5.00	7.50
2,3,6,10,11-S&K covers only	1.50	3.00	4.50
8,9,12-S&K art	2.50	5.00	7.50
V3#1-6(5/53)-S&K cvrs/stories in all(#19-24)	2.00	4.00	6.00
V4#1(6-7/53)-#5(3-4/54)-S&K covers/stories in all(#25-30)	2.00	4.00	6.00

(Black Magic cont'd)   Good   Fine   Mint
V5#1-3(no#4-6)-S&K covers/stories(#31-33)
                                   2.00   4.00   6.00
V6#1(9-10/57)-#6(7-8/58) 1.00   2.00   3.00
V7#1(9-10/58),#2(11-12/58),#3(7-8/60)
                             .65   1.35   2.00
 #4(9-10/60),#5(11-12/60)-Torres art in all
                            1.50   3.00   4.50
  6(1-2/61)   .65   1.35   2.00
V8#1(3-4/61)   .65   1.35   2.00
  2(5-6/61)-E.C. story swipe, Ditko art
                             .80   1.60   2.40
  3(7-8/61)-#5   .65   1.35   2.00
NOTE: *Ditko art-#27-29. Meskin art-#6. S&K
means Simon & Kirby.*

BLACK MAGIC
Oct-Nov, 1973 - #9, Apr-May, 1975
National Periodical Publications

#1-S&K reprints   .25   .50   .75
 2-9-S&K reprints   .15   .30   .45

BLACKMAIL TERROR (See Dick Tracy)

BLACKOUTS (See Broadway Hollywood --)

BLACK PANTHER, THE
January, 1977 - Present
Marvel Comics Group

#1-Kirby cover/art   .20   .40   .60
 2- "   "   "   .15   .30   .45
 3-7   .15   .30

BLACK PHANTOM (See Wisco)
Nov, 1954 - 1955
Magazine Enterprises

#1(A-1#122)   6.00   12.00   18.00
 2   4.00   8.00   12.00

BLACK RIDER (Formerly Western Winners; West-
ern Tales of Black Rider #28-31; Gunsmoke
Western #32 on)
#8, 3/50 - #18, 1/52; #19, 11/53 - #27, 1/55
Marvel/Atlas Comics(CDS #8-17/CPS #19 on)

#8(#1)   5.00   10.00   15.00
 9   2.50   5.00   7.50
10-Origin Black Rider   3.00   6.00   9.00
11-20   2.00   4.00   6.00
21-27: #21,23-Two-Gun Kid story. #24-Arrow-
  head story. #26,27-Kid Colt Outlaw story
                            1.50   3.00   4.50

BLACK RIDER RIDES AGAIN!
Sept, 1957

Atlas Comics (CPS)
                              Good   Fine   Mint
#1-Three Kirby stories + Powell; Severin
   cover   2.50   5.00   7.50

BLACKSTONE (See Wisco Giveaways & Super
Magician Comics)

BLACKSTONE, MASTER MAGICIAN COMICS
Mar-Apr, 1946 - #3, Jul-Aug, 1946
Vital Publications/Street & Smith Publ.

#1   3.00   6.00   9.00
 2,3   2.00   4.00   6.00

BLACKSTONE, THE MAGICIAN (--Detective #3,4)
#2, May, 1948 - #4, Sept, 1948 (No #1)
Marvel Comics (CnPC)

#2-4-The Blonde Phantom in all
                              8.00   16.00   24.00

BLACKSTONE, THE MAGICIAN DETECTIVE FIGHTS
Fall, 1947   CRIME
E.C. Comics

#1   12.00   24.00   36.00

BLACK SWAN COMICS
1945
MLJ Magazines

#1-The Black Hood reprints from Black Hood
   #14   3.00   6.00   9.00

BLACK TARANTULA (See Feature Presentations#5)

BLACK TERROR (See Exciting & America's Best)
1942 - #27, June, 1949
Better Publications/Standard

#1-Black Terror, Crime Crusader begin
                             30.00   60.00   90.00
 2   15.00   30.00   45.00
 3   12.00   24.00   36.00
 4,5   9.00   18.00   27.00
 6-10: The Ghost app. #7   7.00   14.00   21.00
11-19   5.00   10.00   15.00
20-The Scarab app.   5.00   10.00   15.00
21-Miss Masque app.   4.00   8.00   12.00
22-Partial Frazetta art on one Black Terror
   story   6.00   12.00   18.00
23-Robinson/Meskin art   4.00   8.00   12.00
24-½pg. Frazetta art + Meskin art
                              5.00   10.00   15.00
25-27-Robinson/Meskin art 4.00   8.00   12.00
NOTE: *Most issues have Schomburg (Xela) covers. Bondage cover-#17.*

Blackstone #1. © WMG

Blackstone #2. © Vital Publ.

Black Terror #22. © STD

Blaze Carson #1, © MCG   Blazing West #1, © ACG   Blazing Western #1, © Timor Publ.

BLAKE HARPER (See City Surgeon --)

BLAST (Satire Magazine)
Feb, 1971 - #2, May, 1971
G & D Publications

	Good	Fine	Mint
#1-Wrightson & Kaluta art	1.00	2.00	3.00
2-Kaluta art	.35	.70	1.05

BLAST-OFF (Three Rocketeers)
October, 1965
Harvey Publications (Fun Day Funnies)

#1-Two Kirby/Williamson stories; Crandall/
 Williamson, Williamson/Crandall, & Will-
 iamson/Torres/Krenkel story
                       2.25   4.50   6.75

BLAZE CARSON (Rex Hart #6 on) (See Wisco)
Sept, 1948 - #5, June, 1949
Marvel Comics (USA)

#1	2.50	5.00	7.50
2-5	1.50	3.00	4.50

BLAZE THE WONDER COLLIE
#2, Oct, 1949 - #3, Feb, 1950
Marvel Comics

#2(#1),3	1.00	2.00	3.00

BLAZING BATTLE TALES
July, 1975
Seaboard Periodicals (Atlas)

#1-Intro. Sgt. Hawk & the Sky Demon; McWill-
 iams art   .20   .40   .60

BLAZING COMBAT (Magazine) (35¢)
Oct, 1965 - #4, July, 1966   (B&W)
Warren Publishing Co.

#1-Frazetta cover	6.00	12.00	18.00
2-4-All Frazetta covers; #4-Frazetta ½ pg.			
	3.00	6.00	9.00

NOTE: *Above has art by Crandall, Evans, Morr-*
ow, Orlando, Severin, Torres, Toth, Williams-
son, and Wood.

BLAZING COMICS
June, 1944 - #6, 1945; V2#3, April, 1945
Enwil Associates/Rural Home

#1-The Green Turtle, Red Hawk, Black Bucca-
 neer begin; origin Jun-Gal
                       4.00   8.00   12.00
 2   2.50   5.00   7.50

	Good	Fine	Mint
3-6	2.00	4.00	6.00
6(V2#3-inside)-36pgs., Will Rogers; 4½x6"			
	2.00	4.00	6.00

BLAZING SIXGUNS
December, 1952
Avon Periodicals

#1-Kinstler cover/story	3.00	6.00	9.00

BLAZING SIXGUNS
1964
I.W./Super Comics

I.W. Reprint #1,8,9-Kinstler cover #8
                        .65   1.35   2.00
Super Reprint #10,11,13-16(Buffalo Bill,
 Swift Deer),17(1964) .50   1.00   1.50
 #12-Reprints Bullseye #3; S&K art
                       2.50   5.00   7.50
 18-Powell's Straight Arrow
                       1.00   2.00   3.00

BLAZING SIX-GUNS
Feb, 1971 - #2, April, 1971   (52pgs.)
Skywald Comics

#1-The Red Mask, Sundance Kid begin, Avon's
 Geronimo reprint by Kinstler
                        .25   .50   .75
 2-Wild Bill Hickok, J. James, Kit Carson
 reprints   .15   .30   .45

BLAZING WEST (Hooded Horseman #23 on)
Fall, 1948 - #22, Mar-Apr, 1952
American Comics Group(B&I Publ./Michel Publ.)

#1-Origin & 1st app. Injun Jones, Tenderfoot
 & Buffalo Belle; Texas Tim & Ranger begins,
 ends #13   3.00   6.00   9.00
 2,3,5   1.50   3.00   4.50
 4-Origin & 1st app. Little Lobo; Starr art
                       2.00   4.00   6.00
 6-10   1.35   2.75   4.00
 11-13   1.00   2.00   3.00
 14-Origin & 1st app. The Hooded Horseman;
 Whitney cover   1.50   3.00   4.50
 15-22   1.00   2.00   3.00

BLAZING WESTERN
Jan, 1954 - #5, Sept, 1954
Timor Publications

#1	1.00	2.00	3.00
2-5	.65	1.35	2.00

Jan-Feb, 1976 - #5, Sept-Oct, 1976
National Periodical Publications

	Good	Fine	Mint
#1-Kubert cover	.25	.50	.75
2-5	.15	.30	.45

BLONDE PHANTOM (Formerly All-Select #1-11;
Lovers #23 on)(Also see Marvel Mystery &
#12, Wint/46-47 - #22, 3/49   Blackstone)
Marvel Comics (MPC)

#12-Miss America begins, ends #14			
	20.00	40.00	60.00
13-Sub-Mariner begins	15.00	30.00	45.00
14,15	13.50	26.75	40.00
16-Captain America with Bucky app.; Kurtz-			
man's "Hey Look"	13.50	26.75	40.00
17-22	10.00	20.00	30.00

BLONDIE (See Eat Right to Work --)
1942 - 1946
David McKay Publications

Feature Book #12 (Rare)	30.00	60.00	90.00
Feature Book #27-29,31,34(1940)			
	5.00	10.00	15.00
Feature Book #36,38,40,42,43,45,47			
	3.00	6.00	9.00

BLONDIE & DAGWOOD FAMILY
10/63 - #4, 12/65   (68 pgs.)
Harvey Publications (King Features Synd.)

#1-4	.35	.70	1.05

BLONDIE COMICS (-- Monthly #16-141)
Spring, 1947 - #163, 11/65; #164, 8/66 -
#175, 12/67; #177, 2/69 - #222, 11/76
David McKay #1-15/Harvey #16-163/King #164-
175/Charlton #177 on

#1	3.00	6.00	9.00
2-5	2.00	4.00	6.00
6-10	1.50	3.00	4.50
11-20	1.00	2.00	3.00
21-30	.65	1.35	2.00
31-50	.50	1.00	1.50
51-80	.40	.80	1.20
81-100	.30	.60	.90
101-130	.25	.50	.75
131-139	.20	.40	.60
140-(80pgs.)	.40	.80	1.20
141-166(#148,155,157,159,161-163 are 68pgs.)			
	.35	.70	1.05
167-One pg. Williamson ad	.20	.40	.60
168-175,177-222		.15	.30
Blondie, Dagwood & Daisy #1(100pgs.,1953)			

	Good	Fine	Mint
	1.50	3.00	4.50
1950 Giveaway	.80	1.60	2.40
1962, 1964 Giveaway	.35	.70	1.05
N.Y. State Dept. of Mental Hygiene Giveaway-			
('56,'61) Reg. size (diff. issues) 16pgs.			
No #	1.00	2.00	3.00
R-03('73)-Premium, 36pgs. in color; Beetle			
Bailey app.	.20	.40	.60

BLOOD IS THE HARVEST
1950   (32pgs.) (Soft cover)
Catechetical Guild

(Rare) Anti-communism	15.00	30.00	45.00

BLUE BEETLE, THE (Also see Mystery Men &
Weekly Comic Mag.)
Winter, 1939-40 - #60, Aug, 1950
Fox Publ., #1-11, #31-60; Holyoke #12-30

#1-Reprints from Mystery Men #1-5; Blue			
Beetle origin; Yarko the Great reprints			
from Wonderworld #2-5 all by Eisner, Mast-			
er Magician app.; (Blue Beetle in 4 diff.			
costumes)	50.00	100.00	150.00
2	25.00	50.00	75.00
3	15.00	30.00	45.00
4,5: #4-Two Eisner stys.	12.00	24.00	36.00
6-Dynamite Thor begins	8.00	16.00	24.00
7,8-Dynamo app. in both. #8-Last Thor			
	8.00	16.00	24.00
9,10-The Blackbird & The Gorilla app. in			
both	7.00	14.00	21.00
11-The Gladiator app.	7.00	14.00	21.00
12-The Black Fury app.	7.00	14.00	21.00
13-V-Man begins, ends #18; Kubert art			
	7.00	14.00	21.00
14,15-Costumed aide, Sparky called Spunky			
#15-19	7.00	14.00	21.00
16-20: #19-Kubert art	6.00	12.00	18.00
21-26: #24-Intro. & only app. The Halo			
	5.00	10.00	15.00
27-Tamra, Jungle Princess app.			
	3.35	6.75	10.00
28-30	3.35	6.75	10.00
31-40: "The Threat from Saturn" serial in			
#34-37	3.00	6.00	9.00
41-45	2.00	4.00	6.00
46-The Puppeteer app.	2.00	4.00	6.00
47-Kamen/Baker covers/stories begin; The			
Puppeteer app.	6.00	12.00	18.00
48-50	6.00	12.00	18.00
51,53	6.00	12.00	18.00
52-Kamen bondage cover	8.00	16.00	24.00
54-Used in Seduction of the Innocent			
	10.00	20.00	30.00
55,57-Last Kamen ish.	5.00	10.00	15.00

Blonde Phantom #19. © MCG

Blood Is The Harvest . © CG

Blue Beetle #3, © Fox

Blue Beetle #49, © Fox

Blue Bolt #4, © NOVP

Blue Bolt #107, © Star

	Good	Fine	Mint
(Blue Beetle cont'd)			
56-Used in _Seduction of the Innocent_,			
page 145	7.00	14.00	21.00
58-60-No Kamen art	2.00	4.00	6.00

NOTE: _Kamen stories-#47-49,51,53,55-57;
covers-#47,49,51,52._

BLUE BEETLE (Formerly The Thing; becomes
Mr. Muscles #22 on) (See Space Adventures)
#18, Feb, 1955 - #21, Aug, 1955
Charlton Comics

#18,19,21-Pre-1942 reprts.	2.00	4.00	6.00
20-John Mason by Kamen	2.50	5.00	7.50

BLUE BEETLE (Unusual Tales #1-49; becomes
Ghostly Tales #55 on)
V2#1, 6/64 - V2#5, 3-4/65; V3#50, 7/65 -
V3#54, 2-3/66; #1, 6/67 - #5, 11/68
Charlton Comics

V2#1-Origin Dan Garrett-Blue Beetle			
	1.00	2.00	3.00
2-5, V3#50-54	.50	1.00	1.50
#1(1967)-Question series begins by Ditko			
	1.00	2.00	3.00
2-Origin Ted Kord-Blue Beetle; Dan Garrett			
x-over	.65	1.35	2.00
3-5(#1-5-Ditko art)	.50	1.00	1.50

BLUEBIRD
1977 (50¢)
Power Comics

#1,2	.20	.40	.60

BLUE BIRD COMICS
Late 1940's - 1964 (Giveaway)
Various Shoe Stores/Charlton Comics

No#(1947-50)(36pgs.)-Several issues; Human			
Torch, Sub-Mariner app. in some			
	5.00	10.00	15.00
1959-(6 titles)(All #2) Black Fury #1,4,			
Freddy #4, Timmy the Timid Ghost #4, Mask-			
ed Raider #4, Li'l Genius, Wild Bill Hick-			
ok (Charlton)	.65	1.35	2.00
1960-(6 titles)(All #4) Black Fury #8,9,			
Masked Raider, Freddy #8,9, Timmy the			
Timid Ghost #9, Li'l Genius #9 (Charlton)			
	.40	.80	1.20
1961, '62(All #10's)-Atomic Mouse #16, Black			
Fury #12, Freddy, Li'l Genius, Masked			
Raider, Six Gun Heroes, Timmy the Ghost,			
Wild Bill Hickok, Wyatt Earp #3,12,16-18			
(Charlton)	.25	.50	.75
1963-Texas Rangers #17 (Charlton)			
	.20	.40	.60

	Good	Fine	Mint
1964-Mysteries of Unexplored Worlds #18			
(Charlton)	.15	.30	.45
1965-War Heroes #18	.15	.30	.45

NOTE: _More than one issue of each character
could have been published each year. Numbering is sporatic._

BLUE BIRD CHILDREN'S MAGAZINE, THE
1957 (16 pgs.)(Soft cover)(Reg. size)
Graphic Information Service

V1#2-6: Pat, Pete & Blue Bird app.			
	.50	1.00	1.50

BLUE BOLT
June, 1940 - #100 (V10#2), Sept-Oct, 1949
Novelty Press/Premium Group of Comics

V1#1-Origin Blue Bolt by Joe Simon, Sub-Zero			
White Rider & Super Horse, Dick Cole, Won-			
der Boy & Sgt. Spook	65.00	130.00	195.00
2-S&K cover/art	45.00	90.00	135.00
3-5-S&K cover/art; #5-Everett art on Sub-			
Zero begins	30.00	60.00	90.00
6-9-S&K cover/art	25.00	50.00	75.00
10-12	8.00	16.00	24.00
V2#1-Origin Dick Cole & The Twister			
	3.00	6.00	9.00
2-Origin The Twister retold			
	3.00	6.00	9.00
3-5-Intro. Freezum #5	3.00	6.00	9.00
6-Origin Sgt. Spook retold			
	3.00	6.00	9.00
7-12: #7-Lois Blake becomes Blue Bolt's			
costume aide	2.00	4.00	6.00
V3#1-3	2.00	4.00	6.00
4-Blue Bolt abandons costume,			
5-12	2.00	4.00	6.00
V4#1-12	1.50	3.00	4.50
V5#1-8	1.00	2.00	3.00
V6#1-10, V7#1-12	1.00	2.00	3.00
V8#1-12, V9#1-9, V10#1,2	.75	1.50	2.25

BLUE BOLT (--Weird Tales of Terror #111,112
--Weird Tales #113-119; becomes Ghostly Weird
Stories #120 on; cont. of Novelty Blue Bolt)
#102, Nov-Dec, 1949 - #119, May-June, 1953
Star Publications

#102-104-The Chameleon app.; last Target-			
#104.	2.50	5.00	7.50
105-Origin Blue Bolt(from #1) retold by			
Simon; Chameleon & Target app.			
	4.00	8.00	12.00
106-Blue Bolt by S&K begins; Spacehawk re-			
prints from Target by Wolverton begins,			
ends #110; Sub-Zero begins			
	5.50	11.00	16.50

(Blue Bolt cont'd)	Good	Fine	Mint
107-110: #108-Last S&K Blue Bolt reprint			
	4.00	8.00	12.00
111-Reprints Red Rocket, Blue Bolt & The Mask	1.75	3.35	5.00
112-Last Blue Bolt & Torpedo Man app.	1.75	3.35	5.00
113-Wolverton's Spacehawk reprint/Target V3#7	5.00	10.00	15.00
114,116,119: #116-Jungle Jo app.			
	1.75	3.35	5.00
115-Sgt. Spook app.	1.75	3.35	5.00
117-Reprints Jo-Jo & Blue Bolt			
	2.00	4.00	6.00
118-"White Spirit" by Orlando?			
	3.00	6.00	9.00

NOTE: *Disbrow art-#112 on.*

BLUE CIRCLE COMICS
June, 1944 - #6, May, 1945
Enwil Associates/Rural Home

#1-The Blue Circle begins; origin Steel Fist	3.00	6.00	9.00
2-6	1.50	3.00	4.50

BLUE PHANTOM, THE
June-Aug, 1962
Dell Publishing Co.

#1(#01-066-208)-by Fred Fredericks			
	1.00	2.00	3.00

BLUE RIBBON COMICS (-- Mystery Comics #9-18)
Nov, 1939 - #22, March, 1942
MLJ Magazines

#1-Dan Hastings, Ricky the Amazing Boy, Rang-A-Tang the Wonder Dog begin; Little Nemo app.; Jack Cole art	30.00	60.00	90.00
2-Bob Phantom, Silver Fox (both in #3), Rang-A-Tang Club & Cpl. Collins begin; Jack Cole art	15.00	30.00	45.00
3	8.00	16.00	24.00
4-Doc Strong, The Green Falcon, & Hercules begin; origin & 1st app. The Fox & Ty-Gor, Son of the Tiger	12.00	24.00	36.00
5-8: #8-Last Hercules	8.00	16.00	24.00
9-Origin & 1st app. Mr. Justice	40.00	80.00	120.00
10-12: #12-Last Doc Strong	25.00	50.00	75.00
13-Inferno, the Flame Breather begins, ends #19	25.00	50.00	75.00
14,15,17,18: #15-Last Green Falcon	20.00	40.00	60.00
16-Origin & 1st app. Captain Flag	30.00	60.00	90.00

	Good	Fine	Mint
19-22: #20-Last Ty-Gor; #22-Origin Mr. Justice retold	13.50	26.75	40.00

BLUE RIBBON COMICS (See Diary Secrets #2)

BLUE RIBBON COMICS (Diary Secrets #7 on)
2/49 - #6, 8/49   (See Heckle & Jeckle)
Blue Ribbon (St. John)

#1,3-Heckle & Jeckle	1.00	2.00	3.00
2-Diary Secrets; Matt Baker cover, two stories	2.50	5.00	7.50
4(6/49)-Diary Secrets; Matt Baker cover, two stories	2.50	5.00	7.50
5-Diary Secrets-Baker story	2.00	4.00	6.00
6-Dinky Duck(8/49)	.65	1.35	2.00

BLUE STREAK (See Holyoke One-Shot #8)

BLYTHE (See 4-Color Comics #1072)

B-MAN (See Double-Dare Adventures)

BO (Also see Big Shot #32)
June, 1955 - #2, Aug, 1955
Charlton Comics Group

#1,2-(a dog) Newspaper reprints by Frank Beck	1.00	2.00	3.00

BOATNIKS, THE (See Walt Disney Showcase #1)

BOBBY BENSON'S B-BAR-B RIDERS (See Model Fun)
May-June, 1950 - #21, 1953
Magazine Enterprises

#1-Powell art	5.00	10.00	15.00
2	3.00	6.00	9.00
3-5: #4-Lemonade Kid cvr.	2.50	5.00	7.50
6-8,10	2.00	4.00	6.00
9,11,13-Frazetta covers; Ghost Rider in #13-15	8.00	16.00	24.00
12,14-20(A-1#88)	2.00	4.00	6.00
21-Frazetta cover	8.00	16.00	24.00
--in the Tunnel of Gold(5½x8";84pgs.)-Radio giveaway by Hecker-H.O. Company(H.O. Oats) contains only 12 color pgs. of comics, rest in novel form	2.50	5.00	7.50

NOTE: *Powell art in #1-13; cover-#1,5.*

BOBBY COMICS
May, 1946
Universal Phoenix Features

#1-by S. M. Iger	1.00	2.00	3.00

Blue Ribbon Comics #13, © MLJ

Blue Ribbon #5, © STJ

Bobby Benson's--#15, © ME

Bob Colt Western #1, © Faw

Bob Steele Western #2, © Faw

Bomber Comics #4, © Sunrise Times

BOBBY SHELBY COMICS
1949

	Good	Fine	Mint
	1.00	2.00	3.00

BOBBY SHERMAN (TV)
Feb, 1972 - #7, Oct, 1972
Charlton Comics

#1-7-Based on TV show "Getting Together"
| | .15 | .30 | .45 |

BOBBY THATCHER & TREASURE CAVE
1932   (86 pgs.) (B&W; hardcover; 7x9")
Altemus Co.

Reprints; art by Storm   6.00   12.00   18.00

BOB COLT WESTERN
Nov, 1950 - #9, March, 1952
Fawcett Publications

| #1 | 4.00 | 8.00 | 12.00 |
| 2-9 | 2.00 | 4.00 | 6.00 |

BOB HOPE (See Adventures of --)

BOBMAN & TEDDY (See The Great Society)
1966
Parallax Publications

Bob & Ted Kennedy - Political satire
| | 1.35 | 2.75 | 4.00 |

BOB SCULLY, TWO-FISTED HICK DETECTIVE
No date (1930's)   36 pgs.; 9½x12"; B&W;
Humor Publ. Co.   Softcover

By Howard Dell-not reprts.4.00   8.00   12.00

BOB SON OF BATTLE (See 4-Color #729)

BOB STEELE WESTERN
Dec, 1950 - #10, June, 1952
Fawcett Publications

| #1 | 4.00 | 8.00 | 12.00 |
| 2-10 | 2.00 | 4.00 | 6.00 |

BOB SWIFT (Boy Sportsman)
May, 1951 - #5, Jan, 1952
Fawcett Publications

| #1 | 1.00 | 2.00 | 3.00 |
| 2-5 | .60 | 1.20 | 1.80 |

BOMBARDIER (See Bee 29, the Bombardier)

BOMBA, THE JUNGLE BOY
Sept-Oct, 1967 - #7, Sept-Oct, 1968
National Periodical Publications

	Good	Fine	Mint
#1	.35	.70	1.05
2-7	.20	.40	.60

BOMBER COMICS
March, 1944 - #4, Winter, 1944-45
Melverne Herald/Elliot Publ./Farrell/
Sunrise Times

#1-Origin Wonder Boy; Kismet, Man of Fate			
begins	5.00	10.00	15.00
2-4	2.50	5.00	7.50

BONANZA (TV)
June-Aug, 1960 - #37, Aug, 1970
Dell/Gold Key

4-Color #1110,1221,1283, also #01070-207,			
01070-210	.65	1.35	2.00
#1(12/62-G.K.)	.65	1.35	2.00
2-10	.35	.70	1.05
11-37	.20	.40	.60

BONGO (See Story Hour Series)

BONGO & LUMPJAW (See 4-Color #706,886, and
Walt Disney Showcase #3)

BON VOYAGE (See Movie Classics)

BOOK AND RECORD SET
1975   (16 pgs.) (7½x10") ($1.49)
A Power Records Production

#PR-10-Spiderman, PR-11-The Hulk, PR-12-Capt
    America, PR-13-Fantastic-4, PR-14-Franken-
    stein, PR-15-Dracula, PR-16-The Man-Thing
    PR-18-Planet of the Apes, PR-19-Escape
    From the Planet O.T.A., PR-20-Beneath the
    Planet O.T.A., PR-21-Battle for the Planet
    O.T.A. (w/45rpm record) .40   .80   1.20
#PR-17-Curse of the Werewolf; Adams cover re-
    print/Marvel Spotlight #2
    with record....   .50   1.00   1.50
#PR-25-Star Trek; Adams cover
    with record....   .50   1.00   1.50
#PR-27-Batman; Adams cvr/story Superman
    with record....   .50   1.00   1.50
#PR-28-Superman. w/record...40   .80   1.20
#PR-31-Conan the Barbarian; Adams cover
    with record....   .50   1.00   1.50

OOK OF ALL COMICS
945   (196 pgs.)
illiam H. Wise

	Good	Fine	Mint
reen Mask, Puppeteer	4.00	8.00	12.00

OOK OF COMICS
944   (132 Pgs.)
illiam H. Wise

	Good	Fine	Mint
#1-Captain V app.	3.00	6.00	9.00

OOK OF LOVE
1950   (132 pgs.)
ox Features Syndicate

No#-See Fox Giants. Contents can vary and
determines price.

3OOTS AND HER BUDDIES
#5, 1948 - #9, 1949; Dec, 1955 - #3, 1956
Standard Comics/Visual/Argo

#5-8	1.50	3.00	4.50
9-(Scarce)-Frazetta art, 2pgs.			
	5.00	10.00	15.00
1-3(Argo-1955-56)Reprts.	1.00	2.00	3.00

3OOTS & SADDLES (See 4-Color #919,1029,1116)

3ORDER PATROL
May-June, 1951 - #3, Sept-Oct, 1951
P. L. Publishing Co.

#1	1.25	2.50	3.75
2,3	.80	1.60	2.40

3ORIS KARLOFF TALES OF MYSTERY   (--Thriller
#3, April, 1963 - Present   #1,2)
Gold Key

#3-8,10	.50	1.00	1.50
9-Wood story	1.35	2.75	4.00
1-Williamson story, Orlando story, 8pgs.			
	1.50	3.00	4.50
2-Torres, McWilliams + 2 Orlando stories			
	.80	1.60	2.40
3,14,16-20	.35	.70	1.05
5-Crandall art	.65	1.35	2.00
1-Jones art	.65	1.35	2.00
2-40	.25	.50	.75
1-60	.20	.40	.60
1-73,75-79	.15	.30	.45
4-Origin & 1st app. Taurus.20		.40	.60
tory Digest #1(7/70-G.K.)-All text			
	.25	.50	.75

(See Mystery Comics Digest #2,5,8,11,14,
7,20,23,26)

NOTE: *Bolle* stories-#51-54,56,58,59. *McWilliams* stories-#12,14,18,19. *Orlando* stories-#11-15,21.

BORIS KARLOFF THRILLER (TV) (Becomes Boris
Karloff Tales of Mystery #3)
Oct, 1962 - #2, Jan, 1963   (80 pgs.)
Gold Key

	Good	Fine	Mint
#1	1.00	2.00	3.00
2	.65	1.35	2.00

BOUNCER, THE   (Formerly Green Mask?)
1944 - #14, Jan, 1945
Fox Features Syndicate

No#(1944)-Same as #14	3.00	6.00	9.00
#11(#1)(9/44)-Origin	2.50	5.00	7.50
12-14	2.00	4.00	6.00

BOUNTY GUNS (See 4-Color Comics #739)

BOY AND THE PIRATES, THE   (See 4-Color #1117)

BOY COMICS (Captain Battle #1&2; Boy Illustories #43-108)(Stories by Charles Biro)
#3, April, 1942 - #119, March, 1956
Lev Gleason Publications

#3-Origin Crimebuster, Bombshell & Young Robin Hood; Yankee Longago, Case 1001-1008, Swoop Storm, Boy Movies, & Yankee Lon begin; intro. Iron Jaw	60.00	120.00	180.00
4	30.00	60.00	90.00
5	25.00	50.00	75.00
6-Origin Iron Jaw; Little Dynamite begins, ends #39	30.00	60.00	90.00
7-10: #7-Bombshell ends. #10-Case 1001-1008 ends	20.00	40.00	60.00
11-14	10.00	20.00	30.00
15-Death of Iron Jaw	12.50	25.00	37.50
16-20	8.00	16.00	24.00
21-29: #28-Yankee Lon ends	4.00	8.00	12.00
30-Origin Crimebuster retold	7.00	14.00	21.00
31-40: #32-Swoop Storm, Young Robin Hood ends	3.00	6.00	9.00
41-50	2.00	4.00	6.00
51-59: #57-Dilly Duncan begins, ends #71	1.50	3.00	4.50
60-Iron Jaw returns	2.00	4.00	6.00
61-Origin Crimebuster & Iron Jaw retold	2.50	5.00	7.50
62-Death of Iron Jaw explained	1.50	3.00	4.50
63-72	1.35	2.65	4.00
73-Frazetta 1-pg. ad	1.75	3.35	5.00

Boris Karloff--#6, ©GK

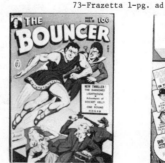

The Bouncer #13, © Fox

Boy Comics #8, © Lev

Boy Commandos #4, © DC

Boy Meets Girl #1, © Lev

Boys' Ranch #4, © Harv

(Boy Comics cont'd)

	Good	Fine	Mint
74-80: #80-1st app. Rocky X of the Rocketeers; becomes "Rocky X" #101; Iron Jaw-Sniffer & the Deadly Dozen begins, ends #118	1.00	2.00	3.00
81-88	1.00	2.00	3.00
89-92-The Claw serial app. in all	1.35	2.75	4.00
93-Claw cameo	1.00	2.00	3.00
94-100	1.00	2.00	3.00
101-107,109-111,119: #111-Crimebuster becomes Chuck Chandler. #119-Last Crimebuster	1.00	2.00	3.00
108,112-118-Kubert stories	1.50	3.00	4.50

(See Giant Boy Book of Comics)
NOTE: *Boy Movies in #3-5,40,41. Iron Jaw app.-#3,4,6,8,10,11,13-15; returns-#60,61,62, 68,69,72-79,81-118. Fuje art-#55, 18pgs.*

BOY COMMANDOS (See Detective Comics)
Winter, 1942-43 - #36, Nov-Dec, 1949
National Periodical Publications

	Good	Fine	Mint
#1-Origin Liberty Belle; The Sandman x-over in Boy Commandos; S&K art, 48pgs.	70.00	140.00	210.00
2-Last Liberty Belle; S&K art, 46pgs.	35.00	70.00	105.00
3-S&K art, 45pgs.	20.00	40.00	60.00
4-S&K art	15.00	30.00	45.00
5	10.00	20.00	30.00
6-10: #6-S&K art	8.00	16.00	24.00
11,13,14,16-20	5.00	10.00	15.00
12,15-S&K art	6.00	12.00	18.00
21,22,24-28,30	2.50	5.00	7.50
23-S&K art, 2 stories	5.00	10.00	15.00
29-S&K story	4.00	8.00	12.00
31-36	2.00	4.00	6.00

NOTE: *Most issues signed by Simon & Kirby are not by them. S&K covers-#1-9.*

BOY COMMANDOS
Sept-Oct, 1973 - #2, Nov-Dec, 1973
National Periodical Publications

#1,2-S&K reprints	.25	.50	.75

BOY DETECTIVE
May-June, 1951 - #4, May, 1952
Avon Periodicals

#1	3.00	6.00	9.00
2-4	2.00	4.00	6.00

BOY EXPLORERS COMICS
1946 - #2, Sept-Oct, 1946
Harvey Publications

	Good	Fine	Mint
#1-Kirby story, 12pgs. + S&K cover	27.50	55.00	82.50
2-(Extremely Rare)-Small size (5⅓x8⅓"-B&W, 32pgs.) Distributed to mail subscribers only. S&K art			

(Sold in San Francisco, 1976 for $900.00)
(Also see All New #15, Flash Gordon #5, and Stuntman #3)

BOY ILLUSTORIES (See Boy Comics)

BOY LOVES GIRL (Boy Meets Girl #1-25)
#26, Aug, 1952 - #57, June, 1956
Lev Gleason Publications

	Good	Fine	Mint
#26(#1)	1.00	2.00	3.00
27-42	.50	1.00	1.50
43-Toth story	1.35	2.65	4.00
44-57	.35	.70	1.05

BOY MEETS GIRL (Boy Loves Girl #26 on)
Feb, 1950 - #25, July, 1952
Lev Gleason Publications

#1-Guardineer art	1.00	2.00	3.00
2-10	.50	1.00	1.50
11-25	.35	.70	1.05

BOYS' AND GIRLS' MARCH OF COMICS (See March of Comics)

BOYS' RANCH (Also see Witches' Western Tales)
10/50 - #6, 8/51 (#1-3, 52pgs.; #46, 36pgs.)
Harvey Publications

#1-Three S&K stories	20.00	40.00	60.00
2-Three S&K stories	12.00	24.00	36.00
3-Two S&K stories + Meskin story	8.00	16.00	24.00
4-S&K art(5pg.)/cover	6.00	12.00	18.00
5,6-S&K splashes & centerspread only; Meskin art	5.00	10.00	15.00
Shoe Store Giveaway #5,6 (Identical to regular issues except S&K centerfold replaced with ad)	4.00	8.00	12.00

NOTE: *Simon & Kirby covers-#1-6.*

BOZO THE CLOWN (TV)
July, 1950 - #4, Oct-Dec, 1963
Dell Publishing Co.

4-Color #285	1.35	2.75	4.00
#2(7-9/51)-#7(10-12/52)	.65	1.35	2.00
4-Color #464,508,551,594	.65	1.35	2.00
#1-4(1963)	.25	.50	.75

BRADY BUNCH, THE (TV)
Feb, 1970 - #2, May, 1970
Dell Publishing Co.

(The Brady Bunch cont'd)	Good	Fine	Mint
.,2	.20	.40	.60

RAIN, THE
ept. 1956 - 1958
ssex Publ. Co./Magazine Enterprises

	1.00	2.00	3.00
2,3	.65	1.35	2.00
4-7	.35	.70	1.05
N Reprints #1,3,4,8,9,10('63),14			
	.35	.70	1.05
N Reprints #2-Reprints Sussex #2 with new			
cover added	.35	.70	1.05
uper Reprint #17,18(no date)			
	.35	.70	1.05

RAIN BOY
pril-June, 1962 - #6, Sept-Nov, 1963
ell Publishing Co.

-Color #1330-Gil Kane art	.80	1.60	2.40
2-6(7-9/62 - 9-11/63)	.40	.80	1.20

RAND ECHH (See Not Brand Echh)

RAND OF EMPIRE (See 4-Color Comics #771)

RAVADOS, THE (See Wild Western Action)
ugust, 1971 (52pgs.) (One Shot)
kywald Publ. Corp.

1-Red Mask, The Durango Kid, Billy Nevada			
reprints	.20	.40	.60

RAVE AND THE BOLD, THE (See Super DC Giant)
ug-Sept, 1955 - Present
ational Periodical Publications/DC Comics

1-Kubert Viking Prince, Silent Knight, Gol-			
den Gladiator begin	40.00	80.00	120.00
2	20.00	40.00	60.00
3,4	15.00	30.00	45.00
5-Robin Hood begins	12.00	24.00	36.00
6-10: #6-Kubert Robin Hood, G. Gladiator			
last app., Silent Knight; no V. Prince			
	10.00	20.00	30.00
1-22: #22-Last Silent Knight			
	7.00	14.00	21.00
23-Kubert Viking Prince origin			
	9.00	18.00	27.00
24-Last Kubert Viking Prince			
	9.00	18.00	27.00
25-27-Suicide Squad	1.50	3.00	4.50
28-Justice League intro.; origin Snapper Carr			
	9.00	18.00	27.00
29,30-Justice League	6.00	12.00	18.00
31-33-Cave Carson	1.50	3.00	4.50

	Good	Fine	Mint
34-Origin Hawkman & Byth by Kubert			
	4.00	8.00	12.00
35,36-Kubert Hawkman; origin Shadow Thief			
#36	3.00	6.00	9.00
37-39-Suicide Squad	1.00	2.00	3.00
40,41-Cave Carson Inside Earth; #40 has			
Kubert art	1.35	2.75	4.00
42,44-Kubert Hawkman	2.00	4.00	6.00
43-Origin Hawkman by Kubert			
	2.50	5.00	7.50
45-49-Infantino Strange Sports Stories			
	.80	1.60	2.40
50-Green Arrow & Jonn' Jonzz'			
	.65	1.35	2.00
51-Aquaman & Hawkman	.65	1.35	2.00
52-Kubert Sgt. Rock, Haunted Tank, Johnny			
Cloud, & Mlle. Marie	1.00	2.00	3.00
53-Toth Atom & Flash	1.00	2.00	3.00
54-Kid Flash, Robin & Aqualad			
	.65	1.35	2.00
55-Metal Men & The Atom	.65	1.35	2.00
56-Flash & Jonn' Jonzz'	.60	1.20	1.80
57-Origin Metamorpho	.60	1.20	1.80
58-Metamorpho	.60	1.20	1.80
59-Batman & Gr. Lantern	.60	1.20	1.80
60-Teen Titans	.60	1.20	1.80
61,62-Starman & Black Canary by Anderson			
	.60	1.20	1.80
63-Supergirl & W. Woman	.60	1.20	1.80
64-Batman & Eclipso	.60	1.20	1.80
65-Flash & Doom Patrol	.60	1.20	1.80
66-Metamorpho & Metal Men	.60	1.20	1.80
67-Infantino Batman & The Flash			
	.60	1.20	1.80
68-Batman & Metamorpho	.60	1.20	1.80
69-Batman & Gr. Lantern	.60	1.20	1.80
70-Batman & Hawkman	.60	1.20	1.80
71-Batman & Gr. Arrow	.50	1.00	1.50
72-Infantino Flash & Spectre			
	.50	1.00	1.50
73-Aquaman-Atom	.50	1.00	1.50
74-Batman-Metal Men	.50	1.00	1.50
75-Batman-The Spectre	.50	1.00	1.50
76-Batman-Plastic Man	.50	1.00	1.50
77-Batman-Atom	.50	1.00	1.50
78-Batman-W. Woman-Batgirl	.50	1.00	1.50
79-Batman-Deadman by Adams	1.35	2.75	4.00
80-Batman-Creeper; Adams art			
	1.35	2.75	4.00
81-Batman-Flash;Adams art	1.35	2.75	4.00
82-Batman-Aquaman; Adams art			
	1.35	2.75	4.00
83-Batman-Teen Titans; Adams art			
	1.35	2.75	4.00
84-Batman-Sgt Rock; Adams	1.35	2.75	4.00
85-Batman-Green Arrow; New costume for Green			
Arrow by Adams	1.35	2.75	4.00

Brain Boy #5, © Dell

Brave & The Bold #6, © DC

Brave & The Bold #30, © DC

53

Brave & The Bold #51, © DC

Brenda Starr V2#3, © SUPR

Brenda Starr V2#5, © SUPR

(Brave and the Bold cont'd)

	Good	Fine	Mint
86-Batman-Deadman; Adams	1.35	2.75	4.00
87-Batman-Wonder Woman	.50	1.00	1.50
88-Batman-Wildcat	.50	1.00	1.50
89-Batman-Phantom Stranger	.50	1.00	1.50
90-Batman-Adam Strange	.50	1.00	1.50
91-Batman-Black Canary	.50	1.00	1.50
92-Batman-Intro. The Bat Squad			
	.35	.70	1.05
93-Batman-House of Mystery; Adams art			
	1.00	2.00	3.00
94-Batman-Teen Titans	.35	.70	1.05
95-Batman-Plastic Man	.35	.70	1.05
96-Batman-Sgt. Rock	.35	.70	1.05
97-Batman-Wildcat; 52pgs.begin, end #102; 1st Deadman reprt/Strange Adv.#205			
	.50	1.00	1.50
98-Batman-Phantom Stranger	.35	.70	1.05
99-Batman-Flash; Adams cover; Kubert Viking Prince	.40	.80	1.20
100-Batman-Green Lantern-Green Arrow-Black Canary-Robin; Adams art	.80	1.60	2.40
101-Batman-Metamorpho; Kubert Viking Prince			
	.35	.70	1.05
102-Batman-Teen Titans; Adams pencils			
	.25	.50	.75
103-Batman-Metal Men	.25	.50	.75
104-Batman-Aparo Deadman	.25	.50	.75
105-Batman-Wonder Woman	.25	.50	.75
106-Batman-Green Arrow	.25	.50	.75
107-Batman-Black Canary	.25	.50	.75
108-Batman-Sgt. Rock	.25	.50	.75
109-Batman-Demon	.25	.50	.75
110-Batman-Wildcat	.25	.50	.75
111-Batman-The Joker	.25	.50	.75
112-Batman-Mr. Miracle; 100pg. issues begin, end #117	.25	.50	.75
113-Batman-Metal Men; Kubert art; Hawkman origin reprint from #34; origin Multi-Man/ Challengers/Unknown#14	.25	.50	.75
114-Batman-Aquaman	.25	.50	.75
115-Batman-Atom; Kubert origin Viking Prince/ #23	.25	.50	.75
116-Batman-Spectre	.25	.50	.75
117-Batman-Sgt. Rock; last 100pg. issue			
	.20	.40	.60
118-Batman-Wildcat-Joker	.20	.40	.60
119-Batman-ManBat	.20	.40	.60
120-Batman-Kamandi-68pgs.	.20	.40	.60
121-Batman-Metal Men	.20	.40	.60
122-Batman-Swamp Thing	.20	.40	.60
123-Batman-Plastic Man-Metamorpho			
	.20	.40	.60
124-Batman-Sgt. Rock	.20	.40	.60
125-Batman-Flash	.20	.40	.60
126-Batman-Aquaman	.15	.30	.45
127-Batman-Wildcat	.15	.30	.45

	Good	Fine	Min
128-Mr. Miracle	.15	.30	.4
129-Batman-Green Arrow-The Atom, Part 1 (Als Two-Face & The Joker)	.15	.30	.4
130-Batman-Green Arrow-The Atom, Part 2 (Als Two-Face & The Joker)	.15	.30	.4
131-Batman-Wonder Woman	.15	.30	.4
132-Batman-Kung-Fu Fighter	.15	.30	.4
133-Batman-Deadman	.15	.30	.4
134-Batman-Green Lantern	.15	.30	.4
135-Batman-Metal Men	.15	.30	.4
136-Batman-Metal Men-Green Arrow			
	.15	.30	.4
137-Batman-The Demon	.15	.30	.4
138-Batman-Mr. Miracle	.15	.30	.4
139-Batman-Hawkman	.15	.30	.4
140-Batman-Wonder Woman(60¢)	.20	.40	.6
141-Batman-Black Canary(vs. The Joker)			
	.20	.40	.6
142-Batman-Aquaman	.20	.40	.6

NOTE: *Adams* stories-#79-86,93,100,102; cove #75,76,79-86,88-90,93,95,99. *Infantino* stor ies-#97,98; covers-#45-49,67,69,70,72; w/*An erson*-#96. *Kubert* &/or *Heath* art-#1-24. *Kub ert* covers-#22-24,34-36,40,42-44,52. *Giant issue*-#112.

BRAVE EAGLE   (See 4-Color #705,770,816,879, 929)

BRAVE ONE, THE   (See 4-Color Comics #773)

BREEZE LAWSON, SKY SHERIFF
Summer, 1948
D. S. Publishing Co.

#1-Edmond Good art	2.50	5.00	7.5

BRENDA LEE STORY, THE
Sept, 1962
Dell Publishing Co.

#01-078-209	1.00	2.00	3.0

BRENDA STARR   (Also see All Great)
#13, #14, 3/48; V2#3, 6/48 - V2#5, 11/48
Four Star/Superior

V1#13	5.00	10.00	15.0
V1#14(3/48)-Kamen bondage cover			
	5.00	10.00	15.0
V2#3,5-Kamen covers	4.00	8.00	12.0
#4-Kamen bondage cover	5.00	10.00	15.0

BRENDA STARR   (-- Reporter)
1954 - #15, 1955
Charlton Comics

Brenda Starr cont'd)	Good	Fine	Mint
1	2.00	4.00	6.00
2-15	1.35	2.75	4.00

BRENDA STARR REPORTER
October, 1963
Dell Publishing Co.

	Good	Fine	Mint
#1	1.00	2.00	3.00

BRER RABBIT (See 4-Color #129, 208,693 and
Walt Disney Showcase #28)

BRER RABBIT IN "A KITE TAIL"
1956 (14 pgs.) (Walt Disney) (Premium)
Pacific Gas & Electric Co.

(Rare)	8.00	16.00	24.00

BRER RABBIT IN "ICE CREAM FOR THE PARTY"
1955 (14 pgs.) (Walt Disney) (Premium)
American Dairy Assn.

(Rare)	3.00	6.00	9.00

BRICK BRADFORD
1948 - 1949 (Ritt & Grey reprints)
King Features Syndicate/Standard

#5-8	3.35	6.75	10.00

BRIDE'S DIARY
#4, May, 1955 - #9, May, 1956
Ajax/Farrell Publ.

#4-9	.50	1.00	1.50

BRIDES IN LOVE (Summer Love #46 on)
Aug, 1956 - #45, Jan, 1965
Charlton Comics

#1	.40	.80	1.20
2-10	.20	.40	.60
11-45		.15	.30

BRIDES ROMANCES
1953 - #23, Dec, 1956
Quality Comics Group

#1	1.50	3.00	4.50
2-10	.65	1.35	2.00
11-23	.40	.80	1.20

BRIDE'S SECRETS
Mar-Apr, 1954 - #19, Mar, 1958
Ajax/Farrell(Excellent Publ.)/Four-Star Comic

#1	1.35	2.75	4.00

	Good	Fine	Mint
2-19	.65	1.35	2.00

BRIDE-TO-BE-ROMANCES (See True --)

BRIGAND, THE (See Fawcett Movie Comics #18)

BRINGING UP FATHER (See Large Feature Comic
#9 and 4-Color Comics #37)

BRINGING UP FATHER
1917 (16½x5½"; cardboard cover; 100pgs.;B&W)
Star Co. (King Features)

(Rare) Daily strip reprints by George McManus- (No price on cover)	25.00	50.00	75.00

BRINGING UP FATHER
1919 - 1934 (by George McManus)
(9½x9½"; cardboard covers; B&W; daily strip
reprints; 52pgs.)
Cupples & Leon

#1	15.00	30.00	45.00
2-10	7.00	14.00	21.00
11-26(Scarcer)	10.00	20.00	30.00
The Big Book #1(1926)-Thick book(hard cover)	20.00	40.00	60.00
The Big Book #2(1929)	15.00	30.00	45.00

NOTE: *The Big Books contain 3 regular issues
rebound.*

BRINGING UP FATHER, THE TROUBLE OF
1921 (9x15")
Embee Publ. Co.

Color Sunday reprints	25.00	50.00	75.00

BROADWAY HOLLYWOOD BLACKOUTS
3/54 - #3, 7-8/54
Stanhall (Trojan)

#1-3	1.50	3.00	4.50

BROADWAY ROMANCES
January, 1949 - #9, 1951
Quality Comics Group

#1-Ward cvr/9pg. story; Gustavson story	4.00	8.00	12.00
2-Ward 9pg. story	2.00	4.00	6.00
3-9	1.00	2.00	3.00

BROKEN ARROW (See 4-Color #855,947)

BROKEN CROSS, THE (See The Crusaders)

Bringing Up Father #7, © C&L   Broadway Hollywood Blackouts #1, © Stanhall   Broadway Romances #2, © Qua

Bruce Gentry #4, © SUPR

Buccaneers #8, © I.W.

Buck Rogers #5, © King

BRONCHO BILL
1939 - 1940; 1949 - 1950
United Features Syndicate/Standard/Visual

	Good	Fine	Mint
Single Series #2('39)	10.00	20.00	30.00
Single Series #19('40)(#2 on cover)			
	7.00	14.00	21.00
#1(1949-Standard)	5.00	10.00	15.00
2	2.50	5.00	7.50
3-6,8-10	2.00	4.00	6.00
7-Bondage cover	2.50	5.00	7.50
11-16	1.75	3.35	5.00

BROTHER POWER, THE GEEK
Sept-Oct, 1968 - #2, Nov-Dec, 1968
National Periodical Publications

#1-Origin The Geek; Simon art			
	.40	.60	1.20
2-Simon art	.20	.40	.60

BROTHERS OF THE SPEAR (Also see Tarzan)
June, 1972 - #17, Feb, 1976
Gold Key

#1	.50	1.00	1.50
2-10	.30	.60	.90
11-17	.20	.40	.60

BROWNIES (See 4-Color #192,244,293,337,365, 398,436,482,522,605)

BRUCE GENTRY
1/58 - #2, 11/48; #3, 1/49 - #8, 1949
Better/Standard/Four Star Publ./Superior #3

#1-Ray Bailey strip reprints begin, end #3; Kamen/Feldstein art; E.C. letters in style of the seal appears as a monogram on stationery	6.00	12.00	18.00
2,3-Feldstein art(#2-5pgs.)			
	4.00	8.00	12.00
4-8	3.00	6.00	9.00

NOTE: *Kamen stories-#4,6; covers-#1-4,6.*

BRUTE, THE
Feb, 1975 - #3, July, 1975
Seaboard Publ. (Atlas)

#1-Origin & 1st app.	.25	.50	.75
2	.15	.30	.45
3-Brunner/Weiss art	.20	.40	.60

BUCCANEER
No date (1963)
I.W. Enterprises

	Good	Fine	Mint
I.W. Reprint #1(reprints Quality #20),#8(reprints #23)	1.00	2.00	3.00
Super Reprint #12('64, reprints #21)			
	1.00	2.00	3.00

BUCCANEERS (Formerly Kid Eternity)
#19, 1/50 - #27, 5/51   (#24-27, 52pgs.)
Quality Comics Group

#19-Captain Daring, Black Roger, Eric Falcon & Spanish Man begin; Crandall story			
	4.00	8.00	12.00
20,23-Crandall story	4.00	8.00	12.00
21-Crandall cover/story	5.00	10.00	15.00
22,24,26: #24-Adam Peril, U.S.N. begins; last Spanish Man	2.50	5.00	7.50
25-Origin & 1st app. Corsair Queen			
	2.50	5.00	7.50
27-Crandall cover/story	5.00	10.00	15.00

BUCCANEERS, THE (See 4-Color Comics #800)

BUCK DUCK
June, 1953 - #4, Dec, 1953
Atlas Comics (ANC)

#1-4 (Funny Animal)	.35	.70	1.05

BUCK JONES (Also see Big Thrill Booklet)
#2, Apr-Jun, 1951 - #8, Oct-Dec, 1952
Dell Publishing Co.

4-Color #299(#1)(1950)	4.00	8.00	12.00
#2(4-6/51)	2.00	4.00	6.00
3-8	1.50	3.00	4.50
4-Color #460,500,546,589	1.50	3.00	4.50
4-Color #652,733,850	1.00	2.00	3.00

BUCK ROGERS (In the 25th Century)
1933   (36 pgs. in color)(6x8")
Kelloggs Corn Flakes Giveaway

(Rare) by Phil Nolan & Dick Calkins; 1st Buck Rogers radio premium	50.00	100.00	150.00

BUCK ROGERS (Also see Famous Funnies & Vicks
Winter/40-41 - #6, 9/43   Comics)
Famous Funnies

#1-Sunday strip reprints by Rick Yager; begins with strip #190	70.00	140.00	210.00
2	50.00	100.00	150.00
3,4	40.00	80.00	120.00
5-Story continues with Famous Funnies #80; ½ Buck Rogers, ½ Sky Roads	30.00	60.00	90.00

Buck Rogers cont'd)   Good   Fine   Mint
5-Reprints of 1939 dailies; contain B.R.
  story "Crater of Doom"(2pgs.) by Calkins
  not reprinted from Famous Funnies
               30.00 60.00 90.00

UCK ROGERS
100, Jan, 1951 - #9, May-June, 1951
oby Press

100(7),#101(8),#9-All Anderson art
            4.00   8.00 12.00

UCK ROGERS
ctober, 1964
old Key

#1(10128-410)   1.35   2.75   4.00

UCKSKIN (See 4-Color #1011,1107)

BUDDIES IN THE U.S. ARMY
1952 - 1953
Avon Periodicals

#1   2.00   4.00   6.00
 2   1.50   3.00   4.50

BUDDY TUCKER & HIS FRIENDS
1906 (11"x17") (In Color)
Cupples & Leon

1905 Sunday strip reprints by R. F. Outcault
            15.00 37.50 60.00

BUFFALO BEE (See 4-Color #957,1002,1061)

BUFFALO BILL (See Super Western Comics)

BUFFALO BILL CODY (See Cody of the Pony Exp.)

BUFFALO BILL, JR. (TV)
Jan, 1956 - #13, Aug-Oct, 1959; 1965
Dell Publishing Co./Gold Key

4-Color #673,742,766,798,828,856(11/57)
             .80   1.60   2.40
#7(2-4/58)-#13   .65   1.35   2.00
 1(6/65-G.K.)   .50   1.00   1.50

BUFFALO BILL'S PICTURE STORIES
1909   (Soft Cover)
Street & Smith Publications

           10.00 20.00 30.00

BUFFALO BILL'S PICTURE STORIES

June-July, 1949 - #2, Aug-Sept, 1949
Street & Smith Publications
           Good   Fine   Mint
#1,2-Wildey art in ea.; Powell in both
           1.50   3.00   4.50

BUGALOOS (TV)
Sept, 1971 - #4, Feb, 1972
Charlton Comics

#1-4   .15   .30
NOTE: #3(1/72) went on sale late in 1972
(after #4) with the 1/73 issues.

BUGHOUSE
March-April, 1954 - #4, Sept-Oct, 1954
Ajax/Farrell (Excellent Publ.)

V1#1   1.75   3.35   5.00
 2-4   1.35   2.75   4.00

BUG MOVIES
1931   (52 pgs.) (B&W)
Dell Publishing Co.

Not reprints; Stookie Allen art
           5.00 10.00 15.00

BUGS BUNNY
1942 - Present
Dell Publishing Co./Gold Key #86 on

Large Feature Comic #8(1942)-(Rarely found in
  Fine-Mint condition) 40.00 110.00 180.00
4-Color #33('43)   30.00 60.00 90.00
4-Color #51   20.00 40.00 60.00
4-Color #88   10.00 20.00 30.00
4-Color #123('46),142,164 6.00 12.00 18.00
4-Color #187,200,217,233 4.00   8.00 12.00
4-Color #250,266,274,281,289,298('50)
            2.50   5.00   7.50
4-Color #307,317(#1),327(#2),338,347,355,366,
  376,393   2.25   4.50   6.75
4-Color #407,420,432 2.00   4.00   6.00
#28-30(1953)   .65   1.35   2.00
 31-50   .50   1.00   1.50
 51-85   .30   .60   .90
 86-88-Bugs Bunny's Showtime-(80pgs.)(25¢)
             .50   1.00   1.50
 89-120   .25   .50   .75
 121-140   .20   .40   .60
 141-170   .15   .30   .45
 171-191   .15   .30
4-Color #498,585   1.00   2.00   3.00
4-Color #647,724,838,1064 .65   1.35   2.00
Christmas Funnies #1('50) 4.00   8.00 12.00
Christmas Funnies #2-5('51-'54) (becomes
  Christmas Party #6) 1.75   3.35   5.00

Buck Rogers #1(GK). © King

Bugs Bunny 4-Color #164. © L. Schlesinger

Bugs Bunny's Trick--#3. © L. Schlesinger

Bulletman #5, © Faw

Bulletman #11, © Faw

Bulls-Eye #5, © Prize

(Bugs Bunny cont'd)

	Good	Fine	Mint
Christmas Funnies #7-9(12/56-12/58)			
	1.50	3.00	4.50
Christmas Party #6('55)(Formerly Christmas			
Funnies #5)(Giant)	1.50	3.00	4.50
County Fair #1('57)(Giant)	1.75	3.35	5.00
Florida Power & Light Giveaway(1960,'68)			
	.40	.80	1.20
Halloween Parade #1('53)(Giant)			
	3.00	6.00	9.00
Halloween Parade #2('54)(Trick 'N' Treat			
Halloween Fun #3 on)	1.50	3.00	4.50
Trick 'N' Treat Halloween Fun #3('55), #4			
(10/56)(Formerly Halloween Fun)			
	1.50	3.00	4.50
Vacation Funnies #1('51)-112 pgs.			
	4.00	8.00	12.00
Vacation Funnies #2-9('52-'59)-100 pgs.			
	1.50	3.00	4.50
Winter Fun #1(12/67)(G.K.)	.50	1.00	1.50

BUGS BUNNY (See The Best of --; Comic Album
#2,6,10,14; Dell Giant #28,32,46; Golden Com-
ics Digest #1,3,5,6,8,10,14,15,17,21,26,30,
35,39,42,47; March of Comics #44,59,75,83,97,
115,132,149,160,179,188,201,220,231,245,259,
273,287,301,315,329,343,363,367,380,392,403;
Super Book #14,26; and Whitman Comic Books)

BUGS BUNNY (Puffed Rice Giveaway)
1949 (32pgs. each, 3-1/8"x6-7/8")
Quaker Cereals

A1-Traps the Counterfeiters, A2-Aboard Mystery Submarine, A3-Rocket to the Moon, A4-
Lion Tamer, A5-Rescues the Beautiful Princess, B1-Buried Treasure, B2-Outwits the
Smugglers, B3-Joins the Marines, B4-Meets
the Dwarf Ghost, B5-Finds Aladdin's Lamp,
C1-Lost in the Frozen North, C2-Secret
Agent, C3-Captured by Cannibals, C4-Fights
the Man From Mars, C5-And the Haunted Cave
each.... 1.50 3.00 4.50

BUGS BUNNY (3-D)
1953 (Pocket size) (15 titles)
Cheerios Giveaway

each.... 1.75 3.35 5.00

BUGS BUNNY & PORKY PIG
Sept, 1965 (100 pgs.)(Soft Cover - Giant)
Gold Key

#1(30025-509) 1.00 2.00 3.00

BULLETMAN (See Master Comics & Fawcett Min.)
1941 - #16, Fall, 1946
Fawcett Publications

	Good	Fine	Mint
#1	70.00	140.00	210.00
2	40.00	80.00	120.00
3	30.00	60.00	90.00
4,5	25.00	50.00	75.00
6-10	20.00	40.00	60.00
11-16 (#13-exist?)	15.00	30.00	45.00

-- Well Known Comics(1942)-Paper cover, glued
binding (Bestmaid/Samuel Lowe giveaway)
22.50 45.00 67.50
NOTE: #2,3,5 have *Mac Raboy* covers.

BULLS-EYE
July-Aug, 1954 - #11, Mar-Apr, 1956
Mainline(Prize)#1-5/Charlton #6-11

#1-S&K cover only	10.00	20.00	30.00
2-S&K cover/story	8.00	16.00	24.00
3-5-S&K cvr/stys(2)	7.00	14.00	21.00
6-11	2.00	4.00	6.00
Great Scott Shoe Store giveaway-Reprints #2			
with new cover	5.00	10.00	15.00

BULLS-EYE COMICS
#11, 1944
Harry 'A' Chesler

#11-Origin K-9, Green Knight's Sidekick,
Lance; The Green Knight, Lady Satan, Yankee Doodle Jones app. 5.00 10.00 15.00

BULLWHIP GRIFFIN (See Movie Comics)

BULLWINKLE (TV) (See March of Comics #233)
3-5/62 - #11, 4/74; #12, 6/76 - Present
Dell/Gold Key

4-Color #1270(3-5/62)	.50	1.00	1.50
#01-090-209(Dell, 7-9/62)	.35	.70	1.05
#1,2(2/63-G.K.)	.35	.70	1.05
#3(4/72)-#11(4/74-G.K.)	.20	.40	.60
12(6/76)-reprints	.20	.40	.60
13(9/76),#14-new stories	.20	.40	.60
15-18	.20	.40	.60
Mother Moose Nursery Pomes #01-530-207			
(5-7/62-Dell)	.40	.80	1.20

BULLWINKLE (TV)
July, 1970 - #7, July, 1971
Charlton Comics

#1	.20	.40	.60
2-7		.15	.30

BUNNY
1967 - #20, Dec, 1971; #21, 11/76
Harvey Publications

Bunny cont'd)	Good	Fine	Mint
1	.15	.30	.45
2-21		.15	.30

BURKE'S LAW (TV)
Jan-Mar, 1964 - #3, Mar-May, 1965
Dell Publishing Co.

	Good	Fine	Mint
1	.20	.40	.60
2,3	.15	.30	.45

BURNING ROMANCES
1950   (132 pgs.)
Fox Feature Publications (Hero Books)

1-See Fox Giants. Contents can vary and
   determines price.

**BUSINESS WEEK PRESENTS - THE AMAZING ADVENT-
URES OF THE MEN FROM PACIFIC PLANTRONICS**
May, 1971   (Oversized)
Business Week Giveaway

AR-444-Twenty pgs. Dick Ayers art in color
.40   .80   1.20

BUSTER BEAR
Dec, 1953 - #10, June, 1955
Quality Comics Group (Arnold Publ.)

#1	.50	1.00	1.50
2-10	.35	.70	1.05
IW Reprint #9,10(Super on inside)			
	.20	.40	.60

BUSTER BROWN
1903 - 1906 (11x17" strip reprints in color)
Frederick A. Stokes Co.

-- & His Resolutions(1903) by R. F. Outcault
25.00 62.50 100.00
-- His Dog Tige & Their Troubles(1904)
20.00 50.00 80.00
-- Pranks(1905)   20.00 50.00 80.00
-- His Dog Tige & Their Jolly Times(1906)
20.00 50.00 80.00
-- My Resolutions(1906)-68pgs., B&W; hard
   cover; Sunday panel reprints
20.00 50.00 80.00
NOTE: *Rarely found in fine or mint condition.*

BUSTER BROWN
1908 - 1917 (11x17" strip reprints in color)
Cuppies & Leon Co./N.Y. Herald Co.

(By R. F. Outcault)
-- Amusing Capers(1908) 15.00 37.50 60.00
-- And His Pets(1909) 15.00 37.50 60.00

	Good	Fine	Mint
-- On His Travels(1910)	15.00	37.50	60.00
-- Happy Days(1911)	15.00	37.50	60.00
-- In Foreign Lands(1912)	15.00	37.50	60.00
-- And the Cat(1917)	12.00	33.50	45.00

NOTE: *Rarely found in fine or mint condition.*

BUSTER BROWN COMICS
1945 - 1959   (#5,9-soft covers)
Brown Shoe Co.

#1	3.35	6.75	10.00
2-10	1.50	3.00	4.50
11-20	.80	1.60	2.40
21-24,26-28	.65	1.35	2.00
25,31,33-37,40,41-Crandall art in all			
	2.00	4.00	6.00

29,30,32-"Interplanetary Police Vs. the Space
Siren" by Crandall 2.00   4.00   6.00
38,39,42,43   .50   1.00   1.50
--Goes to Mars('58, Western Printing)
1.00   2.00   3.00
--In "Buster Makes the Team!"(1959-Custom
Comics)   .65   1.35   2.00
--Of the Safety Patrol('60, Custom Comics)
.65   1.35   2.00
--Out of This World('59-Custom Comics)
.65   1.35   2.00
--Safety Coloring Book(1958)-Slick paper,
16 pgs.   .65   1.35   2.00

BUSTER BUNNY
Nov, 1949 - #15, July, 1953
Standard Comics(Animated Cartoons)/Pines

#1,2-Frazetta 1 pg. text illos. in both
1.75   3.35   5.00
3-15   .50   1.00   1.50

BUSTER CRABBE
Nov, 1951 - #12, 1953
Famous Funnies

#1-Frazetta back cover showing drug pusher
7.00 14.00 21.00
2-Williamson/Evans cover 9.00 18.00 27.00
3-Williamson/Evans cover & story
10.00 20.00 30.00
4-Cover & 1pg. by Frazetta
12.00 24.00 36.00
5-Frazetta cover & 11 pg. story by William-
son/Krenkel/Orlando (per Mr. Williamson)
(Rare)   60.00 120.00 180.00
6,8,10-12   1.75   3.35   5.00
7,9-One pg. of Frazetta in each
2.00   4.00   6.00

Buster Brown (1904), © F.A. Stokes

Buster Brown #11, © Buster Brown

Buster Crabbe #3, © FF

Buzzy #57, © DC

Calling All Boys #14, © PMI

Camp Comics #2, © Dell

BUSTER CRABBE
Dec, 1953 - #4, June, 1954
Lev Gleason Publications

	Good	Fine	Mint
#1	2.50	5.00	7.50
2,3-Toth art	2.50	5.00	7.50
4	1.50	3.00	4.50

BUTCH CASSIDY
June, 1971 - #3, Oct, 1971 (52 pgs.)
Skywald Comics

#1-Red Mask reprint, retitled Maverck;			
Bolle art	.20	.40	.60
2-Whip Wilson reprint	.15	.30	.45
3-Dead Canyon Days reprt/Crack Western #63;			
Sundance Kid app.	.15	.30	.45

BUTCH CASSIDY & THE WILD BUNCH
1951
Avon Periodicals

No#-Kinstler cover/story	3.50	7.00	10.50

BUTCH CASSIDY (See Fun-In #11)

BUZ SAWYER
1948 - 1949
Standard Comics

#1-Roy Crane	3.35	6.75	10.00
2-5	2.00	4.00	6.00

BUZ SAWYER'S PAL, ROSCOE SWEENEY (See Sweeney)

BUZZY
Winter, 1944-45 - #77, Oct, 1959
National Periodical Publ./Detective Comics

#1	3.00	6.00	9.00
2-5	1.50	3.00	4.50
6-10	1.00	2.00	3.00
11-40: #33-Scribbly by Mayer			
	.50	1.00	1.50
41-77	.35	.70	1.05

BUZZY THE CROW (See Harvey Hits #18)

CADET GRAY OF WEST POINT
1958   (Giant)
Dell Publishing Co.

#1-Williamson story-10pgs.	2.50	5.00	7.50

CAIN'S HUNDRED (TV)
May-July, 1962 - #2, Sept-Nov, 1962
Dell Publishing Co.

	Good	Fine	Min
No#(01-094-207),#2	.35	.70	1.0

CALL FROM CHRIST
1952
Catholic Education Society

	1.35	2.75	4.0

CALLING ALL BOYS (Tex Granger #18 on)
Jan, 1946 - #17, May, 1948
Parents' Magazine Institute

#1	2.00	4.00	6.0
2-17	1.00	2.00	3.0

CALLING ALL GIRLS
Sept, 1941 - #44, Nov, 1945? (Movie reviews
Parents' Magazine Institute

#1,2	2.00	4.00	6.00
3-10	1.00	2.00	3.00
11-20	.60	1.20	1.80
21-44	.40	.80	1.20

CALLING ALL KIDS
Dec-Jan, 1945-46 - #26, Aug, 1949
Parents' Magazine/Quality Comics

#1	1.00	2.00	3.0
2	.80	1.60	2.4
3-10	.50	1.00	1.5
11-26	.40	.80	1.2

CALVIN (See Li'l Kids)

CALVIN & THE COLONEL (TV)
1962 - #2, Jul-Sept, 1962
Dell Publishing Co.

4-Color #1354	.40	.80	1.20
#2	.25	.50	.75

CAMERA COMICS
July, 1944 - #9, 1946
U.S. Camera Publishing Corp.

No#(7/44 & 9/44 issues)	1.50	3.00	4.50
#1(10/44)-The Grey Comet	1.50	3.00	4.50
2-9: All ½ photos	1.00	2.00	3.00

CAMP COMICS
Feb, 1942 - #3, April, 1942
Dell Publishing Co.

#1-"Seaman Sy Wheeler" by Kelly, 7 pgs.;			
Bugs Bunny app.	25.00	50.00	75.00
2-Kelly story, 12pgs.; Bugs Bunny app.			
	17.50	35.00	52.50
3-(Scarce)-Kelly story	20.00	40.00	60.00

CAMP RUNAMUCK (TV)
April, 1966
Dell Publishing Co.

	Good	Fine	Mint
#1	.20	.40	.60

CAMPUS LOVES
Dec, 1949 - #5, Aug, 1950
Quality Comics Group (Comic Magazines)

	Good	Fine	Mint
#1-Ward cover, 9pg. story	4.00	8.00	12.00
2-Ward cover/story	2.50	5.00	7.50
3-5-Gustavson art, photo covers in all			
	1.50	3.00	4.50

CAMPUS ROMANCES
Sept-Oct, 1949 - #3, Feb-Mar, 1950
Avon Periodicals

#1	2.00	4.00	6.00
2,3	1.50	3.00	4.50

CANADA DRY PREMIUMS (See Swamp Fox, The)

CANDY
Fall, 1944 - #3, Spring, 1945
William H. Wise & Co.

#1-Two Scoop Scuttle stories by Basil Wolverton	6.00	12.00	18.00
2,3-Scoop Scuttle by Basil Wolverton (2-4 pgs.)	4.50	9.00	13.50

CANDY
Autumn, 1947 - #63, May, 1956
Quality Comics Group

#1	2.00	4.00	6.00
2-10	1.00	2.00	3.00
11-63	.65	1.35	2.00
Super Reprint #2,10,16,17('64),18			
	.50	1.00	1.50

CANNONBALL COMICS
Feb, 1945 - #2, Mar, 1945
Rural Home Publishing Co.

#1-The Crash Kid, Thunderbrand, The Captive Prince & Crime Crusader begin			
	3.00	6.00	9.00
2	2.00	4.00	6.00

CANTEEN KATE (Also see All Picture All True
Love Story & Fightin' Marines)
June, 1952 - #3, Nov, 1952
St. John Publishing Co.

#1-Matt Baker cvr/stories	7.00	14.00	21.00

	Good	Fine	Mint
2,3-Matt Baker cvr/stys.	4.00	8.00	12.00

CAP'N CRUNCH COMICS (See Quaker Oats)
1963; 1965 (16pgs.; Miniature giveaways;
Quaker Oats Co.   2½x5½")

(4 titles)-"The Picture Pirates," "The Fountain of Youth," "I'm Dreaming of a Wide Isthmus," "Bewitched, Betwitched, & Betweaked"('65)   .15   .30   .45

CAPTAIN ACTION
Oct-Nov, 1968 - #5, June-July, 1969
National Periodical Publications

#1-Origin Captain Action; Wood art; Superman cameos	.50	1.00	1.50
2,3,5-Wood inks	.35	.70	1.05
4	.25	.50	.75
-- & Action Boy('67)-Ideal Toy Co. Giveaway			
	.15	.30	.45

CAPTAIN AERO COMICS (Samson #1-6)
V1#7(#1), Dec, 1941 - V2#4(#10), Jan, 1943;
V3#9(#11), Sept, 1943 - V4#3(#17), Oct, 1944;
#21, Dec, 1944 - #26, Aug, 1946 (No #18-20)
Holyoke Publishing Co.

V1#7(#1)-Flag-Man & Solar, Master of Magic, Captain Aero, Cap Stone, Adventurer begin	15.00	30.00	45.00
8(#2)-Pals of Freedom app.			
	8.00	16.00	24.00
9(#3)-Alias X begins; Pals of Freedom app.			
	8.00	16.00	24.00
10(#4)-Origin The Gargoyle; Kubert art			
	9.00	18.00	27.00
11,12(#5,6)-Kubert art; Miss Victory app. in #6	7.00	14.00	21.00
V2#1(#7)	5.00	10.00	15.00
2(#8)-Origin The Red Cross			
	5.00	10.00	15.00
3(#9)-Miss Victory app.	4.00	8.00	12.00
4(#10)	2.50	5.00	7.50
V3#9 - V3#13(#11-15)	2.00	4.00	6.00
V4#2, V4#3(#16,17)	2.00	4.00	6.00
#21-26	2.00	4.00	6.00

CAPTAIN AMERICA (See All-Select, All Winners,
Aurora, Book & Record Set, Giant Comics To
Color, & USA Comics)

CAPTAIN AMERICA COMICS
3/41 - #75, 1/50; #76, 5/54 - #78, 9/54
##74 & 75 titled Captain America's Weird Tales)
Timely #1-75/Atlas #76-78 (CCC/MJMC/CMPS)

Campus Loves #1, © Qua

Candy #13, © Qua

Captain Aero Comics #5, © Hoke

61

Captain America Comics #1, © MCG   Captain America Comics #59, © MCG   Captain America #100, © MCG

(Capt. America cont'd)	Good	Fine	Mint
#1-Origin & 1st app. Captain America & Bucky by S&K; Hurricane, Tuk, the Caveboy begin by S&K; Red Skull app.			
	750.00	1500.00	2250.00
(Prices vary widely on this book)			
2-S&K Hurricane; Tuk by Avison(Kirby splash)			
	300.00	600.00	900.00
3-Red Skull app.	200.00	400.00	600.00
4	150.00	300.00	450.00
5	125.00	250.00	375.00
6-Origin Father Time; Tuk, the Caveboy ends			
	100.00	200.00	300.00
7-10-Last S&K issue; Red Skull in #7 (S&K centerfold #6-10)	90.00	180.00	270.00
11-Last Hurricane, Headline Hunter; Al Avison Captain America begins, ends #20			
	60.00	120.00	180.00
12-The Imp begins, ends #16; Last Father Time	60.00	120.00	180.00
13-Origin The Secret Stamp			
	60.00	120.00	180.00
14,15	50.00	100.00	150.00
16-Red Skull app.	50.00	100.00	150.00
17-The Fighting Yank only app.			
	50.00	100.00	150.00
18,19-Human Torch begins #19; not in #20			
	35.00	70.00	105.00
20-Sub-Mariner app.	30.00	60.00	90.00
21-25	27.50	55.00	82.50
26-30: #27-Last Secret Stamp			
	25.00	50.00	75.00
31-36,38-40	22.50	45.00	67.50
37-Red Skull app.	25.00	50.00	75.00
41-50	20.00	40.00	60.00
51-58,60	17.50	35.00	52.50
59-Origin retold	19.00	38.00	57.00
61-Red Skull app.	17.50	35.00	52.50
62-65,67	15.00	30.00	45.00
66-Origin Golden Girl; Kurtzman's "Hey Look"			
	17.50	35.00	52.50
68-70-Sub-Mariner in all	15.00	30.00	45.00
71-73: #71-Bucky app.	12.00	24.00	36.00
74(1949)-Titled "C.A.'s Weird Tales"; Red Skull app.	15.00	30.00	45.00
75(1/50)-Titled "C.A.'s Weird Tales"; no C.A. app.; horror cover/stories			
	10.00	20.00	30.00
76-78(1954)	10.00	20.00	30.00
Shoestore Giveaway #77	5.00	10.00	15.00

NOTE: *Part Crandall art-#2,3? S&K covers-#1, 2,5-7,9,10. A Canadian 132 pg. issue exists in black & white.*

CAPTAIN AMERICA (Tales of Suspense #1-99; -- and the Falcon #134 on)
#100, April, 1968 - Present
Marvel Comics Group

	Good	Fine	Mint
#100-Flashback on Cap's revival with Avengers & Sub-Mariner	1.35	2.75	4.00
101-108	.80	1.60	2.40
109-Origin Capt.America	1.00	2.00	3.00
110,111,113-Steranko art; #110-Rick becomes Cap's partner	1.50	3.00	4.50
112,114,115	.65	1.35	2.00
116-130	.60	1.20	1.80
131-150	.50	1.00	1.50
151-179	.35	.70	1.05
180-Changes name temporarily to Nomad with origin	.25	.50	.75
181-192	.20	.40	.60
193-217	.15	.30	.45
Giant Size #1(12/75)	.65	1.35	2.00
Special #1(1/71)	1.00	2.00	3.00
Special #2(1/72)	.65	1.35	2.00
Annual #3(4/76), #4(8/77)-Kirby cover/art			
	.40	.80	1.20

NOTE: *Buscema cover/story-#217. Everett inks-#136,137. Kirby art-#100-109,112,193-205; covers-#100-109,112,126,195-197,199-216. Morrow art-#144. Wood inks-#127.*

CAPTAIN AND THE KIDS, THE (See Famous Comics Cartoon Books)

CAPTAIN AND THE KIDS, THE (See Comics on 1938 - 4-Color #881, Feb, 1958   Parade)
United Features Syndicate/Dell Publ. Co.

Single Series #1('38)	15.00	30.00	45.00
Single Series #1(Reprint)(12/39-"Reprint" on cover)	10.00	20.00	30.00
Okay #1	5.00	10.00	15.00
#1(Summer, 1947-Dell)	2.50	5.00	7.50
2-10	1.75	3.35	5.00
11-32(1952)	1.35	2.75	4.00
50th Anniversary ish('48)-Contains a 2pg. history of the strip, including an account of the famous Supreme Court decision allowing Boch the Pulitzer & Hearst to run the same strip under different names.			
	1.50	3.00	4.50
Special Summer issue, Fall issue (1948)			
	1.50	3.00	4.50
4-Color #881	1.00	2.00	3.00

CAPTAIN ATOM
1950 - 1951   (5x7¼")
Nationwide Publishers

#1-7	1.50	3.00	4.50

CAPTAIN ATOM (Strange Sus. Stories #1-77)
#78, Dec, 1965 - #89, Dec, 1967
Charlton Comics

(Captain Atom cont'd)	Good	Fine	Mint
#78-Origin retold	1.35	2.75	4.00
79-81	1.00	2.00	3.00
82-Intro. Nightshade	1.00	2.00	3.00
83-Ted Kord Blue Beetle begins, ends #86,			
84-86,88,89	1.00	2.00	3.00
87-Nightshade begins	1.00	2.00	3.00

NOTE: *All issues have* Ditko *art & stories.*

CAPTAIN BATTLE (Boy #3 on)(See Silver Streak)
Summer, 1941 - #2, Fall, 1941
Comic House/Fun

#1-Origin Blackout; Captain Battle begins			
	25.00	50.00	75.00
2	15.00	30.00	45.00

CAPTAIN BATTLE (2nd Series)
1943 - 1945 (Gleason reprints)
Picture Scoop

#3-Origin Silver Streak	8.00	16.00	24.00
4	6.00	12.00	18.00
5-Origin Blackout retold	6.00	12.00	18.00

CAPTAIN BATTLE, JR.
Fall, 1943 - #2, Winter, 1943-44
Comic House

#1-The Claw vs. The Ghost			
	12.50	25.00	37.50
2-Wolverton's Scoop Scuttle			
	15.00	30.00	45.00

CAPTAIN BRITAIN
10/13/76 - #39, 1977 (Weekly)
Marvel Comics International

#1-Origin; with Capt. Britain's face mask			
inside	1.35	2.75	4.00
2-Origin, conclusion. Britain's Boomerang			
inside	.80	1.60	2.40
3-Vs. Bank Robbers	.50	1.00	1.50
4-7-Vs. Hurricane	.50	1.00	1.50
8-Vs. Bank Robbers	.50	1.00	1.50
9-13-Vs. Dr. Synne	.50	1.00	1.50
14,15-Vs. Mastermind	.50	1.00	1.50
16-20-With Capt. America; #17 misprinted &			
color section reprinted in #18			
	.50	1.00	1.50
21-26-With Capt. America	.40	.80	1.20
27-39	.35	.70	1.05

NOTE: *Distributed in Great Britain only.*

CAPTAIN CANUCK
July, 1975 - Present (Distributed in U.S.)
Comely Comix (Canada)

	Good	Fine	Mint
#1	.35	.70	1.05
2,3	.25	.50	.75

CAPTAIN CARVEL AND HIS CARVEL CRUSADERS
(See The Amazing Advs. of --)

CAPTAIN COURAGEOUS (Banner #3-5)
March, 1942
Ace Magazines

#6-Origin & 1st app. The Sword; Lone Warrior,			
Capt. Courageous app.	15.00	30.00	45.00

CAPT'N CRUNCH COMICS (See Cap'n --)

CAPTAIN DAVY JONES (See 4-Color #598)

CAPTAIN EASY
1939 - 1956
Dell Publ./Standard(Visual Editions)/Argo

Hawley(1939)-Contains reprints from The			
Funnies & 1938 Sunday strips			
	15.00	30.00	45.00
4-Color #24('43)	12.00	24.00	36.00
4-Color #111	5.00	10.00	15.00
#10(Standard, 10/47)	3.00	6.00	9.00
11-17: All-30's & 40's strip reprints			
	2.50	5.00	7.50
Argo #1(4/56)-Reprints	2.00	4.00	6.00

CAPTAIN EASY & WASH TUBBS (See Famous Comics
Cartoon Books)

CAPTAIN FEARLESS COMICS (See Holyoke
One-Shot #6)

CAPTAIN FEARLESS COMICS
August, 1941 - #2, Sept, 1941
Holyoke Publishing Co.

#1-Origin Mr. Miracle, Alias X, Captain Fear-			
less, Citizen Smith, Son of the Unknown			
Soldier; Miss Victory begins			
	17.50	35.00	52.50
2	8.00	16.00	24.00

CAPTAIN FLASH
Nov, 1954 - #4, July, 1955
Sterling Comics

#1-Origin by Mike Sekowsky(not Toth); Tomboy			
begins	4.00	8.00	12.00
2,3	2.50	5.00	7.50
4-Tomboy app.	2.50	5.00	7.50

Captain Battle #2, © Lev

Captain Easy (Hawley), © NEA Services, Inc.

Captain Flash #3, © Sterling Comics

Captain Flight #5, © Four Star

Captain Gallant #2, © CC

Captain Marvel Adv. #1, © Faw

CAPTAIN FLEET
Fall, 1952
Ziff-Davis Publishing Co.

	Good	Fine	Mint
#1	1.20	2.40	3.60

CAPTAIN FLIGHT COMICS
Mar, 1944 - #11, Feb-Mar, 1947
Four Star Publications

	Good	Fine	Mint
#1	3.35	6.75	10.00
2	2.00	4.00	6.00
3-5: #4-Rock Raymond begins, ends #7. #5- Red Rocket begins; the Grenade app.	1.50	3.00	4.50
6-8: #8-Yankee Girl, Black Cobra begin; Intro. Cobra Kid	2.00	4.00	6.00
9-Torpedoman app.; last Yankee Girl; Kinstler story	2.00	4.00	6.00
10-Deep Sea Dawson, Zoom of the Jungle, & Rock Raymond app.; no Red Rocket, Black Cobra	1.50	3.00	4.50
11-Torpedoman, Blue Flame app.; last Black Cobra, Red Rocket	1.50	3.00	4.50

CAPTAIN FORTUNE PRESENTS
1955 - 1959 (16pgs.)(Giveaway - 3¼x7")
Vital Publications

"Davy Crockett in Episodes of teh Creek War,"
"Davy Crockett at the Alamo," "Young Davy
Crockett", In Sherwood Forest Tells Strange
Tales of Robin Hood('57), Tells How Buffalo
Bill Fights the Dog Soldiers('57)

	.50	1.00	1.50

CAPTAIN GALLANT (--of the Foreign Legion)(TV)
1955 - 1956
Charlton Comics

	Good	Fine	Mint
#1-Buster Crabbe	1.75	3.35	5.00
2-4	1.00	2.00	3.00
Heinz Foods Premium(1955, regular size) U.S. Pictorial; contains Buster Crabbe photos; Don Heck art	1.35	2.75	4.00
Non-Heinz version(same as above except pict- ures of show replaces ads)	1.35	2.75	4.00

CAPTAIN HERO (See Jughead As --)

CAPTAIN HOBBY COMICS
Feb, 1948 (Canadian)
Export Publication Ent. Ltd. (Dist. in U.S.
by Kable News Co.)

#1	1.00	2.00	3.00

CAPTAIN HOOK & PETER PAN (See 4-Color #446
and Peter Pan)

CAPTAIN JET
May, 1952 - #5, Jan, 1953
Comic Media/Four Star Publ./Farrell

	Good	Fine	Mint
#1	1.35	2.75	4.00
2-5	.75	1.50	2.25

CAPTAIN KANGAROO (See 4-Color #721,780,872)

CAPTAIN KIDD (Formerly Dagar)
1949
Fox Features Syndicate

#24,25	1.50	3.00	4.50

CAPTAIN MARVEL (See All Hero, America's
Greatest, Fawcett Min., Gift, Marvel Family,
Master #21, Shazam, Whiz, Wisco, & Xmas)

CAPTAIN MARVEL (--Presents the Terrible 5 #
April, 1966 - #4, Nov, 1966 (25¢)
M. F. Enterprises

No#-(#1 on page 5)-Origin	.40	.80	1.20
#2	.20	.40	.60
3-(#3 on page 4)-Fights the Bat, 4	.20	.40	.60

CAPTAIN MARVEL (See Marvel Super-Heroes #12)
May, 1968 - #19, Dec, 1969; #20, June, 1970-
#21, Aug, 1970; #22, Sept, 1972 - Present
Marvel Comics Group

#1	1.75	3.35	5.00
2-5	.80	1.60	2.40
6-10	.50	1.00	1.50
11-Smith/Trimpe cover	.65	1.35	2.00
12-20	.40	.80	1.20
21-24	.35	.70	1.05
25-34,36-Starlin cvr/stys.	.80	1.60	2.40
35	.25	.50	.75
37-Starlin art, 3pgs.	.50	1.00	1.50
38-40	.25	.50	.75
41,43-Wrightson part inks; cover #43	.50	1.00	1.50
42,44-50	.20	.40	.60
51-54	.15	.30	.45
Giant-Size #1(12/75)	.65	1.35	2.00

NOTE: _Alcala_ story-#35.

CAPTAIN MARVEL ADVENTURES
1941 - #150, Nov, 1953
Fawcett Publications

No#(#1)-Captain Marvel & Sivana by Jack Kir- by. The cover was printed on unstable pap- er stock and is rarely found in Fine or Mint condition	500.00	1250.00	2000.00

(Prices vary widely on this book)

(Capt. Marvel cont'd)	Good	Fine	Mint
#2-Art by George Tuska	175.00	350.00	525.00
3	80.00	160.00	240.00
4- 3 Lt. Marvels app.	60.00	120.00	180.00
5	50.00	100.00	150.00
6-10	37.50	75.00	112.50
11-15: #15-comic cards on back cover begin,			
end #26	27.50	55.00	82.50
16,17	22.50	45.00	67.50
18-Origin & 1st app. Mary Marvel & Marvel			
Family; painted cvr.	30.00	60.00	90.00
19,20: #19-Mary Marvel x-over			
	20.00	40.00	60.00
20-With miniature comic still attached to			
cover; miniature's cover same as Whiz #22			
(other variations possible)(See Fawcett			
Miniatures & Mighty Midget)			
	25.00	50.00	75.00
21	13.50	26.75	40.00
22-Mr.Mind serial begins	20.00	40.00	60.00
23-25	15.00	30.00	45.00
26-30	13.50	26.75	40.00
31-35: #35-Origin Radar	10.00	20.00	30.00
36-40: #37-Mary Marvel x-over			
	9.00	18.00	27.00
41-46: #43-Captain Marvel 1st meets Uncle			
Marvel; Mary Batson cameo. #46-Mr. Mind			
serial ends	8.00	16.00	24.00
47-50	6.00	12.00	18.00
51-53,55-60: #52-Origin & 1st app. Sivana Jr.;			
Capt.Marvel Jr. x-over	4.00	8.00	12.00
54-Special oversize 68pg. ish.			
	5.00	10.00	15.00
61-The Cult of the Curse serial begins			
	6.00	12.00	18.00
62-66-Serial ends; Mary Marvel x-over in #65			
	4.00	8.00	12.00
67-79: #69-Billy Batson's Xmas; Uncle Marvel,			
Mary Marvel, Capt. Marvel Jr. x-over. #71-			
3 Lt. Marvels app. #78-Origin Mr. Atom.			
#79-Origin Mr. Tawny	4.00	8.00	12.00
80-Origin retold	5.00	10.00	15.00
81-90: #81,90-Mr. Atom app. #85-Freedom Train			
issue. #86-Mr. Tawny app.			
	3.35	6.75	10.00
91-99: #96-Mr. Tawny app.	2.75	5.50	8.00
100-Origin retold	4.00	8.00	12.00
101-120	2.75	5.50	8.00
121-Origin retold	3.00	6.00	9.00
122-149	2.35	4.75	7.00
150-(Low distribution)	6.00	12.00	18.00
Bond Bread Giveaways(24 pgs.; Pocket size-			
7¼x3½"; soft cover): "-- & the Stolen			
City," "The Boy Who Never Heard of C.M."-			
('50)(reprint) each...15.00		30.00	45.00

CAPTAIN MARVEL ADVENTURES (Also see Whiz)
1945 (6x8") (Full Color, Soft Cover)

Fawcett Publications (Wheaties Giveaway)

	Good	Fine	Mint
"Captain Marvel & the Threads of Life" plus			
2 other stories(32pgs.)	5.00	10.00	15.00

NOTE: *All copies were taped at each corner to a box of Wheaties and are never found in Fine or Mint condition.*

CAPTAIN MARVEL AND THE GOOD HUMOR MAN
1950
Fawcett Publications

	Good	Fine	Mint
No#	10.00	20.00	30.00

CAPTAIN MARVEL AND THE LTS. OF SAFETY
1950 - 1951 (3 issues - no #'s)
Fawcett Publications

"Danger Flies a Kite," "Danger Smashes the Lights," "Takes to Climbing"
	4.00	8.00	12.00

CAPTAIN MARVEL COMIC STORY PAINT BOOK
(See Comic Story Paint Book)

CAPTAIN MARVEL, JR. (See Fawcett Miniatures)

CAPTAIN MARVEL, JR. (See Marvel Family,
Master Comics, and Shazam)
Nov, 1942 - #119, June, 1953 (No #34)
Fawcett Publications

#1-Origin Capt. Marvel Jr. retold (Whiz #25);			
Capt. Nazi app.	85.00	170.00	255.00
2-Vs. Capt. Nazi	45.00	90.00	135.00
3,4	35.00	70.00	105.00
5-Vs. Capt. Nazi	25.00	50.00	75.00
6-10: #8-Vs. Capt. Nazi	20.00	40.00	60.00
11-20: #16-Captain Marvel & Sivana x-over			
	12.00	24.00	36.00
21-30	6.00	12.00	18.00
31-33,35-40: #35-has #34 on inside			
	4.00	8.00	12.00
41-50	2.50	5.00	7.50
51-70	2.50	5.00	7.50
71-119	2.00	4.00	6.00

NOTE: *Mac Raboy covers-#1-10,12,13,16, among others.*

CAPTAIN MARVEL JR. WELL KNOWN COMICS
1944 (12pgs.) (Printed in Blue)(8½x10½")
(Paper cover; glued binding)
Bestmaid/Samuel Lowe (Giveaway)

(Rare)	26.50	53.25	80.00

CAPTAIN MARVEL PRESENTS THE TERRIBLE FIVE
Aug, 1966; V2#5, Sept, 1967 (No #2-4)(25¢)
M. F. Enterprises

Captain Marvel Adv. #9, © Faw

Captain Marvel Adv. #66, © Faw

Captain Marvel Jr. #31, © Faw

Captain Midnight #4, © Faw

Captain Science #4, © YM

Captain Steve Savage #1, © Avon

(Capt. Marvel Presents the Terrible 5 cont'd)

	Good	Fine	Mint
#1	.25	.50	.75
V2#5-(Formerly Capt.Marvel).	20	.40	.60

CAPTAIN MARVEL'S FUN BOOK
1944   (1/2" Thick; Carboard covers)
Samuel Lowe Co.

Contain puzzles, games, magic, etc.
4.00   8.00   12.00

CAPTAIN MARVEL SPECIAL EDITION (See Special
Edition)

CAPTAIN MARVEL STORY BOOK
Summer, 1946 - 1948
Fawcett Publications

| #1 | 15.00 | 30.00 | 45.00 |
| 2-4 | 7.50 | 15.00 | 22.50 |

CAPTAIN MARVEL THRILL BOOK (Large-Size)
1941   (Black & White; Color Cover)
Fawcett Publications

#1-Reprints from Whiz #8,10,& Special
   Edition #1 (Rare) 100.00 300.00 500.00

CAPTAIN MARVEL WELL KNOWN COMICS
1944   (12 pgs.) Printed in red (8½x10½")
(Paper cover; glued binding)
Bestmaid/Samuel Lowe (Giveaway)

(Rare)   30.00 60.00 90.00

CAPTAIN MIDNIGHT (Sweethearts #68 on)
Sept, 1942 - #67, Autumn, 1948
Fawcett Publications

#1-Origin Captain Midnight; Captain Marvel			
cameo on cover	40.00	80.00	120.00
2	17.50	35.00	52.50
3-5	12.00	24.00	36.00
6-10	8.00	16.00	24.00
11-20	5.00	10.00	15.00
21-30	3.00	6.00	9.00
31-40	2.50	5.00	7.50
41-67	2.00	4.00	6.00

              (See Super Book #3)

CAPTAIN NICE (TV)
Nov, 1967   (One Shot)
Gold Key

#1(10211-711)   .25   .50   .75

CAPTAIN PUREHEART (See Archie As --)

CAPTAIN ROCKET
1950
Fox Features Publ.

	Good	Fine	Mint
#1-(Reprinted in Canada by P. L. Publ. in			
Nov, 1951)	2.50	5.00	7.50

CAPTAIN SAVAGE (-- & His Leatherneck Raiders)
Jan, 1968 - #19, Mar, 1970 (See Sgt. Fury #10)
Marvel Comics Group

#1-Sgt. Fury & Howlers cameo			
	.40	.80	1.20
2-Origin Hydra	.20	.40	.60
3-10	.15	.30	.45
11-19(Severin art #8,9,16-19)-#11-Sgt. Fury			
& Howlers x-over	.15	.30	.45

CAPTAIN SCIENCE (Also see Fantastic)
Nov, 1950 - #7, Dec, 1951
Youthful Magazines

#1-Wood story	12.00	24.00	36.00
2,3,6,7	4.00	8.00	12.00
4,5-Wood & Orlando covers & 2 stories each			
	10.00	20.00	30.00

CAPTAIN SILVER'S LOG OF SEA HOUND (See
Sea Hound)

CAPTAIN SINDBAD (Movie Adaptation)(See Movie Comics)

CAPTAIN STEVE SAVAGE
1950 - #13, May-June, 1956
Avon Periodicals

No#(1st series)-Wood art, 22 pgs.			
	8.00	16.00	24.00
#1(4/51)-Reprints No# ish.(Canadian)			
	6.00	12.00	18.00
2-13: #2,9-Kinstler art	1.50	3.00	4.50

NOTE: *Kinstler covers-#3,4,7,8,11.*

#1(1954-2nd series)	1.75	3.35	5.00
2-5,7('55)	1.00	2.00	3.00
6-Reprints No# ish.	3.00	6.00	9.00
8-13	.65	1.35	2.00

CAPTAIN STONE (See Holyoke One-Shot #10)

CAPTAIN STORM
May-June, 1964 - #18, Mar-Apr, 1967
National Periodical Publications

| #1-Origin | .65 | 1.35 | 2.00 |
| 2-18: #12-Kubert cover | .35 | .70 | 1.05 |

CAPTAIN 3-D
December, 1953
Harvey Publications

	Good	Fine	Mint
#1-Kirby/Ditko art	8.00	16.00	24.00

CAPTAIN TOOTSIE & THE SECRET LEGION
1950
Toby Press

#1-Not Beck art	4.00	8.00	12.00
2- " " "	2.50	5.00	7.50

CAPTAIN VENTURE & THE LAND BENEATH THE SEA
Oct, 1968 - #2, Oct, 1969
Gold Key

#1,2	.65	1.35	2.00

CAPTAIN VIDEO (TV)
Feb, 1951 - #6, Dec, 1951
Fawcett Publications

#1-George Evans art	5.00	10.00	15.00
2-6-All Evans art	3.00	6.00	9.00

CAPTAIN WIZARD
1946
Rural Home

#1-Capt. Wizard reprint/Meteor #1			
	2.75	5.50	8.00

CAREER GIRL ROMANCES
Jan, 1965 - #77, 1972
Charlton Comics

V4#24-77	.15	.30

CAR 54, WHERE ARE YOU? (TV)
3-5/62 - #7, 9-11/63; 1964 - 1965
Dell Publishing Co.

4-Color #1257(3-5/62)	.40	.80	1.20
#2(7-9/62)-#7	.20	.40	.60
#2,3(10-12/64),#4(1-3/65)-Reprints #2,3,&4 of 1st series	.20	.40	.60

CARNATION MALTED MILK GIVEAWAYS (See Wisco)

CARNIVAL COMICS
1945
Harry 'A' Chesler/Pershing Square Publ. Co.

#1	1.00	2.00	3.00

CARNIVAL OF COMICS
1954 (Giveaway)

Fleet-Air Shoes

	Good	Fine	Mint
No#-Contains a comic bound with new cover; Several combinations possible; Charlton's Eh! known	.50	1.00	1.50

CAROLINE KENNEDY
1961 (One Shot)
Charlton Comics

	1.50	3.00	4.50

CAROUSEL COMICS
V1#8, April, 1948
F. E. Howard, Toronto

V1#8	.50	1.00	1.50

CARTOON KIDS
1957
Atlas Comics (CPS)

#1	1.00	2.00	3.00

CARTOONS (Magazine)(Also see Drag Cartoons)
1961 - Present (52pgs)(Automobile humor)
Petersen Publ. Co.

#1	.65	1.35	2.00
2-20	.25	.50	.75
21-25	.20	.40	.60
26-Toth art	1.35	2.75	4.00
27-101	.15	.30	.45

CARVEL COMICS (Amaz. Advs. of Capt. Carvel)
1973 (25¢; #3-35¢)
Carvel Corp. (Ice Cream)

#1-3	.15	.30

CASE OF THE SHOPLIFTER'S SHOE (See Feature Book #50(Perry Mason), & McKay)

CASE OF THE WASTED WATER, THE
1974 (Giveaway)
Rheem Water Heating

Neal Adams art	1.00	2.00	3.00

CASE OF THE WINKING BUDDHA, THE
1950 (132 pgs.)(25¢)(B&W 5½x7-5/8")
St. John Publ. Co.

Charles Raab, artist	2.00	4.00	6.00

CASEY-CRIME PHOTOGRAPHER
Aug, 1949 - #4, Feb, 1950
Marvel Comics (BFP)

Captain 3-D #1, © Harv   Captain Tootsie #1, © TOBY

Captain Video #1, © Faw

Casper #4, © STJ   The Cat #1, © MCG   Catholic Comics #7, © CG

(Casey-Crime Photographer cont'd)

	Good	Fine	Mint
#1	1.35	2.75	4.00
2-4	1.00	2.00	3.00

CASEY JONES (See 4-Color Comics #915)

CASPER AND NIGHTMARE (See Harvey Hits #37,45,
1964 - #42, 6/73   (25¢)   56,59)
Harvey Publications

	Good	Fine	Mint
#1	.65	1.35	2.00
2-10	.25	.50	.75
11-42		.15	.30

CASPER AND SPOOKY (See Harvey Hits #20)
Oct, 1972 - #8, 1973
Harvey Publications

#1-8	.15	.30

CASPER AND THE GHOSTLY TRIO
Nov, 1972 - #5, 1973
Harvey Publications

#1-5	.15	.30

CASPER AND WENDY
Sept, 1972 - #8, 1973
Harvey Publications

#1-8	.15	.30

CASPER CAT
1958; 1963
I.W. Enterprises/Super

	Good	Fine	Mint
#1,7-Reprint, Super #14('63)	.20	.40	.60

CASPER HALLOWEEN TRICK OR TREAT
January, 1976
Harvey Publications

#1	.15	.30

CASPER IN SPACE (Formerly Casper Spaceship)
#6, June, 1973
Harvey Publications

#6	.15	.30

CASPER'S GHOSTLAND
April, 1959 - Present   (25¢)
Harvey Publications

	Good	Fine	Mint
#1	2.00	4.00	6.00
2-10	1.35	2.75	4.00

	Good	Fine	Mint
11-20	.65	1.35	2.00
21-40	.35	.70	1.05
41-60	.15	.30	.45
61-97		.15	.30

CASPER SPACESHIP (Casper in Space #6)
Aug, 1972 - #5, April, 1973
Harvey Publications

#1-5	.15	.30

CASPER STRANGE GHOST STORIES
October, 1974 - Present
Harvey Publications

	Good	Fine	Mint
#1	.15	.30	.45
2-15: (#13-40¢)		.15	.30

CASPER, THE FRIENDLY GHOST (See The Friendly
Ghost --, Harvey Hits #61 & Tastee-Freez)

CASPER, THE FRIENDLY GHOST
Sept, 1949 - #5, 1950; Sept, 1950 - #5, 5/51
St. John Publishing Co.

	Good	Fine	Mint
#1(1949)-Origin & 1st app. Baby Huey	8.00	16.00	24.00
2-5	3.00	6.00	9.00
#1(9/50-St.John)	5.00	10.00	15.00
2-5	2.50	5.00	7.50

CASPER, THE FRIENDLY GHOST (Paramount Picture
1953 - #70, 1958   Star --)
Harvey Publications (Family Comics)

	Good	Fine	Mint
#1	5.00	10.00	15.00
2-5	2.00	4.00	6.00
6-20	1.35	2.75	4.00
21-40(1958)	.65	1.35	2.00
41-70(1958)	.50	1.00	1.50
#1(8/58-Harvey)	2.00	4.00	6.00

CASTILIAN (See Movie Classics)

CAT, T.H.E. (TV) (See T.H.E. Cat)

CAT, THE (See Movie Classics)

CAT, THE
Nov, 1972 - #4, June, 1973
Marvel Comics Group

	Good	Fine	Mint
#1-Origin The Cat; Wally Wood inks	.65	1.35	2.00
2-Mooney/Marie Severin art,			
3-Everett inks	.40	.80	1.20
4-Starlin/Weiss art	.50	1.00	1.50

CATHOLIC COMICS (See Heroes All Catholic--)
June, 1946 - V3#10, July, 1949
Catholic Publications

	Good	Fine	Mint
#1	2.00	4.00	6.00
2-12	1.35	2.75	4.00
V2#1-10	.80	1.60	2.40
V3#1-10	.50	1.00	1.50

CATHOLIC PICTORIAL
1947
Catholic Guild

	Good	Fine	Mint
#1-Two Toth stys.(Scarce)	6.00	12.00	18.00

CATMAN COMICS (Crash #1-5)
5/41 - #17, 1/43; #18, 7/43 - #22, 12/43;
#23, 3/44 - #26, 11/44; #27, 4/45 - #30,
12/45; #31, 6/46 - #32, 8/46
Holyoke Publishing Co.

#1(V1#6)-Origin The Deacon & Sidekick Mickey,
  Dr. Diamond & Rag-Man; The Black Widow
  app.; The Catman by Chas. Quinlan & Blaze

	Good	Fine	Mint
Baylor begin	30.00	60.00	90.00
2(V1#7)	15.00	30.00	45.00
3(V1#8)-The Pied Piper begins,			
4(V1#9)	12.00	24.00	36.00
5(V2#10)-Origin Kitten; The Hood begins,			
6,7(V2#11,12)	8.00	16.00	24.00
8(V2#13,3/42)-Origin Little Leaders; Volton by Kubert begins(1st comic book work)			
	12.00	24.00	36.00
9(V2#14)	7.00	14.00	21.00
10(V2#15)-Origin Blackout; Phantom Falcon			
begins	7.00	14.00	21.00
11(V3#1)-20(V3#10)	5.00	10.00	15.00
21-23(V3#13,5/44)	4.00	8.00	12.00
24(V2#12,7/44)	4.00	8.00	12.00
25-The Reckoner begins	3.00	6.00	9.00
26-Origin The Golden Archer; Leatherface			
app.	2.50	5.00	7.50
27-Origin Kitten retold	3.00	6.00	9.00
28-Catman learns Kitten's I.D.; Dr. Macabre,			
Deacon app.	2.50	5.00	7.50
29-32	2.50	5.00	7.50

CAUGHT
Aug, 1956 - #5, April, 1957
Atlas Comics (VPI)

	Good	Fine	Mint
#1	1.00	2.00	3.00
2,4	.65	1.35	2.00
3-Torres story	1.00	2.00	3.00
5-Crandall + Krigstein stories			
	1.75	3.35	5.00

CAVALIER COMICS
1945; 1952 (Early DC reprints)
A. W. Nugent Publ. Co.

	Good	Fine	Mint
#2(1945)-Speed Saunders, Fang Gow			
	2.50	5.00	7.50
#2(1952)	1.00	2.00	3.00

CAVE GIRL
1953 - 1954
Magazine Enterprises

	Good	Fine	Mint
#11(A-1#82)-Origin	8.00	16.00	24.00
12(A-1#96),13(A-1#116),14(A-1#125)-			
Thunda by Powell	6.00	12.00	18.00

NOTE: *Powell covers, stories in all.*

CAVE KIDS
Feb, 1963 - #16, Mar, 1967 (Hanna-Barbera)
Gold Key

#1-5		.15	.30
6-16		.10	.20

CENTURY OF COMICS
1933 (100pgs.)(Probably the 3rd comic book)
Eastern Color Printing Co.

Bought by Wheatena, Milk-O-Malt, John Wanamaker, Kinney Shoe Stores, & others to be
  used as premiums and radio giveaways. No
  publisher listed.

No#-Mutt & Jeff, etc. reprints			
	100.00	200.00	300.00

CHALLENGE OF THE UNKNOWN
#6, Sept, 1950 (Formerly Love Experiences)
Ace Magazines

#6	1.50	3.00	4.50

CHALLENGER, THE
1945 - #4, Oct-Dec, 1946
Interfaith Publications

No#; No date; 32pgs.; Origin the Challenger
  Club; Anti-Fascist with filler Funny

Animal	3.35	6.75	10.00
#2-4-Kubert art	3.35	6.75	10.00

CHALLENGERS OF THE UNKNOWN (See Showcase &
4-5/58 - #77, 12-1/70-71;   Super DC Giant)
#78, 2/73 - #80, 6-7/73; #81, 6-7/77 -
#87, 6-7/78
National Periodical Publications/DC Comics

#1-Two Kirby/Stein stys.	20.00	40.00	60.00

Catman Comics #19, © Hoke

Century of Comics #1, © EAS

Challengers of the Unknown #1, © DC

Chamber of Chills #13, © Harv

Champ Comics #14, © Harv

Champion Comics #5, © Harv

(Challengers of the Unknown cont'd)

	Good	Fine	Mint
2- " " " "	10.00	20.00	30.00
3- " " " "	8.00	16.00	24.00
4-8-Kirby/Wood stories + cover #8	5.00	10.00	15.00
9,10	2.00	4.00	6.00
11-20: #14-Origin Multi-Man. #18-Intro. Cosmo, the Challs Spacepet	1.00	2.00	3.00
21-40: #31-Retells origin of the Challengers	.65	1.35	2.00
41-60: #48-Doom Patrol app. #49-Intro. Challenger Corps. #55-Death of Red Ryan. #51-Sea Devils app.	.50	1.00	1.50
61-63,66-73: #69-Intro. Corinna	.25	.50	.75
64,65-Kirby origin reprint, parts 1 & 2	.40	.80	1.20
74-Deadman by Adams; Wrightson art	1.00	2.00	3.00
75-80	.20	.40	.60
81('77)-87	.15	.30	.45

NOTE: _Adams_ covers-#67,68,70,72,74(inks),81. _Kirby_ reprints-#75-80; covers-#75,77,78. _Kubert_ covers-#64,69,76,79. _Wood_ inks-#2-4,6-8.

CHALLENGE TO THE WORLD
1951
Catechetical Guild

No#	2.00	4.00	6.00

CHAMBER OF CHILLS (-- of Clues #27 on)
#21, June, 1951 - #26, Dec, 1954
Harvey Publications/Witches Tales

#21-24,#5(2/52)	1.50	3.00	4.50
6-17: #8-Powell story	1.00	2.00	3.00
18(7/53)-#23(5/54)-Nostrand art in all	1.75	3.35	5.00
24-26: #25 reprints #5	1.00	2.00	3.00

CHAMBER OF CHILLS
Nov, 1972 - #25, Nov, 1976
Marvel Comics Group

#1-Adkins inks	.35	.70	1.05
2,3-Brak the Barbarian; Brunner art,			
4-Brunner art	.50	1.00	1.50
5-7-Last new story	.20	.40	.60
8-10,12-20,22-25	.15	.30	.45
11-Everett story reprt/Menace #3,			
21-8pg. Everett Venus reprt/Venus #18	.15	.30	.45

NOTE: _Brunner_ cover/story-#2-4. _Everett_ inks-#3.

CHAMBER OF CLUES (Formerly Chamber of Chills)
Feb, 1955 - #28, April, 1955
Harvey Publications

	Good	Fine	Mint
#27-Kerry Drake reprint/#19; Heroine story	3.35	6.75	10.00
28-Kerry Drake	2.00	4.00	6.00

CHAMBER OF DARKNESS (Monsters on the Prowl #9)
Oct, 1969 - #8, Dec, 1970
Marvel Comics Group

#1-Buscema art	.50	1.00	1.50
2-Adams story	.65	1.35	2.00
3-Smith story	.65	1.35	2.00
4-A Conanesque tryout by Smith; reprinted in Conan #16	3.00	6.00	9.00
5,6,8	.25	.50	.75
7-Wrightson story/cover	1.00	2.00	3.00
#1(1/72-25¢ Special)	.35	.70	1.05

NOTE: _Adkins/Everett_ story-#8. _Craig_ story-#5, _Ditko_ reprints-#6-8. _Kirby_ story-#4,5,7. _Kirby/Everett_ cover-#5. _Wrightson_ covers-#7,8.

CHAMP COMICS (Champion #1-10)
#11, Oct, 1940 - #29, March, 1944
Champ Publ./Greenwald/Harvey Publications

#11-Human Meteor cont'd.	8.00	16.50	25.00
12-18: #14-Crandall cvr.	7.00	14.00	21.00
19-The Wasp app.; Kirby cover	7.00	14.00	21.00
20-The Green Ghost app.	7.00	14.00	21.00
21-29: #22-The White Mask app.	6.00	12.00	18.00

CHAMPION (See Gene Autry's --)

CHAMPION COMICS (Champ #11 on)
#2, Dec, 1939 - #10, Aug, 1940 (No #1)
Worth Publ. Co./Harvey Publications

#2-The Champ, The Blazing Scarab, Neptina, Liberty Lads, Jungleman, Bill Handy, Swingtime Sweetie begin	20.00	40.00	60.00
3-5	10.00	20.00	30.00
6-The Human Meteor begins,			
7-10-Kirby covers	12.00	24.00	36.00

CHAMPIONS, THE
October, 1975 - Present
Marvel Comics Group

#1-The Angel, Black Widow, Ghost Rider, Hercules, Ice Man, & Venus (The Champions) begin; Kane/Adkins cover	.50	1.00	1.50
2-5	.25	.50	.75
6-10	.20	.40	.60
11-17	.15	.30	.45

70

CHAMPION SPORTS
Oct-Nov, 1973 - #3, Feb-Mar, 1974
National Periodical Publications

	Good	Fine	Mint
#1-3	.15	.30	.45

CHAOS (See The Crusaders)

CHARLIE CHAN (The Adventures of)
6-7/48 - #5, 2-3/49; #6, 6/55 - #9, 3/56
Crestwood(Prize)#1-5; Charlton #6(6/55) on

	Good	Fine	Mint
#1-S&K cover, Infantino story	4.00	8.00	12.00
2-5-All S&K covers	3.00	6.00	9.00
6(6/55-Charlton)S&K cvr.	2.50	5.00	7.50
7-9	1.75	3.35	5.00

CHARLIE CHAN
Oct-Dec, 1965 - #4, Jul-Sept, 1966
Dell Publishing Co.

| #1-Springer art | .65 | 1.35 | 2.00 |
| 2-4 | .35 | .70 | 1.05 |

CHARLIE CHAPLIN
1917 (9x16", Large Size, Softcover, B&W)
Essanay/M. A. Donohue & Co.

Series 1, #315-Comic Capers. #316-In the			
Movies	8.00	16.00	24.00
Series 1, #317-Up in the Air. #318-In the			
Army	8.00	16.00	24.00
-- Funny Stunts(12½x16-3/8") in color			
	15.00	30.00	45.00

CHARLIE McCARTHY (See Edgar Bergen Presents--)
1947 - 1954
Dell Publishing Co.

4-Color #171,196	1.75	3.50	3.25
#1	1.35	2.75	4.00
2-9	.65	1.35	2.00
4-Color #445,478,527,571	1.00	2.00	3.00

CHARLTON CLASSICS LIBRARY (1776)
V10#1, March, 1973 (One Shot)
Charlton Comics

| 1776 (Title)-Adaptation of teh film musical, | | | |
| "1776" | .25 | .50 | .75 |

CHARLTON PREMIERE (Formerly Marine War Heroes)
V1#19, 7/67; V2#1, 9/67 - #4, 5/68
Charlton Comics

| V1#19-Marine War Heroes | .20 | .40 | .60 |
| V2#1-Trio; intro. Shape, Tyro Team, & Spook- |

	Good	Fine	Mint
man	.20	.40	.60
V2#2-Children of Doom	.20	.40	.60
3-Sinistro Boy Fiend; Blue Beetle Peace-			
maker x-over	.20	.40	.60
4-Unlikely Tales; Ditko art			
	.25	.50	.75

CHARLTON SPORT LIBRARY - PROFESSIONAL FOOTBALL
Winter, 1969-70 (Jan. on cover) (68 pgs.)
Charlton Comics

| #1 | .15 | .30 | .45 |

CHASING THE BLUES
1912 (52pgs.) (7½x10" - B&W) (Hardcover)
Doubleday Page

| by Rube Goldberg | 7.00 | 14.00 | 21.00 |

CHECKMATE (TV)
Oct, 1962 - #2, Dec, 1962
Gold Key

| #1,2 | .20 | .40 | .60 |

CHEERIOS PREMIUMS (Disney)
1947 (32 pgs.)(Pocket size - 16 titles)
Walt Disney Productions

Set "W"-Donald Duck & the Pirates			
	2.50	5.00	7.50
Pluto Joins the F.B.I.			
	2.00	4.00	6.00
Bucky Bug & the Cannibal King			
	2.00	4.00	6.00
Mickey Mouse & the Haunted House			
	2.50	5.00	7.50
Set "X"-Donald Duck, Counter Spy	2.50	5.00	7.50
Goofy Lost in the Desert			
	2.00	4.00	6.00
Br'er Rabbit Outwits Br'er Fox			
	2.00	4.00	6.00
Mickey Mouse at the Rodeo			
	2.50	5.00	7.50
Set "Y"-Donald Duck's Atom Bomb by Carl			
Barks	70.00	140.00	210.00
Br'er Rabbit's Secret			
	2.00	4.00	6.00
Dumbo & the Circus Mystery			
	2.00	4.00	6.00
Mickey Mouse Meets the Wizard			
	2.50	5.00	7.50
Set "Z"-Donald Duck Pilots a Jet Plane (Not			
by Barks)	2.50	5.00	7.50
Pluto Turns Sleuth Hound			
	2.00	4.00	6.00

Charlie Chan #3, © Prize

Charlie Chan #1, © DC

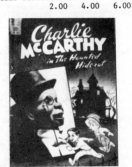
Charlie McCarthy, 4-Color #196, © Dell

Cheerios Premiums (1947), © WDP

Cheyenne Kid #11, © CC

Chief Crazy Horse, © Avon

(Cheerios Premiums cont'd)	Good	Fine	Mint
The Seven Dwarfs & the Enchanted Mtn.			
	2.00	4.00	6.00
Mickey Mouse's Secret Room			
	2.50	5.00	7.50

CHEERIOS 3-D GIVEAWAYS (Disney)
1954 (Pocket size) - 24 titles
Walt Disney Productions
  (Glasses were not in boxes - had to
  order from the company.)

Glasses only....	2.00	4.00	6.00

(Set 1)
#1 Donald Duck & Uncle Scrooge, the Fire-
    fighters
 2 Mickey Mouse & Goofy, Pirate Plunder
 3 Donald Duck's Nephews, the Fabulous
    Inventors
 4 Mickey Mouse, Secret of the Ming Vase
 5 Donald Duck with Huey, Dewey & Louie;
   -- the Seafarers (title on 2nd page)
 6 Mickey Mouse, Moaning Mountain
 7 Donald Duck, Apache Gold
 8 Mickey Mouse, Flight to Nowhere

(per book)......	2.00	4.00	6.00

(Set 2)
#1 Donald Duck, Treasure of Timbuktu
 2 Mickey Mouse & Pluto, Operation China
 3 Donald Duck in the Magic Cows
 4 Mickey Mouse & Goofy, Kid Kokonut
 5 Donald Duck, Mystery Ship
 6 Mickey Mouse, Phantom Sheriff
 7 Donald Duck, Circus Adventures
 8 Mickey Mouse, Arctic Explorers

(per book)......	2.00	4.00	6.00

(Set 3)
#1 Donald Duck & Witch Hazel
 2 Mickey Mouse in Darkest Africa
 3 Donald Duck & Uncle Scrooge, Timber

Trouble	Good	Fine	Mint
4 Mickey Mouse, Rajah's Rescue			
5 Donald Duck in Robot Reporter			
6 Mickey Mouse, Slumbering Sleuth			
7 Donald Duck in the Foreign Legion			
8 Mickey Mouse, Airwalking Wonder			
(per book)......	2.00	4.00	6.00

CHESTER GUMP (See Lemix-Korlix)

CHEWING GUM BOOKLET
1930's-40's? (2x2½", 8pgs., color cover &
illos inside with text (30 booklets known)
Chewing Gum Giveaway

Titles: each in several issues (6 each?)
  The Soldier of Fortune, Reckless Steele,
  Mirtho, the Clown, Operator#7 of the Sec-
  ret Service, Flash Brown the Super-Scien-

tist.	each....	1.00	2.00	3.00

CHEYENNE (TV)
Oct, 1956 - #25, Dec-Jan, 1961-62
Dell Publishing Co.

4-Color #734,772,803	.65	1.35	2.00
#4(8-10/57) - #12	.50	1.00	1.50
13-25	.35	.70	1.05

CHEYENNE AUTUMN (See Movie Classics)

CHEYENNE KID (Wild Frontier #1-7)
#8, 1957 - #99, Nov, 1973
Charlton Comics

#8,9,13,15-20	.40	.80	1.20
10-Three Williamson/Torres stories			
	2.50	5.00	7.50
11,12-Two Williamson/Torres stories each;			
#11-68pgs.	2.00	4.00	6.00
14-Williamson sty, 5pgs.	2.00	4.00	6.00
21-24,27-29	.25	.50	.75
25-Severin cover & 3 stys.1.00	2.00	3.00	
26,30-Severin art	.50	1.00	1.50
31-59	.15	.30	.45
60-99: #66-Wander begins, ends #87. Apache			
Red begins #88, origin #89			
	.15	.30	.45

CHICAGO MAIL ORDER (See C-M-O Comics)

CHICAGO TRIBUNE COMIC BOOK
1940 - 1943 (Similar to Spirit Sections)
Chicago Tribune

#1-Fu Manchu & Kit Carson 5.00	10.00	15.00

CHIEF, THE (Indian Chief #3 on)
1950, 1951
Dell Publishing Co.

(The Chief cont'd)	Good	Fine	Mint
4-Color #290, #2	1.50	3.00	4.50

CHIEF CRAZY HORSE
1950
Avon Periodicals

No#	3.00	6.00	9.00

CHIEF VICTORIO'S APACHE MASSACRE
1951
Avon Periodicals

No#-Williamson/Frazetta story(7pgs.);			
Kinstler cover	10.00	20.00	30.00

CHILDREN'S BIG BOOK
1945 (68 pgs.) (Stiff covers) (25¢)
Dorene Publ. Co.

Comics & Fairy Tales; art by David Icove			
	2.50	5.00	7.50

CHILI (Millie's Rival)
April, 1969 - 1973
Marvel Comics Group

#1		.15	.30
2-25		.10	.20
Special #1(12/71)		.15	.30

CHILLING ADVENTURES IN SORCERY (--As Told By
Sabrina #1,2)(Red Circle Sorcery #6 on)
Sept, 1972 - #5, Feb, 1974
Archie Publications (Red Circle Prod.)

#1,2-Sabrina cameo in both	.35	.70	1.05
3-Morrow art/covers, all	.50	1.00	1.50
4,5-Morrow cvr/art, 5,6pgs.	.40	.80	1.20

CHILLING TALES (Formerly Beware)
#13, Dec, 1952 - #17, Oct, 1953
Youthful Magazines

#13(#1)-17	.80	1.60	2.40

CHILLING TALES OF HORROR (Magazine)
V1#1, 6/69 - V1#7, 12/70; V2#2, 2/71 - V2#5,
10/71 (52 pgs.) (Black & White) (50¢)
Stanley Publications

V1#1	.65	1.35	2.00
2-7: #7-Cameron story	.40	.80	1.20
V2#2-Spirit of Frankenstein reprt/Adv. Into			
Unknown #16;V2#3,5	.30	.65	1.00
V2#4-Reprints 9pg. Feldstein story from Advs.			
Into Unknown #4	.65	1.35	2.00

CHILLY WILLY (See 4-Color #740,852,967,
1017,1074,1122,1177,1212,1281)

CHINA BOY (See Wisco)

CHIP 'N' DALE (Walt Disney)
11/53 - #30, 6-8/62; 9/67 - Present
Dell Publishing Co./Gold Key

	Good	Fine	Mint
4-Color #517,581,636	1.00	2.00	3.00
#4(12-2/55-56) - #10	.50	1.00	1.50
11-30	.35	.70	1.05
#1(G.K. reprints, '67)	.25	.50	.75
2-10	.20	.40	.60
11-20	.15	.30	.45
21-49		.15	.30

NOTE: *All Gold Key issues have reprints
except #32-35,38-41,45-47. #23-28,30-42,45-
47,49 have new covers.*

CHITTY CHITTY BANG BANG (See Movie Comics)

CHOICE COMICS
Dec, 1941 - #3, Feb, 1942
Great Publications

#1-Origin Secret Circle; Atlas the Mighty			
app. Zomba, Jungle Fight, Kangaroo Man,			
& Fire Eater begin	15.00	30.00	45.00
2,3	7.50	15.00	22.50

CHOO CHOO CHARLIE
Dec, 1969
Gold Key

#1-John Stanley art	.50	1.00	1.50

CHOPPERTOONS (Magazine)
Summer, 1971 - #2, Fall, 1971 (52 pgs.)
TRM Publications

#1,2 (Motorcycle humor)	.35	.70	1.05

CHRISTIAN HEROES OF TODAY
1964 (36 pgs.)
David C. Cook

	.50	1.00	1.50

CHRISTMAS (See A-1 #28)

CHRISTMAS ADVENTURE, THE
1963 (16 pgs.)
S. Rose (H.L. Green Giveaway)

	.35	.70	1.05

CHRISTMAS ALBUM (See March of Comics #312)

Chief Victorio's--, © Avon

Children's Big Book, © Dorene Publ.

Choice Comics #3, © GP

Christmas Carnival, © Z-D

Christmas Parade #1('49), © WDP

4-Color #126, © Dell

CHRISTMAS & ARCHIE ($1.00)
Jan, 1975 (68 pgs.) (10½x13¼")
Archie Comics

	Good	Fine	Mint
#1	1.00	2.00	3.00

CHRISTMAS AT THE ROTUNDA (Titled Ford Rotunda
Christmas Book 1957 on) (Regular Size)
Given away every Christmas at one location
1954 - 1961
Ford Motor Co. (Western Printing)

1954-56 issues(no #'s)	1.35	2.75	4.00
1957-61 issues(no #'s)	.65	1.35	2.00

CHRISTMAS BELLS (See March of Comics #297)

CHRISTMAS CARNIVAL
1952 (100 pgs.) (One Shot)
Ziff-Davis Publ. Co.

No#	2.50	5.00	7.50

CHRISTMAS CAROL, A (See March of Comics #33)

CHRISTMAS DREAM, A
1950 (16 pgs.)(Kinney Shoe Store Giveaway)
Promotional Publishing Co.

No#	1.00	2.00	3.00

CHRISTMAS EVE, A (See March of Comics #212)

CHRISTMAS IN DISNEYLAND
Dec, 1957 (25¢) (Disney)
Dell Publishing Co.

#1-Barks art, 18 pgs.	5.00	10.00	15.00

CHRISTMAS JOURNEY THROUGH SPACE
1960
Promotional Publishing Co.

Reprints 1954 issue Jolly Christmas Book with new slick cover	1.00	2.00	3.00

CHRISTMAS PARADE (Walt Disney's)
Dec, 1949 - #9, Dec, 1957 (25¢) (#9-35¢)
Dell Publishing Co.

#1-Barks art-reprinted in G.K. Christmas Parade #5	25.00	50.00	75.00
2-Barks art-reprinted in G.K. Christmas Parade #6	15.00	30.00	45.00
3-7	2.50	5.00	7.50
8,9-(12/56-12/57)-Barks art	6.00	12.00	18.00

CHRISTMAS PARADE (See March of Comics #284
and Dell Giant #26)

CHRISTMAS PARADE (Walt Disney's)
1/63 - #9, 1/72; #1,5:(80pgs)#2-4,6-9(36pgs)
Gold Key

	Good	Fine	Mint
#1-(30018-301)	2.50	5.00	7.50
2-Reprints 4-Color #367 by Barks	4.00	8.00	12.00
3-Reprints 4-Color #178 by Barks	4.00	8.00	12.00
4-Reprints 4-Color #203 by Barks	4.00	8.00	12.00
5-Reprints Christmas Parade #1(Dell) by Barks	4.00	8.00	12.00
6-Reprints Christmas Parade #2(Dell) by Barks	4.00	8.00	12.00
7,9: #7-Pull-out poster	1.50	3.00	4.50
8-Reprints 4-Color #367 by Barks; pull-out poster	4.00	8.00	12.00

CHRISTMAS PARTY (See March of Comics #256)

CHRISTMAS ROUNDUP
1960
Promotional Publishing Co.

Marv Levy cvr/art	.80	1.60	2.40

CHRISTMAS STORY (See March of Comics #326)

CHRISTMAS STORY BOOK (See Woolworth's
Christmas Book)

CHRISTMAS TREASURY, A (See March of Comics
1954 (100 pgs.) #227)
Dell Publishing Co.

#1	2.50	5.00	7.50

CHRISTMAS USA (Through 300 Years)
1956 (Also see Uncle Sam's --)
Promotional Publ. Co. (Giveaway)

Marv Levy cvr/art	.80	1.60	2.40

CHRISTMAS WITH MOTHER GOOSE (See 4-Color
#90,126,172,201,253)

CHRISTMAS WITH SANTA (See March of Comics#92)

CHUCKLE, THE GIGGLY BOOK OF COMIC ANIMALS
1945 (132 pgs.) (One Shot)
R. B. Leffingwell Co.

#1-Funny animal	2.00	4.00	6.00

CHUCK WAGON (See Sheriff Bob Dixon's --)

CICERO'S CAT
July-Aug, 1959 - #2, Sept-Oct, 1959
Dell Publishing Co.

	Good	Fine	Mint
#1,2	1.35	2.75	4.00

CIMARRON STRIP (TV)
January, 1968
Dell Publishing Co.

#1	.25	.50	.75

CINDERELLA (See 4-Color #272,786, & Movie Comics)

CINDERELLA IN "FAIREST OF THE FAIR"
1955   (14 pgs.)   (Walt Disney)
American Dairy Assn.   (Premium)

No#	2.00	4.00	6.00

CINDERELLA LOVE
10-11/49 - #11, 4-5/51; #12, 2/54 - #15,
8/54; #26, 2/55 - #29, 10/55
Ziff-Davis/St. John Publ. Co. #12 on

#1(1st Series)	1.50	3.00	4.50
2-8,10('51)	.65	1.35	2.00
9-Kinstler story	1.00	2.00	3.00
11-Crandall story	1.75	3.35	5.00
12('54)-14	.65	1.35	2.00
15-Matt Baker cover	1.00	2.00	3.00
26-29(2nd Series)-Formerly Romantic Marriage			
	.35	.70	1.05

CINDY (-- Smith #40; Crime Can't Win #41?)
1947 - #40, July, 1950
Timely Comics

#27-Kurtzman art, 3 pgs.	2.50	5.00	7.50
28-31-Kurtzman art	1.75	3.35	5.00
32-40	.40	.80	1.20

NOTE: *Kurtzman's "Hey Look"-#27,29-31;*
"Giggles 'N' Grins"-#28.

CIRCUS (-- the Comic Riot)
June, 1938 - #3, Aug, 1938
Globe Syndicate

#1-Spacehawk (2 pgs.), Disk Eyes by Wolverton (2 pgs.), Pewee Throttle by Cole, Beau Gus, Ken Craig & The Lords of Crillon, Jack Hinton by Eisner, Yan Bragger by Kane	60.00	120.00	180.00
2,3-Eisner, Cole, Wolverton, Bob Kane art in each	30.00	60.00	90.00

CIRCUS BOY (See 4-Color #759,785,813)

CIRCUS COMICS
1945 - #2, June, 1945; Winter, 1948-49
Farm Women's Publishing Co./D.S. Publ.

	Good	Fine	Mint
#1	1.00	2.00	3.00
2	.50	1.00	1.50
1(1948)-D.S. Publ.; 2pgs. Frazetta			
	5.00	10.00	15.00

CIRCUS OF FUN COMICS
1945 - 1947 (A book of games & puzzles)
A. W. Nugent Publishing Co.

#1-3	1.00	2.00	3.00

CIRCUS WORLD (See Movie Classics)

CISCO KID
Winter, 1944 - #3, 1945
Bernard Bailey/Swappers Quarterly

#1-Giunta art	3.00	6.00	9.00
2,3	2.00	4.00	6.00

CISCO KID COMICS (TV)
July, 1951 - #41, Oct-Dec, 1958
Dell Publishing Co.

4-Color #292(#1)-1950	2.50	5.00	7.50
#2(1/51)-#5	1.35	2.75	4.00
6-20	1.00	2.00	3.00
21-41	.65	1.35	2.00

CITIZEN SMITH (See Holyoke One-Shot #9)

CITY OF THE LIVING DEAD (Movie)
1952   (See Fantastic Tales #1)
Avon Periodicals

No#-One pg. Kinstler art	4.00	8.00	12.00

CITY SURGEON (Blake Harper --)
August, 1963
Gold Key

#1(10075-308)	.50	1.00	1.50

CIVIL WAR MUSKET, THE
(Kadets of America Handbook)
1960   (36 pgs.)   (1/2 Size)   (25¢)
Custom Comics, Inc.

No#	1.00	2.00	3.00

CLAIRE VOYANT
1946 - 1947   (Sparling strip reprints)
Leader Publ./Standard/Pentagon Publ.

Cinderella Love #15, © STJ

Circus #1('48), © D.S.

Cisco Kid #25, © Dell

Claire Voyant #3, © STD

Classic Comics #3, © Gil

Classic Comics #16, © Gil

(Claire Voyant cont'd)	Good	Fine	Mint
#1	8.00	16.00	24.00
2,4-Kamen covers	7.00	14.00	21.00

3-Bridal cover by Kamen; contents mentioned in Love and Death, a book by Gershom Legman('49) referenced by Dr. Wertham

| | 10.00 | 20.00 | 30.00 |

CLANCY THE COP
1930 - 1931 (52pgs.)(B&W)(Not reprints)
Dell Publishing Co.

| #1,2-Vep art | 4.00 | 8.00 | 12.00 |

UNDERSTANDING THE CLASSICS
By Charles Heffelfinger

The Classic Comics section of the Price Guide, divided as it is into several categories and subcategories, may appear quite formidable to those unfamiliar with the series. For those who hesitate to wade through the listings section by section, here is a brief background and a few definitions which we hope will simplify the detailed listings which follow.

I. SERIES TITLE. The series commonly known as Classic Comics began as "Classic Comics Presents" in 1941. The first five issues were titled "Classic Comics Presents;" Nos. 6 and 7 were "Classic Comics Library," but basically the first 34 issues were known as "Classic Comics." With No. 35, published in March, 1947, the title was changed to "Classics Illustrated," which was thought to more accurately represent the contents. All reprints and new issues from that date on have the "Classics Illustrated" logo.

II. ORIGINALS VS. REPRINTS. Unlike most comic books, most issues of Classics were reprinted regularly, usually every year or two, since the first time they were issued, much like many paperback books. The resulting multiplicity of editions of each title, with a variety of different covers, interior art, logos, dates, and number of pages, is very confusing to the general public and dealers alike. Basically, though, it is important to be able to distinguish between an **original** or **first edition** and reprints. Virtually all first editions have, usually on the inside cover, a promotional ad for the issue to be published next, while on reprints this ad was removed. There are few exceptions to this. Reprints of No. 55 and 57 published at the time of No. 75 have been found in which the "Coming Next" ad was inadvertently left in. Also, the last two issues, Nos. 168 and 169, which were published after the series changed ownership, do not have the "Coming Next" ad, even though first editions. Some collectors believe No. 169 was published before No. 168 in the U.S.

III. DATING AND REORDER LIST. Nearly all Classics contain, usually on the back cover, a list of titles in the series that were available at the time that issue was published. The publishers kept all titles in print up through the first 57 issues; after that, gaps started appearing in the checklist. The order list on a first edition only goes up to that issue's number or the one preceding or following it. The number of the last title on the list, known as the Highest Reorder Number (HRN) is very important, since in the case of reprints, it often provides the only clue to the date of the comic. Reprints with a HRN between 78 and 161, covering the period from December 1950 to March 1961, carried the date of the first printing of that issue regardless of the actual age of the reprint. Thus it is common to see a Classic with a checklist of titles ending in the 150's with a date in the 1940's, though the comic was actually published in 1959! In such cases, the date of the reprint is the same as that of the last title on the list. (You must have a copy of the first edition of the latter title to obtain the approximate date.) Obviously, a copy of No. 28 with an order list ending in No. 115 was printed much later than the original No. 28.

During the 1940's, most reprints were undated, and starting in September 1963 the actual date of reprinting was used for the first time. Reprints and originals of the first 80 issues can also be distinguished by the price; first editions of Nos. 1-80 all were marked 10 cents on the front cover, while on reprints no price, or simply "15 cents in Canada" was shown.

IV. COVERS. The first 80 issues of Classics had what is known as **line drawing** covers, which were reproduced, like the interior art, from drawings pencilled and inked by the artist. All issues from No. 81 on, however, had **painted** covers, which were reproduced from actual paintings in oil, gauche, or acrylic. Gradually all but 10 of the first 80 issues had their covers replaced with new painted covers, too. Except for minor variations, only four issues had more than one line drawing cover, while about 31 issues had a second painted cover. About 30 issues got new interior art as well, thus resulting in a variety of different issues of the same title. Many collectors try to obtain copies of each different cover and interior art for each title.

If, after reading this, you are still confused, don't worry. Even the publisher apparently kept poor records of the earliest issues, and thus often listed supposedly original dates for reprints that were at variance by as much as a year from the actual date of the original printing of that issue!

CLASSIC COMICS (See America in Action, Stories by Famous Authors, Story of the Commandos, & The World Around Us)

CLASSIC COMICS (--'s Illustrated #35 on)
Oct, 1941 - Winter, 1971
Gilberton Publications

CLASSIC COMICS. Classic Comics first appeared in October 1941 and were issued randomly until July 1945, at which time a monthly schedule was established. Reprints of first editions appeared almost immediately and are described in detail in the reprint listing. The last Classic Comics title was "Mysterious Island," published in February 1947. The first Classics Illustrated was "The Last Days of Pompeii," published in March 1947. The original covers of issues 29, 35, 38, 41, 53, 56, 61, 65, 66, 71, 73, 74, 90 and 93 were never reprinted. The last issue with a line drawing cover was No. 80, "White Fang." Starting in September 1963, the date of reprinting rather than the original printing date was listed inside the front cover. NOTE: All originals (first editions) of Classics have a promotional ad for the next issue, except No. 168 and 169. Reprints rarely have this ad.

	Good	Fine	Mint
#1-The Three Musketeers	75.00	150.00	225.00
2-Ivanhoe	35.00	70.00	105.00
3-The Count of Monte Cristo			
	25.00	50.00	75.00
4-The Last of the Mohicans			
	20.00	40.00	60.00
5-Moby Dick	20.00	40.00	60.00
6-A Tale of Two Cities	16.00	32.00	48.00
7-Robin Hood	16.00	32.00	48.00
8-Arabian Nights	30.00	60.00	90.00
9-Les Miserables	16.50	33.50	50.00
10-Robinson Crusoe	15.00	30.00	45.00
11-Don Quixote	15.00	30.00	45.00
12-Rip Van Winkle & the Headless Horseman			
	20.00	40.00	60.00
13-Dr. Jekyll & Mr. Hyde	15.00	30.00	45.00
14-Westward Ho!	40.00	80.00	120.00
15-Uncle Tom's Cabin	15.00	30.00	45.00
16-Gulliver's Travels	10.00	20.00	30.00
17-The Deerslayer	9.00	18.00	27.00
18-The Hunchback of Notre Dame			
	10.00	20.00	30.00
19-Huckleberry Finn	8.00	16.00	24.00
20-The Corsican Brothers	10.00	20.00	30.00
21-Three Famouse Mysteries-"The Sign of the 4," "The Murders in the Rue Morgue," "The Flayed Hand"	15.00	30.00	45.00

(Classic Comics cont'd)	Good	Fine	Mint
22-The Pathfinder	8.00	16.00	24.00
23-Oliver Twist	8.00	16.00	24.00
24-Connecticut Yankee in King Arthur's Court	8.00	16.00	24.00
25-Two Yrs. Before the Mast	9.00	18.00	27.00
26-Frankenstein	15.00	30.00	45.00
27-The Adventures of Marco Polo	7.00	14.00	21.00
28-Michael Strogoff	9.00	18.00	27.00
29-The Prince & the Pauper	12.00	24.00	36.00
30-The Moonstone	7.00	14.00	21.00
31-The Black Arrow	8.00	16.00	24.00
32-Lorna Doone-Matt Baker art	8.00	16.00	24.00
33-Adventures of Sherlock Holmes	23.50	46.75	70.00
34-Mysterious Island	7.00	14.00	21.00
35-The Last Days of Pompeii - 1st Classics Illustrated	12.00	24.00	36.00
36-Typee	5.00	10.00	15.00
37-The Pioneers	5.00	10.00	15.00
38-The Advs. of Cellini	8.00	16.00	24.00
39-Jane Eyre	7.00	14.00	21.00
40-Mysteries - "The Pit and the Pendulum," "The Advs. of Hans Pfall," "The Fall of the House of Usher"	10.00	20.00	30.00
41-Twenty Yrs. After	10.00	20.00	30.00
42-Swiss Family Robinson	5.00	10.00	15.00
43-Great Expectations	40.00	80.00	120.00
44-Mysteries of Paris	10.00	20.00	30.00
45-Tom Brown's School Days	7.00	14.00	21.00
46-Kidnapped	3.00	6.00	9.00
47-Twenty Thousand Leagues Under the Sea	3.00	6.00	9.00
48-David Copperfield	3.00	6.00	9.00
49-Alice in Wonderland	6.00	12.00	18.00
50-The Advs.of Tom Sawyer	4.00	8.00	12.00
51-The Spy	3.00	6.00	9.00
52-The House of 7 Gables	3.00	6.00	9.00
53-A Christmas Carol	5.00	10.00	15.00
54-The Man in the Iron Mask	2.50	5.00	7.50
55-Silas Marner	2.50	5.00	7.50
56-Toilers of the Sea	7.00	14.00	21.00
57-The Song of Hiawatha	2.00	4.00	6.00
58-The Prairie	3.00	6.00	9.00
59-Wuthering Heights	5.00	10.00	15.00
60-Black Beauty	3.00	6.00	9.00
61-The Woman in White	3.00	6.00	9.00
62-Western Stories - "The Luck of Roaring Camp" and "The Outcasts of Poker Flat"	2.50	5.00	7.50
63-The Man Without a Country	3.00	6.00	9.00

	Good	Fine	Mint
64-Treasure Island	3.00	6.00	9.00
65-Biography of Ben Franklin	2.50	5.00	7.50
66-The Cloister & the Hearth	7.00	14.00	21.00
67-The Scottish Chiefs	2.50	5.00	7.50
68-Julius Caesar	2.50	5.00	7.50
69-Around the World in 80 Days	4.00	8.00	12.00
70-The Pilot	2.00	4.00	6.00
71-The Man Who Laughs	3.00	6.00	9.00
72-The Oregon Trail	2.00	4.00	6.00
73-The Black Tulip	6.00	12.00	18.00
74-Mr. Midshipman Easy	6.00	12.00	18.00
75-The Lady of the Lake	3.00	6.00	9.00
76-The Prisoner of Zenda	2.50	5.00	7.50
77-The Iliad	2.50	5.00	7.50
78-Joan of Arc	2.00	4.00	6.00
79-Cyrano De Bergerac	2.00	4.00	6.00
80-White Fang - last issue with line drawn cover	2.50	5.00	7.50
81-The Odyssey	2.00	4.00	6.00
82-The Master of Ballantrae	2.00	4.00	6.00
83-The Jungle Book	2.00	4.00	6.00
84-The Gold Bug & other stories - "The Gold Bug," "The Tell-Tale Heart," "The Cask of Amontillado"	3.00	6.00	9.00
85-The Sea Wolf	2.00	4.00	6.00
86-Under Two Flags	2.00	4.00	6.00
87-A Midsummer Night's Dream	2.00	4.00	6.00
88-Men of Iron	1.50	3.00	4.50
89-Crime & Punishment	2.00	4.00	6.00
90-Green Mansions	2.00	4.00	6.00
91-The Call of the Wild	2.00	4.00	6.00
92-The Courtship of Miles Standish	2.00	4.00	6.00
93-Pudd'nhead Wilson	1.50	3.00	4.50
94-David Balfour	1.50	3.00	4.50
95-All Quiet on the Western Front	3.00	6.00	9.00
96-Daniel Boone	2.00	4.00	6.00
97-King Solomon's Mines	1.50	3.00	4.50
98-The Red Badge of Courage	1.50	3.00	4.50
99-Hamlet	1.50	3.00	4.50
100-Mutiny on the Bounty	1.25	2.50	3.75
101-William Tell	1.25	2.50	3.75
102-The White Company	1.00	2.00	3.00
103-Men Against the Sea	1.00	2.00	3.00
104-Bring 'em Back Alive	1.00	2.00	3.00
105-From the Earth to the Moon	1.00	2.00	3.00
106-Buffalo Bill	1.50	3.00	4.50
107-The King of the Khyber Rifles	1.00	2.00	3.00

Classic Comics #19, © Gil

Classics Illustrated #41, © Gil

Classics Illustrated #61, © Gil

Classics Illustrated #72, © Gil

Classics Illustrated #83, © Gil

Classics Illustrated #149, © Gil

(Classic Comics cont'd)	Good	Fine	Mint
108-Knights of the Round Table			
	1.00	2.00	3.00
109-Pitcairn's Island	1.00	2.00	3.00
110-A Study in Scarlet	3.00	6.00	9.00
111-The Talisman-Kiefer's last art			
	3.00	6.00	9.00
112-The Adventures of Kit Carson			
	2.50	5.00	7.50
113-The 45 Guardsmen	2.50	5.00	7.50
114-The Red Rover	2.00	4.00	6.00
115-How I Found Livingstone			
	2.00	4.00	6.00
116-The Bottle Imp	2.00	4.00	6.00
117-Captains Courageous	2.00	4.00	6.00
118-Rob Roy	2.50	5.00	7.50
119-Soldiers of Fortune	2.50	5.00	7.50
120-The Hurricane	2.00	4.00	6.00
121-Wild Bill Hickok	3.00	6.00	9.00
122-The Mutineers	1.50	3.00	4.50
123-Fang and Claw	3.00	6.00	9.00
124-The War of the Worlds	1.50	3.00	4.50
125-The Ox-Bow Incident	1.50	3.00	4.50
126-The Downfall	1.50	3.00	4.50
127-The King of the Mtns.	1.50	3.00	4.50
128-Macbeth-A. Blum art	1.50	3.00	4.50
129-Davy Crockett	2.50	5.00	7.50
130-Caesar's Conquests	1.35	2.75	4.00
131-The Covered Wagon	2.50	5.00	7.50
132-The Dark Frigate	2.00	4.00	6.00
133-The Time Machine	2.00	4.00	6.00
134-Romeo & Juliet	1.25	2.50	3.75
135-Waterloo	1.25	2.50	3.75
136-Lord Jim	1.25	2.50	3.75
137-The Little Savage	1.25	2.50	4.00
138-A Journey to the Center of the Earth			
	2.00	4.00	6.00
139-In the Reign of Terror	1.25	2.50	3.75
140-On Jungle Trails	1.00	2.00	3.00
141-Castle Dangerous	1.00	2.00	3.00
142-Abraham Lincoln	2.00	4.00	6.00
143-Kim - Orlando art	1.00	2.00	3.00
144-The First Men in the Moon - Williamson/ Evans art			
	2.50	5.00	7.50
145-The Crisis	1.00	2.00	3.00
146-With Fire & Sword	1.00	2.00	3.00
147-Ben Hur - Orlando art	2.00	4.00	6.00
148-The Buccaneer	1.00	2.00	3.00
149-Off on a Comet	1.00	2.00	3.00
150-The Virginian	2.50	5.00	7.50
151-Won by the Sword	1.00	2.00	3.00
152-Wild Animals I Have Known			
	2.00	4.00	6.00
153-The Invisible Man	1.50	3.00	4.50
154-The Conspiracy of Pontiac			
	1.25	2.50	3.75
155-The Lion of the North	1.00	2.00	3.00
156-The Conquest of Mexico	1.00	2.00	3.00

	Good	Fine	Mint
157-Lives of the Hunted	1.00	2.00	3.00
158-The Conspirators	1.00	2.00	3.00
159-The Octopus	1.00	2.00	3.00
160-The Food of the Gods	1.00	2.00	3.00
161-Cleopatra	3.00	6.00	9.00
162-Robur the Conqueror - Gray Morrow art			
	2.00	4.00	6.00
163-Master of the World	2.00	4.00	6.00
164-The Cossack Chief	1.50	3.00	4.50
165-The Queen's Necklace	2.00	4.00	6.00
166-Tigers & Traitors	1.50	3.00	4.50
167-Faust	4.00	8.00	12.00
168-In Freedom's Cause	1.00	2.00	3.00
169-Negro Americans-The Early Years (Scarce)			
	4.00	8.00	12.00

CLASSIC COMICS REPRINTS. The first reprinting of Classic Comics occurred in April 1943, when Numbers 1, 2, 3 and 5 received their second printing. Two months later (June 1943) No. 4 was reprinted and from then on reprintings were scheduled every few months. Besides Elliot Publishing Company (a Gilberton name) and Gilberton, eight other printers published Classic Comics during the period April 1943 to October 1944. Many of these printers were neighborhood weeklies in the greater New York City area. The known printers are:

Conray Products	The Richmond Courier
Island Publishing	The Long Island Independent
The Nassau Bulletin	Queens County Times
Queens Home News	Sunrise Times

One reason suggested for so many printers was the lack of newsprint available because of World War II. Another was the wholesale purchases by the American Red Cross for distribution to servicemen around the world. Issues 18-22 had several printers for original editions. This was the only period when a publisher other than Elliot or Gilberton printed first editions. Reprints from this period have reorder lists to 10-22 when printed by other publishers. The last two reprints occurred in June 1946 (28) and September 1946 (30). Classic Comics 28-34 were never reprinted as "Comics" as the new look of "Illustrated" was planned for March 1947 with the issuance of "The Last Days of Pompeii."

The following three sections have descriptions of the particular editions appropriate to each period. Specific comments applicable to the editions discussed should be reviewed for a complete understanding of this most complicated printing schedule.

SECTION I

Section I lists Classic Comics Reprints with Highest Reorder Number (HRN) of 15 or lower. These editions represent the first or second reprint of early Classic Comics and are very much in demand. In most cases they are identical to originals, except for the price on the cover (10 cents) and the promotion for the next issue, which occupied the entire back cover up through title number 14.

NOTE: Title Number 11 has not been reported with a HRN of 15 or lower. Letters in Parenthesis after edition refer to printers: "E" for Elliot Publishing Company (a Gilberton front!), "L" for Long Island Independent and "C" for Conray Products.

Title#	Eds./Publishers			
1	2	(E - L)	7.00	14.00	21.00
2	2	(E - L)	7.00	14.00	21.00
3	2	(E - L,C)	7.00	14.00	21.00
4	2	(E - L)	7.00	14.00	21.00
5	2	(E - C)	7.00	14.00	21.00

78

(Classic Comics cont'd)

Title#	Eds./Publishers		Good	Fine	Mint
6	1	(E)	10.00	20.00	30.00
7	1	(E)	10.00	20.00	30.00
8	1	(E)	15.00	30.00	45.00
9	1	(E)	10.00	20.00	30.00
10	1	(E)	7.00	14.00	21.00
12	1	(L)	7.00	14.00	21.00
13	1	(L)	7.00	14.00	21.00
14	1	(L)	15.00	30.00	45.00
15	1	(L)	10.00	20.00	30.00

SECTION II

This section lists Classic Comics reprints with Highest Reorder Numbers (HRN's) between 17 and 22. these editions are from the most confusing period in Gilberton's history. Many editions were being printed at the same time by different printers. In some cases, entire printings were purchased by the American Red Cross and sent overseas to servicemen or placed in the now famous boxes, or both, and hence saw very limited distribution on the newsstands. The first Canadian reprint editions also began showing up during this era. The reprint for title number 20 is unique as it represents the only known edition with a white background for the "Classic Comics" banner. It was printed by the Queen's County Times (T). Other codes used for printers are: Island Publishing (I), Nassau Bulletin (N), Queen's Home News (Q), Sunrise Times (S) and Richmond Courier (R). Another feature of this period was the multiple editions of originals or first printings advertising the subsequent title. This was unique in the printing history of first editions and saw the following: First editions of "The Hunchback of Notre Dame" by Gilberton and Island Publishing; "Corsican Brothers" by Gilberton, Richmond Courier and Long Island Independent; "Three Famous Mysteries" by Gilberton, Richmond Courier and Island Publishing; "Pathfinder" by Gilberton, Island Publishing and Queen's County times, and "Huckleberry Finn" by Gilberton and Island Publishing Company.

Title#	Eds./Publishers		Good	Fine	Mint
1	2	(R - S)	5.00	10.00	15.00
2	2	(R - S)	5.00	10.00	15.00
3	2	(R - S)	5.00	10.00	15.00
4	2	(L - Q)	5.00	10.00	15.00
5	2	(S)	5.00	10.00	15.00
6	2	(L - S)	8.00	16.00	24.00
7	2	(L - N)	8.00	16.00	24.00
8	2	(L - N)	10.00	20.00	30.00
9	2	(N - R)	8.00	16.00	24.00
10	2	(N - Q)	5.00	10.00	15.00
11	2	(N - Q)	5.00	10.00	15.00
12	1	(T)	5.00	10.00	15.00
13	1	(T)	5.00	10.00	15.00
14	1	(Q)	10.00	20.00	30.00
15	1	(N)	8.00	16.00	24.00
16	2	(Q - T)	5.00	10.00	15.00
17	2	(N - T)	5.00	10.00	15.00
18	2	(Q - T)	5.00	10.00	15.00
19	2	(N - T)	5.00	10.00	15.00
20	1	(T)	6.00	12.00	18.00
21	1	(N)	7.00	14.00	21.00

SECTION III

The final section of Classic Comic Reprints is refreshing for its rationality and integrity of printing sequence. All of these editions were published by Gilberton. There was only one edition of each title number. For title numbers 1-20 the Highest Reorder Number (HRN) was (28), for 21-27 the reorder number was (30). All of these editions had identical logos, the now familiar "Classic Comics" one inch black and yellow banner across the top of the front cover. This banner first appeared with title number 9 and replaced the many false starts, in searching for an enduring logo, such as "Classic Comics Presents" (1-5) and "Classic Comics Library" (6,7). Title numbers 8 and 11, while using the logo "Classic Comics" had individualized presentations until later editions formalized the described banner.

Title#	Good	Fine	Mint
1	3.50	7.00	10.50
2	3.50	7.00	10.50
3	3.50	7.00	10.50
4	3.50	7.00	10.50
5	3.50	7.00	10.50
6	5.00	10.00	15.00
6-Ben Franklin Store giveaway, 52pgs. (Rare)	15.00	30.00	45.00
7-Saks 34th Ave. Christmas Giveaway (Diff. cover-same interior art) (Rare)	15.00	30.00	45.00
7-Robin Hood & His Merry Men, The Ill. Story of (Flour giveaway) Circa 1947	15.00	30.00	45.00
7	5.00	10.00	15.00
8	8.00	16.00	24.00
9	5.00	10.00	15.00
10	3.50	7.00	10.50
11	3.50	7.00	10.50
12	3.50	7.00	10.50
13	3.50	7.00	10.50
14	8.00	16.00	24.00
15	5.00	10.00	15.00
16	3.50	7.00	10.50
17	3.50	7.00	10.50
18	3.50	7.00	10.50
19	3.50	7.00	10.50
20	5.00	10.00	15.00
21	6.00	12.00	18.00
22	3.50	7.00	10.50
23	3.50	7.00	10.50
24	3.50	7.00	10.50
25	3.50	7.00	10.50
26	7.00	14.00	21.00
27	3.50	7.00	10.50

CLASSIC COMICS LIBRARY GIFT BOX
(Later boxes titled Classics Illustrated --)

These Gift Boxes first appeared in November 1943. They were (at least according to the advertising) designed with the boys in the service in mind. The buyer was told that "the boys relax with Classic Comics." The boxes held five Classics. They began to sell for 50 cents and ceased publication at a price of 79 cents. The earlier series is worth more and are more colorful.

Classic Comics Reprint #4, © Gil

Ben Franklin Stores Giveaway, © Gil

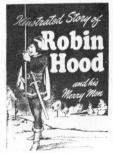

Robin Hood Flour Giveaway('47), © Gil

79

Classic Comics boxes:

	Good	Fine	Mint
Box A,B,C,D	15.00	30.00	45.00
1952 Christmas Box-held #64,76,83 & 98			
(reprints)	10.00	20.00	30.00

NOTE: *These boxes were priced at 50¢. Box A held reprints of #1-5; Box B-#6-10; Box C-#11-15; & Box D-#16-20.*

Classics Illustrated boxes:

	Good	Fine	Mint
Boxes with 59¢ price	10.00	20.00	30.00
Boxes with 69¢ price	8.00	16.00	24.00
Boxes with 79¢ price	7.00	14.00	21.00

NOTE: *Condition of box should be graded, also.*

CLASSICS ILLUSTRATED (Line Drawing Reprints). The first Classics Illustrated reprint was issued in April 1947. At that time Gilberton reprinted issues 1—5. In September 1948, Issues 6—10, 28 and 31 were reprinted, then 14, 15 and 33 in November 1948, and 21 in January 1949. After this period the deluge of reprints began with June 1949 through May 1950 seeing reprints of almost all issues. In all cases but four, the covers bearing the new logo are unchanged from the original comics. The issues changed (13, 18, 29 and 41) were objected to by Dr. Wertham because of violent covers. Several others which had been reprinted were terminated because of "violent" covers. Among these were 20, 36, 40, 43 and 44. No reason is known for not reprinting 11, 35, 53, 56, 61, 65 and 66. Issue 38 was said to be suppressed because of religious bias; 71, 73 and 74 may have been destroyed in the Spring flood in 1951 which damaged much of Gilberton's plant in Brooklyn, New York. Generally, the line drawing reprints continued to be published until 1954-1955, although several continued further and 17 and 37 were reprinted as late as 1966 with line covers. Either because of higher quality control or new color presses, the line drawing reprints from August 1953 (110) to November 1955 (129) are brilliant when compared to earlier reprints and first editions. From a collector's standpoint these reprints, while not as old as others, are more desirable than one with a lower number. Another consideration in valuing line reprints is the contents. In several cases, whole pages of art were clipped; in others panels were omitted and rearranged. Some original 56-page issues were clipped to 48 pages and some 64-page issues to 56, etc. Only a page-by-page comparison with a first edition can show whether or not a reprint has been clipped. The older the reprint the more likely all original art is included. Numbers omitted below have never been reported as line drawing reprints. Editions refers to the number of editions reprinted.

The following listing differentiates LDR's into two sections, April 1947 (36) to October 1949 (64) and April 1950 (70) and later. The first section generally consists of first or extremely early reprintings with the new "Classics Illustrated" logo, clearly more desirable from a collector's standpoint than the later reprintings. To list the LDR's all together does not accurately reflect the everyday activity of market forces and, consequently, they are described here in two sections. The LDR's in Section I generally have all original artwork intact from the first edition. Many are 64 pages in length, as the first edition Classic Comics was, and therefore in demand. The LDR's in Section II generally have pages clipped to get down to a 48-page size and, consequently, are less in demand by collectors.

SECTION I

All issues listed below have HRN ( )'s of 64 or lower. Where issue numbers are not listed, the title does not exist as a Line Drawn Reprint (LDR) in the range specified.

*Indicates cover changed from Classic Comics or first edition.

Title#	Editions	Good	Fine	Mint
1	3	1.50	3.00	4.50
2	3	1.50	3.00	4.50
3	3	1.50	3.00	4.50
4	3	1.50	3.00	4.50
5	3	1.50	3.00	4.50
6	2	1.50	3.00	4.50
7	3	1.50	3.00	4.50
8	2	5.00	10.00	15.00
9	1	2.50	5.00	7.50
10	2	1.50	3.00	4.50
12	2	1.50	3.00	4.50
13*	2	1.50	3.00	4.50
14	1	5.00	10.00	15.00
15	1	2.50	5.00	7.50
16	3	1.50	3.00	4.50
17	2	1.50	3.00	4.50
18*	2	1.50	3.00	4.50
19	2	1.50	3.00	4.50

#		Good	Fine	Mint
20	2	3.50	7.00	10.50
21	2	4.00	8.00	12.00
22	1	1.50	3.00	4.50
23	2	1.50	3.00	4.50
24	2	1.50	3.00	4.50
25	2	1.50	3.00	4.50
26	2	2.50	5.00	7.50
28	1	5.00	10.00	15.00
29*	2	1.50	3.00	4.50
30	1	2.50	5.00	7.50
31	2	1.50	3.00	4.50
32	1	1.50	3.00	4.50
33	1	8.00	16.00	24.00
34	2	1.50	3.00	4.50
36	1	2.50	5.00	7.50
37	1	2.50	5.00	7.50
39	2	2.50	5.00	7.50
40	1	5.00	10.00	15.00
41*	1	1.50	3.00	4.50
42	1	1.50	3.00	4.50
43	1	20.00	40.00	60.00
44	1	5.00	10.00	15.00
45	1	3.50	7.00	10.50
46	1	1.50	3.00	4.50
47	1	1.50	3.00	4.50
48	1	1.50	3.00	4.50
49	1	2.50	5.00	7.50
50	1	2.50	5.00	7.50

SECTION II

All issues listed below have HRN's ( )'s of 70 or higher. Where issue numbers are not listed the title does not exist as a Line Drawn Reprint (LDR) in the range specified.

I*Indicates cover art changed from Classic Comics or first edition.

NOTE: Because of unusually fine brilliance in cover reproduction, CI's LDR's with Highest Reorder Numbers (HRN's) between 110 and 129, inclusive, generally command a premium (10 to 15 per cent) over other editions in this range. This premium should be added only if the item is in fine or better condition. With this exception, as a general rule the lower the HRN, the more desirable the item.

Title#	Editions	Good	Fine	Mint
1	3	1.00	2.00	3.00
2	4	1.00	2.00	3.00
3	3	1.00	2.00	3.00
4	3	1.00	2.00	3.00
5	3	1.00	2.00	3.00
6	3	1.00	2.00	3.00
7	4	1.00	2.00	3.00
8	1	4.00	8.00	12.00
9	2	2.00	4.00	6.00
10	3	1.00	2.00	3.00
12	3	1.00	2.00	3.00
13*	2	1.00	2.00	3.00
15	2	2.00	4.00	6.00
16	2	1.00	2.00	3.00
17	4	1.00	2.00	3.00
18*	3	1.00	2.00	3.00
19	3	1.00	2.00	3.00
20	2	3.00	6.00	9.00
21	2	4.00	8.00	12.00
22	5	1.00	2.00	3.00
23	4	1.00	2.00	3.00
24	3	1.00	2.00	3.00
25	3	1.00	2.00	3.00
26	3	2.00	4.00	6.00
27	3	1.00	2.00	3.00
29*	3	1.00	2.00	3.00
30	1	2.00	4.00	6.00
31	3	1.00	2.00	3.00
32	2	1.00	2.00	3.00
33	2	6.00	12.00	18.00
34	4	1.00	2.00	3.00
37	7	1.00	2.00	3.00
39	3	1.00	2.00	3.00

Title#	Editions	Good	Fine	Mint
40	2	5.00	10.00	15.00
41*	1	1.00	2.00	3.00
42	3	1.00	2.00	3.00
44	1	5.00	10.00	15.00
46	3	1.00	2.00	3.00
47	3	1.00	2.00	3.00
48	1	1.00	2.00	3.00
49	1	2.00	4.00	6.00
50	5	1.00	2.00	3.00
51	2	1.00	2.00	3.00
52	2	1.00	2.00	3.00
54	2	1.00	2.00	3.00
55	2	1.00	2.00	3.00
57	3	1.00	2.00	3.00
58	4	1.00	2.00	3.00
59	2	2.00	4.00	6.00
60	2	2.00	4.00	6.00
62	2	1.00	2.00	3.00
63	1	2.00	4.00	6.00
64	2	1.00	2.00	3.00
67	2	1.00	2.00	3.00
68	2	1.00	2.00	3.00
69	2	1.00	2.00	3.00
70	2	1.00	2.00	3.00
72	2	1.00	2.00	3.00
75	2	1.00	2.00	3.00
76	2	1.00	2.00	3.00
77	2	1.00	2.00	3.00
78	2	1.00	2.00	3.00
79	2	1.00	2.00	3.00
80	2	1.00	2.00	3.00

INTRODUCTION OF NEW ART AND NEW COVERS

The following title numbers were changed as to interior art, covers or both, at period indicated. Where integrity of the Highest Reorder Number (HRN) system is maintained (through 163) this number in parenthesis indentifies the first introduction of the new art/cover. Where HRN identification is not meaningful, the date of the reprint is shown in parenthesis. The month/season and year is shown in these cases, e. g. 11/63: November 1963; R/68: Reissued 1968, etc. Where (62/63) is shown, the reprint allowed no discernable method of determining date of publication, however, all of these editions appeared between July 1961 and September 1963 and are grouped together as 1962 or 1963, i. e. (62/63). Highest reorder number can be 149, 164, 165 or 167. This was a very unstable period for Gilberton which saw them going into bankruptcy and reorganization. Title numbers omitted below are not reported to have changes in either art or covers.

NOTE: Many Classics were extensively changed in terms of interior art by clipping panels and omitting complete pages. Comparisons of title numbers 11, 13, 15 and many other early editions on a page-by-page comparison with a first edition can show whether or not a reprint has been clipped.

("A2" indicates second art, "C2" second cover, etc.)

Title#	A2	C2	C3
1	(150)	(134)	
2	(142)	(136)	
3	(135)	(135)	
4	(150)	(135)	
5	(131)	(131)	(W/69)
6	(132)	(132)	(F/68)
7	(136)	(129)	
8	(62/63)	(62/63)	
9	(161)	(161)	(R/68)
10	(140)	(130)	
11		(110)	(R/68)
12	(150)	(132)	(R/68)
13	(112)	(60)	(112)
15		(117)	(W/69)
16		(155)	
17		(R/68)	
18	(158)	(60)	(140)

(#18 had a fourth cover - (158).)

Title#	A2	C2	C3
19	(131)	(131)	
21		(114)	
22		(11/63)	
23	(62/63)	(136)	

Title#	A2	C2	C3
24	(140)	(140)	
25		(156)	
26		(146)	
27		(154)	
28		(115)	(SU/69)
29		(60)	(128)
30		(155)	
31		(131)	
32		(138)	(R/68)
34		(140)	
35	(161)	(161)	
36		(155)	
37		(R/68)	
38	(62/63)	(62/63)	
39	(62/63)	(142)	(R/68)
41		(62)	(156)
42	(152)	(131)	
45	(161)	(161)	
46		(131)	
47		(128)	(R/68)
48		(121)	
49		(155)	(F/68)
50	(62/63)	(140)	
51		(139)	
52	(142)	(142)	
54	(142)	(142)	
55		(121)	
56	(62/63)	(62/63)	
57		(134)	
58		(146)	
59		(156)	
60	(158)	(158)	(R/68)
61		(156)	
62		(137)	(R/68)
63	(62/63)	(156)	
64		(131)	
65		(131)	
67		(136)	
68	(62/63)	(156)	
69		(136)	
70		(156)	
71	(62/63)	(62/63)	
72		(131)	
75		(139)	
76		(128)	
77		(139)	
78		(128)	(W/69)
79		(133)	
80		(132)	
81		(SP/69)	
82		(F/68)	
83	(R/68)	(R/68)	
90		(148)	
93		(62/63)	
96		(W/69)	
98		(R/68)	
99		(SP/69)	
103		(131)	
112		(W/69)	
134		(W/69)	
144		(F/68)	
147		(F/68)	
149		(F/68)	

CLASSICS ILLUSTRATED (Painted Cover Reprints). In March 1951, with the publication of "The Odyssey," Gilberton introduced their painted covers designed to make the scenes more real or photographic. Shortly thereafter, the early line covers began converting to the "new" style. Initially, interior art remained the same. Sometime later, many were replaced with new art, previously described, indicating contents redrawn by new artists.

This period also saw the reappearance of some issues discontinued before. Numbers 11, 35, 38 and 56 were reprinted with new art and new covers. Issues released prior to an inside date of "Reissued 1967" have a 15 cents cover price. After this the cover price was 25 cents. Of the millions of Classics Illustrated issued, perhaps 90 per cent are of the painted cover variety. Consequently, they constitute an overwhelming portion of this title available on the market. With the exceptions noted below, most numbers are readily available to collectors willing to accept any edition of a particular title. In a few cases in Section I below, complete, first edition artwork is available (such as No. 1 (143), No. 2 (136), No. 4 (141) and No. 7 (129) in the original 64-page size.) Obviously, these represent real "finds" and are much more desirable from a collector's standpoint than painted covers with new art. The last painted reprints, Numbers 2, 5, 50 and 133 were dated Winter 1971.

The painted cover reprints are shown in two sections below. The first section lists the original painted cover reprint for the title shown. In some unusual cases, the painted cover reprint, because of scarcity due to low press runs, etc., will have a higher value than the first edition painted cover.

Some titles have two different painted covers, none had three. When a date or highest reorder number (HRN) is shown in parenthesis in Section II, any later date or higher reorder number brings the value listed.

All covers in Section II are different from those title numbers listed in Section I. In order to assist differentiation between the second painted cover in Section II, the highest reorder number or edition date, is listed in parenthesis. The edition date is shown at the bottom of the inside front cover.

The following codes are used in Section II: W—Winter, F—Fall, R—Reissued, SP—Spring.

When two painted covers exist, those listed in Section I will all have dates or HRN's prior/lower to the date/HRN listed in Section II.

Some painted cover reprints (e. g. 90 & 93) were never reprinted with the original painted cover. Title numbers not listed in Section I or II do not exist as painted cover reprints in the category described.

Title#	Editions	Good	Fine	Mint
1	11	1.00	2.00	3.00
2	12	1.00	2.00	3.00
2 (Twin Circle edition)		1.25	2.50	3.75
3	10	1.00	2.00	3.00
4	10	1.00	2.00	3.00
4 (Twin Circle edition)		1.25	2.50	3.75
5	8	1.00	2.00	3.00
6	10	1.00	2.00	3.00
7	11	1.00	2.00	3.00
8	1	3.00	6.00	12.00
9	3	1.35	2.75	4.00
10	11	1.00	2.00	3.00
10 (Twin Circle edition)		1.25	2.50	3.75
11	5	1.00	2.00	3.00
12	7	1.00	2.00	3.00
13	9	1.00	2.00	3.00
13 (Twin Circle edition)		1.25	2.50	3.75
15	10	1.00	2.00	3.00
16	6	1.00	2.00	3.00
17	2	1.00	2.00	3.00
18	2	1.00	2.00	3.00
19	12	1.00	2.00	3.00
21	1	4.00	8.00	12.00
22	3	1.35	2.75	4.00
23	8	1.00	2.00	3.00
24	8	1.00	2.00	3.00
25	5	1.00	2.00	3.00
26	11	1.00	2.00	3.00
27	4	1.35	2.75	4.00
28	4	1.00	2.00	3.00
29	9	1.00	2.00	3.00
30	5	1.35	2.75	4.00
31	8	1.00	2.00	3.00
32	5	1.00	2.00	3.00
34	6	1.00	2.00	3.00
35	4	1.75	3.35	5.00
36	4	1.75	3.35	5.00
37	1	2.50	5.00	7.50
38	4	1.35	2.75	4.00
39	5	1.75	3.35	5.00
41	4	1.00	2.00	3.00

		Good	Fine	Mint
42	10	1.00	2.00	3.00
45	3	1.35	2.75	4.00
46	11	1.00	2.00	3.00
47	10	1.00	2.00	3.00
48	11	1.00	2.00	3.00
48 (Twin Circle edition)		1.25	2.50	3.75
49	3	1.75	3.35	5.00
50	9	1.00	2.00	3.00
51	5	1.00	2.00	3.00
52	7	1.00	2.00	3.00
54	6	1.00	2.00	3.00
55	8	1.00	2.00	3.00
56	3	1.75	3.35	5.00
57	7	1.00	2.00	3.00
58	5	1.00	2.00	3.00
59	4	1.00	2.00	3.00
60	3	1.75	3.35	5.00
61	3	1.75	3.35	5.00
62	5	1.00	2.00	3.00
63	4	1.00	2.00	3.00
64	10	1.00	2.00	3.00
65	3	1.00	2.00	3.00
65-Ben Franklin Store Giveaway('50-'51)		2.00	4.00	6.00
67	4	1.35	2.75	4.00
68	6	1.00	2.00	3.00
68 (Twin Circle edition)		1.25	2.50	3.75
69	9	1.00	2.00	3.00
70	3	1.35	2.75	4.00
71	2	4.00	8.00	12.00
72	8	1.00	2.00	3.00
75	6	1.00	2.00	3.00
76	6	1.00	2.00	3.00
77	7	1.00	2.00	3.00
78	8	1.00	2.00	3.00
79	3	1.35	2.75	4.00
80	8	1.00	2.00	3.00
81	2	1.00	2.00	3.00
82	1	1.00	2.00	3.00
83	10	.65	1.35	2.00
84	1	2.00	4.00	6.00
85	7	1.00	2.00	3.00
86	6	.65	1.35	2.00
87	4	1.00	2.00	3.00
88	3	1.00	2.00	3.00
89	4	.65	1.35	2.00
91	10	.65	1.35	2.00
92	3	1.00	2.00	3.00
94	2	.65	1.35	2.00
95	2	1.00	2.00	3.00
96	8	.65	1.35	2.00
97	7	.65	1.35	2.00
98	7	.65	1.35	2.00
99	5	.65	1.35	2.00
100	9	.65	1.35	2.00
101	7	.65	1.35	2.00
102	2	1.35	2.75	4.00
103	1	.65	1.35	2.00
104	7	.65	1.35	2.00
105	11	.65	1.35	2.00
106	7	.65	1.35	2.00
107	6	.65	1.35	2.00
108	6	.65	1.35	2.00
109	3	1.00	2.00	3.00
110	1	2.50	5.00	7.50
111	3	.65	1.35	2.00
112	7	.65	1.35	2.00
113	1	1.00	2.00	3.00
114	1	1.35	2.75	4.00
115	1	1.35	2.75	4.00
116	1	1.35	2.75	4.00
117	2	1.35	2.75	4.00
118	1	1.35	2.75	4.00
119	2	1.35	2.75	4.00
120	1	1.35	2.75	4.00

(Classics Illustrated cont'd)

Title#	Editions	Good	Fine	Mint
21	7	1.00	2.00	3.00
22	6	.65	1.35	2.00
23	5	.65	1.35	2.00
24	10	.65	1.35	2.00
25	7	.65	1.35	2.00
26	2	.65	1.35	2.00
26 (Twin Circle edition)	1.25	2.50	3.75	
27	2	.65	1.35	2.00
28	7	.65	1.35	2.00
28 (Twin Circle edition)	1.25	2.50	3.75	
29	1	1.35	2.75	4.00
30	6	.65	1.35	2.00
31	7	.65	1.35	2.00
32	3	.65	1.35	2.00
33	8	.65	1.35	2.00
34	3	1.00	2.00	3.00
35	4	.65	1.35	2.00
36	4	.65	1.35	2.00
37	5	.65	1.35	2.00
38	7	.65	1.35	2.00
39	4	.65	1.35	2.00
40	4	.65	1.35	2.00
41	3	1.00	2.00	3.00
42	6	1.35	2.75	4.00
43	3	.65	1.35	2.00
44	4	.65	1.35	2.00
45	4	.65	1.35	2.00
46	3	1.35	2.75	4.00
47	6	.65	1.35	2.00
48	4	.65	1.35	2.00
49	5	.65	1.35	2.00
50	3	2.00	4.00	6.00
51	3	1.00	2.00	3.00
52	4	.65	1.35	2.00
53	6	.65	1.35	2.00
54	3	2.00	4.00	6.00
55	2	.65	1.35	2.00
56	3	1.00	2.00	3.00
57	2	1.75	3.35	5.00
58	2	1.75	3.35	5.00
59	2	.65	1.35	2.00
60	2	1.00	2.00	3.00
61	2	2.50	5.00	7.50
62	2	1.00	2.00	3.00
63	2	.65	1.35	2.00
64	2	.65	1.35	2.00
65	2	.65	1.35	2.00
66	2	1.00	2.00	3.00
67	2	3.00	6.00	9.00
68		1.00	2.00	3.00
69	1	1.00	2.00	3.00

SECTION II

Title#	Editions	Good	Fine	Mint
5(W/69)	2	.40	.80	1.20
6(F/68)	1	.50	1.00	1.50
9(R/68)	1	.65	1.35	2.00
11(R/68)	1	.50	1.00	1.50
12(R/68)	2	.50	1.00	1.50
15(W/69)	2	.50	1.00	1.50
18(158)	7	.35	.70	1.05
28(169)	1	.65	1.35	2.00
32(R/68)	1	.35	.70	1.05
39(R/68)	1	2.50	5.00	7.50
47(R/68)	2	.50	1.00	1.50
49(F/68)	1	2.50	5.00	7.50
60(R/68)	1	1.50	3.00	4.50
62(R/68)	1	1.50	3.00	4.50
78(W/69)	1	.65	1.35	2.00
81(169)	1	.50	1.00	1.50
82(F/68)	1	.50	1.00	1.50
83(R/68)	1	.50	1.00	1.50
90(Any)	5	.35	.70	1.05

Title#	Editions	Good	Fine	Mint
93(Any)	3	.35	.70	1.05
96(W/69)	1	.50	1.00	1.50
98(R/68)	1	2.50	5.00	7.50
99(SP/69)	1	.50	1.00	1.50
103(131)	4	.65	1.35	2.00
112(W/69)	1	.80	1.60	2.40
134(W/69)	1	.50	1.00	1.50
144(F/68)	2	.50	1.00	1.50
147(F/68)	1	.50	1.00	1.50
149(F/68)	1	.65	1.35	2.00

CLASSICS ILLUSTRATED LIBRARY GIFT BOX (See
Classics Comics --)

CLASSICS ILLUSTRATED EDUCATIONAL SERIES
1951; 1953 (16 pgs.)
Gilberton Corp.

#1-Shelter Through the Ages(Ruberoid Co.)
(1951-15¢) Kiefer art 7.00 14.00 21.00
No#-The Westinghouse Story-The Dreams of a
Man (Westinghouse Co.-1953) H. C. Kiefer
art 7.00 14.00 21.00

Classics Ill. Giants, © Gil

CLASSICS ILLUSTRATED GIANTS
February, 1950 (One Shots - "OS")
Gilberton Publications

These Giant Editions were on sale for two years, beginning in
1950. They were 50 cents on the newsstand and 60 cents by mail.
They are actually four classics in one volume. All the stories are
reprints of the Classics Illustrated Series.

"An Illustrated Library of Great Adventure
Stories" - Reprints of #6,7,8,10
15.00 30.00 45.00
"An Illustrated Library of Exciting Mystery
Stories" - Reprints of #13,30 & others
15.00 30.00 45.00
"An Illustrated Library of Great Indian
Stories" - Reprints of #4,17,22,37
15.00 30.00 45.00

CLASSICS ILLUSTRATED "GOLDEN RECORDS GREAT
LITERATURE SERIES" ($2.49 retail for comic
& record)
Mar, 1966 (All issues)(Record with comic sets)
Gilberton (Comics)/A.A. Records (Records)

SLP-189--Black Beauty, SLP-190--Mutiny on the
Bounty, SLP-191--The Time Machine, SLP-192--
The Call of the Wild
Comic & Record...Each..... 7.50
NOTE: Comics are all dated March, 1966 and
the last reorder number on the back is 167.

CLASSICS ILLUSTRATED JUNIOR
Oct, 1953 - Spring, 1971
Famous Authors Ltd. (Gilberton Publications)

(Classics Ill. Jr. cont'd)
Original editions have ad for the next issue.
Originals (first prints) are worth 50% more
than reprints.

	Good	Fine	Mint
#501-Snow White & the Seven Dwarfs-Alex Blum art & cover	5.00	10.00	15.00
502-The Ugly Duckling	1.00	2.00	3.00
503-Cinderella	.35	.70	1.05
504-The Pied Piper	.35	.70	1.05
505-The Sleeping Beauty	.35	.70	1.05
506-The 3 Little Pigs	.35	.70	1.05
507-Jack & the Beanstalk	.35	.70	1.05
508-Goldilocks & the 3 Bears	.35	.70	1.05
509-Beauty & the Beast	.35	.70	1.05
510-Little Red Riding Hood	.35	.70	1.05
511-Puss-N-Boots	.35	.70	1.05
512-Rumpel Stiltskin	.35	.70	1.05
513-Pinocchio	.35	.70	1.05
514-The Steadfast Tin Soldier	1.00	2.00	3.00
515-Johnny Appleseed	.35	.70	1.05
516-Aladdin & His Lamp	.35	.70	1.05
517-The Emperor's New Clothes	.35	.70	1.05
518-The Golden Goose	.35	.70	1.05
519-Paul Bunyan	.35	.70	1.05
520-Thumbelina	.35	.70	1.05
521-King of the Golden River	.35	.70	1.05
522-The Nightingale	.35	.70	1.05
523-The Gallant Tailor	.35	.70	1.05
524-The Wild Swans	.35	.70	1.05
525-The Little Mermaid	.35	.70	1.05
526-The Frog Prince	.35	.70	1.05
527-The Golden-Haired Giant	.35	.70	1.05
528-The Penny Prince	.35	.70	1.05
529-The Magic Servants	.35	.70	1.05
530-The Golden Bird	.35	.70	1.05
531-Rapunzel	.35	.70	1.05
532-The Dancing Princesses	.35	.70	1.05
533-The Magic Fountain	.35	.70	1.05
534-The Golden Touch	.35	.70	1.05
535-The Wizard of Oz	.35	.70	1.05
536-The Chimney Sweep	.35	.70	1.05
537-The Three Fairies	.35	.70	1.05
538-Silly Hans	.35	.70	1.05
539-The Enchanted Fish	.35	.70	1.05
540-The Tinder-Box	1.00	2.00	3.00
541-Snow White & Rose Red	.35	.70	1.05
542-The Donkey's Tale	1.00	2.00	3.00
543-The House in the Woods	.35	.70	1.05
544-The Golden Fleece	.35	.70	1.05
545-The Glass Mountain	.35	.70	1.05
546-The Elves & the Shoemaker	.35	.70	1.05
547-The Wishing Table	.35	.70	1.05
548-The Magic Pitcher	.35	.70	1.05
549-Simple Kate	.35	.70	1.05
550-The Singing Donkey	.35	.70	1.05
551-The Queen Bee	.35	.70	1.05
552-The 3 Little Dwarfs	.35	.70	1.05
553-King Thrushbeard	.35	.70	1.05
554-The Enchanted Deer	.35	.70	1.05
555-The 3 Golden Apples	.35	.70	1.05
556-The Elf Mound	.35	.70	1.05
557-Silly Willy	.35	.70	1.05
558-The Magic Dish	.35	.70	1.05
559-The Japanese Lantern	.35	.70	1.05
560-The Doll Princess	.35	.70	1.05
561-Hans Humdrum	.35	.70	1.05
562-The Enchanted Pony	.35	.70	1.05
563-The Wishing Well	.35	.70	1.05
564-The Salt Mountain	.35	.70	1.05

	Good	Fine	Mint
565-The Silly Princess	.35	.70	1.05
566-Clumsy Hans	.35	.70	1.05
567-The Bearskin Soldier	.35	.70	1.05
568-The Happy Hedgehog	.35	.70	1.05
569-The Three Giants	.35	.70	1.05
570-The Pearl Princess	.35	.70	1.05
571-How Fire Came to the Indians	.35	.70	1.05
572-The Drummer Boy	.35	.70	1.05
573-The Crystal Ball	.35	.70	1.05
574-Brightboots	.35	.70	1.05
575-The Fearless Prince	.35	.70	1.05
576-The Princess Who Saw Everything	.35	.70	1.05
577-The Runaway Dumpling	.35	.70	1.05

NOTE: *Last reprint - Spring, 1971.*

CLASSICS ILLUSTRATED SPECIAL ISSUE
Dec, 1955 - July, 1962 (100 pgs.)(35¢)
Gilberton Co.   (Came out semi-annually)

	Good	Fine	Mint
129A-The Story of Jesus (titled --Special Edition)"Three Camels" cover	4.00	8.00	12.00
"Jesus on Mountain"cvr.	2.00	4.00	6.00
132A-The Story of America(6/56)	2.00	4.00	6.00
135A-The Ten Commandments(12/56)	3.00	6.00	9.00
138A-Adventures in Science(6/57)-C.C Beck art	3.00	6.00	9.00
141A-The Rough Rider (Teddy Roosevelt)	2.00	4.00	6.00
144A-Blazing the Trail West(6/58)-73pgs. of Evans & Severin art	2.00	4.00	6.00
147A-Crossing the Rockies(12/58)-Crandall/ Evans art	2.00	4.00	6.00
150A-Royal Canadian Police(6/59)-Ingels, Sid Check art	2.00	4.00	6.00
153A-Men, Guns & Cattle(12/59)-Evans art, 26pgs.	2.00	4.00	6.00
156A-The Atomic Age(6/60)-Crandall/Evans, Torres art	2.00	4.00	6.00
159A-Rockets, Jets, Missiles(12/60)-Evans, Morrow art	3.00	6.00	9.00
162A-War Between the States(6/61)-Kirby & Crandall/Evans art	2.00	4.00	6.00
165A-To the Stars(12/61)-Torres & Crandall/ Evans art	2.00	4.00	6.00
166A-World War II('62)-Torres art	2.00	4.00	6.00
167A-Prehistoric World(7/62)-Torres & Crandall/Evans art	3.00	6.00	9.00
No# Special Issue-The United Nations (50¢) Williamson art (Rare)	6.00	12.00	18.00

Claw The Unconquered #1, © DC

CLAW THE UNCONQUERED
5-6/75 - #9, 9-10/76; #10, 4-5/78 - Present
National Periodical Publications/DC Comics

Cloak & Dagger #1, © Z-D

Clue Comics #12, © Hill

The Clutching Hand #1, © ACG

(Claw the Unconq. cont'd)	Good	Fine	Mint
#1	.25	.50	.75
2,3	.20	.40	.60
4-10: #9-Origin	.15	.30	.45

CLAY CODY, GUNSLINGER
Fall, 1957
Pines Comics

#1	.65	1.35	2.00

CLEAN FUN, STARRING "SHOOGAFOOTS JONES"
1944 (24 pgs.)(B&W)(Oversized covers)(10¢)
Specialty Book Co.

Humorous situations involving Negros in the
Deep South   6.00 12.00 18.00

CLEMENTINA THE FLYING PIG (See Dell Jr.
Treasury)

CLEOPATRA (See Ideal, A Classical Comic #1)

CLIFF MERRITT
Giveaway   (2 different)
Brotherhood of Railroad Trainsmen

--And the Very Candid Candidate by Al
  Williamson   .65   1.35 2.00
--Sets the Record Straight by Al Williamson
  (2 different covers-one by Williamson;
  the other-McWilliams)   .65 1.35 2.00

CLIMAX!
July, 1955
Gilmor

#1,2 (Mystery)	.80	1.60	2.40

CLINT & MAC (See 4-Color Comics #889)

CLOAK AND DAGGER
Fall, 1952
Ziff-Davis Publishing Co.

#1	1.75	3.35	5.00

CLOSE SHAVES OF PAULINE PERIL, THE
1970 - #4, March, 1971
Gold Key

#1-4	.15	.30	.45

CLOWN COMICS
1945; May-June, 1946 - #3, Sept-Oct, 1946
Home Comics/Harvey Publications

No# (1945)	1.35	2.75	4.00
#1-3	1.25	2.50	3.75

CLUBHOUSE PRESENTS
June, 1956
Sussex Publ. Co./Magazine Enterprises

	Good	Fine	Mint
#1	.65	1.35	2.00

CLUBHOUSE RASCALS
June, 1956 - #2, Oct, 1956
Sussex Publ. Co. (Magazine Enterprises)

#1,2-The Brain app. #2	.50	1.00	1.50

CLUB "16"
June, 1948 - #4, Dec, 1948
Famous Funnies

#1-4	1.00	2.00	3.00

CLUE COMICS (Real Clue Crime V2#4 on)
Jan, 1943 - #15(V2#3), May, 1947
Hillman Periodicals

#1-Origin The Boy King, Nightmare, Micro-Face, Twilight, & Zippo	25.00	50.00	75.00
2	12.00	24.00	36.00
3	10.00	20.00	30.00
4	8.00	16.00	24.00
5	6.00	12.00	18.00
6-9	4.00	8.00	12.00
10-Origin The Gun Master	4.00	8.00	12.00
11	3.00	6.00	9.00
12-Origin Rackman	4.00	8.00	12.00
V2#1-3: #1-Nightro new origin; Iron Lady app.; Kirby art	5.00	10.00	15.00

CLUTCHING HAND, THE
July-Aug, 1954
American Comics Group

#1	1.50	3.00	4.50

CLYDE BEATTY
October, 1953   (84 pgs.)
Commodore Productions

#1	2.50	5.00	7.50
--African Jungle Book('53)-Richfield Oil Co. giveaway	1.25	2.50	3.75

CLYDE CRASHCUP (TV)
Aug-Oct, 1963 - #5, Sept-Nov, 1964
Dell Publishing Co.

#1-5	.20	.40	.60

C-M-O COMICS
1942
Chicago Mail Order Co.

(C-M-O Comics cont'd) Good Fine Mint

#1-Invisible Terror, Super Ann, & Plymo the
   Rubber Man app. (All costume heroes)
                          5.00 10.00 15.00
   2-Invisible Terror, Super Ann app.
                          4.00   8.00 12.00

COBALT BLUE
1977   (50¢)
Power Comics

#1-3   .20   .40   .60

COCOMALT BIG BOOK OF COMICS
1938   (Regular Size - Full Color)
Harry 'A' Chesler

#1-Biro cover; Little Nemo, Dan Hastings;
   Guardineer art   18.00 36.00 54.00

CODY OF THE PONY EXPRESS (See Colossal
Feature Magazine)
Sept, 1950 - #3, Jan, 1951
Fox Features Syndicate

#1-3   1.50   3.00   4.50

CODY OF THE PONY EXPRESS (Buffalo Bill --)
(Outlaws of the West #11 on)(See Colossal Feat.)
#8, Oct, 1955; #9, Jan, 1956; #10, June, 1956
Charlton Comics

#8-Bullseye on splash page-not Simon & Kirby
                           1.00   2.00   3.00
   9,10   .65   1.35   2.00

COLLECTORS ITEM CLASSICS (See Marvel C.I.C.)

COLOR COMICS (See 4-Color Comics)

COLOSSAL FEATURES MAGAZINE (Formerly I Loved)
(See Cody of the Pony --)
#33, 5/50 - #34, 7/50; #3, 9/50
Fox Features Syndicate

#33,34-Cody of the Pony Express begins
   (Based on serial)   1.50   3.00   4.50
#3-Authentic criminal cases
                          1.50   3.00   4.50

COLOSSAL SHOW, THE (TV)
October, 1969
Gold Key

#1   .20   .40   .60

COLOSSUS COMICS
March, 1940

Sun Publications
                          Good Fine Mint
#1-Tulpa of Tsang(hero) 17.50 35.00 52.50

COLT 45 (TV)
1958 - 11-1/60; #4, 2-4/60 - #9, 5-7/61
Dell Publishing Co.

4-Color #924,1004,1058; #4-9
                           .65   1.35   2.00

COLUMBIA, THE GEM OF THE COMICS
1943
William H. Wise Co.

#1-Joe Palooka, Charlie Chan, Capt. Yank,
   Sparky Watts, Dixie Dugan begin
                          5.00 10.00 15.00
   2-4   4.00   8.00 12.00

COMANCHE (See 4-Color #1350)

COMANCHEROS, THE (See 4-Color #1300)

COMBAT
June, 1952 - #11, April, 1953
Atlas Comics (ANC)

#1   1.00   2.00   3.00
   2-11   .65   1.35   2.00
NOTE: Combat Casey in #7,8,10,11. Krigstein
story-#4.

COMBAT
Oct-Nov, 1961 - #40, Oct, 1973 (No #9)
Dell Publishing Co.

#1   .80   1.60   2.40
   2-7   .40   .80   1.20
   8(4-6/63),#8(7-9/63)   .25   .50   .75
   10-27   .15   .30   .45
   28-40(reprints #1-14)   .15   .30
NOTE: Glanzman covers/stories-#1-27.

COMBAT CASEY (Formerly War Combat)
#6, Jan, 1953 - #34, July, 1957
Atlas Comics (SAI)

#6-9   1.00   2.00   3.00
   10-Battle Brady x-over .65   1.35   2.00
   11-34   .50   1.00   1.50
NOTE: Everett story-#6. Powell story-#29,30,
34.

COMBAT KELLY
Nov, 1951 - #44, Aug, 1957
Atlas Comics (SPI)

#1-Heath art   1.50   3.00   4.50

Cocomalt Big Book--, © Ches

Cody Of The--#10, © CC

Colossus Comics #1, © Sun Publ.

Comedy #14, © MCG   Comedy #1('48), © MCG   Comic Cavalcade #1, © DC

(Combat Kelly cont'd)	Good	Fine	Mint
2-10	.80	1.60	2.40

11-44: #17-Combat Casey app.; #18-Battle
   Brady app. #38-Green Berets story(8/56)

| | .65 | 1.35 | 2.00 |

NOTE: *Berg stories-#21-23,25,28,31,36.*
Whitney story-#5.

COMBAT KELLY (and the Deadly Dozen)
June, 1972 - #9, Oct, 1973
Marvel Comics Group

#1-Intro. Combat Kelly	.20	.40	.60
2,3-Origin C. Kelly #3	.15	.30	.45
4-Sgt. Fury x-over		.15	.30
5-9: #9-Deadly Dozen dies		.10	.20

COMBINED OPERATIONS (See The Story of the
Commandos)

COMEDY CARNIVAL (See Carnival)

COMEDY COMICS (1st Series) (Daring Mystery
#1-8) (Margie #35 on)
#9, April, 1942 - #34, Fall, 1946
Timely Comics

#9-The Fin by Everett, Capt. Dash, Citizen V,
   & The Silver Scorpion app.; Wolverton art

	40.00	80.00	120.00

10-Origin The Fourth Musketeer, Victory Boys;
   Monstro, the Mighty app.

	25.00	50.00	75.00
11-Vagabond app.	3.00	6.00	9.00
12,13,15-32	1.35	2.75	4.00

14-Origin & 1st app. Super Rabbit

	1.75	3.35	5.00
33-Kurtzman art-5pgs.	4.00	8.00	12.00
34-Wolverton art, 5pgs.	4.00	8.00	12.00

COMEDY COMICS (2nd Series)
May, 1948 - #10, 1949
Marvel Comics (ACI)

#1,3,4-Hedy, Tessie, Millie begin; Kurtzman's
   "Hey Look"

	3.00	6.00	9.00
2	1.00	2.00	3.00
5-10	.60	1.20	1.80

COMIC ALBUM
Mar-May, 1958 - #18, June-Aug, 1962
Dell Publishing Co.

#1-Donald Duck	1.50	3.00	4.50
2-Bugs Bunny	.80	1.60	2.40
3-Donald Duck; Barks cvr.	1.00	2.00	3.00
4-Tom & Jerry	.50	1.00	1.50
5-Woody Woodpecker	.40	.80	1.20

	Good	Fine	Mint
6-Bugs Bunny	.40	.80	1.20
7-Popeye	.50	1.00	1.50
8-Tom & Jerry	.40	.80	1.20
9-Woody Woodpecker	.40	.80	1.20
10-Bugs Bunny	.40	.80	1.20
11-Popeye(9-11/60)	.50	1.00	1.50
12-Tom & Jerry	.40	.80	1.20
13-Woody Woodpecker	.40	.80	1.20
14-Bugs Bunny	.40	.80	1.20
15-Popeye	.50	1.00	1.50
16-Flintstones	.30	.65	1.00
17-Space Mouse	.30	.65	1.00
18-Three Stooges	.65	1.35	2.00

COMIC BOOK (Also see Comics From Weatherbird)
1954   (Giveaway)
American Juniors Shoe

Contains a comic rebound with new cover. Several combinations possible. Contents determines price.

COMIC CAPERS
1944 - #6, Summer, 1946
Red Circle Mag./Marvel Comics

#1-Super Rabbit	1.50	3.00	4.50
2-6	1.00	2.00	3.00

COMIC CAVALCADE
Winter, 1942-43 - #63, 6-7/54
(#30, Dec-Jan, 1948 on, contents change)
All-American/National Periodical Publ.

#1-The Flash, Green Lantern, Wonder Woman,
   Wildcat, The Black Pirate by Moldoff(also
   #2), Ghost Patrol, & Red White & Blue begin; Scribbly app., Minute Movies

	75.00	150.00	225.00

2-Mutt & Jeff begin; last Ghost Patrol &
   Black Pirate; Minute Movies

	40.00	80.00	120.00

3-Hop Harrigan & Sargon, the Sorcerer begin;
   The King app.   25.00 50.00 75.00
4-The Gay Ghost, The King, Scribbly, & Red
   Tornado app.   20.00 40.00 60.00

5	17.50	35.00	52.50

6-10: #7-Red Tornado & Black Pirate app.;
   last Scribbly   15.00 30.00 45.00
11,12,14-20: #12-Last Red White & Blue. #15-
   Johnny Peril begins, ends #29

	12.00	24.00	36.00
13-Solomon Grundy app.	20.00	40.00	60.00
21-23	9.00	18.00	27.00

24-Solomon Grundy x-over in Green Lantern

	12.00	24.00	36.00

25-29: #25-Black Canary app. #26,27-Johnny

(Comic Cavalcade cont'd)   Good   Fine   Mint
Peril app. #28-Last Mutt & Jeff. #29-Last
Flash, Wonder Woman, Green Lantern &
Johnny Peril   8.00 16.00 24.00
30-The Fox & the Crow begin,
31-63   1.00   2.00   3.00
NOTE: *Toth art-#26-28(Green Lantern); covers-*
#23,27. Atom app.-#22,23.

COMIC COMICS
1946 - #10, 1947
Fawcett Publications

#1-Capt. Kidd   1.70   3.35   5.00
2-10-Wolverton art, 4pgs. each
                   2.50   5.00   7.50

COMIC CUTS (Also see The Funnies)
1934   (5¢) (Tabloid size in full color)(Not
reprints; published weekly; created for newsstand sale)
H. L. Baker Co., Inc.

V1#7(6/30/34), V1#8(7/14/34),
V1#9(7/28/34)-Idle Jack strips
                 10.00 20.00 30.00

COMIC LAND
March, 1946
Fact and Fiction

#1-Sandusky & the Senator, Sam Stuper, Marvin
the Great, Sir Passer, Phineas Gruff app.;
Irv Tirman & Perry Williams art
                 2.00   4.00   6.00

COMIC MONTHLY
Feb, 1921 - #7, Jul, 1922 (24pgs)(8½x9")(10¢)
(1st monthly newsstand publication;B&W dailies)
Embee Dist. Co.

#1-Polly & Her Pals   40.00 80.00 120.00
2-Mike & Ike   10.00 20.00 30.00
3-S'Matter, Pop?   10.00 20.00 30.00
4-Barney Google   20.00 40.00 60.00
5-Tillie the Toiler 15.00 30.00 45.00
6-Indoor Sports   7.00 14.00 21.00
7-Little Jimmy   7.00 14.00 21.00

COMIC PAGES (Formerly Funny Picture Stories)
V3#4, July, 1939 - V3#6, Dec, 1939
Centaur Publications

V3#4-6   5.00 10.00 15.00

COMICS (See All Good)

COMICS, THE (--Funny Pages #2,3; Funny Pages
April, 1936 - #3, July, 1936   #4 on)

Centaur Publications

                 Good   Fine   Mint
#1-Siegel & Shuster, Kelly art
              25.00 50.00 75.00
2,3   12.00 24.00 36.00
NOTE: *See Taylor's Christmas Tabloid for*
Siegel & Shuster's first pro work.

COMICS, THE
3/1937 - #11, 1938 (Newspaper strip reprints)
Dell Publishing Co.

#1-Wash Tubbs, Tom Mix, Tom Beatty, & Ariz-
ona Kid begin   20.00 40.00 60.00
2   12.00 24.00 36.00
3-11: #3-Alley Oop 10.00 20.00 30.00

COMICS CALENDAR, THE (The 1946 --)
1946 (116 pgs.) (25¢) (Stapled at top)
True Comics Press

Has a "strip" story for every day of the
year; bound at top 10.00 20.00 30.00

COMICS DIGEST (Pocket Size)
Winter, 1942-43 (100 pgs.) (Black & White)
Parents' Magazine Institute

#1-Reprints from True Comics (non-fiction
World War II stories) 2.50   5.00   7.50

COMIC SELECTIONS (Shoe store giveaway)
1944-46 (Reprints from Calling All Girls,
True Comics, True Aviation, & Real Heroes)
Parents' Magazine Press

#1   1.00   2.00   3.00
2-5   .65   1.35   2.00

COMICS FOR KIDS
1945
London Publishing Co./Timely

#1,2   1.35   2.75   4.00

COMICS FROM WEATHER BIRD (Also see Comic Book,
Free Comics To You, Weather Bird & Edward's
1954 - 1957 (Giveaway)   Shoes
Weather Bird Shoes

Contains a comic bound with new cover - Many
combinations possible. Contents would determine price. Some issues do not contain complet
comics, but only parts of comics.
                 .50   1.00   1.50

COMICS MAGAZINE, THE
May, 1936 - #5, Sept, 1936
Quality Comics Group

Comic Monthly #1, © Embee Dist. Co.

The Comics #3, © Dell

The 1946 Comics Calendar, © True Comics

Comics On Parade #53, © UFS

Comics Revue #5, © UFS

Commander Battle #1, © ACG

(Comics Magazine cont'd)

	Good	Fine	Mint
#1	20.00	40.00	60.00
2	12.00	24.00	36.00
3-5	9.00	18.00	27.00

COMICS MAN, THE
1937   (One Shot)

	Good	Fine	Mint
#1	12.00	24.00	36.00

COMICS NOVEL   (Anarcho, Dictator of Death)
1947
Fawcett Publications

#1-All Radar	6.00	12.00	18.00

COMICS ON PARADE (#30 on, continuation of
4/1938 - #104, 2/1955   Single Series)
United Features Syndicate

#1-Tarzan by Foster; Captain & the Kids,
   Little Mary Mixup, Abbie & Slats, Ella
   Cinders, Broncho Bill, Li'l Abner begin

	Good	Fine	Mint
	60.00	120.00	180.00
2	25.00	50.00	75.00
3	20.00	40.00	60.00
4,5	15.00	30.00	45.00
6-10	10.00	20.00	30.00
11-20	8.00	16.00	24.00
21-29-Last Tarzan ish	6.00	12.00	18.00
30-Li'l Abner	4.00	8.00	12.00
31-The Captain & the Kids	3.00	6.00	9.00
32-Nancy & Fritzi Ritz	2.00	4.00	6.00
33-Li'l Abner	4.00	8.00	12.00
34-The Captain & the Kids	3.00	6.00	9.00
35-Nancy & Fritzi Ritz	2.00	4.00	6.00
36-Li'l Abner	4.00	8.00	12.00
37-The Captain & the Kids	3.00	6.00	9.00
38-Nancy & Fritzi Ritz	2.00	4.00	6.00
39-Li'l Abner	4.00	8.00	12.00
40-The Captain & the Kids	3.00	6.00	9.00
41-Nancy & Fritzi Ritz	1.50	3.00	4.50
42-Li'l Abner	3.00	6.00	9.00
43-The Captain & the Kids	3.00	6.00	9.00
44-Nancy & Fritzi Ritz	1.50	3.00	4.50
45-Li'l Abner	3.00	6.00	9.00
46-The Captain & the Kids	3.00	6.00	9.00
47-Nancy & Fritzi Ritz	1.50	3.00	4.50
48-Li'l Abner	3.00	6.00	9.00
49-The Captain & the Kids	3.00	6.00	9.00
50-Nancy & Fritzi Ritz	1.50	3.00	4.50
51-Li'l Abner	2.50	5.00	7.50
52-The Captain & the Kids	1.50	3.00	4.50
53-Nancy & Fritzi Ritz	1.25	2.50	3.75
54-Li'l Abner	2.50	5.00	7.50
55-Nancy & Fritzi Ritz	1.25	2.50	3.75

	Good	Fine	Mint
56-The Captain & the Kids	1.50	3.00	4.50
57-Nancy & Fritzi Ritz	1.25	2.50	3.75
58-Li'l Abner	2.50	5.00	7.50
59-The Captain & the Kids	1.50	3.00	4.50
60-70-Nancy & Fritzi Ritz	1.25	2.50	3.75
71-76-Nancy only	1.25	2.50	3.75
77-104-Nancy & Sluggo	1.25	2.50	3.75

Special Issue, 7/46; Summer, 1948- The Capt.
   & the Kids app.   1.50   3.00   4.50
Bound Volume (Very Rare) includes #1-12;
   bound by publisher in pictorial comic
   boards & distributed at the 1939 World's
   Fair & through mail order from ads in comic books (Also see Tip Top)
                  135.00 270.00 405.00
NOTE: *Li'l Abner reprinted from Tip Top.*

COMICS REVUE
June, 1947 - #5, Jan, 1948
St. John Publ. Co. (United Features Synd.)

#1-Ella Cinders & Blackie	2.00	4.00	6.00
2-Hap Hopper (7/47)	2.00	4.00	6.00
3-Iron Vic (8/47)	2.00	4.00	6.00
4-Ella Cinders (9/47)	2.00	4.00	6.00
5-Gordo #1 (1/48)	2.00	4.00	6.00

COMIC STORY PAINT BOOK
1943   (68 pgs.) (Large Size)
Samuel Lowe Co.

#1055-Captain Marvel & a Captain Marvel Jr.
   story to read & color; 3 panels in color
   per page (reprints) 25.00 50.00 75.00

COMIX BOOK   (B&W Magazine - $1.00)
1974 - #3, Mar, 1975; #4, Feb, 1976
Marvel Comics Group/Krupp Comics Works #4

#1-Underground comic artists; 2pg. Wolverton			
story	1.00	2.00	3.00
2	.65	1.35	2.00
3-Low distribution	1.00	2.00	3.00
4,5	.65	1.35	2.00

NOTE: *Print run #1-3, 200-250M; #4&5, 10M ea.*

COMIX INTERNATIONAL
July, 1974 - #3, 1976   (Full Color)
Warren Magazines

#1-Low distribution; all Corben reprints
   from Warren Magazines 3.00   6.00   9.00
| 2,3 | | 1.75 | 3.35 | 5.00 |

COMMANDER BATTLE AND THE ATOMIC SUB
Jul-Aug, 1954 - #7, Jul-Aug, 1955
American Comics Group (Titan Publ. Co.)

Comic Books
Science Fiction
Collectors Items

P.O. BOX 3791 STATION B   WINNIPEG, MANITOBA R2W 3R6   PHONE (204) 586-7920

STYX COMIC SERVICE was the first service of its kind. It supplies a complete
selection of comics, magazines, science fiction, collectors'
supplies and related items to fans throughout the world.

HOW THE SERVICE WORKS: All materials are sold for cover price. There is a monthly
service charge of $1.50 levied to cover costs of running
each member's personal account. NO OTHER COSTS ARE INVOL-
VED. WE PAY ALL POSTAGE AND SHIPPING COSTS.

Each member of the service is given his or her personal account at the time
of joining. Each member deposits funds into this account and maintains it in order to pay for the materials which are purchased.

Your order is selected each month from a "standing list" of items which you
prepare for us (see below). This list is composed of titles and quantities of
issues desired. ANY QUANTITY of ANY TITLE may be selected. You are GUARANTEED
that each issue of a given title will be supplied in the quantity you desire.
Best of all, once on the service, you will NEVER MISS AN ISSUE OF YOUR FAVOURITE
TITLES. In addition, changes to the list may be sent in at any time.

A mailing is prepared once at the end of each month. At this time, each
member receives a monthly newsletter/magazine which contains items of interest
pertaining to the service and the comics-sf world. In addition, a CLEAR, CONCISE
bill is included, listing all purchases for the month, the total costs, and the
amount of credit remaining in the member's account. This bill is prepared in
TRIPLICATE. One copy is received with the newsletter, one copy is kept by us for
records, and the third copy goes into the parcel being sent so that ALL CONTENTS
ARE EASILY VERIFIED. THUS, EVERYTHING IS TRIPLE-CHECKED FOR YOUR PROTECTION.

Each parcel is prepared with care and patience. The books are wrapped in
plastic and are protected further with paper padding before they are placed in
our specially-designed mailing boxes. Thus, you are ensured of materials which
arrive in THE FINEST POSSIBLE CONDITION.

HOW TO JOIN: 1.) On a piece of paper, place the titles of the items you collect
REGULARLY, together with the quantity of each which you regularly buy. If you wish, our standard publications list may be obtained by sending
25¢ to cover costs of mailing.
2.) Estimate your monthly expense, including the $1.50 service charge. This is
your minimum deposit. You may, if you wish, deposit as far ahead as you desire. Each month you will receive a careful account of your remaining credit.
Accounts must be maintained with a credit balance for service to continue.
3.) Make your cheque or money order payable to "STYX COMIC SERVICE" , and mail
it together with your completed publications listing to the address above.

STYX COMIC SERVICE is by far the best service anywhere. Our system is simple.
There are no fancy discount gimmicks or hidden costs. We aim to provide the BEST,
MOST ECONOMICAL, MOST COMPLETE SERVICE POSSIBLE. We look forward to serving you.

WE ARE INTERESTED IN PURCHASING GROUPS OR COLLECTIONS OF COMIC BOOKS FOR OUR
EXTENSIVE BACK-ISSUE STOCK. PLEASE CONTACT US IF YOU HAVE MATERIALS FOR SALE.

Our Store, located at 1858 ARLINGTON STREET (at Luxton Avenue) in Winnipeg, Manitoba features a complete line of new comics and sf materials, along
with thousands of back issues on hand for immediate inspection. We are open each
day, except Sundays. We look forward to meeting you when you are in the area.
Our BACK ISSUE CATALOGUE is available by mail for $1.00 (refundable with first
order). We look forward to serving you in every way possible, and hope that you
will join our growing list of satisfied customers throughout the world.

(Commander Battle & the Atomic Sub cont'd)

	Good	Fine	Mint
#1 (3-D effect)	2.00	4.00	6.00
2-7	1.00	2.00	3.00
3-D(1954)	3.00	6.00	9.00

COMMANDMENTS OF GOD
1954, 1958
Catechetical Guild

Same contents in both editions; different
covers   1.50   3.00   4.50

COMMANDO ADVENTURES
June, 1957 - #2, Aug, 1957
Atlas Comics (MMC)

#1,2: #1-Severin cover   .75   1.50   2.25

COMMANDO YANK   (See Mighty Midget Comics)

COMPLETE BOOK OF COMICS AND FUNNIES
1944   (196 pgs.)   (One Shot)
Better Publications

#1-Origin Brad Spencer, Wonderman; The Magnet,
   The Silver Knight by Kinstler, & Zudo, the
   Jungle Boy app.   5.00 10.00 15.00

COMPLETE BOOK OF TRUE CRIME COMICS
No date (Mid 1940's) (132 pgs.) (25¢)
William H. Wise & Co.

No#-Contains Crime Does Not Pay rebound
   (includes #22,#1)   15.00 30.00 45.00

COMPLETE COMICS   (Formerly Amazing #1)
Winter, 1944-45
Marvel Comics

#2-The Destroyer, The Whizzer, The Young All-
   ies, & Sergeant Dix   22.50 45.00 67.50

COMPLETE LOVE MAGAZINE (Formerly a pulp with
same title)
V26#2, 5-6/51 - V32#4(#191), 9/56
Ace Periodicals (Periodical House)

V26#2-6(2/52), V27#1-6	.50	1.00	1.50
V28#1-6, V29#1-6	.50	1.00	1.50
V30#1(#176,4/54) - V30#6(#181,1/55)			
	.50	1.00	1.50
V31#1(#182,3/55) - V31#6(#187,1/56)			
	.40	.80	1.20
V32#1(#188,3/56) - V32#4(#191,9/56)			
	.40	.80	1.20

COMPLETE MYSTERY   (True Mystery #5 on)
Aug, 1948 - #4, Feb, 1949 (Full length stories)
Marvel Comics (PrPI)

	Good	Fine	Mint
#1-Seven Dead Men	2.00	4.00	6.00
2-Jigsaw of Doom	1.50	3.00	4.50
3-Fear in the Night-Burgos art			
	1.50	3.00	4.50
4-A Squealer Dies Fast	1.50	3.00	4.50

COMPLETE ROMANCE
1949
Avon Periodicals

#1   1.50   3.00   4.50

CONAN, THE BARBARIAN
Oct, 1970 - Present
Marvel Comics Group

	Good	Fine	Mint
#1-Origin Conan by Barry Smith; Kull app.			
	12.00	24.00	36.00
2	6.00	12.00	18.00
3-(low distribution in some areas)			
	9.00	18.00	27.00
4,5	4.00	8.00	12.00
6-10: #10-52pgs.; Black Knight reprt.; Kull			
by Severin app.	3.00	6.00	9.00
11-13	2.00	4.00	6.00
14,15-Elric app.	2.50	5.00	7.50
16-20: #16-Conan reprint from Savage Tales			
#1	1.50	3.00	4.50
21,22,24: #22-has reprints from #1. #24-Last			
Smith issue	1.50	3.00	4.50
23-1st app. Red Sonja	2.00	4.00	6.00
25-Buscema art begins	1.00	2.00	3.00
26-30	.50	1.00	1.50
31-36,38-40	.40	.80	1.20
37-Adams cover/story	1.00	2.00	3.00
41-43,46,48-50	.35	.70	1.05
44,45-Adams inks; cvr-#45	.40	.80	1.20
47-Wood reprint	.35	.70	1.05
51-60: #57-Ploog story	.25	.50	.75
61-70: #64 reprints/Savage Tales #5; Starlin			
art on Conan	.20	.40	.60
71-82: #78-reprints/Savage Sword of Conan#1			
	.15	.30	.45

NOTE: *Buckler* cover-#40. *Buscema* stories-
#25-36, 38, 39, 41-56, 58-63, 65-68, 70-82; covers-
#26, 36, 44, 52, 56, 58, 59, 64, 72, 78, 79. *Ditko*
story-#40. *Kane* stories-Giant Size #1-4; cov-
ers-#12, 17(w/*Brunner*), 23, 25, 27-32, 34, 35, 38,
39, 41-43, 45-51, 53-55, 57, 60-63, 65-71, Giant
Size #1, 3, 4. *Smith* art-#1-16, 19-21, 23, 24;
layouts only-#21; covers-#1-11, 13-16, 19-22,
24. Issues #3-5, 7-9, 11, 16, 18, 21, 23, 25, 27-30,
35, 37, 38, 42, 45, 52, 57, 58, 65 have original

Complete Book of True Crime, © WHW

Complete Comics #2, © MCG

Conan #1, © MCG

(Conan cont'd)
Robert E. Howard stories adapted. Issues #32-34 adapted from Norvell Page's novel Flame Winds.

	Good	Fine	Mint
-- Book & Record Set	.50	1.00	1.50

Giant Size #1(9/74)-Smith reprint from #3; start adaptation of Howard's "Hour of the Dragon" .90 1.80 2.70
Giant Size #2(12/74)-Smith reprint from #5; Sutton art; Buscema cvr .65 1.35 2.00
Giant Size #3('75; Smith reprint from #6; Sutton art), Giant Size #4(6/75; Smith reprint from #7), Giant Size #5('75; Smith reprint from #14,15; Kirby cover) .50 1.00 1.50
King Size #1(9/73-35¢)-Smith reprints from #2,4 1.50 3.00 4.50
Annual #2(6/76)-50¢ - new stories .40 .80 1.20
Annual #3(12/77) .25 .50 .75

<u>CONAN</u> (See Savage Tales, Savage Sword of--, & Chamber of Darkness #4)

<u>CONFESSIONS ILLUSTRATED</u> (Magazine)
Jan-Feb, 1956 - #2, Spring, 1956
E.C. Comics

#1-Craig, Kamen, Wood, Orlando art
 4.00 8.00 12.00
 2-(Scarce)-Craig, Crandall, Kamen, Orlando art 6.00 12.00 18.00

<u>CONFESSIONS OF LOVE</u> (Conf. of Romance #7)
#12, Oct, 1952 - #6, Aug, 1953
Star Publications

#12,13-Jay Disbrow story 1.35 2.75 4.00
 14,#5,6 .65 1.35 2.00
#4-Disbrow story 1.35 2.75 4.00

<u>CONFESSIONS OF ROMANCE</u> (Formerly Conf.of Love)
#7, Nov, 1953 - #11, Nov, 1954
Star Publications

#7,8,10,11 1.00 2.00 3.00
 9-Wood story 2.50 5.00 7.50

<u>CONFESSIONS OF THE LOVELORN</u> (Formerly Love-
#52, Aug, 1954 - #111, Oct, 1959 lorn)
American Comics Group (Regis Publ./Best Synd. Features)

#52-(3-D effect)Whitney cvr.
 1.00 2.00 3.00
 53-111 .35 .70 1.05
 (The 3/58 issue has Williamson art--$5.00)

<u>CONFIDENTIAL DIARY</u>
#14, Sept, 1962 - #17, Mar, 1963
Charlton Comics

	Good	Fine	Mint
#14-17	.15	.30	.45

<u>CONGO BILL</u>
Aug-Sept, 1954 - #7, Aug-Sept, 1955
National Periodical Publications

#1 3.00 6.00 9.00
2-7 2.00 4.00 6.00

<u>CONQUEROR, THE</u> (See 4-Color Comics #690)

<u>CONQUEROR COMICS</u>
Winter, 1945
Albrecht Publishing Co.

No# 2.00 4.00 6.00

<u>CONQUEST</u>
1953 (6¢)
Store Comics

#1-Richard the Lion Hearted, Beowulf, Swamp Fox 1.00 2.00 3.00

<u>CONQUEST</u>
1955
Famous Funnies

#1-Crandall art, 1 pg. 1.50 3.00 4.50

<u>CONTACT COMICS</u>
July, 1944 - #12, May, 1946
Aviation Press

#1-Black Venus, Flamingo, Golden Eagle, Tommy Tomahawk begin 5.00 10.00 15.00
 2-5: #3-Last Flamingo. #5-The Phantom Flyer app. 2.50 5.00 7.50
 6,11-Kurtzman's Black Venus; #11-Last Golden Eagle, last Tommy Tomahawk; Feldstein art, 4 pgs. 5.00 10.00 15.00
 7-10,12: #12-Sky Rangers, Air Kids, Ace Diamond app. 2.00 4.00 6.00

<u>COO COO COMICS</u> (--the Bird Brain #57 on)
Oct, 1942 - 1952
Nedor Comics/Standard(Animated Cartoons)

#1-Super Mouse origin 2.00 4.00 6.00
 2-10 1.00 2.00 3.00
 11-33 .65 1.35 2.00
 34-40,43,46,48-50-Text illos by Frazetta in all 2.00 4.00 6.00
 41-Two Frazetta stories 5.00 10.00 15.00

Congo Bill #1, © DC

Conqueror Comics #1('45). © Albrecht Publ.

Coo Coo Comics #32. © STD

'Cookie' #2, © ACG   Cosmo Cat #1, © Fox   Cowboy Love #1, © Faw

(Coo Coo Comics cont'd)

	Good	Fine	Mint
42,44,45,47-All contain Frazetta stories & text illos.	4.00	8.00	12.00
51-62	.50	1.00	1.50

"COOKIE"
April, 1946 - #54, Apr-May, 1955
Michel Publ./American Comics Group(Regis Publ.)

#1	1.00	2.00	3.00
2-10	.65	1.35	2.00
11-20	.40	.80	1.20
21-54	.35	.70	1.05

COOL CAT (Formerly Black Magic)
V8#6, 3-4/62 - V9#2, 7-8/62
Prize Publications

V8#6, No#(V9#1), V9#2	.40	.80	1.20

COPPER CANYON (See Fawcett Movie Comics)

CORKY & WHITE SHADOW (See 4-Color #707)

CORLISS ARCHER (See Meet --)

CORPORAL RUSTY DUGAN (See Rusty Dugan)

CORPSES OF DR. SACOTTI, THE (See Ideal A Classical Comic)

CORSAIR, THE (See A-1 Comics #5,7,10)

COSMO CAT
July-Aug, 1946 - 1949; 1959
Fox Publications/Green Publ. Co./Norlen Mag.

#1	1.75	3.35	5.00
2-10	1.00	2.00	3.00
2-4(1957-Green Publ. Co.)	.35	.70	1.05
2-4(1959-Norlen Mag.)	.35	.70	1.05
I.W. Reprint #1	.25	.50	.75

COSMO THE MERRY MARTIAN
Sept, 1958 - #6, Oct, 1959
Archie Publications (Radio Comics)

#1-Bob White art	1.00	2.00	3.00
2-6-Bob White art	.65	1.35	2.00

COTTON WOODS (See 4-Color Comics #837)

COUGAR, THE
April, 1975 - #2, June, 1975
Seaboard Periodicals (Atlas)

#1	.25	.50	.75
2-Origin	.20	.40	.60

COUNTDOWN (See Movie Classics)

COUNT OF MONTE CRISTO, THE (See 4-Color #794)

COURAGE COMICS
1945
J. Edward Slavin

	Good	Fine	Mint
#1,2,77	1.00	2.00	3.00

COURTSHIP OF EDDIE'S FATHER (TV)
January, 1970 - #2, May, 1970
Dell Publishing Co.

#1,2	.20	.40	.60

COVERED WAGONS, HO (See 4-Color #814)

COWBOY ACTION (Western Thrillers #1-4: Quick Trigger Western #12 on)
#5, March, 1955 - #11, March, 1956
Atlas Comics (ACI)

#5-10	1.00	2.00	3.00
11-Williamson story, 4pgs.	2.00	4.00	6.00

COWBOY COMICS (-- Stories #14)
1937 - 1938
Centaur Publishing Co.

#13,14	8.00	12.00	24.00

COWBOY IN AFRICA (TV)
March, 1968
Gold Key

#1(10219-803)	.35	.70	1.05

COWBOY LOVE
July, 1949 - V2#7, 1955
Fawcett Publications/Charlton Comics

V1#1(52pgs.)	1.75	3.35	5.00
V1#2,3	1.00	2.00	3.00
V1#4-27, V1#28,29(4/55)	.50	1.00	1.50
V2#7-Williamson/Evans art	2.50	5.00	7.50

NOTE: *Powell story-#10.*

COWBOY ROMANCES
Oct, 1949 - #3, Mar, 1950
Marvel Comics (IPC)

#1	1.75	3.35	5.00
2,3	1.35	2.75	4.00

COWBOYS AND INDIANS (Formerly Cowboys 'N'
#6, 1949 - #8, 1952   Injuns)
Magazine Enterprises

(Cowboys & Indians cont'd)

	Good	Fine	Mint
#6(A-1#23), 7(A-1#41), 8(A-1#48)			
	1.00	2.00	3.00

COWBOYS 'N' INJUNS COMICS (--& Indians #6 on)
1946 - 1949
Compix/Magazine Enterprises

	Good	Fine	Mint
#1	1.25	2.50	3.75
2-5	.75	1.50	2.25
I.W. Reprint #1,7 (reprinted in Canada by			
Superior, #7)	.50	1.00	1.50

COWBOY WESTERN COMICS (Becomes Wild Bill
1947 - #67, 1/58   Hickok & Jingles #18 on)
Fawcett/Charlton(Capitol Stories)

#1	3.00	6.00	9.00
2-10	1.25	2.50	5.00
11-20	1.20	2.40	3.60
21-30	1.00	2.00	3.00
31-50	.80	1.60	2.40
51-66	.65	1.35	2.00
67-Williamson/Torres story, 5 pgs.			
	2.50	5.00	7.50

COWGIRL ROMANCES (Formerly Jeanie)
#28, Jan, 1950
Marvel Comics (CCC)

#28(#1)	2.00	4.00	6.00

COWGIRL ROMANCES
1950 - #12, Winter, 1952-53
Fiction House Magazines

#1	2.50	5.00	7.50
2-12	1.50	3.00	4.50

COW PUNCHER (-- Comics)
Jan, 1947 - 1949
Avon Periodicals

#1-Clint Cortland, Texas Rancher, Kit West,			
Pioneer Queen begin; Kubert story; Alabam			
stories begin	6.00	12.00	18.00
2-Kubert story; Kamen bondage cover			
	5.00	10.00	15.00
3-7: #3-Kiefer story	4.00	8.00	12.00

COWPUNCHER
1953   (No #) (Reprints Avon's #2)
Realistic Publications

Kubert story	2.50	5.00	7.50

COWSILLS, THE (See Harvey Pop Comics)

CRACKAJACK FUNNIES (Giveaway)
1937   (32 pgs.)(Full Size, Soft Cover, Full
Color) (Before #1?)
Malto-Meal

	Good	Fine	Mint
Features Dan Dunn, G-Man, Speed Bolton, Freck			
les, Buck Jones, Clyde Beatty, The Nebbs, Maj			
or Hoople, Wash Tubbs	16.50	33.25	50.00

CRACKAJACK FUNNIES
June, 1938 - #43, Jan, 1942
Dell Publishing Co.

#1-Dan Dunn, Freckles, Myra North, Wash Tubbs			
Apple Mary, The Nebbs, Don Winslow, Tom			
Mix, Buck Jones begin	33.00	66.50	100.00
2	16.50	33.25	50.00
3	13.50	26.75	40.00
4,5	10.00	20.00	30.00
6-8,10	9.00	18.00	27.00
9-Red Ryder begins	9.00	18.00	27.00
11-14	7.00	14.00	21.00
15-Tarzan text feature begins; not in #26,35			
	8.00	16.00	24.00
16-24	7.00	14.00	21.00
25-The Owl begins; in new costume #26 by			
Frank Thomas	15.00	30.00	45.00
26-30	10.00	20.00	30.00
31-Owl covers begin	8.00	16.00	24.00
32-Origin Owl Girl	10.00	20.00	30.00
33-39: #36-Last Tarzan ish. #39-Andy Panda			
begins	8.00	16.00	24.00
40-43-Last Owl cover #42	7.00	14.00	21.00

NOTE: *McWilliams* art in most issues.

CRACK COMICS (-- Western #63 on)
May, 1940 - #62, Sept, 1949
Quality Comics Group

#1-Origin The Black Condor by Lou Fine, Mad-			
ame Fatal, Red Torpedo & The Space Legion;			
The Clock, Alias the Spider, Wizard Wells,			
& Ned Bryant begin; Powell art			
	125.00	250.00	375.00
2	60.00	120.00	180.00
3	50.00	100.00	150.00
4	35.00	70.00	105.00
5	32.50	65.00	97.50
6-9	30.00	60.00	90.00
10-Tor, the Magic Master begins			
	30.00	60.00	90.00
11-21-Last Condor by Lou Fine			
	25.00	50.00	75.00
22-26,28-30	10.00	20.00	30.00
27-Origin Captain Triumph by Alfred Andriola			
(Kerry Drake artist)	25.00	50.00	75.00
31-39	6.00	12.00	18.00
40-50	4.00	8.00	12.00

Cow Puncher #2, © Avon

Crackajack Funnies #2, © Dell

Crack Comics #6, © DC (Qua)

Crack Comics #17, © DC (Qua)   Crack Western #72, © DC (Qua)   Crash Comics #3, © Tem Publ.

(Crack Comics cont'd)	Good	Fine	Mint
51-62	3.00	6.00	9.00

NOTE: _Black Condor by Fine-#1-24. Crandall_
art-#40-62(Capt. Triumph). McWilliams art-
#15-27.

CRACK WESTERN (Formerly Crack; Jonesy #85 on)
#63, Nov, 1949 - May, 1953
Quality Comics Group

#63-Origin & 1st app. Two-Gun Lil(ends #84),
   Arizona Ames, Frontier Marshal, & Dead
   Canyon Days   3.00   6.00   9.00
 64,65,67,69-Crandall stories; #67-Arizona
   Ames becomes A. Raines. #69-Last Dead Canyon Days   2.00   4.00   6.00
 66,68,72-82: #75,78,81-Crandall covers
                 1.50   3.00   4.50
 70-Origin & 1st app. The Whip
                 1.35   3.35   5.00
 71,83-Crandall cvr/sty. 2.00   4.00   6.00
 84-Crandall story   1.75   3.35   5.00

CRACKED (Magazine)(See Biggest Greatest --)
Feb-Mar, 1958 - Present   (Satire)
Major Magazines

#1-One pg. Williamson   4.00   8.00 12.00
 2-1st Shut-Ups & Bonus Cut-Outs
                 2.00   4.00   6.00
 3-6   1.35   2.75   4.00
 7-Reprints 1st 6 covers on cover
                  .65   1.35   2.00
 8-12,14-17,19,20: #10-Last ish edited by
   Sol Brodsky   .65   1.35   2.00
 13-(No#, 3/60)   .65   1.35   2.00
 18-(No#, 2/61)   .65   1.35   2.00
 21-27(11/62)   .50   1.00   1.50
 27(#28, 2/63, misnumbered) .50   1.00   1.50
 29(5/63),30   .50   1.00   1.50
 31-60   .30   .65   1.00
 61-98,100   .25   .50   .75
 99-Alfred E. Newman featured on cover
                  .25   .50   .75
101-145   .20   .40   .60
Biggest, Greatest Cracked-No#('65)
                  .35   .70   1.05
Biggest, Greatest Cracked #2('66)-#12('76)
                  .25   .50   .75
Extra Special--#1('76),#2('76)
                  .20   .40   .60
Giant -- No#('65)   .50   1.00   1.50
Giant -- #2('66)-#12('76), No#(9/77),
King Sized -- #1('67)   .25   .50   .75
King Sized -- #2('68)-#11('77)
                  .20   .40   .60
Super -- #1('68)   .25   .50   .75
Super -- #2('69)-#10('77) .20   .40   .60

NOTE: _Burgos stories-#1-10. Davis stories-#5,_
11-18,24,80(art); covers-#12-14,16. Elder
stories-#5,6,10-13; cover-#10. Everett stories-
#1-10,23-25,61; cover-#1. Heath stories-#1-3,
6,13,14,17,110; cover-#6. Jaffee story-#5,6.
Morrow story-#8-10. Reinman (Paul) story-#1-4.
Severin art & stories in most all issues #1 on.
Shores (Syd) stories-#3-7. Stone (Chic) stor-
ies-#16,17. Torres story-#7-10. Williamson art-
#1 (1 pg.). Wolverton art-#10(2pgs.), _Giant_
_No#('65)._

CRACKED COLLECTORS' EDITION(Formerly --Special)
#4, 1973 - Present
Major Magazines

	Good	Fine	Mint
#4	.30	.60	.90
5-16	.20	.40	.60

CRACKED SHUT-UPS (Cracked Special #3)
Feb, 1972 - #2, 1972
Major Magazines

#1,2	.25	.50	.75

CRACKED SPECIAL (Formerly Cracked Shut-Ups;
-- Collectors' Edition #4 on)
#3, 1973
Major Magazines

#3	.25	.50	.75

CRASH COMICS (Catman #6 on)
May, 1940 - #5, Nov, 1940
Tem Publishing Co.

#1-The Blue Streak, Strongman (origin), The
   Perfect Human begin; Simon & Kirby art
              30.00 60.00 90.00
 2-Simon & Kirby art 17.50 35.00 52.50
 3- " " " "   12.00 24.00 36.00
 4-Origin & 1st app. The Catman; S&K art
              17.50 35.00 52.50
 5-S&K art   12.00 24.00 36.00
NOTE: _Solar Legion by Kirby_ #1-5 (5pgs. ea.)

CRAZY
Dec, 1953 - #7, July, 1954
Atlas Comics (CSI)

#1-Everett art	2.00	4.00	6.00
2-7	1.50	3.00	4.50

NOTE: _Berg story-#2. Drucker story-#6. Ever-_
ett story-#1,4.

CRAZY (People Who Buy This Magazine Is --)
(Formerly This Magazine Is --)
V3#3, 11/57 - V4#8, 2/59 (Magazine)(Satire)
Charlton Publications

(Crazy cont'd)

	Good	Fine	Mint
V3#3 - V4#7	.50	1.00	1.50
V4#8-Davis art 8 pgs.	1.50	3.00	4.50

CRAZY (Satire)
Feb, 1973 - #3, June, 1973
Marvel Comics Group

	Good	Fine	Mint
#1-3-Not Brand Echh reprints; Kirby reprint-			
#3	.15	.30	.45

CRAZY (Magazine)(Satire)
Oct, 1973 - Present (40¢) (Black & White)
Marvel Comics Group

	Good	Fine	Mint
#1-1pg. Wolverton, Ploog story, Bode art;			
3pg. photo story of Adams & Giordano			
	.40	.80	1.20
2-Adams story; Kurtzman's "Hey Look" reprint			
2 pgs.; Buscema art	.40	.80	1.20
3,5,6,8: #3-Drucker art	.20	.40	.60
4,7-Ploog art	.25	.50	.75
9-16-Eisner art	.15	.30	.45
17-33	.15	.30	.45
Super Special #1(Sum.'75,100pgs.)-Ploog,			
Adams reprint	.50	1.00	1.50

NOTE: *Cardy covers-#7,8. Freas covers-#1,4, 6; art-#7.*

CRAZY, MAN, CRAZY (Magazine) (Satire)
June, 1956
Humor Magazines

	Good	Fine	Mint
V2#2-Three pgs. Wolverton	2.00	4.00	6.00

CREATURE, THE (See Movie Classics)

CREATURES ON THE LOOSE (Tower of Shadows #1-9)
#10, March, 1971 - #37, Sept, 1975
Marvel Comics Group

	Good	Fine	Mint
#10-First King Kull story; Wrightson cover/			
story	3.50	7.00	10.50
11-15: #13-Crandall art	.40	.80	1.20
16-Origin Warrior of Mars	.50	1.00	1.50
17-20	.40	.80	1.20
21,22: Steranko cover; Thongor begins #22,			
ends #29	.30	.65	1.00
23-29	.20	.40	.60
30-Manwolf begins	.15	.30	.45
31-37	.15	.30	.45

NOTE: *Everett inks-#16. Morrow art-#20,21.*

CREEPER, THE (See Beware --)

CREEPY (Magazine)
1964 - Present
Warren Publishing Co.

	Good	Fine	Mint
#1-Frazetta story	2.00	4.00	6.00
2	1.50	3.00	4.50
3-13	1.00	2.00	3.00
14-25	.80	1.60	2.40
26-40	.60	1.20	1.80
41-60	.50	1.00	1.50
61-80	.40	.80	1.20
81-93	.35	.70	1.05
Year Book 1968,'69	1.50	3.00	4.50
Year Book 1970-Adams, Ditko art			
	1.35	2.75	4.00
Annual 1971,'72	.80	1.60	2.40
Annual 1973	.65	1.35	2.00
Annual 1974-All Crandall reprints			
	.65	1.35	2.00

(NOTE: Annuals are included in regular numbering.)

NOTE: *Above books contain many good artists works: Adams, Brunner, Corben, Craig (Taycee) Crandall, Ditko, Evans, Frazetta, Heath, Jeff Jones, Krenkel, McWilliams, Morrow, Orlando, Ploog, Severin, Torres, Toth, Williamson, Wood & Wrightson; covers by Crandall, Davis, Frazetta, Morrow, SanJulian, Todd/Bode; Otto Binder's "Adam Link" stories in #2,4,6,8,9, 12,13,15 with Orlando art.*

CREEPY THINGS
July, 1975 - #6, June, 1976
Charlton Comics

	Good	Fine	Mint
#1	.15	.30	.45
2-6: #3,4-Sutton covers		.15	.30

CRIME AND JUSTICE
March, 1951 - 1955
Capitol Stories/Charlton Comics

	Good	Fine	Mint
#1	1.20	2.40	3.60
2-17,19-26: Shuster cover #19, story #21			
	.60	1.20	1.80
18-Ditko art	.80	1.60	2.40

CRIME AND PUNISHMENT
April, 1948 - #74, Aug, 1955
Lev Gleason Publications

	Good	Fine	Mint
#1	4.00	8.00	12.00
2-5	2.00	4.00	6.00
6-10	1.35	2.75	4.00
11-20	1.00	2.00	3.00
21-30	.80	1.60	2.40
31-45	.65	1.35	2.00
46-One Pg. Frazetta	1.35	2.75	4.00
47-65,68,70-74	.50	1.00	1.50
66-Toth cover + all stys.	3.00	6.00	9.00

Crazy #1('53), © MCG

Creepy #1, © WP

Crime & Punishment #66, © Lev

Crime Detective #3, © Hill

Crime Does Not Pay #28, © Lev

Crime Files #5, © STD

(Crime and Punishment cont'd)

	Good	Fine	Mint
67,69-Drug stories	2.00	4.00	6.00

NOTE: *Guardineer story-#2,3,10. Kinstler cover-#69. McWilliams stories-#41,48,49.*

CRIME CAN'T WIN (Formerly Cindy Smith?)
#41, 1950 - #43, 2/51; #4, 4/51 - #12, 9/53
Marvel/Atlas Comics (CCC)

	Good	Fine	Mint
#41-43	.65	1.35	2.00
#4(4/51)	.65	1.35	2.00
5-12	.50	1.00	1.50

NOTE: *Robinson story-#9,10.*

CRIME CASES (Formerly Willie Comics)
#24, 8/50 - #27, 3/51; #5, 5/51 - #12, 7/52
Marvel/Atlas Comics(CnPC #24-8/MJMC #9-12)

	Good	Fine	Mint
#24-27: Everett art #27	.80	1.60	2.40
#5-12: #11-Robinson story	.65	1.35	2.00

CRIME CLINIC
1951 - #11, Sept-Oct, 1951
Ziff-Davis Publ. Co.

	Good	Fine	Mint
#1	1.00	2.00	3.00
2-11: #11-Painted cover	.60	1.20	1.80

CRIME DETECTIVE COMICS
Mar-Apr, 1948 - V3#8, 1952
Hillman Periodicals

	Good	Fine	Mint
V1#1-7, 10-12	1.00	2.00	3.00
8-Kirby story	2.00	4.00	6.00
9-Used in Seduction of the Innocent			
	5.00	10.00	15.00
V2#1-3, 5-10	.50	1.00	1.50
V2#4-Krigstein story	1.50	3.00	4.00
V3#1-8	.50	1.00	1.50

NOTE: *Krigstein story-V1#5, V2#1,4,7. Powell story-#11.*

CRIME DETECTOR
Jan, 1954 - #5, Sept, 1954
Timor Publications

	Good	Fine	Mint
#1	1.00	2.00	3.00
2-4	.75	1.50	2.25
5-Disbrow story	1.20	2.40	3.60

CRIME DOES NOT PAY (Silver Streak #1-21)
#22, 6/42 - #147, 7/55   (1st Crime Comic)
Comic House/Lev Gleason/Golfing

#22-Origin The War Eagle & only app.; Chip
   Gardner begins; #22 rebound in True Crime,

	Good	Fine	Mint
Complete Book of			
(Scarce)	35.00	70.00	105.00
23 (Scarce)	20.00	40.00	60.00
24-Intro. & 1st app. Mr. Crime			
(Scarce)	15.00	30.00	45.00
25-30	10.00	20.00	30.00
31-40	5.00	10.00	15.00
41-70	2.00	4.00	6.00
71-100: #87-Chip Gardner begins, ends #99,			
102	1.00	2.00	3.00
101-105,107	.80	1.60	2.40
106,114-Frazetta, 1 pg.	1.50	3.00	4.50
108-113,115-130	.65	1.35	2.00
131-140,144-147	.65	1.35	2.00
141-143-One Kubert story in each			
	1.50	3.00	4.50
#1(Golfing-'45)	1.00	2.00	3.00
The Best of--(1944)128pgs. Series contains			
4 rebound issues	12.00	24.00	36.00
1945 issue	10.00	20.00	30.00
1946-48 issues	8.00	16.00	24.00
1949,'50 issues	6.00	12.00	18.00
1951-53 issues	5.00	10.00	15.00

NOTE: *Kubert cover-#143. McWilliams story-#91,93,95,102. Whodunnit by Guardineer-#40-104; Chip Gardner by Bob Fujitani (Fuje)-#88-103.*

CRIME EXPOSED
June, 1948; Dec, 1950 - #14, June, 1952
Marvel/Atlas Comics(PrPI/PPI)

	Good	Fine	Mint
#1(6/48)	1.50	3.00	4.50
1(12/50)	1.00	2.00	3.00
2-11,14	.65	1.35	2.00
12,13-Krigstein stories	1.50	3.00	4.50

CRIMEFIGHTERS
April, 1948 - #10, Nov, 1949
Marvel Comics (CmPS/CCC #4-10)

	Good	Fine	Mint
#1	1.00	2.00	3.00
2-10	.65	1.35	2.00

CRIME FIGHTERS (-- Always Win)
#11, Sept, 1954 - #13, Jan, 1955
Atlas Comics (CnPC)

	Good	Fine	Mint
#11-13	.60	1.20	1.80

CRIME FIGHTING DETECTIVE (Shock Det. Cases
1950 - #19, June, 1952   #20 on)
Star Publishing Co.

	Good	Fine	Mint
#11-19: #17-Young King Cole & Dr. Doom app.			
	.65	1.35	2.00

CRIME FILES
#5, Sept, 1952 - #6, Nov, 1952
Standard Comics

	Good	Fine	Mint
#5,6-Alex Toth art	2.00	4.00	6.00

CRIME ILLUSTRATED (Magazine)
Nov-Dec, 1955 - #2, Spring, 1956
E.C. Comics

	Good	Fine	Mint
#1-Ingels & Crandall art	6.00	12.00	18.00
2- " " " "	5.00	10.00	15.00

NOTE: *Craig story-#2. Crandall stories-#1,2; cover-#2. Evans story-#1. Davis story-#2. Ingels stories-#1,2. Krigstein/Crandall story-#1. Orlando stories-#1,2; cover-#1.*

CRIME INCORPORATED
1950 - #2, Aug, 1950; #3, Aug, 1951
Fox Features Syndicate

No#(1950)-132pgs. - See Fox Giants. Contents can vary and determines price.

#2,3	1.70	3.35	5.00

CRIME MACHINE (Magazine)
Feb, 1971 - #2, May, 1971
Skywald Publications

#1-Two Kubert stories reprint (Avon)			
	1.00	2.00	3.00
2	.65	1.35	2.00

CRIME MUST LOSE!
#4, Oct, 1950 - #12, April, 1952
Sports Action (Atlas Comics)

#4-12	.65	1.35	2.00

CRIME MUST PAY THE PENALTY
1948 - #48, Jan, 1957; 1956 - 1957
Ace Magazines (Current Books)

#33(2/48-Ace Mag.)	1.75	3.35	5.00
#1(1948)	1.75	3.35	5.00
2-10	1.00	2.00	3.00
11-20	.65	1.35	2.00
21-48	.50	1.00	1.50
#1(1955)	.65	1.35	2.00
2-12	.35	.70	1.05

CRIME MUST STOP
October, 1952
Hillman Periodicals

V1#1	.65	1.35	2.00

CRIME MYSTERIES (Secret Mysteries #16 on)
May, 1952 - #15, Sept, 1954
Ribage Publishing Corp. (Trojan Magazines)

	Good	Fine	Mint
#1	1.35	2.75	4.00
2-Marijuana story(7/52)	4.00	8.00	12.00
3,4-One pg. Frazetta	1.50	3.00	4.50
5-15: #13-Woodbridge art	.80	1.60	2.40

CRIME ON THE RUN
1949; June, 1954
St. John Publishing Co./Approved Comics

#8(1949)	.65	1.35	2.00
#8(Reprint-1954)	.35	.70	1.05

CRIME ON THE WATERFRONT (Formerly Famous
#4, May, 1952   Gangsters)
Realistic Publications

#4	1.50	3.00	4.50

CRIME PATROL (International #1-5; International Crime Patrol #6, becomes Crypt of Terror #17 on)
#7, Summer, 1948 - #16, Feb-Mar, 1950
E.C. Comics

#7-14: Ingels art #12	15.00	30.00	45.00
15-Intro. of Crypt Keeper & Crypt of Terror	40.00	80.00	120.00
16-2nd Crypt Keeper app.	30.00	60.00	90.00

CRIME PHOTOGRAPHER (See Casey --)

CRIME REPORTER
Aug, 1948 - #3, Dec, 1948 (Shows Oct.)
St. John Publ. Co.

#1	3.00	6.00	9.00
2-Used in Seduction of the Innocent: "The Children Told Me What the Man Was Going To Do With the Hot Poker" illustration; Baker cover; Tuska story			
	5.00	10.00	15.00
3-Baker cover; Tuska sty.	3.00	6.00	9.00

CRIMES BY WOMEN
June, 1948 - #15, 1949; 1954
Fox Features Syndicate

#1	5.00	10.00	15.00
2-15	3.00	6.00	9.00
#54(M.S.Publ.,'54)-Reprint(formerly My Love Secret)	2.00	4.00	6.00

CRIME SMASHER
Summer, 1948   (One Shot)
Fawcett Publications

Crime Patrol #7, © WMG

Crime Reporter #2, © STJ

Crimes By Women #3, © Fox

Crime SuspenStories #14, © WMG   Crime SuspenStories #23, © WMG   Crusader From Mars #2, © Z-D

	Good	Fine	Mint
(Crime Smasher cont'd)			
#1 (Spy Smasher)	2.50	5.00	7.50

CRIME SMASHERS (Secret Mysteries #16 on)
Oct, 1950 - #15, Sept, 1954
Ribage Publishing Corp.(Trojan Magazines)

	Good	Fine	Mint
#1-Used in Seduction of the Innocent; Sally			
the Sleuth	4.00	8.00	12.00
2-Kubert cover	2.50	5.00	7.50
3-7,9-12,14,15	1.50	3.00	4.50
8-Cocaine drug story	2.50	5.00	7.50
13-One pg. Frazetta	2.00	4.00	6.00

NOTE: Combined with Crime Mysteries with #7;
#8-15 exist?

CRIME SUSPENSTORIES (Formerly Vault of Horror
#15, 10-11/50 - #27, 2-3/55   #12-14)
E.C. Comics

#15   identical to No. 1 in content; No. 1 printed on outside front cover. No. 15 (formerly "The Vault of Horror") printed and blackened out on inside front cover with Vol. 1, No. 1 printed over it. Evidently, several of No. 15 were printed before a decision was made not to drop the V. O. H. & Haunt of Fear series. The print run was stopped on No. 15 and continued on No. 1. All of No. 15 were changed as described above.

	Good	Fine	Mint
	50.00	100.00	150.00
#1	40.00	80.00	120.00
2	25.00	50.00	75.00
3-5	20.00	40.00	60.00
6-10	12.00	24.00	36.00
11,12,14,15	9.00	18.00	27.00
13,16-Williamson art	15.00	30.00	45.00
17-Williamson/Frazetta story, 6pgs.			
	17.50	35.00	52.50
18,19	8.00	16.00	24.00
20-Cover used in Seduction of the Innocent			
	10.00	20.00	30.00
21,23-27	7.00	14.00	21.00
22-Used in Senate investigation on juvenile			
delinquency	8.00	16.00	24.00

NOTE: Craig stories-#1-21; covers-#1-18,20-22. Crandall stories-#18-26. Davis stories-#4,5, 7,9-12,20. Elder stories-#17,18. Evans stories-#15,19,21,23,25,27; covers-#23,24. Feldstein cover-#19. Ingels stories-#1-12,14,15, 27. Kamen stories-#2,4-18,20-27; covers-#25-27. Krigstein stories-#22,24,25,27. Kurtzman stories-#1,3. Orlando stories-#16,22,24,26. Wood stories-#1,3. Issues 11-15 have E.C. "quickie" stories. #25 contains the famous "Are You a Red Dupe?" editorial.

CRIMINALS ON THE RUN (Formerly Young King
8-9/48 - V5#2, 10-11/49   Cole)
Premium Group (Novelty Press)

	Good	Fine	Mint
V4#1-15: #6-Young King Cole & Dr. Doom app.;			
McWilliams art	1.00	2.00	3.00
V5#1,2	.65	1.35	2.00

CROSS AND THE SWITCHBLADE, THE
1972   (35¢) (Religious)
Spire Christian Comics/Fleming H. Revell Co.

	Good	Fine	Mint
No#	.20	.40	.60

CROSSING THE ROCKIES (See Classics Special)

CROWN COMICS
Winter, 1944 - #19, Winter, 1949
Golfing/McCombs Publ.

	Good	Fine	Mint
#1-"The Oblong Box" story	2.50	5.00	7.50
2,3	1.50	3.00	4.50
4-6,8-Voodah app.	3.00	6.00	9.00
7-Feldstein story	4.00	8.00	12.00
9-12,14-19: Voodah in #10-15			
	1.50	3.00	4.50
13-Leonard Starr/Bolle stories			
	2.00	4.00	6.00

CRUSADER FROM MARS (See Tops in Adventure)
Jan-Mar, 1952 - #2, Fall, 1952
Ziff-Davis Publ. Co.

	Good	Fine	Mint
#1	4.00	8.00	12.00
2	3.00	6.00	9.00

CRUSADER RABBIT (See 4-Color #735,805)

CRUSADERS, THE
1974 - Present (36 pgs.) (39¢) (Religious)
Chick Publications

Vol. 1-Operation Bucharest('74). Vol.2-The
  Broken Cross('74). Vol.3-Scarface('74).
    Vol.4-Exorcists('75). Vol.5-Chaos('75).
      each....   .20   .40   .60

CRYIN' LION, THE
Fall, 1944 - #3, Spring, 1945
William H. Wise

#1-3	.65	1.35	2.00

CRYPT OF SHADOWS
Jan, 1973 - #21, Nov, 1975
Marvel Comics Group

	Good	Fine	Mint
#1-Wolverton reprint/Advs. Into Terror #7			
	.30	.65	1.00
2-10	.20	.40	.60
11-21		.15	.30

(Crypt of Shadows cont'd)
NOTE: *Briefer story-#2. Everett story-#6,14 (reprt./Mystery Tales #3). Moldoff story-#8. Powell reprint-#12(uncanny Tales #38),#14(Mystery #4).*

CRYPT OF TERROR (Tales From the Crypt #20 on; formerly Crime Patrol)
#17, Apr-May, 1950 - #19, Aug-Sept, 1950
E.C. Comics

	Good	Fine	Mint
#17	65.00	130.00	195.00
18,19	45.00	90.00	135.00

NOTE: *Craig stories/covers-#17-19. Feldstein stories-#17-19. Ingels story-#19. Kurtzman story-#18. Wood story-#18. Canadian reprints known; see Table of Contents.*

CUPID
Jan, 1950 - #2, Mar, 1950
Marvel Comics (U.S.A)

#1,2	1.00	2.00	3.00

CURIO
1930's (?) (Tabloid size, 16-20 pgs.)
Harry 'A' Chesler

	7.00	14.00	21.00

CURLY KAYOE COMICS
1946 - 1948; 1948 - 1950
United Features Syndicate/Dell Publ. Co.

#1(1946)	2.00	4.00	6.00
2-8	1.00	2.00	3.00
#1(1948)	1.50	3.00	4.50
2-7	1.00	2.00	3.00
4-Color #871(Dell)	1.00	2.00	3.00
United Presents--(Fall, 1948)			
	1.35	2.75	4.00

CUSTER'S LAST FIGHT
1950
Avon Periodicals

No#-Partial reprint of Cowpuncher #1			
	2.00	4.00	6.00

CUTIE PIE
May, 1955 - #5, Aug, 1956
Junior Reader's Guild/Lev Gleason

#1	.65	1.35	2.00
2-5	.35	.70	1.05

CYCLONE COMICS
June, 1940 - #5, Nov, 1940
Bilbara Publishing Co.

	Good	Fine	Mint
#1-Origin Tornado Tom; Volton begins, Mister Q app.	20.00	40.00	60.00
2	10.00	20.00	30.00
3-5	7.00	14.00	21.00

CYNTHIA DOYLE, NURSE IN LOVE
#66, Oct, 1962 - 1963
Charlton Publications

#66-73	.20	.40	.60

DAFFY (-- Duck #18 on)
1953 - Present
Dell Publishing Co./Gold Key #31 on

4-Color #457,536,615('55)	.80	1.60	2.40
#4-11(1956-'57)	.50	1.00	1.50
12-19(1958-'59)	.40	.80	1.20
20-40(1960-'64)	.25	.50	.75
41-60(1964-'68)	.20	.40	.60
61-90(1969-'73)	.15	.30	.45
91-112(1974-'77)		.15	.30

(See March of Comics #277,288,313,331,347, 357,375,387,397,402,413)

DAFFYDILS
1911 (52 pgs.) (6x8") (B&W) (Hardcover)
Cupples & Leon Co.

by Tad	6.00	12.00	18.00

DAFFY TUNES COMICS
June, 1947 - #2, Aug, 1947
Four Star Publications

No#, #2	.25	.50	.75

DAGAR, DESERT HAWK (Capt. Kidd #24; formerly
#14, 2/48 - #23, 4/49 (No#17,18) All Great)
Fox Features Syndicate

#14-Tangi & Safari Cary begin			
	9.00	18.00	27.00
15,16	8.00	16.00	24.00
19-23	7.00	14.00	21.00

NOTE: *Kamen cover-#21.*

DAGAR THE INVINCIBLE (Tales of Sword &
Oct, 1972 - #18, 12/76 Sorcery --)
Gold Key (See Dan Curtis)

#1-Origin; intro. Villains Ostellon & Scorpio	.65	1.35	2.00
2-5: #3-Intro. Graylin, Dagar's Woman; Jarn x-over	.40	.80	1.20
6-1st Dark Gods story	.30	.60	.90
7-10: #9-Intro. Torgus. #10-1st 3 Witches			

Crypt of Terror #17, © WMG

Curly Kayoe Comics #1, © UFS

Dagar, Desert Hawk #14, © Fox

Daisy Handbook #2, © Faw

Dale Evans #1, © DC

The Dalton Boys , © Avon

(Dagar the Invincible cont'd)

	Good	Fine	Mint
story	.30	.60	.90

11-18: #13-Durak & Torgus x-over; story continues in Dr. Spector #15. #14-Dagar's origin retold. #18-Origin retold

	.20	.40	.60

NOTE: *Durak app.-#7,12,13. Tragg app.-#5,11.*

DAGWOOD (Chic Young's)
Sept, 1950 - #140, Nov, 1965
Harvey Publications

#1	3.00	6.00	9.00
2-10	1.50	3.00	4.50
11-30: #30-1pg. Popeye	1.00	2.00	3.00
31-70	.60	1.20	1.80
71-100	.30	.60	.90
101-128,130,135,138	.20	.40	.60
129,131-134,136,137,139,140-All are 68 pg. issues	.25	.50	.75

DAGWOOD SPLITS THE ATOM
1949 (Science comic with King Features characters) (Giveaway)
King Features Syndicate

No#	2.00	4.00	6.00

DAISY AND DONALD (See W. D. Showcase #8)
May, 1973 - Present
Gold Key

#1-Barks reprint from WDC&S #308			
	.20	.40	.60
2,3,5	.15	.30	.45
4-Barks reprt/WDC&S #224	.20	.40	.60
6-10	.15	.30	.45
11-27		.15	.30

DAISY & HER PUPS (Blondie's Dogs)
#21, 7/51 - #27, 7/52; #8, 9/52 - #25, 7/55
Harvey Publications

#21-27: #26,27 have #6 & 7 on cover by #26 & 27 on inside	.65	1.35	2.00
#8-25	.40	.80	1.20

DAISY COMICS
Dec, 1936 (Small size: 5¼x7½")
Eastern Color Printing Co.

Joe Palooka, Buck Rogers (2pgs. from Famous Funnies #18), Napoleon Flying To Fame, Butty & Fally	20.00	40.00	60.00

DAISY DUCK & UNCLE SCROOGE PICNIC TIME
(See Dell Giant #33)

DAISY DUCK & UNCLE SCROOGE SHOW BOAT
(See Dell Giant #55)

DAISY DUCK'S DIARY (See 4-Color #600,659, 743,858,948,1055,1150,1247)

DAISY HANDBOOK
1946 - 1948 (132 pgs.)(50¢)(Pocket-size)
Daisy Manufacturing Co.

	Good	Fine	Mint
#1-Buck Rogers, Red Ryder	15.00	30.00	45.00
2-Captain Marvel & Ibis the Invincible, Boy Commandos, & Robotman; 2 pgs. Wolverton art	15.00	30.00	45.00

DAISY IS RED RYDER GUN BOOK
1955 (132 pgs.)(25¢)(Pocket Size)
Daisy Manufacturing Co.

Boy Commandos, Red Ryder, 1 pg. Wolverton art	10.00	20.00	30.00

DAISY MAE (See Oxydol-Dreft)

DAKOTA LIL (See Fawcett Movie Comics)

DAKTARI (Ivan Tors) (TV)
July, 1967 - #4, 1969
Dell Publishing Co.

#1	.20	.40	.60
2-4	.15	.30	.45

DALE EVANS (See Queen of the West --)

DALE EVANS COMICS
Sept-Oct, 1948 - #24, July-Aug, 1952
National Periodical Publications

#1-Sierra Smith begins by Alex Toth			
	5.00	10.00	15.00
2-11-Alex Toth art	2.50	5.00	7.50
12-24	1.50	3.00	4.50

DALTON BOYS, THE
1951
Avon Periodicals

No#-Kinstler cover	3.00	6.00	9.00

DAN CURTIS GIVEAWAYS
1974 (24 pgs.) (3x6") (In Color)
Dan Curtis Productions

#1-Dark Shadows, #2-Star Trek, #3-The Twilight Zone, #4-Ripley's Believe It Or Not! True Ghost Stories, #5-Turok, Son of Stone, #6-

(Dan Curtis cont'd)   Good Fine Mint
Star Trek, #7-The Occult Files of Dr. Spektor,
#8-Dagar the Invincible, #9-Grimm's Ghost
Stories   Set....   2.00   4.00   6.00

DANDEE
1947
Four Star Publications

                       .50   1.00   1.50

DAN DUNN (See Super Book (No#), & Detective
Dan)

DAN DUNN & GANGSTER'S FRAME-UP
1937   (68 pgs.)(5½x7½")(B&W)(Hardcover)
Whitman Publishing Co.

Reprints   4.00   8.00 12.00

DANDY COMICS (Also see Happy Jack Howard)
Spring, 1947 - #7, Spring, 1948
E.C. Comics

#1   12.00 24.00 36.00
2-7   8.00 16.00 24.00

DANGER
January, 1953 - #12, 1955
Comic Media/Allen Hardy Assoc.

#1-Heck art   1.35   2.75   4.00
2-10   1.00   2.00   3.00
11,12   .65   1.35   2.00

DANGER
#12, June, 1955 - #14, Nov, 1955
Charlton Comics

#12(#1)-Nyoka begins 1.75   3.35   5.00
13,14   1.25   2.50   3.75

DANGER
1964
Super Comics

Super Reprint #10-12:(Black Dwarf; #11-re-
  prints from Johnny Danger),#15,16(Yankee
  Girl & Johnny Rebel),#17(Capt. Courage &
  Enchanted Daggar),#18(no date)(Gun-Master,
  Annie Oakley, The Chameleon)
                 .75   1.50   2.25

DANGER AND ADVENTURE (Formerly Danger)
#15, Feb, 1955 - #27, Feb, 1956
Charlton Comics

#15-No Nyoka   .50   1.00   1.50

                       Good Fine Mint
16-21   .65   1.35   2.00
22-Ibis the Invincible app.
           1.35   2.75   4.00
23-Lance O'Casey app. .65   1.35   2.00
24-27   .40   .80   1.20

DANGER IS OUR BUSINESS!
Dec, 1953 - #10, June, 1955
Toby Press

#1-Williamson/Frazetta story, 6pgs. (Science
  Fiction)   10.00 20.00 30.00
2-10   .80   1.60   2.40
I.W. Reprint #9('64)-Williamson/Frazetta
  story reprint from #1; Kinstler cover
            5.00 10.00 15.00

DANGER IS THEIR BUSINESS (See A-1 Comics #50)

DANGER MAN (See 4-Color Comics #1231)

DANGER TRAIL
July-Aug, 1950 - #5, Mar-Apr, 1951
National Periodical Publications

#1-King Farraday begins, ends #4
            6.00 12.00 18.00
2-5-Toth art in all; Johnny Peril app. #5
            3.00   6.00   9.00

DANIEL BOONE (See The Exploits of --, 4-
Color #1163, The Legends of --, Frontier Scout
--, Fighting --, & March of Comics #306)

DAN'L BOONE
Sept, 1955 - #8, Sept, 1957
Magazine Enterprises/Sussex Publ. Co. #2 on

#1   1.35   2.75   4.00
2-8   .80   1.60   2.40

DANIEL BOONE (TV)(See March of Comics #306)
Jan, 1965 - #15, Apr, 1969
Gold Key

#1('64) (TV)   .50   1.00   1.50
2-15   .25   .50   .75

DANNY BLAZE
Aug, 1955 - #2, Oct, 1955
Charlton Comics

#1,2   1.00   2.00   3.00

DANNY DINGLE (See Single Series #17)

Dandy #1, © WMG

Danger Trail #1, © DC

Dan'l Boone #5, © Sussex

Daredevil #10, © MCG

Daredevil Comics #15, © Lev

Daredevil Comics #108, © Lev

DANNY KAYE'S BAND FUN BOOK
1959
H & A Selmer   (Giveaway)

	Good	Fine	Mint
	1.00	2.00	3.00

DANNY THOMAS SHOW, THE (See 4-Color#1180,1249)

DARBY O'GILL & THE LITTLE PEOPLE (See
4-Color #1024 & Movie Comics)

DAREDEVIL (--& the Black Widow #92-107)
April, 1964 - Present
Marvel Comics Group

	Good	Fine	Mint
#1-Origin D.D	15.00	30.00	45.00
2-F.F. cameo	7.00	14.00	21.00
3-Origin, 1st app. The Owl			
	5.00	10.00	15.00
4,5: #4-dons new costume	3.35	6.75	10.00
6-10: #7-dons new costume	.75	3.35	5.00
11-20: #12-Facts about Ka-Zar's origin;			
Kirby art	1.00	2.00	3.00
21-30	.50	1.00	1.50
31-40	.40	.80	1.20
41-49	.35	.70	1.05
50-52-Smith art	.65	1.35	2.00
53-Origin retold	.35	.70	1.05
54-60	.30	.60	.90
61-80	.25	.50	.75
81-90: #81-Black Widow begins. #83-Smith			
layouts	.25	.50	.75
91-113,115-120	.20	.40	.60
114-1st app. Deathstalker	.25	.50	.75
121-140	.15	.30	.45
141-150		.15	.30
Giant Size #1('75)	.35	.70	1.05
Special #1(9/67)-new art	.80	1.60	2.40
Special #2(2/71)(Wood reprint), #3(1/72)-			
reprints	.40	.80	1.20
Annual #4(10/76)	.30	.60	.90

NOTE: *Buscema stories-#136,137; cover-#142.
Craig inks-#50,52. Everett story & cover-#1,
inks-#21,81,83. Kirby covers-#2-4,5(w/Wood);
layouts-#13. Orlando stories-#2-4. Powell
pencils-#11. Wood stories-#6-10; inks-#11;
covers-#5-11.*

DAREDEVIL COMICS (See Silver Streak)
7/41 - #134, 9/56 (Charles Biro stories)
Lev Gleason Publications
    (#1 titled "Daredevil Battles Hitler")

#1-The Silver Streak, Lance Hale, Dickey
Dean, Pirate Prince & Cloud Curtis team
up with Daredevil and battle Hitler;
Daredevil battles the Claw
                225.00 450.00 675.00

	Good	Fine	Mint
2-London, Pat Patriot, Nightro, Real Amer-			
ican #1, Dickie Dean, Pirate Prince,			
& Times Square begin; intro. & only app.			
The Pioneer, Champion of America			
	100.00	200.00	300.00
3-Origin of 13	60.00	120.00	180.00
4	50.00	100.00	150.00
5-Intro. Sniffer & Jinx; Ghost vs. Claw be-			
gins by Bob Wood	40.00	80.00	120.00
6-10	30.00	60.00	90.00
11	23.50	47.00	70.00
12-Origin of The Claw; Scoop Scuttle by			
Wolverton begins(2-4pgs.), ends #22, not			
in #21	35.00	70.00	105.00
13-Intro. of Little Wise Guys			
	35.00	70.00	105.00
14	17.50	35.00	52.50
15-Death of Meatball	20.00	40.00	60.00
16,17	15.00	30.00	45.00
18-New origin of Daredevil-Not same as Sil-			
ver Streak #6	25.00	50.00	75.00
19,20	12.00	24.00	36.00
21-Reprints cover of Silver Streak #6(on in-			
side) + intro. of The Claw from Silver			
Streak #1	10.00	20.00	30.00
22-30	6.00	12.00	18.00
31-Death of The Claw	9.00	18.00	27.00
32-37	4.00	8.00	12.00
38-Origin of Daredevil retold from #18			
	6.00	12.00	18.00
39,40	4.00	8.00	12.00
41-50: #42-Intro. Kilroy in D.D.			
	3.00	6.00	9.00
51-69-Last Daredevil ish.	2.00	4.00	6.00
70-Little Wise Guys take over book; McWill-			
iams art; Hot Rock Flanagan begins, ends			
#80	1.35	2.75	4.00
71-79,81: #79-Daredevil returns			
	1.35	2.75	4.00
80-Daredevil x-over	1.35	2.75	4.00
82,90-One pg. Frazetta ad in both			
	1.75	3.35	5.00
83-89	1.20	2.40	3.60
91-100	1.00	2.00	3.00
101-134	1.00	2.00	3.00

NOTE: *Wolverton's Scoop Scuttle-#12-20,22.
Bolle art-#125. McWilliams art-#73,75,79.*

DARING ADVENTURES
May, 1954 - 1956
St. John Publishing Co.

	Good	Fine	Mint
#6-Krigstein story	1.75	3.35	5.00
7-10	1.00	2.00	3.00
11-18	.65	1.35	2.00
3-D #1(11/53)-Kubert art	5.00	10.00	15.00

DARING ADVENTURES
1963 - 1964
I.W. Enterprises/Super Comics

	Good	Fine	Mint
Super Reprint #9,10,11('63)-Dynamic Man			
	1.00	2.00	3.00
Super Reprint #12,15('64)-Phantom Lady from Fox(reprints #14,15); #15-Hooded Menace			
	4.00	8.00	12.00
Super Reprint #16('64)-Mr. E, Dynamic Man			
	1.00	2.00	3.00
Super Reprint #17('64)-Green Lama by Raboy from Green Lama #3	1.50	3.00	4.50
Super Reprint #18-Origin Atlas			
	1.00	2.00	3.00

DARING COMICS (Formerly Daring Mystery)
#9, Fall/44 - #12, Fall/45 (Jeanie #13 on)
Timely Comics

#9-Human Torch & Sub-Mariner begin			
	17.50	35.00	52.50
10-The Angel only app.	15.00	30.00	45.00
11,12-The Destroyer app.	15.00	30.00	45.00

DARING CONFESSIONS (Formerly Youthful Hearts)
#4, 1952 - #7, May, 1953
Youthful Magazines

#4-Doug Wildey art	.65	1.35	2.00
5-7: #6-Wildey art	.40	.80	1.20

DARING LOVE (Radiant Love #2 on)
Sept-Oct, 1953
Gillmore Magazines

#1	1.35	2.75	4.00

DARING LOVE (Formerly Youthful Romances)
#15, Dec, 1952
Ribage/Pix

#15	.50	1.00	1.50

DARING MYSTERY COMICS (Comedy #9 on; title changed to Daring with #9)
Jan, 1940 - #8, Jan, 1942
Timely Comics

#1-Origin The Fiery Mask by Joe Simon; Monako, Prince of Magic, John Steele, Soldier of Fortune, Doc Doyle begin; Flash Foster & Barney Mullen, Sea Rover only app.   300.00 600.00 900.00
 2-Origin The Phantom Bullet & only app.; The Laughing Mask & Mr. E only app.; Trojak the Tiger Man begins, ends #6; Zephyr Jones & K-4 & His Sky Devils app., also

	Good	Fine	Mint
#4	160.00	320.00	480.00

3-The Phantom Reporter, Dale of FBI, Breeze Barton, Captain Strong & Marvex, the Super-Robot only app.; The Purple Mask begins   105.00 210.00 315.00
4-Last Purple Mask; Whirlwind Carter begins; Dan Gorman, G-Man app.90.00 180.00 270.00
5-The Falcon begins; The Fiery Mask, Little Hercules app. by Sagendorf in the Segar style   80.00 160.00 240.00
6-Origin of Marvel Boy by S&K & only app.; Flying Flame, Dynaman, & Stuporman only app.; The Fiery Mask by S&K; S&K cover   95.00 190.00 285.00
7-Origin The Blue Diamond, Captain Daring by S&K, The Challenger, The Fin by Everett, The Silver Scorpion & The Thunderer by Burgos; Mr. Millions app.   100.00 200.00 300.00
8-Origin Citizen V; Last Fin, Silver Scorpion, Capt. Daring by Borth, Blue Diamond & The Thunderer; S&K cover; Rudy the Robot only app.   70.00 140.00 210.00
NOTE: *Simon art-#2,3.*

DARK MANSION OF FORBIDDEN LOVE, THE (Becomes Forbidden Tales of Dark Mansion #5 on)
Sept-Oct, 1971 - #4, Mar-Apr, 1972
National Periodical Publications

#1	.40	.80	1.20
2-Adams cover	.50	1.00	1.50
3-Jeff Jones cover	.50	1.00	1.50
4	.25	.50	.75

DARK MYSTERIES
June-July, 1951 - #30, 1955
"Master"-"Merit" Publications

#1-Wood cover/story,8pgs.	6.00	12.00	18.00
2-Wood cover/story w/Harrison, 8pgs.			
	5.00	10.00	15.00
3-10	.80	1.60	2.40
11-30	.60	1.20	1.80

DARK SHADOWS
October, 1957 - 1958
Steinway Comic Publications (Ajax)

#1	.65	1.35	2.00
2,3	.30	.65	1.00

DARK SHADOWS (TV) (See Dan Curtis)
May, 1969 - #35, Feb, 1976
Gold Key

#1(30039-903)-with pull-out poster

Daring Adventures #11, © Super

Daring Mystery #3, © MCG

Dark Mysteries #2, © Master Publ.

Darling Love #1, © AP

A Date With Judy #6, © DC

A Date With Patsy #1, © MCG

(Dark Shadows cont'd)	Good	Fine	Mint
	.40	.80	1.20
2-5: #3-with pull-out poster; #4-photo			
cover	.25	.50	.75
6-10	.20	.40	.60
11-20	.15	.30	.45
21-35		.15	.30
Story Digest #1(6/70)	.25	.50	.75

DARLING LOVE
Oct-Nov, 1949 - #11, 1952 (no month)
Close Up/Archie Publ.(A Darling Magazine)

#1	1.50	3.00	4.50
2-8,10,11	1.00	2.00	3.00
9-Krigstein story	1.75	3.35	5.00

DARLING ROMANCE
Sept-Oct, 1949 - #7, 1951
Close Up (MLJ Publications)

#1	1.50	3.00	4.50
2-7	1.00	2.00	3.00

DASTARDLY & MUTTLEY IN THEIR FLYING MACHINES
(See Fun-In #1-4,6)

DASTARDLY & MUTTLEY KITE FUN BOOK (Giveaway)
1969 (16pgs.;5x7") (Hanna-Barbera's)
Florida Power & Light Co./Sou. Calif. Edison/
Pacific Gas & Electric

	.15	.30	.45

DATE WITH DANGER
#5, 1952 - #6, 1953
Standard Comics

#5,6	.65	1.35	2.00

DATE WITH DEBBI
Jan-Feb, 1969 - #17, Sept-Oct, 1971
National Periodical Publications

#1	.20	.40	.60
2-17	.15	.30	.45

DATE WITH JUDY, A (Radio/TV)
Oct-Nov, 1947 - #79, Oct-Nov, 1960
National Periodical Publications

#1	2.00	4.00	6.00
2-10	1.00	2.00	3.00
11-20	.50	1.00	1.50
21-40	.40	.80	1.20
41-79	.35	.70	1.05

DATE WITH MILLIE, A
Aug, 1956 - #35, 1964
Atlas/Marvel Comics (MPC)

	Good	Fine	Mint
#1	1.35	2.75	4.00
2-10	.65	1.35	2.00
11-20	.30	.65	1.00
21-35	.15	.30	.45

DATE WITH PATSY, A
Sept, 1957
Atlas Comics

#1	.75	1.50	2.25

DAVID AND GOLIATH (See 4-Color #1205)

DAVID CASSIDY
Feb, 1972 - #13, 1973
Charlton Comics

#1	.25	.50	.75
2-13	.15	.30	.45

DAVID LADD'S LIFE STORY (See Movie Classics)

DAVY CROCKETT (See Fighting --, Frontier
Fighters, It's Game Time, & Western Tales)

DAVY CROCKETT (Frontier Fighter --)
1951
Avon Periodicals

No#	2.00	4.00	6.00

DAVY CROCKETT (TV)
May, 1955 - #2, Nov, 1969 (Walt Disney)
Dell Publishing Co./Gold Key

4-Color #631,639	1.35	2.75	4.00
4-Color #664,671(Marsh art)			
	1.50	3.00	4.50
Annual #1('55-25¢-Marsh art-100pgs.)			
	2.50	5.00	7.50
#1(9/63-Gold Key)	.35	.70	1.05
2	.20	.40	.60

DAVY CROCKETT FRONTIER FIGHTER
Aug, 1955 - #8, 1957
Charlton Comics

#1	.80	1.60	2.40
2-8	.50	1.00	1.50
Hunting With --('55, 16pgs.)-Ben Franklin			
Store giveaway(Publ.-S. Rose)			
	.80	1.60	2.40

DAVY CROCKETT IN THE RAID AT PINEY CREEK
1955 (16pgs.)(5x7½")(Premium)(Walt Disney)
Hudson Div. of American Motors

	1.75	3.35	5.00

DAYS OF THE MOB (See In the Days of the Mob)

DAZEY'S DIARY
June-Aug, 1962
Dell Publishing Co.

	Good	Fine	Mint
#01-174-208	.15	.30	.45

DC 100 PG. SUPER SPECTACULAR (50¢)(No #1-3)
1971 - #13, 6/72; #14, 2/73 - #22, 11/73
National Periodical Publications

#4-Weird Mystery Tales-Johnny Peril & Phantom
   Stranger; cover & chapter headings by
   Wrightson; origin Jungle Boy of Jupiter
   | | .65 | 1.35 | 2.00 |
5-Love stories .35 .70 1.05
6-"World's Greatest Super-Heroes"-JLA, JSA,
   Spectre, Johnny Quick, Vigilante, Wildcat
   & Hawkman; Adams wrap-around cover
   | | .65 | 1.35 | 2.00 |
7-Superman #245-Air Wave, Kid Eternity reprints .50 1.00 1.50
8-Batman #238; Adams cover; Atom, Sargon,
   Plastic Man reprints .50 1.00 1.50
9-Our Army at War #242(Sgt. Rock)-Kubert
   cover .50 1.00 1.50
10-Adventure #416(Supergirl)-Features
   "World's Greatest Super-Females", Supergirl, Black Canary, Wonder Woman, Merry
   Girl of 1000 Gimmicks, Phantom Lady(Police)
   .50 1.00 1.50
11-Flash #214-Flash, Quicksilver, Kid Flash,
   Johnny Quick, Flash(old), Metal Men
   .40 .80 1.20
12-Superboy #185-Superboy, Star-Spangled Kid,
   Teen Titans, Kid Eternity, Little Boy Blue,
   Legion of Super Heroes .40 .80 1.20
13-Superman #252-"World's Greatest Flying
   Heroes"-Dr. Fate, Hawkman, Black Condor
   (Crack #18), Spectre, Starman, The Ray
   (Smash #14); wrap-around Adams cover
   .50 1.00 1.50
14-Batman-(reprints Detective #31,32); Dollman, Wonder Woman, The Atom, Wildcat, &
   Blackhawk reprints .50 1.00 1.50
15-Superboy, Boy Commandos, Sandman, & Aquaman reprints; S&K art .40 .80 1.20
16-Sgt. Rock & Capt. Storm reprints
   .40 .80 1.20
17-JLA-Sandman & All-Star #37 reprint
   .40 .80 1.20
18-Superman, Hourman, Captain Triumph, The
   G.A. Atom reprint .40 .80 1.20
19-Tarzan newspaper reprints by Russ Manning
   .40 .80 1.20
20-Batman origin Two-Face; Dr. Mid-Nite,
   Starman, Black Canary, Blackhawk, The
   Spectre reprints .40 .80 1.20
21-Superboy reprints .40 .80 1.20
22-The Flash reprints .40 .80 1.20
NOTE: Anderson story-#11,22. Crandall art-#14.
Drucker reprint-#4. Grandenetti art-#1,16.
Infantino stories-#17,20,22. Kubert stories-
#6,7,16,17; covers-#16,19. Meskin art-#4,22.
Toth stories-#17,20.

DC SPECIAL (Also see Super DC --)
10-12/68 - #15, 11-12/71; #16, Spr/75 - #29,
National Periodical Publ.   8-9/77

#1-All Infantino ish; Flash, Batman, Adam
   Strange reprints .65 1.35 2.00
2-Teen Favorites .40 .80 1.20
3-All Heroine ish. Unpubbed G.A. Black Canary & Wonder Woman sty. .50 1.00 1.50

DC Special #4, © DC

	Good	Fine	Mint
4-Mystery Tales	.35	.70	1.05

5-All Kubert ish. Viking Prince, Sgt. Rock
   reprints .60 1.20 1.80
6-Wild Frontier .40 .80 1.20
7-Strange Sports Stories .35 .70 1.05
8-Wanted .40 .80 1.20
9-Strange Sports Stories .40 .80 1.20
10-Stop! In the Name of the Law; reprints/
   Showcase #1,5 .40 .80 1.20
11-The Monsters Are Here; Neal Adams cover;
   Two Kirby stories .40 .80 1.20
12-Viking Prince; Kubert cover; reprints from
   Brave & the Bold #1,5,9,16; new Kubert
   splashes .65 1.35 2.00
13-Strange Sports Stories .35 .70 1.05
14-Wanted .35 .70 1.05
15-G.A. Plastic Man origin reprint(Police#1)
   & origin Woozy by Cole .80 1.60 2.40
16-Super Heroes Battle Super Gorillas
   .35 .70 1.05
17-Green Lantern .35 .70 1.05
18-Earth Shaking Stories-Flash, Green Lantern, Captain Marvel .35 .70 1.05
19-War Against the Giants .35 .70 1.05
20-Green Lantern .35 .70 1.05
21-War Against the Monsters.25 .50 .75
22-25-The 3 Mustketeers(new) & Robin Hood
   (reprints) .25 .50 .75
26-Enemy Ace reprts/Kubert .25 .50 .75
27-Captain Comet .25 .50 .75
28-Earth Shattering Disaster Stories
   .25 .50 .75
29-Secret Origin of the Justice Society
   .25 .50 .75
NOTE: Adams covers-#3,4,6,11,29. Infantino
stories-#13. Kubert story-#22. Newton story-
#27. Staton story-#29. Toth story-#13.

DC SPECIAL SERIES
Sept, 1977 - Present
National Periodical Publ./DC Comics

#1-Five-Star Super-Hero Spectacular; Adams
   cover; Staton story .35 .70 1.05
2(#1)-Original Swamp Thing Saga, The(9-10/77)
   reprints Swamp Thing #1&2 by Wrightson;
   Wrightson wrap-around cover
   .35 .70 1.05
3(#2)-Sgt. Rock Special(10/77); Kubert
   cover .25 .50 .75
4(#1)-Unexpected Annual, The(10/77)
   .25 .50 .75
5(No#)-Superman Spectacular(11/77, 68pgs.)
   .25 .50 .75
6(No#)-Secret Society of Super-Villains
   Special(11/77) .25 .50 .75
7(No#)-Ghosts Special(12/77)
   .25 .50 .75

(DC Special Series cont'd)

	Good	Fine	Mint
8-Deadman & Sgt. Rock	.25	.50	.75

NOTE: # in () is cover #; the actual # of
#1-4 is on inside.

DC SUPER-STARS
March, 1976 - Present   (50¢)
National Periodical Publications

#1-Teen Titans	.25	.50	.75
2-Adam Strange, Hawkman	.25	.50	.75
3-Superman, Legion of Super-Heroes			
	.25	.50	.75
4-Adam Strange	.25	.50	.75
5-The Flash	.25	.50	.75
6-Adam Strange, Capt. Comet, Tommy Tomorrow,			
Space Cabby	.25	.50	.75
7-Aquaman	.25	.50	.75
8-Adam Strange, Star Rovers, Space Ranger			
	.25	.50	.75
9-Superman, Nighthawk	.25	.50	.75
10-Nine super-heroes & 9 super-villains			
	.25	.50	.75
11-Magic - Morrow cover	.25	.50	.75
12-Superboy	.25	.50	.75
13-Aragones cover/art	.25	.50	.75
14-Secret Origins of Super-Villains			
	.25	.50	.75
15-War Heroes-Kubert cover	.25	.50	.75
16-Star Hunters (1st appearance)-Newton sty/			
cover	.25	.50	.75
17-Secret Origins of Super-Heroes(1st app. &			
origin of The Huntress)-Staton story/cover,			
18-Deadman & The Phantom Stranger			
	.25	.50	.75

D-DAY (Also see Special War Series)
Summer, 1963 - #6, Nov, 1968
Charlton Comics

#1(1963)-Montes/Bache cvr	.20	.40	.60
2(Fall,'64)-3 Wood stories	.50	1.00	1.50
3-6('68)-Montes/Bache art #5			
	.15	.30	.45

DEAD END CRIME STORIES
April, 1949   (52 pgs.)
Kirby Publishing Co.

No#-Powell, Roussos art	1.50	3.00	4.50

DEAD EYE CRIME STORIES
1950
Hillman Periodicals

#1-Roussos art	.80	1.60	2.40

DEAD-EYE WESTERN COMICS
11-12/48 - 1949; #2, 10-11/50 - V3#1, 1952
Hillman Periodicals

	Good	Fine	Mint
V1#1(1948-52pgs.)-Krigstein story			
	2.00	4.00	6.00
No#(3-4/49,52pgs.)	1.00	2.00	3.00
V1#2-22	.80	1.60	2.40
V2#1-2,5-8,10-12	.65	1.35	2.00
3,4-Krigstein art	1.35	2.75	4.00
9-1pg. Frazetta ad	1.35	2.75	4.00
V3#1	.50	1.00	1.50

NOTE: _Kinstleresque_ stories by _McCann_-#12,
V2#1,2,V3#1.

DEADLY HANDS OF KUNG FU, THE
June, 1974 - #32, 2/77 (75¢)(Magazine-B&W)
Marvel Comics Group

#1-Origin Sons of the Tiger; Shang-Chi, Mast-			
er of Kung Fu begins; Bruce Lee photo			
pin-up	1.25	2.50	3.75
2-5	.65	1.35	2.00
6-15	.50	1.00	1.50
16-32	.40	.80	1.20
Special Album Edition #1(Summer, '74)			
	.50	1.00	1.50

NOTE: _Adams_ covers-#1,2-4,11,12,14,17.
Starlin stories-#1,2,15(reprint). _Staton_
stories-#31,32. _Sons of the Tiger_ in #1,3,4,
6-9.

DEAD OF NIGHT
Dec, 1973 - #11, Aug, 1975
Marvel Comics Group

#1-Reprints	.15	.30	.45
2-10: #9-Kirby reprint	.15	.30	
11-Intro. & 1st app. The Scarecrow; Kane/			
Wrightson cover	.15	.30	.45

DEAD WHO WALK, THE
1952
Realistic Comics

No#	2.50	5.00	7.50

DEADWOOD GULCH
1931   (52 pgs.) (B&W)
Dell Publishing Co.

By Gordon Rogers	5.00	10.00	15.00

DEAN MARTIN & JERRY LEWIS (See Adventures of--)

DEAR BEATRICE FAIRFAX
1950 - #9, Sept, 1951 (Vern Greene art)
Best/Standard Comics(King Features)

Dead Eye Western #1, © Hill

The Dead Who Walk #1, © Real

Dear Lonely Heart #1, © Artful

Dearly Beloved #1, © Z-D

Death Valley #1, © ME

The Defenders #1, © MCG

(Dear Beatrice Fairfax cont'd)

	Good	Fine	Mint
#1	1.50	3.00	4.50
2-9	1.00	2.00	3.00

NOTE: *Schomburg line cover-#5; painted cover-#6,7,9.*

DEAR HEART
1956
Ajax

#15	.50	1.00	1.50

DEAR LONELY HEART (-- Illustrated #1-6)
Mar, 1951; #3, 12/51 - #8, 10/52
Artful Publications

#1	.80	1.60	2.40
2-8	.50	1.00	1.50

DEAR LONELY HEARTS
#6, June, 1954 - #8, Oct, 1954
Harwell Publ./Mystery Publ. Co.

#6-8	.50	1.00	1.50

DEARLY BELOVED
Fall, 1952
Ziff-Davis Publishing Co.

#1	1.00	2.00	3.00

DEAR NANCY PARKER
June, 1963 - #2, Sept, 1963
Gold Key

#1,2	.15	.30	.45

DEATH VALLEY
Oct, 1953 - #9, 1955
Comic Media/Magazine Enterprises

#1-Old Scout	1.00	2.00	3.00
2-9	.50	1.00	1.50

DEBBIE DEAN, CAREER GIRL
April, 1945 - #2, 1945
Civil Service Publ.

#1,2-Newspaper reprints by Bert Whitman

	1.75	3.35	5.00

DEBBIE'S DATES
Apr-May, 1969 - #11, Dec-Jan, 1970-71
National Periodical Publications

#1-11: #4-Adams text illo.	.15	.30	.45

DEEP, THE (Movie)
November, 1977
Marvel Comics Group

	Good	Fine	Mint
#1-Infantino story/cover	.15	.30	.45

DEFENDERS, THE (TV)
Sept-Nov, 1962 - #2, Feb-Apr, 1963
Dell Publishing Co.

#12-176-211(#1), 304(#2)	.35	.70	1.05

DEFENDERS, THE (See Marvel Feature)

DEFENDERS, THE (Also see Marvel Feature)
Aug, 1972 - Present
Marvel Comics Group

#1-The Hulk, Doc Strange, & Sub-Mariner begin			
	2.50	5.00	7.50
2	1.20	2.40	3.60
3-5	1.00	2.00	3.00
6-10	.80	1.60	2.40

11-20: #11-X-Men, The Titan app. #13,14-Squadron Sinister app.; Sub-Mariner Leaves, Nighthawk joins. #15,16-Magneto app.; #17-19-Wrecking Crew app.

	.50	1.00	1.50
21-25,30	.35	.70	1.05

26-29-Guardians of the Galaxy app.

	.50	1.00	1.50
31,32-Origin Nighthawk	.25	.50	.75

33-40: #36-Intro. Red Guardian

	.25	.50	.75

41-50: #43-Kirby cover. #44-Hellcat joins. #45-Dr. Strange leaves. #47-Wonderman app.

	.20	.40	.60
51-55	.15	.30	.45

NOTE: *Kirby covers-#43-45. Silver Surfer in #2,3,6,8-11.*

Annual #1(11/76)	.40	.80	1.20
Annual #2(11/77)	.25	.50	.75

Giant Size #1(7/74)-Silver Surfer app.; Starlin art; Everett & Ditko reprint

	.75	1.50	2.25
Giant Size #2(10/74)	.40	.80	1.20
Giant Size #3-Starlin art	.50	1.00	1.50
Giant Size #4(4/75), #5(7/75)			
	.35	.70	1.05

DELECTA OF THE PLANETS (See Fawcett Miniatures & Don Fortune)

DELLA VISION
April, 1955 - #2, June, 1955
Atlas Comics

#1,2	1.50	3.00	4.50

DELL GIANT COMICS
#21, 9/59 - #55, 9/61 (Most 80 pgs., 25¢)
Dell Publishing Co.

	Good	Fine	Mint
#21-Tom & Jerry Picnic Time.	.80	1.60	2.40
22-Huey, Dewey & Louie Back To School(10/59)			
	1.00	2.00	3.00
23-Little Lulu & Tubby Halloween Fun			
	3.00	6.00	9.00
24-Woody Woodpecker Family Fun (11/59)			
	.80	1.60	2.40
25-Tarzan's Jungle World(11/59)-Marsh art			
	2.25	4.50	6.75
26-Christmas Parade-Barks art(Disney)			
	6.00	12.00	18.00
27-Man in Space-Reprints 4-Color #716,866, & 954(100pgs., 35¢)(Disney)			
	1.50	3.00	4.50
28-Bugs Bunny's Winter Fun (2/60)			
	1.00	2.00	3.00
29-Little Lulu & Tubby in Hawaii (4/60)			
	2.50	5.00	7.50
30-Disneyland USA(6/60)-Reprinted in Vacation in Disneyland	1.35	2.75	4.00
31-Huckleberry Hound Summer Fun (7/60)			
	.65	1.35	2.00
32-Bugs Bunny Beach Party			
	1.00	2.00	3.00
33-Daisy Duck & Uncle Scrooge Picnic Time (9/60)	2.00	4.00	6.00
34-Nancy & Sluggo Summer Camp (8/60)			
	.65	1.35	2.00
35-Huey, Dewey & Louie Back To School (10/60)	1.00	2.00	3.00
36-Little Lulu & Witch Hazel Halloween Fun (10/60)	2.00	4.00	6.00
37-Tarzan, King of the Jungle(11/60)-Marsh art	2.25	4.50	6.75
38-Uncle Donald & His Nephews Family Fun (11/60)	1.00	2.00	3.00
39-Walt Disney's Merry Christmas(12/60)-Not by Barks	1.20	2.40	3.60
40-Woody Woodpecker Christmas Parade(12/60)			
	.65	1.35	2.00
41-Yogi Bear's Winter Sports(12/60)			
	.65	1.35	2.00
42-Little Lulu & Tubby in Australia (1961)			
	2.00	4.00	6.00
43-Mighty Mouse in Outer Space (5/61)			
	1.35	2.75	4.00
44-Around the World with Huckleberry & His Friends (7/61)	.65	1.35	2.00
45-Nancy & Sluggo Summer Camp (8/61)			
	.80	1.60	2.40
46-Bugs Bunny Beach Party			
	1.75	3.35	5.00
47-Mickey & Donald in Vacationland (8/61)			
	1.50	3.00	4.50

	Good	Fine	Mint
48-The Flintstones (Bedrock Bedlam)(7/61)			
	.50	1.00	1.50
49-Huey, Dewey & Louie Back To School (9/61)	1.00	2.00	3.00
50-Little Lulu & Witch Hazel Trick 'N' Treat (10/61)	2.00	4.00	6.00
51-Tarzan, King of the Jungle by Jesse Marsh (11/61)	1.75	3.35	5.00
52-Uncle Donald & His Nephews Dude Ranch (11/61)	1.50	3.00	4.50
53-Donald Duck Merry Christmas-Not by Barks (12/61)	1.35	2.75	4.00
54-Woody Woodpecker Christmas Party(12/61) issued after #55	.65	1.35	2.00
55-Daisy Duck & Uncle Scrooge Showboat(9/61)			
	1.35	2.75	4.00

DELL JUNIOR TREASURY (15¢)
June, 1955 - #10, Oct, 1957
Dell Publishing Co.

	Good	Fine	Mint
#1-Alice in Wonderland-reprints 4-Color #331 (52 pgs.)	1.80	3.60	5.25
2-Aladdin & the Wonderful Lamp			
	1.35	2.75	4.00
3-Gulliver's Travels	1.35	2.75	4.00
4-Advs. of Mr. Frog & Miss Mouse			
	1.35	2.75	4.00
5-The Wizard of Oz	1.75	3.35	5.00
6-Heidi (10/56)	1.35	2.75	4.00
7-Santa & the Angel	1.35	2.75	4.00
8-Raggedy Ann & the Camel With the Wrinkled Knees	1.35	2.75	4.00
9-Clementina the Flying Pig			
	1.35	2.75	4.00
10-Advs. of Tom Sawyer	1.50	3.00	4.50

DEMON, THE
Aug-Sept, 1972 - #16, Jan, 1974
National Periodical Publications

	Good	Fine	Mint
#1-Origin; Kirby art in all			
	1.00	2.00	3.00
2-5	.50	1.00	1.50
6-10	.40	.80	1.20
11-16	.35	.70	1.05

DEMON-HUNTER
Sept, 1975
Seaboard Periodicals (Atlas)

	Good	Fine	Mint
#1-Origin	.15	.30	.45

DENNIS THE MENACE (See The Best of --)
Aug, 1953 - Present
Standard Comics/Pines #15-31/Hallden/
Fawcett #32 on

Dell Giant =27. © Dell

Dell Giant =28. © Leon Schlesinger

Dell Jr. Treasury =6. © Dell

Dennis The Menace #1, © Faw   Dennis The Menace Giant #35, © Faw   Dennis The Menace Giant #37, © Faw

(Dennis the Menace cont'd)

	Good	Fine	Mint
#1	7.00	14.00	21.00
2	3.00	6.00	9.00
3-10	2.00	4.00	6.00
11-20	1.50	3.00	4.50
21-40	1.35	2.75	4.00
41-60	1.00	2.00	3.00
61-90	.60	1.20	1.80
91-152	.25	.50	.75
--& Dirt('68)-Soil Conservation giveaway			
	.40	.80	1.20
--Away We Go('70)-Caladayl giveaway			
	.40	.80	1.20
Food & Drug giveaway('61-16pgs.)("Takes a			
Poke at Poison")	.80	1.60	2.40
Fun Book #1('60)(100pgs.)	1.35	2.75	4.00
Takes a Poke at Poison(F.D.A giveaway)-1961			
(revised 11/70)	.50	1.00	1.50

DENNIS THE MENACE (Giants)
(#1 titled Giant Vacation Special; becomes
Bonus Magazine #76 on)
#1-8,18,23,25,30,38, 100pgs.; rest to #41 are
84pgs.; #42-75, 68pgs.
Summer, 1955 - #75, 1970
Standard/Pines/Hallden(Fawcett)

No#-Giant Vacation Special(Summer, 1955-
  Standard)   2.00   4.00   6.00
No#-Christmas issue(Winter/55)
#2-Giant Vacation Special (Summer'56, Pines)
 3-Giant Christmas issue(Winter,'56, Pines)
 4-Giant Vacation Special(Summer'57, Pines)
 5-Giant Christmas issue(Winter'57, Pines)
 6-In Hawaii(Giant Vacation Special)(Sum.'58-
  Pines)-Reprint Summer'60 + 3 more times
 6-Giant Christmas issue(Winter'58)
 7-In Hollywood(Winter'59, Hallden)
 8-In Mexico(Winter'60,100pgs-Hallden/Fawcett)
 9-Goes to Camp(Summer'61, 84pgs., 2nd printing Summer'62)-1st CCA approved ish.
10-X-Mas issue(Winter'61)
             each.... 1.25   2.50   3.75
11-Giant Christmas issue(Winter'62)
12-Triple Feature(Winter'62)
13-Best of Dennis the Menace(Spr'63)-reprints
14-And His Dog Ruff(Summer'63)
15-In Washington, D.C.(Summer'63)
16-Goes to Camp(Summer'63)-reprints #9
17-& His Pal Joey(Winter'63)
18-In Hawaii(reprints #6)
19-Giant Christmas issue(Winter'63)
20-Spring Special(Spring'64)
            each.... 1.00   2.00   3.00
21-The Best of--(Spring'64)-reprints
22-T.V. Special(Spring'64)

	Good	Fine	Mint
23-In Hollywood(Summer'64-100pgs.)reprints#7
24-Goes to Camp(Summer'64)-reprints #9
25-In Mexico - reprints #8
26-In Washington, D.C.(Summer'64)-reprts.#15
27-Giant Christmas issue(Winter'64)
28-Triple Feature(Spring'65)
29-Best of--(Spring'65)-reprints
30-In Hawaii(Summer'65)-reprints #6
31-All Year 'Round(Summer'65)
32-And His Pal Joey!(Summer'65)-reprints #17
33-In California(Summer'65)
34-And His Dog Ruff(Sum.'65)-reprts. all #14
35-Christmas Special(Winter'65)
36-Spring Special(Spring'66)
37-Television Special(Spring'66)
38-In Mexico(Summer'66)-reprints #8
39-Goes to Camp(Summer'66)-reprints #9
40-In Washington, D.C.(Summer'66)-reprts.#15
      each.... .65   1.35   2.00
41-From A to Z(Summer'66)
42-In Hollywood(Summer'66)-reprints #7
43-Christmas Special(Winter'66)
44-Around the Clock(Spring'67)
45-And His Pal Joey!(Spring'67)
46-Triple Feature(Summer'67)-reprints #28
47-In California(Summer'67)-reprints most#33
48-Way Out Stories(Summer'67)
49-All Year 'Round(Fall'67)-reprints #31
50-At the Circus(Summer'67)
51-Christmas Special(Winter'67)
52-Sports Special(Spring'68)-last CCA approved ish
53-Spring Special(Spr'68)-reprints most #36
54-And His Dog Ruff(Summ'68)-reprts.most #14
55-Tall Stories(Spring'68)
56-Television Special(Spring'68)-reprints TV
  show scripts
57-Pet Parade(Summer'68)
58-The Best of--(Summer'68)-reprints
59-Day By Day(Summer'68)
60-In Hollywood(Fall'68)-reprints most #7
61-Christmas Favorites(Winter'68)
62-Fun Book(Winter'68)-reprints most D.T.M
  Fun Book #1
63-& His Wish I Was Book(Winter'69)
64-In Mexico(Spr'69)-reprints most #8
65-Around the Clock(Spring'69)-reprints #44
66-Gags 'n' Games(Summer'69)
67-Goes to Camp(Summer'69)reprints most #16
68-In Hawaii(Summer'69)-part reprint #6
69-The Best of--(Aug'69)-reprints
70-Tangled Tales(Aug'69)
71-Highlights(Sept'69)-reprints
72-In Washington, D.C.(Aug'69)-reprts.most#15
73-Way-Out Stories(Sept'69)-reprints #48
74-Mr. Wilson & His Gang at Christmas (Dec,
  '69)-reprints

(Dennis the Menace (Giants) cont'd)

	Good	Fine	Mint
75-Merry Christmas to You(Dec'69)			
each....	.30	.65	1.00

DENNIS THE MENACE AND HIS DOG RUFF
Summer, 1961
Hallden/Fawcett

#1	1.35	2.75	4.00

DENNIS THE MENACE AND HIS FRIENDS
1969; #5, Jan, 1970 – Present
Fawcett Publications

	Good	Fine	Mint
Dennis T.M. & Joey #1,2(7/69)			
	.50	1.00	1.50
Dennis T.M. & Ruff #1,2(9/69)			
	.50	1.00	1.50
Dennis T.M. & Mr. Wilson #1(10/69)			
	.50	1.00	1.50
Dennis & Margaret #1(Winter, '69)			
	.50	1.00	1.50

#5-10: #5-Dennis T.M. & Margaret. #6-& Joey.
#7-& Ruff. #8-& Mr. Wilson. #9-& Margaret.
#10-& Joey.   .25   .50   .75
11-20: #11-& Ruff. #12-& Mr. Wilson. #13-&
Margaret. #14-& Joey. #15-& Ruff. #16-&
Mr. Wilson. #17-& Margaret. #18-& Joey.
#19-& Ruff. #20-& Mr. Wilson.
                              .25   .50   .75
21-35: #21-& Margaret. #22-& Joey. #23-& Ruff.
#24-& Mr. Wilson. #25-& Margaret. #26-&
Joey. #27-& Ruff. #28-& Mr. Wilson. #29-
& Margaret. #30-& Joey. #31-& Ruff. #32-
& Mr. Wilson. #33-& Margaret. #34-& His
Pal Joey. #35-& Ruff.   .20   .40   .60

D.T.M. & His Pal Joey #1, © Faw

DENNIS THE MENACE AND HIS PAL JOEY
Summer, 1961   (10¢) (See D.T.M. Giants #45)
Fawcett Publications

#1	1.35	2.75	4.00

DENNIS THE MENACE BONUS MAGAZINE
#76, 1970 - Present (#76-124, 68pgs.; #125-
163, 52pgs.; #164 on, 36pgs.)
Fawcett Publications

#76-In the Carribean(1/70)
 77-Sports Special(2/70)-reprints #52
 78-Spring Special(3/70)-reprints most #20
 79-Tall Stories(4/70)-reprints #55
 80-Day By Day(5/70)-reprints #59
 81-Summer Funner(6/70)
 82-In California(6/70)-reprints most #33
 83-Mama Goose(7/70)
 84-At the Circus(7/70)-reprint

	Good	Fine	Mint
85-The Fall Ball(8/70)			
86-Mr. Wilson & His Gang at Christmas(10/70) reprints			
87-Christmas Special(10/70)			
88-In London(1/71)			
89-Spring Fling(2/71)			
90-Highlights(3/71)-reprints			
each....	.35	.70	1.05

91-Fun Book(4/71)-reprints most D.T.M. Fun
Book #1
92-In Hollywood(5/71)-reprints most #7
93-Visits Paris(6/71)
94-Jackpot(6/71)-reprint
95-That's Our Boy(7/71)-reprints
96-(Some numbered #95)-Summer Games(7/71)
97-Comicapers(8/71)
98-Mr. Wilson & His Gang at Christmas(10/71)
99-Christmas Special(10/71)
100-Up in the Air(1/72)
101-Rise and Shine(2/72)
102-Wish-I-Was Book(3/72)-reprints #63
103-Short Stuff Special(4/72)
104-In Mexico(5/72)-reprints most #8
105-Birthday Special(6/72)-reprints part
D.T.M. #1
106-Fast & Funny(6/72)
107-Around the Clock(7/72)-reprints #44
108-Goes to Camp(7/72)-reprints most #9
109-Gags and Games(7/72)-reprints #66 w/new
cover

110-Mr. Wilson & His Gang at Christmas(10/72)			
each....	.25	.50	.75

111-Christmas Special(10/72)
112-Go-Go Special(1/73)
113-Tangled Tales(2/73)-reprints #70
114-In Hawaii(3/73)-reprints #68 w/new cover
115-Ting-A-Ling Special(4/73)
116-In Washington, D.C.(5/73)-reprts.most #15
117-Encore(6/73)-reprints #69 w/new cover
118-Here's How(6/73)
119-The Summer Number(7/73)
120-Strikes Back(7/73)
121-Way-Out Stories(8/73)-reprints #48
122-& Mr. Wilson & His Gang at Christmas(10/73)
123-Christmas Special(10/73)
124-Happy Holidays!(1/74)
125-In London(2/74)-reprts. most #88
126-Sports Special(3/74)-reprints most #52
127-Visits Paris(4/74)-partially reprints #93
128-Visits the Queen(Queen Mary)(5/74)
129-At the Circus(6/74)-part reprint #50
130-In Hollywood(6/74)-reprints half #7
131-What in the World?! (7/74)
132-Follow the Leader(7/74)-reprints
133-That's the Spirit!(8/74)
134-Christmas Special(10/74)
135-& Mr. Wilson & His Gang at Christmas
(10/74)-reprints
136-"Crazy Daze"(1/75)
137-"Up and at 'Em(2/75)
138-Fun Book(3/75)-reprints ½ D.T.M.Fun Book#1
139-Jackpot(4/75)-reprints most #94

140-Big Deal(5/75)			
each....	.20	.40	.60

141-Gags & Games(6/75)-reprints most #109
142-Just Kidding(6/75)-Intro. Hot Dog(Dennis'
cat)
143-Ireland(7/75)
144-In Washington, D.C.(7/75)(Bicentennial)-
reprints most #116
145-Yankee Doodle Dennis 1776-1976(8/75)
146-Christmas Special(10/75)
147-& Mr. Wilson & His Gang at Christmas(10/75)
148-In Florida(1/76)

(Dennis the Menace Bonus Mag. cont'd)

	Good	Fine	Mint
149-The Cookie Kid!(2/76)-reprints			
150-The Daffy Dozen(3/76)			
151-Yearbook(4/76)			
152-The Best of--(5/76)-reprints			
153-Yankee Doodle Dennis 1776-1976(6/76)- reprints #145			
154-Yours Truly Dennis(6/76)-reprints part #101,106			
155-Making Movies!(Summer Special, 7/76)			
156-Pretty Tricky!(7/76)-reprints			
157-Dare-Devil Dennis(8/76)-reprints			
158-Christmas Special(10/76)			
159-& Mr. Wilson & His Gang at Christmas(10/76)			
160-Yearbook(1/77)			
161-Off and Running!(2/77)-reprints ½ D.T.M. Fun Book #1			
162-At Marriott's Great America(3/77)			
163-Cherry Blossom Festival(4/77)			
164-"Just Kid-ding"(5/77)-reprints			
165-The Best of Dennis(6/77)-reprints			
166-Vacation Sensation(6/77)-reprints			
167-At the National Air & Space Museum of the Smithsonian Instit. Washington, D.C.(6/77)			
168-Tough and Tricky(7/77)-reprints			
each....	.15	.30	.45

DENNIS THE MENACE POCKET FULL OF FUN!
Spring, 1969 - Present (196pgs.)(Digest size)
Fawcett Publications (Hallden)

		Good	Fine	Mint
#1-Reprints in all issues		.30	.65	1.00
2-10		.25	.50	.75
11-34		.15	.30	.45

NOTE: #1-28 are 192pgs., #29 on, 160 pgs.
#8,11,15,21,25,29 all contain strip reprints.

DENNIS THE MENACE TELEVISION SPECIAL
Summer, 1961 - #2, Spring, 1962 (Giant)
Fawcett Publications (Hallden Div.)

	Good	Fine	Mint
#1	1.25	2.50	3.75
2	1.00	2.00	3.00

DENNIS THE MENACE TRIPLE FEATURE
Winter, 1961 (Giant)
Fawcett Publications

	Good	Fine	Mint
#1	1.25	2.50	3.75

DEPUTY, THE (See 4-Color #1077,1130,1225)

DEPUTY DAWG (TV)
10-12/61 - #1, 8/65
Dell Publishing Co./Gold Key

	Good	Fine	Mint
4-Color #1238,1299	.35	.70	1.05

	Good	Fine	Mint
#1(10164-508)	.20	.40	.60

DEPUTY DAWG PRESENTS DINKY DUCK AND HASHIMOTO SAM
August, 1965
Gold Key

		Good	Fine	Mint
#1(10159-508)			.15	.30

DESIGN FOR SURVIVAL (Gen. Thomas S. Power's--
1968 (36pgs. in Color)(25¢)
American Security Council Press

		Good	Fine	Mint
No#-Propaganda against the Threat of Communism		1.50	3.00	4.50

DESPERADO (Black Diamond Western #9 on)
1948 - #8, Jul-Aug, 1949
Lev Gleason Publications

	Good	Fine	Mint
#1-Biro art	2.00	4.00	6.00
2-8	1.00	2.00	3.00

DESTINATION MOON (See Fawcett Movie Comics)

DESTRUCTOR, THE
February, 1975 - #4, Aug, 1975
Atlas/Seaboard

	Good	Fine	Mint
#1-Origin; Ditko/Wood art	.40	.80	1.20
2-4: #2,3-Wood/Ditko; #4-Ditko art	.25	.50	.75

DETECTIVE COMICS
March, 1937 - Present
National Periodical Publications/DC Comics

#1-Slam Bradley & Spy by Siegel & Shuster, Speed Saunders by Guardineer, Flat Foot Flannigan by Gustavson, Cosmo, the Phantom of Disguise, Buck Marshall, Bruce Nelson begin; Fu Manchu cover

	Good	Fine	Mint
	225.00	450.00	675.00
2 (Rare)	90.00	180.00	270.00
3 (Rare)	70.00	140.00	210.00
4,5	45.00	90.00	135.00
6,7,9,10	40.00	80.00	120.00
8-Fu Manchu cover	50.00	100.00	150.00
11-17,19	30.00	60.00	90.00
18-Fu Manchu cover	40.00	80.00	120.00
20-The Crimson Avenger begins (intro. & 1st app.)	45.00	90.00	135.00
21,23-25	20.00	40.00	60.00
22-Crimson Avenger cvr.	25.00	50.00	75.00
26	25.00	50.00	75.00

27-1st app. The Batman & Commissioner Gordon

Design For Survival, © American Security Council   Desperado #1, © Lev   Detective Comics #2, © DC

Detective Comics #8, © DC

Detective Comics #22, © DC

Detective Comics #26, © DC

	Good	Fine	Mint

(Detective Comics cont'd) Good Fine Mint
by Bob Kane; #27 reprinted in Famous 1st
Edition   1200.00 2700.00 4200.00
   (Prices vary widely on this book)
28   450.00 900.00 1350.00
29-Batman cover; Doctor Death app.
                  200.00 400.00 600.00
30,32: #30-Dr.Death app.125.00 250.00 375.00
31-Batman cover   175.00 350.00 525.00
33-Origin The Batman; Batman cover
                  300.00 600.00 900.00
34-Steve Malone & Larry Steele begin
                  80.00 160.00 240.00
35-37: Batman covers. #36-Origin Hugo Strange
  #37-Cliff Crosby begins
                  80.00 160.00 240.00
38-Origin & 1st app. Robin the Boy Wonder
                  200.00 400.00 600.00
39   70.00 140.00 210.00
40-Origin & 1st app. Clay Face
                  55.00 110.00 165.00
41-Robin's 1st solo 35.00 70.00 105.00
42-45: #44-Crimson Avenger dons new costume
                  27.50 55.00 82.50
46-50: #48-1st time car called Batmobile.
  #49-Last Clay Face 22.00 44.00 66.00
51-59: #58-1st Penguin app.; last Speed Saunders. #59-Last Steve Malone; 2nd Penguin;
  Wing becomes Crimson Avenger's aide
                  20.00 40.00 60.00
60-Intro. Air Wave 20.00 40.00 60.00
61-63: #63-Last Cliff Crosby; 1st app. Mr.
  Baffle   17.50 35.00 52.50
64-Origin & 1st app. Boy Commandos by Simon
  & Kirby   40.00 80.00 120.00
65-Boy Commandos cover 27.50 55.00 82.50
66-Origin & 1st app. Two-Face
                  20.00 40.00 60.00
67-70: #68-Two-Face app. 14.00 28.00 42.00
71-75: #74-1st Tweedledum & Tweedledee;

	Good	Fine	Mint

S&K art   12.00 24.00 36.00
76-Newsboy Legion & The Sandman x-over in Boy
  Commandos; S&K art 15.00 30.00 45.00
77-80: All S&K art; Two-Face in #80
                  12.00 24.00 36.00
81,82,84-90: #81-1st Cavalier app. #85-Last
  Spy. #82-Last S&K art? #89-Last Crimson
  Avenger   10.00 20.00 30.00
83-1st "Skinny" Alfred 12.00 24.00 36.00
91-100   8.00 16.00 24.00
101-120   7.00 14.00 21.00
121-130   6.00 12.00 18.00
131-137,139: #137-Last Airwave
                  5.00 10.00 15.00
138-Origin Robotman (See Star Spangled #7,
  1st app.)   7.00 14.00 21.00
140-1st app. The Riddler 15.00 30.00 45.00
141-150: #142-2nd Riddler app. #150-Last Boy
  Commandos   4.00 8.00 12.00
151-160: #151-Origin & 1st app. Pow Wow Smith.
  #152-Last Slam Bradley. #153-1st Roy Raymond app. #156(2/50)-The new classic
  Batmobile   3.00 6.00 9.00
161-180   3.00 6.00 9.00
181-210: #187-Two-Face app. #202-Last Robotman & Pow Wow Smith 3.00 6.00 9.00
211-224: #213-Origin Mirror Man
                  2.00 4.00 6.00
225-Intro. & 1st app. Martian Manhunter-the
  1st National Silver Age Hero
                  12.00 24.00 36.00
226-230: #230-1st app. Mad Hatter
                  2.50 5.00 7.50
231,232,234-260: #246-Intro. Diane Meade, J.
  Jones girl. #257-Intro. & 1st app. Lohirly
  Bats   1.75 3.35 5.00
233-Origin & 1st app. Batwoman
                  2.50 5.00 7.50
261-264,266-280: #261-1st app. Dr. Double.

Detective Comics #27, © DC

Detective Comics #35, © DC

Detective Comics #128, © DC

Detective Comics #164, © DC   Detective Eye #2, © Cen   Devil Dogs #1, © S & S

(Detective Comics cont'd)

	Good	Fine	Mint
#267-Origin & 1st app. Bat-Mite	1.00	2.00	3.00
265-Batman's origin retold	1.50	3.00	4.50
281-300: #292-Last Roy Raymond. #293-Aquaman begins, ends #300	.75	1.50	2.25
301-327,329,330: #311-Intro. Zook in John Jones; 1st app. Catman. #326-Last John Jones; intro. Idol-Head of Diabolu. #327-Elongated Man begins	.60	1.20	1.80
328-Death of Alfred	.75	1.50	2.25
331-368,370: #355-Zatanna x-over in Elongated Man. #356-Alfred brought back in Batman. #359-Intro. new Batgirl	.50	1.00	1.50
369-Adams story	1.50	3.00	4.50
371-390: #383-Elongated Man series ends. #387-Reprints 1st Batman story from #27	.35	.70	1.05
391-394,396,398,399,401,403,405,406,409,411-420: #414-52pgs. begin, end #424. #418-Creeper x-over	.35	.70	1.05
395,397,400,402,404,407,408,410-Adams stories. #400-Origin & 1st app. Man-Bat	1.00	2.00	3.00
421-436: #424-Last Batgirl. #425-1st Jason Bard	.25	.50	.75
437-Manhunter begins by Simonson, ends #443	.35	.70	1.05
438-441,443-445: All 100pgs. #441-G.A. Plastic Man reprt. #443-Origin The Creeper reprint. #444-Elongated Man begins	.35	.70	1.05
442-New 12pg. Toth art	.40	.80	1.20
446-460: #446-Hawkman begins, ends #455. #458-Man-Bat begins. #460-Tim Trench begins	.20	.40	.60
461-474	.15	.30	.45
Special Edition(1944)-Giveaway-(68pgs.) Regular comic format	20.00	40.00	60.00

NOTE: _Adams_ covers-#369,370,372,385,389,391, 392,394-422,439. _Anderson_ art-#359,360,377, 390,440,442; covers-#359,361-365,369,371, 431,433. _Ditko_ story-#443. _Infantino_ art-#327-357,361-363,366,367,369,439,442; covers-#327-331,333-347,351-368,371. _Kaluta_ covers-#423,424,426-428,431,434,438. _Kubert_ art-#438,439; covers-#348-350. _Robinson_ stories-part #72&73, 74-76,79,80; covers-#62,64,66-69,72,74,76,79,86,88. _Roussos_ Airwave-#105. _Simon/Kirby_ art-#440,442. _Toth_ art-#424,440-444. _Wrightson_ cover-#425.

DETECTIVE DAN, SECRET OP. 48
1933 (36pgs.)(9½x12"-B&W-Softcover)
Humor Publ. Co.

By Norman Marsh - forerunner of Dan Dunn

	Good	Fine	Mint
	5.00	10.00	15.00

DETECTIVE EYE
Nov, 1940 - #2, Dec, 1940
Centaur Publications

	Good	Fine	Mint
#1-Air Man & The Eye Sees begins; The Maskel Marvel app.	25.00	50.00	75.00
2	15.00	30.00	45.00

DETECTIVE PICTURE STORIES
Dec, 1936 - 1937
Quality Comics Group

	Good	Fine	Mint
#1	25.00	50.00	75.00
2	12.00	24.00	36.00
3-The Clock begins	15.00	30.00	45.00
4,5-Eisner art in each + Kane in #5	15.00	30.00	45.00
6,7	10.00	20.00	30.00

DETECTIVES, THE (See 4-Color#1168,1219,1240)

DEVIL-DOG DUGAN (Tales of the Marines #4 on
July, 1956 - #3, Nov, 1956
Atlas Comics (OPI)

	Good	Fine	Mint
#1-Severin cover	1.00	2.00	3.00
2-Iron Mike McGraw x-over; Severin cover,			
3	.75	1.50	2.25

DEVIL DOGS
1942
Street & Smith Publishers

	Good	Fine	Mint
#1-Boy Rangers	5.00	10.00	15.00

DEVILINA
Feb, 1975 - #2, May, 1975 (Magazine-B&W)
Atlas/Seaboard

	Good	Fine	Mint
#1,2	.75	1.50	2.25

DEVIL KIDS STARRING HOT STUFF
1962 - Present
Harvey Publications (Illustrated Humor)

	Good	Fine	Mint
#1	1.00	2.00	3.00
2	.50	1.00	1.50
3-10	.25	.50	.75
11-30	.15	.30	.45
31-86		.15	.30

DEXTER COMICS
Summer, 1948 - #5, July, 1949
Dearfield Publ.

	Good	Fine	Mint
#1	1.00	2.00	3.00
2-5	.65	1.35	2.00

EXTER THE DEMON (Formerly Melvin the Monster)
6, July, 1957 - #7, Sept, 1957
Atlas Comics (HPC)

	Good	Fine	Mint
6,7	.30	.65	1.00

DIARY CONFESSIONS (Formerly Ideal Romance)
May, 1955 - 1956
Stanmor/Key Publ.

9-14	.40	.80	1.20

DIARY LOVES (G.I. Sweethearts #32 on)
Nov, 1949 - #31, April, 1953
Quality Comics Group

#1-Crandall & Colan art	2.50	5.00	7.50
2-Ward cover, 9pgs.	2.50	5.00	7.50
3,5-7,10	.80	1.60	2.40
4-Crandall art	1.50	3.00	4.50
8,9-Ward art-6,8pgs. + Gustavson-#8			
	2.00	4.00	6.00
11,13,14,17-20	.75	1.50	2.25
12,15,16-Ward art-9,7,?pgs.			
	1.75	3.35	5.00
21-Ward art, 7pgs.	1.75	3.35	5.00
22-31: #31-Whitney art	.40	.80	1.20

NOTE: *Most early issues have photo covers.*

DIARY OF HORROR
December, 1952
Avon Periodicals

#1-One pg. Kinstler	2.50	5.00	7.50

DIARY SECRETS (Formerly Blue Ribbon Comics)
#6, Sept, 1949 - #30, June, 1955
St. John Publishing Co.

No#(#6, 9/49)	1.75	3.35	5.00
#7-10	1.25	2.50	3.75
11-16,18,19,21-30	1.00	2.00	3.00
17,20-Kubert stories	1.75	3.35	5.00
Annual-No#(25¢)	2.00	4.00	6.00

NOTE: *Baker stories/covers most issues.*

DICK COLE (Sport Thrills #11 on)
Dec-Jan, 1948-49 - #10, Jun-Jul, 1950
Premium Group(Novelty)/Star Publications

#1-Sgt. Spook	1.50	3.00	4.50
2	1.00	2.00	3.00
3-10	.75	1.50	2.25
Accepted Reprint #7(V1#6 on cover)-(1950's)			
reprints #9	.50	1.00	1.50

DICKIE DARE
1941

Eastern Color Printing Co.

	Good	Fine	Mint
#1-Caniff art, Everett cover			
	8.00	16.00	24.00
2,3	6.00	12.00	18.00
4-Half Scorchy Smith by Noel Sickles who was very influential in Milton Caniff's development	6.00	12.00	18.00

DICK POWELL (See A-1 Comics #22)

DICK QUICK, ACE REPORTER
Jan-Feb, 1947   (Formerly Picture News)
Lafayette St. Corp.

#10-Krigstein + Milt Gross story			
	1.75	3.35	5.00

DICK'S ADVENTURES IN DREAMLAND (See 4-Color
Comics #245)

DICK TRACY (See Big Thrill Booklet, Lemix-
Korlix, Merry Christmas, Tastee-Freez, Limited
Coll. Ed., Harvey Comics Library, & Super Book
#1,7,13,25)

DICK TRACY
1939 - #24, Dec, 1949
Dell Publishing Co.

Black & White #1(1939)	80.00	160.00	240.00
Black & White #4,8,11,13,15			
	40.00	80.00	120.00
4-Color #1(1939)('35 rpt)	90.00	180.00	270.00
4-Color #6(1940)('37 rpt)	50.00	100.00	150.00
4-Color #8(1940)('38-'39 reprint)			
	40.00	80.00	120.00
Large Feature Comics #3(1941)			
	35.00	70.00	105.00
4-Color #21('41)('38 rpt)	30.00	60.00	90.00
4-Color #34('43)('39-'40 reprint)			
	20.00	40.00	60.00
4-Color #56('44)('40 rpt)	15.00	30.00	45.00
4-Color #96('46)('40 rpt)	8.00	16.00	24.00
4-Color #133('47)('40-'41 reprint)			
	8.00	16.00	24.00
4-Color #163('47)('41 rpt)	6.00	12.00	18.00
4-Color #215('48)-titled "Sparkle Plenty," Tracy reprints	5.00	10.00	15.00
Buster Brown Shoes giveaway-36pgs. in color (1938 reprints)	15.00	30.00	45.00
Gillmore Giveaway-(See Super Book)			
--Hatfull of Fun(no date, 1950-52)-32pgs., 8½x10"-Dick Tracy hat promotion; D. Tracy games, magic tricks. Miller Bros. premium	2.50	5.00	7.50

Diary Loves #2, © Qua

Diary Secrets #6, © STJ

Dick Tracy, 4-Color #34, © N.Y. News Synd.

(Dick Tracy cont'd)   Good   Fine   Mint
Motorola Giveaway('53)-reprints Harvey Comics
  Library #2   3.00   6.00   9.00
Popped Wheat Giveaway('47)-'40 reprint-16pgs.
  in color; Sig Feuchtwanger publ.
                1.20   2.40   3.60
--Presents the Family Fun Book-Tip Top Bread
  Giveaway, no date, #(mid '40's)16pgs. in
  color; Spy Smasher, Ibis, Lance O'Casey
  app.   25.00 50.00 75.00
#1(1/48)('34 reprints) 15.00 30.00 45.00
  2,3   7.00 14.00 21.00
  4-18   5.00 10.00 15.00
  19-24-Not by Gould   3.00   6.00   9.00

DICK TRACY (Cont'd. from Dell series)
#25, Mar, 1950 - #145, April, 1961
Harvey Publications

#25   7.00 14.00 21.00
  26-30: #30-1st app. Gravel Gertie
            6.00 12.00 18.00
  31-50: #36-1st app. B.O. Plenty
            5.00 10.00 15.00
  51-80   3.35   6.75 10.00
  81-140   2.50   5.00   7.50
  141-145 (25¢)   4.00   8.00 12.00
NOTE: *#110-120,141-145 are all reprints from
earlier issues.*

DICK TRACY
May, 1937 - Jan, 1938
David McKay Publications

Feature Book No#, 100pgs. Part reprinted as
  4-Color #1(appeared before Black & Whites,
  1st Dick Tracy comic book)
  (Rare)   250.00 500.00 750.00
Feature Book #4-Reprints No# issue but with
  new cover added   75.00 150.00 225.00
Feature Book #6,9   60.00 120.00 180.00

DICK TRACY & DICK TRACY JR. CAUGHT THE
RACKETEERS, HOW
1933 (88 pgs.) (7x8½") (Hardcover)
Cupples & Leon Co.

#2(#'d on pg.84)-Continuation of Stooge
  Villar book(daily strip reprints from
  8/3/33 thru 11/8/33)
  (Rarer than #1) 40.00 80.00 120.00
  with dust jacket.... 60.00 120.00 180.00

DICK TRACY & DICK TRACY JR. AND HOW THEY
CAPTURED "STOOGE" VILLER (See Treasury Box
of Comics)
1933 (7x8½") Hard cover; One Shot; 100pgs.
Reprints 1932 & 1933 Dick Tracy daily strips

Cupples & Leon Co.
                  Good   Fine   Mint
No#-First app. of "Stooge" Viller
              30.00 60.00 90.00
  with dust jacket.... 40.00 80.00 120.00

DICK TRACY, EXPLOITS OF
1946 (Strip reprints)(Hard Cover)($1.00)
No publisher listed

#1-Reprints the complete case of "The Brow"
  from early 1940's 20.00 40.00 60.00
  with dust jacket.... 25.00 50.00 75.00

DICK TRACY SHEDS LIGHT ON THE MOLE
1949 (16pgs.) (Ray-O-Vac Flashlights Give-
Western Printing Co.   Away

Not by Gould   2.50   5.00   7.50

DICK TURPIN (See Legend of Young --)

DICK WINGATE OF THE U.S. NAVY
1951; 1953
Toby Press/Superior Publ.

No#-U.S. Navy giveaway .65 1.35 2.00
#1(1953)   .65 1.35 2.00

DIE, MONSTER, DIE (See Movie Classics)

DIG 'EM
1973 (16 pgs.) (2-3/8"x6")
Kellogg's Sugar Smacks Giveaway

4 different   .15   .30   .45

DILLY (The Little Wise Guys)
May, 1953 - #3, Sept, 1953
Lev Gleason Publications

#1-3: #2,3-Biro covers 1.00 2.00 3.00

DIME COMICS
1945 (Gleason reprints); 1951
Newsbook Publ. Corp.

#1-Silver Streak app. 4.00 8.00 12.00
  1(1951), #5   1.50 3.00 4.50

DING DONG
1946
Compix/Magazine Enterprises

#1   1.00 2.00 3.00
2-5   .50 1.00 1.50

DINKY DUCK (Paul Terry's--)(See Blue Ribbon

Dick Tracy #7. © N.Y. News Synd.   Dick Tracy Tip Top Bread. © N.Y. News Synd.   Dilly #3. © Lev

Dixie Dugan #3, © McNaught Synd.

Dizzy Dames #1, © ACG

Doc Savage V2#2, © S & S

(Dinky Duck cont'd)
(Comics)
#1/51 - #16, 9/55; #16, Fall, 1956; #17, 5/57-
#19, Summer, 1958
St. John Publishing Co./Pines #16 on

	Good	Fine	Mint
#1	1.00	2.00	3.00
2-10	.50	1.00	1.50
11-16(9/55)	.35	.70	1.05
16(Fall,'56)-#19	.25	.50	.75

DINKY DUCK & HASHIMOTO SAM (See Deputy Dawg
Presents --)

DINO (The Flintstones)
Aug, 1973 - #20, Jan, 1977
Charlton Publications

#1	.15	.30	.45
2-20		.15	.30

DINOSAURUS (See 4-Color Comics #1120)

DIPPY DUCK
October, 1957
Atlas Comics(OPI)

#1-Maneely art	.65	1.35	2.00

DIRTY DOZEN (See Movie Classics)

DISNEYLAND BIRTHDAY PARTY
1958   (25¢)
Dell Publishing Co.

#1-Carl Barks art	5.00	10.00	15.00

DISNEYLAND, USA (See Dell Giant #30)

DIVER DAN
Feb-Apr, 1962 - #2, June-Aug, 1962
Dell Publishing Co.

4-Color #1254, #2	.65	1.35	2.00

DIXIE DUGAN
1942 - 1949
McNaught Syndicate/Columbia/Publication Ent.

#1-Joe Palooka x-over in Dixie Dugan by			
Ham Fisher	4.00	8.00	12.00
2,3	2.00	4.00	6.00
4,5(1945-46)	1.50	3.00	4.50
6-13(1948-49)	1.00	2.00	3.00

DIXIE DUGAN
Nov, 1951 - 1954
Prize Publications (Headline)

	Good	Fine	Mint
V3#1-4	1.00	2.00	3.00
V4#1-4(#5-8)	.50	1.00	1.50

DIZZY DAMES
Sept-Oct, 1952 - #6, Jul-Aug, 1953
American Comics Group (B&M Distr. Co.)

#1	1.00	2.00	3.00
2-6	.50	1.00	1.50

DIZZY DON
1947 - #4, 1947
F. E. Howard Publications (Canada)

#1	.65	1.35	2.00
2-4	.40	.80	1.20

DIZZY DUCK
#32, Nov, 1950 - #39, 1952
Standard Comics

#32-39	.35	.70	1.05

DOBERMAN (See Sgt. Bilko's Private --)

DOBIE GILLIS (See The Many Loves of --)

DOC SAVAGE (-- Comics)
May, 1940 - #20, Oct, 1943
Street & Smith Publications

#1-Doc Savage, Cap Fury, Danny Garrett, Mark Mallory, The Whisperer, Captain Death, Billy the Kid, Sheriff Pete & Treasure Island begin; Norgil, the Magician app.			
	55.00	110.00	165.00
2-Origin & 1st app. Ajax, the Sun Man; Danny Garrett, The Whisperer end			
	27.50	55.00	82.50
3	22.50	45.00	67.50
4-Treasure Island ends	20.00	40.00	60.00
5-Origin & 1st app. Astron, the Crocodile Queen, not in #9 & 11; Norgil, the Magician app.	15.00	30.00	45.00
6-9: #6-Cap Fury ends; origin & only app. Red Falcon in Astron story. #8-Mark Mallory ends. #9-Supersnipe app.			
	12.00	24.00	36.00
10-Origin The Thunderbolt			
	12.00	24.00	36.00
11,12	9.00	18.00	27.00
V2#1-8(#13-20): #16-The Pulp Hero, The Avenger app. #18-Sun Man ends; Nick Carter begins. #20-Astron, the Crocodile Queen ends.	9.00	18.00	27.00

DOC SAVAGE
Nov, 1966
Gold Key

	Good	Fine	Mint
#1-Adaptation of the Thousand-Headed Man;			
James Bama cover	1.35	2.75	4.00

DOC SAVAGE
Oct, 1972 - #8, Jan, 1974
Marvel Comics Group

	Good	Fine	Mint
#1	.50	1.00	1.50
2,3-Steranko covers	.35	.70	1.05
4-8	.25	.50	.75
Giant-Size #1(1975)-Reprints #1 & 2			
	.25	.50	.75

DOC SAVAGE (Magazine)
Aug, 1975 - Present   (Black & White)
Marvel Comics Group

	Good	Fine	Mint
#1-Cover from movie poster	.50	1.00	1.50
2(10/75),3-8	.35	.70	1.05

NOTE: *Buscema story-#3.*

DR. ANTHONY KING, HOLLYWOOD LOVE DOCTOR
Jan, 1952 - #3, May, 1953; #4, May, 1954
Minoan Publishing Corp.

	Good	Fine	Mint
#1	1.20	2.40	3.60
2-4	.80	1.60	2.40

DR. ANTHONY LOVE CLINIC (See Mr. Anthony's--)

DR. BOBBS (See 4-Color Comics #212)

DR. FU MANCHU (See The Mask of --)
1964
I.W. Enterprises

	Good	Fine	Mint
#1-Reprints Avon's "Mask of Dr. Fu Manchu";			
Wood & Orlando art	4.00	8.00	12.00

DOCTOR GRAVES (See The Many Ghosts of --)

DR. JEKYLL AND MR. HYDE (See A Star Presentation)

DR. KILDARE (TV)
1962 - #9, Apr-June, 1965
Dell Publishing Co.

	Good	Fine	Mint
4-Color #1337('62)	.40	.80	1.20
#2-9	.25	.50	.75

DR. MASTERS (See The Adventures of Young--)

DOCTOR SOLAR, MAN OF THE ATOM

Oct, 1962 - #27, April, 1969
Gold Key

	Good	Fine	Mint
#1-Origin Dr. Solar	1.75	3.35	5.00
2-Prof. Harbinger begins	1.00	2.00	3.00
3-5: #5-Intro. Man of the Atom in costume			
	.65	1.35	2.00
6-10	.50	1.00	1.50
11-14,16-27	.40	.80	1.20
15-Origin retold	.40	.80	1.20

NOTE: *Frank Bolle art-#6-19. Bob Fugitani art in early issues. Al McWilliams art-#20-23*

DOCTOR SPEKTOR (See The Occult Files of --)

DOCTOR STRANGE (Strange Tales #1-168)
#169, June, 1968 - #183, Nov, 1969; June,
1974 - Present   (Also see Marvel Premiere)
Marvel Comics Group

	Good	Fine	Mint
#169(#1)	.80	1.60	2.40
170-183: #177-New costume for Dr. Strange			
	.40	.80	1.20
#1(6/74)-Brunner cvr/stys.	.80	1.60	2.40
2-Brunner cvr/stories	.50	1.00	1.50
3-Ditko reprints & Brunner story/cover			
	.40	.80	1.20
4,5-Brunner cvr/stys end	.40	.80	1.20
6-Brunner cover	.35	.70	1.05
7-10	.20	.40	.60
11-21	.15	.30	.45
22-Brunner cover	.20	.40	.60
23-26-Starlin stories; covers-#25,26			
	.20	.40	.60

NOTE: *Alcala story-#19; Brunner covers-#6,22.*

	Good	Fine	Mint
Giant-Size #1(11/75)	.35	.70	1.05
Annual #1('76)	.35	.70	1.05
King Size Annual #1(1/77)	.25	.50	.75

DR. TOM BRENT, YOUNG INTERN
Feb, 1963 - #5, Oct, 1963
Charlton Publications

	Good	Fine	Mint
#1	.20	.40	.60
2-5	.15	.30	.45

DR. VOLTZ (See Mighty Midget Comics)

DR. WHO & THE DALEKS (See Movie Classics)

DO-DO
1951   (5"x7½" Miniature)   (5¢)
Nation Wide Publishers

	Good	Fine	Mint
#1-7	.50	1.00	1.50

DODO & THE FROG, THE (Formerly Funny Stuff)
Sept-Oct, 1954 - #92, 1957

Doctor Solar #1, © GK

Doctor Strange #169, © MCG

Dodo & The Frog #86, © DC

117

Dollman #11, © DC (Qua)

Dollman #21, © DC (Qua)

Donald Duck Firestone, 1949, © WDP

(Dodo & the Frog cont'd)
National Periodical Publ. (Arleigh)

	Good	Fine	Mint
#80-92: Doodles Duck by Sheldon Mayer in many issues	.40	.80	1.20

DOGFACE DOOLEY
1951 - 1953
Magazine Enterprises

#1(A-1#40)	1.00	2.00	3.00
2(A-1#43),3(A-1#49),4(A-1#53),5(A-1#64)	1.00	2.00	3.00
IW Reprint #1('64), Super Reprint #17	.50	1.00	1.50

DOG OF FLANDERS, A (See 4-Color #1088)

DOGPATCH (See Al Capp's -- & Mammy Yokum)

DOINGS OF THE DOO DADS, THE
1922 (34pgs.)(7-3/4"x7-3/4")(B&W)(50¢)
(Red & White cover)(Square binding)
Detroit News (Universal Feat.& Specialty Co.)

Reprints 1921 newspaper strip "Text & Pictures" given away as prize in the Detroit
News Doo Dads contest; by Arch Dale

	6.00	12.00	18.00

DOLLFACE & HER GANG (See 4-Color #309)

DOLL MAN
Autumn, 1941 - #47, Oct, 1953
Quality Comics Group

#1-Dollman & Justice Wright begin	65.00	130.00	195.00
2-The Dragon begins; 5 Crandall stories	30.00	60.00	90.00
3-Dollman by Fuje	22.50	45.00	67.50
4	17.50	35.00	52.50
5	12.00	24.00	36.00
6-10	8.00	16.00	24.00
11-20	6.00	12.00	18.00
21-30	5.00	10.00	15.00
31-36,38-40: Jeb Rivers app. #32-34	4.00	8.00	12.00
37-Origin Dollgirl	5.00	10.00	15.00
41-47	2.50	5.00	7.50
IW Reprint #1('63)-Crandall art	1.35	2.75	4.00
Super Reprint #11('64),15(reprts.#23),17,18: Torchy app.-#15,17	1.50	3.00	4.50

NOTE: _Ward Torchy in #8,9,11,12,14-29; by
Fox-#30,35-47. Crandall stories-#2,7,10,13 &
Super #11,17,18._

DOLLY DILL
1945
Marvel Comics/Newsstand Publ.

	Good	Fine	Mint
#1	1.00	2.00	3.00

DOLLY DILL
1951 - #10, 1951

#1	.65	1.35	2.00
2-10	.40	.80	1.20

DONALD AND MICKEY IN DISNEYLAND
1958 (25¢)
Dell Publishing Co.

#1(Giant)	1.75	3.35	5.00

DONALD AND MICKEY MERRY CHRISTMAS
1943 - 1949 (20 pgs.)(Giveaway) Put out each
Christmas; 1943 issue titled "Firestone Presents Comics". (Disney)
K.K. Publ./Firestone Tire & Rubber Co.

1943-D.Duck reprint from WDC&S #32 by Carl Barks	125.00	250.00	375.00
1944-D.Duck reprint from WDC&S #35 by Barks	100.00	200.00	300.00
1945-"Donald Duck's Best Christmas", 8 pgs. Carl Barks; intro. & 1st app. Grandma Duck	150.00	300.00	450.00
1946-D.Duck in "Santa's Stormy Visit," 8pgs. Carl Barks	100.00	200.00	300.00
1947-D.Duck in "Three Good Little Ducks," 8 pgs. Carl Barks	100.00	200.00	300.00
1948-D.Duck in "Toyland," 8 pgs. Carl Barks	100.00	200.00	300.00
1949-D.Duck in "New Toys," 8 pgs. Carl Barks	100.00	200.00	300.00

DONALD AND THE WHEEL (See 4-Color #1190)

DONALD DUCK (Also see The Wise Little Hen)
1935, 1935 (linen-like text & color pictures;
1st Donald Duck book ever) (9½x13")
Whitman Publishing Co./Grosset & Dunlap/K.K.

#978(1935)-16 pgs.; story book	100.00	200.00	300.00
No#(1936)-36pgs.-Reprints '35 edition with expanded ill. & text	60.00	120.00	180.00
...with dust jacket....	80.00	160.00	240.00

DONALD DUCK (Walt Disney's) (10¢)
1938 (B&W)(8½x11½")(Cardboard covers)
Whitman/K.K. Publications
(Has D.D. smoking pike on front cover)

Donald Duck #978('35), © WDP   Black & White #16, © WDP   4-Color #9, © WDP

	Good	Fine	Mint

(Donald Duck cont'd)

No#-The first Donald Duck comic book; 1936 & 1937 Sunday strip reprints(in black and white)same format as Black & Whites
          200.00 400.00 600.00
(Prices vary widely on this book)

DONALD DUCK (See 4-Color listings for titles)
(Also see Cheerios, Whitman Comic Books)
1940 - Present
Dell Publishing Co./Gold Key #85 on

4-Color #4(1940)Sunday strip reprints by Al Taliaferro   400.00 800.00 1200.00
Black & White #16(1/41?)-Reprints 1940 Sunday strips in B&W   400.00 800.00 1200.00
Black & White #20('41)500.00 1000.00 1500.00
4-Color #9('42)-"Finds Pirate Gold"; 68pgs. by Carl Barks & Jack Hannah
          500.00 1000.00 1500.00
4-Color #29('43)-"Mummy's Ring" by Carl Barks-reprinted in Uncle Scrooge & Donald Duck #1('65) & W.D. Comics Digest #44('73)
          375.00 750.00 1125.00
(Prices vary widely on all above books)
4-Color #62('44)-"Frozen Gold"; 52pgs. by Carl Barks reprinted in The Best of W.D. Comics   175.00 350.00 525.00
4-Color #108-"Terror of the River"; 52pgs. by Carl Barks   100.00 200.00 300.00
4-Color #147-in "Volcano Valley" by Carl Barks   70.00 140.00 210.00
4-Color #159-in "The Ghost of the Grotto"; 52pgs. by Carl Barks-reprinted in Best of Uncle Scrooge & Donald Duck #1('66) & The Best of W.D. Comics; two Barks stories
          60.00 120.00 180.00
4-Color #178-1st Uncle Scrooge by Carl Barks-reprinted in Gold Key Christmas Parade #3 & The Best of W.D. Comics

	Good	Fine	Mint

          60.00 120.00 180.00
4-Color #189-by Carl Barks-reprinted in Best of Donald Duck & Uncle Scrooge #1('64)
          50.00 100.00 150.00
4-Color #199-by Barks   50.00 100.00 150.00
4-Color #203-by Barks-reprinted as Gold Key Christmas Parade #4 30.00 60.00 90.00
4-Color #223-by Barks-reprinted as Best of D. Duck #1('65)   35.00 70.00 105.00
4-Color #238,256-by Barks;#256-reprinted in Best of Donald Duck & Uncle Scrooge #2 ('67) & W.D. Comics Digest #44('73)
          25.00 50.00 75.00
4-Color #263-Two Barks stories
          25.00 50.00 75.00
4-Color #275,282,291-All by Carl Barks; #275, 282 reprinted in W.D. Comics Digest #44 ('73)   20.00 40.00 60.00
4-Color #300,308,318-by Barks; #318 reprinted in W.D. Comics Digest #34
          17.50 35.00 52.50
4-Color #328-by Carl Barks (drug issue)
          20.00 40.00 60.00
4-Color #339,379-not by Barks
           3.00 6.00 9.00
4-Color #348,356,394-Barks covers only
           4.00 8.00 12.00
4-Color #367-by Barks   15.00 30.00 45.00
4-Color #408,422-All by Carl Barks. #367-reprinted as G.K. Christmas Parade #2 & again as #8. #408-reprinted in Best of Donald Duck & Uncle Scrooge #1('64)
          14.00 28.00 42.00
#26(11-12/53)-In "Trick or Treat"(36pgs. of Barks art)-reprinted in Walt Disney Digest #16   12.00 24.00 36.00
27-30-Barks covers only 3.00 6.00 9.00
31-40   1.75 3.35 5.00
41-44,47-50   1.00 2.00 3.00

4-Color #147, © WDP   4-Color #282, © WDP   4-Color #367, © WDP

4-Color #995, © WDP   D.D. Tells About Kites (PG&E), © WDP   Donald Duck & The Boys('48), © WDP

(Donald Duck cont'd)	Good	Fine	Mint
45-Barks art(6pgs.)	4.00	8.00	12.00
46-"Secret of Hondorica" by Barks, 24pgs.-			
reprinted in D.D. #154-6.00		12.00	18.00
51-Half-pg. Barks	1.50	3.00	4.50
52-"Lost Peg-Leg Mine" by Barks, 10pgs.			
	4.00	8.00	12.00
53,55-59	1.00	2.00	3.00
54-"Forbidden Valley" by Barks, 26 pgs.			
	6.00	12.00	18.00
60-"D.D. & the Titanic Ants" by Barks, 20pgs.			
	5.00	10.00	15.00
61-67,69,70	.65	1.35	2.00
68-Barks art, 5pgs.	3.00	6.00	9.00
71,79,81-½pg.Barks reprt.1.50		3.00	4.50
72-78,80,82-97,100: #96-D.D. Album			
	.60	1.20	1.80
98-Reprints #46 (Barks)	2.00	4.00	6.00
99-Xmas Album	.65	1.35	2.00
101-133: #112-1st Moby Duck.25		.50	.75
134-Barks reprint(#52)	.80	1.60	2.40
135-Barks reprints, 19pgs. .65		1.35	2.00
136-153	.20	.40	.60
154-Barks reprint(#46)	.50	1.00	1.50
155,156,158	.20	.40	.60
157-Barks reprint(#45)	.35	.70	1.05
159-Reprints/WDC&S #192	.20	.40	.60
160,164-Barks reprint(#26)	.20	.40	.60
161-163,165-170	.15	.30	.45
171,177-Reprints	.15	.30	.45
172,173,175,176		.15	.30
174-Reprints 4-Color #394	.15	.30	.45
178-187,189,190		.15	.30
188-5pg. Barks reprint	.15	.30	.45

NOTE: *Carl Barks* wrote #117,126,134,135,138
only. Issues 4-Color #189,203,223,238,256,
263,275,348,356,367,394,408,422,#26-30,34,35,
44,51,57,65,70,71,73,78-81,83 all have Barks
covers. #96 titled "Comic Album", #99-"Christmas Album."

DONALD DUCK (Has Soft Cover)
1944 (16 pg. Christmas giveaway)(2 different)
K. K. Publications

Kelly cover reprint	60.00	120.00	180.00

DONALD DUCK ALBUM (See Duck Album & Comic
May-July, 1959 - Oct, 1963   Album #1,3)
Dell Publishing Co./Gold Key

4-Color #995,1099,1140,1182,1239(Barks cover),			
#01204-207('62-Dell)	1.00	2.00	3.00
#1(8/63-G.K.)	.35	.70	1.05
2(10/63)	.20	.40	.60

DONALD DUCK AND THE BOYS (Also see Story Hour
1948 (Hardcover book; 5¼x5½")   Series)
Whitman Publishing Co.

	Good	Fine	Mint
Partial reprint/WDC&S #74 by Barks			
	15.00	30.00	45.00

DONALD DUCK AND THE RED FEATHER
1948 (4 pgs.) (8½x11") (B&W)
Red Feather Giveaway

	2.00	4.00	6.00

DONALD DUCK BEACH PARTY
1954 - 1959; 1965 (25¢)
Dell Publishing Co./Gold Key('65)

#1	2.50	5.00	7.50
2-6	1.35	2.75	4.00
1(G.K. #10158-509 reprints Barks story from			
WDC&S #45)	2.50	5.00	7.50

DONALD DUCK BOOK (See Story Hour Series)

DONALD DUCK COMIC PAINT BOOK (See Black &
White #20)

DONALD DUCK FUN BOOK (Annual)
1953 - 1954 (100 pgs.) (25¢)
Dell Publishing Co.

#1('53), #2('54)	2.00	4.00	6.00

DONALD DUCK IN DISNEYLAND
1955 (Giant)
Dell Publishing Co.

#1	1.75	3.35	5.00

DONALD DUCK IN "THE LITTERBUG"
1963 (15 pgs.) (Disney giveaway)
Keep America Beautiful

	.65	1.35	2.00

DONALD DUCK MARCH OF COMICS
1947 - 1951 (Giveaway)(Disney)
K.K. Publications

No#(#4)-"Maharajah Donald"; 32pgs. by Carl			
Bark-(1947)	500.00	1000.00	1500.00
#20-"Darkest Africa" by Carl Barks-1948			
(24 pgs.)	350.00	700.00	1050.00
#41-"Race to South Seas" by Carl Barks-1949			
(24 pgs.)	250.00	500.00	750.00
#56(1950)-Not Barks	20.00	40.00	60.00

(Donald Duck March of Comics cont'd)

	Good	Fine	Mint
#69(1951)-Not Barks	15.00	30.00	45.00
#263	2.00	4.00	6.00

DONALD DUCK MERRY XMAS (See Dell Giant #53)

DONALD DUCK PICNIC PARTY (See Picnic Party)

DONALD DUCK "PLOTTING PICNICKERS"
1962   (14 pgs.) (Disney)
Fritos Giveaway

	1.00	2.00	3.00

DONALD DUCK'S SURPRISE PARTY
1948 (16 pgs.)(Giveaway for Icy Frost Twins
Walt Disney Productions   Ice Cream Bars)

Kelly art	30.00	60.00	90.00

DONALD DUCK TELLS ABOUT KITES
1954 (Giveaway) (8 pgs.-no cover)(Disney)
Southern California Edison Co./Pacific Gas
and Electric Co.

S.C.E. issue-Barks pencils-8pgs.; inks-7pgs.
   (Rare)   600.00 1200.00 1800.00
P.G.&E. issue-7th page redrawn changing
   middle 3 panels to show P.G.&E. in story
   line(All Barks; last page Barks pencils
   only) (Rare)   450.00 900.00 1350.00
      (Prices vary widely on above books)
NOTE: *These books appeared one month apart
in the fall and were distributed on the West
Coast only.*

DONALD DUCK, THIS IS YOUR LIFE (See 4-Color
Comics #1109)

DONALD DUCK XMAS ALBUM (See Reg. Series #99)

DONALD IN MATHMAGIC LAND (See 4-Color #1051,
#1198)

DONDI (See 4-Color Comics #1176,1276)

DON FORTUNE MAGAZINE
Aug, 1946 - #6, Feb, 1947
Don Fortune Publishing Co.

#1-Delecta of the Planets begins by C.C. Beck			
	2.00	4.00	6.00
2-6	1.50	3.00	4.50

DON NEWCOMBE
1950   (Baseball)
Fawcett Publications

No#	Good 1.50	Fine 3.00	Mint 4.50

DON'T GIVE UP THE SHIP (See 4-Color #1049)

DON WINSLOW OF THE NAVY (See 4-Color #2,22,
& Super Book #5,6)

DON WINSLOW OF THE NAVY (See TV Teens)
Feb, 1943 - #73, Sept, 1955
Fawcett Publications/Charlton #70 on

#1	17.50	35.00	52.50
2	7.00	14.00	21.00
3	5.00	10.00	15.00
4,5	4.00	8.00	12.00
6-10	3.00	6.00	9.00
11-20	2.50	5.00	7.50
21-40	1.75	3.35	5.00
41-64(12/48)	1.35	2.75	4.00
65(1/51)-73: #70,71 & 72 reprints #26,58 & 59			
	1.00	2.00	3.00

DOOM PATROL (My Greatest Adv. #1-85)
3/64 - #121, 9-10/68; 2/73 - #124, 6-7/73
National Periodical Publications

#86	.80	1.60	2.40
87-94: #88-Origin the Chief. #91-Intro.			
Mento. #94-Intro. Beast Boy			
	.40	.80	1.20
100-Origin Beast Boy; Robot-Maniac series			
begins	.40	.80	1.20
101-110: #105-Robot-Maniac series ends. #106-			
Negative Man begins(origin)			
	.35	.70	1.05
111-120	.25	.50	.75
121-Death of Doom Patrol; Orlando cover			
	.25	.50	.75
122-124(reprints)	.15	.30	.45

DOOMSDAY + 1
July, 1975 - #6, May, 1976
Charlton Comics

#1	.25	.50	.75
2-6	.15	.30	.45

DOORWAY TO NIGHTMARE
Jan-Feb, 1978 - Present
DC Comics, Inc.

#1	.15	.30	.45
2-Kaluta cover		.20	.35
3,4: #4-Craig story		.20	.35

DOPEY DUCK COMICS (Wacky Duck #3)

Don Winslow #12, © Faw

Don Winslow #71, © CC

Doom Patrol #90, © DC

Dotty Dripple #1, © ME

Double Comics 1941, © EP

The Double Life--#2, © AP

(Dopey Duck cont'd)
Fall, 1945 - #2, Apr, 1946 (See Super Funnies)
Timely Comics (NPP)

	Good	Fine	Mint
#1,2	1.00	2.00	3.00

DOROTHY LAMOUR-JUNGLE PRINCESS (Formerly Jun-
#2, 6/50 - #3, 8/50   gle Lil)
Fox Features Syndicate

#2,3-Wood story in ea.	5.00	10.00	15.00

DOT DOTLAND (Formerly Little Dot --)
#63, Nov, 1974
Harvey Publications

#63		.15	.30

DOTTY (-- & Her Boy Friends)(Glamorous Rom-
#35, 7/48 - #40, 5/49   ances #41 on)
Ace Magazines (A.A. Wyn)

#35-40	1.00	2.00	3.00

DOTTY DRIPPLE (Horace & Dotty Dripple #25 on)
1944 - #24, June, 1952
Magazine Ent.(Life's Romances)/Harvey #3 on

#1(no date)	1.00	2.00	3.00
No#(no date)-10¢	1.00	2.00	3.00
A-1#1-(no date)(M.E.-'44)	1.00	2.00	3.00
A-1#2-(M.E.-'44)	1.00	2.00	3.00
#3-24	.50	1.00	1.50

DOTTY DRIPPLE
Aug, 1955 - 1958
Dell Publishing Co.

4-Color #646,691,718,746,801,903, #7-11	.50	1.00	1.50

DOUBLE ACTION COMICS
#2, 1/40 (Reg.Size, 68pgs., B&W, color cover)
National Periodical Publications

Contains original stories; no costume heroes;
only one known copy. Same cover as Adventure
#37.   Estimated value.... $1,500.00

DOUBLE COMICS
1940 - 1944   (132 pgs.)
Elliott Publications

1940 issues	25.00	50.00	75.00
1941 issues	15.00	30.00	45.00
1942 issues	10.00	20.00	30.00
1943,44 issues	8.00	16.00	24.00

NOTE: Double Comics consisted of an almost endless
combination of pairs of remaindered, unsold issues of comics
representing most publishers and usually mixed publishers in the
same book; e. g., a Captain America with a Silver Streak, or a
Feature with a Detective, etc., could appear inside the same
cover. The actual contents would have to determine its price.
Prices listed are for average contents. Any containing rare origin
or first issues are worth much more. Covers also vary in same
year. Value would be 30 - 50% of contents.

DOUBLE DARE ADVENTURES
Dec, 1966 - #2, Mar, 1967   (25¢)
Harvey Publications

	Good	Fine	Mint
#1-Origin Bee-Man, Glowing Gladiator, & Mag- ic-Master; Kirby art	.80	1.60	2.40
2-Al Williamson/Crandall art; reprint Alarm- ing Adv. #3('63)	1.00	2.00	3.00

DOUBLE LIFE OF PRIVATE STRONG, THE
June, 1959 - #2, Aug, 1959
Archie Publications/Radio Comics

#1-Origin The Shield by Simon & Kirby	10.00	20.00	30.00
2-S&K Shield	5.00	10.00	15.00

DOUBLE UP
1941   (200 pgs.) (Pocket-Size)
Elliott Publications

#1-Contains rebound copies of digest sized issues of Pocket Comics, Speed Comics, & Spitfire Comics	15.00	30.00	45.00

DOUBLE TROUBLE
1958
St. John Publishing Co.

#1,2	.40	.80	1.20

DOUBLE TROUBLE WITH GOOBER
1952 - 1953
Dell Publishing Co.

4-Color #417,471,516,556	.50	1.00	1.50
#1	.40	.80	1.20

DOVER BOYS (Adventures of the --)
1950
Archie Comics

#1	1.35	2.75	4.00

DOVER THE BIRD
1955
Famous Funnies Publishing Co.

#1	.30	.65	1.00

DOWN WITH CRIME
Nov, 1952 - #7, 1953
Fawcett Publications

	Good	Fine	Mint
#1	1.00	2.00	3.00
2,4-7: #5-Bondage cover	.65	1.35	2.00
3-Heroin drug cover/story	2.50	5.00	7.50

DO YOU BELIEVE IN NIGHTMARES?
Nov, 1957 - #2, Jan, 1958
St. John Publishing Co.

#1-Ditko art	1.75	3.35	5.00
2-Ayers art	.80	1.60	2.40

DRACULA
(See Book & Record --, Tomb of --, & Movie Classics under Universal Presents as well as Dracula)

DRACULA
(See Movie Classics for #1)
9/66 - #4, 3/67; #6, 7/72 - #8, 7/73 (No#5)
Dell Publishing Co.

#2-Origin Dracula(9/66)	.35	.70	1.05
3,4-Intro. Fleeta #4('67)	.25	.50	.75
6-('72)-reprints #2	.25	.50	.75
7,8: #7 reprints #3, 8-#4	.20	.40	.60

DRACULA LIVES! (Magazine)
1973(no month) - #14, 9/75 (B&W) (75¢)
Marvel Comics Group

#1-Buckler art	1.00	2.00	3.00
2-Origin; Adams story/cover; Starlin art	1.00	2.00	3.00
3-Adams cover; story inks	.75	1.50	2.25
4-Ploog story	.65	1.35	2.00
5(V2#1)-#14: #7-Evans story. #9-Alcala art	.50	1.00	1.50
Annual #1('75)-Adams reprt.	.50	1.00	1.50

DRAG CARTOONS (Magazine)
#1, 6-7/63; #2, 12/63 - 1970's
(Later issues-no numbers)
Millar Publ./Professional Serv./Lopez Publ.

#1-Russ Manning + Warren Tufts art	1.25	2.50	3.75
2-Russ Manning art	.65	1.35	2.00
3-5,7,9-11,13-24	.20	.40	.60
6,8-Toth art	.30	.65	1.00
12-Griffin & Toth art	1.00	2.00	3.00
25-49: Wonder Wart-Hog by Gilbert Shelton in all; The Adventures of Bull O' Fuzz & other strips	.50	1.00	1.50
50-60	.15	.30	.45

DRAG 'N' SURF
1969

Charlton Comics

	Good	Fine	Mint
#1	.20	.40	.60

DRAG 'N' WHEELS (Formerly Top Eliminator)
#30, Sept, 1968 - #59, May, 1973
Charlton Comics

#30-59-Scot Jackson feat.		.10	.15

DRAGOON WELLS MASSACRE (See 4-Color #815)

DRAGSTRIP HOTRODDERS (World of Wheels #17 on)
Nov-Dec, 1963 - #16, May-June, 1967
Charlton Comics

#1		.15	.30
2-16		.10	.15

DRAMA OF AMERICA, THE
1973   (224 pgs.)   ($1.95)
Action Text

#1-"Students' Supplement to History"	.65	1.35	2.00

DREAM BOOK OF LOVE (See A-1 Comics #106,114, 123)

DREAM BOOK OF ROMANCE (See A-1 Comics #92, 101,109,124)

DREAM OF LOVE
1958   (Reprints)
I.W. Enterprises

#1,2,8,9	.50	1.00	1.50

DRIFT MARLO
May-July, 1962 - #2, Oct-Dec, 1962
Dell Publishing Co.

#01-232-207, #2(12-232-212)	.40	.80	1.20

DRISCOLL'S BOOK OF PIRATES
1934   (124 pgs.)(B&W)(Hardcover)(7x9")
David McKay Publ.   (Not reprints)

By Montford Amory	5.00	10.00	15.00

DRUM BEAT (See 4-Color Comics #610)

DUCK ALBUM (See Donald Duck Album)
Oct, 1951 - Sept, 1957
Dell Publishing Co.

4-Color #353,450	1.35	2.75	4.00
4-Color #492,531,560,586	1.20	2.40	3.60

Down With Crime #1. © Faw   Do You Believe In Nightmares #1. © STJ   Dracula #2. © Dell

Dumbo, 1941 Giveaway, © WDP   Dumbo Weekly #11, © WDP   Durango Kid #14, © ME

(Duck Album cont'd)	Good	Fine	Mint
4-Color #611,649,686	1.00	2.00	3.00
4-Color #726,782,840	.65	1.35	2.00

DUDLEY
Nov-Dec, 1949 - #3, Mar-Apr, 1950
Feature/Prize Publications

#1-By Boody Rogers	1.00	2.00	3.00
2,3	.65	1.35	2.00

DUDLEY DO-RIGHT (TV)
Aug, 1970 - #7, Aug, 1971 (Jay Ward)
Charlton Comics

#1-7		.15	.30

DUKE OF THE K-9 PATROL
April, 1963
Gold Key

#1(10052-304)	.35	.70	1.05

DUMBO (See 4-Color #17,234,668, Movie Comics, & Walt Disney Showcase #12)

DUMBO (Walt Disney's --)
1941 (K.K. Publ. Giveaway)
Weatherbird Shoes/Ernest Kern Co.(Detroit)

16pgs., 9x10" (Rare)	25.00	50.00	75.00
24pgs., 5½x8½", slick cover in color; B&W interior	8.00	16.00	24.00

DUMBO COMIC PAINT BOOK (See Black & White#19)

DUMBO WEEKLY
1942 (Premium supplied by Diamond D-X Gas
Walt Disney Productions   Stations)

16 known issues - each...	8.00	16.00	24.00

DUNC AND LOO (#1 titled "Around the Block
with Dunc and Loo")
1961 - #8, Oct-Dec, 1963
Dell Publishing Co.

#1	.50	1.00	1.50
2-8	.25	.50	.75

NOTE: *Written by John Stanley; Bill Williams
art.*

DURANGO KID (Also see White Indian)
Oct-Nov, 1949 - #41, 1955
Magazine Enterprises

#1-White Indian by Frazetta begins(origin);
Frazetta art continues through #16

	Good	Fine	Mint
	25.00	50.00	75.00
2-5	12.00	24.00	36.00
6-16-Last Frazetta ish.	10.00	20.00	30.00
17-Origin Durango Kid	5.00	10.00	15.00
18-30	2.00	4.00	6.00
31-41	1.50	3.00	4.50

NOTE: *#6,8,14,15 contain Frazetta stories
not reprinted in White Indian.*

DWIGHT D. EISENHOWER
December, 1969
Dell Publishing Co.

#01-237-912 - Life story	1.50	3.00	4.50

DYNAMIC ADVENTURES
#9, 1964
I.W. Enterprises

#9-Reprints Avon's "Escape From Devil's Island"	1.00	2.00	3.00
No#,no date-Reprts. Risks Unlimited with Rip Carson, Senorita Rio	.65	1.35	2.00

DYNAMIC COMICS (No #4-7)
Oct, 1941 - #25, May, 1948
Harry 'A' Chesler

#1-Origin Major Victory by Charles Sultan(reprinted in Major Victory #1), Dynamic Man & Hale the Magician; The Black Cobra only app.	20.00	40.00	60.00
2-Origin Dynamic Boy & Lady Satan; Intro. the Green Knight & Sidekick Lance Cooper	10.00	20.00	30.00
3	6.00	12.00	18.00
8-Dan Hastings, The Echo, The Master Key, Yankee Boy begin; Yankee Doodle Jones app.	4.00	8.00	12.00
9-Mr. E begins	4.00	8.00	12.00
10-14,16,18-20	2.50	5.00	7.50
15-The Sky Chief app.	2.50	5.00	7.50
17-Used "We'll drain this dame dry" photo in Seduction of the Innocent	5.00	10.00	15.00
21,22,24,25	2.00	4.00	6.00
23-Yankee Girl app.	2.00	4.00	6.00
IW Reprint #1-Yankee Girl('64), #8	.80	1.60	2.40

DYNAMITE (Johnny Dynamite #10 on)
May, 1953 - #9, Dec, 1955?
Comic Media/Allen Hard Publ.

#1-Pete Morisi art	1.00	2.00	3.00
2	.65	1.35	2.00

(Dynamite cont'd)

	Good	Fine	Mint
3-Johnny Dynamite begins by Pete Morisi; F. Robbins art	.80	1.60	2.40
4-9: #9-Morisi art	.65	1.35	2.00

DYNAMO
Aug, 1966 - #4, June, 1967   (25¢)
Tower Comics

	Good	Fine	Mint
#1-Crandall, Ditko art; Weed series begins; NoMan & Lightning cameos; Wood cover & stories	1.35	2.75	4.00
2-4: Wood covers & stories in all	1.00	2.00	3.00

DYNOMUTT (TV)
Nov, 1977 - Present
Marvel Comics Group

	Good	Fine	Mint
#1,2	.15	.30	.45

EAGLE, THE (1st Series)
July, 1941 - #4, Jan, 1942
Fox Features Syndicate

	Good	Fine	Mint
#1-The Eagle begins; Rex Dexter of Mars app.	25.00	50.00	75.00
2-Origin The Spider Queen	15.00	30.00	45.00
3-Origin Joe Spook	10.00	20.00	30.00
4	10.00	20.00	30.00

EAGLE (2nd Series)
Feb-Mar, 1945 - #2, Apr-May, 1945
Rural Home Publ.

	Good	Fine	Mint
#1-Aviation stories	2.00	4.00	6.00
2-Lucky Aces	1.00	2.00	3.00

EARTH MAN ON VENUS (An --)
1951   (Also see Strange Planets)
Avon Periodicals

	Good	Fine	Mint
No#-Wood story, 26pgs.	25.00	50.00	75.00

EASTER BONNET SHOP (See March of Comics #29)

EASTER WITH MOTHER GOOSE (See 4-Color #103, 140,185,220)

EAT RIGHT TO WORK AND WIN
1942   (16 pgs.) (Giveaway)
Swift & Company

Blondie, Henry, Flash Gordon by A. Raymond, Toots & Casper, Thimble Theatre(Popeye), Tillie the Toiler, The Phantom, The Little King, & Bringing Up Father - original strips just for this book - (in daily strip form which shows what foods we should eat & why)

	Good	Fine	Mint
	30.00	60.00	90.00

E.C. CLASSIC REPRINTS
May, 1973 - #12, 1976 (E.C. Comics reprinted in full color minus ads)
East Coast Comix Co.

	Good	Fine	Mint
#1-The Crypt of Terror #1(Tales From the Crypt #46)	3.00	6.00	9.00
2-Weird Science #15('52)	1.50	3.00	4.50
3-Shock SuspenStories #12	.50	1.00	1.50
4-Haunt of Fear #12	.50	1.00	1.50
5-Weird Fantasy #13	.50	1.00	1.50
6-Crime SuspenStories #25	.50	1.00	1.50
7-Vault of Horror #26	.50	1.00	1.50
8-Shock SuspenStories #6	.50	1.00	1.50
9-Two-Fisted Tales #34	.50	1.00	1.50
10-Haunt of Fear #23	.50	1.00	1.50
11-Weird Science #12(#1)	.50	1.00	1.50
12-Shock SuspenStories #2	.50	1.00	1.50

E.C. 3-D CLASSICS (#2 titled "3-D Tales of Terror") (worth less without glasses)
Spring, 1954 - #2, Spring, 1954
E.C. Comics

	Good	Fine	Mint
#1-Reprints: Wood(Mad #3), Krigstein(W.S.#7), Evans(F.C.#13), & Ingels(CSS #5); Kurtzman cover	10.00	20.00	30.00
2-Davis(TFTC #25), Elder(VOH #14), Craig (TFTC #24), & Orlando(TFTC #22) stories; Feldstein cover	7.00	14.00	21.00

NOTE: Stories redrawn to 3-D format. Original stories not necessarily by artists listed. TFTC: Tales From the Crypt; VOH: Vault of Horror.

EDDIE STANKY (Baseball Hero)
1951   (New York Giants)
Fawcett Publications

	Good	Fine	Mint
No#	1.50	3.00	4.50

EDGAR BERGEN PRESENTS CHARLIE McCARTHY
1938   (36 pgs.)(15"x10½")(In Color)
Whitman Publishing Co.(Charlie McCarthy Co.)

	Good	Fine	Mint
#764	12.00	24.00	36.00

EDWARD'S SHOES GIVEAWAY
1954   (Has clown on cover)
Edward's Shoe Store

Contains comic with new cover. Many combinations possible. Contents determines price.

Dynamic #3, © Ches

Dynamo #3, © Tower

An Earth Man On Venus, © Avon

Edgar Bergen Presents--#764, © Whit　　　　Eerie #2, © Avon　　　　Egbert #12, © Qua

(Edward's Shoes Giveaway cont'd)
(Similar to Comics From Weatherbird & Free
Comics To You)

ED WHEELAN'S JOKE BOOK STARRING FAT & SLAT
(See Fat & Slat)

EERIE (Magazine)
#1, Sept, 1965; #2, Mar, 1966 - Present
Warren Publishing Co.

	Good	Fine	Mint
#1			

24 pgs., B&W, small size (5¼x7¼"), low distribution; cover from
inside back cover of Creepy No. 2; stories reprinted from Creepy
No. 7, 8. At least three different versions exist.

First Printing — B&W, 5¼" wide x 7¼" high, evenly trimmed. On
page 18, panel 5, in the upper left-hand corner, the large rear view
of a bald headed man blends into solid black and is unrecogniz-
able. Overall printing quality is poor.

	50.00	100.00	150.00

Second Printing — B&W, 5¼x7¼", with uneven, untrimmed edges
(if one of these were trimmed evenly, the size would be less than
as indicated). The figure of the bald headed man on page 18, panel 5 is cleared and discernible. The staples have a ¼" blue stripe.

	15.00	30.00	45.00

Other unauthorized reproductions for comparison's sake would
be practically worthless. One known version was probably shot
off a first printing copy with some loss of detail; the finer lines
tend to disappear in this version which can be determined by
looking at the lower right-hand corner of page one, first story.
The roof of the house is shaded with straight lines. These lines are
sharp and distinct on original, but broken on this version.

	1.00	2.00	3.00

NOTE: *THE PRICE GUIDE recommends that, before buying,
you consult an expert.*

	Good	Fine	Mint
#2-Frazetta cover	2.50	5.00	7.50
3-Frazetta cover, 1pg.	1.75	3.35	5.00
4-10: #4-Frazetta ½ pg.	1.50	3.00	4.50
11-19	1.20	2.40	3.60
20-25	1.00	2.00	3.00
26-42: #39-1st Dax by Maroto. #42-Williamson			
reprint	.75	1.50	2.25
43-46	.65	1.35	2.00
47-78: #78-The Mummy reprts.	.50	1.00	1.50
79,80-Origin Darklon the Mystic by Starlin			
	.50	1.00	1.50
81-88	.40	.80	1.20
Year Book 1970,71 reprts.	1.35	2.75	4.00
Year Book 1972,73 reprts.	.80	1.60	2.40
Year Book 1974,75 reprts.	.50	1.00	1.50

NOTE: *The above books contain art by many
good artists: Adams, Brunner, Corben, Craig
(Taycee), Crandall, Ditko, Eisner, Evans,
Jeff Jones, Kinstler, Krenkel, McWilliams,
Morrow, Orlando, Ploog, Severin, Starlin,
Torres, Toth, Williamson, Wood, & Wrightson;
covers by Bode', Corben, Davis, Frazetta,
Morrow, & Orlando.*

EERIE (Strange Worlds #18 on)
#1, 1/47; #1, 5-6/51 - #17, 8-9/54
Avon Periodicals

	Good	Fine	Mint
#1(1947)-Kubert art	6.00	12.00	18.00
1(1951)	5.00	10.00	15.00
2-Wood cover & story	5.00	10.00	15.00
3-Wood cover, Kubert + Wood/Orlando story			
	5.00	10.00	15.00
4,5-Wood covers + 1 pg. art			
	3.00	6.00	9.00
6,10-15	1.50	3.00	4.50
7,9-Kubert stories	2.00	4.00	6.00
8-Kinstler story	1.50	3.00	4.50
16-Wood story reprint	3.00	6.00	9.00
17-Wood/Orlando & Kubert story; reprints #3			
minus inside Wood cvr.	3.00	6.00	9.00

EERIE
1964
I.W. Enterprises

IW Reprint #1(Wood cover reprint)('64)			
	1.00	2.00	3.00
IW Reprint #2,6,8(Dr. Drew by Grandenetti-			
Ghost #9)	.80	1.60	2.40
IW Reprint #9-Wood cover	1.00	2.00	3.00

EERIE ADVENTURES
Winter, 1951 - 1953
Ziff-Davis Publ. Co. (Approved)

#1-Powell story	1.75	3.35	5.00
2-7,9-11	.80	1.60	2.40
8-Kinstler story	1.20	2.40	3.60

EERIE TALES (Magazine)
1959 (Black & White)
Hastings Associates

#1-Williamson + Torres, Powell(2), & Morrow			
2 stories	5.00	10.00	15.00

EERIE TALES
1964
Super Comics

Super Reprint #10,11,12,18: Purple Claw in

#11,12	.65	1.35	2.00
15-Wolverton story-Spacehawk reprt/Blue Bolt			
W. Tales #113	1.50	3.00	4.50

EGBERT
Spring, 1946 - #20, 1950
Arnold Publications/Quality Comics Group

#1	2.00	4.00	6.00
2-10	1.00	2.00	3.00
11-20	.65	1.35	2.00

EH! (-- Dig This Crazy Comic)(From Here To Insanity #8 on)
Dec, 1953 - 1954   (Satire)
Charlton Comics

	Good	Fine	Mint
#1	2.50	5.00	7.50
2-7	1.50	3.00	4.50

80 PAGE GIANT (-- Magazine #1-15) (25¢)
8/64 - #15, 10/65; #16, 11/65 - #89, 7/71
National Periodical Publ. (#57-89, 68pgs.)

	Good	Fine	Mint
#1-Superman	2.50	5.00	7.50
2-Jimmy Olsen	1.50	3.00	4.50
3-Lois Lane	1.20	2.40	3.60
4-Flash-G.A. reprint; Infantino art			
	1.00	2.00	3.00
5-Batman	1.00	2.00	3.00
6-Superman	1.00	2.00	3.00
7-Sgt. Rock's Prize Battle Tales; Kubert cover + stories	.80	1.60	2.40
8-More Secret Origins-origins of JLA, Aquaman, Robin, Atom, & Superman; Infantino art	2.00	4.00	6.00
9-Flash(Reprints Flash #123)-Infantino art			
	.80	1.60	2.40
10-Superboy	.80	1.60	2.40
11-Superman	.65	1.35	2.00
12-Batman	.65	1.35	2.00
13-Jimmy Olsen	.65	1.35	2.00
14-Lois Lane	.65	1.35	2.00
15-World's Finest	.65	1.35	2.00

Continued as part of regular series under each title in which that particular book came out, a Giant being published instead of the regular size. Issues No. 16 to No. 89 are listed for your information. See individual titles for prices.

16-JLA #39(11/65)
17-Batman #176
18-Superman #183
19-Our Army at War #164
20-Action #334
21-Flash #160
22-Superboy #129
23-Superman #187
24-Batman #182
25-Jimmy Olsen #95
26-Lois Lane #68
27-Batman #185
28-World's Finest #161
29-JLA #48
30-Batman #187
31-Superman #193
32-Our Army at War #177
33-Action #347
34-Flash #169

35-Superboy #138
36-Superman #197
37-Batman #193
38-Jimmy Olsen #104
39-Lois Lane #77
40-World's Finest #170
41-JLA #58
42-Superman #202
43-Batman #198
44-Our Army at War #190
45-Action #360
46-Flash #178
47-Superboy #147
48-Superman #207
49-Batman #203
50-Jimmy Olsen #113
51-Lois Lane #86
52-World's Finest #179
53-JLA #67
54-Superman #212

55-Batman #208
56-Our Army at War #203
57-Action #373
58-Flash #187
59-Superboy #156
60-Superman #217
61-Batman #213
62-Jimmy Olsen #122
63-Lois Lane #95
64-World's Finest #188
65-JLA #76
66-Superman #222
67-Batman #218
68-Our Army at War #216
69-Adventure #390
70-Flash #196
71-Superboy #165

72-Superman #227
73-Batman #223
74-Jimmy Olsen #131
75-Lois Lane #104
76-World's Finest #197
77-JLA #85
78-Superman #232
79-Batman #228
80-Our Army at War #229
81-Adventure #403
82-Flash #205
83-Superboy #174
84-Superman #239
85-Batman #233
86-Jimmy Olsen #140
87-Lois Lane #113
88-World's Finest #206
89-JLA #93

87TH PRECINCT (TV)
Apr-June, 1962 - #2, July-Sept, 1962
Dell Publishing Co.

	Good	Fine	Mint
4-Color #1309(Krigstein art)			
	1.75	3.35	5.00
#2	1.00	2.00	3.00

EL BOMBO COMICS
1946
Standard Comics/Frances M. McQueeny

No#(1946)	1.75	3.35	5.00
#1(no date)	1.75	3.35	5.00

EL CID (See 4-Color Comics #1259)

EL DORADO (See Movie Classics)

ELLA CINDERS (See Famous Comics Cartoon Book)

ELLA CINDERS
1938 - 1940
United Features Syndicate

Single Series #3('38)	8.00	16.00	24.00
Single Series #21(#2 on cover, #21 on inside)			
#28('40)	7.00	14.00	21.00

ELLA CINDERS (See Comics Revue #1,4)
1948 - #5, 1949
United Features Syndicate

#1	2.00	4.00	6.00
2-5	1.20	2.40	3.60

ELLERY QUEEN
May, 1949 - #4, Nov, 1949

80 Page Giant #1. © DC

El Bombo #1. © STD

Ellery Queen #2. © SUPR

Elmer Fudd, 4-Color #470, © Dell   E-Man #1, © CC   Escape From Devil's Island #1, © Avon

(Ellery Queen cont'd)
Superior Comics Ltd.

	Good	Fine	Mint
#1	5.00	10.00	15.00
2-4	3.00	6.00	9.00

NOTE: _Baker art_; _Kamen covers-#1-3._

ELLERY QUEEN
1-3/52 - #2, Summer/52 (Painted covers)
Ziff-Davis Publishing Co.

#1,2	2.00	4.00	6.00

ELLERY QUEEN (See 4-Color #1165,1243,1289)

ELMER FUDD
May, 1953 - #1293, Mar-May, 1962
Dell Publishing Co.

4-Color #470,558,628,689('56)			
	.65	1.35	2.00
4-Color #725,783,841,888,938,977,1032,1081,			
1131,1171,1222,1293('61)	.50	1.00	1.50

(See Super Book #10,22, & No#)

ELMO
January, 1948
St. John Publishing Co.

#1-Daily newspaper strip reprints			
	1.35	2.75	4.00

ELSIE THE COW
Oct-Nov, 1949 - #3, Jul-Aug, 1950
D.S. Publishing Co.

#1-(36pgs.)	4.00	8.00	12.00
2,3	2.00	4.00	6.00
Borden Milk Giveaway(16pgs., No#),(3 issues, 1957)	1.25	2.50	3.75
Elsie's Fun Book(1950, Borden Milk)			
	1.50	3.00	4.50
Everyday Birthday Fun With--(1957, 20pgs.- 100th Anniversary)	1.25	2.50	3.75

E-MAN
Oct, 1973 - #10, Sept, 1975
Charlton Comics

#1-Origin E-Man by Joe Staton			
	1.35	2.75	4.00
2-Ditko art	1.00	2.00	3.00
3,4: #3-Howard art. #4-Ditko art			
	.65	1.35	2.00
5-Miss Liberty Belle app. by Ditko			
	.50	1.00	1.50
6-10	.50	1.00	1.50

EMERGENCY (Magazine)
June, 1976 - #4, Jan, 1977 (B&W)
Charlton Comics

	Good	Fine	Mint
#1-Adams cover/stories	.50	1.00	1.50
2,3-Adams covers, story-#3			
	.40	.80	1.20
4	.35	.70	1.05

EMERGENCY (TV)
June, 1976 - #4, Dec, 1976
Charlton Comics

#1	.20	.40	.60
2-4	.15	.30	.45

EMERGENCY DOCTOR
Summer, 1963 (One Shot)
Charlton Comics

#1	.15	.30	.45

EMIL & THE DETECTIVES (See Movie Comics)

EMMA PEEL & JOHN STEED (See The Avengers)

ENCHANTMENT VISUALETTES (Magazine)
1949 - V1#5, April, 1950
World Editions

V1#1-4-Contains romance comic strips			
	5.00	10.00	15.00
V1#5-Contains two romance comic strips			
	5.00	10.00	15.00

ENCHANTING LOVE
Oct, 1949 - #6, July, 1950
Kirby Publishing Co.

#1	1.35	2.75	4.00
2-6: #2-Powell art	.75	1.50	2.25

ENEMY ACE (See Star-Spangled War Stories)

ENSIGN O'TOOLE (TV)
Aug-Oct, 1963 - #2, 1964
Dell Publishing Co.

#1,2	.25	.50	.75

ENSIGN PULVER (See Movie Classics)

ERNIE COMICS (All Love Romances #26 on)
Sept, 1948 - #25, Mar, 1949
Current Books/Ace Periodicals

No#(9/48,11/48)	.65	1.35	2.00
#24,25	.50	1.00	1.50

ESCAPADE IN FLORENCE (See Movie Comics)

ESCAPE FROM DEVIL'S ISLAND
1952   (Also see Dynamic Adventures)
Avon Periodicals

	Good	Fine	Mint
#1-Kinstler cover-reprinted as Dynamic Adv.#9			
	3.00	6.00	9.00

ESCAPE TO WITCH MOUNTAIN (See Walt Disney
Showcase #29)

ESPIONAGE (TV)
May-July, 1964 - #2, Aug-Oct, 1964
Dell Publishing Co.

#1,2	.25	.50	.75

ETERNAL BIBLE, THE
1946   (Large Size) (16 pgs. in Color)
Authentic Publications

#1	1.35	2.75	4.00

ETERNALS, THE
July, 1976 - #19, Jan, 1978
Marvel Comics Group

#1	.40	.80	1.20
2-5	.25	.50	.75
6-19	.20	.40	.60
Annual #1(10/77)-Kirby cover/art			
	.25	.50	.75

NOTE: *Kirby covers/stories-#1-6.*

ETTA KETT
#11, Dec, 1948 - #14, Sept, 1949
King Features Syndicate/Standard

#11-14	1.50	3.00	4.50

EVA THE IMP
1957
Red Top Comic/Decker

#1,2	.35	.70	1.05

EVEL KNIEVEL
1974   (16 pgs.) (Giveaway)
Marvel Comics Group (Ideal Toy Corp.)

No#-Sekowsky art	.35	.70	1.05

EVERYBODY'S COMICS
1944 - 1947
Fox Features Syndicate

#1(1944)-The Green Mask, The Puppeteer;

	Good	Fine	Mint
194 pgs.	4.00	8.00	12.00
#1(1946)-Contents vary-Green Lama, The Pupp-			
eteer app.	3.00	6.00	9.00
#1(1946)-Same as the 1945 Ribtickler			
	1.35	2.75	4.00
1947 (132 pgs.)	2.35	4.75	7.00

EVERYTHING HAPPENS TO HARVEY
Sept-Oct, 1953 - #7, Sept-Oct, 1954
National Periodical Publications

#1	1.00	2.00	3.00
2-7	.50	1.00	1.50

EVERYTHING'S ARCHIE
May, 1969 - Present
Archie Publications

#1(Giant)	.80	1.60	2.40
2-10(Giants)	.35	.70	1.05
11-20	.20	.40	.60
21-62		.15	.30

EVERYTHING'S DUCKY (See 4-Color #1251)

EXCITING COMICS
April, 1940 - #69, Sept, 1949
Nedor/Better Publications/Standard Comics

#1-Origin The Mask, Jim Hatfield, Sgt. Bill King, Dan Williams begin			
	30.00	60.00	90.00
2-The Sphinx begins; The Masked Rider app.			
	15.00	30.00	45.00
3	12.00	24.00	36.00
4	10.00	20.00	30.00
5	8.00	16.00	24.00
6-8	7.00	14.00	21.00
9-Origin & 1st app. of The Black Terror & Sidekick Tim	35.00	70.00	105.00
10-13	17.50	35.00	52.50
14-Last Sphinx, Dan Williams			
	10.00	20.00	30.00
14-Origin The Liberator	12.00	24.00	36.00
16-20: #20-The Mask ends	8.00	16.00	24.00
21,23-30: #28-Crime Crusader begins, ends			
#59	7.00	14.00	21.00
22-Origin The Eaglet; The American Eagle begins	8.00	16.00	24.00
31-38	5.00	10.00	15.00
39-Origin Kara, Jungle Princess			
	6.00	12.00	18.00
40-50: #42-The Scarab begins. #49-Last Kara, Jungle Princess	5.00	10.00	15.00
51-Miss Masque begins	6.00	12.00	18.00
52-54	5.00	10.00	15.00
55-Judy of the Jungle begins(origin); 1pg.			

Everybody's Comics #1, © Fox

Exciting Comics #18, © BP

Exciting Comics #57, © BP

Exploits of --#5, © Qua   The Face #2, © CCG   Fairy Tale Parade #6, © Dell

	Good	Fine	Mint
(Exciting Comics cont'd)			
Ingels art	6.00	12.00	18.00
56-58: All airbrush cvrs.	5.00	10.00	15.00
59-Frazetta art in Caniff style; signed Frank			
Frazeta, 9 pgs.	8.00	16.00	24.00
60-66-Rick Howard, the Mystery Rider begins-			
#60	5.00	10.00	15.00
67-69-Last Black Terror	3.50	7.00	10.50

NOTE: _Schomburg (Xela) covers-#56-66. #66-
last airbrush cover._

EXCITING ROMANCES
1949 - 1953
Fawcett Publications

	Good	Fine	Mint
#1	1.00	2.00	3.00
2-12	.65	1.35	2.00

EXCITING ROMANCE STORIES
1949   (132 pgs.)
Fox Features Syndicate

No#-See Fox Giants. Contents can vary and
determines price.

EXCITING WAR
#5, Sept, 1952 - #8, May, 1953; #9, 11/53
Standard Comics (Better Publ.)

	Good	Fine	Mint
#5-7,9	.65	1.35	2.00
8-Toth story	1.50	3.00	4.50

EXORCISTS (See The Crusaders)

EXOTIC ROMANCES (Formerly True War Romances)
#22, Oct, 1955 - #31, Nov, 1956
Quality Comics Group (Comic Magazines)

	Good	Fine	Mint
#22-31	.65	1.35	2.00

EXPLOITS OF DANIEL BOONE
Nov, 1955 - #8, Dec, 1956
Quality Comics Group

	Good	Fine	Mint
#1	2.00	4.00	6.00
2-8	1.35	2.75	4.00

EXPLOITS OF DICK TRACY (See Dick Tracy)

EXPLORER JOE
Winter, 1951 - #2, 10-11/52 (Painted Covers)
Ziff-Davis Publ. Co.

	Good	Fine	Mint
#1	1.35	2.75	4.00
2-Krigstein story	2.00	4.00	6.00

EXPOSED (-- True Crime Cases)
Mar-Apr, 1948 - #9, July-Aug, 1949
D.S. Publishing Co.

	Good	Fine	Mint
#1	1.20	2.40	3.60
2-4,7-9	.65	1.35	2.00
5-Breeze Lawton, Sky Sheriff by Good			
	.65	1.35	2.00
6-Ingels art	2.00	4.00	6.00

NOTE: _Orlando story-#4._

EXTRA   (Magazine)
1949
Magazine Enterprises

	Good	Fine	Mint
#1-Funny Man by Siegel & Shuster, Space Ace,			
Undercover Girl	5.00	10.00	15.00

EXTRA!
Mar-Apr, 1955 - #5, Nov-Dec, 1955
E.C. Comics

	Good	Fine	Mint
#1	4.00	8.00	12.00
2-5	3.00	6.00	9.00

NOTE: _Craig, Crandall, Severin art in all._

FACE, THE (Tony Trent, the Face #3 on)
1941
Columbia Comics Group

	Good	Fine	Mint
#1-The Face	12.00	24.00	36.00
2	6.00	12.00	18.00

FAIRY TALE PARADE (See Famous Fairy Tales)
June-July, 1942 - 1946 (All by Walt Kelly)
Dell Publishing Co.

	Good	Fine	Mint
#1-All by Kelly	100.00	200.00	300.00
2(1943)	60.00	120.00	180.00
3-5	40.00	80.00	120.00
6-9: #7-Kelly cover	30.00	60.00	90.00
4-Color #50('44)	25.00	50.00	75.00
4-Color #69('45)	25.00	50.00	75.00
4-Color #87('45)	20.00	40.00	60.00
4-Color #104,114('46)	15.00	30.00	45.00
4-Color #121('46)-Not Kelly			
	8.00	16.00	24.00

NOTE: _#2-9 partially by Kelly._

FAIRY TALES
#10, 1951 - #11, Jun-Jul, 1951
Ziff-Davis Publ. Co. (Approved Comics)

	Good	Fine	Mint
#10,11	1.50	3.00	4.50

FAITHFUL
November, 1949
Marvel Comics/Lovers' Magazine

	Good	Fine	Mint
#1	1.00	2.00	3.00

FALLING IN LOVE
Sept-Oct, 1955 - #143, Oct-Nov, 1973
Arleigh Publ. Co./National Per. Publ.

	Good	Fine	Mint
#1	1.75	3.35	5.00
2-20	.65	1.35	2.00
21-40	.35	.70	1.05
41-100	.25	.50	.75
101-143		.15	.30

FALL OF THE ROMAN EMPIRE (See Movie Comics)

FAMILY AFFAIR (TV)
Feb, 1970 - #4, Oct, 1970   (25¢)
Gold Key

#1-Pull-out poster	.35	.70	1.05
2-4	.20	.40	.60

FAMILY FUNNIES
#9, Aug-Sept, 1946
Parents' Magazine Institute

#9	1.35	2.75	4.00

FAMILY FUNNIES
Sept, 1950 - 1953
Harvey Publications

#1-Mandrake	2.50	5.00	7.50
2-10: #4-Flash Gordon	2.00	4.00	6.00
11-20	1.35	2.75	4.00
21-35	1.20	2.40	3.60
#1(Black & White)	1.35	2.75	4.00

FAMOUS AUTHORS ILL.   (See Stories by --)

FAMOUS COMICS
No date; Early 1930's (24 pgs.) (no cover)
Zain-Eppy/United Features Syndicate

34 strips reprinted from newspaper strips in
color; Joe Palooka, Hairbreadth Harry, Napol-
eon, The Nebbs, etc.   15.00 30.00 45.00

FAMOUS COMICS   (1st King Features comic book)
1934 (100pgs., daily newspaper reprints)
3½x8½", soft cover) (Came in a box)
King Features Synd. (Whitman Publ. Co.)

#684(#1)-Little Jimmy, Polly & Her Pals &
   Katzenjammer Kids, Barney Google
                12.00 24.00 36.00
#684(#2)-Polly, Little Jimmy, Katzenjammer
   Kids   9.00 18.00 27.00
#684(#3)-Little Annie Rooney, Polly, Katzen-
   jammer Kids   9.00 18.00 27.00

FAMOUS COMICS CARTOON BOOKS
1934 (68pgs.)(8x7¾")(Daily strip reprints)
Whitman Publishing Co.   (B&W: hardbacks)

	Good	Fine	Mint
#1200-The Captain & the Kids			
	10.00	20.00	30.00
#1202-Captain Easy & Wash Tubbs by Roy Crane			
	15.00	30.00	45.00
#1203-Ella Cinders	10.00	20.00	30.00
#1204-Freckles & His Friends			
	8.00	16.00	24.00

FAMOUS CRIMES
June, 1948 - 1953
Fox Features Syndicate

#1-Blue Beetle app. & crime story reprt/Phan-
   tom Lady #16   4.00 8.00 12.00

2-15	1.75	3.35	5.00
16-51	1.35	2.75	4.00

FAMOUS FAIRY TALES
1943 (32pgs.); 1944 (16pgs.) (Soft Covers)
K.K. Publ. Co.   (Giveaway)

1942-Reprints from Fairy Tale Parade #2 & 3;
   Kelly inside art   50.00 100.00 150.00
1944-Kelly inside art 25.00 50.00 75.00

FAMOUS FEATURE STORIES
1938
Dell Publishing Co.

#1-Tarzan, Terry & the Pirates, King of the
   Royal Mtd., Buck Jones, Dick Tracy, Smilin' Jack, Dan Dunn, Don Winslow, G-Man,
   Tailspin Tommy, Mutt & Jeff, & Little Orphan Annie reprints-All illustrated text
          20.00 40.00 60.00

FAMOUS FIRST EDITION (See Limited Collectors
Edition) ($1.00) (10x13½"-Giant Size)
1974 - #8, 8-9/75 (72pgs.;#6-84pgs;#7,8-68pgs)
National Periodical Publications

C-26-Action #1	1.35	2.75	4.00
C-28-Detective #27	1.00	2.00	3.00
C-30-Sensation #1(1974)	.65	1.35	2.00
F-4-Whiz #2(#1)(10-11/74)	.65	1.35	2.00
F-5-Batman #1(F-6 on inside)			
	.65	1.35	2.00
F-6-Wonder Woman #1	.65	1.35	2.00
F-7-All-Star Comics #3	.65	1.35	2.00
F-8-Flash #1 (8-9/75)	.65	1.35	2.00

Hardbound editions w/dust jacket ($5.00)
  (Lyle Stuart, Inc.) C-26,C-28,C-30,F-4,F-6,
  known   2.50 5.00 7.50

Faithful #1, © MCG

Famous Comics (1930's), © UFS

Famous Crimes #3, © Fox

F.F. A Carnival of Comics, © EAS

Famous Funnies, Series 1, © EAS

Famous Funnies #20, © EAS

(Famous First Edition cont'd)
WARNING: The above books are **exact** reprints of the originals that they represent except for the Giant-Size format. None of the originals are Giant-Size. The first five issues were printed with two covers. Reprint information can be found on the outside cover but not on the inside cover which was reprinted exactly like the original (inside & out).

FAMOUS FUNNIES
1933 – #218, July, 1955
Eastern Color/Dell Publ./Eastern Color

	Good	Fine	Mint

A Carnival of Comics (Probably the second comic book), 36 pgs., no date given, no publisher, no number; Contains strip reprints of Mutt & Jeff & others. This book was sold by M. C. Gaines to Wheatena, Milk-O-Malt, John Wanamaker, Kinney Shoe Stores & others to be given away as premiums & radio giveaways (1933).

175.00 350.00 525.00

Series I—(No date-early 1934) (68 pgs.) No publisher given; sold in chain stores 10 cents. 35,000 print run (produced by Eastern Color for Dell Publ. Co.) Contains Sunday strip reprints of Mutt & Jeff, Reg'lar Fellers, Nipper, Hairbreadth Harry, Strange As It Seems, Joe Palooka, Dixie Dugan, the Nebbs, Keeping Up With the Jones, & others. Inside front & back covers & pages 1-16 of Famous Funnies Series I Nos. 49-64 reprinted from **Famous Funnies**, A Carnival of Comics, & most of pages 17-48 reprinted from **Funnies on Parade.** This was the first comic book sold.

150.00 300.00 450.00

No. 1 (7/34-on stands 5/34)—Eastern Color Printing Co. First monthly newsstand comic book. Contains Sunday strip reprints of Toonerville Folks, Mutt & Jeff, Hairbreadth Harry, 'S Matter Pop, Nipper, Dixie Dugan, The Bungle Family, Connie, Ben Webster, Tailspin Tommy, The Nebbs, & others.

	120.00	240.00	360.00
2	40.00	80.00	120.00

3-Buck Rogers Sunday strip reprints by Rick Yager begins, ends #218; not in #131,191-208; the # of the 1st strip reprinted is Page #190, Series #1 55.00 110.00 165.00

4	25.00	50.00	75.00
5	20.00	40.00	60.00
6-10	16.50	33.25	50.00

11,12,14,18-4pgs. of Buck Rogers in each issue, completes stories in Buck Rogers #1

	Good	Fine	Mint

which lacks these pages; #14 has two Buck Rogers panels missing; #18-2pgs. of Buck Rogers reprinted in Daisy Comics #1

	18.00	36.00	54.00
13,15-17,19,20	15.00	30.00	45.00

21,23-30: #27-War on Crime begins
9.00 18.00 27.00

22-4pgs. of Buck Rogers needed to complete stories in Buck Rogers #1
12.00 24.00 36.00

31-34,36,37,39,40	9.00	18.00	27.00

35-2pgs. Buck Rogers omitted in Buck Rogers #2
12.00 24.00 36.00

38-Full color portrait of Buck Rogers
10.00 20.00 30.00

41-60	8.00	16.00	24.00
61-64,66-70	6.00	12.00	18.00

65-2pgs. Kirby art-"Lightnin & the Lone Rider"
7.00 14.00 21.00

71,73,77-80: #80-Buck Rogers story continues from B.R. #5 5.00 10.00 15.00

72,74-76-2pgs. Kirby art in all
6.00 12.00 18.00

81-Origin Invisible Scarlet O'Neil; strip begins #82, ends #167 5.00 10.00 15.00

82-87,90: #82-Buck Rogers cover. #87 has last B.R. full pg. reprint 5.00 10.00 15.00

88-Buck Rogers in "Moon's End" by Calkins, 2pgs. (not reprints). Beginning with #88, all Buck Rogers pages have rearranged panels 6.00 12.00 18.00

89-Origin Fearless Flint, the Flint Man
4.00 8.00 12.00

91-93,95,96,98-110: #105-Series 2 begins (Strip Page #1) 4.00 8.00 12.00

94-Buck Rogers in "Solar Holocaust" by Calkins, 3pgs. (not reprts.) 5.00 10.00 15.00

97-War Bond promotion, B. Rogers by Calkins, 2pgs. (not reprints) 5.00 10.00 15.00

Famous Funnies #209, © EAS

Famous Funnies #213, © EAS

Famous Funnies #214, © EAS

Famous Gangsters #1, © Avon

Fantastic #8, © YM

Fantastic Adventures #17, © Super

(Famous Funnies cont'd)	Good	Fine	Mint
111-130	3.00	6.00	9.00
131-150: #137-Strip page #110½ omitted.			
	2.50	5.00	7.50
151-169	2.00	4.00	6.00

170-Two text illos. by Williamson, his 1st
   comic book work   4.00   8.00 12.00
171-180: #171-Strip pgs. 227,229,230, Series
   2 omitted. #172-Strip pg. 232 omitted
                    2.00   4.00   6.00
181-190: Buck Rogers ends with start of strip
   pg. 302, Series 2   1.35   2.75   4.00
191-197,199-201,203,204,206-208: No Buck
   Rogers   1.00   2.00   3.00
198,202,205-One pg. Frazetta ads; no Buck
   Rogers   2.00   4.00   6.00
209-Buck Rogers begins with strip pg.#480,
   Series 2; Frazetta cover
              25.00 50.00 75.00
210-216: Frazetta covers. #215-Contains Buck
   Rogers strip pg. #515-518, Series 2 followed by pgs. #179-181, Series 3
              25.00 50.00 75.00
217,218-Buck Rogers ends with pg.199, Series
   3   1.35   2.75   4.00

NOTE: **Rick Yager** did the Buck Rogers Sunday strips reprinted in Famous Funnies. The Sundays were formerly done by Russ Keaton & Lt. Dick Calkins did the dailies, but would sometimes assist Yager on a panel or two from time to time. No. 184 is Yager's first full Buck Rogers page. Yager did the strip until 1958 when **Murphy Anderson** took over. **Tuska** art from 4/26/59 — 1965. Virtually every panel was rewritten for Famous Funnies. Not identical to the original Sunday page. The Buck Rogers reprints run continuously through Famous Funnies issue No. 190 (Strip No. 302) with no break in story line. The story line has no continuity after No. 190. The Buck Rogers newspaper strips came out in four series: Series 1, 3/30/30 — 9/21/41 (No. 1 — 600); Series 2, 9/28/41 — 10/21/51 (No. 1 — 525)(Strip No. 110½ (½ pg.) published in only a few newspapers); Series 3, 10/28/51 — 2/9/58 (No. 100 — 428) (No No. 1 — 99); Series 4, 2/16/58 — 6/13/65 (No numbers, dates only).

FAMOUS FUNNIES
1964
Super Comics

Reprint #15-18   .60   1.20   1.80

FAMOUS GANG
1942   (Giveaway)
Firestone Tire & Rubber Co.

Bugs Bunny   7.00 14.00 21.00

FAMOUS GANGSTERS (Crime on the Waterfront #4)
April, 1951 - #3, Feb, 1952
Avon Periodicals/Realistic

#1-Capone, Dillinger; Kinstler art
              2.00   4.00   6.00
2-Wood cover + 1 pg.-Reprints Saint story/
   Saint #7, retitled "Mike Strong"

	Good	Fine	Mint
	2.50	5.00	7.00
3	1.50	3.00	4.50

FAMOUS INDIAN TRIBES
July-Sept, 1962; July, 1972
Dell Publishing Co.

#12-264-209 (The Sioux)	.30	.65	1.00
#2(7/72)-reprints above		.15	.30

FAMOUS STARS
1950 - #4, May-June, 1951; #6, Spring, 1952
Ziff-Davis Publ. Co.

#1-Shelley Winters, Susan Peters, Ava Gard-
   ner, Shirley Temple 2.50   5.00   7.50
2-Betty Hutton, Bing Crosby, Colleen Town-
   send, Gloria Swanson; 2 Everett stories
              2.00   4.00   6.00
3-Farley Granger, Judy Garland's ordeal,
   Alan Ladd   1.75   3.35   5.00
4-Al Jolson, Bob Mitchum, Ella Raines, Richard Conte, Vic Damone; 6 pgs. Crandall
              2.00   4.00   6.00
5-Liz Taylor, Betty Grable, Esther Williams,
   George Brent; Krigstein story
              2.50   5.00   7.50
6-Gene Kelly, Hedy Lamar, June Allyson, Wm.
   Boyd, Janet Leigh, Gary Cooper
              2.00   4.00   6.00

NOTE: *Whitney story-#1,3.*

FAMOUS STORIES (-- Book #2)
1942
Dell Publishing Co.

#1-Treasure Island	7.00	14.00	21.00
2-Tom Sawyer	7.00	14.00	21.00

FAMOUS TV FUNDAY FUNNIES
1961
Harvey Publications

#1-Casper the Ghost 1.00   2.00   3.00

FAMOUS WESTERN BADMEN
#13, Dec, 1952 - #15, 1953
Youthful Magazines

#13-15   .65   1.35   2.00

FANTASTIC (Beware #10 on)
1951 - #9, April, 1952
Youthful Magazines

#1	1.00	2.00	3.00
2-7,9	.65	1.35	2.00

	Good	Fine	Mint
8-Capt. Science by Harrison	1.50	3.00	4.50

FANTASTIC (Fantastic Fears #1-9)
#10, Nov-Dec, 1954 - #11, Jan-Feb, 1955
Ajax/Farrell Publ.

#10,11	.65	1.35	2.00

FANTASTIC ADVENTURES
1963 - 1964   (Reprints)
Super Comics

#9-12,15,16,18: #11-Reprints Disbrow/Blue Bolt			
#118. #16-Briefer art. #18-Reprints/Super-			
ior Stories #1	.65	1.35	2.00
#17-South Sea Girl by Baker			
	1.00	2.00	3.00

FANTASTIC COMICS
Dec, 1939 - #23, Nov, 1941
Fox Features Syndicate

#1-Origin Samson; Stardust, The Super Wizard,			
Space Smith, Sub Saunders, Capt. Kidd be-			
gin	40.00	80.00	120.00
2	25.00	50.00	75.00
3-5	20.00	40.00	60.00
6-9: #6,7-Simon cover	15.00	30.00	45.00
10-Intro. David	13.50	26.75	40.00
11-17	10.00	20.00	30.00
18-Intro. Black Fury & Sidekick Chuck			
	12.00	24.00	36.00
19,20	10.00	20.00	30.00
21-Origin The Banshee	12.00	24.00	36.00
22	10.00	20.00	30.00
23-Origin The Gladiator	12.00	24.00	36.00

NOTE: _Lou Fine_ covers-#1-5.

FANTASTIC FEARS (Fantastic #10 on)
1952 - #9, Sept-Oct, 1954
Ajax/Farrell Publ.

#1	1.50	3.00	4.50
2-4	1.00	2.00	3.00
5-1st Ditko story written by Bruce Hamilton			
reprted in Weird,V2#8	5.00	10.00	15.00
6	.75	1.50	2.25
7(5/53), 8(7/53)	.75	1.50	2.25
7(5-6/54), 8(7-8/54), 9(9-10/54)			
	.75	1.50	2.25

FANTASTIC FOUR (See Book & Record --)
Nov, 1961 - Present
Marvel Comics Group

#1-Origin & 1st app. The Fantastic Four (Reed

	Good	Fine	Mint
Richards-Mr. Fantastic, Johnny Storm-The			
Human Torch, Sue Storm-The Invisible Girl,			
& Ben Grimm-The Thing); origin The Mole			
Man	200.00	400.00	600.00
1-Reprint from the Golden Record Comic Set			
	1.00	2.00	3.00
with record....	1.75	3.35	5.00
2-Vs. The Skrulls	70.00	140.00	210.00
3-Fantastic Four don costumes & establish			
Headquarters	50.00	100.00	150.00
4-1st Silver Age Sub-Mariner app.			
	35.00	70.00	105.00
5-Origin & 1st app. Doctor Doom			
	25.00	50.00	75.00
6-10: #6-Sub-Mariner, Dr. Doom team up			
	15.00	30.00	45.00
11-Origin The Impossible Man			
	10.00	20.00	30.00
12-15: #12-Fant.Four Vs. The Hulk. #13-Intro.			
The Watcher	10.00	20.00	30.00
16-20: #18-Origin The Super Skrull. #19-			
Intro. Rama-Tut. #20-Origin The Molecule			
Man	7.00	14.00	21.00
21-30: #21-Intro. The Hate Monger. #25,26-			
The Thing Vs. The Hulk. #30-Intro. Diablo			
	4.00	8.00	12.00
31-40: #35-Intro. & 1st app. Dragon Man.			
#36-Intro. & 1st app. Madam Medusa & the			
Frightful Four(Sandman, Wizard, & Paste			
Pot Pete). #39-Wood inks on Daredevil			
	3.00	6.00	9.00
41-47: #41-43-Frightful Four app. #44-Intro.			
Gorgan. #45-Intro. The Inhumans			
	2.00	4.00	6.00
48-Intro. & 1st app. The Silver Surfer			
	4.00	8.00	12.00
49,50-Silver Surfer x-over			
	2.50	5.00	7.50
51-60: #52-Intro. The Black Panther; origin-			
#53. Silver Surfer x-over in #55-60,61			
(cameo)	1.50	3.00	4.50
61-1st app. Him (Warlock)	1.50	3.00	4.50
62-70	1.00	2.00	3.00
71,73,75,78-80	.75	1.50	2.25
72,74,76,77: Silver Surfer app.			
	.80	1.60	2.40
81-90: #81-Crystal joins & dons costume.			
#84-87-Dr. Doom app.	.50	1.00	1.50
91-102: #94-Intro. Agatha Harkness. #102-			
Last Kirby issue	.35	.70	1.05
103-120: #112-Hulk Vs. Thing.25	.25	.50	.75
121-140: #121-123-Silver Surfer x-over. #126-			
Origin F.F. retold. #128-4pg. glossy in-			
sert of F.F. Friends & Fiends. #129-Intro.			
Thundra. #130-Sue leaves F.F. #132-Med-			
usa joins. #133-Thundra Vs. Thing			
	.25	.50	.75

Fantastic Comics #4, © Fox

Fantastic Four #1, © MCG

Fantastic Four #4, © MCG

Fantastic Giants #24, © CC

Fantastic Worlds #5, © STD

Fantasy Masterpieces #7, © MCG

(Fantastic Four cont'd)	Good	Fine	Mint
141-154,158-160: #147-Kirbyesque art by Buckler begins. #150-Crystal & Quicksilver's wedding. #151-Origin Thundra. #159-Medusa leaves, Sue rejoins	.20	.40	.60
155-157: Silver Surfer in all	.25	.50	.75
161-180: #164-The Crusader (old Marvel Boy) revived; origin #165. #166-Hulk Vs. F.F. #167-Hulk & Thing Vs. F.F. #175-Return of Impossible Man. #177,178-Frightful Four app.	.15	.30	.45
181-190	.15	.30	.45

NOTE: *Ditko inks-#13. Kirby art-#1-102,108; covers-#1-101,164,173,180. Steranko covers-#130,131.*

	Good	Fine	Mint
Giant-Size #2(8/74) - #4: Formerly G-S Super-Stars	.60	1.20	1.80
Giant-Size #5,6(8/75)	.35	.70	1.05
Special #1('63)-Origin F.F.; Ditko art	7.00	14.00	21.00
Special #2('64)-Dr. Doom origin & x-over	4.00	8.00	12.00
Special #3('65)-Reed & Sue marry	2.00	4.00	6.00
Special #4(11/66)-G.A. Torch x-over & origin retold	1.50	3.00	4.50
Special #5(11/67)-Intro. Pscho-Man; no reprints; Silver Surfer app.	1.00	2.00	3.00
Special #6(11/68)-Intro. Annihilus; no reprints; Birth of Franklin Richards	.65	1.35	2.00
Special #7(11/69), #8(12/70), #9(12/71), #10 ('73)	.50	1.00	1.50
Annual #11(6/76),#12(11/77)	.35	.70	1.05

NOTE: *Buscema stories-#172-175(pencils), Annual #11. Kirby stories-#1-6; covers-#1-7.*

FANTASTIC GIANTS (Konga #1-23)
Sept, 1966 (25¢)
Charlton Comics

	Good	Fine	Mint
V2#24-Origin Konga & Gorgo reprinted; two new Ditko stories	2.00	4.00	6.00

FANTASTIC TALES
1958 (No date) (Reprint)
I.W. Enterprises

	Good	Fine	Mint
#1-Reprints Avon's "City of the Living Dead"	1.00	2.00	3.00

FANTASTIC VOYAGE (See Movie Comics)
Aug, 1969 - #2, Dec, 1969
Gold Key

	Good	Fine	Mint
#1,2(TV)	.35	.70	1.05

FANTASTIC VOYAGES OF SINDBAD, THE
Oct, 1965 - #2, June, 1967
Gold Key

	Good	Fine	Mint
#1,2	1.00	2.00	3.00

FANTASTIC WORLDS
#5, Sept, 1952 - #7, Jan, 1953
Standard Comics

	Good	Fine	Mint
#5-Toth & Anderson art	2.00	4.00	6.00
6-Toth story	2.00	4.00	6.00
7	1.00	2.00	3.00

FANTASY MASTERPIECES (Becomes Marvel Super
2/66 - #11, 10/67 Heroes #12 on)
Marvel Comics Group

	Good	Fine	Mint
#1	.80	1.60	2.40
2	.60	1.20	1.80
3-G.A. Captain America reprints begin; 1st 25¢ ish.	.60	1.20	1.80
4-6-Capt. America reprts.	.60	1.20	1.80
7-Begin G.A. Sub-Mariner, Torch reprint	.40	.80	1.20
8-Torch battles the Sub-Mariner reprint (Marvel Mystery #9)	.40	.80	1.20
9-Origin Human Torch reprint (Marvel Comics #1)	.40	.80	1.20
10-All Winners reprint	.40	.80	1.20
11-Reprint of origin Toro & Black Knight	.40	.80	1.20

FANTASY QUARTERLY
1978 (50¢)
Power Comics

	Good	Fine	Mint
#1	.20	.40	.60

FANTOMAN (Formerly Amazing Adv. Funnies)
#2, Aug, 1940 - #4, Dec, 1940
Centaur Publications

	Good	Fine	Mint
#2-The Fantom of the Fair; reprints; The Arrow app.	15.00	30.00	45.00
3,4	12.00	24.00	36.00

FARGO KID (Formerly Justice Traps the Guilty)
V2#3(#1), 6-7/58 - V11#5, 10-11/58
Prize Publications

	Good	Fine	Mint
V11#3(#1)-Origin Fargo Kid, Severin cover & two Williamson stys.	2.50	5.00	7.50
V11#4,5-Severin cvr/stys.	1.35	2.75	4.00

FARMER'S DAUGHTER, THE
2-3/54 - #3, 6-7/54; 8-9/54 - #4, 2-3/55
Stanhall Publ./Trojan Magazines

(The Farmer's Daughter cont'd)

	Good	Fine	Mint
#1-3('54)(Stanhall)	2.00	4.00	6.00
#1(Trojan)	1.50	3.00	4.50
2-4	1.00	2.00	3.00

FASTEST GUN ALIVE, THE (See 4-Color #741)

FAST FICTION (-- Action)(Stories By Famous
Authors Illustrated #6 on)
March, 1950 - #5, July, 1950
Seaboard Publ./Famous Authors Ill.

#1-Scarlet Pimpernel; Jim Lavery art			
	4.00	8.00	12.00
2-Captain Blood; H. C. Kiefer art			
	3.50	7.00	10.50
3-She, by H. Rider Haggard; Vincent Napoli			
art	6.00	12.00	18.00
4-The 39 Steps; Lavery art			
	3.50	7.00	10.50
5-Beau Geste-Kiefer art	3.50	7.00	10.50

FAST WILLIE JACKSON
October, 1976 - Present
Fitzgerald Periodicals, Inc.

#1		.15	.30
2-7		.10	.20

FAT ALBERT (-- & the Cosby Kids)(TV)
March, 1974 - Present
Gold Key

#1		.15	.30
2-22		.10	.20

FAT AND SLAT (Ed Wheelan)(Gunfighter #5 on)
Summer, 1947 - #4, Spring, 1948
E.C. Comics

#1	12.00	24.00	36.00
2-4	8.00	16.00	24.00

FAT AND SLAT JOKE BOOK
Summer, 1944   (One Shot)
All-American Comics (William H. Wise)

by Ed Wheelan	8.00	16.00	24.00

FATE (See Hand of Fate, & Thrill-O-Rama)

FATMAN, THE HUMAN FLYING SAUCER
April, 1967 - #3, Aug-Sept, 1967
Lightning Comics

#1-Origin Fatman & Tinman by C.C. Beck

	Good	Fine	Mint
	1.75	3.35	5.00
2,3-Beck art	1.00	2.00	3.00

FAUNTLEROY COMICS (Superduck Presents--)
1953
Close-Up/Archie Publications

#1	1.35	2.75	4.00
2,3	.65	1.35	2.00

FAWCETT MINIATURES (See Mighty Midget)
1946 (12-24pgs.)(4x5")(Wheaties Giveaways)
Fawcett Publications

Captain Marvel-"And the Horn of Plenty", &			
The Raiders From Space	2.00	4.00	6.00
Captain Marvel Jr.-"The Case of the Poison			
Press!"	2.00	4.00	6.00
Delecta of the Planets-C.C Beck art. B&W in-			
side; 12pgs.; 3 different			
	10.00	20.00	30.00

FAWCETT MOTION PICTURE COMICS (See M.P.C.)

FAWCETT MOVIE COMICS
1949 - #20, Dec, 1952
Fawcett Publications

No#-"Dakota Lil"-Geo. Montgomery & Rod Cam-			
eron('49)	4.00	8.00	12.00
No#-"Copper Canyon"-Ray Milland & Hedy			
Lamarr('50)	4.50	9.00	13.50
No#-"Destination Moon"-(1950)			
	8.00	16.00	24.00
No#-"Montana"-Errol Flynn & Alexis Smith('50)			
	4.50	9.00	13.50
No#-"Pioneer Marshal"-Monte Hale(1950)			
	4.00	8.00	12.00
No#-"Powder River Rustlers"-Rocky Lane(1950)			
	4.50	9.00	13.50
No#-"Singing Guns"-Vaughn Monroe & Ella			
Raines(1950)	4.50	9.00	13.50
#7-"Gunmen of Abilene"-Rocky Lane; Bob			
Powell art (1950)	5.00	10.00	15.00
8-"King of the Bullwhip"-Lash LaRue; Bob			
Powell art (1950)	5.00	10.00	15.00
9-"The Old Frontier"-Monte Hale; Bob Powell			
art (2/51)	4.00	8.00	12.00
10-"The Missourians"-Monte Hale (4/51)			
	4.00	8.00	12.00
11-"The Thundering Trail"-Lash LaRue (6/51)			
	4.00	8.00	12.00
12-"Rustlers on Horseback"-Rocky Lane (8/51)			
	4.00	8.00	12.00
13-"Warpath"-Edmond O'Brien & Forrest Tucker			
(10/51)	4.00	8.00	12.00
14-"Last Outpost"-Ronald Reagan(12/51)			

Fast Fiction #3. © Famous Authors

Fat & Slat Joke Book. © WHW

Fawcett Movie Comics. © Faw

Fawcett Movie Comics #15, © Faw

Fawcett's Funny Animals #11, © Faw

Feature Book No #, © N.Y. News Synd.

(Fawcett Movie Comics cont'd)

	Good	Fine	Mint
	5.00	10.00	15.00
15-"The Man From Planet X"-Robert Clark; Shaffenberger art (2/52) (Scarce)	10.00	20.00	30.00
16-"10 Tall Men"-Burt Lancaster	3.00	6.00	9.00
17-"Rose of Cimarron"-Jack Buetel & Mala Powers	3.00	6.00	9.00
18-"The Brigand"-Anthony Dexter; art by Shaffenberger	3.00	6.00	9.00
19-"Carbine Williams"-James Stewart; art by Costanza	3.00	6.00	9.00
20-"Ivanhoe"-Liz Taylor	4.00	8.00	12.00

FAWCETT'S FUNNY ANIMALS (#1-26 titled "Funny
12/42 - #91, 2/56   Animals")
Fawcett Publications/Charlton Comics

#1-Capt. Marvel on cover	5.00	10.00	15.00
2-10-Marvel Bunny	2.50	5.00	7.50
11-20-Marvel Bunny	1.75	3.35	5.00
21-40-Marvel Bunny	1.35	2.75	4.00
41-88,90,91	1.00	2.00	3.00
89-Merry Mailman ish	1.35	2.75	4.00

F.B.I., THE
April-June, 1965
Dell Publishing Co.

#1-Sinnott art	.25	.50	.75

F.B.I. STORY, THE (See 4-Color #1069)

FEAR (Adventure Into --)
Nov, 1970 - #31, Dec, 1975
Marvel Comics Group

#1-Reprints Fantasy & Sci-Fi stories	.25	.50	.75
2-5	.20	.40	.60
6-9: #9-Everett art	.20	.40	.60
10-Man-Thing begins; Morrow cover & pencils	1.35	2.75	4.00
11-Adams cover	.65	1.35	2.00
12-Starlin art	.60	1.20	1.80
13-18	.35	.70	1.05
19-Intro. Howard the Duck by Val Mayerick	4.00	8.00	12.00
20-Morbius, the Living Vampire begins, ends #31	.25	.50	.75
21-29,31	.15	.30	.45
30-Evans art	.15	.30	.45

NOTE: Brunner covers-#16,17.

FEAR IN THE NIGHT (See Complete Mystery #3)

FEARLESS FAGAN (See 4-Color Comics #441)

FEATURE BOOK (Dell) (See Black & White and
Large Feature Book)

FEATURE BOOK (All newspaper reprints)
May, 1937 - #57, 1947
David McKay Publications

	Good	Fine	Mint
No#-Popeye & the Jeep (Very Rare)	100.00	200.00	300.00
No#-Dick Tracy-Reprinted as Feature Book #4 (100pgs.) & in part as 4-Color #1 (Very Rare)	250.00	500.00	750.00

NOTE: Above books were advertised together.

#1-King of the Royal Mtd.	35.00	70.00	105.00
2-Popeye(6/37) by Segar	50.00	100.00	150.00
3-Popeye(7/37)-by Segar	35.00	70.00	105.00
4-Dick Tracy(8/37)-Same as No# issue listed but a new cover added	75.00	150.00	225.00
5-Popeye(9/37)by Segar	30.00	60.00	90.00
6-Dick Tracy(10/37)	60.00	120.00	180.00
7-Little Orphan Annie (Rare)	60.00	120.00	180.00
8-Secret Agent X-9-Not by Raymond	16.50	33.25	50.00
9-Dick Tracy (1/38)	60.00	120.00	180.00
10-Popeye(2/38)	30.00	60.00	90.00
11-Little Annie Rooney	15.00	30.00	45.00
12-Blondie(4/38)(Rare)	30.00	60.00	90.00
13-Inspector Wade	7.00	14.00	21.00

Feature Book #5, © King

14-Popeye(6/38)by Segar (Scarce)	40.00	80.00	120.00
15-Barney Baxter(7/38)	12.00	24.00	36.00
16-Red Eagle	7.00	14.00	21.00
17-Gangbusters	10.00	20.00	30.00
18,19-Mandrake	16.50	33.25	50.00
20-Phantom	30.00	60.00	90.00
21-Lone Ranger	16.50	33.25	50.00
22-Phantom	30.00	60.00	90.00
23-Mandrake	16.50	33.25	50.00
24-Lone Ranger(1941)	16.50	33.25	50.00

137

(Feature Book cont'd)   Good   Fine   Mint
25-Flash Gordon-Reprints not by Alex Raymond
                      50.00 100.00 150.00
26-Prince Valiant(1941)-Harold Foster art-
  1st 64 newspaper strips reprinted
              125.00 250.00 375.00
27-29,31,34-Blondie   5.00 10.00 15.00
30,32,35,37,41,44-Katzenjammer Kids
                4.00   8.00 12.00
33-
36,38,40,42,43,45,47-Blondie
                3.00   6.00   9.00
39,53-Phantom   15.00 30.00 45.00
46-Mandrake   10.00 20.00 30.00
48-Maltese Falcon('46) 10.00 20.00 30.00
49,50-Perry Mason   2.50   5.00   7.50
51,54-Rip Kirby by Alex Raymond; origin-#51
             10.00 20.00 30.00
52,55-Mandrake   8.00 16.00 24.00
56,57-Phantom   12.00 24.00 36.00

NOTE: *All Feature Books through #25 are over-*
sized 8½x11-3/4" comics with color covers &
black & white interiors. The covers of the
1st 9 issues are of rough, heavy stock. Be-
ginning with #10, the covers are slick &
thin, and because of their size, are diffi-
cult to handle without damaging. For this
reason, they are seldom found in Fine to Mint
condition. The paper stock, unlike Wow #1 and
Captain Marvel #1 is itself not unstable -
just thin. The page counts, including covers,
are as follows: No#,3&4-100pgs.; #1&2-52pgs.;
#5-25 are all 76 pages, changing to 36 pages
#26 on.

FEATURE COMICS (Formerly Feature Funnies)
#21, June, 1939 - #144, May, 1950
Quality Comics Group

#21-26: #23-Charlie Chan begins
              9.00 18.00 27.00
 27-Origin & 1st app. of Dollman
            75.00 150.00 225.00
28-1st Fine Dollman 25.00 50.00 75.00
29,30   20.00 40.00 60.00
31-Last Clock & Charlie Chan issue
          15.00 30.00 45.00
32-37: #32-Rusty Ryan & Samar begin. #37-
  Last Fine Dollman 15.00 30.00 45.00
38-41: #38-Origin the Ace of Space. #39-Ori-
  gin The Destroying Demon, ends #40. #40-
  Bruce Blackburn in costume
          8.00 16.00 24.00
42-USA, the Spirit of Old Glory begins
          7.00 14.00 21.00
43-50: #44-Dollman by Crandall begins, ends
  #63. #46-Intro. Boyville Brigadiers in
  Rusty Ryan   7.00 14.00 21.00

             Good   Fine   Mint
51-55: #51-Crandall art 5.00 10.00 15.00
56-Marijuana story in "Swing Session"
          7.00 14.00 21.00
57-Spider Widow begins 5.00 10.00 15.00
58-60: #59-Crandall art 5.00 10.00 15.00
61-68   4.00   8.00 12.00
69,70-Phantom Lady x-over in Spider Widow
          6.00 12.00 18.00
71-80   3.00   6.00   9.00
81-100   2.50   5.00   7.50
101-144   2.00   4.00   6.00
NOTE: *Celardo art-#37-43. Crandall stories-*
#37(2). Gustavson art (Rusty Ryan)-#32-47.
Powell art-#64-73.

FEATURE FILMS MAGAZINE
Mar-Apr, 1950 - #5, Nov-Dec, 1950
National Periodical Publications

#1-"Captain China" with John Payne & Gail
  Russell   7.00 14.00 21.00
2-"Riding High" with Bing Crosby
          5.00 10.00 15.00
3-"The Eagle & the Hawk" with John Payne, R.
  Fleming & D. O'Keefe 4.00   8.00 12.00
4-"Fancy Pants"-Bob Hope & Lucille Ball,
5   4.00   8.00 12.00

FEATURE FUNNIES (Feature Comics #21 on)
Oct, 1937 - #20, May, 1939
Quality Comics Group

#1-Joe Palooka, Mickey Finn, The Bungles,
  Jane Arden, Dixie Dugan, Big Top, Ned
  Bryant, Strange As It Seems, & Off the
  Record strip reprints begin
         50.00 100.00 150.00
2-The Clock begins(11/37)-Masked hero
         30.00 60.00 90.00
3   15.00 30.00 45.00
4,5   12.00 24.00 36.00
6-12   8.00 16.00 24.00
13-Espionage, Starring Black X begins
         10.00 20.00 30.00
14-20   8.00 16.00 24.00

FEATURE PRESENTATIONS MAGAZINE (Becomes
Feature Stories Magazine #3 on)
#5, April, 1950 - #6, July, 1950
Fox Features Syndicate

#5(#1)-Black Tarantula 3.00   6.00   9.00
6(#2)-Moby Dick; Wood cover
          4.00   8.00 12.00

FEATURE STORIES MAGAZINE (Formerly Feature
Presentations Magazine #5,6)

Feature Book #42, © King

Feature Comics #27, © DC (Qua)

Feature Presentations Mag. #5, © Fox

138

Feature Stories Mag. #3, © Fox

Felix The Cat, 1931, © King

Fight Comics #46, © FH

(Feature Stories Magazine cont'd)
#3, Aug, 1950 - #4, Oct, 1950
Fox Features Syndicate

	Good	Fine	Mint
#3-Jungle Lul, Zegra app.	4.00	8.00	12.00
4	3.00	6.00	9.00

FEDERAL MEN COMICS
1945 - #5, 1946   (DC reprints from 1930's)
Gerard Publ. Co.

#1-5: #2-Siegel & Shuster	3.35	6.75	10.00

FELIX THE CAT
1927 - 1931 (24pgs.)(1926,'27 color strip re-
McLoughlin Bros.   prints)(8x10¼")

#260-by Otto Messmer	25.00	50.00	75.00

FELIX THE CAT   (See Inky & Dinky & March of
1943 - #12, 7-9/65   Comics)
Dell Publ#1-19/Toby#20-61/Harvey#62-118/Dell

4-Color #15	25.00	50.00	75.00
4-Color #46('44)	15.00	30.00	45.00
4-Color #77('45)	10.00	20.00	30.00
4-Color #119('46)	7.00	14.00	21.00
4-Color #135('46)	6.00	12.00	18.00
4-Color #162('47)	5.00	10.00	15.00
#1(2-3/48)(Dell)	7.00	14.00	21.00
2	3.00	6.00	9.00
3-5	2.50	5.00	7.50
6-19(2-3/51-Dell)	1.75	3.35	5.00

20-30(Toby): #28-2/52 Has #29 on cover, #28

on inside	1.50	3.00	4.50

31-61(6/55)(Toby)-Last Messmer ish.

	1.00	2.00	3.00
62(8/55)-#100(Harvey)	.50	1.00	1.50
101-118(11/61)	.35	.70	1.05
#12-269-211(9-11/62)(Dell)	.65	1.35	2.00
#2-12(7-9/65)(Dell)	.40	.80	1.20
-- & His Friends #1(12/53-Toby)			
	1.00	2.00	3.00
-- & His Friends #2-4	.80	1.60	2.40
3-D Comic Book #1(1953-One Shot)			
	5.00	10.00	15.00

Summer Annual #2('52)-Early '30's Sunday

strip reprints	12.00	24.00	36.00

Summer Annual No#('53,100pgs.,Toby)

	7.00	14.00	21.00
Winter Annual #2('54)	4.00	8.00	12.00

(See March of Comics #24,36,51)
NOTE: *4-Color #15,46,77 are all daily or Sunday newspaper reprints from the 1930's drawn
by Otto Messmer, who created Felix in 1915
for the Sullivan animation studio. He drew
Felix from the beginning under contract to
Pat Sullivan. In 1946 he went to work for*

*Dell & wrote & drew most of the stories thru
the Toby Press issues. He did not work for
Harvey or the 1960's Dells. #107 reprints #71
interior; #110 reprints #56 interior.*

FERDINAND THE BULL
1938 (10¢)(Large size; some color, rest B&W)
Dell Publishing Co.

	Good	Fine	Mint
No#	7.00	14.00	21.00

FIBBER McGEE & MOLLY   (See A-1 Comics #25)

FICTION ILLUSTRATED   (Digest size)
1/76 - Present (4-3/4"x6-3/4")($1.00)
Pyramid Publ. (Byron Preiss Visual Publ.)
Vol.1-Schlomo Raven, Detective begins
Vol.2-Starfawn, Vol.3-Chandler

	.50	1.00	1.50

55 DAYS AT PEKING   (See Movie Comics)

FIGHT AGAINST CRIME (Fight Against the Guilty
May, 1951 - #21, Sept, 1954   #22)
Story Comics

#1	1.00	2.00	3.00
2-4	.60	1.20	1.80
5-Frazetta, 1 pg.	1.35	2.75	4.00
6-11,13-15	.50	1.00	1.50
12-Drug story	1.75	3.35	5.00

14,16-Tothesque art by Ross Andru; #16-Bond-
age cover & E.C. story swipe, also #21

	1.00	2.00	3.00
17-21	.50	1.00	1.50

FIGHT AGAINST THE GUILTY (Formerly Fight
#22, 12/54 - #23, 3/55   Against Crime)
Story Comics

#22-Tothesque art by Ross Andru; E.C. story

swipe	1.00	2.00	3.00
23	.50	1.00	1.50

FIGHT COMICS
Jan, 1940 - #86, Summer, 1953
Fiction House Magazines

#1-Origin Spy Fighter, Starring Saber; cover

by Lou Fine & Eisner	35.00	70.00	105.00
2-Eisner cover	20.00	40.00	60.00

3-Rip Regan, the Powerman begins; Eisner

cover	15.00	30.00	45.00
4,5: #4-Fine cover	10.00	20.00	30.00
6-10	8.00	16.00	24.00
11-14: Rip Regan ends	7.00	14.00	21.00
15-1st Super American	12.00	24.00	36.00
16-Captain Fight begins	12.00	24.00	36.00

(Fight Comics cont'd)	Good	Fine	Mint
17,18	10.00	20.00	30.00

19-Captain Fight ends; origin & 1st app.
  Senorita Rio; Rip Carson, Chute Trooper

	Good	Fine	Mint
begins	8.00	16.00	24.00
20	5.00	10.00	15.00
21-30	4.00	8.00	12.00
31,33-40	3.00	6.00	9.00
32-Tiger Girl begins	5.00	10.00	15.00

41-47,49,50: #44-1st Capt. Fight
	3.00	6.00	9.00

48-Used in Love and Death by Legman
	4.00	8.00	12.00
51-Origin Tiger Girl	4.00	8.00	12.00
52-70	2.50	5.00	7.50
71-78	2.00	4.00	6.00
79-The Space Rangers app.	2.00	4.00	6.00
80-85	2.00	4.00	6.00

86-Two Tigerman stories by Evans
	2.50	5.00	7.50

NOTE: *Bondage cover-#40. Tiger Girl by Baker-#36-60,62-65. Kayo Kirby by Baker-#52-64.*

FIGHT FOR LOVE
1952 (No month)
United Features Syndicate

No#-Abbie and Slats newspaper reprints
	2.00	4.00	6.00

FIGHTING AIR FORCE
1952 - 1959
Superior Comics Ltd.

#1	1.00	2.00	3.00
2-10	.50	1.00	1.50
11-53	.35	.70	1.05

FIGHTIN' AIR FORCE
#3, Feb, 1956 - #53, Feb, 1966
Charlton Comics

V1#3-10,11(68pgs., 3/58)	.40	.80	1.20
12 (100pgs)	.40	.80	1.20

13-50: #50-American Eagle begins
	.20	.40	.60
51-53	.15	.30	.45

FIGHTING AMERICAN
Apr-May, 1954 - #7, Apr-May, 1955
Headline Publications/Prize

#1-Origin Fighting American & Speedboy;
S&K cvr.+ 3 stories	22.50	45.00	67.50
2-Three S&K stories	15.00	30.00	45.00
3,4-Three S&K stories	15.00	30.00	45.00

5-Two S&K stories, Kirby/? story
	12.00	24.00	36.00

	Good	Fine	Mint

6-4pg. reprint of origin, plus 2pgs. by S&K
	10.00	20.00	30.00
7-Kirby story	8.00	16.00	24.00

NOTE: *Simon & Kirby covers on all.*

FIGHTING AMERICAN
Oct, 1966   (25¢)
Harvey Publications

#1-Origin Fighting American & Speedboy by
  S&K-reprint, plus 3 original S&K stories;
1pg. Adams ad	1.75	3.35	5.00

FIGHTIN' ARMY
#16, May, 1956 - #127, 12/76; #128, 9/77
Charlton Comics

#16-30	.25	.50	.75
31-60	.20	.40	.60

61-80-The Lonely War of Willy Schultz be-
gins #75, ends #92	.15	.30	.45

81-128: #89,90,92-Ditko art; Devil Brigadein
#79,82,83	.15	.30	.45

NOTE: *Montes/Bache art #48,49,51,69,75,76.*

FIGHTING DANIEL BOONE
1953
Avon Periodicals

No#-Kinstler cvr/22pgs.	4.00	8.00	12.00

IW Reprint #1-Kinstler cover/story
	1.00	2.00	3.00

FIGHTING DAVY CROCKETT (Formerly Kit Carson)
#9, Oct-Nov, 1955
Avon Periodicals

#9-Kinstler cover	1.50	3.00	4.50

FIGHTIN' 5, THE (Formerly Space War)
July, 1964 - #41, Jan, 1967
Charlton Comics

V2#28-Origin F. Five	.40	.80	1.20
29-39,41	.25	.50	.75
40-Peacemaker begins	.35	.70	1.05

FIGHTING FRONTS!
Aug, 1952 - #5, Jan, 1953
Harvey Publications

#1	.80	1.60	2.40
2-5: #2,3-Powell art	.40	.80	1.20

FIGHTING INDIAN STORIES (See Midget Comics)

Fight Comics #61, © FH

Fighting American #1, © Prize

Fighting Indians--#1, © Avon

Fighting Leathernecks #1, © Toby   Fightin' Marines #15(#1). © STJ   Fighting Yank #27. © BP

FIGHTING INDIANS OF THE WILD WEST!
Mar, 1952 - #2, Nov, 1952
Avon Periodicals

	Good	Fine	Mint
#1-Kinstler art	2.00	4.00	6.00
2-Kinstler art	1.35	2.75	4.00
100pg. Annual(1952,25¢)-Contains three comics			
rebound	2.50	5.00	7.50

FIGHTING LEATHERNECKS
Feb, 1952 - #6, Dec, 1952
Toby Press

#1	.80	1.60	2.40
2-6	.60	1.20	1.80

FIGHTING MAN, THE
May, 1952 - #8, July, 1953
Ajax/Farrell Publications(Excellent Publ.)

#1	1.00	2.00	3.00
2-"Duke's Diary"	.50	1.00	1.50
3-"Gil's Gals"	.65	1.35	2.00
4,5-Full pg. pin-ups by Bob Powell			
	1.75	3.35	5.00
6-8	.50	1.00	1.50
Annual #1(132pgs.)	2.50	5.00	7.50

FIGHTING MAN MANUAL, THE
1952
Ajax/Farrell Publications

#1	1.75	3.35	5.00

FIGHTIN' MARINES (The Texan #1-15)(2 #15's)
#15, Aug, 1951 - #132, Nov, 1976; #133, 10/77
St. John(Approved Comics)/Charlton Comics

#15(#1)	1.35	2.75	4.00
2-9-Canteen Kate by Matt Baker plus Baker			
covers	1.75	3.35	5.00
10,11-Baker covers	.85	1.75	2.50
12-20-Not Baker covers	.65	1.35	2.00
21-24	.50	1.00	1.50
25(68pgs.)	.65	1.35	2.00
26(100pgs.)(8/58)	1.00	2.00	3.00
27-50	.25	.50	.75
51-100: #78-Shotgun Harker & the Chicken			
series begin	.15	.30	.45
101-121		.15	.30
122-Pilot issue for "War" title (Fightin'			
Marines Presents War)		.15	.30
123-133		.15	.30

NOTE: #14 & 16 (CC) reprints St. John issue;
#16 reprints St. John insignia on cover.
Montes/Bache art-#48,53,55,64,65,72-74,77-83.

FIGHTING MARSHAL OF THE WILD WEST
(See The Hawk)

FIGHTIN' NAVY
#74, May, 1956 - #125, Apr-May, 1966
Charlton Comics

	Good	Fine	Mint
#74-125	.15	.30	.45

NOTE: Montes/Bache art-#109.

FIGHTING PRINCE OF DONEGAL, THE (See Movie Comics)

FIGHTIN' TEXAN
#16, Oct, 1952 - #17, Dec, 1952
St. John Publishing Co.

#16,17	.60	1.20	1.80

FIGHTING UNDERSEA COMMANDOS
1952 - #5, April, 1953
Avon Periodicals

#1	1.35	2.75	4.00
2-5	.65	1.35	2.00

FIGHTING WAR STORIES
Aug, 1952 - 1953
Men's Publications

#1	.80	1.60	2.40
2-5	.40	.80	1.20

FIGHTING YANK (See Startling & America's Best)
Sept, 1942 - #29, Aug, 1949
Nedor/Better Publ./Standard

#1-The Fighting Yank begins; Mystico, the			
Wonder Man app.	30.00	60.00	90.00
2	15.00	30.00	45.00
3	12.00	24.00	36.00
4	10.00	20.00	30.00
5,6,8-10	8.00	16.00	24.00
7-The Grim Reaper app.	8.00	16.00	24.00
11-The Oracle app.	5.00	10.00	15.00
12-17	5.00	10.00	15.00
18-The American Eagle app.	4.00	8.00	12.00
19,20	4.00	8.00	12.00
21,22,24-#21-Kara, Jungle Princess app. #22,			
24-Miss Masque app. in each			
	4.00	8.00	12.00
23	4.00	8.00	12.00
25-The Cavalier app.	4.00	8.00	12.00
26,27,29: #27-Robinson/Meskin art			
	4.00	8.00	12.00
28-One pg. Williamson; Robinson/Meskin story			
	4.00	8.00	12.00

NOTE: Many issues have Schomburg (Xela) cvrs.

FIGHT THE ENEMY
Aug, 1966 - #3, Mar, 1967 (25¢)
Tower Comics

(Fight the Enemy cont'd)	Good	Fine	Mint
#1-Lucky 7 & Mike Manly begin; Grandenetti art	.50	1.00	1.50
2,3: ½-pg. Wood art #3; McWilliams art	.35	.70	1.05

FILM FUNNIES
Nov, 1949 - #2, Feb, 1950
Marvel Comics (CPC)

	Good	Fine	Mint
#1	1.75	3.35	5.00
2	1.35	2.75	4.00

FILM STARS ROMANCES
Jan-Feb, 1950 - #3, May-June, 1950
Star Publications

	Good	Fine	Mint
#1-R. Valentino story	1.75	3.35	5.00
2-Liz Taylor/Robert Taylor photo cover,			
3	1.75	3.35	5.00

FIRE BALL XL5 (See Steve Zodiac)

FIREHAIR COMICS (Pioneer West Romances #3-5)
Winter/48-49 - #2, Spr/49; #6, Winter/49-50
thru #11, Spr/52
Fiction House Magazines

	Good	Fine	Mint
#1	3.00	6.00	9.00
2,6-11	2.00	4.00	6.00
IW Reprint #8-Kinstler cover; reprints Rangers #57; Dr. Drew story by Grandenetti (no date)	1.00	2.00	3.00

FIRESTONE (See Donald & Mickey)

FIRESTORM
March, 1978 - Present
DC Comics, Inc.

	Good	Fine	Mint
#1	.15	.30	.45

FIRST AMERICANS, THE (See 4-Color #843)

FIRST CHRISTMAS, THE (3-D)
1953   (25¢)(Oversized - 8¼"x10¼")
Fiction House Magazines(Real Advs.Publ. Co.)

	Good	Fine	Mint
No#-Kelly Freas cover	4.00	8.00	12.00

FIRST ISSUE SPECIAL
April, 1975 - #13, April, 1976
National Periodical Publications

	Good	Fine	Mint
#1-Intro. Atlas by Kirby	.35	.70	1.05
2-Green Team	.15	.30	.45
3-Metamorpho	.20	.40	.60

	Good	Fine	Mint
4-Lady Cop	.20	.40	.60
5-Manhunter by Kirby	.25	.50	.75
6-Dingbats by Kirby	.25	.50	.75
7-The Creeper by Fleisher/Ditko	.35	.70	1.05
8-The Warlord (origin)	.25	.50	.75
9-Dr. Fate; Kubert cover; Simonson art	.25	.50	.75
10-The Outsiders	.20	.40	.60
11-Code Name: Assassin; Redondo art	.20	.40	.60
12-New Starman-Kubert cvr.	.20	.40	.60
13-Return of the New Gods	.20	.40	.60

FIRST KISS
Dec, 1957 - #35, Dec, 1963
Charlton Comics

	Good	Fine	Mint
V1#1	.40	.80	1.20
V1#2-35	.20	.40	.60

FIRST LOVE ILLUSTRATED
Feb, 1949 - #90, Feb, 1963
Harvey Publications(Home Comics)(True Love)

	Good	Fine	Mint
#1	1.35	2.75	4.00
2-10	.65	1.35	2.00
11-34,36,37,39-90	.40	.80	1.20
35-Used in Seduction of the Innocent	2.00	4.00	6.00
38-Nostrand art	.65	1.35	2.00

NOTE: *Powell art-#1,22,33,35,41,50,71-73,76, 82.*

FIRST MEN IN THE MOON (See Movie Comics)

FIRST ROMANCE MAGAZINE
Aug, 1949 - #51, Sept, 1958
Home Comics(Harvey Publ.)/True Love

	Good	Fine	Mint
#1	1.35	2.75	4.00
2-10	.65	1.35	2.00
11-27,29-51	.40	.80	1.20
28-Nostrand art	.65	1.35	2.00

NOTE: *Powell art-#1,25,27,28,46,48.*

FIRST TRIP TO THE MOON (See Space Advs. #20)

5-STAR SUPER-HERO SPEC. (See DC Special Series #1)

FLAME, THE
Summer, 1940 - #8, Jan, 1942
Fox Features Syndicate

#1-Flame stories from WonderWorld #6-9; Origin The Flame; Lou Fine art, 50 pgs.

First Kiss #1. © CC

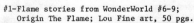

The Flame #2. © Fox

First Romance #1. © Harv

Flaming Love #2, © Qua

The Flash #123, © DC

The Flash #129, © DC

	Good	Fine	Mint
(The Flame cont'd)	60.00	120.00	180.00
2-Two stories by Fine	25.00	50.00	75.00
3-8	12.00	24.00	36.00

FLAME, THE (Formerly Lone Eagle)
#5, Dec-Jan, 1954-55 - #4, Jun-Jul, 1955
Ajax/Farrell Publications

#5(#1)	4.00	8.00	12.00
2-4	2.00	4.00	6.00

FLAMING LOVE
Dec, 1949 - #6, Oct, 1950
Quality Comics Group (Comic Magazines)

#1-Ward cover, 9pgs.	3.00	6.00	9.00
2,4-6 (photo covers)	1.50	3.00	4.50
3-Ward art, 9pgs.	2.00	4.00	6.00

FLAMING WESTERN ROMANCES
Nov-Dec, 1949 - #3, Mar-Apr, 1950
Star Publications

#1	2.00	4.00	6.00
2	1.35	2.75	4.00
3-Robert Taylor, Arlene Dahl photo cover			
with biographies inside			
	1.35	2.75	4.00

FLASH (Miniature)
1946 (One Shot) (Wheaties Giveaway)
National Periodical Publications

#1-Johnny Thunder, Ghost Patrol, The Flash &			
Kubert Hawkman app.	10.00	30.00	50.00

NOTE: *All known copies were taped to Wheaties boxes and never found in Fine & Mint condition.*

FLASH, THE (Formerly Flash Comics) (See Showcase, The Brave & the Bold, World's Finest, & Super Team Family)
#105, Feb-Mar, 1959 - Present
National Periodical Publ./DC Comics, Inc.

#105-Origin Flash(retold), & Mirror Master			
	50.00	100.00	150.00
106-Origin Grodd & Pied Piper			
	20.00	40.00	60.00
107-110: #110-Intro. & origin Kid Flash &			
The Weather Wizard	10.00	20.00	30.00
111,114,115	3.35	6.75	10.00
112-Origin Elongated Man	4.00	8.00	12.00
113-Origin Trickster	4.00	8.00	12.00
116-120: #117-Origin Capt. Boomerang			
	3.00	6.00	9.00
121	2.00	4.00	6.00
122-Origin & 1st app. The Top			
	2.00	4.00	6.00

	Good	Fine	Mint
123-Re-intro. Golden Age Flash; origins of			
both Flashes	2.50	5.00	7.50
124-130: #127-G.A. Flash x-over, J.S.A.			
cameo. #128-Origin Abra Kadabra			
	1.50	3.00	4.50
131-140: #131-Green Lantern x-over. #136-			
1st Dexter Miles. #137-G.A. Flash x-over,			
J.S.A. cameo. #139-Origin Prof. Doom.			
#140-Origin Heat Wave	1.00	2.00	3.00
141-150: #143-Green Lantern x-over			
	.75	1.50	2.25
151-160: #151-G.A. Flash x-over. #160-25¢			
ish G-21: G.A. reprints of Flash & Johnny			
Quick	.50	1.00	1.50
(84pg. Giant G-21)	.60	1.20	1.80
161-170: #167-New facts about Flash's ori-			
gin. #169-25¢ ish G-34. #170-Dr. Mid-Nite,			
Dr. Fate, G.A. Flash x-over			
	.35	.70	1.05
(84pg. Giant G-34)	.40	.80	1.20
171-180: #171-JLA, Green Lantern, Atom			
flashbacks. #173-G.A. Flash x-over. #178-			
25¢ ish G-46	.30	.60	.90
(84pg. Giant G-46)	.40	.80	1.20
181-190: #186-Re-intro. Sargon. #187-25¢ ish			
G-58	.30	.60	.90
(84pg. Giant G-58)	.40	.80	1.20
191-200: #191-Green Lantern x-over. #196-			
25¢ ish G-70	.25	.50	.75
(84pg. Giant G-70)	.35	.70	1.05
201-210: #205-25¢ ish G-82. #208-52pg. be-			
gin, end #213,15,16. #214-Origin Metal			
Men reprint	.25	.50	.75
(84pg. Giant G-82)	.35	.70	1.05
211-216,220: #211-G.A. Flash origin (#104).			
#213-All reprints. #214-50¢ ish DC-11,			
origin Metal Men. #215-G.A. Flash x-over,			
reprint in #216	.20	.40	.60
(Giant DC-11)	.50	1.00	1.50
217-219: Adams stories in all. #217-Green			
Lantern/Green Arrow series begins. #219-			
Last Green Arrow	1.00	2.00	3.00
221-225,227,228	.20	.40	.60
226-Adams story	.65	1.35	2.00
229-232-All 100pgs.	.30	.60	.90
233-250: #243-Death of the Top			
	.15	.30	.45
251-257	.15	.30	.45
Annual #1(10-12/63)-Origin Elongated Man &			
Kid Flash reprint	2.00	4.00	6.00
Annual #2,3	1.20	2.40	3.60

NOTE: *Adams covers-#194,195,202-204,206-208, 211,213,215,246. Anderson inks-#110,111,114, 115,117-119,148-150,188,176,194,200-204,206-208,210; covers-#165,176,196,205,210,212,232. Infantino art-#105-174,178,187,194,196,201, 203,209,210,213-215,229,Annual #1; covers-*

(The Flash cont'd)
#105-164,166-174,176,200,201. Kubert/Infant-
ino story-#108. Kubert covers-#189-191.
Meskin reprint-#229.

FLASH BROWN, THE SUPER-SCIENTIST (See Chewing Gum Booklet)

FLASH COMICS (The Flash #105 on; also see
1/40 - #104, 2-3/49   All-Flash)
National Periodical Publ./All-American

	Good	Fine	Mint
#1-Origin The Flash by Harry Lampert, Hawkman by Garner Fox, The Whip & Johnny Thunder; Cliff Cornwall by Moldoff, Minute Movies begin; Moldoff (Shelly) cover; reprinted in Famous First Edition	250.00	500.00	750.00
2-Rod Rian begins, ends #11	100.00	200.00	300.00
3-The King begins	75.00	150.00	225.00
4-Moldoff (Shelley) Hawkman begins	60.00	120.00	180.00
5	50.00	100.00	150.00
6-10	40.00	80.00	120.00
11-20: #12-Les Watts begins; "Sparks" #16 on. #17-Last Cliff Cornwall	25.00	50.00	75.00
21-23	20.00	40.00	60.00
24-Shiera becomes Hawkgirl	25.00	50.00	75.00
25-30: #28-Last Les Sparks. #29-Origin Ghost Patrol	17.50	35.00	52.50
31-40: #35-Origin Shade	15.00	30.00	45.00
41-50	12.00	24.00	36.00
51-61: #59-Last Minute Movies. #61-Last Moldoff Hawkman	8.00	16.00	24.00
62-Hawkman by Kubert begins	12.00	24.00	36.00
63-70: #66-68-Hop Harrigan in all	8.00	16.00	24.00
71-80: #80-Atom begins	8.00	16.00	24.00
81-85: #81-Little Boy Blue app.	7.00	14.00	21.00
86-Intro. The Black Canary in Johnny Thunder	25.00	50.00	75.00
87-90: #88-Origin Ghost	10.00	20.00	30.00
91,93-103: #98-Atom dons new costume	12.00	24.00	36.00
92-1st solo Black Canary	15.00	30.00	45.00
104-Origin The Flash retold (Rare)	40.00	80.00	120.00

NOTE: *Infantino stories-#90,93-95,99-104.*
Kinstler stories-#87,89(Hawkman). Krigstein
story-#94. Kubert stories-#62-76,83,85,86,88-
104; covers-#63,65,67,70,71,73,75,83,85,86,
88,89,91,94,96,98,100,104.

FLASH GORDON (See Eat Right to Work--, Feature Book #25, McKay, King Comics, March of Comics #118,133,142 & Street Comix)

FLASH GORDON
#10, 1943 - #512, Nov, 1953
Dell Publishing Co.

	Good	Fine	Mint
4-Color #10-by Alex Raymond(1943)-Reprints/ "The Ice Kingdom"	100.00	200.00	300.00
4-Color #84-by Alex Raymond(1945)-Reprints/ "The Fiery Desert"	40.00	80.00	120.00
4-Color #173,190	7.00	14.00	21.00
4-Color #204,247	6.00	12.00	18.00
4-Color #424	5.00	10.00	15.00
#2(5-7/53)(Dell)	3.00	6.00	9.00
4-Color #512	3.00	6.00	9.00
Macy's Giveaway(1943-20pgs.)-Not by Raymond	80.00	160.00	240.00

FLASH GORDON
Oct, 1950 - April, 1951
Harvey Publications

	Good	Fine	Mint
#1-Alex Raymond art	20.00	40.00	60.00
2-4-Alex Raymond	15.00	30.00	45.00
5-(Extremely Rare)-Small size(5½x8½";B&W; 32pgs.)Distributed to mail subscribers only Estimated value...... $700.00			

(Also see All-New #15, Boy Explorers #2, and
Stuntman #3)

FLASH GORDON
June, 1965
Gold Key

	Good	Fine	Mint
#1(1947 reprint)	1.00	2.00	3.00

FLASH GORDON
Sept, 1966 - #18, Jan, 1970
King, #1-11(12/67)/Charlton, #12(2/69) on

	Good	Fine	Mint
#1-Army giveaway("Complimentary" on cover) (Same as regular #1 minus Mandrake story & back cover)	1.75	3.35	5.00
1-Williamson cover & 2 stories; Mandrake app.	1.75	3.35	5.00
2-Bolle, G. Kane art	1.20	2.40	3.60
3-Williamson cover, Estrada art	1.35	2.75	4.00
4-Secret Agent X-9 begins, Williamson cover and art	1.50	3.00	4.50
5-Williamson cover/art	1.50	3.00	4.50
6,8-Crandall art. #6-Crandall cover	1.35	2.75	4.00
7-Raboy art	1.00	2.00	3.00
9,10-Raymond reprint + Buckler story	1.35	2.75	4.00

Flash Comics #23. © DC

Flash Comics #91. © DC

Flash Gordon #1(GK). © King

144

Fly Boy #1, © Z-D   Flying Aces #1, © Key Publ.   Flying A's Range Rider #14, © Dell

	Good	Fine	Mint
(Flash Gordon cont'd)			
11,12-Crandall story; #12-Crandall cover			
	1.35	2.75	4.00
13-Jeff Jones art	1.20	2.40	3.60
14-17: #17-Brick Bradford app.			
	.65	1.35	2.00
18-Kaluta story	1.20	2.40	3.60

FLAT TOP
Nov, 1953 - #5, 1954
Mazie Comics/Harvey Publ.(Magazine Publ.)

#1	.80	1.60	2.40
2-5	.50	1.00	1.50

FLINTSTONES, THE (TV)(See Dell Giant #48 for
#2, 11-12/61 - #60, 9/70 (Hanna-Barbera) #1)
Dell Publ. Co./Gold Key #7 on

#2	.25	.50	.75
3-10	.20	.40	.60
11-30	.15	.30	.45
31-60(9/70): #34-1st app. the Great Gazoo			
		.15	.30
At N.Y. World's Fair('64)-J.W. Books(25¢),			
re-issued in 1965(1965 on cover)			
	.65	1.35	2.00
Bigger & Boulder #1(30013-211)G.K. Giant(25¢)			
84pgs.	.65	1.35	2.00
Bigger & Boulder #2-(25¢)(1966)-reprints			
B&B #1	.35	.70	1.05
Pebbles & Bamm Bamm(100pgs.)-#30028-511(Soft			
cover-25¢)	.25	.50	.75

(See Comic Album #16, Bamm-Bamm & Pebbles
Flintstone, Dell Giant #48, March of Comics
#229,243,271,280,289,299,317,327,341, Pebbles
Flintstone, and Whitman Comic Books.)

FLINTSTONES, THE
Nov, 1970 - #50, Feb, 1977
Charlton Comics

#1	.20	.40	.60
2-7,9-50		.15	.30
8-"Flintstones Summer Vacation", 52pgs.			
(Summer, '71)	.20	.40	.60

(Also see Barney & Bettle Rubble, Dino, The
Great Gazoo, and Pebbles & Bamm-Bamm)

FLINTSTONES, THE (TV)
October, 1977 - Present
Marvel Comics Group

#1,2		.15	.30

FLIP
1954 - #2, June, 1954   (Satire)
Harvey Publications

	Good	Fine	Mint
#1,2-Nostrand art	2.00	4.00	6.00

FLIPPER (TV)
April, 1966 - #3, Nov, 1967
Gold Key

#1-3	.15	.30	.45

FLIPPITY & FLOP
Dec-Jan, 1951-52 - #47, Sept-Nov, 1960
National Per. Publ.(Signal Publ. Co.

#1	1.35	2.75	4.00
2-20	.65	1.35	2.00
21-47	.35	.70	1.05

FLY, ADVENTURES OF THE   (Flyman #31-39)
Aug, 1959 - #30, Oct, 1964; #31, Aug, 1965
Archie Publications

#1-Shield app.; origin the Fly by Simon &			
Kirby	9.00	18.00	27.00
2-Williamson & Simon & Kirby stories			
	6.00	12.00	18.00
3-Origin retold; Davis story			
	4.00	8.00	12.00
4-Adams pencils(1 panel)	2.50	5.00	7.50
5-10: #7-Black Hood app. #8,9-Shield x-over.			
#10-Black Hood app.	1.20	2.40	3.60
11-13,15-20	.65	1.35	2.00
14-Intro. & origin Fly Girl.	.65	1.35	2.00
21-31: #23-Jaguar cameo. #30-Comet x-over in			
Fly Girl	.50	1.00	1.50

FLY BOY
Spring, 1952 - #5, May, 1954 (Painted covers)
Ziff-Davis Publ. Co. (Approved)

#1	1.00	2.00	3.00
2-5	.65	1.35	2.00

FLYING ACES
July, 1955 - 1956
Key Publications

#1	.80	1.60	2.40
2-5	.50	1.00	1.50

FLYING A'S RANGE RIDER (TV)(See 4-Color #404
#2, 6-8/53 - #24, 12-2/59   for #1)
Dell Publishing Co.

#2	1.75	3.35	5.00
3-10	1.00	2.00	3.00
11-16,18-24	.80	1.60	2.40
17-Toth story	1.75	3.35	5.00

FLYING CADET (WW II Plane Photos)
Jan, 1943 - 1947 (½ photos, ½ comics)
Flying Cadet Publishing Co.

	Good	Fine	Mint
V1#1-9	1.20	2.40	3.60
V2#1-8(#10-17)	.80	1.60	2.40

FLYIN' JENNY
1946 - 1947
Pentagon Publ. Co.

No#-1945 strip reprints begin	2.50	5.00	7.50
#2-Baker cover	2.50	5.00	7.50

FLYING MODELS
May, 1954 (16 pgs.) (5¢)
H-K Publ. (Harvey Kurtzman)

V61#3 (Rare)	5.00	10.00	15.00

FLYING NUN (TV)
Feb, 1968 - #4, Nov, 1968
Dell Publishing Co.

#1-4	.15	.30	.45

FLYING NURSES (See Sue & Sally Smith --)

FLYING SAUCERS
1950 - 1953
Avon Periodicals/Realistic

#1-(1950)-21pg. Wood sty.	10.00	20.00	30.00
No#(1952)-cover altered + 2pgs. of Wood art not in original	10.00	20.00	30.00
No#(1953)-reprints above	7.00	14.00	21.00

FLYING SAUCERS (Comics)
April, 1967 - #5, Oct, 1969
Dell Publishing Co.

#1	.50	1.00	1.50
2-5	.35	.70	1.05

FLYMAN (Formerly The Fly #1-30; Mighty Comics Presents #40 on)
#31, May, 1965 - #39, Sept, 1966
Mighty Comics Group(Radio Comics)(Archie)

#31-Comet, Shield, Black Hood	.80	1.60	2.40
32,33-Comet, Shield, Black Hood x-over; re-intro. Wizard, Hangman-#33	.65	1.35	2.00
34-Shield begins	.65	1.35	2.00
35-Origin Black Hood	.65	1.35	2.00
36-Hangman x-over in Shield; re-intro. &			

	Good	Fine	Mint
origin of Web	.65	1.35	2.00
37-Hangman, Wizard x-over in Flyman; last Shield issue	.65	1.35	2.00
38-Web story	.65	1.35	2.00
39-Steel Sterling story	.65	1.35	2.00

FOLLOW THE SUN (TV)
May-July, 1962 - #2, Sept-Nov, 1962
Dell Publishing Co.

#01-280-207(#1), 208(#2)	.40	.80	1.20

FOODINI (See The Great--, Pinhead &--, and
Mar, 1950 - #5, 1950   Jingle Dingle)
Continental Publications (Holyoke)

#1	1.00	2.00	3.00
2-5	.65	1.35	2.00

FOOEY (Magazine) (Satire)
Feb, 1961 - #4, May, 1961
Scoff Publishing Co.

#1-4	.40	.80	1.20

FOOTBALL THRILLS
Fall-Winter, 1951-52 - #2, 1952
Ziff-Davis Publ. Co.

#1,2	1.00	2.00	3.00

FOR A NIGHT OF LOVE
1951
Avon Periodicals

No#-Two stories adapted from the works of Emile Zola	2.50	5.00	7.50

FORBIDDEN LOVE
Mar, 1950 - #4, Sept, 1950
Quality Comics Group

#1-Classic photo cover; Crandall story	8.00	16.00	24.00
2,3	2.00	4.00	6.00
4-Ward/Cuidera art	3.00	6.00	9.00

FORBIDDEN LOVE (See Dark Mansion of --)

FORBIDDEN TALES OF DARK MANSION (Dark Mansion of Forbidden Love #1-4)
#5, May-June, 1972 - #15, Feb-Mar, 1974
National Periodical Publications

#5-15	.25	.50	.75

NOTE: *Alcala* stories-#9-11,13. *Chaykin* stor-
ies-#7,15. *Kaluta* covers-#7-13. *Kane* story-
#13. *Kirby* story-#6. *Redondo* story-#14.

Flyin' Jenny #1, © Pentagon Publ.   Flying Saucers #1, © Avon

For A Night Of Love #1, © Avon

Forbidden Worlds #1, © ACG

Forever People #1, © DC

Four Color #4, © WDP

FORBIDDEN WORLDS (--Presents Herbie #114,116)
7-8/51 - #145, 8/67   (#1-5,52pgs; #6,48pgs)
American Comics Group

	Good	Fine	Mint
#1-10pg. Williamson/Frazetta story			
	15.00	30.00	45.00
2	4.00	8.00	12.00
3-7pg. Williamson/Wood story			
	8.00	16.00	24.00
4	3.00	6.00	9.00
5-8pg. Williamson/Krenkel story			
	7.00	14.00	21.00
6-Williamson inks/Harrison pencils, 8pgs.			
	6.00	12.00	18.00
7-10	1.50	3.00	4.50
11-34-Last pre-code ish.	1.00	2.00	3.00
35-62	.65	1.35	2.00
63,69,76,78-Williamson stories in all			
	2.00	4.00	6.00
64,66-68,70-72,74,75,77,79-86,88-90			
	.50	1.00	1.50
65-"There's a New Moon Tonight" listed in #114 as holding 2nd record fan mail response	.65	1.35	2.00
73-Intro., 1st app. Herbie by Whitney			
	4.00	8.00	12.00
87-Contains story that got record fan mail response "The Train That Vanished"			
	.65	1.35	2.00
91-93,95-100	.50	1.00	1.50
94-Herbie app.	1.50	3.00	4.50
101-109,111-113,115,117-120	.25	.50	.75
110,114,116-Herbie app.; #114 contains list of editor's top 20 ACG stories			
	.80	1.60	2.40
121-124: #124-Magic Agent app.			
	.25	.50	.75
125-Magic Agent app.; intro. & origin Magicman series, ends #141	.35	.70	1.05
126-130	.25	.50	.75
131,132,134-141: #136-Nemesis x-over in Magicman. #140-Mark Midnight app. by Ditko			
	.20	.40	.60
133-Origin & 1st app. Dragonia in Magicman (1-2/66); returns #138	.25	.50	.75
142-145	.20	.40	.60

NOTE: *Buscema story-#75,79,81,82. Ditko story-#137,138,140. Moldoff story-#31. Whitney art in most issues.*

FORD ROTUNDA CHRISTMAS BOOK (See Christmas at the Rotunda)

FOREIGN INTRIGUE
1956
Charlton Comics

#1-Johnny Dynamite begins, ends #15

	Good	Fine	Mint
	1.00	2.00	3.00
2-15	.65	1.35	2.00

FOREVER, DARLING (See 4-Color #681)

FOREVER PEOPLE
Feb-Mar, 1971 - #11, Oct-Nov, 1972
National Periodical Publications

#1-Superman x-over; Jack Kirby art begins			
	2.00	4.00	6.00
2	1.20	2.40	3.60
3-5: #4-G.A. reprints begin			
	1.00	2.00	3.00
6-8,11	.65	1.35	2.00
9,10-Deadman x-over	.65	1.35	2.00

NOTE: *Kirby art & covers-#1-11; #4-9 contain Sandman reprints from Adventure #85,84,75,80, 77,74 in that order.*

FOR LOVERS ONLY
#38, Dec, 1968 - #98, Nov, 1976
Charlton Comics

#38-98			.15	.30

48 FAMOUS AMERICANS
1947   (Giveaway)   (Half-size in color)
J. C. Penney Co.   (Cpr. Edwin H. Stroh)

Simon & Kirby art	5.00	10.00	15.00

FOUR COLOR
1939 - #1354, 1962
Dell Publishing Co.

NOTE: *Four Color only appears on issues #19-25, 1-99. Dell Publishing Co. filed these as Series I, #1-25, and Series II, #1-1354. Later issues were printed with & without ads on back cover. Issues without ads are worth more.*

SERIES I:

	Good	Fine	Mint
#1(no#)-Dick Tracy	90.00	180.00	270.00
2(no#)-Don Winslow(Rare)	35.00	70.00	105.00
3(no#)-Myra North	10.00	20.00	30.00
4-Donald Duck(2/40) by Al Taliaferro (Disney)	400.00	800.00	1200.00
	(Prices vary widely on this book)		
5-Smilin' Jack	25.00	50.00	75.00
6-Dick Tracy (Rare)	50.00	100.00	150.00
7-Gangbusters	10.00	20.00	30.00
8-Dick Tracy	40.00	80.00	120.00
9-Terry & the Pirates-Reprints #5 & The Pirate from Super #9-29	35.00	70.00	105.00
10-Smilin' Jack	25.00	50.00	75.00

Four Color # 8, © N.Y. News Synd.

Four Color #13, © WDP

Four Color #16, © WDP

Four Color cont'd)	Good	Fine	Mint
1-Smitty	13.50	26.75	40.00
2-Little Orphan Annie	20.00	40.00	60.00
3-Reluctant Dragon('41)-Contains 2pgs. of			
photo from film; 2pg. foreword to Fantasia			
by Leopold Stokowski; Donald Duck, Goofy,			
Baby Weems & Mickey Mouse(as the Sorcerer's			
Apprentice) app.	50.00	100.00	150.00
4-Moon Mullins	12.00	24.00	36.00
5-Tillie the Toiler	8.00	16.00	24.00
6-Mickey Mouse(Disney)by Gottfredson			
	325.00	812.50	1300.00
(Prices vary widely on this book)			
	10.00	20.00	30.00
7-Dumbo(1941)-Mickey Mouse, Donald Duck, &			
Pluto app.(Disney)	60.00	120.00	180.00
8-Jiggs & Maggie(1936-'38 reprints)			
	10.00	20.00	30.00
9-Barney Google-(1st issue with Four Color			
on the cover)	15.00	30.00	45.00
20-Tiny Tim	12.00	24.00	36.00
21-Dick Tracy	30.00	60.00	90.00
22-Don Winslow	8.00	16.00	24.00
23-Gangbusters	10.00	20.00	30.00
24-Captain Easy	12.00	24.00	36.00
25-Popeye	35.00	70.00	105.00

SERIES II:

#1-Little Joe	15.00	30.00	45.00
2-Harold Teen	12.00	24.00	36.00
3-Alley Oop	25.00	50.00	75.00
4-Smilin' Jack	20.00	40.00	60.00
5-Raggedy Ann & Andy	20.00	40.00	60.00
6-Smitty	8.00	16.00	24.00
7-Smokey Stover	15.00	30.00	45.00
8-Tillie the Toiler	6.00	12.00	18.00
9-Donald Duck "Finds Pirate Gold" by Carl			
Barks & Jack Hannah (Disney)			
	500.00	1000.00	1500.00
(Prices vary widely on this book)			
10-Flash Gordon by Alex Raymond-Reprints			

	Good	Fine	Mint
from "The Ice Kingdom"			
	100.00	200.00	300.00
11-Wash Tubbs	15.00	30.00	45.00
12-Bambi (Disney)	30.00	60.00	90.00
13-Mr. District Attorney	9.00	18.00	27.00
14-Smilin' Jack	20.00	40.00	60.00
15-Felix the Cat	25.00	50.00	75.00
16-Porky Pig(1942)-"Secret of the Haunted			
House"	30.00	60.00	90.00
17-Popeye	25.00	50.00	75.00
18-Little Orphan Annie's Jr. Commandos			
	15.00	30.00	45.00
19-Thumper Meets the 7 Dwarfs (Disney)-re-			
printed in Silly Symphonies			
	30.00	60.00	90.00
20-Barney Baxter	12.00	24.00	36.00
21-Oswald the Rabbit	16.50	33.25	50.00
22-Tillie the Toiler	5.00	10.00	15.00
23-Raggedy Ann	15.00	30.00	45.00
24-Gangbusters	10.00	20.00	30.00
25-Andy Panda	20.00	40.00	60.00
26-Popeye	20.00	40.00	60.00
27-Mickey Mouse & the 7 Colored Terror			
(Disney)	50.00	100.00	150.00
28-Wash Tubbs	10.00	20.00	30.00
29-Donald Duck-"Mummy's Ring" by Carl Barks			
(Disney)	375.00	750.00	1125.00
(Prices vary widely on this book)			
30-Bambi's Children(1943)-Disney			
	25.00	50.00	75.00
31-Moon Mullins	8.00	16.00	24.00
32-Smitty	5.00	10.00	15.00
33-Bugs Bunny-Public Nuisance #1			
	30.00	60.00	90.00
34-Dick Tracy	20.00	40.00	60.00
35-Smokey Stover	7.00	14.00	21.00
36-Smilin' Jack	8.00	16.00	24.00
37-Bringing Up Father	7.00	14.00	21.00
38-Roy Rogers	20.00	40.00	60.00

Four Color #17, © WDP

Four Color #8, © King

Four Color #23, © J. Gruelle

148

Four Color #31, © N.Y. News Synd.

Four Color #38, © Roy Rogers

Four Color #50, © Dell

(Four Color cont'd)	Good	Fine	Mint
39-Oswald the Rabbit('44)	13.50	26.75	40.00
40-Barney Google	6.00	12.00	18.00
41-Mother Goose & Nursery Rhyme Comics(Kelly			
cover only)	12.00	24.00	36.00
42-Tiny Tim('34 reprts)	6.00	12.00	18.00
43-Popeye('38-'42 rprts)	12.00	24.00	36.00
44-Terry & the Pirates	16.50	33.25	50.00
45-Raggedy Ann	10.00	20.00	30.00
46-Felix the Cat & the Haunted Castle			
	15.00	30.00	45.00
47-Gene Autry	15.00	30.00	45.00
48-Porky Pig of the Mounties by Carl Barks			
(1944)	100.00	200.00	300.00
49-Snow White & the 7 Dwarfs			
	16.50	33.25	50.00
50-Fairy Tale Parade-Walt Kelly art (1944)			
	25.00	50.00	75.00
51-Bugs Bunny	20.00	40.00	60.00
52-Little Orphan Annie	8.00	16.00	24.00
53-Wash Tubbs	6.00	12.00	18.00
54-Andy Panda	12.00	24.00	36.00
55-Tillie the Toiler	4.00	8.00	12.00
56-Dick Tracy	15.00	30.00	45.00
57-Gene Autry	12.00	24.00	36.00
58-Smilin' Jack	8.00	16.00	24.00
59-Mother Goose & Nursery Rhyme Comics by			
Walt Kelly	16.50	33.25	50.00
60-Tiny Folks Funnies	7.00	14.00	21.00
61-Santa Claus Funnies(11/44)-Kelly art			
	20.00	40.00	60.00
62-Donald Duck-"Frozen Gold" by Carl Barks			
(Disney)	175.00	350.00	525.00
63-Roy Rogers	13.50	26.75	40.00
64-Smokey Stover	4.00	8.00	12.00
65-Smitty	4.00	8.00	12.00
66-Gene Autry	12.00	24.00	36.00
67-Oswald the Rabbit	8.00	16.00	24.00
68-Mother Goose by Walt Kelly			
	16.50	33.25	50.00

	Good	Fine	Mint
69-Fairy Tale Parade by Walt Kelly			
	25.00	50.00	75.00
70-Popeye	7.00	14.00	21.00
71-Three Caballeros by Walt Kelly (1945)			
(Disney)	75.00	150.00	225.00
72-Raggedy Ann & Andy	8.00	16.00	24.00
73-The Gumps	3.35	6.75	10.00
74-Little Lulu	70.00	140.00	210.00
75-Gene Autry	8.00	16.00	24.00
76-Little Orphan Annie	7.00	14.00	21.00
77-Felix the Cat	10.00	20.00	30.00
78-Porky Pig & the Bandit Twins			
	8.00	16.00	24.00
79-Mickey Mouse in The Riddle of the Red			
Hat by Carl Barks (Disney)			
	70.00	140.00	210.00
80-Smilin' Jack	6.00	12.00	18.00
81-Moon Mullins	4.00	8.00	12.00
82-Lone Ranger	12.00	24.00	36.00
83-Gene Autry	8.00	16.00	24.00
84-Flash Gordon by Alex Raymond-Reprts. from			
"The Fiery Desert"	40.00	80.00	120.00
85-Andy Panda & the Mad Dog Mystery			
	6.00	12.00	18.00
86-Roy Rogers	9.00	18.00	27.00
87-Fairy Tale Parade by Walt Kelly; Dan			
Noonan cover	20.00	40.00	60.00
88-Bugs Bunny	10.00	20.00	30.00
89-Tillie the Toiler	3.00	6.00	9.00
90-Xmas with Mother Goose by Walt Kelly			
(11/45)	13.50	26.75	40.00
91-Santa Claus Funnies by Walt Kelly (11/45)			
	15.00	30.00	45.00
92-Pinocchio(1945); Donald Duck by Kelly,			
16 pgs.(Disney)	20.00	40.00	60.00
93-Gene Autry	6.00	12.00	18.00
94-Winnie Winkle(1945)	4.00	8.00	12.00
95-Roy Rogers	9.00	18.00	27.00
96-Dick Tracy	8.00	16.00	24.00

Four Color #53, © News Synd.

Four Color #72, © J. Gruelle

Four Color #74, © West

Four Color #104, © Dell

Four Color #111, © NEA Service

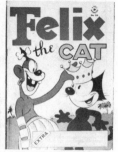

Four Color #119, © King

(Four Color cont'd)	Good	Fine	Mint
97-Little Lulu (1946)	25.00	50.00	75.00
98-Lone Ranger	10.00	20.00	30.00
99-Smitty	3.00	6.00	9.00

(#99-Smitty is last issue to carry "Four
Color" logo on cover; all issues beginning
with #100 are marked "-- O.S."(One Shot)
which can be found in the bottom left-hand
panel on the first page; the numbers following "O.S." relate to the year/month issued.

	Good	Fine	Mint
100-Gene Autry	6.00	12.00	18.00
101-Terry & the Pirates	12.00	24.00	36.00
102-Oswald the Rabbit-Walt Kelly art, 1 pg.			
	8.00	16.00	24.00
103-Easter with Mother Goose by Walt Kelly			
	15.00	30.00	45.00
104-Fairy Tale Parade by Walt Kelly			
	15.00	30.00	45.00
105-Albert the Alligator & Pogo Possum by			
Kelly(4/46)	50.00	100.00	150.00
106-Tillie the Toiler	2.50	5.00	7.50
107-Little Orphan Annie	6.00	12.00	18.00
108-Donald Duck-"Terror of the River" by			
Carl Barks (Disney)	100.00	200.00	300.00
109-Roy Rogers	6.00	12.00	18.00
110-Little Lulu	17.50	35.00	52.50
111-Captain Easy	5.00	10.00	15.00
112-Porky Pig's Adv. in Gopher Gulch			
	6.00	12.00	18.00
113-Popeye	3.00	6.00	9.00
114-Fairy Tale Parade by Walt Kelly			
	15.00	30.00	45.00
115-Little Lulu	17.50	35.00	52.50
116-Mickey Mouse & "The House of Many Myster-			
ies" (Disney)	10.00	20.00	30.00
117-Roy Rogers	5.00	10.00	15.00
118-The Lone Ranger	10.00	20.00	30.00
119-Felix the Cat	7.00	14.00	21.00
120-Little Lulu	13.50	26.75	40.00

	Good	Fine	Mint
121-Fairy Tale Parade-(not Kelly)			
	8.00	16.00	24.00
122-Henry (10/46)	2.00	4.00	6.00
123-Bugs Bunny's Dangerous Venture			
	6.00	12.00	18.00
124-Roy Rogers	5.00	10.00	15.00
125-The Lone Ranger	7.00	14.00	21.00
126-Christmas with Mother Goose by Walt			
Kelly (1946)	12.00	24.00	36.00
127-Popeye	3.00	6.00	9.00
128-Santa Claus Funnies-"Santa & the Angel"			
by Gollub; "A Mouse in the House" by			
Kelly	12.00	24.00	36.00
129-Uncle Remus & Tales of Brer Rabbit(1946)			
(Disney)	10.00	20.00	30.00
130-Andy Panda	3.00	6.00	9.00
131-Little Lulu	13.50	26.75	40.00
132-Tillie the Toiler('47)	2.50	5.00	7.50
133-Dick Tracy	8.00	16.00	24.00
134-Tarzan & the Devil Ogre			
	20.00	40.00	60.00
135-Felix the Cat	6.00	12.00	18.00
136-The Lone Ranger	7.00	14.00	21.00
137-Roy Rogers	5.00	10.00	15.00
138-Smitty	2.50	5.00	7.50
139-Little Lulu (1947)	13.50	26.75	40.00
140-Easter with Mother Goose by Walt Kelly			
	12.00	24.00	36.00
141-Mickey Mouse & the Submarine Pirates			
(Disney)	10.00	20.00	30.00
142-Bugs Bunny & the Haunted Mtn.			
	6.00	12.00	18.00
143-Oswald the Rabbit	3.00	6.00	9.00
144-Roy Rogers (1947)	5.00	10.00	15.00
145-Popeye	3.00	6.00	9.00
146-Little Lulu	13.50	26.75	40.00
147-Donald Duck in "Volcano Valley" by Carl			
Barks (Disney)	70.00	140.00	210.00
148-Albert the Alligator & Pogo Possum by			

Four Color #129, © WDP

Four Color #132, © King

Four Color #141, © WDP

Four Color #149, © N.Y. News Synd.

Four Color #155, © King

Four Color #162, © King

(Four Color cont'd)

	Good	Fine	Mint
Walt Kelly	40.00	80.00	120.00
149-Smilin' Jack	5.00	10.00	15.00
150-Tillie the Toiler (6/47)			
	2.00	4.00	6.00
151-The Lone Ranger	5.00	10.00	15.00
152-Little Orphan Annie	5.00	10.00	15.00
153-Roy Rogers	4.00	8.00	12.00
154-Andy Panda	3.00	6.00	9.00
155-Henry (7/47)	2.00	4.00	6.00
156-Porky Pig & the Phantom			
	4.00	8.00	12.00
157-Mickey Mouse & "The Beanstalk" (Disney)			
	8.00	16.00	24.00
158-Little Lulu	13.50	26.75	40.00
159-Donald Duck in "The Ghost of the Grotto"			
by Carl Barks(Disney)	60.00	120.00	180.00
160-Roy Rogers	4.00	8.00	12.00
161-Tarzan & the Fires of Tohr			
	17.50	35.00	52.50
162-Felix the Cat (9/47)	5.00	10.00	15.00
163-Dick Tracy	6.00	12.00	18.00
164-Bugs Bunny "Finds the Frozen Kingdom"			
	6.00	12.00	18.00
165-Little Lulu	13.50	26.75	40.00
166-Roy Rogers	4.00	8.00	12.00
167-The Lone Ranger	5.00	10.00	15.00
168-Popeye (10/47)	3.00	6.00	9.00
169-Woody Woodpecker-"Manhunter in the North"			
	2.50	5.00	7.50
170-Mickey Mouse on "Spook's Island" (11/47)			
(Disney)-reprinted in M.M. #103			
	8.00	16.00	24.00
171-Charlie McCarthy	1.75	3.35	5.00
172-Christmas with Mother Goose by Walt			
Kelly (11/47)	10.00	20.00	30.00
173-Flash Gordon	7.00	14.00	21.00
174-Winnie Winkle	2.50	5.00	7.50
175-Santa Claus Funnies by Walt Kelly ('47)			
	12.00	24.00	36.00

	Good	Fine	Mint
176-Tillie the Toiler (12/47)			
	2.00	4.00	6.00
177-Roy Rogers	4.00	8.00	12.00
178-Donald Duck in "Christmas on Bear Mtn."			
by Carl Barks; 1st app. Uncle Scrooge			
(Disney)	60.00	120.00	180.00
179-Uncle Wiggily-Walt Kelly cover			
	5.00	10.00	15.00
180-Ozark Ike	2.50	5.00	7.50
181-Mickey Mouse in "Jungle Magic" (Disney)			
	8.00	16.00	24.00
182-Porky Pig (2/48)	4.00	8.00	12.00
183-Oswald the Rabbit	3.00	6.00	9.00
184-Tillie the Toiler	2.00	4.00	6.00
185-Easter with Mother Goose by Walt Kelly			
(1948)	12.00	24.00	36.00
186-Bambi(Disney)-Reprinted as Bambi #3('56)			
	5.00	10.00	15.00
187-Bugs Bunny-"The Dreadful Dragon"			
	4.00	8.00	12.00
188-Woody Woodpecker(5/48)	2.50	5.00	7.50
189-Donald Duck in "The Old Castle's Secret"			
by Carl Barks(Disney)	50.00	100.00	150.00
190-Flash Gordon ('48)	7.00	14.00	21.00
191-Porky Pig "To the Rescue"			
	4.00	8.00	12.00
192-The Brownies by Walt Kelly (7/48)			
	10.00	20.00	30.00
193-Tom & Jerry (1948)	3.00	6.00	9.00
194-Mickey Mouse in "The World Under the Sea"			
(Disney)-Reprinted in M.M. #101			
	8.00	16.00	24.00
195-Tillie the Toiler	1.75	3.50	5.25
196-Charlie McCarthy	1.75	3.50	5.25
197-Spirit of the Border (Zane Grey, 1948)			
	2.50	5.00	7.50
198-Andy Panda	3.00	6.00	9.00
199-Donald Duck in "Sheriff of Bullet Valley"			
by Carl Barks(Disney)	50.00	100.00	150.00

Four Color #168, © King

Four Color #194, © WDP

Four Color #199, © WDP

151

Four Color #200, © L. Schlesinger

Four Color #207, © NEA Service

Four Color #213, © King

(Four Color cont'd)	Good	Fine	Mint
200-Bugs Bunny-Super Sleuth (10/48)			
	4.00	8.00	12.00
201-Christmas with Mother Goose by Walt Kelly			
	8.00	16.00	24.00
202-Woody Woodpecker	2.00	4.00	6.00
203-Donald Duck in "The Golden Christmas Tree" by Carl Barks (Disney)			
	30.00	60.00	90.00
204-Flash Gordon (1948)	6.00	12.00	18.00
205-Santa Claus Funnies by Walt Kelly			
	10.00	20.00	30.00
206-Little Orphan Annie	4.00	8.00	12.00
207-King of the Royal Mtd.	2.50	5.00	7.50
208-Brer Rabbit Does It Again (Disney, 1/49)			
	5.00	10.00	15.00
209-Harold Teen	1.00	2.00	3.00
210-Tippie & Cap Stubbs	1.00	2.00	3.00
211-Little Beaver	2.50	5.00	7.50
212-Dr. Bobbs	1.00	2.00	3.00
213-Tillie the Toiler	1.75	3.50	5.25
214-Mickey Mouse & "His Sky Adventure"(2/49) (Disney)-reprinted in M.M. #105			
	6.00	12.00	18.00
215-Sparkle Plenty (Dick Tracy reprints by Gould)			
	5.00	10.00	15.00
216-Andy Panda	1.75	3.35	5.00
217-Bugs Bunny in "Court Jester"			
	4.00	8.00	12.00
218-The Three Little Pigs (Disney - 3/49)			
	3.00	6.00	9.00
219-Swee'pea	2.50	5.00	7.50
220-Easter with Mother Goose by Walt Kelly			
	9.00	18.00	27.00
221-Uncle Wiggily-Walt Kelly cover in part			
	5.00	10.00	15.00
222-West of the Pecos (Zane Grey)			
	2.50	5.00	7.50
223-Donald Duck "Lost in the Andes" by Carl Barks-(Disney)-(Square egg story-4/49)			

	Good	Fine	Mint
	35.00	70.00	105.00
224-Little Iodine (4/49)	2.00	4.00	6.00
225-Oswald the Rabbit	2.50	5.00	7.50
226-Porky Pig & Spoofy, the Spook			
	3.00	6.00	9.00
227-Seven Dwarfs(Disney)	4.00	8.00	12.00
228-Mark of Zorro ('49)	4.00	8.00	12.00
229-Smokey Stover	2.00	4.00	6.00
230-Sunset Pass(Zane Grey)	2.50	5.00	7.50
231-Mickey Mouse & "The Rajah's Treasure" (Disney)			
	6.00	12.00	18.00
232-Woody Woodpecker(6/49)	2.00	4.00	6.00
233-Bugs Bunny-"Sleepwalking Sleuth"			
	4.00	8.00	12.00
234-Dumbo in "Sky Voyage" (Disney)			
	3.00	6.00	9.00
235-Tiny Tim	1.50	3.00	4.50
236-Heritage of the Desert (Zane Grey-'49)			
	2.50	5.00	7.50
237-Tillie the Toiler	1.75	3.50	5.25
238-Donald Duck in "Voodoo Hoodoo" by Carl Barks (Disney)	25.00	50.00	75.00
239-Adventure Bound(8/49)	1.25	2.50	3.75
240-Andy Panda	1.75	3.35	5.00
241-Porky Pig	3.00	6.00	9.00
242-Tippie & Cap Stubbs	1.00	2.00	3.00
243-Thumper Follows His Nose (Disney)			
	3.00	6.00	9.00
244-The Brownies by Walt Kelly			
	9.00	18.00	27.00
245-Dick's Adventures in Dreamland (9/49)			
	1.75	3.35	5.00
246-Thunder Mountain (Zane Grey)			
	1.50	3.00	4.50
247-Flash Gordon	6.00	12.00	18.00
248-Mickey Mouse & "The Black Sorcerer" (Disney)	6.00	12.00	18.00
249-Woody Woodpecker-"The Globetrotter" (10/49)	2.00	4.00	6.00

Four Color #218, © WDP

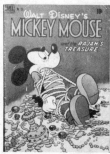

Four Color # 231, © WDP

Four Color #235, © News Synd.

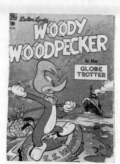

Four Color #249, © Walter Lantz

Four Color #270, © Dell

Four Color #274, © L. Schlesinger

(Four Color cont'd)	Good	Fine	Mint
250-Bugs Bunny	2.50	5.00	7.50
251-Hubert at Camp Moonbeam			
	1.35	2.75	4.00
252-Pinocchio(Disney)-not Kelly; origin			
	5.00	10.00	15.00
253-Christmas with Mother Goose by Walt Kelly			
	8.00	16.00	24.00
254-Santa Claus Funnies by Walt Kelly; Pogo & Albert story by Kelly (11/49)			
	10.00	20.00	30.00
255-The Ranger (Zane Grey - '49)			
	1.50	3.00	4.50
256-Donald Duck in "Luck of the North" by Carl Barks (Disney)	25.00	50.00	75.00
257-Little Iodine	2.00	4.00	6.00
258-Andy Panda & "The Balloon Race"			
	1.75	3.35	5.00
259-Santa & the Angel (Gollub art-condensed from #128) & Santa at the Zoo(12/49)- two books in one	2.50	5.00	7.50
260-Porky Pig-"Hero of the Wild West"(12/49)			
	3.00	6.00	9.00
261-Mickey Mouse & "The Missing Key"(Disney)			
	6.00	12.00	18.00
262-Raggedy Ann & Andy	2.50	5.00	7.50
263-Donald Duck in "Land of the Totem Poles" by Carl Barks(Disney)(Has 2 Barks stories)			
	25.00	50.00	75.00
264-Woody Woodpecker-in "The Magic Lantern"			
	2.00	4.00	6.00
265-King of the Royal Mtd.	2.50	5.00	7.50
266-Bugs Bunny-"Isle of Hercules"(2/50)-re- printed Best of B.B.#1-	2.50	5.00	7.50
267-Little Beaver	1.75	3.35	5.00
268-Mickey Mouse's "Surprise Visitor"-(1950) (Disney)	6.00	12.00	18.00
269-Johnny Mack Brown	3.00	6.00	9.00
270-Drift Fence (Zane Grey-3/50)			
	1.50	3.00	4.50

	Good	Fine	Mint
271-Porky Pig-"Phantom of the Plains"			
	3.00	6.00	9.00
272-Cinderella (Disney)	2.50	5.00	7.50
273-Oswald the Rabbit	2.50	5.00	7.50
274-Bugs Bunny-"Hair Brained Reporter"			
	2.50	5.00	7.50
275-Donald Duck in "Ancient Persia" by Carl Barks(Disney-5/50)	20.00	40.00	60.00
276-Uncle Wiggily	2.50	5.00	7.50
277-Porky Pig-"Desert Adventure" (5/50)			
	3.00	6.00	9.00
278-Wild Bill Elliott	3.00	6.00	9.00
279-Mickey Mouse & Pluto Battle the Giant Ants(Disney)-reprinted in M.M. #102			
	5.00	10.00	15.00
280-Andy Panda	1.75	3.35	5.00
281-Bugs Bunny-"In the Great Circus Mystery"			
	2.50	5.00	7.50
282-Donald Duck and "The Pixilated Parrot" by Carl Barks(Disney)	20.00	40.00	60.00
283-King of the Royal Mounted (7/50)			
	2.50	5.00	7.50
284-Porky Pig-"Kingdom of Nowhere"			
	3.00	6.00	9.00
285-Bozo the Clown & His Minikin Circus (TV)			
	1.35	2.75	4.00
286-Mickey Mouse-"& the Uninvited Guest" (Disney)	5.00	10.00	15.00
287-Gene Autry's Champion	2.00	4.00	6.00
288-Woody Woodpecker-"Klondike Gold"			
	2.00	4.00	6.00
289-Bugs Bunny in Indian Trouble			
	2.50	5.00	7.50
290-The Chief	1.50	3.00	4.50
291-Donald Duck in "The Magic Hourglass" by Carl Barks (Disney)	20.00	40.00	60.00
292-The Cisco Kid	2.50	5.00	7.50
293-The Brownies-Kelly cover/art			
	9.00	18.00	27.00

Four Color #277, © L. Schlesinger

Four Color #279, © WDP

Four Color #292, © Dell

Four Color #297, © Walter Lantz

Four Color #312, © The Lone Ranger

Four Color #313, © WDP

	Good	Fine	Mint
(Four Color cont'd)			
294-Little Beaver	1.75	3.35	5.00
295-Porky Pig in "President Porky" (9/50)	3.00	6.00	9.00
296-Mickey Mouse in "Private Eye for Hire" (Disney)	5.00	10.00	15.00
297-Andy Pandy (10/50)	1.75	3.35	5.00
298-Bugs Bunny "Sheik for a Day"	2.50	5.00	7.50
299-Buck Jones	4.00	8.00	12.00
300-Donald Duck in "Big-Top Bedlam" by Carl Barks(Disney-11/50)	17.50	35.00	52.50
301-The Mysterious Rider (Zane Grey)	1.50	3.00	4.50
302-Santa Claus Funnies (11/50)	2.50	5.00	7.50
303-Porky Pig in "The Land of the Monstrous Flies"	1.75	3.50	5.25
304-Mickey Mouse in "Tom-Tom Island" (Disney-12/50)	4.00	8.00	12.00
305-Woody Woodpecker	1.50	3.00	4.50
306-Raggedy Ann	4.00	8.00	12.00
307-Bugs Bunny-"Lumber Jack Rabbit"	2.25	4.50	6.75
308-Donald Duck in "Dangerous Disguise" by Carl Barks (Disney)	17.50	35.00	52.50
309-Dollface & Her Gang ('51)	1.35	2.75	4.00
310-King of the Royal Mounted (1/51)	1.50	3.00	4.50
311-Porky Pig in "Midget Horses of Hidden Valley"	1.75	3.50	5.25
312-Tonto(#1)	2.50	5.00	7.50
313-Mickey Mouse(#1) in "The Mystery of the Double-Cross Ranch" (Disney)	4.00	8.00	12.00
314-Ambush (Zane Grey)	1.50	3.00	4.50
315-Oswald the Rabbit	1.75	3.50	5.25
316-Rex Allen(#1)	2.50	5.00	7.50
317-Bugs Bunny in "Hair Today Gone Tomorrow"			

	Good	Fine	Mint
(#1)	2.25	4.50	6.75
318-Donald Duck in "No Such Varmint" by Carl Barks(#1)(Disney)	17.50	35.00	52.50
319-Gene Autry's Champion	1.25	2.50	3.75
320-Uncle Wiggily	2.00	4.00	6.00
321-The Little Scouts	1.00	2.00	3.00
322-Porky Pig(#1)	1.75	3.50	5.25
323-Suzie Q. Smith(3/51)	1.20	2.40	3.60
324-I Met a Handsome Cowboy (3/51)	1.75	3.35	5.00
325-Mickey Mouse(#2) in "The Haunted Castle" (Disney-4/61)	4.00	8.00	12.00
326-Andy Panda	1.20	2.40	3.60
327-Bugs Bunny	2.25	4.50	6.75
328-Donald Duck in "Old California"(#2) by Carl Barks-drug issue (Disney-5/51)	20.00	40.00	60.00
329-Trigger (5/51)	2.00	4.00	6.00
330-Porky Pig (#2)	1.75	3.50	5.25
331-Alice in Wonderland (Disney-1951)	2.50	5.00	7.50
332-Little Beaver	1.75	3.35	5.00
333-Wilderness Trek (Zane Grey-5/51)	1.50	3.00	4.50
334-Mickey Mouse & "Yukon Gold" (Disney-6/51)	4.00	8.00	12.00
335-Francis the Mule	1.00	2.00	3.00
336-Woody Woodpecker	1.50	3.00	4.50
337-The Brownies-not by Walt Kelly	2.00	4.00	6.00
338-Bugs Bunny	2.25	4.50	6.75
339-Donald Duck and "The Magic Fountain"-Not by Carl Barks(Disney 7-8/51)	3.00	6.00	9.00
340-King of the Royal Mounted (7/51)	1.50	3.00	4.50
341-Unbirthday Party with Alice in Wonderland (Disney-7/51)	2.50	5.00	7.50
342-Porky Pig	1.25	2.50	3.75

Four Color #336, © Walter Lantz

Four Color #339, © WDP

Four Color #342, © L. Schlesinger

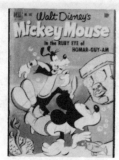

Four Color #343, © WDP

Four Color #347, © L. Schlesinger

Four Color #349, © Dell

(Four Color cont'd)	Good	Fine	Mint
343-Mickey Mouse in "The Ruby Eye of Homar-Guy-Am" (Disney)-reprinted in M.M. #104			
	3.50	7.00	10.50
344-Sgt. Preston (TV)	1.75	3.35	5.00
345-Andy Panda in Scotland Yard (8-10/51)			
	1.20	2.40	3.60
346-Hideout (Zane Grey)	1.50	3.00	4.50
347-Bugs Bunny-"The Frigid Hare" (8-9/51)			
	2.25	4.50	6.75
348-Donald Duck "The Crocodile Collector"-Barks cover only (Disney - 9-10/51)			
	4.00	8.00	12.00
349-Uncle Wiggily	2.00	4.00	6.00
350-Woody Woodpecker	1.50	3.00	4.50
351-Porky Pig-"Grand Canyon Giant" (9-10/51)			
	1.25	2.50	3.75
352-Mickey Mouse-"The Mystery of Painted Valley" (Disney)	3.50	7.00	10.50
353-Duck Album-Barks cover (Disney)			
	1.35	2.75	4.00
354-Raggedy Ann & Andy	2.50	5.00	7.50
355-Bugs Bunny Hot-Rod Hare			
	2.25	4.50	6.75
356-Donald Duck in "Rags to Riches"-Barks cover only (Disney)	4.00	8.00	12.00
357-Comeback (Zane Grey)	1.35	2.75	4.00
358-Andy Panda (11-1/52)	1.20	2.40	3.60
359-Frosty the Snowman	1.00	2.00	3.00
360-Porky Pig-"In Tree of Fortune" (11-12/51)			
	1.25	2.50	3.75
361-Santa Claus Funnies	2.50	5.00	7.50
362-Mickey Mouse & "The Smuggled Diamonds" (Disney)	3.50	7.00	10.50
363-King of the Royal Mtd.	1.50	3.00	4.50
364-Woody Woodpecker	1.00	2.00	3.00
365-The Brownies-not by Kelly			
	2.00	4.00	6.00
366-Bugs Bunny-"Uncle Buckskin Comes to Town" (12-1/52)	2.25	4.50	6.75

	Good	Fine	Mint
367-Donald Duck in "A Christmas for Shacktown" by Carl Barks (Disney- 1-2/52)			
	15.00	30.00	45.00
368-Beany & Cecil (1/52)	1.50	3.00	4.50
369-The Lone Ranger's Famous Horse-Hi-Yo Silver	2.00	4.00	6.00
370-Porky Pig "Trouble in the Big Trees"			
	1.25	2.50	3.75
371-Mickey Mouse-"The Inca Idol Case" ('52) (Disney)	3.50	7.00	10.50
372-Riders of the Purple Sage (Zane Grey)			
	1.35	2.75	4.00
373-Sgt. Preston (TV)	1.75	3.35	5.00
374-Woody Woodpecker	1.00	2.00	3.00
375-John Carter of Mars (E. R. Burroughs)-Jesse Marsh art; origin			
	5.00	10.00	15.00
376-Bugs Bunny	2.25	4.50	6.75
377-Suzie Q. Smith	1.00	2.00	3.00
378-Tom Corbett, Space Cadet(TV)-McWilliams art	2.50	5.00	7.50
379-Donald Duck in "Southern Hospitality"-not by Barks (Disney)	3.00	6.00	9.00
380-Raggedy Ann & Andy	2.50	5.00	7.50
381-Tubby (#1)	7.00	14.00	21.00
382-Snow White & 7 Dwarfs(Disney)-origin; partial reprint of 4-Color #49 (Movie)			
	3.00	6.00	9.00
383-Andy Panda	1.00	2.00	3.00
384-King of the Royal Mounted (3/52)			
	1.50	3.00	4.50
385-Porky Pig-"The Isle of Missing Ships" (3-4/52)	1.25	2.50	3.75
386-Uncle Scrooge #1 by Carl Barks (Disney) in "Only a Poor Old Man"			
	80.00	160.00	240.00
387-Mickey Mouse in "High Tibet" (Disney-4-5/52)	3.50	7.00	10.50
388-Oswald the Rabbit	1.75	3.50	5.25

Four Color #356, © WDP

Four Color #380, © J. Gruelle

Four Color #384, © NEA Service

Four Color #393, © L. Schlesinger

Four Color #399, © L. Schlesinger

Four Color #411, © WDP

(Four Color cont'd)	Good	Fine	Mint
389-Andy Hardy	.80	1.60	2.40
390-Woody Woodpecker	1.00	2.00	3.00
391-Uncle Wiggily	1.50	3.00	4.50
392-Hi-Yo Silver	2.00	4.00	6.00
393-Bugs Bunny	2.25	4.50	6.75
394-Donald Duck in "Malayalaya"-Barks cover only (Disney)	4.00	8.00	12.00
395-Forlorn River (Zane Grey-1952)-First Nevada (5/52)	1.35	2.75	4.00
396-Tales of the Texas Rangers (TV)	1.35	2.75	4.00
397-Sgt. Preston (TV)	1.75	3.35	5.00
398-The Brownies-not by Kelly	2.00	4.00	6.00
399-Porky Pig in "The Lost Gold Mine"	1.25	2.50	3.75
400-Tom Corbett-Space Cadet(TV)-McWilliams art	2.50	5.00	7.50
401-Mickey Mouse & Goofy's Mechanical Wizard (Disney, 6-7/52)	2.50	5.00	7.50
402-Mary Jane & Sniffles	1.20	2.40	3.60
403-Li'l Bad Wolf(Disney-6/52)	1.20	2.40	3.60
404-The Range Rider (TV)	2.00	4.00	6.00
405-Woody Woodpecker	1.00	2.00	3.00
406-Tweety & Sylvester	1.00	2.00	3.00
407-Bugs Bunny "Foreign-Legion Hare"	2.00	4.00	6.00
408-Donald Duck and "The Golden Helmet" by Carl Barks (Disney)	14.00	28.00	42.00
409-Andy Panda (7-9/52)	1.00	2.00	3.00
410-Porky Pig in "The Water Wizard"	1.25	2.50	3.75
411-Mickey Mouse & "The Old Sea Dog" (Disney) (8-9/52)	2.50	5.00	7.50
412-Nevada (Zane Grey)	1.35	2.75	4.00
413-Robin Hood (Disney-Movie, 8/52)	2.00	4.00	6.00
414-Beany & Cecil(TV)('52)	.80	1.60	2.40

	Good	Fine	Mint
415-Rootie Kazootie (TV)	.80	1.60	2.40
416-Woody Woodpecker	1.00	2.00	3.00
417-Double Trouble with Goober	.50	1.00	1.50
418-Rusty Riley-A Boy, A Horse, and A Dog-Frank Godwin art(strip reprints)(8/52)	1.35	2.75	4.00
419-Sgt. Preston (TV)	1.75	3.35	5.00
420-Bugs Bunny-"Mysterious Buckaroo"(8-9/52)	2.00	4.00	6.00
421-Tom Corbett-Space Cadet(TV)-McWilliams art	2.50	5.00	7.50
422-Donald Duck and "The Gilded Man" by Carl Barks (Disney)	14.00	28.00	42.00
423-Rhubarb, Owner of the Brooklyn Ball Club (The Millionaire Cat)	1.00	2.00	3.00
424-Flash Gordon-Test Flight in Space (9/52)	5.00	10.00	15.00
425-Zorro, the Return of	2.50	5.00	7.50
426-Porky Pig in "The Scalawag Leprechaun"	1.25	2.50	3.75
427-Mickey Mouse & "The Wonderful Whizzix" (1952)(Disney)-reprinted in M.M. #100	2.50	5.00	7.50
428-Uncle Wiggily	1.50	3.00	4.50
429-Pluto in "Why Dogs Leave Home" (Disney)	1.75	3.35	5.00
430-Tubby	4.00	8.00	12.00
431-Woody Woodpecker	1.00	2.00	3.00
432-Bugs Bunny & "The Rabbit Olympics"	2.00	4.00	6.00
433-Wildfire (Zane Grey)	1.35	2.75	4.00
434-Rin Tin Tin-"In Dark Danger" (11/52)	1.00	2.00	3.00
435-Frosty the Snowman	1.00	2.00	3.00
436-The Brownies-not by Kelly (11/52)	1.50	3.00	4.50
437-John Carter of Mars (E. R. Burroughs)-art by Marsh	4.00	8.00	12.00

Four Color #430, © West

Four Color #431, © Walter Lantz

Four Color #437, © ERB

Four Color #446, © WDP

Four Color #457, © Dell

Four Color #477, © B. Clampett

(Four Color cont'd)	Good	Fine	Mint
438-Annie Oakley (TV)	1.75	3.35	5.00
439-Little Hiawatha(Disney)(12/52)			
	1.50	3.00	4.50
440-Black Beauty (12/52)	1.25	2.50	3.75
441-Fearless Fagan	1.00	2.00	3.00
442-Peter Pan (Disney)(Movie)			
	2.50	5.00	7.50
443-Ben Bowie	1.35	2.75	4.00
444-Tubby	4.00	8.00	12.00
445-Charlie McCarthy	1.00	2.00	3.00
446-Captain Hook & Peter Pan (Disney)(Movie)			
(1/53)	2.50	5.00	7.50
447-Andy Hardy	.80	1.60	2.40
448-Beany & Cecil (TV)	.80	1.60	2.40
449-Tappan's Burro (Zane Grey, 2-4/53)			
	1.35	2.75	4.00
450-Duck Album (Disney)	1.35	2.75	4.00
451-Rusty Riley-Frank Godwin art(strip re-			
prints)(2/53)	1.35	2.75	4.00
452-Raggedy Ann & Andy('53)			
	2.50	5.00	7.50
453-Suzie Q. Smith(2/53)	1.00	2.00	3.00
454-Krazy Kat-not by Herriman (2/53)			
	1.50	3.00	4.50
455-Johnny Mack Brown (3/53)			
	1.50	3.00	4.50
456-Uncle Scrooge in "Back to the Klondike"			
(#2) by Barks	40.00	80.00	120.00
457-Daffy Duck	.80	1.60	2.40
458-Oswald the Rabbit	1.20	2.40	3.60
459-Rootie Kazootie (TV)	.80	1.60	2.40
460-Buck Jones (4/53)	1.50	3.00	4.50
461-Tubby	4.00	8.00	12.00
462-Little Scouts	.65	1.35	2.00
463-Petunia Pig (4/53)	1.00	2.00	3.00
464-Bozo (4/53)	.65	1.35	2.00
465-Francis the Mule	.65	1.35	2.00
466-Rhubarb, the Millionaire Cat			
	.80	1.60	2.40

	Good	Fine	Mint
467-Desert Gold (Zane Grey, 5-7/53)			
	1.35	2.75	4.00
468-Goofy (Disney)	1.00	2.00	3.00
469-Beetle Bailey (5/53)	.80	1.60	2.40
470-Elmer Fudd	.65	1.35	2.00
471-Goober, Double Trouble with			
	.50	1.00	1.50
472-Wild Bill Elliott (6/53)			
	1.50	3.00	4.50
473-Li'l Bad Wolf (Disney)1.20		2.40	3.60
474-Mary Jane & Sniffles	1.00	2.00	3.00
475-The Two Mouseketeers	.65	1.35	2.00
476-Rin Tin Tin	1.00	2.00	3.00
477-Beany & Cecil (TV)	.80	1.60	2.40
478-Charlie McCarthy	1.00	2.00	3.00
479-Dale Evans	1.75	3.35	5.00
480-Andy Hardy	.80	1.60	2.40
481-Annie Oakley (TV)	1.35	2.75	4.00
482-Brownies-not by Kelly	1.00	2.00	3.00
483-Little Beaver ('53)	1.50	3.00	4.50
484-River Feud (Zane Grey)(8-10/53)			
	1.35	2.75	4.00
485-The Little People-Walt Scott			
	1.35	2.75	4.00
486-Rusty Riley-Frank Godwin strip reprints			
	1.35	2.75	4.00
487-Mowgli, the Jungle Book (Rudyard Kip-			
ling's)	1.35	2.75	4.00
488-John Carter of Mars (Burroughs)-Marsh			
art	4.00	8.00	12.00
489-Tweety & Sylvester	1.00	2.00	3.00
490-Jungle Jim	1.75	3.50	5.25
491-Silvertip (Max Brand)-Kinstler art(8/53)			
	1.75	3.35	5.00
492-Duck Album (Disney)	1.20	2.40	3.60
493-Johnny Mack Brown	1.50	3.00	4.50
494-The Little King	1.50	3.00	4.50
495-Uncle Scrooge(#3)(Disney)-by Carl Barks			
	20.00	40.00	60.00

Four Color #483, © Dell

Four Color #484, © Dell

Four Color #492, © Dell

Four Color #536, © Dell

Four Color #539, © WDP

Four Color #567, © Dell

(Four Color cont'd)	Good	Fine	Mint
496-The Green Hornet(TV)	2.50	5.00	7.50
497-Zorro(Sword of--)	2.50	5.00	7.50
498-Bugs Bunny's Album	1.00	2.00	3.00
499-Spike & Tyke (9/53)	.50	1.00	1.50
500-Buck Jones	1.50	3.00	4.50
501-Francis the Mule	.65	1.35	2.00
502-Rootie Kazootie (TV)	.80	1.60	2.40
503-Uncle Wiggily (10/53)	1.25	2.50	3.75
504-Krazy Kat-not by Herriman			
	1.50	3.00	4.50
505-The Sword & the Rose(Disney)(10/53)(TV)			
	1.75	3.35	5.00
506-The Little Scouts	.65	1.35	2.00
507-Oswald the Rabbit	1.20	2.40	3.60
508-Bozo (10/53)	.65	1.35	2.00
509-Pluto (Disney-10/53)	1.75	3.35	5.00
510-Son of Black Beauty	1.00	2.00	3.00
511-Outlaw Trail (Zane Grey)-Kinstler stories			
	1.50	3.00	4.50
512-Flash Gordon (11/53)	3.00	6.00	9.00
513-Ben Bowie's Mountain Men (11/53)			
	1.00	2.00	3.00
514-Frosty the Snowman	.60	1.20	1.80
515-Andy Hardy	.80	1.60	2.40
516-Goober, Double Trouble with			
	.50	1.00	1.50
517-Chip 'N' Dale (Disney)	1.00	2.00	3.00
518-Rivets (11/53)	.65	1.35	2.00
519-Steve Canyon-not by Milton Caniff			
	2.00	4.00	6.00
520-Wild Bill Elliott	1.50	3.00	4.50
521-Beetle Bailey (12/53)	.80	1.60	2.40
522-The Brownies	1.00	2.00	3.00
523-Rin Tin Tin	1.00	2.00	3.00
524-Tweety & Sylvester	1.00	2.00	3.00
525-Santa Claus Funnies	1.00	2.00	3.00
526-Napoleon	.75	1.50	2.25
527-Charlie McCarthy	1.00	2.00	3.00
528-Dale Evans	1.50	3.00	4.50
529-Little Beaver	1.50	3.00	4.50
530-Beany & Cecil (1/54)	.80	1.60	2.40
531-Duck Album (Disney)	1.20	2.40	3.60
532-The Rustlers (Zane Grey, 2-4/54)			
	1.25	2.50	3.75
533-Raggedy Ann & Andy	2.50	5.00	7.50
534-Western Marshal(Ernest Haycox's)-			
Kinstler art	1.50	3.00	4.50
535-I Love Lucy(TV)('54)	.50	1.00	1.50
536-Daffy (3/54)	.80	1.60	2.40
537-Stormy, the Thoroughbred--(Disney-Movie)			
on top 2/3 of each page; Pluto story on			
bottom 1/3 of each page (2/54)			
	1.50	3.00	4.50
538-Zorro(Mask of--)-Kinstler art			
	2.50	5.00	7.50
539-Ben & Me (Disney)	1.00	2.00	3.00

	Good	Fine	Mint
540-Knights of the Round Table (3/54)(Movie)			
	1.50	3.00	4.50
541-Johnny Mack Brown	1.35	2.75	4.00
542-Super Circus Featuring Mary Hartline (TV)			
(3/54)	1.00	2.00	3.00
543-Uncle Wiggily (3/54)	1.25	2.50	3.75
544-Rob Roy (Disney-Movie)-Russ Manning art			
	1.75	3.35	5.00
545-Pinocchio-Partial reprint of 4-Color #92			
(Disney-Movie)	2.00	4.00	6.00
546-Buck Jones	1.50	3.00	4.50
547-Francis the Mule	.65	1.35	2.00
548-Krazy Kat-not by Herriman (4/54)			
	1.20	2.40	3.60
549-Oswald the Rabbit	1.20	2.40	3.60
550-The Little Scouts	.65	1.35	2.00
551-Bozo (4/54)	.65	1.35	2.00
552-Beetle Bailey	.80	1.60	2.40
553-Suzie Q. Smith	.80	1.60	2.40
554-Rusty Riley (Frank Godwin strip reprints)			
	1.20	2.40	3.60
555-Range War (Zane Grey)	1.25	2.50	3.75
556-Goober, Double Trouble with (5/54)			
	.50	1.00	1.50
557-Ben Bowie & His Mountain Men			
	1.00	2.00	3.00
558-Elmer Fudd (5/54)	.65	1.35	2.00
559-I Love Lucy (TV)	.50	1.00	1.50
560-Duck Album (Disney)	1.20	2.40	3.60
561-Mr. Magoo (5/54)	1.00	2.00	3.00
562-Goofy (Disney)	1.00	2.00	3.00
563-Rhubarb, the Millionaire Cat (6/54)			
	.65	1.35	2.00
564-Li'l Bad Wolf(Disney)	1.20	2.40	3.60
565-Jungle Jim	1.75	3.50	5.25
566-Son of Black Beauty	1.00	2.00	3.00
567-Prince Valiant-by Bob Fuje (Movie)			
	3.50	7.00	10.50
568-Gypsy Colt (Movie)	1.20	2.40	3.60
569-Priscilla's Pop	.80	1.60	2.40
570-Beany & Cecil (TV)	.80	1.60	2.40
571-Charlie McCarthy	1.00	2.00	3.00
572-Silvertip (Max Brand)	1.20	2.40	3.60
573-The Little People by Walt Scott			
	.80	1.60	2.40
574-Zorro (Hand of --)	2.00	4.00	6.00
575-Annie Oakley (TV)	1.35	2.75	4.00
576-Angel (8/54)	.50	1.00	1.50
577-Spike & Tyke	.50	1.00	1.50
578-Steve Canyon (8/54)	1.75	3.50	5.25
579-Francis the Talking Mule			
	.65	1.35	2.00
580-Six Gun Ranch (Luke Short-8/54)			
	1.20	2.40	3.60
581-Chip 'N' Dale (Disney)	1.00	2.00	3.00
582-Mowgli-Jungle Book	1.00	2.00	3.00
583-The Lost Wagon Train (Zane Grey)			
	1.25	2.50	3.75

(Four Color cont'd)

	Good	Fine	Mint
584-Johnny Mack Brown	1.35	2.75	4.00
585-Bugs Bunny's Album	1.00	2.00	3.00
586-Duck Album (Disney)	1.20	2.40	3.60
587-The Little Scouts	.65	1.35	2.00
588-King Richard & the Crusaders(Movie)(10/54)			
Matt Baker art	1.50	3.00	4.50
589-Buck Jones	1.50	3.00	4.50
590-Hansel & Gretel	1.00	2.00	3.00
591-Western Marshal (Ernest Haycox's)-			
Kinstler art	1.50	3.00	4.50
592-Super Circus (TV)	1.00	2.00	3.00
593-Oswald the Rabbit	1.20	2.40	3.60
594-Bozo (10/54)	.65	1.35	2.00
595-Pluto (Disney)	1.00	2.00	3.00
596-Turok, Son of Stone(#1)			
	8.00	16.00	24.00
597-The Little King	.80	1.60	2.40
598-Captain Davy Jones	.80	1.60	2.40
599-Ben Bowie & His Mountain Men (11/54)			
	1.00	2.00	3.00
600-Daisy Duck's Diary (Disney)(11/54)			
	1.20	2.40	3.60
601-Frosty the Snowman	.60	1.20	1.80
602-Mr. Magoo & Gerald McBoing-Boing			
	1.00	2.00	3.00
603-The Two Mouseketeers	.65	1.35	2.00
604-Shadow on the Trail (Zane Grey)			
	1.25	2.50	3.75
605-The Brownies-not by Kelly (12/54)			
	1.00	2.00	3.00
606-Sir Lancelot (not TV)	1.35	2.75	4.00
607-Santa Claus Funnies	1.00	2.00	3.00
608-Silvertip-Valley of Vanishing Men (Max			
Brand)-Kinstler art	1.75	3.35	5.00
609-The Littlest Outlaw (Disney-Movie)(1/55)			
	1.50	3.00	4.50
610-Drum Beat (Movie)	1.35	2.75	4.00
611-Duck Album (Disney)	1.00	2.00	3.00
612-Little Beaver (1/55)	1.20	2.40	3.60
613-Western Marshal (Ernest Haycox's)(2/55)			
Kinstler art	1.50	3.00	4.50
614-20,000 Leagues Under the Sea (Disney)			
(Movie)(2/55)	1.50	3.00	4.50
615-Daffy	.80	1.60	2.40
616-To the Last Man (Zane Grey)			
	1.25	2.50	3.75
617-Zorro (Quest of--)	2.00	4.00	6.00
618-Johnny Mack Brown	1.35	2.75	4.00
619-Krazy Kat-not by Herriman			
	1.20	2.40	3.60
620-Mowgli-Jungle Book	1.00	2.00	3.00
621-Francis the Talking Mule (4/55)			
	.50	1.00	1.50
622-Beetle Bailey	.80	1.60	2.40
623-Oswald the Rabbit	.65	1.35	2.00
624-Treasure Island (Disney-Movie)(4/55)			

	Good	Fine	Mint
	1.50	3.00	4.50
625-Beaver Valley (Disney-Movie)			
	1.00	2.00	3.00
626-Ben Bowie & His Mountain Men			
	1.00	2.00	3.00
627-Goofy (Disney)(5/55)	1.00	2.00	3.00
628-Elmer Fudd	.65	1.35	2.00
629-Lady & the Tramp with Jock (Disney-5/55)			
	1.75	3.35	5.00
630-Priscilla's Pop	.65	1.35	2.00
631-Davy Crockett (Disney-5/55)(--Indian			
Fighter)(TV)	1.35	2.75	4.00
632-Fighting Caravans (Zane Grey)			
	1.25	2.50	3.75
633-The Little People by Walt Scott			
	.80	1.60	2.40
634-Lady & the Tramp Album (Disney-6/55)			
	1.50	3.00	4.50
635-Beany & Cecil (TV)	.80	1.60	2.40
636-Chip 'N' Dale (Disney)	1.00	2.00	3.00
637-Silvertip (Max Brand)-Kinstler art			
	1.75	3.35	5.00
638-Spike and Tyke (8/55)	.50	1.00	1.50
639-Davy Crockett (Disney-7/55)(--At the			
Alamo)(TV)	1.35	2.75	4.00
640-Western Marshal (Ernest Haycox's)			
Kinstler art	1.50	3.00	4.50
641-Steve Canyon ('55)-not by Caniff			
	1.75	3.50	5.25
642-The Two Mouseketeers	.65	1.35	2.00
643-Wild Bill Elliott	1.50	3.00	4.50
644-Sir Walter Raleigh(5/55)-Based on movie			
"The Virgin Queen"	1.50	3.00	4.50
645-Johnny Mack Brown	1.35	2.75	4.00
646-Dotty Dripple & Taffy	.50	1.00	1.50
647-Bugs Bunny Album(9/55)	.65	1.35	2.00
648-Texas Rangers(Jace Pearson's)			
	1.20	2.40	3.60
649-Duck Album (Disney)	1.00	2.00	3.00
650-Prince Valiant - by Bob Fuje			
	2.50	5.00	7.50
651-King Colt(Luke Short)(9/55)-Kinstler art			
	1.20	2.40	3.60
652-Buck Jones	1.00	2.00	3.00
653-Smokey the Bear (10/55)	.80	1.60	2.40
654-Pluto (Disney)	1.00	2.00	3.00
655-Francis the Talking Mule (10/55)			
	.50	1.00	1.50
656-Turok, Son of Stone(#2)(10/55)			
	5.00	10.00	15.00
657-Ben Bowie & His Mountain Men			
	1.00	2.00	3.00
658-Goofy (Disney)	1.00	2.00	3.00
659-Daisy Duck's Diary	1.20	2.40	3.60
660-Little Beaver	1.20	2.40	3.60
661-Frosty the Snowman	.60	1.20	1.80
662-Zoo Parade(TV)-Marlin Perkins (11/55)			

Four Color #627, © WDP

Four Color #642, © Dell

Four Color #643, © Dell

Four Color #668, © WDP

Four Color #706, © WDP

Four Color #719, © Dell

	Good	Fine	Mint
(Four Color cont'd)	.65	1.35	2.00
663-Winky Dink (TV)	.65	1.35	2.00
664-Davy Crockett in the Great Keelboat Race (TV)(Disney)	1.50	3.00	4.50
665-The African Lion (Disney-Movie)(11/55)	1.20	2.40	3.60
666-Santa Claus Funnies	1.00	2.00	3.00
667-Silvertip & the Stolen Stallion (Max Brand-12/55)	1.20	2.40	3.60
668-Dumbo (Disney)(12/55)	1.25	2.50	3.75
668-Dumbo (Disney)(1/58) different cover, same contents	1.25	2.50	3.75
669-Robin Hood (Disney-12/55)(Movie)-reprint of #413	1.00	2.00	3.00
670-Mouse Musketeers(1/56)-Formerly the Two Mouseketeers	.50	1.00	1.50
671-Davy Crockett & the River Pirates (TV) (Disney-12/55)-Jesse Marsh art	1.50	3.00	4.50
672-Quentin Durward(1/56)(Movie)	1.75	3.35	5.00
673-Buffalo Bill, Jr.(TV)	.80	1.60	2.40
674-The Little Rascals	.65	1.35	2.00
675-Steve Donovan, Western Marshal (TV)-Kinstler art	1.50	3.00	4.50
676-Will-Yum!	.65	1.35	2.00
677-Little King	.80	1.60	2.40
678-The Last Hunt (Movie)	1.20	2.40	3.60
679-Gunsmoke (TV)	1.00	2.00	3.00
680-Out Our Way with the Worry Wart(2/56)	.65	1.35	2.00
681-Forever, Darling(Movie)with Lucille Ball & Desi Arnaz (2/56)	1.20	2.40	3.60
682-When Knighthood Was in Flower(Disney-Movie)-reprint of #505	1.35	2.75	4.00
683-Hi & Lois (3/56)	.65	1.35	2.00
684-Helen of Troy (Movie)-Buscema art	1.75	3.50	5.25
685-Johnny Mack Brown	1.35	2.75	4.00
686-Duck Album (Disney)	1.00	2.00	3.00
687-The Indian Fighter (Movie)	1.35	2.75	4.00
688-Alexander the Great (Movie)(5/56)	1.50	3.00	4.50
689-Elmer Fudd (3/56)	.65	1.35	2.00
690-The Conqueror (Movie)	1.00	2.00	3.00
691-Dotty Dripple & Taffy	.50	1.00	1.50
692-The Little People-Walt Scott	.80	1.60	2.40
693-Song of the South (Disney)(1956)-Partial reprint of #129	1.35	2.75	4.00
694-Super Circus (TV)	1.00	2.00	3.00
695-Little Beaver	1.20	2.40	3.60
696-Krazy Kat-not by Herriman (4/56)	1.20	2.40	3.60
697-Oswald the Rabbit	.65	1.35	2.00
698-Francis the Talking Mule			

	Good	Fine	Mint
	.50	1.00	1.50
699-Prince Valiant-by Bob Fuje	2.50	5.00	7.50
700-Water Birds & the Olympic Elk (Disney-Movie)	1.20	2.40	3.60
701-Jiminy Crickett (Disney - 5/56)	1.00	2.00	3.00
702-The Goofy Success Story (Disney)	1.00	2.00	3.00
703-Scamp (Disney)	.65	1.35	2.00
704-Priscilla's Pop(5/56)	.65	1.35	2.00
705-Brave Eagle	1.00	2.00	3.00
706-Bongo & Lumpjaw(Disney)	1.00	2.00	3.00
707-Corky & White Shadow (Disney-5/56)-Mickey Mouse Club (TV)	1.00	2.00	3.00
708-Smokey the Bear	.80	1.60	2.40
709-The Searchers (Movie)	1.20	2.40	3.60
710-Francis the Mule	.50	1.00	1.50
711-MGM's Mouse Musketeers	.50	1.00	1.50
712-The Great Locomotive Chase(Disney-Movie) (9/56)	1.50	3.00	4.50
713-The Animal World (Movie-8/56)	1.20	2.40	3.60
714-Spin & Marty(TV)(Disney)-Mickey Mouse Club (6/56)	1.00	2.00	3.00
715-Timmy (8/56)	.50	1.00	1.50
716-Man in Space (Disney-Movie)	1.25	2.50	3.75
717-Moby Dick (Movie)	1.50	3.00	4.50
718-Dotty Dripple & Taffy	.50	1.00	1.50
719-Prince Valiant - by Bob Fuje	2.00	4.00	6.00
720-Gunsmoke (TV)	.65	1.35	2.00
721-Capt. Kangaroo (TV)	.65	1.35	2.00
722-Johnny Mack Brown	1.35	2.75	4.00
723-Santiago (Movie)-Kinstler art	1.75	3.50	5.25
724-Bugs Bunny's Album	.65	1.35	2.00
725-Elmer Fudd (9/56)	.50	1.00	1.50
726-Duck Album	.65	1.35	2.00
727-The Nature of Things(TV)(Disney)-Jesse Marsh art	1.50	3.00	4.50
728-Mouse Musketeers	.50	1.00	1.50
729-Bob, Son of Battle	.80	1.60	2.40
730-Smokey Stover	1.20	2.40	3.60
731-Silvertip-the Fighting Four (Max Brand) Kinstler art	1.75	3.35	5.00
732-Zorro, the Challenge of (10/56)	2.00	4.00	6.00
733-Buck Jones	1.00	2.00	3.00
734-Cheyenne (TV)(10/56)	.65	1.35	2.00
735-Crusader Rabbit	.65	1.35	2.00
736-Pluto (Disney)	.80	1.60	2.40
737-Steve Canyon	1.75	3.50	5.25
738-Westward Ho, the Wagons (Disney-Movie)	1.35	2.75	4.00

(Four Color cont'd)   Good Fine Mint

	Good	Fine	Mint
739-Bounty Guns(Luke Short)-Drucker art	1.20	2.40	3.60
740-Chilly Willy(Walter Lantz)	.50	1.00	1.50
741-The Fastest Gun Alive (Movie)(9/56)	1.75	3.35	5.00
742-Buffalo Bill, Jr.(TV)	.80	1.60	2.40
743-Daisy Duck's Diary (Disney-11/56)	1.20	2.40	3.60
744-Little Beaver	1.20	2.40	3.60
745-Francis the Famous Talking Mule	.50	1.00	1.50
746-Dotty Dripple & Taffy	.50	1.00	1.50
747-Goofy (Disney)	.80	1.60	2.40
748-Frosty the Snowman (11/56)	.50	1.00	1.50
749-Secrets of Life (Disney-Movie)	1.35	2.75	4.00
750-The Great Cat Family (Disney-Movie)	1.50	3.00	4.50
751-Our Miss Brooks (TV)	.80	1.60	2.40
752-Mandrake the Magician	1.75	3.35	5.00
753-Walt Scott's Little People (11/56)	.80	1.60	2.40
754-Smokey the Bear	.80	1.60	2.40
755-The Littlest Snowman (12/56)	.65	1.35	2.00
756-Santa Claus Funnies	1.00	2.00	3.00
757-The True Story of Jesse James (Movie)	1.75	3.35	5.00
758-Bear Country (Disney-Movie)	1.35	2.75	4.00
759-Circus Boy (TV)	1.00	2.00	3.00
760-The Hardy Boys(TV)(Disney)-Mickey Mouse Club	1.00	2.00	3.00
761-Howdy Doody(TV)(1/57)	.80	1.60	2.40
762-The Sharkfighters (Movie)(1/57)(Scarce)	2.00	4.00	6.00
763-Grandma Duck's Farm Friends (Disney)	1.35	2.75	4.00
764-MGM's Mouse Musketeers	.50	1.00	1.50
765-Will-Yum!	.50	1.00	1.50
766-Buffalo Bill, Jr. (TV)	.80	1.60	2.40
767-Spin & Marty (TV)(Disney)-Mickey Mouse Club (2/57)	1.00	2.00	3.00
768-Steve Donovan, Western Marshal (TV) Kinstler stories	1.50	3.00	4.50
769-Gunsmoke (TV)	.65	1.35	2.00
770-Brave Eagle	1.00	2.00	3.00
771-Brand of Empire(Luke Short-3/57)-Drucker art	1.20	2.40	3.60
772-Cheyenne (TV)	.65	1.35	2.00
773-The Brave One(Movie)	1.25	2.50	3.75
774-Hi & Lois (3/57)	.65	1.35	2.00
775-Sir Lancelot(TV)-Buscema art	2.00	4.00	6.00
776-Johnny Mack Brown	1.35	2.75	4.00

	Good	Fine	Mint
777-Scamp (Disney)	.65	1.35	2.00
778-The Little Rascals	.65	1.35	2.00
779-Lee Hunter, Indian Fighter (3/57)	.80	1.60	2.40
780-Capt. Kangaroo (TV)	.65	1.35	2.00
781-Fury (TV)(3/57)	.80	1.60	2.40
782-Duck Album (Disney)	.65	1.35	2.00
783-Elmer Fudd	.50	1.00	1.50
784-Around the World in 80 Days (Movie-2/57)	1.75	3.35	5.00
785-Circus Boy (TV)(4/57)	1.00	2.00	3.00
786-Cinderella (Disney)(3/57)-Partial reprint of #272	1.35	2.75	4.00
787-Little Hiawatha (Disney-4/57)	1.35	2.75	4.00
788-Prince Valiant - by Bob Fuje	2.00	4.00	6.00
789-Silvertip-Valley Thieves(Max Brand)(4/57)	1.20	2.40	3.60
790-The Wings of Eagles (Movie)-Toth art	2.00	4.00	6.00
791-The 77th Bengal Lancers (TV)	1.00	2.00	3.00
792-Oswald the Rabbit	.65	1.35	2.00
793-Morty Meekle	.65	1.35	2.00
794-The Count of Monte Cristo (5/57)(Movie) Buscema art	2.00	4.00	6.00
795-Jiminy Cricket(Disney)	1.00	2.00	3.00
796-Ludwig Bemelman's Madeleine & Genevieve	1.20	2.40	3.60
797-Gunsmoke (TV)	.65	1.35	2.00
798-Buffalo Bill, Jr. (TV)	.80	1.60	2.40
799-Priscilla's Pop	.80	1.60	2.40
800-The Buccaneers	1.35	2.75	4.00
801-Dotty Dripple & Taffy	.50	1.00	1.50
802-Goofy (Disney, 5/57)	.80	1.60	2.40
803-Cheyenne (TV)	.65	1.35	2.00
804-Steve Canyon (1957)	1.75	3.50	5.25
805-Crusader Rabbit	.65	1.35	2.00
806-Scamp (Disney)(6/57)	.65	1.35	2.00
807-Savage Range (Luke Short)-Drucker art	1.20	2.40	3.60
808-Spin & Marty (TV)(Disney)-Mickey Mouse Club	1.00	2.00	3.00
809-The Little People-Walt Scott	.80	1.60	2.40
810-Francis the Mule	.50	1.00	1.50
811-Howdy Doody(TV)(7/57)	.80	1.60	2.40
812-The Big Land (Movie)	1.35	2.75	4.00
813-Circus Boy (TV)	1.00	2.00	3.00
814-Covered Wagons, Ho! (Disney)-Donald Duck (6/57)	1.35	2.75	4.00
815-Dragoon Wells Massacre (Movie)	1.35	2.75	4.00
816-Brave Eagle	.80	1.60	2.40
817-Little Beaver	1.20	2.40	3.60
818-Smokey the Bear (6/57)	.80	1.60	2.40

Four Color #741, © Dell

Four Color #804, © Dell

Four Color #822, © WDP

Four Color #826, © WDP   Four Color #829, © Dell   Four Color #869, © WDP

(Four Color cont'd)	Good	Fine	Mint
819-Mickey Mouse in Magicland (Disney)(7/57)			
	1.00	2.00	3.00
820-The Oklahoman (Movie)	1.35	2.75	4.00
821-Wringle Wrangle (Disney)-Based on movie "Westward Ho, the Wagons"-Marsh art			
	1.75	3.35	5.00
822-Paul Revere's Ride with Johnny Tremain (TV)(Disney)-Toth art	1.75	3.35	5.00
823-Timmy	.50	1.00	1.50
824-The Pride & the Passion (Movie)(8/57)			
	1.35	2.75	4.00
825-The Little Rascals	.60	1.20	1.80
826-Spin & Marty & Annette(TV)(Disney)-Mickey Mouse Club	1.00	2.00	3.00
827-Smokey Stover (8/57)	1.20	2.40	3.60
828-Buffalo Bill, Jr. (TV)	.80	1.60	2.40
829-Tales of the Pony Express (TV)(8/57)			
	1.00	2.00	3.00
830-The Hardy Boys (TV)(Disney)-Mickey Mouse Club (8/57)	1.00	2.00	3.00
831-No Sleep 'Til Dawn (Movie)(9/57)			
	1.25	2.50	3.75
832-Lolly & Pepper	.40	.80	1.20
833-Scamp (Disney)(9/57)	.65	1.35	2.00
834-Johnny Mack Brown	1.35	2.75	4.00
835-Silvertip-The Fake Rider (Max Brand)			
	1.20	2.40	3.60
836-Man in Flight (Disney)(9/57)			
	1.00	2.00	3.00
837-All-American Athlete Cotton Woods			
	.50	1.00	1.50
838-Bugs Bunny's Life Story Album (9/57)			
	.65	1.35	2.00
839-The Vigilantes (Movie)	1.35	2.75	4.00
840-Duck Album (Disney)	.65	1.35	2.00
841-Elmer Fudd	.50	1.00	1.50
842-The Nature of Things (Disney-Movie)('57) Jesse Marsh art (TV Series)			
	1.50	3.00	4.50
843-The First Americans (Disney)-Jesse Marsh art	1.35	2.75	4.00
844-Gunsmoke (TV)	.65	1.35	2.00
845-The Land Unknown (Movie)-Alex Toth art			
	2.50	5.00	7.50
846-Gun Glory (Movie) by Alex Toth			
	1.75	3.50	5.25
847-Perri(Squirrels)(Disney-Movie)-Two different cvrs. published	1.25	2.50	3.75
848-Marauder's Moon(Movie)	1.20	2.40	3.60
849-Prince Valiant-by Bob Fuje			
	2.00	4.00	6.00
850-Buck Jones	1.00	2.00	3.00
851-The Story of Mankind (Movie)(1/58)			
	1.25	2.50	3.75
852-Chilly Willy (2/58)	.50	1.00	1.50
853-Pluto (Disney)(10/57)	.80	1.60	2.40

	Good	Fine	Mint
854-The Hunchback of Notre Dame (Movie)			
	2.50	5.00	7.50
855-Broken Arrow (TV)	.80	1.60	2.40
856-Buffalo Bill, Jr.(TV)	.80	1.60	2.40
857-The Goofy Adventure Story (Disney-11/57)			
	.80	1.60	2.40
858-Daisy Duck's Diary (Disney)(11/57)			
	1.00	2.00	3.00
859-Topper & Neil (11/57)	.65	1.35	2.00
860-Hugh O'Brian Famous Marshal Wyatt Earp (TV)-Manning art	1.20	2.40	3.60
861-Frosty the Snowman	.50	1.00	1.50
862-The Truth About Mother Goose (Movie-Disney)(11/57)	1.50	3.00	4.50
863-Francis the Mule	.50	1.00	1.50
864-The Littlest Snowman	.65	1.35	2.00
865-Andy Burnett(TV)(Disney)(12/57)			
	1.35	2.75	4.00
866-Mars & Beyond (Disney-Movie)			
	1.35	2.75	4.00
867-Santa Claus Funnies	1.00	2.00	3.00
868-Walt Scott's Little People (12/57)			
	.80	1.60	2.40
869-Old Yeller (Disney-Movie)(1/58)			
	1.35	2.75	4.00
870-Little Beaver (1/58)	1.20	2.40	3.60
871-Curly Kayoe	1.00	2.00	3.00
872-Capt. Kangaroo (TV)	.65	1.35	2.00
873-Grandma Duck's Farm Friends (Disney)			
	1.00	2.00	3.00
874-Old Ironsides (Disney-Movie with J. Tremain)(1/58)	1.35	2.75	4.00
875-Trumpets West(Luke Short-2/58)			
	1.20	2.40	3.60
876-Tales of Wells Fargo (TV)(2/58)			
	1.25	2.50	3.75
877-Frontier Doctor with Rex Allen(TV)-Alex Toth art	1.75	3.35	5.00
878-Peanuts-Schulz cover only (2/58)			
	1.50	3.00	4.50
879-Brave Eagle (2/58)	.80	1.60	2.40
880-Steve Donovan, Western Marshal-Drucker art	1.00	2.00	3.00
881-The Capt. & the Kids	1.00	2.00	3.00
882-Zorro(Disney)-1st Disney issue by Alex Toth(TV) (2/58)	2.00	4.00	6.00
883-The Little Rascals	.60	1.20	1.80
884-Hawkeye & the Last of the Mohicans (TV)			
	1.20	2.40	3.60
885-Fury (TV)(3/58)	.80	1.60	2.40
886-Bongo & Lumpjaw(Disney)			
	1.00	2.00	3.00
887-The Hardy Boys(Disney)(TV)-Mickey Mouse Club (1/58)	1.00	2.00	3.00
888-Elmer Fudd (3/58)	.50	1.00	1.50
889-Clint & Mac (Disney)-Alex Toth art (TV) (3/58)	2.00	4.00	6.00

	Good	Fine	Mint
890-Hugh O'Brian Famous Marshal Wyatt Earp (TV)-by Russ Manning	1.20	2.40	3.60
891-Light in the Forest(Disney-Movie)(3/58)	1.35	2.75	4.00
892-Maverick (TV)(4/58)	1.00	2.00	3.00
893-Jim Bowie (TV)	1.00	2.00	3.00
894-Oswald the Rabbit	.65	1.35	2.00
895-Wagon Train (TV)(3/58)	.80	1.60	2.40
896-Tinker Bell (Disney)	2.00	4.00	6.00
897-Jiminy Cricket(Disney)	1.00	2.00	3.00
898-Silvertip's Trap(Max Brand)-Kinstler art (5/58)	1.75	3.35	5.00
899-Goofy (Disney)	.80	1.60	2.40
900-Prince Valiant - by Bob Fuje	2.00	4.00	6.00
901-Little Hiawatha (Disney)	1.25	2.50	3.75
902-Will-Yum!	.50	1.00	1.50
903-Dotty Dripple & Taffy	.50	1.00	1.50
904-Lee Hunter, Indian Fighter	.80	1.60	2.40
905-Annette(TV)(Disney)-Mickey Mouse Club	1.50	3.00	4.50
906-Francis the Mule	.50	1.00	1.50
907-Sugarfoot(TV)Toth art	1.75	3.35	5.00
908-The Little People-Walt Scott (5/58)	.80	1.60	2.40
909-Smitty & Herby	1.00	2.00	3.00
910-The Vikings (Movie)-Buscema art	1.50	3.00	4.50
911-The Gray Ghost of the Confederacy (TV) (Movie)	1.25	2.50	3.75
912-Leave It to Beaver(TV)	.50	1.00	1.50
913-The Left-Handed Gun (Movie)(7/58)	1.35	2.75	4.00
914-No Time For Sergeants (Movie)	1.00	2.00	3.00
915-Casey Jones (TV)	.35	.70	1.05
916-Red Ryder	1.20	2.40	3.60
917-The Life of Riley(TV)	.65	1.35	2.00
918-Beep Beep, the Roadrunner(7/58)-Two different back cvrs. publ.	.80	1.60	2.40
919-Boots & Saddles (TV)	.50	1.00	1.50
920-Zorro(Disney)(TV)-Alex Toth art (6/58)	2.00	4.00	6.00
921-Hugh O'Brian Famous Marshal Wyatt Earp (TV)-Manning art	1.20	2.40	3.60
922-Johnny Mack Brown by Russ Manning	1.35	2.75	4.00
923-Timmy	.50	1.00	1.50
924-Colt 45 (TV)(8/58)	.65	1.35	2.00
925-Last of the Fast Guns (Movie)(8/58)	1.20	2.40	3.60
926-Peter Pan (Disney)-reprint of #442	1.35	2.75	4.00
927-Top Gun (Luke Short)	1.20	2.40	3.60
928-Sea Hunt (TV)	.80	1.60	2.40
929-Brave Eagle	.80	1.60	2.40
930-Maverick (TV)(7/58)	1.00	2.00	3.00
931-Have Gun, Will Travel (TV)	.60	1.20	1.80
932-Smokey the Bear-origin	.80	1.60	2.40
933-Zorro(Disney)-by Alex Toth (9/58)	2.00	4.00	6.00
934-The Restless Gun (TV)	.80	1.60	2.40
935-King of the Royal Mtd.	1.35	2.75	4.00
936-The Little Rascals	.60	1.20	1.80
937-Ruff and Reddy(TV)(Hanna-Barbera)(9/58)	.40	.80	1.20
938-Elmer Fudd (9/58)	.50	1.00	1.50
939-Steve Canyon - not by Caniff	1.75	3.50	5.25
940-Lolly & Pepper	.40	.80	1.20
941-Pluto (Disney)(10/58)	.80	1.60	2.40
942-Pony Express (TV)	1.00	2.00	3.00
943-White Wilderness (Disney-Movie)(10/58)	1.35	2.75	4.00
944-The 7th Voyage of Sindbad(Movie)(9/58) Buscema art	3.50	7.00	10.50
945-Maverick (TV)	1.00	2.00	3.00
946-The Big Country(Movie)	1.20	2.40	3.60
947-Broken Arrow (TV)	.80	1.60	2.40
948-Daisy Duck's Diary (Disney)(11/58)	1.00	2.00	3.00
949-Lowell Thomas' High Adventures (TV)	.65	1.35	2.00
950-Frosty the Snowman	.50	1.00	1.50
951-The Lennon Sisters Life Story - 36pgs. Toth art	1.75	3.50	5.25
952-Goofy (Disney)(11/58)	.80	1.60	2.40
953-Francis the Mule	.50	1.00	1.50
954-Man in Space (Disney-Movie)	1.00	2.00	3.00
955-Hi & Lois (11/58)	.65	1.35	2.00
956-Ricky Nelson (TV)	1.00	2.00	3.00
957-Buffalo Bee (TV)	.40	.80	1.20
958-Santa Claus Funnies	.65	1.35	2.00
959-Walt Scott's Christmas Stories-(Little People)(1951-56 strip reprints)	.80	1.60	2.40
960-Zorro(Disney)(TV)(12/58)-Toth art	2.00	4.00	6.00
961-Jace Pearson's Tales of the Texas Rangers (TV)-Toth art	1.75	3.50	5.25
962-Maverick (TV)(1/59)	1.00	2.00	3.00
963-Johnny Mack Brown	1.35	2.75	4.00
964-The Hardy Boys(TV)(Disney)-Mickey Mouse Club (1/59)	1.00	2.00	3.00
965-Grandma Duck's Farm Friends (Disney) (1/59)	1.00	2.00	3.00
966-Tonka-Starring Sal Mineo(Disney-Movie)	1.35	2.75	4.00
967-Chilly Willy (2/59)	.50	1.00	1.50
967-Johnny Mack Brown	1.35	2.75	4.00

Four Color #893, © Dell

Four Color #939, © Dell

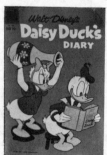

Four Color #948, © WDP

Four Color #971, © Dell   Four Color #982, © WDP   Four Color #1037, © WDP

	Good	Fine	Mint
(Four Color cont'd)			
968-Tales of Wells Fargo (TV)	1.00	2.00	3.00
969-Peanuts (2/59)	1.50	3.00	4.50
970-Lawman (TV)	.65	1.35	2.00
971-Wagon Train (TV)	.80	1.60	2.40
972-Tom Thumb (Movie)-George Pal	1.50	3.00	4.50
973-Sleeping Beauty & the Prince (Disney) (5/59)	1.50	3.00	4.50
974-Spanky & Alfalfa, the Little Rascals (3/59)	.50	1.00	1.50
975-Fury (TV)	.80	1.60	2.40
976-Zorro (Disney)(TV)-Toth art	2.00	4.00	6.00
977-Elmer Fudd	.50	1.00	1.50
978-Lolly & Pepper	.40	.80	1.20
979-Oswald the Rabbit	.65	1.35	2.00
980-Maverick (TV)(4-6/59)	1.00	2.00	3.00
981-Ruff & Reddy (TV)(Hanna-Barbera)	.40	.80	1.20
982-Tinker Bell(TV-Disney)	2.00	4.00	6.00
983-Have Gun, Will Travel (TV)(4-6/59)	.60	1.20	1.80
984-Sleeping Beauty's Fairy Godmothers (Disney)	1.50	3.00	4.50
985-Shaggy Dog(Disney-Movie)(5/59)	1.25	2.50	3.75
986-Restless Gun (TV)	.80	1.60	2.40
987-Goofy (Disney)(7/59)	.80	1.60	2.40
988-Little Hiawatha (Disney)	1.25	2.50	3.75
989-Jiminy Cricket (Disney)(5-7/59)	1.00	2.00	3.00
990-Huckleberry Hound (TV)(Hanna-Barbera)	.50	1.00	1.50
991-Francis the Mule	.50	1.00	1.50
992-Sugarfoot(TV)Toth art	1.75	3.35	5.00
993-Jim Bowie (TV)	.80	1.60	2.40
994-Sea Hunt (TV)	.80	1.60	2.40
995-Donald Duck Album (Disney)(5-7/59)	1.00	2.00	3.00
996-Nevada (Zane Grey)	1.25	2.50	3.75
997-Walt Disney Presents-Tales of Texas John Slaughter(TV)(Disney)	1.00	2.00	3.00
998-Ricky Nelson (TV)	1.00	2.00	3.00
999-Leave It To Beaver (TV)	.50	1.00	1.50
1000-The Gray Ghost of the Confederacy(Movie) (6-8/59)	1.00	2.00	3.00
1001-Lowell Thomas' High Adventure (TV) (8-10/59)	.65	1.35	2.00
1002-Buffalo Bee (TV)	.40	.80	1.20
1003-Zorro (TV)(Disney)	1.35	2.75	4.00
1004-Colt 45 (TV)(6-8/59)	.65	1.35	2.00
1005-Maverick (TV)	1.00	2.00	3.00
1006-Hercules (Movie)-Buscema art	2.00	4.00	6.00
1007-John Paul Jones (Movie)(7-9/59)			

	Good	Fine	Mint
	1.20	2.40	3.60
1008-Beep Beep, the Road Runner (7-9/59)	.80	1.60	2.40
1009-The Rifleman (TV)	1.00	2.00	3.00
1010-Grandma Duck's Farm Friends (Disney) by Carl Barks	3.00	6.00	9.00
1011-Buckskin (TV)	.80	1.60	2.40
1012-Last Train from Gun Hill(Movie)(7/59)	1.35	2.75	4.00
1013-Bat Masterson(TV)(8/59)	.65	1.35	2.00
1014-The Lennon Sisters - Toth art	1.75	3.50	5.25
1015-Peanuts-cvr.by Schulz	1.50	3.00	4.50
1016-Smokey the Bear	.50	1.00	1.50
1017-Chilly Willy	.50	1.00	1.50
1018-Rio Bravo(Movie)(6/59)-Toth art	2.00	4.00	6.00
1019-Wagon Train (TV)	.80	1.60	2.40
1020-Jungle Jim	1.20	2.40	3.60
1021-Jace Pearson's Tales of the Texas Rangers (TV)	.90	1.80	2.70
1022-Timmy	.50	1.00	1.50
1023-Tales of Wells Fargo (TV)(8-10/59)	1.00	2.00	3.00
1024-Darby O'Gill & the Little People(Disney-Movie)-Toth art	2.00	4.00	6.00
1025-Vacation in Disneyland (8-10/59)-Carl Barks art	4.00	8.00	12.00
1026-Spin & Marty(TV)(Disney)-Mickey Mouse Club (9-11/59)	.65	1.35	2.00
1027-The Texan (TV)	1.00	2.00	3.00
1028-Rawhide (TV)	.65	1.35	2.00
1029-Boots & Saddles (TV)	.50	1.00	1.50
1030-Spanky & Alfalfa, the Little Rascals	.50	1.00	1.50
1031-Fury (TV)	.65	1.35	2.00
1032-Elmer Fudd	.50	1.00	1.50
1033-Steve Canyon - not by Caniff	1.75	3.50	5.25
1034-Nancy & Sluggo Summer Camp (9-11/59)	.60	1.20	1.80
1035-Lawman (TV)	.65	1.35	2.00
1036-The Big Circus(Movie)	1.00	2.00	3.00
1037-Zorro(Disney)(TV)-Tufts art	1.35	2.75	4.00
1038-Ruff & Reddy (TV)(Hanna-Barbera)(1959)	.40	.80	1.20
1039-Pluto(Disney)(11-1/60)	.80	1.60	2.40
1040-Quick Draw McGraw(TV)(Hanna-Barbera) (12-2/60)	.40	.80	1.20
1041-Sea Hunt(TV)-Toth art	1.75	3.35	5.00
1042-The Three Chipmunks (Alvin, Simon & Theodore)(10-12/59)	.35	.70	1.05
1043-The Three Stooges	1.20	2.40	3.60
1044-Have Gun, Will Travel (TV)(10-12/59)	.60	1.20	1.80
1045-The Restless Gun (TV)	.80	1.60	2.40

(Four Color cont'd)

	Good	Fine	Mint
1046-Beep Beep, the Road Runner (11-1/60)			
	.80	1.60	2.40
1047-Gyro Gearloose(Disney)-by Carl Barks			
	3.00	6.00	9.00
1048-The Horse Soldiers (Movie)			
	1.35	2.75	4.00
1049-Don't Give Up the Ship (Movie)(8/59)			
	1.35	2.75	4.00
1050-Huckleberry Hound (TV)(Hanna-Barbera)			
(10-12/59)	.50	1.00	1.50
1051-Donald in Mathmagic Land(Disney-Movie)			
	1.25	2.50	3.75
1052-Ben Hur (Movie)(11/59)-by Russ Manning			
	1.75	3.50	5.25
1053-Goofy(Disney)(11-1/60)	.80	1.60	2.40
1054-Huckleberry Hound Winter Fun(TV)(Hanna-			
Barbera)(12/59)	.40	.80	1.20
1055-Daisy Duck's Diary(Disney)-by Carl Barks			
(11-1/60)	3.00	6.00	9.00
1056-Yellowstone Kelly (Movie)(11-1/60)			
	1.35	2.75	4.00
1057-Mickey Mouse Album (Disney)			
	.65	1.35	2.00
1058-Colt 45 (TV)(11-1/60)	.65	1.35	2.00
1059-Sugarfoot (TV)	.65	1.35	2.00
1060-Journey to the Center of the Earth(Movie)			
	1.75	3.35	5.00
1061-Buffalo Bee (TV)	.40	.80	1.20
1062-Walt Scott's Christmas Stories-Little			
People(strip reprints)	.80	1.60	2.40
1063-Santa Claus Funnies	.65	1.35	2.00
1064-Bugs Bunny's Merry Christmas (12/59)			
	.65	1.35	2.00
1065-Frosty the Snowman	.50	1.00	1.50
1066-77 Sunset Strip(TV)-Toth art (1-3/60)			
	1.75	3.35	5.00
1067-Yogi Bear (TV)(Hanna-Barbera)			
	.40	.80	1.20
1068-Francis the Talking Mule (11/59-1/60)			
	.50	1.00	1.50
1069-The FBI Story (Movie)-Toth art			
	1.75	3.35	5.00
1070-Solomon & Sheba(Movie)	1.20	2.40	3.60
1071-The Real McCoys (TV)	.40	.80	1.20
1072-Blythe (Marge's)	.65	1.35	2.00
1073-Grandma Duck's Farm Friends-by Carl Barks			
(Disney)	3.00	6.00	9.00
1074-Chilly Willy	.50	1.00	1.50
1075-Tales of Wells Fargo (TV)(2-4/60)			
	1.00	2.00	3.00
1076-The Rebel (TV)	.80	1.60	2.40
1077-The Deputy(TV)-Buscema art			
	1.35	2.75	4.00
1078-The Three Stooges	1.20	2.40	3.60
1079-Spanky & Alfalfa, the Little Rascals			
	.50	1.00	1.50
1080-Fury (TV)	.65	1.35	2.00

	Good	Fine	Mint
1081-Elmer Fudd	.50	1.00	1.50
1082-Spin & Marty (Disney)	.65	1.35	2.00
1083-Men Into Space(TV)-Anderson art			
	1.35	2.75	4.00
1084-Speedy Gonzales	.75	1.50	2.25
1085-The Time Machine (Movie-3/60)-Alex Toth			
art	2.00	4.00	6.00
1086-Lolly & Pepper	.40	.80	1.20
1087-Peter Gunn (TV)	.80	1.60	2.40
1088-A Dog of Flanders(Movie)(4/60)			
	1.20	2.40	3.60
1089-Restless Gun (TV)	.80	1.60	2.40
1090-Francis the Mule	.50	1.00	1.50
1091-Jacky's Diary(4-6/60)	.50	1.00	1.50
1092-Toby Tyler (Disney-Movie)(3/60)			
	1.35	2.75	4.00
1093-MacKenzie's Raiders (Movie)(6-8/60)			
	1.20	2.40	3.60
1094-Goofy (Disney)	.80	1.60	2.40
1095-Gyro Gearloose (Disney)-Carl Barks art			
(4-6/60)	3.00	6.00	9.00
1096-The Texan (TV)	1.00	2.00	3.00
1097-Rawhide(TV)-Manning art.	.65	1.35	2.00
1098-Sugarfoot (TV)	.65	1.35	2.00
1099-Donald Duck Album (Disney)(5-7/60)			
	1.00	2.00	3.00
1100-Annette's Life Story (Disney-Movie)			
	1.50	3.00	4.50
1101-Kidnapped(Disney-Movie)(5/60)			
	1.35	2.75	4.00
1102-Wanted: Dead or Alive (TV)(5-7/60)			
	1.00	2.00	3.00
1103-Leave It To Beaver(TV)	.50	1.00	1.50
1104-Yogi Bear Goes to College (TV)(Hanna-			
Barbera)(6-8/60)	.40	.80	1.20
1105-Oh, Susanna(TV)-Toth art			
	1.75	3.35	5.00
1106-77 Sunset Strip(TV)-Toth art(6-8/60)			
	1.75	3.35	5.00
1107-Buckskin (Movie)	1.20	2.40	3.60
1108-The Troubleshooters(TV).	.80	1.60	2.40
1109-This Is Your Life, Donald Duck (Disney)			
(8-10/60)-Gyro flashback written by Carl			
Barks	1.25	2.50	3.75
1110-Bonanza (TV)(6-8/60)	.65	1.35	2.00
1111-Shotgun Slade (TV)	.80	1.60	2.40
1112-Pixie & Dixie & Mr. Jinks (TV)(Hanna-			
Barbera)(7-9/60)	.50	1.00	1.50
1113-Tales of Wells Fargo (TV)			
	1.00	2.00	3.00
1114-Huckleberry Finn (Movie)(7/60)			
	1.35	2.75	4.00
1115-Ricky Nelson (TV)-Manning art			
	1.50	3.00	4.50
1116-Boots & Saddles (TV)	.50	1.00	1.50
1117-The Boy & the Pirates (Movie)			
	1.35	2.75	4.00

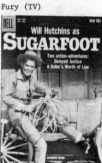

Four Color #1059, © Dell

Four Color #1071, © Dell

Four Color #1114, © Dell

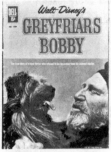

Four Color #1139, © Dell   Four Color #1150, © WDP   Four Color #1189, © WDP

(Four Color cont'd)	Good	Fine	Mint
1118-The Sword & the Dragon (Movie)(6/60)			
	1.35	2.75	4.00
1119-Smokey the Bear	.50	1.00	1.50
1120-Dinosaurus (Movie)	1.35	2.75	4.00
1121-Hercules Unchained (Movie)(8/60)			
Crandall/Evans art	2.00	4.00	6.00
1122-Chilly Willy	.50	1.00	1.50
1123-Tombstone Territory(TV)			
	1.00	2.00	3.00
1124-Whirlybirds (TV)	.65	1.35	2.00
1125-Laramie (TV)	.80	1.60	2.40
1126-Hotel DeParee-Sundance (TV)(8-10/60)			
	.65	1.35	2.00
1127-The Three Stooges	1.20	2.40	3.60
1128-Rocky & His Friends(Jay Ward)(8-10/60)			
	.50	1.00	1.50
1129-Pollyanna(Disney-Movie)(8/60)			
	1.35	2.75	4.00
1130-The Deputy (TV)-Buscema art			
	1.00	2.00	3.00
1131-Elmer Fudd (9-11/60)	.50	1.00	1.50
1132-Space Mouse (8-10/60)	.65	1.35	2.00
1133-Fury (TV)	.65	1.35	2.00
1134-Real McCoys (TV)-Toth art			
	1.50	3.00	4.50
1135-Mouse Musketeers	.40	.80	1.20
1136-Jungle Cat(Disney-Movie)(9-11/60)			
	1.35	2.75	4.00
1137-The Little Rascals	.50	1.00	1.50
1138-The Rebel (TV)	.80	1.60	2.40
1139-Spartacus (Movie)(11/60)-Buscema art			
	2.00	4.00	6.00
1140-Donald Duck Album (Disney)(10-12/60)			
	1.00	2.00	3.00
1141-Huckleberry Hound for President (TV)			
(Hanna-Barbera)(10/60)	.40	.80	1.20
1142-Johnny Ringo (TV)	.65	1.35	2.00
1143-Pluto (Disney)	.80	1.60	2.40
1144-The Story of Ruth (Movie)			
	1.35	2.75	4.00
1145-The Lost World (Movie)-Gil Kane art			
	1.35	2.75	4.00
1146-The Restless Gun (TV)	.80	1.60	2.40
1147-Sugarfoot (TV)	.65	1.35	2.00
1148-I Aim at the Stars-the Wernher Von Braun			
Story(Movie)(11-1/61)	1.35	2.75	4.00
1149-Goofy(Disney)(11-1/61)	.80	1.60	2.40
1150-Daisy Duck's Diary (Disney)(12-1/61) by			
Carl Barks	3.00	6.00	9.00
1151-Mickey Mouse Album (Disney)(11-1/61)			
	.65	1.35	2.00
1152-Rocky & His Friends(Jay Ward)(TV)			
(12-2/61)	.50	1.00	1.50
1153-Frosty the Snowman	.40	.80	1.20
1154-Santa Claus Funnies	.65	1.35	2.00
1155-North to Alaska(Movie)1.35		2.75	4.00
1156-Swiss Family Robinson (Disney-Movie)			

	Good	Fine	Mint
(12/60)	1.35	2.75	4.00
1157-Master of the World (Movie)(7/61)			
	1.35	2.75	4.00
1158-3 Worlds of Gulliver (2 issues with diff-			
erent covers)(Movie)	1.35	2.75	4.00
1159-77 Sunset Strip(TV)-Toth art			
	1.75	3.35	5.00
1160-Rawhide (TV)	.65	1.35	2.00
1161-Grandma Duck's Farm Friends (Disney) by			
Carl Barks (2-4/61)	3.00	6.00	9.00
1162-Yogi Bear Joins the Marines(TV)(Hanna-			
Barbera)(5-7/61)	.40	.80	1.20
1163-Daniel Boone (3-5/61)	.65	1.35	2.00
1164-Wanted: Dead or Alive (TV)			
	.80	1.60	2.40
1165-Ellery Queen	1.35	2.75	4.00
1166-Rocky & His Friends (Jay Ward)(TV)			
(3-5/61)	.50	1.00	1.50
1167-Tales of Wells Fargo (TV)			
	1.00	2.00	3.00
1168-The Detectives (TV)	.80	1.60	2.40
1169-New Adventures of Sherlock Holmes			
	1.25	2.50	3.75
1170-The Three Stooges	1.20	2.40	3.60
1171-Elmer Fudd	.50	1.00	1.50
1172-Fury (TV)	.65	1.35	2.00
1173-The Twilight Zone by Reed Crandall (TV)			
(5/61)	2.00	4.00	6.00
1174-The Little Rascals	.50	1.00	1.50
1175-MGM's Mouse Musketeers (3-5/61)			
	.40	.80	1.20
1176-Dondi (Movie)-origin	1.00	2.00	3.00
1177-Chilly Willy (4-6/61)	.50	1.00	1.50
1178-Ten Who Dared (Disney-Movie)(12/60)			
	1.25	2.50	3.75
1179-The Swamp Fox (TV)(Disney)(3-5/61)			
	1.00	2.00	3.00
1180-The Danny Thomas Show (TV)-Manning art			
	1.35	2.75	4.00
1181-Texas John Slaughter (TV)(Disney)			
(4-6/61)	1.00	2.00	3.00
1182-Donald Duck Album (Disney)(5-7/61)			
	1.00	2.00	3.00
1183-101 Dalmatians (Disney-Movie)(3/61)			
	1.25	2.50	3.75
1184-Gyro Gearloose by Carl Barks (Disney)			
	3.00	6.00	9.00
1185-Sweetie Pie	.50	1.00	1.50
1186-Yak Yak (#1) by Jack Davis			
	2.00	4.00	6.00
1187-The 3 Stooges(6/61)	1.20	2.40	3.60
1188-Atlantis the Lost Continent (Movie)(5/61)			
	1.35	2.75	4.00
1189-Greyfriars Bobby (Disney-Movie)(11/61)			
	1.35	2.75	4.00
1190-Donald & the Wheel (Disney-Movie)(11/61)			
	1.35	2.75	4.00

(Four Color cont'd)

	Good	Fine	Mint
1191-Leave It To Beaver(TV)	.50	1.00	1.50
1192-Ricky Nelson (TV)-Manning art	1.50	3.00	4.50
1193-The Real McCoys (TV)	.40	.80	1.20
1194-Pepe (Movie)(4/61)	1.00	2.00	3.00
1195-National Velvet (TV)	.65	1.35	2.00
1196-Pixie & Dixie & Mr. Jinks (TV)(Hanna-Barbera)(7-9/61)	.50	1.00	1.50
1197-The Aquanauts (TV)	.80	1.60	2.40
1198-Donald in Mathmagic Land - reprint of #1051(Disney-Movie)	1.00	2.00	3.00
1199-The Absent-Minded Professor(Disney-Movie)(4/61)	1.25	2.50	3.75
1200-Hennessey (TV)(8-10/61)-Gil Kane art	.80	1.60	2.40
1201-Goofy(Disney)(8-10/61)	.80	1.60	2.40
1202-Rawhide (TV)	.65	1.35	2.00
1203-Pinocchio(Disney)(3/62)	1.00	2.00	3.00
1204-Scamp (Disney)	.65	1.35	2.00
1205-David & Goliath (Movie)(7/61)	1.35	2.75	4.00
1206-Lolly & Pepper(9-11/61)	.40	.80	1.20
1207-The Rebel(TV)Toth art	.80	1.60	2.40
1208-Rocky & His Friends(Jay Ward)(TV)	.50	1.00	1.50
1209-Sugarfoot (TV)	.65	1.35	2.00
1210-The Parent Trap (Disney-Movie)(8/61)	1.35	2.75	4.00
1211-77 Sunset Strip(TV)-Manning art	1.20	2.40	3.60
1212-Chilly Willy (7-9/61)	.50	1.00	1.50
1213-Mysterious Island (Movie)	1.35	2.75	4.00
1214-Smokey the Bear	.50	1.00	1.50
1215-Tales of Wells Fargo(TV)(10-12/61)	1.00	2.00	3.00
1216-Whirlybirds (TV)	.65	1.35	2.00
1218-Fury (TV)	.65	1.35	2.00
1219-The Detectives (TV)	.80	1.60	2.40
1220-Gunslinger (TV)	.80	1.60	2.40
1221-Bonanza(TV)(9-11/61)	.65	1.35	2.00
1222-Elmer Fudd (9-11/61)	.50	1.00	1.50
1223-Laramie (TV)	.80	1.60	2.40
1224-The Little Rascals	.50	1.00	1.50
1225-The Deputy (TV)	.80	1.60	2.40
1226-Nikki, Wild Dog of the North (Disney-Movie)(9/61)	1.35	2.75	4.00
1227-Morgan the Pirate (Movie)	1.75	3.35	5.00
1229-Thief of Baghdad (Movie)-Evans art	2.50	5.00	7.50
1230-Voyage to the Bottom of the Sea (Movie)	1.20	2.40	3.60
1231-Danger Man (TV)	.65	1.35	2.00
1232-On the Double (Movie)	1.20	2.40	3.60
1233-Tammy Tell Me True (Movie)(1961)			

	Good	Fine	Mint
	1.35	2.75	4.00
1234-The Phantom Planet (Movie)(1961)	1.50	3.00	4.50
1235-Mister Magoo (12-2/62)	.65	1.35	2.00
1235-Mister Magoo(3-5/65)2nd printing-reprints of '61 issue	.35	.70	1.05
1236-King of Kings (Movie)	1.25	2.50	3.75
1237-The Untouchables (TV)-not by Toth	.65	1.35	2.00
1238-Deputy Dawg (TV)	.35	.70	1.05
1239-Donald Duck Album (Disney)(10-12/61) Barks cover	1.00	2.00	3.00
1240-The Detectives (TV)	.80	1.60	2.40
1241-Sweetie Pie	.50	1.00	1.50
1242-King Leonardo (TV) (11-1/62)	.50	1.00	1.50
1243-Ellery Queen	1.20	2.40	3.60
1244-Space Mouse (11-1/62)	.65	1.35	2.00
1245-New Adventures of Sherlock Holmes	1.25	2.50	3.75
1246-Mickey Mouse Album (Disney)(11-1/62)	.65	1.35	2.00
1247-Daisy Duck's Diary (Disney)(12-2/62)	1.00	2.00	3.00
1248-Pluto (Disney)	.80	1.60	2.40
1249-The Danny Thomas Show(TV)-Manning art	1.35	2.75	4.00
1250-The Four Horsemen of the Apocalypse (Movie)	1.35	2.75	4.00
1251-Everything's Ducky (Movie)(1961)	1.20	2.40	3.60
1252-Andy Griffith (TV)	.65	1.35	2.00
1253-Space Man (1-3/62)	.65	1.35	2.00
1254-Diver Dan(TV)(2-4/62)	.65	1.35	2.00
1255-The Wonders of Aladdin(Movie)(1961)	1.35	2.75	4.00
1256-Kona, Monarch of Monster Isle (2-4/62)	1.75	3.35	5.00
1257-Car 54, Where Are You? (TV)(3-5/62)	.40	.80	1.20
1258-The Frogmen-Evans art	1.50	3.00	4.50
1259-El Cid (Movie)(1961)	1.75	3.35	5.00
1260-The Horsemasters (TV,Movie-Disney)(12-2/62)	1.25	2.50	3.75
1261-Rawhide (TV)	.65	1.35	2.00
1262-The Rebel (TV)	.80	1.60	2.40
1263-77 Sunset Strip(TV)-Manning art(12-2/62)	1.20	2.40	3.60
1264-Pixie & Dixie & Mr. Jinks (TV)(Hanna-Barbera)	.50	1.00	1.50
1265-The Real McCoys (TV)	.40	.80	1.20
1266-Spike & Tyke (12-2/62)	.35	.70	1.05
1267-Gyro Gearloose by Carl Barks, 4pgs. (Disney)(12-2/62)	3.00	6.00	9.00
1268-Oswald the Rabbit	.65	1.35	2.00
1269-Rawhide (TV)	.65	1.35	2.00
1270-Bullwinkle & Rocky(Jay Ward)(TV)(3-5/62)			

Four Color #1198, © WDP

Four Color #1210, © WDP

Four Color #1234, © Dell

Four Color #1311, © Jay Ward

Four Color #1350, © WDP

Four Favorites #9, © Ace

(Four Color cont'd)	Good	Fine	Mint
	.50	1.00	1.50
1271-Yogi Bear Birthday Party(TV)(Hanna-Barbera)(11/61)	.25	.50	.75
1272-Frosty the Snowman	.40	.80	1.20
1273-Hans Brinker (Disney-Movie)(1962)	1.35	2.75	4.00
1274-Santa Claus Funnies	.65	1.35	2.00
1275-Rocky & His Friends(Jay Ward)(TV) (12-2/62)	.50	1.00	1.50
1276-Dondi	1.00	2.00	3.00
1278-King Leonardo(TV)	.50	1.00	1.50
1279-Grandma Duck's Farm Friends (Disney) (2-4/62)	1.00	2.00	3.00
1280-Hennessey (TV)	.50	1.00	1.50
1281-Chilly Willy (4-6/62)	.50	1.00	1.50
1282-Babes in Toyland (Disney-Movie)(1/62)	1.35	2.75	4.00
1283-Bonanza (TV)(2-4/62)	.65	1.35	2.00
1284-Laramie (TV)-Heath art	.80	1.60	2.40
1285-Leave It To Beaver (TV)	.50	1.00	1.50
1286-The Untouchables (TV)	.65	1.35	2.00
1287-Man From Wells Fargo (TV)	.65	1.35	2.00
1288-The Twilight Zone (TV)(4/62)-Evans/Crandall art	2.00	4.00	6.00
1289-Ellery Queen	1.20	2.40	3.60
1290-Mouse Musketeers	.40	.80	1.20
1291-77 Sunset Strip (TV)-Manning art	1.20	2.40	3.60
1293-Elmer Fudd(3-5/62)	.50	1.00	1.50
1294-Ripcord (TV)	.65	1.35	2.00
1295-Mister Ed(TV)(3-5/62)	.35	.70	1.05
1296-Fury (3-5/62)	.65	1.35	2.00
1297-Spanky, Alfalfa & the Little Rascals	.50	1.00	1.50
1298-The Hathaways (TV)	.40	.80	1.20
1299-Deputy Dawg (TV)	.35	.70	1.05
1300-The Comancheros (Movie)(1961)	1.35	2.75	4.00
1301-Adventures in Paradise (TV)(2-4/62)	.65	1.35	2.00
1302-Johnny Jason, Teen Reporter (2-4/62)	.35	.70	1.05
1303-Lad: A Dog (Movie)	1.00	2.00	3.00
1304-Nellie the Nurse(3-5/62)-John Stanley art	1.35	2.75	4.00
1305-Mister Magoo (3-5/62)	.65	1.35	2.00
1306-Target: the Corrupters (TV)(3-5/62)	.50	1.00	1.50
1307-Margie (TV)(3-5/62)	.40	.80	1.20
1308-Tales of the Wizard of Oz (TV)(3-5/62)	1.35	2.75	4.00
1309-87th Precinct (TV)(4-6/62)-Krigstein art	1.75	3.35	5.00
1310-Huck & Yogi Winter Sports (TV)(Hanna-Barbera)(3-62)	.50	1.00	1.50

	Good	Fine	Mint
1311-Rocky & His Friends(Jay Ward)(TV)	.50	1.00	1.50
1312-National Velvet (TV)	.65	1.35	2.00
1313-Moon Pilot (Disney-Movie)(3/62)	1.35	2.75	4.00
1324-The Underwater City (Movie)-Evans art	1.75	3.35	5.00
1328-The Underwater City (Movie)-Evans art (1961)	1.75	3.35	5.00
1329-Gyro Gearloose-Barks cover	1.75	3.35	5.00
1330-Brain Boy-G.Kane art	.80	1.60	2.40
1332-Bachelor Father (TV)	.65	1.35	2.00
1333-Short Ribs	.65	1.35	2.00
1335-Aggie Mack	.80	1.60	2.40
1336-On Stage - not by Leonard Starr	.80	1.60	2.40
1337-Dr. Kildare (TV)	.40	.80	1.20
1341-Andy Griffith (TV)	.65	1.35	2.00
1348-Yak Yak-by Jack Davis	2.00	4.00	6.00
1349-Yogi Bear Visits the U.N.(TV)(Hanna-Barbera)(1/62)	.25	.50	.75
1350-Comanche(Disney-Movie)(1962)-Reprints 4-Color #966(title change from "Tonka" to "Comanche")(4-6/62)	1.00	2.00	3.00
1354-Calvin & the Colonel (TV)	.40	.80	1.20

NOTE: *Missing numbers probably do not exist.*

FOUR FAVORITES
Sept, 1941 - #32, Dec, 1947
Ace Magazines

	Good	Fine	Mint
#1-Vulcan, Lash Lightning, Magno the Magnetic Man & The Raven begin	25.00	50.00	75.00
2-The Black Ace only app.	12.00	24.00	36.00
3-Last Vulcan	10.00	20.00	30.00
4,5: #4-The Raven ends; Unknown Soldier begins. #5-Captain Courageous begins	8.00	16.00	24.00
6-11: #9-11-Kurtzman art	6.00	12.00	18.00
12-20	5.00	10.00	15.00
21	2.50	5.00	7.50
22-Captain Courageous drops costume	2.50	5.00	7.50
23-26-Last Magno	2.50	5.00	7.50
27-32	1.35	2.75	4.00

FOUR HORSEMEN OF THE APOCALYPSE, THE
(See 4-Color Comics #1250)

FOUR MOST (-- Boys #37-41)
Winter, 1941-42 - V8#5, 9-10/49; 1950
Novelty Publications

V1#1-The Target, The Cadet & Dick Cole, Wond-

(Four Most cont'd)	Good	Fine	Mint
er Boy begin	7.00	14.00	21.00
2	4.00	8.00	12.00
3,4	3.00	6.00	9.00
V2#1-4, V3#1-4	1.50	3.00	4.50
V4#1-4	1.00	2.00	3.00
V5#1-The Target & Targeteers app.,			
2-4	1.00	2.00	3.00
V6#1-White Rider & Super Horse begins,			
2-6	1.00	2.00	3.00
V7#1-6-Last Dick Cole	1.00	2.00	3.00
V8#1-5	1.00	2.00	3.00
#37-41(1950)	.65	1.35	2.00

FOUR STAR BATTLE TALES
Feb-Mar, 1973 - #5, Nov-Dec, 1973
National Periodical Publications

#1-All reprints	.15	.30	.45
2-4		.15	.30
5-Krigstein reprint	.15	.30	.45

NOTE: _Drucker reprints-#1,3-5. Kubert reprint-#4, cover-#2._

FOUR STAR SPECTACULAR
Mar-Apr, 1976 - #6, Jan-Feb, 1977 (68 pgs.)
National Periodical Publications

#1	.20	.40	.60
2-6	.15	.30	.45

NOTE: _All contain DC Superhero reprints. #6 has a Blackhawk G.A. reprint._

FOUR TEENERS
April, 1948 (Love comic)
A. A. Wyn

#34	.65	1.35	2.00

FOX AND THE CROW (Stanley & His Monster#109)
Dec-Jan, 1951-52 - #108, Feb-Mar, 1968
National Periodical Publications

#1	5.00	10.00	15.00
2-5	2.50	5.00	7.50
6-10	1.75	3.35	5.00
11-20	1.35	2.75	4.00
21-60	.65	1.35	2.00
61-108	.35	.70	1.05

NOTE: _Many covers by Mort Drucker._

FOX GIANTS

Each of these contain four remaindered Fox books minus covers. Since these missing covers often had the first page of the first story, most Giants therefore are incomplete. The value can be determined at 30-50% the listed price of each individual title included in the Giant.

FOXHOLE
Sept-Oct, 1954 - 1955
Simon & Kirby Publ.(Prize)/Charlton Comics

	Good	Fine	Mint
#1-Kirby cover	1.35	2.75	4.00
2-Kirby cvr/2 stories	1.50	3.00	4.50
3,5-Kirby cvrs. only	1.00	2.00	3.00
4,7-10	.50	1.00	1.50
6-Kirby cvr/2 stories	1.35	2.75	4.00
11-18	.35	.70	1.05
Super Reprints #10-12,15-18			
	.50	1.00	1.50

NOTE: _Kirby art-#11,12,18. Powell art-#15,16._

FOXY FAGAN
1946 - #7, Summer, 1948
Dearfield Publishing Co.

#1-Foxy Fagan & Little Buck begin			
	1.00	2.00	3.00
2-7	.50	1.00	1.50

FOXY GRANDPA
1901 - 1916 (Hardcover; strip reprints)
N.Y.Herald/Frederick A.Stokes Co./M.A. Donahue & Co./Bunny Publ.

1901-9x15" in color-N. Y. Herald			
	20.00	50.00	80.00
1902-"Latest Larks of--", 32pgs. in color,			
9½x15½"	20.00	50.00	80.00
1903-"Latest Advs.", 9x15", 24pgs. in color,			
Hammersly Co.	20.00	50.00	80.00
1903-"--'s New Advs.", 10x15", 30pgs. in			
color, Stokes	20.00	50.00	80.00
1904-"Up to Date", 10x15", 28pgs. in color,			
Stokes	20.00	50.00	80.00
1905-"The Latest Advs. of", 9x15", 24pgs.,			
B&W, M.A.Donahue Co.	8.00	20.00	32.00
1905-"Merry Pranks of", 9½x15½", 24pgs. in			
color, Donahue			
1905-"Latest Larks of", 9½x15½", 32pgs. in			
color, Donahue			
1906-"Frolics", 10x15", 30pgs. in color,			
Stokes	15.00	37.50	60.00
1908?-"Triumphs", 10x15"			
1908?-"& Little Brother", 10x15"			
1908?-"& Flip Flaps", 10x15"			
	8.00	20.00	32.00
1914-9½x15½", 24pgs., 6 color cartoons/page,			
Bunny Publ.			
1916-"Merry Book", 10x15" 30pgs. in color,			
Stokes	10.00	20.00	30.00

Four Most #3, © NOVP

Foxy Grandpa, 1904, © M.A. Donahue

Frank Buck #71, © Fox

Frankenstein #1, © MCG

Freckles #5, © NEA Service

FOXY GRANDPA SPARKLETS SERIES
1908   (6½x7-3/4"; 24 pgs. in color)
Donahue & Co.

	Good	Fine	Mint
--"Rides the Goat",--"And His Boys",			
--"Playing Ball",--"Fun on the Farm",			
--"Fancy Shooting",--"Show the Boys Up Sports",			
--"Plays Santa Claus"			
each....	15.00	37.50	60.00

FRACTURED FAIRY TALES
Oct, 1962
Gold Key

#1(10022-210)	.35	.70	1.05

FRANCIS THE FAMOUS TALKING MULE (All based
on movie)(See 4-Color #335,465,501,547,579,
621,655,698,710,745,810,863,906,953,991,1068,
1090)

FRANK BUCK (Formerly My True Love)
#70, May, 1950 - #3, Sept, 1950
Fox Features Syndicate

#70,71-Wood stories each	4.00	8.00	12.00
72,3	1.75	3.35	5.00

FRANKENSTEIN (See Movie Classics)
8-10/64; #2, 9/66 - #4, 3/67
Dell Publishing Co.

#1(12-283-410)('64)	.50	1.00	1.50
2-Intro. & origin Super-Hero character(9/66),			
3,4	.20	.40	.60

FRANKENSTEIN COMICS
1945 - V5#5(#33), Oct-Nov, 1954
Prize Publications (Crestwood/Feature)

#1-Frankenstein begins by Dick Briefer			
(origin)	7.00	14.00	21.00
2	4.00	8.00	12.00
3-10: #8-(7-8/47)-Superman satire			
	3.00	6.00	9.00
11-17(1948)-Last humor issue			
	2.50	5.00	7.50
18(3/51)-New origin, horror series begins			
	1.50	3.00	4.50
19	1.50	3.00	4.50
20(V3#4, 8-9/52)	1.50	3.00	4.50
21(V3#5),22(V3#6)	1.50	3.00	4.50
23(V4#1)-#28(V4#6)	1.20	2.40	3.60
29(V5#1)-#33(V5#5)	1.20	2.40	3.60

FRANKENSTEIN (The Monster of--)(See Book &
Jan, 1973 - #18, Sept, 1975   Record--)
Marvel Comics Group

	Good	Fine	Mint
#1-Ploog art begins	.50	1.00	1.50
2-6-Last Ploog art	.35	.70	1.05
7-17	.20	.40	.60
18-Wrightson cover	.25	.50	.75

FRANKENSTEIN, JR. (--& the Impossibles)(TV)
January, 1967   (Hanna-Barbera)
Gold Key

#1	.15	.30	.45

FRANKIE (--& Lana)(Formerly Movie Tunes;
Frankie Fuddle #16 on)
#4, Spring, 1947 - 1948
Marvel Comics (MgPC)

#4-8	.60	1.20	1.80
9-15	.40	.80	1.20

FRANKIE DOODLE (See Single Series #7 and
Sparkler #2)

FRANKIE FUDDLE (Formerly Frankie & Lana)
1949
Marvel Comics

#16,17	.40	.80	1.20

FRANK LUTHER'S SILLY PILLY COMICS
1950   (10¢)   (See Jingle Dingle --)
Children's Comics

#1-Characters from radio, records, & TV			
	.65	1.35	2.00

FRANK MERRIWELL AT YALE
June, 1955 - #3, Oct, 1955
Charlton Comics

#1	.80	1.60	2.40
2,3	.50	1.00	1.50

FRANTIC (Magazine) (See Zany & Ratfink)
Oct, 1958 - V2#2, April, 1959   (Satire)
Pierce Publishing Co.

V1#1,2	.80	1.60	2.40
V2#1,2	.40	.80	1.20

FRECKLES AND HIS FRIENDS (See Famous Comics
Cartoon Book)

FRECKLES AND HIS FRIENDS
#5, 11/47 - #12, 8/49; 11/55 - 1956
Standard Comics/Argo

#5	2.00	4.00	6.00
6-12-Reprints	1.75	3.35	5.00

(Freckles & His Friends cont'd)

	Good	Fine	Mint
NOTE: *#8&9 contain a printing oddity. The negatives were elongated in the engraving process, probably to conform to page dimensions on the filler pages. Those pages only look normal when viewed at a 45 degree angle.*

	Good	Fine	Mint
#1(Argo,'55)-reprints	1.50	3.00	4.50
2,3	1.00	2.00	3.00

FREDDY (See Blue Bird)
March, 1958 - #47, Feb, 1965
Charlton Comics

V2#12-47	.20	.40	.60

FREDDY
May-July, 1963 - #3, Oct-Dec, 1964
Dell Publishing Co.

#1-3	.15	.30	.45

FREE COMICS TO YOU FROM (--name of shoe store)
(Has clown on cover & another with a rabbit)
Circa 1956   (Like comics from Weather Bird
Shoe Store Giveaway   & Edward's Shoes)

Contains a comic bound with new cover - several combinations possible; contents determines price.

FREEDOM AGENT (Also see John Steele)
April, 1963
Gold Key

#1(10054-304)	.60	1.20	1.80

FREEDOM FIGHTERS (See Justice League#107,108)
Mar-Apr, 1976 - #15, Jul-Aug, 1978
National Periodical Publications/DC Comics

#1-Uncle Sam, The Ray, Black Condor, Doll Man, Human Bomb, & Phantom Lady begin

	.25	.50	.75
2,3	.15	.30	.45
4-Redondo art, Kubert cvr	.15	.30	.45
5-15		.15	.30

FREEDOM TRAIN
1948   (Giveaway)
Street & Smith Publ.

	1.00	2.00	3.00

FRENZY (Magazine) (Satire)
April, 1958 - #6, March, 1959
Picture Magazine

#1	1.00	2.00	3.00
2-6	.65	1.35	2.00

FRIDAY FOSTER
October, 1972
Dell Publishing Co.

#1	.35	.70	1.05

FRIENDLY GHOST, CASPER, THE
1958 - Present
Harvey Publications

#1	4.00	8.00	12.00
2	2.00	4.00	6.00
3-10	1.50	3.00	4.50
11-20	1.00	2.00	3.00
21-50	.50	1.00	1.50
51-100	.30	.60	.90

	Good	Fine	Mint
101-150	.15	.30	.45
151-195		.15	.30

American Dental Assoc. giveaway-Small size

(1967, 16pgs.)	.25	.50	.75

FRIGHT
June, 1975 (August on inside)
Atlas/Seaboard Periodicals

#1-Origin The Son of Dracula; Frank Thorne

cover/art	.20	.40	.60

FRISKY ANIMALS (Formerly Frisky Fables)
#44, 1951 - #55, Sept, 1953
Star Publications

#44-55-Super Cat	.25	.50	.75

FRISKY ANIMALS ON PARADE (Formerly Parade;
#2, 11/57 - #3, 1958   Becomes Superspook)
Ajax-Farrell Publ. (Four Star Comic Corp.)

#2,3	.25	.50	.75

FRISKY FABLES (Frisky Animals #44 on)
Spring, 1945 - #43, Oct, 1950
Premium Group/Novelty/Star Publ.

V1#1	1.75	3.35	5.00
2,3(1945)	1.20	2.40	3.60
4-7(1946)	.80	1.60	2.40
V2#1-12(1947)	.65	1.35	2.00
V3#1-12(1948)	.50	1.00	1.50
#32-43(V4#1-12)(1949-50): #39-L.B. Cole cvr.
	.25	.50	.75

FRITZI RITZ (See Single Series #5,1(reprint)
United Comics & Comics on Parade)

Fritzi Ritz #7, © UFS

FRITZI RITZ
Fall/48-#54,6/57; #55,9-11/57 - #59, 9-11/58
United Features Synd./St. John/Dell #55 on

No#(1948)-Special fall ish.

	2.50	5.00	7.50
2-5	1.20	2.40	3.60
6-10	.80	1.60	2.40
11-28,30-33,35-59	.65	1.35	2.00
29-5pg. Abbie & Slats; 1pg. Mamie by Russell
Patterson	.80	1.60	2.40
34-Li'l Abner dressed as a woman (transvestism) cameo	.80	1.60	2.40

FROGMAN COMICS
Jan-Feb, 1952 - #11, May, 1953
Hillman Periodicals

Frogman Comics #1, © Hill

Frontier Romances #1, © Avon

Frontline Combat #8, © WMG

(Frogman Comics cont'd)	Good	Fine	Mint
#1	1.00	2.00	3.00
2-4,6-11	.60	1.20	1.80
5-Krigstein story	1.75	3.35	5.00

FROGMEN, THE
#1258, Feb-Apr, 1962 - #12, Feb-Mar, 1965
Dell Publishing Co.

4-Color #1258-Evans art	1.35	2.75	4.00
#2,3-Evans art; partial Frazetta inks in			
both	1.75	3.35	5.00
4,6-12	.60	1.20	1.80
5-Toth art	1.50	3.00	4.50

FROM BEYOND THE UNKNOWN
10-11/69 - #25, 11-12/73 (#7-11,64pgs;#12-17,
National Periodical Publ.   52pgs.)

#1	.35	.70	1.05
2-5	.20	.40	.60
6-10: #7-Intro. Col. Glenn Merrit; Anderson			
art #7,8	.20	.40	.60
11-25: Star Rovers reprints begin #18,19.			
Space Museum in #23-25	.15	.30	.45

NOTE: _Adams_ covers-#3,6,8,9. _Anderson_ covers-
#2,5,10,11,15-17,22; reprints-#3,4,6-8,10,11,
13-16,24,25. _Infantino_ reprints-#1-5,7-19,23-
25. _Kaluta_ cover-#18. _Kubert_ covers-#1,7,12-
14. _Toth_ reprint-#2. _Wood_ inks-#13.

FROM HERE TO INSANITY (Magazine) (Eh #1-7)
(See Frantic & Frenzy) (Satire)
#8, Feb, 1955 - V3#1, 1956
Charlton Comics

#8-10-comic format	2.00	4.00	6.00
11,12-All Kirby except 4 pgs.			
	4.00	8.00	12.00
V3#1(1956)-5pgs. Wolverton, 3pgs. Ditko			
	1.75	3.35	5.00

FRONTIER DAYS
1956   (Giveaway)
Robin Hood Shoe Store (Brown Shoe)

#1	.35	.70	1.05

FRONTIER DOCTOR (See 4-Color Comics #877)

FRONTIER FIGHTERS
Sept-Oct, 1955 - #8, Nov-Dec, 1956
National Periodical Publications

#1-Davy Crockett, Buffalo Bill by Kubert,			
Kit Carson begin	4.00	8.00	12.00
2-8	2.00	4.00	6.00

NOTE: _Buffalo Bill by Kubert in all._

FRONTIER ROMANCES
Nov-Dec, 1949 - #2, Jan-Feb, 1950
Avon Periodicals/I.W.

	Good	Fine	Mint
#1-"Spanking scene" illustrated in _Seduction_			
of the Innocent	5.00	10.00	15.00
2	1.50	3.00	4.50
#1-IW (reprints Avon's #1)	1.50	3.00	4.50
IW Reprint #9	.65	1.35	2.00

FRONTIER SCOUT, DAN'L BOONE
#10, Jan, 1956 - 1965
Charlton Comics

#10-13	.50	1.00	1.50
V2#14(3/65)	.20	.40	.60

FRONTIER TRAIL (The Rider #1-5)
#6, May, 1958
Ajax/Farrell Publ.

#6	.40	.80	1.20

FRONTIER WESTERN
Feb, 1956 - #10, Aug, 1957
Atlas Comics (PrPI)

#1	1.35	2.75	4.00
2,3,6-Williamson stories, 4pgs. each			
	2.00	4.00	6.00
4,7,9,10	.75	1.50	2.25
5-Crandall & Davis stys.	1.75	3.35	5.00
8-Crandall, Morrow, & Wildey stories			
	1.35	2.75	4.00

NOTE: _Drucker_ story-#4. _Ringo Kid_ in #4.

FRONTIER COMBAT
July-Aug, 1951 - #15, Jan, 1954
E.C. Comics

#1-Kurtzman cover	35.00	70.00	105.00
2- " "	25.00	50.00	75.00
3- " "	17.50	35.00	52.50
4-10	12.00	24.00	36.00
11-15	7.00	14.00	21.00

NOTE: _Davis stories in all; covers-#11,12.
Evans_ stories-#10-15. _Heath_ story-#1. _Kubert_
story-#14. _Kurtzman_ stories-#1-5; covers-
#1-9. _Severin_ stories-#5-7,9,13,15. _Severin/
Elder_ stories-#2-11; cover-#10. _Toth_ stories-
#8,12. _Wood_ stories-#1-4,6-10,12-15; covers-
#13-15. _Special issues:_ #7(Iwo Jima), #9
(Civil War), #12(Air Force). (Canadian re-
prints known; see Table of Contents.)

FRONT PAGE COMIC BOOK
1945
Harvey Publications

(Front Page cont'd)

	Good	Fine	Mint
#1-Kubert art; Man in Black by Powell	5.00	10.00	15.00

FROSTY THE SNOWMAN
1951 - 1961
Dell Publishing Co.

	Good	Fine	Mint
4-Color #359,435	1.00	2.00	3.00
4-Color #514,601,661	.60	1.20	1.80
4-Color #748,861,950,1065	.50	1.00	1.50
4-Color #1153,1272	.40	.80	1.20

FRUITMAN SPECIAL
Dec, 1969   (68 pgs.)
Harvey Publications

#1-Funny Super Hero	.20	.40	.60

F-TROOP (TV)
Aug, 1966 - #7, Aug, 1967
Dell Publishing Co.

#1	.25	.50	.75
2-7	.15	.30	.45

FUGITIVES FROM JUSTICE
Feb, 1952 - #5, Oct, 1952
St. John Publishing Co.

#1	2.00	4.00	6.00
2,4-Vic Flint strip reprints	1.35	2.75	4.00
3-Used in Seduction of the Innocent; Vic Flint reprints	5.00	10.00	15.00
5	.75	1.50	2.25

FULL COLOR COMICS
1946
Fox Features Syndicate

No#	1.75	3.35	5.00

FULL OF FUN
Aug, 1957 - #2, Nov, 1957; 1964
Red Top(Decker Publ.)(Farrell)/I.W. Ent.

#1(1957)	.40	.80	1.20
2-reprints Bingo, the Monkey Doodle Boy	.40	.80	1.20
8-I.W. Reprint('64)	.35	.70	1.05

FUN AT CHRISTMAS (See March of Comics #138)

FUN CLUB COMICS (See Interstate Theatres--)

FUN COMICS (Mighty Bear #13 on)

Jan, 1953 - #12, Oct, 1953
Star Publications

	Good	Fine	Mint
#9(Giant)	.65	1.35	2.00
10-12	.65	1.35	2.00

FUNDAY FUNNIES (See Famous TV --, and Harvey Hits #35)

FUN-IN (Hanna-Barbera)
Feb, 1970 - #10, 1/72; #11, 4/74 - #15, 12/74
Gold Key

#1-4,6-Dastardly & Muttley in Their Flying Machines-Perils of Penelope Pitstop in #1-4; It's the Wolf in all; Cattanooga Cats in #2-4	.15	.30
5,7-Motormouse & Autocat-Dastardly & Muttley in both; It's the Wolf in #7	.10	.20
8,10-The Harlem Globetrotters-Dastardly & Muttley in #10	.10	.20
9-Where's Huddles?-Dastardly & Muttley, Motormouse & Autocat app.	.10	.20
11-Butch Cassidy	.10	.20
12,15-Speed Buggy; #15-52pgs.	.15	.30
13-The Hair Bear Bunch	.10	.20
14-Inch High Private Eye	.10	.20

NOTE: 52pg. issues had 16pgs. of adv. added.

FUNKY PHANTOM, THE (TV)
Dec, 1971 - #13, Mar, 1975   (Hanna-Barbera)
Gold Key

#1	.15	.30	.45
2-13		.15	.30

FUNLAND COMICS
1945
Croyden Publishers

#1	1.00	2.00	3.00

FUNNIES, THE (Also see Comic Cuts)
1929 - #36, 10/18/30 (10¢; 5¢ #22 on)(16pgs.)
Full tabloid size in color (not reprints)
Published every Saturday
Dell Publishing Co.

#1-My Big Brudder, Johnathan, Jazzbo & Jim, Foxy Grandpa, Sniffy, Jimmy Jams & other strips begin; first four-color comic newsstand publication; also contains magic, puzzles & stories	40.00	80.00	120.00
2-21(1930, 30¢)	15.00	30.00	45.00
22(no#-7/12/30-5¢)	10.00	20.00	30.00
23(no#-7/19/30-5¢), #24(no#-7/26/30-5¢), 25(no#-8/2/30), #26(no#-8/9/30),			

Front Page #1. © Harv   Fugitives From Justice #1. © STJ

The Funnies #4(1929). © Dell

173

The Funnies #17, © Dell

The Funnies #36, © Dell

Funny Films #4, © ACG

	Good	Fine	Mint
(The Funnies cont'd)			

27(no#-8/16/30), #28(no#-8/23/30),
29(no#-8/30/30), #30(no#-9/6/30),
31(no#-9/13/30), #32(no#-9/20/30),
33(no#-9/27/30), #34(no#-10/4/30),
35(no#-10/11/30), #36(no#, no date-10/18/30)

	Good	Fine	Mint
each....	10.00	20.00	30.00

FUNNIES, THE (New Funnies #65 on)
Oct, 1936 - #64, May, 1942
Dell Publishing Co.

#1-Tailspin Tommy, Mutt & Jeff, Alley Oop,
Capt. Easy, Don Dixon begin

	Good	Fine	Mint
	40.00	80.00	120.00
2	20.00	40.00	60.00
3	15.00	30.00	45.00
4	10.00	20.00	30.00
5	9.00	18.00	27.00
6-10	8.00	16.00	24.00
11-29	7.00	14.00	21.00

30-John Carter of Mars begins by Edgar Rice

Burroughs	15.00	30.00	45.00

31-44: #33-John Coleman Burroughs art begins

on John Carter	10.00	20.00	30.00

45-Origin Phantasmo, the Master of the World
& intro. his sidekick Whizzer McGee

	10.00	20.00	30.00

46-The Black Knight begins,

47-50	9.00	18.00	27.00

51-56-Last ERB John Carter of Mars

	9.00	18.00	27.00

57-Intro. & origin Captain Midnight

	15.00	30.00	45.00
58-60	9.00	18.00	27.00

61-Andy Panda begins by Walter Lantz,

62-64-Last C. Midnight	10.00	20.00	30.00

NOTE: *McWilliams art in many issues on "Rex
King of the Deep."*

FUNNIES ANNUAL, THE
1959 (B&W) (Tabloid-Size) ($1.00)
Avon Periodicals

#1-(Rare)-Features the best newspaper comic
strips of the year: Archie, Snuffy Smith,
Beetle Baily, Henry, Blondie, Steve Canyon,
Buz Sawyer, The Little King, Hi & Lois,
Popeye & others. Also has a chronological
history of the comics from 2000 B.C. to

1959.	4.00	8.00	12.00

FUNNIES ON PARADE (Premium)
1933 (Probably the 1st comic book)(32pgs.)
No date or publisher listed
Eastern Color Printing Co.

No#-Contains Sunday page reprints of Mutt &

	Good	Fine	Mint

Jeff, Joe Palooka, Hairbreadth Harry, Reg'-
lar Fellers, Skippy, & others (10,000
print run). This book was printed for
Proctor & Gamble to be given away & came
out before Famous Funnies or Century of

Comics.	175.00	350.00	525.00

Funnies On Parade, © Eas

FUNNY ANIMALS (See Fawcett's Funny Animals)

FUNNYBONE
1944 (132 pgs.)
La Salle Publishing Co.

	1.00	2.00	3.00

FUNNY BOOK (-- Magazine)(Hocus Pocus #9)
Dec, 1942 - #8, June-July, 1946
Parents' Magazine Press

#1-Funny animal	1.75	3.35	5.00
2-8	1.00	2.00	3.00

FUNNY COMIC TUNES (See Funny Tunes)

FUNNY FABLES
Sept, 1957 - #2, Nov, 1957
Decker Publications (Red Top Comics)

V2#1,2	.20	.40	.60

FUNNY FILMS
Sept-Oct, 1949 - #29, May-June, 1954
American Comics Group(Michel Publ/Titan Publ)

#1	1.75	3.35	5.00
2-10	1.00	2.00	3.00
11-29	.65	1.35	2.00

FUNNY FOLKS (Hollywood--, on cvr. only#17-30;
becomes Hollywood Funny Folks #31 on)
4-5/45 - #30, 1/51
National Periodical Publications

	Good	Fine	Mint
#1	2.50	5.00	7.50
2-5	1.35	2.75	4.00
6-10	1.00	2.00	3.00
11-30	.50	1.00	1.50

FUNNY FROLICS
Summer, 1945 - #5, Dec, 1946
Timely/Marvel Comics(SPI)

#1-4	.80	1.60	2.40
5-Kurtzman art	2.00	4.00	6.00

FUNNY FUNNIES
1943   (68 pgs.)
Nedor Publishers

#1	2.00	4.00	6.00

FUNNYMAN
Dec, 1947; #1, Jan, 1948 - #7, Aug, 1948
Magazine Enterprises

No#(12/47)-Prepublication B&W undistributed
copy by Siegel & Shuster-(5-3/4x8"),16pgs;
Sold in San Francisco in 1976 for $300.00

#1-By Siegel & Shuster	5.00	10.00	15.00
2-5-By Siegel & Shuster	2.50	5.00	7.50
6,7-(#7 exist?)	1.70	3.35	5.00

FUNNY MOVIES (See 3-D Funny Movies)

FUNNY PAGES (The Comics #1; Comics Funny
#4, Sept, 1936 - #45, 1942   Pages #2,3)
Centaur Publications

#4,5	8.00	16.00	24.00
6-The Clock begins(2pg. strip), ends #11			
	10.00	20.00	30.00
7-11	8.00	16.00	24.00
12-20(V2#1-9)	7.00	14.00	21.00
21-1st app. of the Arrow by Gustavson			
(V2#10)	15.00	30.00	45.00
22,23(V2#11,12)	10.00	20.00	30.00
24-33(V3#1-10)	10.00	20.00	30.00
34-The Owl & The Phantom Rider app.; origin			
Mantoka, Maker of Magic by Jack Cole			
	12.00	24.00	36.00
35-42-Last Arrow	10.00	20.00	30.00
43-45	8.00	16.00	24.00

FUNNY PICTURE STORIES (Becomes Comic Pages
Nov, 1936 - V3#3, May, 1939   with V3#4)
Centaur Publications

	Good	Fine	Mint
V1#1-The Clock begins	20.00	40.00	60.00
2	10.00	20.00	30.00
3,5-11	7.00	14.00	21.00
4-Eisner art	8.00	16.00	24.00
V2#1-Jack Strand begins	6.00	12.00	18.00
2-11	5.00	10.00	15.00
V3#1-3	5.00	10.00	15.00

FUNNY STUFF (Becomes The Dodo & the Frog #80)
Summer, 1944 - #79, July-Aug, 1954
All-American/National Periodical Publ.

#1-The 3 Mouseketeers & The "Terrific What-			
zit" begin	4.00	8.00	12.00
2-5	2.00	4.00	6.00
6-15	1.35	2.75	4.00
16-30	.80	1.60	2.40
31-79-Dodo & the Frog	.50	1.00	1.50
Wheaties Giveaway(1946, 6½x8¼")			
	2.50	5.00	7.50

FUNNY 3-D
December, 1953
Harvey Publications

#1	3.35	6.75	10.00

FUNNY TUNES (Animated Funny Comic Tunes #16-
#22; Funny Comic Tunes #23, on covers only;
Formerly Human Torch; Oscar #24 on)
#16, Summer, 1944 - #23, Fall, 1946
U.S.A. Comics Magazine Corp. (Timely)

#16-22	1.00	2.00	3.00
23-Kurtzman art	2.00	4.00	6.00

FUNNY TUNES
Aug-Sept, 1953 - #3, Dec-Jan, 1953-54
Avon Periodicals

#1-Space Mouse	1.35	2.75	4.00
2,3-Space Mouse-#3	.80	1.60	2.40

FUNNY WORLD
1947 - 1948
Marbak Press

#1-3-Newspaper strip reprints			
	1.35	2.75	4.00

FUN TIME
1953 - #4, Winter, 1953-54
Ace Periodicals

#1,2	.50	1.00	1.50
3,4(100 pgs. each)	1.00	2.00	3.00

FUN WITH SANTA CLAUS (See March of Comics
#11,108,325)

Funny Funnies #1, © Nedor

Funnyman #1, © ME

Funny Stuff #62, © DC

Action Comics No. 7, 1938
The second Superman cover
© DC

Adventure Comics No. 79, 1942
Simon & Kirby cover art. © DC

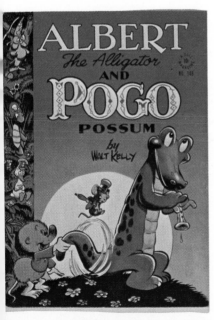

4-Color No. 148, 1947
By Walt Kelly
© Oscar Lebeck

All Star Comics No. 13, 1942
© DC

Blood Is The Harvest, 1950
© Catechetical Guild

Buster Crabbe No. 5, 1952
Frank Frazetta cover
© Buster Crabbe

Captain America No. 12, 1942
© MCG

Captain Marvel Jr. No. 7, 1943
Mac Raboy cover art
© Faw

Future World #1, © Geo. Dougherty   Gabby Hayes #4, © Faw   Gang Busters #23, © DC

FURY (Straight Arrow's Horse--)(See A-1 #119)

FURY (TV)
Aug, 1957 - 1962
Dell Publishing Co./Gold Key

	Good	Fine	Mint
4-Color #781,885,975	.80	1.60	2.40
4-Color #1031,1080,1133,1172,1218,1296,			
#01292-208(#1-'62)	.65	1.35	2.00
#10020-211(11/62-G.K.)	.60	1.20	1.80

(See March of Comics #200)

FUTURE COMICS
June, 1940 - #4, Sept, 1940
David McKay Publications

#1-The Lone Ranger, The Phantom & Little Nemo begin	16.50	33.25	50.00
2-4	10.00	20.00	30.00

FUTURE WORLD COMICS
Summer, 1946 - #2, Fall, 1946
George W. Dougherty

#1,2	1.35	2.75	4.00

G-8 (See G-Eight)

GABBY (Formerly Ken Shannon)
#11, July, 1953; #2, 9/53 - #9, 9/54
Quality Comics Group

#11(#1)(7/53)	1.00	2.00	3.00
2-9	.65	1.35	2.00

GABBY GOB (See Harvey Hits #85,90,99,103,106)

GABBY HAYES WESTERN
Nov, 1948 - #50, Jan, 1953; 12/54 - #59, 1/57
Fawcett/Toby Press/Charlton Comics #51 on

#1	6.00	12.00	18.00
2-10	2.50	5.00	7.50
11-20	2.00	4.00	6.00
21-50	1.75	3.35	5.00
51-59(Charlton '54-57)	1.35	2.75	4.00
#1(Toby)(12/53)	2.00	4.00	6.00
Quaker Oats Giveaway #1-5(1951)			
	1.75	3.35	5.00

GAGS
7/37; 7/42 (13-3/4"x10-3/4")
United Features Synd./Triangle Publ. #9

#1(7/37)-52pgs.;20pgs. Grin & Bear It, Fellow Citizen	4.00	8.00	12.00
#1#9-(36pgs., 15¢)	2.00	4.00	6.00

GAG STRIPS
Aug, 1942 (13-3/4"x10-3/4")(36pgs.)(15¢)
Triangle Publications

	Good	Fine	Mint
V1#1-Comic strips by 24 different cartoonists			
	2.50	5.00	7.50

GALLANT MEN, THE (TV)
October, 1963
Gold Key

#1(10085-310)-Manning art	.65	1.35	2.00

GALLEGHER, BOY REPORTER (TV)
May, 1965 (Disney)
Gold Key

#1(10149-505)	.50	1.00	1.50

GANDY GOOSE
3/53 - #5, 11/53; #5, Fall/56 - #6, Summer/58
St. John Publ. Co./Pines #5,6

#1	.60	1.20	1.80
2-5(1953)(St.John)	.30	.60	.90
5,6(Pines,'56-58)	.30	.60	.90

GANG BUSTERS
1398 - 1943
David McKay/Dell Publishing Co.

Feature Book #17(McKay)('38)			
	10.00	20.00	30.00
Black & White #10('39) (Scarce)			
	20.00	40.00	60.00
Black & White #17('40)	12.00	24.00	36.00
4-Color #7(1940)	10.00	20.00	30.00
4-Color #23,24('42-43)	10.00	20.00	30.00

GANG BUSTERS (Radio/TV)
Dec-Jan, 1947-48 - #67, Dec-Jan, 1958-59
National Periodical Publications

#1	4.00	8.00	12.00
2	2.00	4.00	6.00
3-10	1.35	2.75	4.00
11-13,15,16,18-30	1.00	2.00	3.00
14,17-Frazetta story in both, 8pgs. each			
	8.00	16.00	24.00
31-Toth story	1.75	3.35	5.00
32-67	.75	1.50	2.25

GANGSTERS AND GUN MOLLS
Sept, 1951 - #4, June, 1952
Avon Periodicals/Realistic Comics

#1-Wood art, 1pg.	5.00	10.00	15.00
2-Check story, 8pgs. + Kamenesque story			

(Gangsters & G.M. cont'd)	Good	Fine	Mint
	4.00	8.00	12.00
3,4	3.00	6.00	9.00

GANGSTERS CAN'T WIN
1948 - 1951
D. S. Publishing Co.

	Good	Fine	Mint
#1	1.75	3.35	5.00
2,3	1.20	2.40	3.60
4-Drug story	2.00	4.00	6.00
5-10	1.00	2.00	3.00
11-24	.65	1.35	2.00

GANG WORLD
#5, Nov, 1952 - #6, Jan, 1953
Standard Comics

#5,6: #5-Bondage cover	.80	1.60	2.40

GARRISON'S GORILLAS (TV)
Jan, 1968 - #5, Oct, 1969
Dell Publishing Co.

#1-5: #5-reprints #1	.20	.40	.60

GASOLINE ALLEY (Hardcover)
1929 (B&W daily strip reprints)(7x8-3/4")
Reilly & Lee Publishers

By King (84 pgs.)	8.00	16.00	24.00

GASOLINE ALLEY
Sept, 1950 - #2, 1950 (Newspaper reprints)
Star Publications

#1-Contains 1 pg. intro. history of the strip
(The Life of Skeezix); reprints 15 scenes
of highlights from 1921-35, + an adventure
from 1935 & 36 strips; a 2-page filler is
included on the life of the creator Frank
King, with photo of the cartoonist

	5.00	10.00	15.00
2	2.50	5.00	7.50

(See Super Book #21)

GASP!
March, 1967 - #4, Aug, 1967
American Comics Group

#1-L.S.D. story	.50	1.00	1.50
2-4	.25	.50	.75

GAY COMICS (Honeymoon #41)
1944 (no month) - #40, Oct, 1949
Timely Comics/USA Comic Mag. Co. #17-24

#1-Wolverton's Powerhouse Pepper; Tessie the Typist begins	8.00	16.00	24.00

	Good	Fine	Mint
2-10	2.00	4.00	6.00
11-16	1.20	2.40	3.60
17-29-Wolverton art in all; Kurtzman in #24,			
29	4.00	8.00	12.00
30,31,33,36,37-Kurtzman's "Hey Look"			
	1.75	3.35	5.00
32,35,38-40	.75	1.50	2.25
34-Three Kurtzman's "Hey Looks"			
	2.50	5.00	7.50

GAY COMICS (Also see Tickle & Smile Comics)
1955 (52pgs.; 5x7¼") (7¢)
Modern Store Publ.

#1	.35	.70	1.05

GAY PURR-EE (See Movie Comics)

GEEK, THE (See Brother Power --)

G-8 AND HIS BATTLE ACES
October, 1966
Gold Key

#1(10184-610)	1.35	2.75	4.00

GEM COMICS
April, 1942; 1945
Spotlight Publishers

#1(1942)	2.50	5.00	7.50
#1(1945)-Little Mohee, Steve Strong			
	2.00	4.00	6.00

GENE AUTRY (See March of Comics #25,28,39, 54,78,90,104,120,135,150)

GENE AUTRY COMICS (Dell takes over with #11)
1941 - 1944 (68 pgs.)
Fawcett Publications

#1 (Rare)	40.00	80.00	120.00
2-5	20.00	40.00	60.00
6-10	13.50	26.75	40.00

GENE AUTRY COMICS (-- & Champion #102 on)
June, 1946 - #121, Jan, 1959
Dell Publishing Co.

#11,12(1943-44)-Continuation of Fawcett			
series	15.00	30.00	45.00
4-Color #47(1944)	15.00	30.00	45.00
4-Color #57('44),66('45)	12.00	24.00	36.00
4-Color #75,83('45)	8.00	16.00	24.00
4-Color #93,100('45)	6.00	12.00	18.00
#1(5-6/46)	10.00	20.00	30.00
2(7-8/46)	6.00	12.00	18.00

Gangsters Can't Win #1, © D.S.

Gasoline Alley #2, © Star

Gene Autry #2, © Gene Autry (Faw)

177

Gene Autry's -#116, © Gene Autry

Georgie #10, © MCG

Geronimo #4, © Avon

(Gene Autry cont'd)	Good	Fine	Mint
3-10	3.35	6.75	10.00
11-30	2.00	4.00	6.00
31-60	1.25	2.50	3.75
61-80	1.00	2.00	3.00
81-121: #118-Manning art	.80	1.60	2.40

Pillsbury Premium('47)-36pgs., 6½x7½"-
  Games, Comics, Puzzles 4.00   8.00 12.00
2½"x6-3/4" Quaker Oats Giveaway (5 different-
  1950)   each.... 2.00   4.00   6.00
3-D Giveaway (5 different-1953, pocket-size)
                   2.00   4.00   6.00
NOTE: *Jesse Marsh art: 4-Color #66,75,93,
100, #1-25,27-37,39,40.*

GENE AUTRY TIM (Formerly Superman-Tim)
(Becomes Tim in Space)
1950   (½ Size) (Black & White Giveaway)
Tim Stores

Several issues	3.00	6.00	9.00

GENE AUTRY'S CHAMPION
1950; #3, Aug-Oct, 1951 - #19, Aug, 1955
Dell Publishing Co.

4-Color #287('50)	2.00	4.00	6.00
4-Color #319('51), #3	1.25	2.50	3.75
#4-19	.80	1.60	2.40

GENERAL DOUGLAS MACARTHUR
1951
Fox Features Syndicate

No#	2.50	5.00	7.50

GENTLE BEN (TV)
Feb, 1968 - #5, Oct, 1969
Dell Publishing Co.

#1	.20	.40	.60
2-5: #5-reprints #1	.15	.30	.45

GEORGE OF THE JUNGLE (TV)
Feb, 1969 - #2, Oct, 1969 (Jay Ward)
Gold Key

#1,2	.25	.50	.75

GEORGIE (-- & Judy #24 on)
Spring, 1945 - #39, Oct, 1952
Timely Comics/GPI #1-34

#1-Dave Berg art	1.75	3.35	5.00
2-8	1.00	2.00	3.00
9,10-Kurtzman's "Hey Look"			
	1.50	3.00	4.50
11,12	.50	1.00	1.50

	Good	Fine	Mint
13-Kurtzman's "Hey Look", 3pgs.			
	2.00	4.00	6.00
14-Wolverton art(1pg.) & Kurtzman's "Hey			
Look"	2.50	5.00	7.50
15,16,18-39	.50	1.00	1.50
17-Kurtzman's "Hey Look", 1 pg.			
	1.50	3.00	4.50

GERALD McBOING-BOING AND THE NEARSIGHTED MR.
MAGOO (Mr. Magoo #6)
Aug-Oct, 1952 - #5, Aug-Oct, 1953
Dell Publishing Co.

#1	1.35	2.75	4.00
2-5	.65	1.35	2.00

GERONIMO
1950 - #4, Feb, 1952
Avon Periodicals

#1-Indian Fighter-Maneely art			
	2.50	5.00	7.50
2-On the Warpath; Kit West app.; Kinstler			
cover/story	2.00	4.00	6.00
3-And His Apache Murderers; Kinstler cover/			
two stories	2.00	4.00	6.00
4-Savage Raids of; Kinstler cover			
	1.75	3.35	5.00

GERONIMO JONES
Sept, 1971 - #9, Jan, 1973
Charlton Comics

#1		.15	.30
2-9		.10	.15

GET LOST
Feb-Mar, 1954 - #3, June-July, 1954 (Satire)
Mikeross Publications

#1	2.50	5.00	7.50
2-Has 4pg. E.C. parady featuring the "Sewer			
Keeper"	1.75	3.50	5.25
3	1.50	3.00	4.50

GET SMART (TV)
June, 1966 - #8, Sept, 1967
Dell Publishing Co.

#1	.25	.50	.75
2-Ditko art	.20	.40	.60
3-8	.15	.30	.45

GHOST
1951 - 1954
Fiction House Magazines

#1	2.50	5.00	7.50

(Ghost cont'd)	Good	Fine	Mint
2-9	1.75	3.35	5.00
10,11-Dr. Drew by Grandenetti in each-			
Reprinted from <u>Rangers</u>; Evans story-#11			
	2.35	4.75	7.00

GHOST BREAKERS (Also see (CC) Sherlock
Holmes & Racket Squad in Action)
Sept, 1948 - #2, Nov, 1948 (52 pgs.)
Street & Smith Publications

#1,2-Powell art; Dr. Neff (magician) app.			
	2.50	5.00	7.50

GHOST CASTLE (See Tales of --)

GHOSTLY HAUNTS (Formerly Ghost Manor)
#20, 9/71 - #53, 12/76; #54, 9/77 - #55, 10/77
Charlton Comics

#20,21		.15	.30
22-41,43-55: #27-Dr. Graves x-over. #39-ori-			
gin & 1st app. Destiny Fox	.10	.20	
42-Newton cover/story	.15	.30	.45

NOTE: <u>Ditko</u> stories-#22-25,27,28,32-34,36-39,
44; covers-#22-27,30,33-38. <u>Howard</u> story-#42.
<u>Sutton</u> cover-#39.

GHOSTLY TALES (Blue Beetle #50-54)
#55,4-5/66 - #124,12/76; #125,9/77 - #126,10/77
Charlton Comics

#55-Intro. Dr. Greaves	.20	.40	.60
56-70: Dr. Graves ends	.15	.30	.45
71-113,115-126		.15	.30
114-Newton story	.15	.30	.45

NOTE: <u>Ditko</u> stories-#55,57,58,60,61,67,69,70,
72,73,75-89,92,95,97,99,100-110,112-114,115,
120; covers-#67,69,77,78,83,84,86-90,92-97,
99,107,122. <u>Howard</u> stories-#95,98,117; covers-
#98,107,120,121. <u>Newton</u> cover-#115. <u>Sutton</u>
story-#112,113.

GHOSTLY WEIRD STORIES (Formerly Blue Bolt
#120, 1953 - #124, Sept, 1954   Weird)
Star Publications

#120,121-Jo-Jo reprints	2.00	4.00	6.00
122-The Mask, Rulah reprt	2.00	4.00	6.00
123	1.50	3.00	4.50
124-Torpedo Man	1.50	3.00	4.50

NOTE: <u>Disbrow</u> art-#120-124.

GHOST MANOR (Ghostly Haunts #20 on)
July, 1968 - #19, July, 1971
Charlton Comics

#1	.20	.40	.60

	Good	Fine	Mint
2-10		.15	.30	.45
11-19			.15	.30

NOTE: <u>Ditko</u> stories-#13-16,18,19; covers-#15,
18,19.

GHOST MANOR (2nd Series)
Oct, 1971 - #32, Dec, 1976; #33, Sept, 1977
Charlton Comics

#1	.15	.30	.45
2-7,9,10		.15	.30
8-Wood story	.15	.30	.45
11-17,19,20		.10	.20
18,22-Newton cover/art	.15	.30	.45
21-E-Man, Blue Beetle, Capt. Atom cameos			
	.15	.30	.45
23-33		.10	.20

NOTE: <u>Ditko</u> stories-#1-5,7,8,12,13,15-18,20-
22,29; covers-#2-7,28. <u>Howard</u> story-#21.

GHOST RIDER (See A-1 Comics)
1950 - 1954
Magazine Enterprises

#1(A-1#27)-Origin G.R.	17.50	35.00	52.50
#2(A-1#29),3(A-1#31),4(A-1#34),5(A-1#37)-All			
Frazetta covers only	15.00	30.00	45.00
#6(A-1#44),7(A-1#51),8(A-1#57),9(A-1#69),10			
(A-1#71),11(A-1#75),12(A-1#80),13(A-1#84)			
14(A-1#112)	4.00	8.00	12.00

NOTE: <u>Dick Ayers</u> art in all.

GHOST RIDER (See Night Rider)
Feb, 1967 - #7, Nov, 1967
Marvel Comics Group

#1-Origin G.R.; Kid Colt reprint			
	.50	1.00	1.50
2-7	.35	.70	1.05

GHOST RIDER (See Marvel Spotlight)
Sept, 1973 - Present   (Super-Hero)
Marvel Comics Group

#1	.50	1.00	1.50
2-5	.35	.70	1.05
6-9	.25	.50	.75
10-Ploog art	.35	.70	1.05
11-20	.20	.40	.60
21-27	.15	.30	.45

NOTE: <u>Kirby</u> covers-#22,23. <u>Mooney</u> art-#6,8.
<u>Newton</u> story-#23.

GHOSTS
Sept-Oct, 1971 - Present (#1-5, 52pgs.)
National Periodical Publications/DC Comics

Ghost Breakers #1, © S & S

Ghostly Weird Stories #124, © Star

Ghost Rider #1, ©ME

Ghost Rider #1('73), © MCG

Ghost Stories #6, © Dell

Giant Comics Edition #14, © STJ

(Ghosts cont'd)	Good	Fine	Mint
1	.40	.80	1.20
2-Wood art	.25	.50	.75
3-10	.20	.40	.60
11-30	.15	.30	.45
31-40: #40-68pgs.		.15	.30

NOTE: *Alcala stories-#9,15,17-19,21,23-25,28, 33,34. Kaluta cover-#7. Redondo story-#13,45.*

GHOSTS SPECIAL (See DC Special Series #7)

GHOST STORIES (See Amazing Ghost Stories)

GHOST STORIES
9-11/62; #2, 4-6/63 - #37, 10/73
Dell Publishing Co.

1-12-295-211-Written by J. Stanley	1.00	2.00	3.00
2-10	.25	.50	.75
11-37	.20	.40	.60

NOTE: *#21-34,36,37 all reprint earlier issues.*

GHOUL TALES (Magazine)
Nov, 1970 - #5, July, 1971 (52pgs.)(B&W)
Stanley Publications

1-Aragon pre-code reprints; Mr. Mystery as host; bondage cover	.50	1.00	1.50
2-(1/71)Reprint/Climax#1	.35	.70	1.05
3-(3/71)	.35	.70	1.05
4-(5/71)Reprints story "The Way to a Man's Heart" used in Seduction of the Innocent	1.35	2.75	4.00
5-ACG reprints	.35	.70	1.05

NOTE: *#1-4 contain pre-code Aragon reprints.*

GIANT BOY BOOK OF COMICS (See Boy)
1945 (Hardcover) (240 pgs.)
Newsbook Publications (Gleason)

1- Crimebuster & Young Robin Hood	15.00	30.00	45.00

GIANT COMIC ALBUM
1972 (52pgs.)(11x14", B&W)(59¢)
King Features Syndicate

Newspaper reprints: Little Iodine, Katzenjammer Kids, Henry, Mandrake the Magician ('59 Falk), Popeye, Beetle Bailey, Barney Google, Blondie, Flash Gordon ('68-69 Dan Barry), & Snuffy Smith	1.00	2.00	3.00

GIANT COMICS
Summer, 1957 - #3, Winter, 1957 (100pgs)(25¢)
Charlton Comics

1-Atomic Mouse, Hoppy app.	.35	.70	1.05

	Good	Fine	Mint
2,3-Atomic Mouse, Rabbit, Christmas Book	.35	.70	1.05

GIANT COMICS (See Wham-O Giant Comics)

GIANT COMICS EDITION
1940's (132 pgs.)
United Features Syndicate

1-Abbie & Slats, Abbott & Costello, Jim Hardy, Ella Cinders, Iron Vic	3.00	6.00	9.00
2-No Jim Hardy	2.50	5.00	7.50

GIANT COMICS EDITION (See Terry-Toons)
1947 - 1950 (All 100-164 pgs.) (25¢)
St. John Publishing Co.

1-Mighty Mouse	2.50	5.00	7.50
2	1.35	2.75	4.00
3-Terry-Toons Album-100pgs.	2.00	4.00	6.00
5-Police Case Book(4/49)-Contents varies; contains remaindered St. John books - some volumes contain 5 copies rather than 4, with 160 pages. Matt Baker cover	2.50	5.00	7.50
5A-Terry-Toons Album, 132pgs.	2.00	4.00	6.00
6,11-Western Picture Stories	2.00	4.00	6.00
7-Contains a teen-age romance + 3 Mopsy comics	2.00	4.00	6.00
8,12	1.75	3.35	5.00
9-Romance confession stories; Four Kubert stories	3.00	6.00	9.00
10-Terry-Toons	2.00	4.00	6.00
13-Romance	2.00	4.00	6.00
14-Mighty Mouse Album	2.00	4.00	6.00
15-Romances(4 love comics)	2.00	4.00	6.00
16-Little Audrey, Abbott & Costello, Casper	2.00	4.00	6.00

NOTE: *The above books contain remaindered comics and contents could vary with each issue.*

GIANT COMICS TO COLOR
1975 - 1976 (16x11") (69¢)
Whitman Publishing Co.

1714-Wonder Woman "The Menace of the Mole Men"(1975)
1715-Shazam! "Double Trouble"(1975)
1716-Superman "Luthor's Lost Land"(1975)
1717-Batman "Comedy of Tears"(1975)
1642-Spider-Man "Weather Forecast: Danger" (1976)
1663-Captain America "The Challenge of Super

(Giant Comics to Color cont'd)

	Good	Fine	Mint
Sport"(1976)			
1664-Superman "Braniac's Biggest Plot"(1976)			
1671-Batman "Four Birds of a Feather"(1976)			
	.35	.70	1.05

GIANT GRAB BAG OF COMICS   (See Archie All-Star Specials)

GIANTS (See Thrilling True Stories of --)

GIANT-SIZE (Avengers, Captain America, Captain Marvel, Conan, Daredevil, Defenders, Fantastic Four, Hulk, Invaders, Iron Man, Kid Colt, Man-Thing, Master of Kung Fu, Power Man, Spider-Man, Super-Villain Team-Up, Thor, Werewolf, and X-Men are listed under their own titles.)

GIANT-SIZE CHILLERS (G-S Dracula #2)
June, 1974; Feb, 1975 - #3, Aug, 1975 (35¢)
Marvel Comic Group

#1-(6/74)-Tomb of Dracula(52pgs.)-Origin & 1st app. Lilith, Dracula's daughter			
	.40	.80	1.20
1-(2/75)(50¢)(68pgs.)-Alcala story			
	.40	.80	1.20
2-(5/75)	.35	.70	1.05
3-(8/75)-Wrightson cover/story; Smith reprint	.50	1.00	1.50

NOTE: *Everett reprint-#2/Advs. Into Weird Worlds #10.*

GIANT SIZE CREATURES (G-S Werewolf #2)
July, 1974   (52pgs.) (35¢)
Marvel Comics Group

#1-Werewolf, Tigra app.; Crandall reprint			
	.40	.80	1.20

GIANT-SIZE DRACULA (Formerly G-S Chillers)
#2, Sept, 1974 - #5, June, 1975   (50¢)
Marvel Comics Group

#2	.50	1.00	1.50
3-Wolverton reprt/Uncanny Tales #6			
	.40	.80	1.20
4,5	.30	.60	.90

GIANT-SIZE SUPER HEROES (G-S Spider-Man #2 on)
June, 1974   (35¢)
Marvel Comics Group

#1-Spider-Man vs. Morbius & Man-Wolf			
	.50	1.00	1.50

GIANT-SIZE SUPER-STARS (G-S Fantastic-4 #2)
May, 1974   (35¢)
Marvel Comics Group

#1-Fantastic-4, Thing, Hulk by Buckler; Kirbyesque art	.65	1.35	2.00

GIANT SPECTACULAR COMICS (See Archie All-Star Specials)

GIANT SUMMER FUN BOOK (See Terry-Toons --)

GIANTS (Baseball) (See New York --)

G.I. COMBAT
Oct, 1952 - #43, Dec, 1956
Quality Comics Group

	Good	Fine	Min
#1-Crandall cover	4.00	8.00	12.00
2-4,7-10	2.00	4.00	6.00
5,6-Crandall stories + Cover-#5			
	2.50	5.00	7.50
11-20	1.50	3.00	4.50
21-33,35-43	1.20	2.40	3.60
34-Crandall story	1.35	2.75	5.00

G.I. COMBAT
#44, Jan, 1957 - Present
National Periodical Publications/DC Comics

	Good	Fine	Min
#44	2.50	5.00	7.50
45	1.50	3.00	4.50
46-50	1.00	2.00	3.00
51-60	.90	1.80	2.70
61-66,68-80	.80	1.60	2.40
67-1st Tank Killer	.90	1.80	2.70
81-86,88-100: #83-1st Big Al, Little Al, & Charlie Cigar	.50	1.00	1.50
87-1st Haunted Tank	1.00	2.00	3.00
101-113,115-120	.35	.70	1.05
114-Origin Haunted Tank	.65	1.35	2.00
121-137,139,140	.20	.40	.60
138-Intro. The Losers (Capt. Storm, Gunner/ Sarge, Johnny Cloud) in H.T.	.25	.50	.75
141-150,152,154	.15	.30	.45
151,153-Medal of Honor series by Maurer	.20	.40	.60
155-170	.15	.30	.45
171-205		.15	.30

Note: *Adams covers-#168,201,202. Drucker stories-#48,61,63,66,71,72,76,134,140,141,144,148,153. Evans stories-#135,138,158,164,166. Kubert/Heath stories in many issues. Morrow art-#159-161(2pgs.). Redondo story-#189. Wildey story-#153. Johnny Cloud app.-#112, 115,120. Mlle. Marie app.-#123,132,200. Sgt Rock app.-#111-113,115,120,125,141,146,147, 149,200. USS Stevens by Glanzman-#145,150-53, 157.*

G.I. COMICS
1945

#37-49	.80	1.60	2.40

GIDGET (TV)
April, 1966 - #2, Dec, 1966
Dell Publishing Co.

#1,2	.15	.30	.45

GIFT COMICS (50¢)
1941 - #4, 1949 (#1-3, 324pgs.; #4, 152pgs.)
Fawcett Publications

#1-Captain Marvel, Bulletman, Golden Arrow, Ibis the Invincible, Mr. Scarlet, & Spy Smasher app.	90.00	180.00	270.00
2	75.00	150.00	225.00
3	33.00	66.50	100.00
4-The Marvel Family, Captain Marvel, etc. Each issue can vary in contents	20.00	40.00	60.00

GIFTS FROM SANTA (See March of Comics #137)

GIGGLE COMICS (Spencer Spook #99)
Oct, 1943 - #98, Dec, 1954
Creston #1-63/American Comics Group #64 on

#1	2.00	4.00	6.00

Gift #1, © Faw

G.I. Joe #39, © Z-D

Girls' Love Stories #3, © DC

(Giggle Comics cont'd)	Good	Fine	Mint
2-5	1.00	2.00	3.00
6-20: #9-1st Superkatt	.65	1.35	2.00
21-40	.50	1.00	1.50
41-98: #55,60-Milt Gross art			
	.40	.80	1.20

G-I IN BATTLE (G-I #1 only)
Aug, 1952 - #9, July, 1953; 1/57 - #6, 5/58
Ajax-Farrell Publ./Four Star

#1	1.00	2.00	3.00
2-9	.50	1.00	1.50
Annual (1953)-100pgs.	1.50	3.00	4.50
#1('57-Ajax)	.65	1.35	2.00
2-6	.35	.70	1.05

G.I. JANE
May, 1953 - #13, Aug-Sept, 1955
Trojan Magazines

#1	1.35	2.75	4.00
2-13	1.00	2.00	3.00

G.I. JOE (Also see Advs. of-- & Showcase#53,
1950 - #51, June, 1957   54)
Ziff-Davis Publ. Co.

#10(#1)	1.00	2.00	3.00
11-14('51-'52)	.60	1.20	1.80
V2#6-17,19,20: #7-Powell story, 8 pgs.			
	.50	1.00	1.50
18-(100pg. Giant-'52)	1.50	3.00	4.50
21-51	.40	.80	1.20

G.I. JOE (America's Moveable Fighting Man)
1967 (32 pgs.) (5-1/8"x8-3/8")
Custom Comics

Shaffenberger art	.20	.40	.60

G.I. JUNIORS (See Harvey Hits #86,91,95,98,
101,104,107,112,114,116,118,120,122)

GIL THORP
May-July, 1963
Dell Publishing Co.

#1	1.00	2.00	3.00

GINGER
1951 - 1954
Archie Publications

#1	1.35	2.75	4.00
2-10	.65	1.35	2.00

GIRL COMICS (Girl Confessions #13 on)
1949 - #12, Jan, 1952
Marvel/Atlas Comics(CnPC)

	Good	Fine	Mint
#1	2.50	5.00	7.50
2-11	1.75	3.35	5.00
12-Krigstein story	2.00	4.00	6.00

GIRL CONFESSIONS (Formerly Girl Comics)
#13, Mar, 1952 - #35, Aug, 1954
Atlas Comics (CnPC/ZPC)

#13-35	.65	1.35	2.00

GIRL FROM U.N.C.L.E., THE (TV)
Oct, 1966 - #5, Oct, 1967
Gold Key

#1-McWilliams art	.65	1.35	2.00
2-5-Leonard Swift-Courier #5			
	.35	.70	1.05

GIRLS' FUN & FASHION MAGAZINE (Formerly Polly
V5#44, 1/50 - V5#47, 7/50   Pigtails)
Parents' Magazine Institute

V5#44-47	.50	1.00	1.50

GIRLS IN LOVE
May, 1950 - #57, Dec, 1956
Fawcett #1/Quality Comics Group

#1	1.00	2.00	3.00
2-10	.65	1.35	2.00
11-57	.50	1.00	1.50

GIRLS IN WHITE (See Harvey Comics Hits #58)

GIRLS' LIFE
Jan, 1954 - #6, 1954
Atlas Comics (BFP)

#1-Patsy Walker	1.00	2.00	3.00
2-6	.50	1.00	1.50

GIRLS' LOVE STORIES
Aug-Sept, 1949 - #180, Nov-Dec, 1973
National Per. Publ.(Signal Publ. #28-65/
Arleigh #83-117)

#1-Toth + Kinstler art, 8 pgs. each			
	4.00	8.00	12.00
2	2.00	4.00	6.00
3-10	1.50	3.00	4.50
11-20	1.00	2.00	3.00
21-50	.65	1.35	2.00
51-146:#113-117-April O'Day app.			
	.25	.50	.75
147-151-"Confessions" serial.	.15	.30	.45
152-180		.10	.20

GIRLS' ROMANCES
Feb-Mar, 1950 - #160, Sept, 1971
National Per. Publ. (Signal Publ. #32-79/
Arleigh #84)

	Good	Fine	Mint
#1	4.00	8.00	12.00
2	2.00	4.00	6.00
3-10	1.50	3.00	4.50
11-20	1.00	2.00	3.00
21-50	.65	1.35	2.00
51-100	.25	.50	.75
101-133		.15	.30
134-Adams cover	.25	.50	.75

G.I. SWEETHEARTS (Formerly Diary Loves)
June, 1952 - #45, May, 1955
Quality Comics Group

#22-45	.65	1.35	2.00

G.I. TALES (Sgt. Barney Barker #1-3)
#4, Feb, 1957 - #6, July, 1957
Atlas Comics (MCI)

#4,5	.50	1.00	1.50
6-Orlando, Powell, & Woodbridge stories			
	.80	1.60	2.40

G.I. WAR BRIDES
1954 - #8, June, 1955
Superior Publishers Ltd.

#1	1.00	2.00	3.00
2-8	.60	1.20	1.80

G.I. WAR TALES
Mar-Apr, 1973 - #4, Oct-Nov, 1973
National Periodical Publications

#1-Reprints		.15	.30
2-Adams reprint	.15	.30	.45
3-Reprints		.10	.20
4-Krigstein art reprint	.15	.30	.45

NOTE: *Drucker reprints-#3,4. Kubert stories-
#2,3.*

GJDRKZLXCBWQ COMICS
Oct, 1973 (36pgs.)(50¢)(Small Size-B&W)
Glenn Bray

Wolverton art	.35	.70	1.05

GLAMOROUS ROMANCES (Formerly Dotty)
#41, Sept, 1949 - #90, Oct, 1956
Ace Magazines (A.A. Wyn)

#41-90	.50	1.00	1.50

GNOME MOBILE, THE (See Movie Comics)

GOD IS
1975
Spire Christian Comics(Fleming H.Revell Co.)

	Good	Fine	Mint
By Al Hartley	.15	.30	.45

GOD'S HEROES IN AMERICA
1956 (No#) (68 pgs.) (25¢)
Catechetical Guild Educational Society

No#	1.50	3.00	4.50

GOD'S SMUGGLER (Religious)
1972   (35¢)
Spire Christian Comics/Fleming H. Revell Co.

#1	.15	.30	.45

GODZILLA
August, 1977 - Present
Marvel Comics Group

#1	.25	.50	.75
2-6	.15	.30	.45

GO-GO
June, 1966 - #9, Oct, 1967
Charlton Comics

#1-Miss Bikini Luv begins	.35	.70	1.05
2	.20	.40	.60
3-Blooperman begins, ends #6,			
4	.40	.80	1.20
5-Super Hero & TV satire by J. Aparo &			
Grass Green begin	1.00	2.00	3.00
6-9	.35	.70	1.05

GO-GO AND ANIMAL (See Tippy's Friends --)

GOING STEADY (Formerly Teen-Age Temptations
#10, 1954 - #13, 6/55;   #1-10)
V3#4, 9-10/60 - #6, 1-2/61
St. John Publishing Co./Prize(Headline)

#10(1954)	.40	.80	1.20
11(2/55)-#13	.35	.70	1.05
V3#4-6(1960-61)	.20	.40	.60

GOING STEADY WITH BETTY
Nov-Dec, 1949
Avon Periodicals

#1	1.75	3.35	5.00

GOLDEN ARROW (See Fawcett Miniatures)

Girls' Romances #1, © DC

G.I. War Brides #1, © Supr

Golden Arrow #3, © Faw

GOLDEN ARROW (-- Western #6)
1942 - #6, Spring, 1947
Fawcett Publications

	Good	Fine	Mint
#1-Golden Arrow begins	10.00	20.00	30.00
2	6.00	12.00	18.00
3-6:#6-Krigstein story	3.00	6.00	9.00

GOLDEN ARROW WELL KNOWN COMICS
1944   (12 pgs.) (8½x10½")
Paper cover; Glued binding
Bestmaid/Samuel Lowe (Giveaway)

	Good	Fine	Mint
	15.00	30.00	45.00

GOLDEN COMICS DIGEST
May, 1969 -#48, Jan, 1976
Gold Key

NOTE: *Whitman editions exist of many titles
and are generally valued less.*

	Good	Fine	Mint
#1-Tom & Jerry, Woody Woodpecker, Bugs Bunny	1.50	3.00	4.50
2-Hanna-Barbera TV Fun Favorites	.35	.70	1.05
3-Tom & Jerry, Woody Woodpecker	.50	1.00	1.50
4-Tarzan-Manning & Marsh art	1.00	2.00	3.00
5,8-Tom & Jerry, Woody Woodpecker, Bugs Bunny	.50	1.00	1.50
6-Bugs Bunny	.50	1.00	1.50
7-Hanna-Barbera TV Fun Favorites	.35	.70	1.05
9-Tarzan	1.00	2.00	3.00
10-Bugs Bunny	.40	.80	1.20
11-Hanna-Barbera TV Fun Favorites,			
12-Tom & Jerry, Bugs, W.Woodpecker Journey to the Sun	.25	.50	.75
13-Tom & Jerry	.25	.50	.75
14-Bugs Bunny Fun Packed Funnies	.25	.50	.75
15-Tom & Jerry, W. Woodpecker, B. Bunny	.25	.50	.75
16-W. Woodpecker Cartoon Special	.25	.50	.75
17-Bugs Bunny	.25	.50	.75
18-Tom & Jerry	.25	.50	.75
19-Little Lulu	1.00	2.00	3.00
20-W. Woodpecker Falltime Funtime	.25	.50	.75
21-Bugs Bunny Showtime	.25	.50	.75
22-Tom & Jerry Winter Wingding	.25	.50	.75
23-Little Lulu & Tubby Fun Fling	1.00	2.00	3.00
24-W. Woodpecker Fun Festival	.25	.50	.75
25,28-Tom & Jerry	.25	.50	.75
26-Bugs Bunny Halloween Hulla-Boo-Loo; Dr. Spektor article, also #25	.25	.50	.75
27-Little Lulu & Tubby in Hawaii	1.00	2.00	3.00
29-Little Lulu & Tubby	1.00	2.00	3.00
30-Bugs Bunny Vacation Funnies	.25	.50	.75
31-Turok, Son of Stone-reprints 4-Color #596, 656	.80	1.60	2.40
32-W. Woodpecker Summer Fun.	.25	.50	.75
33-Little Lulu & Tubby Halloween Fun; Dr. Spektor app.	1.00	2.00	3.00
34-Tom & Jerry Snowtime Funtime	.25	.50	.75
35-Bugs Bunny Winter Funnies			

	Good	Fine	Mint
	.25	.50	.75
36-Little Lulu & Her Friends	1.00	2.00	3.00
37-W. Woodpecker County Fair	.25	.50	.75
38-The Pink Panther	.20	.40	.60
39-Bugs Bunny Summer Fun	.20	.40	.60
40-Little Lulu & Tubby Trick or Treat - all by Stanley	1.00	2.00	3.00
41-Tom & Jerry Winter Carnival	.20	.40	.60
42-Bugs Bunny	.20	.40	.60
43-Little Lulu in Paris	1.00	2.00	3.00
44-W. Woodpecker Family Fun Festival	.20	.40	.60
45-The Pink Panther	.20	.40	.60
46-Little Lulu & Tubby	1.00	2.00	3.00
47-Bugs Bunny	.20	.40	.60
48-The Lone Ranger	.20	.40	.60

NOTE: *#1-30, 164 pgs.; #31 on, 132 pgs.*

Golden Lad #1, © Spark Publ.

GOLDEN LAD
July, 1945 - #5, June, 1946
Spark Publications

	Good	Fine	Mint
#1-Origin Golden Lad & Swift Arrow	7.00	14.00	21.00
2-Mort Meskin art	4.00	8.00	12.00
3-Mort Meskin art	3.00	6.00	9.00
4	3.00	6.00	9.00
5-Origin Golden Girl; Shaman & Flame app.	5.00	10.00	15.00

GOLDEN LEGACY
1966 - 1972 (Black History)   (25¢)
Fitzgerald Publishing Co.

#1-Toussaint L'Ouverture ('66)
 2-Harriet Tubman ('67)
 3-Crispus Attucks & the Minutemen ('67)
 4-Benjamin Banneker ('68)
 5-Matthew Henson ('69)
 6-Alexander Dumas & Family ('69)
 7-Frederick Douglass, Part 1 ('69)
 8-Frederick Douglass, Part 2 ('70)
 9-Robert Smalls ('70)
10-J. Cinque & the Amistad Mutiny ('70)
11-The Life of Alexander Pushkin ('71)
12-Black Cowboys ('72)
13-The Life of Martin Luther King, Jr. ('72)
14-Men of Action: White, Marshall J. Wilkins ('72)
15-Ancient African Kingdoms ('72)

	Good	Fine	Mint
each....	.35	.70	1.05
#11,14('76)-reprints		.15	.30

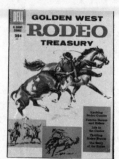

Golden West Rodeo Treasury #1, © Dell   Goofy #2, © STD   Gorgo #3, © CC

GOLDEN LOVE STORIES (Formerly Golden West
#4, April, 1950   Love)
Kirby Publishing Co.

	Good	Fine	Mint
#4-Powell art; cover features picture of Glenn			
Ford & Janet Leigh	1.75	3.35	5.00

GOLDEN PICTURE STORY BOOK
Dec, 1961 (52pgs.; 50¢; Large Size)(Disney)
Racine Press (Western)

#ST-1-Huckleberry Hound	1.00	2.00	3.00
ST-2-Yogi Bear	1.00	2.00	3.00
ST-3-Babes in Toyland (Walt Disney's --)			
	2.00	4.00	6.00
ST-4-(--of Disney Ducks)-Walt Disney's Won-			
derful World of Ducks(Donald Duck, Uncle			
Scrooge, Donald's Nephews, Grandma Duck,			
Ludwig Von Drake, & Gyro Gearloose stor-			
ies)	3.00	6.00	9.00

GOLDEN WEST LOVE (Golden Love Stories #4)
Sept-Oct, 1949 - #3, Feb, 1950
Kirby Publishing Co.

#1-Powell art	2.00	4.00	6.00
2,3-Powell art	1.50	3.00	4.50

GOLDEN WEST RODEO TREASURY
1957 (25¢-Giant)
Dell Publishing Co.

#1	2.50	5.00	7.50

GOLDILOCKS (See March of Comics #1)

GOLDILOCKS & THE THREE BEARS
1943 (Giveaway)
K. K. Publications

	4.00	8.00	12.00

GOLD KEY SPOTLIGHT
May, 1976 - Present
Gold Key

#1-Tom, Dick & Harriet		.15	.30
2-Wacky Advs. of Cracky		.15	.30
3-Wacky Witch		.15	.30
4-Tom, Dick & Harriet		.15	.30
5-Wacky Advs. of Cracky		.15	.30
6-Dagar the Invincible-Santos art; origin			
Demonomicon	.15	.30	.45
7			
8-The Occult Files of Dr. Spector-Santos art			
	.15	.30	.45
9-Tragg	.15	.30	.45
10-O.G. Whiz		.15	.30

GOLD MEDAL COMICS
1945 (132 pgs.)
Cambridge House

	Good	Fine	Mint
#1-Captain Truth	4.00	8.00	12.00
2-5	2.00	4.00	6.00

GOMER PYLE (TV)
July, 1966 - #3, Jan, 1967
Gold Key

#1-3	.20	.40	.60

GOODBYE, MR. CHIPS (See Movie Comics)

GOOFY
May, 1953 - Sept-Nov, 1962
Dell Publishing Co.

4-Color #468,562,627,658,702			
	1.00	2.00	3.00
4-Color #747,802,857,899,952,987,1053,1094,			
1149,1201	.80	1.60	2.40
#12-308-211(Dell,9-11/62)	.40	.80	1.20

GOOFY COMICS
June, 1943 - 1953
Nedor Publ. Co. #1-14/Standard #18-48(Animat-
ed Cartoons)

#1	2.00	4.00	6.00
2	1.00	2.00	3.00
3-19	.65	1.35	2.00
20-35-Frazetta text illos in all			
	1.75	3.35	5.00
36-48	.40	.80	1.20

GOOSE (Humor Magazine)
Sept, 1976 - #3, 1976 (52pgs.) (75¢)
Cousins Publ. (Fawcett)

#1-3	.20	.40	.60

GORDO (See Comics Revue #5)

GORGO (Based on movie) (See Return of --)
May, 1961 - #23, Sept, 1965
Charlton Comics

#1-Ditko art, 22pgs.	3.35	6.75	10.00
2,3-Ditko cvr.& stories	2.00	4.00	6.00
4-10: #4-Ditko cover	1.50	3.00	4.50
11,13-16-Ditko art	1.00	2.00	3.00
12,17-23: #12-Reptisaurus x-over; Montes/			
Bache art-#17-23	.80	1.60	2.40
Gorgo's Revenge('62)-Becomes Return of Gorgo			
	1.50	3.00	4.50

185

GOTHIC ROMANCES
January, 1975 (B&W Magazine) (75¢)
Atlas/Seaboard Publ.

	Good	Fine	Mint
#1-Adams art	.35	.70	1.05

GOVERNOR & J.J., THE (TV)
Feb, 1970 - #3, Aug, 1970
Gold Key

#1	.20	.40	.60
2,3	.15	.30	.45

GRANDMA DUCK (See 4-Color #763,873,965,
1010,1073,1161,1279)

GRAND PRIX (Formerly Hot Rod Racers)
1967 - #44, May, 1972
Charlton Comics

#16-44: Features Rick Roberts		
	.15	.30

GRAY GHOST, THE (See 4-Color #911,1000)

GREAT ACTION COMICS
1958 (Reprints)
I.W. Enterprises

#1-Captain Truth	1.00	2.00	3.00
8,9-Phantom Lady #15 & ?-3.00	6.00	9.00	

GREAT AMERICAN COMICS PRESENTS - THE SECRET
VOICE
1945 (10¢)
Peter George 4-Star Publ./Amer.Features Synd.

#1-All anti-Nazi	4.00	8.00	12.00

GREAT CAT FAMILY, THE (See 4-Color #750)

GREAT COMICS
Nov, 1941 - #3, Jan, 1942
Great Publications

#1-Origin The Great Zarro; Madame Strange			
begins; Captain Power & The Defender app.			
	15.00	30.00	45.00
2	9.00	18.00	27.00
3-Futuro Takes Hitler to Hell			
	12.00	24.00	36.00

GREAT COMICS
1945
Novack Publishing Co.

#1-The Defenders, Capt. Power app.; Cole			
cover	3.00	6.00	9.00

GREAT DOGPATCH MYSTERY (See Mammy Yokum &
the --)
GREAT EXPLOITS
Oct, 1957
Decker Publ./Red Top

	Good	Fine	Mint
#1-Two Krigstein stories (re-issue on cover)			
reprts/Daring Advs.#6	1.00	2.00	3.00

GREAT FOODINI, THE (See Foodini)

GREAT GAZOO, THE (The Flintstones)
Aug, 1973 - #20, Jan, 1977 (Hanna-Barbera)
Charlton Comics

#1	.15	.30
2-20	.10	.20

GREAT GRAPE APE, THE
Sept, 1976 - #2, Nov, 1976 (Hanna-Barbera)
Charlton Comics

#1,2	.10	.20

GREAT LOCOMOTIVE CHASE, THE(See 4-Color #712)

GREAT LOVER ROMANCES
March, 1951 - #22, May, 1955
Toby Press

#1-Jon Juan reprt/JJ #1 by Schomburg			
	1.50	3.00	4.50
2-5,7,9-22	.40	.80	1.20
6- Kurtzman art	1.75	3.35	5.00
8-Five full pgs. of "Pin-Up Pete" by Powell			
	1.75	3.35	5.00

GREAT RACE, THE (See Movie Classics)

GREAT SCOTT SHOE STORE (See Bulls-Eye)

GREAT SOCIETY, THE (Political Satire)
1966 ($1.00) (Also see Bobman & Teddy)
Parallax

Along Ranger; Captain Marvelous; Colonel
America; Phantasm; Super LBJ; Wonderbird
1.00 2.00 3.00

GREAT WEST (Magazine)
1969 (52 pgs.) (Black & White)
M. F. Enterprises

V1#1	.25	.50	.75

GREAT WESTERN
Jan-Mar, 1954 - #11, Oct-Dec, 1954
Magazine Enterprises

Great American Comics--#1, © Amer. Feat.

Great Comics #1('41), © GP

Great Exploits #1, © Decker

Green Giant #1, © Pelican Publ.

Green Hornet #9, © Harv

Green Hornet #15, © Harv

(Great Western cont'd)	Good	Fine	Mint
#8(A-1#93)-origin The Ghost Rider	3.00	6.00	9.00
#9(A-1#105),10(A-1#113),11(A-1#127)- Ghost Rider in #9-11, Durango Kid in all	2.00	4.00	6.00
IW Reprint #1,2,9: Straight Arrow app. in #1,2	.65	1.35	2.00
IW Reprint #8-Origin Ghost Rider(Tim Holt #11); Tim Holt app.; Bolle art	1.75	3.35	5.00

GREEN BERET, THE   (See Tales of --)

GREEN GIANT COMICS
1940   (no price on cover)
Pelican Publications (Funnies, Inc.?)

#1-Dr. Nerod, Green Giant & Master Mystic app. (Rare)	90.00	180.00	270.00

NOTE: *Three copies found in estate that produced the Motion Picture Funnies Weekly issues. Contains 5 pgs. reprinted from Motion Picture Funnies Weekly.*

GREEN HORNET   (TV)
Feb, 1967 - #3, Aug, 1967
Gold Key

#1	1.25	2.50	3.75
2,3	.65	1.35	2.00

GREEN HORNET   (See 4-Color Comics #496)

GREEN HORNET COMICS   (-- Fights Crime #37)
Dec, 1940 - #47, Sept, 1949
Helnit Publ.(Holyoke)#1/Harvey Publ.

#1-Green Hornet begins	60.00	120.00	180.00
2	30.00	60.00	90.00

	Good	Fine	Mint
3	20.00	40.00	60.00
4	15.00	30.00	45.00
5	12.00	24.00	36.00
6	10.00	20.00	30.00
7-Origin The Zebra; Robin Hood & Spirit of 76 begin	15.00	30.00	45.00
8-10	9.00	18.00	27.00
11,12-Mr. Q in both	7.00	14.00	21.00
13-20: #20-Kubert art	6.00	12.00	18.00
21-30: #30-Kubert art	5.00	10.00	15.00
31-The Man in Black Called Fate begins	5.00	10.00	15.00
32-36	5.00	10.00	15.00
37-Shock Gibson app.; S&K Kid Adonis reprtd. from Stuntman #3	7.00	14.00	21.00
38-Shock Gibson, Kid Adonis app.	5.00	10.00	15.00
39-Stuntman story by S&K	10.00	20.00	30.00
40,41	3.00	6.00	9.00
42-47-Kerry Drake in all	3.00	6.00	9.00

NOTE: *Powell art-#7-10,31-34 (Man in Black).*

GREEN JET COMICS, THE
1950   (5½x8½", 16pgs., in color) Soft cover
Metropolitan Printing Co.   (Giveaway)

#1-Green Lama by Raboy	15.00	30.00	45.00
2-No Green Lama	1.50	3.00	4.50

GREEN LAMA   (Also see Green Jet #1)
Dec, 1944 - #8, March, 1946
Spark Publications

#1-Intro. The Green Lama, Lt. Hercules & The Boy Champions; Mac Raboy art #1-8	20.00	40.00	60.00
2	12.00	24.00	36.00
3-8: #4-Robinson story	9.00	18.00	27.00

The Green Jet #1, © Metro. Print. Co.

Green Lama #7, © Spark Publ.

Green Lantern #1('41), © DC

Green Lantern #15, © DC

Green Lantern #8, © DC

Green Lantern #77, © DC

GREEN LANTERN (1st Series)(See All-American)
Autumn, 1941 - #38, May-June, 1949
National Periodical Publ./All-American

	Good	Fine	Mint
#1-Origin retold	100.00	200.00	300.00
2	60.00	120.00	180.00
3	40.00	80.00	120.00
4	30.00	60.00	90.00
5	27.50	55.00	82.50
6,7	25.00	50.00	75.00
8-Hop Harrigan begins	25.00	50.00	75.00
9	20.00	40.00	60.00
10-Origin Vandal Savage	20.00	40.00	60.00
11-20: #12-Origin Gambler	16.50	33.25	50.00
21-30: #27-Origin Sky Pirate	13.50	26.75	40.00
31-38: #37-Sargon the Sorcerer app.	12.00	24.00	36.00

NOTE: Book-length stories #2-8. Toth art-#28,
30,31,34-38; covers-#30,34,36-38.

GREEN LANTERN(2nd Series)(See Showcase,Flash)
7-8/60 - #89, 4-5/72; #90, 8-9/76 - Present
National Periodical Publications/DC Comics

#1-Origin retold; Gil Kane art begins	20.00	40.00	60.00
2-1st Pieface	10.00	20.00	30.00
3-5: #5-Origin & 1st app. Hector Hammond; 1st 5700 A.D. story	5.00	10.00	15.00
6-10: #7-Origin Sinestro. #9-1st Jordan Brothers	3.00	6.00	9.00
11-20: #13-Flash x-over. #14-Origin Sonar. #16-Origin Star Sapphire. #20-Flash x-over	1.75	3.35	5.00
21-30: #21-Origin Dr. Polaris. #23-1st Tatooed Man. #24-Origin Shark. #29-JLA cameo; 1st Blackhand	1.20	2.40	3.60
31-40: #40-G.A. Green Lantern x-over; origin The Guardians	.75	1.50	2.25
41-50: #42-Zatanna x-over. #43-Flash x-over. #45-G.A. Green Lantern x-over	.50	1.00	1.50
51-75: #52,61-G.A. Green Lantern x-over. #67-G.A. Green Lantern origin retold. #69-Wood inks	.35	.70	1.05
76-Begin Green Lantern/Green Arrow series by Neal Adams	6.00	12.00	18.00
77	3.00	6.00	9.00
78-80	2.50	5.00	7.50
81-83	2.00	4.00	6.00
84-Adams/Wrightson story	2.00	4.00	6.00
85,86-DC drug books	2.50	5.00	7.50
87,89: #89-G.A. Green Lantern stories, 52pgs.	1.50	3.00	4.50
88('72)	.25	.50	.75
90('76)-100	.15	.30	.45

NOTE: Adams stories-#76-87,89; covers-#63,
76-89. Anderson inks-#1,4,9,10,16,21,71,73,
74,87,88;cover inks-#2,9,10,12,14-16,19-44,
52-56,59,61,69. Infantino stories-#53,88;
cover-#53. Gil Kane stories-#1-61,68-75,85,
87,88; covers-#1-52,54-61,67-75. Toth re-
print-#86.

GREEN MASK, THE (The Bouncer #11 on?)
Summer, 1940 - V2#6, Oct-Nov, 1946
Fox Features Syndicate

	Good	Fine	Mint
V1#1-Origin The Green Mask & Domino; reprints/ Mystery Men #1-3,5-7	30.00	60.00	90.00
2	15.00	30.00	45.00
3	10.00	20.00	30.00
4-Navy Jones begins	10.00	20.00	30.00
5	10.00	20.00	30.00
6-The Nightbird begins	8.00	16.00	24.00
7-9	5.00	10.00	15.00
10-Origin One Round Hogan & Rocket Kelly,			
11	5.00	10.00	15.00
V2#1-6	4.00	8.00	12.00
#1(1955-2nd Series)	2.50	5.00	7.50

Green Mask #5, © Fox

GREEN PLANET, THE
1962   (One Shot)
Charlton Comics

No#	.40	.80	1.20

GREETINGS FROM SANTA (See March of Comics #48)

GREYFRIARS BOBBY (See 4-Color Comics #1189)

GRIM GHOST, THE
Jan, 1975 -#3, July, 1975
Atlas/Seaboard Publ.

#1-Origin	.25	.50	.75
2,3-Heath cover	.15	.30	.45

188

GRIMM'S GHOST STORIES (See Dan Curtis)
Jan, 1972 - Present
Gold Key

	Good	Fine	Mint
#1	.25	.50	.75
2-4,6,7,9,10	.20	.40	.60
5,8-Williamson story	.35	.70	1.05
11-16,18-20	.15	.30	.45
17-Crandall story	.25	.50	.75
21-35: #25-Bolle art; .#32,34-reprints			
	.15	.30	.45
36-42		.15	.30

GRIN (The American Funny Book) (Magazine)
Nov, 1972 -#3, April, 1973 (52pgs.)(Satire)
APAG House Pubs

#1	.25	.50	.75
2,3	.20	.40	.60

GRIN & BEAR IT (See Large Feat. Comic #28)

GRIT GRADY (See Holyoke One-Shot #1)

GROOVY (Cartoon Comics-not CCA approved)
March, 1968 - #3, July, 1968
Marvel Comics Group

#1-3	.15	.30	.45

GUADALCANAL DIARY
1945 (One Shot)
David McKay Publishing Co.

No#	2.50	5.00	7.50

GUERRILLA WAR (Formerly Jungle War Stories)
#12, Jul-Sept, 1965 - #14, Mar, 1966
Dell Publishing Co.

#12-14	.15	.30	.45

GUILTY (See Justice Traps the --)

GULF FUNNY WEEKLY (In full color)
1933 - #422, 5/23/41 (4pgs; tabloid size to
2/3/39; 2/10/39 on, reg. comic book size);
early issues undated (Giveaway)
Gulf Oil Company

#1-30	1.75	3.35	5.00
31-100	1.25	2.50	3.75
101-196	1.00	2.00	3.00
197-Wings Winfair begins(1/29/37);by Fred Meagher beginning in '38	15.00	30.00	45.00
198-300(Last tabloid size)	5.00	10.00	15.00
301-350 (Reg. size)	3.00	6.00	9.00
351-422	2.00	4.00	6.00

GULLIVER'S TRAVELS (See Dell Jr.Treasury #3)
Sept-Nov, 1965 - #3, May, 1966
Dell Publishing Co.

	Good	Fine	Mint
#1-3	.65	1.35	2.00

GUMPS, THE
1918 - #8, 1931 (9½x9½") (Black & White)
Cupples & Leon Co./Landfield-Kupfer #4('27)on

1918-(5-3/4"x14")-48pgs. dailies	10.00	20.00	30.00
No#(1924)by Sidney Smith	8.00	16.00	24.00
#2,3	6.00	12.00	18.00
4-7: #6-(10x10")48pgs.	5.00	10.00	15.00
8-(10x14")32pgs. B&W	5.00	10.00	15.00

GUMPS, THE (-- in Radioland)
1937 (95pgs.) (Mostly text)
Pebco Tooth Paste Premium

	8.00	16.00	24.00

GUMPS, THE (Also see Merry Christmas --)
Mar-Apr, 1947 - #5, Nov-Dec, 1947
Dell Publ. Co./All-American/National

4-Color #73(Dell)	3.35	6.75	10.00
#1(1947)	3.00	6.00	9.00
2-5	2.00	4.00	6.00

GUNFIGHTER (Fat & Slat #1-4)(Becomes Haunt
of Fear #15 on)
#5, Summer, 1948 - #14, Mar-Apr, 1950
E.C. Comics

#5,6-Moon Girl in ea.	20.00	40.00	60.00
7-14	20.00	40.00	60.00

NOTE: _Craig & H.C. Kiefer art in most issues.
Feldstein/Craig story-#10. Feldstein stories-
#7-11. Ingels stories-#5-14; covers-#7-12.
Wood stories-#13,14._

GUNFIGHTERS, THE
1963 - 1964
Super Comics (Reprints)

#10,11(Billy the Kid),12(Swift Arrow), 15(Straight Arrow),16,18-All reprints			
	.65	1.35	2.00

GUNFIGHTERS, THE (Formerly Kid Montana)
#51, 10/66 - #52, 10/67
Charlton Comics

#51,52	.15	.30	.45

GUN GLORY (See 4-Color Comics #846)

The Gumps #4 (C&L), © News Synd.

Gunfighter #10, © WMG   Gunfighter #13, © WMG

Guns Against Gangsters #1, © Novp   Gunsmoke #6, © P.L. Publ.   Gunsmoke #27, © Dell

GUNHAWK, THE (Whip Wilson #10,11)
#12, Nov, 1950 - #18, Dec, 1951
Marvel Comics/Atlas (MCI)

	Good	Fine	Mint
#12-18	1.50	3.00	4.50

GUNHAWKS, THE (The Gunhawk #7)
October, 1972 - #7, October, 1973
Marvel Comics Group

#1-Reno Jones, Kid Cassidy	.20	.40	.60
2-5	.15	.30	.45
6-Kid Cassidy dies. #7-Reno Jones solo		.15	.30

GUNMASTER (Judo Master #89 on; formerly
Six-Gun Heroes) (Two #89's)
9/64; 3-4/66 - #89, 10/67
Charlton Comics

V1#1	.50	1.00	1.50
2-4,V5#84-86	.30	.60	.90
V5#87-89	.20	.40	.60

NOTE: *Vol. 5 was originally cancelled with
#88(3-4/66). #89 on became Judo Master, then
later in 1967, Charlton issued #89 as a Gun-
master one-shot.*

GUNS AGAINST GANGSTERS
1948 - 1949
Curtis Publications/Novelty Press

#1	1.35	2.75	4.00
2-6: #4-Toni Gayle	1.00	2.00	3.00
V2#1-Toni Gayle(bondage cover)			
	1.75	3.35	5.00
2	1.00	2.00	3.00

GUNSLINGER (See 4-Color Comics #1220)

GUNSLINGER (Formerly Tex Dawson --)
#2, April, 1973 - #3, June, 1973
Marvel Comics Group

#2,3		.15	.30

GUNSMOKE
Apr-May, 1949 - #16, Jan, 1952
P. L. Publishing Co.

#1-Gunsmoke, Masked Marvel begin, both by			
Ingels #1	4.00	8.00	12.00
2-Ingels cover/story	3.00	6.00	9.00
3-6	2.00	4.00	6.00
7-16	1.00	2.00	3.00

NOTE: *Ingels covers-#1-6; bondage-#1,3.*

GUNSMOKE (TV)

1955 - #27, Jun-Jul, 1961; 2/69 - #6, 2/70
Dell Publishing Co./Gold Key

	Good	Fine	Mint
4-Color #679	1.00	2.00	3.00
4-Color #720,769,797,844	.65	1.35	2.00
#6(11/57), #7	.40	.80	1.20
8,9,11,12-Williamson stories in all, 4pgs.			
each	1.50	3.00	4.50
10-Williamson/Crandall story, 4pgs.			
	1.50	3.00	4.50
13-27	.35	.70	1.05
Gunsmoke Film Story (11/62-G.K. Giant)			
#30008-211	.40	.80	1.20
#1(G.K.)	.20	.40	.60
2-6('69-70)	.15	.30	.45

GUNSMOKE TRAIL
June, 1957 - #4, 1957
Ajax-Farrell Publ./Four Star Comic Corp.

#1	1.00	2.00	3.00
2-4	.40	.80	1.20

GUNSMOKE WESTERN (Formerly Western Tales of
Dec, 1955 - #77, 7/63   Black Rider)
Atlas Comics,#32-35(CPS/NPI); Marvel, #36 on

#32,34,35,37-39	1.00	2.00	3.00
33,36-Williamson stories in both, 5 & 4 pgs.			
+ Drucker #33	1.75	3.50	5.25
40-Williamson/Mayo story, 4pgs.			
	1.75	3.50	5.25
41,42,45-49,51-60: #49,52-Kid From Texas			
story. #57-1st Two Gun Kid by Severin.			
#60-Sam Hawk app. in Kid Colt			
	.60	1.20	1.80
43,44-Torres story	.90	1.80	2.70
50,61-Crandall story	1.20	2.40	3.60
62-71,73-77	.50	1.00	1.50
72-Origin Kid Colt Outlaw	.50	1.00	1.50

NOTE: *Davis art-#50,52,54,55;cover-#54. Ditko
story-#66. Kirby stories-#59,62,63,65-67,69,
71,73,77; cover-#56(w/Ditko),57,58,63,66,68,
69,71-77. Wildey story-#42,57. Kid Colt in
all. Two-Gun Kid in #57,59,60-62,63,66. Wyatt
Earp in #45,48,49,52,54,55,58.*

GUNS OF FACT & FICTION (See A-1 Comics #13)

GUN THAT WON THE WEST, THE
1956 (28 pgs.) (Regular size) (Giveaway)
Winchester-Western Division & Olin Mathieson
Chemical Corp.

No#-Painted cover	1.00	2.00	3.00

GYPSY COLT (See 4-Color Comics #568)

190

GYRO GEARLOOSE (See Walt Disney Showcase #18)
Nov, 1959 - May-July, 1962   (Disney)
Dell Publishing Co.

	Good	Fine	Mint
4-Color #1047,1095,1184,1267-All by Carl Barks			
	3.00	6.00	9.00
4-Color #1329, #01329-207(5-7/62)-Barks cover			
only	1.75	3.35	5.00

HA HA COMICS (Teepee.Tim #100 on)
Oct, 1943 - #99, Jan, 1955
Creston Publ. #1-61/American Comics Group

#1	3.00	6.00	9.00
2-5	1.00	2.00	3.00
6-20	.65	1.35	2.00
21-40	.50	1.00	1.50
41-99	.40	.80	1.20

HAIR BEAR BUNCH, THE (TV) (See Fun-In #13)
Feb, 1972 - #9, Feb, 1974 (Hanna-Barbera)
Gold Key

#1-9		.15	.30

HALLELUJAH TRAIL, THE (See Movie Classics)

HAND OF FATE (Formerly Mr. Risk)
#8, Dec, 1951 - #26, March, 1955
Ace Magazines

#8	.90	1.80	2.70
9-24,26	.65	1.35	2.00
25(11/54),25(12/54)	.65	1.35	2.00

NOTE: Cameron art-#20-23,25(both). Nostrand
art-#25.

HANDS OF THE DRAGON
June, 1975
Seaboard Periodicals (Atlas)

#1-Origin	.25	.50	.75

HANGMAN COMICS (Special #1; Black Hood #9 on)
#2, Spring, 1942 - #8, Fall, 1943
MLJ Magazines

#2-The Hangman, Boy Buddies begin			
	30.00	60.00	90.00
3-8	16.50	33.25	50.00

HANK
1946
Pentagon Publications

No#-Coulton Waugh's newspaper reprint			
	.50	1.00	1.50

HANNA-BARBERA (See Golden Comics Dig. #2,7,11)

HANNA-BARBERA BAND WAGON
Oct, 1962 - #3, April, 1963
Gold Key

	Good	Fine	Mint
#1,2-Giants, 84pgs.	.35	.70	1.05
3-Regular size	.25	.50	.75

HANNA-BARBERA HI-ADVENTURE HEROES (See Hi --)

HANNA-BARBERA PARADE
Sept, 1971 - #10, Dec, 1972
Charlton Comics

#1,2,4-10	.35	.70	1.05
3-"Summer Picnic"-52pgs.	.25	.50	.75

NOTE: #4 (1/72) went on sale late in 1972
with the Jan. 1973 issues.

HANNA-BARBERA SUPER TV HEROES
April, 1968 - #7, Oct, 1969 (Hanna-Barbera)
Gold Key

#1-The Birdman, The Herculoids, Moby Dick,			
Samson & Goliath, & The Mighty Mightor			
begin	.40	.80	1.20
2-The Galaxy Trio only app.; Shazzan begins-			
no Samson & Goliath	.25	.50	.75
3-7: #3-The Space Ghost app.; also #3,6,7,			
no Herculoids; no Samson & Goliath in #4-7			
	.40	.80	1.20

HANS AND FRITZ
1917 (16pgs)(10x13½" B&W Sunday strip reprts)
The Saalfield Publishing Co.

By R. Dirks, 16 pgs.	15.00	30.00	45.00

HANS BRINKER (See 4-Color Comics #1273)

HANS CHRISTIAN ANDERSON
1953   (100 pgs.-Special Issue)
Ziff-Davis Publ. Co.

No#-Danny Kaye (movie)	2.50	5.00	7.50

HANSEL & GRETEL (See 4-Color #590)

HAP HAZARD COMICS (Real Love #25 on)
1944 - #24, Feb, 1949
Ace Magazines (Readers' Research)

#1	1.50	3.00	4.50
2-10	1.00	2.00	3.00
11-13,15-24	.65	1.35	2.00
14-Feldstein cover(4/47)	2.00	4.00	6.00

HAP HOPPER (See Comics Revue #2)

HAPPIEST MILLIONAIRE, THE (See Movie Comics)

Ha Ha Comics #1, © ACG

Hangman Comics #8, © MLJ

Hank #1, © Pentagon Publ.

Happy Comics #12, © Std   Happy Houlihans #1, © WMG   Harold Teen (1929)(C&L), © Chicago Tribune

HAPPI TIM   (See March of Comics #182)

HAPPY COMICS   (Happy Rabbit #41 on)
1943 - #40, Dec, 1950
Nedor Publ./Standard Comics(Animated Cartoons)

	Good	Fine	Mint
#1	2.00	4.00	6.00
2-10	.80	1.60	2.40
11-19	.50	1.00	1.50
20-31,34-37-Frazetta text illos in all; 2 in			
#34	1.35	2.75	4.00
32-Frazetta story, 7pgs.	4.00	8.00	12.00
33-Two Frazetta stories, 6pgs. each (Scarce)			
	7.00	14.00	21.00
38-40	.35	.70	1.05

HAPPY HOLIDAY   (See March of Comics #181)

HAPPY HOOLIGAN   (See Alphonse --)
1903 (18pgs.)(Sunday strip reprints in color)
Hearsts New York American-Journal

Book 1-by Fred Opper	20.00	50.00	80.00
50pg. Edition(1903)-10x15" in color			
	25.00	62.50	100.00

HAPPY HOOLIGAN   (Handy --)
1908 (32pgs. in color)(10x15",cardboard cvrs)
Frederick A. Stokes Co.

	15.00	37.50	60.00

HAPPY HOOLIGAN   (Story of --)
1932   (16pgs.) (9½x12")(Softcover)
McLoughlin Bros.

#281-Three-color text, pictures on heavy			
paper	5.00	10.00	15.00

HAPPY HOULIHANS   (Saddle Justice #3 on)
Fall, 1947 - #2, Winter, 1947-48
E.C. Comics

#1-Origin Moon Girl	15.00	30.00	45.00
2	7.00	14.00	21.00

HAPPY JACK
August, 1957
Red Top (Decker)

V1#1	1.00	2.00	3.00

HAPPY JACK HOWARD
1957
Red Top(Farrell)/Decker

No#-Reprints Handy Andy story from E.C.			
Dandy Comics #5, renamed "Happy Jack"			
	1.00	2.00	3.00

HAPPY RABBIT   (Formerly Happy Comics)
#41, Feb, 1950 - #48, April, 1952
Standard Comics (Animated Cartoons)

	Good	Fine	Mint
#41-48	.25	.50	.75

HAPPY TIME XMAS BOOK
1952   (Christmas Giveaway)
F. W. Woolworth Co.

	1.75	3.35	5.00

HARDY BOYS, THE   (See 4-Color #760,830,887,
964-Disney)

HARDY BOYS, THE   (TV)
April, 1970 - #4, Jan, 1971
Gold Key

#1-4	.25	.50	.75

HARLEM GLOBETROTTERS   (TV)(See Fun-In #8,10)
April, 1972 - #12, Jan, 1975 (Hanna-Barbera)
Gold Key

#1-12		.10	.20

NOTE: #4,8 and 12 contain 16 extra pages of
advertising.

HAROLD TEEN   (See 4-Color #2,209, & Treasure
Box of Famous Comics)

HAROLD TEEN   (Adv. of --)
1929-31   (36-52pgs.) (Paper covers)
Cupples & Leon Co.

B&W daily strip reprints by Carl Ed			
	10.00	20.00	30.00

HARVEY
Oct, 1970; #2, 12/70; #3, 6/72 - #6, 12/72
Marvel Comics Group

#1-6		.10	.20

HARVEY COLLECTORS COMICS (Richie Rich Coll-
ectors Comics #10 on)
Sept, 1975 - #9, 1976   (52 pgs.) (35¢)
Harvey Publications

#1	.15	.30	.45
2-9		.15	.30

NOTE: All reprints: Casper-#2,3, Richie Rich-
#1,6,8, Wendy-#4.

HARVEY COMICS HITS
Oct, 1951 - #61, Oct, 1952
Harvey Publications

(Harvey Com. Hits cont'd)	Good	Fine	Mint
#51-The Phantom	6.00	12.00	18.00
52-Steve Canyon	4.00	8.00	12.00
53-Mandrake the Magician	5.00	10.00	15.00
54-Tim Tyler's Tales of Jungle Terror			
	3.35	6.75	10.00
55-Mary Worth	2.50	5.00	7.50
56-The Phantom	5.00	10.00	15.00
57-Rip Kirby by Alex Raymond-"Kidnap Racket"			
	10.00	20.00	30.00
58-Girls in White	1.75	3.35	5.00
59-Tales of the Invisible Scarlet O'Neil			
	5.00	10.00	15.00
60			
61-Casper the Friendly Ghost			
	1.75	3.50	5.25

HARVEY COMICS LIBRARY
April, 1952 - #2, 1952
Harvey Publications

#1-Teen-Age Dope Slaves as exposed by Rex Morgan, M.D.; used in Seduction of the Innocent	70.00	140.00	210.00
(Prices vary widely on this book)			
2-Sparkle Plenty (Dick Tracy in "Blackmail Terror")	5.00	10.00	15.00

HARVEY HITS
Sept, 1957 - #122, Nov, 1967
Harvey Publications

#1-The Phantom	5.00	10.00	15.00
2-Rags Rabbit(10/57)	.65	1.35	2.00
3-Richie Rich(11/57)-1st app.			
	8.00	16.00	24.00
4-Little Dot's Uncles	.65	1.35	2.00
5			
6-The Phantom-Kirby cvr.	3.00	6.00	9.00
7-Wendy the Witch	.65	1.35	2.00
8-Sad Sack	.65	1.35	2.00
9-Richie Rich	1.35	2.75	4.00
10-Little Lotta	.65	1.35	2.00
11-Little Audrey Summer Fun(7/58)			
	.65	1.35	2.00
12-The Phantom-Kirby cvr.	3.00	6.00	9.00
13			
14-Herman & Katnip(10/58)	.65	1.35	2.00
15-The Phantom(1958)	2.50	5.00	7.50
16-Wendy the Witch	.50	1.00	1.50
17-Sad Sack's Army Life	.35	.70	1.05
18-Buzzy & the Crow	.50	1.00	1.50
19-Sad Sack Army Life	.35	.70	1.05
20-Casper & Spooky	.50	1.00	1.50
21-Wendy the Witch	.50	1.00	1.50
22-Sad Sack's Army Life	.35	.70	1.05
22-Baby Huey-the Baby Giant	.50	1.00	1.50
23-Wendy the Witch	.50	1.00	1.50

	Good	Fine	Mint
24-Little Dot's Uncles	.50	1.00	1.50
25-Herman & Kapnip	.50	1.00	1.50
26-The Phantom(11/59)	2.50	5.00	7.50
27-Wendy the Good Little Witch			
	.50	1.00	1.50
28-Sad Sack's Army Life	.35	.70	1.05
29-Harvey-Toon('60)-Casper, Buzzy			
	.50	1.00	1.50
30			
31-Herman & Kapnip	.50	1.00	1.50
32			
33			
34-Harvey-Toon	.35	.70	1.05
35-Funday Funnies	.35	.70	1.05
36-The Phantom(1960)	2.00	4.00	6.00
37-Casper & Nightmare	.50	1.00	1.50
38			
39-Sad Sack's Army Life	.35	.70	1.05
40			
41-Herman & Katnip	.50	1.00	1.50
42			
43-Sad Sack's Army Life	.35	.70	1.05
44-The Phantom	2.00	4.00	6.00
45-Casper & Nightmare	.50	1.00	1.50
46-Harvey-Toon	.50	1.00	1.50
47-Sad Sack's Army Life(8/61)			
	.35	.70	1.05
48-The Phantom(1961)	2.00	4.00	6.00
49-Little Audrey	.50	1.00	1.50
50-Stumbo the Giant	.25	.50	.75
51-Sad Sack's Army Life	.20	.40	.60
52-Little Audrey	.25	.50	.75
53-Little Audrey	.25	.50	.75
54			
55-Sad Sack's Army Life	.20	.40	.60
56-Casper & Nightmare	.25	.50	.75
57-Stumbo the Giant	.25	.50	.75
58-Sad Sack's Army Life	.20	.40	.60
59-Casper & Nightmare	.25	.50	.75
60-Stumbo the Giant(9/62)	.25	.50	.75
61-Sad Sack	.20	.40	.60
62			
63-Stumbo the Giant	.25	.50	.75
64-Sad Sack's Army Life	.20	.40	.60
65			
66			
67			
68			
69			
70-Sad Sack's Army Life	.20	.40	.60
71-Nightmare	.20	.40	.60
72-Stumbo	.20	.40	.60
73-Little Sad Sack	.20	.40	.60
74-Sad Sack's Muttsy	.20	.40	.60
75-Sad Sack's Funny Friends	.20	.40	.60
76-Little Sad Sack	.20	.40	.60
77-Sad Sack's Muttsy	.20	.40	.60

Harvey Comics Hits #54, © Harv

Harvey Comics Library #1, © Harv

Harvey Hits #2, © Harv

Haunted Thrills #1, © Ajax

Haunt of Fear #5, © WMG

Haunt Of Fear #20, © WMG

(Harvey Hits cont'd)	Good	Fine	Mint
78-Stumbo the Giant	.20	.40	.60
79			
80-Sad Sack's Muttsy	.20	.40	.60
81			
82-Sad Sack's Muttsy	.20	.40	.60
83-Little Sad Sack	.20	.40	.60
84-Muttsy-the Talking Dog(1965)			
	.20	.40	.60
85-Gabby Gob	.20	.40	.60
86-G.I. Juniors	.20	.40	.60
87-Muttsy-the Talking Dog	.20	.40	.60
88-Stumbo the Giant	.20	.40	.60
89-Sad Sack's Muttsy	.20	.40	.60
90-Gabby Gob	.20	.40	.60
91-G.I. Juniors	.20	.40	.60
92-Muttsy-the Talking Dog (1965)			
	.20	.40	.60
93-Sadie Sack	.20	.40	.60
94			
95-G.I. Juniors	.20	.40	.60
96-Sad Sack's Muttsy(9/65)	.20	.40	.60
97-Gabby Gob	.20	.40	.60
98-G.I. Juniors	.20	.40	.60
99-Sad Sack's Muttsy(12/65)	.20	.40	.60
100			
101-G.I. Juniors	.15	.30	.45
102-Sad Sack's Muttsy	.15	.30	.45
103-Gabby Gob	.15	.30	.45
104-G.I. Juniors	.15	.30	.45
105-Sad Sack's Muttsy	.15	.30	.45
106-Gabby Gob	.15	.30	.45
107-G.I. Juniors(1966)	.15	.30	.45
108-Sad Sack's Muttsy	.15	.30	.45
109			
110			
111-Sad Sack's Muttsy	.15	.30	.45
112-G.I. Juniors	.15	.30	.45
113-Sad Sack's Muttsy	.15	.30	.45
114-G.I. Juniors	.15	.30	.45
115-Sad Sack's Muttsy	.15	.30	.45
116-G.I. Juniors	.15	.30	.45
117-Sad Sack's Muttsy	.15	.30	.45
118-G.I. Juniors	.15	.30	.45
119-Sad Sack's Muttsy	.15	.30	.45
120-G.I. Juniors	.15	.30	.45
121-Sad Sack's Muttsy	.15	.30	.45
122-G.I. Juniors	.15	.30	.45

HARVEY POP COMICS (Teen Humor)
Oct, 1968 - #2, Nov, 1969
Harvey Publications

#1,2-The Cowsills	.20	.40	.60

HARVEY 3-D HITS (See Sad Sack)

HARVEY TOON (See Harvey Hits #29,34,46)

HATARI (See Movie Classics)

HATHAWAYS, THE (See 4-Color Comics #1298)

HAUNTED (See This Mag Is Haunted)

HAUNTED (-- Library #21 on)
9/71 - #30, 11/76; #31, 9/77 - #32, 10/77
Charlton Comics

	Good	Fine	Mint
#1	.15	.30	.45
2-16,18-20,22-32		.10	.20
17,21-Newton story	.15	.30	.45

NOTE: *Ditko* art-#1-5,7,8,13,15,16,18; covers-#1-7. *Howard* story-#18. *Newton* covers-#21,22.

HAUNTED LOVE
April, 1973 - #11, Sept, 1975
Charlton Comics

#1-Tom Sutton love story, 16 pgs.			
	.15	.30	.45
2,3,6-11		.10	.20
4,5-Ditko stories	.15	.30	.45

NOTE: *Howard* story-#8. *Newton* cover-#8,9.

HAUNTED THRILLS
June, 1952 - #21, Nov, 1954
Ajax/Farrell Publications

#1	1.35	2.75	4.00
2-5	.80	1.60	2.40
6-21	.65	1.35	2.00

HAUNT OF FEAR (Formerly Gunfighter)
#15, May-June, 1950 - #28, Nov-Dec, 1954
E.C. Comics

#15(1950)	75.00	150.00	225.00
16	40.00	80.00	120.00
17-Origin of Crypt of Terror, Vault of Horror, & Haunt of Fear	30.00	60.00	90.00
#4	23.50	46.75	70.00
5-10	16.50	33.25	50.00
11-13,15-18,20	13.50	26.75	40.00
14-Origin Old Witch by Ingels			
	16.50	33.25	50.00
19-Used in *Seduction of the Innocent*			
	16.50	33.25	50.00
21-28	10.00	20.00	30.00

(*Canadian reprints known; see Table of Contents.*

NOTE: *Craig* stories-#15-17,5,7,10,12,13; covers-#15-17,5-7. *Crandall* stories-#20,21,26,27. *Davis* stories-#4-26,28. *Evans* stories-#15-19, 22-25,27. *Feldstein* stories-#15-17,20; covers-#4,8-10. *Ingels* stories-#16,4-28; covers-#11-28. *Kamen* stories-#16,4,6,7,9-11,13-19, 21-28. *Krigstein* story-#28. *Kurtzman* stories-

(Haunt of Fear cont'd)
#15/1,17/3. <u>*Orlando*</u> *stories-#9,12.* <u>*Wood*</u> *stories-#15,16,4-6.*

HAUNT OF HORROR, THE (Magazine) (75¢)
May, 1974 - #5, Jan, 1975 (B&W)
Cadence Comics Publ. (Marvel)

	Good	Fine	Mint
#1-Alcala art	.65	1.35	2.00
2-Origin & 1st app. Gabriel the Devil Hunter;			
Satana begins	.40	.80	1.20
3	.40	.80	1.20
4-Adams art	.50	1.00	1.50
5-Two Evans stories	.40	.80	1.20

HAVE GUN, WILL TRAVEL (TV)
1958 - #14, July-Sept, 1962
Dell Publishing Co.

	Good	Fine	Mint
4-Color #931,983,1044	.60	1.20	1.80
#4-14	.35	.70	1.05

HAWAIIAN EYE (TV)
July, 1963
Gold Key

	Good	Fine	Mint
#1(10073-307)	.35	.70	1.05

HAWAIIAN ILLUSTRATED LEGENDS SERIES
1975 (B&W)(Cover printed w/blue,yellow,green)
Hogarth Press

#1-Kalelealuaka, the Mysterious Warrior			
	.25	.50	.75
2,3	.20	.40	.60

HAWK, THE (Also see Approved Comics)
Winter, 1951 - #12, May, 1955
Ziff-Davis/St. John Publ. Co. #3 on

#1-Anderson art	3.35	6.75	10.00
2-Kubert art	2.50	5.00	7.50
3-8,10-12: #8-reprints #3 with different			
cover. #10-reprts. 1 story/#2			
	1.20	2.40	3.60
9-Kubert story reprt/#2	2.00	4.00	6.00
3-D#1(11/53)-Baker cover	4.00	8.00	12.00

HAWK & THE DOVE, THE (See Showcase)
Aug-Sept, 1968 - #6, June-July, 1969
National Periodical Publications

#1-Ditko cover/art	.65	1.35	2.00
2- " " "	.50	1.00	1.50
3-6: #5-Teen Titans cameo	.40	.80	1.20
NOTE: <u>*Gil Kane*</u> *art/cover-#3-6.*

HAWKEYE & THE LAST OF THE MOHICANS
(See 4-Color Comics #884)

HAWKMAN (See The Brave & the Bold, Mystery
in Space, Atom & Hawkman)
April-May, 1964 - #27, Aug-Sept, 1968
National Periodical Publications

	Good	Fine	Mint
#1	2.50	5.00	7.50
2	1.50	3.00	4.50
3-5: #4-Zatanna x-over	1.35	2.75	4.00
6-10: #9-Atom cameo	1.00	2.00	3.00
11-15	.65	1.35	2.00
16-27: Adam Strange x-over #18; cameo #19.			
#25-G.A. Hawkman reprint.50	1.00	1.50
NOTE: <u>*Anderson*</u> *stories-#1-21; covers-#1-21.*
<u>*Kubert*</u> *cover-#27.*

HAWKSHAW THE DETECTIVE (See Okay)
1917 (10½x13½") (Sunday strip reprints)
(Black & White) (24 pgs.)
The Saalfield Publishing Co.

By Gus Mager	5.00	10.00	15.00

HAWTHORN-MELODY FARMS DAIRY COMICS
No Date ('50's) (Giveaway)
Everybody's Publishing Co.

Cheerie Chick, Tuffy Turtle, Robin Koo Koo,			
Donald & Longhorn Legends 1.00	2.00	3.00

HEADLINE COMICS (-- Crime #32-39)
2/43 - #22, 11-12/46; 1947 - #77, 10/56
Prize Publications

#1-Yank & Doodle x-over in Junior Rangers			
	5.00	10.00	15.00
2	2.50	5.00	7.50
3	2.00	4.00	6.00
4-10	1.50	3.00	4.50
11,12,17,18	1.25	2.50	3.75
13-15-Blue Streak in all	1.50	3.00	4.50
16-Origin Atomic Man	1.50	3.00	4.50
19-21-S&K art	3.35	6.75	10.00
22	1.50	3.00	4.50
23,24-(100% S&K)	4.00	8.00	12.00
25-35-S&K covers/stories	3.00	6.00	9.00
36-S&K story	2.50	5.00	7.50
37-1pg. S&K, Severin art	1.75	3.35	5.00
38,40-Meskin art	1.50	3.00	4.50
39,41-43,45-55	.75	1.50	2.25
44-S&K cover, Severin/Elder story, Meskin			
story	2.50	5.00	7.50
56-58-S&K art	2.00	4.00	6.00
59-77	.65	1.35	2.00

The Hawk & The Dove #1, © DC

Hawkman #26, © DC

Headline Comics #1, © Prize

Heart Throbs #1, © Qua

Heart Throbs #10, © Qua

Hello Pal Comics #3, © Harv

HEAP, THE
Sept, 1971   (52 pgs.)
Skywald Publications

	Good	Fine	Mint
#1-Kinstler story reprint from Strange Worlds #8	.25	.50	.75

HEART AND SOUL
1954
Mikeross Publications

	Good	Fine	Mint
#1,2	.35	.70	1.05

HEART THROBS (Love Stories #147 on)
Aug, 1949 - #146, Oct, 1972
Quality/National #47(4-5/57)on(Arleigh#48-101)

#1-Ward cover, 9pgs. + Gustavson art			
	4.00	8.00	12.00
2-Ward cover, 9pgs. + Gustavson art,			
3-Ward cover, story	2.00	4.00	6.00
4,6,8-Ward art, 80g, 9pg, 8pg.			
	1.50	3.00	4.50
5,7,9	.65	1.35	2.00
10-Ward art, 6pgs.	1.50	3.00	4.50
11-20	.50	1.00	1.50
21-Ward cover	1.00	2.00	3.00
22-39	.35	.70	1.05
40-Reprints 7pgs./#21	.35	.70	1.05
41-70	.25	.50	.75
71-119,121-146: #102-123:Serial-Three Girls, Their Lives, Their Loves.15	.30	.45	
120-Adams cover	.30	.60	.90

HEAVY METAL (Magazine) ($1.50)
April, 1977 - Present
HM Communications

#1	1.00	2.00	3.00
2-5	.50	1.00	1.50

HECKLE AND JECKLE (See Blue Ribbon Comics)
10/51 - #24, 10/55; #25, Fall/56 - #34, 6/59
St. John Publ. Co. #1-24/Pines #25 on

#1	1.75	3.35	5.00
2-10	.80	1.60	2.40
11-20	.40	.80	1.20
21-34	.30	.60	.90

HECKLE AND JECKLE (TV)(See New Terrytoons)
Nov, 1962 - #4, Aug, 1963
Gold Key

#1-4	.15	.30	.45
	(See March of Comics #379)		

HECKLE AND JECKLE (TV)

May, 1966 - #2, Oct, 1966; #3, Aug, 1967
Dell Publishing Co.

	Good	Fine	Mint
#1-3		.15	.30

HECTOR COMICS
1953 - 1954
Key Publications

#1-3	.50	1.00	1.50

HECTOR HEATHCOTE (TV)
March, 1964
Gold Key

#1(10111-403)	.15	.30	.45

HEDY DEVINE COMICS (Formerly USA #17?)
(Hedy of Hollywood #36 on)
#22, Aug, 1947 - #50, Sept, 1952
Marvel Comics (RCM)

#22	1.00	2.00	3.00
23-Wolverton art(1pg.) + Kurtzman's "Hey Look", 2pgs.	3.00	6.00	9.00
24,25,27-30-"Hey Look" by Kurtzman, 1-3pgs., 26-"Giggles & Grins" by Kurtzman			
	2.00	4.00	6.00
31-34,36-50	.65	1.35	2.00
35-Four pgs. "Rusty" by Kurtzman			
	2.50	5.00	7.50

HEDY-MILLIE-TESSIE COMEDY (See Comedy)

HEDY WOLFE
August, 1957
Atlas Publishing Co. (Emgee)

#1	.80	1.60	2.40

HEE HAW (TV)
July, 1970 - #7, Aug, 1971
Charlton Press

#1-7		.10	.20

HEIDI (See Dell Jr. Treasury #6)

HELEN OF TROY (See 4-Color Comics #684)

HELLO PAL COMICS (Short Story Comics)
Jan, 1943 - #3, May, 1943
Harvey Publications

#1-Rocketman & Rocketgirl begin; Yank & Doodle Jones app.; Mickey Rooney cover			
	7.00	14.00	21.00
2-Charlie McCarthy cover	5.00	10.00	15.00
3-Bob Hope cover	5.00	10.00	15.00

HELL-RIDER (Magazine)
Aug, 1971 - #2, Oct, 1971   (B&W)
Skywald Publications

	Good	Fine	Mint
#1-Origin # 1st app.; Butterfly & Wildbunch			
begins	1.00	2.00	3.00
2	.65	1.35	2.00

NOTE: #3 advertised in Psycho #5 but did not
come out (Morrow cover). Buckler art-#1,2.

HELP! (Magazine)
8/60 - #12, 9/61; V2#1(#13), 2/62 - V2#8(#20),
2/64; #21, 10/64 - #26, 9/65
Edited by Harvey Kurtzman
General Promotions/Warren Publishing Co.

V1#1	4.00	8.00	12.00
2-4	1.35	2.75	4.00
5,9-Little Nemo reprint by Winsor McCay			
(3pgs. & 2pgs.)	1.75	3.35	5.00
6-8,10,12	1.35	2.75	4.00
11-Krazy Kat by George Herriman(2pgs.)			
	1.50	3.00	4.50
V2#1(#13, 2/62)-Spirit reprint by Eisner			
(7pgs.)	2.50	5.00	7.50
2-8(#14-20): #2-The Humor of Charles Dana			
Gibson(6pgs.). #5-Miss Lace by Caniff			
(5pgs.). #6-Skippy by P. Crosby(6pgs.).			
#8-Mutt & Jeff by Ham Fisher(4pgs.)			
	1.75	3.35	5.00
21-(75¢ Annual-10/64)	1.35	2.75	4.00
22(1/65)-Robert Crumb-Fritz the Cat(2pgs.)			
in Public Gallery(Early Underground Comix			
Development)	2.50	5.00	7.50
23,26	1.20	2.40	3.60
24-Fritz the Cat, 2pgs.	2.50	5.00	7.50
25-Sketchbook-Life in Bulgaria			
	2.00	4.00	6.00

NOTE: Robert Crumb art-#22,24,25. Gilbert
Sheldon's Wonder Warthog-V2#4(16),V2#6(18),
V2#8(20),22-26. Covers feature photos of:
#1-Sid Caesar, #2-Ernie Kovacs, #3-Jerry Lew-
is, #4-Mort Sahl, #5-Dave Garroway, #6-Jona-
than Winters, #7-Tom Poston, #8-Hugh Downs,
#9-Phil Ford/Mime Hines, #10-Jackie Gleason.

HE-MAN
Fall, 1952
Ziff-Davis Publ. Co. (Approved Comics)

#1-Kinstler cvr.	1.75	3.35	5.00

HE-MAN
1954 - #2, July, 1954
Toby Press

#1	2.00	4.00	6.00
2	1.00	2.00	3.00

HENNESSEY (See 4-Color Comics #1200,1280)

HENRY
1935 (52pgs.)(Daily B&W strip reprints)
David McKay Publications

	Good	Fine	Mint
#1-by Carl Anderson	4.00	8.00	12.00

HENRY
1946 - #65, Apr-June, 1961
Dell Publishing Co.

4-Color #122,155	2.00	4.00	6.00
#1	2.00	4.00	6.00
2	.65	1.35	2.00
3-10	.50	1.00	1.50
11-20	.40	.80	1.20
21-65	.30	.60	.90

HENRY (See March of Comics #43,58,84,101,
112,129,147,162,178,189)

HENRY ALDRICH COMICS
Aug-Sept, 1950 - #22, 1954
Dell Publishing Co.

#1-Series written by John Stanley; Bill			
Williams art	2.50	5.00	7.50
2-5	1.50	3.00	4.50
6-22	1.00	2.00	3.00

HENRY BREWSTER
Feb, 1966 - V2#7, Sept, 1967 (All Giants)
Country Wide (M.F. Ent.)

#1-6(12/66)-Powell art in most			
	.25	.50	.75
V2#7	.20	.40	.60

HERBIE (See Forbidden Worlds)
April-May, 1964 - #23, Feb, 1967
American Comics Group

#1	5.00	10.00	15.00
2-5	2.50	5.00	7.50
6,7,9,10	2.00	4.00	6.00
8-Origin	3.00	6.00	9.00
11-22	1.50	3.00	4.50
23-Reprts.1st sty/F.W.#73	2.00	4.00	6.00

NOTE: All have Whitney art/covers.

HERBIE GOES TO MONTE CARLO, -- RIDES AGAIN
(See Walt Disney Showcase #24,41)

HERCULES
Oct, 1967 - #13, Sept, 1969; Dec, 1968
Charlton Comics

#1-Thane of Bagarth series begins

He-Man #1, © Z-D

Henry Aldrich #2, © Dell

Herbie #4, © ACG

Heroes, Inc. #1, © Wally Wood   Heroic Comics #8, © Eas   Heroic Comics #55, © Eas

(Hercules cont'd)	Good	Fine	Mint
	.50	1.00	1.50
2-13	.35	.70	1.05
8-(Low distribution)-35¢ magazine format			
(B&W)(12/68)-reprints	2.50	5.00	7.50

HERCULES (See The Mighty ---)

HERCULES UNBOUND
Oct-Nov, 1975 - #12, Aug-Sept, 1977
National Periodical Publications

#1-Wood inks	.25	.50	.75
2-5	.15	.30	.45
6,8,9-Wood inks	.20	.40	.60
7-Simonson art	.20	.40	.60
10-12		.15	.30

HERCULES UNCHAINED (See 4-Color #1006,1121)

HERE COMES SANTA (See March of Comics #30, 213,340)

HERE'S HOWIE!
Jan-Feb, 1952 - #20, Mar-Apr, 1955
National Periodical Publications

#1	2.50	5.00	7.50
2-5	1.75	3.35	5.00
6-10	.80	1.60	2.40
11-20	.50	1.00	1.50

HERMAN & KATNIP (See Harvey Hits#14,25,31,41)

HERO FOR HIRE (Power Man #17 on)
June, 1972 - #16, Dec, 1973
Marvel Comics Group

#1-Origin Luke Cage	.80	1.60	2.40
2,3	.50	1.00	1.50
4-10	.40	.80	1.20
11-16	.25	.50	.75

HEROES ALL CATHOLIC ACTION ILLUSTRATED
V4#9, 11/45 - V4#10, 3/46 (16pgs)(Soft cover)
Heroes All Co.

V4#9,10	.80	1.60	2.40

HEROES, INC. PRESENTS CANNON
1969 - #2, 1976
Wally Wood/CPL/Gang Publ. #2

No#-Wood/Ditko art	2.50	5.00	7.50
2-Wood cover (8½x10½")(B&W)($2.00)-Ditko &			
Wood stories	1.00	2.00	3.00

NOTE: *First issue not distributed by publisher; it is rumored that 9,000 copies were stored in a warehouse and stolen.*

HEROES OF THE WILD FRONTIER (Formerly Baffling Mysteries)
#26, 3/55 - #2, 4/56
Ace Periodicals

	Good	Fine	Mint
#26(#1),27,28	.50	1.00	1.50
#2	.35	.70	1.05

HEROIC COMICS (Reg'lar Fellas #1-15; New Heroic #41 on)
Aug, 1940 - #97, June, 1955
Eastern Color Printing Co./Famous Funnies

#1-Origin Hydroman by Bill Everett & the			
Purple Zombie	35.00	70.00	105.00
2	20.00	40.00	60.00
3,4	15.00	30.00	45.00
5,6	12.00	24.00	36.00
7-Origin Man O'Metal, 1 pg.			
	12.00	24.00	36.00
8-10	7.00	14.00	21.00
11,13	6.00	12.00	18.00
12-Origin Music Master	8.00	16.00	24.00
14-Hydroman x-over in Rainbow Boy; also in			
#15. Origin Rainbow Boy			
	8.00	16.00	24.00
15-Intro. Downbeat	7.00	14.00	21.00
16-Hydroman & Man O'War begin			
	5.00	10.00	15.00
17-20: #17-Rainbow Boy x-over in Hydroman.			
#19-Rainbow Boy x-over in Hydroman & vice			
versa	5.00	10.00	15.00
21-30: #23-Rainbow Boy x-over in Hydroman			
	2.50	5.00	7.50
31,34,40	1.35	2.75	4.00
32,33,35-38,41-Toth art	1.75	3.35	5.00
39-Ingels art	1.75	3.35	5.00
42,49-Toth art	1.50	3.00	4.50
43-48,50	1.00	2.00	3.00
51-Williamson story; Kiefer cover			
	3.00	6.00	9.00
52-55,57,59-64	.80	1.60	2.40
56,58-Toth cover	1.00	2.00	3.00
65-Williamson/Frazetta story; Evans story,			
2pgs.	4.00	8.00	12.00
66,67,75,94-Frazetta(2pgs.) in each			
	1.75	3.35	5.00
70,71,86,87-Frazetta (3-4 pgs.),			
73-Two Frazetta stories, 2pgs. each			
	2.50	5.00	7.50
68,74,76-80,84,85,88-93,95-97			
	.50	1.00	1.50
69,72-Two Frazetta stories(6&8pgs. total)			
	4.00	8.00	12.00
81,82-1pg. Frazetta art	1.35	2.75	4.00
83-½pg. Frazetta art	1.35	2.75	4.00

NOTE: *Everett stories (Hydroman)-#1-7; covers-#1-7,62,63.*

HEY THERE, IT'S YOGI BEAR (See Movie Comics)

HI-ADVENTURE HEROES (Hanna-Barbera)
May, 1969 - #2, Aug, 1969
Gold Key

	Good	Fine	Mint
#1-Three Musketeers, Gulliver, Arabian			
Knights stories	.25	.50	.75
2-Three Musketeers, Micro-Venture, Arabian			
Knights	.20	.40	.60

HI AND LOIS (See 4-Color #683,774,955)

HI AND LOIS
Nov, 1969 - #11, July, 1971
Charlton Comics

	Good	Fine	Mint
#1	.20	.40	.60
2-11		.15	.30

HICKORY
Oct, 1949 - #6, Aug, 1950
Quality Comics Group

	Good	Fine	Mint
#1-SAHL art/covers	3.00	6.00	9.00
2,4-6	2.00	4.00	6.00
3-Wardesque cover by SAHL			
	2.50	5.00	7.50

HIDDEN CREW, THE (See The United States A.F.)

HIDE-OUT (See 4-Color Comics #346)

HIDING PLACE, THE (Religious)
1973   (35¢)
Spire Christian Comics/Fleming H. Revell Co.

	Good	Fine	Mint
#1	.15	.30	.45

HIGH ADVENTURE
Oct, 1957
Red Top(Decker)Comics (Farrell)

	Good	Fine	Mint
#1-Krigstein reprint from Explorer Joe			
(re-issue on cover)	.65	1.35	2.00

HIGH ADVENTURE (See 4-Color #949,1001)

HIGH CHAPPARAL (TV)
August, 1968
Gold Key

	Good	Fine	Mint
#1(10226-808)	.25	.50	.75

HIGH SCHOOL CONFIDENTIAL DIARY
June, 1960 - #11, Mar, 1962
Charlton Comics

	Good	Fine	Mint
#1	.15	.30	.45
2-11		.15	.30

HI-HO COMICS
1946
Four Star Publications

	Good	Fine	Mint
#1-Cole cover	1.35	2.75	4.00
2,3	.80	1.60	2.40

HI-JINX
July-Aug, 1947 - 1949
B&I Publ. Co.(American Comics Group)/Creston/
LaSalle

	Good	Fine	Mint
#1-3	1.00	2.00	3.00
4-7-Milt Gross	1.00	2.00	3.00
132pg. issue, no#, no date (LaSalle)			
	1.50	3.00	4.50

HI-LITE COMICS
Fall, 1945
E. R. Ross Publishing Co.

	Good	Fine	Mint
#1-Miss Shady	3.35	6.75	10.00

HILLBILLY COMICS
Aug, 1955 - #4, July, 1956   (Satire)
Charlton Comics

	Good	Fine	Mint
#1	.65	1.35	2.00
2-4	.50	1.00	1.50

HIP-IT-TY HOP (See March of Comics #15)

HI-SCHOOL ROMANCES (-- Romance #1-15)
Oct, 1949 - #71, Jan, 1958
Harvey Publications/True Love(Home Comics)

	Good	Fine	Mint
#1-Powell art-most issues	1.00	2.00	3.00
2-20	.40	.80	1.20
21-71	.25	.50	.75
--Datebook #1(25¢,Giant,11/62) Powell, Baker			
art	1.50	3.00	4.50

NOTE: *Powell art-#11,14,22,33,45,58.*

HIS NAME IS SAVAGE (Magazine format)
#1, June, 1968   (One Shot)
Adventure House Press

	Good	Fine	Mint
#1-Gil Kane art	2.00	4.00	6.00

HI-SPOT COMICS (Red Ryder #1 & 3 on)
#2, Nov, 1940
Hawley Publications

	Good	Fine	Mint
#2-David Innes of Pellucidar; art by J. C.			
Burroughs; written by Edgar R. Burroughs			
(Rare)	120.00	240.00	360.00

Hickory #4, © Qua

Hi-School Romance Date Book #1, © Harv

Hi-Spot Comics #2, © Hawley Publ.

Hit Comics #6, © Qua

Hit Comics #33, © Qua

Holiday Comics #1, © Faw

HIT COMICS
July, 1940 - #65, July, 1950
Quality Comics Group

	Good	Fine	Mint
#1-Origin Neon, the Unknown & Hercules; Intro. The Red Bee; Blaze Barton, the Strange Twins, X-5 Super Agent, Casey Jones, Jack & Jill(ends #7), & Bob & Swab begin	140.00	280.00	420.00
2-The Old Witch begins, ends #14	60.00	120.00	180.00
3-Casey Jones ends	50.00	100.00	150.00
4-Super Agent(ends #17), & Betty Bates(ends #65) begin; X-5 ends	40.00	80.00	120.00
5-(classic cover)	50.00	100.00	150.00
6-10: #10-Old Witch by Crandall, 4pgs.	30.00	60.00	90.00
11-17: #13-Bob & Swab, Blaze Barton ends. #17-Last Neon; Crandall Hercules in all	26.50	53.25	80.00
18-Origin Stormy Foster, the Great Defender; The Ghost of Flanders begins; Crandall cover	30.00	60.00	90.00
19,20	25.00	50.00	75.00
21-24: #21-Last Hercules. #24-Last Red Bee & Strange Twins	20.00	40.00	60.00
25-Origin Kid Eternity by Moldoff	25.00	50.00	75.00
26-Blackhawk x-over in Kid Eternity	16.50	33.25	50.00
27-29: #28-Intro. Her Highness in Kid Eternity	10.00	20.00	30.00
30,31-"Bill the Magnificent" by Kurtzman, 11pgs. in each	8.25	16.50	24.75
32-40: #34-Last Stormy Foster	5.50	11.00	16.50
41-50	4.00	8.00	12.00
51-60-Last Kid Eternity	3.00	6.00	9.00
61,62,65: #61-Jeb Rivers begins	2.00	4.00	6.00
63-Crandall cover/story	3.00	6.00	9.00
64-Crandall art	3.00	6.00	9.00

NOTE: _Crandall_ stories-#11-17(Hercules),#23, 24(Stormy Foster); covers-#18-20,23,24. _Fine_ covers-#1-17; story-#22 only.

HI-YO SILVER (See Lone Ranger's Famous Horse --, March of Comics #215, & The Lone Ranger)

HOCUS POCUS (Formerly Funny Book)
#9, Aug-Sept, 1946
Parents' Magazine Press

	Good	Fine	Mint
#9	1.00	2.00	3.00

HOGAN'S HEROES (TV)
June, 1966 - #9, Oct, 1969
Dell Publishing Co.

	Good	Fine	Mint
#1	.20	.40	.60
2,4-9: #9-reprints #1		.15	.30
3-Ditko/Trapani story	.25	.50	.75

HOLIDAY COMICS
1942 (196 pgs.) (25¢)
Fawcett Publications

	Good	Fine	Mint
#1-Reprints three Fawcett comics: Capt. Marvel, Nyoka & Whiz	50.00	100.00	150.00

HOLIDAY COMICS
January, 1951 - 1952
Star Publications

	Good	Fine	Mint
#1-8-Funny animal contents (Frisky Fables)	.65	1.35	2.00

HOLI-DAY SURPRISE (Formerly Summer Fun)
1967 (25¢)
Charlton Comics

	Good	Fine	Mint
V2#55-Giant		.15	.30

HOLLYWOOD COMICS
1944
New Age Publications

	Good	Fine	Mint
#1	2.50	5.00	7.50

HOLLYWOOD CONFESSIONS
October, 1949 - #2, Dec, 1949
St. John Publishing Co.

	Good	Fine	Mint
#1-Kubert cover/3 stys.	3.35	6.75	10.00
2-Kubert cvr/sty.(Scarce)	5.00	10.00	15.00

HOLLYWOOD DIARY
1949 - 1950
Quality Comics Group

	Good	Fine	Mint
#1	2.00	4.00	6.00
2-5: #2-Photo cover	1.75	3.35	5.00

HOLLYWOOD FILM STORIES
April, 1950 - #4, 1950
Feature Publications/Prize

	Good	Fine	Mint
#1	2.50	5.00	7.50
2-4	2.00	4.00	6.00

HOLLYWOOD FUNNY FOLKS (Formerly Funny Folks; Nutsy Squirrel #61 on)
#31, Feb, 1951 - #60, Jul-Aug, 1954
National Periodical Publications

	Good	Fine	Mint
#31-40	.65	1.35	2.00
41-60	.35	.70	1.05

HOLLYWOOD LOVE DOCTOR (See Doctor Anthony
King --)

HOLLYWOOD PICTORIAL (Romances on cover)
#3, Jan, 1950
St. John Publishing Co.

	Good	Fine	Mint
#3	1.50	3.00	4.50

*(Becomes a movie magazine - Hollywood Pictor-
ial Western with #4.)*

HOLLYWOOD ROMANCES
1949; #48, Nov, 1968 - #59, June, 1971
Charlton Comics

#48-50(1949)	.65	1.35	2.00
48-59: #56-"Born to Heart Break" begins			
		.10	.20

HOLLYWOOD SECRETS
Nov, 1949 - #6, Sept, 1950
Quality Comics Group

#1-Ward cover, 9pgs.	5.00	10.00	15.00
2-Crandall art, Ward cover/story			
	3.00	6.00	9.00
3-6: #3-photo cover	1.75	3.35	5.00
-- of Romance, I.W. Reprint #9			
	.35	.70	1.05

HOLYOKE ONE-SHOT
1944 - 1945   (All reprints)
Holyoke Publishing Co. (Tem Publ.)

#1-Grit Grady (on cover only), Miss Victory,			
Alias X(origin)-All reprints from Captain			
Fearless	2.00	4.00	6.00
2-Rusty Dugan (Corporal); Capt. Fearless			
(origin), Mr. Miracle (origin), app.			
	2.00	4.00	6.00
3-Miss Victory-Crash #4 reprints; Cat Man-			
(origin), Solar Legion by Kirby app.;			
Miss Victory on cover only (1945)			
	5.00	10.00	15.00
4-Mr. Miracle-The Blue Streak app.			
	1.50	3.00	4.50
5-U.S. Border Patrol Comics(Sgt. Dick Carter			
of the --) Miss Victory (story matches			
cover #3), Citizen Smith, & Mr. Miracle			
app.	1.50	3.00	4.50
6-Capt.Fearless, Alias X, Capt.Stone(splash			
used as cover-#10); Diamond Jim & Rusty			
Dugan(splash from cover-#2)			
	2.00	4.00	6.00
7-Z-2, Strong Man, Blue Streak(story matches			
cover-#8)-Reprints from Crash #2			
	3.00	6.00	9.00
8-Blue Streak, Strong Man(story matches cov-			

er-#7)-Crash reprints   1.50   3.00   4.50

9-Citizen Smith-The Blue Streak, Solar Leg-			
ion by Kirby, & Strongman, the Perfect			
Human app.; reprints from Crash #4 & 5;			
Citizen Smith on cover only-from story in			
#5(1944-before #3)	4.00	8.00	12.00
10-Captain Stone(Crash reprints); Solar Leg-			
ion by S&K	4.00	8.00	12.00

HOMER COBB (See Adventures of --)

HOMER HOOPER
July, 1953 - #3, Sept, 1953
Atlas Comics

#1-3	.40	.80	1.20

HOMER, THE HAPPY GHOST (See Adventures of--)
3/55 - #22, 11/58; V2#1, 11/69 - V2#5, 7/70
Atlas(ACI/PPI/WPI)/Marvel Comics

V1#1	.65	1.35	2.00
2-22	.35	.70	1.05
V2#1-V2#5(1969-70)		.10	.20

HOME RUN (See A-1 Comics #89)

HONEYMOON (Formerly Gay Comics)
#41, January, 1950
A Lover's Magazine(USA) (Marvel)

#41	.50	1.00	1.50

HONEYMOON ROMANCE
April, 1950   (25¢) (Digest Size)
Artful Publications

#1	1.75	3.35	5.00

HONEY WEST (TV)
Sept, 1966
Gold Key

#1(10186-609)	.50	1.00	1.50

HONG KONG PHOOEY (Hanna-Barbera)
June, 1975 - #9, Nov, 1976
Charlton Comics

#1-9		.10	.20

HOODED HORSEMAN, THE (Formerly Blazing West)
#23, 5-6/52 - #27, 1-2/53; #18, 12-1/54-55 -
#27, 6-7/56
American Comics Group (Michel Publ.)

#23(5-6/52)-Hooded Horseman, Injun Jones

Hollywood Secrets #2, © Qua

Holyoke One-Shot #1, © Hoke

The Hooded Menace, © Avon

201

Hoot Gibson #3, © Fox   Hopalong Cassidy #15, © Faw   Horrific #1, © Comic Media

(The Hooded Horseman cont'd)

	Good	Fine	Mint
continues	1.35	2.75	4.00
24-27(1-2/53)	1.00	2.00	3.00
#18(11-12/54)(Formerly Out of the Night),			
19	1.00	2.00	3.00
20-Origin Johnny Injun	1.00	2.00	3.00
21-25,27(6-7/56)	.80	1.60	2.40
26-Origin & 1st app. Cowboy Sahib; 11pgs.			
Starr art	1.00	2.00	3.00

NOTE: _Whitney stories/covers-#20-22._

HOODED MENACE, THE (Also see Daring Advs.)
1951   (One Shot)
Realistic/Avon Periodicals

No#-Based on a band of hooded outlaws in the
Pacific Northwest, 1900-1906; reprinted in
Daring Advs. #15   12.00 24.00 36.00

HOOT GIBSON WESTERN
#3, Sept, 1950 - #9, 1951
Fox Features Syndicate

#3(#1)-Wood story	5.00	10.00	15.00
4-9	3.00	6.00	9.00
Western Roundup('50)(25¢-132pgs.)			
	4.00	8.00	12.00

HOPALONG CASSIDY (Also see Master Comics)
1943 - #91, July, 1954
Fawcett Publications

#1	15.00	30.00	45.00
2	8.00	16.00	24.00
3-5	6.00	12.00	18.00
6-14	4.00	8.00	12.00
15-30	3.00	6.00	9.00
31-50	2.00	4.00	6.00
51-91	1.35	2.75	4.00
Grape Nuts Flakes giveaway(1950)			
	2.00	4.00	6.00
--in the Strange Legacy	3.00	6.00	9.00
--Gives a Helping Hand(1951,52pgs.)B&W,Samuel			
Lowe Co. #517-5	2.00	4.00	6.00
--& the Mad Barber(1951)-Bond Bread giveaway			
(7"x5")	3.00	6.00	9.00
--Meets the Brend Brothers Bandits			
	3.00	6.00	9.00

HOPALONG CASSIDY
Feb, 1954 - #135, May-June, 1959
National Periodical Publications

#86-135	1.50	3.00	4.50

NOTE: _Gil Kane art-1956 up._

HOPE SHIP

June-Aug, 1963
Dell Publishing Co.

	Good	Fine	Mint
#1	.65	1.35	2.00

HOPPY THE MARVEL BUNNY
Dec, 1945 - 1947 (See Fawcett Funny Animal)
Fawcett Publications

#1	3.00	6.00	9.00
2-15	1.50	3.00	4.50

HORACE & DOTTY DRIPPLE (Dotty Dripple #1-24)
#25, Aug, 1952 - #43, Oct, 1955
Harvey Publications

#25-43	.40	.80	1.20

HORIZONTAL LIEUTENANT, THE(See Movie Classics)

HORRIFIC (Terrific #14 on)
Sept, 1952 - #13, Sept, 1954
Artful/Comic Media/Harwell/Mystery

#1	1.35	2.75	4.00
2-10	.80	1.60	2.40
11-13	.50	1.00	1.50

HORROR FROM THE TOMB (Mysterious Stories #2)
Sept, 1954
Premier Magazine Co.

#1-Woodbridge/Torres sty.	1.75	3.35	5.00

HORRORS OF MYSTERY
1953
Star Publications

#13-15	1.00	2.00	3.00

HORRORS OF THE UNDERWORLD
#14, 1953 - #15, April, 1954
Star Publications

#14,15	1.50	3.00	4.50

HORRORS OF WAR
1953
Star Publications

#11,12: Disbrow art-#11	1.50	3.00	4.50

HORROR TALES (Magazine)
V1#7, 6/69 - V6#6, 12/74; V7#2, 5/76 - Present
(V1-V6, 52pgs; V7,V8#2, 112pgs; V8#4 on, 68pgs)
(No V5#3, V7#1, V8#1,3)
Eerie Publications

V1#7-9	.35	.70	1.05

(Horror Tales cont'd)

	Good	Fine	Mint
V2#1-6('70),V3#1-6('71)	.25	.50	.75
V4#1-3,5,6('72)	.25	.50	.75
V4#4-LSD story reprint/Weird V3#5	.50	1.00	1.50
V5#1,2,4,5(6/73),5(10/73)	.25	.50	.75
V6#1-6('74),V7#2-4('76)	.25	.50	.75
V8#2,4,5('77)	.25	.50	.75

NOTE: *Bondage covers-V6#1,3.*

HORSE FEATHERS COMICS
Nov, 1945
Lev Gleason Publications

	Good	Fine	Mint
#1-Wolverton's Scoop Scuttle	6.00	12.00	18.00
2-4	2.00	4.00	6.00

HORSEMASTERS, THE (See 4-Color #1260)

HORSE SOLDIERS, THE (See 4-Color #1048)

HORSE WITHOUT A HEAD, THE (See Movie Comics)

HOT DOG
June-July, 1954 - #4, Dec-Jan, 1954-55
Magazine Enterprises

#1(A-1#107), 2(A-1#110), 3(A-1#115),			
4(A-1#136)	.65	1.35	2.00

HOTEL DEPAREE-SUNDANCE (See 4-Color #1126)

HOT ROD AND SPEEDWAY COMICS
Feb-Mar, 1952 - #5, Apr-May, 1953
Hillman Periodicals

#1	1.00	2.00	3.00
2-Krigstein story	1.00	2.00	3.00
3-5	.65	1.35	2.00

HOT ROD CARTOONS (Magazine)
Nov, 1964 - 1974   (35¢)
Petersen Publ. Co.

#1	1.50	3.00	4.50
2-5,8,9	.65	1.35	2.00
6,7,10-12,15-Toth art	1.00	2.00	3.00
13,14,16-20	.25	.50	.75
21-46,48-59	.20	.40	.60
47-Toth art, 2pgs.	.65	1.35	2.00
60-Robert Williams art	.65	1.35	2.00

HOT ROD COMICS
Nov, 1951 - V2#7, Feb, 1953
Fawcett Publications

V1#1-Powell art	1.00	2.00	3.00

	Good	Fine	Mint
2-6	.65	1.35	2.00
V2#7	.50	1.00	1.50

"HOT ROD" KING
Fall, 1952
Ziff-Davis Publ. Co.

#1-Giacoia art	.80	1.60	2.40

HOT ROD RACERS (Grand Prix #16 on)
Dec, 1964 - #15, 1967
Charlton Comics

#1	.15	.30	.45
2-15		.15	.30

HOT RODS AND RACING CARS
Nov, 1951 - #120, June, 1973
Charlton Comics (Motor Mag. #1)

#1	1.00	2.00	3.00
2-10	.50	1.00	1.50
11-50	.20	.40	.60
51-120		.10	.20

HOT SHOT CHARLIE
1947   (Lee Elias)
Hillman Periodicals

#1	.65	1.35	2.00

HOT STUFF CREEPY CAVES
Nov, 1974 - Present
Harvey Publications

#1-7		.10	.20

HOT STUFF SIZZLERS
1960 - Present   (25¢)
Harvey Publications

#1	.50	1.00	1.50
2-20	.25	.50	.75
21-57		.15	.30

HOT STUFF, THE LITTLE DEVIL
Oct, 1957 - Present
Harvey Publications (Illustrated Humor)

#1	1.75	3.35	5.00
2-5	.80	1.60	2.40
6-20	.35	.70	1.05
21-60	.20	.40	.60
61-142		.15	.30
Shoestore Giveaway('63)	.25	.50	.75

Hot Rod & Speedway #1, © Hill

Hot Rod King #1, © Z-D

Hot Rods & Racing Cars #57, © CC

House Of Mystery #1, © DC

House Of Mystery #7, © DC

House of Secrets #2, © DC

HOT WHEELS (TV)
Mar-Apr, 1970 - #6, Jan-Feb, 1971
National Periodical Publications

	Good	Fine	Mint
#1	.65	1.35	2.00
2-5: Toth art-#1-5; covers-#1,4,5			
	.50	1.00	1.50
6-Adams cover/story	1.00	2.00	3.00

HOUSE OF MYSTERY (See Limited Collectors' Edition & Super DC Giant)

HOUSE OF MYSTERY
Dec-Jan, 1951-52 - Present
National Periodical Publications/DC Comics

	Good	Fine	Mint
#1	10.00	20.00	30.00
2,3	5.00	10.00	15.00
4-15	3.35	6.75	10.00
16-34-Last pre-code ish	2.00	4.00	6.00
35-60	1.20	2.40	3.60
61,66,72-Kirby stories	1.75	3.35	5.00
62-65,67-71,73-75	.60	1.20	1.80
76,82,84,85-Kirby stys.	1.25	2.50	3.75
77-81,83,86-100	.40	.80	1.20
101-108,110-119	.35	.70	1.05
109,120-Toth art + Kubert #109			
	1.00	2.00	3.00
121-140	.25	.50	.75
141,142	.25	.50	.75
143-J'onn J'onzz, Manhunter begins, ends #173 (6/64)	.65	1.35	2.00
144-148,150	.20	.40	.60
149-Toth story	.65	1.35	2.00
151-155,157,159	.20	.40	.60
156-Origin Robby Reed in Dial H for Hero(begins; ends #173)	.25	.50	.75
158-Origin & last app. Diabolu Idol-Head in J'onn J'onzz	.25	.50	.75
160-Intro. Marco Xavier (Martian Manhunter) & Vulture Crime Organization in J'onn J'onzz (7/66), ends #173; Plastic Man x-over			
	.25	.50	.75
161-168,170	.20	.40	.60
169-Origin & 1st app. Gem Girl in Dial H for Hero	.20	.40	.60
171-177: #174-Mystery format begins			
	.15	.30	.45
178-Adams story	1.00	2.00	3.00
179-Adams/Orlando + Wrightson (1st pro work)			
	1.25	2.50	3.75
180,181,183: Wrightson stys.+ Wood in #180,183			
	.80	1.60	2.40
182-Toth reprint	.20	.40	.60
184-Kane/Wood + Toth story	.65	1.35	2.00
185-Williamson/Kaluta story; 3pgs. Wood art			
	1.00	2.00	3.00
186-Adams + Wrightson	1.25	2.50	3.75

	Good	Fine	Mint
187,190-Toth reprints	.60	1.20	1.80
188-Wrightson story	1.00	2.00	3.00
189-Wood story	.60	1.20	1.80
191,195-Wrightson story + Redondo #195			
	1.00	2.00	3.00
192,193,198,200	.20	.40	.60
194,196-Toth reprints	.60	1.20	1.80
197-Redondo story	.60	1.20	1.80
199-Wood & Kirby story	.80	1.60	2.40
201,205,206,208-210	.15	.30	.45
202,203,207,211: Redondo art in all			
	.25	.50	.75
204-Wrightson art, 9pgs.	.80	1.60	2.40
212,213,215,216,218,220,222,223,225			
	.15	.30	.45
214,217,219-Redondo stories	.20	.40	.60
221-Wrightson/Kaluta story	.40	.80	1.20
224-Adams inks + Wrightson stories; begin 100 pg. issues; Phantom Stranger reprint			
	.65	1.35	2.00
226-Wrightson + Redondo stories; Phantom Stranger reprint	.40	.80	1.20
227-Redondo story	.25	.50	.75
228-Adams + Wrightson stys.	.65	1.35	2.00
229-Wrightson(reprint) + Redondo story; Toth story; last 100pg ish	.35	.70	1.05
230-235,237-240,242,243: #230-68pgs.			
	.15	.30	.45
236-Adams inks, Ditko sty.	.20	.40	.60
241-Redondo story	.20	.40	.60
244-Wrightson Spectre app.	.20	.40	.60
245-250		.15	.30
251-($1.00 size)-Wood art	.35	.70	1.05
252-256	.35	.70	1.05

NOTE: *Adams covers*-#175-192,196,197,199,251-254. *Alcala stories*-#209,211-215,217,219,220, 222,224-228. *Ditko story*-#254,258. *Drucker story*-#37. *Howard story*-#254. *Infantino stories*-#110,111. *Bob Kane story*-#84. *Kaluta story*-#109,195,200,202; *covers*-#200-202,210, 212,233. *Kirby story*-#63,194,199; *covers*-#76, 78,79,85. *Morrow stories*-#192,196,255. *Orlando art*-#175(2pgs.). *Reese story*-#195,200,205 (inks). *Starlin art*-#207(2pgs.). *Wrightson covers*-#193-195,204,207,209,211,213,214,217, 221,231,236,255,256.

HOUSE OF SECRETS
Nov-Dec, 1956 - #80, Sept-Oct, 1966;
#81, Aug-Sept, 1969 - Present
National Periodical Publications/DC Comics

	Good	Fine	Mint
#1-Drucker story	9.00	18.00	27.00
2	5.00	10.00	15.00
3-Kirby cover/story	4.00	8.00	12.00
4,8-Kirby art	3.50	7.00	10.50
5-7,9,10	3.00	6.00	9.00

(House of Secrets cont'd)	Good	Fine	Mint
11,12-Kirby cover/story	2.50	5.00	7.50
13-20	1.75	3.35	5.00
21-47,49,50: #23-Origin Mark Merlin			
	1.20	2.40	3.60
48-Toth story	1.35	2.75	4.00
51-60,62: #58-Origin Mark Merlin retold			
	.50	1.00	1.50
61-First Eclipso	.50	1.00	1.50
63-67-Toth stories	1.00	2.00	3.00
68-80: #73-Mark Merlin ends, Prince Ra-Man begins. #80-Eclipso, Prince Ra-Man end			
	.25	.50	.75
81,84,86-89: #81-Mystery format begins			
	.20	.40	.60
82-Adams story(inks)	.65	1.35	2.00
83-Toth story	.50	1.00	1.50
85-Adams story(inks); Disney satire by Reese			
	.65	1.35	2.00
90-Buckler(1st art in comics)/Adams story			
	.65	1.35	2.00
91-Wood story	.50	1.00	1.50
92-Intro. Swamp Thing; Wrightson story (6-7/71)	7.00	14.00	21.00
93,96-98-Toth reprints + Wood-#96			
	.65	1.35	2.00
94-Wrightson story + Toth #94 (reprint)			
	.80	1.60	2.40
95,99,102,104-Redondo stys.	.25	.50	.75
100,101,103,105-112,114,115	.20	.40	.60
113,116-Redondo stories	.25	.50	.75
117,119,120	.20	.40	.60
118-Evans story	.25	.50	.75
121,122,124-130	.15	.30	.45
123-12pgs. Toth art	.25	.50	.75
131-134,136-138	.15	.30	.45
135,139-Wrightson covers; Redondo story-#139			
	.20	.40	.60
140-Origin the Patchworkman; Redondo & Wrightson art	.35	.70	1.05
141-151		.20	.35

NOTE: _Adams covers-#81,82,84-88,90,91. Alcala stories-#100,104-107,109,115,117,119,120,122, 125. Anderson story-#91. Ditko story-#139. Finley story-#7. Infantino story-#53. Kaluta story-#87,98; covers-#98,99,101,102,151. Bob Kane stories-#15,18,21. Kirby cover-#11. Kubert story-#39(with Meskin?). Morrow stories-#86,89,90; covers-#89,147,148. Redondo cover-#95. Starlin cover-#150. Wrightson covers-#92-94,96,99,100,103,106,107,135,139._

HOUSE OF TERROR (3-D)
October, 1953
St. John Publishing Co.

#1-Kubert art	5.00	10.00	15.00

HOUSE OF YANG, THE (See Yang)
July, 1975 - #6, June, 1976
Charlton Comics

	Good	Fine	Mint
#1	.20	.40	.60
2-6		.15	.30

HOWARD THE DUCK (See Fear, Man-Thing & Marvel Treasury Ed.)
Jan, 1976 - Present
Marvel Comics Group

#1-Brunner cvr/art-Spiderman x-over	4.00	8.00	12.00
2-Brunner cvr/art + Starlin	1.75	3.35	5.00
3-Buscema art	.65	1.35	2.00
4,5-Colan art	.50	1.00	1.50
6-9	.25	.50	.75
10-13-Leialoha art	.20	.40	.60
14,15	.20	.40	.60
16-Album ish.	.25	.50	.75
17-20	.20	.40	.60
Annual #1(9/77)	.25	.50	.75

HOW BOYS AND GIRLS CAN HELP WIN THE WAR
1942 (One Shot) (10c)
The Parents' Magazine Institute

#1	3.00	6.00	9.00

HOWDY DOODY (TV)
1949 - #37, Apr-June, 1956
Dell Publishing Co.

#1	2.50	5.00	7.50
2-5	1.50	3.00	4.50
6-10	1.00	2.00	3.00
11-37	.80	1.60	2.40
4-Color #761,811	.80	1.60	2.40

HOW IT BEGAN (See Single Series #15)

HOW SANTA GOT HIS RED SUIT (See March of Comics #2)

HOW STALIN HOPES HE WILL DESTROY AMERICA
1951 (Giveaway)
Joe Lowe Co.

	2.50	5.00	7.50

HOW THE WEST WAS WON (See Movie Comics)

H.R. PUFNSTUF (TV)
Oct, 1970 - #8, July, 1972
Gold Key

#1-8		.10	.20

(See March of Comics #360)

House Of Secrets #92. © DC

House Of Terror #1. © STJ

How Boys & Girls--('42). © PMI

205

Human Torch #1, © MCG   Human Torch #4, © MCG   Human Torch #38, © MCG

HUBERT (See 4-Color Comics #251)

HUCK & YOGI WINTER SPORTS(See 4-Color #1310)

HUCK FINN (See New Advs. of --)

HUCKLEBERRY FINN (See 4-Color Comics #1114)

HUCKLEBERRY HOUND (See Dell Giant #31,44,
March of Comics #199,214,235, Whitman Comic
Books & Golden Picture Story Book)

HUCKLEBERRY HOUND (TV)
May-July, 1959 - #43, Oct, 1970(Hanna-Barbera)
Dell/Gold Key #15 on

	Good	Fine	Mint
4-Color #990,1050	.50	1.00	1.50
#3(1-2/60)-#17	.15	.30	.45
18-20: All titled Huckleberry Hound Chuckle-			
berry Tales; #18,19-84pgs.			
	.15	.30	.45
21-43	.15	.30	.45
4-Color #1054,1141	.40	.80	1.20

HUCKLEBERRY HOUND (TV)
Nov, 1970 - #8, Jan, 1972 (Hanna-Barbera)
Charlton Comics

#1-8	.10	.20

HUCKLEBERRY HOUND CHUCKLEBERRY TALES
(See #18-20 in regular series)

HUEY, DEWEY, & LOUIE BACK TO SCHOOL
1958 (25¢) (See Dell Giant #22,35,49)
Dell Publishing Co.

#1-Giant	1.00	2.00	3.00

HUEY, DEWEY, AND LOUIE JUNIOR WOODCHUCKS
Aug, 1966 - Present (Disney)
Gold Key

#1-Written by Carl Barks	1.35	2.75	4.00
2,3-written by C. Barks	1.00	2.00	3.00
4,5-Barks reprints	.80	1.60	2.40
6-9,11-17-written by Barks	.40	.80	1.20
10-Barks reprt/WDC&S #238	.40	.80	1.20
18-21,24,27-30	.15	.30	.45
22,23,25,26-Barks reprints	.20	.40	.60
31-47: #41-Reprints	.15		.30

HUGH O'BRIAN FAMOUS MARSHAL WYATT EARP
1957 - 1958; #4, 9-11/58 - #20, 1962
Dell Publishing Co.

4-Color #860,890,921-All Manning art
		1.20	2.40	3.60

	Good	Fine	Mint
#4-12-Manning art	.80	1.60	2.40
13-20	.65	1.35	2.00

HULK, THE (See The Incredible-- & Rampaging--)

HUMAN FLY
1963 - 1964 (Reprints)
I.W. Enterprises/Super

IW Reprint #1-Reprints Blue Beetle #44('46)
	1.00	2.00	3.00
Super Reprint #10-Reprints Blue Beetle #46
('47) | 1.00 | 2.00 | 3.00 |

HUMAN FLY, THE
Sept, 1977 - Present
Marvel Comics Group

#1	.20	.40	.60
2-5	.15	.30	.45

HUMAN TORCH, THE (Formerly Red Raven #1)
(See Marvel Mystery)
#2, Fall/40 - #15, Spr/44(becomes Funny
Tunes); #16, Fall/44 - #35, 3/49(becomes
Love Tales); #36, 4/54 - #38, 8/54
Timely Comics #1-35(SnPC#16-35)/Atlas #36-38

#2(#1)-Origin Toro; The Falcon, The Fiery			
Mask, Mantor the Magician, & Microman			
only app.; Human Torch, Sub-Mariner by			
Everett begin	325.00	650.00	975.00
(Prices vary widely on this book)			
3(#2)	150.00	300.00	450.00
4(#3)-The Patriot app.; last Everett Sub-			
Mariner	100.00	200.00	300.00
5(#4)-The Patriot app. (Summer, 1941)			
	80.00	160.00	240.00
5-Human Torch battles Sub-Mariner(Fall,'41)			
	125.00	250.00	375.00
6,7,9	40.00	80.00	120.00
8-Human Torch battles Sub-Mariner; Wolver-			
ton art(1pg.)	80.00	160.00	240.00
10-Human Torch battles Sub-Mariner; Wolver-			
ton art(1pg.)	60.00	120.00	180.00
11-15	30.00	60.00	90.00
16-20	25.00	50.00	75.00
21-30	16.50	33.25	50.00
31-Namora x-over in Sub-Mariner			
	13.50	26.75	40.00
32-Sungirl, Namora app.	13.50	26.75	40.00
33-Capt. America x-over in Sub-Mariner			
	13.50	26.75	40.00
34-Sungirl solo	13.50	26.75	40.00
35-Captain America & Sungirl app.(1949)			
	13.50	26.75	40.00
36-38(1954)-Sub-Mariner in all issues except			

Human Torch cont'd)	Good	Fine	Mint
#34 & #35	10.00	20.00	30.00

NOTE: *Since there is a ½-year delay between #15 & 16, it is believed that Funny Tunes #16 continued after H.T. #15.*

HUMAN TORCH, THE
Sept, 1974 - #8, Nov, 1975
Marvel Comics Group

#1	.35	.70	1.05
2-8	.20	.40	.60

HUMBUG (Satire by Harvey Kurtzman)
Aug, 1957 - #11, Oct, 1958
Humbug Publications

#1-Wood, Davis art	5.00	10.00	15.00
2-9-Heath art-#2,4-8	3.00	6.00	9.00
10,11-Magazine format; #11-Kurtzman, Davis, & Elder art	3.00	6.00	9.00
Bound Volume(#1-9)-Sold by distributor	20.00	40.00	60.00

HUMDINGER
May-June, 1946 - 1947
Novelty Press/Premium Group

#1-Jerkwater Line, Mickey Starlight by Don Rico, Dink begin	1.75	3.35	5.00
2-6,V2#1,2	.75	1.50	2.25

HUMOR (See All Humor Comics)

HUMPHREY COMICS
Oct, 1948 - #40, 1954
Harvey Publications

#1-Joe Palooka's pal (reprints); Powell art	1.75	3.35	5.00
2,3	1.00	2.00	3.00
4-Boy Heroes app.	2.50	5.00	7.50
5-10	1.00	2.00	3.00
11-20	.65	1.35	2.00
21-40	.50	1.00	1.50

HUNCHBACK OF NOTRE DAME, THE
(See 4-Color Comics #854)

HUNK
Aug, 1961 - 1963
Charlton Comics

#1-11		.15	.30

HUNTED (Formerly My Love Memoirs)
#13, July, 1950 - #2, Sept, 1950
Fox Features Syndicate

	Good	Fine	Mint
#13(#1), 2	1.35	2.75	4.00

HURRICANE COMICS
1945
Cambridge House

#1-(Humor)	1.35	2.75	4.00

HYPER MYSTERY COMICS
May, 1940 - #2, June, 1940
Hyper Publications

#1-Hyper, the Phenomenal begins	16.50	33.25	50.00
2	12.00	24.00	36.00

I AIM AT THE STARS (See 4-Color #1148)

IBIS, THE INVINCIBLE (See Fawcett Min. & Whiz)
1942 - #6, Spring, 1948
Fawcett Publications

#1-Origin Ibis; Raboy cover	45.00	90.00	135.00
2	20.00	40.00	60.00
3-Wolverton art #3-6(4pgs. each)	15.00	30.00	45.00
4-6	12.00	24.00	36.00

IDAHO
June-Aug, 1963 - #8, July-Sept, 1965
Dell Publishing Co.

#1	.65	1.35	2.00
2-8	.35	.70	1.05

IDEAL, A CLASSICAL COMIC (2nd Series)
July, 1948 - #5, Mar, 1949
Timely Comics

#1-Antony & Cleopatra	4.00	8.00	12.00
2-The Corpses of Dr. Sacotti	4.00	8.00	12.00
3-Joan of Arc	3.35	6.75	10.00
4-Richard the Lion-hearted; titled "-- the World's Greatest Comics"; The Witness app.	4.00	8.00	12.00
5-Ideal Love & Romance	3.00	6.00	9.00

(Feature-length stories in all)

IDEAL COMICS (1st Series) (Willie #5 on)
Fall, 1944 - #4, Spring, 1946
Timely Comics (MgPC)

#1-4-Super Rabbit	1.35	2.75	4.00

IDEAL LOVE & ROMANCE (See Ideal, A Classical Comic)

Humbug #1, © Humbug Publ.

Hyper Mystery #1, © Hyper Publ.

Ibis The Invincible #1, © Faw

If The Devil Would Talk, © CG

I Loved #30, © Fox

The Incredible Hulk #2, © MCG

IDEAL ROMANCE (Diary Confessions #9 on)
April, 1954 - #7, Dec, 1954
Key Publications

	Good	Fine	Mint
#3	1.00	2.00	3.00
4-7	.65	1.35	2.00

IDEAL ROMANCES
1950
Stanmor

#6	.65	1.35	2.00

I DREAM OF JEANNIE (TV)
1966 - #2, Dec, 1966
Dell Publishing Co.

#1,2	.15	.30	.45

IF THE DEVIL WOULD TALK
1950   (32 pgs.) (Soft cover)
Roman Catholic Catechetical Guild

No# (Rare)	4.00	8.00	12.00

ILLUSTRATED GAGS (See Single Series #16)

ILLUSTRATED LIBRARY OF --, AN (See Classics
Illustrated Giants)

ILLUSTRATED STORIES OF THE OPERAS
1943   (16pgs.;B&W)(25¢)(cover-B&W & Red)
Baily (Bernard) Publ. Co.

No#-Faust (part reprinted in Cisco Kid #1)	4.00	8.00	12.00
No#-Aida	4.00	8.00	12.00

ILLUSTRATED STORY OF ROBIN HOOD & HIS MERRY
MEN, THE (See Robin Hood)

ILLUSTRATED TARZAN BOOK, THE (See Tarzan
Book)

ILLUSTRATED WEEKENDER COMIC
1945
Harry 'A' Chesler

#2-Mr. E, Echo, Sky Chief app.	2.00	4.00	6.00

I LOVED (Formerly Rulah; Colossal Feat.Mag.
#28, 7/49 - #32, 3/50   #33 on)
Fox Features Syndicate

#28-32	1.20	2.40	3.60

I LOVE LUCY COMICS (TV)

Summer, 1953; 8-10/54 - #35, 4-6/62
Dell Publishing Co.

	Good	Fine	Mint
3-D(Summer, '53)	4.00	8.00	12.00
4-Color #535,559	.50	1.00	1.50
#3-10	.30	.60	.90
11-35	.20	.40	.60

I LOVE YOU
June, 1950 - #6, 1951
Fawcett Publications

#1	1.50	3.00	4.50
2-6	.80	1.60	2.40

I LOVE YOU (Formerly In Love)
#7, Sept, 1955 - #121, Dec, 1976
Charlton Comics

#7-Kirby cvr, Powell sty.	1.00	2.00	3.00
8-20	.65	1.35	2.00
21-50	.25	.50	.75
51-121: #113-Jonnie Love app.			
		.10	.20

I'M A COP
1954
Magazine Enterprises

#1(A-1#111)	1.75	3.35	5.00
2(A-1#126),3(A-1#128),4	1.00	2.00	3.00

I'M DICKENS-HE'S FENSTER (TV)
May-July, 1963 - #2, Aug-Oct, 1963
Dell Publishing Co.

#1,2	.25	.50	.75

I MET A HANDSOME COWBOY (See 4-Color #324)

IMPACT
Mar-Apr, 1955 - #5, Nov-Dec, 1955
E.C. Comics

#1	6.00	12.00	18.00
2-5: #4-Crandall story	4.00	8.00	12.00

NOTE: *Crandall* stories-#1-4. *Davis* stories-
#2-4; covers-#1-5. *Evans* stories-#1,4,5.
Ingels stories in all. *Kamen* story-#3. *Krigstein* story-#1,5. *Orlando* story-#2,5.

INCREDIBLE HULK, THE (See Aurora, Book & Record Set, & Rampaging --)
5/62 - #6, 3/63; #102, 4/68 - Present
Marvel Comics Group

#1-Origin	80.00	160.00	240.00
2	30.00	60.00	90.00

(Incredible Hulk cont'd)	Good	Fine	Mint
3-Origin retold	16.50	33.25	50.00
4-6: #6-Intro. Teen Brigade			
	12.00	24.00	36.00
102-Origin retold	1.75	3.35	5.00
103-110	.80	1.60	2.40
111-120	.60	1.20	1.80
121-130	.40	.80	1.20
131-140	.35	.70	1.05
141-1st app. Doc Samson	.50	1.00	1.50
142-150	.30	.60	.90
151-160	.25	.50	.75
161-176,179,180	.25	.50	.75
177,178-Warlock app.	.50	1.00	1.50
181-1st app. Wolverine	.40	.80	1.20
182-200	.20	.40	.60
201-219	.15	.30	.45
Giant-Size #1('75)	.40	.80	1.20
Special #1(10/68)-New material; Steranko			
cover	1.35	2.75	4.00
Special #2(10/69)-Origin retold			
	.65	1.35	2.00
Special #3(1/71),#4(1/72)	.40	.80	1.20
Annual #5(10/76)	.35	.70	1.05
Annual #6(11/77)	.25	.50	.75

NOTE: *Buscema* cover-#202. *Ditko* stories-#2,6; *covers*-#2,6. *Kirby* stories-#1-5; *covers*-#1-5, *Annual* #5. *Starlin* cover-#217. *Staton* stories-#207-209. *Wrightson* cover-#197.

INCREDIBLE MR. LIMPET, THE (See Movie Classics)

INCREDIBLE SCIENCE FICTION (Formerly Weird
#-8/55 - #33, 1-2/56   Science-Fantasy)
E.C. Comics

#30,33	15.00	30.00	45.00
31,32-Williamson/Krenkel in both; Krenkel			
story-#31	20.00	40.00	60.00

NOTE: *Davis* stories-#30,32,33; *covers*-#30-32. *Krigstein* stories in all. *Orlando* stories-#30,32,33("Judgement Day" reprint). *Wood* stories in all; cover-#33.

INDIAN BRAVES (Baffling Mysteries #5 on)
March, 1951 - #4, Sept, 1951
Ace Magazines

#1	1.00	2.00	3.00
2-4	.65	1.35	2.00
I.W. Reprint #1(no date)	.40	.80	1.20

INDIAN CHIEF (White Eagle--)(Formerly The
1951 - #33, Jan-Mar, 1959   Chief)
Dell Publishing Co.

#3-11: #6-White Eagle app.	1.00	2.00	3.00

	Good	Fine	Mint
12-1st White Eagle(10-12/53)-Not same as			
earlier character	1.20	2.40	3.60
13-29	.80	1.60	2.40
30-33-Buscema stories	1.00	2.00	3.00

INDIAN CHIEF (See March of Comics #94,110,
127,140,159,170,187)

INDIAN FIGHTER, THE (See 4-Color #687)

INDIAN FIGHTER
May, 1950 - #11, Jan, 1952
Youthful Magazines

#1	1.35	2.75	4.00
2-11	.65	1.35	2.00

INDIAN LEGENDS OF THE NIAGARA (See American
Graphics)

INDIANS
Spring, 1950 - 1953
Fiction House Magazines (Wings Publ. Co.)

#1-Manzar, White Indian, Long Bow & Orphan of			
the Storm begin	2.00	4.00	6.00
2-Starlight begins	1.00	2.00	3.00
3-5	1.00	2.00	3.00
6-17	.80	1.60	2.40

INDIANS OF THE WILD WEST
Circa 1958? (No date)
I.W. Enterprises

#9-Reprints	.50	1.00	1.50

INDIANS ON THE WARPATH
No date; (132 pgs.) (No Indian stories)
St. John Publishing Co.

No#-Funnies, crime stories; photos of Gene			
Autry, Roy Rogers from movies with			
captions	2.50	5.00	7.50

INDIAN TRIBES (See Famous Indian Tribes)

INDIAN WARRIORS (Formerly White Rider --)
#7, June, 1951 - #11, 1952
Star Publications

#7-11: #11-White Rider & Superhorse app.			
	1.00	2.00	3.00
3-D #1 (12/53)	4.00	8.00	12.00
Accepted Reprint(No#)(inside cover shows			
White Rider & Superhorse #11)-Reprints			
cover/#7; origin White Rider & --			
	.40	.80	1.20

Incredible Science Fiction #30. © WMG

Indian Chief #15. © Dell

Indian Fighter #3. © YM

Inside Crime #3, © Fox   International Comics #1, © WMG   Intimate #1, © CC

INDOORS-OUTDOORS (See Wisco)

INDOOR SPORTS
No Date (64pgs.)(6x9";B&W reprints;Hardcover)
National Specials Co.

	Good	Fine	Mint
By Tad	3.00	6.00	9.00

INFERIOR 5, THE (See Showcase)
Mar-Apr, 1967 - #10, Sept-Oct, 1968; #11,
Aug-Sept, 1972 - #12, Oct-Nov, 1972
National Periodical Publications

#1	.40	.80	1.20
2-Plastic Man app.	.40	.80	1.20
3-5	.25	.50	.75
6-9	.20	.40	.60
10-Superman x-over	.25	.50	.75
11,12-Orlando cover/art; both reprints Show-
case #62,63	.20	.40	.60

INFORMER, THE
April, 1954 - #5, Dec, 1954
Feature Television Productions

#1-Sekowsky art begins	1.00	2.00	3.00
2-5	.60	1.20	1.80

INHUMANS, THE (See Amazing Advs.)
Oct, 1975 - #12, Aug, 1977
Marvel Comics Group

#1	.50	1.00	1.50
2-5	.25	.50	.75
6-12: #9-reprints	.15	.30	.45

NOTE: *Gil Kane* art-#5-7.

INKY & DINKY (Felix's Nephews)
Sept, 1957 - #7, Oct, 1958
Harvey Publications

#1	1.00	2.00	3.00
2-7	.50	1.00	1.50

IN LOVE (I Love You #7 on)
Sept, 1954 - #6, July, 1955
Prime Publ./Mainline(Prize)/Charlton #5 on

#1-Simon & Kirby art	3.35	6.75	10.00
2-2pgs. S&K art	1.35	2.75	4.00
3,4-S&K art	2.00	4.00	6.00
5-S&K cover only	1.35	2.75	4.00
6-No S&K art	.50	1.00	1.50

IN LOVE WITH JESUS
1952 (Giveaway)
Catechetical Educational Society

	Good	Fine	Mint
	1.75	3.35	5.00

IN SEARCH OF THE CASTAWAYS (See Movie Comics)

INSIDE CRIME (Formerly My Intimate Affair)
1950; #3, July, 1950 - #2, Sept, 1950
Fox Features Syndicate (Hero Books)

No#	1.50	3.00	4.50
#3-Wood story, 10pgs.	4.00	8.00	12.00
#2(9/50)	1.20	2.40	3.60

INSPECTOR, THE
July, 1974 - Present
Gold Key

#1	.15	.30	.45
2-5		.15	.30
6-18		.10	.20

INSPECTOR WADE (See Feature Book #13, McKay)

INTERNATIONAL COMICS (-- Crime Patrol #6)
Spring, 1947 - #5, Nov-Dec, 1947
E.C. Comics

#1	15.00	30.00	45.00
2-5	12.00	24.00	36.00

INTERNATIONAL CRIME PATROL (Formerly Interna-
tional Comics #1-5; becomes Crime Patrol #7 c
Spring, 1948
E.C. Comics

#6-Moon Girl app.	20.00	40.00	60.00

INTERSTATE THEATRES' FUN CLUB COMICS
Mid 1940's (10¢ on cover)(B&W cover)(Premium
Interstate Theatres

Cover features MLJ characters looking at a
copy of Top-Notch Comics, but contains an
early Detective Comic on inside; many combinations possible   6.00   12.00   18.00

IN THE DAYS OF THE MOB (Magazine)
Fall, 1971 (Black & White)
Hampshire Dist. Ltd. (National)

#1-Jack Kirby art; has John Dillinger wanted
poster inside	1.00	2.00	3.00

IN THE PRESENCE OF MINE ENEMIES
1973 (35¢)
Spire Christian/Fleming H. Revell Co.

	.15	.30	.45

INTIMATE
December, 1957
Charlton Comics

	Good	Fine	Mint
#1	.35	.70	1.05

INTIMATE CONFESSIONS
1950   (132 pgs.)
Fox Features Syndicate

no#-See Fox Giants. Contents could vary and
    determines price.

INTIMATE CONFESSIONS
July-Aug, 1951 - #8, Mar, 1953
Realistic Comics

#1-Kinster story; cover reprinted from paper-			
back showing lady of the night with Las			
Vegas background	12.00	24.00	36.00
2	2.00	4.00	6.00
3,8-Kinstler story	2.50	5.00	7.50
4-7	1.50	3.00	4.50

INTIMATE CONFESSIONS
1964
C.W. Enterprises/Super Comics

C.W. Reprint #9	.65	1.35	2.00
Super Reprint #12,18	.65	1.35	2.00

INTIMATE LOVE
1950 - #28, Aug, 1954
Standard Comics

#5,6	1.00	2.00	3.00
7,8-Severin/Elder story	1.50	3.00	4.50
9,10: #10-Celardo story	.65	1.35	2.00
11-20,23-25,27,28	.60	1.20	1.80
21,22,26-Toth art	2.00	4.00	6.00

INTIMATE ROMANCES
1950 - 1954
Standard Comics

#1	1.00	2.00	3.00
2-19	.50	1.00	1.50

INTIMATE SECRETS OF ROMANCE
Sept, 1953 - #2, April, 1954
Star Publications

#1	1.00	2.00	3.00
2	.50	1.00	1.50

INTRIGUE
January, 1955
Quality Comics Group

	Good	Fine	Mint
#1(Horror)-Jack Cole art	3.00	6.00	9.00

INVADERS, THE (TV)
Oct, 1967 - #4, Oct, 1968
Gold Key

#1	.50	1.00	1.50
2-4	.30	.60	.90

INVADERS, THE
August, 1975 - Present
Marvel Comics Group

#1-Captain America, Sub-Mariner & Human Torch			
begin	.80	1.60	2.40
2	.50	1.00	1.50
3-5	.40	.80	1.20
6-10: #7-Intro. Union Jack.	.35	.70	1.05
11-Origin Spitfire	.40	.80	1.20
12-19: #19-New Union Jack app.			
	.25	.50	.75
20-Reprints Sub-Mariner story/Motion Picture			
Funnies Weekly with brief write-up about			
MPFW	.50	1.00	1.50
21-24: #24-Burgos & Everett reprint			
	.20	.40	.60
Annual #1(9/77)-Schomburg, Rico stories;			
Schomburg cover	.35	.70	1.05

NOTE: _Kirby covers-#5,6,8,9,12,14-16._
Giant-Size--#1(6/75)(50¢)-Captain America,
  Sub-Mariner, Human Torch reprint from Sub-
  Mariner #1('41)   .50   1.00   1.50

INVISIBLE BOY
March, 1954
St. John Publishing Co.

#2-Origin	2.50	5.00	7.50

INVISIBLE MAN, THE (See Superior Stories #1)

INVISIBLE SCARLET O'NEIL
Dec, 1950 - #3, April, 1951
Famous Funnies (Harvey)

#1	6.00	12.00	18.00
2,3	4.00	8.00	12.00

(See Harvey Comics Hits #59)

IRON FIST
November, 1975 - #15, Sept, 1977
Marvel Comics Group

#1-McWilliams art	.50	1.00	1.50
2	.35	.70	1.05
3-5	.25	.50	.75
6-10	.20	.40	.60
11-15	.15	.30	.45

Intimate Confessions #1, © Real

Invisible Scarlet O'Neil #1, © Harv

Iron Jaw #1, © Seaboard Publ.

Iron Man #1, © MCG   Iron Man & Submariner #1, © MCG   Is This Tomorrow?, © CG

IRON HORSE (TV)
March, 1967 - #2, June, 1967
Dell Publishing Co.

	Good	Fine	Mint
#1,2	.40	.80	1.20

IRON JAW (Also see The Barbarians)
January, 1975 - #4, July, 1975
Atlas/Seaboard Publ.

#1-Adams cover	.40	.80	1.20
2-Adams cover	.25	.50	.75
3,4-Origin	.20	.40	.60

IRON MAN
May, 1968 - Present
Marvel Comics Group

#1-Origin	4.00	8.00	12.00
2	2.00	4.00	6.00
3-5	1.00	2.00	3.00
6-10	.65	1.35	2.00
11-20	.50	1.00	1.50
21-40: #22-Death of Janice Cord			
	.35	.70	1.05
41-46,48-50	.25	.50	.75
47-Origin retold; Smith art	.65	1.35	2.00
51,52	.25	.50	.75
53-Starlin pencils	.35	.70	1.05
54-Everett Sub-Mariner in part			
	.25	.50	.75
55,56-Starlin art	.50	1.00	1.50
57-70	.25	.50	.75
71,73-80: #76 reprts.#9	.20	.40	.60
72-Brunner draws himself & wife, pg. 14,			
panel 1	.25	.50	.75
81-86,89,90	.15	.30	.45
87-1st app. Blizzard	.20	.40	.60
88-Origin Blizzard	.20	.40	.60
91-99,101-106	.15	.30	.45
100-Starlin cover	.20	.40	.60

NOTE: *Craig* pencils-#2-4,15,24,25; inks-#1-
19,26-28; covers-#2-4. *Kirby* covers-#80,90,
92,94,95

Giant Size #1('75)	.40	.80	1.20
Special #1(8/70)	.80	1.60	2.40
Special #2(11/71)	.50	1.00	1.50
Annual #3(6/76)-Manthing app.			
	.35	.70	1.05
Annual #4(8/77)-Newton sty.	.35	.70	1.05

IRON MAN AND SUBMARINER
April, 1968   (One Shot)
Marvel Comics Group

#1-Craig inks-Iron Man	1.35	2.75	4.00

IRON VIC (See Comics Revue #3)
1940; Aug, 1947 - #3, 1947

United Features Syndicate/St. John Publ. Co.

	Good	Fine	Mint
Single Series #22	6.00	12.00	18.00
#2,3(St. John)	1.00	2.00	3.00

ISIS (TV) (Also see Shazam)
Oct-Nov, 1976 - #8, Dec-Jan, 1977-78
National Periodical Publications/DC Comics

#1-Wood inks	.20	.40	.60
2-8	.15	.30	.45

ISLAND AT THE TOP OF THE WORLD (See Walt
Disney Showcase #27)

ISLAND OF DR. MOREAU, THE (Movie)
October, 1977
Marvel Comics Group

#1	.20	.40	.60

I SPY (TV)
Aug, 1966 - #6, Sept, 1968
Gold Key

#1	.50	1.00	1.50
2-6	.30	.60	.90

IS THIS TOMORROW?
1947   (One Shot)   (3 editions)
Catechetical Guild

#1-Theme of communists taking over the USA			
	16.50	26.75	40.00

IT! (See Supernatural Thrillers #1 and
Astonishing Tales #21-24)

IT HAPPENS IN THE BEST FAMILIES
1920   (48 pgs.)   (B&W Sundays)
Powers Photo Engraving Co.

By Briggs	6.00	12.00	18.00

IT REALLY HAPPENED
1944 - #11, Oct, 1947
William H. Wise #1,2/Standard(Visual Editions

#1	1.75	3.50	5.25
2-7,9-11	1.00	2.00	3.00
8-Story of Roy Rogers	1.25	2.50	3.75

NOTE: *Guardineer* story-#7(2); *Schomburg* cov-
er-#6.9.

IT'S ABOUT TIME (TV)
January, 1967
Gold Key

#1(10195-701)	.15	.30	.45

IT'S A DUCK'S LIFE
Feb, 1950 - #11, Feb, 1952
Marvel Comics/Atlas(MMC)

	Good	Fine	Mint
#1-Buck Duck, Super Rabbit begin			
	1.50	3.00	4.50
2-11	1.00	2.00	3.00

IT'S FUN TO STAY ALIVE. (Giveaway)
1948 (16 pgs.) (Heavy stock paper)
Ohio Auto Dealers Association

Featuring: Bugs Bunny, The Berrys, Dixie
Dugan, Elmer, Tim Tyler, Bruce Gentry, Abbie
& Slats, Joe Jinks, The Toodles, & Cokey
| | 4.00 | 8.00 | 12.00 |

IT'S GAME TIME
Sept-Oct, 1955 - #4, Mar-Apr, 1956
National Periodical Publications

#1-(Scarce)-Davy Crockett app. in puzzle			
	3.00	6.00	9.00
2-4 (Scarce)	2.50	5.00	7.50

IT'S LOVE, LOVE, LOVE
November, 1957   (10¢)
St. John Publishing Co.

#1	.65	1.35	2.00

IVANHOE (See Fawcett Movie Comics #20)

IVANHOE
July-Sept, 1963
Dell Publishing Co.

#1(12-373-309)	.65	1.35	2.00

IWO JIMA (See A Spectacular Feature)

JACE PEARSON (See Texas Rangers)

JACK ARMSTRONG
Nov, 1947 - #13, Sept, 1949
Parents' Magazine Institute

#1	4.00	8.00	12.00
2-5	2.00	4.00	6.00
6-13	1.50	3.00	4.50

JACKIE GLEASON
1948; Sept, 1955 - #5, Dec, 1955
St. John Publishing Co.

#1,2(1948)	2.35	4.75	7.00
1(1955)	1.50	3.00	4.50
2-5	.65	1.35	2.00

JACKIE GLEASON & THE HONEYMOONERS (TV)
June-July, 1956 - #12, April-May, 1959
National Periodical Publications

	Good	Fine	Mint
#1	2.00	4.00	6.00
2-12	1.00	2.00	3.00

JACKIE JOKERS (See Richie Rich & --)
March, 1973 - #2, 1973
Harvey Publications

#1,2		.15	.30

JACKIE ROBINSON (Famous Plays of --)
May, 1950 - #6, 1952   (Baseball hero)
Fawcett Publications

#1	4.00	8.00	12.00
2-6	3.00	6.00	9.00

JACK IN THE BOX (Yellow Jacket #1-10)
Feb, 1946; #11, 1946 - #16, 1947
Frank Comunale/Charlton Comics #12 on

#1-Stitches, Marty Mouse & Nutsy McKrow			
	1.35	2.75	4.00
11-Yellowjacket	1.50	3.00	4.50
12,14-16	1.00	2.00	3.00
13-Wolverton art	6.00	12.00	18.00

JACKPOT COMICS (Jolly Jingles #10 on)
Spring, 1941 - #9, Spring, 1943
MLJ Magazines

#1-The Black Hood, Mr. Justice, Steel Sterling			
& Sgt. Boyle begin	50.00	100.00	150.00
2	25.00	50.00	75.00
3,5	16.50	33.25	50.00
4-Archie begins (on sale 12/41)			
	20.00	40.00	60.00
6-9	13.50	26.75	40.00

JACK Q FROST (See Unearthly Spectaculars)

JACK THE GIANT KILLER (See Movie Classics)

JACK THE GIANT KILLER (New Advs. of --)
Aug-Sept, 1953
Bimfort & Co.

V1#1	1.20	2.40	3.60

JACKY'S DIARY (See 4-Color Comics #1091)

JAGUAR, THE (See The Advs. of --)

JAMBOREE
Feb, 1946 - #3, April, 1946
Round Publishing Co.

It's Game Time #1, © DC

Jackie Gleason #3, © DC

Jackpot Comics #2, © MLJ

Jann Of The Jungle #10, © MCG

Jeanie Comics #16, © MCG

Jesse James #20, © Avon

(Jamboree cont'd)	Good	Fine	Mint
#1-3	.80	1.60	2.40

JANE ARDEN (See Pageant of Comics)
March, 1948 - #2, June, 1948
St. John (United Features Syndicate)

#1-Newspaper reprints	4.00	8.00	12.00
2	3.00	6.00	9.00

JANN OF THE JUNGLE (Jungle Tales #1-7)
#8, Nov, 1955 - #17, June, 1957
Atlas Comics (CSI)

#8(#1)	3.00	6.00	9.00
9,11-15	2.00	4.00	6.00
10-Williamson/Colleta cvr	3.00	6.00	9.00
16,17-Three Williamson/Mayo stories, 5 pgs.			
each	4.00	8.00	12.00

JASON & THE ARGONAUTS (See Movie Classics)

JEANIE COMICS (Cowgirl Romances #28)(Formerly
#13, April, 1947 - #27, 1949   Daring)
Marvel Comics/Atlas(CPC)

#13	1.00	2.00	3.00
14,15	.65	1.35	2.00
16-Used in Love and Death by Legman; Kurtz-			
man's "Hey Look"	2.50	5.00	7.50
17-19,22-Kurtzman's "Hey Look", 1-3 pgs. ea.			
	1.75	3.35	5.00
20,21,23-27	.50	1.00	1.50

JEEP COMICS
Winter, 1944 - #3, Mar-Apr, 1948
R. B. Leffingwell & Co.

#1-3-Capt. Power in #1,2; Criss Cross & Jeep			
& Peep(costumed)in all	1.75	3.35	5.00
#1-29(Giveaway)-Tarzan strip reprints in all;			
distributed to U.S. Armed Forces in early			
to mid '40's	3.00	6.00	9.00

JEFF JORDAN, U.S. AGENT
Dec, 1947 - Jan, 1948
D. S. Publishing Co.

#1	1.75	3.35	5.00

JERRY DRUMMER
1957
Charlton Comics

V2#10,11, V3#12	.25	.50	.75

JERRY LEWIS (See Advs. of --)

JESSE JAMES (See 4-Color #757 & The Legend
of --)

JESSE JAMES (Also see Badmen of the West)
Aug, 1950 - #29, Aug-Sept, 1956
Avon Periodicals

	Good	Fine	Mint
#1-"Alabam" reprints begin by Kubert, end #3			
	5.00	10.00	15.00
2-Three Kubert stories	4.00	8.00	12.00
3-Kubert Alabam story reprt/Cowpuncher #2			
	3.00	6.00	9.00
4-No Kubert	1.75	3.50	5.25
5,6-Three Kubert Jesse James stories + 1pg.			
Wood-#5	4.00	8.00	12.00
7-Two Kubert Jesse James stories			
	3.35	6.75	10.00
8-Three Kinstler stories	2.50	5.00	7.50
9,10-No Kubert	1.75	3.35	5.00
11-14	1.50	3.00	4.50
15-Kinstler reprt/#3	1.75	3.35	5.00
16-Kinstler reprt/#3, & Sheriff Bob Dixon's			
Chuck Wagon #1 with name changed to Sher-			
iff Tom Wilson	1.75	3.35	5.00
17-Jesse James reprt/#4; Kinstler cover idea			
from Kubert splash in #6			
	1.75	3.35	5.00
18-Kubert Jesse James reprint/#5			
	1.75	3.35	5.00
19-Kubert Jesse James rpt.	1.75	3.35	5.00
20-Williamson/Frazetta story; reprint-Chief			
Vic. Apache Massacre; Kubert Jesse James			
reprint/#6	6.00	12.00	18.00
21-Two J.James reprts/#4, Kinstler/#4			
	1.75	3.50	5.25
22,23-No Kubert	1.35	2.75	4.00
24-New McCarty strip by Kinstler + Kinstler			
reprt/#9	1.50	3.00	4.50
25-New McCarty, Jesse James strip by Kinst-			
ler; Kinstler J. James reprt/#7,#9			
	1.50	3.00	4.50
26,27-New McCarty J. James strip + a Kinst-			
ler/McCann J. James reprt.			
	1.50	3.00	4.50
28-Reprints most of Red Mountain, Featuring			
Quantrells Raiders	1.35	2.75	4.00
29	1.35	2.75	4.00
Annual(No#, 1952-25¢)"--Brings Six-Gun Just-			
ice to the West"(100pgs.)-3 earlier iss-			
ues rebound. Kubert, Kinstler art			
	5.00	10.00	15.00

NOTE: *Mostly reprints #10 on.* Kinstler *stor-
ies-#3,4,7,8,15(reprt),16(2 stories),21-27;
covers-#3,4,9,17,18,20,21,24-27*

JESSE JAMES
July, 1953
Realistic Publications

No#-Reprints Avon's #1, same cover, colors			
different	2.00	4.00	6.00

JEST (Kayo #12) (Formerly Snap)
1944
Harry 'A' Chesler

	Good	Fine	Mint
#10-Johnny Rebel & Yankee Boy app. in text			
	1.75	3.35	5.00
11-Little Nemo in Adventure Land			
	1.75	3.35	5.00

JESTER
1945
Harry 'A' Chesler

#10	1.50	3.00	4.50

JET (Jet Powers #2-4) (Space Ace #5)
1950 - 1951
Magazine Enterprises

#1(A-1#30)-Powell art begins			
	5.00	10.00	15.00
2(A-1#32)	3.00	6.00	9.00
3(A-1#35)-Williamson sty	7.00	14.00	21.00
4(A-1#38)-Williamson/Wood story			
	8.00	16.00	24.00

JET ACES
1952 - 1953
Fiction House Magazines

#1	1.35	2.75	4.00
2-4	.80	1.60	2.40

JET DREAM (-- & Her Stuntgirl Counterspies)
June, 1968
Gold Key

#1	.40	.80	1.20

JET FIGHTERS
#5, Nov, 1952 - #7, March, 1953
Standard Magazines

#5,7-Toth art	1.75	3.35	5.00
6	.65	1.35	2.00

JETMAN
1950's
Superior Publ. Ltd.

#1	1.35	2.75	4.00

JET POWER (-- Powers #1)(See Jet)
1963
I.W. Enterprises

#1,2(Powell art)-reprints Jet #1 & 2			
	1.00	2.00	3.00

JET PUP (See 3-D Features)

JETSONS, THE (TV)
Jan, 1963 - #36, Oct, 1970 (Hanna-Barbera)
Gold Key

	Good	Fine	Mint
#1	.20	.40	.60
2-36		.15	.30
(See March of Comics #276,330,348)			

JETSONS, THE (TV) (Hanna-Barbera)
Nov, 1970 - #20, Dec, 1973
Charlton Comics

#1-20		.10	.20

JETTA OF THE 21ST CENTURY
#5, 1952 - 1953 (Teen-Age Archie type)
Standard Comics

#5-7	1.00	2.00	3.00

JIGGS & MAGGIE (See 4-Color #18)

JIGGS & MAGGIE
#11, 1949 - #26, Dec-Jan, 1953-54
Standard Comics/Harvey Publications

#11	2.50	5.00	7.50
12-20: #16-Wood text illos.			
	2.00	4.00	6.00
21-25	1.35	2.75	4.00
26-(3-D story)	3.00	6.00	9.00

NOTE: *Sunday page reprints by McManus loosely blended into story continuity. Advertised on covers as "All New".*

JIGSAW (Big Hero Adventures)
Sept, 1966 - #2, Dec, 1966
Harvey Publications (Funday Funnies)

#1-Origin; Crandall art	.80	1.60	2.40
2-Man From S.R.A.M.	.40	.80	1.20

JIGSAW OF DOOM (See Complete Mystery #2)

JIM BOWIE
1953 - #19, April, 1957
Charlton Comics

#1	.65	1.35	2.00
2-19	.35	.70	1.05

JIM BOWIE (See 4-Color #893,993 & Western Tales)

JIM DANDY
May, 1956 - #3, Sept, 1956 (Charles Biro)

Jet Aces #1, © FH   Jet Power #2, © I.W.

Jim Bowie #17, © CC

Jimmy Wakely #2, © DC

Jim Ray's Aviation--#1, © Vital Publ.

Jingle Jangle #2, © Eas

(Jim Dandy cont'd)
Dandy Magazine (Lev Gleason)

	Good	Fine	Mint
#1	1.00	2.00	3.00
2,3	.40	.80	1.20

JIM HARDY (Also see Treasury of Comics &
1939 - 1940; 1947; 1/48   Sparkler)
United Feat. Synd./Spotlight Publ./St. John

Single Series #6	9.00	18.00	27.00
Single Series #27('40)	7.00	14.00	21.00
#1('47)-Spotlight Publ.	2.00	4.00	6.00
2	1.50	3.00	4.50
1(1/48)-St. John-(Feat. Windy & Paddles)			
	1.50	3.00	4.50

JIM HARDY
1944; 1948 (132 pgs.)(25¢)(Giant)
(Tip Top, Sparkler reprints)
Spotlight/United Features Syndicate

(1944)-Origin Mirror Man; Triple Terror app.			
	6.00	12.00	18.00
(1948)	2.50	5.00	7.50

JIMINY CRICKET (See 4-Color #701,795,897,
989 & Walt Disney Showcase #37)

JIMMY (James Swinnerton)
1905 (10x15") (40 pgs. in color)
N. Y. American & Journal

	15.00	37.50	60.00

JIMMY DURANTE (See A-1 Comics #18,20)

JIMMY OLSEN (See Superman's Pal --)

JIMMY WAKELY
Sept-Oct, 1949 - #18, July-Aug, 1952
National Periodical Publications

#1-Alex Toth art; Kit Colby Girl Sheriff be-			
gins	8.00	16.00	24.00
2-Toth art	5.00	10.00	15.00
3,4,6,7-Frazetta art in all, 3pgs. each;			
Kurtzman in #4; Toth in all			
	6.00	12.00	18.00
5,8-15,18-Toth art; #12,14-Kubert art, 3 &			
2pgs.	4.00	8.00	12.00
16,17	2.50	5.00	7.50

JIM RAY'S AVIATION SKETCH BOOK
Feb, 1946 - #2, May-June, 1946
Vital Publishers

#1,2-Picture stories about planes and pilots			
	2.00	4.00	6.00

JIM SOLAR (See Wisco/Klarer)

JINGLE BELLS (See March of Comics #65)

JINGLE DINGLE CHRISTMAS STOCKING COMICS
V2#1, 1951 (no date listed)(100pgs;Giant-Size)
Stanhall Publications (Pub-annually)(25¢)

	Good	Fine	Mint
V2#1-Foodini & Pinhead, Silly Pilly plus			
games & puzzles	1.00	2.00	3.00

JINGLE JANGLE COMICS (Also see Puzzle Fun)
Feb, 1942 - #42, Dec, 1949
Eastern Color Printing Co.

#1-Pie-Face Prince of Old Pretzelburg, &			
Jingle Jangle Tales by George Carlson,			
Hortense, & Benny Bear begin			
	20.00	40.00	60.00
2,3-No Pie-Face Prince	8.00	16.00	24.00
4-Pie-Face Prince cover	10.00	20.00	30.00
5	7.00	14.00	21.00
6-10	6.00	12.00	18.00
11-15	4.00	8.00	12.00
16-30: #17,18-No Pie-Face Prince			
	3.00	6.00	9.00
31-42	2.00	4.00	6.00

NOTE: *George Carlson art(2 stories) in all
except #2,3,17,18; covers-#1-6.*

JING PALS
1946
Victory Magazine Corporation

#1-3	1.00	2.00	3.00

JINKS, PIXIE, AND DIXIE (See Whitman Comic--)
1965   (Giveaway) (Hanna-Barbera)
Florida Power & Light

	.15	.30	.45

JOAN OF ARC (See A-1 Comics #21 & Ideal A
Classical Comic)

JOE COLLEGE
1949 - #2, Winter, 1950
Hillman Periodicals

#1,2-Powell art	1.20	2.40	3.60

JOE JINKS (See Single Series #12)

JOE LOUIS
Sept, 1950 - #2, Nov, 1950
Fawcett Publications

#1	5.00	10.00	15.00
2	3.00	6.00	9.00

JOE PALOOKA
1933 (B&W daily strip reprints)(48pgs.)
Cupples & Leon Co.

	Good	Fine	Mint
#1-by Fisher	9.00	18.00	27.00

JOE PALOOKA (1st Series)
1942 - 1944
Columbia Comics Corp.

#1	10.00	20.00	30.00
2	5.00	10.00	15.00
3,4	4.00	8.00	12.00

JOE PALOOKA (2nd Series)(Battle Adv. #68-73)
Nov, 1945 - #118, 1961
Harvey Publications

#1	6.00	12.00	18.00
2	3.35	6.75	10.00
3,4,6	2.75	5.50	8.25
5-Boy Explorers by S&K + Powell art(7-8/46)			
	7.00	14.00	21.00
7-1st Powell Flyin' Fool, ends #25,			
8-10	2.50	5.00	7.50
11-14,16-20	2.00	4.00	6.00
15-Origin Humphrey	2.50	5.00	7.50
21-60: #44-Joe Palooka marries Ann Howe			
	1.35	2.75	4.00
61-80	1.00	2.00	3.00
81-115	.75	1.50	2.25
16-118 (Giant issues; reprint, 1960-61)			
Kirby art-#116	1.75	3.35	5.00
Joe Palooka Fights His Way Back(1945 Give-away, 24pgs.) Family Comics			
	10.00	20.00	30.00
--Visits the Lost City(1945)(One-Shot)(No#) (50¢)-160pg. continuous story strip re-print. Has biography & photo of Ham Fisher			
	15.00	30.00	45.00

NOTE: *Powell art #26-53 at least.*

JOE YANK
March, 1952 - 1954
Standard Comics (Visual Editions)

#5	1.00	2.00	3.00
6-Toth + Severin/Elder story			
	1.75	3.35	5.00
7,8	.65	1.35	2.00
9-16	.50	1.00	1.50

JOHN CARTER OF MARS (See 4-Color #375,437,488)

JOHN CARTER OF MARS
April, 1964 - #3, Oct, 1964
Gold Key

	Good	Fine	Mint
#1(10104-404)-Reprints 4-Color #375; Jesse Marsh art	2.00	4.00	6.00
2(407), 3(410)-Reprints 4-Color #437 & 488; Marsh art	1.50	3.00	4.50

JOHN CARTER OF MARS
1970 (72pgs.)(Soft cover;10½x16½";B&W)
House of Greystroke

1941-42 Sunday strip reprints; John Coleman Burroughs art	4.00	8.00	12.00

JOHN CARTER, WARLORD OF MARS
June, 1977 - Present
Marvel Comics Group

#1	.35	.70	1.05
2-8	.20	.40	.60
Annual #1(10/77)	.50	1.00	1.50

JOHN F. KENNEDY, CHAMPION OF FREEDOM
1964 (no month) (25¢)
Worden & Childs

No#	2.00	4.00	6.00

JOHN F. KENNEDY LIFE STORY
Aug-Oct, 1964; Nov, 1965; June, 1966 (12¢)
Dell Publishing Co.

#12-378-410	2.00	4.00	6.00
#12-378-511 (reprint)	1.00	2.00	3.00
#12-378-606 (reprint)	1.00	2.00	3.00

JOHN FORCE (See Magic Agent)

JOHN HIX SCRAP BOOK, THE
Late 1930's (no date)(68pgs.-Reg. size)(10¢)
Eastern Color Printing Co.(McNaught Synd.)

No#(#1)-Strange As It Seems (resembles Single Series books)	6.00	12.00	18.00
#2-Strange As It Seems	5.00	10.00	15.00

JOHNNY DANGER
1950
Toby Press

#1	1.50	3.00	4.50

JOHNNY DANGER PRIVATE DETECTIVE
1954 (Reprinted in Danger #11 (Super))
Toby Press

#1	1.20	2.40	3.60

Joe Palooka #2, © CCG

John Carter #1(GK), © ERB

John Hix Scrap Book #1, © Eas

Johnny Law #1, © Lev   John Wayne #8, © Toby   Jo-Jo Comics #12, © Fox

JOHNNY DYNAMITE (Formerly Dynamite #1-9)
1955 - 1956
Charlton Comics

	Good	Fine	Mint
#10-12	.90	1.80	2.70

JOHNNY HAZARD
#5, Aug, 1948 - #8, May, 1949
Best Books (Standard Comics)

#5-Strip reprints by Frank Robbins
	2.50	5.00	7.50
6,8-Strip reprints by Frank Robbins			
	2.00	4.00	6.00
7-New art, not Robbins	1.50	3.00	4.50
#35	1.75	3.35	5.00

JOHNNY JASON (-- Teen Reporter)
Feb-Apr, 1962 - #2, June-Aug, 1962
Dell Publishing Co.

4-Color #1302,#2(01380-208)	.35	.70	1.05

JOHNNY LAW, SKY RANGER
April, 1955 - #3, Aug, 1955; #4, Nov, 1955
Good Comics (Lev Gleason)

#1-Edmond Good art	2.00	4.00	6.00
2-4	1.50	3.00	4.50

JOHNNY MACK BROWN
#2, Oct-Dec, 1950 - #10, Sept-Nov, 1952
Dell Publishing Co.

4-Color #269('50)-Marsh art
	3.00	6.00	9.00
#2(1950)-Marsh art	2.00	4.00	6.00
3-10: Marsh art #3-9	1.50	3.00	4.50
4-Color #455,493	1.50	3.00	4.50
4-Color #541,584,618,645,685,722,776,834,922,			
963,967	1.35	2.75	4.00

JOHNNY RINGO (See 4-Color #1142)

JOHNNY STARBOARD (See Wisco)

JOHNNY THUNDER
Feb-Mar, 1973 - #3, July-Aug, 1973
National Periodical Publications

#1-Johnny Thunder & Nighthawk reprints begin
	.25	.50	.75
2-Trigger Twins app., #3	.20	.40	.60

NOTE: *Drucker stories-#2,3. Infantino story-*
#2. Toth stories-#1,3. Also see All-American
& All-Star Western.

JOHN PAUL JONES

Sept, 1959 - 1959
Dell Publishing Co.

	Good	Fine	Mint
4-Color #1007, #1	1.20	2.40	3.60

JOHN STEED & EMMA PEEL (See The Avengers)

JOHN STEELE SECRET AGENT
Dec, 1964 (Freedom Agent)
Gold Key

#1	.50	1.00	1.50

JOHN WAYNE ADVENTURE COMICS (See Oxydol-Dreft)
Winter, 1949 - #31, May, 1955
Toby Press

#1	5.00	10.00	15.00
2-Two Williamson/Frazetta stories(one reprt/ Billy the Kid #1), 6 & 2 pgs.,			
3,4-Two Williamson/Frazetta stories, 16pgs. total each	9.00	18.00	27.00
5-Kurtzman art-(Alfred "L" Newman in Potshot Pete)	2.50	5.00	7.50
6,7-Williamson/Frazetta story in both; Kurtzman art in #6	9.00	18.00	27.00
8-Two Williamson/Frazetta stories, 12 & 9 pgs.	10.00	20.00	30.00
9-11,13-15	1.35	2.75	4.00
12-Kurtzman art	2.00	4.00	6.00
16-Williamson/Frazetta reprint from Billy the Kid #1	4.00	8.00	12.00
17,19-24,26-28,30	1.20	2.40	3.60
18-Williamson/Frazetta stories reprts./John Wayne #4&8	6.00	12.00	18.00
25-Williamson/Frazetta reprinted from Billy the Kid #3	6.00	12.00	18.00
29-Williamson/Frazetta story reprint from #4	6.00	12.00	18.00
31-Williamson/Frazetta story reprint from #2	6.00	12.00	18.00

NOTE: *Williamsonish art in later issues by*
Gerald McCann.

JO-JO COMICS (--Congo King #7-29; My Desire
#30 on) (Also see Jungle Jo)
1945 - #29, July, 1949 (2 #7's; no #13)
Fox Features Syndicate

No#(1945)-Funny animal	1.20	2.40	3.60
#2(4-5/47)-6-Funny animal	1.00	2.00	3.00
7(7/47)-Jo-Jo, Congo King begins			
	12.00	24.00	36.00
7(#8)-(9/47)	10.00	20.00	30.00
8-10(#9-11): #8-Tanee begins			
	10.00	20.00	30.00
11,12(#12,13)	8.00	16.00	24.00
14-16	8.00	16.00	24.00

(Jo-Jo cont'd)	Good	Fine	Mint
17-Kamen cover	9.00	18.00	27.00
18-20	7.00	14.00	21.00
21-29	6.00	12.00	18.00

NOTE: *Many bondage covers & art by Baker/ Kamen/Feldstein. #7's have Princesses Gwenna, Geesa, Yolda & Safra before settling down on Tanee.*

JO-JOY (Adventures of --)
1945 - 1953   (Christmas gift comic)
W. T. Grant Dept. Stores

1945-53 issues	.80	1.20	2.40

JOKEBOOK COMICS DIGEST ANNUAL
Oct, 1977 - Present (192pgs.-Digest Size)
Archie Publications

#1-Reprints	.40	.80	1.20

JOKER, THE (See Batman & Detective)
May, 1975 - #9, Sept-Oct, 1976
National Periodical Publications

#1-Two-Face app.	.25	.50	.75
2-5: #3-The Creeper app. #4-Green Arrow, Black Canary app.	.20	.40	.60
6-9: #9-Catwoman app.	.15	.30	.45

JOKER COMICS (Adventures Into Terror #43 on)
April, 1942 - #42, March, 1950
Timely/Marvel Comics #36 on

#1-1st app. Powerhouse Pepper by Wolverton; Stuporman app. from Daring	40.00	80.00	120.00
2-Wolverton art cont'd.	20.00	40.00	60.00
3-5- " " "	12.00	24.00	36.00
6-10- " " "	9.00	18.00	27.00
11-20- " " "	5.00	10.00	15.00
21-27,29,30-Wolverton cont'd. & Kurtzman's "Hey Look" in #23-27	4.00	8.00	12.00
28,32,34,37-42	.80	1.60	2.40
31-Last Powerhouse Pepper; not in #28	4.00	8.00	12.00
33,35,36-Kurtzman's "Hey Look"	2.00	4.00	6.00

JOLLY CHRISTMAS, A (See March of Comics #269)

JOLLY CHRISTMAS BOOK (See Christmas Journey Through Space)
1951; 1954; 1955   (36pgs.; 24pgs.)
Promotional Publ. Co.

1951-Slightly oversized; no slick cover (Woolworth giveaway)-Marv Levy cover/art

	Good	Fine	Mint
	1.75	3.35	5.00
1954-Regular size-reprints '51 issue; slick cover added (24pgs., no ads)(Hot Shoppes giveaway)	1.75	3.35	5.00
1955-Regular size (J.M. McDonald Co. give-away)	1.35	2.75	4.00

JOLLY COMICS
1947
Four Star Publishing Co.

#1	.80	1.60	2.40

JOLLY JINGLES (Formerly Jackpot)
1944 - 1945
MLJ Magazines

#10-Super Duck begins	2.00	4.00	6.00
11-25	1.20	2.40	3.60

JONAH HEX
Mar-Apr, 1977 - Present
National Periodical Publications/DC Comics

#1	.20	.40	.60
2-10: #10-Morrow cover	.15	.30	.45

JONESY (Formerly Crack Western)
#85, 8/53; #2, 10/53 - #8, 1954
Comic Favorite/Quality Comics Group

#85(#1)	.40	.80	1.20
#2-8	.30	.60	.90

JON JUAN (Also see Great Lover Romances)
Spring, 1950
Toby Press

#1-All Schomburg art (signed Al Reid) - written by Siegel	4.00	8.00	12.00

JONNY QUEST (TV)
Dec, 1964   (Hanna-Barbera)
Gold Key

#1(10139-412)	.35	.70	1.05

JOSEPH & HIS BRETHREN (See The Living Bible)

JOSIE (She's --#1-13)(-- & the Pussycats #45 on)
Feb, 1963 - Present
Archie Publ./Radio Comics

#1	1.00	2.00	3.00
2-10	.50	1.00	1.50
11-49,51-54	.25	.50	.75
50-Meet William Hanna & Joseph Barbera, the			

Jo-Jo Comics #16, © Fox

Jo-Jo Comics #20, © Fox

Joker Comics #2, © MCG

Journey Into Mystery #86, © MCG

Journey Into Mystery #109, © MCG

Journey Into Unknown Worlds #52, © MCG

(Josie cont'd)	Good	Fine	Mint
cartoon producers	.25	.50	.75
55-74(Giants)(52pgs.)	.25	.50	.75
75-96		.15	.30

JOURNAL OF CRIME
1949   (132 pgs.)
Fox Features Syndicate

No#-See Fox Giants. Contents can vary and determines price.

JOURNEY INTO FEAR
May, 1951 - #21, Sept, 1954
Superior-Dynamic Publications

	Good	Fine	Mint
#1-Two Baker stories	2.00	4.00	6.00
2-21	1.00	2.00	3.00

JOURNEY INTO MYSTERY (1st Series)(Thor #126
6/52 - #48,8/57; #49,11/58 - #125,2/66   on)
Atlas(CPS #1-48/AMI #49-82/Marvel #83 on)

#1	26.50	53.25	80.00
2	13.50	26.75	40.00
3,4	10.00	20.00	30.00
5-10: #5-Briefer story	5.00	10.00	15.00
11-20,22-Last pre-code ish			
	2.50	5.00	7.50
21-Kubert story	3.35	6.75	10.00
23-32,35-38,40,41	1.75	3.35	5.00
33,34-Williamson story in both + Krigstein			
story in #34	3.35	6.75	10.00
39-Wood story	3.35	6.75	10.00
42-Torres story	1.75	3.50	5.25
43,44-Williamson/Mayo story in both			
	2.50	5.00	7.50
45,47-49,52,53	1.35	2.75	4.00
46-Torres & Krigstein sty.	2.00	4.00	6.00
50-Davis story	2.00	4.00	6.00
51-Kirby/Wood story	1.75	3.35	5.00
54-Williamson story	2.50	5.00	7.50
55-73: #62-1st app. Xemu(Titan)-called "The			
Hulk" in #62. #66-Return of Xemu			
	1.35	2.75	4.00
74-82-Contents change to Fantasy with #74			
	1.00	2.00	3.00
83-Reprint from the Golden Record Comic Set			
	1.00	2.00	3.00
with the record...	2.00	4.00	6.00
83-Origin & 1st app. The Mighty Thor by			
Kirby(8/62)	75.00	150.00	225.00
84	20.00	40.00	60.00
85-1st app. Loki & Heimdall			
	15.00	30.00	45.00
86-1st app. Odin	8.00	16.00	24.00
87-90	6.00	12.00	18.00
91-100: #97-Tales of Asgard series begins			

	Good	Fine	Mint
	4.00	8.00	12.00
101-110: #108-Doctor Strange x-over			
	1.75	3.35	5.00
111,113-125	1.00	2.00	3.00
112-Thor Vs. Hulk	1.50	3.00	4.50
Annual #1('65)-1st app. Hercules; Kirby			
cover/story	2.50	5.00	7.50

NOTE: *Crandall* story-#41. *Ditko* stories-#50, 53. *Ditko/Kirby* art in all issues #50-82. *Everett* story-#9(reprt.),40; covers-#5,6,37, 39,40,44,45. *Russ Heath* cover-#51. *Kirby* stories-#83-89,93,97,101-125; covers-#50-82 (w/Ditko),83,84,86,87,89,90,92,94,97-125. *Morrow* story-#42. *Orlando* story-#16,30,45,57

JOURNEY INTO MYSTERY (2nd Series)
Oct, 1972 - #19, Oct, 1975
Marvel Comics Group

#1-Robert Howard adaptation; Kane art; Star-			
lin/Ploog story	.40	.80	1.20
2-Robert Bloch adaptation; Starlin/Ploog			
art; Adams inks	.35	.70	1.05
3-Bloch adaptation	.25	.50	.75
4-H.P. Lovecraft adapt.	.25	.50	.75
5-Last new story	.20	.40	.60
6-19: #16-Orlando reprt.	.15	.30	.45

NOTE: *Ditko* reprints-#7,10,12,15,19. *Everett* reprint-#9. *Kirby* reprints-#7,13,18,19; cover-#7. *Orlando* reprint-#16. *Wildey* reprints-#9,14.

JOURNEY INTO UNKNOWN WORLDS (Formerly Teen)
#36, Sept, 1950 - #59, Aug, 1957
Atlas Comics (WFP)

#36(#1)-Science fiction	5.00	10.00	15.00
37(#2)- " "	4.00	8.00	12.00
38(#3)- " "	3.00	6.00	9.00
#4-6,8,9,10(All horror)	2.00	4.00	6.00
7,14,15-Wolverton art	7.00	14.00	21.00
11,12-Krigstein stories	1.75	3.50	5.25
13,16-20	1.00	2.00	3.00
21-33,36-42	.80	1.60	2.40
34-Kubert + Torres story	1.75	3.35	5.00
35-Torres story	1.50	3.00	4.50
43-Krigstein story	1.35	2.75	4.00
44-Davis story	1.50	3.00	4.50
45,55,59-Williamson stories in all with Mayo			
#55,59+Crandall Sty#55	2.50	5.00	7.50
46,47,49,52,56-58	.80	1.60	2.40
48,51-Wood + Crandall #48	2.00	4.00	6.00
50-Davis story	1.50	3.00	4.50
53-Crandall story	1.20	2.40	3.60
54-Torres story	1.00	2.00	3.00

NOTE: *Ditko* story-#50,51; cover-#31. *Everett* story-#11,14,41,47,48,55; covers-#17,47,50,

(Journey Into Unknown Worlds cont'd)
53-55,59. *Morrow story-#48*. *Orlando story-#44,57*. *Powell stories-#53,54*.

JOURNEY OF DISCOVERY WITH MARK STEEL
(See Mark Steel)

JOURNEY TO THE CENTER OF THE EARTH (See 4-Color Comics #1060)

JUDGE COLT
Oct, 1969 - #4, Sept, 1970
Gold Key

	Good	Fine	Mint
#1-4	.25	.50	.75

JUDGE PARKER
1956
Argo

#1	1.50	3.00	4.50
2	1.20	2.40	3.60

JUDO JOE
Aug, 1953 - #3, Dec, 1953
Jay-Jay Corp.

#1-Drug story	2.00	4.00	6.00
2,3	1.00	2.00	3.00

JUDOMASTER (Gun Master #84-90)(See Special
#89, 5-6/66 - #98, 12/67   War Series)
Charlton Comics   (Two #89's)

#89-98: #91-Sarge Steel begins. #93-Intro.			
Tiger	.60	1.20	1.80

JUDY CANOVA (Formerly My Experience)
May, 1950 - #3, Sept, 1950
Fox Features Syndicate

#23(#1),24	2.00	4.00	6.00
3-Wood story?	2.50	5.00	7.50

JUDY GARLAND (See Famous Stars)

JUDY JOINS THE WAVES
1951   (For U.S. Navy)
Toby Press

No#	.80	1.60	2.40

JUGHEAD (Formerly Archie's Pal --)
#127, Dec, 1965 - Present
Archie Publications

#127-130	.50	1.00	1.50
131,133,135-160	.35	.70	1.05

	Good	Fine	Mint
132-Shield cover, #134-Shield cover & app.			
	.40	.80	1.20
161-200	.20	.40	.60
201-240	.15	.30	.45
241-271		.15	.30

JUGHEAD AS CAPTAIN HERO
Oct, 1966 - #7, Nov, 1967
Archie Publications

#1	.65	1.35	2.00
2-7	.35	.70	1.05

JUGHEAD JONES COMICS DIGEST
June, 1977 - Present   (160 pgs.)
Archie Publications

#1-Capt. Hero reprint	.35	.70	1.05
2(9/77)-#3	.25	.50	.75

JUGHEAD'S EAT-OUT COMIC BOOK MAGAZINE
(See Archie Giant Series Mag. #170)

JUGHEAD'S FANTASY
Aug, 1960 - #3, Dec, 1960
Archie Publications

#1	1.50	3.00	4.50
2,3	.65	1.35	2.00

JUGHEAD'S FOLLY
1957
Archie Publications (Close-Up)

#1	2.00	4.00	6.00

JUGHEAD'S JOKES
Aug, 1967 - Present
#1-8,38 on-reg.size;#9-23, 68pgs;#24-37,52pgs.
Archie Publications

#1	1.00	2.00	3.00
2-10	.65	1.35	2.00
11-30	.25	.50	.75
31-56		.15	.30

JUGHEAD WITH ARCHIE (-- Plus Betty &
Veronica & Reggie Too #1,2)
March, 1974 - Present   (Digest Size-160 pgs.)
Archie Publications

#1	.60	1.20	1.80
2-10	.25	.50	.75
11-23: Capt. Hero reprint in #14-16; Pure-heart the Powerful #18,21,22; Capt. Pure-heart reprts. in #17,19	.20	.40	.60

Judo Master #92. © CC

Judy Canova #3. © Fox

Jumbo Comics #8, © FH

Jumbo Comics #17, © FH   Jumbo Comics #99, © FH   Jungle Adventures #15, © Super

JUKE BOX COMICS
March, 1948 - #6, 1949
Famous Funnies

	Good	Fine	Mint
#1-Toth art	4.00	8.00	12.00
2-6	2.50	5.00	7.50

JUMBO COMICS (#1-8 oversized-10½x14½"; B&W)
9/38 - #167, 4/53 (#1-3, 68 pgs;#4-8, 52 pgs)
Fiction House Magazines(Real Adv. Publ. Co.)

#1-(Rare)-Origin Sheena, Queen of the Jungle
   by Meskin; The Hawk by Eisner, The Hunchback by Dick Briefer(ends #8)begin; 1st
   comic art by Jack Kirby (Count of Monte
   Cristo & Wilton of the West); Mickey Mouse
   appears(1 panel) with brief biography of
   Walt Disney.   140.00 350.00 560.00
2-Diary of Dr. Hayward by Kirby (also #3)
   plus 2 other stories; contains strip from
   Universal Film featuring Edgar Bergen &
   Charlie McCarthy   70.00 175.00 280.00
3-Last Kirby ish.   50.00 125.00 200.00
4-Origin The Hawk by Eisner; Wilton of the
   West by Fine(ends #14); Count of Monte
   Cristo by Fine(ends #15); The Diary of
   Dr. Hayward by Fine(cont'd. #8,9)
                         50.00 125.00 200.00
5   40.00 100.00 160.00
6-8-Last B&W issue. #8 was a N.Y. World's
   Fair Special Ed.   30.00 75.00 120.00
9-Stuart Taylor begins by Fine; Fine cover;
   1st color issue-8¼x10¼"
                         30.00 60.00 90.00
10-14   25.00 50.00 75.00
15-Lightning begins   16.50 33.25 50.00
16-20   13.50 26.75 40.00
21-30: #22-1st Tom, Dick & Harry; origin The
   Hawk retold   9.00 18.00 27.00
31-40: #35 shows V2#11 (correct # does not
   appear)   7.00 14.00 21.00
41-50   6.00 12.00 18.00
51-60   4.50   9.00 13.50
61-70: #68-Sky Girl begins, ends #130
                          3.50   7.00 10.50
71-80   3.00   6.00   9.00
81-93,95-100: #89-2x5 becomes a private eye
                          2.75   5.50   8.25
94-Used in Love and Death by Legman
                          4.00   8.00 12.00
101-110   2.50   5.00   7.50
111-140: #131-Long Bow, Indian Boy begins,
   ends #159   2.00   4.00   6.00
141-158   1.75   3.50   5.25
159-163: Space Scouts serial in all; #163-
   Suicide Smith app.   1.75   3.50   5.25
164-The Star Pirate begins 1.75 3.50   5.25
165-167: The Space Rangers app. #165,167

	Good	Fine	Mint
	1.75	3.50	5.25

NOTE: Hawk by Eisner-#10-15; Eisner covers-
#6,12,13,15. Sheena by Meskin-#1,4; by Powell-
#2,3,5-28; by Crandall-#41-51. Sky Girl by
Matt Baker-#69-78,80-124. Bailey art-#3-8.
Briefer art-#1-8. Fine covers-#9-11. Bob Kane
art-#1-8.

JUNGLE ACTION
Oct, 1954 - #6, Aug, 1955
Atlas Comics (IPC)

	Good	Fine	Mint
#1-Leopard Girl app.	3.00	6.00	9.00
2,4-6	2.00	4.00	6.00
3-Leopard Girl app.	2.50	5.00	7.50

JUNGLE ACTION
Oct, 1972 - #24, Nov, 1976
Marvel Comics Group

	Good	Fine	Mint
#1-Lorna, Jann reprints	.25	.50	.75
2-4: #3-Tharn reprints	.15	.30	.45
5-Black Panther begins	.35	.70	1.05
6-10-All new stories	.25	.50	.75
11-24: All new stories. #18-Kirby cover. #23-reprint/#22, Buscema cvr.	.20	.40	.60

JUNGLE ADVENTURES
1963 - 1964   (Reprints)
Super Comics

	Good	Fine	Mint
#10,12(Rulah),15(Kaanga/Jungle #152)	1.50	3.00	4.50
17(Jo-Jo)	1.50	3.00	4.50
18-Reprints/White Princess of the Jungle #1; No Kinstler art; origin of both White Princess & Cap'n Courage	2.00	4.00	6.00

JUNGLE ADVENTURES
March, 1971 - #3, June, 1971
Skywald Comics

	Good	Fine	Mint
#1-Zangar origin; reprints of Jo-Jo, Blue Gorilla(origin)/White Princess #3, Kinstler story/White Princess #2	.35	.70	1.05
2-Zangar, Sheena/Sheena #17 & Jumbo #162, Jo-Jo, origin Slave Girl Princess reprints	.35	.70	1.05
3-Zangar, Jo-Jo, White Princess reprints	.35	.70	1.05

JUNGLE BOOK, THE (See Movie Comics)

JUNGLE CAT (See 4-Color Comics #1136)

JUNGLE COMICS
Jan, 1940 - #163, Summer, 1954

(Jungle Comics cont'd)
Fiction House Magazines

	Good	Fine	Mint
#1-Origin The White Panther, Kaanga, Lord of the Jungle, Tabu, Wizard of the Jungle; Wambi, the Jungle Boy & Camilla begin	65.00	130.00	195.00
2-Fantomah, Mystery Woman of the Jungle begins	35.00	70.00	105.00
3,4	23.50	46.75	70.00
5	18.00	36.00	54.00
6-10	15.00	30.00	45.00
11-20	9.00	18.00	27.00
21-30: #25 shows V2#1(correct # does not appear). #27-New origin Fantomah, Daughter of the Pharoahs; Camilla dons new costume	7.00	14.00	21.00
31-40	6.00	12.00	18.00
41-50: #42-Kaanga by Crandall	4.00	8.00	12.00
51-60	3.00	6.00	9.00
61-70	2.50	5.00	7.50
71-110: #79-New origin Tabu	2.25	4.50	6.75
111-150: #135-Desert Panther begins in Terry Thunder(origin), not in #137; ends(dies) #138	2.00	4.00	6.00
151-163: #152-Tiger Girl begins. #158-Sheena app.	1.75	3.35	5.00
IW Reprint #1,9: #9-reprints #151	1.35	2.75	4.00

NOTE: _Kaanga by John Celardo_ #90-110; _by Maurice Whitman_ #124-163. _Tabu by Whitman_ #94-110. _Crandall_ art-#25-37,42,49-61. _Eisner_ cover-#2,5. _Fine_ cover-#1,3. _Bondage covers_ are common.

JUNGLE GIRL   (See Lorna, --)

JUNGLE GIRL   (Nyoka, -- #2 on)
Autumn, 1942
Fawcett Publications

#1	22.50	45.00	67.50

JUNGLE JIM
Jan, 1949 - #20, April, 1951
Standard Comics (Best Books)

#11-20	1.50	3.00	4.50

JUNGLE JIM
1953 - #1020, Aug-Oct, 1959
Dell Publishing Co.

4-Color #490,565('53-54)	1.35	3.50	5.25
#3(10-12/54)-#5	1.35	2.75	4.00
6-20(4-6/59)	1.00	2.00	3.00

	Good	Fine	Mint
4-Color #1020(#21)	1.20	2.40	3.60

JUNGLE JIM
December, 1967
King Features Syndicate

#5-Reprints Dell #5; Wood cover	.40	.80	1.20

JUNGLE JIM   (Continued from Dell)
#22, Feb, 1969 - #28, Feb, 1970 (No #21)
Charlton Comics

#22-Dan Flagg begins, ends #23; Wood & Ditko art	.60	1.20	1.80
23-28: #23-Wood cvr. #24-Jungle People begin. #27-Wood, Ditko art. #28-Ditko	.35	.70	1.05

Jungle Jo No #, © Fox

JUNGLE JO
Mar, 1950 - #6, Mar, 1951
Fox Features Syndicate (Hero Books)

No#-Jo-Jo blanked out, leaving Congo King; came out after Jo-Jo #29(intended as Jo-Jo #30?)	5.00	10.00	15.00
#1-Tangi begins	5.00	10.00	15.00
2-6	4.00	8.00	12.00

JUNGLE LIL   (Dorothy Lamour, Jungle Princess #2 on)(Also see Feature Stories Magazine)
April, 1950
Fox Features Syndicate/Hero Books

#1	6.00	12.00	18.00

JUNGLE TALES   (Jann of the Jungle #8 on)
Sept, 1954 - #7, Sept, 1955
Atlas Comics (CSI)

Jungle Comics #78, © FH

Jungle Comics #87, © FH

Jungle Jim #14, © Dell

223

Jungle Tales Of Tarzan #1, © ERB

Junior #10, © Fox

Junior Miss #1, © MCG

(Jungle Tales cont'd)	Good	Fine	Mint
#1-Jann of the Jungle	2.50	5.00	7.50
2-7	2.00	4.00	6.00

JUNGLE TALES OF TARZAN
Dec, 1964 - #5, 1965
Charlton Comics

#1	2.00	4.00	6.00
2-4	1.35	2.75	4.00

5-(Very Rare)-Cardboard covers in color;
   Glanzman art-This series was unauthorized
   & killed after #5 was printed - all but a
   few issues of #5 were destroyed.
                 Estimated value..... $350.00
NOTE: *Glanzman didn't get his art back; was
told had to be destroyed with other Tarzan
art.*

JUNGLE TERROR (See Harvey Comics Hits #54)

JUNGLE THRILLS (Terrors of the Jungle #17)
#16, Feb, 1952
Fox Features Syndicate/Star Publications

#16-Phantom Lady & Rulah story-reprint/All
   Top #15   8.00 16.00 24.00
3-D#1(12/53)-Jungle Lil & Jungle Jo appears
                         5.00 10.00 15.00

JUNGLE TWINS, THE (Tono & Kono)
April, 1972 - #17, Nov, 1975
Gold Key

#1	.20	.40	.60
2-5	.15	.30	.45
6-17		.15	.30

JUNGLE WAR STORIES (Guerrilla War #12 on)
July-Sept, 1962 - #11, Apr-June, 1965
Dell Publishing Co.

#01-384-209	.35	.70	1.05
#2-11	.25	.50	.75

JUNIE PROM
Winter, 1947-48 - #7, August, 1949
Dearfield Publishing Co.

#1	1.20	2.40	3.60
2-7	.80	1.60	2.40

JUNIOR COMICS
#9, Sept, 1947 - #16, July, 1948
Fox Features Syndicate

#9-16-Feldstein cvr/stys 10.00 20.00 30.00

JUNIOR FUNNIES (Formerly Tiny Tot Funnies #9)
#10, Aug, 1951 - #13, Feb, 1952
Harvey Publications (King Features Synd.)

	Good	Fine	Mint
#10-13: Partial reprints-Blondie, Popeye, Fe-			
lix, Katzenjammer Kids	1.00	2.00	3.00

JUNIOR HOP COMICS (Junior Hopp)
1952 - #3, July, 1952
Atlas Comics/SPM Publ.

#1,2	1.00	2.00	3.00
3-Dave Berg art	1.00	2.00	3.00

JUNIOR MEDICS OF AMERICA, THE
1957   (15¢)
E. R. Squire & Sons

#1359	.65	1.35	2.00

JUNIOR MISS
Winter, 1944 - #39, August, 1950
Timely/Marvel Comics(CnPC)

#1-Frank Sinatra life story

	2.50	5.00	7.50
2-10	1.35	2.75	4.00
11-20	1.00	2.00	3.00
21-38	.60	1.20	1.80
39-Kurtzman art	1.50	3.00	4.50

JUNIOR PARTNERS (Formerly Oral Roberts' True
#120, 8/59 - V3#12, 12/61   Stories)
Oral Roberts Evangelistic Assn.

#120(#1)	1.00	2.00	3.00
#2(9/59)	.65	1.35	2.00
3-12(7/60)	.50	1.00	1.50
V2#1(8/60)-5(12/60)	.25	.50	.75
V3#1(1/61)-12	.20	.40	.60

JUNIOR TREASURY (See Dell Junior --)

JUNIOR WOODCHUCKS (See Huey, Dewey & Louie--)

JUSTICE COMICS (Tales of Justice #63 on;
Formerly Wacky Duck)
#7, Fall/47 - #9, 6/48; #4, 8/48 - #57, 12/55
Atlas(NPP #7-19/CnPC #20-23/MgMC #24-37/
Male #38-62

#7-9('47-48)	1.35	2.75	4.00
4-10	.80	1.60	2.40
11-30: #22,25-Robinson art	.50	1.00	1.50
31-57	.40	.80	1.20

NOTE: *Everett story-#53.*

JUSTICE, INC. (The Avenger)
May-June, 1975 - #4, Nov-Dec, 1975
National Periodical Publications

	Good	Fine	Mint
#1-McWilliams sty.; origin	.20	.40	.60
2-4	.15	.30	.45

NOTE: *Kirby* covers-#2,3; *stories-#2-4.*
Kubert covers-#1,4.

JUSTICE LEAGUE OF AMERICA (See Brave & Bold)
Oct-Nov, 1960 - Present
National Periodical Publications/DC Comics

#1-Origin Despero	20.00	40.00	60.00
2	10.00	20.00	30.00
3-Origin Kanjarro	7.00	14.00	21.00
4,5: #4-Green Arrow joins JLA. #5-Origin Dr.			
Destiny	5.00	10.00	15.00
6-8,10: #6-Origin Prof. Amos Fortune. #10-			
Origin Felix Faust	3.00	6.00	9.00
9-Origin J.L.A.	4.00	8.00	12.00
11-13,15: #12-Origin Dr. Light. #13-Speedy			
app.	2.00	4.00	6.00
14-Atom joins JLA	2.50	5.00	7.50
16-20: #17-Adam Strange flashback			
	1.75	3.35	5.00
21,22: #21-Re-intro. of JSA. #22-JSA x-over			
	1.75	3.35	5.00
23-28: #28-Robin app.	1.00	2.00	3.00
29,30-JSA x-over	1.50	3.00	4.50
31-Hawkman joins JLA, Hawkgirl cameo			
	1.20	2.40	3.60
32-Origin Brain Storm	1.20	2.40	3.60
33-36,40	.75	1.50	2.25
37,38-JSA x-over	1.35	2.75	4.00
39-25¢ Giant G-16	1.00	2.00	3.00
41-Origin The Key	.80	1.60	2.40
42-45: #42-Metamorpho app.	.60	1.20	1.80
46,47-JSA x-over	.75	1.50	2.25
48-25¢ Giant G-29	.80	1.60	2.40
50-Robin app.	.60	1.20	1.80
51-54,56,57,59,60	.50	1.00	1.50
55-Intro. Earth 2 Robin	.60	1.20	1.80
58-25¢ Giant G-41	.60	1.20	1.80
61-63,66,68-70: #69-Wonder Woman quits. #70-			
Creeper x-over	.40	.80	1.20
64,65-JSA x-over; intro. Red Tornado #65			
	.50	1.00	1.50
67-25¢ Giant G-53	.50	1.00	1.50
71,72,75,77-80: #71-Manhunter leaves JLA.			
#78-Re-intro. Vigilante. #79-Vigilante			
x-over	.35	.70	1.05
73,74-JSA x-over; #73-Black Canary leaves			
JSA & joins JLA	.40	.80	1.20
76-25¢ Giant G-65	.40	.80	1.20
81,84,86-90	.35	.70	1.05
82-JSA x-over; origin Brainstorm			
	.50	1.00	1.50

	Good	Fine	Mint
83-JSA x-over; death of Spectre(revived later)			
	.50	1.00	1.50
85-25¢ Giant G-77	.40	.80	1.20
91-JSA x-over; Hourman reprint; 52pgs. begin,			
end #99	.35	.70	1.05
92-JSA x-over; Flash reprt.	.35	.70	1.05
93-25¢ Giant G-89	.40	.80	1.20
94-Origin Sandman(Adv.#40)& Starman(Adv.#61);			
Deadman x-over; Adams art			
	1.35	2.75	4.00
95-Origin Dr. Fate & Dr. Midnight reprint			
(More Fun #67, All-American #25)			
	.40	.80	1.20
96-Origin Hourman reprint(Adventure #48)			
	.40	.80	1.20
97-Origin JLA retold	.35	.70	1.05
98-100: #98-G.A. Sargon, Starman reprint.			
#99-G.A. Sandman, Atom reprint. #100-JSA,			
7 Soldiers x-over	.25	.50	.75
101,102-JSA, 7 Soldiers & others x-over			
	.35	.70	1.05
103-106: #103-Phantom Stranger joins. #105-			
Elongated Man joins. #106-New Red Tornado			
joins	.25	.50	.75
107,108-JSA & G.A. Uncle Sam, Black Condor,			
The Ray, Dollman, Phantom Lady, & The			
Human Bomb x-over	.35	.70	1.05
109-Hawkman resigns	.25	.50	.75
110-116: All 100pg. issues; JSA Tale #110 &			
Toth reprint. #113-JSA/JLA team up.			
	.20	.40	.60
117-120: #117-Hawkman rejoins			
	.20	.40	.60
121-Adam Strange marries Alanna			
	.20	.40	.60
122,125-130: #128-Wonder Woman rejoins. #129-			
Death of Red Tornado	.15	.30	.45
123,124-JSA x-over	.20	.40	.60
131,132	.15	.30	.45
133,134-Part 2&3 of Desparo	.20	.40	.60
135,136:JSA & G.A. Bulletman, Bulletgirl, Spy			
Smasher, Mr. Scarlet, Pinky & Ibis x-over			
in all	.20	.40	.60
137-Same as above + Superman battles G.A.			
Capt. Marvel	.25	.50	.75
138-Adams covers; #139-begin 52pg. ishs.			
	.20	.40	.60
140-150	.20	.40	.60

NOTE: *Adams* covers-#63,66,67,70,74,79,81,82,
86-89,91,92,94,96-98,138,139. *Anderson* cov-
ers-#1-4,10,12-14,16,17,19,24,75-77,80,83-85,
95,138,139. *Infantino* story-#110(reprint);
covers-#56-58,90. *Krigstein* story-#96(reprint-
Sensation #84). *Kubert* covers-#72,73. *Sekowsky* stories-#57,60.

Justice League #2, © DC

Justice League #8, © DC

Justice League #22, © DC

Justice Traps The Guilty #4, © Prize   Kaanga #15, © FH   Katy Keene #5, © AP

JUSTICE MACHINE
1978   (50¢)
Power Comics

	Good	Fine	Mint
#1	.20	.40	.60

JUSTICE TRAPS THE GUILTY (Fargo Kid V11#3 on)
Oct-Nov, 1947 - V11#2(#92), Apr-May, 1958
Prize/Headline Publications

	Good	Fine	Mint
V2#1-S&K cover/stories	7.00	14.00	21.00
2-5-S&K cover/stories	3.50	7.00	10.50
6-S&K cover/story, + Feldstein story			
	4.00	8.00	12.00
7,9-S&K cover/story	2.00	4.00	6.00
8,10-S&K cover/story + Krigstein story			
	2.50	5.00	7.50
11,18,19-S&K covers	1.50	3.00	4.50
12-17,20-No S&K	1.00	2.00	3.00
21-23-S&K covers	1.50	3.00	4.50
24-50	1.00	2.00	3.00
51-70	.50	1.00	1.50
71-92	.35	.70	1.05

NOTE: *Elder* story-#18. *Meskin* story-#27.

JUST KIDS
1932   (16pgs.)   (9½x12") (Soft cover)
McLoughlin Bros.

	Good	Fine	Mint
#283-Three-color text, pictures on heavy paper	4.00	8.00	12.00

JUST MARRIED
January, 1958 - Present
Charlton Comics

	Good	Fine	Mint
#1	.50	1.00	1.50
2-20	.20	.40	.60
21-50	.15	.30	.45
51-114		.10	.20

KA'A'NGA COMICS (-- Jungle King)
Spring, 1949 - #20, Summer, 1954
Fiction House Magazines(Glen-Kel Publ. Co.)

	Good	Fine	Mint
#1-Ka'a'nga, Lord of the Jungle begins			
	7.00	14.00	21.00
2-4	4.00	8.00	12.00
5-Camilla app.	2.50	5.00	7.50
6-10: #9-Tabu, Wizard of the Jungle app.			
	2.00	4.00	6.00
11-15	1.50	3.00	4.50
16-Sheena app.	2.00	4.00	6.00
17-20	1.35	2.75	4.00
IW Reprint #1(reprts.#18)	.65	1.35	2.00
IW Reprint #8(reprts.#10)	.65	1.35	2.00

KAMANDI, THE LAST BOY ON EARTH
Oct-Nov, 1972 - Present

National Periodical Publications/DC Comics

	Good	Fine	Mint
#1-Origin	1.00	2.00	3.00
2-5	.65	1.35	2.00
6-10	.50	1.00	1.50
11-20	.40	.80	1.20
21-31	.30	.60	.90
32-Giant, origin from #1	.35	.70	1.05
33-40-Last Kirby issue	.20	.40	.60
41-54	.15	.30	.45

NOTE: *Alcala* stories-#47-52. *Kirby* stories-#1-40; covers-#1-33. *Kubert* covers-#34-41.

KARATE KID (See Action, Adventure & Superboy)
Mar-Apr, 1976 - #15, Jul-Aug, 1978
National Periodical Publications/DC Comics

	Good	Fine	Mint
#1-Estrada/Staton art	.20	.40	.60
2-15	.15	.30	.45

NOTE: *Staton* stories-#6-9.

KASCO COMICS
1949   (Giveaway)(Reg. Size)(Soft Cover)
Kasko Grainfeed

	Good	Fine	Mint
#2-Similar to Katy Keene; Bill Woggan art			
	6.00	12.00	18.00

KATHY
September, 1949 - 1953
Standard Comics

	Good	Fine	Mint
#1	.80	1.60	2.40
2-5	.50	1.00	1.50
6-16	.40	.80	1.20

KATHY
Oct, 1959 - #27, Feb, 1964
Atlas Comics/Marvel (ZPC)

	Good	Fine	Mint
#1	.40	.80	1.20
2-27	.20	.40	.60

KAT KARSON
No Date   (Reprint)
I.W. Enterprises

	Good	Fine	Mint
#1-Funny animals	.35	.70	1.05

KATY KEENE (Also see Kasco Komics, Laugh, Pep, Suzie, & Wilbur)
1950 - 1961
Archie Publ./Close Up/Radio Comics

	Good	Fine	Mint
#1-Bill Woggon art begins	10.00	20.00	30.00
2	6.00	12.00	18.00
3-5	5.00	10.00	15.00
6-10	3.35	6.75	10.00

(Katy Keene cont'd)	Good	Fine	Mint
11-20	2.50	5.00	7.50
21-30,32-40	2.00	4.00	6.00
31-3-D issue(1953)	4.00	8.00	12.00
41-62	1.35	2.75	4.00
Annual #1('54)	6.00	12.00	18.00
Annual #2-6('55-'59)	3.35	6.75	10.00
3-D#1(1953-Large size)	5.00	10.00	15.00
Charm #1(9/58)	2.00	4.00	6.00
Glamour #1(1957)	2.50	5.00	7.50
Spectacular #1('56)	3.00	6.00	9.00

KATY KEENE FASHION BOOK
1955 - #23, Winter, 1958
Radio Comics/Archie Publications

	Good	Fine	Mint
#1	5.00	10.00	15.00
2-10	2.50	5.00	7.50
11-23	1.50	3.00	4.50

KATY KEENE HOLIDAY FUN (See Archie Giant
Series Mag. #7,12)

KATY KEENE PINUP PARADE
1955 - #16, Summer, 1961 (25¢)
Radio Comics/Archie Publications

	Good	Fine	Mint
#1	5.00	10.00	15.00
2-16	2.00	4.00	6.00

KATZENJAMMER KIDS, THE
1903 (50 pgs.) (10x15½") (In Color)
New York American & Journal

	Good	Fine	Mint
1903 (Rare)	25.00	62.50	100.00
1905-Tricks of --(10x15)	20.00	50.00	80.00
1906-Stokes-10x16",32pgs. in color			
	20.00	50.00	80.00
1910-The Komical--(10x15)16.50		33.25	50.00
1921-Embee Dist. Co., 10x16", 20pgs. in color			
	15.00	37.50	60.00

KATZENJAMMER KIDS, THE
Summer, 1947 - #27, Feb-Mar, 1954
David McKay Publ./Standard #12-21(Spring,
'50-53)/Harvey #22, 4/53 on

	Good	Fine	Mint
Feature Book #30,32,35,37('45),41,44('46)			
	4.00	8.00	12.00
#1(1947)	3.00	6.00	9.00
2-11	2.00	4.00	6.00
12-14(Standard)	1.75	3.35	5.00
15-21(Standard)	1.00	2.00	3.00
22-27(Harvey)	1.25	2.50	3.75

KAYO (Formerly Jest?)
March, 1945
Harry 'A' Chesler

	Good	Fine	Mint
#12-Green Knight, Capt. Glory, Little Nemo			
(not by McCay)	1.75	3.35	5.00

KA-ZAR
Aug, 1970 - #3, March, 1971 (Giant-Size)
Marvel Comics Group

	Good	Fine	Mint
#1-Reprints earlier Ka-Zar stories; Avengers			
x-over in Hercules	.50	1.00	1.50
2,3-Ka-Zar origin #2; Angel in both			
	.35	.70	1.05

KA-ZAR
Jan, 1974 - #20, Feb, 1977 (Regular size)
Marvel Comics Group

	Good	Fine	Mint
#1	.40	.80	1.20
2-10: #4-Brunner cover	.25	.50	.75
11-20	.20	.40	.60

NOTE: *Alcala inks-#6,8. Kirby cover-#12.*

KEEN COMICS
V2#1, May, 1939 - V2#3, Nov, 1939
Centaur Publications

	Good	Fine	Mint
V2#1	10.00	20.00	30.00
V2#2,3: #3-Burgos art	8.00	16.00	24.00

KEEN DETECTIVE FUNNIES
Dec, 1937 - V3#9, Sept, 1940
Centaur Publications

	Good	Fine	Mint
V1#1	25.00	50.00	75.00
2	15.00	30.00	45.00
3-11: The Clock in #8,9			
	12.00	24.00	36.00
V2#1,2-The Eye Sees begins; ends V3#8			
	9.00	18.00	27.00
3-TNT Todd begins	10.00	20.00	30.00
4,5-The Clock in #5	9.00	18.00	27.00
6,8-12	9.00	18.00	27.00
7-The Masked Marvel begins			
	12.00	24.00	36.00
V3#1-6	8.00	16.00	24.00
7-Origin Air Man	12.00	24.00	36.00
8,9	9.00	18.00	27.00

KEEN TEENS
1945
Life's Romances Publ./Leader/Mag. Ent.

	Good	Fine	Mint
No#-14pgs. Claire Voyant(cont'd. in other No#			
issue), movie photos, Dotty Dripple, Gert-			
ie O'Grady & Sissy	4.00	8.00	12.00
No#-16pgs. Claire Voyant & 16pgs. movie			
photos	4.00	8.00	12.00
#3-5(M.E.)	1.00	2.00	3.00

Katy Keene Fashion Book #22,© AP

Katy Keene Pin-Up Parade #3,© AP

Keen Detective Funnies #11,© Cen

Ken Maynard #1, © Faw

Kerry Drake #23, © Harv

Kid Carrots #1, © STJ

KEEPING UP WITH THE JONESES
1920 - #2, 1921 (48pgs;9½x9½";B&W daily strip
Cupples & Leon Co.   reprints)

	Good	Fine	Mint
#1,2-By Pop Momand	4.00	8.00	12.00

KELLYS, THE (Formerly Rusty; Spy Cases #26 on)
#23, Jan, 1950 - #25, June, 1950
Marvel Comics (HPC)

	Good	Fine	Mint
#23-25	.80	1.60	2.40

KEN MAYNARD WESTERN
Sept, 1950 - #8, Feb, 1952
Fawcett Publications

	Good	Fine	Mint
#1-with photos	6.00	12.00	18.00
2	3.00	6.00	9.00
3-8	1.50	3.00	4.50

KEN SHANNON (Gabby #11)
Oct, 1951 - #15, 1953 (A Private Eye)
Quality Comics Group

	Good	Fine	Mint
#1	5.00	10.00	15.00
2	2.50	5.00	7.50
3-9	2.00	4.00	6.00
10-Crandall cover	1.50	3.00	4.50
11-15	1.20	2.40	3.60

NOTE: *Jack Cole stories-#1-9. Crandall stor-
ies-#3-5,9; covers-#5,9,10. #11-15 published
after title change to Gabby.*

KEN STUART
1948
Publication

	Good	Fine	Mint
#1-Frank Borth art	1.75	3.50	5.25

KENT BLAKE OF THE SECRET SERVICE (War)
May, 1951 - #14, July, 1953
Marvel/Atlas Comics(20CC)

	Good	Fine	Mint
#1	1.20	2.40	3.60
2-14	.65	1.35	2.00

KERRY DRAKE (-- Racket Buster #32,33)
1944; #6, 1/48 - #33, 8/52
Life's Romances/Magazine Ent.#1-5/Harvey#6 on

	Good	Fine	Mint
No#(1944)	4.00	8.00	12.00
2-5(1944)	3.00	6.00	9.00
6,8	3.00	6.00	9.00
7-Kubert story	4.00	8.00	12.00
9,10-Two-part marijuana story	4.00	8.00	12.00
11-15: #13-Powell art	2.50	5.00	7.50
16-18,20-33	2.00	4.00	6.00

	Good	Fine	Mint
19-Drug story	4.00	8.00	12.00

--In the Case of the Sleeping City-(1951-Pub-
lishers Synd.)(16pg. Giveaway-for armed

forces) soft cover	1.35	2.75	4.00

KERRY DRAKE (Also see Green Hornet)
Jan, 1956 - #2, Mar, 1956
Argo

	Good	Fine	Mint
#1,2-Newspaper reprints	2.00	4.00	6.00

KEWPIES
1949
Will Eisner Publications

	Good	Fine	Mint
#1-Eisner & Feiffer art	5.00	10.00	15.00

KEY COMICS
Jan, 1944 - #5, Aug, 1946
Consolidated Magazines

	Good	Fine	Mint
#1-The Key, Will-O-The Wisp begin	2.50	5.00	7.50
2-5	1.75	3.50	5.25

KEY COMICS
1951 - 1956 (32 pgs.) (Giveaway)
Key Clothing Co./Peterson Clothing

Contains a comic from different publishers
bound with new cover. Cover changed each year.
Many combinations possible. Distributed in
Nebraska, Iowa, & Kansas. Contents would determine price.

KEY RING COMICS
1941 (16pgs.) (Sold 5 for 10¢)
Dell Publishing Co.

	Good	Fine	Mint
#1-Origin Greg Gilday reprint from War Comics			
#2	2.00	4.00	6.00

KID CARROTS
Sept, 1953
St. John Publishing Co.

	Good	Fine	Mint
#1	.65	1.35	2.00

KID COLT OUTLAW (-- Hero of the West #1-?)
(Also see Wisco)
Aug, 1948 - #139, 3/68; #140, 11/69 - Present
#1-102, Marvel/Atlas(LMC); #103 on, Marvel

	Good	Fine	Mint
#1	8.00	16.00	24.00
2	4.00	8.00	12.00
3-5	3.00	6.00	9.00
6-10	2.00	4.00	6.00

(Kid Colt Outlaw cont'd)	Good	Fine	Mint
11-Origin	3.00	6.00	9.00
12-30	1.50	3.00	4.50
31-47,49,50	1.00	2.00	3.00
48-Kubert art	1.35	2.75	4.00
51-53,55,56	.90	1.80	2.70
54-Williamson/Maneely cover only			
	1.50	3.00	4.50
57-60,66: 4pg. Williamson stories in all.			
#59-Reprint Rawhide Kid #79			
	1.75	3.50	5.25
61-64,67-78,80,82-85	.60	1.20	1.80
65-Crandall story	1.20	2.40	3.60
79-Origin retold	1.00	2.00	3.00
81,87-Davis stys.reprint	1.20	2.40	3.60
86-Kirby story reprint	.80	1.60	2.40
88,89-Williamson stories in both(4pgs.).#89-			
redrawn Matt Slade #2	1.50	3.00	4.50
90-92,94-118,120	.40	.80	1.20
93,119-Kirby story	.50	1.00	1.50
121-140: #121-Rawhide Kid x-over. #125-Two-Gun			
Kid x-over. #130-132-68pg. issues with one			
new story each; #130-Origin. #132-Last			
Jack Keller ish. #140-Reprints begin			
	.25	.50	.75
141-146,148-160: #141-New Two-Gun Kid story.			
#156-Giant; reprints	.20	.40	.60
147-Williamson story reprt.	.25	.50	.75
161-169,171	.15	.30	.45
170,172-Williamson story reprints; origin re-			
told #170	.15	.30	.45
173-221		.15	.30
Giant Size #1(1/75), 2(4/75), 3(7/75)			
	.25	.50	.75

NOTE: _Crandall_ story reprint-#140,167. _Ever-ett_ inks-#137. _Kirby_ covers-#87,92-95,97,99-112,114-117,121-123,197(reprint). _Morrow_ story-#173(reprint). _Whitney_ reprint-#141. _Woodbridge_ story-#64. _Black Rider_ in #33,35-37,41,74,86. _Iron Mask_ in #110,114,121,127. _Sam Hawk_ in #84,101,111,121,146,174,181,188.

KID COWBOY
1950 - 1955   (Painted covers)
Ziff-Davis Publ./St. John (Approved Comics)

#1-Lucy Belle begins	1.00	2.00	3.00
2-14, #4(4/54-Approved)	.50	1.00	1.50

KIDDIE KAPERS
Oct, 1957; 1963 - 1964
Decker Publ. (Red Top-Farrell)

#1(no date)	.35	.70	1.05
#1(10/57)(Decker)-Little Bit reprints from			
Kiddie Karnival	.35	.70	1.05
Super Reprint #10('63),#14('63),#15,17('64),			
#18('64)	.15	.30	.45

KIDDIE KARNIVAL
1952   (100pgs.)   (One Shot)
Ziff-David Publ. Co. (Approved Comics)

	Good	Fine	Mint
No#-Rebound Little Bit #1,2			
	1.00	2.00	3.00

KID ETERNITY (Becomes Buccaneers) (See Hit)
Spring, 1946 - #18, 1949
Quality Comics Group

#1	9.00	18.00	27.00
2	5.00	10.00	15.00
3-Mac Raboy story	7.00	14.00	21.00
4-10	2.50	5.00	7.50
11-18	1.75	3.35	5.00

KID FROM DODGE CITY, THE
July, 1957 - #2, Sept, 1957
Atlas Comics (MMC)

#1	1.20	2.40	3.60
2-Everett cover	.80	1.60	2.40

KID FROM TEXAS, THE (A Texas Ranger)
June, 1957 - #2, Aug, 1957
Atlas Comics (CSI)

#1-Powell story	1.20	2.40	3.60
2	.80	1.60	2.40

KID KOKO
1958
I.W. Enterprises

Reprint #1,2-(reprints M.E.'s Koko & Kola			
#4, 1947)	.50	1.00	1.50

KID KOMICS (-- Movie Comics #11)
Feb, 1943 - #10, Spring, 1946
Timely Comics

#1-Origin Captain Wonder & sidekick Tim			
Mullrooney; intro. Subbie, the Sea-Going			
Lad, Pinto Pete, & Trixy Trouble; Knuck-			
les & Whitewash Jones only app. Wolver-			
ton art, 7pgs.	60.00	120.00	180.00
2-The Young Allies, Red Hawk, & Tommy Tyme			
begin; last Captain Wonder & Subbie			
	40.00	80.00	120.00
3-The Vision & Daredevils app.			
	25.00	50.00	75.00
4-The Destroyer begins; Sub-Mariner app.;			
Red Hawk & Tommy Tyme end			
	20.00	40.00	60.00
5,6	13.50	26.75	40.00
7-10: The Whizzer app. #7; Destroyer not in			
#7,8; #10-Last Destroyer, Young Allies &			
Whizzer	10.00	20.00	30.00

Kid Colt Outlaw #1, © MCG

Kid Eternity #1, © Qua

Kid Komics #1, © MCG

Kid Slade Gunfighter #5, © MCG

The Killers #1, © ME

King Comics #12, © DMP

KID MONTANA (The Gunfighters #51 on)
V2#9, 11/57 - #50, 3/65
Charlton Comics

	Good	Fine	Mint
V2#9,10	.25	.50	.75
#11-20	.20	.40	.60
21-50	.15	.30	.45

NOTE: *Title change to Montana Kid on cover only on #44; remained Kid Montana on inside.*

KID MOVIE KOMICS (Formerly Kid Komics; Rusty
#11, Summer, 1946   #12 on)
Timely Comics

#11-Silly Seal & Ziggy Pig; 2pgs. Kurtzman "Hey Look" + 6pg. sty.	3.00	6.00	9.00

KIDNAPPED (See 4-Color #1101 & Movie Comics)

KIDNAP RACKET (See Harvey Comics Hits #57)

KID SLADE GUNFIGHTER (Formerly Matt Slade--)
#5, Jan, 1957 - #8, July, 1957
Atlas Comics (SPI)

#5	1.00	2.00	3.00
6,8	.65	1.35	2.00
7-Williamson/Mayo story, 4 pgs.	1.75	3.50	5.25

KID ZOO COMICS
July, 1948
Street & Smith Publications

#1	.65	1.35	2.00

KILLERS, THE
1947 - 1948
Magazine Enterprises

#1-Mr. Zin, the Hatchet Killer-Mentioned in Seduction of the Innocent, pgs. 179,180	6.00	12.00	18.00
2-(Rare)-Hashish story; Whitney, Ingels art	4.00	8.00	12.00

KILROYS, THE
June-July, 1947 - #54, June-July, 1955
B&I Publ. Co. #1-19/American Comics Group

#1	2.00	4.00	6.00
2-5	1.00	2.00	3.00
6-10	.65	1.35	2.00
11-30	.35	.70	1.05
31-47,50-54	.20	.40	.60
48,49-(3-D effect)	.40	.80	1.20

KING COLT (See 4-Color Comics #651)

KING COMICS (Strip Reprints)
April, 1936 - #159, Feb, 1952(Winter on cvr)
David McKay Publications/Standard #159

	Good	Fine	Mint
#1-Flash Gordon by Alex Raymond; Brick Bradford, Mandrake, the Magician & Popeye begin	140.00	280.00	420.00
2	60.00	120.00	180.00
3	40.00	80.00	120.00
4	25.00	50.00	75.00
5	20.00	40.00	60.00
6-10	16.50	33.25	50.00
11-20	12.00	24.00	36.00
21-30	10.00	20.00	30.00
31-40: #33-Last Segar Popeye	9.00	18.00	27.00
41-49	7.00	14.00	21.00
50-The Lone Ranger begins	7.00	14.00	21.00
51-60: #59-Barney Baxter begins	6.00	12.00	18.00
61-The Phantom begins	5.00	10.00	15.00
62-90	5.00	10.00	15.00
91-100	5.00	10.00	15.00
101-115-Last Raymond ish.	4.00	8.00	12.00
116-145	3.00	6.00	9.00
146,147-Prince Valiant in both,			
148-159	2.00	4.00	6.00

KING KONG (See Movie Comics)

KING LEONARDO & HIS SHORT SUBJECTS (TV)
1962 - #4, Sept, 1963
Dell Publishing Co./Gold Key

4-Color #1242,1278	.50	1.00	1.50
#01390-207(5-7/62)(Dell)	.35	.70	1.05
#1-4(10/62-'63)	.35	.70	1.05

KING LOUIE & MOWGLI
May, 1968   (Disney)
Gold Key

#1(10223-805)	.25	.50	.75

KING OF BAD MEN OF DEADWOOD
1950
Avon Periodicals

No#-Kinstler cover	2.50	5.00	7.50

KING OF DIAMONDS (TV)
July-Sept, 1962
Dell Publishing Co.

#01-391-209	.50	1.00	1.50

KING OF KINGS (See 4-Color Comics #1236)

KING OF THE ROYAL MOUNTED (See Black & White
#9, Feature Book #1(McKay),& Super Book #2,6)

KING OF THE ROYAL MOUNTED
1937   (64pgs.;5½x7½";B&W daily reprints)
Whitman Publ. Co.   (Hardcover)
                         Good   Fine   Mint
                         5.00 10.00 15.00

KING OF THE ROYAL MOUNTED   (Zane Grey's)
#8, June-Aug, 1952 - #28, Mar-May, 1958
Dell Publishing Co.

	Good	Fine	Mint
4-Color #207('48),265,283	2.50	5.00	7.50
4-Color #310,340,363,384	1.50	3.00	4.50
#8-28('58)	1.35	2.75	4.00
4-Color #935('58)	1.35	2.75	4.00

NOTE: 4-Color #207,265,283,310,340,363,384
are all newspaper reprints with Jim Gary art.
#8 on are all Dell originals.

KING RICHARD & THE CRUSADERS (See 4-Color#588)

KING SOLOMON'S MINES
1951   (Movie)
Avon Periodicals

No#(#1 on 1st page)   5.00 10.00 15.00

KISS (See Marvel Comics Super Special)

KIT CARSON (See Frontier Fighters)

KIT CARSON (Formerly All True Detective
Cases #4; Fighting Davy Crockett #9)
6/51 - #3, 12/51; #5, 11-12/54 - #8, 9/55
Avon Periodicals

No#(#1)	2.00	4.00	6.00
#2(1951)	1.50	3.00	4.50
5-8	1.35	2.75	4.00
IW Reprint #10('63)	.65	1.35	2.00

NOTE: Kinstler covers-#3,5,6.

KIT CARSON & THE BLACKFEET WARRIORS
1953
Realistic

No#   1.50   3.00   4.50

KIT KARTER
1962
Dell Publishing Co.

#1   .25   .50   .75

KITTY
Oct, 1948

St. John Publishing Co.
                         Good   Fine   Mint
#1-Lily Renee art   1.00   2.00   3.00

KLARER GIVEAWAYS (See Wisco)

KNIGHTS OF THE ROUND TABLE (See 4-Color #540)

KNIGHTS OF THE ROUND TABLE
#10, April, 1957
Pines Comics

#10   .50   1.00   1.50

KNIGHTS OF THE ROUND TABLE
Nov-Jan, 1964
Dell Publishing Co.

#1(12-397-401)   .50   1.00   1.50

KNOCK KNOCK
1936   (32 pgs.) (B&W)
Gerona Publications

#1-Bob Dunn art   7.00 14.00 21.00

KNOCKOUT ADVENTURES
1954
Fiction House Magazines

#1-Reprints/Fight Comics #53
                         2.00   4.00   6.00

KNOW YOUR MASS
1958   (100pg. Giant) (35¢)
Catechetical Guild

#303-In color   1.50   3.00   4.50

KOBRA
Feb-Mar, 1976 - #7, Mar-Apr, 1977
National Periodical Publications

#1-Art plotted by Kirby .25   .50   .75
2-7   .20   .40   .60

KOKEY KOALA
May, 1952
Toby Press

#1   .80   1.60   2.40

KOKO & KOLA
Fall, 1946 - #5, May, 1947; #6, 1950
Compix/Magazine Enterprises

#1-5,6(A-1#28)   1.00   2.00   3.00

King Of The Bad Men-, © Avon   Kit Carson #3, © Avon   Kokey Koala #1, © Toby

Kona #14, © Dell   Konga #5, © CC   Korak #3, © ERB

KO KOMICS
October, 1945
Gerona Publications

	Good	Fine	Mint
#1-The Duke of Darkness & The Menace (hero)			
	4.00	8.00	12.00

KOMIC KARTOONS
Fall, 1945 - #2, Winter, 1945
Timely Comics

	Good	Fine	Mint
#1,2	1.50	3.00	4.50

KOMIK PAGES
April, 1945
Harry 'A' Chesler, Jr. (Our Army, Inc.)

#10(#1 on inside)-Land O' Nod by Rick Yager
(2pgs.), Animal Crackers, Foxy GrandPa,
Tom, Dick & Mary, Cheerio Minstrels, Red
Starr + other 1-2 pg. strips; Cole art
2.00   4.00   6.00

KONA (-- Monarch of Monster Isle)
Feb-Apr, 1962 - #21, Jan-Mar, 1967
Dell Publishing Co.

4-Color #1256	1.75	3.35	5.00
#2-10: #4-Anak begins	.65	1.35	2.00
11-21	.50	1.00	1.50

KONGA (Fantastic Giants #24)(See Return of--)
1961 - #23, Nov, 1965
Charlton Comics

#1-Based on movie	3.35	6.75	10.00
2-5	1.75	3.50	5.25
6-15	1.00	2.00	3.00
16-23	.80	1.60	2.40

NOTE: _Ditko_ stories-#1,3-15; covers-#4,6-9.
Montes & Bache art-#16-23.

KONGA'S REVENGE (Formerly Return of --)
#2, Summer, 1963 - #3, Fall, 1954; Dec, 1968
Charlton Comics

#2,3: #2-Ditko cover/sty	1.35	2.75	4.00
#1('68)-Reprints Konga's Revenge #3			
	1.00	2.00	3.00

KONG THE UNTAMED
June-July, 1975 - #5, Feb-Mar, 1976
National Periodical Publications

#1	.35	.70	1.05
2-5	.25	.50	.75

NOTE: _Alcala_ stories-#1-3. _Wrightson_ covers-
#1,2.

KOOKIE
Feb-Apr, 1962 - #2, May-July, 1962
Dell Publishing Co.

	Good	Fine	Mint
#1,2-Written by John Stanley; Bill Williams			
art	.65	1.35	2.00

KORAK, SON OF TARZAN (Edgar Rice Burroughs)
Jan, 1964 - #45, Jan, 1972
Gold Key

#1-Russ Manning art	2.50	5.00	7.50
2-11-Russ Manning art	1.50	3.00	4.50
12-21: #14-Jon of the Kalahari ends. #15-			
Mabu, Jungle Boy begins; Manning art #21			
	.80	1.60	2.40
22-30	.65	1.35	2.00
31-45	.50	1.00	1.50

KORAK, SON OF TARZAN (Tarzan Family #60 on)
#46, 5-6/72 - #56, 2-3/74; #57, 5-6/75 - #59,
9-10/75 (Edgar Rice Burroughs)
National Periodical Publications

#46-(52pgs.)-Carson of Venus begins(origin);			
Pellucidar feature	.65	1.35	2.00
47,48,50	.50	1.00	1.50
49-Origin Korak retold	.50	1.00	1.50
51-56-Carson of Venus ends.	.35	.70	1.05
57-59	.25	.50	.75

NOTE: _Anderson_ stories-#52-55. _Kaluta_ stor-
ies-#46-56. All have covers by _Joe Kubert_.
Manning strip reprints-#57-59.

KORG: 70,000 B.C.
May, 1975 - #9, Nov, 1976 (Hanna-Barbera)
Charlton Comics

#1	.25	.50	.75
2-9	.15	.30	.45

KORNER KID COMICS
1947
Four Star Publications

#1	.65	1.35	2.00

KOSHER COMICS
1966   ($1.00)
Parallax

"Supermax" & "Tishman of the Apes"
1.35   2.75   4.00

KRAZY KAT
1946   (Hardcover)
Holt

(Krazy Kat cont'd)

	Good	Fine	Mint
Reprints daily & Sunday strips by Herriman

	Good	Fine	Mint
	30.00	60.00	90.00
with dust jacket(Rare)..	50.00	100.00	150.00

KRAZY KAT (--& Ignatz the Mouse early issues)
May-June, 1951 - Jan, 1964 (None by Herriman)
Dell Publishing Co./Gold Key

#1(1951)	2.00	4.00	6.00
2-5,4-Color#454,504	1.50	3.00	4.50
4-Color #548,619,696	1.20	2.40	3.60
#1(10098-401)(1/64-G.K.)	.65	1.35	2.00

KRAZY KAT (See March of Comics #72,87)

KRAZY KOMICS (1st Series)
July, 1942 - #26, 1946
Timely Comics(USA #1-21/JPC #22-26)

#1	5.00	10.00	15.00
2-10	2.50	5.00	7.50
11,13,14	1.35	2.75	4.00
12-Timely's entire art staff drew themselves into a Creeper story	2.00	4.00	6.00
15-Has "Super Soldier" by Pfc. Stan Lee	1.75	3.35	5.00
16-24,26	1.35	2.75	4.00
25-Kurtzman story, 6pgs.	3.00	6.00	9.00

KRAZY KOMICS (2nd Series)(Also see Ziggy Pig)
Aug, 1948 - #26, 1950
Timely/Marvel Comics

#1-Wolverton(10pgs.)&Kurtzman(8pgs.)stories	12.00	24.00	36.00
2-Wolverton art	5.00	10.00	15.00
3-10	1.35	2.75	4.00
11-26	1.00	2.00	3.00

KRAZY KROW
Summer, 1945 - #7, 1946
Marvel Comics (ZPC)

#1	1.00	2.00	3.00
2-5	.50	1.00	1.50
6,7	.40	.80	1.20
IW Reprint #1('57), #2('58), #7	.25	.50	.75

KRAZYLIFE
1945 (No month)
Fox Features Syndicate

#1-Funny animal	.80	1.60	2.40

KRIM-KO COMICS
1936 - 1939 (4 pg. Giveaway) (Weekly)
Krim-ko Chocolate Drink

	Good	Fine	Mint
Lola, Secret Agent; 184 issues-all original stories each....	1.50	3.00	4.50

KULL & THE BARBARIANS (Magazine)
May, 1975 - #3, Sept, 1975 (B&W)($1.00)
Marvel Comics Group

#1-Wood reprt./Kull #1, 2pg. Adams	1.00	2.00	3.00
2-Red Sonja begins; Adams inks; Wrightson + Adams art	.65	1.35	2.00
3-Origin Red Sonja; Adams inks	.65	1.35	2.00

KULL THE CONQUEROR (--the Destroyer #11 on)
6/71 - #2, 8/71; #3, 7/72 - #15, 8/74;
#16, 8/76 - Present
Marvel Comics Group

#1-Wood/Ross Andru art; origin Kull	2.00	4.00	6.00
2,3	1.00	2.00	3.00
4,5	.80	1.60	2.40
6-9	.65	1.35	2.00
10-15-Ploog stories	.50	1.00	1.50
16-24	.15	.30	.45

NOTE: #1,2,7-9,11 are based on Robert E. Howard stories. Alcala inks-#17,18,20. Severin stories-#2-9.

KUNG FU (See Deadly Hands of --, & Master of --)

KUNG FU FIGHTER (See Richard Dragon --)

LAD: A DOG
1961 - #2, July-Sept, 1962
Dell Publishing Co.

4-Color #1303 (movie)	1.00	2.00	3.00
#2	.50	1.00	1.50

LADY AND THE TRAMP (See 4-Color #629,634, & Movie Classics & Comics)

LADY AND THE TRAMP IN "BUTTER LATE THAN NEVER"
1955 (14 pgs.) (Walt Disney)
American Dairy Assn. (Premium)

	1.75	3.35	5.00

LADY BOUNTIFUL
1917 (10x13½") (24pgs.) (B&W)
Saalfield Publ. Co.

by Gene Carr	6.00	12.00	18.00

Krazy Komics #2('42). © MCG

Krazylife #1, © Fox

Kull & The Barbarians #1, © MCG

Lady Luck #88, © Will Eisner   Lance O'Casey #3, © Faw   Large Feature Comic #1, © Dell

LADY LUCK (Formerly Smash #1-85)
Dec, 1949 - #90, Aug, 1950
Quality Comics Group

	Good	Fine	Mint
#86(#1)	10.00	20.00	30.00
87-90	8.00	16.00	24.00

LAFFY-DAFFY COMICS
Feb, 1945 - #2, March, 1945
Rural Home Publ. Co.

#1,2	.60	1.20	1.80

LANA (Little Lana #8 on)
Aug, 1948 - #7, Aug, 1949
Marvel Comics (MjMC)

#1	1.35	2.75	4.00
2-Kurtzman's "Hey Look"	1.75	3.35	5.00
3-7	.65	1.35	2.00

LANCELOT & GUINEVERE (See Movie Classics)

LANCELOT LINK, SECRET CHIMP (TV)
April, 1971 - #8, Feb, 1973
Gold Key

#1	.15	.30	.45
2-8		.15	.30

LANCE O'CASEY (See Mighty Midget Comics)
Spr, 1946 - #3, Fall, 1946; #4, Summer, 1948
Fawcett Publications

#1	4.00	8.00	12.00
2-4	2.00	4.00	6.00

LANCER (TV)
Feb, 1969 - #3, 1969
Gold Key

#1	.20	.40	.60
2,3	.15	.30	.45

LAND OF THE GIANTS (TV)
Nov, 1968 - #5, Sept, 1969
Gold Key

#1	.25	.50	.75
2-5	.20	.40	.60

LAND OF THE LOST COMICS (Radio)
July-Aug, 1946 - #9, Spring, 1948
E.C. Comics

#1	10.00	20.00	30.00
2-9	7.00	14.00	21.00

LAND UNKNOWN, THE (See 4-Color #845)

LARAMIE (TV)
Aug, 1960 - July, 1962
Dell Publishing Co.

	Good	Fine	Mint
4-Color #1125,1223,1284	.80	1.60	2.40
#01-418-207	.80	1.60	2.40

LAREDO (TV)
June, 1966
Gold Key

#1(10179-606)	.25	.50	.75

LARGE FEATURE COMIC (Continuation of Black & White)(Black & White interior)
1941 - 1943 (8½x11-3/8" with thin slick color covers; 52 pgs.
Dell Publishing Co.

#25-Smilin' Jack	15.00	30.00	45.00
26-Smitty	10.00	20.00	30.00
27-Terry & the Pirates	25.00	50.00	75.00
28-Grin & Bear It	5.00	10.00	15.00
29-Moon Mullins	9.00	18.00	27.00
30-Tillie the Toiler	8.00	16.00	24.00
1-Peter Rabbit by Cady	25.00	50.00	75.00
2-Winnie Winkle	7.00	14.00	21.00
3-Dick Tracy	35.00	70.00	105.00
4-Tiny Tim	15.00	30.00	45.00
5-Toots & Casper	5.00	10.00	15.00
6-Terry & the Pirates	25.00	50.00	75.00
7-Pluto Saves the Ship (Disney) written by Carl Barks, Jack Hannah & Nick George	65.00	130.00	195.00
8-Bugs Bunny('42)	60.00	120.00	180.00
9-Bringing Up Father	7.00	14.00	21.00
10-Popeye (Thimble Theatre)	22.00	44.00	66.00
11-Barney Google & Snuffy Smith	10.00	20.00	30.00
12-Private Buck	5.00	10.00	15.00

LARRY DOBY, BASEBALL HERO
1950   (Cleveland Indians)
Fawcett Publications

No#	2.50	5.00	7.50

LARS OF MARS
May-June, 1951 - #11, July-Aug, 1951
Ziff-Davis Publ. Co.

#10,11-Anderson stories (3) in each	4.00	8.00	12.00

LASH LARUE WESTERN
June, 1949 - #46, Jan, 1954
Fawcett Publications

(Lash Larue Western cont'd)

	Good	Fine	Mint
#1	10.00	20.00	30.00
2-10	4.00	8.00	12.00
11-20	2.50	5.00	7.50
21-46	2.00	4.00	6.00

LASH LARUE WESTERN
#47, 1954 - #84, June, 1961
Charlton Comics

#47-67,69,70	1.35	2.75	4.00
68-(68pgs.)	1.75	3.35	5.00
71-84	1.00	2.00	3.00

LASSIE (M-G-M's -- #1-36)
1950 - #70, July, 1969
Dell Publ. Co./Gold Key #59(10/62) on

#1	2.00	4.00	6.00
2-10	1.00	2.00	3.00

11-19: #12-Rocky Langford (Lassie's master)
marries Gerry Lawrence. #15-1st app.

Timbu	.65	1.35	2.00
20-22-Matt Baker stories	1.50	3.00	4.50

23-40: #39-1st app. Timmy as Lassie picks up

her TV family	.40	.80	1.20

41-70: #63-Last Timmy. #64-Reprints/#19.
#65-Forest Ranger Corey Stuart begins,
ends #69. #70-Forest Rangers Bob Ericson
& Scott Turner app.(Lassie's new masters)

	.35	.70	1.05

The Adventures of --(Red Heart Dog Food

Giveaway, 1949)	1.35	2.75	4.00

Florida Power & Light Giveaway(1973)

	.20	.40	.60

Kite Fun Book('73)(No#)-Pacific Gas & Elec.
Co. & Sou. Calif. Edison (16pgs.,5x7")

	3.00	6.00	9.00

*(See March of Comics #210,217,230,254,266,
278,296,308,324,334,346,358,370,381,394,411)*

LAST HUNT, THE (See 4-Color Comics #678)

LAST OF THE COMANCHES
1953 (Movie)
Avon Periodicals

No#-Kinstler cover/story	4.00	8.00	12.00

LAST OF THE ERIES, THE (See American Graphics)

LAST OF THE FAST GUNS, THE (See 4-Color #925)

LAST TRAIN FROM GUN HILL (See 4-Color #1012)

LATEST ADVENTURES OF FOXY GRANDPA (See Foxy--)

LATEST COMICS (Super Duper #3?)
March, 1945
Spotlight Publ./Palace Promotions(Jubilee)

	Good	Fine	Mint
#1-Super Duper	1.00	2.00	3.00
2-Bee-29 (no date)	1.00	2.00	3.00

LAUGH COMICS (Formerly Black Hood #1-19)
#20, Fall, 1946 - Present (Laugh #226 on)
Archie Publications (Close-Up)

#20-Archie begins	7.00	14.00	21.00
21-23,25	4.00	8.00	12.00
24-"Pipsy" by Kirby,6pgs.	5.00	10.00	15.00
26-30	3.00	6.00	9.00
31-40	2.50	5.00	7.50
41-70	1.75	3.35	5.00
71-100	1.00	2.00	3.00
101-126	.60	1.20	1.80

127,129,130,131,133,135,140-142,144-Jaguar

app. + The Fly-#129	.65	1.35	2.00

128,132,134,136,137,139-Fly app.

	.65	1.35	2.00
138-Flyman & Flygirl app.	.65	1.35	2.00
143-Flygirl app.	.65	1.35	2.00
145-160	.50	1.00	1.50
161-180	.30	.60	.90
181-220	.20	.40	.60
221-260	.15	.30	.45
261-321		.15	.30

NOTE: *Josie app.-#145,160,164. Katy Keene
app.-#59,65,82,88,90,99,103,107,110,111,113,
114,116,121,122,124,130.*

LAUGH COMICS DIGEST
8/74; #2, 9/75; #3, 3/76 - Present (160 pgs.)
Archie Publications(Close-Up #1,3 on)

#1	.35	.70	1.05
2-13	.25	.50	.75

LAUGH COMIX (Formerly Top Notch Laugh;
Becomes Suzie #49 on)
#46, Summer, 1944 - #48, Winter, 1944-45
MLJ Magazines

#46-48-Wilbur & Suzie	2.50	5.00	7.50

LAUGH-IN MAGAZINE (Magazine)
Oct, 1968 - #12, Oct, 1969 (50¢) (Satire)
Laufer Publ. Co.

V1#1	.35	.70	1.05
2-12	.25	.50	.75

LAUREL & HARDY(See March of Comics #302,314)

LAUREL AND HARDY (-- Comics)
1949 - #28, 1951

Lars Of Mars #11. © Z-D

Lassie #36. © Dell

Laugh Comics #21. © AP

Lawbreakers Always Lose #1, © MCG

Law-Crime #1, © Essenkay Publ.

Leading Comics #11, © DC

(Laurel & Hardy cont'd)
St. John Publishing Co.

	Good	Fine	Mint
#1	4.00	8.00	12.00
2-10	2.00	4.00	6.00
11-28	1.35	2.75	4.00

LAUREL AND HARDY (TV)
Oct, 1962 - #4, Sept-Nov, 1963
Dell Publishing Co.

#12-423-210(8-10/62)	1.00	2.00	3.00
#2-4(Dell)	.65	1.35	2.00

LAUREL AND HARDY
Jan, 1967 - #2, Oct, 1967 (Larry Harmon's)
Gold Key

#1,2	.40	.80	1.20

LAUREL AND HARDY (-- Comics)
July-Aug, 1972 (Larry Harmon's)
National Periodical Publications

#1	.25	.50	.75

LAW AGAINST CRIME (See Law-Crime)

LAWBREAKERS (-- Suspense Stories #6 on)
Mar, 1951 - #5, Mar, 1952
Law and Order Magazines (Charlton Comics)

#1	1.00	2.00	3.00
2,3,5	.65	1.35	2.00
4-Drug story	2.00	4.00	6.00

LAWBREAKERS ALWAYS LOSE!
Spring, 1948 - #10, Oct, 1949
Marvel Comics (CBS)

#1-Kurtzman art, 2 pgs.	2.50	5.00	7.50
2-5	1.00	2.00	3.00
6-10	.80	1.60	2.40

LAWBREAKERS SUSPENSE STORIES (Formerly Law-
breakers; Strange Suspense Stories #16 on)
June, 1952 - #15, Nov, 1953
Capitol Stories/Charlton Comics

#6-15	.65	1.35	2.00

LAW-CRIME (Law Against Crime on inside)
April, 1948 - #3, Aug, 1948
Essenkay Publishing Co.

#1-(½ funny animal, ½ crime)			
	2.00	4.00	6.00
2,3	1.35	2.75	4.00

LAWMAN (TV)
1958 - #11, Apr-June, 1962
Dell Publishing Co.

	Good	Fine	Mint
4-Color #970,1035('58-60)	.65	1.35	2.00
#3-11	.50	1.00	1.50

LAWRENCE (See Movie Classics)

LEADING COMICS (-- Screen Comics #34 on)
Winter, 1941-42 - #33, 10-11/48
National Periodical Publications

#1-Origin The Seven Soldiers of Victory;
   Crimson Avenger, Green Arrow & Speedy,
   Shining Knight, The Vigilante, Star Span-
   gled Kid & Stripsey begin

	Good	Fine	Mint
	60.00	120.00	180.00
2-Meskin art	30.00	60.00	90.00
3	23.50	46.75	70.00
4	20.00	40.00	60.00
5	16.50	33.25	50.00
6-10	13.50	26.75	40.00
11-14(Spring,1945)	10.00	20.00	30.00
15-Content change to funny animal,			
16-30: #23-1st app. Peter Porkchops			
	1.20	2.40	3.60
31-33	.65	1.35	2.00

LEADING SCREEN COMICS (Formerly Leading Comics)
#34, 12-1/48-49 - #77, 8-9/55
National Periodical Publications

#34-77	.50	1.00	1.50

LEATHERNECK THE MARINE (See Mighty Midget
Comics)

LEAVE IT TO BEAVER (TV)
1958 - May-July, 1962
Dell Publishing Co.

4-Color #912,999,1103,1191,1285,			
#01-428-207	.50	1.00	1.50

LEAVE IT TO BINKY (Binky #72 on)(See Super
DC Giant & Showcase)
Feb-Mar, 1948 - #60, Dec-Jan, 1958; #61,
June-July, 1968 - #71, Apr-May, 1970
National Periodical Publications

#1	2.50	5.00	7.50
2-10	1.35	2.75	4.00
11-20	1.00	2.00	3.00
21-60	.65	1.35	2.00
61-71	.35	.70	1.05

LEE HUNTER, INDIAN FIGHTER (See 4-Color
Comics #779,904)

LEFT-HANDED GUN, THE (See 4-Color #913)

LEGEND OF CUSTER, THE (TV)
January, 1968
Dell Publishing Co.

	Good	Fine	Mint
#1	.65	1.35	2.00

LEGEND OF JESSE JAMES, THE (TV)
February, 1966
Gold Key

#10172-602	.65	1.35	2.00

LEGEND OF LOBO, THE (See Movie Comics)

LEGEND OF YOUNG DICK TURPIN, THE (TV)
May, 1966   (Disney TV episode)
Gold Key

#1(10176-605)	.80	1.60	2.40

LEGENDS OF DANIEL BOONE, THE
Oct-Nov, 1955 - #8, Dec-Jan, 1956-57
National Periodical Publications

#1	2.50	5.00	7.50
2-8	1.50	3.00	4.50

LEGION OF MONSTERS (Magazine)
September, 1975   (Black & White)
Marvel Comics Group

#1-Adams cover; Morrow art; origin & only app.	.50	1.00	1.50

LEGION OF SUPER-HEROES (See Action, Adventure,
2/73 - #4, 7-8/73   & Superboy)
National Periodical Publications

#1-Legion & Tommy Tomorrow reprints begin	.50	1.00	1.50
2-4	.35	.70	1.05

LEMIX-KORLIX (Kool-Aid)
1935   (48 pgs.) (15"x8")
Lemix-Korlix Giveaways

#1,2-Tarzan	25.00	50.00	75.00
3-Terry	20.00	40.00	60.00
4-Dick Tracy	25.00	50.00	75.00
5-Chester Gump	13.50	26.75	40.00

LENNON SISTERS LIFE STORY, THE (See 4-Color
Comics #951,1014)

LEO THE LION
No Date   (10¢)

I.W. Enterprises

	Good	Fine	Mint
#1-Reprint	.20	.40	.60

LEROY
Nov, 1949 - 1950
Standard Comics

#1	.65	1.35	2.00
2-6	.35	.70	1.05

LET'S PRETEND
May-June, 1950 - #3, Sept-Oct, 1950
D.S. Publishing Co.

#1	1.75	3.35	5.00
2,3	1.00	2.00	3.00

LET'S READ THE NEWSPAPER
1974
Charlton Press

Feat. Quincy by Ted Sheares.	.15	.30	.45

LET'S TAKE A TRIP (TV)
Spring, 1958   (CBS TV Presents)
Pines

#1-Marv Levy cover/art	.35	.70	1.05

LETTERS TO SANTA (See March of Comics #228)

LIBERTY COMICS (Miss Liberty #1)
1945 - 1946   (MLJ reprints)
Green Publishing Co.

#4	4.00	8.00	12.00
10-Hangman & Boy Buddies app.; Suzie & Wilbur begin; reprt. of Hangman #8	4.00	8.00	12.00
11	3.00	6.00	9.00
12-Black Hood app.	3.00	6.00	9.00
14,15-Patty of Airliner & Leonard Star in both	1.50	3.00	4.50
V2#2(1946)	1.50	3.00	4.50

LIBERTY GUARDS
No Date (1946?)
Chicago Mail Order

No#-Reprints Man of War #1 with cover of Liberty Scouts #1	10.00	20.00	30.00

LIBERTY SCOUTS (See Man of War & Liberty
June, 1941 - #3, Fall, 1941   Guards)
Centaur Publications

#2(#1)-Origin The Fire-Man, Man of War, The

The Legends Of Daniel Boone #1. © DC

Legion Of Super-Heroes #1. © DC

Let's Pretend #2. © D.S.

Life Story #17, © Faw

Life With Archie #25, © AP

Lightning Comics V3#1, © Ace

	Good	Fine	Mint
(Liberty Scouts cont'd)			
Sentinel; Vapo-Man & Liberty Scouts begin	25.00	50.00	75.00
3(#2)	16.50	33.25	50.00

LIDSVILLE (TV)
Oct, 1972 - #5, Oct, 1973
Gold Key

	Good	Fine	Mint
#1		.15	.30
2-5		.10	.20

LIEUTENANT, THE (TV)
April-June, 1964
Dell Publishing Co.

	Good	Fine	Mint
#1	.20	.40	.60

LT. ROBIN CRUSOE, U.S.N. (See Movie Comics
and Walt Disney Showcase #26)

LIFE OF CHRIST, THE
1958   (100 pgs.) (35¢)
Catechetical Guild Educational Society

	Good	Fine	Mint
#301-Book-length story	1.00	2.00	3.00

LIFE OF CHRIST VISUALIZED
1942 - 1943
Standard Publishers

	Good	Fine	Mint
#1-3	2.00	4.00	6.00

LIFE OF PAUL (See The Living Bible)

LIFE OF RILEY, THE (See 4-Color Comics #917)

LIFE OF THE BLESSED VIRGIN
1950
Catechetical Guild

	Good	Fine	Mint
No#	2.00	4.00	6.00

LIFE'S LITTLE JOKES
No Date (1924) (52pgs.) (B&W)
MS Publ. Co.

	Good	Fine	Mint
By Rube Goldberg	6.00	12.00	18.00

LIFE STORIES OF AMERICAN PRESIDENTS
Nov, 1957   (25¢)
Dell Publishing Co.

	Good	Fine	Mint
#1-Buscema art	2.50	5.00	7.50

LIFE STORY
April, 1949 - V8#43, Oct, 1952
Fawcett Publications

	Good	Fine	Mint
V1#1	1.75	3.35	5.00
2-6	1.00	2.00	3.00
V2#7-12	.65	1.35	2.00
V3#13-Wood story	1.75	3.35	5.00
V3#14-18, V4#19-24	.40	.80	1.20
V5#25-30, V6#31-36	.25	.50	.75
V7#37-42, V8#43	.25	.50	.75

LIFE WITH ARCHIE
Sept, 1958 - Present
Archie Publications

	Good	Fine	Mint
#1	5.00	10.00	15.00
2	2.50	5.00	7.50
3-5	1.50	3.00	4.50
6-10	1.00	2.00	3.00
11-25	.50	1.00	1.50
26-41	.40	.80	1.20
42-45: #42-Pureheart begins	.35	.70	1.05
46-Origin Pureheart	.40	.80	1.20
47-50: #50-United 3 begin	.35	.70	1.05
51-59-Pureheart ends	.25	.50	.75
60-100: #60-Archie band begins	.20	.40	.60
101-150	.15	.30	.45
151-188		.15	.30

LIFE WITH MILLIE
Nov, 1958 - #20, Dec, 1962
Atlas/Marvel (Male)

	Good	Fine	Mint
#1	1.50	3.00	4.50
2-10	.80	1.60	2.40
11-20	.50	1.00	1.50

LIFE WITH SNARKY PARKER (TV)
August, 1950
Fox Features Syndicate

	Good	Fine	Mint
#1	2.00	4.00	6.00

LIGHT IN THE FOREST (See 4-Color #891)

LIGHTNING COMICS (Sure-Fire #1-4)(No V3#2)
June, 1940 - #14, June, 1942   (2 #3's)
Ace Magazines

	Good	Fine	Mint
V1#1-Origin Flash Lightning; X-The Phantom Fed, Ace McCoy, Buck Steele, Marvo the Magician, The Raven(not in #2) begin	26.50	53.25	80.00
2	16.50	33.25	50.00
3(9/40)	13.50	26.75	40.00
3(#4,10/40)No# on cover, #3 on inside	12.00	24.00	36.00
5	10.00	20.00	30.00
6-Dr. Nemesis begins	8.00	16.00	24.00

Lightning Comics cont'd)   Good Fine Mint
V2#1-6: #2-"Flash Lightning" becomes
  "Lash --"   8.00 16.00 24.00
V3#1-Intro. Lightning Girl & The Sword
                    8.00 16.00 24.00

LI'L (See Little)

LILY OF THE ALLEY IN THE FUNNIES
No Date (1920's?)(10½x15½")(In Color)(28pgs.)
Whitman Publishers

No. W936 - by T. Burke   7.00 14.00 21.00

LIMITED COLLECTORS' EDITION (See Famous 1st
Edition & Rudolph the Red Nosed Reindeer; be-
comes All-New Coll. Edition)
(80pgs. 68pgs.#35-41; 60pgs.#42 on) ($1.00)
C-21, Sum,'73 - #C-52,10-11/77   (10x13½")
National Periodical Publications

C-21: Shazam + Captain Marvel Jr. reprint by
  Raboy   .65 1.35 2.00
C-22: Tarzan-complete origin reprinted from
  #207-210   .80 1.60 2.40
C-23: House of Mystery-Wrightson, Adams,
  Wood, Toth, Orlando art .50 1.00 1.50
C-25: Batman; Adams cvr/art.65 1.35 2.00
C-27: Shazam   .50 1.00 1.50
C-29: Tarzan-Reprints "Return of Tarzan"
  from #219-223   .90 1.80 2.70
C-31: Superman-Origin retold; Adams art
                .65 1.35 2.00
C-32: Ghosts (new stories) .40 .80 1.20
C-33: Rudolph (new stories).40 .80 1.20
C-34: Xmas with the Super-Heroes; unpublish-
  ed Angel & Ape story by Oksner & Wood
                .50 1.00 1.50
C-35: Shazam-cover features TV's Captain Mar-
  vel, Jackson Bostwick .50 1.00 1.50
C-36: The Bible-all new adaptation beginning
  with Genesis by Kubert, Redondo & Mayer
                .65 1.35 2.00
C-37: Batman   .50 1.00 1.50
C-38: Superman; 1pg. Adams .50 1.00 1.50
C-39: Secret Origins/Super Villains; Adams
  story reprint   .65 1.35 2.00
C-40: Dick Tracy by Gould featuring Flattop;
  newspaper reprints from 12/21/43-5/17/44
                .65 1.35 2.00
C-41: Super Friends-Toth art
                .50 1.00 1.50
C-42: Rudolph   .35 .70 1.05
C-43: Christmas with the Super-Heroes; Wright-
  son, S&K, Adams art .60 1.20 1.80
C-44: Batman   .50 1.00 1.50
C-45: Secret Origins/Super Villains
                .50 1.00 1.50

                  Good Fine Mint
C-46: Justice League of America
                .50 1.00 1.50
C-47: Superman Salutes the Bicentennial
                .40 .80 1.20
C-48: The Superman-Flash Race
                .50 1.00 1.50
C-49: Superboy & the Legion of Super-Heroes
                .50 1.00 1.50
C-50: Rudolph   .35 .70 1.05
C-51: Batman-Adams cvr/sty .40 .80 1.20
C-52: The Best of DC-Adams cover
                .40 .80 1.20
NOTE: *All reprints with exception of some
special features & covers.*

LINDA (Phantom Lady #5 on)
Apr-May, 1954 - #4, Oct-Nov, 1955
Ajax-Farrell Publ. Co.

#1   1.50 3.00 4.50
2   1.00 2.00 3.00
3,4-Kamen art   1.50 3.00 4.50

LINDA CARTER, STUDENT NURSE
Sept, 1961 - #9, Jan, 1963
Atlas Comics (AMI)

#1   .35 .70 1.05
2-9   .20 .40 .60

LINDA LARK (--Student Nurse #1; --Nurse#7,8)
Oct-Dec, 1961 - #8, Aug-Oct, 1963
Dell Publishing Co.

#1   .25 .50 .75
2-8   .15 .30 .45

LINUS, THE LIONHEARTED (TV)
September, 1965
Gold Key

#1(10155-509)   .20 .40 .60

LION, THE (See Movie Comics)

LION OF SPARTA (See Movie Classics)

LIPPY THE LION AND HARDY HAR HAR (TV)
March, 1963   (Hanna-Barbera)
Gold Key

#1(10049-303)   .20 .40 .60

LI'L ABNER (See Comics on Parade)
1939 - 1948
United Features Syndicate

Linda #1, © Ajax   Linda Carter #1, © MCG   Li'l Abner #75, © UFS

Little Ambrose #1, © AP   Little Annie Rooney #1, © Std   Little Audrey #18, © STJ

(Li'l Abner cont'd)	Good	Fine	Mint
Single Series #4('39)	15.00	30.00	45.00
Single Series #18('40)(#18 on inside, #2 on cover)	12.00	24.00	36.00

LI'L ABNER (Al Capp's)(See Oxydol-Dreft)
#61, Dec, 1947 - #97, Jan, 1955
Toby Press/Harvey Publ./Toby Press #70 on

#61(#1)Wolverton art	6.00	12.00	18.00
62-65,68: #68-Fosdick	4.50	9.00	13.50
66,67,69,70	3.50	7.00	10.50
71-74,76,80,95: #95-Fosdick	3.00	6.00	9.00
75,77-79,86,91-All with Kurtzman art	4.00	8.00	12.00
81-85,87-90,92-94,96,97: #93-reprints #71	2.00	4.00	6.00
-- & the Creatures from Drop-Outer Space (Giveaway)(No#)	2.50	5.00	7.50
-- Joins the Navy(1950)(Toby Press Premium)	3.00	6.00	9.00
-- by Al Capp Giveaway(Circa 1955, no date)	2.75	5.50	8.00

NOTE: *Kurtzman art-#75,77-79,86,91(reprints #77. Powell story-#61. Wolverton art-#61. #68,95 have full length Fearless Fosdick stories.*

LI'L ABNER
1951
Toby Press

#1	2.50	5.00	7.50

LI'L ABNER'S DOGPATCH (See Al Capp's --)

LITTLE AL OF THE F.B.I.
#10, 1950(no month) - #11, April-May, 1951
Ziff-Davis Publications

#10(1950), 11(1951)-Painted covers by Norman Saunders	1.00	2.00	3.00

LITTLE AL OF THE SECRET SERVICE
1950 - #10, 1951
Ziff-Davis Publications

#1	1.00	2.00	3.00
2-10	.65	1.35	2.00

LITTLE AMBROSE
Sept, 1958
Archie Publications

#1	2.00	4.00	6.00

LITTLE ANGEL

#5, Sept, 1954; #6, 9/55 - #16, 9/59
Standard(Visual Editions)/Pines

	Good	Fine	Mint
#5-16	.35	.70	1.0

LITTLE ANNIE ROONEY
1935 (48 pgs.) (B&W dailies) (25¢)
David McKay Publications

Book #1-Daily strip reprints by Darrell McClure	12.00	24.00	36.00

LITTLE ANNIE ROONEY
1938; Aug, 1948 - #3, Oct, 1948
David McKay/St. John/Standard

Feature Book #11(McKay, '38)	15.00	30.00	45.00
#1(St. John)	2.00	4.00	6.00
2,3	1.50	3.00	4.50

LITTLE ARCHIE (The Advs. of --)
1956 - Present (Giants #3-84)
Archie Publications

#1	5.00	10.00	15.00
2-5	2.50	5.00	7.50
6-10	1.50	3.00	4.50
11-20	1.20	2.40	3.60
21-40: Little Pureheart begins #40, ends #42,44	.65	1.35	2.00
41-60: #42-Intro. The Little Archies. #59-Little Sabrina begins	.40	.80	1.20
61-100	.20	.40	.60
101-125		.15	.30
--In Animal Land #1('57)	2.00	4.00	6.00
--In Animal Land #17(Winter, 1957-58)-#19 (Summer,'58)-Formerly Li'l Jinx	1.00	2.00	3.00

LITTLE ARCHIE COMICS DIGEST ANNUAL
Oct, 1977 - Present (Digest) (192 pgs.)
Archie Publications

#1-Reprints	.20	.40	.60

LITTLE ARCHIE MYSTERY
1963 - #2, Oct, 1963
Archie Publications

#1	3.00	6.00	9.00
2	1.50	3.00	4.50

LITTLE ASPIRIN (See Wisco)
July, 1949 - #3, Dec, 1949 (52 pgs.)
Marvel Comics (CnPC)

#1-4pgs. Kurtzman art	2.50	5.00	7.50

ittle Aspirin cont'd)	Good	Fine	Mint
2- " " "	1.75	3.35	5.00
3-No Kurtzman	.65	1.35	2.00

ITTLE AUDREY (See Harvey Hits #11,49,52,53)
948 - 1956
c. John Publ./Harvey Publ. #25 on

1	4.00	8.00	12.00
2-5	2.00	4.00	6.00
5-10	1.35	2.75	4.00
1-20	1.00	2.00	3.00
1-53	.40	.80	1.20

ITTLE AUDREY (-- Yearbook)
950 (260 pgs.) (50¢)
c. John Publishing Co.

ontains 8 complete 1949 comics rebound;
ittle Audrey, Abbott & Costello, Pinocchio,
oon Mullins, Three Stooges(from Jubilee), &
ittle Annie Rooney app. (Rare)
          10.00 20.00 30.00

ITTLE AUDREY (See Playful --)

ITTLE AUDREY & MELVIN
ay, 1962 - Present
arvey Publications

1	2.00	4.00	6.00
2-5	1.00	2.00	3.00
6-10	.80	1.60	2.40
1-25	.35	.70	1.05
6-61	.15	.30	.45

ITTLE AUDREY TV FUNTIME
962 - #33, Oct, 1971
arvey Publications

1	1.00	2.00	3.00
2-5	.50	1.00	1.50
6-10	.35	.70	1.05
1-33	.15	.30	.45

ITTLE BAD WOLF (See 4-Color #403,473,564,
  Walt Disney Showcase #21)

ITTLE BEAVER
948 - #8, Jan, 1953
ell Publishing Co.

-Color #211('48)	2.50	5.00	7.50
-Color #267,294,332	1.75	3.35	5.00
-Color #483,529	1.50	3.00	4.50
-Color #612,660,695,744,817,870	1.20	2.40	3.60
3(10/51)-#8	1.00	2.00	3.00

LITTLE BIT
March, 1949 - #2, 1949
Jubilee/St. John Publishing Co.

	Good	Fine	Mint
#1,2	1.00	2.00	3.00

LITTLE DOT (See Tastee-Freez Comics)
9/53 - #150, 7/73; #151 - #164, 4/77
Harvey Publications

#1	2.50	5.00	7.50
2-5	1.35	2.75	4.00
6-10	.65	1.35	2.00
11-20	.35	.70	1.05
21-50	.25	.50	.75
51-100	.20	.40	.60
101-150	.15	.30	.45
161-164		.15	.30

LITTLE DOT DOTLAND (Dot Dotland #63)
July, 1962 - #62, Sept, 1974
Harvey Publications

#1	.65	1.35	2.00
2-10	.25	.50	.75
11-20	.15	.30	.45
21-62		.15	.30

LITTLE DOT'S UNCLES & AUNTS (See Harvey Hits
May, 1962 - Present   #4,24)
Harvey Publications

#1	.65	1.35	2.00
2-10	.25	.50	.75
11-20	.15	.30	.45
21-50		.15	.30

LITTLE EVA
May, 1952 - #31, Nov, 1956
St. John Publishing Co.

#1	2.00	4.00	6.00
2-10	1.20	2.40	3.60
11-31	.80	1.60	2.40
3-D#1,2(25¢)(10/53-11/53)	3.00	6.00	9.00
IW Reprint #1,2,7,8	.35	.70	1.05
Super Reprint #10,12('63),14,16,18('64)			
	.35	.70	1.05

LITTLE FIR TREE, THE
1942 (8½x11") (12 pgs. with cover)
W. T. Grant Co. (Christmas giveaway)

8 pg. Kelly story reprint/Santa Claus Funnies
  not signed.
    (One copy sold for $300.00 in 1977)

Little Beaver 4-Color #267. © Dell

Little Dot #1. © Harv

Little Eva #1, © I.W.

Little Ghost #1, © STJ   Little Iodine #2, © Dell   Little Lana #8, © MCG

LI'L GENIUS (Summer Fun #54 on)(See Blue Bird)
1954 - #52, Jan, 1965; #53, Oct, 1965
Charlton Comics

	Good	Fine	Mint
#1	.65	1.35	2.00
2-20	.35	.70	1.05
21-53	.15	.30	.45

LI'L GHOST
Feb, 1958 - #3, Mar, 1959
St. John Publishing Co./Fago #2 on

#1	.40	.80	1.20
2,3	.25	.50	.75

LITTLE GIANT COMICS
7/38 - #2, 8/38 (132pgs.) (6-3/4"x4-1/2")
Centaur Publications

#1,2 (B&W)	15.00	30.00	45.00

LITTLE GIANT DETECTIVE FUNNIES
10/38 - #3, 2/39 (132 pgs.) (6-3/4"x4-1/2")
Centaur Publications

#1	15.00	30.00	45.00
2,3	10.00	20.00	30.00
4(1/39)-B&W-no cover, 36pgs. 6½x9½"	10.00	20.00	30.00

LITTLE GIANT MOVIE FUNNIES
8/38 - #2, 10/38 (132 pgs.)(6-3/4"x4-1/2")
Centaur Publications

#1-Reprints of Ed Wheelan's "Minute Movies"	15.00	30.00	45.00
2- " " " "	10.00	30.00	45.00

LITTLE GROUCHO (--Grouchy #2)(See Tippy Terry)
Feb-Mar, 1955 - #2, June-July, 1955
Reston Publ. Co.

#16,1	.50	1.00	1.50
#2(6-7/55)	.35	.70	1.05

LITTLE HIAWATHA(See 4-Color #439,787,901,988)

LITTLE IKE
April, 1953 - #4, Oct, 1953
St. John Publishing Co.

#1	.65	1.35	2.00
2-4	.40	.80	1.20

LITTLE IODINE
April, 1949 - #57, July-Sept, 1962
Dell Publishing Co.

4-Color #224,257	2.00	4.00	6.00

	Good	Fine	Mi
#1	2.50	5.00	7.
2-10	1.35	2.75	4.
11-20	1.00	2.00	3.
21-30	.65	1.35	2.
31-40	.50	1.00	1.
41-57	.40	.80	1.

LITTLE JACK FROST
1951
Avon Periodicals

#1	2.00	4.00	6.

LI'L JINX (Little Archie in Animal Land #1
1953 - #16, Sept, 1957; Nov, 1956
Archie Publications

#1	1.50	3.00	4.
2-16	.80	1.60	2.
1(11/56)	1.20	2.40	3.

LI'L JINX (See Archie Giant Series Mag.)

LI'L JINX CHRISTMAS BAG (See Archie Giant
Series Mag. #195,206,219)

LI'L JINX GIANT LAUGH-OUT
#33, Sept, 1971 - #43, Nov, 1973 (52pgs.)
Archie Publications

#33-43		.15	.30
(See Archie Giant Series Mag. #176,185)			

LITTLE JOE (See 4-Color Comics #1)

LITTLE JOE
1953
St. John Publishing Co.

#1		.65	1.35	2.

LITTLE JOHNNY & THE TEDDY BEARS
1907 (10x14") (32 pgs. in color)
Reilly & Britton Co.

By J. R. Bray	15.00	37.50	60.

LI'L KIDS
Aug, 1970 - #12, June, 1973
Marvel Comics Group

#1			.15
2-12: #10,11-Calvin app.			.10

LITTLE KING (See 4-Color #494,597,677)

LITTLE LANA (Formerly Lana)
#8, Nov, 1949 - #9, Mar, 1950

242

ittle Lana cont'd)
arvel Comics (MjMC)

	Good	Fine	Mint
8,9	.65	1.35	2.00

ITTLE LENNY
une, 1949 - #3, Nov, 1949
arvel Comics (CDS)

1	.65	1.35	2.00
2,3	.40	.80	1.20

ITTLE LIZZIE
une, 1949 - #5, April, 1950
arvel Comics (PrPI)

1	1.00	2.00	3.00
2-5	.65	1.35	2.00

ITTLE LOTTA (See Harvey Hits #10)
ov, 1955 - Present
arvey Publications

1	2.50	5.00	7.50
2-5	1.35	2.75	4.00
6-10	1.00	2.00	3.00
1-30	.50	1.00	1.50
1-60	.20	.40	.60
1-121(5/76)		.15	.30

ITTLE LOTTA FOODLAND
eptember, 1963
arvey Publications

1	1.00	2.00	3.00

ITTLE LOTTA FOODTOWN
963 - #9, 1965
arvey Publications

1	1.00	2.00	3.00
2-9	.50	1.00	1.50

ITTLE LOTTA IN FOODLAND
968 - #38, Oct, 1971
arvey Publications

1	.20	.40	.60
2-38	.15	.30	.45

ITTLE LULU (Marge's --)
June, 1945 - Present
ell Publishing Co./Gold Key, 12/62 on

-Color #74('45)	70.00	140.00	210.00
-Color #97('46)	25.00	50.00	75.00

(Above two books done entirely by John Stanley - cover, pencils, & inks.)

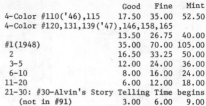

	Good	Fine	Mint
4-Color #110('46),115	17.50	35.00	52.50
4-Color #120,131,139('47),146,158,165			
	13.50	26.75	40.00
#1(1948)	35.00	70.00	105.00
2	16.50	33.25	50.00
3-5	12.00	24.00	36.00
6-10	8.00	16.00	24.00
11-20	6.00	12.00	18.00
21-30: #30-Alvin's Story Telling Time begins			
(not in #91)	3.00	6.00	9.00

Little Lulu 4-Color #97, © West

	Good	Fine	Mint
31-38,40	3.00	6.00	9.00
39-Intro. Witch Hazel in "That Awful Witch			
Hazel"	4.00	8.00	12.00
41-60: #45-2nd Witch Hazel app. #49-Gives			
Stanley & others credit			
	2.50	5.00	7.50
61-80: #80-Intro. Little Itch(2/55)			
	2.00	4.00	6.00
81-100	1.75	3.35	5.00
101-130	1.20	2.40	3.60
131-164,167-170; #165 & 166 listed below as			
Giant issues	.65	1.35	2.00
171-205	.35	.70	1.05
206-Last issue to carry Marge's name,			
207-220	.20	.40	.60
221-242		.20	.35
--& Alvin Story Telling Time #1(3/59)-re-			
prints/#2,5,3,11,30,10,21,17,8,14,16			
	3.35	6.75	10.00
--& Her Friends #4(3/56) 100 pgs.			
	3.35	6.75	10.00
--& Her Special Friends #3(3/55), 100pgs.			
	3.35	6.75	10.00
--& Tubby Annual #1(1953)-reprints from			
4-Color #165,4C-74,4C-146,4C-97,4C-158,			
4C-139,4C-131	12.00	24.00	36.00
--& Tubby Annual #2(1954)-Reprints/4C-139,6,			
4C-115,4C-74,5,4C-97,3,4C-146,18			

Little Lizzie #5, © MCG

Little Lotta #1, © Harv

Little Lulu #34, © West

Little Lulu & Tubby Annual #1, © West   Little Miss Muffet #13, © King   Little Orphan Annie #4(C&L), © News Synd

(Little Lulu cont'd)	Good	Fine	Mint
	8.00	16.00	24.00
--& Tubby at Summer Camp #5(1957)			
	3.00	6.00	9.00
--& Tubby at Summer Camp #2(10/58)			
	3.00	6.00	9.00
--& Tubby Halloween Fun #6(1957)			
	1.75	3.35	5.00
--& Tubby Halloween Fun #2(1958)			
	1.75	3.35	5.00
--& Tubby Halloween Fun #23(1959)(Dell Giant)			
	3.00	6.00	9.00
--& Tubby in Alaska #1(7/59)			
	3.00	6.00	9.00
--& Tubby in Australia #42(1961)			
	2.00	4.00	6.00
--& Tubby in Hawaii #29(4/60)			
	2.50	5.00	7.50
--& Tubby in Japan (12¢)(5-7/62) #01476-207			
	1.75	3.35	5.00
--& Tubby Witch Hazel Halloween Fun #36(1960)			
	2.00	4.00	6.00
--& Witch Hazel Trick & Treat #50(1961)			
	2.00	4.00	6.00
--Christmas Diary #166(1962-63)(Gold Key)			
	1.50	3.00	4.50
--in Paris #165(1962-G.K.)	2.00	4.00	6.00
--on Vacation #1(1954)-Reprints/4C-110,14,			
4C-146,5,4C-97,4,4C-158,3,1			
	6.00	12.00	18.00
--Summer Camp #1(1967-G.K.)-reprints '57-58			
	1.00	2.00	3.00
--Trick 'N' Treat #1 (12¢)(12/62-Gold Key)			
	2.00	4.00	6.00

NOTE: *All Giants by Stanley except Christmas Diary #166, In Paris #165.*

LITTLE LULU (See Golden Comics Digest #19, 23,27,29,33,36,40,43,46 & March of Comics #251,267,275,293,307,323,335,349,355,369,385, 406,417)

LITTLE MARY MIXUP (See Single Series #10,26)

LITTLE MAX COMICS (Joe Palooka's Pal)
Oct, 1949 - #73, 1961
Harvey Publications

#1	1.35	2.75	4.00
2-10	.65	1.35	2.00
11-20	.40	.80	1.20
21-73	.25	.50	.75

LI'L MENACE
Dec, 1958 - #2, Feb, 1959
Fago Magazine Co.

#1-Peter Rabbit app.	.50	1.00	1.50

	Good	Fine	Mint
2- " " (Vincent Fago's)			
	.35	.70	1.05

LITTLE MISS MUFFET
Dec, 1948 - #13, March, 1949
Standard Comics/King Features Synd.

#11-13-Strip reprints; Fanny Cory art			
	1.50	3.00	4.50

LITTLE MISS SUNBEAM COMICS
#2, Aug-Sept, 1950 - #4, Dec-Jan, 1950-51
Magazine Enterprises

#2-4	1.35	2.75	4.00
Bread Giveaway #1-4(Quality Bakers, 1949-50)			
(14 pgs. ea.)	1.35	2.75	4.00

LITTLE MONSTERS, THE
Nov, 1964 - Present
Gold Key

#1	.25	.50	.75
2-10	.15	.30	.45
11-20		.15	.30
21-43: #34-36-reprints	.10	.20	

LITTLE NEMO (See Cocomalt, Future Comics, Help, Jest, Kayo, Punch, Red Seal, & Superworld; most by Winsor McCay Jr., son of famous artist)

LITTLE NEMO (-- in Slumberland)
1906, 1909 (Sunday strip reprints in color)
(Cardboard covers)
Doffield & Co.(1906)/Cupples & Leon Co.(1909)

1906-11x16½" in color by Winsor McCay (30pgs)			
(Very Rare)	185.00	342.50	500.00
1909-10x14" in color by Winsor McCay			
(Very Rare)	150.00	300.00	450.00

LITTLE NEMO (-- in Slumberland)
1945 (28 pgs.) (11x7¼") (B&W)
McCay Features/Nostalgia Press('69)

Reprints from 1905 & 1911 by Winsor McCay

	8.00	16.00	24.00
1969-70 exact reprint	2.00	4.00	6.00

LITTLE ORHPAN ANNIE (See Merry Christmas--, Super Book #11,23, & Treasury Box of Famous Comics)

LITTLE ORPHAN ANNIE
1926 - 1934 (Daily strip reprints)(7x8-3/4")
Cupples & Leon Co.   (B&W)

(Little Orphan Annie cont'd)

	Good	Fine	Mint
(Hardcover Editions, 96 pgs.)			
#1(1926)-Little Orphan Annie	15.00	30.00	45.00
2('27)-In the Circus	10.00	20.00	30.00
3('28)-The Haunted House	10.00	20.00	30.00
4('29)-Bucking the World	10.00	20.00	30.00
5('30)-Never Say Die	10.00	20.00	30.00
6('31)-Shipwrecked	10.00	20.00	30.00
7('32)-A Willing Helper	8.00	16.00	24.00
8('33)-In Cosmic City	8.00	16.00	24.00
9('34)-Uncle Dan	10.00	20.00	30.00

NOTE: *Hardcovers with dust jackets are worth 20-50% more; the earlier the book, the higher the percentage. Each book reprints dailies from the previous year.*

LITTLE ORPHAN ANNIE & THE BIG TOWN GUNMAN
1937   (64pgs.;5½x7½";B&W daily reprints)
Whitman Publishing Co.   (Hardcover)

	5.00	10.00	15.00

LITTLE ORPHAN ANNIE
1937 - 1948
David McKay Publ./Dell Publishing Co.

	Good	Fine	Mint
Feature Book(McKay)#7-('37) (Rare)	60.00	120.00	180.00
4-Color #12(1941)	20.00	40.00	60.00
4-Color #18('43)	15.00	30.00	45.00
4-Color #52('44)	8.00	16.00	24.00
4-Color #76('45)	7.00	14.00	21.00
4-Color #107('46)	6.00	12.00	18.00
4-Color #152('47)	5.00	10.00	15.00
4-Color #206('49)	4.00	8.00	12.00
#1(3-5/48)	10.00	20.00	30.00
2,3	5.00	10.00	15.00
4	4.00	8.00	12.00

Junior Commandos Giveaway(Same cover as 4-
    Color #18, K.K. Publ.(Big Shoe Store);
    same back cover as '47 Popped Wheat give-
    away; 16pgs.   15.00   30.00   45.00
Popped Wheat Giveaway('47)-16pgs. full color;
    '38,'40 reprints   1.00   2.00   3.00
Quaker Giveaway(1940)   5.00   10.00   15.00
Quaker Giveaway(1941,'42)"Advs. of," "The
    Kidnappers," "The Rescue"
        each....   4.00   8.00   12.00
Sparkies Giveaway(Full color-20pgs.)
    (1941-42)(2 different) 2.50   5.00   7.50

LI'L PALS
Sept, 1972 - #5, May, 1973
Marvel Comics Group

	Good	Fine	Mint
#1-5		.10	.20

LITTLE PAN
#6, Dec-Jan, 1947 - #8, Apr-May, 1947
Fox Features Syndicate

#6-8	1.00	2.00	3.00

LITTLE PEOPLE (See 4-Color #485,573,633,692,
753,809,868,908,959,1024,1062)

LITTLE RASCALS (See 4-Color #674,778,825,
883,936,974,1030,1079,1137,1174,1224,1297)

LI'L RASCAL TWINS
1957 - #17, Mar, 1959
Charlton Comics

#6-17-Li'l Genius & Tomboy	.15	.30	.45

LITTLE ROQUEFORT
June, 1952 - #9, 10/53; #10, Summer, 1958
St. John Publishing Co./Pines #10

#1	1.00	2.00	3.00
2-10	.50	1.00	1.50

LITTLE SAD SACK (See Harvey Hits #73,76,83)
Oct, 1964 - #19, 1967
Harvey Publications

#1-Richie Rich app.	.40	.80	1.20
2-19		.15	.30

LITTLE SAMMY SNEEZE
1905   (28 pgs.) (11x16½") (In Color)
New York Herald Co.

By Winsor McCay   100.00 200.00 300.00
NOTE: *Rarely occurs in Fine-Mint condition.*

LITTLE SCOUTS
1951 - #587, Oct, 1954
Dell Publishing Co.

4-Color #321('51)	1.00	2.00	3.00
#2(10-12/51)-#6(10-12/52)	.65	1.35	2.00
4-Color #462,506,550,587	.65	1.35	2.00

LITTLE SPUNKY
No Date (1963?) (10¢)
I.W. Enterprises

#1-Reprint	.25	.50	.75

Little Orphan Annie #3(Dell). © News Synd

Little Sammy Sneeze. © N.Y. Herald

Little Scouts #2. © Dell

The Living Bible #1, © Living Bible   The Lone Ranger #83, © Lone Ranger   The Lone Ranger Merita Giveaway, © Lone Ranger

LITTLE STOOGES, THE (The Three Stooges' Sons)
Sept, 1972 - #7, Mar, 1974
Gold Key

	Good	Fine	Mint
#1-Norman Maurer cover/stories in all			
	.20	.40	.60
2-7	.15	.30	.45

LITTLEST OUTLAW (See 4-Color Comics #609)

LITTLEST SNOWMAN, THE
1956; 1964
Dell Publishing Co./Gold Key

4-Color #755,864	.65	1.35	2.00
#1(1964)(Gold Key)	.40	.80	1.20

LI'L TOMBOY
V14#93, Mar, 1957 - #108, May, 1959
Charlton Comics

V14#93-#108	.15	.30	.45

LI'L WILLIE
July, 1949 - #21, Aug-Sept, 1949
Marvel Comics (MgPC)

#20,21	.50	1.00	1.50

LIVING BIBLE, THE
Fall, 1945 - 1946
Living Bible Corp.

#1-Life of Paul	2.00	4.00	6.00
2-Joseph & His Brethren	1.35	2.75	4.00
3	1.35	2.75	4.00

LOBO
Dec, 1965 - #2, Oct, 1966
Dell Publishing Co.

#1,2	.25	.50	.75

LOCO (Magazine) (Satire)
Aug, 1958 - V1#3, Jan, 1959
Satire Publications

V1#1-Chic Stone art	1.00	2.00	3.00
V1#2,3-Severin art, 2pgs. Davis #3			
	.50	1.00	1.50

LOGAN'S RUN
Jan, 1977 - #7, July, 1977
Marvel Comics Group

#1	.35	.70	1.05
2-7	.20	.40	.60

LOIS LANE (See Superman's Girlfriend --)

LOLLY AND PEPPER
1957 - July, 1962
Dell Publishing Co.

	Good	Fine	Mint
4-Color #832,940,978,1086,1206,			
#01-459,207	.40	.80	1.20

LOMAX (See Police Action)

LONE EAGLE (The Flame #5 on)
Apr-May, 1954 - #4, Oct-Nov, 1954
Ajax/Farrell Publications

#1	1.35	2.75	4.00
2-4	.80	1.60	2.40

LONELY HEART
#9, March, 1955 - #14, Feb, 1956
Ajax/Farrell Publ. (Excellent Publ.)

#9-14	.40	.80	1.20

LONE RANGER, THE
1939 - 1947
Dell Publishing Co.

Black & White #3('39)-Heigh-Yo Silver; text with ill. by Robert Weisman			
	25.00	50.00	75.00
Black & White #7('39)-Hi-Yo Silver the Lone Ranger to the Rescue	40.00	80.00	120.00
4-Color #82('45)	12.00	24.00	36.00
4-Color #98('45),#118('46)			
	10.00	20.00	30.00
4-Color #125('46),#136('47)			
	7.00	14.00	21.00
4-Color #151,167('47)	5.00	10.00	15.00

LONE RANGER COMICS, THE (10¢)
1939 (Ice Cream mail order)(68pgs. in Color)
Lone Ranger, Inc.   (Regular size)

(Scarce)-not by Vallely	40.00	80.00	120.00

LONE RANGER, THE (#1-37 strip reprints)
Jan-Feb, 1948 - #145, May-July, 1962
Dell Publishing Co.

#1	16.50	33.25	50.00
2	10.00	20.00	30.00
3-7,9,10	6.00	12.00	18.00
8-Origin retold	7.00	14.00	21.00
11-17,19,20	4.00	8.00	12.00
18-Origin retold	5.00	10.00	15.00
21,22,24-30	3.00	6.00	9.00
23-Origin retold	5.00	10.00	15.00

The Lone Ranger cont'd)	Good	Fine	Mint
31-37-Last newspaper reprint ish; new outfit			
	2.00	4.00	6.00
38-60	1.75	3.35	5.00
61-80	1.50	3.00	4.50
81-111	1.20	2.40	3.60
12-1st Clayton Moore cvr.	1.20	2.40	3.60
13-117	1.20	2.40	3.60
18-Orign Lone Ranger, Tonto, & Silver retold-Special anniversary issue			
	2.50	5.00	7.50
19-145	1.00	2.00	3.00
Cheerios Giveaways #1-"The Lone Ranger, Hi Mask & How He Met Tonto". #2-"The Lone Ranger & the Story of Silver" (1945)			
each....	1.75	3.35	5.00
Doll Giveaway(Gabriel Ind.)(1973, 3½x5")			
	.25	.50	.75
--Golden West #3('55,100pgs.)			
	2.00	4.00	6.00
How the L.R. Captured Silver Book(1936)-Silvercup Bread giveaway	10.00	20.00	30.00
--In Milk for Big Mike(1955, Dairy Association giveaway)	1.50	3.00	4.50
Merita Bread giveaway('54,16pgs.,5x7½")-"How To Be a L.R. Health Safety Scout"			
	2.00	4.00	6.00
--Movie Story('56,100pgs.)-Origin Lone Ranger in text	3.00	6.00	9.00
Western Treasury #1('53)-Origin of Lone Ranger	4.00	8.00	12.00
Western Treasury #2('54)(Becomes Golden West #3)	2.50	5.00	7.50

LONE RANGER, THE (See March of Comics #165, 174,193,208,225,238,310,322,338,350, Feature Book #21,24, McKay, & Aurora)

LONE RANGER, THE
9/64 - #16, 12/69; #17, 11/72; #18, 9/74 - #28, 3/77
Gold Key

#1	.50	1.00	1.50
2-17: Small Bear reprints in #6-12			
	.20	.40	.60
18-28	.15	.30	.45
Golden West #1(30029-610)-Giant, '66-reprints most Golden West #3	.65	1.35	2.00

LONE RANGER'S FAMOUS HORSE HI-YO SILVER, THE
#3, July-Sept, 1952 - #36, Oct, 1960
Dell Publishing Co.

4-Color #369,392	2.00	4.00	6.00
#3-10	1.35	2.75	4.00
11-36	.80	1.60	2.40

LONE RIDER
April, 1951 - #26, July, 1955
Ajax/Farrell Publications

	Good	Fine	Mint
#1	1.75	3.35	5.00
2-5	1.00	2.00	3.00
6-10	.65	1.35	2.00
11-26	.50	1.00	1.50

LONG BOW, INDIAN BOY
1951 - 1953
Fiction House Magazines(Real Adventures Publ.)

#1	1.35	2.75	4.00
2-9	.65	1.35	2.00

LONGEST DAY (See Movie Classics)

LONG JOHN SILVER & THE PIRATES (Formerly Terry & the Pirates)
#30, Aug, 1956 - #32, March, 1957
Charlton Comics

#30-32	1.20	2.40	3.60

LOONEY TUNES & MERRIE MELODIES COMICS
("Looney Tunes" #166 (8/55) on)
1941 - #246, July-Sept, 1962
Dell Publishing Co.

#1-Porky Pig, Bugs Bunny, Elmer Fudd begin			
	100.00	200,00	300.00
2	50.00	100.00	150.00
3-Kandi the Cave Kid by Walt Kelly; also in #4,5,8,11	40.00	80.00	120.00
4	25.00	50.00	75.00
5	20.00	40.00	60.00
6-10	15.00	30.00	45.00
11-20: #20-Pat, Patsy & Pete by Kelly begin, end-#25	12.00	24.00	36.00
21-30	8.00	16.00	24.00
31-40	6.00	12.00	18.00
41-50	4.00	8.00	12.00
51-60	3.00	6.00	9.00
61-80	2.00	4.00	6.00
81-100	1.50	3.00	4.50
101-150	1.00	2.00	3.00
151-200	.65	1.35	2.00
201-246	.40	.80	1.20

LOONEY TUNES (2nd Series)
April, 1975 - Present
Gold Key

#1	.20	.40	.60
2-17		.15	.30

Long John Silver #32, © CC

Looney Tunes #19, © Dell

Looney Tunes #25, © Dell

Lorna The Jungle Girl #7, © MCG   Lost Worlds #6, © Std   Love Classics #1, © MCG

LOONY SPORTS (Magazine)
Spring, 1975   (68 pgs.)
3-Strikes Publishing

	Good	Fine	Mint
#1-Sports satire	.35	.70	1.05

LOOY DOT DOPE   (See Single Series #13)

LORD JIM   (See Movie Comics)

LORNA THE JUNGLE GIRL   (--Jungle Queen #1-5)
June, 1953 - #26, Aug, 1957
Atlas Comics (OMC #1-11/NPI #12-26)

#1	4.00	8.00	12.00
2-5: #2-Intro. & 1st app. Greg Knight			
	3.00	6.00	9.00
6-15	2.50	5.00	7.50
16,17,19-26	2.00	4.00	6.00
18-Williamson/Colleta cvr.	2.50	5.00	7.50

LOST IN SPACE   (Space Family Robinson--,
on Space Station One)(Formerly Space Family
#37, Oct, 1973 - Present   Robinson)
Gold Key

#37-54		.20	.35

LOST WORLD, THE   (See 4-Color Comics #1145)

LOST WORLDS
#5, Oct, 1952 - #6, Dec, 1952
Standard Comics

#5-Toth + Sekowsky art	2.00	4.00	6.00
6-Sekowsky art	1.35	2.75	4.00

LOU GEHRIG (See The Pride of the Yankees)

LOVE ADVENTURES (Actual Confessions #13)
Oct, 1949 - #12, 1952
Marvel/Atlas Comics (MPI)

#1	1.00	2.00	3.00
2-12	.65	1.35	2.00

LOVE AND MARRIAGE
March, 1952 - #16, Sept, 1954
Superior Comics Ltd.

#1	1.35	2.75	4.00
2-16	.65	1.35	2.00
IW Reprint #1,2,8,11,14	.15	.30	.45
Super Reprint #15,17('64)	.15	.30	.45

LOVE AND ROMANCE
Sept, 1971 - #24, Sept, 1975
Charlton Comics

	Good	Fine	Mint
#1		.15	.30
2-24		.10	.20

LOVE AT FIRST SIGHT
Oct, 1949 - #42, Aug, 1956
Ace Magazines(RAR Publ.Co./Periodical House)

#1	1.00	2.00	3.00
2-10	.50	1.00	1.50
11-42	.30	.60	.90
#6(1960)		.15	.30

LOVE BUG, THE   (See Movie Comics)

LOVE CLASSICS
Nov, 1949 - #2, Jan, 1950
A Lover's Magazine/Marvel Comics

#1,2	1.00	2.00	3.00

Love Confessions #4, © Qua

LOVE CONFESSIONS
Oct, 1949 - #53, 1956 (some issues: photo
Quality Comics Group   covers)

#1-Ward cover, 9pgs. + Gustavson story			
	4.00	8.00	12.00
2-Gustavson story	1.35	2.75	4.00
3	1.00	2.00	3.00
4-Crandall story	1.50	3.00	4.50
5-7pgs. Ward art	2.00	4.00	6.00
6,7,9,10	.80	1.60	2.40
8-Ward story	1.75	3.35	5.00
11-18	.75	1.50	2.25
19-Ward story	1.50	3.00	4.50
20-53	.50	1.00	1.50

LOVE DIARY
July, 1949 - #47, 1954
Our Publishing Co./Toytown/Patches

(Love Diary cont'd)	Good	Fine	Mint
#1-Krigstein story	3.00	6.00	9.00
2,3-Krigstein & Mort Leav story in each			
	2.00	4.00	6.00
4-8	1.00	2.00	3.00
9,10-Everett story	1.35	2.75	4.00
11-Mort Leav story	1.00	2.00	3.00
12-20	.65	1.35	2.00
21-47	.50	1.00	1.50

LOVE DIARY
Sept, 1949
Quality Comics Group

	Good	Fine	Mint
#1-Ward cover/story	4.00	8.00	12.00

LOVE DIARY
July, 1958 - Present
Charlton Comics

#1	.35	.70	1.05
2-20	.15	.30	.45
21-97		.10	.20

LOVE DOCTOR (See Dr. Anthony King --)

LOVE DRAMAS
Oct, 1949 - #2, Jan, 1950
Marvel Comics (IPS)

#1-Jack Kamen art	2.00	4.00	6.00
2	1.00	2.00	3.00

LOVE EXPERIENCES(Challenge of the Unknown #6)
10/49 - #5, 1950; #6, 4/51 - #35, 12/55
Ace Periodicals(A.A.Wyn/Periodical House)

#1	1.00	2.00	3.00
2-5	.50	1.00	1.50
6-10	.30	.60	.90
11-35	.20	.40	.60

LOVE EXPRESSIONS
1949 ?
Ace Magazines

#1	1.00	2.00	3.00

LOVE JOURNAL
#10, Oct, 1951 - #24, May, 1954
Our Publishing Co.

#10	.65	1.35	2.00
11-24	.35	.70	1.05

LOVELAND
Nov, 1949 - 1950
Mutual Mag./Eye Publ. (Atlas)

	Good	Fine	Mint
#1,2	.65	1.35	2.00

LOVE LESSONS
Oct, 1949 - #5, June, 1950
Harvey Comics/Key Publ. #5

#1-Same cover as Love Letters #1			
	1.00	2.00	3.00
2-5: #2-Powell story	.65	1.35	2.00

LOVE LETTERS
1949
Harvey Comics

#1-Cover reprinted as Love Lessons #1			
	1.00	2.00	3.00

LOVE LETTERS
Nov, 1949 - #50, Oct, 1956
Quality Comics Group

#1-Ward cover	3.00	6.00	9.00
2-Ward cover, Gustavson story			
	2.00	4.00	6.00
3,5-10	1.00	2.00	3.00
4-Ward art, 9pgs.	2.00	4.00	6.00
11-9pgs. Ward art reprinted/Broadway Romances			
#2 & retitled	1.75	3.35	5.00
12-15,18-20	.75	1.50	2.25
16,17-Ward art, 6 & 9pgs.	1.50	3.00	4.50
21-50	.50	1.00	1.50

NOTE: *Photo covers-#9,16.*

LOVE LIFE
1951
Approved Comics (Ziff-Davis)

#1	.65	1.35	2.00

LOVELORN (Confessions of the Lovelorn #52 on)
Aug-Sept, 1949 - #51, July, 1954
American Comics Group(Michel Publ./Regis Publ.)

#1	1.20	2.40	3.60
2-10: Whitney art #5	.65	1.35	2.00
11-48,50: #18-2pgs. Drucker	.40	.80	1.20
49,51-Has 3-D effect	1.00	2.00	3.00

LOVE MEMORIES
1949 (no month) - #4, July, 1950
Fawcett Publications

#1	1.35	2.75	4.00
2-4	.65	1.35	2.00

LOVE MYSTERY
June, 1950 - #3, Oct, 1950

Love Diary #2, © Our Publ.

Love Letters #2, © Qua

Lovelorn #3, © ACG

Love Problems, © Fox

Love Stories Of Mary Worth #1, © Harv

Love Trails #1, © MCG

(Love Mystery cont'd)
Fawcett Publications

	Good	Fine	Mint
#1,2-Geo. Evans art ea.	2.00	4.00	6.00
3-Powell art	1.50	3.00	4.50

LOVE PROBLEMS
1949   (132 pgs.)
Fox Features Syndicate

No#-See Fox Giants. Contents can vary and
determines price.

LOVE PROBLEMS & ADVICE ILLUSTRATED
(See True --)

LOVE ROMANCES
#7, July, 1949 - #106, July, 1963
Timely/Marvel/Atlas(TCI #7-71/Male #72-106)

#7	1.00	2.00	3.00
8-Kubert story	1.50	3.00	4.50
9-20	.40	.80	1.20
21,24-Krigstein stories	1.50	3.00	4.50
22,23,25-37,39,40	.25	.50	.75
38-Krigstein story	1.35	2.75	4.00
41-48,50,51-97: #80,85,88-Kirby covers			
	.25	.50	.75
49-Toth art, 6pgs.	1.20	2.40	3.60
98-Four Kirby stories	1.75	3.35	5.00
99-Kirby story	1.00	2.00	3.00
105,106-Kirby story	1.00	2.00	3.00

LOVERS   (Formerly Blonde Phantom)
#23, May, 1949 - #85, June, 1957
Marvel Comics #23,24, Marvel/Atlas #25 on(ANC)

#23-25	.65	1.35	2.00
26-29	.40	.80	1.20
30-36,38-85	.25	.50	.75
37-Krigstein story	1.35	2.75	4.00

LOVERS' LANE
Oct, 1949 - #40, May, 1954
Lev Gleason Publications

#1	1.00	2.00	3.00
2,3,5-10	.60	1.20	1.80
4-Fuje art, 9pgs.	.65	1.35	2.00
11-19	.35	.70	1.05
20-Frazetta 1 pg. ad	1.00	2.00	3.00
21-38,40	.25	.50	.75
39-Story narrated by Frank Sinatra			
	.40	.80	1.20

LOVE SCANDALS
2/50 - #5, 10/50 (#4,5-photo covers)
Quality Comics Group

	Good	Fine	Min
#1-Ward cover, 9 pgs. art	3.00	6.00	9.0
2,3	1.00	2.00	3.0
4-Ward art, 18pgs. + Gill Fox story			
	2.50	5.00	7.5
5-C. Cuidera story	1.35	2.75	4.0

LOVE SECRETS
Oct, 1949 - #55, Oct, 1956
Quality Comics Group

#1	2.00	4.00	6.0
2-10	1.00	2.00	3.0
11-55	.60	1.20	1.8

LOVE STORIES
#6, 1950 - #18, Aug, 1954
Fox Features Syndicate/Star Publ. #15 on

#6,8-Wood stories	3.00	6.00	9.0
7,9-18	1.00	2.00	3.0

LOVE STORIES   (Formerly Heart Throbs)
#147, Nov, 1972 - #152, Oct-Nov, 1973
National Periodical Publications

#147-152		.10	.2(

LOVE STORIES OF MARY WORTH (See Harvey Hits
Sept, 1949 - #4, Mar, 1950   #55)
Harvey Publications

#1-1940's newspaper reprints-#1-4			
	2.50	5.00	7.5(
2-4	1.75	3.35	5.0(

LOVE TALES   (Formerly The Human Torch #35)
#36, May, 1949 - #75, Sept, 1957
Marvel/Atlas Comics(ZPC #36-50/MMC #67-75)

#36	.65	1.35	2.0(
37-51,53-75	.35	.70	1.0!
52-Krigstein story	1.35	2.75	4.0(

LOVE, 10 STORIES
July, 1955
Charlton Comics

#6	.25	.50	.7!

LOVE TRAILS
Dec, 1949   (52 pgs.)
A Lover's Magazine(CDS)(Marvel)

#1	1.00	2.00	3.0(

LOWELL THOMAS' HIGH ADVENTURE   (See 4-Color
Comics #949,1001)

250

T. (See Lieutenant)

LUCKY COMICS
Jan, 1944; #2, Sum, 1945 – #5, Sum, 1946
Consolidated Magazines

	Good	Fine	Mint
1-Lucky Starr, Bobbie	2.00	4.00	6.00
2-5	1.35	2.75	4.00

LUCKY DUCK
5, Jan, 1953 – #8, Sept, 1953
Standard Comics (Literary Ent.)

5-8	.65	1.35	2.00

LUCKY FIGHTS IT THROUGH
1949 (16pgs.)(Soft Cover, in color)(Giveaway)
Educational Comics

Extremely Rare)-Kurtzman art; V.D. prevent-
ion 25.00 50.00 75.00
NOTE: *Subtitled "The Story of That Ignorant,
Ignorant Cowboy." Prepared for Communications Materials Center, Columbia University.*

LUCKY "7" COMICS
1944
Howard Publishers Ltd.

1-Congo Raider, Punch Powers	2.35	4.75	7.00

LUCKY STAR
1950 – #7, 1951; #8, 1953 – #14, 1955
(5"x7¼") (Full Color)
Nation Wide Publ. Co.

1-Nostrand art begins	1.00	2.00	3.00
2-7 (52 pgs.)	1.35	2.75	4.00
8-14 (36 pgs.)	1.35	2.75	4.00
Given Away with Lucky Star Western Wear by the Juvenile Mfg. Co.	1.00	2.00	3.00

LUCY SHOW, THE (TV)
June, 1963 – #5, June, 1964
Gold Key

1	.20	.40	.60
2-5	.15	.30	.45

LUCY, THE REAL GONE GAL(Meet Miss Pepper#5 on)
June, 1953 – #4, Dec, 1953
St. John Publishing Co.

1-4: #3-Drucker art	1.00	2.00	3.00

LUDWIG BEMELMAN'S MADELEINE & GENEVIEVE
(See 4-Color Comics #796)

LUDWIG VON DRAKE (Walt Disney)
Nov-Dec, 1961 – #4, June-Aug, 1962
Dell Publishing Co.

	Good	Fine	Mint
#1	.80	1.60	2.40
2-4	.40	.80	1.20
-- Fish Stampede(15pgs., 1962, Fritos Give-away)	1.00	2.00	3.00

LUKE CAGE (See Hero For Hire)

LUKE SHORT'S WESTERN STORIES
April, 1954 – 1958
Dell Publishing Co.

#1(4/54)	1.75	3.35	5.00
4-Color #580(8/54), #2(10/54)	1.20	2.40	3.60
4-Color #651,739,771,807,848,875,927	1.20	2.40	3.60

LUNATICKLE (Magazine) (Satire)
Feb, 1956 – #2, April, 1956
Whitstone Publ.

#1,2-Kubert art	1.00	2.00	3.00

LYNDON B. JOHNSON
March, 1965
Dell Publishing Co.

#12-445-503	1.50	3.00	4.50

MACKENZIE'S RAIDERS (See 4-Color #1093)

MACO TOYS COMIC
1959 (36 pgs.) (Full Color) (Giveaway)
Maco Toys/Charlton Comics

#1-All military stories featuring Maco Toys	.50	1.00	1.50

MAD
Oct-Nov, 1952 – Present
(#24 on, Magazine format)(Kurtzman editor #1-
28, Feldstein #29 on)
E.C. Comics

#1-Wood, Davis, Elder start as regulars	60.00	120.00	180.00
2-Davis cover	30.00	60.00	90.00
3	17.50	35.00	52.50
4	15.00	30.00	45.00
5-(Scarce)-low distribution; Elder cover	50.00	100.00	150.00
6-10	12.00	24.00	36.00
11-15	8.00	16.00	24.00
16-23: #22-all by Elder	6.00	12.00	18.00

Lucky Star #5. © Nation Wide

Lucy #1. © STJ

Ludwig Von Drake #1. © WDP

Mad #6, © EC

Mad #17, © EC

Mad Hatter #1, © O.W. Comics

(Mad cont'd)	Good	Fine	Mint
24-1st magazine issue(25¢); Kurtzman logo & border on cover	12.00	24.00	36.00
25-Jaffee starts as regular writer	5.00	10.00	15.00
26-Wood cover	4.00	8.00	12.00
27-Davis cover	4.00	8.00	12.00
28-Elder cvr; Heath back cvr; last issue edited by Kurtzman	4.00	8.00	12.00
29-Wood cvr; Kamen story; Don Martin starts as regular; Feldstein editing begins	4.00	8.00	12.00
30-1st A.E. Neuman cover by Mingo; Crandall inside cover; last Elder story; Bob Clarke starts as regular	4.00	8.00	12.00
31-Freas starts as regular; last Davis art until #99	3.00	6.00	9.00
32-Orlando, Drucker, Woodbridge start as regulars; Wood back cover	3.00	6.00	9.00
33-Orlando back cover	3.00	6.00	9.00
34-Berg starts as regular	2.50	5.00	7.50
35-Mingo wraparound cover; Crandall story	2.50	5.00	7.50
36-40	2.00	4.00	6.00
41-50	1.75	3.35	5.00
51-60: #60-Two Clarke cvrs; Prohias starts as regular	1.00	2.00	3.00
61-70: #64-Rickard starts as regular. #68-Martin cover	.90	1.80	2.70
71-80: #76-Aragones starts as regular	.65	1.35	2.00
81-90: #86-1st Fold-in. #89-One strip by Walt Kelly. #90-Frazetta back cvr; 1pg. Wood story	.60	1.20	1.80
91-100: #91-Jaffee starts as story artist. #99-Davis art resumes	.50	1.00	1.50
101-120: #106-Frazetta back cover	.40	.80	1.20
121-140: #130-Torres starts as regular. #122-Drucker & Mingo cvr. #128-Last Orlando. #135,139-Davis covers	.35	.70	1.05
141-170: #143-2pgs. Wood art. #165-Martin cvr. #169-Drucker cover	.25	.50	.75
171-200: #173,178-Davis cvrs. #176-Drucker cvr. #182-Bob Jones starts as regular. #187-Harry North starts as regular	.20	.40	.60

NOTE: _Jules Feiffer_ story(reprint)-#42. _Freas-most covers & back covers-#40-74. Heath stories-#14,27. Krigstein stories-#12,17,24,26. Kurtzman covers-#1,3,4,6-10,13,14,16,18. John Severin art-#1-6,9,10. Wolverton cover-#11; stories-#11,17,29,31,36,40,82,137._

MAD (See --Follies, --Special, More Trash from--, & The Worst from--)

MAD ABOUT MILLIE

April, 1969 - #17, Dec, 1970
Marvel Comics Group

	Good	Fine	Mint
#1	.15	.30	.45
2-17		.10	.20
Annual #1('71),2,3		.15	.30

MAD FOLLIES (Special)
1963 - #7, 1969
E.C. Comics

No#(1963)-Paperback book covers			
	4.00	8.00	12.00
#2(1964)-Calendar	2.00	4.00	6.00
3(1965)-Mischief Stickers	1.50	3.00	4.50
4(1966)-Mobile; reprints Frazetta back cvr/ Mad #90	1.50	3.00	4.50
5(1967)-Stencils	1.50	3.00	4.50
6(1968)-Mischief Stickers	1.25	2.50	3.75
7(1969)-Nasty Cards	1.25	2.50	3.75

NOTE: _Clarke_ cover-#4. _Mingo_ covers-#1-3.

MAD HATTER, THE (Costume Hero)
Jan-Feb, 1946 - #2, Sept-Oct, 1946
O.W. Comics Corp.

#1-Freddy the Firefly begins; Giunta art, 2-Has ad for E.C.'s Animal Fables #1			
	2.50	5.00	7.50

MADHOUSE
1954; 1957
Ajax/Farrell Publ.(Excellent Publ./4-Star)

#1(1954)	4.00	8.00	12.00
2-4	2.00	4.00	6.00
1(1957)	1.20	2.40	3.60
2-4	.65	1.35	2.00

MADHOUSE (Formerly Madhouse Glads)
#95, 9/74 - #97, 1/75; #98, 8/75 - Present
Red Circle Productions/Archie Publications

#95-97: Horror stories. #97-Intro. Henry Hobson; Morrow art	.20	.40	.60
98-110-Satire/humor stys.	.20	.40	.60
Annual #8(1970-71)-#12(1974-75)-Formerly Madhouse Ma-ad Annual	.25	.50	.75
--Comics Digest #1('75-76)-#3('77-78)	.25	.50	.75

NOTE: _McWilliams_ art-#97. _Morrow_ covers-#95-97. See Archie Comics Digest #1,13.

MADHOUSE GLADS (Formerly Madhouse Ma-ad; Madhouse #95 on)
#75, Oct, 1970 - #94, Aug, 1974(#78-92, 52pgs)
Archie Publications

(Madhouse Glads cont'd)	Good	Fine	Mint
#75		.15	.30
76-94		.10	.20

MADHOUSE MA-AD (--Jokes #67-70; --Freak-Out #71-74)(Formerly Archie's Madhouse)(Becomes Madhouse Glads #75 on)
#67, Apr, 1969 - #74, Sept, 1970
Archie Publications

#67-74		.15	.30
--Annual #7(1969-70)-formerly Archie's Madhouse Annual; becomes Madhouse Annual	.15	.30	.45

MAD MONSTER PARTY (See Movie Classics)

MAD SPECIAL
Fall, 1970 - Present
E.C. Publications, Inc.

Fall '70(#1)-Bonus-Voodoo Doll; contains 17pgs. new material	1.00	2.00	3.00
Spring '71(#2)-Wall Nuts: 17pgs. new material	.65	1.35	2.00
#3-Protest Stickers	.65	1.35	2.00
4-8: #4-Mini Posters. #5-Mad Flag. #7-Presidential candidate posters, Wild Shocking Message posters. #8-TV Guise	.65	1.35	2.00
9(1972)-24pg. color comic insert from Mad comics	.65	1.35	2.00
10,11,13: #10-Nonsense Stickers(Don Martin). #11-33-1/3 RPM record. #13-Sickie Stickers	.40	.80	1.20
12-32pg. color comic insert; reprints from Mad comics	.65	1.35	2.00
14-Vital Message posters & Art Depreciation paintings	.40	.80	1.20
15-17	.40	.80	1.20
18-32pg. color comic insert; reprints from Mad comics	.50	1.00	1.50
19-21	.40	.80	1.20

MAGIC AGENT (See Unknown Worlds)
Jan-Feb, 1961 - #3, May-June, 1961
American Comics Group

#1-Origin & 1st app. John Force	.65	1.35	2.00
2,3	.35	.70	1.05

MAGIC COMICS
August, 1939 - #123, Nov-Dec, 1949
David McKay Publications

#1-Mandrake the Magician, Henry, Popeye (not by Segar) begin	25.00	50.00	75.00

	Good	Fine	Mint
2	12.00	24.00	36.00
3	10.00	20.00	30.00
4	8.00	16.00	24.00
5	7.00	14.00	21.00
6-10	6.00	12.00	18.00
11-16,18-20	5.00	10.00	15.00
17-The Lone Ranger begins	5.00	10.00	15.00
21-30	4.00	8.00	12.00
31-40	3.00	6.00	9.00
41-50	2.50	5.00	7.50
51-60	2.00	4.00	6.00
61-70	1.75	3.35	5.00
71-100	1.35	2.75	4.00
101-106,109-123	1.20	2.40	3.60
107,108-Flash Gordon in each, not by Raymond	3.00	6.00	9.00

MAGICA DE SPELL (See Walt Disney Showcase#30)

MAGIC SWORD, THE (See Movie Classics)

MAGILLA GORILLA (TV) (Hanna-Barbera)
May, 1964 - #10, Dec, 1968
Gold Key/Charlton

#1(Gold Key)		.15	.30
2,4-10		.10	.20
3-Vs. Yogi Bear for President		.10	.20

MAGILLA GORILLA (TV)
Nov, 1970 - #5, July, 1971   (Hanna-Barbera)

#1-5		.10	.20

MAGNUS, ROBOT FIGHTER (-- 4000 A.D.)
Feb, 1963 - #46, Jan, 1977
Gold Key

#1-Origin Magnus; Aliens series begins	3.35	6.75	10.00
2,3	1.75	3.35	5.00
4-10	1.20	2.40	3.60
11-20	.75	1.50	2.25
21-30: #22-Reprint of origin from #1. #28-Last new material issue; Aliens series ends	.25	.50	.75
31-46: #43,45-reprints	.15	.30	.45

NOTE: *Russ Manning* art-#1-22. *Russ Manning reprints-#29-43.*

MAID OF THE MIST (See American Graphics)

MAJOR HOOPLE COMICS
1942
Nedor Publications

#1-Mary Worth, Phantom Soldier by Moldoff

Magic Comics #3, © DMP

Magic Comics #25, © DMP

Magnus Robot Fighter #7, © GK

Major Victory #2, © Ches

Man #15, © MCG

Manhunt! #1, © ME

(Major Hoople cont'd)	Good	Fine	Mint
app.	7.00	14.00	21.00

MAJOR INAPAK THE SPACE ACE
1951   (20 pgs.) (Giveaway)
Magazine Enterprises (Inapac Foods)

| #1-Bob Powell art | .65 | 1.35 | 2.00 |

NOTE: *Many copies found in warehouse in 1975.*

MAJOR VICTORY COMICS
1944 - #3, Summer, 1945
H.Clay Glover/Service Publ/Harry 'A' Chesler

#1-Origin Major Victory by C. Sultan (reprint			
from Dynamic #1); Spider Woman 1st app.			
	8.00	16.00	24.00
2-Dynamic Boy app.	4.00	8.00	12.00
3-Rocket Boy app.	3.35	6.75	10.00

MALTESE FALCON (See Feature Book #48(McKay))

MALU IN THE LAND OF ADVENTURE
1964
I.W. Enterprises

#1-Reprints Avon's Slave Girl Princess #1			
	2.00	4.00	6.00

MAMMOTH COMICS
1937   (80 pgs.) (Black & White)
Whitman Publishing Co.

#1-Terry & the Pirates, Dick Tracy, Little			
Orphan Annie, Wash Tubbs, & other reprints			
	30.00	60.00	90.00

MAMMY YOKUM & THE GREAT DOGPATCH MYSTERY
1951   (Giveaway)
Toby Press

| Li'l Abner | 2.50 | 5.00 | 7.50 |

MAN-BAT (Also see Detective #400)
Dec-Jan, 1975-76 - #2, Feb-Mar, 1976
National Periodical Publications

| #1-Ditko art | .35 | .70 | 1.05 |
| 2 | .20 | .40 | .60 |

MAN COMICS
Dec, 1949 - #28, Sept, 1953
Marvel/Atlas Comics(NPI)

#1	1.20	2.40	3.60
2-5	.65	1.35	2.00
6-15	.50	1.00	1.50
16-21,23-28	.40	.80	1.20
22-Krigstein story	1.35	2.75	4.00

NOTE: *Everett* cover-#25. *Kubertesque story
by Bob Brown*-#3.

MANDRAKE THE MAGICIAN (See Feature Book #18, 19,23,46,52,55)

MANDRAKE THE MAGICIAN (See Harvey C. Hits#53)
1956; Sept, 1966 - #10, Nov, 1967
Dell Publishing Co./King Comics

	Good	Fine	Mint
4-Color #752('56)	1.75	3.35	5.00
#1(King)-Begin S.O.S. Phantom series, ends			
#3	1.00	2.00	3.00
2-5: #4-Girl Phantom app. #5-Brick Bradford			
app., also #6	.65	1.35	2.00
6-7,9: #7-Origin Lothar. #9-Brick Bradford			
app.	.40	.80	1.20
8-Jeff Jones story	.80	1.60	2.40
10-Rip Kirby app.; 14pgs. art by Raymond			
	1.00	2.00	3.00

MAN FROM U.N.C.L.E., THE (TV)
Feb, 1965 - #22, April, 1969
Gold Key

#1	.65	1.35	2.00
2	.40	.80	1.20
3-10: #7-Jet Dream begins	.35	.70	1.05
11-22: #21,22-reprints	.20	.40	.60

MAN FROM WELLS FARGO (TV)
July, 1962
Dell Publishing Co.

| 4-Color #1287, #01-495-207 | .65 | 1.35 | 2.00 |

MANHUNT! (Becomes Red Fox #15 on)
Oct, 1947 - 1953
Magazine Enterprises

#1-Red Fox by L.E. Cole, Undercover Girl,			
Space Ace begin	6.00	12.00	18.00
2-8: #6,8-Space Ace ends	4.00	8.00	12.00
9-Trail Colt app.	4.00	8.00	12.00
10-Ingels story	5.00	10.00	15.00
11-Frazetta art, 7pgs.; Trail Colt app.; The			
Duke, Scotland Yard begin			
	10.00	20.00	30.00
12	3.00	6.00	9.00
13(A-1#63)-Frazetta, reprint from Trail Colt			
#1, 7pgs.	8.00	16.00	24.00
14(A-1#77)-bondage cover	4.00	8.00	12.00

NOTE: *Guardineer* art-#1-5. *Whitney art*-#2-14;
covers-#1-6.

MAN IN BLACK (See Thrill-O-Rama)
Sept, 1957 - 1958
Harvey Publications

(Man in Black cont'd)	Good	Fine	Mint
#1-Bob Powell cover/art	3.00	6.00	9.00
2-5: Powell cover/art	2.00	4.00	6.00

MAN IN FLIGHT (See 4-Color Comics #836)

MAN IN SPACE (See Dell Giant #27 & 4-Color Comics #716,954)

MAN OF PEACE, POPE PIUS XII
1950
Catechetical Guild

		1.75	3.35	5.00

MAN OF WAR (See Liberty Scouts & Liberty
Nov, 1941 - #2, Jan, 1942   Guards)
Centaur Publications

#1-The Fire-Man, Man of War, The Sentinel, &			
Vapo-Man begin	25.00	50.00	75.00
2-The Ferret app.	16.50	33.25	50.00

MAN O' MARS
1953; 1964
Fiction House Magazines

#1-Space Rangers	3.00	6.00	9.00
IW Reprint #1/Man O'Mars #1; Murphy Anderson			
art	1.75	3.35	5.00

MAN-THING, THE (See Book & Record and Fear)
Jan, 1974 - #22, Oct, 1975
Marvel Comics Group

#1-Howard the Duck app.	2.00	4.00	6.00
2-4	1.00	2.00	3.00
5-Ploog art	.80	1.60	2.40
6-11-Ploog art	.50	1.00	1.50
12-20	.25	.50	.75
21-Origin by Mooney	.20	.40	.60
22-Howard the Duck cameo	.40	.80	1.20
Giant Size #1(8/74)-Ploog cover/story			
	.65	1.35	2.00
Giant Size #2,3	.50	1.00	1.50
Giant Size #4-Howard the Duck by Brunner			
	3.00	6.00	9.00
Giant Size #5-Howard the Duck by Brunner			
	2.50	5.00	7.50

NOTE: *Alcala story-#14, Giant Size #3. Brunner
cover-#1, Giant Size #4. Mooney stories-#18,
20-22. Ploog Man-Thing-#5-11.*

MAN WITH THE X-RAY EYES, THE (See X, --,
under Movie Comics)

MANY GHOSTS OF DR. GRAVES, THE
5/67 - #60, 12/76; #61, 9/77 - #62, 10/77

Charlton Comics

	Good	Fine	Mint
#1	.35	.70	1.05
2-10	.20	.40	.60
11-20	.15	.30	.45
21-44		.15	.30
45-1st Newton comic book work			
	.50	1.00	1.50
46,48,50-62	.15	.30	.45
47,49-Newton stories	.15	.30	.45

NOTE: *Ditko stories-#1,7,9,11-13,15-18,20-22,
24,26,27,29-35,37,38,40-43,47,48,51,52,53,55;
covers-#11,12,16-18,22,24,26-35,38,58. Newton
covers-#49,52. Sutton cover/art-#42.*

MANY LOVES OF DOBIE GILLIS (TV)
June-July, 1960 - #26, Oct, 1964
National Periodical Publications

#1	1.00	2.00	3.00
2-10	.50	1.00	1.50
11-26	.35	.70	1.05

MARAUDER'S MOON (See 4-Color Comics #848)

MARCH OF COMICS (Boys' and Girls' --)
(K.K. Giveaway) (#1-4, No#'s)
1946 - Present (Founded by Sig Feuchtwanger)
K.K. Publications/Western Publ. Co.

Early issues were full size, 32 pages, and were printed
with and without an extra cover of slick stock, just for
the advertiser. The binding was stapled if the slick cover
was added; otherwise the pages were glued together at
the spine. 1948—1951 issues were full size, 24 pages,
pulp covers. Starting in 1952 they were half-size and 32
pages with slick covers. 1959 and later issues had only
16 pages plus covers. 1952—1959 issues read oblong;
1960 and later issues read upright.

#1(No#)-Goldilocks(1946)	8.00	16.00	24.00
2(No#)-How Santa Got His Red Suit(1946) -			
Walt Kelly back cover	10.00	20.00	30.00
3(No#)-Our Gang(Walt Kelly)(1947)			
	30.00	60.00	90.00
4(No#)-Donald Duck by Carl Barks, "Maharajah			
Donald", 32pgs.; Kelly cover			
	500.00	1000.00	1500.00
5-Andy Panda	10.00	20.00	30.00
6-Popular Fairy Tales-Walt Kelly cover; two			
Noonan stories	12.00	24.00	36.00
7-Oswald the Rabbit; Kelly cover			
	12.00	24.00	36.00
8-Mickey Mouse, 32pgs.	40.00	80.00	120.00
9-The Story of the Gloomy Bunny			
	5.00	10.00	15.00
10-Out of Santa's Bag	5.00	10.00	15.00
11-Fun With Santa Claus	4.00	8.00	12.00
12-Santa's Toys	4.00	8.00	12.00

Man Of War #1, © Cen

Man O'Mars #1, © FH

March Of Comics #3, © MGM (Loew's Inc.)

March Of Comics #5, © Walter Lantz

March Of Comics #8, © WDP

March Of Comics #16, © Walter Lantz

(March of Comics cont'd)	Good	Fine	Mint
13-Santa's Surprise	4.00	8.00	12.00
14-Santa's Candy Kitchen	4.00	8.00	12.00
15-Hip-It-Ty Top & the Big Bass Viol			
	4.00	8.00	12.00
16-Woody Woodpecker('47)	8.00	16.00	24.00
17-Roy Rogers(1948)	9.00	18.00	27.00
18-Popular Fairy Tales	7.00	14.00	21.00
19-Uncle Wiggily	7.00	14.00	21.00
20-Donald Duck by Carl Barks. "Darkest Africa", 24pgs.; Kelly cover			
	350.00	700.00	1050.00
21-Tom and Jerry	7.00	14.00	21.00
22-Andy Panda	7.00	14.00	21.00
23-Raggedy Ann; Kerr art	8.00	16.00	24.00
24-Felix the Cat,'32 reprints by Otto Messmer			
	10.00	20.00	30.00
25-Gene Autry	8.00	16.00	24.00
26-Our Gang-Walt Kelly	20.00	40.00	60.00
27-Mickey Mouse	25.00	50.00	75.00
28-Gene Autry	7.00	14.00	21.00
29-Easter Bonnet Shop	2.50	5.00	7.50
30-Here Comes Santa	3.00	6.00	9.00
31-Santa's Busy Corner	3.00	6.00	9.00
32-No book produced			
33-A Christmas Carol	3.00	6.00	9.00
34-Woody Woodpecker	5.00	10.00	15.00
35-Roy Rogers(1948)	7.00	14.00	21.00
36-Felix the Cat(1949)-by Messmer			
	7.00	14.00	21.00
37-Popeye	6.00	12.00	18.00
38-Oswald the Rabbit	5.00	10.00	15.00
39-Gene Autry	7.00	14.00	21.00
40-Andy and Woody	5.00	10.00	15.00
41-Donald Duck by Carl Barks. "Race to the South Seas", 24pgs.; Kelly cover			
	250.00	500.00	750.00
42-Porky Pig	5.00	10.00	15.00
43-Henry	3.00	6.00	9.00
44-Bugs Bunny	5.00	10.00	15.00

	Good	Fine	Mint
45-Mickey Mouse	20.00	40.00	60.00
46-Tom and Jerry	5.00	10.00	15.00
47-Roy Rogers	7.00	14.00	21.00
48-Greetings from Santa	2.50	5.00	7.50
49-Santa Is Here	2.50	5.00	7.50
50-Santa's Workshop('49)	2.50	5.00	7.50
51-Felix the Cat(1950)-by Messmer			
	7.00	14.00	21.00
52-Popeye	6.00	12.00	18.00
53-Oswald the Rabbit	5.00	10.00	15.00
54-Gene Autry	6.00	12.00	18.00
55-Andy and Woody	4.00	8.00	12.00
56-Donald Duck-not by Barks; Barks art on back cover	20.00	40.00	60.00
57-Porky Pig	4.00	8.00	12.00
58-Henry	2.50	5.00	7.50
59-Bugs Bunny	4.00	8.00	12.00
60-Mickey Mouse	15.00	30.00	45.00
61-Tom and Jerry	3.50	7.00	10.50
62-Roy Rogers	5.00	10.00	15.00
63-Welcome Santa	2.00	4.00	6.00
64-Santa's Helpers	2.00	4.00	6.00
65-Jingle Bells(1950)	2.00	4.00	6.00
66-Popeye(1951)	4.00	8.00	12.00
67-Oswald the Rabbit	3.50	7.00	10.50
68-Roy Rogers	4.00	8.00	12.00
69-Donald Duck-not Barks	15.00	30.00	45.00
70-Tom and Jerry	3.00	6.00	9.00
71-Porky Pig	4.00	8.00	12.00
72-Krazy Kat	5.00	10.00	15.00
73-Roy Rogers	4.00	8.00	12.00
74-Mickey Mouse(1951)	9.00	18.00	27.00
75-Bugs Bunny	3.50	7.00	10.50
76-Andy and Woody	3.00	6.00	9.00
77-Roy Rogers	4.00	8.00	12.00
78-Gene Autry(1951)-Last regular size issue			
	4.00	8.00	12.00
79-Andy Panda(1952)-5"x7" size			
	2.50	5.00	7.50

March Of Comics #19, © K.K. Publ.

March Of Comics #35, © Roy Rogers

March Of Comics #51, © King

March Of Comics #63, © K.K. Publ.

March Of Comics #98, © ERB

March Of Comics #133, © King

(March of Comics cont'd)	Good	Fine	Mint
80-Popeye	3.00	6.00	9.00
81-Oswald the Rabbit	2.50	5.00	7.50
82-Tarzan	5.00	10.00	15.00
83-Bugs Bunny	2.50	5.00	7.50
84-Henry	2.00	4.00	6.00
85-Woody Woodpecker	2.00	4.00	6.00
86-Roy Rogers	3.50	7.00	10.50
87-Krazy Kat	3.50	7.00	10.50
88-Tom and Jerry	2.00	4.00	6.00
89-Porky Pig	2.50	5.00	7.50
90-Gene Autry	3.50	7.00	10.50
91-Roy Rogers & Santa	3.50	7.00	10.50
92-Christmas with Santa	1.75	3.35	5.00
93-Woody Woodpecker('53)	2.00	4.00	6.00
94-Indian Chief	2.50	5.00	7.50
95-Oswald the Rabbit	2.00	4.00	6.00
96-Popeye	2.50	5.00	7.50
97-Bugs Bunny	2.50	5.00	7.50
98-Tarzan	5.00	10.00	15.00
99-Porky Pig	2.50	5.00	7.50
100-Roy Rogers	3.00	6.00	9.00
101-Henry	1.50	3.00	4.50
102-Tom Corbett	2.50	5.00	7.50
103-Tom and Jerry	1.75	3.35	5.00
104-Gene Autry	3.00	6.00	9.00
105-Roy Rogers	3.00	6.00	9.00
106-Santa's Helpers	1.35	2.75	4.00
107-Santa's Christmas Book - not published			
108-Fun With Santa('53)	1.35	2.75	4.00
109-Woody Woodpecker('54)	1.35	2.75	4.00
110-Indian Chief	1.75	3.35	5.00
111-Oswald the Rabbit	1.75	3.35	5.00
112-Henry	1.00	2.00	3.00
113-Porky Pig	1.50	3.00	4.50
114-Tarzan(Russ Manning)	5.00	10.00	15.00
115-Bugs Bunny	2.00	4.00	6.00
116-Roy Rogers	2.50	5.00	7.50
117-Popeye	2.00	4.00	6.00
118-Flash Gordon	6.00	12.00	18.00
119-Tom and Jerry	1.50	3.00	4.50
120-Gene Autry	2.50	5.00	7.50
121-Roy Rogers	2.50	5.00	7.50
122-Santa's Surprise('54)	1.35	2.75	4.00
123-Santa's Christmas Book	1.35	2.75	4.00
124-Woody Woodpecker('55)	1.50	3.00	4.50
125-Tarzan	4.00	8.00	12.00
126-Oswald the Rabbit	1.50	3.00	4.50
127-Indian Chief	1.50	3.00	4.50
128-Tom and Jerry	1.50	3.00	4.50
129-Henry	1.25	2.50	3.75
130-Porky Pig	1.50	3.00	4.50
131-Roy Rogers	2.50	5.00	7.50
132-Bugs Bunny	1.50	3.00	4.50
133-Flash Gordon	4.00	8.00	12.00
134-Popeye	1.75	3.35	5.00
135-Gene Autry	2.00	4.00	6.00
136-Roy Rogers	2.00	4.00	6.00

	Good	Fine	Mint
137-Gifts from Santa	1.25	2.50	3.75
138-Fun at Christmas('55)	1.25	2.50	3.75
139-Woody Woodpecker('56)	1.50	3.00	4.50
140-Indian Chief	1.50	3.00	4.50
141-Oswald the Rabbit	1.50	3.00	4.50
142-Flash Gordon	4.00	8.00	12.00
143-Porky Pig	1.50	3.00	4.50
144-Tarzan(Russ Manning)	4.00	8.00	12.00
145-Tom and Jerry	1.25	2.50	3.75
146-Roy Rogers	2.00	4.00	6.00
147-Henry	1.00	2.00	3.00
148-Popeye	1.75	3.35	5.00
149-Bugs Bunny	1.50	3.00	4.50
150-Gene Autry	2.00	4.00	6.00
151-Roy Rogers	2.00	4.00	6.00
152-The Night Before Christmas			
	1.00	2.00	3.00
153-Merry Christmas('56)	1.00	2.00	3.00
154-Tom and Jerry('57)	1.25	2.50	3.75
155-Tarzan	3.00	6.00	9.00
156-Oswald the Rabbit	1.25	2.50	3.75
157-Popeye	1.50	3.00	4.50
158-Woody Woodpecker	1.25	2.50	3.75
159-Indian Chief	1.50	3.00	4.50
160-Bugs Bunny	1.50	3.00	4.50
161-Roy Rogers	1.75	3.35	5.00
162-Henry	1.00	2.00	3.00
163-Rin Tin Tin	1.50	3.00	4.50
164-Porky Pig	1.25	2.50	3.75
165-The Lone Ranger	3.00	6.00	9.00
166-Santa and His Reindeer	1.00	2.00	3.00
167-Roy Rogers and Santa	1.75	3.35	5.00
168-Santa's Workshop('57)	1.00	2.00	3.00
169-Popeye('58)	1.25	2.50	3.75
170-Indian Chief	1.50	3.00	4.50
171-Oswald the Rabbit	1.25	2.50	3.75
172-Tarzan	3.00	6.00	9.00
173-Tom and Jerry	1.25	2.50	3.75
174-The Lone Ranger	2.50	5.00	7.50
175-Porky Pig	1.25	2.50	3.75
176-Roy Rogers	1.50	3.00	4.50
177-Woody Woodpecker	1.25	2.50	3.75
178-Henry	1.25	2.50	3.75
179-Bugs Bunny	1.25	2.50	3.75
180-Rin Tin Tin	1.35	2.75	4.00
181-Happy Holiday	.75	1.50	2.25
182-Happi Tim	.75	1.50	2.25
183-Welcome Santa(1958)	.75	1.50	2.25
184-Woody Woodpecker('59)	1.00	2.00	3.00
185-Tarzan	3.00	6.00	9.00
186-Oswald the Rabbit	1.00	2.00	3.00
187-Indian Chief	1.25	2.50	3.75
188-Bugs Bunny	1.00	2.00	3.00
189-Henry	1.00	2.00	3.00
190-Tom and Jerry	1.00	2.00	3.00
191-Roy Rogers	1.50	3.00	4.50
192-Porky Pig	1.00	2.00	3.00

	Good	Fine	Mint
193-The Lone Ranger	2.00	4.00	6.00
194-Popeye	1.20	2.40	3.60
195-Rin Tin Tin	1.35	2.75	4.00
196-Sears Special - not published			
197-Santa Is Coming	.65	1.35	2.00
198-Santa's Helpers(1959)	.65	1.35	2.00
199-Huckleberry Hound('60)	.50	1.00	1.50
200-Fury	.65	1.35	2.00
201-Bugs Bunny	.75	1.50	2.25
202-Space Explorer	1.00	2.00	3.00
203-Woody Woodpecker	.75	1.50	2.25
204-Tarzan	2.00	4.00	6.00
205-Mighty Mouse	1.25	2.50	3.75
206-Roy Rogers	1.50	3.00	4.50
207-Tom and Jerry	.75	1.50	2.25
208-The Lone Ranger	2.00	4.00	6.00
209-Porky Pig	.75	1.50	2.25
210-Lassie	1.00	2.00	3.00
211-Sears Special - not published			
212-Christmas Eve	.65	1.35	2.00
213-Here Comes Santa('60)	.65	1.35	2.00
214-Huckleberry Hound('61)	.50	1.00	1.50
215-Hi Yo Silver	1.50	3.00	4.50
216-Rocky & His Friends	.65	1.35	2.00
217-Lassie	.65	1.35	2.00
218-Porky Pig	.75	1.50	2.25
219-Journey to the Sun	.80	1.60	2.40
220-Bugs Bunny	.75	1.50	2.25
221-Roy and Dale	1.50	3.00	4.50
222-Woody Woodpecker	.75	1.50	2.25
223-Tarzan	2.50	5.00	7.50
224-Tom and Jerry	.75	1.50	2.25
225-The Lone Ranger	1.50	3.00	4.50
226-Sears Special - not published			
227-Christmas Treasury	.65	1.35	2.00
228-Letters to Santa('61)	.65	1.35	2.00
229-The Flintstones('62)	.60	1.20	1.80
230-Lassie	.65	1.35	2.00
231-Bugs Bunny	.75	1.50	2.25
232-The Three Stooges	1.20	2.40	3.60
233-Bullwinkle	.65	1.35	2.00
234-Smokey the Bear	.50	1.00	1.50
235-Huckleberry Hound	.50	1.00	1.50
236-Roy and Dale	1.20	2.40	3.60
237-Mighty Mouse	1.00	2.00	3.00
238-The Lone Ranger	1.50	3.00	4.50
239-Woody Woodpecker	.75	1.50	2.25
240-Tarzan	2.00	4.00	6.00
241-Santa Claus Around the World	.65	1.35	2.00
242-Santa's Toyland('62)	.65	1.35	2.00
243-The Flintstones('63)	.60	1.20	1.80
244-Mister Ed	.60	1.20	1.80
245-Bugs Bunny	.75	1.50	2.25
246-Popeye	1.00	2.00	3.00
247-Mighty Mouse	1.00	2.00	3.00
248-The Three Stooges	1.20	2.40	3.60

	Good	Fine	Mint
249-Woody Woodpecker	.60	1.20	1.80
250-Roy and Dale	1.50	3.00	4.50
251-Little Lulu by Stanley	5.00	10.00	15.00
252-Tarzan	2.00	4.00	6.00
253-Yogi Bear	.50	1.00	1.50
254-Lassie	.65	1.35	2.00
255-Santa's Christmas List	.65	1.35	2.00
256-Christmas Party('63)	.65	1.35	2.00
257-Mighty Mouse	1.00	2.00	3.00
258-The Sword in the Stone (Disney)	1.50	3.00	4.50
259-Bugs Bunny	.75	1.50	2.25
260-Mister Ed	.50	1.00	1.50
261-Woody Woodpecker	.75	1.50	2.25
262-Tarzan	2.00	4.00	6.00
263-Donald Duck-not Barks	2.00	4.00	6.00
264-Popeye	1.00	2.00	3.00
265-Yogi Bear	.50	1.00	1.50
266-Lassie	.65	1.35	2.00
267-Little Lulu	4.00	8.00	12.00
268-The Three Stooges	1.00	2.00	3.00
269-A Jolly Christmas	.65	1.35	2.00
270-Santa's Little Helpers	.65	1.35	2.00
271-The Flintstones('65)	.50	1.00	1.50
272-Tarzan	1.75	3.35	5.00
273-Bugs Bunny	.75	1.50	2.25
274-Popeye	.75	1.50	2.25
275-Little Lulu	3.00	6.00	9.00
276-The Jetsons	.50	1.00	1.50
277-Daffy Duck	.50	1.00	1.50
278-Lassie	.65	1.35	2.00
279-Yogi Bear	.50	1.00	1.50
280-The Flintstones('65)	.45	.90	1.35
281-Tom and Jerry	.45	.90	1.35
282-Mister Ed	.45	.90	1.35
283-Santa's Visit	.65	1.35	2.00
284-Christmas Parade('65)	.65	1.35	2.00
285-Astro Boy	.65	1.35	2.00
286-Tarzan	1.75	3.35	5.00
287-Bugs Bunny	.50	1.00	1.50
288-Daffy Duck	.50	1.00	1.50
289-The Flintstones	.50	1.00	1.50
290-Mister Ed	.50	1.00	1.50
291-Yogi Bear	.50	1.00	1.50
292-The Three Stooges	1.00	2.00	3.00
293-Little Lulu	2.00	4.00	6.00
294-Popeye	.60	1.20	1.80
295-Tom and Jerry	.40	.80	1.20
296-Lassie	.65	1.35	2.00
297-Christmas Bells	.65	1.35	2.00
298-Santa's Sleigh('66)	.65	1.35	2.00
299-The Flintstones('67)	.40	.80	1.20
300-Tarzan	1.50	3.00	4.50
301-Bugs Bunny	.50	1.00	1.50
302-Laurel and Hardy	1.00	2.00	3.00
303-Daffy Duck	.40	.80	1.20
304-The Three Stooges	1.00	2.00	3.00

March Of Comics #190, © MGM (Loew's Inc.)

March Of Comics #208, © Lone Ranger

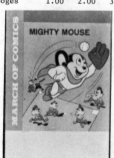

March Of Comics #247, © Terrytoons

March Of Comics #251, © West

March Of Comics #263, © WDP

March Of Comics #323, © West

(March of Comics cont'd)	Good	Fine	Mint
305-Tom and Jerry	.40	.80	1.20
306-Daniel Boone	.75	1.50	2.25
307-Little Lulu	1.50	3.00	4.50
308-Lassie	.65	1.35	2.00
309-Yogi Bear	.40	.80	1.20
310-The Lone Ranger	1.50	3.00	4.50
311-Santa's Show	.65	1.35	2.00
312-Christmas Album('67)	.65	1.35	2.00
313-Daffy Duck('68)	.40	.80	1.20
314-Laurel and Hardy	1.00	2.00	3.00
315-Bugs Bunny	.50	1.00	1.50
316-The Three Stooges	1.00	2.00	3.00
317-The Flintstones	.40	.80	1.20
318-Tarzan	1.50	3.00	4.50
319-Yogi Bear	.40	.80	1.20
320-Space Family Robinson	1.00	2.00	3.00
321-Tom and Jerry	.40	.80	1.20
322-The Lone Ranger	1.50	3.00	4.50
323-Little Lulu-not Stanley			
	1.50	3.00	4.50
324-Lassie	.65	1.35	2.00
325-Fun With Santa	.50	1.00	1.50
326-Christmas Story('68)	.50	1.00	1.50
327-The Flintstones('69)	.40	.80	1.20
328-Space Family Robinson	1.00	2.00	3.00
329-Bugs Bunny	.50	1.00	1.50
330-The Jetsons	.40	.80	1.20
331-Daffy Duck	.40	.80	1.20
332-Tarzan	1.50	3.00	4.50
333-Tom and Jerry	.40	.80	1.20
334-Lassie	.50	1.00	1.50
335-Little Lulu	1.50	3.00	4.50
336-The Three Stooges	1.00	2.00	3.00
337-Yogi Bear	.40	.80	1.20
338-The Lone Ranger	1.35	2.75	4.00
339-(Did not come out)			
340-Here Comes Santa('69)	.50	1.00	1.50
341-The Flintstones	.30	.60	.90
342-Tarzan	1.50	3.00	4.50
343-Bugs Bunny	.40	.80	1.20
344-Yogi Bear	.40	.80	1.20
345-Tom and Jerry	.40	.80	1.20
346-Lassie	.40	.80	1.20
347-Daffy Duck	.40	.80	1.20
348-The Jetsons	.40	.80	1.20
349-Little Lulu-not Stanley			
	1.00	2.00	3.00
350-The Lone Ranger	1.00	2.00	3.00
351-Beep-Beep, the Road Runner			
	.40	.80	1.20
352-Space Family Robinson	.80	1.60	2.40
353-Beep-Beep, the Road Runner (1971)			
	.40	.80	1.20
354-Tarzan('71)	1.20	2.40	3.60
355-Little Lulu-not Stanley			
	1.00	2.00	3.00
346-Scooby Doo, Where Are You?			

	Good	Fine	Mint
	.40	.80	1.20
357-Daffy Duck & Porky Pig	.40	.80	1.20
358-Lassie	.50	1.00	1.50
359-Baby Snoots	.40	.80	1.20
360-H.R. Pufnstuf (TV)	.40	.80	1.20
361-Tom and Jerry	.35	.70	1.05
362-Smokey the Bear	.35	.70	1.05
363-Bugs Bunny & Yosemite Sam			
	.35	.70	1.05
364-The Banana Splits	.35	.70	1.05
365-Tom and Jerry('72)	.35	.70	1.05
366-Tarzan	.80	1.60	2.40
367-Bugs Bunny & Porky Pig	.35	.70	1.05
368-Scooby Doo(4/72)	.35	.70	1.05
369-Little Lulu-not Stanley	.65	1.35	2.00
370-Lassie	.50	1.00	1.50
371-Baby Snoots	.30	.60	.90
372-Smokey the Bear	.30	.60	.90
373-The Three Stooges	.40	.80	1.20
374-Wacky Witch	.30	.60	.90
375-Beep-Beep & Daffy Duck	.30	.60	.90
376-The Pink Panther('72)	.30	.60	.90
377-Baby Snoots('73)	.25	.50	.75
378-Turok, Son of Stone	.60	1.20	1.80
379-Heckle & Jeckle New Terrytoons			
	.25	.50	.75
380-Bugs Bunny & Yosemite Sam			
	.25	.50	.75
381-Lassie	.25	.50	.75
382-Scooby Doo, Where Are You?			
	.35	.70	1.05
383-Smokey the Bear	.25	.50	.75
384-Pink Panther	.25	.50	.75
385-Little Lulu	.60	1.20	1.80
386-Wacky Witch	.20	.40	.60
387-Beep-Beep & Daffy Duck	.20	.40	.60
388-Tom and Jerry('73)	.20	.40	.60
389-Little Lulu-not Stanley	.60	1.20	1.80
390-Pink Panther	.20	.40	.60
391-Scooby Doo	.20	.40	.60
392-Bugs Bunny & Yosemite Sam			
	.20	.40	.60
393-New Terrytoons(Heckle & Jeckle)			
	.20	.40	.60
394-Lassie	.25	.50	.75
395-Woodsy Owl	.20	.40	.60
396-Baby Snoots	.20	.40	.60
397-Beep-Beep & Daffy Duck	.20	.40	.60
398-Wacky Witch	.20	.40	.60
399-Turok, Son of Stone	.40	.80	1.20
400-Tom and Jerry	.20	.40	.60
401-Baby Snoots('75)(Reprints #371)			
	.20	.40	.60
402-Daffy Duck(Reprints#313)	.20	.40	.60
403-Bugs Bunny(Reprints#343)	.20	.40	.60
404-Space Family Robinson(Reprints #328)			
	.40	.80	1.20

(March of Comics cont'd)	Good	Fine	Mint
405-Cracky	.20	.40	.60
406-Little Lulu(Reprts.#355)	.40	.80	1.20
407-Smokey the Bear(Reprints #362)			
	.20	.40	.60
408-Turok, Son of Stone	.40	.80	1.20
409-Pink Panther	.20	.40	.60
410-Wacky Witch	.20	.40	.60
411-Lassie(Reprints #324)	.25	.50	.75
412-New Terrytoons('75)	.20	.40	.60
413-Daffy Duck('76)(Reprints #331)			
	.20	.40	.60
414-Space Family Robinson(Reprints #328)			
	.35	.70	1.05
415-Bugs Bunny(Reprints#329)	.20	.40	.60
416-Road Runner(Reprts.#353)	.20	.40	.60
417-Little Lulu(Reprts.#323)	.25	.50	.75
418-Pink Panther(Reprt.#384)	.20	.40	.60
419-Baby Snoots(Reprts.#377)	.20	.40	.60
420-Woody Woodpecker	.20	.40	.60
421-Tweety & Sylvester	.20	.40	.60
422-Wacky Witch(Reprts.#386)	.20	.40	.60
423-Little Monsters	.20	.40	.60
424-Cracky(12/76)	.15	.30	.45
425-Daffy Duck	.15	.30	.45
426-Underdog	.15	.30	.45
427-Little Lulu	.20	.40	.60
428-Bugs Bunny	.15	.30	.45
429-The Pink Panther	.15	.30	.45
430-Beep-Beep, the Road Runner			
	.15	.30	.45
431-Baby Snoots	.15	.30	.45
432-Lassie	.15	.30	.45
433-Tweety & Sylvester	.15	.30	.45
434-Wacky Witch	.15	.30	.45

MARCH OF CRIME (My Love Affair #1-6)
1948 (132pgs); #7, 7/50 - #2, 9/50; #3, 9/51
Fox Features Syndicate

No#(1948,132pgs.)-See Fox Giants. Contents can vary and determines price.			
#7(#1)-(7/50)-Wood story	5.00	10.00	15.00
2(9/50)-Wood story	5.00	10.00	15.00
3(9/51)	1.00	2.00	3.00

MARCO POLO
1962 (Movie Classic)
Charlton Comics

No#	2.00	4.00	6.00

MARGARET O'BRIEN, THE ADVENTURES OF
1947 (20pgs. in Color; Slick Cover; Reg.Size)
Bambury Fashions (Clothes) (Premium)

In "The Big City"-movie adaptation			
	2.50	5.00	7.50

MARGIE (See My Little --)

MARGIE (TV)
Mar-May, 1962 - #2, July-Sept, 1962
Dell Publishing Co.

	Good	Fine	Mint
4-Color #1307, #2	.40	.80	1.20

MARGIE COMICS (Formerly Comedy)(Reno Browne
#35, Winter/46-47 - #49, 1949   #50 on)
Marvel Comics (ACI)

#35-38,42,45,47-49	.65	1.35	2.00
39-41,43,44,46-Kurtzman's "Hey Look"			
	1.50	3.00	4.50

MARINES (See Tell It To the --)

MARINES ATTACK
Aug, 1964 - #9, Feb, 1966
Charlton Comics

#1	.20	.40	.60
2-9	.15	.30	.45

MARINES AT WAR (Tales of the Marines #4)
#5, April, 1957 - #7, Aug, 1957
Atlas Comics (OPI)

#5-7: #5-Drucker story. #7-Orlando story			
	.50	1.00	1.50

MARINES IN ACTION
June, 1955 - #14, Sept, 1957
Atlas News Co.

#1-Rock Murdock, Boot Camp Brady begin			
	1.00	3.00	3.00
2-14: #9-Berg art	.50	1.00	1.50

MARINES IN BATTLE
Aug, 1954 - #25, Sept, 1958
Atlas Comics(ACI #1-12/WPI #13-25)

#1-Heath cover; Iron Mike McGraw by Heath; history or U.S. Marine Corps. begins			
	1.00	2.00	3.00
2-10	.65	1.35	2.00
11-16,18-24: #23-Rock Murdock app.			
	.50	1.00	1.50
17-Williamson story, 3pgs.	2.00	4.00	6.00
25-Torres story	1.00	2.00	3.00

NOTE: *Everett story-#4; cover-#21. Orlando story-#14.*

MARINE WAR HEROES (Charlton Premiere #19)
Jan, 1964 - #18, Mar, 1967
Charlton Comics

Margie #35, © MCG

Marines In Action #1, © MCG

Margaret O'Brien-, © Bambury Fashions

Mark Trail's Adv. Book--#1, © Hallden

M.A.R.S. Patrol #5, © GK

Martin Kane--#4, © Fox

(Marine War Heroes cont'd)	Good	Fine	Mint
#1	.20	.40	.60
2-18	.15	.30	.45

NOTE: _Montes/Bache stories-#1,14,18; cover-#1._

MARK OF ZORRO (See 4-Color Comics #228)

MARK STEEL
1967, 1968, 1972 (24pgs.) (Color)
American Iron & Steel Institute

1967,1968-"Journey of Discovery with--"			
Neal Adams art	1.35	2.75	4.00
1972-"-- Fights Pollution"	1.00	2.00	3.00

MARK TRAIL
Oct, 1955 - #5, Summer, 1959
Standard Magazines (Hall Syndicate)

#1-Sunday strip reprints	2.00	4.00	6.00
2-5	1.50	3.00	4.50
--Adventure Book of Nature #1(Summer, 1958)-			
(Pines, 100pg. Giant-contains 78 Sunday			
strip reprints)	2.00	4.00	6.00

MARMADUKE MONK
No Date; 1963 (10¢)
I.W. Enterprises/Super Comics

#1-I.W. Reprint	.25	.50	.75
#14-(Super Reprint-'63)	.25	.50	.75

MARMADUKE MOUSE
Spring, 1946 - #65, Dec, 1956
Quality Comics Group (Arnold Publ.)

#1	1.75	3.35	5.00
2-30	.65	1.35	2.00
31-65	.40	.80	1.20
Super Reprint #14('63)	.25	.50	.75

MARS & BEYOND (See 4-Color Comics #866)

M.A.R.S. PATROL TOTAL WAR (Total War #1,2)
#3, Sept, 1966 - #10, Aug, 1969
Gold Key

#3-Wood art	1.00	2.00	3.00
4-10	.35	.70	1.05

MARTHA WAYNE (See The Story of --)

MARTIN KANE PRIVATE EYE (Formerly My Secret
#4, June, 1950 - #2, Aug, 1950   Affair)
Fox Features Syndicate

#4(#1)-Wood cover	2.50	5.00	7.50
2 -5pg. Orlando story	2.00	4.00	6.00

MARTY MOUSE
No Date (1958?)   (10¢)
I.W. Enterprises

	Good	Fine	Mint
#1-Reprint	.20	.40	.60

MARVEL ADVENTURE
December, 1975 - #6, Oct, 1976
Marvel Comics Group

#1-Daredevil reprints	.20	.40	.60
2-6	.15	.30	.45

MARVEL BOY (Astonishing #3 on)
Dec, 1950 - #2, Feb, 1951
Marvel Comics (20CC)

#1-Origin Marvel Boy by Russ Heath			
	8.00	16.00	24.00
2-Everett art	6.00	12.00	18.00

MARVEL CHILLERS
Oct, 1975 - #7, Oct, 1976
Marvel Comics Group

#1-Intro. Modred the Mystic.	35	.70	1.05
2	.25	.50	.75
3-Tigra, the Were-Woman begins(origin),			
ends #7	.20	.40	.60
4-7: #7-Kirby cover	.15	.30	.45

MARVEL CLASSICS COMICS
1976 - Present
Marvel Comics Group

#1-Dr. Jekyll and Mr. Hyde; Redondo story			
	.65	1.35	2.00
2-Time Machine-Nino art	.50	1.00	1.50
3-Hunchback of Notre Dame	.50	1.00	1.50
4-20,000 Leagues Under the Sea			
5-Black Beauty			
6-Gulliver's Travels			
7-Tom Sawyer			
8-Moby Dick-Nino art			
9-Dracula-Redondo story			
10-Red Badge of Courage			
each....	.35	.70	1.05
11-Mysterious Island			
12-The Three Musketeers-Nino art			
13-Last of the Mohicans			
14-War of the Worlds			
15-Treasure Island			
16-Ivanhoe			
17-The Count of Monte Cristo			
18-The Odyssey			
19-Robinson Crusoe			
20-Frankenstein			
each....	.25	.50	.75

(Marvel Classics Comics cont'd)

	Good	Fine	Mint
21-Master of the World			
22-Food of the Gods			
23-The Moonstone			
24-She			
25-The Invisible Man			
26-The Illiad-Buscema cover			
27-Kidnapped			
28-The Pit and the Pendùlum			
29-Prisoner of Zenda			
30-Arabian Nights			
31-A Christmas Carol			
32-The Prince and the Pauper			
each....	.20	.40	.60

MARVEL COLLECTORS ITEM CLASSICS
(Marvel's Greatest #23 on)
1965 - #22, Aug, 1969
Marvel Comics Group

#1	1.75	3.35	5.00
2-4	1.00	2.00	3.00
5-10	.65	1.35	2.00
11-22	.40	.80	1.20

MARVEL COMICS (Marvel Mystery #2 on)
November, 1939
Timely Comics (Funnies, Inc.)

NOTE: The first issue was originally dated October 1939. Most copies have a black circle stamped over the date (on cover & inside) with "November" printed over it. However, some copies do not have the November overprint. Most No. 1's have printing defects, i. e. tilted pages which caused trimming into the panels usually on right side and bottom.

#1-Origin Sub-Mariner by Bill Everett (based on an idea by Mickey Spillaine); 1st 8pgs. reprinted from Motion Picture Funnies Weekly #1; Human Torch by Carl Burgos, Kazar the Great, & Jungle Terror (only app.); Intro. The Angel, The Masked Raider (ends #12)   2500.00 6250.00 10,000.00
(Prices vary widely on this book)

MARVEL COMICS SUPER SPECIAL
Sept, 1977   (Magazine) ($1.50)
Marvel Comics Group

#1-Kiss, 40pgs. comics plus photos & features
    .65 1.35 2.00

MARVEL DOUBLE FEATURE
Dec, 1973 - #21, Mar, 1977
Marvel Comics Group

#1-Captain America & Iron Man reprints begin
    .40 .80 1.20
2-5   .35 .70 1.05

6-21: #18-Kirby cover	Good .20	Fine .40	Mint .60

MARVEL FAMILY (Also see Capt. Marvel #18)
Dec, 1945 - #89, Jan, 1954
Fawcett Publications

1-Origin Captain Marvel, Captain Marvel Jr., Mary Marvel, & Uncle Marvel retold; Black Adam origin & 1st app.	40.00	80.00	120.00
2	20.00	40.00	60.00
3	15.00	30.00	45.00
4,5	9.00	18.00	27.00
6-10: #7-Shazam app.	7.00	14.00	21.00
11-20	5.00	10.00	15.00
21-30	4.00	8.00	12.00
31-40	3.00	6.00	9.00
41-89	2.50	5.00	7.50

MARVEL FEATURE (See Marvel Two-In-One)
Dec, 1971 - #12, Nov, 1973   (#1,2-25¢)
Marvel Comics Group

#1-Origin The Defenders; Sub-Mariner, The Hulk & Dr. Strange; G.A. Sub-Mariner reprint, Adams cover	1.75	3.35	5.00
2-G.A. Sub-Mariner reprt.	1.00	2.00	3.00
3-Defender series ends	1.00	2.00	3.00
4-Begin Ant-Man series	.40	.80	1.20
5-7	.35	.70	1.05
8-Origin The Wasp; Starlin art; reprint	.40	.80	1.20
9,10-Last Ant-Man	.25	.50	.75
11,12-Thing team-ups; Starlin art	.35	.70	1.05

MARVEL FEATURE (Also see Red Sonja)
Nov, 1975 - #8, Jan, 1977
Marvel Comics Group

#1-Red Sonja begins; Adams reprint/Savage Sword of Conan #1	.40	.80	1.20
2,3	.25	.50	.75
4-8	.20	.40	.60

MARVEL MINI-BOOKS
1966   (50 pgs.)(5/8"x7/8")(6 different)
Marvel Comics Group

Captain America, Spiderman, Sgt. Fury, Hulk, Millie the Model, Thor   .65 1.35 2.00

MARVEL MOVIE PREMIERE (Magazine)
Sept, 1975   (One Shot) (Black & White)
Marvel Comics Group

#1-Burroughs "The Land That Time Forgot" adaptation   .65 1.35 2.00

Marvel Comics #1, © MCG   The Marvel Family #14, © Faw   Marvel Feature #3, © MCG

Marvel Mystery #5, © MCG   Marvel Mystery #13, © MCG   Marvel Mystery #85, © MCG

MARVEL MYSTERY COMICS (Formerly Marvel Comics)(Marvel Tales #93 on)
#2, Dec, 1939 - #92, June, 1949
Timely Comics/Marvel Comics

	Good	Fine	Mint
#2-American Ace begins, ends #3; Human Torch by Burgos, Sub-Mariner continues	600.00	1200.00	1800.00
3	400.00	800.00	1200.00
4-Intro. Electro, the Marvel of the Age (ends #19), The Ferret, Mystery Detective (ends #9)	300.00	600.00	900.00
5-(Rare)	600.00	1200.00	1800.00
6,7	200.00	400.00	600.00
8-Human Torch & Sub-Mariner battle	250.00	500.00	750.00
9-Human Torch & Sub-Mariner battle	300.00	600.00	900.00
10-Human Torch & Sub-Mariner battle, conclusion; Terry Vance, the Schoolboy Sleuth begins, ends #57	175.00	350.00	525.00
11,12: #12-Kirby cover	100.00	200.00	300.00
13-Intro. & 1st app. The Vision by S&K	120.00	240.00	360.00
14,15	75.00	150.00	225.00
16-Intro. & 1st app. Toro, Torch's sidekick	75.00	150.00	225.00
17-Human Torch/Sub-Mariner x-over	75.00	150.00	225.00
18,19	60.00	120.00	180.00
20-Origin The Angel in text; last S&K Vision	50.00	100.00	150.00
21-Intro. & 1st app. The Patriot; not in #46-48	40.00	80.00	120.00
22-25	35.00	70.00	105.00
26-30: #27-Kazar ends. #28-Jimmy Jupiter in the Land of Nowhere begins, ends #48	30.00	60.00	90.00
31-40	26.50	53.25	80.00
41-48-Last Vision	23.50	46.75	70.00
49-Origin Miss America	25.00	50.00	75.00
50-Mary becomes Miss Patriot,			
51-60	20.00	40.00	60.00
61-70	16.50	33.25	50.00
71-75: #74-Last Patriot. #75-Young Allies begin	13.50	26.75	40.00
76-81: #76-10 Chapter Miss America serial begins, ends #85. #79-Last Angel	13.50	26.75	40.00
82-Origin Namora; Captain America app.	20.00	40.00	60.00
83,85: #83-Last Young Allies. #85-Last Miss America	13.50	26.75	40.00
84-Blonde Phantom begins; Captain America app.	16.50	33.25	50.00
86,87,89-Captain America app. in all. Sungirl in #89	12.00	24.00	36.00
88-Human Torch & Sungirl x-over; Captain			

	Good	Fine	Mint
America app.	12.00	24.00	36.00
90,91: #90-Capt. America app. #91-Venus app., Blonde Phantom & Sub-Mariner end	12.00	24.00	36.00
92-Origin Human Torch retold; Captain America app.; no Sub-Mariner	20.00	40.00	60.00
128pg issue, B&W (25¢)-1942-printed in N.Y.	100.00	200.00	300.00

MARVELOUS WIZARD OF OZ (M.G.M.'s --)
Nov, 1975 (Oversize) ($1.50)
Marvel Comics Group/National Per. Publ.

#1-Adaptation of MGM's movie (See Marvel Treasury of --)	.80	1.60	2.40

MARVEL PREMIERE
April, 1972 - Present
Marvel Comics Group

#1-Origin Warlock by Gil Kane/Dan Adkins	1.00	2.00	3.00
2-Warlock ends; Kirby Yellow Claw reprint	.65	1.35	2.00
3-Dr. Strange series begins, Smith pencils	1.00	2.00	3.00
4-Smith art	.65	1.35	2.00
5-10: #10-Death of the Ancient One	.50	1.00	1.50
11-14: #11-Origin reprint by Ditko. #14-Intro. God; Last Dr. Strange	.40	.80	1.20
15-Iron Fist begins(origin), ends #25	.60	1.20	1.80
16-20	.35	.70	1.05
21-28: #26-Hercules app. #27-Satana app. #28-Legion of Monsters	.25	.50	.75
29,30-Liberty Legion	.20	.40	.60
31-Woodgod	.20	.40	.60
32-Monark Starstalker	.20	.40	.60
33,34-Soloman Kane	.15	.30	.45
35-Origin, 1st app. 3-D Man.	.20	.40	.60
36,37- 3-D Man	.15	.30	.45
38-Ploog story	.15	.30	.45
39-Torpedo	.15	.30	.45

NOTE: _Adams_ stories(inks)-#10,13. _Brunner_ stories-#4,6,9-14; covers-#9-14. _Chaykin_ stories-#32-34. _Kirby_ covers-#29,35. _Ploog_ cover-#7. _Starlin_ story-#8.

MARVEL PRESENTS
October, 1975 - #12, Aug, 1977
Marvel Comics Group

#1-Bloodstone app.,also #2	.35	.70	1.05
2	.25	.50	.75
3-Guardians of the Galaxy	.20	.40	.60
4-7,9-12	.15	.30	.45
8-Reprts. Silver Surfer#2	.15	.30	.45

MARVEL PREVIEW (Magazine)
1975 - Present   (B&W) ($1.00)
Marvel Comics Group

	Good	Fine	Mint
#1-Man Gods From Beyond the Stars; Adams cover; Nino art	1.00	2.00	3.00
2-Origin & 1st app. The Punisher & Dominic Fortune; Morrow cover	.65	1.35	2.00
3-Blade the Vampire	.50	1.00	1.50
4-Star-Lord & Sword in the Star (origins & 1st app.)	.50	1.00	1.50
5,6-Sherlock Holmes	.60	1.20	1.80
7-Satana	.40	.80	1.20
8-Legion of Monsters	.40	.80	1.20
9-Man-God	.40	.80	1.20
10-Thor the Mighty; Starlin art	.40	.80	1.20
11-Starlord	.40	.80	1.20
12-Haunt of Horrow	.40	.80	1.20

NOTE: _Morrow covers-#2-4. Ploog art-#8._

MARVEL'S GREATEST COMICS
(Marvel Collectors Item Classics #1-22)
#23, Oct, 1969 - Present
Marvel Comics Group

	Good	Fine	Mint
#23,24-Dr. Strange, Fantastic Four, Iron Man, Watcher	.40	.80	1.20
25-28-Capt. America, Dr. Strange, Iron Man, Fantastic Four	.40	.80	1.20
29-34	.40	.80	1.20
35-Silver Surfer & Fantastic-4 reprts.begin			
36-50	.25	.50	.75
51-60	.20	.40	.60
61-75: #75-Kirby cover	.15	.30	.45

MARVELS OF SCIENCE
March, 1946 - #4, June, 1946
Charlton Comics

	Good	Fine	Mint
#1-(1st Charlton comic)	2.50	5.00	7.50
2-4	1.75	3.35	5.00

MARVEL SPECIAL EDITION (Also see Special Coll-
1975 - Present (84pgs.)   ectors' Edition)
Marvel Comics Group   (Oversized)

	Good	Fine	Mint
#1-Spiderman reprints	.80	1.60	2.40
1-Star Wars(1977)-reprints Star Wars #1-3	.65	1.35	2.00
2-Star Wars(1978)-reprints Star Wars #4-6	.65	1.35	2.00

NOTE: _Chaykin covers/stories-#1(1977),#2._

MARVEL SPECTACULAR
Aug, 1973 - #19, Nov, 1975
Marvel Comics Group

	Good	Fine	Mint
#1-Thor reprints begin by Kirby	.40	.80	1.20
2-5	.25	.50	.75
6-10	.20	.40	.60
11-19	.15	.30	.45

MARVEL SPOTLIGHT
Nov, 1971 - #33, April, 1977
Marvel Comics Group

	Good	Fine	Mint
#1-Origin Red Wolf; Wood inks, Adams cover	.65	1.35	2.00
2-Venus reprint by Everett; origin Werewolf by Ploog; Adams cover	.80	1.60	2.40
3,4-Werewolf ends #4	.50	1.00	1.50
5-Origin Ghost Rider	.50	1.00	1.50
6-8-Last Ploog ish.	.50	1.00	1.50
9-11-Last Ghost Rider	.35	.70	1.05
12-Origin The Son of Satan - begin series, 13-20	.25	.50	.75
21-27: #25-Sinbad. #26-Scarecrow. #27-Sub-Mariner	.15	.30	.45
28,29-Moon Night app.	.15	.30	.45
30	.15	.30	.45
31-Nick Fury app.	.15	.30	.45
32-1st app. Spider-Woman	.15	.30	.45
33-Deathlok	.15	.30	.45

NOTE: _Buscema story-#30. Kirby cover-#29.
Mooney stories-#8,10(inks),14-17,24. Ploog
stories-#2-8; covers-#2-9._

MARVEL SUPER ACTION (Magazine)
January, 1976   (One Shot) (Black & White)
Marvel Comics Group

	Good	Fine	Mint
#1-Origin & 1st app. Dominic Fortune; The Punisher & Weird World app.; The Huntress; Evans & Ploog art	.50	1.00	1.50

MARVEL SUPER-ACTION
May, 1977 - Present
Marvel Comics Group

	Good	Fine	Mint
#1-Capt. America reprints by Kirby begin	.20	.40	.60
2-5	.15	.30	.45

MARVEL SUPER HEROES (Fantasy Masterpieces
#12, 12/67 - #31, 11/71   #1-11)
#32, Sept, 1972 - Present
Marvel Comics Group

	Good	Fine	Mint
#12-Origin & 1st app. Capt. Marvel of the Kree; G.A. Torch, Destroyer, Capt. America, Black Knight, Sub-Mariner reprints	1.00	2.00	3.00

13-G.A. Black Knight, Torch, Vision, Capt.

Marvel Premiere #1, © MCG

Marvels Of Science #1, © CC

Marvel Super Heroes #12, © MCG

Marvel Tales #1, © MCG

Marvel Tales #104, © MCG

Marvel Team-Up #1, © MCG

(Marvel Super Heroes cont'd)

	Good	Fine	Mint
America, Sub-Mariner reprints; Capt. Marvel app.	.60	1.20	1.80
14-G.A. Sub-Mariner, Torch, Mercury, Black Knight, Capt. America reprints; Spiderman app.	.60	1.20	1.80
15-Black Bolt cameo in Medusa; G.A. Black Knight, Sub-Mariner, Black Marvel, Capt. America reprints	.60	1.20	1.80
16-Origin & 1st app. Phantom Eagle; G.A. Torch, Capt. America, Bl. Knight, Patriot, Sub-Mariner reprints	.50	1.00	1.50
17-Origin Black Knight; G.A. Torch, Sub-Mariner, All-Winners Squad reprints	.50	1.00	1.50
18-Origin Guardians of the Galaxy; G.A. Sub-Mariner, All-Winners Squad reprints	.65	1.35	2.00
19-G.A. Torch, Marvel Boy, Black Knight, Sub-Mariner reprints; Smith/Trimple cover	.50	1.00	1.50
20-G.A. Sub-Mariner, Torch, Capt. America reprints; Dr. Doom app.	.50	1.00	1.50
21-Avengers, Sub-Mariner, Hulk, X-Men reprints	.40	.80	1.20
22-Daredevil & X-Men reprt.	.35	.70	1.05
23-X-Men & Daredevil reprint; new Watcher story	.35	.70	1.05
24-Daredevil & X-Men reprt.	.35	.70	1.05
25-27-Hulk, X-Men & Daredevil reprints	.35	.70	1.05
28-Daredevil & Iron Man reprints; Iron Man origin retold	.35	.70	1.05
29-31-Iron Man & Daredevil reprints	.35	.70	1.05
32-40-All Sub-Mariner/Hulk reprints	.15	.30	.45
41-46,48-50	.15	.30	.45
47-Starlin cover	.20	.40	.60
51-55	.15	.30	.45
56-61-Hulk reprints	.15	.30	.45
62-69	.15	.30	.45

NOTE: *Everett* inks-#14,15. New *Kirby* covers-#22,27.

MARVEL SUPER HEROES SPECIAL
October, 1966
Marvel Comics Group

#1-Reprints origin Daredevil; G.A. Sub-Mariner & Torch app.	1.35	2.75	4.00

MARVEL TALES (Marvel Mystery #1-92)
#93, Aug, 1949 - #159, Aug, 1957
Marvel/Atlas Comics (MCI)

	Good	Fine	Mint
#93	6.00	12.00	18.00
94-Classic Everett story	4.00	8.00	12.00

	Good	Fine	Mint
95,96	3.00	6.00	9.00
97-Sun Girl, 2pgs.	4.00	8.00	12.00
98-Krigstein story	4.00	8.00	12.00
99,101,103,105	2.50	5.00	7.50
102-Wolverton's End of the World story, 6pgs.	8.00	16.00	24.00
104-Wolverton story	7.00	14.00	21.00
106,107-Krigstein stories	2.50	5.00	7.50
108-121,123-131-Last pre-code issue	1.35	2.75	4.00
122-Krigstein, Kubert sty.	2.50	5.00	7.50
132,133,135-141,143	1.20	2.40	3.60
134-Krigstein, Kubert sty.	2.50	5.00	7.50
142-Krigstein story	2.00	4.00	6.00
144-Williamson/Krenkel story, 3pgs.	2.00	4.00	6.00
145,146,148-151,153-155,158	.80	1.60	2.40
147,156-Torres stories	1.50	3.00	4.50
152-Wood, Morrow art	2.00	4.00	6.00
157,159-Krigstein stories	1.50	3.00	4.50

NOTE: *Ditko* story-#145,147. *Drucker* stories-#127,135,146. *Everett* stories-#104,106,108, 131,151,153; covers-#111,117,127,143,148-151, 153. *Gil Kane* art-#117. *Morrow* stories-#150, 152,156. *Orlando* stories-#149,151,157. *Powell* story-#154. *Whitney* story-#107. *Wildey* story-#138.

MARVEL TALES
1964 - Present
Marvel Comics Group

	Good	Fine	Mint
#1-Origin Spider-Man, Hulk, Ant/Giant Man, Iron Man, Thor & Sgt.Fury-All reprints	5.00	10.00	15.00
2-Origin X-Men, Dr. Strange, Avengers reprinted	2.50	5.00	7.50
3	1.75	3.35	5.00
4,5	1.00	2.00	3.00
6-12,14;15	.60	1.20	1.80
13-Reprints origin Marvel Boy from Marvel Boy #1	.75	1.50	2.25
16-23: Last 68pg. ish.	.40	.80	1.20
24-30	.35	.70	1.05
31-60	.25	.50	.75
61-70: #63-Mooney story	.20	.40	.60
71-74,76-80	.15	.30	.45
75-Origin Spider-Man reprt.	.20	.40	.60
81-87	.15	.30	.45

MARVEL TEAM-UP
March, 1972 - Present
Marvel Comics Group

#1-Spider-Man, H-T	1.75	3.35	5.00
2,3-SpM/H-T x-over	.80	1.60	2.40

(Marvel Team-Up cont'd)   Good   Fine   Mint
4-10: #4-SpM/X-Men. #5-SpM/Vision. #6-SpM/
   Thing. #7-SpM/Thor. #8-SpM/The Cat. #9-
   SpM/Iron-Man. #10-SpM/Torch
                  .65   1.35   2.00
11-20: #11-SpM/Inhumans. #12-SpM/Werewolf.
   #13-SpM/Capt.America. #12-SpM/S-M. #15-
   SpM/Ghost Rider(new). #16-SpM/Capt.Marvel.
   #17-SpM/Mr. Fantastic. #18-H-T/Hulk. #19-
   SpM/Ka-Zar. #20-SpM/Black Panther
                  .40   .80   1.20
21-30: #21-SpM/Dr. Strange. #22-SpM/Hawkeye.
   #23-SpM/H-T/Iceman. #24-SpM/Brother Voodoo.
   #25-SpM/Daredevil. #26-H-T/Thor. #27-SpM/
   Hulk. #28-SpM/Hercules. #29-H-T/Iron Man.
   #30-SpM/Falcon   .30   .60   .90
31-40: #31-SpM/Iron Fist. #32-H-T/Son of Satan. #33-SpM/Nighthawk. #34-SpM/S-M/Valkyr-
   ie. #35-H-T/Dr. Strange. #36-SpM/S-M/Fran-
   kenstein. #37-SpM/Man-Wolf. #38-SpM/Beast.
   #39-SpM/H-T. #40-SpM/Sons of the Tiger/H-T
                  .20   .40   .60
41-50: #41-SpM/Scarlet Witch. #42-SpM/The
   Vision. #43-SpM/Dr. Doom. #44-SpM/Moondra-
   gon. #45-SpM/Killraven. #46-SpM/Deathlok.
   #47-SpM/Thing. #48-SpM/Iron Man. #49,50-
   SpM/Dr. Strange/Iron Man
                  .15   .30   .45
51-60: #51-SpM/Dr. Strange/Iron Man. #52-SpM/
   Capt. America. #53-SpM/Woodgod/Hulk. #54-
   SpM/Woodgod/Hulk. #55-SpM/Warlock. #56-SpM/
   Daredevil. #57-SpM/Black Widow. #58-SpM/
   Ghost Rider. #59-SpM/Yellowjacket/The Wasp.
   #60-SpM/The Wasp   .15   .30   .45
61-65: #61-SpM/H-T. #62-SpM/Ms. Marvel. #63-
   SpM/Iron Fist. #64-SpM/Daughters of the
   Dragon. #65-SpM/Capt. Britain(1st U.S. app.)
                  .15   .30   .45
Annual #1(1/77)   .25   .50   .75
Annual #2   .20   .40   .60
NOTE: *Kane art in #4-6,13,14,16-19,23. "H-T"*
mean Human Torch; "SpM" means Spider-Man;
"S-M" means Sub-Mariner.

MARVEL TREASURY EDITION   ($1.50)
Sept, 1974 - Present (100 pgs.) (Oversized)
Marvel Comics Group

#1-Spider-Man reprints   1.35   2.75   4.00
  2-Fantastic Four   1.00   2.00   3.00
  3-The Mighty Thor   1.00   2.00   3.00
  4-Conan-Smith reprints, Smith cover
              1.20   2.40   3.60
  5-The Hulk (origin)   1.00   2.00   3.00
  6-Doctor Strange-Brunner cover/art; Ditko
    art; Adams reprt.inks 1.00   2.00   3.00
  7-Avengers-Kirby cover 1.00   2.00   3.00
  8-Christmas stories-Spider-Man, Hulk, Nick

Fury   .65   1.35   2.00
9   .65   1.35   2.00
10-Thor reprints-Kirby   .65   1.35   2.00
11-Fantastic 4 reprts-Kirby .65 1.35   2.00
12-Howard the Duck-reprts. .65   1.35   2.00
13-Giant Superhero Holiday Grab-Bag
              .50   1.00   1.50
14-Spider-Man   .50   1.00   1.50
15-Conan-Smith, Buscema, Adams reprints
              .50   1.00   1.50
16   .50   1.00   1.50

MARVEL TREASURY OF OZ (See MGM's Marvelous--)
1975   (Over-Sized) ($1.50)
Marvel Comics Group

#1-The Marvelous Land of Oz; Alcala art
              .80   1.60   2.40

MARVEL TREASURY SPECIAL
1974; 1976   (84 pgs.) ($1.50) (Over-Sized)
Marvel Comics Group

Vol.1-Spider-Man, Torch, Sub-Mariner, Avengers
   "Giant Superhero Holiday Grab-Bag"; Smith
   art   .80   1.60   2.40
Vol.1-Captain America's Bicentennial Battles
   (6/76)-Kirby art; Smith inks
              .80   1.60   2.40

MARVEL TRIPLE ACTION
2/72 - #24, 3/75; #25, 8/75 - Present
Marvel Comics Group

#1   .60   1.20   1.80
2-5   .40   .80   1.20
6,8-10   .35   .70   1.05
7-Starlin cover   .40   .80   1.20
11-15,17-20   .25   .50   .75
16-Wood inks   .30   .60   .90
21-30   .20   .40   .60
31-39   .15   .30   .45
Giant-Size #1(5/75)   .35   .70   1.05
Giant-Size #2(7/75)   .25   .50   .75
NOTE: *Fantastic Four reprints-#1-4; Avengers*
reprints-#5-12.

MARVEL TWO-IN-ONE
Jan, 1974 - Present
Marvel Comics Group

#1-Thing team-ups begin   .60   1.20   1.80
2-4: #2-Kane art   .35   .70   1.05
5-Guardians of the Galaxy .40   .80   1.20
6-10   .25   .50   .50.7
11-20   .20   .40   .60
21-35   .15   .30   .45

Marvel Triple Action #1, © MCG

Mary Marvel #4, © Faw

Mary Worth #1, © Argo

Mask Comics #1, © RH

Masked Marvel #1, © Cen

Masked Raider #1, © CC

(Marvel 2-in-1 cont'd)
NOTE: *Buscema cover-#30. Kirby covers-#25,27.*

	Good	Fine	Mint
Annual #1(6/76)-Liberty Legion app.	.35	.70	1.05
Annual #2(2/77)-Starlin cover/story	.25	.50	.75

MARVIN MOUSE
Sept, 1957
Atlas Comics (BPC)

	Good	Fine	Mint
#1-Everett/Maneely art	1.50	3.00	4.50

MARY JANE & SNIFFLES (See 4-Color #402,474)

MARY MARVEL COMICS (Monte Hale #29 on)(Also
see Capt. Marvel #18, Marvel Family, & Shazam)
Dec, 1945 - #28, Sept, 1948
Fawcett Publications

#1	30.00	60.00	90.00
2	15.00	30.00	45.00
3	13.50	26.75	40.00
4	12.00	24.00	36.00
5	9.00	18.00	27.00
6,7	8.00	16.00	24.00
8-Bulletgirl x-over in Mary Marvel			
	8.00	16.00	24.00
9,10	6.00	12.00	18.00
11-20	5.00	10.00	15.00
21-28	4.00	8.00	12.00

MARY POPPINS (See Walt Disney Showcase #17
and Movie Comics)

MARY WORTH (See Love Stories of --)
March, 1956
Argo

#1	1.75	3.35	5.00

MASK COMICS
2-3/45 - #2, 4-5/45; #2, Fall, 1945
Rural Home Publications

	Good	Fine	Mint
#1-L.B. Cole cvr/story	5.00	10.00	15.00
2-Black Rider, The Boy Magician & The Collector; L.B.Cole cover	4.00	8.00	12.00
2(Fall,'45)-No Publ.-same as regular #2; L.B. Cole cover	2.50	5.00	7.50

MASKED BANDIT, THE
1952
Avon Periodicals

No#-Kinstler art	2.00	4.00	6.00

MASKED MARVEL
Sept, 1940 - #3, Dec, 1940
Centaur Publications

#1-The Masked Marvel begins			
	20.00	40.00	60.00
2,3	13.50	26.75	40.00

MASKED RAIDER, THE (See Blue Bird)
June, 1955 - #30, June, 1961
Charlton Comics

#1	1.00	2.00	3.00
2-10	.40	.80	1.20
11-14,16-30: #22-Rocky Lane app.	.25	.50	.50
15-Williamson story, 7pgs.	1.75	3.35	5.00

MASKED RANGER
April, 1954 - #9, Aug, 1955
Premier Magazines

#1-Woodbridge story	2.00	4.00	6.00
2,3-Crimson Avenger app.	1.35	2.75	4.00

Masked Ranger #1, © Premier Mag.

Mask Of Dr. Fu Manchu #1, © Avon

Master Comics #12, © Faw

Master Comics #21, © Faw   Master Comics #43, © Faw   Matt Slade Gunfighter #1, © MCG

(Masked Ranger cont'd)	Good	Fine	Mint
4-8	1.35	2.75	4.00
9-Torres story	2.00	4.00	6.00

NOTE: _Woodbridge covers/stories-#1,4-8._

MASK OF DR. FU MANCHU, THE (See Dr. Fu Manchu)
1951
Avon Periodicals

#1-Wood cover + 26 pgs.	35.00	70.00	105.00

MASQUE OF THE RED DEATH (See Movie Classics)

MASTER COMICS (#1-6 over-sized issues)
March, 1940 - #133, April, 1953
Fawcett Publications

#1-Origin Masterman; The Devil's Dagger, El
Carim, Master of Magic, Rick O'Shay, Mor-
ton Murch, White Rajah, Shipwreck Roberts,
Frontier Marshall, Streak Sloan, Mr. Clue
begin.(All features end #6)

	Good	Fine	Mint
	120.00	300.00	480.00
2	50.00	125.00	200.00
3-5	30.00	75.00	120.00
6-Last Masterman	30.00	60.00	90.00

7-(10/40)-Bulletman, Zorro, the Mystery Man
(ends #22), Lee Granger, Jungle King, &
Buck Jones begin; only app. The War Bird
& Mark Swift & the Tim Retarder

	60.00	120.00	180.00

8-The Red Gaucho(ends #13), Captain Vent-
ure(ends #22) & The Planet Princess begin

	30.00	60.00	90.00
9,10: #10-Lee Granger ends			
	25.00	50.00	75.00
11-Origin Minute-Man	55.00	110.00	165.00
12	35.00	70.00	105.00
13-Origin Bulletgirl	50.00	100.00	150.00
14-16: #14-Companions Three begin, ends #31			
	30.00	60.00	90.00
17-20: #17-Raboy art on Bulletman begins			
	35.00	70.00	105.00

21-(Scarce)-Captain Marvel x-over in Bulletman; Capt. Nazi origin

	150.00	300.00	450.00

22-Captain Marvel Jr. x-over in Bulletman;
Capt. Nazi app.

	125.00	250.00	375.00
23-Captain Marvel Jr. begins, vs. Capt. Nazi			
	90.00	180.00	270.00
24,25,29	35.00	70.00	105.00
26-28,30-Captain Marvel Jr. vs. Capt. Nazi			
	35.00	70.00	105.00

31,32: #32-Last El Carim & Buck Jones. Balbo,
the Boy Magician intro. in El Carim

	25.00	50.00	75.00

33-Balbo, the Boy Magician(ends #47), Hopalong Cassidy(ends #49) begins

	Good	Fine	Mint
	25.00	50.00	75.00
34-Capt. Marvel Jr. vs. Capt. Nazi			
	25.00	50.00	75.00
35	25.00	50.00	75.00
36-40	20.00	40.00	60.00

41-Bulletman, Capt. Marvel Jr. & Bulletgirl
x-over in Minute-Man; only app. Crime
Crusaders Club(Capt. Marvel Jr., Minute-
Man, Bulletman & Bulletgirl)-Only team
in Fawcett Comics

	16.50	33.25	50.00

42-49: #48-Intro. Bulletboy; Capt. Marvel
cameo in Minute-Man. #49-Last Minute-Man

	12.00	24.00	36.00

50-Radar, Nyoka the Jungle Girl begin. Capt.
Marvel x-over in Radar; origin Radar

	8.00	16.00	24.00
51-58	4.00	8.00	12.00

59-62: Nyoka serial "Terrible Tiara" in all;
#61-Capt. Marvel Jr. 1st meets Uncle
Marvel

	5.00	10.00	15.00
63-80	4.00	8.00	12.00

81-100: #88-Hopalong Cassidy begins(ends #94).
#95-Tom Mix begins(ends #133)

	3.00	6.00	9.00
101-106-Last Bulletman	2.50	5.00	7.50
107-133	2.00	4.00	6.00

NOTE: _Mac Raboy_ stories-#17-39,40 in part,
42; covers-#21-49,52,56,58,59.

MASTER DETECTIVE
1964   (Reprint)
Super Comics

#10,17(Young King Cole), #18			
	.40	.80	1.20

MASTER OF KUNG FU (Formerly Spec. Marvel Ed.)
#17, April, 1974 - Present
Marvel Comics Group

#17-Starlin art	.50	1.00	1.50
18-20: Gulacy art. #19-Man-Thing app.			
	.40	.80	1.20
21,23,32,36,37	.25	.50	.75
24-Starlin art	.50	1.00	1.50
25-31,33-35-Gulacy art	.35	.70	1.05
38-40	.35	.70	1.05
41	.20	.40	.60
42-50-Gulacy art	.30	.60	.90
51-Gulacy cover	.15	.30	.45
Giant Size #1(9/74)	.60	1.20	1.80
Giant Size #2-4(6/75): #4-Reprints 2 Kirby			
stys/Yellow Claw #2	.40	.80	1.20
Annual #1(4/76)	.35	.70	1.05

MASTERS OF TERROR (Magazine)
July, 1975 - #2, 1975   (Black & White)
Marvel Comics Group

(Masters of Terror cont'd)   Good   Fine   Mint
#1-Brunner, Smith art; Morrow cover; Adams
  reprint inks; Starlin pencils
                    .50   1.00   1.50
2   .35   .70   1.05

MASTER OF THE WORLD (See 4-Color #1157)

MATT SLADE GUNFIGHTER (Kid Slade #5 on)
May, 1956 - #4, Nov, 1956
Atlas Comics (SPI)

#1-Williamson/Torres art 2.50 5.00 7.50
 2-Williamson story   2.00 4.00 6.00
 3,4   .75 1.50 2.25

MAUD
1906   (32pgs. in color)(10x15½")
Frederick A. Stokes Co.   (Cardboard covers)

By Fred Opper   15.00 37.50 60.00

MAVERICK (TV)
1958 - #19, Apr-June, 1962
Dell Publishing Co.

4-Color #892,930,945,962,980,1005
             1.00 2.00 3.00
#7-19   .65 1.35 2.00

MAVERICK MARSHAL
Nov, 1958 - #7, May, 1960
Charlton Comics

#1   .35   .70 1.05
2-7   .20   .40   .60

MAX BRAND (See Silvertip)

MAYA (See Movie Classics)
March, 1968
Gold Key

#1(10218-803)(TV)   .25   .50   .75

MAZIE (-- & Her Friends)(See Tastee-Freez)
1950 - 1958
Mazie Comics(Magaizne Publ.)/Harvey Publ.

#1   1.00 2.00 3.00
 2-10   .50 1.00 1.50
 11-28   .25   .50   .75

MAZIE (5¢)
1950 - 1951   (5"x7¼"-Miniature)
Nation Wide Publishers

#1-7   .40   .80 1.20

McCRORY'S TOYLAND BRINGS YOU SANTA'S
PRIVATE EYES
1956   (16 pgs.)
Promotional Publ. Co.   (Giveaway)
                 Good Fine Mint
Has 9-pg. story + 7pgs. toy ads
                  .50 1.00 1.50

McHALE'S NAVY (TV) (See Movie Classics)
May-July, 1963 - #3, Nov-Jan, 1963-64
Dell Publishing Co.

#1-3   .20   .40   .60

McKEEVER & THE COLONEL (TV)
Feb-Apr, 1963 - #3, Aug-Oct, 1963
Dell Publishing Co.

#1-3   .15   .30   .45

McLINTOCK (See Movie Comics)

MD
April-May, 1955 - #5, Dec-Jan, 1955-56
E.C. Comics

#1   3.00 6.00 9.00
 2-5   2.50 5.00 7.50
NOTE: *Crandall, Evans, Ingels, Orlando* stories in all issues; *Craig* covers-#1-5.

MEDAL OF HONOR COMICS
Spring, 1946
A. S. Curtis

#1   2.00 4.00 6.00

MEET ANGEL (Formerly Angel & the Ape)
#7, Nov-Dec, 1969
National Periodical Publications

#7   .15   .30   .45

MEET CORLISS ARCHER (My Live #4 on)
March, 1948 - #3, July, 1948
Fox Features Syndicate

#1-Feldstein cover/art 7.00 14.00 21.00
 2-Feldstein cover only 5.00 10.00 15.00
 3-Part Feldstein cover only
             4.00 8.00 12.00

MEET HERCULES (See Three Stooges)

MEET MERTON
1954 - #4, June, 1954
Toby Press

#1-Dave Berg art   .65 1.35 2.00

Maverick #9, © Dell   Mazie #13, © Nation Wide

Meet Corliss Archer #3, © Fox

Melvin Monster #2, © Dell

Menace #1, © MCG

Men's Adventures #4, © MCG

	Good	Fine	Mint
(Meet Merton cont'd)			
2-4: Dave Berg art	.35	.70	1.05
IW Reprint #9	.25	.50	.75
Super Reprint #11('63),18	.25	.50	.75

MEET MISS BLISS
May, 1955 - #3, Sept, 1955
Atlas Comics (LMC)

#1	1.00	2.00	3.00
2,3	.80	1.60	2.40

MEET MISS PEPPER (Formerly Lucy --)
#5, April, 1954 - #6, June, 1954
St. John Publishing Co.

#5-Kubert/Maurer art	6.00	12.00	18.00
6-Kubert art	5.00	10.00	15.00

MEL ALLEN'S SPORTS COMICS
Nov, 1949 - 1950
Standard Comics

#1(#5 on cover)-Tuska art	.80	1.60	2.40
2-6	.40	.80	1.20

MELVIN MONSTER
April-June, 1965 - #10, Oct, 1969
Dell Publishing Co.

#1-by John Stanley	.65	1.35	2.00
2-10-All by Stanley	.40	.80	1.20

MELVIN THE MONSTER (Dexter the Demon #6 on)
July, 1956 - #5, June, 1957
Atlas Comics (HPC)

#1-5	.40	.80	1.20

MENACE
March, 1953 - #11, May, 1954
Atlas Comics (HPC)

#1-Everett, Heath stories	1.50	3.00	4.50
2-4,6-Everett, Heath stories			
	1.00	2.00	3.00
5-Origin & 1st app. The Zombie by Everett			
(reprinted in Tales of Zombie #1)			
	1.00	2.00	3.00
7,8,10,11	.90	1.80	2.70
9-Everett story reprinted in Vampire Tales			
#1	1.00	2.00	3.00

NOTE: *Everett covers-#1,5. Powell art-#11.*

MEN AGAINST CRIME (Also see Mr. Risk)
1950 - #7, Oct, 1951
Ace Magazines

	Good	Fine	Mint
#1	1.00	2.00	3.00
2-7: #2,3-Mr. Risk app.	.50	1.00	1.50

MEN FROM PACIFIC PLANTRONICS, THE
(See Business Week --)

MEN, GUNS, & CATTLE (See Classics Special)

MEN IN ACTION (Battle Brady #10 on)
April, 1952 - #9, Dec, 1952
Atlas Comics (IPS)

#1	1.00	2.00	3.00
2-6,8,9	.50	1.00	1.50
7-Krigstein story	1.50	3.00	4.50

MEN IN ACTION
1957 - 1958
Ajax/Farrell Publications

#1	.65	1.35	2.00
2-9	.35	.70	1.05

MEN INTO SPACE (See 4-Color Comics #1083)

MEN OF BATTLE (See New --)

MEN OF WAR
August, 1977 - Present
DC Comics, Inc.

#1	.20	.40	.60
2-4	.15	.30	.45

NOTE: *Kubert covers-#2,3,4.*

MEN'S ADVENTURES (Formerly True Adventures)
#4, Aug, 1950 - #28, July, 1954
Marvel/Atlas Comics (CCC)

#4(#1)	1.75	3.35	5.00
5-10	1.00	2.00	3.00
11-20	.75	1.50	2.25
21,22,24-26	.90	1.80	2.70
23-Crandall art	1.50	3.00	4.50
27,28-Captain America, Human Torch, & Sub-			
Mariner app. in ea.	10.00	20.00	30.00

NOTE: *Everett story-#25; cover-#22. Advent-
ure-#4-10; War-#11-20; Horror-#21-26.*

MEN WHO MOVE THE NATION
(Giveaway - Black & White)

Neal Adams art	1.50	3.00	4.50

MERLIN JONES AS THE MONKEY'S UNCLE (See
Movie Comics & The Misadventures of -- under
Movie Comics)

270

MERRILL'S MARAUDERS (See Movie Classics)

MERRY CHRISTMAS, A
1948   (No#)   (Giveaway)
K.K. Publications (Child Life Shoes)

	Good	Fine	Mint
	1.75	3.35	5.00

MERRY CHRISTMAS (See Donald Duck --, Dell
Giant #39, & March of Comics #153)

MERRY CHRISTMAS FROM MICKEY MOUSE
1939   (16 pgs. - Color & B&W)
K.K. Publications (Shoe store giveaway)

Donald Duck & Pluto app.; text with art
(Rare)   110.00 220.00 330.00

MERRY CHRISTMAS FROM SEARS TOYLAND
1939   (16 pgs.) (In Color)
Sear Roebuck Giveaway)

Dick Tracy, Little Orphan Annie, The Gumps,
Terry & the Pirates   10.00 20.00 30.00

MERRY COMICS
December, 1945
Carlton Publishing Co.

No#-Boogeyman app.	1.35	2.75	4.00

MERRY COMICS
1947
Four Star Publications

#1	.80	1.60	2.40

MERRY-GO-ROUND COMICS
1944(132pgs.)(25¢); 1946; Sept-Oct, 1947
LaSalle Publ. Co./Croyden Publ./Rotary Litho.

#1(1944)(LaSalle)	2.75	5.50	8.00
#21	1.35	2.75	4.00
#1(1946-Croyden)	1.00	2.00	3.00
V1#1(9-10/47-52pgs.)(Rotary Litho. Co. Ltd.,			
Canada	1.00	2.00	3.00

MERRY MAILMAN
1955
Charlton Comics

#1	.65	1.35	2.00

MERRY MOUSE
June, 1953 - #4, Jan-Feb, 1954
Avon Periodicals

#1-4	.65	1.35	2.00

METAL MEN (See Showcase & Brave & the Bold)
4-5/63 - #41, 12-1/69-70; #42, 2-3/73 - #44,
7-8/73; #45, 4-5/76 - #56, 2-3/78
National Periodical Publications/DC Comics

	Good	Fine	Mint
#1	2.00	4.00	6.00
2-5	1.00	2.00	3.00
6-10	.50	1.00	1.50
11-26	.35	.70	1.05
27-Origin Metal Men	.40	.80	1.20
28-41(1970)	.20	.40	.60
42-44(1973)-Reprints	.15	.30	.45
45('76)-49-Simonson art in all			
	.20	.40	.60
50-56	.15	.30	.45

NOTE: _Kane_ stories/covers-#30,31. _Staton_
stories-#52-55.

METAMORPHO (See Brave & the Bold, Action,
First Issue Special, & World's Finest)
July-Aug, 1965 - #17, Mar-Apr, 1968
National Periodical Publications

#1	1.50	3.00	4.50
2-5	.65	1.35	2.00
6-9	.50	1.00	1.50
10-Origin 1st app. Element Girl(1-2/67)			
	.50	1.00	1.50
11-17	.35	.70	1.05

NOTE: _Orlando_ story pencils-#5-11; covers-
#5-9,11.

METEOR COMICS
Nov, 1945
L. L. Baird (Croyden)

#1-Captain Wizard, Impossible Man, Race Wil-			
kins app.; origin Baldy Bean, Capt. Wiz-			
ard's sidekick	3.35	6.75	10.00

MGM'S MARVELOUS WIZARD OF OZ (See Marvelous--)

MICKEY AND DONALD IN VACATIONLAND (See Dell
Giant #47)

MICKEY & THE BEANSTALK (See Story Hour Series)

MICKEY & THE SLEUTH (See Walt Disney Showcase
#38,39)

MICKEY FINN
1942 - 1952
McNaught Syndicate #5 on (Columbia)

#1	6.00	12.00	18.00
2	3.00	6.00	9.00
3-Charlie Chan app.	2.00	4.00	6.00

Merry Christmas From M.M.('39). © WDP

Metamorpho #1. © DC

Mickey Finn #11. © McNaught Synd.

Mickey Mouse Book #4('34, McKay), © WDP   Mickey Mouse 4-Color #27, © WDP   Mickey Mouse 4-Color #261, © WDP

(Mickey Finn cont'd)	Good	Fine	Mint
4	1.75	3.35	5.00
5-15(1949)	1.00	2.00	3.00
V3#1,2(1952)	1.00	2.00	3.00

MICKEY MOUSE
1931 - 1934 (48pgs.)(10x9-3/4")(Cardboard cvrs)
David McKay Publications

#1('31)	80.00	160.00	240.00
2('32)	70.00	140.00	210.00
3('33)-All color Sunday reprints; pgs.#5-17, #32-48 reissued in Whitman #948			
	100.00	200.00	300.00
4('34)	60.00	120.00	180.00

NOTE: *Each book reprints strips from previous year - dailies in B&W in #1,2,4; Sundays in color in #3.*

MICKEY MOUSE
1933 (Copyright date, printing date unknown)
30 pgs.; 10x8-3/4"; Cardboard covers
Whitman Publishing Co.

#948-1932 Sunday strips in color
NOTE: Some copies are known to have been
bound with a second front cover upside-
down instead of the regular back cover;
both covers have the same art, but different right & left margins.
                                80.00 160.00 240.00
NOTE: *The above book is an exact, but abbrev-
iated reissue of David McKay #3 but with ½"
of border trimmed from the top and bottom.*

MICKEY MOUSE (See Cheerios giveaways Merry
Christmas From --, & The Best of Walt Disney
Comics)

MICKEY MOUSE
1941 - Present
Dell Publishing Co./Gold Key #85 on

4-Color #16(1941)-1st M.M. comic book-"vs.
the Phantom Blot" by Gottfredson
                        325.00 812.50 1300.00
              (Prices vary widely on this book)
4-Color #27(1943)-"7 Colored Terror"
                        50.00 100.00 150.00
4-Color #79(1945)-By Carl Barks(1 story)
                        70.00 140.00 210.00

4-Color #116(1946)	10.00	20.00	30.00
4-Color #141(1947)	10.00	20.00	30.00
4-Color #157('47),170,181,194('48)			
	8.00	16.00	24.00
4-Color #214('49),231,248,261			
	6.00	12.00	18.00

4-Color #268-Reprints/WDC&S #22-24 by Gottfredson (Surprise Visitor)

	Good	Fine	Mint
	6.00	12.00	18.00
4-Color #279,286,296	5.00	10.00	15.00
4-Color #304,313(#1),325(#2),334			
	4.00	8.00	12.00
4-Color #343,352,362,371,387			
	3.50	7.00	10.50
4-Color #401,411,427('52)	2.50	5.00	7.50
4-Color #819-M.M. in Magicland			
	1.00	2.00	3.00
4-Color #1057,1151,1246(1959-61)-Album			
	.65	1.35	2.00
#28-34	1.00	2.00	3.00
35-50	.65	1.35	2.00
51-80	.50	1.00	1.50
81-99: #93,95-titled "Mickey Mouse Club Album"	.40	.80	1.20
100-105: Reprints 4-Color #427,194,279,170, 343,214 in that order	1.00	2.00	3.00
106-130	.35	.70	1.05
131-146	.25	.50	.75
147-Reprints "The Phantom Fires" from WDC&S #200-202	.50	1.00	1.50
148-Reprints "The Mystery of Lonely Valley" from WDC&S #208-210	.50	1.00	1.50
149-158	.15	.30	.45
159-Reprints "The Sunken City" from WDC&S #205-207	.35	.70	1.05
160-170: #162-170-reprints	.15	.30	.45
171-178		.20	.35
Album #01-518-210(Dell), #1(10082-309)(9/63-Gold Key)	.50	1.00	1.50
Almanac #1('57)-Barks art	4.00	8.00	12.00
--& Goofy Explore Energy(1976, Walt Disney Educational Media)		.15	.30

Birthday Party #1('53)(25th Anniversary)
Reprints entire 48 pgs. of Gottfredson's
"M.M in Love Trouble" from WDC&S #36-39.
Quality equal to original. Also reprints
one story each from 4-Color #27,79 & 181
plus 6 panels of highlights in the career
of M.M.   10.00 20.00 30.00
Club #1(1/64-G.K.)(TV)   1.00 2.00 3.00
Club Parade #1(12/55)-Reprints 4-Color #16
with some art redrawn & recolored with
night scenes turned into day; quality much
poorer than original 5.00 10.00 15.00
In Fantasy Land #1('57) 1.75 3.35 5.00
In Frontier Land #1('56)-M.M. Club ish.
                        1.75 3.35 5.00
Surprise Party #1(30037-901, G.K.)(1/69)
40th Anniversary   .80 1.60 2.40

MICKEY MOUSE AND GOOFY "BICEP BUNGLE"
1952   (14 pgs.) (Fritos Giveaway)
Walt Disney Productions

                        1.50 3.00 4.50

MICKEY MOUSE BOOK
1930   (2 printings)
Bibo & Lang

	Good	Fine	Mint
Very 1st Disney book; origin of Mickey
Mouse (1st Printing) 175.00 350.00 525.00

MICKEY MOUSE CLUB MAGAZINE(See Walt Disney--)

MICKEY MOUSE CLUB SPECIAL
Oct, 1977   (224 pgs.)
Gold Key

	Good	Fine	Mint
#1	.40	.80	1.20

MICKEY MOUSE MAGAZINE
Vol.1#1, Jan, 1933 - Vol.1#9, Sept, 1933
#1-3 published by Kamen-Blair(Kay Kamen, Inc.)
Walt Disney Productions

(Very Rare)-Distributed by leading stores
thru their local threatres. 1st few issues
had 5¢ listed on the cover, later ones had
no price.

	Good	Fine	Mint
V1#1	150.00	300.00	450.00
2-9	60.00	120.00	180.00

MICKEY MOUSE MAGAZINE
V1#1, Nov, 1933 - V2#12, Oct, 1935
Mills giveaways issued by different dairies
Walt Disney Productions

	Good	Fine	Mint
V1#1	30.00	60.00	90.00
2-12	15.00	30.00	45.00
V2#1-12	12.00	24.00	36.00

MICKEY MOUSE MAGAZINE (No V3#1)
(Becomes Walt Disney's Comics & Stories)
Summer, 1935 - V5#12, Sept, 1940
K.K. Publications

	Good	Fine	Mint
V1#1-John Stanley cover & interior art	65.00	130.00	195.00
2	30.00	60.00	90.00
3	16.50	33.25	50.00
4-6	13.50	26.75	40.00
7-12	10.00	20.00	30.00
V2#1-13	8.00	16.00	24.00
V3#2-12-(Gottfredson Mickey Mouse reprints begin V3#?)	8.00	16.00	24.00
V4#1-12	8.00	16.00	24.00
V5#1-8	15.00	30.00	45.00
9-Regular comic book size begins	25.00	50.00	75.00
10,11	25.00	50.00	75.00
V5#12-(Comic book format)(Rare)-strip reprints	200.00	400.00	600.00
V4#1(Giveaway)	12.00	24.00	36.00

MICKEY MOUSE MARCH OF COMICS
1947 - 1951   (Giveaway)
K.K. Publications

	Good	Fine	Mint
#8(1947)-32pgs.	40.00	80.00	120.00
27(1948)	25.00	50.00	75.00
45(1949)	20.00	40.00	60.00
60(1950)	15.00	30.00	45.00
74(1951)	9.00	18.00	27.00

MICKEY MOUSE SUMMER FUN (Summer Fun #2)
1958
Dell Publishing Co.

	Good	Fine	Mint
#1	2.00	4.00	6.00

MICKEY MOUSE'S SUMMER VACATION (See Story
Hour Series)

MICROBOTS, THE
Dec, 1971   (One Shot)
Gold Key

#1(10271-112)	.15	.30	.45

MIDGET COMICS (Fighting Indian Stories)
Feb, 1950 - #2, Apr, 1950 (5-3/8"x7-3/8")
St. John Publishing Co.

#1,2-Tex West, Cowboy Marshal	1.00	2.00	3.00

MIDNIGHT
1957 - #6, June, 1958
Ajax/Farrell Publ. (Four Star Comic Corp.)

#1-Reprints from Voodoo & Strange Fantasy with some changes	.65	1.35	2.00
2-6	.50	1.00	1.50

MIDNIGHT MYSTERY
Jan-Feb, 1961 - #7, Oct, 1961
American Comics Group

#1	.65	1.35	2.00
2-7	.35	.70	1.05

MIDNIGHT TALES
Dec, 1972 - #18, May, 1976
Charlton Press

V1#1	.15	.30	.45
2-10,15-18		.10	.20
11-14-Newton stories	.15	.30	.45

NOTE: _Howard_ stories(Wood imitator)-#1-12,14,
15,17,18; covers-#1-18.

Mickey Mouse V2#1 Dairy Giv.('34), © WDP   Mickey Mouse Magazine V5#9, © WDP

Midnight Mystery #2, © ACG

Mighty Atom #6, © ME   Mighty Comics #41, © AP   The Mighty Heroes #1, © Dell

MIGHTY ATOM (-- & the Pixies #6)(Formerly
The Pixies #1-5)
#6, 1949; Nov, 1957 - #6, Aug-Sept, 1958
Magazines Enterprises

	Good	Fine	Mint
#6(1949-M.E.)No month(1st Series)	1.00	2.00	3.00
#1-6(2nd Series)-Pixies reprints	.50	1.00	1.50
IW Reprint #1(no date)	.35	.70	1.05
Giveaway('59)-Evans art	1.20	2.40	3.60

MIGHTY BEAR (Formerly Fun Comics)
#13, Jan, 1954 - #14, Mar, 1954; 1957
Star Publ.#13,14/Ajax-Farrell(Four Star)

#13,14	.35	.70	1.05
No#(1957)(Ajax)	.25	.50	.75
#2(11/57)Four Star(Ajax)	.25	.50	.75

MIGHTY COMICS (-- Presents)(Formerly Flyman)
#40, Nov, 1966 - #50, Oct, 1967
Radio Comics (Archie)

#40-Web	.40	.80	1.20
41-Shield, Black Hood	.40	.80	1.20
42-Black Hood	.40	.80	1.20
43-Shield & Web	.40	.80	1.20
44-Black Hood, Steel Sterling & The Shield	.40	.80	1.20
45-Shield & Hangman	.40	.80	1.20
46-Steel Sterling & Web	.40	.80	1.20
47-Bl. Hood & Mr. Justice	.40	.80	1.20
48-Shield & Hangman; Wizard x-over in Shield	.40	.80	1.20
49-Steel Sterling & Fox; Black Hood x-over in Steel Sterling	.40	.80	1.20
50-Black Hood & Web; Inferno x-over in Web	.40	.80	1.20

MIGHTY CRUSADERS, THE
Nov, 1965 - #7, Oct, 1966
Mighty Comics Group(Radio Comics)(Archie)

#1-Origin The Shield	1.35	2.75	4.00
2-Origin Comet	.65	1.35	2.00
3-Origin Fly-Man	.50	1.00	1.50
4-Fireball, Inferno, Firefly, Web, Fox, Bob Phantom, Blackjack, Hangman, Zambini, Kardak, Steel Sterling, Mr. Justice, Wizard, Capt.Flag, Jaguar x-over.	.75	1.50	2.25
5-Intro. Ultra-Men(Fox, Web, Capt. Flag) & Terrific Three(Jaguar, Mr. Justice, Steel Sterling)	.50	1.00	1.50
6,7: #7-Steel Sterling feature; origin Fly-Girl	.50	1.00	1.50

MIGHTY GHOST
#4, 1958

Ajax/Farrell Publ.

	Good	Fine	Mint
#4	.35	.70	1.05

MIGHTY HERCULES, THE (TV)
July, 1963 - #2, Oct, 1963
Gold Key

#1,2(10072-307,311)	.25	.50	.75

MIGHTY HEROES, THE (TV) (Funny)
Mar, 1967 - #4, July, 1967
Dell Publishing Co.

#1-Reprints 1957 Heckle & Jeckle		.20	.40
2,3		.10	.20
4-Two '58 Mighty Mouse reprints	.15	.30	.45

MIGHTY MARVEL WESTERN, THE
10/68 - #46, 9/76 (#1-14,68pgs; #15,16,52pgs)
Marvel Comics Group

#1-Begin Kid Colt, Rawhide Kid, Two-Gun Kid reprints	.20	.40	.60
2-10	.15	.30	.45
11-20		.15	.30
21-30: #24-Kid Colt reprints end. #25-Matt Slade reprints begin		.15	.30
31,33-36,38-46		.15	.30
32-Origin reprint/Ringo Kid #23; Williamson reprt/Kid Slade #7	.15	.30	.45
37-5pg. Williamson reprint	.15	.30	.45

NOTE: #21-24 Jack Davis reprints. Kirby reprints #1-3,6,9,12,14,16,26,29,32,41,43,44;
cover-#29. No Matt Slade-#43.

MIGHTY MIDGET COMICS, THE (Miniature)
No Date; Circa 1943 (5"x3-3/4")
Black & White & Red)(Sold 2 for 5¢)
Samuel E. Lowe & Co.

Bulletman #11(1943)	2.50	5.00	7.50
Captain Marvel #11(2 issues; one issue has ad on back for C.M. comics & is believed to be the small comic glued to cover of Capt.Marvel #20)-Golden Arrow, Spysmasher, Ibis, Lance O'Casey x-over	2.50	5.00	7.50
Captain Marvel Jr. #11	2.50	5.00	7.50
Golden Arrow #11	1.50	3.00	4.50
Ibis the Invincible #11	2.00	4.00	6.00
Spy Smasher #11	2.00	4.00	6.00

NOTE: The above books came in a box called
"box full of books" and was distributed with
other Samuel Lowe puzzles, paper dolls, coloring books, etc. They are not titled Mighty

(Mighty Midget cont'd)	Good	Fine	Mint

Midget Comics. All have a war bond seal on back cover. These books came in a "Mighty Midget" counter display rack.

	Good	Fine	Mint
Balbo, the Boy Magician #12	2.00	4.00	6.00
Bulletman #12	2.00	4.00	6.00
Commando Yank #12	2.00	4.00	6.00
Dr. Voltz the Human Generator	1.50	3.00	4.50
Lance O'Casey #12	1.75	3.35	5.00
Leatherneck the Marine	1.50	3.00	4.50
Minute Man #12	2.00	4.00	6.00
Mister Q	1.50	3.00	4.50
Mr. Scarlet & Pinky #12	2.00	4.00	6.00
Pat Wilton & His Flying Fortress	1.00	2.00	3.00
The Phantom Eagle #12	2.00	4.00	6.00
Tornado Tom-reprints from Cyclone #1-3; origin	2.50	5.00	7.50

MIGHTY MOUSE (See Adventures of --, Dell Giant #43, Giant Comics Edition, March of Comics #205,237,247,257, Oxydol-Dreft, Paul Terry's, & Terry-Toons Comics)

MIGHTY MOUSE (1st Series)
Fall, 1946 - #4, Summer, 1947
Timely/Marvel Comics

#1	6.00	12.00	18.00
2-4	4.00	8.00	12.00

MIGHTY MOUSE (2nd Series)
Aug, 1947 - #83, June, 1959
St. John Publishing Co./Pines

#1	5.00	10.00	15.00
2-10	2.50	5.00	7.50
11-19	1.50	3.00	4.50
20-25(52pgs.)	1.35	2.75	4.00
26-37	1.00	2.00	3.00
38-45(100pgs.)	2.00	4.00	6.00
46-83	.80	1.60	2.40
Album(No#,date)-Giant Comics Edition, 100pgs. on cover but contains 148 pgs.	2.50	5.00	7.50
Album #2(11/52-St. John)	2.50	5.00	7.50
Fun Club Magazine #1(Fall '57-Pines)	1.75	3.35	5.00
Fun Club Magazine #2-6(Winter '58-Pines)	1.35	2.75	4.00
3-D #1-1st printing-9/53, stiff covers (St. John)	5.00	10.00	15.00
3-D #1-2nd printing-10/53-slick, glossy covers, slightly smaller	4.00	8.00	12.00
3-D #2(11/53),#3(12/53)-St. John	3.00	6.00	9.00

MIGHTY MOUSE ADVENTURES (Advs.of--#2 on, 1st
Nov, 1951   Series)
St. John Publishing Co.

	Good	Fine	Mint
#1	3.00	6.00	9.00

MIGHTY MOUSE (TV)(3rd Series)(Formerly Adventures of Mighty Mouse)
#161, Oct, 1964 - #172, Oct, 1968
Gold Key/Dell Publishing Co.

#161(10/64)-#165(9/65) Gold Key	.65	1.35	2.00
#166(3/66)-#172(10/68)Dell	.65	1.35	2.00

MIGHTY SAMSON
7/64 - #20, 11/67; #21, 8/72 - #31, 3/76
Gold Key

#1-Origin	1.00	2.00	3.00
2-5	.50	1.00	1.50
6-10: #7-Tom Morrow begins, ends #20	.35	.70	1.05
11-20	.25	.50	.75
21-31: #21,22-reprints	.15	.30	.45

MIGHTY THOR (See Thor)

MIKE BARNETT, MAN AGAINST CRIME
1952
Fawcett Publications

#1	1.20	2.40	3.60
2-4,6	.80	1.60	2.40
5-"Market for Morphine"	4.00	8.00	12.00

MIKE SHAYNE PRIVATE EYE
Nov-Jan, 1962 - #3, Sept-Nov, 1962
Dell Publishing Co.

#1-3	.25	.50	.75

MILITARY COMICS (Becomes Modern #44 on)
Aug, 1941 - #43, Oct, 1945
Quality Comics Group

#1-Origin Blackhawk by C. Cuidera, Miss America, The Death Patrol by Jack Cole(also #2-4), & The Blue Tracer by Guardineer; X of the Underground, The Yankee Eagle, Q-Boat & Shot & Shell, Archie Atkins, Loops & Banks by Bud Ernest (Bob Powell) begin	165.00	330.00	495.00
2-Secret War News begins (by McWilliams #7); Cole art	75.00	150.00	225.00
3-Origin Chop Chop	50.00	100.00	150.00
4	60.00	80.00	120.00
5-The Sniper begins; Miss America in cost-			

Mighty Mouse #21, © Terry Toons

Mighty Mouse 3-D #1, © Terry Toons

Military Comics #8, © DC(Qua)

Military Comics #22, © DC (Qua)

Millie The Model Annual #1, © MCG

Milt Gross Funnies #1, © Rotary

(Military Comics cont'd)	Good	Fine	Mint
ume #4-7	30.00	60.00	90.00
6-10: #8-X of the Underground begins(ends #13). #9-The Phantom Clipper begins (ends #16)	25.00	50.00	75.00
11	20.00	40.00	60.00
12-Blackhawk by Crandall, Cuidera & Kotzky	25.00	50.00	75.00
13-15: #14-Private Dogtag begins(ends #83)	20.00	40.00	60.00
16-20: #16-Blue Tracer ends	16.50	33.25	50.00
21-30: #22-Last Crandall Blackhawk	13.50	26.75	40.00
31-43	10.00	20.00	30.00

NOTE: _Crandall stories-#6-38; covers-#13-22._
Eisner covers-#9,10,12. Ward Blackhawk-#30,
31(15pgs.each); cover-#29,30.

MILLIE, THE LOVABLE MONSTER
Sept-Nov, 1962 - #6, Jan, 1973
Dell Publishing Co.

#12-523-211, #2(8-10/63)	.20	.40	.60
#3(8-10/64), #4(7/72), #5(10/72), #6(1/73)		.15	.30

NOTE: _Woggon stories-#3,6; cover-#3._

MILLIE THE MODEL (See Modeling With --, A Date With --, & Life With --)
1945 - #207, 1974
Marvel/Atlas/Marvel Comics(SPI/Male/VPI)

#1	7.00	14.00	21.00
2	3.00	6.00	9.00
3-7	2.00	4.00	6.00
8,10-Kurtzman's "Hey Look"	2.00	4.00	6.00
9-Powerhouse Pepper by Wolverton, 4pgs.	5.00	10.00	15.00
11-Kurtzman art	1.35	2.75	4.00
12,15,17-30	.65	1.35	2.00
13,14,16-Kurtzman's "Hey Look"	1.20	2.40	3.60
31-60	.35	.70	1.05
61-100	.20	.40	.60
101-207: #192-52pgs.		.15	.30
Annual #1(1962)	.65	1.35	2.00
Annual #2-10(11/71)	.35	.70	1.05
Queen-Size #11('73), #12(9/74)	.20	.40	.60

MILT GROSS FUNNIES
Aug, 1947 - #2, Sept, 1947
Rotary Lithograph Co.

#1,2	2.50	5.00	7.50

MILTON THE MONSTER & FEARLESS FLY (TV)
May, 1966
Gold Key

	Good	Fine	Mint
#1(10175-605)	.15	.30	.45

MINUTE MAN (See Mighty Midget Comics)
1941 - #3, Spring, 1942
Fawcett Publications

#1	30.00	60.00	90.00
2,3	16.50	33.25	50.00

MINUTE MAN
No Date (B&W-16pgs.-paper cover Blue & Red)
Sovereign Service Station giveaway

American history	.50	1.00	1.50

MIRACLE COMICS
Feb, 1940 - #4, March, 1941
Hillman Periodicals

#1-Sky Wizard, Master of Space, Dash Dixon, Man of Might, Dusty Doyle, Pinkie Parker, The Kid Cop, K-7, Secret Agent, The Scorpion, & Blandu, Jungle Queen begin; Masked Angel only app.	15.00	30.00	45.00
2-4: #3-Bill Colt, the Ghost Rider begins. #4-The Veiled Prophet & Bullet Bob app.	8.00	16.00	24.00

MIRACLE OF THE WHITE STALLIONS, THE
(See Movie Comics)

MIRTH OF A NATION
#5, 1941   (Small size)
William Wise & Co. (Harry 'A' Chesler)

#5-Art by Harry 'A' Chesler, Jr. + a strip called Private Chesler	3.00	6.00	9.00

MIRTHO, THE CLOWN   (See Chewing Gum Booklet)

MISADVENTURES OF MERLIN JONES, THE
(See Movie Comics & Merlin Jones as the Monkey's Uncle under Movie Comics)

MISS AMERICA COMICS (Miss America Mag. #2 on)
1944   (One Shot)
Marvel Comics (MAP)

#1	30.00	60.00	90.00

MISS AMERICA MAGAZINE (Formerly Miss America)
V1#2, Nov, 1944 - #98, 1957
Miss America Publ. Corp./Marvel/Atlas(MAP)

Miss America Magazine #24, © MCG

Miss Beverly Hills #1, © DC

Miss Fury #1, © Tarpe' Mills

(Miss America Mag. cont'd)
	Good	Fine	Mint
V1#2: Photo cover of teenage girl in Miss America costume; Miss America, Patsy Walker(intro.)comic stories + movie reviews & stories; intro. Buzz Baxter & Hedy Wolfe	30.00	60.00	90.00
3-5-Miss America stories + Patsy Walker	12.00	24.00	36.00
6-Patsy Walker only	1.50	3.00	4.50
7-10	1.00	2.00	3.00
11-40: #24-Kamen story	.60	1.20	1.80
41-98	.35	.70	1.05

MISS BEVERLY HILLS OF HOLLYWOOD
Mar-Apr, 1949 - #11, Oct-Nov, 1950
National Periodical Publications

#1	4.00	8.00	12.00
2-11	2.50	5.00	7.50

MISS CAIRO JONES
1945
Croyden Publishers

#1-Bob Oksner daily newspaper reprints (1st strip story)	4.00	8.00	12.00

MISS FURY COMICS (Newspaper strip reprints)
Winter, 1942-43 - #8, Winter, 1946
Timely Comics

#1-Origin Miss Fury by Tarpe' Mills(68pgs.) in costume w/pin-ups	125.00	250.00	375.00
2-60pgs; In costume w/pin-ups	60.00	120.00	180.00
3-60pgs; In costume w/pin-ups	50.00	100.00	150.00
4-52pgs; Costume, 2pgs. w/pin-ups	40.00	80.00	120.00
5-52pgs; In costume w/pin-ups			

	Good	Fine	Mint
	40.00	80.00	120.00
6-52pgs; Not in costume in inside stories, w/pin-ups	25.00	50.00	75.00
7,8-36pgs; In costume lpg. ea., no pin-ups	25.00	50.00	75.00

MISSION IMPOSSIBLE (TV)
May, 1967 - #5, Oct, 1969
Dell Publishing Co.

#1	.35	.70	1.05
2-5	.20	.40	.60

MISS LIBERTY (Becomes Liberty)
1944 (MLJ Reprints)
Burten Publishing Co.

#1-The Shield & Dusty, The Wizard, & Roy, the Super Boy app. Reprint/Shield-Wizard #13	7.00	14.00	21.00

MISS MELODY LANE OF BROADWAY
Feb-Mar, 1950 - #4, Sept-Oct, 1950
National Periodical Publications

#1	3.00	6.00	9.00
2-4	2.00	4.00	6.00

MISS PEACH
Oct-Dec, 1963; 1969
Dell Publishing Co.

#1-John Stanley art	1.00	2.00	3.00
-- Tells You How To Grow('69,25¢)-Mell Lazarus art; also given away (36pgs.)	1.00	2.00	3.00

MISS PEPPER (See Meet Miss Pepper)

MISS SUNBEAM (See Little Miss --)

Miss Fury #4, © Tarpe' Mills

Miss Liberty, © Burten Publ.

Miss Peach #1, © Dell

Mister Ed #1, © GK   Mister Miracle #1, © DC   Mister Mystery #7, © Aragon Publ.

MISS VICTORY (See Holyoke One-Shot #3)
1945
Holyoke Publishing Co. (Tem)

	Good	Fine	Mint
#1	3.00	6.00	9.00
2	2.00	4.00	6.00

MR. & MRS.
1922 (48 pgs.) (B&W)
Whitman Publishing Co.

By Briggs	6.00	12.00	18.00

MR. & MRS. BEANS (See Single Series #11)

MR. & MRS. J. EVIL SCIENTIST
Nov, 1963 - #6, Oct, 1966 (Hanna-Barbera)
Gold Key

#1(11093-311)	.20	.40	.60
2-6	.15	.30	.45

MR. ANTHONY'S LOVE CLINIC
Nov, 1949 - #5, Apr-May, 1950
Hillman Periodicals

#1	1.35	2.75	4.00
2-5	.65	1.35	2.00

MR. DISTRICT ATTORNEY
Jan-Feb, 1948 - #67, Jan-Feb, 1959
National Periodical Publications

#1	3.00	6.00	9.00
2-10	1.50	3.00	4.50
11-40	1.20	2.40	3.60
41-67	.80	1.60	2.40

MR. DISTRICT ATTORNEY (See 4-Color #13)

MISTER ED, THE TALKING HORSE (TV)
Mar-May, 1962 - #6, Feb, 1964
Dell Publishing Co./Gold Key

4-Color #1295	.35	.70	1.05
#1(11/62)-#6 (G.K.)	.25	.50	.75

(See March of Comics #244,260,282,290)

MR. MAGOO (TV)(The Nearsighted --, --& Gerald McBoing Boing 1954 issues; Formerly Ger-
#6, 11-1/53-54; 1963 - 1965   ald--)
Dell Publishing Co.

#6	1.00	2.00	3.00
4-Color #561,602('54)	1.00	2.00	3.00
4-Color #1235,1305('61)	.65	1.35	2.00
#3-5(9-11/63)	.40	.80	1.20
4-Color #1235(12-536-505)(3-5/65)-2nd Print-			
ing	.35	.70	1.05

MISTER MIRACLE
3-4/71 - #18, 2-3/74; #19, 9/77 - Present
National Periodical Publications/DC Comics

	Good	Fine	Mint
#1	1.75	3.35	5.00
2	1.00	2.00	3.00
3	.90	1.80	2.70
4-Boy Commando reprints begin,			
5-Young Scott Free begins	.65	1.35	2.00
6-8	.65	1.35	2.00
9-Origin Mr. Miracle	.65	1.35	2.00
10-14,16-18	.40	.80	1.20
15-Origin Shilo Norman	.40	.80	1.20
19-22	.15	.30	.45

NOTE: #4-8 contain Simon & Kirby Boy Commando
reprints from Detective #82,76, Boy Commandos
#1,3, Detective #64 in that order. Kirby art
& cover in all issues.

MR. MIRACLE (See Holyoke One-Shot #4)

MR. MUSCLES (Formerly Blue Beetle #18-21)
#22, Mar, 1956 - #23, May-June, 1956
Charlton Comics

#22,23	.75	1.50	2.25

MISTER MYSTERY
Sept, 1951 - #19, Oct, 1954
Mr. Publ.(Media Publ.)#1-3/SPM Publ./
Stanmore (Aragon)

#1-Kurtzman story	1.75	3.35	5.00
2	1.20	2.40	3.60
3	1.00	2.00	3.00
4,6: Bondage covers + torture -#6			
	1.35	2.75	5.00
5,8	.80	1.60	2.40
7-"The Brain Bats of Venus" by Wolverton;			
used for Weird Tales of the Future #7			
	12.00	18.00	36.00
9,10-Nostrand art	1.50	3.00	4.50
11-Wolverton swiped from Weird Mysteries #2			
with editing	8.00	16.00	24.00
12-Classic injury to eye cover			
	5.00	10.00	15.00
13,15,17,19	.80	1.60	2.40
16-Bondage cover	1.00	2.00	3.00
18-"Robot Woman" by Wolverton cut up & re-			
printed from Weird Mysteries #2			
	8.00	16.00	24.00

MISTER Q (See Mighty Midget Comics)

MR. RISK (Formerly All Romances; becomes
Hand of Fate #8 on) (See Men Against Crime)
#7, Oct, 1950 - #2, Dec, 1950
Ace Magazines

(Mr. Risk cont'd)	Good	Fine	Mint
#7,2	.65	1.35	2.00

MR. SCARLET & PINKY (See Mighty Midget Comics)

MR. UNIVERSE
1951
Mr. Publications (Comic Media)

#1	1.35	2.75	4.00
2-5	.80	1.60	2.40

MITZI COMICS
Spring, 1948 - #4, Winter, 1948
Timely Comics

#1-Kurtzman's "Hey Look" + 3pgs. "Giggles 'n' Grins"	2.50	5.00	7.50
2-4	.80	1.60	2.40

MITZI'S BOY FRIEND (Becomes Mitzi's Romances)
#2, June, 1948 - #7, April, 1949
Marvel Comics

#2-7	.60	1.20	1.80

MITZI'S ROMANCES (Formerly Mitzi's Boy --)
#8, June, 1949 - #10, Dec, 1949
Timely/Marvel Comics

#8-10	.60	1.20	1.80

MOBY DICK (See 4-Color #717 & Feature
Presentations #6)

MOBY DUCK (See Walt Disney Showcase #2,11)
10/67 - #11, 10/70; #12, 1/74 - Present
Gold Key   (Disney)

#1	.65	1.35	2.00
2-5	.40	.80	1.20
6-15	.20	.40	.60
16-29	.15	.30	.45

MODEL FUN (With Bobby Benson)
#4, Spring, 1955 - #5, July, 1955
Harle Publications

#4,5-Bobby Benson	.80	1.60	2.40

MODELING WITH MILLIE
1961 - #54, June, 1967
Atlas/Marvel Comics Group (Male Publ.)

#1	1.00	2.00	3.00
2-10	.50	1.00	1.50
11-30	.25	.50	.75
31-54		.20	.35

MODERN COMICS (Military #1-43)
#44, Nov, 1945 - #102, Oct, 1950
Quality Comics Group

	Good	Fine	Mint
#44	8.00	16.00	24.00
45-52: #49-1st app. Fear, Lady Adventuress	6.00	12.00	18.00
53-Torchy by Ward begins	8.00	16.00	24.00
54-60	6.00	12.00	18.00
61-80	5.00	10.00	15.00
81-101	4.00	8.00	12.00
102-(Scarce)	5.00	10.00	15.00

NOTE: *Crandall Blackhawk-#46-51,54,56-102.
Ward Blackhawk-#52,53,55 (15pgs. each). Torchy
in #53-102; by Ward only in early issues.*

MODERN LOVE
June-July, 1949 - #8, Aug-Sept, 1950
E.C. Comics

#1	30.00	60.00	90.00
2-Craig/Feldstein cover	20.00	40.00	60.00
3	15.00	30.00	45.00
4-6 (Scarce)	25.00	50.00	75.00
7,8	15.00	30.00	45.00

NOTE: *Feldstein art in most issues. Ingels
art in #1,2,4-7. (Canadian reprints known;
See Table of Contents)*

MOD LOVE
1967   (36 pgs.) (50¢)
Western Publishing Co.

#1	.20	.40	.60

MODNIKS, THE
Aug, 1967 - #2, Aug, 1970
Gold Key

#10206-708(#1),2		.10	.20

MOD SQUAD (TV)
Jan, 1969 - #8, April, 1971
Dell Publishing Co.

#1	.15	.30	.45
2-8: #8 reprints #2		.15	.30

MOD WHEELS
March, 1971 - #18, Oct, 1975
Gold Key

#1		.15	.30
2-18		.10	.20

MOE & SHMOE COMICS
Spring, 1948 - #2, Summer, 1948
O. S. Publ. Co.

Model Fun #4, © Harle Publ.

Modern Comics #51, © DC (Qua)

Modern Love #4, © WMG

The Monkees #10, © Dell

The Monster #2, © FH

Monster Crime #1, © Hill

	Good	Fine	Mint
(Moe & Shmoe cont'd)			
#1,2	1.00	2.00	3.00

MOLLY MANTON'S ROMANCES (My Love #3)
Sept, 1949 - #2, Nov, 1949
Marvel Comics

	Good	Fine	Mint
#1	1.00	2.00	3.00
2	.50	1.00	1.50

MOLLY O'DAY (Super Sleuth)
Feb, 1945
Avon Periodicals

	Good	Fine	Mint
#1-Molly O'Day, The Enchanted Dagger by C. Sultan?, Capt'n Courage, Corporal Grant app. (Scarce)	8.00	16.00	24.00

MONKEES, THE (TV)
March, 1967 - #17, Oct, 1969
Dell Publishing Co.

	Good	Fine	Mint
#1	.65	1.35	2.00
2-17: #17 reprints #1	.35	.70	1.05

MONKEY & THE BEAR, THE
Sept, 1953 - #3, Jan, 1954
Atlas Comics (ZPC)

	Good	Fine	Mint
#1-3	.35	.70	1.05

MONKEYSHINES COMICS
Summer, 1944 - #26, May, 1949
Ace Periodicals/Publishers Specialists/
Current Books

	Good	Fine	Mint
#1	1.35	2.75	4.00
2-10	1.00	2.00	3.00
11-26	.65	1.35	2.00

MONKEY SHINES OF MARSELEEN
1909 (11½x17") (28 pgs. in 2 colors)
Cupples & Leon Co.

	Good	Fine	Mint
By Norman E. Jennett	12.00	24.00	36.00

MONKEY'S UNCLE, THE (See Movie Comics under
Merlin Jones as the --)

MONROES, THE (TV)
April, 1967
Dell Publishing Co.

	Good	Fine	Mint
#1	.15	.30	.45

MONSTER
1953
Fiction House Magazines

	Good	Fine	Mint
#1-Dr. Drew by Grandenetti-Reprint from Rangers Comics	3.00	6.00	9.00
2	2.00	4.00	6.00

MONSTER CRIME COMICS
October, 1952
Hillman Periodicals

	Good	Fine	Mint
#1-(Rare)	7.00	14.00	21.00

MONSTER HOWLS (Magazine)
Dec, 1966 (Satire) (35¢) (68 pgs.)
Humor-Vision

	Good	Fine	Mint
#1	.35	.70	1.05

MONSTER HUNTERS
August, 1975 - #9, Jan, 1977; #10, Oct, 1977
Charlton Comics

	Good	Fine	Mint
#1-Howard art, Newton cvr.	.20	.40	.60
2-10	.15	.30	.45

NOTE: _Ditko_ story-#2. _Sutton_ story-#2,4;
cover-#2,4.

MONSTER OF FRANKENSTEIN (See Frankenstein)

MONSTERS ON THE PROWL (Chamber of Darkness
#1-8) (#13,14-52pgs.)
#9, 2/71 - #27, 11/73; #28, 6/74 - #30, 10/74
Marvel Comics Group

	Good	Fine	Mint
#9-Smith inks	.65	1.35	2.00
10-13,15	.25	.50	.75
14,17-30-All reprints	.15	.30	.45
16-Kull app.	1.00	2.00	3.00

NOTE: _Kirby_ reprints-#10-17,21,23,25,27,28,
30; covers-#9,25. _Kirby/Ditko_ reprints-#17,
18-20,22,24,26,29. _Marie/John Severin_ art-
#16(Kull). #9-13,15-contain _one_ new story.
Woodesque art by Reese-#11.

MONSTERS UNLEASHED (Magazine)
July, 1973 - #11, April, 1975 (B&W)
Marvel Comics Group

	Good	Fine	Mint
#1-Morrow cover	1.00	2.00	3.00
2-The Frankenstein Monster begins; Brunner reprint	.65	1.35	2.00
3-Adams cover; The Man-Thing begins (origin reprint by Morrow); Adams art	.65	1.35	2.00
4-Intro. & only app. Satana, the Devil's daughter-Krigstein reprt.	.65	1.35	2.00
5	.65	1.35	2.00
6-Ploog story	.65	1.35	2.00
7-Williamson reprint	.50	1.00	1.50

(Monsters Unl. cont'd)	Good	Fine	Mint
8-Adams reprint	.50	1.00	1.50
9-1st app. Wendigo	.40	.80	1.20
10,11: #11-Brunner cover	.40	.80	1.20
Annual #1(Summer, '75)	.40	.80	1.20

MONTANA KID, THE (See Kid Montana)

MONTE HALE WESTERN (Mary Marvel #1-28)
#29, Oct, 1948 - #88, 1955
Fawcett Publications/Charlton #51 on

	Good	Fine	Mint
#29(#1)	5.00	10.00	15.00
30-50	2.50	5.00	7.50
51-86,88	1.50	3.00	4.50
87-Wolverton reprint	2.00	4.00	6.00

MONTY HALL OF THE U.S. MARINES (See With the
August, 1951 - 1953   Marines--)
Toby Press

#1	1.00	2.00	3.00
2-6,8-11	.50	1.00	1.50
7-Powell Pin-Up Pete feature			
	2.00	4.00	6.00

A MOON, A GIRL...ROMANCE (Becomes Weird
Fantasy #13 on; formerly Moon Girl #1-8)
#9, Sept-Oct, 1949 - #12, Mar-Apr, 1950
E.C. Comics

#9-Moon Girl cameo	30.00	60.00	90.00
10,11	20.00	40.00	60.00
12-(Scarce)	27.50	55.00	82.50

NOTE: *Feldstein, Ingels art in all. Canadian
reprints known; see Table of Contents.*

MOON GIRL AND THE PRINCE (#1)
(Moon Girl #2-6; Moon Girl Fights Crime #7,8;
Becomes A Moon, A Girl, Romance #9 on)
Fall, 1947 - #8, Summer, 1949
E.C. Comics

#1-Origin Moon Girl by Moldoff(44 pgs.);			
Intro. Assistant, Star			
	35.00	70.00	105.00
2	20.00	40.00	60.00
3,4-Moon Girl vs. a vampire #4			
	15.00	30.00	45.00
5-E.C.'s 1st horror story			
	40.00	80.00	120.00
6-8 (Scarce)	25.00	50.00	75.00

*(#2 & #3 are 52pgs., #4 on, 36pgs. Canadian
reprints known; see Table of Contents.)*

MOON MULLINS
1927 - 1933 (48pgs.)(Daily B&W strip reprints)
Cupples & Leon Co.

	Good	Fine	Mint
Series 1('27)-By Willard	15.00	30.00	45.00
Series 2('28), Series 3('29), Series 4('30)			
	10.00	20.00	30.00
Series 5('31), 6('32), 7('33)			
	8.00	16.00	24.00
Big Book #1('30)-B&W	20.00	40.00	60.00

MOON MULLINS (See Superbook #3)
1941 - 1945
Dell Publishing Co.

Moon Mullins #1(STJ), © N.Y. News Synd.

4-Color #14(1941)	12.00	24.00	36.00
Large Feature Comic #29(1941)			
	9.00	18.00	27.00
4-Color #31(1943)	8.00	16.00	24.00
4-Color #81(1945)	4.00	8.00	12.00

MOON MULLINS
Dec-Jan, 1947-48 - #8, 1949   (52 pgs.)
Michel Publ. (St. John)

#1-Willard reprt., alternating Sunday & daily			
newspaper reprints	3.00	6.00	9.00
2-8-Willard reprint + Milt Gross-#8			
	2.00	4.00	6.00

MOON PILOT (See 4-Color Comics #1313)

MOON-SPINNERS, THE (See Movie Comics)

MOPSY (See TV Teens & Pageant of Comics)
Feb, 1948 - #19, Sept, 1953
St. John Publ. Co.

#1-Partial reprints; also reprints "Some			
Punkins" by Neher	3.00	6.00	9.00
2-19(1953)	2.00	4.00	6.00

Monte Hale #31, © Faw

Monty Hall--#7, © Toby

Moon Girl #7, © WMG

More Fun #7, © DC

More Fun #30, © DC

More Fun #59, © DC

MORE FUN COMICS (Formerly New Fun #1-6)
#7, 1/36 - #127, 4-5/49
National Periodical Publications

	Good	Fine	Mint
#7(1/36),#8(2/36)-Both oversized; lpg. Kelly in each	45.00	90.00	135.00
9(3-4/36)-11(7/36) Last soft cover & Henri Duval by Siegel & Shuster	33.00	66.50	100.00
12(8/36)-1st slick cover, V2#1(9/36,#13), V2#2(10/36,#14)-Dr. Occult in costume begins, ends #17	30.00	60.00	90.00
V2#3(11/36,#15),16(V2#4),17(V2#5) cover numbering begins #16	25.00	50.00	75.00
18-20(V2#8,5/37)	20.00	40.00	60.00
21(V2#9)-24(V2#12,9/37)	15.00	30.00	45.00
25(V3#1,10/37)-27(V3#3,12/37)	15.00	30.00	45.00
28-30: #30-1st non-funny cover	15.00	30.00	45.00
31-35: #32-Last Dr. Occult	13.50	26.75	40.00
36-40: #36-The Masked Ranger begins, ends #41	12.00	24.00	36.00
41-50	10.00	20.00	30.00
51-1st app. The Spectre(in costume) in one panel ad at end of Buccaneer story	20.00	40.00	60.00
52-Origin The Spectre(out of costume), Part 1 by Bernard Baily; last Wing Brady (Very Rare)	750.00	1500.00	2250.00
53-Origin The Spectre(out of costume), Part 2; Capt. Desmo begins (Rare)	500.00	1000.00	1500.00

(Prices vary widely on above 2 books)

54-The Spectre in costume; last King Carter	175.00	350.00	525.00
55-Intro. & 1st app. Dr. Fate; last Bulldog Martin	125.00	250.00	375.00
56-60: #56-Congo Bill begins	80.00	160.00	240.00
61-66: #63-Last St. Bob Neal. #64-Lance Larkin begins	60.00	120.00	180.00
67-Origin Dr. Fate; last Congo Bill & Biff Bronson	80.00	160.00	240.00
68-70: #68-Clip Carson begins. #70-Last Lance Larkin	50.00	100.00	150.00
71-Origin & 1st app. Johnny Quick	60.00	120.00	180.00
72-Dr. Fate's new helmet; last Sgt. Carey, Sgt. O'Malley & Capt. Desmo	40.00	80.00	120.00
73-Origin & 1st app. Aquaman; intro. Green Arrow	80.00	160.00	240.00
74-80: #76-Last Clip Carson; intro. Speedy	35.00	70.00	105.00

	Good	Fine	Mint
81-88: #85-Johnny Quick by Kubert begins, ends #97. #87-Last Radio Squad	25.00	50.00	75.00
89-Origin Green Arrow & Speedy Team-up	30.00	60.00	90.00
90-100: #93-Dover & Clover begin. #97-Kubert art. #98-Last Dr.Fate	15.00	30.00	45.00
101-Origin & 1st app. Superboy; last Spectre issue	70.00	140.00	210.00
102	25.00	50.00	75.00
103	20.00	40.00	60.00
104-107: #107-Last Johnny Quick & Superboy	18.00	36.00	54.00
108-120: #108-Genius Jones begins	2.50	5.00	7.50
121-124,126,127	1.50	3.00	4.50
125-(Scarce)-Superman on cover	10.00	20.00	30.00

NOTE: *The Spectre-#52-55,57-60,62-67. Dr.*
Fate-#55,56,61,68-76. The Green Arrow &
Speedy-#77-85,88-97,99,101; w/Dover & Clover-
#98,103. Johnny Quick-#86,87,100. Superboy-
#101,105; w/Dover & Clover-#102-107. Genius
Jones-#108-127.

More Fun #125, © DC

MORE SEYMOUR (See Seymour My Son)
Oct, 1963
Archie Publications

#1	.65	1.35	2.00

MORE TRASH FROM MAD (Annual)
1958 - #12, 1969
E.C. Comics

No#(1958)-8pgs. color Mad reprint from #20	5.00	10.00	15.00
#2(1959)-Market Product Labels	4.00	8.00	12.00

(More Trash From Mad cont'd)

	Good	Fine	Mint
3(1960)-Text book cvrs.	3.00	6.00	9.00
4(1961)-Sing along with Mad booklet			
	2.50	5.00	7.50
5(1962)-Window stickers-reprint from Mad			
#39	2.00	4.00	6.00
6(1963)-TV Guise booklet	2.00	4.00	6.00
7(1964)-Alfred E. Newman commemorative			
stamps	1.75	3.35	5.00
8(1965)-Life size poster-A.E. Newman			
	1.75	3.35	5.00
9,10('66,'67)-Mischief sticker			
	1.75	3.35	5.00
11(1968)-Campaign poster & bumper sticker			
	1.75	3.35	5.00
12(1969)-Pocket medals	1.75	3.35	5.00

NOTE: *Kelly Freas* covers-#1,2,4. *Mingo* cov-
ers-#3,5-9.

MORGAN THE PIRATE (See 4-Color Comics #1227)

MORLOCK 2001 (--& the Midnight Men #3)
Feb, 1974 - #3, July, 1975
Atlas/Seaboard Publ.

#1-Origin	.25	.50	.75
2	.20	.40	.60
3-Ditko/Wrightson story; origin The Midnight			
Man & The Midnight Men	.25	.50	.75

MORTIE (Mazie's Friend)
Dec, 1952 - #3, June, 1953
Magazine Publishers/Harvey Publications

#1-3	.65	1.35	2.00

MORTY MEEKLE (See 4-Color Comics #793)

MOSES & THE TEN COMMANDMENTS
1957 (100 pgs.) (25¢)
Dell Publishing Co.

#1-Not based on movie; Dell's adaptation			
	1.50	3.00	4.50

MOTHER GOOSE (See Christmas With Mother
Goose & 4-Color #41,59,68, & 862)

MOTION PICTURE COMICS (See Faw. Movie Comics)
1950 - #114, Jan, 1953
Fawcett Publications

#101-"The Vanishing Westerner"-Monte Hale			
('50)	5.00	10.00	15.00
102-"Code of the Silver Sage"-Rocky Lane			
(1/51)	5.00	10.00	15.00
103-"Covered Wagon Raid"-Rockey Lane(3/51)			
	5.00	10.00	15.00

	Good	Fine	Mint
104-"Vigilante Hideout"-Rocky Lane (5/51)			
	5.00	10.00	15.00
105-"Red Badge of Courage"-Audie Murphy;			
Bob Powell art(7/51)	6.00	12.00	18.00
106-"The Texas Rangers"-George Montgomery			
(9/51)	5.00	10.00	15.00
107-"Frisco Tronado"-Rocky Lane (11/51)			
	5.00	10.00	15.00
108-"Mask of the Avenger"-John Derek			
	5.00	10.00	15.00
109-"Rough Rider of Durango"-Rocky Lane			
	5.00	10.00	15.00
110-"When Worlds Collide"-George Evans art			
(1951) (Scarce)	10.00	20.00	30.00
111-"The Vanishing Outpost"-Lash LaRue			
	5.00	10.00	15.00
112-"Brave Warrior"-Jon Hall & Jay Silver-			
heels	4.00	8.00	12.00
113-"Walk East on Beacon"-George Murphy;			
Shaffenberger art	4.00	8.00	12.00
114-"Cripple Creek"-George Montgomery			
(1/53)	4.00	8.00	12.00

MOTION PICTURE FUNNIES WEEKLY
1939 (36 pgs.)(Giveaway)(Black & White)
(No month given; last panel in Sub-Mariner
story dated 4/39) (Also see Green Giant &
Invaders #20)
First Funnies, Inc.

#1-Origin & 1st app. Sub-Mariner by Bill			
Everett(8pgs.)-Reprinted in Marvel Myst-			
ery #1 with color added over the craft			
tint which was used to shade the black &			
white version; Spy Ring, American Ace			
(reprinted in Marvel Mystery #3) app.			
(Extremely Rare)-only five(5) known			
copies	2000.00	4000.00	6000.00

NOTE: The only five known copies (with a sixth suspected) were
discovered in 1974 in the estate of the deceased publisher. Covers
only to issues No. 2-4 were also found which evidently were
printed in advance along with No. 1. No. 1 was to be distributed
only through motion picture movie houses. However it is believed
that only advanced copies were sent out and the motion picture
houses not going for the idea. Possible distribution at local
theatres in Boston suspected. The last panel of Sub-Mariner
contains a rectangular box with "Continued Next Week" printed
in it. When reprinted in M. Mystery, the box was left in with
lettering omitted.

MOUNTAIN MEN (See Ben Bowie)

MOUSE MUSKETEERS (Formerly The Two Mouseketeers)
Jan, 1956 - 1962 (M-G-M)
Dell Publishing Co.

4-Color #670,711,728,764	.50	1.00	1.50
#8-21(4/57-3/60)	.35	.70	1.05
4-Color #1135,1175,1290	.40	.80	1.20

Mortie #1, © Harv

Motion Picture Comics #104, © Faw

Motion Picture Funnies Weekly #1, © MCG

Dracula The Mummy--, © Dell

Circus World, © Dell

El Dorado, © Dell

MOUSE ON THE MOON, THE (See Movie Classics)

MOVIE CLASSICS
January, 1953 - Dec, 1969
Dell Publishing Co.

(Before 1962, most movie adaptations were part of the 4-Color Series)

	Good	Fine	Mint
Around the World Under the Sea-#12-030-612 (12/66-Dell)	1.00	2.00	3.00
Bambi-#3(4/56-Dell)-Disney; reprints 4-Color #186	1.35	2.75	4.00
Battle of the Bulge-#12-056-606(6/66-Dell)	.65	1.35	2.00
Beach Blanket Bingo-#12-058-509(Dell)	1.00	2.00	3.00
Bon Voyage-#01-068-212(12/62-Dell)-Disney	1.00	2.00	3.00
Castilian, The-#12-110-401(Dell)	.65	1.35	2.00
Cat, The-#12-109-612(12/66-Dell)	.65	1.35	2.00
Cheyenne Autumn-#12-112-506(4-6/65-Dell)	1.35	2.75	4.00
Circus World, Samuel Bronston's-#12-115-411 (Dell)	1.00	2.00	3.00
Countdown-#12-150-710(10/67-Dell)	.65	1.35	2.00
Creature, The-#1(12-142-302)12-2/62-63-Dell)	1.00	2.00	3.00
Creature, The-#12-142-410(10/64-Dell)	.65	1.35	2.00
David Ladd's Life Story-#12173-212(10-12/62-Dell)	1.00	2.00	3.00
Die, Monster, Die-#12-175-603(3/66-Dell)	1.00	2.00	3.00
Dirty Dozen-#12-180-710(10/67-Dell)	1.00	2.00	3.00
Dr. Who & the Daleks-#12-190-612(12/66-Dell)	.65	1.35	2.00
Dracula-#12-231-212(10-12/62-Dell)	1.00	2.00	3.00
El Dorado-#12-240-710(10/67-Dell)	1.00	2.00	3.00
Ensign Pulver-#12-257-410(8-10/64-Dell)	.65	1.35	2.00
Frankenstein-#12-283-304(3-5/63-Dell)	1.00	2.00	3.00
Great Race, The-#12-299-603(3/66-Dell)	.80	1.60	2.40
Hallelujah Trail, The-#12-307-602(2/66-Dell) (Says 1/66 inside)	1.00	2.00	3.00
Hatari-#12-340-301(1/63-Dell)	.80	1.60	2.40
Horizontal Lieutenant, The-#01-348-210(10/62-Dell)	.80	1.60	2.40
Incredible Mr. Limpet, The-#12-370-408(Dell)	.80	1.60	2.40

	Good	Fine	Mint
Jack the Giant Killer-#12-374-301(1/63-Dell)	1.35	2.75	4.00
Jason & the Argonauts-#12-376-310(8-10/63-Dell)	1.75	3.35	5.00
Lady and the Tramp-#1(6/55-Dell Giant,100pgs) Disney	1.00	2.00	3.00
Lancelot & Guinevere-#12-416-310(10/63-Dell)	1.00	2.00	3.00
Lawrence-#12-426-308(8/63-Dell)-Story of Lawrence of Arabia-Movie ad on back cover; not exactly like movie	1.00	2.00	3.00
Lion of Sparta-#12-439-301(1/63-Dell)	.80	1.60	2.40
Longest Day, The-('62-Dell).65	1.35	2.00	
Mad Monster Party-#12-460-801(9/67-Dell)	.50	1.00	1.50
Magic Sword, The-#01-496-209(9/62-Dell)	1.35	2.75	4.00
Masque of the Red Death-#12-490-410(8-10/64-Dell)	1.00	2.00	3.00
Maya-#12-495-612(12/66-Dell)	.65	1.35	2.00
McHale's Navy-#12-500-412(10-12/64-Dell)	.65	1.35	2.00
Merrill's Marauders-#12-510-301(1/63-Dell)	.65	1.35	2.00
Mouse on the Moon, The-#12-530-312(10-12/63-Dell)	1.00	2.00	3.00
Mummy, The-#12-537-211(9-11/62-Dell) 2 different back cvr. ishs.	1.00	2.00	3.00
Music Man, The-#12-538-301(1/63-Dell)	.80	1.60	2.40
Naked Prey, The-#12-545-612(12/66-Dell)	.80	1.60	2.40
Night of the Grizzly, The-#12-558-612(12/66-Dell)	.65	1.35	2.00
None But the Brave-#12-565-506(4-6/65-Dell)	.80	1.60	2.40
Operation Bikini-#12-597-310(10/63-Dell)	.65	1.35	2.00
Operation Crossbow-#12-590-512(10-12/65-Dell)	.50	1.00	1.50
Peter Pan Treasure Chest-#1(1/53-Dell)-Disney; contains movie adaptation plus other stories	7.00	14.00	21.00
Prince & the Pauper, The-#01-654-207(5-7/62-Dell)-Disney	1.00	2.00	3.00
Raven, The-#12-680-309(9/63-Dell)	1.00	2.00	3.00
Ring of Bright Water-#01-701-910(10/69-Dell, inside #12-701-909)	.65	1.35	2.00
Runaway, The-#12-707-412(10-12/64-Dell)	.65	1.35	2.00
Santa Claus Conquers the Martians-#12-725-603 (3/66-Dell)	.65	1.35	2.00
Six Black Horses-#12-750-301(1/63-Dell)	.65	1.35	2.00

(Movie Classics cont'd)   Good   Fine   Mint

Ski Party-#12-743-511(9-11/65-Dell)
                1.00   2.00   3.00

Sleeping Beauty-#1(1959-Dell Giant,100 pgs.)
  Disney   1.00   2.00   3.00

Smoky-#12-746-702(2/67-Dell)
                .65   1.35   2.00

Sons of Katie Elder-#12-748-511(9-11/65-Dell)
                .65   1.35   2.00

Sword of Lancelot-(1963-Dell)
               1.35   2.75   4.00

Tales of Terror-#12-793-302(2/63-Dell)
                1.00   2.00   3.00

Taras Bulba-(1962-Dell) 2.00   4.00   6.00

Three Stooges Meet Hercules-#01828-208(8/62-Dell)
               1.75   3.35   5.00

Tomb of Ligeia-#12-830-506(4-6/65-Dell)
                1.00   2.00   3.00

Treasure Island-#01-845-211(7-9/62-Dell)-Disney; reprts.4-Color#624 .65   1.35   2.00

Twice Told Tales-#12-840-401(11-1/63-64-Dell)
                1.00   2.00   3.00

Two on a Guillotine-#12-850-506(4-6/65-Dell)
                .65   1.35   2.00

Universal Presents-Dracula-The Mummy & Other Stories-#02-530-311(9-11/63-Dell Giant, 84pgs.)-reprints Dracula #12-231-212, The Mummy #12-537-211, & part of Ghost Stories #1   1.35   2.75   4.00

Valley of Gwangi-#01-880-912(12/69-Dell)
               1.35   2.75   4.00

War Gods of the Deep-#12-900-509(7-9/65-Dell)
                1.00   2.00   3.00

War Wagon, The-#12-533-709(9/67-Dell)
                1.00   2.00   3.00

Who's Minding the Mint?-#12-924-708(8/67-Dell)
                .50   1.00   1.50

Wolfman, The-#12-922-308(6-8/63-Dell)
                1.00   2.00   3.00

Wolfman, The-#1(12-922-410)(8-10/64-Dell)-
  2nd printing(reprints #12-922-308)
                .40   .80   1.20

Zulu-#12-950-410(8-10/64-Dell)
                .80   1.60   2.40

MOVIE COMICS (See Fawcett Movie Comics)

MOVIE COMICS
April, 1939 - #6, Sept, 1939
National Periodical Publications

#1-"Gunga Din","Son of Frankenstein","The Great Man Votes","Fisherman's Wharf", & "Scouts to the Rescue" part I; Wheelan "Minute Movies" begin-50.00 100.00 150.00
 2-"Stagecoach","The Saint Strikes Back", "King of the Turf","Scouts to the Rescue" part II,"Arizona Legion"

                Good   Fine   Mint
                30.00 60.00 90.00

 3-"East Side of Heaven","Mystery in the White Room","Four Feathers","Mexican Rose" with Gene Autry,"Spirit of Culver","Many Secrets","The Mikado" 30.00 60.00 90.00

 4-"Captain Fury", Gene Autry in "Blue Montana Skies","Streets of N.Y." with Jackie Cooper, "Oregon Trail" part I with Johnny Mack Brown, "Big Town Czar" with Barton MacLane, & "Star Reporter" with Warren Hull   30.00 60.00 90.00

 5-"Man in the Iron Mask","Five Came Back", "Wolf Call","The Girl & the Gambler","The House of Fear","The Family Next Door", "Oregon Trail" part II
                30.00 60.00 90.00

 6-"The Phantom Creeps","Chumps at Oxford", & "The Oregon Trail" part III
                35.00 70.00 105.00

MOVIE COMICS
Dec, 1946 - 1947
Fiction House Magazines

#1-Big Town & Johnny Danger begin-Celardo art   4.00   8.00 12.00
 2-"White Tie & Tails" with William Bendix; Mitzi of the Movies begins by Matt Baker, ends #4   3.00   6.00   9.00
 3-Andy Hardy   3.00   6.00   9.00
 4-Slave Girl by M.Baker 4.00   8.00 12.00

MOVIE COMICS
Oct, 1962 - March, 1972
Gold Key/Whitman

Alice in Wonderland-#10144-503(3/65-G.Key)
  Disney; partial reprint of 4-Color #331
                .50   1.00   1.50

Aristocats, The-#1(30045-103)(3/71-G.Key)
  Disney; with pull-out poster(25c)
                .35   .70   1.05

Bambi #1(10087-309)(9/63-G.Key)-Disney; reprints 4-Color #186 .50   1.00   1.50

Bambi #2(10087-607)(7/66-G.Key)-Disney; reprints 4-Color #186 .40   .80   1.20

Beneath the Planet of the Apes-#30044-012 (12/70-G.Key)-with pull-out poster
                1.00   2.00   3.00

Big Red-#10026-211(11/62-G.Key)-Disney
                .65   1.35   2.00

Big Red-#10026-503(3/65-G.Key)-Disney; reprints #10026-211 .65   1.35   2.00

Blackbeard's Ghost-#10222-806(6/68-G.Key)
  Disney   .80   1.60   2.40

Bullwhip Griffin-#10181-706(3/67-G.Key)-
  Disney   .65   1.35   2.00

The Three Stooges--, © Dell

Movie #1, © FH

55 Days At Peking, © GK

285

Lt. Robin Crusoe, © GK   Those Magnificent--, © GK   Toby Tyler, © GK

(Movie Comics cont'd)

	Good	Fine	Mint
Captain Sindbad-#10077-309(9/63-G.Key)-			
Manning art	1.35	2.75	4.00
Chitty Chitty Bang Bang-#1(30038-902)(2/69-			
G.Key)-with pull-out poster			
	1.35	2.75	4.00
Cinderella-#10152-508(8/65-G.Key)-Disney; re-			
prints 4-Color #786	.65	1.35	2.00
Darby O'Gill & the Little People-#1(10251-001)			
(1/70-G.Key)-Disney; reprint 4-Color			
#1024 (Toth)	1.20	2.40	3.60
Dumbo #1(10090-310)(10/63-G.Key)-Disney; re-			
prints 4-Color #668	.50	1.00	1.50
Emil & the Detectives-#10120-502(2/65-G.Key)			
Disney	.80	1.60	2.40
Escapade in Florence-#1(10043-301)(1/63-G.			
Key)-Disney; starring Annette			
	1.00	2.00	3.00
Fall of the Roman Empire-#10118-407(7/64-			
G.Key)	1.00	2.00	3.00
Fantastic Voyage-#10178-702(2/67-G.Key)-Wood/			
Adkins art	1.35	2.75	4.00
55 Days at Peking-#10081-309(9/63-G.Key)			
	.80	1.60	2.40
Fighting Prince of Donegal, The-#10193-701			
(1/67-G.Key)-Disney	1.00	2.00	3.00
First Men in the Moon-#10132-503(3/65-G.Key)			
	.80	1.60	2.40
Gay Purr-ee-#1(30017-301)(1/63-G.Key Giant,			
84pgs.)	.65	1.35	2.00
Gnome Mobile, The-#10207-710(10/67-G.Key)			
Disney	.65	1.35	2.00
Goodbye, Mr. Chips-#10246-006(6/70-G.Key)			
	.50	1.00	1.50
Happiest Millionaire, The-#10221-804(4/68-			
G.Key)-Disney	.65	1.35	2.00
Hey There, It's Yogi Bear-#10122-409(9/64-			
G.Key)-Hanna-Barbera	.35	.70	1.05
Horse Without a Head, The-#10109-401(1/64-			
G.Key)-Disney	.65	1.35	2.00
How the West Was Won-#1(10074-307)(7/63-			
G.Key)	1.00	2.00	3.00
In Search of the Castaways-#10048-303(3/63-			
G.Key)-Disney	.80	1.60	2.40
Jungle Book, The-#1(6022-801)(1/68-Whitman)			
Disney; large size(10x13½") (59¢)			
	1.00	2.00	3.00
Jungle Book, The-#1(30033-803)(3/68-G.Key)-			
Disney; same contents as Whitman #1			
	.50	1.00	1.50
Kidnapped-#10080-306(6/63-G.Key)-Disney; re-			
prints 4-Color #1101	.50	1.00	1.50
King Kong-#1(30036-809)(9/68-G.Key Giant,			
68pgs.)-painted cover	2.00	4.00	6.00
Lady and the Tramp-#10042-301(1/63-G.Key)-			
Disney; reprints 4-Color #629			
	.65	1.35	2.00
Lady and the Tramp-#1(1967-G.Key Giant 25¢)-			

	Good	Fine	Mint
Disney; reprints part of Dell #1			
	.35	.70	1.05
Lady and the Tramp-#2(10042-203)(3/72-G.Key)			
Disney; reprints 4-Color #629			
	.50	1.00	1.50
Legend of Lobo, The-#1(10059-303)(3/63-G.Key)			
Disney	.65	1.35	2.00
Lt. Robin Crusoe, U.S.N.-#10191-610(10/66-			
G.Key)-Disney	.65	1.35	2.00
Lion, The-#10035-301(1/63-G.Key)			
	.65	1.35	2.00
Lord Jim-#10156-509(9/65-G.Key)			
	.65	1.35	.200
Love Bug, The-#10237-906(6/69-G.Key)-Disney			
	.65	1.35	2.00
Mary Poppins-#10136-501(1/65-G.Key)-Disney			
	1.00	2.00	3.00
Mary Poppins-#30023-501(1/65-G.Key Giant,			
68 pgs.)-Disney	1.75	3.35	5.00
McLintock-#10110-403(3/64-G.Key)			
	.65	1.35	2.00
Merlin Jones as the Monkey's Uncle-#10115-510			
(10/65-G.Key)-Disney	.65	1.35	2.00
Miracle of the White Stallions, The-#10065-			
306(6/63-G.Key)-Disney	.65	1.35	2.00
Misadventures of Merlin Jones, The-#10115-405			
(5/64-G.Key)-Disney	.65	1.35	2.00
Moon-Spinners, The-#10124-410(10/64-G.Key)			
Disney	1.00	2.00	3.00
Mutiny on the Bounty-#1(10040-302)(2/63-			
G.Key)	.80	1.60	2.40
Nikki, Wild Dog of the North-#10141-412			
(12/64-G.Key)-Disney; reprints 4-Color			
#1226	.65	1.35	2.00
Old Yeller-#10168-601(1/66-G.Key)-Disney;			
reprints 4-Color #869	.65	1.35	2.00
Old Yeller-(1968-G.Key)-Disney; reprint			
	.50	1.00	1.50
One Hundred & One Dalmations-#1(10247-002)			
(2/70-G.Key)-Disney; reprints 4-Color			
#1183	.65	1.35	2.00
Peter Pan-#1(10086-309)(9/63-G.Key)-Disney;			
reprints 4-Color #442	.65	1.35	2.00
Peter Pan-#2(10086-909)(9/69-G.Key)-Disney;			
reprints 4-Color #442	.35	.70	1.05
P.T. 109-#10123-409(9/64-G.Key)-John F.			
Kennedy	1.20	2.40	3.60
Rio Conchos-#10143-503(3/65-G.Key)			
	.65	1.35	2.00
Robin Hood-#10163-506(6/65-G.Key)-Disney;			
reprints 4-Color #413	.65	1.35	2.00
Shaggy Dog & the Absent-Minded Professor-			
#30032-708(8/67-G.Key Giant, 68pgs.)-			
Disney; reprints 4-Color #985,1199			
	.65	1.35	2.00
Sleeping Beauty-#1(30042-009)(9/70-G.Key)-			
Disney; reprints 4-Color #973; with pull-			
out poster	.40	.80	1.20

(Movie Comics cont'd)

	Good	Fine	Mint
Snow White & the Seven Dwarfs-#1(10091-310) (10/63-G.Key)-Disney; reprints 4-Color #382	.65	1.35	2.00
Snow White & the Seven Dwarfs-#10091-709 (9/67-G.Key)-Disney; reprints 4-Color #382	.50	1.00	1.50
Son of Flubber-#1(10057-304)(4/63-G.Key)- Disney; sequel to "The Absent-Minded Professor"	.65	1.35	2.00
Summer Magic-#10076-309(9/63-G.Key)-Disney; Manning art	1.50	3.00	4.50
Swiss Family Robinson-#10236-904(4/69-G.Key) Disney; reprints 4-Color #1156	.65	1.35	2.00
Sword in the Stone, The-#30019-402(2/64-G.Key Giant, 84pgs.)-Disney	1.00	2.00	3.00
That Darn Cat-#10171-602(2/66-G.Key)-Disney	.80	1.60	2.40
Those Magnificent Men in Their Flying Machines-#10162-510(10/65-G.Key)	.80	1.60	2.40
Three Stooges in Orbit-#30016-211(11/62-G. Key Giant, 32pgs.)-all photos from movie	2.00	4.00	6.00
Tiger Walks, A-#10117-406(6/64-G.Key)-Disney; Torres art	1.35	2.75	4.00
Toby Tyler-#10142-502(2/65-G.Key)-Disney; reprints 4-Color #1092	.60	1.20	1.80
Treasure Island-#1(10200-703)(3/67-G.Key)- Disney; reprts.4C-#624	.50	1.00	1.50
20,000 Leagues Under the Sea-#1(10095-312) (12/63-G.Key)-Disney; reprints 4-Color #614	.65	1.35	2.00
Wonderful Adventures of Pinocchio, The-#1 (10089-310)(10/63-G.Key)-Disney; reprints 4-Color #545	.50	1.00	1.50
Wonderful Adventures of Pinocchio, The-#10089-109(9/71-G.Key)-Disney; reprints 4-Color #545	.35	.70	1.05
Wonderful World of the Brothers Grimm-#1 (10008-210)(10/62-G.Key)	.80	1.60	2.40
X, the Man with the X-Ray Eyes-#10083-309 (9/63-G.Key)	.80	1.60	2.40
Yellow Submarine-#35000-902(2/69-G.Key Giant 68 pgs.)with pull-out poster; The Beatles cartoon movie	7.00	14.00	21.00

MOVIE LOVE (See Personal Love)
Feb, 1950 - #21, June, 1953
Famous Funnies

	Good	Fine	Mint
#1	1.75	3.35	5.00
2-7,9	1.20	2.40	3.60
8-Williamson/Frazetta story, 6 pgs.	25.00	50.00	75.00
10-Frazetta story, 6 pgs. (Rare)	30.00	60.00	90.00

	Good	Fine	Mint
11-16	1.00	2.00	3.00
17-1pg. Frazetta ad	1.50	3.00	4.50
18-21	1.00	2.00	3.00

NOTE: *Each issue has a full-length movie adaptation with photo covers.*

MOVIE THRILLERS
1949
Magazine Enterprises

	Good	Fine	Mint
#1-"Rope of Sand" with Burt Lancaster	5.00	10.00	15.00

MOVIE TOWN ANIMAL ANTICS (Formerly Animal Antics; Raccoon Kids #52 on)
#20, May-June, 1949 - #51, Jul-Aug, 1954
National Periodical Publications

	Good	Fine	Mint
#20-51-Raccoon Kids continue	.65	1.35	2.00

MOVIE TUNES (Frankie #4 on)(Also see Animated--)
Spring, 1946 - #3, Fall, 1946
Marvel Comics (MgPC)

	Good	Fine	Mint
#1-Super Rabbit	1.50	3.00	4.50
2,3-Super Rabbit	.80	1.60	2.40

MOWGLI JUNGLE BOOK (See 4-Color #487,582,620)

MR. (See Mister)

MS. MARVEL
January, 1977 - Present
Marvel Comics Group

	Good	Fine	Mint
#1-Buscema art	.40	.80	1.20
2-Origin	.25	.50	.75
3-5	.20	.40	.60
6-13	.15	.30	.45

NOTE: *Buscema stories-#1-3; covers-#2,4,7,8. Starlin cover-#12.*

MUGGSY MOUSE
1951 - 1954
Magazine Enterprises

	Good	Fine	Mint
#1(A-1#33),2(A-1#36),3(A-1#39), 4(A-1#95)	.50	1.00	1.50
Super Reprint #14('63)	.20	.40	.60
I.W. Reprint #1,2(no date)	.20	.40	.60

MUGGY-DOO, BOY CAT
July, 1953 - #4, Jan, 1954
Standard Publications

	Good	Fine	Mint
#1-4	.65	1.35	2.00

Movie Love =1. © FF

Movie Thrillers =1. © ME

Muggsy Mouse =1. © ME

Murder, Inc. =4. © Fox

Mutiny =1. © Aragon

Mutt & Jeff =13(C&L). © Ball Synd.

(Muggy-Doo cont'd)	Good	Fine	Mint
Super Reprint #12('63),#16('64)			
	.20	.40	.60

MUMMY, THE (See Movie Classics)

MUNSTERS, THE (TV)
Jan, 1965 - #16, Jan, 1968
Gold Key

#1(10134-501)	.50	1.00	1.50
2-16	.20	.40	.60

MURDER, INC. (My Private Life #16 on)
1/48 - #15, 12/49;(No #10, 2 #9's); 6/50 -
#3, 8/51
Fox Features Syndicate

#1(1st Series)	5.00	10.00	15.00
2-7,9(3/49),9(4/49),11-15			
	2.50	5.00	7.50
8-Used in Seduction of the Innocent			
	4.00	8.00	12.00
5(6/50)(2nd Series)-Formerly My Desire			
	2.00	4.00	6.00
3(8/51)	1.50	3.00	4.50

MURDEROUS GANGSTERS
July, 1951 - #4, June, 1952
Avon Periodicals/Realistic #3 on

#1-Pretty Boy Floyd, Leggs Diamond; 1 pg.			
Wood	4.00	8.00	12.00
2-Baby Face Nelson; 1pg. Wood,			
3,4	2.00	4.00	6.00

MURDER TALES (Magazine)
V1#10, 11/70 - V1#11, 1/71   (52pgs.)
World Famous Publications

V1#10-1pg. Frazetta ad	1.00	2.00	3.00
11-Guardineer reprint	.50	1.00	1.50

MUSHMOUSE AND PUNKIN PUSS (TV)
Sept, 1965   (Hanna-Barbera)
Gold Key

#1(10153-509)		.10	.20

MUSIC MAN, THE (See Movie Classics)

MUTINY (Stormy Tales of Seven Seas)
Oct, 1954 - #3, Feb, 1955
Aragon Magazines

#1	1.00	2.00	3.00
2-Capt. Mutiny, #3	.65	1.35	2.00

MUTINY ON THE BOUNTY (See Movie Comics)

MUTT & JEFF (-- Cartoon, The)
1911 - 1914 (5-3/4x15-1/2")(Hardcover-B&W)
Ball Publications Co.

	Good	Fine	Mint
#1(1911)by Bud Fisher	20.00	40.00	60.00
2(1911),3-5(1914)	15.00	30.00	45.00

NOTE: *Above books were reprinted for several years after issued.*

MUTT & JEFF
1916 - 1933 (B&W dailies)(16x11" large hard-
Cupples & Leon Co.   cover comic;48pgs.)

#6-10-by Bud Fisher	10.00	20.00	30.00
11-22	8.00	16.00	24.00
No#(1920)(16x11",20pgs. reprints 1919 Sunday			
strips)(Advs.of--)	8.00	16.00	24.00
Big Book #1-(1928)-Thick book(hardcovers)			
w/dust jacket	20.00	40.00	60.00
Big Book #2-(1929)-Thick book (hardcovers)			
w/dust jacket	20.00	40.00	60.00

NOTE: *The Big Books contain three previous issues rebound.*

MUTT & JEFF
1921   (9x15")
Embee Publ. Co.

Sunday strips in color	25.00	50.00	75.00

MUTT AND JEFF
Summer, 1940 - #148, Nov, 1965
All American/National #1-103(6/58)/Dell #104-
115(10-12/59)/Harvey #116(2/60)-148

#1(No#)-Lost Wheels	30.00	60.00	90.00
2(No#)-Charging Bull	15.00	30.00	45.00
3(No#)-Bucking Broncos	10.00	20.00	30.00
4,5	8.00	16.00	24.00
6-10	5.00	10.00	15.00
11-20	2.50	5.00	7.50
21-30	1.75	3.35	5.00
31-74-Last Fisher ish.	1.00	2.00	3.00
75-100	.65	1.35	2.00
101-148	.50	1.00	1.50
--Jokes #1-3(1960-61, Harvey, 84 pgs.)			
	.65	1.35	2.00
--New Jokes #1-4(10/63-'65, Harvey, 68pgs.)			
	.40	.80	1.20

NOTE: *Issues #1-74 by Bud Fisher. #86 on by Al Smith. Issues from 1963 on have Fisher reprints. Clarification: early issues signed by Fisher are mostly drawn by Smith.*

MUTTSY, THE TALKING DOG (See Harvey Hits
Magazine #84,87,92)

MY CONFESSIONS (My Confession #7; formerly
Western True Crime; A Spec. Feat. Mag. #11 on)

(My Confessions cont'd)
#7, Aug, 1949 - #10, Jan-Feb, 1950
Fox Features Syndicate

	Good	Fine	Mint
#7-Wood story, 10pgs.	4.00	8.00	12.00
8-Wood story	3.00	6.00	9.00
9,10	1.00	2.00	3.00

MY DATE COMICS
July, 1947 - V1#4, Jan, 1948
Hillman Periodicals

#1-4-S&K + Dan Barry art	3.00	6.00	9.00

MY DESIRE (Formerly Jo-Jo)(Murder, Inc. #5 on)
#30, Aug, 1949 - #4, April, 1950
Fox Features Syndicate

#30,31(#1,2)	1.35	2.75	4.00
32(12/49)-Wood story	3.00	6.00	9.00
3,4	1.00	2.00	3.00

MY DIARY
December, 1949
Marvel Comics (A Lovers Mag.)

#1	1.00	2.00	3.00

MY DOG TIGE (Buster Brown's Dog)
1957   (Giveaway)
Buster Brown Shoes

	1.00	2.00	3.00

MY EXPERIENCE (Formerly All Top; Judy Canova
#19, Sept, 1949 - #22, Mar, 1950   #23 on)
Fox Feaures Syndicate

#19-Wood story	4.00	8.00	12.00
20	1.00	2.00	3.00
21-Two Wood stories	4.00	8.00	12.00
22-Wood story, 9pgs.	3.00	6.00	9.00

MY FAVORITE MARTIAN (TV)
Jan, 1964 - #15, Feb-Apr, 1968
Gold Key

#1-Russ Manning art	.80	1.60	2.40
2-15	.25	.50	.75

MY FRIEND IRMA (Radio/TV)
#3, June, 1950 - #47, Sept, 1954; #48, 2/55
Marvel/Atlas Comics(BFP)

#3	1.35	2.75	4.00
4-Kurtzman story, 10pgs.	5.00	10.00	15.00
5-"Egghead Doodle" by Kurtzman, 4pgs.			
	3.00	6.00	9.00

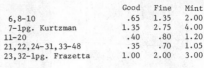

	Good	Fine	Mint
6,8-10	.65	1.35	2.00
7-1pg. Kurtzman	1.35	2.75	4.00
11-20	.40	.80	1.20
21,22,24-31,33-48	.35	.70	1.05
23,32-1pg. Frazetta	1.00	2.00	3.00

MY GIRL PEARL
April, 1955 - #6, 9/57; #7, 8/60 - #16, 1961
Atlas Comics

#1	.50	1.00	1.50
2-16	.25	.50	.75

My Greatest Adventure #20, © DC

MY GREATEST ADVENTURE (Doom Patrol #86 on)
Jan-Feb, 1955 - #85, Feb, 1964
National Periodical Publications

#1-Before CCA	8.00	16.00	24.00
2-5	4.00	8.00	12.00
6-10	2.00	4.00	6.00
11-16,19,22-27,29,30	1.35	2.75	4.00
17,18-Kirby story/cvr-#18	2.00	4.00	6.00
20,21,28-Kirby art	1.50	3.00	4.50
31-57,59	.65	1.35	2.00
58,60,61,77-Toth art	1.00	2.00	3.00
62-76,78,79	.35	.70	1.05
80-Intro. Doom Patrol	.65	1.35	2.00
81,85-Toth art	.50	1.00	1.50
82-84	.35	.70	1.05

NOTE: _Anderson_ _story-#42._

MY GREATEST THRILLS IN BASEBALL
       (16 pg. Giveaway)
Mission of California

By Mickey Mantle	1.00	2.00	3.00

MY GREAT LOVE
Oct, 1949 - #4, Apr, 1950
Fox Features Syndicate

My Date #4, © Hill

My Desire #3, © Fox

My Experience #21, © Fox

My Great Love #2, © Fox

My Life #4, © Fox

My Little Margie #27, © CC

(My Great Love cont'd)	Good	Fine	Mint
#1	1.35	2.75	4.00
2-4	1.00	2.00	3.00

MY INTIMATE AFFAIR (Inside Crime #3)
1950
Fox Features Syndicate

	Good	Fine	Mint
#1,2	1.00	2.00	3.00

MY LIFE (Meet Corliss Archer #1-3)
#4, Sept, 1948 - #15, July, 1950
Fox Features Syndicate

#4,6-Kamen/Feldstein art?	2.50	5.00	7.50
5,7-15	1.00	2.00	3.00

MY LITTLE MARGIE (TV)
1954 - #54, Nov, 1964
Charlton Comics

#1	.65	1.35	2.00
2-20	.25	.50	.75
21-53	.15	.30	.45
54-Beatles on cover; lead story spoofs the Beatle haircut craze of the '60's			
	1.75	3.35	5.00

MY LITTLE MARGIE'S BOY FRIENDS
1955 - 1961
Charlton Comics

#1	.50	1.00	1.50
2-20	.25	.50	.75
21-38	.15	.30	.45

MY LITTLE MARGIE'S FASHIONS
Feb, 1959 - #5, 1959
Charlton Comics

#1	.35	.70	1.05

	Good	Fine	Mint
2-5	.20	.40	.60

MY LOVE (Formerly Molly Manton's Romances
July, 1949 - #3, Jan, 1950   #1 & 2)
Marvel Comics (CDS)

#1(7/49)	1.20	2.40	3.60
3(1/50)	.65	1.35	2.00

MY LOVE
Sept, 1969 - #39, Mar, 1976
Marvel Comics Group

#1-9		.10	.20
10-Williamson reprint (My Own Romance #71); Kirby story	.20	.40	.60
11-20: #14-Morrow art		.10	.20
21-39: #23-Steranko reprint(Our Love Story#5).			
#38,39-Reprints		.10	.20
Special (12/71)		.10	.20

MY LOVE AFFAIR (March of Crime #7)
July, 1949 - #6, May, 1950
Fox Features Syndicate

#1	1.35	2.75	4.00
2,4	1.00	2.00	3.00
3,5,6-Wood stories	3.00	6.00	9.00

MY LOVE LIFE (Formerly Zegra)
#6, June, 1949 - #12, June, 1950
Fox Features Syndicate

#6-12	1.00	2.00	3.00

MY LOVE MEMOIRS (Formerly Woman Outlaws; Hunt-
#9, 11/49 - #12, 5/50   ed #13 on)
Fox Features Syndicate

My Love Memoirs #11, © Fox

My Love Secret #26, © Fox

My Love Story #3, © Fox

My Romance #1. © MCG

My Secret Confession #1. © Sterling

My Secret Life #23. © Fox

(My Love Memoirs cont'd)

	Good	Fine	Mint
#9,11,12-Wood stories	3.00	6.00	9.00
10	1.00	2.00	3.00

MY LOVE SECRET (Formerly Phantom Lady)(Animal
#24, 6/49 - #30, 6/50; 1954   Crackers #31)
Fox Features Syndicate/M.S.Distr.

#24,25,27,29,30	1.00	2.00	3.00
26,28-Wood stories	3.00	6.00	9.00
#53-(Reprint, M.S.Distr.)1954? no date given;			
formerly Western Thrillers #52 (Crimes By			
Women #54)	1.00	2.00	3.00

MY LOVE STORY
Sept, 1949 - #4, Mar, 1950
Fox Features Syndicate

#1	1.35	2.75	4.00
2	1.00	2.00	3.00
3,4-Wood stories	3.00	6.00	9.00

MY LOVE STORY
April, 1956 - #9, Aug, 1957
Atlas Comics (GPS)

#1-Two Colletta stories	.40	.80	1.20
2-9	.25	.50	.75

MY ONLY LOVE
July, 1975 - #9, Nov, 1976
Charlton Comics

#1,2,4-9		.10	.20
3-Toth art		.15	.30

MY OWN ROMANCE (Formerly My Romance)
#3, May, 1949 - #76, July, 1960
Marvel/Atlas(MjPC/RCM #3-59/ZPC #60-76)

#3-5	.65	1.35	2.00
6-20	.35	.70	1.05
21-70,72-76	.15	.30	.45
71-Williamson story	1.75	3.35	5.00

MY PAST CONFESSIONS (Formerly Western Thrill-
#8, Oct, 1949 - #11, April, 1950   ers)
Fox Features Syndicate

#8-10	1.00	2.00	3.00
11-Wood story	3.00	6.00	9.00

MY PERSONAL PROBLEM
Nov, 1955 - #3, Sept, 1956; Oct, 1957 - 1958
Ajax/Farrell/Steinway Comic

#1-3	1.00	2.00	3.00
#1(10/57),2('58)-Steinway	.35	.70	1.05

MY PRIVATE LIFE (Formerly Murder, Inc.)
#16, Feb, 1950
Fox Features Syndicate

	Good	Fine	Mint
#16	1.00	2.00	3.00

MYRA NORTH (See 4-Color Comics #3)

MY ROMANCE (My Own Romance #3 on)
Sept, 1948 - #3, Jan, 1949
Marvel Comics (RCM)

#1-3	1.00	2.00	3.00

MY ROMANTIC ADVENTURES (Formerly Romantic Ad-
#70, 10/56 - #137, 2/64   ventures)
American Comics Group

#70-85	.35	.70	1.05
86-3pg. Williamson story(2/58)			
	2.00	4.00	6.00
87-137	.15	.30	.45

NOTE: *Whitney* stories-#102,105.

MY SECRET
Aug, 1949 - #3, Oct, 1949
Superior Comics, Ltd.

#1	1.35	2.75	4.00
2,3	1.00	2.00	3.00

MY SECRET AFFAIR (Martin Kane #4)
Dec, 1949 - #3, April, 1950
Hero Book (Fox Features Syndicate)

#1-Harrison/Wood story, 10pgs.			
	5.00	10.00	15.00
2-Wood story (poor)	2.00	4.00	6.00
3-Wood story	3.00	6.00	9.00

MY SECRET CONFESSION
September, 1955
Sterling Comics

#1-Sekowsky art	1.00	2.00	3.00

MY SECRET LIFE (Formerly Western Outlaws;
Romeo Tubbs #28 on)
#22, July, 1949 - #27, May, 1950
Fox Features Syndicate

#22	1.35	2.75	4.00
23-Wood story, 6pgs.	3.00	6.00	9.00
24-27	1.00	2.00	3.00

MY SECRET LIFE
#20, Nov, 1957 - #47, 1962
Charlton Comics

(My Secret Life cont'd)	Good	Fine	Mint
#20-47	.20	.40	.60

MY SECRET MARRIAGE
May, 1953 - #24, July, 1956
Superior Comics, Ltd.

#1	1.35	2.75	4.00
2-24	.80	1.60	2.40
IW Reprint #9	.20	.40	.60

MY SECRET ROMANCE (A Star Presentation #3)
Jan, 1950 - #2, March, 1950
Hero Book (Fox Features Syndicate)

#1,2-Wood art	3.00	6.00	9.00

MY SECRET STORY (Sabu #30 on)
#26, Oct, 1949 - #29, April, 1950
Fox Features Syndicate

#26-29	1.00	2.00	3.00

MYSTERIES (-- Weird & Strange)
May, 1953 - #11, Jan, 1955
Superior/Dynamic Publ.(Randall Publ. Ltd.)

#1	1.35	2.75	4.00
2	.65	1.35	2.00
3-11	.50	1.00	1.50

MYSTERIES OF SCOTLAND YARD (See A-1 #121)

MYSTERIES OF UNEXPLORED WORLDS(See Blue Bird)
(Son of Vulcan V2#49 on)
April, 1956 - #48, Sept, 1965
Charlton Comics

#1	1.35	2.75	4.00
2-10	.80	1.60	2.40
11-20	.50	1.00	1.50
21-30	.35	.70	1.05
31-45	.25	.50	.75
46-Son of Vulcan origin & series begins			
	.50	1.00	1.50
47,48	.35	.70	1.05

NOTE: *Ditko art-#2,3-5,6-10,19,21-24,26;
covers-#2-6,10,19,21-24.*

MYSTERIOUS ADVENTURES
March, 1951 - #25, Aug, 1955
Story Comics

#1	1.35	2.75	4.00
2	.80	1.60	2.40
3,4,6-10	.65	1.35	2.00
5-Bondage cover	1.00	2.00	3.00
11-25: #23-Disbrow art	.60	1.20	1.80

MYSTERIOUS ISLAND (See 4-Color Comics #1213)

MYSTERIOUS ISLE
Nov-Jan, 1964   (Jules Verne)
Dell Publishing Co.

	Good	Fine	Mint
#1	1.00	2.00	3.00

MYSTERIOUS STORIES (Horror From the Tomb #1)
1954 - 1956
Premier Group

#2-Woodbridge cover	1.35	2.75	4.00
3-Woodbridge cvr/story	1.35	2.75	4.00
4-7: #6-Woodbridge cover	1.00	2.00	3.00

MYSTERIOUS SUSPENSE
October, 1968
Charlton Comics

#1-The Question app. by Ditko			
	1.50	3.00	4.50

MYSTERIOUS TRAVELER (See Tales of the --)

MYSTERIOUS TRAVELER COMICS (Radio)
Nov, 1948 - #4, 1949
Trans-World Publications

#1	2.50	5.00	7.50
2-4	1.50	3.00	4.50

MYSTERY COMICS
1944 - #4, 1944
Better Publications

#1-The Magnet, The Silver Knight, Brad Spen- cer, Wonderman, Dick Devins, King of Fut- uria, & Zudo, the Jungle Boy begin			
	10.00	20.00	30.00
2	6.00	12.00	18.00
3-Lance Lewis, Space Detective begins,			
4	5.00	10.00	15.00

MYSTERY COMICS
1952 - 1953
Standard Publications

#8-12	.65	1.35	2.00

MYSTERY COMICS DIGEST
March, 1972 - #26, Nov, 1975
Gold Key

#1-Ripley's-reprint of Ripley's #1; origin Ra-Ka-Tep the Mummy; Wood art			
	1.00	2.00	3.00
2-Boris Karloff-Wood art; 1st app. Werewolf			

Mysteries Of Unex-#41, © CC

Mysterious Stories #7, © Premier Group

Mysterious Traveler #13, © CC

Mystery In Space #34, © DC

Mystery Men #15, © Fox

Mystery Tales #44, © MCG

	Good	Fine	Mint
(Mystery Com. Dig. cont'd)			
Count Wulfstein	.65	1.35	2.00
3-Twilight Zone-Crandall, Toth & George Evans art; 1st app. Tragg & Simbar the Lion Lord	.65	1.35	2.00
4-Ripley's Believe I.O.N.-1st app. Baron Tibor, the Vampire	.35	.70	1.05
5-Boris Karloff Tales of Mystery-1st app. Dr. Spektor	.35	.70	1.05
6-Twilight Zone-1st app. U.S. Marshal Reid & Sir Duane	.35	.70	1.05
7-Ripley's Believe I.O.N.-origin The Lurker in the Swamp; 1st app. Duroc	.35	.70	1.05
8-Boris Karloff T.O.M.	.35	.70	1.05
9-Twilight Zone-Williamson, Crandall, McWilliams art; 2nd Tragg app.	.65	1.35	2.00
10,13,16-Ripley's--	.25	.50	.75
11,14-Boris Karloff--	.25	.50	.75
12,15-Twilight Zone	.25	.50	.75
16,19,22,25-Ripley's--	.25	.50	.75
17-Boris Karloff T.O.M.-Williamson reprint	.50	1.00	1.50
18,21,24-Twilight Zone	.25	.50	.75
20,23,26-Boris Karloff--	.25	.50	.75

NOTE: *Dr. Spektor app.-#5,10-12,21. Durak app.-#15. Duroc app.-#14(later called Durak). King George 1st app.-#8.*

MYSTERY IN SPACE (#1-4, 52pgs.)
Apr-May, 1951 - #110, Sept, 1966
National Periodical Publications

	Good	Fine	Mint
#1-Frazetta art, 8pgs.; Knights of the Galaxy begins, ends #8	40.00	80.00	120.00
2	15.00	30.00	45.00
3	10.00	20.00	30.00
4-5	7.00	14.00	21.00
6-10: #7-Toth art	5.00	10.00	15.00
11-15: #13-Toth art	4.00	8.00	12.00
16-18,20-25: Interplanetary Insurance feature by Infantino in all. #24-Last precode issue	4.00	8.00	12.00
19-Virgil Finley story	5.00	10.00	15.00
26-Space Cabbie begins	2.50	5.00	7.50
27-34,36-40	2.50	5.00	7.50
35-Kubert art	3.00	6.00	9.00
41-52: #47-Space Cabbie feature ends	1.50	3.00	4.50
53-1st Adam Strange app.	10.00	20.00	30.00
54	5.00	10.00	15.00
55	4.00	8.00	12.00
56-60	3.00	6.00	9.00
61-70: #63-Origin Vandor. #66-1st Star Rovers. #68-Origin Dust Devil	2.00	4.00	6.00
71-74,76-80	1.50	3.00	4.50
75-JLA x-over in Adam Strange			

	Good	Fine	Mint
	1.50	3.00	4.50
81-86	1.00	2.00	3.00
87-90-Hawkman in all	.80	1.60	2.40
91-102: #91-End Infantino art on Adam Strange. #92-Space Ranger begins. #94,98-Adam Strange/Space Ranger team-up. #102-Adam Strange ends	.35	.70	1.05
103-Origin Ultra, the Multi-Alien; Space Ranger ends	.35	.70	1.05
104-110	.25	.50	.75

NOTE: *Anderson stories-#2,4,8-10,12-17,19, 45-48,51,57,61-64,70,76,87-98; covers-#9,10, 15-25,87,89,105-108,110. Drucker stories-#13, 14. Infantino stories-#1-8,11,14-25,27-46,48, 49,51,53-91,103; covers-#60-86,88,90,91,105, 107. Gil Kane stories-#100-102; cover-#101. Simon & Kirby art-#4(2pgs.).*

MYSTERY MEN COMICS
Aug, 1939 - #31, Feb, 1942
Fox Features Syndicate

	Good	Fine	Mint
#1-Intro. & 1st app. The Blue Beetle, The Green Mask, Rex Dexter of Mars, Zanzibar, Lt. Drake, D-13, Secret Agent, Chen Chang, Wing Turner, & Captain Denny Scott	60.00	120.00	180.00
2	30.00	60.00	90.00
3	26.50	53.25	80.00
4-Capt. Savage begins	25.00	50.00	75.00
5	20.00	40.00	60.00
6-8	15.00	30.00	45.00
9-The Moth begins	13.50	26.75	40.00
10,11-Intro. Domino	12.00	24.00	36.00
12,13,15-18	10.00	20.00	30.00
14-Intro. Lynx & sidekick Blackie	12.00	24.00	36.00
19-Intro. & 1st app. Miss X(ends #21)	12.00	24.00	36.00
20-25	10.00	20.00	30.00
26-The Wraith begins	10.00	20.00	30.00
27-31	10.00	20.00	30.00

NOTE: *Lou Fine covers-#1-5,8,9. Simon cover-#10.*

MYSTERY TALES
March, 1952 - #54, Aug, 1957
Atlas Comics (20CC)

	Good	Fine	Mint
#1	2.00	4.00	6.00
2	1.20	2.40	3.60
3-10: #10-Gil Kane art	1.00	2.00	3.00
11-19,21: Last precode ish	.80	1.60	2.40
20-Torres art	1.50	3.00	4.50
22-43,45,49	.65	1.35	2.00
44,51-Williamson/Mayo stories	2.00	4.00	6.00

(Mystery Tales cont'd)	Good	Fine	Mint
46-Williamson/Krenkel sty.	2.00	4.00	6.00
47-Crandall + Powell art	1.35	2.75	4.00
50-Torres + Morrow story	1.35	2.75	4.00
52,53	.65	1.35	2.00
54-Crandall story	1.00	2.00	3.00

NOTE: _Crandall_ story-#54. _Ditko_ story-#45.
Everett stories-#2,28,29,35,43; covers-#9,11,
14,38,46,48-51,53. _Kinstler_ story-#15. _Krig-
stein_ stories-#2,36,39. _Orlando_ story-#51.
Powell story-#21,29,37,48. _Robinson_ story-#7
(with Lee),42. _Wildey_ story-#37. #26-No code
on cover.

MYSTERY TALES
1964
Super Comics

Super Reprint #16,17('64)	.35	.70	1.05
Super Reprint #18-Kubert art/Strange Terrors			
#4	.65	1.35	2.00

MYSTIC (3rd Series)
March, 1951 - #61, Aug, 1957
Marvel/Atlas Comics(CSI)

#1	2.00	4.00	6.00
2,3,5,7-10	1.35	2.75	4.00
4,6-Wolverton art	8.00	16.00	24.00
11-20	1.00	2.00	3.00
21-36-Last precode ish.	.80	1.60	2.40
37-51,53-57,61	.65	1.35	2.00
52-Wood & Crandall art	2.00	4.00	6.00
58,59-Krigstein stories	1.50	3.00	4.50
60-Williamson/Mayo story, 4pgs.			
	2.00	4.00	6.00

NOTE: _Drucker_ story-#52,56. _Everett_ stories-
#9,40,44,53,57; covers-#18,42,53-55,61. _Infan-
tino_ story-#12. _Kane_ art-#1,8. _Morrow_ story-
#51. _Orlando_ stories-#57,61. _Whitney_ story-#33.

MYSTICAL TALES
June, 1956 - #8, Aug, 1957
Atlas Comics (EPI)

#1-Everett cover/story	1.75	3.35	5.00
2-4-Crandall art	1.75	3.35	5.00
5-Williamson story,4pgs.	2.00	4.00	6.00
6-Torres story	1.50	3.00	4.50
7-Torres + Orlando story	1.75	3.35	5.00
8-Krigstein, Check story	1.50	3.00	4.50

NOTE: _Everett_ covers-#4,6,7. _Krigstein_ story-
#6,8. _Orlando_ stories-#1,2,8. _Powell_ story-
#1,4.

MYSTIC COMICS (1st Series)
March, 1940 - #10, Aug, 1942
Timely Comics

	Good	Fine	Mint
#1-Origin The Blue Blaze, The Dynamic Man, & Flexo, the Rubber Man; Zephyr Jones, 3X's & Deep Sea Demon app.; The Magician begins			
	250.00	500.00	750.00
2-The Invisible Man & Master Mind Excello begin; Space Rangers, Zara of the Jungle, Taxi Taylor app.	135.00	270.00	405.00
3-Origin Hercules, who last appears in #4			
	100.00	200.00	300.00
4-Origin The Thin Man & The Black Widow; Merzak, the Mystic app.; last Flexo Dynamic Man, Invisible Man & Blue Blaze.(Some issues have date sticker on cover)			
	115.00	230.00	345.00
5-Origin The Black Marvel, The Blazing Skull, The Sub-Earth Man, Super Slave & The Terror; The Moon Man & Black Widow app.	100.00	200.00	300.00
6-Origin The Challenger & The Destroyer	80.00	160.00	240.00
7-The Witness begins(origin); origin Davey & the Demon; last Black Widow; Simon & Kirby cover	70.00	140.00	210.00
8	60.00	120.00	180.00
9-Gary Gaunt app.; last Black Marvel, Mystic & Blazing Skull	60.00	120.00	180.00
10-Father Time, World of Wonder, & Red Skeleton app.; last Challenger & Terror			
	50.00	100.00	150.00

MYSTIC COMICS (2nd Series)
Oct, 1944 - #4, Winter, 1944-45
Timely Comics

#1-The Angel, The Destroyer, The Human Torch, Terry Vance, the Schoolboy Sleuth, & Tommy Tyme begin	20.00	40.00	60.00
2,3: #2-Last Human Torch & Terry Vance; #3-last Angel(2 stories) & Tommy Tyme			
	12.00	24.00	36.00
4-The Young Allies app.	12.00	24.00	36.00

MY STORY, TRUE ROMANCES IN PICTURES
#5, May, 1949 - #12, Aug, 1940 (Formerly Zago)
Hero Books (Fox Features Syndicate)

#5	1.20	2.40	3.60
5-8,11,12	1.00	2.00	3.00
9,10-Wood stories	3.00	6.00	9.00

MY TRUE LOVE (Frank Buck #70 on)
#66, Sept, 1949 - #69, March, 1950
Fox Features Syndicate

#66-69	1.00	2.00	3.00

NAKED PREY, THE (See Movie Classics)

Mystic #6('51), © MCG

Mystic Comics #3, © MCG

My Story #9, © Fox

Namora #3, © MCG

National Comics #4, © DC (Qua)

National Comics #28, © DC (Qua)

NAMORA
Autumn, 1948 - #3, Dec, 1948
Marfel Comics

	Good	Fine	Mint
#1-Sub-Mariner x-over in Namora; Everett art
	25.00	50.00	75.00
2-The Blonde Phantom app. in Sub-Mariner story
	20.00	40.00	60.00
3-Sub-Mariner app.; Everett art
	15.00	30.00	45.00

NANCY AND SLUGGO
1949 - #23, 1954
United Features Syndicate

#16(#1)	1.35	2.75	4.00
17-23	1.00	2.00	3.00

NANCY & SLUGGO (Nancy #157-173; formerly Spar-
#121, 4/55 - #192, 10/63   kler Comics
St. John/Dell #146-187/Gold Key #188 on

#121(4/55)-#145(7/57)-St. John
	.80	1.60	2.40
146(9/57)-Peanuts begins, ends #192(Dell)
	.80	1.60	2.40
147-161(Dell)	.80	1.60	2.40
162-180-John Stanley art	1.00	2.00	3.00
181-187(3-4/62)(Dell)	.60	1.20	1.80
188(10/62)-192(G.Key)	.50	1.00	1.50
4-Color #1034-Summer Camp	.60	1.20	1.80
--Travel Time #1('58-Dell)(25¢)
	1.00	2.00	3.00

(See Dell Giant #34,45)

NANNY AND THE PROFESSOR (TV)
Aug, 1970 - #2, Oct, 1970
Dell Publishing Co.

#1(01-546-008), #2		.15	.30

NAPOLEON & SAMANTHA (See Walt Disney Show-
case #10)

NAPOLEON & UNCLE ELBY
1942   (68 pgs.)   (One Shot)
Eastern Color Printing Co.

#1	10.00	20.00	30.00
1945-American Book-Strafford Press(128pgs.)
(8x10½"-B&W reprints-Hardcover)
	7.00	14.00	21.00

NAPOLEON & UNCLE ELBY
1954
Dell Publishing Co.

4-Color #526, #1		.75	1.50	2.25

NATIONAL COMICS
July, 1940 - #75, 1949
Quality Comics Group

	Good	Fine	Mint
#1-Origin Uncle Sam, Merlin, the Magician (ends #26), & Wonder Boy's sidekick Buddy; Cyclone, Wonder Boy(ends #26), Kid Patrol, Sally O'Neal Policewoman, Pen Miller(ends #22), Kid Dixon, Prop Powers(ends #26), & Paul Bunyan(ends #22) begin
	120.00	240.00	360.00
2	60.00	120.00	180.00
3	50.00	100.00	150.00
4-Last Cyclone	35.00	70.00	105.00
5-Quick Silver by Jack Cole begins; origin Uncle Sam	40.00	80.00	120.00
6-11: #8-Jack & Jill begins(ends #22)
	30.00	60.00	90.00
12-20-Lou Fine art	25.00	50.00	75.00
21,22	20.00	40.00	60.00
23-The Unknown & Destroyer 171 begin
	17.50	35.00	52.50
24-26,28,30	15.00	30.00	45.00
27-G-2, the Unknown begins(ends #46)
	15.00	30.00	45.00
29-Origin The Unknown	15.00	30.00	45.00
31-33: #33-Chic Carter begins(ends #47)
	8.00	16.00	24.00
34-40: #35-Last Kid Patrol
	7.00	14.00	21.00
41-47,49,50: #42-The Barker begins
	4.00	8.00	12.00
48-Origin The Whistler	5.00	10.00	15.00
51-Sally O'Neil by Ward, 8pgs.
	5.00	10.00	15.00
52-60	3.00	6.00	9.00
61-67: #67-Format change; Quicksilver app.
	2.50	5.00	7.50
68-75: #72-The Barker ends
	2.00	4.00	6.00

NOTE: *Cole Quicksilver-#13. Crandall Uncle Sam-#11,13(w/Fine),25,26; covers-#24-26,30-33. Crandall Paul Benjamin-#11-13. Fine Uncle Sam-#12,13(w/Crandall)-20; covers-#1-22. Guardineer Quicksilver-#27. Gustafson Quicksilver-#14-26. McWilliams art-#23-28, 57. Zolnerwich Uncle Sam-#1-3.*

NATIONAL CRUMB, THE (Magazine-Size)
August, 1975   (52 pgs.)   (Satire)
Mayfair Publications

#1		.35	.70	1.05

NATIONAL VELVET (TV)
May-July, 1961 - Mar, 1963
Dell Publishing Co./Gold Key

(National Velvet cont'd)	Good	Fine	Mint
4-Color #1195,1312	.65	1.35	2.00
#01556-207,210	.65	1.35	2.00
#1(12/62),#2(3/63)-G.Key	.35	.70	1.05

NATURE BOY
#3, March, 1956 – #5, Feb, 1957
Charlton Comics

#3-Origin; Blue Beetle story; Buscema story			
	2.50	5.00	7.50
4,5-Buscema stories each	1.75	3.35	5.00

NATURE OF THINGS (See 4-Color #727,842)

NAVY ACTION (Sailor Sweeney #12-14)
Aug, 1954 – #11, 4/56; #15, 1/57 – #18, 8/57
Atlas Comics (CDS)

#1-Powell story	1.35	2.75	4.00
2-11	.65	1.35	2.00
15-18: #1 -Devil Dog Dugan app.			
	.65	1.35	2.00

NOTE: *Berg story-#9. Drucker story-#7,17.*

NAVY COMBAT
June, 1955 – #20, Oct, 1958
Atlas Comics (MPI)

#1-Torpedo Taylor begins by D. Heck			
	1.35	2.75	4.00
2-10	.65	1.35	2.00
11-13,15,16,18-20	.50	1.00	1.50
14-Torres story	1.20	2.40	3.60
17-Williamson story,4pgs.	2.00	4.00	6.00

NOTE: *Everett stories-#3,20; covers-#10,15.*

NAVY HEROES
1945
Almanac Publishing Co.

#1-Heavy in propaganda	2.00	4.00	6.00

NAVY: HISTORY & TRADITION
1958 - 1961 (No#) (Giveaway)
Stokes Walesby Co./Dept. of Navy

1772-1778, 1778-1817, 1817-1865, 1865-1936,			
1940-1945	1.35	2.75	4.00
1961-Navy Actions of the Civil War(6 known			
issues in all)			
each....	1.35	2.75	4.00

NAVY PATROL
May, 1955 – #4, Nov, 1955
Key Publications

#1	1.00	2.00	3.00

	Good	Fine	Mint
2-4	.50	1.00	1.50

NAVY TALES
Jan, 1957 – #4, July, 1957
Atlas Comics (CDS)

#1-Everett cover	1.35	2.75	4.00
2-Williamson/Mayo story, 5pgs. + Crandall			
story	2.50	5.00	7.50
3,4: #3-Krigstein story. #4-Crandall story			
	1.35	2.75	4.00

NAVY TASK FORCE
Feb, 1954 – #8, April, 1956
Stanmor Publications/Aragon Mag. #4-8

#1	1.00	2.00	3.00
2-8	.50	1.00	1.50

NAVY WAR HEROES
Jan, 1964 – #7, Mar-Apr, 1965
Charlton Comics

#1	.15	.30	.45
2-7		.15	.30

NAZA (Stone Age Warrior)
Nov-Jan, 1964 – #9, March, 1966
Dell Publishing Co.

#1(12-555-401)	1.00	2.00	3.00
2-9	.50	1.00	1.50

NEBBS, THE
1928 (Daily B&W strip reprints, 48 pgs.)
Cupples & Leon Co.

By Sol Hess; Carlson art	5.00	10.00	15.00

NEBBS, THE
1941 - 1945
Dell Publishing Co./Croyden Publishers

Black & White #23('41)	6.00	12.00	18.00
#1(1945) reprints	2.50	5.00	7.50

NEGRO (See All-Negro)

NEGRO HEROES (Reprints from True, Real
Heroes, & Calling All Girls)
Spring, 1947 – #2, Summer, 1948
Parents' Magazine Institute

#1 (Scarce)	20.00	40.00	60.00
2 (Scarce)	10.00	20.00	30.00

NEGRO ROMANCE (Negro Romances #4)
June, 1950 – #3, Oct, 1950

Navy Heroes #1, © Almanac Publ.

Navy History --1817-1865, © Stokes Walesby

Negro Romance #1, © Faw

Nellie The Nurse #1, © MCG

New Adventure Comics #12, © DC

New Adventure Comics #16, © DC

(Negro Romance cont'd)
Fawcett Publications

	Good	Fine	Mint
#1-Evans art (Scarce)	40.00	80.00	120.00
2,3 (Scarce)	25.00	50.00	75.00

NEGRO ROMANCES (Formerly Negro Romance)
#4, May, 1955
Charlton Comics

#4 (Scarce)-Reprints Fawcett #2			
	15.00	30.00	45.00

NELLIE THE NURSE
1945 - #36, Oct, 1952; 1957
Marvel/Atlas Comics(SPI/LMC)

#1	2.00	4.00	6.00
2-4	1.00	2.00	3.00
5-Kurtzman's "Hey Look"	2.00	4.00	6.00
6-8,10	.50	1.00	1.50
9-Wolverton art, 1pg.	2.00	4.00	6.00
11,14-16,18-Kurtzman's "Hey Look"			
	1.75	3.35	5.00
12-"Giggles 'n' Grins" by Kurtzman			
	1.35	2.75	4.00
13,17,19-27,29-36	.35	.70	1.05
28-Kurtzman's Rusty reprt.	1.75	3.35	5.00
#1('57)-Leading Mag.(Atlas)	.35	.70	1.05

NELLIE THE NURSE (See 4-Color Comics #1304)

NEUTRO
Jan, 1967
Dell Publishing Co.

#1	.50	1.00	1.50

NEVADA (See Zane Grey's Stories of the West#1)

NEVER AGAIN (Navy Stories)
Aug, 1955 - #8, July, 1956
Charlton Comics

#1	1.75	3.35	5.00
2-8	1.20	2.40	3.60

NEW ADVENTURE COMICS (Formerly New Comics;
becomes Adventure Comics #31 on)
V1#12, Jan, 1937 - #30, Sept, 1938
National Periodical Publications

V1#12	25.00	50.00	75.00
V2#1(2/37,#13)	20.00	40.00	60.00
14(V2#2)-#20(V2#8): #15-1st Adventure logo.			
#17-Nadir, Master of Magic begins, ends			
#30	20.00	40.00	60.00
21(V2#9),#22(V2#10,2/37)			

	Good	Fine	Mint
	15.00	30.00	45.00
23-30: #29-Federal Men by Siegel & Shuster			
begins; last New Adventure			
	15.00	30.00	45.00

NEW ADVENTURE OF SNOW WHITE AND THE SEVEN
DWARFS, A (See Snow White Bendix Giveaway)

NEW ADVENTURES OF CHARLIE CHAN, THE
May-June, 1958 - #6, Mar-Apr, 1959
National Periodical Publications

#1	1.50	3.00	4.50
2-6-Sid Greene art	1.00	2.00	3.00

NEW ADVENTURES OF HUCK FINN, THE (TV)
September, 1968 (Hanna-Barbera)
Gold Key

#1-"The Curse of Thut"	.25	.50	.75

NEW ADVENTURES OF PETER PAN (Disney)
1953 (36pgs.) (Admiral giveaway)(5x7¼")
Western Publishing Co.

	2.50	5.00	7.50

NEW ADVENTURES OF PINOCCHIO
Oct-Dec, 1962 - #3, 1963
Dell Publishing Co.

#12-562-212	.50	1.00	1.50
#2,3	.35	.70	1.05

NEW ADVENTURES OF ROBIN HOOD (See Robin Hood)

NEW ADVENTURES OF SHERLOCK HOLMES (See
4-Color Comics #1169,1245)

NEW BOOK OF COMICS
1936, 1938 (100pgs.) (Reprints)
National Periodical Publications

#1	50.00	100.00	150.00
2-Dr. Occult by Siegel & Shuster; #1&2 re-			
prts. New Comics & More Fun			
	30.00	60.00	90.00

NEW COMICS (New Adventure #12 on)
Dec, 1935 - #11, Dec, 1936 (#1-6, soft cover)
National Periodical Publications

V1#1-Billy the Kid, Sagebrush 'n' Cactus,
Jibby Jones, Needles, The Vikings, Sir
Loin of Beef, Now-When I Was a Boy, &
other 1-2pg. strips. 2pgs. Kelly art
(Gulliver's Travels). (Also see More-

	Good	Fine	Mint
Fun #6)	135.00	270.00	405.00
2	65.00	130.00	195.00
3-5	40.00	80.00	120.00
NOTE: *#1-5 rarely occur in mint condition.*			
6-11	25.00	50.00	75.00

NEW FUN COMICS (More Fun #7 on)
Feb, 1935 - #6, Oct, 1935 (Large Size)
National Periodical Publications

	Good	Fine	Mint
V1#1	166.50	333.25	500.00
2(3/35) (Very Rare)	100.00	200.00	300.00
3-5(8/35)	60.00	120.00	180.00
6(10/35)-1st Dr. Occult by Siegel & Shuster; 1st comic book art by Walt Kelly, 1 pg; Last "New Fun" title. "New Comics" #1 begins in Dec. which is reason for title change to More Fun; Henri Duval (ends #9), Leger Reuths by Siegel & Shuster begins	80.00	160.00	240.00

NEW FUNNIES (The Funnies, #1-64; #259,260, 272,273 titled New TV--; #261-271-TV Funnies)
#65, July, 1942 - #288, Mar-Apr, 1962
Dell Publishing Co.

	Good	Fine	Mint
#65(#1)-Andy Panda, Felix the Cat, Raggedy Ann, Oswald the Rabbit, & Li'l Eight Ball begin	50.00	100.00	150.00
66-70: #67-Billy & Bonnie Bee by Frank Thomas begins	20.00	40.00	60.00
71-75,80,81: #72-Kelly illos	10.00	20.00	30.00
76-Andy Panda-(Carl Barks & Pabian art)	70.00	140.00	210.00
77-79-Andy Panda in a World of Real People ends, becomes all funny animal	10.00	20.00	30.00
82-Brownies by Kelly?	12.00	24.00	36.00
83-85-Kelly text illos	8.00	16.00	24.00
86-90	3.35	6.75	10.00
91-100	2.75	5.50	8.00
101-120	1.75	3.35	5.00
121-150	1.00	2.00	3.00
151-200: #182-Origin & 1st app. Nuthead & Splinter	.65	1.35	2.00
201-288	.35	.70	1.05
NOTE: *Early issues written by John Stanley.*			

NEW GODS, THE (Orion of--#2,3)(See 1st Issue Spec.)
Feb-Mar, 1971 - #11, Oct-Nov, 1972;
#12, July, 1977 - Present
National Periodical Publications/DC Comics

	Good	Fine	Mint
#1	2.00	4.00	6.00
2	1.35	2.75	4.00
3,4-Origin Manhunter reprinted in #4			

	Good	Fine	Mint
	1.00	2.00	3.00
5-8: #5-Young Gods feature. #7-Origin Orion.			
#7,8-Young Gods app.	.90	1.80	2.70
9-11	.65	1.35	2.00
12-14-Newton/Atkins art	.25	.50	.75
15-17	.20	.40	.60
NOTE: *#4-9 contain Manhunter reprints by Simon & Kirby from Adventure #73,74,75,76,77, & 78 in that order. Kirby art/covers in #1-11. Starlin cover-#17.*			

NEW HEROIC (See Heroic)

NEWLYWEDS & THEIR BABY'S COMIC PICTURES, THE
1917 (22pgs.)(14x10",oblong,cardboard covers)
Saalfield Publ. Co.

By George McManus. Reprints "Newlyweds" (Baby Snookums strips) mainly from 1916. Blue cover; says for painting and crayoning, but some pages in color.   20.00 40.00 60.00

NEW MEN OF BATTLE, THE
No#   1949   (Cardboard covers)
Catechetical Guild

	Good	Fine	Mint
No#(V8#1-V8#6)-192pgs., contains 6 issues of Topix rebound	1.50	3.00	4.50
No#(V8#7-V8#11)-160pgs., contains 5 issues of Topix	1.50	3.00	4.50

NEW PEOPLE, THE (TV)
Jan, 1970 - #2, May, 1970
Dell Publishing Co.

	Good	Fine	Mint
#1,2	.15	.30	.45

NEW ROMANCES
#5, May, 1951 - #19, Dec, 1953
Standard Comics

	Good	Fine	Mint
#5	.80	1.60	2.40
6-Moreira art	.65	1.35	2.00
7-Tuska art	.65	1.35	2.00
8-10,12-15,18,19	.40	.80	1.20
11,16,17-Toth art	1.50	3.00	4.50

NEW TERRYTOONS (TV)
6-8/60 - #8, 3-5/62; 10/62 - Present
Dell Publishing Co./Gold Key

	Good	Fine	Mint
#1('60-Dell)	.35	.70	1.05
2-8 ('62)	.20	.40	.60
1(30010-210)(3/62,G.Key, 84 pgs.)	.15	.30	.45
2(30010-301)-84pgs.	.15	.30	.45
3-16		.15	.30

New Comics #2. © DC

New Fun Comics #1, © DC

New Funnies #86. © Dell

N.Y. World's Fair 1940. © DC

Nickel Comics #1. © Faw

Nightmare #13. © STJ

	Good	Fine	Mint
(New Terrytoons cont'd)			
17-47		.10	.20

NOTE: *Reprints: #4-12,38,40,47. (See March of Comics #393,412)*

NEW TV FUNNIES (See New Funnies)

NEW YORK GIANTS (See Thrilling True Story of the Baseball Giants)

NEW YORK WORLD'S FAIR
1939, 1940   (100 pgs.)
National Periodical Publications

	Good	Fine	Mint
1939-Superman, Sandman, Zatara, Slam Bradley, Pep Morgan begin; Ginger Snap by Bob Kane app.	200.00	400.00	600.00
1940-Slam Bradley, Batman, Hourman, Johnny Thunder app.	125.00	250.00	375.00

NOTE: The 1939 edition was published at 25 cents. Since all other comics were 10 cents, it didn't sell. Remaining copies were repriced with 15 cents stickers placed over the 25 cents price. Four variations on the 15 cents stickers known. It was advertised in other DC comics at 25 cents. Everyone who sent a quarter through the mail for it received a free Superman No. 1 to make up the dime difference. The 1940 edition was priced at 15 cents.

NICKEL COMICS
1938   (Pocket size - 7½x5½") (132 pgs.)
Dell Publishing Co.

	Good	Fine	Mint
#1-"Bobby & Chip" by Otto Messmer, Felix the Cat artist. Contains some English reprints	20.00	40.00	60.00

NICKEL COMICS
5/40 - #8, 8/40   (36pgs.) (Bi-Weekly) (5¢)
Fawcett Publications

	Good	Fine	Mint
#1-Origin Bulletman	75.00	150.00	225.00
2	40.00	80.00	120.00
3	30.00	60.00	90.00
4-The Red Gaucho begins	25.00	50.00	75.00
5-8	25.00	50.00	75.00

NOTE: *Covers on some issues by C. C. Beck. Jack Binder cover-#1.*

NICK FURY, AGENT OF SHIELD (See Shield)
June, 1968 - #18, March, 1971
Marvel Comics Group

	Good	Fine	Mint
#1	1.50	3.00	4.50
2,3	1.00	2.00	3.00
4-Origin retold	1.00	2.00	3.00
5-Steranko story	1.00	2.00	3.00
6-11: #9-Hate Monger begins(ends #11). #11-Smith cover	.50	1.00	1.50
12-Smith cover/art	.65	1.35	2.00
13-15	.40	.80	1.20

	Good	Fine	Mint
16-18-All reprints	.25	.50	.75

NOTE: *Craig inks-#10. Kirby reprints-#18. Steranko stories-#1-3,5; covers-#1-7.*

NICK HALIDAY
May, 1956
Argo

	Good	Fine	Mint
#1-Daily & Sunday strip reprints be Petree	1.75	3.35	5.00

NIGHT BEFORE CHRISTMAS, THE (See March of Comics #152)

NIGHTMARE
Summer, 1952 - #2, Fall, 1952; #3, 1953
Ziff-Davis(Approved Comics)/St. John #3

	Good	Fine	Mint
#1-Kinstler art	2.00	4.00	6.00
2-Kinstler story-Poe's "Pit & the Pendulum"	1.50	3.00	4.50
3-Kinstler story	1.50	3.00	4.50

NIGHTMARE (Formerly Weird Horrors #1-9)
(Amazing Ghost Stories #14 on)
#10, Dec, 1953 - #13, Aug, 1954
St. John Publishing Co.

	Good	Fine	Mint
#10-Reprints Z-D Weird Thrillers #2 with new Kubert cover + 2pgs. Kinstler, Toth & Anderson stories	2.00	4.00	6.00
11-Krigstein story	1.50	3.00	4.50
12-Kubert cover	1.50	3.00	4.50
13-Reprints Z-D Weird Thrillers #3 with new cover(Kubert) + Powell story	1.35	2.75	4.00

NIGHTMARE (Magazine)
Dec, 1970 - #23, Feb, 1975 (B&W)(68pgs.)
Skywald Publishing Corp.

	Good	Fine	Mint
#1-Everett art	1.00	2.00	3.00
2-5	.65	1.35	2.00
6,7,9,10: #9,10-Wolverton back covers	.65	1.35	2.00
8-Features E.C. movie "Tales From the Crypt"; reprints some E.C. comic panels	1.50	3.00	4.50
11-20	.25	.50	.75
21-(1974 Summer Special)	.35	.70	1.05
22-Tomb of Horror ish.	.35	.70	1.05
23-(1975 Winter Special)	.35	.70	1.05
Annual #1(1972)	.50	1.00	1.50
Winter Special #1(1973)	.50	1.00	1.50
Yearbook-No#(1974)	.35	.70	1.05

NOTE: *Jones art-#6,21. Kaluta art-#6,21. Wildey art-#6,'74 Year Book.*

NIGHTMARE & CASPER (See Harvey Hits #71)
1963   (25¢)
Harvey Publications

	Good	Fine	Mint
#1	.40	.80	1.20
2-5	.25	.50	.75

NIGHTMARES (See Do You Believe In --)

NIGHT NURSE
Nov, 1972 - #4, May, 1973
Marvel Comics Group

	Good	Fine	Mint
#1-4		.10	.20

NIGHT OF MYSTERY
1953   (No Month)   (One Shot)
Avon Periodicals

No#-Kinstler art, 1pg.	2.50	5.00	7.50

NIGHT OF THE GRIZZLY, THE (See Movie Classics)

NIGHT RIDER
Oct, 1974 - #6, Aug, 1975
Marvel Comics Group

	Good	Fine	Mint
#1	.20	.40	.60
2-6		.15	.30

NOTE: *#1-6 reprints Ghost Rider #1-6.*

NIGHTWITCH
1977 - Present   (50¢)
Power Comics

	Good	Fine	Mint
#1,2	.20	.40	.60

NIKKI, WILD DOG OF THE NORTH (See 4-Color
#1226 & Movie Comics)

NIPPY'S POP
1917   (Sunday strip reprints-B&W)(10½x13½")
The Saalfield Publishing Co.

32pgs.	4.00	8.00	12.00

NOAH'S ARK
1975
Spire Christian Comics/Fleming H. Revell Co.

By Al Hartley	.15	.30	.45

NOMAN
Nov, 1966 - #2, March, 1967
Tower Comics

#1-Wood/Williamson cover; Lightning begins;
Dynamo cameo; Kane pencils

	Good	Fine	Mint
	1.00	2.00	3.00
2-Wood cover only; Dynamo x-over; Whitney stories-#1,2	1.00	2.00	3.00

NONE BUT THE BRAVE (See Movie Classics)

NOODNIK COMICS (See Pinky the Egghead)
1953; #2, Feb, 1954 - #5, Aug, 1954
Comic Media/Mystery/Biltmore

	Good	Fine	Mint
3-D(1953)(Comic Media)(#1)	4.00	8.00	12.00
#2-5	.65	1.35	2.00

NORTH TO ALASKA (See 4-Color Comics #1155)

NORTHWEST MOUNTIES
Oct, 1948 - #12, 1949; #12, Aug, 1954
Jubilee Publications/St. John

	Good	Fine	Mint
#1	2.00	4.00	6.00
2-12	1.35	2.75	4.00
12(8/54)-St. John	1.35	2.75	4.00

NOTE: *Matt Baker art in most issues.*

NO SLEEP 'TIL DAWN (See 4-Color #831)

NOT BRAND ECHH
Aug, 1967 - #13, May, 1969 (#9-13, 68pgs.)
Marvel Comics Group

	Good	Fine	Mint
#1	.65	1.35	2.00
2-4	.35	.70	1.05
5-Origin & intro. Forbush Man	.35	.70	1.05
6-13-Avengers satire #12	.25	.50	.75

NOTE: *Kirby art-#1,3,5-7; cover-#1. Archie
satire-#9.*

NO TIME FOR SERGEANTS (TV)
July, 1958 - #3, Aug-Oct, 1965
Dell Publishing Co.

	Good	Fine	Mint
4-Color #914 (Movie)	1.00	2.00	3.00
#1(2-4/65)-#3 (TV)	.35	.70	1.05

NOVA
Sept, 1976 - Present
Marvel Comics Group

	Good	Fine	Mint
#1-Origin	.90	1.80	2.70
2	.40	.80	1.20
3-5	.30	.60	.90
6-10	.25	.50	.75
11-17	.15	.30	.45

NOTE: *John Buscema stories-#1-4. Sal Buscema
#5 on. Kirby covers-#4,5,7.*

Night Of Mystery #1. © Avon

Noman =1. © TC

Not Brand Echh =1. © MCG

Nurse Betsy Crane #1. © CC

Nutsy Squirrel #66. © DC

Nyoka #2. © Faw

NUKLA
Oct-Dec, 1965 - #4, Sept, 1966
Dell Publishing Co.

	Good	Fine	Mint
#1-Origin Nukla	.65	1.35	2.00
2,3	.40	.80	1.20
4-Ditko art	.65	1.35	2.00

NURSE BETSY CRANE
Aug, 1961 - #27, Mar, 1964
Charlton Comics

V2#12-27		.10	.20

NURSE HELEN GRANT (The Romances of)
August, 1957
Atlas Comics (VPI)

#1	.25	.50	.75

NURSE LINDA LARK (See Linda Lark)

NURSERY RHYMES
1951
Ziff-Davis Publ. Co.

#2-10-Howie Post art #10	1.00	2.00	3.00

NURSES, THE (TV)
April, 1963 - #3, Oct, 1963
Gold Key

#1	.20	.40	.60
2,3	.15	.30	.45

NUTS! (Satire)
March, 1954 - #5, Nov, 1954
Premiere Comics Group

#1	2.50	5.00	7.50
2-5: #5-Capt. Marvel parody			
	1.75	3.35	5.00

NUTS (Magazine) (Satire)
Feb, 1958 - #2, April, 1958
Health Knowledge

#1,2	1.00	2.00	3.00

NUTS & JOLTS (See Black & White #22)

NUTSY SQUIRREL (Formerly Hollywood Funny
#61, 9-10/54 - #72, 11/57   Folks)
National Periodical Publications

#61-72	1.00	2.00	3.00

NUTTY COMICS

Winter, 1946
Fawcett Publications

	Good	Fine	Mint
#1-Capt. Kidd story; Wolverton art			
	2.50	5.00	7.50

NUTTY COMICS
1945 - #8, June-July, 1947
Harvey Publications (Home Comics)

No#-Helpful Hank, Bozo Bear & others			
	1.00	2.00	3.00
#2-4	.40	.80	1.20
5-8: #5-Rags Rabbit begins	.40	.80	1.20

NUTTY LIFE
#2, Summer, 1946
Fox Features Syndicate

#2	1.35	2.75	4.00

NYOKA, THE JUNGLE GIRL (Formerly Jungle Girl)
#2, Winter, 1945 - #77, June, 1953
Fawcett Publications

#2	15.00	30.00	45.00
3	10.00	20.00	30.00
4-10	7.00	14.00	21.00
11-20	5.00	10.00	15.00
21-30	4.00	8.00	12.00
31-50	2.50	5.00	7.50
51-60	2.00	4.00	6.00
61-77	1.50	3.00	4.50

NOTE: *Krigstein* stories-#11,13,14,17,18.

NYOKA, THE JUNGLE GIRL (Zoo Funnies #1-12)
1955 - #22, Nov, 1957
Charlton Comics

#13-22	1.75	3.35	5.00

OAKEY DOAKES
1942   (One Shot)
Eastern Color Printing Co.

#1	12.00	24.00	36.00

OBIE
1953   (6¢)
Store Comics

#1	.25	.50	.75

OCCULT FILES OF DOCTOR SPEKTOR, THE
May, 1973 - #24, Feb, 1977
Gold Key (Also see Mystery Comics Digest #5)

#1-1st app. Lakota; Baron Tibor begins			
	.40	.80	1.20

301

(Occult Files of Dr. Spektor cont'd)

	Good	Fine	Mint
2-5: #3-Ra-Ka-Tep, the Mummy begins. #4-Intro. Elliott Kane; Duroc(later called Durak) app. #5-Hyde begins; 1st app. Count Dracula	.20	.40	.60
6-10: #6-Origin Simbar, the Lion Lord; 1st app. Frankenstein Monster. #7-Flashbacks to Tragg #8 & Dagar #1; establishes blood-link between Tragg, Dagar, & Spektor. #8-1st app. Cindy Bask(Kane's girlfriend). #9-Dr. Solar app.	.15	.30	.45
11-13: #11-1st app. Spektor as Werewolf. #12-1st app. Dr. Tong & Lu-Sai	.15	.30	.45
14-Dr. Solar app.	.15	.30	.45
15-17: #15-Xorkon app.; Durak flashback(Digest #14). #16-Durak app. #17-1st app. Anne Sara, Spektor's cousin	.15	.30	
18-Rutland, Vermont story. The Owl, Dr. Solar, Lurker, Hyde, Frankenstein Monster, Dracula, Count Wulfstein, Ra-Ka-Tep, Simbar, The Purple Zombie app.	.15	.30	
19-22: #19-Tragg cameo. #21-Lurker guest-stars	.15	.30	
23-Dr. Solar cameo	.15	.30	
24-Dr. Tong app.	.15	.30	

ODELL'S ADVENTURES IN 3-D (See Adventures in --)

OFFICIAL SOUPY SALES COMIC (See Soupy Sales)

OFFICIAL TRUE CRIME CASES (Formerly All-Winner #21; All-True Crime Cases #26 on)
#22, Spring, 1947 - #25, Winter, 1947-48
Timely/Marvel(OCI)

#22-25: #24-Burgos art	.80	1.60	2.40

O.G. WHIZ
Feb, 1971 - #6, May, 1972
Gold Key

#1,2-John Stanley script, pencils, inks, & lettering	.50	1.00	1.50
3-6	.25	.50	.75

OH, BROTHER! (Teen Comedy)
Jan, 1953 - #5, Oct, 1953
Stanhall Publ./Trojan/Standard #5

#1	.65	1.35	2.00
2-5	.40	.80	1.20

OH SUSANNA (See 4-Color Comics #1105)

OKAY COMICS

1940
United Features Syndicate

	Good	Fine	Mint
#1-Captain & the Kids & Hawkshaw the Detective reprints	10.00	20.00	30.00

OK COMICS
July, 1940 - #2, 1940
United Features Syndicate

	Good	Fine	Mint
#1-Little Giant, Phantom Knight, Sunset Smith & The Teller Twins begin	15.00	30.00	45.00
2 (Rare)	15.00	30.00	45.00

OKLAHOMA KID
June, 1957 - #4, 1958
Ajax/Farrell Publ.

#1	1.35	2.75	4.00
2-4	.80	1.60	2.40

OKLAHOMAN, THE (See 4-Color Comics #820)

OLD GLORY COMICS
1944 (Giveaway)
Chesapeake & Ohio Railway

Capt. Fearless reprint	2.00	4.00	6.00

OLD IRONSIDES (See 4-Color Comics #874)

OLD YELLER (See 4-Color #869, Movie Comics, and Walt Disney Showcase #25)

OMAC (One Man Army, -- Corps #4 on)
Sept-Oct, 1974 - #8, Nov-Dec, 1975
National Periodical Publications

#1	.50	1.00	1.50
2-8	.25	.50	.75

NOTE: *Kirby* art-#1-8; covers-#1-7. *Kubert* cover-#8.

O'MALLEY AND THE ALLEY CATS
April, 1971 - #9, Jan, 1974 (Disney)
Gold Key

#1	.20	.40	.60
2-9		.15	.30

OMEGA THE UNKNOWN
March, 1976 - #10, Sept, 1977
Marvel Comics Group

#1	.25	.50	.75
2-10: #2-Hulk app.	.15	.30	.45

Official True Crime Cases #25. © MCG

OK Comics #2. © UFS

Oklahoma Kid #1. © Ajax

100 Pages Of Comics #101, © Dell

Operation Peril #1, © ACG

Oswald 4-Color #273, © Walter Lantz

ONE HUNDRED AND ONE DALMATIANS (See 4-Color
#1183, Movie Comics, & W. Disney Showcase #9)

100 PAGES OF COMICS
1937   (Stiff covers)
Dell Publishing Co.
                      Good   Fine   Mint
#101(Found on back cover)-Alley Oop, Wash
   Tubbs, Capt. Easy, Og Son of Fire, Apple
   Mary, Tom Mix, Dan Dunn, Tailspin Tommy,
   Doctor Doom   32.50 65.00 97.50

100-PAGE SUPER SPECTACULAR (See DC --)

$1,000,000 DUCK (See W. Disney Showcase #5)

ONE MILLION YEARS AGO (See Tor)

ONE SHOT (See 4-Color --)

1001 HOURS OF FUN
1942   (52pgs.)(11¼x8-3/8")(Like Large Feat-
Dell Publishing Co.   ure Comics)

Puzzles & games; by A.W. Nugent
                      4.00   8.00   12.00

ON STAGE (See 4-Color Comics #1336)

ON THE AIR
1947   (Giveaway)
NBC Network Comic

(Scarce)   1.00   2.00   3.00

ON THE DOUBLE (See 4-Color Comics #1232)

ON THE LINKS
Dec, 1926   (48 pgs.) (9x10")
Associated Feature Service

Daily strip reprints 7.00   14.00   21.00

ON THE SPOT (Pretty Boy Floyd --)
Fall, 1948
Fawcett Publications

No#   4.00   8.00   12.00

OPERATION BIKINI (See Movie Classics)

OPERATION BUCHAREST (See The Crusaders)

OPERATION CROSSBOW (See Movie Classics)

OPERATION PERIL
Oct-Nov, 1950 - 1953
American Comics Group

                      Good   Fine   Mint
#1-Time Travelers, Danny Danger (by Leonard
   Starr) & Typhoon Tyler (by Ogden Whitney)
   begin   2.00   4.00   6.00
2-5: #3-Horror story 1.35   2.75   4.00
6-12-Last Time Travelers; change to war
   format; #7-All horror 1.00 2.00   3.00
13-16   .65   1.35   2.00
NOTE: *Whitney stories-#1,2,8-10; covers-#1,
8,9.*

OPERATOR #7 OF THE SECRET SERVICE
(See Chewing Gum Booklet)

ORAL ROBERTS' TRUE STORIES (15¢)(Junior
Partners #120 on) (No#, #102 - 25¢)
1956(no month) - #119, 7/59
TelePix Publ.(Oral Roberts' Evangelistic Assn/
Healing Waters)

V1#1(1956)-(Not code approved)-"The Miracle
   Touch"   2.00   4.00   6.00
#102-(only issue approved by code)(10/56)
                     2.00   4.00   6.00
103-119: #115-(#114 on inside)
                     1.50   3.00   4.50

ORIGINAL SWAMP THING SAGA, THE (See DC
Special Series #2)

OSCAR (Formerly Animated Funny Comic Tunes;
Awful -- #12 on)
#24, Spring, 1947 - #11, June, 1949
Marvel Comics

#24(1947)   1.00   2.00   3.00
 25(1947)-Wolverton art + Kurtzman's "Hey
   Look"   3.00   6.00   9.00
#3-9,11   .80   1.60   2.40
10-Kurtzman's "Hey Look" 2.00 4.00   6.00

OSWALD THE RABBIT
1943 - 1962   (Walter Lantz)
Dell Publishing Co.

4-Color #21('43)   16.50   33.25   50.00
4-Color #39('43)   13.50   26.75   40.00
4-Color #67('44)   8.00   16.00   24.00
4-Color #102('46)-Kelly art, 1pg.
                      8.00   16.00   24.00
4-Color #143,183   3.00   6.00   9.00
4-Color #225,273   2.50   5.00   7.50
4-Color #315,388   1.75   3.50   5.25
4-Color #458,507,549,593 1.20 2.40   3.60
4-Color #623,697,792,894,979,1268
                       .65   1.35   2.00

303

OSWALD THE RABBIT (See March of Comics #7, 38,53,67,81,95,111,126,141,156,171,186, & Super Book #8,20)

OUR ARMY AT WAR (Sgt. Rock #302 on)
Aug, 1952 - #301, Feb, 1977
National Periodical Publications

	Good	Fine	Mint
#1	8.00	16.00	24.00
2,3,5	4.00	8.00	12.00
4-Krigstein story	5.00	10.00	15.00
6,7	3.00	6.00	9.00
8-10-Krigstein stories	4.00	8.00	12.00
11,14-Krigstein stories	3.00	6.00	9.00
12,15-20	2.00	4.00	6.00
13-Krigstein cover/story	3.50	7.00	10.50
21-30	1.50	3.00	4.50
31-60	1.00	2.00	3.00
61-70	.80	1.60	2.40
71-80	.65	1.35	2.00
81-1st Sgt. Rock app. by Andru & Esposito in Easy Co. story	3.00	6.00	9.00
82-Sgt. Rock cameo in Easy Co. story(6 panels)			
83-1st Kubert Sgt. Rock	1.75	3.35	5.00
84-90,92-100	.50	1.00	1.50
91-All Sgt. Rock issue	.65	1.35	2.00
101-120	.40	.80	1.20
121-150	.30	.60	.90
151-Intro. Enemy Ace by Kubert	1.35	2.75	4.00
152-163,165-170: #153,155-Enemy Ace stories. #157-2pg.pin-up. #162,163-Viking Prince x-over in Sgt. Rock	.80	1.60	2.40
164-Giant G-19	1.00	2.00	3.00
165-176,178-181	.25	.50	.75
177-80pg. Giant G-32	.35	.70	1.05
182,183,186-Neal Adams art	.65	1.35	2.00
184,185,187-189,191-199: #189-Intro. The Teenage Underground Fighters of Unit 3	.20	.40	.60
190-80pg. Giant G-44	.35	.70	1.05
200-12pg. Rock story told in verse; Krigstein reprint; Evans story	.25	.50	.75
201-Krigstein reprint/#14	.25	.50	.75
202,206-215	.20	.40	.60
203-80pg. Giant G-56-All reprints, no Sgt. Rock	.25	.50	.75
204,205-All reprints, no Sgt. Rock	.20	.40	.60
216-80pg. Giant G-68	.30	.60	.90
217-228	.20	.40	.60
229-80pg. Giant G-80	.30	.60	.90
230-234,236-239	.15	.30	.45
235,241-Toth art	.20	.40	.60
240-Adams art	.20	.40	.60
242-50¢ ish. DC-9	.25	.50	.75
243-248,250-253	.15	.30	.45
249-Wood art	.25	.50	.75

	Good	Fine	Mint
254-Toth art	.15	.30	.45
255-301		.20	.40

NOTE: *Alcala* story-#251. *Drucker* stories-#27, 67,68,79,82,83,164,177,203,212,244,269,275, 280. *Evans* stories-#165-175,200,266,269,270, 274,276,278,280. *Kubert* stories-#38,59,67,68 & most issues from #83 on. *Maurer* stories-#233,237,239. *Medal of Honor* by *Maurer*-#233, 237,239,240,280,284,288,290,291,295. *U.S.S. Stevens* by *Glanzman*-#218,220,222,223,225,227, 230-32,238,240,241,244,247,248,256-59,261, 265-67,271,282,283,298.

OUR FIGHTING FORCES
Oct-Nov, 1954 - Present
National Periodical Publications/DC Comics

	Good	Fine	Mint
#1	6.00	12.00	18.00
2-5	3.00	6.00	9.00
6-9	2.00	4.00	6.00
10-Wood story	2.50	5.00	7.50
11-30	1.35	2.75	4.00
31-40	1.00	2.00	3.00
41-44	.50	1.00	1.50
45-Gunner & Sarge begin(ends #94)	.50	1.00	1.50
46-50	.40	.80	1.20
51-90	.25	.50	.75
91-100: #95-Devil-Dog begins, ends #98. #99-Capt. Hunter begins, ends #106	.20	.40	.60
101-122: #106-Hunters Hellcats begin. #116-Mlle. Marie app. #121-Intro. Heller	.15	.30	.45
123-Losers(Capt. Storm, Gunner/Sarge, Johnny Cloud) begin	.15	.30	.45
124-133,135-145	.15	.30	.45
134,146-Toth art		.20	.40
147-177		.20	.40

NOTE: *Adams* cover-#147. *Drucker* stories-#39, 42,43. *Evans* story-#149,165-173(Losers). *Infantino* story-#135. *Kirby* story-#151-162; covers-#152-159. *Kubert* art in many issues. *Maurer* story-#135. *Redondo* story-#166. *Medal of Honor* by *Maurer*-#135. *U.S.S. Stevens* by *Glanzman*-#125-28,134,138-41,143,144.

OUR FIGHTING MEN IN ACTION
1957 - 1958
Ajax/Farrell Publ. (Four Star Comic Corp.)

	Good	Fine	Mint
#1	.80	1.60	2.40
2-6	.40	.80	1.20

OUR FLAG COMICS
Aug, 1941 - #5, April, 1942
Ace Magazines

Our Flag Comics #2. © Ace

Our Gang Comics #11. © Loew's Inc.

Our Army At War #123. © DC

Our Gang Comics #32. © Loew's Inc.

The Outer Limits #2. © Dell

The Outlaw Kid #1. © MCG

(Our Flag Comics cont'd)	Good	Fine	Mint
#1-Captain Victory & the Unknown Soldier			
begin	40.00	80.00	120.00
2-Origin The Flag	25.00	50.00	75.00
3-5	20.00	40.00	60.00

OUR GANG COMICS (With Tom & Jerry #39-59;
becomes Tom & Jerry #60 on)
Sept-Oct, 1942 - #59, June, 1949
Dell Publishing Co.

	Good	Fine	Mint
#1-Our Gang & Barney Bear by Kelly, Tom & Jerry, Pete Smith, Flip & Dip, The Milky Way begin	90.00	180.00	270.00
2	40.00	80.00	120.00
3-5	30.00	60.00	90.00
6-Bumbazine & Albert only app. by Kelly	40.00	80.00	120.00
7-No Kelly story	17.50	35.00	52.50
8-Benny Burro begins by Barks	40.00	80.00	120.00
9-Two Barks stories-B.Burro & Happy Hound; No Kelly story	30.00	60.00	90.00
10-B.Burro by Barks	30.00	60.00	90.00
11-1st Barney Bear & Benny Burro by Barks; Happy Hound by Barks	25.00	50.00	75.00
12-20	17.50	35.00	52.50
21-30	12.00	24.00	36.00
31-36-Last Barks ish.	7.00	14.00	21.00
37-50	2.00	4.00	6.00
51-57	1.50	3.00	4.50
58,59-No Kelly art or Our Gang story	1.00	2.00	3.00

NOTE: #31-36 contain Barks art in part only.
(See March of Comics #3,26.)

OUR LADY FATIMA
1955   (15¢)
Catechetical Guild Educational Society

No#	1.50	3.00	4.50

OUR LOVE
1949 - #2, Jan, 1950
Marvel Comics (SPC)

#1,2	1.00	2.00	3.00

OUR LOVE STORY
Oct, 1969 - #38, 1975
Marvel Comics Group

#1		.20	.35
2-4,6-13		.10	.20
5-Steranko art	2.00	4.00	6.00
14-New story by Gary Fredrich & Tarpe' Mills (Miss Fury artist)	.65	1.35	2.00
15-38		.10	.20

OUR MISS BROOKS (See 4-Color Comics #751)

OUR SECRET
1950
Superior Comics Ltd.

	Good	Fine	Mint
#5-8	1.00	2.00	3.00

OUTBURSTS OF EVERETT TRUE
1921   (32 pgs.) (B&W)
Saalfield Publ. Co.

1907 (2-panel strips reprint)			
	5.00	10.00	15.00

OUTER LIMITS, THE (TV)
Jan-Mar, 1964 - #18, Oct, 1969
Dell Publishing Co.

#1	.50	1.00	1.50
2	.25	.50	.75
3-10	.20	.40	.60
11-18: #17 reprints #1; #18-#2			
	.15	.30	.45

OUTER SPACE
May, 1958 - #25, Dec, 1959
Charlton Comics

#17-Williamson/Wood art swiped; not by the above artists	.65	1.35	2.00
18-20: Ditko art	.65	1.35	2.00
21-25: #21-Ditko cover	.50	1.00	1.50
V2#1(11/68)-Ditko art	.35	.70	1.05
V3#2-Ditko cover	.25	.50	.75

OUTLAW (See Return of the --)

OUTLAW FIGHTERS
Aug, 1954 - #5, April, 1955
Atlas Comics (IPC)

#1	1.00	2.00	3.00
2-5	.65	1.35	2.00

OUTLAW KID, THE (1st Series)
Sept, 1954 - #19, Sept, 1957
Atlas Comics(CCC #1-11/EPI #12-19)

#1-Black Rider app.	2.00	4.00	6.00
2-7,9: #2-Bl.Rider app.	1.00	2.00	3.00
8,10-Williamson stories in both, 4pgs. ea.	2.00	4.00	6.00
11-17,19	.80	1.60	2.40
18-Williamson story	2.00	4.00	6.00

NOTE: Wildey stories-#1,4,5,7,10,15,18.

OUTLAW KID, THE (2nd Series)
Aug, 1970 - #30, Oct, 1975

(The Outlaw Kid cont'd)
Marvel Comics Group

	Good	Fine	Mint
#1,2-Reprints; Wildey art	.20	.40	.60
3-Williamson story reprt.	.15	.30	.45
4-8		.15	.30
9-Williamson story reprt.	.15	.30	.45
10-Origin Outlaw Kid-new material begins		.15	.30
11,12-Bounty Hawk cameo #11, x-over in #12,			
13-26,29,30		.15	.30
27-Origin reprint/#10		.15	.30
28-Williamson reprint		.15	.30

NOTE: *Berg* story-#7. *Wildey stories-#3,6,7,*
19,21,22,26.

OUTLAWS
Feb-Mar, 1948 - #9, June-July, 1949
D.S. Publishing Co.

#1-Used in Seduction of the Innocent			
	3.00	6.00	9.00
2-Ingels story	2.00	4.00	6.00
3-6: #3-Not Frazetta	1.00	2.00	3.00
7,8-Ingels story in ea.	2.00	4.00	6.00
9-Frazetta story, 7pgs.	9.00	18.00	27.00

OUTLAWS
#10, 5/52 - #13, 9/53; #14, 4/54
Star Publishing Co.

#10-14	.65	1.35	2.00

OUTLAWS OF THE WEST (Formerly Cody of the
Pony Express #10)
#11, July, 1957 - #81, May, 1970
Charlton Comics

#11-13,15-17,19,20	.50	1.00	1.50
14-68pgs. (15¢)	.65	1.35	2.00
18-Ditko art	.75	1.50	2.25
21-50	.25	.50	.75
51-70: #54-Kid Montana app. #65-Captain			
Doom begins. #68-Kid Montana begins			
	.15	.30	.45
71-81: #73-Origin & 1st app. The Sharp Shoot-			
er, last app.-#74. #75-Last Capt. Doom.			
#80,81-Ditko art		.15	.30

OUTLAWS OF THE WILD WEST
1952 (132 pgs.) (25¢)
Avon Periodicals

#1-Wood back cover; Kubert art(3 Jesse James			
reprints)	4.00	8.00	12.00

OUT OF SANTA'S BAG (See March of Comics #10)

OUT OF THE NIGHT (The Hooded Horseman #18 on)
Feb-Mar, 1952 - #17, Oct-Nov, 1954
American Comics Group (Creston/Scope)

	Good	Fine	Mint
#1-Williamson story, 9pgs. + Torres story			
	6.00	12.00	18.00
2-Williamson story,5pgs.	4.00	8.00	12.00
3,5-10	.80	1.60	2.40
4-Williamson story,7pgs.	4.00	8.00	12.00
11-17	.65	1.35	2.00

OUT OF THE SHADOWS
June, 1950 - 1951
Avon Periodicals

#1-Kubert art	4.00	8.00	12.00
2-7	2.00	4.00	6.00

OUT OF THE SHADOWS
#5, July, 1952 - #14, Aug, 1954
Standard Comics/Visual Editions

#5,12,14-Toth stories + Moreira art-#5			
	1.50	3.00	4.50
6-8,10,13	.65	1.35	2.00
9-Two Crandall stories	1.75	3.35	5.00
11-Toth art, 2pgs.	1.00	2.00	3.00

OUT OF THIS WORLD
June, 1950 (One Shot)
Avon Periodicals

#1-Two Kubert stories(one reprt/Eerie #1-'47			
+ Crom the Barbarian by Giunta (origin)			
	9.00	18.00	27.00

OUT OF THIS WORLD ADVENTURES (Pulp)
July, 1950 - #2, Dec, 1950; #2, April, 1951
Avon Periodicals

#1-Has Avon's Out of This World #1 comic in-			
sert	6.00	12.00	18.00
2-Has Avon's Strange Worlds #1			
	5.00	10.00	15.00
2(4/51)-Has Avon's Flying Saucers #1			
	6.00	12.00	18.00

NOTE: *Comic book inserts can vary.*

OUT OF THIS WORLD
1957 - #16, Dec-Jan, 1960
Charlton Comics

#1	1.35	2.75	4.00
2	.65	1.35	2.00
3-6: #3,4-Ditko stories each			
	1.50	3.00	4.50
7,8-68pgs.(15¢-Ditko art)	1.75	3.35	5.00
9-12-Ditko stories	1.35	2.75	4.00

Outlaws #2. © DS   Out Of This World(Pulp) #1. © Avon   Out Of This World #8. © CC

Ozark Ike #14, © Std

Ozzie & Babs #1, © Faw

Pancho Villa, © Avon

	Good	Fine	Mint
Out of This World cont'd)			
3-16	.40	.80	1.20

NOTE: *Ditko covers-#3-5,11.*

OUT OUR WAY WITH WORRY WART (See 4-Color#680)

OWL, THE
April, 1967; #2, April, 1968
Gold Key

#1,2	.20	.40	.60

OXYDOL-DREFT
1950 (Set of 6 pocket-size giveaways-Distributed through the mail as a set)
Oxydol-Dreft

#1-Li'l Abner, #2-Daisy Mae, #3-Shmoo
	3.00	6.00	9.00
#4-John Wayne-Williamson/Frazetta cover from			
John Wayne #3	3.50	7.00	10.50
#5-Archie	2.50	5.00	7.50
#6-Terrytoons Mighty Mouse	2.00	4.00	6.00

NOTE: *Set is worth more with original envelope.*

OZ (See MGM's Marvelous-- & Marvel Treasury--)

OZARK IKE
2/48; 11/48 - #24, 12/51; #25, 9/52
Dell Publishing Co./Standard Comics

4-Color #180(1948-Dell)	2.50	5.00	7.50
#B11, B12	2.50	5.00	7.50
#13-15	2.50	5.00	7.50
16-25	2.00	4.00	6.00

OZZIE & BABS
#1947 - #13, Fall, 1949
Fawcett Publications

#1	1.00	2.00	3.00
2-13	.50	1.00	1.50

OZZIE & HARRIET (See The Adventures of--)

PACIFIC GAS & ELECTRIC (See Donald Duck)

PAGEANT OF COMICS (See Jane Arden & Mopsy)
Sept, 1947 - #2, Oct, 1947
Archer St. John

#1-Mopsy strip reprints	3.00	6.00	9.00
2-Jane Arden strip reprints			
	3.00	6.00	9.00

PANCHO VILLA
1950
Avon Periodicals

	Good	Fine	Mint
No#-Kinstler cover	4.00	8.00	12.00

PANHANDLE PETE AND JENNIFER (TV)
July, 1951 - #3, Nov, 1951
J. Charles Laue Publishing Co.

#1-3	1.00	2.00	3.00

PANIC (Companion to Mad)
Feb-Mar, 1954 - #12, Dec-Jan, 1955-56
E.C. Comics

#1	6.00	12.00	18.00
2-4: #3-Kelly parody	4.00	8.00	12.00
5-12	3.00	6.00	9.00

NOTE: *Davis stories-#1-12; cover-#12. Elder stories-#1-12. Feldstein covers-#1-3,5. Kamen story-#1. Orlando stories-#1-9. Wolverton cover-#4. Wood stories-#2-9,11,12.*

PANIC (Magazine) (Satire)
7/58 - #6, 7/59; V2#10, 12/65 - V2#12, 1966
Panic Publications

#1	1.35	2.75	4.00
2-6	1.00	2.00	3.00
V2#10-12: Reprints earlier issues			
	.50	1.00	1.50

NOTE: *Davis art-#3(2pgs.),4,5,10; cover-#10. Elder art-#5. Powell art-V2#10. Torres art-#1-5.*

PARADE (See Hanna-Barbera --)

PARADE COMICS (Frisky Animals on Parade #2 on)
Sept, 1957
Ajax/Farrell Publ. (World Famous Publ.)

#1	.25	.50	.75

NOTE: *Cover title: Frisky Animals on Parade.*

PARAMOUNT ANIMATED COMICS
Feb, 1953 - #21, 1956
Harvey Publications

#1	1.75	3.35	5.00
2-6	1.35	2.75	4.00
7-Baby Huey begins	2.00	4.00	6.00
8-21	1.00	2.00	3.00

PARENT TRAP, THE (See 4-Color Comics #1210)

PAROLE BREAKERS
Dec, 1952 - #3, July, 1952
Avon Periodicals/Realistic

#1	3.35	6.75	10.00

(Parole Breakers cont'd)	Good	Fine	Mint
2-Kubert story	4.00	8.00	12.00
3-Kinstler cover	2.50	5.00	7.50

PARTRIDGE FAMILY, THE (TV)
March, 1971 - #20, Nov, 1973
Charlton Comics

	Good	Fine	Mint
#1-4,6-20		.15	.30
5-Partridge Family Summer Special (52pgs.)			
	.15	.30	.45

PASSION, THE
1955
Catechetical Guild

	1.50	3.00	4.50

PAT BOONE
Sept-Oct, 1959 - #5, May-June, 1960
National Periodical Publications

#1	2.50	5.00	7.50
2-5	1.50	3.00	4.50

PATCHES
Mar-Apr, 1945 - #11, Nov, 1947
Rural Home/Patches Publ. (Orbit)

#1-L.B. Cole cover	1.35	2.75	4.00
2-11	1.00	2.00	3.00

PATORUZU (See Adventures of --)

PATSY & HEDY
1952 - #110, Feb, 1967
Atlas Comics/Marvel(GPI/Male)

#1	1.75	3.35	5.00
2-10	1.00	2.00	3.00
11-20	.50	1.00	1.50
21-50	.25	.50	.75
51-110		.20	.40
Annual #1('63)	1.00	2.00	3.00

PATSY & HER PALS
1953 - #29, Aug, 1957
Atlas Comics (PPI)

#1	1.75	3.35	5.00
2-10	.65	1.35	2.00
11-29	.40	.80	1.20

PATSY WALKER (Also see Girls' Life & Miss America Magazine)
Oct, 1945 - #124, Dec, 1965
Marvel/Atlas Comics(BPC)

	Good	Fine	Min
#1	7.00	14.00	21.0
2	3.35	6.75	10.0
3-10	2.00	4.00	6.0
11,12,15,16,18,23,24,26-29			
	1.35	2.75	4.0
13,14,17,19-22-Kurtzman's "Hey Look"			
	2.00	4.00	6.0
25-Rusty by Kurtzman	2.50	5.00	7.5
30-60	.65	1.35	2.0
61-100	.35	.70	1.0
101-124	.15	.30	.4
Fashion Parade #1('66,68pgs)			
	.65	1.35	2.0

PAT THE BRAT
June, 1953; Summer, 1955 - #35, Nov, 1959
Archie Publications (Radio)

No#(6/53)	1.75	3.35	5.0
#1(Summer,'55)	1.35	2.75	4.0
2-10	.65	1.35	2.0
11-35	.40	.80	1.2

PATTY POWERS
1956
Atlas Comics

#5-7	.40	.80	1.2

PAT WILTON (See Mighty Midget Comics)

PAULINE PERIL (See The Close Shaves of --)

PAUL REVERE'S RIDE (See 4-Color #822)

PAUL TERRY'S ADVENTURES OF MIGHTY MOUSE
(See Adventures of --)

PAUL TERRY'S COMICS (Formerly Terry-Toons Comics; becomes Adv. of Mighty Mouse #126 on
#85, Mar, 1951 - #125, May, 1955
St. John Publishing Co.

#85-125-Mighty Mouse	.80	1.60	2.4

PAUL TERRY'S MIGHTY MOUSE ADVENTURE STORIES
1953 (384pgs.) (50¢) (Cardboard covers)
St. John Publishing Co.

No#	5.00	10.00	15.0

PAWNEE BILL
February, 1951 - #3, July, 1951
Story Comics

#1	1.50	3.00	4.5
2,3: #3-Origin Golden Warrior; Cameron art			

Parole Breakers #1, © Avon

Patsy & Her Pals #22, © MCG

Patsy Walker #17, © MCG

Pep Comics #6, © MLJ   Pep Comics #22, © MLJ   Pep Comics #38, © MLJ

	Good	Fine	Mint
(Pawnee Bill cont'd)	1.00	2.00	3.00

PAY-OFF (This Is the --, --Crime, --Detect-
ive Stories)
July-Aug, 1948 - #5, Mar-Apr, 1949 (52 pgs.)
D. S. Publishing Co.

#1	1.20	2.40	3.60
2-5	.80	1.60	2.40

PEACEMAKER, THE
Mar, 1967 - #5, Nov, 1967
Charlton Comics

#1-Fightin' Five begins	.50	1.00	1.50
2,3,5	.30	.60	.90
4-Origin The Peacemaker	.40	.80	1.20

PEANUTS (Charlie Brown)
2/58 - #13, 1962; 5/63 - #4, 2/64
Dell Publishing Co./Gold Key

4-Color #878,969,1015('59)	1.50	3.00	4.50
#4(2-4/60)	1.35	2.75	4.00
5-13	1.00	2.00	3.00
1(G.K.)	.65	1.35	2.00
2-4	.50	1.00	1.50
#1('53-'54)-Reprints United Features' Strange
As It Seems, Willie, Fernand
	4.00	8.00	12.00

PEBBLES & BAMM BAMM (TV)
Jan, 1972 - #36, Dec, 1976 (Hanna-Barbera)
Charlton Comics

#1	.15	.30	.45
2-36		.15	.30

PEBBLES FLINTSTONE (TV)
Sept, 1963 (Hanna-Barbera)
Gold Key

#1(10088-309)	.15	.30	.45

PECKS BAD BOY & COUSIN CYNTHIA
1907 - 1908 (Strip reprints)(11¼x15-3/4")
Thompson of Chicago (by Walt McDougal)

--& Cousin Cynthia('07)-In color
	15.00	37.50	60.00
--& His Chums('08)-Hardcover-in full color
16pgs.	15.00	37.50	60.00
Advs. of--in Pictures('08)-In color-Stanton
& Van V. Liet Co.	15.00	37.50	60.00

PEDRO
1950
Fox Features Syndicate

	Good	Fine	Mint
#18(#1),2	.80	1.60	2.40

PEE-WEE PIXIES (See The Pixies)

PENALTY (See Crime Must Pay the --)

PENNY
1947 - 1949
Avon Periodicals

#1-Photo & biography of creator; newspaper
reprints	2.00	4.00	6.00
2-6	1.35	2.75	4.00

PEP COMICS
Jan, 1940 - Present
MLJ Magazines/Archie Publ. #57 on

#1-Intro. The Shield by Irving Novick(1st
   patriotic hero); origin The Comet by Jack
   Cole, The Queen of Diamond & Kayo Ward;
   The Rocket, The Press Guardian(The Falcon
   #1 only), Sergeant Boyle, Fu Chang, &
   Bentley of Scotland Yard

	100.00	200.00	300.00
2-Origin The Rocket	50.00	100.00	150.00
3	35.00	70.00	105.00
4-Wizard cameo	35.00	70.00	105.00
5-Wizard cameo in Shield story
	30.00	60.00	90.00
6-10: #8-Last Cole Comet
	25.00	50.00	75.00
11-Dusty, Shield's sidekick begins; last
Press Guardian, Fu Chang
	20.00	40.00	60.00
12-Origin Fireball; last Rocket & Queen of
Diamonds	25.00	50.00	75.00
13-15	20.00	40.00	60.00
16-Origin Madam Satan	25.00	50.00	75.00
17-Origin The Hangman; death of The Comet
	75.00	150.00	225.00
18-20-Last Fireball	17.50	35.00	52.50
21-Last Madam Satan	16.50	33.25	50.00
22-Intro. & 1st app. Archie, Betty, &
Jughead(12/41)	35.00	70.00	105.00
23-29	15.00	30.00	45.00
30-Capt. Commando begins	15.00	30.00	45.00
31-40: #36-1st Archie cover
	12.00	24.00	36.00
41-47: #47-Last Hangman issue. #41 on are
all Archie covers	8.00	16.00	24.00
48-Black Hood begins(5/44); ends #51,59,60
	6.00	12.00	18.00
49-60: #52-Suzie begins. #54-Capt. Commando
app. #56-Last Capt. Commando. #59-Suzie
ends. #60-Katy Keene begins
	5.00	10.00	15.00

(Pep Comics cont'd)	Good	Fine	Mint

61-65: #62-1st app. Li'l Jinx. #65-Last
  Shield ish.   3.00 6.00 9.00
66-100: #66-G-Man Club becomes Archie Club
  (2/48)   2.00 4.00 6.00
101-149: #139,140-Katy Keene app.
              1.50 3.00 4.50
150,152,157,159-Jaguar stories in all
             .65 1.35 2.00
151,154,160-The Fly stories in all
             .65 1.35 2.00
153,155,156,158-Flygirl stories in all
             .65 1.35 2.00
161,162,164-Katy Keene by Bill Woggan
             .65 1.35 2.00
163,169-200   .50 1.00 1.50
168-Jaguar app.   .65 1.35 2.00
201-240   .20   .40   .60
241-300   .15   .30   .45
301-332   .15   .30

PEPE (See 4-Color Comics #1194)

PERCY & FERDIE
1921 (48 pgs.) (B&W Dailies)
Cupples & Leon Co.

By H. A. McGill   6.00 12.00 18.00

PERFECT CRIME, THE
Oct, 1949 - 1953
Cross Publications

#1-Powell art   1.50 3.00 4.50
2-7,9,10: #4-Powell art. #5-Wildey art. #7-
  Steve Duncan begins, ends #30
             1.00 2.00 3.00
8-Heroin drug story 2.00 4.00 6.00
11-33   .65 1.35 2.00

PERFECT LOVE
#2, Oct-Nov, 1951 - #10, 1952
Ziff-Davis/Approved

#2   .80 1.60 2.40
3-7,9,10   .60 1.20 1.80
8-Kinstler story   1.00 2.00 3.00

PERRI (See 4-Color Comics #847)

PERRY MASON (See Feature Book #49,50,McKay)

PERRY MASON MYSTERY MAGAZINE (TV)
June-Aug, 1964 - #2, Oct-Dec, 1964
Dell Publishing Co.

#1,2   .40   .80 1.20

PERSONAL LOVE (Also see Movie Love)
Jan, 1950 - #33, June, 1955
Famous Funnies

	Good	Fine	Mint

#1   1.50 3.00 4.50
2-7,9,10   1.00 2.00 3.00
8-7pg. Kinstler story 1.75 3.35 5.00
11-Toth story   2.50 5.00 7.50
12-15,18-23   .80 1.60 2.40
16,17-1pg. Frazetta 2.00 4.00 6.00
24,25,27,28-Frazetta stories in all-8,7,8 &
  6pgs. ea.; Everett story-#24
           25.00 50.00 75.00
26,29-31,33   .65 1.35 2.00
32-Classic Frazetta story, 8pgs.
           40.00 80.00 120.00

PERSONAL LOVE
V1#1, Sept, 1957 - V3#1, Sept-Oct, 1959
Prize Publ. (Headline)

V1#1   .50 1.00 1.50
2-6(7-8/58)   .35   .70 1.05
V2#1(9-10/58)-V2#6(7-8/59) .30   .60   .90
V3#1   .20   .40   .60

PETER COTTONTAIL
Jan, 1954; Feb, 1954 - #2, Mar, 1954
Key Publications

#1(1/54)-not 3-D   1.00 2.00 3.00
1(3-D)(2/54)-Written by Bruce Hamilton
            4.00 8.00 12.00
2-Reprints 3-D #1 by not 3-D
            1.00 2.00 3.00

PETER GUNN (See 4-Color Comics #1087)

PETER PAN (See New Adventures of--, 4-Color
#442,446,926 & Movie Classics & Comics)

PETER PAN TREASURE CHEST (See Movie Classics)

PETER PANDA
Aug-Sept, 1953 - #31, Aug-Sept, 1958
National Periodical Publications

#1   2.00 4.00 6.00
2-10   1.00 2.00 3.00
11-31   .50 1.00 1.50

PETER PARKER (See The Spectacular Spider-Man)

PETER PAT (See Single Series #8)

PETER PAUL'S 4 IN 1 JUMBO COMIC BOOK
No Date (1953)
Capitol Stories

The Perfect Crime #24. © Cross Publ.

Personal Love #32. © FF

Peter Cottontail 3-D =1. © Key Publ.

Peter Paul's--#1, © Capitol Stories   Peter Wheat No #(#1), © Bakers Assoc.   Peter Wheat News #20, © Bakers Assoc.

(Peter Paul's 4-in-1 Jumbo Comic cont'd)

	Good	Fine	Mint
#1-Contains 4 comics bound; Space Adventures, Space Western, Crime & Justice, Racket Squad in Action	3.00	6.00	9.00

PETER PIG
#5, May, 1953 - #6, Aug, 1953
Standard Comics

	Good	Fine	Mint
#5,6	.25	.50	.75

PETER PORKCHOPS
Nov-Dec, 1949 - #61, Sept-Oct, 1959
National Periodical Publications

	Good	Fine	Mint
#1	3.00	6.00	9.00
2-10	1.50	3.00	4.50
11-30	1.00	2.00	3.00
31-61	.65	1.35	2.00

PETER POTAMUS (TV)
Jan, 1965   (Hanna-Barbera)
Gold Key

	Good	Fine	Mint
#1		.15	.30

PETER RABBIT (See Large Feature Comic #1)

PETER RABBIT
1922 - 1923   (9¼x6¼") (Soft Cover)
John H. Eggers Co. The House of Little Books
Publishers

#B1-B4(Set of 4 books which came in a card-
   board box) Each book reprints ½ of a Sunday page per page & contains 8 B&W & 2
   color pages; by Harrison Cady
            each.... 15.00 30.00 45.00

PETER RABBIT (Adventures of --)
1947 - #34, Aug-Sept, 1956
Avon Periodicals

#1(1947)-Reprints 1943-44 Sunday strips; con-
   tains a biography & drawing of Cady
                8.00 16.00 24.00
2-5(1949)-Last Cady ish. 5.00 10.00 15.00
6-10(1950-51)   1.50   3.00   4.50
11(11/51)-#34('56)-Avon's character
                1.50   3.00   4.50
--Easter Parade(Giant) 2.50   5.00   7.50
--Jumbo Book(1954-Giant size,25¢)-6pgs.-Jesse
   James by Kinstler 2.50   5.00   7.50

PETER RABBIT
1958
Fago Magazine Co.

	Good	Fine	Mint
#1	1.00	2.00	3.00

PETER, THE LITTLE PEST (#4 titled Petey)
Nov, 1969 - #4, May, 1970
Marvel Comics Group

#1	.15	.30	.45
2-4('69)-Reprints Dexter the Demon & Melvin the Monster		.15	.30

PETER WHEAT (The Adventures of --)
1948 - 1952 (16pgs. in color; soft covers)
Bakers Associates Giveaway

No#(#1)-States on last page, end of 1st Adventure of--; Kelly art
                15.00 30.00 45.00
No#(5 issues)-Kelly art 12.00 24.00 36.00
#7-10-All Kelly art 10.00 20.00 30.00
11-20- "   "   "   9.00 18.00 27.00
21-30 "   "   "   8.00 16.00 24.00
31-40   6.00 12.00 18.00
41-66   5.00 10.00 15.00
NOTE: *Al Hubbard* art #34? on; written by *Del Connell.*

PETER WHEAT NEWS
1948 - #20, 1949   (4pgs. in color)
Bakers Associates

Vol.1-All have 2pgs. Peter Wheat by Kelly
                10.00 20.00 30.00
2-10   8.00 16.00 24.00
11-20   5.00 10.00 15.00
NOTE: *Early issues have no date.*

PETTICOAT JUNCTION (TV)
Oct-Dec, 1964 - #5, Oct-Dec, 1965
Dell Publishing Co.

#1	.20	.40	.60
2-5	.15	.30	.45

PETUNIA (See 4-Color Comics #463)

PHANTASMO (See Black & White #18)

PHANTOM, THE
1939 - 1949
David McKay Publishing Co.

Feature Book #20,22	30.00	60.00	90.00
Feature Book #39,53	15.00	30.00	45.00
Feature Book #56,57('49)	12.00	24.00	36.00

PHANTOM, THE (See Eat Right to Work--,
Harvey Comics Hits #51,56 & Harvey Hits #1,
6,12,15,26,36,44,48)

PHANTOM, THE (No #29)
Nov, 1962 - #17, July, 1966; #18, Sept, 1966-
#28, Dec, 1967; #30, Feb, 1969 - #74, 1/77
Gold Key(#1-17)/King(#18-28)/Charlton(#30 on

	Good	Fine	Mint
#1	1.50	3.00	4.50
2-King, Queen & Jack begins; ends #11			
	1.00	2.00	3.00
3-5	.80	1.60	2.40
6-10	.65	1.35	2.00
11-17-Track Hunter begins #12			
	.50	1.00	1.50
18-Flash Gordon begins; Wood art			
	1.00	2.00	3.00
19,20-Flash Gordon ends	.65	1.35	2.00
21-24,26,27: #22,23-Mandrake app. #26-Brick			
Bradford app.	.50	1.00	1.50
25-Jeff Jones art, 1pg. Williamson ad			
	.50	1.00	1.50
28(No#)-Brick Bradford app.	.50	1.00	1.50
30-40: #36,39-Ditko art	.25	.50	.75
41-66: #62-Bolle cover	.15	.30	.45
67-Newton cvr/stys. begin	.25	.50	.75
68-74	.20	.40	.60
R-06('73)-Premium, 36pgs. in color-Mandrake			
app.	.50	1.00	1.50

PHANTOM BLOT, THE (Disney)
Oct, 1964 - #7, Nov, 1966
Gold Key

#1	1.00	2.00	3.00
2-1st Super-Goof	.80	1.60	2.40
3-7	.60	1.20	1.80

PHANTOM EAGLE (See Mighty Midget Comics)

PHANTOM LADY (1st Series) (My Love Secret
#24 on; Also see All Top, Daring Adventures,
& Jungle Thrills)
Aug, 1947 - #23, April, 1949
Fox Features Syndicate

#13(#1)-Phantom Lady by Matt Baker begins;			
The Blue Beetle app.	70.00	140.00	210.00
14(#2)	40.00	80.00	120.00
15,16	35.00	70.00	105.00
17-Classic bondage cover; used in Seduction			
of the Innocent	80.00	160.00	240.00
18-23	25.00	50.00	75.00

NOTE: *Matt Baker covers/stories in all.*

PHANTOM LADY (2nd Series)(See Terrific Comics)
12-1/55 - #4, 6/55   (Formerly Linda)
Ajax/Farrell Publ.

V1#5(#1)-by Matt Baker	15.00	30.00	45.00
V1#2-4-Red Rocket in#3,4	8.00	16.00	24.00

PHANTOM PLANET, THE (See 4-Color #1234)

PHANTOM STRANGER, THE (1st Series)
Aug-Sept, 1952 - 1953
National Periodical Publications

	Good	Fine	Mint
#1	7.00	14.00	21.00
2-6	5.00	10.00	15.00

PHANTOM STRANGER, THE (2nd Series)(See Show-
5-6/69 - #41, 2-3/76   case)
National Periodical Publications

#1	1.00	2.00	3.00
2,3,5-10	.50	1.00	1.50
4-Neal Adams art	1.20	2.40	3.60
11-19: Last 25¢ ish. #15-Toth art(reprint)			
	.40	.80	1.20
20-22	.35	.70	1.05
23-Spawn of Frankenstein begins by Kaluta,			
ends #25	.65	1.35	2.00
24,25	.50	1.00	1.50
26-30	.25	.50	.75
31-The Black Orchid begins (Dezuniga art)			
	.30	.60	.90
32,35,36-Black Orchid by Redondo			
	.30	.60	.90
33-Deadman app.	.25	.50	.75
34,37,38	.20	.40	.60
39-41-Deadman in all	.25	.50	.75

NOTE: *Adams covers-#3-19. Kaluta cover-#26.*
Meskin reprints-#15,16,18. Black Orchid by
Carrilo-#38-41. Dr. 13 solo in #13,18,20.
Frankenstein by Kaluta-#23-25; by Baily-#27-
30. No Black Orchid-#33,34.

PHANTOM WITCH DOCTOR
1952
Avon Periodicals

#1-Kinstler cover, 7pgs.	5.00	10.00	15.00

PHIL RIZZUTO (Baseball Hero)
1951   (New York Yankees)
Fawcett Publications

No#	3.00	6.00	9.00

PHOENIX
Jan, 1975 - #4, Oct, 1975
Atlas/Seaboard Publ.

#1-Origin	.25	.50	.75
2,3: #3-Origin & only app. The Dark Avenger			
	.20	.40	.60
4-New origin/costume The Protector (former-			
ly Phoenix)	.20	.40	.60

Phantom Lady #21. © DC (Fox)

Phantom Lady #5. © DC (Ajax)

Phantom Stranger #1. © DC

Pictorial Confessions #2, © STJ

Picture News #6, © Lafayette St. Corp.

P.S.F.T.B.-Life Of Christ Ed., © WMG

ICNIC PARTY (Walt Disney's)(Vacation Parade
955 - 1957   #1-5)
ell Publishing Co.

	Good	Fine	Mint
6,7-Uncle Scrooge	1.75	3.35	5.00
8-Carl Barks art	4.00	8.00	12.00

ICTORIAL CONFESSIONS
ept, 1949 - #3, Dec, 1949
t. John Publishing Co.

1-Baker art	2.50	5.00	7.50
2-Baker stys; photo cvr.	1.50	3.00	4.50
3-Kubert, Baker art	3.00	6.00	9.00

ICTORIAL LOVE STORIES (Formerly Tim McCoy)
22, Oct, 1949
harlton Comics

22	.80	1.60	2.40

ICTORIAL LOVE STORIES
ctober, 1952
t. John Publ. Co.

1-Baker cover/story	2.00	4.00	6.00

ICTORIAL ROMANCES
949 - #24, March, 1954
t. John Publishing Co.

1	2.00	4.00	6.00
2,4-10	1.50	3.00	4.50
3-Kubert story	2.50	5.00	7.50
4-18	1.00	2.00	3.00
9,20(7/53)-100pgs. ea.	2.00	4.00	6.00
1-24	1.00	2.00	3.00

NOTE: *Matt Baker art in most issues.*

PICTURE NEWS (Dick Quick #10 on)
Jan, 1946 - #9, Sept, 1946
Lafayette Street Corp.

1-Milt Gross begins, ends #6; 4pg. Kirby			
story	2.50	5.00	7.50
2-5	1.00	2.00	3.00
6-9	.80	1.60	2.40

PICTURE PARADE (Picture Progress #5 on)
Sept, 1953 - V1#4, Dec, 1953   (28 pgs.)
Gilberton Corp.

V1#1-Andy's Atomic Adventures
   2-
   3-Adventures of the Lost One (11/53)
   4-A Christmas Adventure

	1.00	2.00	3.00

PICTURE PROGRESS (Formerly Picture Parade)
V1#5, 1/54 - V3#2, 10/55   (28-36 pgs.)
Gilberton Corp.

	Good	Fine	Mint
V1#5-News in Review 1953			
6-The Birth of America			
7-The Four Seasons			
8-Paul Revere's Ride			
9-The Hawaiian Islands(5/54)			
V2#1-The Story of Flight(9/54)			
2-The Meaning of Elections			
3-Louis Pasteur			
4-The Star Spangled Banner			
5-News in Review 1954			
6-Alaska: The Great Land			
7-Life in the Circus			
V2#8-The Time of the Cave Man			
9-Summer Fun(5/55)			
each....	.65	1.35	2.00
V3#1-The Man Who Discovered America			
2-The Lewis & Clark Expedition			
each....	.65	1.35	2.00
No#-The American Indian	.65	1.35	2.00

PICTURE SCOPE JUNGLE ADVENTURES
1954   (32pgs.) (3-D?)
Star Publishing Co.

No#-Disbrow art/script	3.00	6.00	9.00

PICTURE STORIES FROM AMERICAN HISTORY
1945 - 1947   (64 - 52 pgs.)
National/All-American/E.C. Comics

#1-4	3.35	6.75	10.00

PICTURE STORIES FROM SCIENCE
Spring, 1947 - #2, Fall, 1947
E. C. Comics

#1,2	4.00	8.00	12.00

PICTURE STORIES FROM THE BIBLE
1942-43 & 1944-46
National/All-American/E.C. Comics

#1-4(Old Test.)(DC)	4.00	8.00	12.00
Complete Old Testament Edition, 232 pgs.(DC)			
1943-contains #1-4	5.00	10.00	15.00
Complete Old Testament Edition, 232 pgs.,			
Hardbound, in color with dust jacket;			
published by Bible Pictures Ltd.(1945)			
	8.00	16.00	24.00

NOTE: *Both Old & New Testaments published in
England by Bible Pictures Ltd. in hardback,
1943, in color, 376 pages.*

#1,2(Old Test. reprints in comic book form)			
(52pgs. ea.-E.C.)	3.00	6.00	9.00

(Picture Stories From the Bible cont'd)

	Good	Fine	Mint
1-3(New Test.)(52pgs. ea.)(1944-46)			
	3.00	6.00	9.00

The Life of Christ Edition-(1944)-Contains
#1 & 2 of the New Testament Edition
4.00 8.00 12.00
Complete New Testament Edition, 144pgs.(E.C.)
(1946)(Contains #1-3) 5.00 10.00 15.00
1(New Test. reprint in comic book form)
(52pgs., E.C.)   3.00 6.00 9.00

PICTURE STORIES FROM WORLD HISTORY
Spring, 1947 - #2, Fall, 1947 (52-48pgs.)
E.C. Comics

#1,2	4.00	8.00	12.00

PINHEAD & FOODINI (Also see The Great Foodini)
July, 1951 - #4, Jan, 1952   (TV)
Fawcett Publications

#1-4	1.35	2.75	4.00

PINK PANTHER & THE INSPECTOR, THE (TV)
April, 1971 - Present
Gold Key

#1	.25	.50	.75
2-10	.20	.40	.60
11-30: Warren Tufts art #16 on			
	.15	.30	.45
31-48		.15	.30
Kite Fun Book-(16pgs., 1972)-Sou. Calif.			
Edison Co. giveaway	1.00	2.00	3.00

NOTE: *Pink Panther began as a movie cartoon.
(See Golden Comics Digest #38,45 & March of
Comics #376,384,390,409)*

PINKY LEE (See The Adventures of --)

PINKY THE EGGHEAD
1963   (Reprints from Noodnik)
I.W./Super Comics

I.W. Reprint #1,2(no date)	.15	.30	.45
Super Reprint #14	.15	.30	.45

PINOCCHIO (See 4-Color #92,252,545,1203,
Movie Comics under Wonderful Advs. of-- &
World's Greatest Stories #2, New Advs. of--)

PINOCCHIO
1940   (10 pgs.) (Linen-like paper)
Montgomery Ward (Giveaway)

	7.00	14.00	21.00

PINOCCHIO LEARNS ABOUT KITES
(Also see Donald Duck & Brer Rabbit)
1954   (8pgs.) (Walt Disney-Premium)
Pacific Gas & Electric Co.

	Good	Fine	Min
(Very Rare)	10.00	20.00	30.0

PIN-UP PETE (Also see Monty Hall --)
1952
Toby Press

#1-Powell pin-ups	4.00	8.00	12.0

PIONEER MARHSALL (See Fawcett Movie Comics

PIONEER PICTURE STORIES
Dec, 1941 - #9, Dec, 1943
Street & Smith Publications

#1	2.00	4.00	6.0
2-9	1.35	2.75	4.0

PIONEER WEST ROMANCES (Firehair #1,2,6-11)
#3, Summer, 1949 - #5, Fall, 1949
Fiction House Magazines

#3-Firehair continues	2.00	4.00	6.0
4,5	1.50	3.00	4.5

PIPSQUEAK (The Adventures of --)
1953 - #39, July, 1960
Archie Publications (Radio Comics)

#1	1.35	2.75	4.0
2-10	.65	1.35	2.0
11-39	.40	.80	1.2

PIRACY
Oct-Nov, 1954 - #7, Oct-Nov, 1955
E.C. Comics

#1-Williamson/Torres art	10.00	20.00	30.0
2-Williamson/Torres art	8.00	16.00	24.0
3-7	7.00	14.00	21.0

NOTE: *Crandall stories in all; covers-#2-4.
Davis stories-#1,2,6. Evans stories-#3-7;
cover-#7. Ingels stories-#3-7. Krigstein
stories-#3-5,7; covers-#5,6. Wood stories-
#1,2; cover-#1.*

PIRANA (See Thrill-O-Rama #2,3)

PIRATE OF THE GULF, THE (See Superior Stor
ies #2)

PIRATES COMICS
Feb-Mar, 1950 - #4, Aug-Sept, 1950
Hillman Periodicals

P.S. From World History #1, © WMG

Pioneer West Romances #4, © FH

Piracy #4, © WMG

Planet Comics #36, © FH

Planet Comics #41, © FH

Plastic Man #3, © DC (Qua)

Pirates Comics cont'd)	Good	Fine	Mint
1	1.35	2.75	4.00
2-4: #4-Berg art	1.00	2.00	3.00

IXIE & DIXIE & MR. JINKS (TV)
uly-Sept, 1960 - Feb, 1963 (Hanna-Barbera)
ell Publishing Co./Gold Key

-Color #1112,1196,1264	.50	1.00	1.50
01-631-207(Dell)	.35	.70	1.05
1(2/63-G.K.)	.25	.50	.75

IXIE PUZZLE ROCKET TO ADVENTURELAND
ov, 1952
von Periodicals

1	1.20	2.40	3.60

IXIES, THE (Advs. of --)(Mighty Atom #6 on)
inter, 1946 - #4, 1947; #5, 1948
lagazine Enterprises

1-Mighty Atom	1.75	3.35	5.00
2-5-Mighty Atom	1.00	2.00	3.00
W Reprint #1('58),#8-(Pee-Wee Pixies),#10-			
IW on cover, Super on inside	.50	1.00	1.50

LANET COMICS
an, 1940 - #73, 1954
iction House Magazines

1-Origin Auro, Lord of Jupiter; Flint Baker			
& The Red Comet begin; Eisner/Fine cover			
	90.00	180.00	270.00
2-(Scarce)	60.00	120.00	180.00
3	50.00	100.00	150.00
4-Gale Allen and the Girl Squadron begins;			
Fine cover	40.00	80.00	120.00
5,6-(Scarce)	35.00	70.00	105.00
7-11	27.50	55.00	82.50
12-The Star Pirate begins	25.00	50.00	75.00
13-15: #13-Reff Ryan begins. #15-Mars, God			
of War begins	25.00	50.00	75.00
16-20	20.00	40.00	60.00
21-The Lost World & Hunt Bowman begin			
	25.00	50.00	75.00
22-25	16.50	33.25	50.00
26-The Space Rangers begin			
	15.00	30.00	45.00
27-30	13.50	26.75	40.00
31-35: #33-Origin Star Pirates Wonder Boots,			
reprinted in #52. #35-Mysta of the Moon			
begins	12.00	24.00	36.00
36-45: #41-New origin of "Auro, Lord of Jup-			
iter". #42-Last Gale Allen. #43-Futura			
begins	10.00	20.00	30.00
46-60	7.00	14.00	21.00
61-64	6.00	12.00	18.00

	Good	Fine	Mint
65-70-All partial reprints of earlier issues			
	4.50	9.00	13.50
71-73-No series stories	4.00	8.00	12.00
IW Reprint #1(no date)-reprints #70, which			
reprints part of #41	1.75	3.35	5.00
IW Reprint #8(reprts.#72),#9-Reprts.#73			
	1.75	3.35	5.00

NOTE: #33-38,40-51-Star Pirate by Anderson.
Eisner covers-#1-5. Evans art-#50-64(Lost
World). Ingels art-#24-31,56-61(Auro, Lord
of Jupiter). Mysta of the Moon by Maurice
Whitman-#51,52; by Matt Baker-#53-59. Star
Pirate by M. Whitman-#54-56.

PLANET OF THE APES (Magazine)(See Book&Record)
8/74 - #29, 2/77 (B&W; based on movies)
Marvel Comics Group

#1-Ploog art	1.00	2.00	3.00
2-Ploog art	.60	1.20	1.80
3-10	.50	1.00	1.50
11-20	.40	.80	1.20
21-29	.35	.70	1.05

NOTE: Alcala art-#7-11,17-22,24. Ploog art-
#1-8,11,13,14,19. Sutton art-#12,15,17,19,
20,23,24.

PLANET OF VAMPIRES
Feb, 1975 - #3, June, 1975
Seaboard Publications (Atlas)

#1-Adams cover	.25	.50	.75
2-Adams cvr, #3-Heath art	.20	.40	.60

PLASTIC MAN (Also see Police)
1943 - #64, 11/56
Vital Publ. #1,2/Quality Comics #3 on

No#(#1)-"The Game of Death"; Jack Cole art			
begins	70.00	140.00	210.00
No#(#2)-"The Gay Nineties Nightmare"			
	40.00	80.00	120.00
#3	30.00	60.00	90.00
4	25.00	50.00	75.00
5	20.00	40.00	60.00
6-10	13.50	26.75	40.00
11-20	10.00	20.00	30.00
21-30	8.00	16.00	24.00
31-40	6.00	12.00	18.00
41-64	4.00	8.00	12.00
Super Reprint #11('63),#16(reprints #21, Cole			
art),#18('64-Spirit app. by Eisner)			
	1.75	3.35	5.00

PLASTIC MAN (See DC Special #15 & Brave & the
11-12/66 - #10, 5-6/68;   Bold)
#11, 2-3/76 - #20, 10-11/77
National Periodical Publications/DC Comics

315

(Plastic Man cont'd)	Good	Fine	Mint
#1-Gil Kane cover	1.00	2.00	3.00
2-5('68)	.50	1.00	1.50
6-10('68)	.40	.80	1.20
11('76)-20	.15	.30	.45

PLAYFUL LITTLE AUDREY
May, 1957 - Present
Harvey Publications

	Good	Fine	Mint
#1	2.50	5.00	7.50
2-5	1.35	2.75	4.00
6-10	.80	1.60	2.40
11-30	.40	.80	1.20
31-50	.20	.40	.60
51-121(5/76)		.15	.30
Clubhouse #1('63)	.80	1.60	2.40

PLOP!
Sept-Oct, 1973 - #24, Nov-Dec, 1976
National Periodical Publications

	Good	Fine	Mint
#1-Wrightson story	.65	1.35	2.00
2-4	.35	.70	1.05
5-Wrightson story	.40	.80	1.20
6-10	.25	.50	.75
11-20	.20	.40	.60
21-24-Giant Size, 52pgs.	.20	.40	.60

NOTE: _Alcala stories-#1-3. Ditko story-#16._
Orlando art-#21,22. Toth story-#11. Wolverton
art-#4(1pg.),22; covers-#1-12,14,17. Wood
art-#14,16,18-24; covers-#13,15,16,18,19.

PLUTO
1942 - 1961   (Walt Disney)
Dell Publishing Co.

Large Feature Comic #7(1942)

	Good	Fine	Mint
	65.00	130.00	195.00
4-Color #429,509	1.75	3.35	5.00
4-Color #595,654	1.00	2.00	3.00
4-Color #736,853,941,1039,1143,1248			
	.80	1.60	2.40

  (See Walt Disney Showcase #4,7,13,20,23)

POCAHONTAS
1941 - #2, 1942
Pocahontas Fuel Company

	Good	Fine	Mint
No#(#1), #2	4.00	8.00	12.00

POCKET COMICS   (Pocket size - 100 pgs.)
Aug, 1941 - #4, Jan, 1942
Harvey Publications

#1-Origin The Black Cat, Cadet Blakey the
  Spirit of 76, The Phantom Sphinx, The Red
  Blazer, & The Zebra; Phantom Ranger, Brit-

	Good	Fine	Mint
ish Agent 99, Spin Hawkins, Satan, Lord			
of Evil begin	25.00	50.00	75.00
2	16.50	33.25	50.00
3,4	15.00	30.00	45.00

POGO PARADE   (Annual)
1953   (100 pgs.)
Dell Publishing Co.

	Good	Fine	Mint
#1-Kelly art(Reprints Pogo from Animal Comics			
in this order: #11,13,21,14,27,16,23,9,18,			
15,17)	20.00	40.00	60.00

POGO POSSUM   (Also see Animal Comics)
1949 - 1954
Dell Publishing Co.

	Good	Fine	Mint
4-Color #105(1946-Kelly	50.00	100.00	150.00
4-Color #148-Kelly	40.00	80.00	120.00
#1-Kelly art in all	30.00	60.00	90.00
2	16.50	33.25	50.00
3-5	13.50	26.75	40.00
6-10	10.00	20.00	30.00
11-16	7.00	14.00	21.00

NOTE: _#1-4,9-13 (52pgs.); #5-8,14-16 (36pgs.)_

POLICE ACTION
Jan, 1954 - #7, Nov, 1954
Atlas News Co.

	Good	Fine	Mint
#1	1.00	2.00	3.00
2-7: #7-Powell story	.60	1.20	1.80

POLICE ACTION
Feb, 1975 - #3, June, 1975
Atlas/Seaboard Publ.

	Good	Fine	Mint
#1-Lomax, N.Y.P.D., Luke Malone begin;			
McWilliams art	.20	.40	.60
2,3: #2-Origin Luke Malone, Manhunter			
	.15	.30	.45

NOTE: _Ploog art in all._

POLICE AGAINST CRIME
April, 1954 - #9, Aug, 1955
Premiere Magazines/Ace Periodicals

	Good	Fine	Mint
#1	.80	1.60	2.40
2-9	.40	.80	1.20

POLICE BADGE #479   (Spy Thrillers #1-4)
#5, Sept, 1955
Atlas Comics (CPI)

	Good	Fine	Mint
#5	1.00	2.00	3.00

POLICE CASE BOOK (See Giant Comics Editions)

Plop! #1, © DC

Pogo #15, © Walt Kelly

Police Action #4, © MCG

Police Comics #1, © DC (Qua)

Police Comics #2, © DC (Qua)

Police Comics #10, © DC (Qua)

POLICE CASES (See Authentic -- & Record
Book of --)

POLICE COMICS
Aug, 1941 - #1?7, Oct, 1953
Quality Comics Group (Comic Magazines)

	Good	Fine	Mint
#1-Origin Plastic Man by Jack Cole, The Human Bomb by Gustavson, & #711; Intro. Chic Carter by W. Eisner, The Firebrand by R. Crandall, The Mouthpiece, Phantom Lady, & The Sword	175.00	350.00	525.00
2	80.00	160.00	240.00
3	70.00	140.00	210.00
4	60.00	120.00	180.00
5-Plastic Man forced to smoke marijuana	60.00	120.00	180.00
6,7	50.00	100.00	150.00
8-Origin Manhunter	60.00	120.00	180.00
9,10	40.00	80.00	120.00
11-Origin The Spirit by Will Eisner-strip reprint('40)	90.00	180.00	270.00
12-Intro. Ebony	40.00	80.00	120.00
13-Intro. Woozy Winks; last Firebrand	40.00	80.00	120.00
14-19: #15-Last #711; Destiny begins	25.00	50.00	75.00
20-The Raven x-over in Phantom Lady; features Jack Cole himself	25.00	50.00	75.00
21,22-Raven & Spider Widow x-over in Phantom Lady #21, cameo in Phantom Lady #22	20.00	40.00	60.00
23-30: #23-Last Phantom Lady. #24-Chic Carter becomes The Sword, only ish. #24-26-Flatfoot Burns by Kurtzman in all	17.50	35.00	52.50
31-41-Last Spirit reprint by Eisner	13.50	26.75	40.00
42-50-(#50 on cvr, #49 on inside, 1/46)	7.00	14.00	21.00
51-60: #58-Last Human Bomb	5.00	10.00	15.00
61,62,64-90	5.00	10.00	15.00
63-(Some issues have #65 printed on cover, but #63 on inside)	5.00	10.00	15.00
91-102: #101-Last Manhunter. #102-Last Plastic Man. #1-102 all by Jack Cole	5.00	10.00	15.00
103-Content change to crime - Ken Shannon	3.00	6.00	9.00
104-112,114-127-Crandall art most issues	2.00	4.00	6.00
113-Crandall cover, 2 stories, 9pgs. each	2.50	5.00	7.50

NOTE: *Most Spirit stories signed by Eisner
are not by him; all are reprints.* Cole *covers-
#20,24-26,28,29,31,36-38.* Crandall *Firebrand-
#1-13.* Grandenetti *Spirit-#94-102. No Spirit
in #89,91,93.*

POLICE LINE-UP
Aug, 1951 - #4, July, 1952
Realistic Comics/Avon Periodicals

	Good	Fine	Mint
#1-Wood art, 1pg. + part cover	2.50	5.00	7.50
2,4	1.50	3.00	4.50
3-Kubert reprints(3 stories & part/cover)	2.50	5.00	7.50

POLICE THRILLS
1954
Ajax/Farrell Publ.

#1	1.00	2.00	3.00

POLICE TRAP
Aug-Sept, 1954 - #6, Sept, 1955
Mainline #1-4(Prize)/Charlton #5

#1-S&K cover	2.50	5.00	7.50
2,3-S&K covers	1.50	3.00	4.50
4	.80	1.60	2.40
5,6-S&K cover/story	2.50	5.00	7.50

POLICE TRAP
1963 - 1964
Super Comics

Reprint #11('63),#16-18('64)	.50	1.00	1.50

POLL PARROT
Poll Parrot Shoe Store/International Shoe
1950 - 1951; 1959 - 1962
K.K. Publications (Giveaway)

#1-4-Howdy Doody('50)	1.35	2.75	4.00
#2('59)-#16('61): #8-Mixed Up Mission('60). #16---& the Rajah's Ruby('62)	.65	1.35	2.00

POLLY & HER PALS (See Comic Monthly #1)

POLLYANNA (See 4-Color Comics #1129)

POLLY PIGTAILS (Girls' Fun & Fashion Mag.
Jan, 1946 - V4#43, 10-11/49   #44 on)
Parents' Magazine Institute/Polly Pigtails

#1	2.00	4.00	6.00
2-5	1.50	3.00	4.50
6-10	1.20	2.40	3.60
11-30	.80	1.60	2.40
31-43	.50	1.00	1.50

PONYTAIL
7-9/62 - #12, 10-12/65; #13, 11/69 - #20, 1/71
Dell Publishing Co./Charlton #13 on

(Ponytail cont'd)	Good	Fine	Mint
No#(#1)	.25	.50	.75
#2-12	.20	.40	.60
13-20	.15	.30	.45

POPEYE (See Eat Right to Work--, Comic Album
#7,11,15, & March of Comics #37,52,66,80,96,
117,134,148,157,169,194,246,264,274,294)

POPEYE (See Thimble Theatre)
1935 (25¢) (48 pgs.) (By Segar) (B&W)
David McKay Publications

#1-Daily strip serial reprints-"The Gold			
Mine Thieves"	40.00	80.00	120.00
2-Daily strip reprints	30.00	60.00	90.00

NOTE: *Popeye first entered Thimble Theatre
in 1929.*

POPEYE
1937 (All color drawings + text taken from
Segar; probably not by him)
Whitman Publishing Co.

-- Borrows a Baby Nurse(72pgs.)
-- & His Jungle Pet(72pgs.)
        each.... 20.00 40.00 60.00
-- Goes Duck Hunting(24pgs.)
-- Tricks Wimpy & Rough-House(24pgs.)
-- Plays Nursemaid to Sweet Pea(24pgs.)
-- Calls on Olive Oyl(24pgs.)
        each.... 15.00 30.00 45.00

POPEYE
1937 - 1939 (All by Segar)
David McKay Publications

Feature Book-No#	100.00	200.00	300.00
Feature Book #2 (52pgs.)	50.00	100.00	150.00
Feature Book #3 (100pgs)	35.00	70.00	105.00
Feature Book #5,10(76pgs)	30.00	60.00	90.00
Feature Book #14 (76pgs.) (Scarce)			
	40.00	80.00	120.00

POPEYE (Strip reprints through 4-Color #70)
1941 - 1947; #1, 2-4/48 - #65, 7-9/62; #66,
10/62 - #80, 5/66; #81, 8/66 - #92, 12/67;
#94, 2/69 - #138, 1/77 (No #93)
Dell #1-65/Gold Key #66-80/King #81-92/
Charlton #94 on

Black & White #24('41)-Half by Segar			
	30.00	60.00	90.00
4-Color #25('41)-by Segar			
	35.00	70.00	105.00
Large Feature Comic #10('43)			
	20.00	40.00	60.00
4-Color #17('43)by Segar	25.00	50.00	75.00

	Good	Fine	Mint
4-Color #26('43)by Segar	20.00	40.00	60.00
4-Color #43('44)	12.00	24.00	36.00
4-Color #70('45)	7.00	14.00	21.00
4-Color #113('46-original strips begin),127,			
145('47),168	3.00	6.00	9.00
#1(2-4/48)(Dell)	7.00	14.00	21.00
2	4.00	8.00	12.00
3-10	2.50	5.00	7.50
11-20	1.75	3.50	5.25
21-40	1.35	2.75	4.00
41-50	.80	1.60	2.40
51-60	.60	1.20	1.80
61-65,68-80	.40	.80	1.20
66,67-both 84pgs.	.50	1.00	1.50
81-92,94-100	.15	.30	.45
101-138		.20	.35
Bold Detergent giveaway(Same as reg. issue			
#94)	.35	.70	1.05
--& Business & Office Careers('73)(32pg.Give-			
away, reg.size)#E-10	.35	.70	1.05
--& Health Careers, & Environmental Careers			
('72, 32pg. Giveaway, reg. size, in color)			
George Wildman art	.35	.70	1.05
--& Manufacturing Careers(1973 giveaway)			
	.35	.70	1.05
R-07-Premium, 32pgs. in color; Little King			
app.	.35	.70	1.05

POPEYE CARTOON BOOK
1934 (36pgs. plus cover)(8½x11")(Cardboard
The Saalfield Publ. Co.   covers)

#2095-1933 strip reprints in color by Segar			
	80.00	160.00	240.00

POPPO OF THE POPCORN THEATRE
10/29/55 - 1956 (Published weekly)
Fuller Publishing Co. (Publishers Weekly)

#1	1.50	3.00	4.50
2-13	1.00	2.00	3.00

NOTE: *By Charles Biro. 10¢ cover price, given
away by super markets such as IGA.*

POP-POP COMICS
No date (Circa 1945)
R. B. Leffingwell Co.

#1	1.35	2.75	4.00

POPSICLE PETE FUN BOOK
1947, 1948
Joe Lowe Corp.

No#-36pgs. in color; Sammy 'n' Claras, The
King Who Couldn't Sleep & Popsicle Pete
stories, games, cut-outs
                  2.50   5.00   7.50

Popeye 4-Color #25, © King

Popeye #10 (Dell), © King

Popular Comics #17, © Dell

Popular Comics #35, © Dell

Porky Pig 4-Color #271, © L. Schlesinger

Power Comics #1, © Hoke

(Popsicle Pete Fun Book cont'd)

	Good	Fine	Mint
Adventure Book('48)	2.00	4.00	6.00

POPULAR COMICS
Feb, 1936 - #145, July-Sept, 1948
Dell Publishing Co.

	Good	Fine	Mint
#1-Terry & the Pirate, Gasoline Alley, Dick Tracy, Moon Mullins, The Gumps begin (All strip reprints)	50.00	100.00	150.00
2	25.00	50.00	75.00
3	20.00	40.00	60.00
4	15.00	30.00	45.00
5	12.00	24.00	36.00
6-10	10.00	20.00	30.00
11-20	9.00	18.00	27.00
21-27-Last Terry & the Pirates	9.00	18.00	27.00
28-37	7.00	14.00	21.00
38-43-Tarzan in all	10.00	20.00	30.00
44-Masked Pilot begins	5.00	10.00	15.00
45	5.00	10.00	15.00
46-Origin Martan, the Marvel Man	6.00	12.00	18.00
47-50	5.00	10.00	15.00
51-Origin The Voice(The Invisible Detective) strip begins	6.00	12.00	18.00
52-59	5.00	10.00	15.00
60-Origin Professor Supermind and Son	6.00	12.00	18.00
61,62,64-71	5.00	10.00	15.00
63-Smilin' Jack begins	5.00	10.00	15.00
72-The Owl & Terry & the Pirates begin; Smokey Stover reprts.begin	5.00	10.00	15.00
73-75	5.00	10.00	15.00
76-78-Capt. Midnight in all	5.00	10.00	15.00
79-86-Last Owl	5.00	10.00	15.00
87-100: #98-Felix the Cat, Smokey Stover reprints begin	3.00	6.00	9.00
101-130	2.50	5.00	7.50
131-145	2.00	4.00	6.00

POPULAR FAIRY TALES (See March of Comics #6,18)

POPULAR ROMANCE
#5, Dec, 1949 - #29, 1954
Better-Standard Publications

#5-Tuska art	.65	1.35	2.00
6-17,19-21,23,24,26,28,29	.50	1.00	1.50
18-Tuska art	.65	1.35	2.00
22,25,27-Toth stories	1.50	3.00	4.50

POPULAR TEEN-AGERS (Secrets of Love)(--Romances #9)
1950 - #23, Nov, 1954
Star Publications

	Good	Fine	Mint
#5-12,16-23	1.00	2.00	3.00
13-Disbrow story	1.50	3.00	4.50
14-Harrison/Wood story; two spanking scenes			
	2.50	5.00	7.50
15-Wood stories	2.50	5.00	7.50

PORE LI'L MOSE
1902 (30pgs.-10½x15"-in full color)
New York Herald Publ. by Grand Union Tea
Cupples & Leon

By R. F. Outcault; lpg. strips about early Negroes	25.00	62.50	100.00

PORKY PIG
1942 - Present
Dell Publishing Co.

4-Color #16(1942)	30.00	60.00	90.00
4-Color #48-Carl Barks art (1944)	100.00	200.00	300.00
4-Color #78('45)	8.00	16.00	24.00
4-Color #112('46)	6.00	12.00	18.00
4-Color #156,182,191('49)	4.00	8.00	12.00
4-Color #226,241('49),260,271,277,284,295 ('50)	3.00	6.00	9.00
4-Color #303,311,322,330	1.75	3.50	5.25
4-Color #342,351,360,370,385,399('52),410, 426	1.25	2.50	3.75
#25-30	.50	1.00	1.50
31-50	.40	.80	1.20
51-81(3-4/62)	.30	.60	.90
#1(1/65-G.K.)(2nd Series)	.35	.70	1.05
2-10	.20	.40	.60
11-30	.15	.30	.45
31-78		.15	.30

PORKY PIG (See March of Comics #42,57,71,89, 99,113,130,143,164,175,192,209,218,367, and Super Book #6,18,30)

PORKY'S BOOK OF TRICKS
1942 (48 pgs.) (8½x5½")
K.K. Publications (Giveaway)

7pg. comic story, text stories, + games & puzzles	20.00	40.00	60.00

POWDER RIVER RUSTLERS (See Faw. Movie Comics)

POWER COMICS
1945
Holyoke Publ. Co./Narrative Publ.

#1	2.50	5.00	7.50
2-4: #2-Dr. Mephisto begins	1.50	3.00	4.50

POWER COMICS
1976 - Present   (50¢)
Power Comics

	Good	Fine	Mint
#1-Nightwitch, 2-Cobolt Blue, 3-Nightwitch, 4-Northern Light, 5-Bluebird, 6-Nightwitch and Bluebird, 7- each....	.20	.40	.60

POWERHOUSE PEPPER COMICS   (See Gay Comics)
#1, 1943; #2, May, 1948 - #5, Nov, 1948
Marvel Comics (20CC)

#1-Wolverton art begins	35.00	70.00	105.00
2-4-All by Wolverton	20.00	40.00	60.00
5-Wolverton art(Scarce)	25.00	50.00	75.00

POWER MAN   (Formerly Hero for Hire)
#17, Feb, 1974 - Present
Marvel Comics Group

#17-Iron Man app.	.25	.50	.75
18-30	.20	.40	.60
31-Part Adams inks	.25	.50	.75
32-48: #36-Reprint. #43-Nino art	.15	.30	.45
Giant-Size #1('75)	.35	.70	1.05
Annual #1(11/76)	.25	.50	.75

POW MAGAZINE   (Bob Sproul's)(Satire Magazine)
Aug, 1966 - #3, Feb, 1967   (30¢)
Humor-Vision

#1	.65	1.35	2.00
2-Jones art	.65	1.35	2.00
3-Wrightson art	1.00	2.00	3.00

PREHISTORIC WORLD (See Classics Special)

PREMIERE   (See Charlton Premiere)

PRETTY BOY FLOYD   (See On the Spot)

PREZ
Aug-Sept, 1973 - #4, Feb-Mar, 1974
National Periodical Publications

#1-Origin	.15	.30	.45
2-4		.15	.30

PRIDE AND THE PASSION, THE (See 4-Color #824)

PRIDE OF THE YANKEES, THE
1949   (The Life of Lou Gehrig)
Magazine Enterprises

No#-Ogden Whitney art	4.00	8.00	12.00

PRIMUS (TV)
Feb, 1972 - #7, Oct, 1972
Charlton Comics

	Good	Fine	Mint
#1-5,7-Staton art in all	.20	.40	.60
2-Drug book	.25	.50	.75

PRINCE & THE PAUPER, THE (See Movie Classics)

PRINCE VALIANT   (See Feature Book #26, McKay)

PRINCE VALIANT   (See 4-Color #567,650,699,719, 788,849,900)

PRINCE VALIANT
1973   (32 pgs.) (In Color)
Charlton Comics (King Features Giveaway)

R-08-Hal Foster art; Flash Gordon, Brick Bradford app. Small Williamson illo. on cover/ Flash Gordon #4	6.00	12.00	18.00

NOTE: *One of a set of eight comics received after buying $45.00 worth of merchandise. Used as a reading skills aid.*

PRISCILLA'S POP (See 4-Color #569,630,704,799)

PRISON BARS   (See Behind --)

PRISON BREAK!
Sept, 1951 - #5, Sept, 1952
Avon Periodicals/Realistic #4 on

#1-Wood cover + 1pg.; has reprt/Saint #7 retitled Michael Strong Private Eye	4.00	8.00	12.00
2-Wood cover/Kubert story + 2pgs. Wood art	4.00	8.00	12.00
3-5: #4,5-Kinstler covers. #5-Infantino art	2.50	5.00	7.50

PRISON RIOT
1952
Avon Periodicals

#1-Kinstler cover	2.50	5.00	7.50

PRISON TO PRAISE
1974
Logos International

True story of Merlin R. Corothers	.15	.30	.45

PRIVATE BUCK   (See Large Feature Comic #12 & Black & White #21)

Powerhouse Pepper #5, © MCG

The Pride Of The Yankees, © ME

Prison Break! #1, © Avon

Prize Comics #2. © Prize

Prize Comics #27. © Prize

Prize Comics Western #72. © Prize

PRIVATE EYE
Jan, 1951 - #8, March, 1952
Atlas Comics (MCI)

	Good	Fine	Mint
#1	1.35	2.75	4.00
2-8: #8-Rocky Jorden--	.80	1.60	2.40

PRIVATE EYE (See Mike Shayne --)

PRIVATE SECRETARY
Dec-Feb, 1962-63 - #2, Mar-May, 1963
Dell Publishing Co.

#1,2	.20	.40	.60

PRIVATE STRONG (See The Double Life of --)

PRIZE COMICS (-- Western #69 on)
March, 1940 - #68, Feb-Mar, 1948
Prize Publications

#1-Origin Power Nelson, The Futureman & Jup-
iter, Master Magician; Ted O'Neal, Secret
Agent M-11, Jaxon of the Jungle, Bucky
Brady & Storm Curtis begin

	Good	Fine	Mint
	30.00	60.00	90.00
2-The Black Owl begins	17.50	35.00	52.50
3	12.00	24.00	36.00
4	9.00	18.00	27.00

5,6: Dr. Dekkar, Master on Monsters app. in
each 8.00 16.00 24.00
7-Black Owl by S&K; Dr. Frost, Frankenstein,
The Green Lama, Captain Gallant, & Twist
Turner begin; Kirby cover
15.00 30.00 45.00

8,9-Black Owl & Ted O'Neil by S&K			
	13.50	26.75	40.00
10,12,14-20	8.00	16.00	24.00
11-Origin Bulldog Denny	8.00	16.00	24.00
13-Origin Yank & Doodle	12.00	24.00	36.00
21-24	5.00	10.00	15.00
25-30	4.00	8.00	12.00
31-33	2.50	5.00	7.50

34-Origin Airmale, Yank & Doodle & The Black
Owl 4.00 8.00 12.00
35-Flying Fist & Bingo begin,
36-40: #37-Intro. Stampy, Airmale's sidekick
3.00 6.00 9.00
41-50: #48-Prince Ra begins
2.50 5.00 7.50
51-68: #55-No Frankenstein
2.00 4.00 6.00

PRIZE COMICS WESTERN (Prize #1-68)
#69, 1949 - #119, Nov-Dec, 1956
Prize Publications (Feature)

#69	3.35	6.75	10.00

	Good	Fine	Mint
70-73,75-78,80,81,83,84	2.00	4.00	6.00
74,79-Kurtzman stories	3.35	6.75	10.00

82-1st app. The Preacher by Mart Bailey
2.50 5.00 7.50
85-American Eagle by John Severin begins
(1-2/50) 4.00 8.00 12.00

86-98,100-105	2.50	5.00	7.50

99-Three Severin & Elder stories
3.35 6.75 10.00

106-108,110-112	2.50	5.00	7.50

109-Severin/Williamson story
4.00 8.00 12.00
113-Two Williamson/Severin stories
5.00 10.00 15.00
114-119: Drifter series in all; by Mort
Meskin #114-118 2.00 4.00 6.00
NOTE: *Kirby* covers-#75,83. *Severin & Elder*
stories-#79,81,82,87-92,98(2 ea.); cover-#98.
Severin stories-#72,75,83-86,96,97,100-105;
covers-most #85-109.

PRIZE MYSTERY
May, 1955 - #3, 1955
Key Publications

#1-3	1.00	2.00	3.00

PROFESSIONAL FOOTBALL (See Charlton Sport Library)

PSYCHO (Magazine)
Jan, 1971 - #24, Mar, 1975 (68pgs.) (B&W)
Skywald Publishing Corp.

#1-All reprints	.65	1.35	2.00

2-Origin & 1st app. The Heap, & Frankenstein
series by Adkins .50 1.00 1.50

3-5	.50	1.00	1.50
6-10	.40	.80	1.20
11-23	.25	.50	.75
24-1975 Winter Special	.35	.70	1.05
Annual #1('72)	.50	1.00	1.50
Fall Special('74)	.35	.70	1.05
Yearbook(1974-No#)	.35	.70	1.05

NOTE: *Boris* cover-#3,5. *Buckler* story-#4,5.
Everett story-#3,4,6. *Jones* stories-#4,6;
cover-#12. *Kaluta* story-#13. *Morrow* story-#1.
Reese story-#5. *Wildey* story-#5:

PSYCHOANALYSIS
Mar-Apr, 1955 - #4, Sept-Oct, 1955
E.C. Comics

#1-4-Kamen art in all 3.00 6.00 9.00

P.T. 109 (See Movie Comics)

PUBLIC DEFENDER IN ACTION
#7, Mar, 1956 - #12, 1957
Charlton Comics

	Good	Fine	Mint
#7-12	.25	.50	.75

PUBLIC ENEMIES
1948 - 1949
D.S. Publishing Co.

	Good	Fine	Mint
#1	1.50	3.00	4.50
2-Used in Seduction of the Innocent			
	4.00	8.00	12.00
3-9	1.00	2.00	3.00

PUDGY PIG
Aug-Sept, 1958 - #2, Nov, 1958
Charlton Comics

	Good	Fine	Mint
#1,2	.15	.30	.45

PUNCH & JUDY COMICS
1944 - V3#9, Dec, 1951
Hillman Periodicals

	Good	Fine	Mint
V1#1(60pgs.)	2.00	4.00	6.00
2-12(7/46)	1.35	2.75	4.00
V2#1,3-10	1.00	2.00	3.00
V2#2,11,12-Two Kirby stories each			
	5.00	10.00	15.00
V3#1-Two Kirby stories	5.00	10.00	15.00
2-Kirby story	4.00	8.00	12.00
3-9	.80	1.60	2.40

PUNCH COMICS
Dec, 1941 - #26, Dec, 1947
Harry 'A' Chesler

	Good	Fine	Mint
#1-Mr. E, The Sky Chief, Hale, the Magician, Kitty Kelly begin	17.50	35.00	52.50
2-Captain Glory app.	10.00	20.00	30.00
3	8.00	16.00	24.00
4	6.00	12.00	18.00
5	5.00	10.00	15.00
6-8	4.00	8.00	12.00
9-Rocketman & The Master Key begin			
	4.00	8.00	12.00
10-Sky Chief app.	3.00	6.00	9.00
11,12: #11-Sky Chief app. #12-Rocket Boy & Capt. Glory app.	2.50	5.00	7.50
13,14,16-20	2.00	4.00	6.00
15-Rocketman & Rocketgirl app.			
	2.50	5.00	7.50
21-26: #23-Little Nemo-not by McCay			
	1.75	3.35	5.00

PUPPET COMICS
Spring, 1946

George W. Dougherty Co.

	Good	Fine	Mint
#1,2	1.00	2.00	3.00

PUPPETOONS (George Pal's)
Dec, 1945 - #18, Dec, 1947; #19, 1950
Fawcett Publications

	Good	Fine	Mint
#1-Capt. Marvel on cover	5.00	10.00	15.00
2-10	2.00	4.00	6.00
11-19	1.50	3.00	4.50

PURPLE CLAW, THE (Also see Tales of Horror)
Jan, 1953 - #3, 1953
Minoan Publishing Co./Toby Press

#1	2.50	5.00	7.50
2,3	1.50	3.00	4.50
IW Reprint #8(reprts.#1)	1.25	2.50	3.75

PUSSYCAT (Magazine)
1968 (B&W reprints from men's magazines)
Marvel Comics Group

#1-Ward, Everett, Wood art			
	4.00	8.00	12.00

PUZZLE FUN COMICS (Also see Jingle Jangle)
Spring, 1946 - #2, Summer, 1946; 1957
George W. Dougherty Co./National Per. Publ.

#1(1946)	5.00	10.00	15.00
2	3.00	6.00	9.00
1(National,'57)	.65	1.35	2.00

NOTE: *#1,2('46) each contain a George Carlson cover + a 6pg. story "Alec in Fumbleland"; also many puzzles in each.*

QUAKER OATS (Also see Cap'n Crunch)
1965   (Giveaway) (2½x5½") (16 pgs.)
Quaker Oats Co.

"Plenty of Glutton","Lava Come-Back","Kite Tale","A Witch in Time"	.20	.40	.60

QUEEN OF THE WEST, DALE EVANS
July, 1953 - #22, Jan, 1959
Dell Publishing Co.

4-Color #479('53)	1.75	3.35	5.00
4-Color #528('54)	1.50	3.00	4.50
#1	2.00	4.00	6.00
2-10-Manning art	1.50	3.00	4.50
11,19,21-No Manning	.65	1.35	2.00
12-18,20,22-Manning art	1.20	2.40	3.60

QUENTIN DURWARD (See 4-Color Comics #672)

Punch Comics #13, © Ches

Puppetoons #19, © Faw

The Purple Claw #1, © Toby

Race For The Moon #1, © Harv

Racket Squad In Action # 12, © CC

Raggedy Ann #22, © J. Gruelle

QUESTION, THE (See Mysterious Suspense)

QUICK-DRAW McDRAW (TV) (Hanna-Barbera)
12-2/60 - #14, 7/64
Dell Publ. Co./Gold Key #12 on

	Good	Fine	Mint
4-Color #1040	.40	.80	1.20
#2(4-6/60)-#6	.25	.50	.75
7-11	.20	.40	.60

12-14-All titled "Q-D McG. Fun-Type Roundup";
  #12,13-84pgs.   .35   .70   1.05
      (See Whitman Comic Books)

QUICK-DRAW McGRAW (TV)
Nov, 1970 - #8, Jan, 1972 (Hanna-Barbera)
Charlton Comics

#1-8   .10   .20

QUICK-TRIGGER WESTERN (Formerly Cowboy Action)
#12, May, 1956 - #19, Sept, 1957
Atlas Comics(ACI #12/WPI #13-19)

#12-Baker art	1.50	3.00	4.50
13-Williamson sty,5pgs.	2.00	4.00	6.00

14-Everett, Crandall, Torres, Heath stories
                    1.75   3.35   5.00
15-Torres, Crandall	1.35	2.75	4.00
16-Orlando + Kirby story	1.25	2.50	3.75
17-Crandall story	1.25	2.50	3.75
18-Baker story	1.00	2.00	3.00
19	.80	1.60	2.40

NOTE: _Morrow_ story-#18. _Severin_ cover-#13,17.

QUINCY
1973 (36 pgs.) (Premium)
Charlton Publ. (King Features)

R-05-Henry app.(for small children)
                    .10   .20   .30

RACCOON KIDS, THE (Formerly Movietown Animal
#52, 6-7/55 - #64, 11/57   Antics)
National Periodical Publ. (Arleigh #63,64)

#52-64   .50   1.00   1.50

RACE FOR THE MOON
March, 1958 - #3, Nov, 1958
Harvey Publications

#1-Powell art; ½-pg. S&K art; cover from Gal-
   axy Science Fiction(5/53)-Pulp)
                    2.50   5.00   7.50
  2-Three Kirby/Williamson stories
                    5.00   10.00 15.00
  3-Four Kirby/Williamson stories
                    6.00   12.00 18.00

RACKET SQUAD IN ACTION
May-June, 1952 - #29, March, 1958
Capitol Stories/Charlton Comics

	Good	Fine	Mint
#1	1.00	2.00	3.00
2	.60	1.20	1.80

  3-6-Dr. Neff, Ghost Breaker app.
                    .60   1.20   1.80
7-10	.50	1.00	1.50
11,13-28	.35	.70	1.05
12-Ditko cover	.65	1.35	2.00
29-(68pgs.)(15c)	.50	1.00	1.50

RADIANT LOVE (Formerly Daring Love #1)
#2, Dec, 1953 - #6, Aug, 1954
Gilmor Magazines

#2-6   1.00   2.00   3.00

RAGGEDY ANN AND ANDY (See March of Comics#23)
1942 - #39, 8/49; 1955 - #4, 3/66
Dell Publishing Co.

4-Color #5(1942)	20.00	40.00	60.00
4-Color #23(1943)	15.00	30.00	45.00
4-Color #45(1943)	10.00	20.00	30.00
4-Color #72(1945)	8.00	16.00	24.00
#1(6/46)	10.00	20.00	30.00

  2,3: #3-Egbert Elephant by Dan Noonan begins
                    6.00   12.00 18.00
4-10	5.00	10.00	15.00
11-20	4.00	8.00	12.00
21-39	2.50	5.00	7.50

4-Color #262,306,354,380,452,533
                    2.50   5.00   7.50
Giant #1('55)Tales From--	3.00	6.00	9.00
#1(10-12/64,Dell)	.65	1.35	2.00
2,3(10-12/65),#4(3/66)	.35	.70	1.05

NOTE: _Kelly_ art("Animal Mother Goose")-#1-34,
36,37; cover-#28. Peterkin Pottle by _John_
Stanley in #32-38.

RAGGEDY ANN AND ANDY
Dec, 1971 - #6, Sept, 1973
Gold Key

#1	.25	.50	.75
2-6	.20	.40	.60

RAGGEDY ANN & THE CAMEL WITH THE WRINKLED
KNEES (See Dell Jr. Treasury #8)

RAGMAN
Aug-Sept, 1976 - #5, June-July, 1977
National Periodical Publications

#1-Origin	.50	1.00	1.50
2-Origin; Kubert cvr/sty.	.25	.50	.75

(Ragman cont'd)   Good Fine Mint
3-5   .20   .40   .60
NOTE: *Kubert stories-#1,2,4,5; covers-#1,2,3,5.*

RAGS RABBIT (See Harvey Hits#2 & Tastee Freez)
1951 - #18, March, 1954
Harvey Publications

#11-18   .50   1.00 1.50

RALPH KINER, HOME RUN KING
1950   (Pittsburgh Pirates)
Fawcett Publications

No#   3.00 6.00 9.00

RAMAR OF THE JUNGLE
1954 - 1956
Toby Press #1,2/Charlton #3-5

#1   2.50 5.00 7.50
2-5   1.50 3.00 4.50

RAMPAGING HULK, THE (Magazine)
January, 1977   (B&W) ($1.00)
Marvel Comics Group

#1-Bloodstone featured   .65   1.35 2.00
2-4   .50   1.00 1.50
NOTE: *Alcala inks-#1-4. Buscema story-#1.
Starlin story-#4; covers-#4,5.*

RANGE BUSTERS
Sept, 1950 - #8, 1951
Fox Features Syndicate

#1   2.00 4.00 6.00
2-8   1.35 2.75 4.00

RANGE BUSTERS
1953?
Charlton Publications

#9,10   .50   1.00 1.50

RANGELAND LOVE
Dec, 1949
Atlas Comics (CDS)

#1   1.35 2.75 4.00

RANGER, THE (See 4-Color Comics #255)

RANGE RIDER (See Flying A's --)

RANGE RIDER, THE (See 4-Color Comics #404)

RANGE ROMANCES

Dec, 1949 - #5, Aug, 1950
Comic Magazines (Quality Comics)
                               Good Fine Mint
#1-Gustavson cover/story   4.00 8.00 12.00
2-Crandall story/cover; "spanking" scene
                               4.00 8.00 12.00
3-Crandall, Gustavson story
                               3.00 6.00 9.00
4-Crandall story   2.50 5.00 7.50
5   1.75 3.35 5.00

RANGERS COMICS (-- of Freedom #1-7)
Oct, 1941 - #69, Winter, 1952-53
Fiction House Magazines (Flying stories)

#1-Intro. Ranger Girl & The Rangers of Free-
   com; ends #4, cover app. only-#5
                               30.00 60.00 90.00
2   20.00 40.00 60.00
3   15.00 30.00 45.00
4,5-Sky Rangers begin-#5
                               10.00 20.00 30.00
6,7   7.00 14.00 21.00
8-12-Commando Rangers begin-#11
                               7.00 14.00 21.00
13-Commando Ranger begins-not same as Comm.
   Rangers   7.00 14.00 21.00
14-20   6.00 12.00 18.00
21-Firehair begins   6.00 12.00 18.00
22-27,29,30: #23-Kazanda begins, ends #28.
   #30-Crusoe Island begins, ends #40
                               5.00 10.00 15.00
28-Origin Tiger Man   5.00 10.00 15.00
31-40   4.00 8.00 12.00
41-46   3.00 6.00 9.00
47-56-"Eisnerish" Dr. Drew by Grandenetti
                               3.00 6.00 9.00
57-60-Straight Dr. Drew by Grandenetti
                               2.50 5.00 7.50
61-66: #64-Suicide Smith begins
                               2.00 4.00 6.00
67-The Space Rangers begin, end #69,
68,69   2.00 4.00 6.00
NOTE: *A very large percentage of above have
bondage, discipline, etc. covers. Firehair
art by Lee Elias-#21-28; by Bob Lubbers-#30-
37. Glory Forbes by Matt Baker-#36-48. "I
Confess" by Evans-#47-52. Tiger Man art by
John Celardo-#36-39; by Evans-#40-45,48,52.
Werewolf Hunter by Evans-#39.*

RANGO (TV)
August, 1967
Dell Publishing Co.

#1   .25   .50   .75

Ramar Of The Jungle #4. © CC

Rangers Comics #5. © FH

Rangers Comics #32. © FH

Rawhide Kid #11, © MCG

Real Clue Crime V2#6, © Hill

Real Fact #5, © DC

RATFINK (See Frantic & Zany)
October, 1964
Canrom, Inc.

	Good	Fine	Mint
#1-Woodbridge art	.65	1.35	2.00

RAT PATROL, THE (TV)
March, 1967 - #6, Oct, 1969
Dell Publishing Co.

#1	.25	.50	.75
2-6	.15	.30	.45

RAVEN, THE (See Movie Classics)

RAWHIDE (TV)
9-11/59 - 6-8/62; 7/63 - #2, 1/64
Dell Publishing Co./Gold Key

4-Color #1028,1097,1160,1202,1261,1269			
	.65	1.35	2.00
#01-684-208(8/62-Dell)	.50	1.00	1.50
#1(10071-307,G.K.),#2	.35	.70	1.05

RAWHIDE KID
3/55 - #16, 9/57; #17, 8/60 - Present
Atlas/Marvel Comics(CnPC #1-16/AMI #17-30)

#1	6.00	12.00	18.00
2	3.00	6.00	9.00
3-5	2.50	5.00	7.50
6,8-10	1.75	3.35	5.00
7-Williamson story,4pgs.	2.50	5.00	7.50
11-15	1.35	2.75	4.00
16-Torres art	1.50	3.00	4.50
17-Origin by J. Kirby	2.00	4.00	6.00
18-30	.65	1.35	2.00
31,32,36-44: #40-Two-Gun Kid x-over. #42-1st			
Larry Lieber issue	.60	1.20	1.80
33-35-Davis stories	1.00	2.00	3.00
45-Origin retold	1.35	2.75	4.00
46-Toth story	1.35	2.75	4.00
47-70: #50-Kid Colt x-over. #64-Kid Colt			
story. #66-Two-Gun Kid story. #67-Kid			
Colt story	.25	.50	.75
71-78	.20	.40	.60
79-Williamson story reprint/Kid Colt #59,			
4pgs.	.20	.40	.60
80-85	.15	.30	.45
86-Origin reprint; Williamson story reprint/			
Ringo Kid #13, 4pgs.	.20	.40	.60
87-94: #89,90-Kid Colt x-over; #93-52pgs.			
	.20	.35	
95-Williamson reprint	.15	.30	.45
96-110: #105-Western Kid reprt.	.20	.35	
111-Williamson reprint	.15	.30	.45
112-115-Last new story	.20	.35	
116-143: #125-Davis reprint	.15	.30	

	Good	Fine	Mint
Special #1(9/71)-Reprints	.25	.50	.75

NOTE: _Davis reprint-#125._ _Everett story-#65,
66,88._ _Kirby_ _story-#17-32,34,42,43,84,86,109,
#1(Special); covers-#17-35,40,41,43-47.
Torres_ _reprint-#99._ _Whitney_ _story-#66._

REAL ADVENTURE COMICS
April, 1955
Gillmore Magazines

#1	.65	1.35	2.00

REAL CLUE CRIME STORIES (Formerly Clue)
1947 - V8#3, May, 1953
Hillman Periodicals

V2#4(#1)-S&K art	3.00	6.00	9.00
5-7-S&K art	2.50	5.00	7.50
8-12	1.00	2.00	3.00
V3#1-12,V4#1-8,10-12	.80	1.60	2.40
V4#9-Krigstein art	1.50	3.00	4.50
V5#1-5,7,8,10,12	.65	1.35	2.00
V5#6,9,11-Krigstein art	1.35	2.75	4.00
V6#1-5,8,9,11	.65	1.35	2.00
V6#6,7,10,12-Krigstein art			
	1.25	2.50	3.75
V7#1-3,5,7-11,V8#1-3	.65	1.35	2.00
V7#4,12-Krigstein art	1.25	2.50	3.75
V7#6-McWilliams art; 1pg. Frazetta ad			
	1.00	2.00	3.00

REAL EXPERIENCES (Formerly Tiny Tessie)
#25, January, 1950
Atlas Comics (20CC)

#25	.35	.70	1.05

REAL FACT COMICS
Mar-Apr, 1946 - #21, July-Aug, 1949
National Periodical Publications

#1-S&K art	4.00	8.00	12.00
2-S&K art	2.50	5.00	7.50
3	1.50	3.00	4.50
4-"Just Imagine" begins by Virgil Finley,			
ends #12(2pgs. ea.)	2.00	4.00	6.00
5-Batman app.	6.00	12.00	18.00
6-Origin & 1st app. Tommy Tomorrow			
	3.00	6.00	9.00
7-(#6 on inside)	1.75	3.35	5.00
8-2nd app. T.Tomorrow	1.75	3.35	5.00
9-S&K art	2.50	5.00	7.50
10-Vigilante by Meskin	2.50	5.00	7.50
11,12,14,15,17-19: #11-Kinstler art			
	1.35	2.75	4.00
13-T.Tomorrow cover/story	1.35	2.75	4.00
16-Tommy Tomorrow app.	1.35	2.75	4.00

(Real Fact Comics cont'd)	Good	Fine	Mint
20-Kubert story	2.00	4.00	6.00
21-Kubert art(2pgs.)	1.50	3.00	4.50

REAL FUN OF DRIVING!!, THE
1967   (Reg. Size)
Chrysler Corp.

12pg. Shaffenberger story	.15	.30	.45

REAL FUNNIES
1943
Nedor Publishing Co.

#1	2.50	5.00	7.50
2,3	1.50	3.00	4.50

REAL HEROES COMICS
Sept, 1941 - #16, Oct, 1946
Parents' Magazine Institute

#1	2.50	5.00	7.50
2-10	1.50	3.00	4.50
11-16	.80	1.60	2.40

REAL HIT
1944   (Savings Bond premium)
Fox Features Publications

#1-Blue Beetle reprint	4.00	8.00	12.00

REALISTIC ROMANCES
July-Aug, 1951 - #17, Aug-Sept, 1954
Realistic Comics/Avon Periodicals

#1-Kinstler story	2.50	5.00	7.50
2-5,7-15,17: #17-Kinstler cover			
	1.50	3.00	4.50
6-Kinstler story	2.00	4.00	6.00
16-Kinstler marijuana sty.	3.00	6.00	9.00
IW Reprint #8,9	.35	.70	1.05

REAL LIFE COMICS
Sept, 1941 - #59, Sept, 1952
Nedor/Better/Standard Publications

#1	5.00	10.00	15.00
2	2.00	4.00	6.00
3-10	1.35	2.75	4.00
11-20	1.00	2.00	3.00
21-49	.80	1.60	2.40
50,52-Frazetta story in each(5&4pgs.) + Severin/Elder story-#52	6.00	12.00	18.00
51,53-57: Severin/Elder story in each			
	1.50	3.00	4.50
58-Two Severin/Elder stys.	2.00	4.00	6.00
59-1pg. Frazetta	1.50	3.00	4.50

NOTE: *Some issues had two titles.*

REAL LIFE SECRETS
1949 - #5, May, 1950
Ace Periodicals

	Good	Fine	Mint
#1	.80	1.60	2.40
2-5	.50	1.00	1.50

REAL LIFE STORY OF FESS PARKER (Magazine)
1955
Dell Publishing Co.

#1	1.35	2.75	4.00

REAL LIFE TALES OF SUSPENSE (See Suspense)

REAL LOVE (Formerly Hap Hazard)
#25, April, 1949 - #75, 1956
Ace Periodicals (A.A.Wyn)

#25-35	.50	1.00	1.50
36-75	.35	.70	1.05

REAL McCOYS, THE (TV)
1960 - 1962
Dell Publishing Co.

4-Color #1071,1193,1265	.40	.80	1.20
4-Color #1134-Toth art	1.50	3.00	4.50
#01689-207(5-7/62)	.30	.60	.90

REAL SCREEN COMICS (#1 titled Real Screen
Funnies; TV Screen Cartoons #129-138)
Spring, 1945 - #128, July-Aug, 1959
National Periodical Publications

#1-The Fox & the Crow begin			
	9.00	18.00	27.00
2-5	5.00	10.00	15.00
6-15	2.50	5.00	7.50
16-30	1.75	3.35	5.00
31-50	1.35	2.75	4.00
51-100	.80	1.60	2.40
101-128	.50	1.00	1.50

REAL SECRETS
1949
Ace Periodicals

#1	1.00	2.00	3.00

REAL SPORTS COMICS
Oct-Nov, 1948
Hillman Periodicals

#1-12pg. Powell story	1.00	2.00	3.00

REAL WESTERN HERO (Formerly Wow #1-69;
becomes Western Hero #76 on)

Real Life Comics #9, © Std

Real Screen Comics #33, © DC

Real Sports #1, © Hill

Red Band #4, © Enwil Assoc.   Red Dragon #5, © S & S   Reddy Kilowatt #1, © WMG

(Real West. Hero cont'd)
#70, Sept, 1948 - #75, March, 1949
Fawcett Publications

	Good	Fine	Mint
#70-Featuring Tom Mix, Gabby Hayes, Monte Hale & Hopalong Cassidy			
	6.00	12.00	18.00
71-75	3.00	6.00	9.00

REAL WEST ROMANCES
Apr-May, 1949 - V2#1, Apr-May, 1950
Crestwood Publishing Co./Prize Publ.

V1#1-S&K art	3.00	6.00	9.00
2,3-Kirby pencils only	1.75	3.35	5.00
4-7-S&K art	2.25	4.50	6.75
V2#1-Kirby pencils only	1.75	3.35	5.00

NOTE: _Meskin_ story-V1#5. _Severin & Elder_
stories-V1#3-6, V2#1. _Leonard Starr_ story-#1-3.

REBEL, THE (See 4-Color #1076,1138,1207,1262)

RECKLESS STEELE (See Chewing Gum Booklet)

RECORD BOOK OF FAMOUS POLICE CASES
1949   (132 pgs.) (25¢)
St. John Publishing Co.

No#-Three Kubert stories; Matt Baker cover			
	4.00	8.00	12.00

RED ARROW
1951 - #3, Oct, 1951
P.L. Publishing Co.

#1	1.00	2.00	3.00
2,3	.65	1.35	2.00

RED BALL COMIC BOOK
1947   (Red Ball Shoes giveaway)
Parents' Magazine Institute

Reprints from True Comics	.65	1.35	2.00

RED BAND COMICS
Feb, 1945 - #4, May, 1945
Enwil Associates

#1	4.00	8.00	12.00
2-Origin Boogeyman & Santanas			
	2.50	5.00	7.50
3,4-Captain Wizard app. in both-Identical contents in each	2.50	5.00	7.50

RED CIRCLE COMICS
Jan, 1945 - #4, April, 1945
Rural Home Publications (Enwil)

#1-The Prankster & Red Riot begin

	Good	Fine	Mint
	3.00	6.00	9.00
2-4-Starr art	2.00	4.00	6.00

RED CIRCLE SORCERY (Chilling Advs. in Sorcery
#6, Apr/74 - #11, Feb/75   #1-5)
Red Circle Productions (Archie)

#6-11	.20	.40	.60

NOTE: _McWilliams_ story-#10. _Morrow_ stories-
#6-8,10,11; covers-#6-11. _Toth_ stories-#8,9.
Wood story-#10.

RED DRAGON (1st Series)(Trail Blazers #1-4)
#5, Jan, 1943 - #9, Jan, 1944
Street & Smith Publications

#5-Origin Red Rover, the Crimson Crimebuster; Rex King, Man of Adventure, Captain Jack Commando, & The Minute Man begin			
	10.00	20.00	30.00
6-Origin The Black Crusader & Red Dragon (3/43)	8.00	16.00	24.00
7	6.00	12.00	18.00
8-The Red Knight app.	6.00	12.00	18.00
9-Origin Chuck Magnon, Immortal Man			
	6.00	12.00	18.00

RED DRAGON (2nd Series)
Nov, 1947 - #7, July, 1948
Street & Smith Publications

#1-Red Dragon begins; Ed Cartier art	8.00	16.00	24.00
2-Powell art	5.00	10.00	15.00
3-Elliman, Nigel app.; Powell art,			
4-6: #4-Powell story	4.00	8.00	12.00
7-Powell, Maneely art	4.00	8.00	12.00

REDDY GOOSE
1959 - #15, Jan, 1962   (Giveaway)
International Shoe Co. (Western Printing)

#3-15	.20	.40	.60

REDDY KILOWATT   (5¢)
1946 - #2, 1947 (no month)(16pgs;soft cover)
Educational Comics (E.C.)

#1-Reddy Made Magic (Rare)	7.00	14.00	21.00
2-Edison, the Man Who Changed the World (3/4"smaller than #1) (Rare)			
	7.00	14.00	21.00

RED EAGLE (See Feature Book #16, McKay)

RED FOX (Manhunt #1-14)
1954
Magazine Enterprises

(Red Fox cont'd)   Good   Fine   Mint
#15(A-1#108)-Undercover Girl app.
                2.50   5.00   7.50

RED GOOSE COMIC SELECTIONS (See Comic Sel.)

RED HAWK (See A-1 Comics #90)

RED ICEBERG, THE
1960   (10¢)
Impact Publ.

Communist propaganda   2.00   4.00   6.00

RED MASK (Formerly Tim Holt)
#42, June-July, 1954 - #54, 1957
Magazine Enterprises

#42-Ghost Rider begins, ends #50; Black Phan-
   tom begins, ends #50,54
                2.50   5.00   7.50
43-50   2.00   4.00   6.00
51-1st app. The Presto Kid
                2.00   4.00   6.00
52-Origin The Presto Kid 2.00   4.00   6.00
53,54   1.75   3.35   5.00
IW Reprint #1(reprts./#52),#2(reprts./#51),#8
  (no date; Kinstler cvr)1.00   2.00   3.00
NOTE: *Bolle stories in all.*

RED MOUNTAIN FEATURING QUANTRELL'S RAIDERS
1952   (Movie)(Also see Jesse James #28)
Avon Periodicals

(Scarce)-Alan Ladd; Kinstler cover/art
                4.00   8.00   12.00

RED RABBIT
Jan, 1947 - #22, Aug-Sept, 1951
Dearfield Comic/J. Charles Laue Publ. Co.

#1   1.00   2.00   3.00
 2-10   .65   1.35   2.00
11-22   .35   .70   1.05

RED RAVEN COMICS (Human Torch #2 on)
August, 1940
Timely Comics

#1-Origin Red Raven; Comet Pierce & Mercury
  by Kirby, The Human Top & The Eternal
  Brain; intro. Magar, the Mystic & only app;
  Kirby cover   600.00 1200.00 1800.00
     (Prices vary widely on this book)

RED RYDER COMICS (Hi Spot #2)
#1, Sept, 1940;   #3, 8/41 - #151, 4/57
Hawley Publ.#1-4/Dell Publishing Co. #5 on

Red Mountain-, © Avon

Red Rabbit #19, © Charles Laue

Red Raven #1, © MCG

                         Good   Fine   Mint
#1-Red Ryder strip reprints by Harmon; 1st
  meeting of Red & Little Beaver
           50.00 100.00 150.00
3-(Scarce)-Alley Oop, Freckles & His Friends,
  Dan Dunn, Capt. Easy, King of Royal Mtd.,
  Red Ryder strip reprints begin
           25.00   50.00   75.00

Red Ryder #128, © Dell

4,5   17.50   35.00   52.50
6-10   13.50   26.75   40.00
11-20   7.00   14.00   21.00
21-32-Last Alley Oop, Dan Dunn, Capt. Easy,
  Freckles   5.00   10.00   15.00
33-40   4.00   8.00   12.00
41-49-Last Red Ryder strip reprint
            2.50   5.00   7.50
50-60-New stories on Red Ryder begin
            2.00   4.00   6.00
61-80: #73-Last King of the Royal Mtd. strip
  reprints by Jim Gary 1.75   3.50   5.25
81-100   1.50   3.00   4.50
101-120   1.35   2.75   4.00
121-144   1.25   2.50   3.75
145-Title changed to Red Ryder Ranch Magazine
  with photos   1.00   2.00   3.00
146-148   1.00   2.00   3.00
149,150,151-Title changed to Red Ryder Ranch
  Comics   1.00   2.00   3.00
4-Color #916   1.20   2.40   3.60
Red Ryder Victory Patrol-Superbook #2('43)
  Giveaway(reprts.#43,44)5.00 10.00 15.00
Wells Lamont Corp. giveaway('50)-16pgs. in
  color; reg. size; soft cover; 1941 reprts.
           17.50   35.00   52.50
NOTE: *Fred Harmon covers-#1-98,107-118.
Photo covers-#108-117. #119-painted covers
begin(not by Harmon).*

RED RYDER PAINT BOOK
1941   (144 pgs.) (8½x11½")

Red Seal #22, © Ches

Red Warrior #1, © MCG

Reform School Girl!, © Real

(Red Ryder Paint Book cont'd)
Whitman Publishing Co.

	Good	Fine	Mint
Reprints 1940 daily strips			
	10.00	20.00	30.00

RED SEAL
Oct, 1945 - #22, Dec, 1947
Harry 'A' Chesler

	Good	Fine	Mint
#14-The Black Dwarf begins; Little Nemo app.			
	4.00	8.00	12.00
15-17: #16-Veiled Avenger & Barry Kuda app.			
#17-Lady Satan, Yankee Girl & Sky Chief			
app.	4.00	8.00	12.00
18,20-Lady Satan & Sky Chief app.			
	4.00	8.00	12.00
19-No Black Dwarf-on cover only; Zor, El			
Tigre app.	4.00	8.00	12.00
21-Lady Satan & Black Dwarf app.,			
22-Zor, Rocketman app.	4.00	8.00	12.00

REDSKIN
Sept, 1950 - #12, Oct, 1952
Youthful Magazines

#1	1.00	2.00	3.00
2-12	.65	1.35	2.00

RED SONJA (Also see Marvel Feature)
Jan, 1977 - Present
Marvel Comics Group

#1	.40	.80	1.20
2,3	.25	.50	.75
4-7	.20	.40	.60

RED WARRIOR
Jan, 1951 - #6, Dec, 1951
Marvel/Atlas Comics (TCI)

#1	1.50	3.00	4.50
2-6	1.00	2.00	3.00

RED WOLF
May, 1972 - #9, Sept, 1973
Marvel Comics Group

#1	.20	.40	.60
2-9: #9-Origin sidekick, Lobo (wolf)			
	.15	.30	.45

REFORM SCHOOL GIRL!
1951
Realistic Comics

No#-Used in Seduction of the Innocent
(Rare)   120.00 240.00 360.00
(Prices vary widely on this book)

REGGIE (Formerly Archie's Rival--; Reggie & #15, 9/63 - #18, 11/65   Me #19 on)
Archie Publications

	Good	Fine	Mint
#15(9/63),16(10/64)	1.00	2.00	3.00
17(8/65),18(11/65)	1.00	2.00	3.00

NOTE: *Cover title #15,16 is Archie's Rival--.*

REGGIE AND ME (Formerly Reggie)
#19, 1967 - Present (#50-68, 52pgs.)
Archie Publications

#19-23-Evilheart app.	.50	1.00	1.50
24-50	.25	.50	.75
51-101		.15	.30

REGGIE'S JOKES (See Reggie's Wise Guy Jokes)

REGGIE'S WISE GUY JOKES
Aug, 1968 - Present (#5 on are Giants)
Archie Publications

#1	.50	1.00	1.50
2-4	.20	.40	.60
5-28 (All Giants)	.15	.30	.45
29-43		.15	.30

REGISTERED NURSE
Summer, 1963
Charlton Comics

#1-Reprints Nurse Betsy Crane & Cynthia Doyle			
	.20	.40	.60

REG'LAR FELLERS
1921 - 1929
Cupples & Leon/MS Publishing Co.

#1(1921)-48pgs. B&W dailies (Cupples & Leon)			
	7.00	14.00	21.00
1925, 48pgs. B&W dailies (MS Publ.)			
	7.00	14.00	21.00
Softcover(1929)-B&W reprints, 32pgs.			
	7.00	14.00	21.00
Hardcover(1929)-B&W reprints, 96 pgs.			
	10.00	20.00	30.00

REG'LAR FELLERS (See Treasure Box of Famous--)
#5, Nov, 1947 - #6, Mar, 1948
Visual Editions (Standard)

#5,6	2.00	4.00	6.00

REG'LAR FELLERS HEROIC (See Heroic)

RELUCTANT DRAGON, THE   (See 4-Color #13)

REMEMBER PEARL HARBOR
1942

(Remember Pearl Harbor cont'd)

	Good	Fine	Mint
No#	3.00	6.00	9.00

RENO BROWNE, HOLLYWOOD'S GREATEST COWGIRL
(Formerly Margie; Apache Kid #53 on)
#50, April, 1950 - #52, Sept, 1950
Marvel Comics (MPC)

#50-52	2.50	5.00	7.50

REPTILICUS (Reptisaurus #3 on)
Aug, 1961 - #2, Oct, 1961
Charlton Comics

#1(Movie), #2	1.00	2.00	3.00

REPTISAURUS THE TERRIBLE (Reptilicus #1,2)
Jan, 1962 - #8, Dec, 1962; Summer, 1963
Charlton Comics

V2#3-8	.75	1.50	2.25
Special Edition #1('63)	.75	1.50	2.25

RESCUERS, THE (See Walt Disney Showcase #40)

RESTLESS GUN, THE (See 4-Color #934,986,1045, 1089,1146)

RETURN OF GORGO, THE (Formerly Gorgo's Revenge)
#2, Summer, 1963 - #3, Fall, 1964
Charlton Comics

#2,3	1.00	2.00	3.00

RETURN OF KONGA, THE (Konga's Revenge #2 on)
1962
Charlton Comics

No#	1.00	2.00	3.00

RETURN OF THE OUTLAW
Feb, 1953 - #11, 1955
Toby Press (Minoan)

#1-Billy the Kid	1.00	2.00	3.00
2-11	.50	1.00	1.50

REVEALING LOVE STORIES
1950   (132 pgs.)
Fox Features Syndicate

No#-See Fox Giants. Contents can vary and
determines price.

REVEALING ROMANCES
Sept, 1949 - #6, Aug, 1950
Ace Magazines

	Good	Fine	Mint
#1	.80	1.60	2.40
2-6	.40	.80	1.20

REX ALLEN COMICS (Also see 4-Color #877)
#2, Sept, 1951 - #31, Dec-Jan, 1958-59
Dell Publishing Co.

4-Color #316('51)	2.50	5.00	7.50
#2-10	1.50	3.00	4.50
11-20	1.00	2.00	3.00
21-23,25-31	1.00	2.00	3.00
24-Toth art	2.00	4.00	6.00

NOTE: _Manning art-#20,27-30._

REX DEXTER OF MARS
Autumn, 1940
Fox Features Syndicate

#1-Rex Dexter, Patty O'Day, & Zanzibar app.; Briefer art	35.00	70.00	105.00

REX HART (Formerly Blaze Carson; Whip Wilson
#6, 8/49 - #8, 2/50   #9 on)
Timely/Marvel Comics (USA)

#6-Black Rider app.	1.75	3.35	5.00
7,8: #8-Blaze the Wonder Collie app. in text	1.25	2.50	3.75

REX MORGAN, M.D. (Also see Harvey Comics
Dec, 1955 - #3, 1956   Library)
Argo Publ.

#1-Reprints R.M. daily newspaper strips & daily panel reprints of "These Women" by D'Alessio & "Timeout" by Jeff Keate	2.00	4.00	6.00
2,3	1.35	2.75	4.00

REX THE WONDER DOG (See The Adventures of--)

RHUBARB, THE MILLIONAIRE CAT (See 4-Color #423,466,563)

RIBTICKLER (Also see Everybody's Comics)
1945 - #9, Aug, 1947; 1957 - 1959
Fox Feat. Synd./Green Publ.('57)/Norlen('59)

No#(1945)-Chicago Nite Life News-Marvel Mutt app.(194pgs.-50¢)	1.35	2.75	4.00
#1	1.35	2.75	4.00
2-9: #7-Cosmo Cat app.	1.00	2.00	3.00
3,8(Green Publ.-'57)	.40	.80	1.20
3,7,8(Norlen Mag.-'59)	.40	.80	1.20

RICHARD DRAGON, KUNG-FU FIGHTER
Apr-May, 1975 - #18, Nov-Dec, 1977
National Periodical Publications/DC Comics

Reptilicus #1, © CC

Return Of The Outlaw #6, © Toby

Rex Dexter Of Mars #1, © Fox

(Richard Dragon, Kung-Fu Fighter cont'd)

	Good	Fine	Mint
#1	.40	.80	1.20
2-Starlin art	.40	.80	1.20
3-Kirby story	.40	.80	1.20
4-8,11-Wood inks	.25	.50	.75
9,12-18	.20	.40	.60

RICHARD THE LION-HEARTED(See Ideal a Classic--)

RICHIE RICH (See Super Richie)

RICHIE RICH (-- The Poor Little Rich Boy)
Nov, 1960 - Present   (See Harvey Hits #3,9)
Harvey Publications

	Good	Fine	Mint
#1	10.00	20.00	30.00
2	6.00	12.00	18.00
3-5	4.00	8.00	12.00
6-10	2.50	5.00	7.50
11-20	1.75	3.35	4.00
21-40	1.00	2.00	3.00
41-60	.65	1.35	2.00
61-80	.35	.70	1.05
81-100	.20	.40	.60
101-162		.15	.30

RICHIE RICH AND BILLY BELLHOPS
October, 1977 - Present
Harvey Publications

		Fine	Mint
#1		.15	.30

RICHIE RICH AND CADBURY
October, 1977 - Present
Harvey Publications

		Fine	Mint
#1		.15	.30

RICHIE RICH AND CASPER
Aug, 1974 - Present
Harvey Publications

	Good	Fine	Mint
#1	.25	.50	.75
2-5	.15	.30	.45
6-20		.15	.30

RICHIE RICH AND DOLLAR THE DOG
Sept, 1977 - Present
Harvey Publications

		Fine	Mint
#1		.15	.30

RICHIE RICH AND DOT
Oct, 1974
Harvey Publications

	Good	Fine	Mint
#1	.25	.50	.75

RICHIE RICH AND GLORIA GLAD
Sept, 1977 - Present
Harvey Publications

		Fine	Mint
#1		.15	.30

RICHIE RICH & JACKIE JOKERS (See Jackie --)
Nov, 1973 - Present
Harvey Publications

	Good	Fine	Mint
#1	.35	.70	1.05
2-5	.20	.40	.60
6-24		.15	.30

RICHIE RICH AND TIMMY TIME
Sept, 1977 - Present
Harvey Publications

	Good	Fine	Mint
#1		.15	.30

RICHIE RICH BANK BOOKS
Oct, 1972 - Present

	Good	Fine	Mint
#1	.40	.80	1.20
2-5	.20	.40	.60
6-33		.15	.30

RICHIE RICH BEST OF THE YEARS
October, 1977   (Digest) (128 pgs.)
Harvey Publications

	Good	Fine	Mint
#1-Reprints	.20	.40	.60

RICHIE RICH BILLIONS
Oct, 1974 - Present   (35¢ - 40¢)
Harvey Publications

	Good	Fine	Mint
#1	.25	.50	.75
2-5	.15	.30	.45
6-21		.15	.30

RICHIE RICH CASH
Sept, 1974 - Present
Harvey Publications

	Good	Fine	Mint
#1	.25	.50	.75
2-5	.15	.30	.45
6-21		.15	.30

RICHIE RICH, CASPER & WENDY NATIONAL LEAGUE
June, 1976   (52 pgs.)
Harvey Publications

	Good	Fine	Mint
#1	.15	.30	.45

RICHIE RICH COLLECTORS COMICS(Formerly Harvey
#10, Feb, 1977 - Present   Coll. Comics)
Harvey Publications

		Fine	Mint
#10-14		.15	.30

RICHIE RICH DIGEST STORIES
Oct, 1977   (Digest) (132 pgs.)
Harvey Publications

	Good	Fine	Mint
#1-Reprints	.20	.40	.60

RICHIE RICH DIAMONDS
Aug, 1972 - Present
Harvey Publications

	Good	Fine	Mint
#1	.40	.80	1.20
2-5	.20	.40	.60
6-34		.15	.30

RICHIE RICH DOLLARS & CENTS
Aug, 1963 - Present   (25¢-40¢)
Harvey Publications

	Good	Fine	Mint
#1	2.50	5.00	7.50
2	1.35	2.75	4.00
3-10	1.00	2.00	3.00
11-20	.65	1.35	2.00
21-30	.35	.70	1.05
31-50	.20	.40	.60
51-83(#76-40¢)		.15	.30

RICHIE RICH FORTUNES
Sept, 1971 - Present
Harvey Publications

	Good	Fine	Mint
#1	.40	.80	1.20

(Richie Rich Fort. cont'd)	Good	Fine	Mint
2-5	.20	.40	.60
6-10	.15	.30	.45
11-38		.15	.30

RICHIE RICH GEMS
Sept, 1974 - Present
Harvey Publications

	Good	Fine	Mint
#1	.25	.50	.75
2-5	.15	.30	.45
6-21		.15	.30

RICHIE RICH GOLD AND SILVER
Sept, 1975 - Present
Harvey Publications

	Good	Fine	Mint
#1	.15	.30	.45
2-16		.15	.30

RICHIE RICH INVENTIONS
Oct, 1977 - Present
Harvey Publications

	Good	Fine	Mint
#1		.15	.30

RICHIE RICH JACKPOTS
Oct, 1972 - Present
Harvey Publications

	Good	Fine	Mint
#1	.40	.80	1.20
2-5	.20	.40	.60
6-32		.15	.30

RICHIE RICH MILLIONS
Sept, 1961 - Present
Harvey Publications

	Good	Fine	Mint
#1	3.00	6.00	9.00
2	1.50	3.00	4.50
3-10	1.20	2.40	3.60
11-20	.80	1.60	2.40
21-30	.40	.80	1.20
31-50	.20	.40	.60
51-87		.15	.30

RICHIE RICH MONEY WORLD
Sept, 1972 - Present
Harvey Publications

	Good	Fine	Mint
#1	.40	.80	1.20
2-5	.20	.40	.60
6-33		.15	.30

RICHIE RICH PROFITS
Oct, 1974 - Present
Harvey Publications

	Good	Fine	Mint
#1	.25	.50	.75
2-5	.15	.30	.45
6-20		.15	.30

RICHIE RICH RICHES
July, 1972 - Present
Harvey Publications

	Good	Fine	Mint
#1	.40	.80	1.20
2-5	.20	.40	.60
6-34		.15	.30

RICHIE RICH SUCCESS STORIES
1964 - Present
Harvey Publications

	Good	Fine	Mint
#1	2.00	4.00	6.00
2-5	1.00	2.00	3.00

	Good	Fine	Mint
6-10	.50	1.00	1.50
11-30	.20	.40	.60
31-78		.15	.30

RICHIE RICH VACATIONS DIGEST
Nov, 1977   (Digest) (132 pgs.)
Harvey Publications

	Good	Fine	Mint
#1-Reprints	.20	.40	.60

RICHIE RICH VAULTS OF MYSTERY
Nov, 1974 - Present
Harvey Publications

	Good	Fine	Mint
#1	.25	.50	.75
2-10	.15	.30	.45
11-20		.15	.30

RICHIE RICH ZILLIONZ
Oct, 1976 - Present   (68 pgs.)
Harvey Publications

	Good	Fine	Mint
#1-7		.15	.30

RICKY
Sept, 1953
Standard Comics (Visual Editions)

	Good	Fine	Mint
#5	.25	.50	.75

RICKY NELSON   (TV)
1959 - 1961
Dell Publishing Co.

	Good	Fine	Mint
4-Color #956,998	1.00	2.00	3.00
4-Color #1115,1192-Manning art	1.50	3.00	4.50
#1-5	.50	1.00	1.50

The Rider #1, © Ajax

RIDER, THE   (Frontier Trail #6)
March, 1957 - #5, 1958
Ajax/Farrell Publ.(Four Star Comic Corp.)

	Good	Fine	Mint
#1	.65	1.35	2.00
2-5	.35	.70	1.05

RIFLEMAN, THE   (TV)
July-Sept, 1959 - #20, Sept, 1964
Dell Publ. Co./Gold Key

	Good	Fine	Mint
4-Color #1009, #2	1.00	2.00	3.00
#3-Toth art-4pgs.	1.20	2.40	3.60
4-20	.40	.80	1.20

RIMA, THE JUNGLE GIRL
Apr-May, 1974 - #7, Apr-May, 1975
National Periodical Publications

Rin Tin Tin #7. © Dell   Rip Hunter #17. © DC   Ripley's B.I.O.N. #1. © Harv

(Rima cont'd)	Good	Fine	Mint
#1-Origin, part 1	.40	.80	1.20
2,3-Origin, part 2,3	.25	.50	.75
4-Origin-conclusion	.25	.50	.75
5-7: #7-Origin & only app. Space Marshal			
	.25	.50	.75

NOTE: _Kubert covers-#1-7. Nino_ art-#1-4.
Redondo art-#1-7.

RING OF BRIGHT WATER (See Movie Classics)

RINGO KID, THE (2nd Series)
Jan, 1970 - #30, Nov, 1976
Marvel Comics Group

#1(1970)-Williamson story reprint from #10,			
1956	.20	.40	.60
2-19,21-30		.15	.30
20-Williamson reprt./#1	.15	.30	.45

NOTE: _Wildey reprint-#13._

RINGO KID WESTERN, THE (1st Series)
August, 1954 - #21, Sept, 1957
Atlas Comics(HPC)/Marvel Comics

#1-Maneely, Sinnott art	2.00	4.00	6.00
2-9: #2-Black Rider app.	1.25	2.50	3.75
10,13-Williamson sty,4pgs.	2.00	4.00	6.00
11,12,14-21	.80	1.60	2.40

RIN TIN TIN (See March of Comics#163,180,195)

RIN TIN TIN (TV) (-- & Rusty #21 on)
Nov, 1952 - #38, May-July, 1961; 1963
Dell Publishing Co./Gold Key

4-Color #434,476,523	1.00	2.00	3.00
#4(6-8/54) - #10	.50	1.00	1.50
11-38	.35	.70	1.05
#1(11/63-G.K.)--& Rusty	.35	.70	1.05

RIO BRAVO (See 4-Color Comics #1018)

RIO CONCHOS (See Movie Comics)

RIOT (Satire)
April, 1954 - #3, 8/54; #4, 2/56 - #6, 6/56
Atlas Comics(ACI #1-5/WPI #6)

#1-Russ Heath art	2.00	4.00	6.00
2-6: #4,6-Everett art. #4-6-Severin stories			
	1.50	3.00	4.50

RIPCORD (See 4-Color Comics #1294)

RIP HUNTER TIME MASTER (See Showcase)
Mar-Apr, 1961 - #29, Nov-Dec, 1965
National Periodical Publications

	Good	Fine	Mint
#1	2.00	4.00	6.00
2	1.35	2.75	4.00
3-5	.80	1.60	2.40
6,7-Toth art in ea.	.65	1.35	2.00
8-15	.50	1.00	1.50
16-29: #29-G.Kane cover	.40	.80	1.20

RIP KIRBY (See Feature Book #51,54 & Harvey
Comics Hits #57 & Street Comix)

RIPLEY'S BELIEVE IT OR NOT!
Sept, 1953 - #4, March, 1954
Harvey Publications

#1	2.00	4.00	6.00
2-4	1.35	2.75	4.00
J.C.Penney giveaway('48)	2.00	4.00	6.00

RIPLEY'S BELIEVE IT OR NOT! (Formerly True
#4, 4/67 - Present   War Stories
Gold Key   #1(#3))

#4-McWilliams art	.65	1.35	2.00
5-10: #5-subtitled "True War Stories". #8-			
Orlando art	.65	1.35	2.00
11-20	.35	.70	1.05
21-40	.20	.40	.60
41-60	.15	.30	.45
61-74		.15	.30

RIPLEY'S BELIEVE IT OR NOT! (See Mystery
Comics Digest #1,4,7,10,13,16,19,22,25)

RIPLEY'S BELIEVE IT OR NOT TRUE GHOST
STORIES (Becomes --True War Stories)
June, 1965 - #2, Oct, 1966 (See Dan Curtis)
Gold Key

#1-Williamson, Wood & Evans stories			
	1.50	3.00	4.50
2-Orlando story	.75	1.50	2.25

RIPLEY'S BELIEVE IT OR NOT TRUE WAR STORIES
(Formerly --True Ghost Stories; becomes Rip-
ley's Believe It Or Not #4)
November, 1966
Gold Key

#1(#3)		.65	1.35	2.00

RIPLEY'S BELIEVE IT OR NOT! TRUE WEIRD
June, 1966 - #2, Aug, 1966 (B&W Magazine)
Ripley Enterprises

#1,2-Comic stories & text	.40	.80	1.20

RIP RAIDER
1944

(Rip Raider cont'd)	Good	Fine	Mint
No#	1.50	3.00	4.50

RIVETS (See 4-Color Comics #518)

RIVETS (A dog)
Jan, 1956 - #3, May, 1956
Argo Publ.

#1-Reprints Sunday & daily newspaper strips			
	1.00	2.00	3.00
2,3	.75	1.50	2.25

ROAD RUNNER, THE (See Beep Beep --)

ROAD RUNNER KITE FUN BOOK
1971   (8 pgs.) (Giveaway)
Pacific Gas & Electric Co.(Western Printing)

No#	3.00	6.00	9.00

ROBIN (See Aurora)

ROBIN HOOD (See 4-Color #413,669, Movie Comics, The Advs. of--, & New Advs. of--)

ROBIN HOOD (-- & His Merry Men, The Illustrated Story of --) (See Classic Comics #7)

ROBIN HOOD (New Adventures of --)
1952 (36pgs.) "New Adventures of Robin Hood",
"Ghosts of Waylea Castle" & "The Miller's
Ransom" (Flour Giveaways) (5x7¼")
Walt Disney Productions

each......	1.50	3.00	4.50

ROBIN HOOD (Adventures of -- #8)
#52, Nov, 1955 - #7, Sept, 1957
Magazine Enterprises (Sussex Publ. Co.)

#52-Origin Robin Hood & Sir Gallant of the			
Round Rable	1.20	2.40	3.60
53, #3-7	1.20	2.40	3.60

NOTE: *Bolle art in all. Powell art-#6,7.*
IW Reprint #1,2(reprts#4), 9(reprts#52)('63)			
	.65	1.35	2.00
Super Reprint #10(reprts.#53 or 3),11,15(re-			
prts.#5),17('64)	.65	1.35	2.00

ROBIN HOOD
No date (Circa 1955)
Shoe Store Giveaway (Robin Hood Stores)

#1-7-Reed Crandall art	2.00	4.00	6.00

ROBIN HOOD (Not Disney)
May-July, 1963 - #7, Nov-Jan, 1964-65

Dell Publishing Co.
	Good	Fine	Mint
#1	.35	.70	1.05
2-7	.20	.40	.60

ROBIN HOOD   ($1.50)
1973 (Disney)(8½x11")(Cardboard covers)
Western Publishing Co.   (52pgs.)

#96151-"Robin Hood", based on movie, #96152- "The Mystery of Sherwood Forest," #96153- "In King Richard's Service," #96154-"The Wizard's King" each... .80 1.60 2.40			

ROBIN HOOD AND HIS MERRY MEN
#28, April, 1956 - #38, Aug, 1958
Charlton Comics

#28-38: #38-Ditko sty,5pgs..65	1.35	2.00

ROBIN HOOD TALES (National Periodical #7 on)
Feb, 1956 - #6, Nov-Dec, 1956
Quality Comics Group (Comic Magazines)

#1	2.00	4.00	6.00
2-6: #4,5-Baker art	1.35	2.75	4.00
Frontier Days giveaway('56)			
	1.00	2.00	3.00

ROBIN HOOD TALES (Cont'd. from Quality)
#7, Jan-Feb, 1957 - #14, Mar-Apr, 1958
National Periodical Publications

#7-14	1.75	3.35	5.00

ROBINSON CRUSOE
Nov-Jan, 1964
Dell Publishing Co.

#1	.35	.70	1.05

ROBOTMEN OF THE LOST PLANET
1952   (Also see Space Thrillers)
Avon Periodicals

#1	12.00	24.00	36.00

ROB ROY (See 4-Color Comics #544)

ROCK AND ROLLO
V2#14, Oct, 1957 - #19, 1958
Charlton Comics

#14-19	.15	.30	.45

ROCKET COMICS
Feb, 1940 - #3, May, 1940
Hillman Periodicals

Robin Hood Flour Giv., © WDP

Robotmen Of The Lost Planet #1, © Avon

Robin Hood #1, © Qua

Rocketman #1, © Ajax

Rocket To The Moon #1, © Avon

Rocky Lane Western #24, © Faw

(Rocket Comics cont'd)	Good	Fine	Mint
#1-Rocket Riley & Red Roberts, Phantom Rang-er, The Steel Shark, Electro Man, The De-fender, Man With a Thousand Faces begin	16.50	33.25	50.00
2,3	10.00	20.00	30.00

ROCKET KELLY
1944; Fall, 1945 - #5, 1947
Fox Features Syndicate

No#(1944)	2.00	4.00	6.00
#1	2.00	4.00	6.00
2-The Puppeteer app.(a costumed hero), 3-5	1.75	3.35	5.00

ROCKETMAN
June, 1952
Ajax/Farrell Publications

#1-Rocketman & Cosmo	2.00	4.00	6.00

ROCKETS AND RANGE RIDERS
1957 (16 pgs.) (Giveaway)
Richfield Oil Corp.

Toth art	2.00	4.00	6.00

ROCKET SHIP X
Sept, 1951
Fox Features Syndicate

#1	6.00	12.00	18.00

ROCKET TO ADVENTURE LAND (See Pixie Puzzle--)

ROCKET TO THE MOON
1951
Avon Periodicals

No#-Orlando cover/story; adapts Otis Aldebert Kline's "Maza of the Moon"; used in Seduct-ion of the Innocent	10.00	20.00	30.00

ROCK HAPPENING
1969
Harvey Publications

#1,2		.15	.30

ROCKY AND BULLWINKLE KITE FUN BOOK
1963; 1970 (8pgs; 16pgs)(Soft Cover)(Giveaway)
Pacific Gas & Electric Co./Sou. Calif. Edison

No#-8pgs.(PG&E)(1963)	2.50	5.00	7.50
No#-16pgs.(SCEC)(1970)	2.00	4.00	6.00

ROCKY AND HIS FIENDISH FRIENDS (TV)
Oct, 1962 - #5, Sept, 1963 (Jay Ward)
Gold Key

	Good	Fine	Mint
#1-3(84pgs.)	.35	.70	1.05
4,5(Reg. size)	.20	.40	.60

ROCKY AND HIS FRIENDS (See 4-Color #1128,1152, 1166,1208,1275,1311 & March of Comics #216)

ROCKY JONES SPACE RANGER
1955
Charlton Comics

#15-18	.80	1.60	2.40

ROCKY LANE WESTERN (See Black Jack)
May, 1949 - #87, Nov, 1959
Fawcett Publications/Charlton #55 on

#1	6.00	12.00	18.00
2	4.00	8.00	12.00
3-10	3.00	6.00	9.00
11-30	2.50	5.00	7.50
31-50	2.00	4.00	6.00
51-78,80-87	1.50	3.00	4.50
79-Giant edition,68pgs.	2.00	4.00	6.00

ROD CAMERON WESTERN
Feb, 1950 - #20, April, 1953
Fawcett Publications

#1	6.00	12.00	18.00
2	3.00	6.00	9.00
3-10	2.50	5.00	7.50
11-20	2.00	4.00	6.00

RODEO RYAN (See A-1 Comics #8)

ROGER BEAN, R.G. (Regular Guy)
1915 - 1917 (34pgs.; B&W; 4-3/4"x16"; Cardboard covers)(#1&4 bound on side, #3 bound
The Indiana News Co.   at top)

#1-By Chic Jackson	5.00	10.00	15.00
2-4	4.00	8.00	12.00

ROGER DODGER (Also in Exciting #57 on)
#5, Aug, 1952
Standard Comics

#5	.65	1.35	2.00

ROLY POLY COMIC BOOK
1945 - 1946 (MLJ Reprints)
Green Publishing Co.

#1-Red Rube & Steel Sterling begin	4.00	8.00	12.00
6-The Blue Circle & The Steel Fist app.	2.00	4.00	6.00

(Roly Poly cont'd)	Good	Fine	Mint
10-Origin Red Rube retold; Steel Sterling			
story(Zip #41)	2.50	5.00	7.50
11,12,14-The Black Hood in all			
	2.50	5.00	7.50
15-The Blue Circle & The Steel Fist app.			
	2.00	4.00	6.00

ROMANCE (See True Stories of --)

ROMANCE DIARY
Dec, 1949
Marvel Comics (CDS)

#1	1.00	2.00	3.00

ROMANCE & CONFESSION STORIES(See Giant Comics)

ROMANCE OF FLYING, THE
1941-42   (World War II photos)
David McKay Publications

No#-Illustration with text. 8pgs. of photos
  of The Doolittle Tokyo Raiders
	2.00	4.00	6.00

ROMANCES OF MOLLY MANTON (See Molly Manton)

ROMANCES OF NURSE HELEN GRANT(See Helen Grant)

ROMANCES OF THE WEST
Nov, 1949 - #2, March, 1950
Marvel Comics (SPC)

#1-Movie photo of Calamity Jane & Sam Bass
	1.35	2.75	5.00
2	1.00	2.00	3.00

ROMANCE STORIES OF TRUE LOVE
#45, May, 1957 - #50, Mar, 1958
Harvey Publications

#45-50	.25	.50	.75

ROMANCE TALES
#8, Jan, 1950 - #9, March, 1950
Marvel Comics (CDS)

#8,9	.50	1.00	1.50

ROMANCE TRAIL
July-Aug, 1949 - #7, July-Aug, 1950
National Periodical Publications

#1	3.00	6.00	9.00
2-7	1.75	3.35	5.00

ROMAN HOLIDAYS, THE (TV)

Feb, 1973 - #4, Nov, 1973   (Hanna-Barbera)
Gold Key

	Good	Fine	Mint
#1-4		.15	.30

ROMANTIC ADVENTURES (My-- #49-69, covers only
3-4/49 - #69, 9/56   (My-- #70 on)
American Comics Group (B&I Publ. Co.)

#1-Wood art?	1.50	3.00	4.50
2	.80	1.60	2.40
3-13,15,16,18-69	.40	.80	1.20
14,17-Whitney art	.40	.80	1.20

ROMANTIC CONFESSIONS
Oct, 1949 - V2#9, Aug-Sept, 1952
Hillman Periodicals

V1#1-McWilliams art	1.20	2.40	3.60
V1#2-12	.50	1.00	1.50
V2#1,2,4-8	.40	.80	1.20
V2#3-Krigstein story	1.75	3.35	5.00
V2#9-1pg. Frazetta ad	1.50	3.00	4.50

ROMANTIC HEARTS
June, 1951; Mar, 1953 - #12, 1954
Story Comics/Master Publ./Star Comics

#2(6/51)(Story Comics)	.50	1.00	1.50
#1(3/53)	1.00	2.00	3.00
2-4,6-12	.65	1.35	2.00
5-Kubert story	1.75	3.35	5.00

ROMANTIC LOVE
#4, June, 1950
Quality Comics Group

#4(6/50)	1.20	2.40	3.60
IW Reprint #2,3,8	.20	.40	.60

ROMANTIC LOVE
Sept-Oct, 1949 - #23, Sept-Oct, 1954
Avon Periodicals/Realistic

#1	2.50	5.00	7.50
2-19,21,22	1.50	3.00	4.50
20-Kinstler cover/story	2.00	4.00	6.00
23-Kinstler cover	1.75	3.35	5.00
No#(1-3/53)(Realistic reprint)			
	1.35	2.75	4.00

ROMANTIC MARRIAGE (Cinderella Love #26 on)
Nov-Dec, 1950 - #25, Nov, 1954
Ziff-Davis/St. John #13 on

#1	1.35	2.75	4.00
2-10	.80	1.60	2.40
11-25	.50	1.00	1.50

Romantic Adventures #1, © ACG

Romantic Confessions #1, © Hill

Romantic Marriage #1, © Z-D

Romantic Secrets #1, © Faw

Roundup #1, © DS

Roy Rogers #66, © Roy Rogers

ROMANTIC PICTURE NOVELETTES
1946   (Mary Worth reprints)
Magazine Enterprises

	Good	Fine	Mint
#1	2.50	5.00	7.50

ROMANTIC SECRETS (Becomes Time For Love)
Sept, 1949 - #38, 1/53; #5, 10/55 - #51, 9/64
Fawcett/Charlton Comics #5(10/55) on

#1	1.50	3.00	4.50
2-5	.80	1.60	2.40
6-8,10-20	.50	1.00	1.50
9-Evans story	.80	1.60	2.40
21-38('53)	.40	.80	1.20
#5(10/55)-#51('64)-Charlton	.15	.30	.45
NOTE: Powell art-#29,33,36.

ROMANTIC STORY
Nov, 1949 - #130, Nov, 1973
Fawcett/Charlton Comics

#1	1.75	3.35	5.00
2-5	1.00	2.00	3.00
6-14,16-20	.80	1.60	2.40
15-Evans story	1.00	2.00	3.00
21-39,41-50	.40	.80	1.20
40-(100pgs.)	2.00	4.00	6.00
51-80	.20	.40	.60
81-130		.15	.30

ROMANTIC THRILLS
1950   (Giant)
Fox Features Syndicate

No#-Wood story	4.00	8.00	12.00

ROMANTIC WESTERN
Winter, 1949 - #3, June, 1950
Fawcett Publications

#1	1.75	3.35	5.00
2-Williamson story + McWilliams story			
	2.50	5.00	7.50
3	1.35	2.75	4.00

ROMEO TUBBS (Formerly My Secret Life)
#28, July, 1950; #1, 1950
Fox Features Syndicate

#28,1	1.00	2.00	3.00

RONALD McDONALD
Sept, 1970 - #4, March, 1971
Charlton Press (King Features Synd.)

#1	.15	.30
2-4	.10	.20

ROOKIE COP
Nov, 1955 - #33, Aug, 1957
Charlton Comics

	Good	Fine	Mint
#27-33	.50	1.00	1.50

ROOM 222 (TV)
Jan, 1970 - #4, Jan, 1971
Dell Publishing Co.

#1,2,4: #4 reprts. #1	.15	.30	.45
3-Marijuana story	.40	.80	1.20

ROOTIE KAZOOTIE (See 3-D-ell)
1952 - 1954
Dell Publishing Co.

4-Color #415,459,502	.80	1.60	2.40
#4(4-6/54)-#6(10/12/54)	.50	1.00	1.50

ROUNDUP (Western Crime)
July-Aug, 1948 - #5, Mar-Apr, 1949
D.S. Publishing Co.

#1	1.35	2.75	4.00
2-5	1.00	2.00	3.00

ROY CAMPANELLA, BASEBALL HERO
1950
Fawcett Publications

No#	3.00	6.00	9.00

ROY ROGERS (See March of Comics #17,35,47,62,
68,73,77,86,91,100,105,116,121,131,136,146,
151,161,167,176,191,206,221,236,250)

ROY ROGERS AND TRIGGER
April, 1967
Gold Key

#1-Reprints	.25	.50	.75

ROY ROGERS COMICS
1944 - 1948
Dell Publishing Co.

4-Color #38('44)	20.00	40.00	60.00
4-Color #63('45)	13.50	26.75	40.00
4-Color #86,95('45)	9.00	18.00	27.00
4-Color #109('46)	6.00	12.00	18.00
4-Color #117,124,137,144	5.00	10.00	15.00
4-Color #153,160,166,177	4.00	8.00	12.00

ROY ROGERS COMICS (See Trigger)
Jan, 1948 - #145, Sept-Oct, 1961
Dell Publishing Co.

#1	12.00	24.00	36.00

337

(Roy Rogers cont'd)	Good	Fine	Mint
2	7.00	14.00	21.00
3-10	3.35	6.75	10.00
11-20	2.50	5.00	7.50
21-30	2.00	4.00	6.00
31-40	1.75	3.50	5.25
41-55: #49-Trigger feature ends; Charley's Tales begins. #55-Last ish. w/back cover picture	1.50	3.00	4.50
56-70	1.35	2.75	4.00
71-91	1.00	2.00	3.00
92-Titled changed to Roy Rogers and Trigger (8/55)	.90	1.80	2.70
93-110,112-118	.90	1.80	2.70
111,119-124-Toth art	1.75	3.35	5.00
125-145	.80	1.60	2.40
-- & the Man From Dodge City(Dodge giveaway, 16pgs.,'54)Frontier, Inc. (5x7¼")	2.50	5.00	7.50
-- Riders Club Comics(16pgs.,'52)	2.50	5.00	7.50

NOTE: _Buscema_ stories,2ea.-#74-108. _Manning_ art-#123,124,132-144. _Marsh_ art-#110.

ROY ROGERS' TRIGGER
#2, Sept-Nov, 1941 - #17, June-Aug, 1955
Dell Publishing Co.

	Good	Fine	Mint
4-Color #329(5/51)	2.00	4.00	6.00
#2-5	1.35	2.75	4.00
6-17	1.00	2.00	3.00

RUDOLPH, THE RED NOSED REINDEER (See Limited Collectors Edition #33,50)

RUDOLPH, THE RED NOSED REINDEER
1939
Montgomery Ward   (Giveaway)

Possible 1st app. in print
	10.00	20.00	30.00

RUDOLPH, THE RED NOSED REINDEER
1950 - #13, Winter, 1963-64; 1972-73
(Issues are not numbered) (15 known issues)
National Periodical Publications

	Good	Fine	Mint
1950-54 issues	1.75	3.35	5.00
1955-63 issues	1.35	2.75	4.00
1972, C-24(1973)80pgs.; oversized 10x13½"	.40	.80	1.20

RUFF & REDDY (TV) (Hanna-Barbera)
Sept, 1958 - #12, Jan-Mar, 1962
Dell Publishing Co./Gold Key

4-Color #937,981,1038	.40	.80	1.20
#4(1-3/60)-#12	.25	.50	.75

NOTE: _Existence of #1('66-Gold Key) suspected_

RUGGED ACTION (Str. Stor. of Suspense #5 on)
Dec, 1954 - #4, June, 1955
Atlas Comics (CSI)

	Good	Fine	Mint
#1	1.20	2.40	3.60
2-4	.75	1.50	2.25

RULAH JUNGLE GODDESS (Formerly Zoot; I Loved #28 on) (Also see Terrors of the Jungle)
#17, Aug, 1948 - #27, June, 1949
Fox Features Syndicate

#17	12.00	24.00	36.00
18-20	9.00	18.00	27.00
21-Used in Seduction of the Innocent, pg. 389	10.00	20.00	30.00
22-27	8.00	16.00	24.00

NOTE: _Kamen_ covers-#17-19,21,22.

RUNAWAY, THE (See Movie Classics)

RUN BABY RUN
1974   (39¢)
Logos International

By Tony Tallarico from Nicky Cruz's book
	.20	.40

RUN, BUDDY, RUN (TV)
June, 1967
Gold Key

#1(10204-706)	.20	.40	.60

RUSTY (Formerly Kid Movie Comics; The Kelley
#12, 4/47 - #22, 9/49   #23 o
Marvel Comics (HPC)

#12,13,18,19	.80	1.60	2.40
14-Wolverton's Powerhouse Pepper(4pgs.) + Kurtzman's "Hey Look"	4.00	8.00	12.00
15-17-Kurtzman's "Hey Look", 20-Kurtzman, 5pgs.	3.00	6.00	9.00
21,22-Kurtzman, 17&22pgs.	5.00	10.00	15.00

RUSTY, BOY DETECTIVE
Mar, 1955 - #5, Nov, 1955
Good Comics/Lev Gleason

#1-5-Bob Wood, Carl Hubbell art	1.50	3.00	4.50

RUSTY DUGAN (See Holyoke One-Shot #2)

RUSTY RILEY (See 4-Color #418,451,486,554)

Roy Rogers Dodge Giv('54), © Roy Rogers

Rudolph ('39 Montgomery Ward), © Mont. Ward

Rulah Jungle Goddess #17, © Fox

338

Sabu #30, © Fox

Saddle Justice #5, © WMG

Sad Sack #1, © Harv

SAARI, THE JUNGLE GODDESS
Nov, 1951
P.L. Publishing Co.

	Good	Fine	Mint
1	5.00	10.00	15.00

SABRINA'S CHRISTMAS MAGIC (See Archie Giant
Series Mag. #196,207,220,231,243,455)

SABRINA, THE TEEN-AGE WITCH (TV)
(See Archie's TV Laugh-Out)(Giants #1-17)
April, 1971 - Present
Archie Publications

1		.15	.30	.45
2-43: #3,4-Archie's Group x-over	.10		.20	

SABU, "ELEPHANT BOY"(Formerly My Secret Story)
#30, June, 1950 - #2, Aug, 1950
Fox Features Syndicate

30(#1)-Wood story	4.00	8.00	12.00
2-Photo cover; Wood art	4.00	8.00	12.00

SADDLE JUSTICE (Happy Houlihans #1,2;
becomes Saddle Romances #9 on)
#3, Spring, 1948 - #8, Sept-Oct, 1949
E.C. Comics

3-8-Ingels art #4-8	20.00	40.00	60.00

NOTE: *Craig & Feldstein* art in most issues.
Canadian reprts. known; see Table of Contents.

SADDLE ROMANCES (Saddle Justice #3-8;
continued as Weird Science #12 on)
#9, Nov-Dec, 1949 - #11, Mar-Apr, 1950
E.C. Comics

#9-11: Ingels art in all; #10-Wood story		20.00	40.00	60.00

NOTE: *Canadian reprints known; see Table of
Contents.*

SADIE SACK (See Harvey Hits #93)

SAD SACK AND THE SARGE
Sept, 1957 - Present
Harvey Publications

	Good	Fine	Mint
#1	2.00	4.00	6.00
2-10	1.00	2.00	3.00
11-20	.50	1.00	1.50
21-50	.20	.40	.60
51-129		.15	.30

SAD SACK COMICS (See Tastee Freez & Harvey
Sept, 1949 - Present   Hits #8,61)
Harvey Publications

	Good	Fine	Mint
#1	6.00	12.00	18.00
2-10	2.50	5.00	7.50
11-30	1.50	3.00	4.50
31-50	.75	1.50	2.25
51-100	.40	.80	1.20
101-150	.20	.40	.60
151-260		.15	.30
3-D#1(1/54-titled "Harvey 3-D Hits")			
	3.00	6.00	9.00
Armed Forces Complimentary copies, HD#3-15,23			
('56-59),#32,33-38('61)	.20	.40	.60

SAD SACK GOES HOME
1951 (16 pgs. in color)
Harvey Publications

	Good	Fine	Mint
No#-by George Baker	1.00	2.00	3.00

SAD SACK FUN AROUND THE WORLD
1974 (no month)
Harvey Publications

#1-About Great Britain		.15	.30

SAD SACK LAUGH SPECIAL
Winter, 1958-59 - #93, Feb, 1977
Harvey Publications

	Good	Fine	Mint
#1	1.75	3.35	5.00
2-10	.80	1.60	2.40
11-30	.40	.80	1.20
31-50	.15	.30	.45
51-93		.15	.30

SAD SACK NAVY, GOBS 'N' GALS
Aug, 1972 - #8, Oct, 1973
Harvey Publications

#1-8		.15	.30

SAD SACK'S ARMY LIFE (See Harvey Hits #17,
19,22,28,39,43,47,51,55,58,64,70)

SAD SACK'S ARMY LIFE (--Parade #1-57,--Today
1963 - Present   #58 on)
Harvey Publications

	Good	Fine	Mint
#1	1.00	2.00	3.00
2-10	.50	1.00	1.50
11-30	.20	.40	.60
31-62		.15	.30

SAD SACK'S FUNNY FRIENDS (See Harvey Hits #75)
1955 - #75, Oct, 1969
Harvey Publications

	Good	Fine	Mint
#1	2.00	4.00	6.00

(Sad Sack's Funny Friends cont'd)

	Good	Fine	Mint
2-10	1.00	2.00	3.00
11-20	.65	1.35	2.00
21-30	.35	.70	1.05
31-50	.20	.40	.60
51-75		.15	.30

SAD SACK'S MUTTSY (See Harvey Hits #74,77,80,
82,89,96,99,102,105,108,111,113,115,117,119,121)

SAD SACK USA (-- Vacation #8)
Nov, 1972 - #7, Nov, 1973; #8, Oct, 1974
Harvey Publications

#1-8		.15	.30

SAD SACK WITH SARGE & SADIE
Sept, 1972 - #8, 1973
Harvey Publications

#1-8		.15	.30

SAD SAD SACK WORLD
1964 - #46, Dec, 1973
Harvey Publications

#1	.50	1.00	1.50
2-10	.20	.40	.60
11-46		.15	.30

SAGA OF BIG RED, THE
Sept, 1976   ($1.25) (In Color)
Omaha World-Herald

No#-by Win Mumma; story of the Nebraska Cornhuskers(sports)	.40	.80	1.20

SAILOR SWEENEY (Navy Action #1-11, 15 on)
#12, July, 1956 - #14, Nov, 1956
Atlas Comics (CDS)

#12-14: #12-Shores art. #13-Severin cover

	.65	1.35	2.00

SAINT, THE
Aug, 1947 - #12, Mar, 1952
Avon Periodicals

#1-Kamen bondage cvr/stories

	10.00	20.00	30.00
2-5	6.00	12.00	18.00
6-Miss Fury app., 14pgs.	12.00	24.00	36.00
7-9(12/50): Saint strip reprints in #8-12; #9-Kinstler cover	4.00	8.00	12.00
10-Wood art, 1pg.	3.00	6.00	9.00
11,12	3.00	6.00	9.00

NOTE: *Lucky Dale, Girl Detective in #1,4,6.*

SAM HILL PRIVATE EYE
1950 - #7, 1951
Close-Up

	Good	Fine	Mint
#1	1.20	2.40	3.60
2-7	.80	1.60	2.40

SAMSON (1st Series) (Capt. Aero #7 on)
Fall, 1940 - #6, Sept, 1941
Fox Features Syndicate

#1-Will Eisner art	25.00	50.00	75.00
2	15.00	30.00	45.00
3-Navy Jones app.	12.00	24.00	36.00
4-Yarko the Great, Master Magician begins; Fine cover	10.00	20.00	30.00
5	10.00	20.00	30.00
6-Origin The Topper	10.00	20.00	30.00

SAMSON (2nd Series) (See Spec. Feat. Mag.)
#12, April, 1955 - #14, Aug, 1955
Ajax/Farrell Publications (Four Star)

#12-14-Wonder Boy in #12,13; Rocket Man in #13	1.75	3.35	5.00

SAMSON (See Mighty Samson)

SAMSON & DELILAH (See A Spectacular Feat. Mag.

SAMUEL BRONSTON'S CIRCUS WORLD (See Movie
Comics under Circus World)

SANDMAN, THE
Winter, 1974; #2, 4-5/75 - #6, 12-1/75-76
National Periodical Publications

#1	.50	1.00	1.50
2,3-Chua art in each	.25	.50	.75
4,5	.20	.40	.60
6-Wood art	.25	.50	.75

NOTE: *Kirby stories-#1,4-6; covers-#1-6.*

SANDS OF THE SOUTH PACIFIC
January, 1953
Toby Press

#1	1.35	2.75	4.00

SANTA AND HIS REINDEER (See March of Comics
#166)

SANTA AND POLLYANNA PLAY THE GLAD GAME
1960   (15 pgs.) (Disney giveaway)
Sales Promotion

	.80	1.60	2.40

The Saint #11, © Avon

Samson #1, © Fox

The Sandman #1, © DC

Santa Claus Funnies #1('52), © Dell   Santa Claus Funnies 4-Color #61, © Dell   Santa Claus Funnies 4-Color #205, © Dell

SANTA AND THE ANGEL (See 4-Color #259 &
Dell Jr. Treasury #7)

SANTA & THE BUCCANEERS
1959
Promotional Publ. Co. (Giveaway)

	Good	Fine	Mint
Reprints 1952 Santa & the Pirates			
	.35	.70	1.05

SANTA & THE PIRATES
1952
Promotional Publ. Co. (Giveaway)

Marv Levy cover/art	.65	1.35	2.00

SANTA AT THE ZOO (See 4-Color Comics #259)

SANTA CLAUS AROUND THE WORLD (See March of
Comics #241)

SANTA CLAUS CONQUERS THE MARTIANS (See Movie Classics)

SANTA CLAUS FUNNIES
1942 - 1962
Dell Publishing Co.

	Good	Fine	Mint
No#(1942)-Kelly art	30.00	60.00	90.00
#2(1943)-Kelly art	25.00	50.00	75.00
4-Color #61('44)-Kelly	20.00	40.00	60.00
4-Color #91('45)-Kelly	15.00	30.00	45.00
4-Color #128('46),175('47)-Kelly art			
	12.00	24.00	36.00
4-Color #205,254-Kelly	10.00	20.00	30.00
4-Color #302,361	2.50	5.00	7.50
4-Color #525,607,666,756,867			
	1.00	2.00	3.00
4-Color #958,1063,1154,1274			
	.65	1.35	2.00
#1(1952-Dell Giant)(Dan Noonan-A Christmas			
Carol adaptation)	3.00	6.00	9.00

NOTE: *Most issues contain only one Kelly
story.*

SANTA CLAUS PARADE
1951; 1952; 1955   (25¢)
Ziff-Davis(Approved Comics)/St. John Publ.

No#(1951)-116pgs.(Ziff-Davis)(XMas Special)			
	2.00	4.00	6.00
#2(12/52-Z-D)100pgs.; Dave Berg art			
	2.00	4.00	6.00
V1#3(1/66-St. John)100pgs.	1.50	3.00	4.50

SANTA IS COMING (See March of Comics #197)

SANTA IS HERE (See March of Comics #49)

SANTA ON THE JOLLY ROGER
1965
Promotional Publ. Co. (Giveaway)

	Good	Fine	Mint
Marv Levy cover/art	.20	.40	.60

SANTA'S BUSY CORNER (See March of Comics #31)

SANTA'S CANDY KITCHEN(See March of Comics #14)

SANTA'S CHRISTMAS BOOK (See March of Comics
#123)

SANTA'S CHRISTMAS COMICS
Dec, 1952   (100 pgs.)
Standard Comics (Best Books)

No#	1.75	3.35	5.00

SANTA'S CHRISTMAS LIST (See March of Comics
#255)

SANTA'S CIRCUS
1964   (½-Size)
Promotional Publ. Co. (Giveaway)

Marv Levy cover/art	.20	.40	.60

SANTA'S HELPERS (See March of Comics #64,
106,198)

SANTA'S LITTLE HELPERS (See March of Comics
#270)

SANTA'S RODEO
1964   (½-Size)
Promotional Publ. Co. (Giveaway)

Marv Levy story only	.20	.40	.60

SANTA'S SHOW (See March of Comics #311)

SANTA'S SLEIGH (See March of Comics #298)

SANTA'S STORIES
1953   (Regular size, soft cover)
K.K. Publications (Klines Dept. Store)

Kelly art	6.00	12.00	18.00

SANTA'S SURPRISE (See March of Comics #13,22)

SANTA'S TINKER TOTS
1958
Charlton Comics

#1-Based on "The Tinker Tots Keep Christmas"			
	.20	.40	.60

341

SANTA'S TOYLAND (See March of Comics #242)

SANTA'S TOYTOWN FUN BOOK
1952
Promotional Publ. Co. (Giveaway)

	Good	Fine	Mint
Marv Levy cover only	.65	1.35	2.00

SANTA'S TOYS (See March of Comics #12)

SANTA'S VISIT (See March of Comics #283)

SANTA'S WORKSHOP (See March of Comics #50,168)

SANTIAGO (See 4-Color Comics #723)

SARGE SNORKEL (Beetle Bailey)
Oct, 1973 - #17, Dec, 1976
Charlton Comics

#1-17	.10	.20

SARGE STEEL (Becomes Secret Agent #9 on)
Dec, 1964 - #8, Mar-Apr, 1966
Charlton Comics

#1-Origin	.35	.70	1.05
2-8	.20	.40	.60

SAVAGE COMBAT TALES
Feb, 1975 - #3, July, 1975
Atlas/Seaboard Publ.

#1-Sgt. Stryker's Death Squad begins(origin);			
McWilliams cvr/art	.20	.40	.60
2,3: #2-Toth, McWilliams art; intro., only			
app. Warhawk	.15	.30	.45

SAVAGE RAIDS OF GERONIMO (See Geronimo #4)

SAVAGE RANGE (See 4-Color Comics #807)

SAVAGE SWORD OF CONAN, THE (Magazine)
Aug, 1974 - Present (Black & White)
Marvel Comics Group

#1-Smith reprint + Buscema/Adams/Krenkel art;			
origin Blackmark by G. Kane(part 1) & Red			
Sonja	2.00	4.00	6.00
2-Adams cover/story inks	1.00	2.00	3.00
3-Smith art; Adams story	1.00	2.00	3.00
4-Adams story reprint	1.00	2.00	3.00
5,6,8-10	.65	1.35	2.00
7-Smith art	.80	1.60	2.40
11-13,15	.65	1.35	2.00
14-Adams art	.80	1.60	2.40
16-Smith pencils	.80	1.60	2.40
17-25	.50	1.00	1.50

	Good	Fine	Mint
Annual #1('75)-B&W, Smith reprints(Conan #10, 13)	.65	1.35	2.00

NOTE: *Alcala stories-#2,4,7,12, inks-#15-19.*
Boris covers-#1,4,5,7,9,10,12,15. Brunner
cover-#8. Buscema stories-#1-5,7,10-12,15-24.
Chaykin story-#18. Corben story-#4. Finley
story-#16. Kaluta story-#11,18; covers-#11,
18. Krenkel story-#9,11,14,16. Morrow story-
#7. Newton story-#6. Nino cover/art-#6. #8 &
#10 contain a Robert E. Howard Conan adapta-
tion.

SAVAGE TALES (Magazine) (B&W)
5/71; #2, 10/73; #3, 2/74 - #12, Summer/75
Marvel Comics Group

#1-Origin & 1st app. The Man-Thing(reprt.)by			
Morrow; Conan the Barbarian(reprt.)by			
Barry Smith, Femizons by Romita begin;			
Ka-Zar app.	13.50	26.75	40.00
2-Smith, Brunner, Morrow, Williamson, Wright			
son art (reprt.-Creatures on the Loose#10)			
King Kull app.	4.00	8.00	12.00
3-Smith, Brunner, Steranko, Williamson art			
	2.50	5.00	7.50
4,5-Adams covers; last Conan (Smith reprt./			
#4)+ Kane/Adams story. #5-Brak the Barbar-			
ian begins, ends #8	1.20	2.40	3.60
6-Ka-Zar begins; Williamson reprint; Adams			
cover	.80	1.60	2.40
7-Buscema/Adams story	.80	1.60	2.40
8-Shanna, the She-Devil begins, ends #10;			
Adams cover/story	.65	1.35	2.00
9,11	.65	1.35	2.00
10-Adams story inks	.80	1.60	2.40
Annual #1(Sum.'75)(#12 on inside)-B&W; Smith			
reprt./Astonishing Tales.	.65	1.35	2.00

NOTE: *Kaluta cover-#9. Starlin story-#4,5.*

SCAMP (Walt Disney)
5/56 - #1204, 8-10/61; 11/67 - Present
Dell Publishing Co./Gold Key

4-Color #703,777,806('57),833			
	.65	1.35	2.00
#5(3-5/58)-#10('59)	.40	.80	1.20
11-16(12-2/61)	.25	.50	.75
4-Color #1204('61)	.65	1.35	2.00
#1('67, G.K.)-reprts.begin	.20	.40	.60
2-10('69)	.15	.30	.45
16-38	.20	.35	

NOTE: *New stories-#20(in part),22-25,27,30,*
31,34,37,38. New covers-#11,12,14,15,17-25,
27,29-31,34,36-38.

SCAR FACE (See The Crusaders)

Sarge Steel #1, © CC

Savage Tales #1, © MCG

The Scarecrow #1, © WDP

SCARECROW, THE (-- of Romney Marsh #1)
April, 1964 - #3, Oct, 1965 (Disney TV Show)
Gold Key

	Good	Fine	Mint
#10112-404 (#1)	.65	1.35	2.00
#2,3	.40	.80	1.20

SCARLET O'NEIL (See Harvey Comics Hits #59)

SCARY TALES
August, 1975 - #9, Jan, 1977; #10, Oct, 1977
Charlton Comics

#1-Origin & 1st app. Countess Von Bludd, not
   in #2   .15   .30   .45
2-10: #3-Ditko story. #4-Sutton cover
                          .15   .30

SCHOOL DAY ROMANCES (-- of Teen-Agers #4)
Nov-Dec, 1949 - #4, May-June, 1950
Star Publications

#1-4   2.00   4.00   6.00

SCHWINN BICYCLE BOOK (--Bike Thrills, 1959)
1949; 1952; 1959
Schwinn Bicycle Co.

1949   2.00   4.00   6.00
1952-Believe It or Not type facts; comic
    format(32pgs.)   1.00   2.00   3.00
1959   1.00   2.00   3.00

SCIENCE COMICS (1st Series)
Feb, 1940 - #8, Sept, 1940
Fox Features Syndicate

#1-Origin Dynamo-(called Electro in #1), The
   Eagle, & Navy Jones; Marga, the Panther
   Woman, Cosmic Carson & Perisphere Payne,
   Dr. Doom begin   50.00 100.00 150.00
2   30.00 60.00 90.00
3   20.00 40.00 60.00
4-Kirby art   25.00 50.00 75.00
5-8   15.00 30.00 45.00
NOTE: *Cosmic Carson by Kirby-#4 only. Lou*
Fine covers-#1,2 only.

SCIENCE COMICS (2nd Series)
January, 1946 - #5, 1946
Fox Features Syndicate

#1,2,4,5   1.50   3.00   4.50
 3-Feldstein art, 6pgs.   2.50   5.00   7.50

SCIENCE COMICS
March, 1951
Export Publication Ent., Toronto, Canada
Distr. in U.S. by Kable News Co.

	Good	Fine	Mint
#1-Science adventure stories + some true			
science features	1.00	2.00	3.00

SCIENCE FICTION SPACE ADVENTURES
(See Space Adventures)

SCOOBY DOO (-- Where Are You? #1-16,26;
-- Mystery Comics #17-25, 27 on) (TV)
Mar, 1970 - #30, Feb, 1975
Gold Key

#1   .20   .40
2-30   .15   .30
   (See March of Comics #356,382,391)

SCOOBY-DOO
Oct, 1977 - Present
Marvel Comics Group

#1,2   .20   .35

SCOOBY DOO, WHERE ARE YOU? (TV)
April, 1975 - #11, Dec, 1976 (Hanna-Barbera)
Charlton Comics

#1   .15   .30
2-11   .10   .20

SCOOP
Nov, 1941 - 1946
Harry 'A' Chesler (Holyoke)

#1-Intro. Rocketman & Rocketgirl; origin The
   Master Key; Dan Hastings begins; cover/
   stories by Charles Sultan
                      16.50 33.25 50.00
2-Rocket Boy app.   8.00   16.00 24.00
3-8   5.00   10.00 15.00

SCOOTER (See Swing with --)

SCOOTER
April, 1946
Rucker Publ. Ltd. (Canadian)

#1   1.00   2.00   3.00

SCORPION, THE
Feb, 1975 - #3, July, 1975
Atlas/Seaboard Publ.

#1-Intro.; Chaykin art   .35   .70   1.05
2,3: #2-Chaykin art   .20   .40   .60

SCOTLAND YARD (Inspector Farnsworth of --)
1955 - #4, March, 1956
Charlton Comics

Schwinn Bicycle Book ('52). © Schwinn

Science Comics #1. © Fox

Scoop #1. © Ches

343

Sea Devils #12, © DC   Season's Greetings('35), © Hallmark   Secret Diary Of Eerie Advs., © Avon

(Scotland Yard cont'd)	Good	Fine	Mint
#1	1.35	2.75	4.00
2-4	.80	1.60	2.40

SCREAM (-- Comics)
Fall, 1944 - #19, April, 1948
Humor Publications/Current Books

#1	1.00	2.00	3.00
2-19	.65	1.35	2.00

SCREAM (Magazine)
Aug, 1973 - #11, Feb, 1975 (68 pgs.) (B&W)
Skywald Publishing Corp.

#1	.35	.70	1.05
2-5: #3(12/73)#3 found only on pg. 22			
	.25	.50	.75
6-11	.20	.40	.60

SCRIBBLY
Aug-Sept, 1948 - #15, Dec-Jan, 1950-51
National Periodical Publications

#1	7.00	14.00	21.00
2-5	4.00	8.00	12.00
6-10	2.50	5.00	7.50
11-15	2.00	4.00	6.00

NOTE: *Sheldon Mayer art in all.*

SEA DEVILS (See Showcase)
Sept-Oct, 1961 - #35, May-June, 1967
National Periodical Publications

#1	2.00	4.00	6.00
2	1.35	2.75	4.00
3-5	1.00	2.00	3.00
6-10	.65	1.35	2.00
11,12,14-20	.50	1.00	1.50
13-Kubert + Colan art	.65	1.35	2.00
21,23-35	.35	.70	1.05
22-Intro. International Sea Devils; origin & 1st app. Capt. X & Man Fish			
	.35	.70	1.05

NOTE: *Heath covers-#1-11,14-16; story-#11.*

SEA HOUND, THE (Capt. Silver's Log of--)
July-Aug, 1945 - #4, Jan-Feb, 1946
Avon Periodicals

#1	2.50	5.00	7.50
2-4	1.75	3.35	5.00

SEA HOUND, THE
#3, July, 1949
Capt. Silver Syndicate

#3	1.00	2.00	3.00

SEA HUNT (TV)
1958 - 10-12/59; #4, 1-3/60 - #13, 4-6/62
Dell Publishing Co.

	Good	Fine	Mint
4-Color #928,994,#4-13: Manning art #4-6, 8-11,13	.80	1.60	2.40
4-Color #1041-Toth art	1.75	3.35	5.00

SEARCH FOR LOVE
Feb-Mar, 1950 - #2, Apr-May, 1950
American Comics Group

#1,2	1.00	2.00	3.00

SEARCHERS (See 4-Color Comics #709)

SEARS (See Merry Christmas from --)

SEASON'S GREETINGS
1935 (6¼x5¼") (14pgs. in color)
Hallmark (King Features)

Cover feat. Mickey Mouse, Popeye, Jiggs & Skippy. "The Night Before Christmas" told one panel per page, each panel by a famous artist featuring their character. Art by Alex Raymond, Gottfriedson, Swinnerton, Segar, Chic Young, Milt Gross, Sullivan, Herriman, McManus, Percy Crosby & others (22 artists in all)   20.00 40.00 60.00

SECRET AGENT (Formerly Sarge Steel)
Oct, 1966 - V2#10, Oct, 1967
Charlton Comics

V2#9-Sarge Steel begins	.20	.40	.60
10-Tiffany Sinn, CIA app.-from Career Girl Romances #39	.20	.40	.60

SECRET AGENT (TV)
Nov, 1966 - #2, Jan, 1968
Gold Key

#1,2	.40	.80	1.20

SECRET AGENT X-9
1934; Book 1(80pgs.), Book 2(120pgs.)(8x7½")
David McKay Publications

Book 1, Book 2-Alex Raymond dailies			
	40.00	80.00	120.00

SECRET AGENT X-9 (See Feature Book #8,McKay)

SECRET AGENT Z-2 (See Z-2)

SECRET DIARY OF EERIE ADVENTURES
1953 (One Shot) (Giant-100pgs.)
Avon Periodicals

(Secret Diary of Eerie Advs. cont'd)

	Good	Fine	Mint
Kubert art	5.00	10.00	15.00

SECRET HEARTS
Sept-Oct, 1949 – #154, 1974
National Per. Publ.(Beverly)(Arleigh #50-113)

#1	2.00	4.00	6.00
2-10	1.00	2.00	3.00
11-30	.65	1.35	2.00
31-50	.35	.70	1.05
51-109	.20	.40	.60
10-"Reach for Happiness" serial begins; ends			
#138	.20	.40	.60
11-119,121-133,135-138	.15	.30	.45
120,134-Adams covers	.35	.70	1.05
139,140		.15	.30
141,142-"20 Miles to Heartbreak", Chapter 2&3			
(See Young Love for Chapter 1&4); Toth +			
Colletta art	.20	.40	.60
143-148,150-154: #144-Morrow art			
		.15	.30
149-Toth art	.15	.30	.45

SECRET LOVE
12/55 – #3, 8/56; 4/57 – #5, 2/58; #6, 6/58
Ajax-Farrell/Four Star Comic Corp. #2 on

#1(12/55-Ajax)	.80	1.60	2.40
2,3	.40	.80	1.20
1(4/57-Ajax)	.50	1.00	1.50
2-6	.25	.50	.75

SECRET LOVE (See Sinister House of --)

SECRET LOVES
Nov, 1949 – #6, Sept, 1950
Comic Magazines/Quality Comics Group

#1	2.00	4.00	6.00
2-Ward cover	2.50	5.00	7.50
3-6	1.00	2.00	3.00

SECRET MISSIONS
Feb, 1950
St. John Publishing Co.

#1-Kubert cover	3.00	6.00	9.00

SECRET MYSTERIES (Formerly Crime Mysteries
& Crime Smashers)
#17, Mar, 1954; #16, 11/54 – #19, 7/55
Ribage/Merit Publishing Corp.

#17(3/54)	1.00	2.00	3.00
16(Crime stories)	1.00	2.00	3.00
17-19(Horror stories)	1.00	2.00	3.00

SECRET ORIGINS
Feb-Mar, 1973 – #6, 1-2/74; #7, 10-11/74
National Periodical Publications

	Good	Fine	Mint
#1-Origin Superman, Batman, The Ghost, The			
Flash(Showcase #4); Infantino + Kubert			
art	.60	1.20	1.80
2-Origin new Green Lantern, the new Atom, &			
Supergirl; Kane art	.35	.70	1.05
3-Origin Wonder Woman, Wildcat			
	.35	.70	1.05
4-Origin Vigilante, Kid Eternity			
	.25	.50	.75
5-Origin The Spectre	.25	.50	.75
6-Origin Blackhawk & Legion of Super Heroes			
	.25	.50	.75
7-Origin Robin, Aquaman	.25	.50	.75

SECRET ORIGINS ANNUAL (See 80 Pg. Giant #8)
Aug-Oct, 1961
National Periodical Publications

#1('61)-Origin Adam Strange(Showcase #17),Gr.			
Lantern(G.L.#1), Challs(partial/Showcase			
#6, 6pgs. Kirby art), J'onn J'onzz(Det.			
#225), New Flash(Showcase #4), Green Arrow			
(1pg. text), Superman-Batman team, & Wond-			
er Woman	6.00	12.00	18.00

SECRET ORIGINS OF THE SUPER-HEROES
January, 1978   (One Shot)
DC Comics, Inc.

Lightray, Black Canary, & Dr. Fate app.			
	.20	.40	.60

SECRET ROMANCE
Oct, 1968 – #41, Nov, 1976
Charlton Comics

#1		.15	.30
2-41: #9-Reese art		.10	.20

NOTE: *Beyond the Stars app. #9,11,12,14.*

SECRET ROMANCES
April, 1951 – #27, July, 1955
Superior Publications Ltd.

#1	1.35	2.75	4.00
2-27	.80	1.60	2.40

SECRET SERVICE (See Kent Blake of the --)

SECRET SIX
Apr-May, 1968 – #7, Apr-May, 1969
National Periodical Publications

#1-Origin	.35	.70	1.05
2-7	.20	.40	.60

Secret Hearts #1, © DC

Secret Loves #2, © Qua

Secret Mysteries #16, © Ribage

Select Detective #1, © DS

Sensation Comics #8, © DC

Sensation Comics #92, © DC

SECRET SOCIETY OF SUPER-VILLAINS
May-June, 1976 - Present
National Periodical Publications/DC Comics

	Good	Fine	Mint
#1	.25	.50	.75
2-5	.20	.40	.60
6-12	.15	.30	.45

SECRET SOCIETY OF SUPER-VILLAINS SPECIAL
(See DC Special Series #6)

SECRETS OF HAUNTED HOUSE
4-5/75 - #5, 12-1/75-76; #6, 6-7/77 - Present
National Periodical Publications/DC Comics

#1	.20	.40	.60
2-11: #4-Redondo art. #5-Wrightson cover. #9-Ditko story. #11-Kaluta cover			
	.15	.30	.45
Special (3/78)	.20	.40	.60

SECRETS OF LIFE (See 4-Color Comics #749)

SECRETS OF LOVE (See Popular Teen-Agers --)

SECRETS OF LOVE & MARRIAGE
1956 - V2#25, June, 1961
Charlton Comics

V2#1-6	.25	.50	.75
V2#7-9-(All 68pgs.)	.20	.40	.60
10-25	.15	.30	.45

SECRETS OF MAGIC (See Wisco)

SECRETS OF SINISTER HOUSE (Sinister House of Secret Love #1-4)
#5, June-July, 1972 - #18, June-July, 1974
National Periodical Publications

#5	.20	.40	.60
6,8,9	.15	.30	.45
7-Redondo story	.20	.40	.60
10-Adams story(inks)	.65	1.35	2.00
11-16,18		.20	.35
17-Toth reprint	.15	.30	.45

NOTE: *Alcala* stories-#13,14. *Ambrose Bierce* adaptation-#14.

SECRETS OF TRUE LOVE
Feb, 1958
St. John Publishing Co.

#1	.65	1.35	2.00

SECRETS OF YOUNG BRIDES
#5, 9/57 - #44, 9/64; 7/75 - #9, 11/76
Charlton Comics

	Good	Fine	Mint
#5	.20	.40	.60
6-44	.15	.30	.45
#1-9		.15	.30

SECRET SQUIRREL (TV)
Oct, 1966 (Hanna-Barbera)
Gold Key

#1	.15	.30	.45
Florida Power & Light Giveaway('66)			
	.15	.30	.45

SECRET STORY ROMANCES (Becomes True Tales of Love?
Nov, 1953 - #18, Dec, 1955
Atlas Comics (TCI)

#1	.65	1.35	2.00
2-18	.30	.60	.90

SECRET VOICE, THE (See Great American Comics

SELECT DETECTIVE
Aug-Sept, 1948 - #3, Dec-Jan, 1948-49
D.S. Publishing Co.

#1-Matt Baker art	1.75	3.35	5.00
2,3	1.00	2.00	3.00

SENSATIONAL POLICE CASES
1952; 1954
Avon Periodicals

No#-100pg. issue(1952,25¢)-Kubert & Kinstler art	3.35	6.75	10.00
#1(1954)	1.75	3.35	5.00
2-5	1.35	2.75	4.00

SENSATIONAL POLICE CASES
No Date (1963?)
I.W. Enterprises

Reprint #5-Reprints Police Break #5('52)Avon
Infantino art .65 1.35 2.00

SENSATION COMICS (-- Mystery #110 on)
Jan, 1942 - #109, May-June, 1952
National Per. Publ./All-American

	Good	Fine	Mint
#1-Origin Mr. Terrific, Wildcat, The Gay Ghost, & Little Boy Blue; Wonder Woman, The Black Pirate begin; intro. Justice & Fair Play Club; #1 reprinted in Famous 1st Editions	125.00	250.00	375.00
2	60.00	120.00	180.00
3	40.00	80.00	120.00
4	30.00	60.00	90.00
5-Intro. Justin, Black Pirate's son	25.00	50.00	75.00

(Sensation Comics cont'd)	Good	Fine	Mint
6-10	20.00	40.00	60.00
11-20	17.50	35.00	52.50
21-30	12.00	24.00	36.00
31-33	8.00	16.00	24.00
34-Sargon, the Sorcerer begins, ends #36;			
begins again #52	8.00	16.00	24.00
35-40	7.00	14.00	21.00
41-50: #43-The Whip app.	5.00	10.00	15.00
51-60: #56,57-Sargon by Kubert			
	4.00	8.00	12.00
61-70: #63-Last Mr. Terrific. #65,66-Wildcat			
by Kubert. #68-Origin Huntress			
	4.00	8.00	12.00
71-80	4.00	8.00	12.00
81-Used in Seduction of the Innocent; Krig-			
stein art	6.00	12.00	18.00
82-90: #83-Last Sargon. #86-The Atom app.			
#90-Last Wildcat	3.35	6.75	10.00
91-94: #91-Streak begins	3.35	6.75	10.00
95-106: (Scarce) Wonder Woman ends. #99-1st			
app. Astra, Girl of the Future, ends #106			
	5.00	10.00	15.00
107,108 (Scarce)	4.00	8.00	12.00
109 (Scarce)-J. Peril by Toth			
	5.00	10.00	15.00

NOTE: *Krigstein stories(Wildcat)-#81,84.*
Moldoff Black Pirate-#1-25. Wonder Woman by
H. C. Peter, all issues except #21.

SENSATION MYSTERY (Sensation #1-109)
#110, Jul-Aug, 1952 - #117, Sept-Oct, 1953
National Periodical Publications

#110-113-Johnny Peril continues, ends #117			
	2.00	4.00	6.00
114-117-Toth J. Peril in all			
	2.50	5.00	7.50

NOTE: *Anderson stories-#111,113,116. Giunta*
story-#112. G.Kane covers-#112,113. Infantino
stories-#111,112,114,116; cover-#116.

SERGEANT BARNEY BARKER (G.I. Tales #4 on)
Aug, 1956 - #3, Dec, 1956
Atlas Comics (MCI)

#1-Four Severin stories	1.50	3.00	4.50
2,3-" " "	1.00	2.00	3.00

SGT. BILKO (Phil Silvers) (TV)
May-June, 1957 - #18, Mar-Apr, 1960
National Periodical Publications

#1	2.00	4.00	6.00
2-5	1.20	2.40	3.60
6-18	.80	1.60	2.40

SGT. BILKO'S PRIVATE DOBERMAN (TV)

July-Aug, 1958 - #11, Feb-Mar, 1960
National Periodical Publications

	Good	Fine	Mint
#1	1.75	3.35	5.00
2-5	.80	1.60	2.40
6-11	.40	.80	1.20

SGT. DICK CARTER (See U.S. Border Patrol)

SGT. FURY (& His Howling Commandos)
May, 1963 - Present
Marvel Comics Group

#1-1st app. Sgt. Fury; Kirby art			
	12.00	24.00	36.00
2-Kirby art	6.00	12.00	18.00
3-5: #3-Reed Richards x-over. #4-Death of			
Junior Juniper. #5-1st Baron Strucker app;			
Kirby art	2.50	5.00	7.50
6,7-Kirby art	2.00	4.00	6.00
8-10: #8-Baron Zemo, 1st Percival Pinkerton			
app. #10-1st app. Capt. Savage (the Skipp-			
er)	1.50	3.00	4.50
11,12,14-20: #14-1st Blitz Squad. #18-Death			
of Pamela Hawley	.75	1.50	2.25
13-Captain America app.; Kirby art			
	1.50	3.00	4.50
21-30: #25-Red Skull app. #27-1st Eric Koenig			
app.	.50	1.00	1.50
31-40: #34-Origin Howling Commandos			
	.35	.70	1.05
41-60: #44-Flashback of Howlers 1st mission			
	.25	.50	.75
61-100: #64-Capt. Savage & Raiders x-over.			
#76-Fury's Father app. in WWI story. #98-			
Deadly Dozen x-over. #100-Captain America,			
Fantastic Four cameos	.20	.40	.60
101-Origin retold	.20	.40	.60
102-120: #113-Reprints	.15	.30	.45
121-143-Reprints		.20	.35
Annual #1('65)	1.00	2.00	3.00
Special #2-7('66-11/71)	.40	.80	1.20

NOTE: *Ditko inks-#15. Kirby stories-Special*
#5. Severin story-#44-46, inks-#49-79. Re-
prints in #80,82,85,87,89,91,93,95,99,101,
103,105,107,109,111.

SGT. PRESTON OF THE YUKON (TV)
1951 - #29, Nov-Jan, 1958-59
Dell Publishing Co.

4-Color #344,373,397('52),419			
	1.75	3.35	5.00
#5-29: #13-Origin	1.20	2.40	3.60

SERGEANT PRESTON OF THE YUKON
1956   (4 comic booklets)(7x2½" & 5x2½")
Giveaways with Quaker Cereals

Sensation Comics #108, © DC

Sgt. Fury #19, © MCG

Sergeant Preston #22, © Dell

Seven Seas #1, © Univ. Phoenix   Shadow Comics #9, © S & S   Shadow Comics V6#11, © S & S

(Sgt. Preston cont'd)	Good	Fine	Mint
each......	2.00	4.00	6.00

SGT. ROCK (Formerly Our Army at War)
#302, March, 1977 - Present
National Periodical Publications

		Fine	Mint
#302-312		.20	.40

SGT. ROCK SPECIAL (See DC Special Series #3)

SGT. ROCK'S PRIZE BATTLE TALES
March, 1964   (One Shot) (Giant)
National Periodical Publications

#1	1.35	2.75	4.00

SEVEN DEAD MEN (See Complete Mystery #1)

SEVEN DWARFS (See 4-Color #227,382)

SEVEN SEAS COMICS
Apr, 1946 - #6, 1947 (no month)
Universal Phoenix Features/Leader #6

#1-South Sea Girl by Matt Baker, Capt. Cut-			
lass begin	7.00	14.00	21.00
2,4-6	5.00	10.00	15.00
3-6pg. Feldstein story	6.00	12.00	18.00

NOTE: Baker stories-#1-6; covers-#3-6.

1776 (See Charlton Classic Library)

7TH VOYAGE OF SINBAD, THE (See 4-Color #944)

77 SUNSET STRIP (TV)
Jan-Mar, 1960 - #2, Feb, 1963
Dell Publ. Co./Gold Key

4-Color #1066,1106,1159-Toth art			
	1.75	3.35	5.00
4-Color #1211,1263,1291-Manning art;			
#01742-209(9/62)-Manning	1.20	2.40	3.60
#1(11/62-G.K.), #2-Manning art in each			
	.80	1.60	2.40

77TH BENGAL LANCERS, THE (See 4-Color #791)

SEYMOUR, MY SON (See More Seymour)
Sept, 1963
Archie Publications (Radio Comics)

#1	.65	1.35	2.00

SHADE, THE CHANGING MAN
June-July, 1977 - Present
National Periodical Publications/DC Comics

#1	.20	.40	.60

	Good	Fine	Mint
2-5-Ditko cover/art	.15	.30	.45

SHADOW, THE
Aug, 1964 - #8, Sept, 1965
Archie Comics (Radio Comics)

#1	1.00	2.00	3.00
2-8	.50	1.00	1.50

SHADOW, THE
Oct-Nov, 1973 - #12, Aug-Sept, 1975
National Periodical Publications

#1-Kaluta art begins	.80	1.60	2.40
2	.50	1.00	1.50
3-Kaluta/Wrightson story	.65	1.35	2.00
4,6-Kaluta art ends	.35	.70	1.05
5,7-12	.20	.40	.60

NOTE: Cruz art-#11,12. Kaluta stories-#1-4,6,
covers-#1-4,6,10,11. Kubert cover-#9. Robbins
art-#5,7-9.

SHADOW COMICS
March, 1940 - #107, Nov, 1950
Street & Smith Publications

NOTE: The Shadow began on radio in 1929 and
was featured in pulps beginning in 1931.

V1#1-Shadow, Doc Savage, Bill Barnes, Nick			
Carter, Frank Merriwell, Iron Munra, the			
Astonishing Man begin			
	60.00	120.00	180.00
2-The Avenger begins, ends #6; Capt. Fury			
only app.	30.00	60.00	90.00
3(No#,5/40)-Norgil the Magician app.(also			
#9);Doc Savage ends	25.00	50.00	75.00
4,5: #4-The Three Musketeers begins, ends			
#8	20.00	40.00	60.00
6-9: #7-Origin & 1st app. Hooded Wasp &			
Wasplet; series ends V3#8			
	15.00	30.00	45.00
10-Origin The Iron Ghost, ends #11; The			
Dead End Kids begins, ends #13			
	15.00	30.00	45.00
11-Origin The Hooded Wasp & Wasplet retold			
	12.00	24.00	36.00
12	10.00	20.00	30.00
V2#1,2	8.00	16.00	24.00
3-Origin Supersnipe	8.00	16.00	24.00
4,5: #4-Little Nemo story			
	8.00	16.00	24.00
6-Blackstone, the Magician app.,			
7-9	7.00	14.00	21.00
10-Supersnipe app.	7.00	14.00	21.00
11,12	7.00	14.00	21.00
V3#1-12: #10-Doc Savage begins, not in V5#5,			
V6#10-12,V8#4	6.00	12.00	18.00

348

(Shadow Comics cont'd)	Good	Fine	Mint
V4#1-12	5.00	10.00	15.00
V5#1-12	4.50	9.00	13.50
V6#1-8	4.00	8.00	12.00
9-Intro Shadow, Jr.	4.00	8.00	12.00
10-12	4.00	8.00	12.00
V7#1-12: #2,5-Shadow, Jr. app.; Powell art			
	4.00	8.00	12.00
V8#1-12-Powell art	4.00	8.00	12.00
V9#1-5(#107)	3.00	6.00	9.00

NOTE: *Powell art in most issues beginning V6#11.*

SHADOWS FROM BEYOND (Formerly Unusual Tales)
October, 1966
Charlton Comics

V2#50		.15	.30

SHAGGY DOG & THE ABSENT-MINDED PROFESSOR
(See 4-Color #985 & Movie Comics)

SHANNA, THE SHE-DEVIL
Dec, 1972 - #5, Aug, 1973
Marvel Comics Group

#1-Steranko cover	.35	.70	1.05
2-5: #2-Steranko cover	.20	.40	.60

SHARK FIGHTERS, THE (See 4-Color #762)

SHARP COMICS (Slightly large size)
Winter, 1945-46 - V1#2, Spring, 1946 (52pgs.)
H. C. Blackerby

V1#1-Origin Dick Royce Planetarian			
	5.00	10.00	15.00
2-Origin The Pioneer, Michael Morgan, Dick Royce, Sir Gallagher, Planetarian, Steve Hagen, Weeny and Pop app.			
	5.00	10.00	15.00

SHARPY FOX
1958; 1963
I.W. Enterprises/Super

#1,2-IW Reprint('58)	.20	.40	.60
#14-Super Reprint('63)	.20	.40	.60

SHAZAM (See Giant Comics to Color & Limited Collector's Edition)

SHAZAM!
Feb, 1973 - #36, July-Aug, 1978
National Periodical Publications/DC Comics

#1-1st revival of the original Captain Marvel, by C.C Beck; Capt. Marvel Jr. & Mary

	Good	Fine	Mint
Marvel x-over	.50	1.00	1.50
2-5	.25	.50	.75
6,7,9,10-Last Beck ish.	.25	.50	.75
8-100pgs.; reprints Capt. Marvel Jr. by Raboy; origin/C.M.#80; origin Mary Marvel/			
C.M.#18	.35	.70	1.05
11-Shaffenberger art begins.	.20	.40	.60
12-17-All 100pgs.	.25	.50	.75
18-24-(reg. size)	.20	.40	.60
25-1st app. Isis	.15	.30	.45
26-36: #35-Newton story		.15	.30

SHEENA, QUEEN OF THE JUNGLE (See 3-D --)
Spring, 1942 - #18, Winter, 1952-53
Fiction House Magazines

#1-Sheena begins	40.00	80.00	120.00
2	20.00	40.00	60.00
3(1942)	15.00	30.00	45.00
4(1952)	7.00	14.00	21.00
5-10	6.00	12.00	18.00
11-18	4.00	8.00	12.00
IW Reprint #9-reprts.#17	1.75	3.35	5.00

SHERIFF BOB DIXON'S CHUCK WAGON
Nov, 1950
Avon Periodicals

#1-Kinstler art	2.00	4.00	6.00

SHERIFF OF COCHISE, THE
1957   (20 pgs.) (TV Show)
Mobil Giveaway

Kurt Shaffenberger art	1.35	2.75	4.00

SHERIFF OF TOMBSTONE
Nov, 1958 - #17, Sept, 1961
Charlton Comics

V1#1-Williamson/Severin cover			
	1.50	3.00	4.50
2-17	.35	.70	1.05

SHERLOCK HOLMES (See 4-Color #1169,1245 &
Spectacular Stories)

SHERLOCK HOLMES (All New Baffling Advs. of)
1955 - 1956
Charlton Comics

#1-Dr. Neff, Ghost Breaker app.			
(#1 only-26pgs.)	2.50	5.00	7.50
2	1.75	3.35	5.00

SHERLOCK HOLMES
Sept-Oct, 1975
National Periodical Publications

Sheena #1, © FH

Sheriff Of Cochise Mobil Giv.

Sheriff Of Tombstone #1, © CC

Shield Wizard #8, © MLJ

Shocking Mystery Cases #59, © Star

Shock SuspenStories #7, © WMG

	Good	Fine	Mint
(Sherlock Holmes cont'd)			
#1-Cruz art; Simonson cvr.	.35	.70	1.05

SHERRY THE SHOWGIRL
July, 1956 - #7, Aug, 1957
Atlas Comics

#1	.65	1.35	2.00
2-7	.35	.70	1.05

SHIELD (Nick Fury & His Agents of --)
Feb, 1973 - #5, Oct, 1973 (See Nick Fury)
Marvel Comics Group

#1-Steranko cover	.35	.70	1.05
2- " "	.25	.50	.75
3-5: #1-5 all contain reprints from Strange Tales #146-155; #3-5-cover reprints			
	.15	.30	.45

SHIELD WIZARD COMICS
Summer, 1940 - #13, Spring, 1944
MLJ Magazines

#1-Origin The Shield & The Wizard by Irving Novick	65.00	130.00	195.00
2-Origin The Shield retold; intro. Wizard's sidekick, Roy	30.00	60.00	90.00
3,4	23.50	46.75	70.00
5-Dusty, the Boy Detective begins	20.00	40.00	60.00
6-8: #6-Roy the Super Boy begins	15.00	30.00	45.00
9,10	13.50	26.75	40.00
11-13	12.00	24.00	36.00

SHIP AHOY
Nov, 1944
Spotlight Publishers

#1-Feldstein story	2.00	4.00	6.00

SHMOO (See Al Capp's-- & Washable Jones &--)

SHOCK (Magazine)
(Reprints from Horror Comics)(Black & White)
May, 1969 - V3#4, Sept, 1971
Stanley Publications

V1#1-Cover reprint/Weird Tales of the Future #7 by Bernard Baily	.35	.70	1.05
2-Wolverton reprint; cover reprt/Weird Chills #1	.35	.70	1.05
3,5,6	.20	.40	.60
4-Harrison/Williamson reprint/Forbidden Worlds #6	.35	.70	1.05
V2#2, V1#8, V2#4-6, V3#1-4	.20	.40	.60

SHOCK DETECTIVE CASES (Formerly Crime Fighting Det.)
#20, 9/52 - #23, 3/53
Star Publications

	Good	Fine	Mint
#20-23	1.00	2.00	3.00

SHOCK ILLUSTRATED (Magazine format)
Sept-Oct, 1955 - #3, Spring, 1956
E.C. Comics

#1-All by Kamen	4.00	8.00	12.00
2-Williamson story redrawn from Crime SuspenStories #13 + Ingels, Crandall & Evans	5.00	10.00	15.00
3-(Very Rare)-Only 100-200 known copies bound & distributed	275.00	550.00	825.00
(Prices vary widely on this book)			

SHOCKING MYSTERY CASES (Formerly Thrilling Crime Cases)
#50, 9/52 - #60, 10/54
Star Publications

#50-60: #50,51-Disbrow art	1.00	2.00	3.00

SHOCK SUSPENSTORIES
Feb-Mar, 1952 - #18, Dec-Jan, 1954-55
E.C. Comics

#1-Feldstein cover	40.00	80.00	120.00
2	20.00	40.00	60.00
3,4	13.50	26.75	40.00
5-7	12.00	24.00	36.00
8-Williamson story	16.50	33.25	50.00
9-12	10.00	20.00	30.00
13-Frazetta's only solo story for E.C., 7pgs.	23.50	46.75	70.00
14-18	8.00	16.00	24.00

NOTE: *Craig* story-#11; cover-#11. *Crandall* stories-#9-13,15-18. *Davis* stories-#1-5. *Evans* stories-#7,8,14-18; covers-#16-18. *Feldstein* covers-#1,7-9,12. *Ingels* stories-#1,2,6. *Kamen* stories in all. *Krigstein* stories-#14,18. *Orlando* stories-#1,3-7,9,10,12, 16,17. *Wood* stories-#2-15; covers-#2-6,14. #16 contains the famous "Red Dupe" editorial.

SHOOK UP (Magazine) (Satire)
Nov, 1958
Dodsworth Publ. Co.

V1#1	.65	1.35	2.00

SHORT RIBS (See 4-Color Comics #1333)

SHORT STORY COMICS (See Hello Pal, --)

SHORTY SHINER
June, 1956 - #3, Oct, 1956
Dandy Magazine (Charles Biro)

	Good	Fine	Mint
#1	1.00	2.00	3.00
2,3	.50	1.00	1.50

SHOTGUN SLADE (See 4-Color Comics #1111)

SHOWCASE
3-4/56 - #93, 9/70; #94, 9/77 - Present
National Periodical Publications/DC Comics

	Good	Fine	Mint
#1-Fire Fighters	40.00	80.00	120.00
2-King of the Wild; Kubert art	20.00	40.00	60.00
3-The Frogmen	15.00	30.00	45.00
4-Origin The Flash(Silver Age) & The Turtle; Kubert art	150.00	300.00	450.00
5-Manhunters	10.00	20.00	30.00
6-Origin Challengers by Kirby-partly reprinted in Secret Origins #1 & Challs./Unknown #64,65	25.00	50.00	75.00
7-Challengers by Kirby/reprt. Challs./Unknown #75	16.50	33.25	50.00
8-The Flash; origin Capt. Cold	50.00	100.00	150.00
9,10-Lois Lane	15.00	30.00	45.00
11,12-Challengers by Kirby	16.50	33.25	50.00
13-The Flash; origin Mr. Element	30.00	60.00	90.00
14-The Flash; origin Dr. Alchemy, former Mr. Element	40.00	80.00	120.00
15,16-Space Ranger	8.00	16.00	24.00
17-Adam Strange	23.50	46.75	70.00
18,19-Adam Strange	16.50	33.25	50.00
20,21-Rip Hunter. #21-Sekowsky cover/art	5.00	10.00	15.00
22-Origin & 1st app. Silver Age Green Lantern by Gil Kane	20.00	40.00	60.00
23,24-Green Lantern	10.00	20.00	30.00
25-Rip Hunter by Kubert	3.00	6.00	9.00
26-Rip Hunter by Kubert	3.00	6.00	9.00
27-29-Sea Devils by Heath, cover/art	2.00	4.00	6.00
30-Origin Aquaman	2.25	4.50	6.75
31-33-Aquaman	1.75	3.35	5.00
34-Origin & 1st app. Silver Age Atom by Kane	3.00	6.00	9.00
35,36-The Atom by G.Kane	2.00	4.00	6.00
37-40-Metal Men	1.20	2.40	3.60
41,42-Tommy Tomorrow	.65	1.35	2.00
43-Dr. No(James Bond); Nodel art; originally done for Classics Ill. Series?	1.35	2.75	4.00
44-Tommy Tomorrow	.65	1.35	2.00
45-Sgt. Rock; Heath cover	.65	1.35	2.00

	Good	Fine	Mint
46,47-Tommy Tomorrow	.65	1.35	2.00
48,49-Cave Carson	.65	1.35	2.00
50,51-I Spy(Danger Trail reprints by Infantino), Anderson cover inks; King Farady story(not reprint-#50)	.50	1.00	1.50
52-Cave Carson	.50	1.00	1.50
53,54-G.I.Joe-Heath art	.50	1.00	1.50
55,56-Dr. Fate & Hourman	.65	1.35	2.00
57,58-Enemy Ace by Kubert	.80	1.60	2.40
59-Teen Titans	.50	1.00	1.50
60,61,64-The Spectre by Anderson	.90	1.80	2.70
62,63,65-Inferior Five	.35	.70	1.05
66,67-B'wana Beast	.35	.70	1.05
68,69-Maniaks	.25	.50	.75
70-Binky	.25	.50	.75
71-Maniaks	.25	.50	.75
72-Top Gun(Johnny Thunder reprints)-Toth art	.40	.80	1.20
73-Creeper by Ditko	1.00	2.00	3.00
74-Anthro	.40	.80	1.20
75-Hawk & the Dove by Ditko	.65	1.35	2.00
76-Bat Lash	.50	1.00	1.50
77-Angel & Ape	.35	.70	1.05
78-Johnny Double	.35	.70	1.05
79-Dolphin	.50	1.00	1.50
80-Phantom Stranger-Neal Adams cover	.80	1.60	2.40
81-Windy & Willy	.25	.50	.75
82-Nightmaster by Grandenetti; Kubert cover	.50	1.00	1.50
83,84-Nightmster by Wrightson in ea.; Kubert covers	2.00	4.00	6.00
85-87-Firehair-Kubert art	.80	1.60	2.40
88-90-Jason's Quest	.25	.50	.75
91-93-Manhunter 2070	.25	.50	.75
94-96-The Doom Patrol	.15	.30	.45
97-99-Power Girl	.15	.30	.45
100-(52pgs.)-Feat. most Showcase characters	.20	.40	.60
101-103-Hawkman	.20	.40	.60
104-106-The World of Krypton	.20	.40	.60

NOTE: _Anderson covers-#34-36(inks) & art-#50, 55,56,60,61,64. Grandenetti story-#80. Infantino art/covers-#4,8,13,14. Kane art-#22-24, 34-36; covers-#17-19,22-24,31,34-36. Kirby covers-#6,7,11,12. Kubert art-#2,25,26,45,53, 54,72; inks-#4; covers-#25,26,53,54,57,58,82, 83-87. Orlando art/covers-#62,63. Staton stories-#95-98._

SHOWGIRLS
June, 1957 - #4, Dec, 1957
Atlas Comics

	Good	Fine	Mint
#1-Millie, Sherry, Chili, Pearl & Hazel begin	1.35	2.75	4.00

Showcase #12, © DC

Showcase #14, © DC

Showcase #73, © DC

Silly Symphonies #2, © WDP

Silver Streak Comics #5, © Lev

Silver Streak Comics #11, © Lev

(Showgirls cont'd)	Good	Fine	Mint
2-4	1.00	2.00	3.00

SICK (Magazine) (Satire)
Aug, 1960 - Present
Feature Publ./Headline Publ./Crestwood Publ.
Co./Hewfred Publ./Pyramid Comm./Charlton Publ.

V1#1-Torres art	2.50	5.00	7.50
2-5-Torres art in all	1.75	3.35	5.00
6	1.35	2.75	4.00
V2#1-8(#7-14)	.80	1.60	2.40
V3#1-8(#15-22)	.50	1.00	1.50
V4#1-5(#23-27)	.50	1.00	1.50
#28-40	.25	.50	.75
41-105	.20	.40	.60
Annual 1971	.25	.50	.75
Annual #2	.25	.50	.75

NOTE: *Davis covers/stories in most issues of
#16-27,30-32,34,35. Simon art-#1-3. Torres
art-V2#7, V4#2. Civil War Blackouts-#23,24.*

SILK HAT HARRY'S DIVORCE SUIT
1912   (5-3/4"x15½")   (B&W)
M. A. Donoghue & Co.

Newspaper reprints by Tad (Thomas Dorgan)
                        8.00 16.00 24.00

SILLY PILLY   (See Frank Luther's --)

SILLY SYMPHONIES (Walt Disney)
Sept, 1952 - 1959   (All Giants)
Dell Publishing Co.

#1-Reprints 3 Little Pigs & M.Mouse in "The			
Brave Little Tailor"	5.00	10.00	15.00
2-Mickey Mouse "The Sorcerer's Apprentice"			
	4.00	8.00	12.00
3-(4-Color #71)(not Duck portion),(4-Color			
#157)	5.00	10.00	15.00
4-(4-Color #234)	2.00	4.00	6.00
5-(4-Color Cinderella)	3.00	6.00	9.00
6,9	3.00	6.00	9.00
7-(4-Color #13)	5.00	10.00	15.00
8-(4-Color #19)	4.00	8.00	12.00

NOTE: *All reprints.*

SILLY TUNES
Fall, 1945 - #7, April, 1947
Timely Comics

#1	2.00	4.00	6.00
2-7	1.50	3.00	4.50

SILVER (See Lone Ranger's Horse --)

SILVER KID WESTERN

Oct, 1954 - 1955
Key/Stanmor Publications

	Good	Fine	Mint
#1	1.00	2.00	3.00
2-5	.50	1.00	1.50
IW Reprint #1,2	.35	.70	1.05

SILVER STREAK COMICS
Dec, 1939 - May, 1942; 1946
Comic House Publ./Newsbook Publ.

#1-Inrto. The Claw(reprt. Daredevil #21),Red			
Reeves, Boy Magician, & Captain Fearless;			
The Wasp, Mister Midnight begin; Spirit			
Man app.	140.00	280.00	420.00
2-Simon cover	60.00	120.00	180.00
3-1st app. & origin Silver Streak; Dickie			
Dean, the Boy Inventor, Lance Hale, Ace			
Powers, Bill Wayne, & The Planet Patrol			
begin	80.00	160.00	240.00
4-Sky Wolf begins; Silver Streak by Jack			
Cole; Intro. Jackie, Lance Hale's sidekick			
	40.00	80.00	120.00
5-Jack Cole cvr/story	50.00	100.00	150.00
6-(Rare)-Origin & 1st app. Daredevil by Jack			
Binder; Cole cover	300.00	600.00	900.00
(Prices vary widely on this book)			
7-Claw vs. Daredevil by Jack Cole & 3 other			
Cole stys.(38pgs.)	125.00	250.00	375.00
8-Claw vs. Daredevil by Cole; last Cole			
Silver Streak	70.00	140.00	210.00
9-Claw vs. Daredevil by Cole			
	50.00	100.00	150.00
10-Origin Captain Battle; Claw vs. Daredevil			
by Cole	35.00	70.00	105.00
11-Intro. Mercury, Silver Streak's sidekick;			
conclusion Claw vs. Daredevil by Rico			
	30.00	60.00	90.00
12-14: #12-Intro. Hale. #13-Origin Thun-Dohr			
	27.50	55.00	82.50
15-17-Last Daredevil ish	25.00	50.00	75.00
18-The Saint begins	15.00	30.00	45.00
19-21(1942): #20,21 have Wolverton's Scoop			
Scuttle	13.50	26.75	40.00
22-24(1946)-reprints	8.00	16.00	24.00
No#(11/46)(Newsbook Publ.)-Reprints SS story			
from #4-7 + 2 Captain Fearless stories-			
all in color	20.00	40.00	60.00

NOTE: *Jack Cole art: (Daredevil)-#6-10,
(Dickie Dean)-#3-10, (Pirate Prince)-#7, (Silver Streak)-#4-8, (Silver Streak cover)-#5.
Mac Raboy Lance Hale-#6. Don Rico Daredevil-
#11-17. Simon Silver Streak-#3. Bob Wood Sil-
ver Streak-#9. Claw covers-#1,2,6-8; by Cole-
#6-8.*

SILVER SURFER (See Fantastic Four)
Aug, 1968 - #18, Sept, 1970 (#1-7, 68pgs.)
Marvel Comics Group

(Silver Surfer cont'd)	Good	Fine	Mint
#1-Origin Silver Surfer by John Buscema; Watcher begins, ends #7	10.00	20.00	30.00
2	5.00	10.00	15.00
3-1st app. Mephisto	3.50	7.00	10.50
4-Low distribution	6.00	12.00	18.00
5-7-Last giant size. #5-The Stranger app.			
	2.50	5.00	7.50
8-10: #6-Brunner inks	2.00	4.00	6.00
11-18: #18-Kirby art/cvr	1.50	3.00	4.50

SILVERTIP (Max Brand)
1953 - 1958
Dell Publishing Co.

4-Color #491,608,637,731,898-Kinstler art			
	1.75	3.35	5.00
4-Color #572,667,789,835	1.20	2.40	3.60

SINBAD, JR. (TV Cartoon)
Sept-Nov, 1965 - #3, May, 1966
Dell Publishing Co.

#1-3	.25	.50	.75

SINDBAD (See Movie Comics: Capt. Sindbad; & Fantastic Voyages of Sindbad)

SINGING GUNS (See Fawcett Movie Comics)

SINGLE SERIES (Comics on Parade #30 on)
1938 - 1940 (Also see John Hix --)
United Features Syndicate

#1-Captain & the Kids	15.00	30.00	45.00
2-Broncho Bill(1939)	10.00	20.00	30.00
3-Ella Cinders	8.00	16.00	24.00
4-Li'l Abner(1939)	15.00	30.00	45.00
5-Fritzi Ritz	6.00	12.00	18.00
6-Jim Hardy by Dick Moores			
	9.00	18.00	27.00
7-Frankie Doodle	7.00	14.00	21.00
8-Peter Pat	6.00	12.00	18.00
9-Strange As It Seems	5.00	10.00	15.00
10-Little Mary Mixup	5.00	10.00	15.00
11-Mr. & Mrs. Beans	4.00	8.00	12.00
12-Joe Jinks	5.00	10.00	15.00
13-Looy Dot Dope	5.00	10.00	15.00
14-Billy Make Believe	6.00	12.00	18.00
15-How It Began('39)	6.00	12.00	18.00
16-Illustrated Gags('40)	3.00	6.00	9.00
17-Danny Dingle	4.00	8.00	12.00
18-Li'l Abner	12.00	24.00	36.00
19-Broncho Bill(#2 on cvr)	7.00	14.00	21.00
20-Tarzan by Hal Foster	100.00	200.00	300.00
21-Ella Cinders(#2 on cvr)	7.00	14.00	21.00
22-Iron Vic	6.00	12.00	18.00
23-Tailspin Tommy by Hal Forrest			
	8.00	16.00	24.00

	Good	Fine	Mint
24-Alice in Wonderland	10.00	20.00	30.00
25-Abbie & Slats	8.00	16.00	24.00
26-Little Mary Mixup	6.00	12.00	18.00
27-Jim Hardy by Dick Moores			
	7.00	14.00	21.00
28-Ella Cinders & Abbie & Slats			
	8.00	16.00	24.00
1-Captain & the Kids (1939 reprint)			
	10.00	20.00	30.00
1-Fritzi Ritz(1939 reprint) 2nd edition			
	6.00	12.00	18.00

NOTE: *Some issues given away at the 1939-40
New York World's Fair(#6).*

SINISTER HOUSE OF SECRET LOVE, THE
(Secrets of Sinister House #5 on)
Oct-Nov, 1971 - #4, Apr-May, 1972
National Periodical Publications

#1	.35	.70	1.05
2,4	.25	.50	.75
3-Toth story, 36pgs.	.40	.80	1.20

SIR LANCELOT (See 4-Color Comics #606,775)

SIR WALTER RALEIGH (See 4-Color #644)

6 BLACK HORSES (See Movie Classics)

SIX-GUN HEROES
March, 1950 - #23, Nov, 1953
Fawcett Publications

#1-Rocky Lane, Hopalong Cassidy, Smiley Burnette begin	5.00	10.00	15.00
2	3.00	6.00	9.00
3-10: #6-Lash Larue begins			
	2.50	5.00	7.50
11-23	1.75	3.50	5.25

SIX-GUN HEROES (Cont'd. from Fawcett)
(Becomes Gunmasters #84 on)
Jan, 1954 - #83, Mar-Apr, 1965
Charlton Comics

V4#24-46: Tom Mix, Lash Larue	1.00	2.00	3.00
47-Williamson story, 2pgs. + Torres			
	2.00	4.00	6.00
48,50-75,82	.30	.60	.90
49-Williamson sty,5pgs.	1.75	3.50	5.25
76-81,83-Gunmaster in all			
	.35	.70	1.05

SIXGUN RANCH (See 4-Color Comics #580)

Silver Surfer #11. © MCG

Single Series #20. © ERB

Six-Gun Heroes #23. © CC

Skeleton Hand #1, © ACG

Skippy's Own Book Of Comics, © Percy Crosby

Skyman #1, © CCG

SIX-GUN WESTERN
Jan, 1957 - 1958
Atlas Comics (CDS)

	Good	Fine	Mint
#1-Crandall art	2.00	4.00	6.00
2,3,7-Williamson stories in all; Powell			
story in #3	2.00	4.00	6.00
4-Woodbridge story	1.00	2.00	3.00
5,6,8-10	.80	1.60	2.40
11-Williamson story	2.00	4.00	6.00

SIX MILLION DOLLAR MAN (Magazine)
June, 1976 - Present (B&W)
Charlton Comics

#1-Adams cover/art	.50	1.00	1.50
2-Adams cover	.40	.80	1.20
3-8	.35	.70	1.05

SIX MILLION DOLLAR MAN
June, 1976 - #4, Jan, 1977; #5, Oct, 1977
Charlton Comics

#1-Staton cover/stories	.25	.50	.75
2-Adams cover	.20	.40	.60
3-5	.15	.30	.45

SKATING SKILLS
1957 (36 pgs.) (5x7") (10¢)
Custom Comics, Inc.
Chicago Roller Skates

Resembles old ACG cover + interior art
	.50	1.00	1.50

SKEEZIX
1925 - 1928 (Strip reprints) (Soft covers)
Reilly & Lee Co. (Pictures & text)

-- and Pal(1925)	7.00	14.00	21.00
-- at the Circus(1926)	7.00	14.00	21.00
-- & Uncle Walt(1927)	7.00	14.00	21.00
-- Out West(1928)	7.00	14.00	21.00
Hardback Editions...	10.00	20.00	30.00

SKELETON HAND(--In Secrets of the Supernatural)
Sept-Oct, 1952 - #6, July-Aug, 1953
American Comics Group (B&M Dist. Co.)

#1	1.35	2.75	4.00
2-6	.80	1.60	2.40

SKI PARTY (See Movie Classics)

SKIPPY
1925 (68pgs.) (Hardcover-in color) (8½x11")
Greenberg Publ.

	Good	Fine	Mint
Panel & strips	10.00	20.00	30.00

SKIPPY'S OWN BOOK OF COMICS
1934 (52 pgs.) (Giveaway)
No publisher listed

No#-Strip reprints by Percy Crosby			
	100.00	200.00	300.00

Published by Max C. Gaines for Phillip's Dental Magnesia to be
advertised on the Skippy Radio Show and given away with the
purchase of a tube of Phillip's Tooth Paste. 500,000 copies
printed. This is the first four-color comic book of reprints about
one character.

SKULL THE SLAYER
August, 1975 - #8, Nov, 1976
Marvel Comics Group

#1-Origin	.20	.40	.60
2-5	.15	.30	.45
6-8		.20	.35

SKY BLAZERS (Radio)
Sept, 1940 - #2, Nov, 1940
Hawley Publications

#1-Sky Pirates, Ace Archer, Flying Aces			
begin	8.00	16.00	24.00
2	5.00	10.00	15.00

SKY KING "RUNAWAY TRAIN"
1964 (16 pgs.) (Regular size)
National Biscuit Co.

	.50	1.00	1.50

SKYMAN (See Big Shot)
1941 - #4, 1948
Columbia Comics Group

#1-Origin Skyman, The Face app.; Whitney art			
	20.00	40.00	60.00
2-Yankee Doodle	10.00	20.00	30.00
3,4	8.00	16.00	24.00

SKY PILOT
1950 (Painted covers by Norman Saunders)
Ziff-Davis Publ. Co.

#10,11-Frank Borth art	1.50	3.00	4.50

SKY RANGER (See Johnny Law --)

SKYROCKET
1944
Harry 'A' Chesler

#1-Atlas the Dragon, Dr. Vampire, Skyrocket			
app.	4.00	8.00	12.00

SKY SHERIFF (See Breeze Lawson --)

SLAM BANG COMICS (Western Desperado #8)
March, 1940 - #7, Sept, 1940
Fawcett Publications

	Good	Fine	Mint
#1-Diamond Jack, Mark Swift & The Time Re-			
tarder, Lee Granger, Jungle King begin			
	30.00	60.00	90.00
2	15.00	30.00	45.00
3	12.00	24.00	36.00
4-7	10.00	20.00	30.00

SLAM BANG COMICS
No date
Post Cereal Giveaway

#9-Dynamic Man, Echo, Mr. E, Yankee Boy app.			
	2.00	4.00	6.00

SLAPSTICK COMICS
1946   (36 pgs.)
Comic Magazine Publishers

#1-Firetop feature	1.75	3.35	5.00

SLAVE GIRL COMICS (See Malu --)
Feb, 1949 - #2, Apr, 1949
Avon Periodicals

#1	15.00	30.00	45.00
2	10.00	20.00	30.00

SLEEPING BEAUTY (See 4-Color #973,984, Movie Classics & Comics)

SLICK CHICK COMICS
1947
Leader Enterprises

#1-Kamen art	2.50	5.00	7.50
2,3	2.00	4.00	6.00

SLIM MORGAN (See Wisco)

SLUGGER (of the Little Wise Guys)
April, 1956
Lev Gleason Publications

#1	1.00	2.00	3.00

SMASH COMICS (Lady Luck #86 on)
Aug, 1939 - #85, Oct, 1949
Quality Comics Group

#1-Origin Hugh Hazard & His Iron Man, Bozo			
the Robot, Espionage, Starring Black X by			
Eisner & Invisible Justice; Chic Carter &			
Wings Wendell begin	40.00	80.00	120.00

	Good	Fine	Mint
2-The Lone Star Rider app.			
	20.00	40.00	60.00
3	15.00	30.00	45.00
4,5	12.00	24.00	36.00
6-12	10.00	20.00	30.00
13-Magno begins; last Eisner issue			
	10.00	20.00	30.00
14-Intro. The Ray by Lou Fine & others			
	80.00	160.00	240.00
15-17	35.00	70.00	105.00
18-Origin Midnight by Jack Cole			
	50.00	100.00	150.00
19-22: Last Fine Ray; The Jester begins-#22			
	25.00	50.00	75.00
23,24: #24-The Sword app.; last Chic Carter;			
Wings Wendell dons costume #24,25			
	20.00	40.00	60.00
25-Origin Wildfire	23.50	46.75	70.00
26-29,31	20.00	40.00	60.00
30-Classic Lou Fine Ray	25.00	50.00	75.00
32,34: Ray by Rudy Palais; also #33			
	15.00	30.00	45.00
33-Origin The Marksman	16.50	33.25	50.00
35-37	13.50	27.00	40.50
38-The Yankee Eagle begins; last Midnight by			
Jack Cole	13.50	27.00	40.50
39,40-Last Ray issue	12.00	24.00	36.00
41,43-50	5.00	10.00	15.00
42-Lady Luck begins	6.00	12.00	18.00
51-60	4.00	8.00	12.00
61-70	3.35	6.75	10.00
71-85	3.00	6.00	9.00

NOTE: *Cole* stories-(Midnight)#18-38,88-85;
covers-#38,60,61. *Crandall* stories-(Ray)#23-
29,35-38; covers-#36,39,40,43,44,46. *Fine*
stories-(Ray)#14-22,30,31. *Fuji* story-#30.
Guardineer stories-(The Marksman)#39-?. *Gustavson* stories-(The Jester)#22-46; (Magno)#13-
21; (Midnight)#39(Cole inks). *Kotzky* stories-
(Espionage)#33-38; covers-#45,47. *Powell* stor-
ies-(Abdul the Arab)#13-24.

SMASH HIT SPORTS COMICS
1949
Essankay Publishing Co.

V2#1		.65	1.35	2.00

SMATTER POP?
1927   (48 pgs.) (B&W)
E. I. Company

By C.M. Payne		6.00	12.00	18.00

SMILE COMICS (Also see Tickle & Gay Comics)
1955   (52 pgs.) (5x7¾") (7¢)
Modern Store Publ.

Slam Bang Comics #1, © Faw

Slave Girl Comics #1, © Avon

Smash Comics #8, © DC (Qua)

Smiley Burnette #4, © Faw   Smilin' Jack #2(Dell), © N.Y. News Synd.   Smitty 4-Color #32, © N.Y. News Synd.

(Smile Comics cont'd)	Good	Fine	Mint
#1	.50	1.00	1.50

SMILEY BURNETTE WESTERN
March, 1950 - #4, Oct, 1950
Fawcett Publications

	Good	Fine	Mint
#1	4.00	8.00	12.00
2-4	2.50	5.00	7.50

SMILIN' JACK   (See Super Book #1,2,7,19)
1941 - #8, Oct-Dec, 1949
Dell Publishing Co.

	Good	Fine	Mint
Black & White#12,14('41)	15.00	30.00	45.00
4-Color #5,10('40)	25.00	50.00	75.00
Large Feature Comic #25('41)			
	15.00	30.00	45.00
4-Color #4,14('42-'43)	20.00	40.00	60.00
4-Color #36,58('43-'44)	8.00	16.00	24.00
4-Color #80('45)	6.00	12.00	18.00
4-Color #149('47)	5.00	10.00	15.00
#1(1949)	5.00	10.00	15.00
2-8(1949)	3.00	6.00	9.00
Popped Wheat Giveaway-(1936,38,40 reprints) 16pgs. in full color(1947)			
	1.00	2.00	3.00
Shoe Store Giveaway-('36 reprints)-16pgs.			
	3.00	6.00	9.00
Sparked Wheat Giveaway(1942)-16pgs. in full color			
	2.50	5.00	7.50

SMILING SPOOK SPUNKY   (See Spunky)

SMITTY
1928 - 1931 (B&W newspaper strip reprints-
7"x8½")(10"x10")(Soft covers, 32pgs.)
Cupples & Leon Co.

1928-Smitty, 1929-At the Ball Game, 1930-The
Flying Office Boy, 1931-The Jockey

each....	8.00	16.00	24.00
Hardback Editions (50-96pgs.)			
each....	12.00	24.00	36.00

SMITTY   (See Treasure Box of Famous Comics &
1940 - 1949   Super Book #2&4)
Dell Publishing Co.

	Good	Fine	Mint
4-Color #11(1940)	13.50	26.75	40.00
Large Feature Comic #26('41)			
	10.00	20.00	30.00
4-Color #6('42)	8.00	16.00	24.00
4-Color #32('43)	5.00	10.00	15.00
4-Color #65('45)	4.00	8.00	12.00
4-Color #99('46)	3.00	6.00	9.00
4-Color #138('47)	2.50	5.00	7.50
#1(1948)	2.50	5.00	7.50

	Good	Fine	Mint
2-4('1949)	1.75	3.35	5.00
5-7(1949)	1.35	2.75	4.00
4-Color #909	1.00	2.00	3.00

SMOKEY BEAR   (TV)
Feb, 1970 - #13, Mar, 1973
Gold Key

		Good	Fine	Mint
#1			.15	.30
2-13			.10	.20

(See March of Comics #362,372,383,407)

SMOKEY STOVER   (See Super Book #5,17,29)

SMOKEY STOVER FIREFIGHTER OF FOO
1937 (64pgs.-5½x7½"-B&W reprints)(Hardcover)
Whitman Publ. Co.

	Good	Fine	Mint
	4.00	8.00	12.00

SMOKEY STOVER
1942 - 1943
Dell Publishing Co.

	Good	Fine	Mint
4-Color #7('42-reprints)	15.00	30.00	45.00
4-Color #35('43)	7.00	14.00	21.00
4-Color #64('44)	4.00	8.00	12.00
4-Color #229	2.00	4.00	6.00
4-Color #730,827	1.20	2.40	3.60
General Motors giveaway('53)			
	2.00	4.00	6.00
National Fire Protection giveaway('53)-16pgs.			
	2.00	4.00	6.00

SMOKEY THE BEAR
Oct, 1955 - 1961
Dell Publishing Co.

	Good	Fine	Mint
4-Color #653,708,754,818,932			
	.80	1.60	2.40
4-Color #1016,1119,1214	.50	1.00	1.50
True Story of --, The('59)-U.S. Forest Service giveaway-Publ. by Western Printing Co. (reprinted in '64 & '69) Reprints 1st 16pgs. 4-Color #932	.50	1.00	1.50

(See March of Comics #234)

SMOKY   (See Movie Classics)

SNAFU
Nov, 1955 - #3, March, 1956
Atlas Comics (RCM)

	Good	Fine	Mint
#1-Heath/Severin art	2.00	4.00	6.00
2,3-Severin art	1.35	2.75	4.00

SNAGGLEPUSS   (TV)
Oct, 1962 - #4, Sept, 1963   (Hanna-Barbera)

(Snagglepuss cont'd)
Gold Key

	Good	Fine	Mint
#1	.15	.30	.45
2-4		.15	.30

SNAP (Jest #10?)
1944
Harry 'A' Chesler

#9-Manhunter, The Voice	2.00	4.00	6.00

SNAPPY COMICS
1945
Cima Publ. Co. (Prize Publ.)

#1-Airmale app.	1.50	3.00	4.50

SNARKY PARKER (See Life with --)

SNIFFY THE PUP
#5, Nov, 1949 - #18, Sept, 1953
Standard Publications (Animated Cartoons)

#5-Two Frazetta text illustrations			
	1.35	2.75	4.00
6-10	.65	1.35	2.00
11-18	.50	1.00	1.50

SNOOPER AND BLABBER DETECTIVES (TV)
Nov, 1962 - #3, May, 1963 (Hanna-Barbera)
Gold Key

#1-3		.20	.40

(See Whitman Comic Books)

SNOW FOR CHRISTMAS
1957   (16 pgs.)   (Giveaway)
W. T. Grant Co.

	1.00	2.00	3.00

SNOW WHITE (See 4-Color #49,227,382 & Movie Comics)

SNOW WHITE AND THE SEVEN DWARFS
1952   (32 pgs.) (5x7½") (Disney)
Bendix Washing Machines

	4.00	8.00	12.00

SNOW WHITE AND THE 7 DWARFS IN "MILKY WAY"
1955   (16pgs.)   (Disney Premium)
American Dairy Association

	3.00	6.00	9.00

SNOW WHITE AND THE SEVEN DWARFS

1958   (16 pgs.)   (Disney Premium)
Western Printing Co.

	Good	Fine	Mint
"Mystery of the Missing Magic"			
	2.50	5.00	7.50

SOJOURN   ($1.50)
Sept, 1977 - Present (Full tabloid size)
White Cliffs Publ. Co.   (Color & B&W)

#1-Tor by Kubert, Eagle by Severin, E.V. Race, Private Investigator by Doug Wildey, T.C. Mars by S. Aragones begin plus other strips			
	.50	1.00	1.50

SOLDIER & MARINE COMICS
#11, Dec, 1954 - V2#9, Dec, 1956
Charlton Comics (Toby Press of Conn. V1#11)

V1#11(12/54)-#13(4/55)	.65	1.35	2.00
V1#14(6/55),#15,V2#9	.65	1.35	2.00

SOLDIER COMICS
Jan, 1952 - #11, Sept, 1953
Fawcett Publications

#1	1.20	2.40	3.60
2-5	.80	1.60	2.40
6-11	.40	.80	1.20

SOLDIER OF FORTUNE (See Chewing Gum Booklet)

SOLDIERS OF FORTUNE
Feb-Mar, 1951 - #13, Feb-Mar, 1953
American Comics Group(Creston Publ. Corp.)

#1-Capt. Crossbones by Shelly, Ace Carter, Lance Larsen begin	1.75	3.35	5.00
2-10	1.00	2.00	3.00
11-13(War format)	.80	1.60	2.40
Giant(1951)	1.50	3.00	4.50

NOTE: *Shelly* art-#1-3,5. *Whitney* art-#6,8-13; covers-#1-3,6.

SOLOMON AND SHEBA (See 4-Color #1070)

SONG OF THE SOUTH (See 4-Color #693 & Brer Rabbit)

SON OF BLACK BEAUTY (See 4-Color #510,566)

SON OF FLUBBER (See Movie Comics)

SON OF SATAN
Dec, 1975 - #8, Feb, 1977
Marvel Comics Group

#1-Starlin art	.40	.80	1.20

Snow White Bendix Giv.('52), © WDP

Song Of The South 4-Color #693, © WDP

Son Of Sinbad #1, © STJ

Space Action #1, © Ace

Space Adventures #58, © CC

Space Detective #2, © Avon

	Good	Fine	Mint
(Son of Satan cont'd)			
2-Origin The Professor	.20	.40	.60
3-8	.15	.30	.45

SON OF SINBAD
February, 1950
St. John Publishing Co.

	Good	Fine	Mint
#1-Kubert cover/art	10.00	20.00	30.00

SON OF TOMAHAWK (See Tomahawk)

SON OF VULCAN (Mysteries of Unexplored
Worlds #1-48; Thunderbolt, V3#51 on)
Nov, 1965 - V2#50, Jan, 1966
Charlton Comics

	Good	Fine	Mint
#49,50	.50	1.00	1.50

SONS OF KATIE ELDER (See Movie Classics)

SORCERY (See Chilling Adventures in-- & Red
Circle --)

SORORITY SECRETS
July, 1954
Toby Press

	Good	Fine	Mint
#1	1.00	2.00	3.00

SOUPY SALES COMIC BOOK (The Official --)
1965
Archie Publications

	Good	Fine	Mint
#1	1.35	2.75	4.00

SPACE ACE (Jet #1; Jet Powers #2-4)
1952
Magazine Enterprises

	Good	Fine	Mint
#5(A-1#61)-Guardineer art	4.00	8.00	12.00

SPACE ACTION
June, 1952 - #3, Oct, 1952
Ace Magazines (Junior Books)

	Good	Fine	Mint
#1	1.50	3.00	4.50
2,3	1.00	2.00	3.00

SPACE ADVENTURES
1952 - #59, 11/64; V3#60, 10/67; V1#1,
5/68 - V1#8, 7/69
Capitol Stories/Charlton Comics

	Good	Fine	Mint
#1	3.00	6.00	9.00
2-12	1.35	2.75	4.00
13,14-Blue Beetle (Fox reprints, 10-11/54 -			
#14, 12-1/54-55)	3.00	6.00	9.00

	Good	Fine	Mint
15,17-19: #18-Rocky Jones	1.00	2.00	3.00
16-Krigstein story; Rocky Jones app.			
	1.50	3.00	4.50
20-Reprints Fawcett's "Destination Moon"			
	2.50	5.00	7.50
21-32: #23-Reprints Fawcett's "Space Trip to			
the Moon"	.65	1.35	2.00
33-Origin & 1st app. Captain Atom by Steve			
Ditko	2.50	5.00	7.50
34-40,42-All Capt. Atom	1.75	3.35	5.00
41,43,46-59	.25	.50	.75
44,45-Mercury Man in ea.	.40	.80	1.20
V2#60(10/67)-Origin Paul Mann & The Saucers			
from the Future	.20	.40	.60
#1('68)	.20	.40	.60
2-8		.20	.35

NOTE: _Ditko_ stories-#10,11,16,24,25,27,29,31,
32,34,35,38,40,#2('68); cover-#10. _Shuster_
story-#11.

SPACE BUSTERS
Spring, 1952 - #3, Fall, 1952 (Painted covers
Ziff-Davis Publ. Co.   by Norman Saunders)

	Good	Fine	Mint
#1-Krigstein art	4.00	8.00	12.00
2,3	2.50	5.00	7.50

NOTE: _Anderson_ stories-#2.

SPACE CADET (See Tom Corbett, --)

SPACE COMICS
#4, Mar-Apr, 1954 - #5, May-June, 1954
Avon Periodicals

	Good	Fine	Mint
#4,5-Space Mouse, Peter Rabbit, Super Pup, &			
Merry Mouse app.	.80	1.60	2.40
IW Reprint #8-No date-Space Mouse reprints			
	.35	.70	1.05

SPACE DETECTIVE
July, 1951 - #4, July, 1952
Avon Periodicals

	Good	Fine	Mint
#1-Rod Hathway, Space Det. begins, ends #4;			
Wood cover/3 stories, 23pgs.; Drug story			
	16.50	33.25	50.00
2-Tales from the Shadow Squad begins; Wood/			
Orlando cover	5.00	10.00	15.00
3,4: #3-Kinstler cover	2.50	5.00	7.50
IW Reprint #1(reprts.#2),8(reprts.cover #1 &			
part Famous Funnies #191)			
	1.00	2.00	3.00
IW Reprint #9	1.00	2.00	3.00

SPACE EXPLORER (See March of Comics #202)

SPACE FAMILY ROBINSON (--Lost in Space #15
on) (Lost in Space #37 on)
Dec, 1962 - #36, Oct, 1969
Gold Key

	Good	Fine	Mint
#1	3.00	6.00	9.00
2(3/63)	1.00	2.00	3.00
3-10	.60	1.20	1.80
11-20	.35	.70	1.05
21-36	.20	.40	.60

NOTE: *Idea created by Carl Barks.*

SPACE FAMILY ROBINSON (See March of Comics
#320,328,352,404)

SPACE GHOST (TV)
March, 1967 (Hanna-Barbera)
Gold Key

#1(10199-703)	.35	.70	1.05

SPACE KAT-ETS (In 3-D)
Dec, 1953 (25¢)
Power Publishing Co.

#1	4.00	8.00	12.00

SPACEMAN (See Speed Carter --)

SPACE MAN
1962 - #8, 3-5/64; #9, 7/72 - #10, 10/72
Dell Publishing Co./Gold Key

4-Color #1253(1-3/62)	.65	1.35	2.00
#2,3	.35	.70	1.05
4-8	.25	.50	.75
9-Reprints #1253	.15	.30	.45
10-Reprints #2	.15	.30	.45

SPACE MOUSE (Also see Space Comics)
April, 1953 - #5, Apr-May, 1954
Avon Periodicals

#1	1.35	2.75	4.00
2-5	.65	1.35	2.00

SPACE MOUSE (See Comic Album #17)
Aug-Oct, 1960 - #5, Nov, 1963 (Walter Lantz)
Dell Publ. Co./Gold Key

4-Color #1132,1244	.65	1.35	2.00
#1(11/62)-#5(G.K.)	.35	.70	1.05

SPACE MYSTERIES
1964
I.W. Enterprises

Reprint #1,8,9	.65	1.35	2.00

SPACE: 1999
Nov, 1975 - #7, Nov, 1976
Charlton Comics

	Good	Fine	Mint
#1-Staton art; origin Moonbase Alpha	.35	.70	1.05
2-Staton art	.25	.50	.75
3-7: #5,6-Morrow art	.15	.30	.45

SPACE: 1999 (Magazine)
November, 1975 - #8, Nov, 1976
Charlton Comics

#1-Origin Moonbase Alpha; Morrow cover/art	.65	1.35	2.00
2,3-Morrow cover/art	.40	.80	1.20
4-8(#7 shows #6 on inside)	.40	.80	1.20

SPACE PATROL
Summer, 1952 - #2, Fall, 1952 (Painted covers
Ziff-Davis Publ. Co.   by Norman Saunders)

#1-Krigstein stories	5.00	10.00	15.00
2-Krigstein stories	3.50	7.00	10.50

SPACE SQUADRON (Space Worlds #6)
June, 1951 - #5, Feb, 1952
Marvel/Atlas Comics (ACI)

#1	2.00	4.00	6.00
2-5	1.00	2.00	3.00

SPACE THRILLERS
1954 (Giant) (25¢)
Avon Periodicals

No#-Robotmen of the Lost Planet; contains 3
rebound comics of The Saint & Strange
Worlds. Contents could vary.
5.00 10.00 15.00

SPACE TRIP TO THE MOON (See Space Advs. #23)

SPACE WAR (Fightin' Five #28 on)
Oct, 1959 - #27, Mar, 1964
Charlton Comics

V1#1,2	.65	1.35	2.00
3-5,7,9-27	.35	.70	1.05
6,8-Ditko story	.80	1.60	2.40

SPACE WESTERN
#40, Oct, 1952 - #45, Aug, 1953
Charlton Comics (Capitol Stories)

#40	4.00	8.00	12.00
41-45	3.00	6.00	9.00

Space Family Robinson #2, © GK

Space War #27, © CC

Space Western #42, © CC

Sparkler #37, © UFS

Sparkling Stars #20, © Hoke

Sparky Watts #3, © CCG

SPACE WORLDS (Space Squadron #1-5)
#6, April, 1952
Atlas Comics (Male)

	Good	Fine	Mint
#6	.80	1.60	2.40

SPANKY & ALFALFA THE LITTLE RASCALS (See
The Little Rascals)

SPARKIE, RADIO PIXIE (Big John & Sparkie #4)
Winter, 1951 - #3, 1952
Ziff-Davis Publ. Co.

#1-3	1.35	2.75	4.00

SPARKLE COMICS
Oct-Nov, 1948 - #33, Dec-Jan, 1953-54
United Features Syndicate/Ziff-Davis Publ.

#1-Li'l Abner, Nancy, Captain & the Kids	1.35	2.75	4.00
2-10	1.00	2.00	3.00
11-33	.65	1.35	2.00

SPARKLE PLENTY (See 4-Color #215 & Harvey
Comics Library #2)

SPARKLER COMICS (1st Series)
1940
United Feature Comic Group

#1-Jim Hardy	8.00	16.00	24.00
2-Frankie Doodle	4.00	8.00	12.00

SPARKLER COMICS (2nd Series)(Nancy & Sluggo
July, 1940 - #120, Jan, 1955   #121 on)
United Features Syndicate

#1-Origin Sparkman; Tarzan(by Hogarth in all
issues), Captain & the Kids, Ella Cinders,
Danny Dingle, Dynamite Dunn, Nancy, Abbie
& Slats, Frankie Doodle, Broncho Bill be-

gin	30.00	60.00	90.00
2	15.00	30.00	45.00
3	12.00	24.00	36.00
4	10.00	20.00	30.00
5-10	8.00	16.00	24.00
11-13,15-20: #12-Sparkman new costume			
	7.00	14.00	21.00
14-Hogarth Tarzan cover	10.00	20.00	30.00
21-27,29,30: #22-Race Riley & the Commandos			
strips begin, end #44	6.00	12.00	18.00
28,31,34,37,39-Tarzan covers by Hogarth			
	9.00	18.00	27.00
32,33,35,36,38,40	5.00	10.00	15.00
41,43,45,46,48,49	3.00	6.00	9.00
42,44,47,50-Tarzan covers	7.00	14.00	21.00
51,52,54-70: #57-Li'l Abner begins			
	2.50	5.00	7.50

	Good	Fine	Mint
53-Tarzan cover	5.00	10.00	15.00
71-80	2.00	4.00	6.00
81,82,84-90	1.50	3.00	4.50
83-Tarzan cover; last Li'l Abner			
	2.50	5.00	7.50
91-96,98-100	1.50	3.00	4.50
97-Origin Casey Ruggles by Warren Tufts			
	1.75	3.35	5.00
101-107,109-112,114-120	1.25	2.50	3.75
108,113-Toth art	2.00	4.00	6.00

SPARKLING LOVE
June, 1950; 1953
Avon Periodicals/Realistic(1953)

#1(Avon)-Kubert art	4.00	8.00	12.00
No#(1953-reprint)-Kubert story			
	2.00	4.00	6.00

SPARKLING STARS
June, 1944 - #33, March, 1948
Holyoke Publishing Co.

#1-Hell's Angels	3.00	6.00	9.00
2-10	1.50	3.00	4.50
11-19,21-33	1.00	2.00	3.00
20-Origin Tiger Boy	1.50	3.00	4.50

SPARKMAN
1945   (One Shot)
United Features Syndicate

#1-Origin Sparkman	7.00	14.00	21.00

SPARKY WATTS
1942 - 1949
Columbia Comic Group

#1-Skyman & The Face app.(1942)			
	7.00	14.00	21.00
2(1943)	5.00	10.00	15.00
3(1944)	4.00	8.00	12.00
4(1944)-Origin	4.00	8.00	12.00
5('47)-Skyman app.	2.50	5.00	7.50
6(1947)	2.50	5.00	7.50
7,8(1948)	2.00	4.00	6.00
9,10(1949)	2.00	4.00	6.00

SPARTACUS (See 4-Color Comics #1139)

SPECIAL AGENT (See Steve Saunders --)

SPECIAL COLLECTOR'S EDITION
Dec, 1975   (10½x13½")
Marvel Comics Group

#1-Kung Fu, Iron Fist & Sons of the Tiger			
	.65	1.35	2.00

SPECIAL COMICS (Hangman #2 on)
Winter, 1941-42
MLJ Magazines

	Good	Fine	Mint
#1-Origin The Boy Buddies(Shield & Wizard x-over); death of The Comet; origin The Hangman retold	70.00	140.00	210.00

SPECIAL EDITION (See Gorgo, Reptisaurus)

SPECIAL EDITION COMICS
1940   (One Shot)
Fawcett Publications

#1-Captain Marvel (came out before Captain
   Marvel #1)   275.00 550.00 825.00
   (Prices vary widely on this book)

SPECIAL MARVEL EDITION (Master of Kung Fu #17
Jan, 1971 - #16, Feb, 1974   on)
Marvel Comics Group

#1-Thor begin(reprint)	.40	.80	1.20
2-4-Last Thor(reprints)	.30	.60	.90
5-14: Sgt. Fury reprints; #11 reprints/Sgt. Fury #13(Capt.America)	.20	.40	.60
15-Master of Kung Fu begins; Starlin art	.75	1.50	2.25
16-Starlin art	.50	1.00	1.50

SPECIAL WAR SERIES
Aug, 1965 - #4, Nov, 1965
Charlton Comics

V4#1-D-Day	.15	.30	.45
2-Attack!	.15	.30	.45
3-War & Attack	.15	.30	.45
4-Judomaster	.65	1.35	2.00

SPECTACULAR ADVENTURES
12/49 - #2, 2/50 (just "Adventures" on inside)
St. John Publishing Co.

#1	3.50	7.00	10.50
2-Slave Girl; L.Starr art	3.50	7.00	10.50

SPECTACULAR FEATURES MAGAZINE, A (Formerly
My Confessions)
#11, April, 1950 - #12, June, 1950
Fox Features Syndicate

#11-Samson & Delilah	4.00	8.00	12.00
12-Iwo Jima	2.50	5.00	7.50

SPECTACULAR SPIDER-MAN, THE (See Marvel
Treasury Edition & Marvel Special Edition)

SPECTACULAR SPIDER-MAN, THE (Magazine)
July, 1968 - #2, Nov, 1968   (35¢)
Marvel Comics Group

	Good	Fine	Mint
#1-(Black & White)	2.00	4.00	6.00
2-(Color)	1.50	3.00	4.50

SPECTACULAR SPIDER-MAN, THE (Peter Parker)
Dec, 1976 - Present
Marvel Comics Group

#1	.40	.80	1.20
2-5	.20	.40	.60
6-14	.15	.30	.45

SPECTACULAR STORIES (-- Magazine) (Formerly
A Star Presentation)
#4, July, 1950
Fox Features Syndicate (Hero Books)

#4-Sherlock Holmes	2.50	5.00	7.50

SPECTRE, THE (See Adventure, Showcase, More
11-12/67 - #10, 5-6/69   Fun)
National Periodical Publications

#1-Anderson cover/art	1.00	2.00	3.00
2-5-Neal Adams cover/art #3; Wildcat x-over	1.50	3.00	4.50
6-8,10: #7-Hourman app.	.75	1.50	2.25
9-Wrightson story	1.50	3.00	4.50

NOTE: *Anderson inks-#6-8.*

SPEED BUGGY (Also see Fun-In #12,15)
July, 1975 - #9, Nov, 1976 (Hanna-Barbera)
Charlton Comics

#1-9		.15	.30

SPEED CARTER SPACEMAN
Sept, 1953 - #8, Nov, 1954
Atlas Comics (CnPC)

#1,2	1.75	3.35	5.00
3-8	1.20	2.40	3.60

SPEED COMICS (New Speed; #14-16 pocket size,
Oct, 1939 - #44, Jan-Feb, 1947   100 pgs.)
Brookwood Publ./Speed Publ./Harvey Publ.

#1-Origin Shock Gibson; Ted Parrish, the Man with 1000 Faces begins; Bob Powell art	40.00	80.00	120.00
2-Powell art	20.00	40.00	60.00
3	13.50	26.75	40.00
4	12.00	24.00	36.00
5	10.00	20.00	30.00
6-12: #7-Mars Mason begins, ends #11. #12-			

Special #1, © MLJ

Spectacular Feat--#11, © Fox

Speed Comics #3, © Harv

Spellbound #29, © MCG

Spirit 8/4/40, © Will Eisner

Spirit 10/31/43, © Will Eisner

	Good	Fine	Mint
(Speed Comics cont'd)			
The Wasp begins; Major Colt app. (Capt. Colt #12)	10.00	20.00	30.00
13-Intro. Captain Freedom & Young Defenders; Girl Commandos, Pat Parker, War Nurse begins; Major Colt app.	16.50	33.25	50.00
14-16: #15-Pat Parker dons costume, last in costume #23; no Girl Commandos	9.00	18.00	27.00
17-Black Cat begins(origin)Reprint/Pocket #1-not in #40,41	15.00	30.00	45.00
18-20	8.00	16.00	24.00
21,22,25-30	7.00	14.00	21.00
23-Origin Girl Commandos	10.00	20.00	30.00
24-Pat Parker Team-up with Girl Commandos	7.00	14.00	21.00
31-44	6.00	12.00	18.00

NOTE: _Kubert_ stories-#7-11(Mars Mason),37,38, 42-44. _Powell_ Shock Gibson-#44.

SPEED DEMONS
1957 - 1958
Charlton Comics

	Good	Fine	Mint
#5-10	.20	.40	.60

SPEED SMITH THE HOT ROD KING
Spring, 1952
Ziff-Davis Publ. Co.

	Good	Fine	Mint
#1	1.00	2.00	3.00

SPEEDY GONZALES (See 4-Color Comics #1084)

SPEEDY RABBIT
No date (1958?); 1963
I.W. Enterprises/Super Comics

IW Reprint #1	.35	.70	1.05
Super Reprint #14('63)	.35	.70	1.05

SPELLBOUND (Tales to Hold You--#1, Stories--)
3/52 - #23, 6/54; #24, 10/55 - #34, 6/57
Atlas Comics(ACI #1-14/Male #15-23/BPC #24-34)

#1	2.00	4.00	6.00
2-10	1.20	2.40	3.60
11-31	.80	1.60	2.40
32,33-Torres stories	1.25	2.50	3.75
34-Williamson/Mayo story, 4pgs.	2.00	4.00	6.00

NOTE: _Ditko_ story-#29. _Everett_ stories-#2,5, 31; covers-#2,7,14,30. _Infantino_ story-#15. _Krigstein_ stories-#6,17. _Orlando_ story-#25. _Powell_ stories-#20,32.

SPENCER SPOOK (Formerly Giggle)
Jan-Feb, 1955 - #100, Mar-Apr, 1955
American Comics Group

	Good	Fine	Mint
#99,100	.35	.70	1.05

SPIDER-MAN (See Amazing --)

SPIDEY SUPER STORIES (Spider-Man)
Oct, 1974 - Present (35c) (No ads)
Marvel/Children's TV Workshop

#1-(Stories simplified)	.25	.50	.75
2-5	.20	.40	.60
6-10	.15	.30	.45
11-30		.15	.30

SPIKE & TYKE (M.G.M.)
Sept, 1953 - #1266, Dec-Feb, 1961-62
Dell Publishing Co.

4-Color #499,577,638	.50	1.00	1.50
#4-10	.25	.50	.75
11-24(12-2/60-61)	.20	.40	.60
4-Color #1266	.35	.70	1.05

SPIN & MARTY (TV) (Walt Disney's)
June, 1956 - #1082, Mar-May, 1960
Dell Publishing Co.

4-Color #714,767,808,826	1.00	2.00	3.00
#5(3-5/58)-#10(6-8/59)	.65	1.35	2.00
4-Color #1026,1082	.65	1.35	2.00

SPINE-TINGLING TALES
May, 1975 - #4, Jan, 1976
Gold Key

#1-Reprints 1st Tragg/Mystery Comics Digest#3	.15	.30	.45
2-Origin Ra-Ka-Tep reprt./Mystery C.Digest #1; Dr. Spektor/#12	.15	.30	
3-All Durak ish. reprts.	.15	.30	
4-Baron Tibor's 1st app. reprt./Mystery Com. Digest #4	.15	.30	

SPIRIT, THE (Weekly Comic Book)
Distributed thru various newspapers
June 2, 1940 - 1952 (16pgs.) (No cover)
Will Eisner

	Good	Fine	Mint
6/2/40(#1)-Origin by Will Eisner, reprinted in Police #11; Lady Luck & Mr. Mystic by Powell begin	50.00	100.00	150.00
6/9/40(#2)-Eisner art	13.50	27.00	40.50
6/16/40(#3)-Eisner art	12.00	24.00	36.00
6/23/40(#4), 6/30/40(#5)-All Eisner	10.00	20.00	30.00
7/7/40-8/40-All Eisner	8.00	16.00	24.00
9/40-12/40-All Eisner	7.00	14.00	21.00
1941-All Eisner	5.00	10.00	15.00
1942-Jan-March issues by Eisner			

(The Spirit cont'd)	Good	Fine	Mint
	4.00	8.00	12.00

1942-April-Dec issues-not Eisner; Many by
Lou Fine in 1942-43   2.50   5.00   7.50
1943,'44 issues-Not Eisner; 10/3/43-Last
Powell Mr. Mystic; 5/14/44-Last Mr. Mystic   2.00   4.00   6.00
1945 issues-Not Eisner 2.00   4.00   6.00
1945-Last 2 Dec. issues by Eisner
                      4.00   8.00 12.00
1946 issues-All Eisner; 3/3/46-Last Lady
Luck   3.50   7.00 10.50
1947-'50 issues-All Eisner3.50 7.00 10.50
1951-Jan-April issues by Eisner
                      3.00   6.00   9.00
1951-May-Dec. issues not by Eisner
                      2.00   4.00   6.00
1952 issues   3.00   6.00   9.00
1952 issues with Denny Colt in Outer Space
by Wally Wood   10.00 20.00 30.00
Large Tabloid pages from 1946 on (Eisner)
        each....   6.00 12.00 18.00
NOTE: *Spirit sections came out in both large
and small format. Also see* Three Comics Mag.

SPIRIT, THE (1st Series)
1944 - #22, Aug, 1950
Quality Comics Group (Vital)

No#(#1)-"Wanted Dead or Alive"
                     25.00 50.00 75.00
No#(#2)-"Crime Doesn't Pay"
                     15.00 30.00 45.00
No#(#3)-"Murder Runs Wild"
                     13.50 26.75 40.00
#4,5   12.00 24.00 36.00
6-10   8.00 16.00 24.00
11,12,15,17   6.00 12.00 18.00
13,14,16-Eisner/Grandenetti covers
                      8.00 16.00 24.00
18-21: Strip reprints by Eisner & Grandenetti;
Eisner/Grandenetti covers
                     16.50 33.25 50.00
22-Classic Eisner cover 20.00 40.00 60.00
Super Reprint #11,12-Not Eisner; Sunday strip
reprints   1.75   3.35   5.00
NOTE: *Crandall cover-#11; Super #11 reprints
Quality Spirit #19.*

SPIRIT, THE (2nd Series)
Spring, 1952 - 1954
Fiction House Magazines

#1-Not Eisner   10.00 20.00 30.00
2-Two Eisner stories 12.00 24.00 36.00
3   5.00 10.00 15.00
4-One Eisner story/cvr 10.00 20.00 30.00
5-Four Eisner stories 13.50 26.75 40.00

SPIRIT, THE
Oct, 1966 - #2, March, 1967
Harvey Publications
	Good	Fine	Mint
#1-Eisner reprints + 2 new pgs.
                      4.00   8.00 12.00
2-Eisner reprints + 2 new pgs.
                      3.50   7.00 10.50
NOTE: *Existence of a #3 suspected; sent to
mail subscribers only.*

SPIRIT, THE (Underground)
Jan, 1973 - #2, Sept, 1973   (Black & White)
Kitchen Sink Enterprises

#1-New Eisner cover, 4pgs. new Eisner art +
reprints   1.75   3.50   5.25
2-New Eisner cover, 4pgs. new Eisner art +
reprints   1.75   3.50   5.25

SPIRIT, THE (Magazine)
April, 1974 - Present
Warren Publishing Co.

#1-Eisner reprts. begin 1.35 2.75 4.00
2-5   1.00   2.00   3.00
6-9,11-14   .75   1.50   2.25
10-Origin   .80   1.60   2.40
Special #1('75)-All Eisner art
                       .50   1.00   1.50
NOTE: *Covers pencilled by Eisner only; one
color story reprinted in #1-10.*

SPIRIT WORLD (Magazine)
Fall, 1971   (Black & White)
National Periodical Publications

#1-Kirby art/Adams cover 1.35 2.75 4.00

SPITFIRE
1944 - 1945   (Female undercover agent)
Malverne Herald (Elliot)(J.R. Mahon)

#132,133   3.00   6.00   9.00

SPITFIRE COMICS (Also see Double Up)
Aug, 1942 - #2   (Pocket size - 100pgs.)
Harvey Publications

#1-Origin The Clown, The Fly-Man, The Spit-
fire & The Magician from Bagdad
                     15.00 30.00 45.00
2   8.00 16.00 24.00

SPOOF!
Oct, 1970; #2, Nov, 1972 - #5, May, 1973
Marvel Comics Group

Spirit #15, © Will Eisner (Qua)

Spirit #4, © Will Eisner (FH)

Spook Suspense & Mystery #28, © Star   Sport Thrills #14, © Star   Spotlight Comics #2, © Ches

(Spoof! cont'd)	Good	Fine	Mint
#1	.15	.30	.45
2-5		.15	.30

SPOOK (-- Detective Cases #22; -- Tales of
Suspense & Mystery #23-30)
#22, Jan, 1953 - #30, Oct, 1954
Novelty-Star Publications

	Good	Fine	Mint
#22(1/53)	1.35	2.75	4.00
23-27,30-Sgt. Spook	1.00	2.00	3.00
28,29-Jo-Jo, Rulah app.	2.00	4.00	6.00

NOTE: _Disbrow art-#26,28-30; #30 reprint/_
Blue Bolt Weird Tales #114.

SPOOK COMICS
1946
Baily Publications/Star

#1-Mr. Lucifer app.	1.00	2.00	3.00

SPOOKY (The Tuff Little Ghost)
Nov, 1956 - Present
Harvey Publications

#1	2.00	4.00	6.00
2-10(1956-57)	.80	1.60	2.40
11-20(1957-58)	.40	.80	1.20
21-40(1958-59)	.25	.50	.75
41-100	.15	.30	.45
101-156		.10	.20

SPOOKY HAUNTED HOUSE
Oct, 1972 - #15, Feb, 1975
Harvey Publications

#1	.15	.30	.45
2-15		.10	.20

SPOOKY MYSTERIES
No date (1946)   (10¢)
Your Guide Publ. Co.

No#-Mr. Spooky, Super Snooper, Pinky, Girl
   Detective app.   1.50   3.00   4.50

SPOOKY SPOOKTOWN
June, 1962 - Present
Harvey Publications

#1-Casper, Spooky	1.50	3.00	4.50
2-10	.65	1.35	2.00
11-20	.35	.70	1.05
21-40	.20	.40	.60
41-66		.20	.35

SPORT COMICS
Oct, 1940 - 1947
Street & Smith Publications

	Good	Fine	Mint
#1-Life story of Lou Gehrig	3.00	6.00	9.00
2,3	2.00	4.00	6.00
4-12(1943)	1.35	2.75	4.00
V2-V4, #1-12	1.00	2.00	3.00

SPORT LIBRARY (See Charlton Sport --)

SPORTS ACTION (Formerly Sport Stars)
#2, Feb, 1950 - #14, Sept, 1952
Marvel/Atlas Comics (ACI #2,3/SAI #4-14)

#2	.75	1.50	2.75
3-12,14	.50	1.00	1.50
13-Krigstein art	1.35	2.75	4.00

SPORT STARS
2-3/46 - #4, 8-9/46 (½ comic, ½ photo mag.)
Parents' Magazine Institute (Sport Stars)

#1-"How Tarzan Got That Way" story of Johnny			
Weissmuller	2.50	5.00	7.50
2-Baseball greats	1.00	2.00	3.00
3,4	1.00	2.00	3.00

SPORT STARS (Sports Action #2)
Nov, 1949
Marvel Comics (ACI)

#1-Knute Rockne	1.50	3.00	4.50

SPORT THRILLS (Formerly Dick Cole)
#11, Nov, 1949 - #15, Nov, 1951
Star Publications

#11-Last app. Dick Cole	1.00	2.00	3.00
12-15	.80	1.60	2.40

SPOTLIGHT COMICS
Nov, 1944 - #3, 1945
Harry 'A' Chesler (Our Army, Inc.)

#1-The Black Dwarf, The Veiled Avenger, &			
Barry Kuda begin	7.00	14.00	21.00
2,3	5.00	10.00	15.00

SPOTTY THE PUP
#3, Dec-Jan, 1953-54
Avon Periodicals

#3	.25	.50	.75

SPUNKY (-- Junior Cowboy)(-- Comics #2 on)
April, 1949 - #7, Nov, 1951
Standard Comics

#1,2-Text illos by Frazetta

(Spunky cont'd)	Good	Fine	Mint
	2.00	4.00	6.00
3-7	.35	.70	1.05

SPUNKY THE SMILING SPOOK
Aug, 1957 - #4, May, 1958
Ajax/Farrell (World Famous Comics/Four Star
Comic Corp.)

#1-Reprints from Frisky Fables			
	.35	.70	1.05
2-4	.20	.40	.60

SPY AND COUNTERSPY (Spy Hunters #3 on)
Aug-Sept, 1949 - #2, Oct-Nov, 1949
American Comics Group

#1-Origin, 1st app. Jonathan Kent, Counterspy			
	1.20	2.40	3.60
2	.80	1.60	2.40

SPY CASES (Formerly The Kellys)
#26, Sept, 1950 - #19, Oct, 1953
Marvel/Atlas Comics (Hercules Publ.)

#26-28(1950)	1.20	2.40	3.60
4-10	.80	1.60	2.40
11-19	.60	1.20	1.80

SPY FIGHTERS
March, 1951 - #15, July, 1953
Marvel/Atlas Comics (CSI)

#1	1.35	2.75	4.00
2-15	.80	1.60	2.40

SPY-HUNTERS (Formerly Spy & Counterspy)
#3, 12-1/49-50 - #24, 6-7/53
American Comics Group

#3-Jonathan Kent begins, ends #10,			
4-10: #8-Starr story	.80	1.60	2.40
11-15,17-24	.65	1.35	2.00
16-9pg. Williamson story	2.00	4.00	6.00

NOTE: _Whitney covers-#8,16; story-#6,16._

SPYMAN (Top Secret Adventures on cover)
Sept, 1966 - #3, Feb, 1967
Harvey Publications

#1	.65	1.35	2.00
2,3	.40	.80	1.20

SPY SMASHER (See Fawcett Miniatures)
1941 - #11, Feb, 1943
Fawcett Publications

#1-Spy Smasher begins	70.00	140.00	210.00
2	30.00	60.00	90.00

	Good	Fine	Mint
3-5	25.00	50.00	75.00
6-11	20.00	40.00	60.00

SPY SMASHER WELL KNOWN COMICS
1944 (12pgs.)(Printed in green)(8½x10½")
(Paper cover; glued binding)
Bestmaid/Samuel Lowe (Giveaway)

(Rare)	25.00	50.00	75.00

SPY THRILLERS (Police Badge #479 #5)
Nov, 1954 - #4, May, 1955
Atlas Comics (PrPI)

#1	1.20	2.40	3.60
2-4	.65	1.35	2.00

SQUEEKS
Oct, 1953 - 1954
Lev Gleason Publications

#1-Biro cover	1.00	2.00	3.00
2-5: #2,3-Biro covers	.65	1.35	2.00

STALKER
June-July, 1975 - #4, Dec-Jan, 1975-76
National Periodical Publications

#1-Ditko/Wood cover-stories begin			
	.40	.80	1.20
2-4	.25	.50	.75

STAMP COMICS
Oct, 1951 - #7, Oct, 1952 (#1 - 15¢)
Youthful Magazines/Stamp Comics, Inc.

#1-6: #3,4-Kiefer, Wildey stories			
	1.00	2.00	3.00
7-Roy Krenkel, 4pgs.	1.50	3.00	4.50

NOTE: _Promotes stamp collecting; gives stories behind various commemorative stamps._

STANLEY & HIS MONSTER (Formerly The Fox & the
#109, 4-5/68 - #114, 2-3/69   Crow)
National Periodical Publications

#109-114	.15	.30	.45

STAR COMICS
2/37 - #22(V2#6), 7/39 (#1-6, Large Size)
Harry 'A' Chesler/Centaur Publications

V1#1-Dan Hastings begins	15.00	30.00	45.00
2-5: #5-Little Nemo	10.00	20.00	30.00
6-10	8.00	16.00	24.00
11-15	7.00	14.00	21.00
16-The Phantom Rider begins			

Spy Cases #11, © MCG   Spy Smasher #5, © Faw   Star Comics #16, © Ches

A Star Presentation #3, © Fox   Stars and Stripes #2, © Cen   Star Spangled Comics #17, © DC

(Star Comics cont'd)	Good	Fine	Mint
	7.00	14.00	21.00
17-22(V2#1-6)	6.00	12.00	18.00

STAR FEATURE COMICS
1963
I.W. Enterprises

Reprint #9-Stunt-Man Stetson app.			
	.65	1.35	2.00

STARFIRE
Aug-Sept, 1976 - #8, Oct-Nov, 1977
National Per.Publ./DC   (not approved by code)

#1-Origin	.25	.50	.75
2-8	.20	.40	.60

STAR HUNTERS
Oct, 1977 - Present
National Periodical Publications/DC Comics

#1-Newton cover/art	.20	.40	.60
2	.15	.30	.45

STARK TERROR (Magazine) (50¢)
Dec, 1970 - #5, Aug, 1971 (52 pgs.) (B&W)
Stanley Publications

#1	.65	1.35	2.00
2-4(Gillmor/Aragon reprts)	.35	.70	1.05
5-(ACG reprints)	.35	.70	1.05

STARLET O'HARA IN HOLLYWOOD
1949 - #4, Sept, 1949
Standard Comics

#1	2.50	5.00	7.50
2-4-by Bob Oksner	2.00	4.00	6.00

STAR PRESENTATION, A (Formerly My Secret
Romance #1,2; Spectacular Stories #4)
#3, May, 1950 (Also see This Is Suspense)
Fox Features Syndicate (Hero Books)

#3-Dr. Jekyll & Mr. Hyde by Wood & Harrison			
(reprinted in Startling Terror Tales #10);			
Wood cover	10.00	20.00	30.00

STAR RANGER
Feb, 1937 - #12, 1938 (Large size-#1-6)
Centaur Publications

#1-Ace & Deuce, Air Plunder			
	16.50	33.25	50.00
2-8,V2#9-12(small size)	7.00	14.00	21.00

STAR RANGER FUNNIES
V1#15, Oct, 1958; V2#2, April, 1939
Centaur Publications

	Good	Fine	Mint
V1#15-6pg. Eisner western story			
	9.00	18.00	27.00
V2#2	6.00	12.00	18.00

STARR FLAGG, UNDERCOVER GIRL(See Undercover--)

STARS AND STRIPES COMICS
Feb, 1941 - #6, Dec, 1941
Centaur Publications

#2(#1)-The Shark, The Iron Skull, A Man, The			
Amazing Man, Mighty Man, Minimidget begin;			
The Voice & Dash Darwell, the Human Meteor			
app.	30.00	60.00	90.00
3-Origin Dr. Synthe; The Black Panther app.			
	25.00	50.00	75.00
4-The Stars and Stripes origin			
	17.50	35.00	52.50
5(#5 on cover, inside)	15.00	30.00	45.00
6(#5 on cover, #6 on inside)			
	15.00	30.00	45.00

STAR SPANGLED COMICS (--War Stories #131 on)
Oct, 1941 - #130, July, 1952
National Periodical Publications

#1-Origin Tarantula; Captain X of the R.A.F.,			
Star Spangled Kid & Armstrong of the Army			
begin	60.00	120.00	180.00
2	30.00	60.00	90.00
3-5	17.50	35.00	52.50
6-Last Armstrong/Army	15.00	30.00	45.00
7-Origin The Guardian by S&K, & Robotman by			
Jimmy Thompson; The Newsboy Legion & TNT			
begin; last Capt.X	90.00	180.00	270.00
8-Origin TNT & Dan the Dyna-Mite			
	50.00	100.00	150.00
9,10	35.00	70.00	105.00
11-17	21.50	55.00	82.50
18-Origin Star Spangled Kid			
	30.00	60.00	90.00
19-Last Tarantula	25.00	50.00	75.00
20-Liberty Belle begins	25.00	50.00	75.00
21-29-Last S&K issue; #23-Last TNT			
	16.50	33.25	50.00
30-40	7.00	14.00	21.00
41-50	6.00	12.00	18.00
51-64: Last Newsboy Legion & The Guardian;			
#53 by S&K	5.00	10.00	15.00
65-Robin begins	6.00	12.00	18.00
66-68,70-80	4.00	8.00	12.00
69-Origin Tomahawk	5.00	10.00	15.00
81-Origin Merry, Girl of 1000 Gimmicks			
	3.00	6.00	9.00

(Star Spangled cont'd)	Good	Fine	Mint
82-Last Star Spangled Kid	2.50	5.00	7.50
83-Capt. Compass begins, ends #130			
	2.50	5.00	7.50
84-100: #91-Federal Men begin, end #93. #94- Manhunters Around the World begin, end #121	2.25	4.50	6.75
101-112,114-121	2.00	4.00	6.00
113-Frazetta story,10pgs.	10.00	20.00	30.00
122-Ghost Breaker begins(origin), ends #130			
	1.75	3.35	5.00
123-130	1.75	3.35	5.00

NOTE: *Most all issues after #29 signed Simon & Kirby are not by them.*

STAR SPANGLED WAR STORIES (Star Spangled Comics #1-130; The Unknown Soldier #205 on)
#131, 8/52 - #133, 10/52; #3, 11/52 - #204, 2-3/77   (See Showcase)
National Periodical Publications

#131(#1)	6.00	12.00	18.00
132,133	3.00	6.00	9.00
#3-10	2.50	5.00	7.50
11-20: #4-Devil Dog Dugan app.			
	2.00	4.00	6.00
21-50	1.50	3.00	4.50
51-90: #84-Origin Mlle. Marie. #90-G.I.'s vs. dinosaurs begin	.80	1.60	2.40
91-120	.50	1.00	1.50
121-133,135-137-Last dinosaur story; Heath Birdman-#129,131	.35	.70	1.05
134,144-Adams story + Kubert #144			
	1.00	2.00	3.00
138-Enemy Ace begins by Joe Kubert, ends #161			
	.65	1.35	2.00
139-143,145-148,152,153,155	.50	1.00	1.50
149,150-Viking Prince by Kubert			
	.65	1.35	2.00
151-1st Unknown Soldier	.35	.70	1.05
154-Origin Unknown Soldier	.35	.70	1.05
156-1st Battle Album	.20	.40	.60
157-161-Last Enemy Ace	.20	.40	.60
162-180,184-204: #164-Toth story. #166-The Young Commandos app.	.15	.30	.45
181-183-Enemy Ace vs. Balloon Buster serial app.	.15	.30	.45

NOTE: *Anderson cover-#120. Drucker stories- #66,73-84. John Giunta story-#72. Grandenetti story-#24. Infantino stories-#21,37,163(re- print); covers-#118,121. Kaluta cover-#167. Krigstein story-#34. Kubert stories-#6-138 (most issues),200. Maurer story-#160. Sutton story-#168. Wildey story-#161. Suicide Squad in #110,116-18,120,121,127. U.S.S. Stevens by Glanzman-#171,172,174.*

STARSTREAM (Adventures in Science Fiction)

1976   (68pgs.) (Cardboard covers) (79¢)
Whitman/Western Publishing Co.

	Good	Fine	Mint
#1-Bolle art	.35	.70	1.05
2-4-McWilliams & Bolle art.	.35	.70	1.05

STAR STUDDED
1945 (25¢; 132pgs.); 1945 (196pgs.)
Cambridge House/Superior Publishers

#1-Captain Combat, Ghost Woman, Commandette, & Red Rogue app.	5.00	10.00	15.00
No#-The Cadet, Edison Bell, Hoot Gibson, Jun- gle Lil(196pgs.); copies vary-Blue Beetle in some	4.00	8.00	12.00

STARTLING COMICS
June, 1940 - #53, May, 1948
Better Publications (Nedor)

#1-Origin Captain Future, Mystico, the Wonder Man; The Masked Rider begins	40.00	80.00	120.00
2	20.00	40.00	60.00
3	15.00	30.00	45.00
4	12.00	24.00	36.00
5-9	9.00	18.00	27.00
10-Origin & 1st app. The Fighting Yank	30.00	60.00	90.00
11-15	12.00	24.00	36.00
16-Origin The Four Comrades; not in #32,35	15.00	30.00	45.00
17-Last Masked Rider & Mystico	8.00	16.00	24.00
18-Origin Pyroman	20.00	40.00	60.00
19	8.00	16.00	24.00
20-The Oracle begins; not in #26,28,33,34	8.00	16.00	24.00
21-Origin The Ape, Oracle's enemy,			
22-30	6.00	12.00	18.00
31-33	4.00	8.00	12.00
34-Origin The Scarab & only app.	4.00	8.00	12.00
35-40: #36-Last Four Comrades. #40-Last Capt. Future & Oracle	4.00	8.00	12.00
41-Front Page Peggy begins	4.00	8.00	12.00
42,43-Last Pyroman	4.00	8.00	12.00
44-Lance Lewis, Space Detective begins; Ingels cover	3.00	6.00	9.00
45-Tygra begins(origin)	4.00	8.00	12.00
46-Ingels cover/story	4.00	8.00	12.00
47-53: #49-Last Fighting Yank. #50-52-Sea- Eagle app.	3.00	6.00	9.00

NOTE: *Ingels covers-#43,45,46(airbrush). Schomburg (Xela) covers-#43,47-53.*

STARTLING TERROR TALES
5/52 - #14, 2/53; #4, 4/53 - #11, 1954
Star Publications

Star Spangled Comics #95, © DC

Startling Comics #17, © BP

Startling Comics #45, © BP

Star Trek #1, © GK   Star Wars #1, © MCG   Steve Canyon #1, © M. Caniff

(Startling Terror cont'd)	Good	Fine	Mint
#10-Wood/Harrison art(reprints A Star Presentation #3)	3.50	7.00	10.50
11,12,14 (1st Series)	1.25	2.50	3.75
13-Jo-Jo reprint; Disbrow art	1.50	3.00	4.50
#4-11('53-'54)(2nd Series)	.75	1.50	2.25

NOTE: *L. B. Cole covers-#10-14(early).*

STAR TREK (TV) (See Dan Curtis)
July, 1967 - Present
Gold Key

#1	4.00	8.00	12.00
2-5	2.00	4.00	6.00
6-10	1.35	2.75	4.00
11-20	.75	1.50	2.25
21-30	.35	.70	1.05
31-40	.20	.40	.60
41-50	.15	.30	.45

NOTE: *McWilliams art-#38,40,41. #29 reprints #1; #35 reprts. #4; #37 reprts. #5; #45 reprts. #7.*

-- the Enterprise Logs #1(8/76)-Whitman, 224pgs.($1.95)-Reprints #1-8 + 7pgs. by McWilliams	1.50	3.00	4.50
-- the Enterprise Logs #2('76)-Reprts.#9-17	1.00	2.00	3.00
-- the Enterprise Logs #3('77)-Reprts.#18-28	.80	1.60	2.40
-- the Enterprise Logs #4(Wint.'77)-Reprts. #29-37	.80	1.60	2.40

STAR WARS (Movie)
July, 1977 - Present
Marvel Comics Group

#1	1.50	3.00	4.50
2	.50	1.00	1.50
3-7	.20	.40	.60
#1-4(reprints)		.20	.35

NOTE: *Chaykin stories-#1-7; cover-#1. Leialoha art-#2.*

STAR VENTURE
1964
I.W. Enterprises

Reprint #9	.75	1.50	2.25

STEEL, THE INDESTRUCTIBLE MAN
March, 1978
DC Comics, Inc.

#1	.15	.30	.45

STEVE CANYON
Feb, 1948 - #6, Dec, 1948 (Reprints)
Harvey Publications

	Good	Fine	Mint
#1-Origin Steve Canyon	12.00	24.00	36.00
2-6(Caniff art #1-6)	7.00	14.00	21.00
Strictly For the Smart Birds-16pgs., 1951-Information Comics Div.(Harvey) Premium	7.00	14.00	21.00

STEVE CANYON
1959 (96pgs.; no text; 6-3/4"x9"; hardcover; black & white inside)
Grosset & Dunlap

#100100-Reprints 2 stories from strip(1953, 1957)	1.75	3.35	5.00
#100100(Softcover edition)	1.00	2.00	3.00

STEVE CANYON (See 4-Color #519,578,641,737, 804,939,1033 & Harvey Comics Hits #52)

STEVE DONOVAN, WESTERN MARSHAL (TV)
1956
Dell Publishing Co.

4-Color #675,768-Kinstler art	1.50	3.00	4.50
4-Color #880, #1	1.00	2.00	3.00

STEVE ROPER
April, 1948 - #5, Dec, 1948
Famous Funnies

#1-Contains 1944 daily newspaper reprints	2.50	5.00	7.50
2-5	1.75	3.35	5.00

STEVE SAUNDERS SPECIAL AGENT
Dec, 1947 - #8, Sept, 1949
Parents' Magazine Institute

#1	1.20	2.40	3.60
2-8	1.00	2.00	3.00

STEVE SAVAGE (See Captain --)

STEVE ZODIAC & THE FIRE BALL XL-5 (TV)
January, 1964
Gold Key

#1(10108-401)	.35	.70	1.05

STEVIE
1952 - #6, April, 1954
Harvey Magazine Publ./Mazie(Magazine Publ.)

#1	.60	1.20	1.80
2-6	.35	.70	1.05

STONEY BURKE (TV)
June-Aug, 1963 - #2, Sept-Nov, 1963
Dell Publishing Co.

(Stoney Burke cont'd)	Good	Fine	Mint
#1,2	.35	.70	1.05

STONY CRAIG
1946 (No#)
Pentagon Publishing Co.

Reprints Bell Syndicate's "Sgt. Stony Craig" newspaper strips	2.50	5.00	7.50

STORIES BY FAMOUS AUTHORS ILLUSTRATED
Fall, 1950 - #13, May, 1951 (Fast Fiction#1-5)
Seaboard Publ./Famous Authors Ill.

	Good	Fine	Mint
#1-Scarlet Pimpernel-Baroness Orczy	3.00	6.00	9.00
2-Capt. Blood-Rafael Sabatini	3.00	6.00	9.00
3-She, by Haggard	4.00	8.00	12.00
4-The 39 Steps-John Buchan	3.00	6.00	9.00
5-Beau Geste-P.C. Wren	3.00	6.00	9.00

NOTE: The above five issues are exact reprints of **Fast Fiction** Nos. 1-5 except for the title change and new Kiefer covers on Nos. 1 and 2. The above five issues were released before **Famous Authors** No. 6.

6-Macbeth, by Shakespeare; Kiefer art(8/50)	3.00	6.00	9.00
7-The Window; Kiefer art	3.50	7.00	10.50
8-Hamlet, by Shakespeare; Kiefer art	3.00	6.00	9.00
9-Nicholas Nickleby, by Dickens; G. Schrotter art	3.00	6.00	9.00
10-Romeo & Juliet, by Shakespeare; Kiefer art	3.00	6.00	9.00
11-Ben-Hur; Schrotter art	3.50	7.00	10.50
12-LaSvengali; " "	3.00	6.00	9.00
13-Scaramouche; Kiefer "	3.00	6.00	9.00

STORIES OF CHRISTMAS
1942 (32 pgs.) (Paper cover) (Giveaway)
K.K. Publications

Adaptation of "A Christmas Carol"	4.00	8.00	12.00

STORIES OF ROMANCE
#5, 1956 - #13, Aug, 1957
Atlas Comics (LMC)

#5-13	.30	.60	.90

STORMY (See 4-Color Comics #537)

STORY HOUR SERIES (Disney)
1948(32pgs.); 1952-53(36pgs.) (4-3/4"x6½")
Given away with subscription to Walt Disney's
Comics & Stories

Whitman Publishing Co.

	Good	Fine	Mint
#800-Donald Duck in "Bringing Up the Boys";			
1948 Soft Cover	4.00	8.00	12.00
1953	2.00	4.00	6.00
#801-Mickey Mouse's Summer Vacation			
1948 Soft Cover	2.50	5.00	7.50
1951,1952 edition	1.50	3.00	4.50
#803-Bongo			
1948 Soft Cover	2.00	4.00	6.00
#804-Mickey and the Beanstalk			
1948 Soft Cover	2.50	5.00	7.50
1948 Hard Cover Edition of each...$2-$3 more			

STORY OF CHECKS, THE
1972 (5th edition)
Federal Reserve Bank of New York

Severin art	.25	.50	.75

STORY OF JESUS (See Classics Special)

STORY OF MANKIND, THE (See 4-Color #851)

STORY OF MARTHA WAYNE, THE
April, 1956
Argo Publ.

#1-Newspaper reprints	1.50	3.00	4.50

STORY OF RUTH, THE (See 4-Color #1144)

STORY OF THE COMMANDOS, THE (Combined Opera-
1943 (68pgs.) (B&W) (15c) tions)
Long Island Independent (Distr.by Gilberton)

No#-All text (no comics); photos & illustra-tions; ads for Classics Comics on back cover (Rare)	10.00	20.00	30.00

STORY OF THE GLOOMY BUNNY, THE (See March of Comics #9)

STRAIGHT ARROW
Feb-Mar, 1950 - #55, Mar, 1956
Magazine Enterprises

#1-Whitney art	7.00	14.00	21.00
2-Red Hawk begins by Powell, ends #55	3.50	7.00	10.50
3-Frazetta cover	10.00	20.00	30.00
4-10	2.00	4.00	6.00
11-20	1.50	3.00	4.50
21,23-40	1.35	2.75	4.00
22-Frazetta cover	9.00	18.00	27.00
41-55	1.20	2.40	3.60

NOTE: *Powell art in all except #25.*

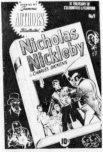

Stories By Famous--#9, © Fam Authors

The Story Of The Commandos, © Long Is.

Straight Arrow #21, © ME

Strange Adventures #19, © DC

Strange Confessions #1, © Z-D

Strange Journey #2, © Ajax

STRAIGHT ARROW'S FURY (See A-1 Comics #119)

STRANGE
March, 1957 - #6, May, 1958
Ajax-Farrell Publ. (Four Star Comic Corp.)

	Good	Fine	Mint
#1	.80	1.60	2.40
2-6	.50	1.00	1.50

STRANGE ADVENTURES
8-9/50 - #244, 10-11/73 (#1-12, 52pgs.)
National Periodical Publications

#1-Adaptation of "Destination Moon"; Kris
   KL-99 & Darwin Jones begin
	20.00	40.00	60.00
2	10.00	20.00	30.00
3,4: Kirby art ea.	8.00	16.00	24.00
5-8: #7-Origin Kris KL-99			
	6.00	12.00	18.00
9-Intro. & origin Captain Comet (6/51)			
	15.00	30.00	45.00
10-15	5.00	10.00	15.00
16-20	4.00	8.00	12.00
21-38	3.00	6.00	9.00
39-Used in Seduction of the Innocent			
	4.00	8.00	12.00
40-49-Last Capt. Comet	2.50	5.00	7.50
50-53-Last pre-code ish.	1.50	3.00	4.50
54-100	1.20	2.40	3.60
101-110: #104-Space Museum begins by Sekowsky			
	.80	1.60	2.40
111-116,118-120: #114-Star Hawkins begins,			
ends #185	.75	1.50	2.25
117-Origin Atomic Knights	3.00	6.00	9.00
121-140: #124-Origin Faceless Creature			
	.60	1.20	1.80
141-160: #159-Star Rovers app. #160-Last Atom-			
ic Knights	.40	.80	1.20
161-179: #161-Last Space Museum. #163-Star			
Rovers app. #177-Origin Immortal Man			
	.30	.60	.90
180-Origin Animal Man	.35	.70	1.05
181-186,188-204	.25	.50	.75
187-Origin The Enchantress	.25	.50	.75
205-Origin Deadman by Infantino; by Neal			
Adams #206 on	4.00	8.00	12.00
206	3.00	6.00	9.00
207-210	2.50	5.00	7.50
211-216-Last Deadman	1.50	3.00	4.50
217-Adam Strange & Atomic Knights reprints			
begin	.25	.50	.75
218-236: #222-New Adam Strange story. #231-			
Last Atomic Knights reprint. #236-Star			
Rovers app.; last Giant issue			
	.20	.40	.60
237-244-Last Adam Strange reprint			
	.15	.30	.45

NOTE: *Adams* stories-#206-216; covers-#207-
218,228,235. *Anderson* stories-#8-52,94,96,
97,99,115,117,119-163; covers or reprints-
#217-233,235-239,241-243. *Ditko* story-#188,
189. *Drucker* stories-#42,43,45. *Finlay* stor-
ies-#2,3,6,7(#210,229 reprints). *Infantino*
stories-#10-101,106-151,154,157-163,180; covers or reprints-#197,199-211,218-221,223-244.
Kaluta cover-#240. *Gil Kane* stories-#8-116,
124,125,130,138,146-157,173-186; reprints-
#204,222,227-231. *Krigstein* story-#32,33.
Kubert stories-#55(2pgs.),226; covers-#219,
225-227,232,234. *Morrow* cover-#230. *Powell*
story-#4. *Mike Sekowsky* stories-#97-162; cov-
er-#206; reprints-#217-219. *Simon & Kirby*-#2
(2pg. reprint). *Toth* stories-#8,12,18,19.
Wood-#154(inks).

STRANGE AS IT SEEMS
1932 (64 pgs.; B&W; square binding)
Blue-Star Publishing Co.
	Good	Fine	Mint
#1-Newspaper reprints	15.00	30.00	45.00

NOTE: *Published with and without No.1 and
price on cover.*

STRANGE AS IT SEEMS
1939
United Features Syndicate

	Good	Fine	Mint
Single Series #9, #1,2	4.00	8.00	12.00

STRANGE CONFESSIONS
Jan-Mar, 1952 - #4, Fall, 1952
Ziff-Davis Publ. Co. (Approved)

#1-Photo cover	2.00	4.00	6.00
2-4	1.20	2.40	3.60

STRANGE FANTASY
Aug, 1952 - #14, Oct-Nov, 1954
Harvey Publ./Ajax-Farrell #2 on

#1-The Black Cat app.	2.50	5.00	7.50
2,5-8,10-14	.80	1.60	2.40
3-Rulah app.	2.50	5.00	7.50
4-Rocket Man app.	1.75	3.50	5.25
9-Some copies have a 32pg. Black Cat comic			
on inside. With......	1.75	3.50	5.25
Without...	.80	1.60	2.40

STRANGE GALAXY (Magazine)
V1#8, Feb, 1971 - #11, Aug, 1971 (B&W)
Eerie Publications

V1#8-Cover reprinted from Fantastic V19#3			
(2/70)(a pulp)	.35	.70	1.05
9-11	.35	.70	1.05

370

STRANGE JOURNEY
Sept, 1957 - #4, June, 1958 (Farrell reprints)
America's Best (Steinway Publ.)(Ajax/Farrell)

	Good	Fine	Mint
#1	1.00	2.00	3.00
2-4	.50	1.00	1.50

STRANGE LOVE
1950   (132 pgs.)
Hero Books/Fox Features Syndicate

No#-Photo cover. See Fox Giants. Contents
can vary and determines price.

STRANGE MYSTERIES
Sept, 1951 - #21, Dec, 1954
Superior/Dynamic Publications

	Good	Fine	Mint
#1	2.00	4.00	6.00
2-5	1.00	2.00	3.00
6-8,10	.65	1.35	2.00
9-Bondage cover	.80	1.60	2.40
11-21	.50	1.00	1.50

STRANGE MYSTERIES
1963 - 1964
I.W. Enterprises/Super Comics

IW Reprint #9   .35   .70 1.05
Super Reprint #10-12,15-17('63-'64): #12-re-
  prints Tales of Horrow #5(3/53) less cov-
  er   .35   .70 1.05
Super Reprint #18-Reprint of Witchcraft #1;
  Kubert story   .65 1.35 2.00

STRANGE PLANETS
1958; 1963-64
I.W. Enterprises/Super Comics

IW Reprint #1(no date)-E.C. Incredible S/F
  #30 + cover/Strange Worlds #3
                       5.00 10.00 15.00
IW Reprint #8   1.00 2.00 3.00
IW Reprint #9-Orlando/Wood story(Strange
  Worlds #4); cover from Flying Saucers #1
                       2.50 5.00 7.50
Super Reprint #10-Wood story from Space Det-
  ective #1 minus cvr. 2.50 5.00 7.50
Super Reprint #11-25pg. Wood story from An
  Earthman on Venus   3.50 7.00 10.50
Super Reprint #12-Wood/Orlando story from
  Rocket to the Moon   2.50 5.00 7.50
Super Reprint #15-Reprints Atlas stories;
  Heath art   1.00 2.00 3.00
Super Reprint #16-Avon's Strange Worlds #6;
  Kinstler art   1.20 2.40 3.60
Super Reprint #17   1.00 2.00 3.00
Super Reprint #18-Reprints Daring Adventures;

	Good	Fine	Mint
Space Busters, Explorer Joe, The Son of Robin Hood; Krigstein art	1.35	2.75	4.00

STRANGE SPORTS STORIES (See Br.& Bold,DC Spec.)
Sept-Oct, 1973 - #6, July-Aug, 1974
National Periodical Publications

#1	.20	.40	.60
2-6		.15	.30

STRANGE STORIES FROM ANOTHER WORLD
(Unknown World #1)
#2, Aug, 1952 - #5, Feb, 1953
Fawcett Publications

#2-5-Painted covers   1.50 3.00 4.50

STRANGE STORIES OF SUSPENSE(Rugged Action#1-4)
#5, Oct, 1955 - #16, Aug, 1957
Atlas Comics (CSI)

#5(#1)   1.75 3.35 5.00
 6,7,9   1.00 2.00 3.00
 8-Williamson/Mayo story, #10-Williamson/
   Crandall + Torres sty. 2.00 4.00 6.00
11,13,16   .80 1.60 2.40
12-Torres story   1.20 2.40 3.60
14-Williamson story   2.00 4.00 6.00
15-Krigstein story   1.35 2.75 4.00
NOTE: *Everett story-#6,7; covers-#11,12.*
Morrow story-#13.

STRANGE STORY
June-July, 1946   (52 pgs.)
Harvey Publications

#1-The Man in Black Called Fate by Powell
                       3.00 6.00 9.00

STRANGE SUSPENSE STORIES (Lawbreakers Suspense Stories #6-15; Captain Atom V1#78 on)
6/52 - #5, 2/53; #16, 1/54 - #77, 10/65;
V3#1, 10/67 - V1#9, 9/69
Fawcett Publ./Charlton Comics

#1(Fawcett)-Powell art 2.50 5.00 7.50
 2-5: #2-4-George Evans horror stories
                       1.50 3.00 4.50
16(1/54)-#23-Last pre-code issue
                       1.00 2.00 3.00
24-35,37-67-Contents change to science fiction   .40   .80 1.20
36-68pgs., Ditko stories 1.00 2.00 3.00
68-74   .25   .50   .75
75-Origin Captain Atom by Ditko
                       1.50 3.00 4.50

Strange Mysteries #1, © Supr

Strange Planets #16, © Super   Strange Suspense Stories #66, © CC

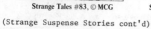

Strange Tales #83, © MCG   Strange Tales Of The Unusual #8, © MCG   Strange Terrors #1, © STJ

(Strange Suspense Stories cont'd)

	Good	Fine	Mint
76,77-Captain Atom	1.00	2.00	3.00
V3#1(10/67)-4	.20	.40	.60
V1#2-9: Everett cover-#13	.15	.30	.45

NOTE: *Ditko stories-#18,20,22,31-35,37,39,41, 45,47,50-52,57,76,77,2('68); covers-#18-20.*

STRANGE TALES (Dr. Strange #169 on)
6/51 - #168, 5/68; #169, 9/73 - #188, 11/76
Atlas(CCPC #1-67/ZPC #68-79/VPI #80-107)/
Marvel #108 on

#1	30.00	60.00	90.00
2	15.00	30.00	45.00
3-5	8.00	16.00	24.00
6-9	6.00	12.00	18.00
10-Krigstein story	7.00	14.00	21.00
11-14,16-20	4.00	8.00	12.00
15-Krigstein story	5.00	10.00	15.00
21,23-32,34	2.50	5.00	7.50
22-Krigstein story	3.00	6.00	9.00
33-Davis story	3.50	7.00	10.50
35-41,43,44,46-52,54,55,57,59,60	1.50	3.00	4.50
42,45,59,61-Krigstein stories	2.00	4.00	6.00
53-Torres, Crandall stys.	2.50	5.00	7.50
56-Crandall story	2.00	4.00	6.00
58,64-Williamson story in each, with Mayo-#58	2.50	5.00	7.50
62-Torres story	1.75	3.50	5.25
63,65,66	1.20	2.40	3.60
67-80-Ditko/Kirby in all	1.35	2.75	4.00
81-90- " " " "	1.00	2.00	3.00
91-100-Kirby art in all	1.00	2.00	3.00
97-Aunt May app.; Kirby art	2.00	4.00	6.00
101-Human Torch begins by Jack Kirby(10/62)	12.00	24.00	36.00
102	7.00	14.00	21.00
103-105	5.00	10.00	15.00
106-109	3.00	6.00	9.00
110-1st app. Dr. Strange by Ditko	5.00	10.00	15.00
111-113	1.50	3.00	4.50
114-Acrobat disguised as Captain America-1st app. since the G.A.; Intro. & 1st app. Victoria Bentley	2.00	4.00	6.00
115-Origin Dr. Strange	4.00	8.00	12.00
116-120	1.20	2.40	3.60
121-125	.80	1.60	2.40
126-129,131-134: Thing/Torch team-up in all; last Human Torch-#134	.65	1.35	2.00
130-The Beatles app.	1.50	3.00	4.50
135-Origin Nick Fury, Agent of Shield by Kirby	1.00	2.00	3.00
136-150: #146-Last Ditko Dr. Strange who is in consecutive stories since #113			

	Good	Fine	Mint
	.50	1.00	1.50
151-168-Steranko art(inks #151-161)	.65	1.35	2.00
169,170-Brother Voodoo origin in ea.; series ends #173	.20	.40	.60
171-177: #174-Origin The Golem. #177-Brunner cover	.20	.40	.60
178-181-Warlock by Starlin	.60	1.20	1.80
182-188	.15	.30	.45
Annual #1(1962)-Reprints from Str. Tales #73 76,78, Tales of Suspense #7,9, Tales to Astonish #1,6,7, & Journey Into Mystery #53,55,59	8.00	16.00	24.00
Annual #2(1963)-Reprints from Str. Tales #67 Str. Worlds(Atlas) #1-3, World of Fantasy #16; Human Torch vs. Spider-Man by Ditko/ Kirby cover	6.00	12.00	18.00

NOTE: *Briefer story-#17. Davis cover-#71. Ditko stories-#50,110,111,114-146. Everett stories-#40-42,45,73,147-152,164(inks); covers-#24,50,51. Jack Katz app.-#26. Kirby Human Torch-#101-104,108,109,114,120; Nick Fury(pencils)-#135,141-143; (layouts)-#136-140,144-153; other Kirby stories-#73,153; layouts-#135-140,144-153; covers-#68-70,72-92,94,101-140. Orlando stories-#41,44,46,49, 52. Powell stories-#44,49. Starlin stories/ covers-#178-181. Woodbridge story-#59. Fantastic Four cameo-#101-134.*

STRANGE TALES OF THE UNUSUAL
Dec, 1955 - #11, Sept, 1957
Atlas Comics (ACI #1-4/WPI #5-12)

#1-Powell story	1.50	3.00	4.50
2,4,6,8,11	.80	1.60	2.40
3-Williamson story,4pgs.	2.50	5.00	7.50
5-Crandall, Ditko stys.	1.35	2.75	4.00
7-Kirby + Orlando	1.00	2.00	3.00
9-Krigstein story	1.35	2.75	4.00
10-Torres + Morrow story	.80	1.60	2.40

NOTE: *Everett story-#2; cover-#11. Orlando story-#7.*

STRANGE TERRORS
June, 1952 - #7, June, 1953
St. John Publishing Co.

#1-Bondage cover	1.75	3.50	5.25
2	1.20	2.40	3.60
3-Kubert story	2.00	4.00	6.00
4-Kubert story(reprinted in Mystery Tales #18); Ekgren cover; has charicature of Jerry Iger	2.00	4.00	6.00
5-Kubert story	2.00	4.00	6.00
6-Giant, 100pgs.; Cameron story(3/53)	2.00	4.00	6.00

(Strange Terrors cont'd)	Good	Fine	Mint
7-Giant, 100pgs.; Kubert story/cover			
	3.00	6.00	9.00

STRANGE WORLD OF YOUR DREAMS
Aug, 1952 - #4, Jan-Feb, 1953
Prize Publications

#1-S&K art	7.00	14.00	21.00
2,3-S&K art	6.00	12.00	18.00
4-S&K cover, Meskin sty.	4.00	8.00	12.00

STRANGE WORLDS (#18 continued from Avon's
11/50 - #22, 9-10/55   Eerie #1-17)
Avon Periodicals

#1-Kenton of the Star Patrol by Kubert; Crom
  the Barbarian by John Giunta
                        12.00 24.00 36.00
2-Wood story-mentioned in Seduction of the
  Innocent; Crom the Barbarian by Giunta;
  Dara of the Vikings app.
                        10.00 20.00 30.00
3-Wood/Orlando story(Kenton), Wood/William-
  son/Frazetta/Krenkel/Orlando story(7pgs.);
  Malu Slave Girl Princess app.; Kinstler
  cover   30.00 60.00 90.00
4,5-Orlando/Wood story in ea.(Kenton); origin The Enchanted Daggar #4; Wood cover-
  #4,5   10.00 20.00 30.00
6-Two Kinstler stories; Orlando/Wood cover,
  Check story   4.00   8.00 12.00
7,9,10: #9-Kinstler sty. 2.00 4.00   6.00
8-Kubert + Kinstler sty. 3.50 7.00 10.50
18-Reprints "Attack on Planet Mars" by
  Kubert   3.50   7.00 10.50
19-Reprints Avon's Robotmen of the Lost Planet   3.50   7.00 10.50
20-22-War stories in all 1.35 2.75   4.00
IW Reprint #5-Kinstler story reprint/Avon's
  #9   1.00   2.00   3.00

STRANGE WORLDS
Dec, 1958 - #5, July-Aug, 1959
Marvel Comics(MPI #1,2/Male #3,5)

#1-Kirby & Ditko art	2.50	5.00	7.50
2	1.50	3.00	4.50
3-Two Kirby stories	2.00	4.00	6.00
4-Williamson story	3.50	7.00	10.50
5-Ditko story	1.35	2.75	4.00

NOTE: Buscema story-#3, Ditko stories-#1-5;
cover-#2. Kirby story-#1,3; covers-#1,3-5.

STREET COMIX   (50¢)
1973   (36 pgs.) (B&W) (20,000 print run)
Street Enterprises/King Features

	Good	Fine	Mint
#1-Rip Kirby	.25	.50	.75
2-Flash Gordon	.25	.50	.75

STRICTLY PRIVATE
1942
Eastern Color Printing Co.

#1,2	10.00	20.00	30.00

STRONG MAN
Mar-Apr, 1955 - #4, Sept-Oct, 1955
Magazine Enterprises

#1(A-1#130)-Powell art   4.00   8.00 12.00
  2(A-1#132), 3(A-1#134), 4(A-1#139)-Powell
  art   3.00   6.00   9.00

STUMBO THE GIANT (See Harvey Hits #50,57,
60,63,72,78,88)

STUMBO TINYTOWN
Oct, 1963 - 1965
Harvey Publications

#1	.50	1.00	1.50
2-13	.25	.50	.75

STUNTMAN COMICS
4-5/46 - #2, 6-7/46; #3, 10-11/46
Harvey Publications

#1-Origin Stuntman by S&K reprinted in Black
  Cat #9   40.00 80.00 120.00
2-S&K art   26.50 53.25 80.00
3-(Extremely Rare)-Small size(5½x8½"; B&W;
  32pgs.)Distributed to mail subscribers only. S&K art. Kid Adonis by S&K reprinted
  in Green Hornet #37. (Sold in San Francisco, 1976 for $700.00)
(Also see All-New #15, Boy Explorers #2, and
Flash Gordon #5)

SUBMARINE ATTACK
#11, May, 1958 - #60, Feb, 1967
Charlton Comics

#11-20	.20	.40	.60
21-60	.15	.30	.45

NOTE: Montes/Bache art-#38,40,41.

SUB-MARINER (See All-Winners, Blonde Phantom,
Daring, Human Torch, Marvel Mystery, Motion
Picture Funnies Weekly, & Namora)

SUB-MARINER, THE (2nd Series)
May, 1968 - #72, Sept, 1974 (#43-52pgs.)
Marvel Comics Group

Strange Worlds #18, © Avon

Stuntman #1, © Harv

Sub-Mariner Comics #1, © MCG

Sub-Mariner Comics #26, © MCG

Sub-Mariner Comics #35, © MCG

Sugar & Spike #1, © DC

(Sub-Mariner cont'd)	Good	Fine	Mint
#1-Origin Sub-Mariner	2.00	4.00	6.00
2	1.00	2.00	3.00
3-5: #5-1st Tiger Shark	.80	1.60	2.40
6-10	.50	1.00	1.50
11-18,20	.40	.80	1.20
19-1st app. Sting Ray	.50	1.00	1.50
21-30: #30-Capt. Marvel app.	.25	.50	.75
31-33,35,37,39,40: #35-Avengers app. #37-			
Death of Lady Dorma	.25	.50	.75
34-Silver Surfer, Hulk app..	.35	.70	1.05
36-Wrightson inks	.50	1.00	1.50
38-Origin	.40	.80	1.20
41-Sub-Mariner vs. H.Torch	.35	.70	1.05
42-49	.25	.50	.75
50-55,57-59-All Everett art.	.35	.70	1.05
61-Last artwork by Everett; 1st 4pgs. com-			
pleted by Mortimer & Mooney			
	.40	.80	1.20
62-1st Tales of Atlantis, ends #66; Chaykin			
art	.20	.40	.60
63-72	.15	.30	.45

NOTE: *Chaykin stories-#62-64. Craig inks-*
#19-21.

Special #1(1971)	.65	1.35	2.00
Annual #2(1/72)	.35	.70	1.05

SUB-MARINER COMICS (1st Series) (Best Love
#33 on)
Spring, 1941 - #32, June, 1949; #33, April,
1954 - #42, Oct, 1955
Timely, #1-32(MPC)/Atlas, #33-42(CCC)

#1-The Sub-Mariner by Everett & The Angel			
begin	250.00	500.00	750.00
2-Everett art	120.00	240.00	360.00
3	80.00	160.00	240.00
4-1pg. Wolverton art	60.00	120.00	180.00
5	50.00	100.00	150.00
6-10: #9-Wolverton art, 4pgs.			
	35.00	70.00	105.00
11-20	25.00	50.00	75.00
21-Last Angel app.	16.50	33.25	50.00
22-Young Allies app.	16.50	33.25	50.00
23-The Human Torch, Namora x-over			
	16.50	33.25	50.00
24-Namora x-over	16.50	33.25	50.00
25-The Blonde Phantom begins, ends #29,31;			
Kurtzman art; Namora x-over			
	16.50	33.25	50.00
26,27	16.50	33.25	50.00
28-Namora cover + story by Everett			
	16.50	33.25	50.00
29-31: #29-The Human Torch app. #31-Capt.			
America app.	16.50	33.25	50.00
32-Origin Sub-Mariner	20.00	40.00	60.00
33-Origin Sub-Mariner; The Human Torch app.			
Namora x-over in Sub-Mariner, #33-42			

	Good	Fine	Mint
	16.50	33.25	50.00
34,35-Human Torch in ea.	10.00	20.00	30.00
36-42	10.00	20.00	30.00

NOTE: *Angel by Gustavson-#1,2.*

SUE & SALLY SMITH (Flying Nurses)
1963
Charlton Comics

V2#48-54		.15	.30

SUGAR & SPIKE
Apr-May, 1956 - #98, Oct-Nov, 1971
National Periodical Publications

#1 (Scarce)	12.00	24.00	36.00
2	5.00	10.00	15.00
3-5	4.00	8.00	12.00
6-10	3.00	6.00	9.00
11-20	2.00	4.00	6.00
21-40	1.00	2.00	3.00
41-98: #85-68pgs., reprints #72. #72-Origin			
& 1st app. Bernie the Brain. #96-68pgs.			
#97,98-52pgs.	.50	1.00	1.50

NOTE: *All written and drawn by Sheldon Mayer.*

SUGAR BEAR
No date   (16 pgs.)   (2½x4½")
Post Cereal Giveaway

"The Almost Take Over of the Post Office"			
	.15	.30	.45
"The Race Across the Atlantic"			
	.15	.30	.45

SUGAR BOWL COMICS
May, 1948 - 1949
Famous Funnies

#1-Toth cover	2.00	4.00	6.00
2,4,5	1.50	3.00	4.50
3-Toth story	2.00	4.00	6.00

SUGARFOOT (See 4-Color #907,992,1059,1098,
1147,1209)

SUMMER FUN (Walt Disney's--)(Formerly Mickey
#2, 1959   Mouse--)
Dell Publishing Co.

#2-Two Barks stories	4.00	8.00	12.00

SUMMER FUN (Formerly Li'l Genius; Holiday
#54, Oct, 1966   (Giant)   Surprise #55)
Charlton Comics

#54		.15	.30

SUMMER LOVE (Formerly Brides in Love)
V2#46, 10/65 - V2#48, Nov, 1968
Charlton Comics

	Good	Fine	Mint
V2#46-Beatle cover/story	1.50	3.00	4.50
47-Beatle story	1.35	2.75	4.00
48		.15	.30

SUMMER MAGIC (See Movie Comics)

SUNDANCE (See 4-Color Comics #1126)

SUNDANCE KID
June, 1971 - #3, Sept, 1971   (52 pgs.)
Skywald Publications

#1-Durango Kid; 2 Kirby Bullseye reprints	.35	.70	1.05
2-Swift Arrow, Durango Kid, Bullseye by S&K; Meskin + 1pg. origin	.20	.40	.60
3-Durango Kid, Billy the Kid, Red Hawk reprints	.15	.30	.45

SUNDAY FUNNIES
1950
Harvey Publications

#1	1.00	2.00	3.00

SUN FUN KOMIKS
1939   (Black, white & red)
Sun Publications

#1	5.00	10.00	15.00

SUN GIRL
Aug, 1948 - #3, Dec, 1948
Marvel Comics

#1-Sun Girl begins; Miss America app.	20.00	40.00	60.00
2-The Blonde Phantom begins, 3	15.00	30.00	45.00

SUNNY, AMERICA'S SWEETHEART
#11, Dec, 1947 - #14, June, 1948
Fox Features Syndicate

#11-14-Feldstein cvr/stys	10.00	20.00	30.00
IW Reprint #9-Feldstein	2.50	5.00	7.50

SUNSET CARSON
Feb, 1951 - #4, 1951
Charlton Comics

#1	1.50	3.00	4.50
2-4	.80	1.60	2.40

SUPER ANIMALS PRESENTS PIDGY & THE
MAGIC GLASSES
Dec, 1953
Star Publications

	Good	Fine	Mint
3-D #1	2.50	5.00	7.50

SUPER BOOK OF COMICS
(32pgs.; later issues-16pgs.)(Omar Bread &
Pan-Am Motor Oil Co. giveaways)
1943 - 1946   (Some numbers repeated)
Dell Publishing Co.

	Good	Fine	Mint
#1-Smilin'Jack(Omar)	4.00	8.00	12.00
1-Dick Tracy	8.00	16.00	24.00
2-Red Ryder Victory Patrol	6.00	12.00	18.00
2-King of the Royal Mtd.	3.50	7.00	10.50
2-Smitty	3.00	6.00	9.00
2-Smilin' Jack(Omar)	4.00	8.00	12.00
3-Captain Midnight	7.00	14.00	21.00
3-Terry & the Pirates	6.00	12.00	18.00
3-Moon Mullins	2.50	5.00	7.50
4-Smitty	3.00	6.00	9.00
4-Andy Panda	3.00	6.00	9.00
5-Don Winslow	3.50	7.00	10.50
5-Smokey Stover(Omar)	3.00	6.00	9.00
5-Terry & the Pirates	6.00	12.00	18.00
6-Don Winslow-McWilliams art	3.50	7.00	10.50
6-King of the Royal Mtd.	3.50	7.00	10.50
6-Porky Pig	3.00	6.00	9.00
7-Dick Tracy	8.00	16.00	24.00
7-Smilin' Jack(Omar)	3.50	7.00	10.50
8-Oswald the Rabbit	2.50	5.00	7.50
9-Alley Oop	3.00	6.00	9.00
9-Terry & the Pirates	5.00	10.00	15.00
10-Elmer Fudd(Omar)	2.00	4.00	6.00
11-Little Orphan Annie	3.00	6.00	9.00
12-Woody Woodpecker	2.50	5.00	7.50
13-Dick Tracy(16pgs)(Omar)	8.00	16.00	24.00
14-Bugs Bunny(Omar)	3.00	6.00	9.00
15-Andy Panda	2.00	4.00	6.00
16-Terry & the Pirates	5.00	10.00	15.00
17-Smokey Stover	3.00	6.00	9.00
18-Porky Pig(Omar)	3.00	6.00	9.00
19-Smilin' Jack(Omar)	3.50	7.00	10.50
20-Oswald the Rabbit(Omar)	3.00	6.00	9.00
21-Gasoline Alley(Omar)	3.00	6.00	9.00
22-Elmer Fudd	2.00	4.00	6.00
23-Little Orphan Annie(Omar)	3.50	7.00	10.50
24-Woody Woodpecker(Omar)	2.00	4.00	6.00
25-Dick Tracy	7.00	14.00	21.00
26-Bugs Bunny(Omar)	2.00	4.00	6.00
27-Andy Panda	1.50	3.00	4.50
28-Terry & the Pirates(1946)(Omar)	5.00	10.00	15.00

Sun Girl #3, © MCG

Sunny #13, © Fox

Super Book #26, © L. Schlesinger

Superboy #38, © DC

Supercar #2, © GK

Super Comics #5, © Dell

(Super Book cont'd)	Good	Fine	Mint
29-Smokey Stover	2.00	4.00	6.00
30-Porky Pig(Omar)	2.00	4.00	6.00
No#-Bugs Bunny('48)	2.00	4.00	6.00
No#-Dan Dunn('39 reprint)	2.00	4.00	6.00
No#-Dick Tracy	6.00	12.00	18.00
No#-Elmer Fudd('46)	2.00	4.00	6.00
No#-Woody Woodpecker	2.00	4.00	6.00

SUPERBOY (-- & the Legion of Super Heroes
with #197) (See More Fun & Aurora)
Mar-Apr, 1949 - Present
National Periodical Publications/DC Comics

#1 (Scarce)	80.00	160.00	240.00
2	40.00	80.00	120.00
3-5	25.00	50.00	75.00
6-10	16.50	33.25	50.00
11-20	9.00	18.00	27.00
21-30	6.00	12.00	18.00
31-40	4.00	8.00	12.00
41-60	2.50	5.00	7.50
61-67,69,70	2.00	4.00	6.00
68-Origin & 1st app. original Bizarro			
(10-11/58)	2.00	4.00	6.00
71-77,79,80: #76-1st Supermonkey			
	1.35	2.75	4.00
78-Origin Mr. Mxyzptlk	2.50	5.00	7.50
81,83-97,99,100: #86-Intro. Pete Ross. #89-			
Intro. Mon-el. #90-Pete Ross learns Super-			
boy's I.D.	1.00	2.00	3.00
82-1st Bizarro Krypto	1.20	2.40	3.60
98-Intro. & origin Ultra Boy			
	1.20	2.40	3.60
101-103,105-120	.65	1.35	2.00
104-Origin Phantom Zone	.80	1.60	2.40
121-140: #129-25¢ Giant G-22. #138-Giant G-35			
	.35	.70	1.05
(80pg. Giant G-22,G-35)	.50	1.00	1.50
141-190: #147,156,165,174-All Giants G-47,			
G-59,G-71,G-83. #147-Origin The Legion of			
Super Heroes. #184-Origin Dial H for Hero.			
#185-100pg. Super Spec. #12			
	.25	.50	.75
(Giants G-47,59,71,83)	.35	.70	1.05
(100pg. Super Spec.#12)	.50	1.00	1.50
191-196,198,199	.25	.50	.75
197-Legion begins	.25	.50	.75
200-Bouncing Boy & Duo Damsel marry			
	.35	.70	1.05
201,202,204,206,207,209	.25	.50	.75
203-Invisible Kid dies	.35	.70	1.05
205-100pgs.	.40	.80	1.20
208-68pgs.	.35	.70	1.05
210-Origin Karate Kid	.35	.70	1.05
211-215,217-220	.20	.40	.60
216-1st app. Tyrol	.25	.50	.75
221-230	.15	.30	.45

	Good	Fine	Mint
231-$1.00 ish	.35	.70	1.05
232-237	.35	.70	1.05
238-Starlin pencils	.35	.70	1.05
Annual #1(6/64)	1.50	3.00	4.50

NOTE: *Adams covers-#143,145,146,148-155,157-
161,163,164,166-168,172,173,175,176,178.
Chaykin pencils-#240. Infantino cover-#171.
Simonson pencils-#237. Staton story-#227.
Wood inks-#152-155,157-161. Legion app.-#172,
173,176,183,184,188,190,191,193,195. See 80-
Page Giant #10.*

SUPER BRAT
January, 1954 - #4, July, 1954
Toby Press

#1-4(1954): #4-Li'l Teevy by Mel Lazarus			
	.50	1.00	1.50
IW Reprint #1,2,3,7,8('58)	.25	.50	.75
IW(Super) Reprint #10('63)	.25	.50	.75

SUPERCAR (TV)
Nov, 1962 - #4, Aug, 1963
Gold Key

#1-Crandall cover	1.00	2.00	3.00
2-4-Crandall covers	.65	1.35	2.00

SUPER CAT
1953 - 1954; Sept, 1957 - #4, May, 1958
Ajax/Farrell Publ. (Four Star Comic Corp.)

#56-58(1st Series)	.35	.70	1.05
#1-4('57-58-Ajax)(2nd Series)			
	.25	.50	.75

SUPER CIRCUS
January, 1951 - #5, 1951
Cross Publishing Co.

#1	.80	1.60	2.40
2-5	.40	.80	1.20

SUPER CIRCUS (TV)
March, 1954 - April, 1956
Dell Publishing Co.

4-Color #542,592,694('54-'56)			
	1.00	2.00	3.00

SUPER COMICS
May, 1938 - #121, Feb-Mar, 1949
Dell Publishing Co.

#1-Terry & the Pirates, The Gumps, Dick			
Tracy, Little Orphan Annie, Gasoline Alley,			
Little Joe, Smilin' Jack begin			
	50.00	100.00	150.00

(Super Comics cont'd)	Good	Fine	Mint
2	25.00	50.00	75.00
3	16.50	33.25	50.00
4	13.50	26.75	40.00
5-10	12.00	24.00	36.00
11-20	10.00	20.00	30.00
21-Origin Magic Morro	9.00	18.00	27.00
22-30	9.00	18.00	27.00
31-40	8.00	16.00	24.00
41-50: #43-Terry & the Pirates ends			
	6.00	12.00	18.00
51-60	5.00	10.00	15.00
61-70	4.00	8.00	12.00
71-100	3.00	6.00	9.00
101-115-Last Dick Tracy	2.50	5.00	7.50
116-121	1.35	2.75	4.00

SUPER COPS, THE
July, 1974   (One Shot)
Red Circle Productions (Archie)

#1-Morrow cover/story	.20	.40	.60

SUPER CRACKED (See Cracked)

SUPER DC GIANT (25¢) (No #1-12)
#13, 9-10/70 - #26, 7-8/71; #27, Fall, 1976
National Periodical Publications

S-13-Binky	.20	.40	.60
S-14-Top Guns of the West; Kubert cover; Trigger Twins, Johnny Thunder, Wyoming Kid reprints	.25	.50	.75
S-15-Western comics; Kubert cover; Pow Wow Smith, Vigilante, Buffalo Bill reprints	.25	.50	.75
S-16-Best of the Brave & the Bold; Kubert art	.35	.70	1.05
S-17-Love 1970	.25	.50	.75
S-18-Three Mouseketeers; Dizzy Dog, Doodles Duck, Bo Bunny reprts.	.20	.40	.60
S-19-Jerry Lewis; 3 stories inked by Adams	.50	1.00	1.50
S-20-House of Mystery-Neal Adams cover; 3 Kirby stories reprinted	.30	.60	.90
S-21-Love 1971	.25	.50	.75
S-22-Top Guns of the West	.25	.50	.75
S-23-Unexpected, The	.25	.50	.75
S-24-Supergirl	.35	.70	1.05
S-25-Challengers of the Unknown-All Kirby/Wood reprints	.35	.70	1.05
S-26-Aquaman('71)	.35	.70	1.05
#27-Strange Flying Saucer Adventures(Fall, '76)	.25	.50	.75

SUPER DOOPER
1946   (Soft cover) (10¢)
Able Publ. Co. (Giveaway)

	Good	Fine	Mint
#1-4,6,7	.65	1.35	2.00
5-Capt. Freedom & Shock Gibson			
	1.75	3.35	5.00

SUPER DUCK COMICS (The Cockeyed Wonder)
Fall, 1944 - #94, Dec, 1960
MLJ Mag. #1-4/Close-Up #5 on (Archie)

#1-Origin	5.00	10.00	15.00
2-10	2.50	5.00	7.50
11-20	1.50	3.00	4.50
21-40	1.00	2.00	3.00
41-94	.75	1.50	2.25

SUPER DUPER
1941
Harvey Publications

#5-Captain Freedom & Shock Gibson app.			
	7.00	14.00	21.00
8,11	4.00	8.00	12.00

SUPER DUPER COMICS (Formerly Latest Comics?)
May-June, 1947
F. E. Howard Publ.

#3-Mr. Monster app.	1.00	2.00	3.00

SUPER FRIENDS (TV)
Nov, 1976 - Present
National Periodical Publications/DC Comics

#1-Superman, Batman, Wonder Woman, Aquaman, Robin, Wendy, Marvin & Wonder Dog begin			
	.20	.40	.60
2-9		.20	.35

SUPER FUN
January, 1956
Gillmor Magazines

#1-Comics, puzzles, cut-outs by A. W. Nugent			
	1.35	2.75	4.00

SUPER FUNNIES (-- Western Funnies #3,4)
Dec, 1953 - #4, 1954   (Satire)
Superior Comics Publishers Ltd. (Canada)

#1(3-D)-Dopey Duck	3.00	6.00	9.00
2	.50	1.00	1.50
3,4-(Western-Phantom Ranger)			
	.50	1.00	1.50

SUPERGEAR COMICS
1976   (4 pgs.)
Jacobs Corp. (Giveaway)

Super Comics #25, © Dell

Super Duck #2, © MLJ

Super Fun #1, © Gillmor

Superior Stories #1, © Nesbit

Super Magician V2#7, © S & S

Superman #1, © DC

(Supergear Comics cont'd) Good Fine Mint
3pg. Lois Lane & Steve Lombard app.
                              .20   .40   .60

SUPERGIRL (See Super DC Giant, Adventure,
Action & Superman Family)
11/72 - #9, 12-1/73-74; #10, 9-10/74
National Periodical Publications

#1   .35   .70 1.05
  2-5: #5-Zatanna origin reprint
                              .25   .50   .75
  6-10   .20   .40   .60
NOTE: _Anderson art-#5. Zatanna in #1-3,5,7;_
Wonder Woman-#9; Prez-#10.

SUPER GOOF (Walt Disney)
Oct, 1965 - Present
Gold Key

#1   .50 1.00 1.50
  2-10   .35   .70 1.05
11-20   .20   .40   .60
21-44   .15   .30   .45
NOTE: _Reprints in #16,24,28,29,37,38,43._

SUPER GREEN BERET (Tod Holton --)
April, 1967 - #2, June, 1967 (68pgs.)
Lightning Comics (Milson Publ. Co.)

#1,2   .65 1.35 2.00

SUPER HEROES (See Marvel --)

SUPER HEROES
Jan, 1967 - #4, June, 1967
Dell Publishing Co.

#1   .50 1.00 1.50
  2-4   .30   .60   .90

SUPER HEROES BATTLE SUPER-GORILLAS
Winter, 1976-77   (One Shot)
National Periodical Publications

#1-Superman, Batman, Flash stories
                              .25   .50   .75

SUPERHEROES VS. SUPERVILLAINS
1966
Archie Publications

#1-Reprints from Archie Superhero comics
                              .65 1.35 2.00

SUPERIOR STORIES
May-June, 1955 - #4, Nov-Dec, 1955
Nesbit Publishing Co.

                              Good Fine Mint
#1-The Invisible Man app. 1.75 3.50 5.25
  2-The Pirate of the Gulf by J. H. Ingrahams
                        1.00 2.00 3.00
  3-Wreck of the Grosvenor 1.00 2.00 3.00
  4-O'Henry's "The Texas Rangers"
                        1.00 2.00 3.00

SUPER MAGIC (Super Magician #2 on)
May, 1941
Street and Smith Publications

V1#1-Blackstone, the Magician app.; origin &
   1st app. Rex King(Black Fury); Eisner
   cover   20.00 40.00 60.00

SUPER MAGICIAN COMICS (Super Magic #1)
#2, Sept, 1941 - V5#8, Feb-Mar, 1947
Street and Smith Publications

V1#2-Rex King, Man of Adventure app.
                        7.00 14.00 21.00
   3-Tao-Anwar, Boy Magician begins
                        6.00 12.00 18.00
   4-Origin Transo   5.00 10.00 15.00
   5-12: #11-Supersnipe app.
                        4.00   8.00 12.00
V2#1-12: #1-The Shadow app.; #5-Origin Tigerman #8-Red Dragon begins
                        1.75   3.35   5.00
V3#1-12: #5-Origin Mr. Twilight
                        1.35   2.75   4.00
V4#1-12: #12-Elliman Nigel begins
                        1.20   2.40   3.60
V5#1-6   1.20   2.40   3.60
   7,8-Red Dragon by Cartier
                        2.75   5.50   8.00

SUPERMAN (See Action Comics, All-Star Comics, Book & Record Set, Giant Comics To Color,
& World's Finest Comics)

SUPERMAN
Summer, 1939 - Present
National Periodical Publications/DC Comics

#1(No#)-1st four Action stories reprinted;
   Origin Superman by Siegel & Shuster; has
   a new 2pg. origin plus 4pgs. omitted in
   Action story   1000.00 2000.00 3000.00
     (Prices vary widely on this book)
  2-All daily strip reprints
                      300.00 600.00 900.00
  3-2nd story reprint from Action #6
                      250.00 500.00 750.00

(Superman cont'd)

	Good	Fine	Mint
4	160.00	320.00	480.00
5	125.00	250.00	375.00
6-10	75.00	150.00	225.00
11-15: #13-Jimmy Olsen app.	40.00	80.00	120.00
16-25	25.00	50.00	75.00

26-29: #28-Lois Lane Girl Reporter series
  begins, ends #40,42   17.50 35.00 52.50
30-Origin & 1st app. Mr. Mxyztplk (pronounced
  "Mix-it-plk"); name later became Mxyzptlk
  ("Mix-yez-pit-1-ick") 25.00 50.00 75.00

31-40	12.00	24.00	36.00
41-50	9.00	18.00	27.00
51,52	7.00	14.00	21.00

53-Origin Superman retold
      16.50 33.25 50.00
54-60   7.00 14.00 21.00
61-Origin Superman retold; origin Green Cryp-
  tonite(1st Kryptonite story)
      9.00 18.00 27.00

| 62-70 | 6.00 | 12.00 | 18.00 |

71-75: Some #75's have #74 on cover
      5.00 10.00 15.00
76-Batman x-over; Superman & Batman learn
  each other's I.D.   8.00 16.00 24.00

77-80	5.00	10.00	15.00
81-90	4.00	8.00	12.00
91-100	3.00	6.00	9.00
101-120	2.50	5.00	7.50

121-130: #123-1st app. Supergirl. #128-1st
  use of Red Kryptonite. #129-Origin &
  1st app. Lori Lemaris, the Mermaid
      2.00 4.00 6.00
131-150: #146-Superman's life story. #147-1st
  app. Legion of Super-Villains
      1.50 3.00 4.50
151-164: #158-1st app. Flamebird & Nightwing
      1.25 2.50 3.75
165-Origin Sally Selwyn   1.50 3.00 4.50
166,168-180   1.00 2.00 3.00
167-New origin Braniac   1.50 3.00 4.50
181,182,184-186,188-192,194-196,198-200: #181-
  1st 2965 story/series   .50 1.00 1.50
183(G-18),187(G-23),193(G-31),197(G-36) - All
  Giants   .60 1.20 1.80
201,203-206,208-211,213-216,218-221,223-226,
  228-231,234-238,241-244 .30 .60 .90
202(G-42),207(G-48),212(G-54),217(G-60),222
  (G-66),227(G-72),232(G-78),239(G-84) -
  All Giants   .50 1.00 1.50
233-1st app. Morgan Edge, Clark Kent switch
  from newspaper reporter to TV newscaster,
240-Kaluta story   .40 .80 1.20
245,252-DC 100pg. Super Spec. #7,13; #252-Ray,
  Black Condor, Starman Hawkman app.
      .60 1.20 1.80
246-248,250,251,253,255-263: #253-2pg. Finley

	Good	Fine	Mint
art	.25	.50	.75

249,254-Adams stories. #249-1st app. Terra-
  Man by Adams(inks) 1.00 2.00 3.00
264-1st app. Steve Lombard .25 .50 .75
265-271,273-277,279-283,285-299
      .20 .40 .60
272,278,284-All 100pgs. .40 .80 1.20
300-Retells origin   .20 .40 .60
301-319   .15 .30 .45

Annual #1(10/60)	6.00	12.00	18.00
Annual #2(1960)	3.00	6.00	9.00
Annual #3(1961)	2.50	5.00	7.50

Annual #4(1961)-Legionairres origins, #5
      1.75 3.35 5.00
Annual #6('62)-Reprints Legion/Adventure#247,
Annual #7('63), #8('64) 1.50 3.00 4.50
The Amazing World of Metropolis Edition-
  (14x10½";$2.00)-Reprints origin
      1.35 2.75 4.00
Pizza Hut Giveaway(12/77)-Exact reprints of
  #97,113   .20 .40 .60
--Special Edition #5(U.S. Navy giveaway,'45)
  52pgs.,regular comic book format
      20.00 40.00 60.00
(See Aurora giveaway)
NOTE: Adams stories-#249(inks),254; covers-
#204-208,210,212-215,219,231,233-237,240-243,
249-252,254,263,306-308,313,314,317. Anderson
stories-#233-270. Wayne Boring art-late 1940's-
early 1960's. Infantino stories-#242,245; cov-
ers-#199,216,238. Kubert cover-#216. Morrow
story-#238.

SUPERMAN & THE GREAT CLEVELAND FIRE(Giveaway)
1948   (4pgs., no cover) (Hospital Fund)
National Periodical Publications

(Rare)(Only one known copy)-in full color
      40.00 80.00 120.00

SUPERMAN COSTUME COMIC
1954   (One Shot)
National Periodical Publications

#1 (Scarce)   8.00 16.00 24.00

SUPERMAN FAMILY, THE (Formerly Superman's Pal
#164, 4-5/74 - Present   Jimmy Olsen)
National Periodical Publications/DC Comics

#164   .40 .80 1.20
165-176-(100-68pgs.) .30 .60 .90
177-181-(52pgs.) .20 .40 .60
182($1.00 ish.begin)-#187 .40 .80 1.20
NOTE: Adams covers-#182-185. Anderson story-
#187.

Superman #8, © DC

Superman #63, © DC

The Great Cleveland Fire, © DC

Superman's Christmas Adv.('40), © DC   Lois Lane #12, © DC   Superman Tim (1948-Illo), © DC

SUPERMAN (Miniature)
1953; 1955 - 1956 (3 issues)No#'s)(32pgs.ea.)
The pages are numbered in the 1st ish: 1-32;
2nd: 1A-32A, & 3rd: 1B-32B
National Periodical Publications

	Good	Fine	Mint
No date-Py-Co-Pay Tooth Powder giveaway (8pgs.; Circa late '40's-early '50's)	8.00	16.00	24.00
#1-The Superman Time Capsule (Kellogg's Sugar Smacks)	6.00	12.00	18.00
1A-Duel in Space	5.00	10.00	15.00
1B-The Super Show of Metropolis (also #1-32, no B)	5.00	10.00	15.00

NOTE: *Numbering variations exist. Each title could have any combination-#1,1A, or 1B.*

SUPERMAN RECORD COMIC
1966   (One Shot)
National Periodical Publications

	Good	Fine	Mint
#1	.50	1.00	1.50

SUPERMAN'S CHRISTMAS ADVENTURE
1940, 1944 (16pgs.) (Giveaway)
Distr. by Nehi drinks, Bailey Store, Ivey-
Keith Co., Kennedy's Boys Shop, Macy's Store
National Periodical Publications

#1(1940)-by Burnley	90.00	180.00	270.00
No#(1944)	65.00	130.00	195.00

SUPERMAN SCRAPBOOK
1940   (10"x17")
Saalfield

Contains Sundays #135,163-172,198,199 + origin from Action #1	16.50	33.25	50.00

SUPERMAN'S GIRLFRIEND LOIS LANE (See 80 Pg. Giants #3,14, Showcase & Superman Family)

SUPERMAN'S GIRLFRIEND LOIS LANE
3-4/58 - #136, 1-2/74; #137, 9-10/74
National Periodical Publications

#1	25.00	50.00	75.00
2	13.50	26.75	40.00
3	10.00	20.00	30.00
4,5	7.00	14.00	21.00
6-10	5.00	10.00	15.00
11-20: #14-Supergirl x-over	3.50	7.00	10.00
21-30: #29-Aquaman, Batman, Green Arrow cameo	1.75	3.35	5.00
31-50	1.00	2.00	3.00
51-67,69,70	.50	1.00	1.50
68-(Giant G-26)	.65	1.35	2.00

	Good	Fine	Mint
70-76,78	.30	.60	.90
77-(Giant G-39)	.50	1.00	1.50
79-Adams covers begin, end #95,108	.50	1.00	1.50
80-85,87-94: #89-Batman x-over; all Adams covers	.50	1.00	1.50
86-(Giant G-51)-Adams cvr.	.40	.80	1.20
95-(Giant G-63)-Wonder Woman x-over; Adams cover	.40	.80	1.20
96-103,106,107,109,110	.25	.50	.75
104-(Giant G-75)	.40	.80	1.20
105-Origin & 1st app. The Rose & the Thorn, 108-Adams cover	.25	.50	.75
111,112,114-120: #111-Morrow story	.20	.40	.60
113-(Giant G-87)	.35	.70	1.05
121-140: #123-G.A. Batman reprt. #136-Wonder Woman x-over	.15	.30	.45
Annual #1(8-10/62)	1.35	2.75	4.00
Annual #2(8-10/63)	.65	1.35	2.00

SUPERMAN'S PAL JIMMY OLSEN (Superman Family #164 on) (See 80 Pg. Giants)
Sept-Oct, 1954 - #163, Feb-Mar, 1974
National Periodical Publications

#1	40.00	80.00	120.00
2	20.00	40.00	60.00
3	15.00	30.00	45.00
4,5	10.00	20.00	30.00
6-10	6.00	12.00	18.00
11-20	4.00	8.00	12.00
21-30	2.00	4.00	6.00
31-40: #31-Origin Elastic Lad. #33-1pg. biography of Jack Larson(T.V. Jimmy Olsen)	1.50	3.00	4.50
41-50	1.00	2.00	3.00
51-70	.65	1.35	2.00
71-78,80-90	.50	1.00	1.50
79(9/64)-Titled The Red-headed Beetle of 1000 B.C.	1.00	2.00	3.00
91-94,96-103,105-110	.40	.80	1.20
95(G-25),104(G-38)-Giants	.50	1.00	1.50
111,112,114-121,123-130,132	.30	.60	.90
113(G-50),122(G-62),131(G-74)-Giants	.50	1.00	1.50
133-Newsboy Legion by Kirby begins	.80	1.60	2.40
134-139	.50	1.00	1.50
140-(Giant G-86)	.35	.70	1.05
141-Newsboy Legion reprints by S&K begin	.50	1.00	1.50
142-148-N.L. reprints	.50	1.00	1.50
149,150-G.A. Plastic Man reprint in both	.25	.50	.75
151-163	.15	.30	.45

NOTE: *Issues #141-148 contain Simon & Kirby Newsboy Legion reprints from Star Spangled*

(Superman's Pal Jimmy Olsen cont'd)
#7,8,9,10,11,12,13,14 in that order. _Adams_
covers-#109-112,115,117,118,120,121,132,134-
136,146-148. _Kirby_ *stories-#133-139,141-148;*
covers-#133,139,142,143,146. _Kirby/Adams_ *cov-*
ers-#137,138,141,144,145.

SUPERMAN SPECTACULAR (See DC Spec.Series #5)

SUPERMAN 3-D (See 3-D --)

SUPERMAN-TIM (Becomes Gene Autry-Tim)
1945 - 50 (½-Size) (B&W Giveaway)
Superman-Tim Stores/National Per. Publ.

	Good	Fine	Mint
Issues with a Superman story			
	15.00	30.00	45.00
Issues with a Superman text illos			
	10.00	20.00	30.00
Issues without Superman	7.00	14.00	21.00

SUPERMAN VS. SPIDER-MAN
April, 1976 (100pgs.) ($2.00) (Over-sized)
National Periodical Publications

Single longest story ever done in one issue			
of a comic book	1.00	2.00	3.00

SUPERMAN WORKBOOK
1945   (One Shot) (68 pgs.) (B&W)
National Per.Publ./Juvenile Group Foundation

	12.00	24.00	36.00

SUPERMOUSE (-- The Big Cheese)
Dec, 1948 - #45, Fall, 1958
Standard Comics/Pines #12 on(Literary Ent.)

#1-3,5,6-Text illos by Frazetta in all			
	2.00	4.00	6.00
4-7pg. text story with Frazetta illos			
	2.50	5.00	7.50
7-10	1.35	2.75	4.00
11-20	.80	1.60	2.40
21-45	.50	1.00	1.50
#1-Summer Holiday issue-Summer'57(Pines)			
(100pgs.)	1.00	2.00	3.00
2-Giant Summer issue-Summer '58(Pines)			
(100pgs.)	.75	1.50	2.25

SUPER-MYSTERY COMICS
July, 1940 - V8#6, July, 1949
Ace Magazines

V1#1-Magno, the Magnetic Man & Vulcan begin			
	35.00	70.00	105.00
2	16.50	33.25	50.00
3-The Black Spider begins			
	16.50	33.25	50.00

	Good	Fine	Mint
4-Origin Davy	16.50	33.25	50.00
5-Intro. The Clown	15.00	30.00	45.00
6	12.00	24.00	36.00
V2#1-Origin Buckskin	12.00	24.00	36.00
2-6	10.00	20.00	30.00
V3#1,2	8.00	16.00	24.00
3-Intro. The Lancer; Dr. Nemesis & The			
Sword begin; cover & 2 stories by Kurtz-			
man(Mr. Risk & Paul Revere Jr.)			
	10.00	20.00	30.00
4-Kurtzman story	8.00	16.00	24.00
5-Two Kurtzman stys.	9.00	18.00	27.00
6-Mr. Risk app.; Kurtzman's Paul Revere			
Jr.	9.00	18.00	27.00
V4#1-6	4.00	8.00	12.00
V5#1-6	3.00	6.00	9.00
V6#1-5: #4-Last Magno; Mr. Risk app. in #2,			
4-6	2.00	4.00	6.00
V7#1-6, V8#1-6	2.00	4.00	6.00

SUPERNATURAL THRILLERS
12/72 - #6, 11/73;   #7, 7/74 - #15, 10/75
Marvel Comics Group

#1-It!	.40	.80	1.20
2-The Invisible Man	.35	.70	1.05
3-The Valley of the Worm	.50	1.00	1.50
4-Dr. Jekyll & Mr. Hyde	.20	.40	.60
5-The Living Mummy	.15	.30	.45
6-The Headless Horseman	.15	.30	.45
7-The Living Mummy begins	.15	.30	.45
8-15	.15	.30	.45

NOTE: _Brunner_ *cover-#11.* _Robert E. Howard_
story-#3. _Steranko_ *covers-#1,2.*

SUPER PUP
#4, Mar-Apr, 1954 - #5, 1954
Avon Periodicals

#4,5	.50	1.00	1.50

SUPER RABBIT (See Wisco)
Fall, 1943 - #14, 1949
Timely Comics (CmPI)

#1	2.50	5.00	7.50
2,3	1.35	2.75	4.00
4,5,7-10,12-14	1.00	2.00	3.00
6-Origin	1.20	2.40	3.60
11-Kurtzman's "Hey Look"	1.75	3.35	5.00
IW Reprint #1,2('58),7,10('63)			
	.40	.80	1.20

SUPER RICHIE
Sept, 1975 - Present
Harvey Publications

Superman Tim (1949-Illo), © DC

Supermouse #1, © Std

Super Mystery V2#1, © Ace

Supersnipe Comics V2#1, © S & S   Superworld #2, © Hugo Gernsback   Suspense #8, © Hoke

(Super Richie cont'd)	Good	Fine	Mint
#1	.15	.30	.45
2-12		.15	.30

SUPERSNIPE COMICS (Army & Navy #1-5)
Oct, 1942 - V5#1, Aug-Sept, 1949
Street & Smith Publications

	Good	Fine	Mint
V1#6-Rex King Man of Adventure by Jack Binder begins; Supersnipe continues from Army & Navy #5; Bill Ward art	6.00	12.00	18.00
7-12: #9-Doc Savage x-over in Supersnipe #11-Little Nemo app.	5.00	10.00	15.00
V2#1-12	4.00	8.00	12.00
V3#1-12	3.00	6.00	9.00
V4#1-12, V5#1	2.00	4.00	6.00

NOTE: _Doc Savage in some issues._

SUPERSPOOK (Formerly Frisky Animals on Parade)
1958
Ajax/Farrell Publications

#4	.35	.70	1.05

SUPER SPY (See Wham)
Oct, 1940 - #2, Nov, 1940
Centaur Publications

#1-Origin The Sparkler	15.00	30.00	45.00
2	10.00	20.00	30.00

SUPER-TEAM FAMILY
10-11/75 - #15, 3-4/78   (#1-3, 68pgs.)
National Periodical Publications/DC Comics

#1-Reprints; Adams, Wood, Infantino art	.40	.80	1.20
2,3: #2-The Creeper app.; Adams reprt. #3-Brunner cover, Wood art; Adams reprint	.25	.50	.75
4-7-Reprints	.20	.40	.60
8-Challs. of Unknown reprints begin	.20	.40	.60
9,10,12-15	.15	.30	.45
11-Weiss art	.15	.30	.45

SUPER TV HEROES (See Hanna-Barbera --)

SUPER-VILLAIN TEAM-UP
August, 1975 - #14, Oct, 1977
Marvel Comics Group

#1-Sub-Mariner app.	.40	.80	1.20
2-5: #4-Mooney art	.25	.50	.75
6-Starlin cover	.25	.50	.75
7-14	.15	.30	.45

NOTE: _Everett pencils-#1._
Giant-Size #1(10/74, 68pgs.)-Craig inks

	Good	Fine	Mint
	.50	1.00	1.50
Giant-Size #2(7/75- 68pgs.)-Dr. Doom, Sub-Mariner app.	.40	.80	1.20

SUPER WESTERN COMICS
Aug, 1950 - #9, Dec, 1951
Youthful Magazines

#1-Buffalo Bill begins; Powell art	.80	1.60	2.40
2-9	.50	1.00	1.50

SUPER WESTERN FUNNIES (See Super Funnies)

SUPERWORLD COMICS
April, 1940 - #3, Aug, 1940
Hugo Gernsback (Komos Publ.)

#1-Origin Hip Knox, Super Hypnotist; Mitey Powers & Buzz Allen, the Invisible Avenger, Little Nemo begin	23.50	46.75	70.00
2-Marvo 1,2 Go+, the Super Boy of the Year 2680	16.50	33.25	50.00
3	12.00	24.00	36.00

SURE FIRE (See Lightning & Veri Best --)

SURF 'N' WHEELS
Nov, 1969 - #20, 1972
Charlton Comics

#1-20?		.10	.20

SURF'TOONS (Magazine)
1965   (50¢)
Petersen Publishing Co.

#1('65)(no month)	.35	.70	1.05
Many issues, no #'s	.25	.50	.75

SURPRISE ADVENTURES
1955 - #5, July, 1955
Sterling Comic Group

#3-5: #5-Sekowsky art	.65	1.35	2.00

SUSPENSE COMICS
Dec, 1943 - #12, Sept, 1946
Holyoke Publications

#1-The Grey Mask begins	5.00	10.00	15.00
2-Intro. The Mask	3.50	7.00	10.50
3-10: #3,5-Schomburg cvr.	2.50	5.00	7.50
11,12	2.00	4.00	6.00

SUSPENSE COMICS (Radio)(Real Life Tales of--
12/49 - #29, 4/53 (#1-7,17,18-52pgs.)   #1,2)
Marvel/Atlas Comics(CnPC #1-1/BFP #11-29)

(Suspense Comics cont'd)	Good	Fine	Mint
#1-Powell art	3.00	6.00	9.00
2-Crime stories	1.50	3.00	4.50
3-Change to horror	1.50	3.00	4.50
4,6-17,19-21,23-29	1.00	2.00	3.00
5,18,22-Krigstein story	1.50	3.00	4.50

NOTE: *Briefer story-#27. Everett stories-#5,
6,19,28; covers-#21,22. Robinson story-#29.
Whitney stories-#15,16,22.*

SUSPENSE DETECTIVE
June, 1952 - #5, Feb, 1953
Fawcett Publications

#1	1.50	3.00	4.50
2-5: #4-Bondage cover	1.00	2.00	3.00

SUSPENSE STORIES (See Strange Suspense Stor.)

SUZIE COMICS (Formerly Laugh Comics)
1945 - 1954
MLJ Mag./Close-Up #51 on (Archie)

#49	5.00	10.00	15.00
50-55	2.50	5.00	7.50
56-65	1.75	3.35	5.00
66-80	1.35	2.75	4.00
81-100	1.00	2.00	3.00

NOTE: *Katy Keene in #62,64,66,85,94-96.*

SUZIE Q. SMITH (See 4-Color #323,377,453,553)

SWAMP FOX, THE (See 4-Color Comics #1179)

SWAMP FOX, THE
1960 (14 pgs.) (Canada Dry Premiums)
Walt Disney Productions

Titles: A. Tory Masquerade, B. Rindau Rampage,
  C. Turnabout Tactics   .80   1.60   2.40

SWAMP THING (See House of Secrets #92)
Oct-Nov, 1972 - #24, Aug-Sept, 1976
National Periodical Publications

#1-Cover/stories by Wrightson begin			
	3.00	6.00	9.00
2-Intro. Patchworkman; continues #3			
	1.50	3.00	4.50
3-5	1.20	2.40	3.60
6-10: #7-Batman app. #10-Last Wrightson			
issue	.90	1.80	2.70
11-15-Redondo art	.50	1.00	1.50
16-23-Redondo art; S.T. reverts back to Dr.			
Holland-#23	.35	.70	1.05
24	.20	.40	.60

   (Also see DC Special Series #2)

SWAT MALONE
Sept, 1955
Swat Malone Enterprises

	Good	Fine	Mint
V1#1-Hy Fleishman art	1.00	2.00	3.00

SWEENEY (Buz Sawyer's Pal, Roscoe --)
1949
Standard Comics

#4,5-Crane art #5	1.75	3.35	5.00

SWEE'PEA (See 4-Color Comics #219)

SWEETHEART DIARY
1949 - 1969
Fawcett/Charlton Publications

#1	1.75	3.35	5.00
2-20	.65	1.35	2.00
21-50	.35	.70	1.05
51-107		.15	.30

SWEETHEART LOVE STORIES
Oct, 1955
Charlton Comics

#32	.20	.40	.60

SWEETHEARTS (Formerly Captain Midnight)
#68, Oct, 1948 - #125, Sept, 1954
Fawcett/Charlton

#68	1.00	2.00	3.00
69-80	.65	1.35	2.00
81-84,86-102,104-125	.25	.50	.75
85,103-George Evans art	.65	1.35	2.00

SWEETHEARTS
V2#24, 1956 - #134, June, 1973
Charlton Comics

V2#24('56) - 50	.20	.40	.60
51-134		.15	.30

SWEETIE PIE (See 4-Color #1185,1241)

SWEETIE PIE
Dec, 1955 - #15, Fall, 1957
Ajax/Pines (Literary Ent.)

#1-by Napine Seltzer	.50	1.00	1.50
2-15	.25	.50	.75

SWEET LOVE
1949
Home Comics (Harvey)

Suzie #73, © MLJ

Swamp Thing #1, © DC

Sweetheart Diary #1, © Faw

Swift Arrow #2, © Ajax   Best Seller #1, © UFS   Tales Calculated To-#1, © AP

(Sweet Love cont'd)	Good	Fine	Mint
#1	1.00	2.00	3.00
2-5	.50	1.00	1.50

SWEET ROMANCE
October, 1968
Charlton Comics

#1		.10	.20

SWEET SIXTEEN
Aug-Sept, 1946 - #13, Jan, 1948
Parents' Magazine Institute

#1-Van Johnson's life story			
	1.50	3.00	4.50
2-13	1.00	2.00	3.00

SWIFT ARROW
Feb-Mar, 1954 - #5, Oct-Nov, 1954; 1957
Ajax/Farrell Publications

#1(1954)(1st Series)	1.00	2.00	3.00
2-5	.65	1.35	2.00
1(2nd Series)(Swift Arrow's Gunfighters #4)			
	1.00	2.00	3.00
2,3(9/57)-Lone Rider begins #2			
	.50	1.00	1.50

SWIFT ARROW'S GUNFIGHTERS (Formerly Swift
#4, Nov, 1957   Arrow)
Ajax/Farrell Publ. (Four Star Comic Corp.)

#4	.50	1.00	1.50

SWING WITH SCOOTER
June-July, 1966 - #36, Oct-Nov, 1972
National Periodical Publications

#1	.50	1.00	1.50
2-10	.25	.50	.75
11-20	.15	.30	.45
21-32,35,36		.20	.35
33-Interview with David Cassidy			
	.20	.40	.60
34-Interview with Rick Ely(Doc Savage)			
	.20	.40	.60

NOTE: *Orlando covers-#1,2,10,11,13; stories-
#1-3,6,11. #20,33,34-68pgs.; #35-52pgs.*

SWISS FAMILY ROBINSON (See 4-Color #1156 &
Movie Comics)

SWORD & THE DRAGON, THE (See 4-Color #1118)

SWORD & THE ROSE, THE (See 4-Color #505,682)

SWORD IN THE STONE, THE (See March of Comics
#258 & Movie Comics)

SWORD OF LANCELOT (See Movie Classics)

SWORD OF SORCERY (See Wonder Woman #201)
Feb-Mar, 1973 - #5, Nov-Dec, 1973
National Periodical Publications

		Good	Fine	Mint
#1-Leiber Fafhrd & The Gray Mouser; Adams/				
Bunkers inks; also #2; Kaluta cover				
		.65	1.35	2.00
2-Wrightson cover inks		.50	1.00	1.50
3-Wrightson story		.65	1.35	2.00
4		.40	.80	1.20
5-Starlin art		.60	1.20	1.80

NOTE: *Chaykin art-#2,3.*

TAFFY
Mar-Apr, 1945 - #12, 1948
Rural Home/Orbit Publ.

#1-Origin of Wonderworm + 7 chapter WWII			
Funny Animal Adv.	1.35	2.75	4.00
2-12	.65	1.35	2.00

TAILSPIN
November, 1944
Spotlight Publishers

No#-Firebird app.	2.00	4.00	6.00

TAILSPIN TOMMY STORY & PICTURE BOOK
1931? (No date)(Color strip reprints)(10½x10")
McLoughlin Bros.

#266-by Forrest	10.00	20.00	30.00

TAILSPIN TOMMY
1932   (86 pgs.) (Hardcover)
Cupples & Leon Co.

(Rare)-B&W strip reprints from 1930 by Hal			
Forrest & Glenn Claffin	16.50	33.25	50.00

TAILSPIN TOMMY
1937 - 1940
United Features Synd./Service Publ. Co.

Single Series #23('40)	8.00	16.00	24.00
Best Seller #1('46)-Service Publ. Co.			
	6.00	12.00	18.00

TALES CALCULATED TO DRIVE YOU BATS
Nov, 1961 - #7, Nov, 1962
Archie Publications

#1		3.00	6.00	9.00
2		1.50	3.00	4.50
3-6		1.00	2.00	3.00
7-Story line change	.65	1.35	2.00	
1-('66-25¢)(reprts.#1,2)	1.00	2.00	3.00	

TALES FROM THE CRYPT (Formerly The Crypt of Terror #17-19)
#20, Oct-Nov, 1950 - #46, Feb-Mar, 1955
E.C. Comics

	Good	Fine	Mint
#20	40.00	80.00	120.00
21-Kurtzman reprt/Haunt of Fear #15/1	25.00	50.00	75.00
22-30: #22-Moon Girl cameo 1 panel	15.00	30.00	45.00
31-Williamson story	17.50	35.00	52.50
32,34-40	10.00	20.00	30.00
33-Origin The Crypt Keeper	15.00	30.00	45.00
41-46	10.00	20.00	30.00

NOTE: *Craig* stories-#20,22-24; cover-#20. *Crandall* stories-#38,44. *Davis* stories-#23, 24-46; covers-#29-46. *Elder* stories-#37,38. *Evans* stories-#32-34,36,40,41,43,46. *Feldstein* stories-#20-23; covers-#21-25,28. *Ingels* stories in all. *Kamen* stories-#20,22, 25,27-31,33-36,39,41-45. *Krigstein* stories-#40,42,45. *Kurtzman* story-#21. *Orlando* stories-#27-30,35,37,39,46. *Wood* stories-#21,24, 25; covers-#26,27. *Canadian reprints known; see Table of Contents.*

TALES FROM THE CRYPT (Magazine)
#10, July, 1968 (35¢) (B&W)
Eerie Publications

#10-Contains Farrell reprints from 1950's	.35	.70	1.05

TALES FROM THE GREAT BOOK
Feb, 1955 - #4, Jan, 1956
Famous Funnies

#1	1.00	2.00	3.00
2-4: #4-Lehti art	.65	1.35	2.00

TALES FROM THE TOMB
Oct, 1962 - #2, Dec, 1962
Dell Publishing Co.

#1(02-810-210)(Giant)-All stories written by John Stanley	1.75	3.50	5.25
2	1.75	3.50	5.25

TALES FROM THE TOMB (Magazine) (52 pgs.)
V1#6, July, 1969 - V6#6, Dec, 1974
Eerie Publications

V1#6	.50	1.00	1.50
7,8	.40	.80	1.20
V2#1-3,5,6	.35	.70	1.05
4-LSD story reprt./Weird V3#5	.35	.70	1.05

	Good	Fine	Mint
V3#1-Rulah reprint	.35	.70	1.05
2-6('70),V4#1-6('72),V5#1-6('73), V6#1-6('74)	.20	.40	.60

TALES OF ASGARD
Oct, 1968 (One Shot) (68 pgs.)
Marvel Comics Group

#1-Thor reprints from Journey into Mystery #97-106; new Kirby cvr.	.80	1.60	2.40

TALES OF DEMON DICK & BUNKER BILL
1934 (78 pgs.) (5x10½") (B&W) (Hardcover)
Whitman Publishing Co.

#793-by Dick Spencer	5.00	10.00	15.00

TALES OF EVIL
Feb, 1975 - #3, June, 1975
Atlas/Seaboard Publ.

#1	.20	.40	.60
2-Intro. The Bog Beast	.15	.30	.45
3-Origin The Man-Monster	.15	.30	.45

TALES OF GHOST CASTLE
May-June, 1975 - #3, Sept-Oct, 1975
National Periodical Publications

#1-2pg. Redondo art	.20	.40	.60
2,3	.15	.30	.45

TALES OF HORROR
June, 1952 - #13, Oct, 1954
Toby Press/Minoan Publ. Corp.

#1	1.50	3.00	4.50
2-8	1.00	2.00	3.00
9-Origin Purple Claw	2.00	4.00	6.00
10-13-Purple Claw	1.50	3.00	4.50

TALES OF JUSTICE (Formerly Justice)
#58, Feb, 1956 - #67, Aug, 1957
Atlas Comics (MjMC #63-66/Male #67)

#58,59-Krigstein stories	1.50	3.00	4.50
60-63,65	.60	1.20	1.80
64-Crandall story	1.50	3.00	4.50
66-Torres + Orlando sty.	1.00	2.00	3.00
67-Crandall story	1.50	3.00	4.50

NOTE: *Everett* story-#60. *Orlando* stories-#65,66.

TALES OF SUSPENSE (Capt. America #100 on)
Jan, 1959 - #99, March, 1968
Atlas(WPI #1,2/Male #3-12/VPI #13-40)/Marvel #41 on

Tales From The Crypt #34, © WMG

Tales From The Tomb #1, © Dell

Tales Of Horror #1, © Toby

Tales Of Suspense #72, © MCG

Tales Of Terror Annual #2, © WMG

Tales Of The Unexpected #84, © DC

(Tales of Suspense cont'd)	Good	Fine	Mint
#1-Williamson sty.,5pgs.	20.00	40.00	60.00
2,3	10.00	20.00	30.00
4-Williamson story,4pgs.	8.00	16.00	24.00
5-10	4.00	8.00	12.00
11,13-22	2.50	5.00	7.50
12-Crandall story	3.00	6.00	9.00
23-38	1.50	3.00	4.50
39-Origin & 1st app. Iron Man; 1st Iron Man			
story-Kirby layouts	35.00	70.00	105.00
40-Iron Man in new armor	10.00	20.00	30.00
41	7.00	14.00	21.00
42-45: #45-Intro. & 1st app. Happy & Pepper			
	4.00	8.00	12.00
46,47	2.50	5.00	7.50
48-New Iron Man	2.50	5.00	7.50
49-51	1.50	3.00	4.50
52-1st app. The Black Widow			
	1.75	3.50	5.25
53-Origin The Watcher(5/64); Black Widow			
app.	1.50	3.00	4.50
54-56	1.35	2.75	4.00
57-Origin Hawkeye(9/64)	1.35	2.75	4.00
58-Captain America begins(10/64)			
	1.50	3.00	4.50
59-Iron Man + Captain America features begin,			
	1.00	2.00	3.00
60,61,64	.75	1.35	2.25
62-Origin Mandarin(2/65)	.80	1.60	2.40
63-Origin Captain America(3/65),			
65-1st Red Skull(6/65)	1.00	2.00	3.00
66-Origin Red Skull	1.00	2.00	3.00
67-99	.75	1.35	2.25

NOTE: *Craig inks(Iron Man)-#99. Crandall
story-#12. Davis story-#38. Ditko Iron Man-
#47-49. Ditko/Kirby art in most all issues
#1-35,37. Kirby Captain America-#59-75,77-
86,92-99; layouts-#69-75,77; covers-#58-72,
74,76,78,80,82,84,86,92,94,96. Kirby pencils
(Iron Man)-#40,41,43; covers-#39-44,46-56.
Wood inks(Iron Man)-#71.*

TALES OF SWORD & SORCERY (See Dagar)

TALES OF TERROR
1952 (no month) - #6, Aug, 1953
Toby Press Publications

#1	1.35	2.75	4.00
2-6	1.00	2.00	3.00

TALES OF TERROR (See Movie Classics)

TALES OF TERROR (Magazine)
Summer, 1964
Eerie Publications

#1	.75	1.50	2.25

TALES OF TERROR ANNUAL
1951 - 1953   (25¢)
E.C. Comics

	Good	Fine	Mint
#1(1951) (Rare)	250.00	500.00	750.00
2(1952) (Scarce)	135.00	270.00	405.00
3(1953)	80.00	160.00	240.00

No. 1 contains both horror and science fiction stories which came
out in 1950. No. 2 contains horror and science fiction stories
which came out in 1951, and No. 3, 1952 stories. All E. C.
annuals contain four complete books that didn't sell on the
stands which were rebound in the annual format, minus the
covers, and sold from the E. C. office for the most part. The
contents of each book will vary in same year.

TALES OF TERROR ILLUSTRATED (See Terror Ill.)

TALES OF TEXAS JOHN SLAUGHTER(See 4-Color#997)

TALES OF THE GREEN BERET
Jan, 1967 - #5, Oct, 1969
Dell Publishing Co.

#1	.25	.50	.75
2-5: #5 reprint #1	.20	.40	.60

NOTE: *Glanzman art-#1-4.*

TALES OF THE INVISIBLE (See Harvey Comics
Hits #59)

TALES OF THE KILLERS (Magazine)
V1#10, 12/70 - V1#11, 2/71 (52pgs.)(B&W)
World Famous Periodicals

V1#10-1pg. Frazetta	1.20	2.40	3.60
11	.80	1.60	2.40

TALES OF THE MARINES (Devil-Dog Dugan #3)
Feb, 1957   (Marines at War #5 on)
Atlas Comics (OPI)

#4-Powell art	.65	1.35	2.00

TALES OF THE MYSTERIOUS TRAVELER
Aug, 1956 - #13, June, 1959
Charlton Comics

#1-Ditko art	3.00	6.00	9.00
2-10-Ditko art	2.00	4.00	6.00
11,12-Ditko covers only	1.50	3.00	4.50
13-No Ditko	1.00	2.00	3.00

TALES OF THE PONY EXPRESS(See 4-Color#829,942)

TALES OF THE TEXAS RANGERS (Jace Pearson's)
1952 - 1959
Dell Publishing Co./Nesbit Publ.

4-Color #396	1.35	2.75	4.00

(Tales of Texas Rangers cont'd)

	Good	Fine	Mint
#2(5-7/53)	1.35	2.75	4.00
3-10	1.00	2.00	3.00
4-Color #648(9/55)	1.20	2.40	3.60
#11-22	1.00	2.00	3.00
4-Color #961-Toth art	1.75	3.50	5.25
4-Color #1021	.90	1.80	2.70

TALES OF THE UNEXPECTED (The Unexpected #105 on)
2-3/56 - #104, 12-1/68 (See Super DC Giant)
National Periodical Publications

		Good	Fine	Mint
#1		8.00	16.00	24.00
2		4.00	8.00	12.00
3-10		2.50	5.00	7.50
11,12,14,15		1.50	3.00	4.50
13,15-18,22,23: Kirby or S&K art. #16-Character named "Thor" with a magic hammer-not like later Thor		2.00	4.00	6.00
19-22,24-39: #24-Cameron story		.75	1.50	2.25
40-Space Ranger begins, ends #82		2.00	4.00	6.00
41-50		.80	1.60	2.40
51-70		.50	1.00	1.50
71-100: #91-1st Automan(also in #94,97)		.30	.60	.90
101-104		.20	.40	.60

NOTE: _Adams cover-#104. Anderson story-#50._
Bob Kane story-#48. Kirby cover-#22.

TALES OF THE WEST (See 3-D ---)

TALES OF THE WIZARD OF OZ (See 4-Color #1308)

TALES OF THE ZOMBIE (Magazine)
8/73 - #10, 3/75   (75¢) (B&W)
Marvel Comics Group

	Good	Fine	Mint
V1#1-Reprint/Menace #5; origin	.65	1.35	2.00
2,3	.50	1.00	1.50
V2#1(#4),5-7,9,10	.35	.70	1.05
8-Kaluta story	.50	1.00	1.50
Annual #1(Sum,'75)(B&W)	.35	.70	1.05

NOTE: _Alcala stories-#6-9._

TALES OF VOODOO (Magazine)
V1#11, Nov, 1968 - V7#6, Nov, 1974
Eerie Publications

	Good	Fine	Mint
V1#11	.65	1.35	2.00
V2#1(3/69)-V2#4(9/69)	.35	.70	1.05
V3#1-6('70)	.25	.50	.75
V4#1-6('71), V5#1-6('72), V6#1-6('73), V7#1-6('74)	.20	.40	.60
Annual #1	1.00	2.00	3.00

TALES OF WELLS FARGO (See 4-Color #876,968, 1023,1075,1113,1167,1215)

TALES TO ASTONISH (The Hulk #102 on)
Jan, 1959 - #101, March, 1968
Atlas(MAP#1/ZPC#2-14/VPI#15-42)/Marvel#43 on

	Good	Fine	Mint
#1-Jack Davis story	20.00	40.00	60.00
2	10.00	20.00	30.00
3	7.00	14.00	21.00
4	5.00	10.00	15.00
5-Williamson story,4pgs.	6.00	12.00	18.00
6-10	3.00	6.00	9.00
11-20	2.00	4.00	6.00
21-26,28-34	1.35	2.75	4.00
27-1st Antman app.(1/62)	40.00	80.00	120.00
35-2nd Antman-begin series	16.50	33.25	50.00
36	7.00	14.00	21.00
37-40	4.00	8.00	12.00
41-43	2.50	5.00	7.50
44-Origin The Wasp	3.00	6.00	9.00
45-48,50	2.00	4.00	6.00
49-Antman becomes Giant Man; origin The Human Top	2.50	5.00	7.50
51-60: #60-Giant Man & Hulk double feature begins	1.20	2.40	3.60
61-70: #65-New Giant Man costume. #69-Last Giant Man. #70-Sub-Mariner begins	.75	1.50	2.25
71-80	.60	1.20	1.80
81-92	.50	1.00	1.50
93-Silver Surfer app.	.75	1.50	2.25
94-101: #100-Hulk battles Sub-Mariner	.40	.80	1.20

NOTE: _Ditko/Kirby art in most issues #1-34. Ditko Hulk-#60-67, Giant Man-#61. Everett Hulk-#78-84, Sub-Mariner-#87-91,94-96; inks-#79,85-91,94. Grandenetti pencils(Sub-Mariner) #86. Kirby stories-#27,35-40,44,49-70; layouts-#71-84(Hulk); pencils(Sub-Mariner)-#82,83; covers-#50-70,73,75,77(w/Romita),78(s/Colan), 79,81,85(all w/Everett),90. Powell Hulk-#73, 74, Giant-Man-#64._

TALES TO HOLD YOU SPELLBOUND (See Spellbound)

TALKING KOMICS
1957   (20 pgs.) (Slick Covers)
Belda Record & Publ. Co.

Each comic contained a record that followed the story - much like the Golden Record sets. Known titles: Chirpy Cricket, Lonesome Octopus, Sleepy Santa, Grumpy Shark, Flying Turtle, Happy Grasshopper

	Good	Fine	Mint
with records........	.75	1.50	2.25

Tales To Astonish #4. © MCG

Tales To Astonish #38. © MCG

Tally-Ho Comics, © Swappers Quart.

387

Target Comics #7, © Novp

Target Comics V2#12, © Novp

Tarzan #9(Dell), © ERB

TALLY-HO COMICS
December, 1944
Swappers Quarterly (Baily Publ. Co.)

	Good	Fine	Mint
Frazetta's 1st work as Giunta's assistant	20.00	40.00	60.00

TAMMY, TELL ME TRUE (See 4-Color #1233)

TARANTULA (See Weird Suspense)

TARAS BULBA (See Movie Classics)

TARGET COMICS (--Western Romances #106 on)
Feb, 1940 - V10#3, Aug-Sept, 1949
Novelty Publications

	Good	Fine	Mint
V1#1-Origin & 1st app. Manowar, The White Streak by Burgos; Bulls-Eye Bill by Everett	40.00	80.00	120.00
2	20.00	40.00	60.00
3	15.00	30.00	45.00
4-Jack Cole art	15.00	30.00	45.00
5-Origin The White Streak in text; Space Hawk by Wolverton begins	50.00	100.00	150.00
6-The Chameleon begins; White Streak origin cont'd. in text	30.00	60.00	90.00
7-Wolverton cover	70.00	140.00	210.00
8,9,12	25.00	50.00	75.00
10-Intro. & 1st app. The Target; Kirby cover	40.00	80.00	120.00
11-Origin The Target & The Targeteers	35.00	70.00	105.00
V2#1,2	15.00	30.00	45.00
3,5	12.00	24.00	36.00
4-The Cadet begins	12.00	24.00	36.00
6-10-Red Seal with White Streak in all	12.00	24.00	36.00
11,12	10.00	20.00	30.00
V3#1-10-Last Wolverton issue	10.00	20.00	30.00
11,12	2.50	5.00	7.50
V4#1-5,7-12	1.75	3.50	5.25
6-Targetoons by Wolverton, 1pg.	2.00	4.00	6.00
V5#1-12	1.35	2.75	4.00
V6#1-12	1.20	2.40	3.60
V7#1-12	1.00	2.00	3.00
V8#1-5,7-12	1.00	2.00	3.00
6-Krigstein art	1.50	3.00	4.50
V9#1-12, V10#1-3	1.00	2.00	3.00

NOTE: *Jack Cole art-#1-8.*

TARGET: THE CORRUPTORS (TV)
#1306, Mar-May, 1962 - #3, 1962
Dell Publishing Co.

	Good	Fine	Mint
4-Color #1306, #2,3	.50	1.00	1.50

TARGET WESTERN ROMANCES (Formerly Target)
#106, 10-11/49 - #107, 12-1/49-50
Star Publications

	Good	Fine	Mint
#106,107	1.20	2.40	3.60

TARGITT
March, 1975 - #3, July, 1975
Atlas/Seaboard Publ.

#1-Origin; Nostrand art in all	.20	.40	.60
2,3: #2-1st in costume	.15	.30	.45

TARZAN (See Aurora, Comics on Parade, DC 100-Pg. Super Spec., Golden Comics Digest #4, 9, Jungle Tales of --, Lemix-Korlix, Limited Coll. Ed., Sparkler, & Tip Top)

TARZAN
1939 - 1947
Dell Publishing Co./United Features Synd.

	Good	Fine	Mint
Black & White #5('39)-by Hal Foster; reprints 1st dailies from '29	100.00	200.00	300.00
Single Series #20('40)-by Hal Foster	100.00	200.00	300.00
4-Color #134('46)	20.00	40.00	60.00
4-Color #161('47)	17.50	35.00	52.50

TARZAN (-- of the Apes #138 on)
Jan-Feb, 1948 - #206, Feb, 1972
Dell Publishing Co./Gold Key #132 on

#1-Jesse Marsh art begins; Two Against the Jungle begins, ends #24	30.00	60.00	90.00
2	16.50	33.25	50.00
3-5	10.00	20.00	30.00
6-10	8.00	16.00	24.00
11-20	5.00	10.00	15.00
21-24,26-30	3.50	7.00	10.50
25-1st "Brothers of the Spear" episode; series ends #156,160,161,196-206	4.00	8.00	12.00
31-40	2.50	5.00	7.50
41-50	2.00	4.00	6.00
51-60	1.75	3.35	5.00
61,62,64-70	1.50	3.00	4.50
63-Two Tarzan stories, 1 by Manning	1.75	3.35	5.00
71-100	1.35	2.75	4.00
101-120	1.20	2.40	3.60
121-140	.90	1.80	2.70
141-154	.65	1.35	2.00
155-Origin Tarzan	1.00	2.00	3.00
156-177: #157-Bantu, Dog of the Arande begins, ends #159,195. #162-No Manning	.40	.80	1.20

388

(Tarzan cont'd)   Good Fine Mint
178-Tarzan origin reprt/#155; Leopard Girl
    app.   .40   .80   1.20
179-206   .35   .70   1.05
Story Digest #1(G.K)(6/70) .65 1.35 2.00
NOTE: *#162,165,168,171 are TV issues. #1-153-
all have Marsh art on Tarzan. #154-161,163,
164,166,167,172-177 all have Manning art on
Tarzan. #178,202 have Manning Tarzan reprints.
No "Brothers of the Spear" in #1-24,157-159,
162-195. #39-126,128-156 all have Russ Manning
art on "Brothers of the Spear;" #196-201,204,
205 all have Manning B.O.T.S. reprints; #25-
38,127 all have Jesse Marsh art on B.O.T.S.
#206 has a Marsh B.O.T.S. reprint. Doug Wildey
art-#179-187.*

TARZAN (Continuation of G.K. series)
#207, April, 1972 - #258, Feb, 1977
National Periodical Publications

#207-Origin Tarzan by Joe Kubert, part 1.
    John Carter begins(origin); 52pg. ish.
    through #209   .75 1.50 2.25
208,209-Origin Tarzan, parts 2-4. #209-Last
    John Carter   .50 1.00 1.50
210,211-Kubert art   .50 1.00 1.50
212-214: Adaptations from "Jungle Tales of
    Tarzan". #213-Beyond the Farthest Star be-
    gins, ends #218 .35   .70 1.05
215-218,224,225-All by Kubert
                  .35   .70 1.05
219-223: Adapts "The Return of Tarzan" by
    Kubert   .30   .60   .90
226-Manning art   .30   .60   .90
227-229   .25   .50   .75
230-100pgs; Kubert, Kaluta art; Korak be-
    gins, ends #234; Carson of Venus app.
                  .35   .70 1.05
231-234: Adapts "Tarzan and the Lion Man;"
    all 100pgs.; Rex, the Wonder Dog reprts.-
    #232,233   .25   .50   .75
235-Last Kubert issue; 100pgs.
                  .25   .50   .75
236,237,239   .20   .40   .60
238-68pgs.   .25   .50   .75
240-243: Adapts "Tarzan & the Castaways",
244-249   .20   .40   .60
250-256: Adapts "Tarzan the Untamed"; #252,
    253-reprints #213 .15   .30   .45
257,258   .15   .30   .45
Comic Digest #1(50¢)-160pgs., Digest Size
    (DC), Fall, 1972 - Kubert cover, Manning
    art   .80 1.60 2.40
NOTE: *Foster strip reprints-#208,209,211,221.
Anderson stories-#207,209,217,218. Chaykin
story-#216. Finley reprint-#212. Infantino
stories-#230 on. Kubert covers-#207-249,253.*

Manning strip reprints-#230-235,238. Morrow
story-#208.

TARZAN BOOK (The Illustrated --)
1929   (80 pgs.) (7x9")
Grosset & Dunlap

#1-(Rare)-Contains 1st B&W Tarzan newspaper
    comics from 1929. Cloth reinforced spine
    & dust jacket (50¢)   Good Fine Mint
    with dust jacket..... 60.00 120.00 180.00
    without dust jacket.. 35.00 70.00 105.00
2nd Printing(1934)-76pgs.(25¢); 4 Foster
    pages dropped; paper spine, circle in low-
    er right cover with 25¢ price. The 25¢ is
    barely visible on some copies.
                 20.00 40.00 60.00
1967-House of Greystoke reprint-7x10"; using
    the complete 300 illustrations/text from
    the 1929 edition minus the original indic-
    ia, foreword, etc. Initial version bound
    in gold paper & sold for $5.00. Officially
    titled Burroughs Bibliophile #2. A very few
    additional copies were bound in heavier
    blue paper.
    Gold binding.... 5.00 7.50 10.00
    Blue binding.... 6.00 9.00 12.00

TARZAN FAMILY (Formerly Korak)
#60, Nov-Dec, 1975 - #66, Nov-Dec, 1976
#60-62, 68pgs.; #63 on, 52pgs.
National Periodical Publications

#60-Korak begins; Kaluta reprt.
                  .25   .50   .75
61-65-All Kaluta reprts. .20   .40   .60
66   .20   .40   .60
NOTE: *Carson of Venus reprints-#60-65. New
John Carter-#62-64(65,66-reprints). New Korak-
#62-66. Pellucidar feature-#66. Foster Sunday
reprints-#60('32),63. Kaluta Carson of Venus-
#62-65. Kubert covers-#60-64. Manning strip
reprints-#60-64. Morrow reprint-#66.*

TARZAN KING OF THE JUNGLE (See Dell Giant
#37,51)

TARZAN, LORD OF THE JUNGLE
1965   (Giant) (Soft cover) (25¢)
Gold Key

#1-Marsh reprints   1.50 3.00 4.50

TARZAN, LORD OF THE JUNGLE
June, 1977 - Present
Marvel Comics Group

#1   .20   .40   .60
2-8   .15   .30   .45

Tarzan Book #1, © ERB

Tarzan King Of The Jungle #37, © ERB

Tarzan Lord Of The Jungle #1, © ERB

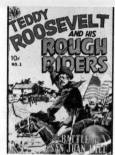

Teddy Roosevelt--#1, © Avon   Teen-Age Brides #1, © Harv   Teen-Age Hotrodders #1, © CC

(Tarzan cont'd)	Good	Fine	Mint
Annual #1(10/77)	.25	.50	.75

NOTE: *John Buscema covers/stories-#1-8; Annual #1(10/77)-J. Buscema cover/art.*

TARZAN MARCH OF COMICS (See March of Comics #82,98,114,125,144,155,172,185,204,223,240, 252,262,272,286,300,318,332,354,366)

TARZAN'S JUNGLE ANNUAL
Aug, 1952 - 1957 (25¢) (Two #5's)
Dell Publishing Co.

#1	3.50	7.00	10.50
2-7: Manning art #3,5-7	2.00	4.00	6.00

NOTE: *All have Marsh art.*

TARZAN'S JUNGLE WORLD (See Dell Giant #25)

TASMANIAN DEVIL & HIS TASTY FRIENDS
Nov, 1962
Gold Key

#1-Bugs Bunny & Elmer Fudd x-over			
	.35	.70	1.05

TASTEE-FREEZ COMICS
1957 (36 pgs.) (10¢) (6 different)
Harvey Comics

#1-Little Dot, #2-Rags Rabbit, #3-Casper,			
#4-Sad Sack, #5-Mazie	1.50	3.00	4.50
#6-Dick Tracy	3.00	6.00	9.00

TAYLOR'S CHRISTMAS TABLOID
Mid 1930's, Cleveland, Ohio
Dept. Store Giveaway

No#(Very Rare)-Among the earliest pro work
of Siegel & Shuster; one full color page
called "The Battle in the Stratosphere";
Shuster art throughout
        Estimated value...... $225.00

T. CASEY BRENNAN'S MYSTIC TALES
1977 (50¢)
Power Comics

#1	.20	.40	.60

TEDDY ROOSEVELT & HIS ROUGH RIDERS
1950
Avon Periodicals

#1-Kinstler cover	2.50	5.00	7.50

TEDDY ROOSEVELT ROUGH RIDER (See Classics Special)

TEE AND VEE CROSLEY IN TELEVISION LAND COMICS
1951 (52pgs.)(8x11")(Soft cover)(in color)
Crosley Division, Avco Mfg. Corp.

Many stories, puzzles, cut-outs,	Good	Fine	Mint
games, etc.	1.00	2.00	3.00

TEENA
1948 - 1949
Magazine Enterprises/Standard Comics

A-1#11,12,15	1.00	2.00	3.00
20-22(Standard)	.80	1.60	2.40

TEEN-AGE BRIDES
Aug, 1953 - #7, Aug, 1954
Harvey/Home Comics

#1	1.00	2.00	3.00
2-7: #2,6-Powell art	.60	1.20	1.80

TEEN-AGE CONFESSIONS (See Teen Confessions)

TEEN-AGE CONFIDENTIAL CONFESSIONS
July, 1960 - #22, 1964
Charlton Comics

#1	.50	1.00	1.50
2-22	.15	.30	.45

TEEN-AGE DIARY SECRETS
#4, Sept, 1949 - #8, Feb, 1950
St. John Publishing Co.

#4-8	1.75	3.50	5.25

NOTE: *Baker in some, probably all.*

TEEN-AGE DOPE SLAVES (See Harvey Comics Library #1)

TEENAGE HOTRODDERS (Top Eliminator #25 on)
April, 1963 - #24, July, 1967
Charlton Comics

#1	.15	.30	.45
2-24		.15	.30

TEEN-AGE LOVE
1950 (132 pgs.)
Fox Publications (Hero)

No#-See Fox Giants. Contents can vary and
determines price.

TEEN-AGE LOVE
V2#4, 7/58 - #96, Dec, 1973
Charlton Comics

V2#4	.25	.50	.75

(Teen-Age Love cont'd)	Good	Fine	Mint
10(9/59)-30		.20	.40
31-96: #61&62-Origin Jonnie Love & begin			
series		.10	.20

TEEN-AGE ROMANCES
Jan, 1949 - #86, Mar, 1962
St. John Publ. Co.(Approved Comics)/Marvel
(ZPC) #65 on

	Good	Fine	Mint
#1-Baker cover/stories	3.00	6.00	9.00
2-10	1.75	3.35	5.00
11-20	1.35	2.75	4.00
21-45	1.20	2.40	3.60
46-60	.40	.80	1.20
61-86	.25	.50	.75

NOTE: *Matt Baker covers & stories in most all issues.*

TEEN-AGE TALK
1964
I.W. Enterprises

Reprint #5,8,9	.25	.50	.75

TEEN-AGE TEMPTATIONS (Going Steady #10 on)
10/52 - #10, 10/54 (See True Love Pict.)
St. John Publishing Co.

	Good	Fine	Mint
#1-Baker cover/story; has story called "Reform School Girl" by Estrada	3.35	6.75	10.00
2-10-Baker cover/stories	1.75	3.50	5.25

TEEN BEAM (Teen Beat #1)
#2, Jan-Feb, 1968
National Periodical Publications

#2	.20	.40	.60

TEEN BEAT (Teen Beam #2)
Nov-Dec, 1967
National Periodical Publications

#1-Photos & text only	.35	.70	1.05

TEEN COMICS (Formerly All Teen; Journey Into
Unknown Worlds #36 on)
#21, 1947 - #35, May, 1950
Marvel Comics (WFP)

#21,24,26,28,30-Kurtzman's "Hey Look"	1.50	3.00	4.50
22,23,25,27,29,31-35	.65	1.35	2.00

TEEN CONFESSIONS
August, 1959 - #97, Nov, 1976
Charlton Comics

	Good	Fine	Mint
#1	.50	1.00	1.50
2-88,91-97: #86-88-Jonnie Love app.		.20	.35
89,90-Newton covers	.15	.30	.45

TEENIE WEENIES, THE
1950 - 1951 (Newspaper reprints)
Ziff-Davis Publ. Co.

#10,11	2.00	4.00	6.00

TEEN-IN (Tippy Teen)
Summer, 1968 - #4, Fall, 1969
Tower Comics

No#(Summer,'68), No#(Spring,'69),			
#3,4		.20	.35

TEEN LIFE (Formerly Young Life)
#3, Winter, 1945 - #5, Fall, 1945
New Age/Quality Comics Group

#3-5	.65	1.35	2.00

TEEN ROMANCES
1964
Super Comics

#15,16-Reprints	.15	.30	.45

TEEN SECRET DIARY
1959 - #9, Feb, 1961; 1972
Charlton Comics

#1	.35	.70	1.05
2-9(2/61)	.15	.30	.45
#1(1972)		.15	.30

TEEN TALK (See Teen)

TEEN TITANS (See Brave & the Bold & Showcase)
1-2/66 - #43, 1-2/73; #44, 11/76 - Present
National Periodical Publications/DC Comics

#1	2.00	4.00	6.00
2	1.00	2.00	3.00
3-5: #4-Speedy app.	.65	1.35	2.00
6-10	.50	1.00	1.50
11-18: #11-Speedy app.	.40	.80	1.20
19-Wood art; Speedy begins as regular			
	.40	.80	1.20
20-22: Adams art in all; #21-Hawk & Dove app.			
#22-Origin Wonder Girl	.80	1.60	2.40
23-Wonder Girl dons new costume,			
24	.30	.60	.90
25-Flash, Aquaman, Batman, Green Arrow, Green Lantern, Superman, & Hawk & Dove guests			

Teen-Age Romances #43. © STJ

Teen-Age Temptations #1. © STJ

Teen Beam #2. © DC

Tegra #1, © Fox

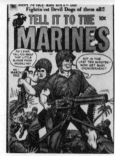
Tell It To The Marines #1, © Toby

Terrific #6, © Hoke

(Teen Titans cont'd)	Good	Fine	Mint
	.30	.60	.90

26-30: #29-Ocean Master app. #29-Hawk & Dove
& Ocean Master app. #30-Aquagirl app.

	.30	.60	.90

31-43: #31-Hawk & Dove app. #36-Superboy
story. #38-Green Arrow/Speedy reprint;
Aquaman/Aqualad story. #39-Hawk & Dove

story (#36-39, 52pgs.)	.25	.50	.75
44-53	.15	.30	.45

TEEPEE TIM (Formerly Ha Ha Comics)
#100, Feb-Mar, 1955 - #102, June-July, 1955
American Comics Group

#100-102	.20	.40	.60

TEGRA JUNGLE PRINCESS (Zegra #2 on)
August, 1948
Fox Features Syndicate

#1-Blue Beetle, Rocket Kelly app.			
	9.00	18.00	27.00

TELEVISION (See TV)

TELEVISION COMICS
1949 - #8, Nov, 1950
Standard Comics(Animated Cartoons)

#1	1.35	2.75	4.00
2-4,6-8	.65	1.35	2.00
5-1st app. Willy Nilly	.80	1.60	2.40

TELEVISION PUPPET SHOW
1950 - #2, Nov, 1950
Avon Periodicals

#1,2	1.50	3.00	4.50

TELEVISION TEENS MOPSY (See T.V. Teens)

TELL IT TO THE MARINES
Mar, 1952 - #15, July, 1955
Toby Press Publications

#1	1.00	2.00	3.00
2-15	.50	1.00	1.50
IW Reprint #1,9	.25	.50	.75
Super Reprint #16('64)	.25	.50	.75

TEN COMMANDMENTS (See Moses & the-- & Classics Special)

TENDER LOVE STORIES
Feb, 1971 - #4, July, 1971 (All 52pgs.) (25¢)
Skywald Publ. Corp.

	Good	Fine	Mint
#1-4		.15	.30

TENDER ROMANCE
December, 1953 - #2, 1954
Key Publications (Gilmour Magazines)

#1,2	1.00	2.00	3.00

TENNIS (For Speed, Stamina, Strength, Skill)
1956 (16 pgs.) (Soft cover) (10¢)
Tennis Educational Foundation
Derus Productions

Book #1-Endorsed by Gene Tunney, Ralph Kiner,
etc. showing how tennis has helped them.

	.65	1.35	2.00

TENSE SUSPENSE
Dec, 1958 - #2, Feb, 1959
Fago Publications

#1,2	.65	1.35	2.00

TEN STORY LOVE (Formerly a pulp magazine
with same title)
V29#6, 1/52 - V36#5(#210), 9/56
Ace Periodicals

V29#6	.50	1.00	1.50
V30#6, V31, V32#1,2	.40	.80	1.20
V32#3(6/53)-V32#6(12/53)	.40	.80	1.20
V33, V34#1-4	.40	.80	1.20
V34#5(#197, 8/54), V34#6(#198), V35#1(#199)-			
V35#6(#204, 9/55), V36#1(#205, 11/55)-V36#5			
(#210, 9/56)	.35	.70	1.05

TEN WHO DARED (See 4-Color Comics #1178)

TERRIFIC COMICS
Jan, 1944 - #6, Nov, 1944
Holyoke Publishing Co.

#1-Kid Terrific	4.50	9.00	13.50
2-The Boomerang begins	3.00	6.00	9.00
3-Diana becomes Boomerang's costumed aide,			
4,6	2.50	5.00	7.50
5-The Reckoner begins; Boomerang & Diana by			
L.B. Cole & Ed Wheelan's "Comics" McCorm-			
ick, called the world's #1 comic book fan;			
Bondage cover	5.00	10.00	15.00

TERRIFIC COMICS (Horrific #1-13)
#14, May, 1955 - #18, July, 1955
Mystery Publ. (Ajax/Farrell)

#14-16-No Phantom Lady	1.35	2.75	4.00
17,18-Phantom Lady & Wonder Boy in both			
	5.00	10.00	15.00

TERRIFYING TALES (Terrors of the Jungle#4-10)
1954
Novelty-Star Publications

	Good	Fine	Mint
#11-15-Rulah, Jo-Jo; #12-reprint/Jo-Jo #19			
	3.50	7.00	10.50

TERROR ILLUSTRATED (Adult Tales of --)
Nov-Dec, 1955 - #2, Spring, 1956 (Magazine)
E.C. Comics

#1	6.00	12.00	18.00
2	5.00	10.00	15.00

NOTE: *Craig* story-#1. *Crandall* stories-#1,2;
covers-#1,2. *Evans* stories-#1,2. *Ingels* stor-
ies-#1,2.

TERRORS OF THE JUNGLE (Terrifying Tales
#11 on; formerly Jungle Thrills)
#17, May, 1952 - #10, 1954
Novelty-Star Publications

#17-Reprints Rulah #21	4.00	8.00	12.00
18-Jo-Jo reprints	4.00	8.00	12.00
19-21(1953)-Jo-Jo app.	4.00	8.00	12.00
4-10	3.50	7.00	10.50

NOTE: *Disbrow art-#1*,7,9.

TERRORS OF THE UNIVERSE
1953
Novelty-Star Publications

#8.9	2.00	4.00	6.00

TERROR TALES (See Beware Terror Tales)

TERROR TALES (Magazine)
V1#7, 1969 - V6#6, Dec, 1974; V7#1, 4/76 -
Present (V1-V6, 52pgs.; V7 on, 68pgs.)
Eerie Publications

V1#7	.40	.80	1.20
V1#8-11('69)	.35	.70	1.05
V2#1-6('70), V3#1-6('71), V4#1-6('72),			
V5#1-6('73), V6#1-6('74)	.25	.50	.75
V7#1,4(no V7#2),V8#1-3('77)	.25	.50	.75
V7#3-LSD story reprt./Weird V3#5			
	.25	.50	.75

TERRY AND THE PIRATES (See Lemix-Korlix &
Super Comics)

TERRY AND THE PIRATES
1939 - 1953 (By Milton Caniff)
Dell Publishing Co.

Black & White #2('39) 50.00 100.00 150.00
Black & White #6('39)-1936 dailies

	Good	Fine	Mint
	35.00	70.00	105.00
4-Color #9(1940)	35.00	70.00	105.00
Large Feature Comic #27('41), #6('42)			
	25.00	50.00	75.00
4-Color #44('43)	16.50	33.25	50.00
4-Color #101('45)	12.00	24.00	36.00
Buster Brown Shoes giveaway(1938, 32pgs.)			
in color	20.00	40.00	60.00
Canada Dry Premiums-Books #1-3; 2"x5",36pgs.			
(Harvey, 1953)	2.50	5.00	7.50
Family Album(1942)	5.00	10.00	15.00
Gillmore Giveaway('38-24pgs.)			
	4.00	8.00	12.00
Popped Wheat Giveaway('38)-reprints in full			
color	1.50	3.00	4.50
Sparked Wheat Giveaway('42)-16pgs. in full			
color	2.50	5.00	7.50

TERRY AND THE PIRATES (See Superbook #3,5,
9,16,28, & Merry Christmas --)

TERRY AND THE PIRATES (Long John Silvers
#30 on) (Reprints of daily strips)
#3, 4/47 - #26, 4/51; #26, 1955 - #28, 1955
Harvey Publ./Charlton #27-29 (Two #26's)

#3(#1)-Boy Explorers by S&K; Terry & Pirates			
begin by Caniff	15.00	30.00	45.00
4-S&K Boy Explorers	10.00	20.00	30.00
5-10: #7-9-Powell art	5.00	10.00	15.00
11-20	4.00	8.00	12.00
21-26(4/51)-Last Caniff ish.			
	3.50	7.00	10.50
26-28('55)-Not by Caniff	2.00	4.00	6.00

TERRY BEARS COMICS (TerryToons, The-- #4)
June, 1952 - #3, Oct, 1952
St. John/Pines #4

#1-3	1.00	2.00	3.00

TERRY-TOONS COMICS (1st Series) (Becomes
Paul Terry's Comics #87 on; later issues
titled "Paul Terry's--")(See Giant Comics Ed.)
Oct, 1942 - #84, Feb, 1951
Timely/Marvel #1-59(7/47)/St.John #60(8/47)on

#1	10.00	20.00	30.00
2	5.00	10.00	15.00
3-5	3.50	7.00	10.50
6-20	1.75	3.50	5.25
21-37	1.35	2.75	4.00
38-1st Mighty Mouse	6.00	12.00	18.00
39-59(8/47): #50-1st app. Heckle & Jeckle			
	1.25	2.50	3.75
60(8/47)-#8	1.00	2.00	3.00

Terrors Of The Jungle #18. © Star

Terry & The Pirates #18. © News Synd.

Terry-Toons #43. © Terry Toons

Texas Rangers In Action #30, © CC

Tex Granger #24, © PMI

Tex Ritter #1, © Faw

TERRY-TOONS COMICS (2nd Series)
June, 1952 - #9, Nov, 1953
St. John Publishing Co./Pines

	Good	Fine	Mint
#1	1.50	3.00	4.50
2-9	1.00	2.00	3.00
Giant Summer Fun Book #101,102(Summer,'57 -			
Summer,'58)	1.00	2.00	3.00

TERRYTOONS, THE TERRY BEARS (Formerly Terry
#4, Summer, 1958   Bears)
Pines Comics

#4	.25	.50	.75

TESSIE THE TYPIST (Tiny Tessie #24)
Summer, 1944 - #23, 1948
Timely/Marvel Comics (20CC)

#1-Doc Rockblock & others by Wolverton			
	9.00	18.00	27.00
2-Wolverton's Powerhouse Pepper			
	5.00	10.00	15.00
3-No Wolverton	1.00	2.00	3.00
4-8-Wolverton art; Kurtzman's "Hey Look"-#6			
	4.00	8.00	12.00
9-14-Wolverton's Powerhouse Pepper + Kurtz-			
man's "Hey Look" (not in #10,11,13)			
	3.50	7.00	10.50
15-18-Kurtzman's "Hey Look" + Giggles 'n'			
Grins #15	2.00	4.00	6.00
19-23	.80	1.60	2.40

TEXAN, THE (Fightin' Marines #15 on)
Aug, 1948 - #15, Oct, 1951 (Two #15's)
St. John Publishing Co.

#1-Buckskin Belle; Tuska art			
	2.00	4.00	6.00
2-15	1.35	2.75	4.00
NOTE: *Matt Baker art in all.*

TEXAN, THE (See 4-Color Comics #1027,1096)

TEXAS JOHN SLAUGHTER (See 4-Color #997,1181)

TEXAS KID
Jan, 1951 - #10, July, 1952
Marvel/Atlas Comics (LMC)

#1-Tuska art	2.00	4.00	6.00
2-10	1.20	2.40	3.60

TEXAS RANGERS, THE (See Superior Stories #4
and Tales of --)

TEXAS RANGERS IN ACTION (See Blue Bird Comics)
#5, July, 1956 - #79, Aug, 1970
Charlton Comics

	Good	Fine	Mint
#5-10	.60	1.20	1.80
11-Three Williamson stories, 5,5,& 8 pgs.			
	3.00	6.00	9.00
12,14-20	.35	.70	1.05
13-Williamson story, 5pgs.	1.75	3.50	5.25
21-59	.25	.50	.75
60-Rileys Rangers begin	.20	.40	.60
61-70: #66-1st app. The Man Called Loco,			
origin-#67	.15	.30	.45
71-79		.15	.30

TEXAS SLIM (See A-1 Comics #4-6,9)

TEX DAWSON, GUN-SLINGER (Gunslinger #2 on)
Jan, 1973
Marvel Comics Group

#1-Steranko cover; Williamson reprint; Tex			
Dawson reprts. begin	.20	.40	.60

TEX FARNUM (See Wisco)

TEX FARRELL
Mar-Apr, 1948
D.S. Publishing Co.

#1-Shelly cover	1.50	3.00	4.50

TEX GRANGER (Formerly Calling All Boys)
#18, June, 1948 - #24, Sept, 1949
Parents' Magazine Institute/Commended

#18-24	.80	1.60	2.40

TEX MORGAN
Aug, 1948 - #9, Feb, 1950
Marvel Comics (CCC)

#1	2.50	5.00	7.50
2-9	1.75	3.50	5.25

TEX RITTER WESTERN
Oct, 1950 - #46, May, 1959
Fawcett, #1-20(1/54)/Charlton #21 on

#1	6.00	12.00	18.00
2	3.00	6.00	9.00
3-10	2.50	5.00	7.50
11-20	2.00	4.00	6.00
21-38,40-46	1.35	2.75	4.00
39-Williamson art(1/58)	2.00	4.00	6.00

TEX TAYLOR (See Wisco)
Sept, 1948 - #9, March, 1950
Marvel Comics (HPC)

#1	2.50	5.00	7.50
2-9	1.75	3.50	5.25

THAT'S MY POP! GOES NUTS FOR FAIR
1939   (76 pgs.) (B&W)
Bystander Press

	Good	Fine	Mint
No#-by Milt Gross	7.00	14.00	21.00

THAT DARN CAT (See Movie Comics & Walt Disney Showcase #19)

THAT THE WORLD MAY BELIEVE
No date   (Graymoor Friars distr.)
Catechetical Guild

	1.00	2.00	3.00

THAT WILKIN BOY (Meet Bingo --)
Jan, 1969 - Present
Archie Publications

#1	.25	.50	.75
2-10	.20	.40	.60
11-26(last giant issue)	.15	.30	.45
27-42		.15	.30

T.H.E. CAT (TV)
Oct, 1966 - #4, Oct, 1967
Dell Publishing Co.

#1	.35	.70	1.05
2-4	.20	.40	.60

THERE'S A NEW WORLD COMING
1974
Spire Christian Comics/Fleming H. Revell Co.

	.15	.30	.45

THEY RING THE BELL
1946
Fox Features Syndicate

#1	1.50	3.00	4.50

THIEF OF BAGHDAD (See 4-Color Comics #1229)

THIMBLE THEATRE STARRING POPEYE
1931, 1932   (52pgs.) (25¢) (B&W) (Rare)
Sonnet Publishing Co.

#1-Daily strip serial reprints in both by			
Segar	50.00	100.00	150.00
2	35.00	70.00	105.00

NOTE: *Probably the first Popeye reprint book.*

THIMK (Magazine) (Satire)
May, 1958 - #6, May, 1959
Counterpart

#1	1.35	2.75	4.00

	Good	Fine	Mint
2-6	.65	1.35	2.00

THING!, THE (Blue Beetle #18 on)
Feb, 1952 - #17, Nov, 1954
Song Hits #1/Capitol Stories/Charlton

#1	2.00	4.00	6.00
2-11	1.50	3.00	4.50
12-15,17-Ditko cover & stories #13-15	2.50	5.00	7.50
16-Used in Seduction of the Innocent	3.00	6.00	9.00
17-Ditko cover	1.75	3.50	5.25

THIRTEEN (-- Going on 18)
Nov-Jan, 1961-62 - #29, Jan, 1971
Dell Publishing Co.

#1	1.35	2.75	4.00
2-10	.65	1.35	2.00
11-29	.35	.70	1.05

NOTE: *John Stanley art/script-#3-29.*

THIRTY SECONDS OVER TOKYO
1943   (Movie)
David McKay Co.

No#	2.50	5.00	7.50

THIS IS SUSPENSE!
1952 - 1955
Charlton Comics

#1	1.00	2.00	3.00
2-22,25,26	.50	1.00	1.50
23-Wood story reprt./A Star Presentation #3- "Dr. Jekyll & Mr. Hyde"	3.00	6.00	9.00
24-Evans story	1.35	2.75	4.00

THIS IS THE PAYOFF (See Pay-Off)

THIS IS WAR
#5, July, 1952 - #9, May, 1953
Standard Comics

#5,6,9-Toth art	1.50	3.00	4.50
7,8	.80	1.60	2.40

THIS IS YOUR LIFE, DONALD DUCK (See 4-Color Comics #1109)

THIS MAGAZINE IS CRAZY (Crazy V3#3 on)
V3#2, 7/57   (68pgs.) (25¢) (Satire)
Charlton Publ. (Humor Magazines)

V3#2	.65	1.35	2.00

Texas Kid #1, © MCG

Thimble Theatre #2('32), © Sonnet

The Thing #15, © CC

Thor #128, © MCG   3-D-Ell #1, © Dell   3-D Love #1, © Mikeross Publ.

THIS MAGAZINE IS HAUNTED
Oct, 1951 - V3#21, Nov, 1954
Fawcett Publications/Charlton #14 on

	Good	Fine	Mint
#1-Evans art	2.50	5.00	7.50
2,5-Evans art	1.50	3.00	4.50
3,4,6-13	1.00	2.00	3.00
14,18-20	.65	1.35	2.00
15-17,21-Ditko stories	1.20	2.40	3.60

NOTE: _Ditko_ cover-V3#16. _Powell_ stories-#5,
11,17.

THIS MAGAZINE IS HAUNTED (2nd Series)(Form-
erly Zaza the Mystic)
V2#12, July, 1957 - V2#16, April, 1958
Charlton Comics

V2#12-16-Ditko cover/stories in all	1.00	2.00	3.00

THIS MAGAZINE IS WILD (See Wild)

THIS WAS YOUR LIFE (Religious)
1964   (3½x5½") (40pgs.) (Bl.,white & red)
Jack T. Chick Publ.

	.15	.30	.45

THOR (Formerly Journey Into Mystery)
March, 1966 - Present
Marvel Comics Group

#126	1.20	2.40	3.60
127-140	.80	1.60	2.40
141-147,150: #146-Inhumans begin, end #151			
	.50	1.00	1.50
148,149-Origin Black Bolt in ea.			
	.80	1.60	2.40
151-157,159,160	.50	1.00	1.50
158-Reprints origin(#83)	.60	1.20	1.80
161-164,167-179-Last Kirby ish.			
	.50	1.00	1.50
165,166-Warlock app.	.75	1.50	2.25
180,181-Adams art	1.00	2.00	3.00
182-192,194-200	.40	.80	1.20
193-Silver Surfer x-over	.75	1.50	2.25
201-226: #225-Intro. Firelord			
	.30	.60	.90
227-230-Buckler art	.40	.80	1.20
231-250	.20	.40	.60
251-267	.15	.30	.45
Giant-Size #1('75)	.35	.70	1.05
Special #2(9/66)	1.00	2.00	3.00
Special #3,4('67-12/71)(See Journey Into			
Mystery for #1)	.80	1.60	2.40
Annual #5(11/76)	.25	.50	.75
Annual #6(10/77)	.20	.40	.60

NOTE: _Adams_ covers-#179-181. _Buscema_ stories-
#182-226,246-253,254(reprint),256-259,Annual
#5. _Everett_ inks-#143,170-175; cover-#241(w/
Romita). _Kirby_ stories-#126-177,179; covers-
#126-169,171,177,250,251,253,255,257,258,
Annual #5.

THOSE MAGNIFICENT MEN IN THEIR FLYING
MACHINES (See Movie Comics)

THREE BEARS, THE (See Surprise Books)

THREE CABALLEROS (See 4-Color Comics #71)

THREE CHIPMUNKS, THE (See 4-Color #1042)

THREE COMICS MAGAZINE
1944
Quality Comics Group

	Good	Fine	Mint
#1-Lady Luck, Mr. Mystic, The Spirit app.			
(3 Spirit sections bound together)			
	8.00	16.00	24.00

3-D (NOTE: _All 3-D comics are worth more_
(about 50%) with glasses, and slightly less
if glasses are loose.)

3-D ACTION
Jan, 1954   (Oversized) (15¢)
Atlas Comics (ACI)

#1-Battle Brady	4.00	8.00	12.00

3-D ANIMAL FUN (See Animal Fun)

3-D BATMAN
1953, Reprinted in 1966
National Periodical Publications

1953-Reprints Batman #48	10.00	20.00	30.00
1966-Tommy Tomorrow app.	2.50	5.00	7.50

3-D CIRCUS
1953   (25¢)
Fiction House Magazines

#1 (with glasses)	4.00	8.00	12.00

3-D COMICS (See Tor, 3-D, & Mighty Mouse)

3-D DOLLY
Dec, 1953
Harvey Publications

#1 (with glasses)	4.00	8.00	12.00

3-D-ELL
1953   (3-D comics) (25¢)
Dell Publishing Co.

(3-D-ell cont'd)	Good	Fine	Mint
#1,2-Rootie Kazootie	4.00	8.00	12.00
3-Flukey Luke	3.50	7.00	10.50

3-D FEATURES PRESENT JET PUP
Oct-Dec, 1953
Dimensions Public

#1 (with glasses)-Two stories by Irving Spector	4.00	8.00	12.00

3-D FUNNY MOVIES
1953   (25¢)
Comic Media

#1 (with glasses)	4.00	8.00	12.00

3-D LOVE
December, 1953   (25¢)
Steriographic Publ. (Mikeross Publ.)

#1 (with glasses)	4.00	8.00	12.00

3-D NOODNICK (See Noodnick)

3-D ROMANCE
January, 1954   (25¢)
Steriographic Publ. (Mikeross Publ.)

#1 (with glasses)	4.00	8.00	12.00

3-D SHEENA, JUNGLE QUEEN
1953
Fiction House Magazines

#1	7.00	14.00	21.00

3-D SUPERMAN
1953   (Large size)
National Periodical Publications

Origin Superman (with glasses)			
	12.00	24.00	36.00

3-D TALES OF TERROR (See E.C. 3-D Classics)

3-D TALES OF THE WEST
Jan, 1954   (Oversized)   (15¢)
Atlas Comics (CPS)

#1 (3-D)	4.00	8.00	12.00

3-D THREE STOOGES (See Three Stooges)

3-D WHACK (See Whack)

THREE DIMENSION COMICS (See Mighty Mouse & E.C. 3-D Classics)

3 FUNMAKERS, THE
1908   (64 pgs.)   (10"x15")
Stokes and Company

	Good	Fine	Mint
Maude, Katzenjammer Kids, Happy Hooligan (1904-06 Sunday strip reprints in color)			
	12.00	30.00	48.00

THREE LITTLE PIGS (See 4-Color Comics #218)

3 LITTLE PIGS, THE (See W.D. Showcase #15,21)
May, 1964 - #2, Sept, 1968   (Walt Disney)
Gold Key

#1(5/64)-reprints 4-Color #218	.40	.80	1.20
2(9/68)	.25	.50	.75

THREE MOUSEKETEERS, THE (1st Series)
Mar-Apr, 1956 - #26, Oct-Dec, 1960; May-June, 1970 - #7, May-June, 1971
National Periodical Publications

#1	1.50	3.00	4.50
2-10	1.00	2.00	3.00
11-26	.50	1.00	1.50

THREE MOUSEKETEERS, THE (2nd Series)
May-June, 1970 - #7, May-June, 1971
National Periodical Publications

#1-4		.15	.30
5-7(68pgs.)	.15	.30	.45
(See Super DC Giant)			

THREE NURSES
V3#18, May, 1963 - V3#23, Mar, 1964
Charlton Comics

V3#18-23		.15	.30

THREE RASCALS
1958; 1963
I.W. Enterprises

IW Reprint #1(Says Super Comics on inside) (M.E.'s Clubhouse Rascals), #2('58), #10('63)-reprints #1	.35	.70	1.05

THREE RING COMICS
March, 1945
Spotlight Publishers

#1	1.00	2.00	3.00

THREE ROCKETEERS (See Blast-Off)

3-D Tales Of The West #1, © MCG

The Three Mouseketeers #24, © DC

Three Stooges #32, © GK

Thrilling Comics #7, © Std

Thrilling Comics #58, © Std

Thrills Of Tomorrow #20, © Harv

THREE STOOGES (See Comic Album #18, The
Little Stooges, March of Comics #232,248,
268,292,304,316,336,373, & Movie Classics
& Comics)

THREE STOOGES
2/49 - #2, 5/49;   9/53 - #4, 3/54?
Jubilee #1,2/St. John #1(9/53) on
	Good	Fine	Mint
#1-(Scarce)-(1949)Kubert art			
	6.00	12.00	18.00
2-(Scarce)-Kubert, Maurer art			
	4.00	8.00	12.00
1(9/53)-Hollywood Stunt Girl by Kubert,7pgs.			
	5.00	10.00	15.00
2,3(3-D)(10-11/53)	3.50	7.00	10.50
4(3/54)	2.00	4.00	6.00
NOTE: All issues have Kubert-Maurer art.

THREE STOOGES
Oct-Nov, 1959 - #55, June, 1972
Dell Publishing Co./Gold Key #10(10/62) on

4-Color #1043,1078,1127,1170,1187, #6('61)-			
#9(01-827-208)	1.20	2.40	3.60
#10-14,16-20	.80	1.60	2.40
15-Go Around the World in a Daze-Movie issue	1.35	2.75	4.00
21-55	.50	1.00	1.50

3 WORLDS OF GULLIVER (See 4-Color #1158)

THRILL COMICS (Becomes Whiz #2)
1940   (B&W)
Fawcett Publications

#1-Captain Thunder only app.
    Estimated value....... $10,000.00
NOTE: The existence of this book is known,
but exact contents, size, etc. not known. Up
to possibly 10 copies were printed & circulated within the office. For some reason, the
title was changed to Whiz Comics and Captain
Thunder changed to Captain Marvel.

THRILLING ADVENTURES IN STAMPS
1953   (25¢) (Formerly Stamps Comics)
Stamp Comics

V1#8	.35	.70	1.05

THRILLING ADVENTURE STORIES
Feb, 1975 - #2, July-Aug, 1975 (B&W, 68pgs.)
Atlas/Seaboard Publ.

#1-Tigerman, Kromag the Killer begin; Heath			
story	.65	1.35	2.00
2-Toth + Severin story, Adams cover			
	.65	1.35	2.00

THRILLING COMICS
Feb, 1940 - #80, April, 1951
Nedor/Better/Standard Comics
	Good	Fine	Mint
#1-Origin Doc Strange; Nickie Norton begins			
	30.00	60.00	90.00
2-The Rio Kid & The Woman in Red begin			
	15.00	30.00	45.00
3-The Ghost & Lone Eagle begin			
	12.00	24.00	36.00
4-10	9.00	18.00	27.00
11-18,20	7.00	14.00	21.00
19-Origin The American Crusader, ends #39,41			
	15.00	30.00	45.00
21-30: #24-Intro. Mike, Doc Strange's side-			
kick. #29-Last Rio Kid	6.00	12.00	18.00
31-40: #36-Commando Cubs begin			
	3.00	6.00	9.00
41-52-The Ghost ends	2.50	5.00	7.50
53-The Phantom Detective begins; The Cavalier			
app.; no Commando Cubs	2.50	5.00	7.50
54-The Cavalier app.; no Commando Cubs			
	2.50	5.00	7.50
55-Lone Eagle ends	2.50	5.00	7.50
56-Princess Pantha begins	5.00	10.00	15.00
57-60	4.00	8.00	12.00
61-65: #61-The Lone Eagle app. #62-Last Phan-			
tom Detective. #63-Last Commando Cubs;			
Captain Eagle app.	4.00	8.00	12.00
66-Frazetta text illo	5.00	10.00	15.00
67,70-73: Frazetta story in each, 5-7pgs.;			
#71-Last Princess Pantha?; Tara app. #72-			
Sea Eagle app.	7.00	14.00	21.00
68,69-Two Frazetta stories, 8&6pgs.; 9&7pgs.			
	10.00	20.00	30.00
74-76	2.00	4.00	6.00
77-80-Western stories	1.50	3.00	4.50
NOTE: Krigstein story-#79. Schomburg (Xela)
covers-#60-69(line or painted). Woman in Red
not in #19,23,31-33,39-45. #72 exists as a
Canadian reprint with no Frazetta story.

THRILLING CRIME CASES (Shocking Myst. Cases
#41, 6-7/50 - #49, 1952   #50 on)
Star Publications

#41-49-L.B. Cole covers; The Cameleon app.			
	2.00	4.00	6.00

THRILLING ROMANCES
1950 - #26, June, 1954
Standard Comics

#7-7pgs.Severin/Elder art	2.50	5.00	7.50
10-4pgs.Severin/Elder art	1.75	3.35	5.00
8,9,11,12,14-21,23,26	.80	1.60	2.40
13-Severin art	1.20	2.40	3.60
22,24,25-Toth art	2.00	4.00	6.00

THRILLING TRUE STORY OF THE BASEBALL GIANTS
1952 (2nd issue titled -- Baseball Yankees)
Fawcett Publications

	Good	Fine	Mint
Each......	3.00	6.00	9.00

THRILL-O-RAMA
Oct, 1965 - #3, Dec, 1966
Harvey Publications (Fun Films)

#1-Fate(Man in Black) by Powell app.; Doug Wildey story	.80	1.60	2.40
2-Pirana begins; Williamson 2pgs.; Fate(Man in Black) by Powell app.	.50	1.00	1.50
3-Man in Black(Fate) app.	.40	.80	1.20

THRILLS OF TOMORROW (Formerly Tomb of Terror)
#17, Oct, 1954 - #20, 1955
Harvey Publications

#17,18-Powell art(horror); #17-reprts. Witches Tales #7. #18-reprints Tomb of Terror

#1	.80	1.60	2.40
19,20-Stuntman by S&K (reprints from Stuntman); #19 has origin	9.00	18.00	27.00

THUMPER (See 4-Color Comics #19 & #243)

THUN'DA
1952 - 1953
Magazines Enterprises

#1(A-1#47)-Cave Girl; Frank Frazetta cover/ art	120.00	240.00	360.00
2(A-1#56)	8.00	16.00	24.00
3(A-1#73), #4(A-1#78), #5(A-1#83), #6(A-1#86) Powell cvr/stys #2-5	7.00	14.00	21.00

THUNDER AGENTS
11/65 - #17, 12/67; #18, 9/68, #19, 11/68,
#20, 11/69 (#1-16, 68pgs.; #17 on, 52pgs.)
Tower Comics

#1-Origin & 1st app. Dynamo, Noman, Menthor, & The Thunder Squad; 1st app. The Iron Maiden	2.50	5.00	7.50
2-Death of Egghead	1.50	3.00	4.50
3-5: #4-Guy Gilbert becomes Lightning who joins Thunder Squad; Iron Maiden app.	1.25	2.50	3.75
6-10: #7-Death of Menthor. #8-Origin & 1st app. The Raven	1.00	2.00	3.00
11-15: #13-Undersea Agent app.; no Raven story	.65	1.35	2.00
16-19	.50	1.00	1.50
20-All reprints	.35	.70	1.05

NOTE: *Crandall* story-#1,4,5(pencil),18; cover-#18. *Ditko* story-#6,7(inks),12(pencils),
16,18. *Kane* story-#1,5(pencils),6(pencils),
14,16; covers-#14,15. *Whitney* stories-#10,
13,15,17,18; cover-#17. *Wood* story-#1-11,
(w/*Ditko*-#12,18),(inks-#9,16,17),5-17,19,20
(reprint); cover-#1-8,10-13(#10 w/*Williamson*).

THUNDERBOLT (See The Atomic --)

THUNDERBOLT (Peter Cannon --)(Formerly Son of Vulcan #50)
Jan, 1966; #51, 3-4/66 - #60, 11/67
Charlton Comics

	Good	Fine	Mint
#1-Origin	.65	1.35	2.00
51	.40	.80	1.20
52-58: #56-Sentinels begin. #58-Last Thunderbolt	.35	.70	1.05
59,60: #60-Prankster app.	.25	.50	.75

THUNDER MOUNTAIN (See 4-Color Comics #246)

TICK TOCK TALES
Jan, 1946 - #34, 1951
Magazine Enterprises

#1-The Pixies	1.35	2.75	4.00
2-10	.65	1.35	2.00
11-34	.40	.80	1.20

TICKLE COMICS (Also see Gay & Smile Comics)
1955 (52pgs.) (5x7¼") (7¢)
Modern Store Publ.

#1	.65	1.35	2.00

TIGER
March, 1970 - #6, Jan, 1971 (15¢)
Charlton Press (King Features)

#1	.15	.30	.45
2-6		.15	.30
R-01(1973)-36pg. Premium in color; Quincy app.		.15	.30

TIGER BOY (See Unearthly Spectaculars)

TIGER GIRL
Sept, 1968
Gold Key

#1(10227-809)	1.00	2.00	3.00

TIGER-MAN
April, 1975 - #3, Sept, 1975
Seaboard Periodicals (Atlas)

#1	.25	.50	.75
2,3-Ditko story in each	.15	.30	.45

Thun'da #2(A-1#56). © ME

Thunder Agents #10. © TC

Tick Tock Tales #1. © ME

Tillie The Toiler #5(C&L), © King

Tim Holt #11, © ME

Tim McCoy #16, © CC

TIGER WALKS, A (See Movie Comics)

TILLIE AND TED-TINKERTOTLAND
1945
W. T. Grant Co.

	Good	Fine	Mint
	1.35	2.75	4.00

TILLIE THE TOILER
1926 - 1933 (B&W daily strip reprints)(48pgs)
Cupples & Leon Co.

	Good	Fine	Mint
#1	6.00	12.00	18.00
2-8	5.00	10.00	15.00

NOTE: *First strip app. was January, 1921.*

TILLIE THE TOILER (See Comic Monthly)
1941 - 1950
Dell Publishing Co.

	Good	Fine	Mint
4-Color #15(1941)	8.00	16.00	24.00
Large Feature Comic #30(1941)	8.00	16.00	24.00
4-Color #8(1942)	6.00	12.00	18.00
4-Color #22(1943)	5.00	10.00	15.00
4-Color #55(1944)	4.00	8.00	12.00
4-Color #89(1945)	3.00	6.00	9.00
4-Color #106('45),132('46)	2.50	5.00	7.50
4-Color #150,176,184	2.00	4.00	6.00
4-Color #195,213,237	1.75	3.50	5.25

TIME FOR LOVE (Formerly Romantic Secrets)
V2#53, Oct, 1966 - #47, May, 1976
Charlton Comics

		Fine	Mint
V2#53(10/66),#2(12/67)		.15	.30
#3-47		.10	.20

TIMELESS TOPIX (See Topix)

TIME MACHINE, THE (See 4-Color Comics #1085)

TIME TO RUN
1975
Spire Christian Comics(Fleming H. Revell Co.)

By Al Hartley (from Billy Graham movie)
	.15	.30	.45

TIME TUNNEL, THE (TV)
Feb, 1967 - #2, July, 1967
Gold Key

#1,2	.65	1.35	2.00

TIM HOLT (Becomes Red Mask #42 on)
1948 - #41, May, 1954
Magazine Enterprises

	Good	Fine	Mint
#1(A-1#14)	12.00	24.00	36.00
2(A-1#17), 3(A-1#19)	6.00	12.00	18.00
4-10: #6-1st app. Calico Kid			
	4.00	8.00	12.00
11-Origin & 1st app. Ghost Rider; series begins in Tim Holt	15.00	30.00	45.00
12-16	2.50	5.00	7.50
17-Frazetta cover	12.00	24.00	36.00
18,19	2.50	5.00	7.50
20-Origin Red Mask	3.00	6.00	9.00
21,23-Frazetta covers	9.00	18.00	27.00
22,24-41-Last Ghost Rider	2.00	4.00	6.00

NOTE: *Bolle art in most issues.*

TIM IN SPACE (Formerly Gene Autry Tim)
1950   (1/2 size giveaway) (B&W)
Tim Stores

	.80	1.60	2.40

TIM McCOY (Pictorial Love Stories #22)
#16, Oct, 1948 - #21, Aug-Sept, 1949
Charlton Comics

	Good	Fine	Mint
#16-21	4.00	8.00	12.00

TIM McCOY, POLICE CAR 17
1934   (32 pgs.) (11x14") (B&W)
Whitman Publishing Co.

	Good	Fine	Mint
1933 movie in pictures	6.00	12.00	18.00

TIMMY (See 4-Color #715,823,923,1022)

TIMMY THE TIMID GHOST (See Blue Bird)
1957 - #45, 9/66; Oct, 1967 - #23, July, 1971
Charlton Comics

	Good	Fine	Mint
#1(1957)(1st Series)	.65	1.35	2.00
2-5	.35	.70	1.05
6-10	.20	.40	.60
11(4/58)(Giant)	.20	.40	.60
12-45('66)		.15	.30
#1(11/67)-Bluebird		.15	.30
2-23		.10	.20
Shoe Store Giveaway	.20	.40	.60

TIM TYLER (See Harvey Comics Hits #54)

TIM TYLER
1942; 1973
Better Publications/CC

#1	3.35	6.75	10.00
R-04(--Luck, 1973)Premium, 36pgs. in color-Felix the Cat app.	.20	.40	.60

TIM TYLER COWBOY
#11, Nov, 1948 - #18, 1950
Standard Comics

	Good	Fine	Mint
#11-18	1.75	3.35	5.00

TINKER BELL (See 4-Color #896,982 & Walt
Disney Showcase #37)

TINY FOLKS FUNNIES (See 4-Color Comics #60)

TINY TESSIE (Tessie #1-23; Real Experiences
#24, Oct, 1949   #25)
Marvel Comics (20CC)

#24	.50	1.00	1.50

TINY TIM
1941 - 1949
Dell Publishing Co.

Large Feature Comic #4('41)			
	15.00	30.00	45.00
4-Color #20(1941)	12.00	24.00	36.00
4-Color #42(1943)	6.00	12.00	18.00
4-Color #235	1.50	3.00	4.50

TINY TOT COMICS
1946 - #10, Nov-Dec, 1947
E.C. Comics

#1	8.00	16.00	24.00
2-10	6.00	12.00	18.00

TINY TOT FUNNIES (Becomes Junior Funnies)
June, 1951
Harvey Publ. (King Features Synd.)

#9-Flash Gordon, Mandrake	2.50	5.00	7.50

TINY TOTS COMICS
1943   (Not reprints)
Dell Publishing Co.

#1-Two Kelly stories	20.00	40.00	60.00

TIPPY & CAP STUBBS (See 4-Color #210,242)

TIPPY'S FRIENDS GO-GO & ANIMAL
July, 1966 - #15, Oct, 1969   (25¢)
Tower Comics

#1	.15	.30	.45
2-15: #12-15 titled "Tippy's Friend Go-Go"			
		.10	.20

TIPPY TEEN
Nov, 1965 - #27, Feb, 1970   (25¢)

Tower Comics

	Good	Fine	Mint
#1	.15	.30	.45
2-27		.10	.20
Special Collectors' Edition(1969-No#)(25¢)			
	.15	.30	.45

TIPPY TERRY
1963
Super/I.W. Enterprises

Super Reprint #14('63)-Little Grouchy reprts.			
	.35	.70	1.05
I.W. Reprint #1(no date)	.35	.70	1.05

TIP TOP COMICS
April, 1936 - #225, May-July, 1961
United Features/St. John/Dell Publ. Co.

#1-Tarzan by H. Foster, Li'l Abner begin;			
strip reprints	70.00	140.00	210.00
2	30.00	60.00	90.00
3	20.00	40.00	60.00
4	15.00	30.00	45.00
5-10	12.00	24.00	36.00
11-20	10.00	20.00	30.00
21-40: #36-Kurtzman panel	7.00	14.00	21.00
41-50: #41-Has 1st Tarzan Sunday			
	6.00	12.00	18.00
51-53	5.00	10.00	15.00
54-Origin Mirror Man & Triple Terror			
	7.00	14.00	21.00
55,56,58,60	5.00	10.00	15.00
57,59,62-Tarzan by Hogarth	8.00	16.00	24.00
61-Last Tarzan by Foster	5.00	10.00	15.00
63-80: #65,67,68,70,73-No Tarzan			
	4.00	8.00	12.00
81-90	3.00	6.00	9.00
91-100	2.00	4.00	6.00
101-140: #111-Li'l Abner app. #118-No Tarzan.			
#132-No Tarzan	1.75	3.35	5.00
141-170: #157-Last Li'l Abner			
	1.35	2.75	4.00
171-188-Tarzan reprints by B. Lubbers in all.			
#176-Peanuts by Shulz begins			
	1.35	2.75	4.00
189-225	.80	1.60	2.40
Bound Volumes (Very Rare) sold at 1939 World's			
Fair; bound by publ. in pictorial comic			
boards. (Also see Comics on Parade)			
Bound issues #1-12	133.00	266.50	400.00
Bound issues #13-24	100.00	200.00	300.00
Bound issues #25-36	66.50	133.25	200.00

NOTE: *Tarzan covers-#3.9,13,16,18,21,24,27,30,
32-34,36,37,39,41,43,45,47,50 (all worth 10-
20% more). Tarzan by Foster-#1-40,44-50; by
Rex Maxon-#41-43; by Burne Hogarth-#57,59,62.*

Tiny Tot Comics #5, © WMG

Tip Top Comics #11, © UFS

Tip Top Comics #17, © UFS

T-Man #16, © Qua   Tomahawk #92, © DC   Tom & Jerry #77, © Loew's Inc.

TIP TOPPER COMICS
1949 - 1954
United Features Syndicate

	Good	Fine	Mint
#1-Li'l Abner, Abbie & Slats			
	1.35	2.75	4.00
2-5	1.00	2.00	3.00
6-25	.65	1.35	2.00
26-28-Twin Earths	2.00	4.00	6.00

T-MAN
Sept, 1951 - #38, Dec, 1956
Quality Comics Group

#1-Jack Cole art	2.00	4.00	6.00
2,3,5,8-10	1.35	2.75	4.00
4-Crandall cover/story	2.00	4.00	6.00
6-Crandall cover	1.50	3.00	4.50
7-Crandall story	1.75	3.35	5.00
11-38	1.00	2.00	3.00

TNT COMICS
Feb, 1946
Charles Publishing Co.

#1-Yellowjacket app.	2.00	4.00	6.00

TOBY TYLER (See Movie Comics & 4-Color #1092)

TODAY'S BRIDE
Nov, 1955 - #4, Nov, 1956
Ajax/Farrell Publishing Co.

#1	1.00	2.00	3.00
2-4	.65	1.35	2.00

TODAY'S ROMANCE
#5, March, 1952 - #6, May, 1952
Standard Comics

#5,6	.50	1.00	1.50

TOKA (Jungle King)
Aug-Oct, 1964 - #10, Jan, 1967
Dell Publishing Co.

#1	.65	1.35	2.00
2	.40	.80	1.20
3-10	.30	.60	.90

TOMAHAWK (Son of -- #131-140 on cover)
Sept-Oct, 1950 - #140, May-June, 1972
National Periodical Publications

#1	10.00	20.00	30.00
2-Frazetta/Williamson story, 4pgs.			
	8.00	16.00	24.00
3-10	3.50	7.00	10.50

	Good	Fine	Mint
11-20	2.00	4.00	6.00
21-27,30	1.20	2.40	3.60
28-1st app. Lord Shilling(arch-foe)			
	1.35	2.75	4.00
29-Frazetta reprint/Jimmy Wakely #3, 3pgs.			
	6.00	12.00	18.00
31-50	.80	1.60	2.40
51-56,58-70	.60	1.20	1.80
57-Frazetta reprint/Jimmy Wakely #6, 3pgs.			
	5.00	10.00	15.00
71-80	.25	.50	.75
81-1st app. Miss Liberty	.35	.70	1.05
82,84,85,87-95	.25	.50	.75
83-Origin Tomahawk's Rangers			
	.30	.60	.90
86-Last Lord Shilling; origin King Colosso (Giant Ape)	.25	.50	.75
96-Origin & 1st app. The Hood, Alias Lady Shilling	.25	.50	.75
97-106,108,109	.20	.40	.60
107-Origin & 1st app. Thunder-Man			
	.20	.40	.60
110-The Hood & Miss Liberty app.			
	.20	.40	.60
111-The Hood & Thunder-Man team-up			
	.15	.30	.45
112-130	.15	.30	.45
131-Frazetta reprint/Jimmy Wakely #7, 3pgs.; origin Firehair retold	.35	.70	1.05
132,134,136-6pg. Kubert	.20	.40	.60
133,135,137,138,140	.15	.30	.45
139-Frazetta reprint/Star Spangled #113			
	.25	.50	.75

NOTE: *Adams* covers-#116-119,121,123-130. *Firehair* by *Kubert*-#131-134,136. *Maurer* story-#138.

TOM AND JERRY (See Comic Album #4,8,12, Dell Giant #21, Golden Comics Digest #1,5,8, 13,15,18,22,25,28,34, & March of Comics #21, 46,61,70,88,103,119,128,145,154,173,190,207, 224,281,295,305,321,333,345,361,365,388,400)

TOM AND JERRY COMICS (M.G.M.)(Our Gang #1-59) #193, 6/48 - #291, 2/75; #292, 3/77 - Present
Dell Publ. Co./Gold Key #213 on

4-Color #193	3.00	6.00	9.00
#60-80	1.35	2.75	4.00
81-100	.75	1.50	2.25
101-130	.50	1.00	1.50
131-160	.35	.70	1.05
161-200	.25	.50	.75
201-212(7-9/62)	.20	.40	.60
213-215-All titled "--Funhouse". #213,214-84pgs.	.40	.80	1.20
216-230	.20	.40	.60

(Tom & Jerry cont'd)	Good	Fine	Mint
31-270	.15	.30	.45
71-301: #286-"Tom & Jerry"		.15	.30
ack to School #1(9/56)	1.35	2.75	4.00
ouse From T.R.A.P.#1(7/66)-Giant, Gold Key			
		.40	.80	1.20
icnic Time #1(7/58)	1.00	2.00	3.00
ummer Fun #1(7/54)-Droopy written by Carl			
Barks	2.50	5.00	7.50
ummer Fun #2-4(7/57)	1.00	2.00	3.00
ummer Fun #1(G.K.-reprints,'67)-Reprints			
Barks' Droopy/Winter Carnival #2			
		.40	.80	1.20
oy Fair #1(100pgs.-'58)	1.00	2.00	3.00
inter Carnival #1('52)-Droopy written by			
Barks	3.00	6.00	9.00
inter Carnival #2('53)-Droopy written by			
Barks (Giant)	2.00	4.00	6.00
inter Fun #3-7('54-'58)	.80	1.60	2.40

NOTE: #60-87,98-121,268,277,289 are 52pgs.

OMB OF DARKNESS (Formerly Beware)
9, July, 1974 - #23, Nov, 1976
arvel Comics Group

	Good	Fine	Mint
9-19: #17-Woodbridge reprt./Astonishing #62			
	.15	.30	.45
0-Everett Venus reprt./Venus #19			
	.15	.30	.45
1-23: #23-Everett reprt.	.15	.30	

OMB OF DRACULA (See Giant-Size Dracula)
oril, 1972 - Present
arvel Comics Group

	Good	Fine	Mint
1	1.35	2.75	4.00
2-5: #3-Intro. Dr. Rachel Van Helsing			
	.65	1.35	2.00
6-9: #6-Intro. Inspector Chelm			
	.50	1.00	1.50
0-1st app. Blade the Vampire Slayer			
	.60	1.20	1.80
1,12,14-20: #12-Brunner cover pencils			
	.35	.70	1.05
3-Origin Blade the Vampire Slayer			
	.50	1.00	1.50
1-Origin Dr. Sun	.30	.60	.90
2-24,26-28,30	.25	.50	.75
5-Origin & 1st app. Hannibal King			
	.30	.60	.90
9-Origin Taj	.30	.60	.90
1-40: #33-Origin Quincy Harker			
	.20	.40	.60
1,42,44-49	.15	.30	.45
3-Wrightson cover	.20	.40	.60
0-Silver Surfer app.	.20	.40	.60
1-53,55-60	.15	.30	.45
4-Birth Dracula's Son	.20	.40	.60

	Good	Fine	Mint
61,62	.15	.30	.45

TOMB OF LIGEIA (See Movie Classics)

TOMB OF TERROR (Thrills of Tomorrow #17 on)
June, 1952 - #16, July, 1954
Harvey Publications

	Good	Fine	Mint
#1	2.00	4.00	6.00
2-12,14-16	1.20	2.40	3.60
13-Special S/F ish.	1.50	3.00	4.50

NOTE: *Nostrand art-#8,9(2pgs.),10-12,15,16.*
Powell art-#1,3,4(1pg.),5,9-16.

TOMBSTONE TERRITORY (See 4-Color #1123)

TOM CAT
July, 1956 - #7, May, 1957
Charlton Comics

	Good	Fine	Mint
#1-7(CDC)	.20	.40	.60

TOM CORBETT SPACE CADET (TV)
1952 - #11, Sept-Nov, 1954
Dell Publishing Co.

	Good	Fine	Mint
4-Color #378,400,421-All by McWilliams			
	2.50	5.00	7.50
#4-11	2.00	4.00	6.00

TOM CORBETT SPACE CADET (See March of Comics #102)

TOM CORBETT SPACE CADET
May-June, 1955 - V3#1, Nov-Dec, 1955
Prize Publications

	Good	Fine	Mint
V2#1-3	1.35	2.75	4.00
V3#1	1.00	2.00	3.00

TOM LANDRY & THE DALLAS COWBOYS
1973 (35¢)
Spire Christian Comics/Fleming H. Revell Co.

	Good	Fine	Mint
#1	.15	.30	.45

TOM MIX (-- Commando Comics #10-12)
Sept, 1940 - #12, Nov, 1942 (36pgs.)
Given away for 2 Ralston box tops
Ralston-Purina Co.

	Good	Fine	Mint
#1-Origin(life)Tom Mix; Fred Meagher art			
	35.00	70.00	105.00
2	25.00	50.00	75.00
3-9	17.50	35.00	52.50
10-Origin Tom Mix Commando Unit; Speed O'Dare			
begins	12.00	24.00	36.00

Tomb Of Terror #7, © Harv

Tom Corbett #4, © Dell

Tom Mix Ralston #1, © Tom Mix

Tom Mix Western #45, © Tom Mix　　Tonto #24, © Lone Ranger　　Toonerville Trolley 1921, © C&L

(Tom Mix cont'd)	Good	Fine	Mint
11,12	12.00	24.00	36.00

TOM MIX NATIONAL CHICLE GUM CO.
(See Big Thrill Booklet) (46 titles known)
1934 (8pgs.)(2 inside ill. with text)
National Chicle Gum Co.   (2-3/8"x2-3/4")

each........	4.00	8.00	12.00

NOTE: *Like Big Thrill Gum Booklets; color on cover only.*

TOM MIX WESTERN (Also see Master Comics)
Jan, 1948 - #61, May, 1953
Fawcett Publications

#1	14.00	28.00	42.00
2	8.00	16.00	24.00
3-5	6.00	12.00	18.00
6-10	5.00	10.00	15.00
11-20	3.00	6.00	9.00
21-40	2.50	5.00	7.50
41-61	2.00	4.00	6.00

TOMMY OF THE BIG TOP
1948 - 1949
King Features Synd./Standard Comics

#10-12	.80	1.60	2.40

TOM SAWYER (See Famous Stories & Advs.of --)

TOM SAWYER & HUCK FINN
1925   (48 pgs. in color)
Stoll & Edwards Co.

By Dwiggins	8.00	16.00	24.00

TOM SAWYER COMICS
1951 ?   (Soft Cover)
Giveaway

Contains a coverless Hopalong Cassidy from
1951; other combinations possible.

	1.00	2.00	3.00

TOM TERRIFIC! (TV)
Summer, 1957 - #6, Fall, 1958
Pines Comics

#1	1.00	2.00	3.00
2-6	.65	1.35	2.00

TOM THUMB (See 4-Color Comics #972)

TOM-TOM, THE JUNGLE BOY
1947; Nov, 1957 - #3, Mar, 1958
Magazine Enterprises

	Good	Fine	Mint
#1-3(1947)	.65	1.35	2.00
1(1957)(& Itchi the Monk),2,3('58)			
	.35	.70	1.05
IW Reprint #1,2,8,10	.25	.50	.75

TONKA (See 4-Color Comics #966)

TONTO (The Lone Ranger's Companion --)
#2, Feb-Apr, 1951 - #33, Nov, 1958
Dell Publishing Co.

4-Color #312(1951)	2.50	5.00	7.50
#2,3	1.50	3.00	4.50
4-10	1.20	2.40	3.60
11-20	1.00	2.00	3.00
21-33	.80	1.60	2.40

(See Aurora Comic Booklets)

TONY TRENT (The Face #1,2)
1948 - 1949
Big Shot/Columbia Comics Group

#3,4: #3-The Face app.	2.00	4.00	6.00

TOODLES, THE
1-2/51 - #10, 7-8/51; 1956 (Newspaper reprts)
Ziff-Davis(Approved Comics)/Argo

#1	1.35	2.75	4.00
2-9	.80	1.60	2.40

10-Painted cover, some newspaper reprints

#1(Argo, 3/56)	1.00	2.00	3.00

TOONERVILLE TROLLEY
1921   (Daily strip reprints)(B&W)(48pgs.)
Cupples & Leon Co.

#1-By Fontaine Fox	12.00	24.00	36.00

TOOTS & CASPER (See Large Feature Comic #5)

TOP
1945
Consolidated Book (Lev Gleason)

#2001	3.00	6.00	9.00

TOP ADVENTURE COMICS
1964   (Reprints)
I.W. Enterprises

#1-Reprints/Explorer Joe #2; Krigstein art			
	1.00	2.00	3.00
2-Black Dwarf	1.35	2.75	4.00

TOP CAT (TV) (Hanna-Barbera)
Dec-Feb, 1961-62 - #31, Sept, 1970
Dell Publishing Co./Gold Key #4 on

	Good	Fine	Mint
#1	.40	.80	1.20
2-5	.25	.50	.75
6-10	.20	.40	.60
11-31		.20	.35

TOP CAT (TV) (Hanna-Barbera)
Nov, 1970 - #20, Nov, 1973
Charlton Comics

#1		.20	.35
2-20		.10	.20

NOTE: #8(1/72) went on sale late in 1972 between #14 & #15 with the Jan., 1973 issues.

TOP COMICS
July, 1967 (All rebound issues)
K.K. Publications/Gold Key

#1-Beagle Boys, Bugs Bunny, Chip 'n' Dale,
Daffy Duck, Flintstones, Flipper, Huckle-
berry Hound, Huey, Dewey & Louie, Junior
Woodchucks, The Jetsons, Lassie, The
Little Monsters, Moby Duck, Porky Pig(has
Gold Key label - says Top Comics on inside)
Scamp, Super Goof, Three Stooges, Tom &
Jerry, Top Cat(#21), Tweety & Sylvester,
Walt Disney Comics & Stories(#322), Woody
Woodpecker, Yogi Bear, Zorro known; each
character given own book.

	.40	.80	1.20
#1-Uncle Scrooge(#70)	1.50	3.00	4.50
#1-Donald Duck(not Barks), Mickey Mouse, Tar-
zan	1.00	2.00	3.00

#2-Bugs Bunny, Daffy Duck, Donald Duck(not
Barks), Mickey Mouse, Porky Pig, Super
Goof, Three Stooges, Tom & Jerry, Tweety
& Sylvester, Walt Disney's C&S(reprints
#325), Woody Woodpecker, Zorro

	.35	.70	1.05
#2-Snow White & 7 Dwarfs(6/67-'44 reprint),
Uncle Scrooge(Barks art)(#71)	1.00	2.00	3.00
#3-Donald Duck	.50	1.00	1.50
#3-Uncle Scrooge(#72)	1.00	2.00	3.00
#3-The Flintstones, Mickey Mouse(reprts.#115),
Tom & Jerry, Woody Woodpecker, Yogi Bear	.25	.50	.75
#4-The Flintstones, Mickey Mouse, Woody Wood-
pecker	.25	.50	.75

NOTE: Each book in this series is identical
to its counterpart except for cover, and
came out at same time. The number in parenthesis is the original issue it contains.

TOP DETECTIVE COMICS
1964 (Reprints)
I.W. Enterprises

	Good	Fine	Mint
#9-Young King Cole & Dr. Drew(not Granden-
etti)	.35	.70	1.05

TOP ELIMINATOR (Formerly Teenage Hotrodders;
Drag 'n' Wheels #30 on)
#25, Sept, 1967 - #29, July, 1968
Charlton Comics

#26-29	.15	.30	.45

TOP FLIGHT COMICS
1947; July, 1949
Four Star Publications/St. John Publ.

#1	1.00	2.00	3.00
1(7/49)-Hector the Inspector
.50	1.00	1.50

TOP GUN (See 4-Color Comics #927)

TOP GUNS (See Super DC Giant & Showcase #72)

TOPIX (--Comics)(Timeless Topix-early issues)
1943 - V10#15, 1/28/52 (Weekly-later issues)
Catechetical Guild Educational Society

V1-V4	1.00	2.00	3.00
V5#1-15	.65	1.35	2.00
V6#1-14,V7#1-17(5/1/49)	.50	1.00	1.50
V8#1-10	.35	.70	1.05
V8#11(12/5/49)-Soft cover, publ. weekly			
	.35	.70	1.05
V8#12-Ingels art	1.20	2.40	3.60
V8#13-18(2/13/50),#19-30(5/15/50)			
	.35	.70	1.05
V9#1-15,V10#1-15	.35	.70	1.05

TOP JUNGLE COMICS
1964 (Reprint)
I.W. Enterprises

| #1(no date)-Reprints White Princess of the
Jungle #3, minus cvr.	1.00	2.00	3.00

TOP LOVE STORIES
Jan, 1951 - #19, Mar, 1954
Star Publications

#3-10,13,16,17,19	.75	1.50	2.25
11,12,14,15,18-Disbrow stories			
	1.00	2.00	3.00

NOTE: L. B. Cole cover-#15.

Top Adventure #2, © I.W.

Topix V5#8, © CG

Top Love Stories #6, © Star

Top-Notch Comics #8, © MLJ

Top-Notch Comics #25, © MLJ

Tor 3-D(Oct.), © STJ

TOP-NOTCH COMICS(--Laugh #28-45; Laugh #46 on)
Dec, 1939 - #45, June, 1944
MLJ Magazines

	Good	Fine	Mint
#1-Origin The Wizard; Kardak, the Mystic Mag- ician begins; J. Cole art			
	50.00	100.00	150.00
2-Jack Cole art	25.00	50.00	75.00
3-Bob Phantom begins	20.00	40.00	60.00
4	15.00	30.00	45.00
5	13.50	26.75	40.00
6	12.00	24.00	36.00
7-Kalthar, the Giant Man x-over in Kardak; The Shield x-over in Wizard; The Wizard dons new costume	25.00	50.00	75.00
8-Origin The Firefly & Roy, the Super Boy	25.00	50.00	75.00
9-Origin & 1st app. The Black Hood			
	50.00	100.00	150.00
10	25.00	50.00	75.00
11-20	15.00	30.00	45.00
21-30: #23,24-No Wizard, Roy app. in each. #25-Last Bob Phantom, Roy app. #26-Roy app. #27-Last Firefly. #28-Suzie begins. #29-Last Kardak	12.00	24.00	36.00
31-40: #34,38,39-Black Hood series ends			
	8.00	16.00	24.00
41,43-Black Hood app.	2.50	5.00	7.50
42,44,45	2.00	4.00	6.00

TOPPER & NEIL   (See 4-Color Comics #859)

TOPPS COMICS
1947
Four Star Publications

#1	.65	1.35	2.00

TOPS
1949   (Large Size) (10"x13")
Consolidated Book Co. (Lev Gleason)

#1,2-(Rare)-Crandall/Lubbers, Biro art			
	20.00	40.00	60.00

TOPS COMICS
1944   (132 pgs.) (10¢)
Consolidated Book Publishers

No#(Color cover, inside in red shade & some in full color)-Ace Kelly by Rick Yager, Black Orchid, Don on the Farm, Dinky Dinkerton (Rare)	7.00	14.00	21.00

NOTE: This book is printed in such a way that when the staple
is removed, the strips on the left side of the book correspond with
the same strips on the right side. Therefore, if strips are removed
from the book, each strip can be folded into a complete comic
section of its own.

TOP SECRET
January, 1952
Hillman Publ.

	Good	Fine	Mint
#1	1.00	2.00	3.00

TOP SECRET ADVENTURES   (See Spyman)

TOP SECRETS   (-- of the F.B.I.)
1947 - #10, July-Aug, 1949
Street & Smith Publications

#1-Powell cover/stories	2.00	4.00	6.00
2-10-Powell cvrs/stories	1.50	3.00	4.50

TOPS IN ADVENTURE
Fall, 1952   (132 pgs.)
Ziff-Davis Publ. Co.

#1-Crusader from Mars & The Hawk; Powell art			
	2.50	5.00	7.50

TOPS IN HUMOR
1944   (Small size) (7½x5")
Consolidated Book Publishers

#2001(#1)-Origin The Jack O' Spades, Ace Kelly by Rick Yager, Black Orchid(female crime fighter) app.	5.00	10.00	15.00
#2	3.00	6.00	9.00

TOP SPOT COMICS
1945
Top Spot Publ. Co.

#1-The Menace, Duke of Darkness app.			
	2.50	5.00	7.50

TOPSY-TURVY
April, 1945
R. B. Leffingwell Publ.

#1	1.00	2.00	3.00

TOR   (#1 titled "One Million Years Ago")(No#2)
#1, Sept, 1953; #3, May, 1954 - #5, Oct, 1954
St. John Publishing Co.

#1-Origin; Kubert art	25.00	50.00	75.00
3-5-Kubert art; Danny Dreams by Toth-#3			
	16.50	33.25	50.00
3-D #2(10/53)-Kubert	7.00	14.00	21.00
3-D #2(10/53)-Oversized, otherwise same contents	7.00	14.00	21.00
3-D #2(11/53)-Kubert	7.00	14.00	21.00

NOTE: All 3-D's have Powell art.

406

TOR
May-June, 1975 – #6, Mar-Apr, 1976
National Periodical Publications

	Good	Fine	Mint
#1-New origin by Kubert	.20	.40	.60
2-Origin reprt./St.John#1	.15	.30	.45
3-6	.15	.30	.45

NOTE: *All Kubert cover/stories; reprints-#2-6.*

TORCHY (--Blond Bombshell)(See Modern, Military & Dollman)
11/49 – #6, 9/50
Quality Comics Group

	Good	Fine	Mint
#1-Bill Ward cover, Gill Fox stories	70.00	140.00	210.00
2,3-Fox cover/stories	25.00	50.00	75.00
4-Fox cover, 3 stories + 1 Ward story	30.00	60.00	90.00
5,6-Ward covers, 9pgs. + 3 Fox stories in each	40.00	80.00	120.00
Super Reprint #16('64)-Reprints #4 with new cover	5.00	10.00	15.00

TORMENTED, THE
July, 1954 – #2, Sept, 1954
Sterling Comics

#1,2	1.00	2.00	3.00

TORNADO TOM (See Mighty Midget Comics)

TOTAL WAR (M.A.R.S. Patrol #3 on)
July, 1965 – #2, Oct, 1965
Gold Key

#1,2-Wood art	1.35	2.75	4.00

TOUGH KID SQUAD COMICS
March, 1942
Marvel Comics

#1-Origin The Human Top & The Tough Kid Squad; The Flying Flame app.	80.00	160.00	240.00

TOWER OF SHADOWS (Creatures on the Loose
Sept, 1969 – #9, Jan, 1971 #10 on)
Marvel Comics Group

#1-Steranko, Craig story	1.00	2.00	3.00
2-Neal Adams story	.65	1.35	2.00
3-Smith story	.65	1.35	2.00
4-Kirby/Everett cover	.50	1.00	1.50
5-Smith, Wood story	.80	1.60	2.40
6,7-Wood stories	.65	1.35	2.00
8,9-Wrightson covers	.50	1.00	1.50
Special #1(12/71)-Adams sty.	.50	1.00	1.50

NOTE: *Issues #1-9 contain new stories with* some pre-Marvel age reprints in #6-9. *H.P. Lovecraft adaptation-#4.*

TOWN & COUNTRY
May, 1940

	Good	Fine	Mint
Origin The Falcon	12.00	24.00	36.00

TOWN THAT FORGOT SANTA, THE
1961 (24 pgs.) (Giveaway)
W. T. Grant Co.

No#	1.00	2.00	3.00

TOYLAND COMICS
Jan, 1947 – 1947
Fiction House Magazine

#1	2.00	4.00	6.00
2-4	1.35	2.75	4.00
148pg. Issue	2.00	4.00	6.00

NOTE: *All above contain strips by Al Walker.*

TOY TOWN COMICS
1945 – 1946
Toytown/Orbit Publ./B. Antin/Swapper Quart.

#1-Mertie Mouse	1.00	2.00	3.00
2-7	.50	1.00	1.50

TRAGG & THE SKY GODS (See Mystery Comics
Digest #3 & Spine Tingling Tales)
June, 1975 – #8, Feb, 1977
Gold Key

#1-Origin	.25	.50	.75
2-8: #4-Sabre-Fang app. #8-Ostellon app.	.15	.30	.45

NOTE: *Santos art-#1,2; covers-#3-7.*

TRAIL BLAZERS (Red Dragon #5 on)
1941 – 1942
Street & Smith Publications

#1	4.00	8.00	12.00
2-4	2.50	5.00	7.50

TRAIL COLT
1949
Magazine Enterprises

#1(A-1#24)-7pg. Frazetta story reprinted in Manhunt #13; Ingels cover (Scarce)	10.00	20.00	30.00
2(A-1#26)-Undercover Girl; Ingels cover	8.00	16.00	24.00

Torchy #2, © DC (Qua)   Torchy #4, © DC (Qua)

Tough Kid Squad #1, © MCG

Treasure Box--(Box), © C&L

Treasure Box (Smitty), © N.Y. News Synd.

Treasure Comics #1, © Prize

TRAPPED!
Oct, 1954 - #4, 1955
Periodical House Magazines (Ace)

	Good	Fine	Mint
#1-4	.65	1.35	2.00

TRAVELS OF JAIMIE McPHEETERS, THE (TV)
December, 1963
Gold Key

#1	.35	.70	1.05

TREASURE BOX OF FAMOUS COMICS
Mid 1930's   (32 pgs.) (6-7/8"x8-1/2")
Cupples & Leon Co.

Box + 5 titles: Reg'lar Fellers, Little
Orphan Annie, Smitty, Harold Teen, Dick
Tracy & Dick Tracy Jr. (These are abbrev-
iated version of hardcover editions)
          (Set)...... 90.00 180.00 270.00

TREASURE CHEST (Catholic Guild)
3/12/46 - V27#8, 7/72 (Educational comics)
George A. Pflaum (not publ. during summer)

V1#1	1.00	2.00	3.00
2-12: #5-Dr. Styx app. by Baily			
	.50	1.00	1.50
V2, V3	.40	.80	1.20
V4#1-20(9/9/48) - 5/31/49)	.35	.70	1.05
V5#1-20(9/6/49) - 5/31/50)	.20	.40	.60
V6#1-20(9/14/50-5/31/51)	.20	.40	.60
V7#1-20(9/13/51-6/5/52)	.20	.40	.60
V8#1-20(9/11/52-6/4/53)	.20	.40	.60
V9#1-20('53-'54)	.20	.40	.60
V10#1-20('54-'55)	.20	.40	.60
V11('55-'56), V12('56-'57)	.15	.30	.45
V13-V20('57-'65)	.15	.30	.45
V13#2,6,8,11-Ingels story 1.00	2.00	3.00	
V21-V25('65-'70)-(2 V24#5's 11/7/68 & 11/21/ 68)(No V24#6)	.15	.30	.45
V21#10-Ingels story	1.00	2.00	3.00
V26,V27#1-8-(V26,27-68pgs)	.15	.30	.45
Summer Edition V1#1-6('66), V2#1-6('67)			
		.15	.30

NOTE: *Anderson story*-V18#13. *Borth stories*-
V13#2,6,11. Crandall stories (R=Reprints)-
*V7#20,V16#7,9,12,14,17,20; V17#1,2,4,5,14,16,
20; V18#1,7,9,10,17,19; V19#4,11,13,16,19;
V20#1,2,6,9,10,12,14-16,20; V21#1-3,5,8,9,11,
13,16,17; V22#3,7,9-11,14,16,20; V23#3,6,9,
13,16; V24#8,10; V25#16; V27#1,3-5(R),6(R),
8(2pg); covers-V16#7, V19#4, V21#5,9, V22#7,
11, V23#9,16.*

TREASURE CHEST OF THE WORLD'S BEST COMICS
1945   (500 pgs.) (Hardcover)
Superior, Toronto, Canada

		Good	Fine	Mint

Contains Blue Beetle, Capt. Combat, John
Wayne, Dynamic Man, Nemo, Li'l Abner; Contents can vary - represents random binding of
extra books   7.00 14.00 21.00

TREASURE COMICS
June-July, 1945 - #12, Fall, 1947
Prize Publications (American Boys' Comics)

#1-Paul Bunyan, Marco Polo, Highwayman & Carrot Topp begin	2.50	5.00	7.50
2-4,12	1.35	2.75	4.00
5,6,11-Krigstein art	2.50	5.00	7.50
7,8-Frazetta, 5pgs. ea.	7.00	14.00	21.00
9,10-Jr. Rangers by Kirby in ea.; #10-Kirby cover	3.50	7.00	10.50

TREASURE ISLAND (See 4-Color #624 & Movie
Classics & Comics)

TREASURE OF COMICS
1947; #2, July, 1947 - #4, Sept, 1947
St. John Publishing Co.

No#(#1)-Abbie 'n' Slats (No# on cover, #1 on inside)	3.00	6.00	9.00
#2-Jim Hardy	2.00	4.00	6.00
3-Bill Bumlin	2.00	4.00	6.00
4-Abbie 'n' Slats	2.00	4.00	6.00

TREASURY OF COMICS
Mar, 1948 - #5, 1948; 1949 (500 pgs.)
St. John Publishing Co.

#1	4.00	8.00	12.00
2(#2 on cvr,#1 on inside)	3.00	6.00	9.00
3-5	2.50	5.00	7.50
#1-(500pgs.)-Abbie & Slats, Abbott & Costello, Little Annie Rooney, Little Audrey, Jim Hardy, Ella Cinders (16 books bound togeth- er - $1.00)	8.00	16.00	24.00

TREASURY OF DOGS, A
Oct, 1956   (Giant)
Dell Publishing Co.

#1	2.00	4.00	6.00

TREASURY OF HORSES, A
1955   (Giant)
Dell Publishing Co.

#1	2.00	4.00	6.00

TRIALS OF LULU AND LEANDER, THE
1906   (32 pgs. in color) (10x16")
William A. Stokes Co.

(See Roy Rogers --)

Trials of Lulu & Leander cont'd)

	Good	Fine	Mint
y F. M. Howarth	15.00	30.00	45.00

RIGGER (See Roy Rogers --)

RIGGER TWINS
ar-Apr, 1973   (One Shot)
ational Periodical Publications

1-Trigger Twins & Pow Wow Smith reprints; Infantino art		.20	.35

RIPLE GIANT COMICS (See Archie All-Star Spec.

RIPLE THREAT
inter, 1945
pecial Action/Holyoke/Gerona Publ.

1-Duke of Darkness, King O'Leary	2.50	5.00	7.50

ROUBLE SHOOTERS, THE (See 4-Color #1108)

RUE ADVENTURES (Formerly True Western)
3, May, 1950   (Men's Adventures #4 on)
arvel Comics (CCC)

	Good	Fine	Mint
3	1.35	2.75	4.00

RUE ANIMAL PICTURE STORIES
inter, 1947 - #2, Spr-Summer, 1947
rue Comics Press

1,2	.75	1.50	2.25

RUE AVIATION PICTURE STORIES (Aviation
dventures & Model Building #16)
942 - #15, Sept-Oct, 1946
arents' Magazine Institute

1-(titled --Aviation Comics Digest)(Not digest size)	1.75	3.35	5.00
2-14	1.00	2.00	3.00
5-(titled "True Aviation Advs. & Model Building")	1.00	2.00	3.00

RUE BRIDE'S EXPERIENCES
pril, 1955 - #15, Sept, 1955
rue Love (Harvey)

#11-15	.50	1.00	1.50

TRUE BRIDE-TO-BE ROMANCES
Aug, 1953 - #28, Feb, 1958
Home Comics/True Love(Harvey)

#1	1.00	2.00	3.00

	Good	Fine	Mint
2-5	.80	1.60	2.40
6-15	.50	1.00	1.50
16,18-22,24-28	.35	.70	1.05
17-S&K cover, Powell sty.	1.00	2.00	3.00
23-Powell story	.50	1.00	1.50

TRUE COMICS
April, 1941 - #84, Aug, 1950
True Comics/Parents' Magazine Press

#1	4.00	8.00	12.00
2-10	2.00	4.00	6.00
11-30	1.35	2.75	4.00
31-50	1.00	2.00	3.00
51-81,83,84	.65	1.35	2.00
82-Distr. to subscribers through the mail only (Rare)	3.00	6.00	9.00

NOTE: #80-84 have soft covers & combined with
Tex Granger, Jack Armstrong, & Calling All
Kids. #68-78 featured true FBI adventures.

TRUE COMICS AND ADVENTURE STORIES
1965   (Giant) (25¢)
Parents' Magazine Institute

#1	.75	1.50	2.25

TRUE COMPLETE MYSTERY
#5, April, 1949 - #7, Aug, 1949
Marvel Comics

#5-7	1.50	3.00	4.50

TRUE CONFESSIONS
1949
Fawcett Publications

#1	1.50	3.00	4.50

TRUE CONFIDENCES
Fall, 1949 - #4, June, 1950
Fawcett Publications

#1	1.50	3.00	4.50
2-4-Bob Powell art #4	1.00	2.00	3.00

TRUE CRIME CASES
1944; Vl#6, 6-7/49 - V2#1, 8-10/49
St. John Publishing Co.

1944-(100pgs.)	5.00	10.00	15.00
V1#6, V2#1	1.35	2.75	4.00

TRUE CRIME COMICS (See Complete Book of --)
1942
Comic House Publications/William H. Wise

True Aviation-#15, © PMI

True Comics #58, © PMI

True Crime #2, © Mag. Village

409

True Love Pictorial #3, © STJ   True Sport Pic. Stories V4#7, © S & S   Truthful Love #2, © YM

(True Crime Comics cont'd)	Good	Fine	Mint
#1-The War Eagle	6.00	12.00	18.00

TRUE CRIME COMICS
#2, May, 1947; #3, 7-8/48 - #6, 6-7/49;
V2#1 - 8-9/49
Magazine Village

#2-Jack Cole cover & stories; used in <u>Seduct-
ion of the Innocent</u>; drug story
	17.50	35.00	52.50
3-Cole cover/stories; heroin drug story			
	12.00	24.00	36.00
4-6: #4-Jack Cole cover. #5-Reprints #3 min-
us drug story	3.00	6.00	9.00

V2#1-Used in <u>Seduction of the Innocent</u>, pgs.
81,82; Toth, Wood(3pgs.), Roussos story;
Cole reprint from #2 + Cole cover
| | 7.00 | 14.00 | 21.00 |

TRUE GHOST STORIES   (See Ripley's --)

TRUE LIFE ROMANCES
Dec, 1955   (<u>Romances</u> on inside)
Ajax/Farrell Publications

| #1 | 1.00 | 2.00 | 3.00 |

TRUE LIFE SECRETS
#3, July-Aug, 1951 - #28, Sept, 1955
Romantic Love Stories/Charlton

#3	1.00	2.00	3.00
4-10	.65	1.35	2.00
11-28	.40	.80	1.20

TRUE LIFE TALES
#8, Oct, 1949 - #2, Jan, 1950
Marvel Comics (CCC)

| #8(10/49) | .80 | 1.60 | 2.40 |
| 2(1/50)-Photo cover | .80 | 1.60 | 2.40 |

TRUE LOVE CONFESSIONS
May, 1954 - #11, Jan, 1956
Premier Magazines

| #1 | 1.00 | 2.00 | 3.00 |
| 2-11 | .75 | 1.50 | 2.25 |

TRUE LOVE PICTORIAL
1952 - #11, Aug, 1954
St. John Publishing Co.

| #1 | 1.50 | 3.00 | 4.50 |
| 2 | 1.20 | 2.40 | 3.60 |
| 3-5(All 100pgs.): #5-formerly TeenAge Temp-
tations (4/53); Kubert stories-#3,5; Baker | | | |

stories-#3-5	2.50	5.00	7.50
6,7-Baker cover/stories	1.50	3.00	4.50
8-11-Baker cover/story	1.25	2.50	3.75

TRUE LOVE PROBLEMS & ADVICE ILLUSTRATED
June, 1949 - #44, Mar, 1957
McCombs/Harvey Publ./Home Comics

V1#1-Powell art	1.20	2.40	3.60
2-10	.65	1.35	2.00
11-37,39-44	.35	.70	1.0
38-S&K cover	1.00	2.00	3.00

TRUE MYSTERIES
June, 1949
Marvel Comics

| #6 | 1.00 | 2.00 | 3.00 |

TRUE SECRETS
#4, Feb, 1951 - #40, Sept, 1956
Marvel/Atlas Comics (MPI)

#4	.65	1.35	2.00
5-21,23-40	.35	.70	1.05
22-Everett story	.80	1.60	2.40

TRUE SPORT PICTURE STORIES
1941 - V5#2, July-Aug, 1949
Street & Smith Publications

V1#4-12(1941-42)	1.50	3.00	4.50
V2#1-12(1943-44)	1.00	2.00	3.00
V3#1-12(1945-46)	.65	1.35	2.00
V4#1-12(1947-48), V5#1,2	.50	1.00	1.50

NOTE: <u>Powell</u> art-V3#10, V4#1,2,4,6,12, V5#2.

TRUE STORIES OF ROMANCE
Jan, 1950 - #3, May, 1950
Fawcett Publications

| #1 | 1.00 | 2.00 | 3.00 |
| 2,3 | .65 | 1.35 | 2.00 |

TRUE STORY OF JESSE JAMES, THE
(See 4-Color Comics #757)

TRUE SWEETHEART SECRETS
May, 1950 - #10, Nov, 1952
Fawcett Publications

| #1 | 1.00 | 2.00 | 3.00 |
| 2-10: #5-Powell art | .50 | 1.00 | 1.50 |

TRUE TALES OF LOVE   (Formerly Secret Story
#22, 4/56 - #31, 9/57   Romances
Atlas Comics (TCI)

(True Tales/Love cont'd)	Good	Fine	Mint
22	.35	.70	1.05
23-31: Colleta art in most.	.20	.40	.60

TRUE 3-D
ec, 1953 - #2, Feb, 1954
arvey Publications

	Good	Fine	Mint
1-Nostrand, Powell art	4.00	8.00	12.00
2	4.00	8.00	12.00

TRUE-TO-LIFE ROMANCES
3, April, 1950 - #23, Oct, 1954
tar Publ. #3/Quality Comics Group

3(4/50)	1.00	2.00	3.00
4-9,12,16,18,22,23	1.00	2.00	3.00
0-11,14,17,19-21-Disbrow stories			
	1.35	2.75	4.00
3-Kamen, Disbrow stys.	1.75	3.25	5.25
5-Wood, Disbrow stys.	2.50	5.00	7.50

TRUE WAR EXPERIENCES
ug, 1952 - #4, Dec, 1952
arvey Publications

1	1.00	2.00	3.00
2-4	.65	1.35	2.00

TRUE WAR ROMANCES
ept, 1952 - #21, June, 1955
uality Comics Group

1-Photo cover	2.00	4.00	6.00
2-21	1.00	2.00	3.00

TRUE WAR STORIES (See Ripley's --)

TRUE WEST
949

1-Billy the Kid	1.50	3.00	4.50

TRUE WESTERN (True Adventures #3)
ec, 1949 - #2, Mar, 1950
arvel Comics (MMC)

1,2	2.00	4.00	6.00

TRUE WEST ROMANCE
952
uality Comics Group

21	.80	1.60	2.40

TRUMP (Magazine format)
an, 1957 - #2, Mar, 1957

HMH Publishing Co.

	Good	Fine	Mint
#1-Harvey Kurtzman satire	9.00	18.00	27.00
2 " " "	7.00	14.00	21.00

NOTE: *Davis, Elder, Heath, Jaffee* art-#1,2;
Wood-#1. #2-article by Mel Brooks.

TRUMPETS WEST (See 4-Color Comics #875)

TRUTH ABOUT CRIME
1949   (132 pgs.)
Fox Features Syndicate

No#-See Fox Giants. Contents can vary and
determines price.

TRUTH ABOUT MOTHER GOOSE (See 4-Color #862)

TRUTH BEHIND THE TRIAL OF CARDINAL
MINDSZENTY, THE
1949   (24 pgs.)
Catechetical Guild Educational Society

	2.00	4.00	6.00

TRUTHFUL LOVE (Formerly Youthful Love)
#2, July, 1950
Youthful Magazines

#2	.50	1.00	1.50

TUBBY (Marge's --) (Little Lulu)
1952 - #49, Dec-Feb, 1961-62
Dell Publishing Co./Gold Key

4-Color #381-Stanley art	7.00	14.00	21.00
4-Color #430,444,461-All by Stanley			
	4.00	8.00	12.00
#5-Stanley art	4.00	8.00	12.00
6-10	3.00	6.00	9.00
11-20: #18-Stanley art	2.50	5.00	7.50
21-30	2.00	4.00	6.00
31-49	1.35	2.75	4.00

And His Clubhouse Pals #1(1956)-4pgs. art by
  Stanley; wrote Gran'pa Feeb stories

	3.00	6.00	9.00

& the Little Men From Mars #30020-410(10/64-
  G.Key, 25¢)-68pgs. 1.50 3.00 4.50

TUFF GHOSTS (Starring Spooky)
July, 1962 - #42, June, 1972
Harvey Publications

#1	.50	1.00	1.50
2-5	.20	.40	.60
6-42		.10	.20

True 3-D #1, © Harv

True War Experiences #1, © Harv

Tubby #49, © West

411

Turok #36, © GK

Tweety & Sylvester #2, © Warner Bros.

Twilight Zone #7, © GK

TUFFY
1949 - 1950
Standard Comics

	Good	Fine	Mint
#1-By Sid Hoff	1.20	2.40	3.60
2-10	.65	1.35	2.00

TUFFY TURTLE
No date
I.W. Enterprises

	Good	Fine	Mint
#1-Reprint	.35	.70	1.05

TUROK, SON OF STONE (See Golden Comics
Digest #33, March of Comics #378,399,408, &
Dec, 1954 - Present   Dan Curtis)
Dell Publ. Co. #1-29/Gold Key #30 on

	Good	Fine	Mint
4-Color #596(12/54)	8.00	16.00	24.00
4-Color #656(10/55)	5.00	10.00	15.00
#3-10	2.50	5.00	7.50
11-20	1.75	3.35	5.00
21-30	1.25	2.50	3.75
31-40	.75	1.50	2.25
41-50	.50	1.00	1.50
51-60	.35	.70	1.05
61-70	.25	.50	.75
71-83	.20	.40	.60
84-Origin & 1st app. Hutel	.20	.40	.60
85-112	.15	.30	.45
Giant #1(30031-611)(11/61)	1.50	3.00	4.50

TV CASPER & COMPANY
Aug, 1963 - #44, 1973   (25¢)
Harvey Publications

	Good	Fine	Mint
#1	.50	1.00	1.50
2-5	.20	.40	.60
6-44		.15	.30

TV FUNDAY FUNNIES (See Famous TV --)

TV FUNNIES (See New Funnies)

TV FUNTIME (See Little Audrey)

TV LAUGHOUT (See Archie's --)

TV SCREEN CARTOONS (Formerly Real Screen)
#129, 9-10/59 - #138, 1-2/61
National Periodical Publications

	Good	Fine	Mint
#129-138	.35	.70	1.05

TV TEENS
Feb, 1954 - V2#13, July, 1956
Charlton Comics

	Good	Fine	Mint
V1#14,15: #14-Ozzie & Babs	.50	1.00	1.50
V2#3-7-Don Winslow	.65	1.35	2.00
V2#8(7/55)-#13-Mopsy	.65	1.35	2.00

TWEETY AND SYLVESTER (1st Series)
June, 1952 - #37, June-Aug, 1962
Dell Publishing Co.

4-Color #406,489,524	1.00	2.00	3.00
#4-20	.40	.80	1.20
21-37	.25	.50	.75

TWEETY AND SYLVESTER (2nd Series)
Nov, 1963; #2, Nov, 1965 - Present
Gold Key

#1	.35	.70	1.05
2-10	.15	.30	.45
11-30		.20	.35
31-76		.10	.20

12 O'CLOCK HIGH (TV)
Jan-Mar, 1965 - #2, Apr-June, 1965
Dell Publishing Co.

#1,2	.35	.70	1.05

20,000 LEAGUES UNDER THE SEA (See 4-Color
Comics #614 & Movie Comics)

TWICE TOLD TALES (See Movie Classics)

TWILIGHT ZONE, THE (TV) (See Dan Curtis)
1961 - Present
Dell Publishing Co./Gold Key

4-Color #1173,1288-Crandall art	2.00	4.00	6.00
#01-860-207,#12-860-210(Dell 5-7/62,8-10/62)	1.00	2.00	3.00
#1(Gold Key-11/62)-Williamson/Evans story, 10pgs. + Crandall sty.	1.50	3.00	4.50
2-5	.80	1.60	2.40
6-11,16-20	.50	1.00	1.50
12-Williamson story	1.00	2.00	3.00
13,15-Crandall story	.80	1.60	2.40
14-Williamson + Orlando + Crandall	1.00	2.00	3.00
21-Crandall reprint	.35	.70	1.05
22-24	.25	.50	.75
25-Evans/Crandall reprint	.35	.70	1.05
26-Crandall, Evans reprts.	.35	.70	1.05
27-Two Evans stys.reprts.	.35	.70	1.05
28-31	.20	.40	.60
32-Evans reprint	.20	.40	.60
33-50,52-70	.15	.30	.45
51-Williamson story	.20	.40	.60

(Twilight Zone cont'd)

	Good	Fine	Mint
71(reprint)-#81		.20	.35

NOTE: *Bolle* story-#50. *McWilliams* story-#59. *Orlando* stories-#19,20,22,23. *Sekowsky* story-#3. (See *Mystery Comics Digest* #3,6,9,12,15,18,21,24)

TWINKLE COMICS
May, 1945
Spotlight Publishers

	Good	Fine	Mint
#1	1.25	2.50	3.75

TWIST, THE
Sept, 1962
Dell Publishing Co.

	Good	Fine	Mint
#01864-209	.40	.80	1.20

TWO BIT THE WACKY WOODPECKER (See Wacky--)
1953 - #3, May, 1953
Toby Press

	Good	Fine	Mint
#1-3	.40	.80	1.20

TWO-FISTED TALES(Formerly Haunt of Fear#15-17)
#18, Nov-Dec, 1950 - #41, Feb-Mar, 1955
E.C. Comics

	Good	Fine	Mint
#18(#1)-Kurtzman cover	55.00	110.00	165.00
19-Kurtzman cover	26.50	46.75	80.00
20-Kurtzman cover	25.00	50.00	75.00
21,22- " "	17.50	35.00	52.50
23-25- " "	12.00	24.00	36.00
26-41	10.00	20.00	30.00
Two-Fisted Annual, 1952	70.00	140.00	210.00
Two-Fisted Annual, 1953	55.00	110.00	165.00

NOTE: *Berg* story-#29. *Craig* stories-#18,19,32. *Crandall* stories-#35,36. *Davis* stories-#20-36,40; covers-#30,34,35,41,Annual #2. *Evans* stories-#34,40,41; cover-#40. *Feldstein* story-#18. *Krigstein* story-#41. *Kubert* stories-#32,33. *Kurtzman* stories-#18-25; covers-#18-29,31,Annual #1. *Severin* stories-#26,28,29,31,34-41(#37-39 are *all-Severin* issues); covers-#36-39. *Severin/Elder* stories-#19-29,31,33,36. *Wood* stories-#18-28,30-35,41; covers-#32,33. *Special Issues:* #26(ChangJin Reservoir), #31(Civil War), #35(Civil War). *Canadian reprints known; see Table of Contents.*

TWO-GUN KID
3/48 - #10, 11/49; 12/53 - #59, 4/61; #60, 11/62 - #92, 3/68; #93, 7/70 - #136, 4/77
Marvel/Atlas Comics(MCI #1-10/HPC #11-59/Marvel #60 on)

	Good	Fine	Mint
#1	8.00	16.00	24.00

	Good	Fine	Mint
2	4.00	8.00	12.00
3-10	2.50	5.00	7.50
11-24,26-29	1.35	2.75	4.00
25,30-Williamson story in both, 5 & 4 pgs.			
	2.00	4.00	6.00
31-33,35,37-40	1.00	2.00	3.00
34-Crandall story	1.35	2.75	4.00
36,41,42,48-origin in all	1.00	2.00	3.00
43,44,47,49,50	.65	1.35	2.00
45,46-Davis stories	1.25	2.50	3.75
51-5pg. Williamson story	1.50	3.00	4.50
52,57-Three Severin stories in each			
	.90	1.80	2.70
53-56,59	.50	1.00	1.50
58,60-New origin	.65	1.35	2.00
61-80: #64-Intro.Boom-Boom	.25	.50	.75
81-100: #85-Rawhide Kid x-over. #89-Kid Colt,			
Rawhide Kid x-over. #92,98-Last new story.			
#99-Three Severin reprts.	.20	.40	.60
101-Origin retold(#58)	.15	.30	.45
102-109,111-136		.20	.35
110-Williamson reprint		.20	.35

NOTE: *Davis* covers-#45-47. *Everett* stories-#82,91. *Kirby* stories-#54,55,57-62,75-77,90,95,101,119,120,129; covers-#10,52,54-65,67-72,74-76,116. *Powell* story-#38,102,104. *Whitney* stories-#87,89-91,98-113,124,129; covers-#87,89,91,113. *Black Rider* in #11,12. *Kid Colt* in #13,14,16-18,21.

TWO-GUN WESTERN (1st Series)
#5, Nov, 1950 - #14, June, 1952
Marvel/Atlas Comics (MPC)

	Good	Fine	Mint
#5-Intro. & origin Apache Kid by Buscema			
	2.00	4.00	6.00
6-14	1.50	3.00	4.50

NOTE: *Crandall* story-#8. *Powell* story-#7. *Wildey* story-#8.

2-GUN WESTERN (2nd Series) (Formerly Billy Buckskin; Two-Gun Western #5 on)
#4, May, 1957
Atlas Comics (MgPC)

	Good	Fine	Mint
#4-Apache Kid; Ditko art	1.35	2.75	4.00

TWO-GUN WESTERN (Formerly 2-Gun Western)
#5, July, 1956 - #12, Sept, 1957
Atlas Comics (MgPC)

	Good	Fine	Mint
#5-8,12	.80	1.60	2.40
9,11-Williamson story in both, 5pgs. each			
	1.50	3.00	4.50
10-Crandall story	1.25	2.50	3.75

NOTE: *Morrow* story-#9. *Powell* story-#11.

Two-Fisted Tales #28, © WMG

Two-Fisted Tales #35, © WMG

2-Gun Western #4, © MCG

Uncanny Tales #50, © MCG

Uncle Charlie's Fables #2, © Lev

Uncle Sam #1, © DC (Qua)

TWO MOUSEKETEERS, THE (See 4-Color #475,603, 642)

TWO ON A GUILLOTINE (See Movie Classics)

2001: A SPACE ODYSSEY (Marvel Treasury Special)
Oct, 1976   (One Shot) (Over-Sized)
Marvel Comics Group

	Good	Fine	Mint
#1-Kirby & Giacoia art	.65	1.35	2.00

2001: A SPACE ODYSSEY (Mister Machine #11 on)
Dec, 1976 - #10, Sept, 1977 (Regular size)
Marvel Comics Group

#1-Kirby cover/story	.25	.50	.75
2- " " "	.20	.40	.60
3-10	.15	.30	.45

UFO FLYING SAUCERS
Oct, 1968 - #13, Jan, 1977 (#2 on, 36pgs.)
Gold Key

#1(30035-810)(68pgs.)	.50	1.00	1.50
2(11/70),3(11/72),4(11/74)	.25	.50	.75
5(2/75)-#13: Bolle stories #4 on			
	.25	.50	.75

UNBIRTHDAY PARTY WITH ALICE IN WONDERLAND
(See 4-Color Comics #341)

UNCANNY TALES
June, 1952 - #57, Sept, 1957
Atlas Comics (PrPI)

#1-Crandall reprint	3.00	6.00	9.00
2-5,7,9,10	1.75	3.35	5.00
6-Wolverton story	6.00	12.00	18.00
8-Toth art	2.00	4.00	6.00
11-20	1.20	2.40	3.60
21-27	1.00	2.00	3.00
28-Last pre-code issue; Kubert art			
	1.75	3.35	5.00
29-49	.80	1.60	2.40
50,53,55-Torres story	1.35	2.75	4.00
51,57-Williamson story	2.00	4.00	6.00
52,54,56	.65	1.35	2.00

NOTE: _Drucker story-#37,42,45. Everett stories-#12,36,47,48; covers-#50,52,53. Krenkel story-#19. Krigstein stories-#42,54,56. Moldoff art-#23. Morrow story-#46. Orlando stories-#49,50,53. Powell stories-#12,18,38,50, 53,56. Robinson stories-#3,13. Wildey story-#48._

UNCANNY TALES
Dec, 1973 - #12, Oct, 1975
Marvel Comics Group

	Good	Fine	Mint
#1	.15	.30	.45
2-12		.15	.30

NOTE: _Ditko reprints-#7,11. Everett covers-#7,11._

UNCLE CHARLIE'S FABLES
1951 - #5, Sept, 1952
Lev Gleason Publications

#1-Norman Maurer art; has Biro's picture			
	2.00	4.00	6.00
2-5	1.35	2.75	4.00

UNCLE DONALD & HIS NEPHEWS DUDE RANCH
(See Dell Giant #52)

UNCLE DONALD & HIS NEPHEWS FAMILY FUN
(See Dell Giant #38)

UNCLE JOE'S FUNNIES
1938
Centaur Publications

#1-Games/puzzles, some interior art; Bill Everett cover	9.00	18.00	27.00

UNCLE MILTY
Dec, 1950 - #4, June, 1950
Victoria Publications/True Cross

#1-Milton Berle	2.50	5.00	7.50
2-4	1.50	3.00	4.50

UNCLE REMUS & HIS TALES OF BRER RABBIT
(See 4-Color Comics #129,208,693)

UNCLE SAM (Blackhawk #9 on)
Fall, 1941 - #8, Fall, 1943
Quality Comics Group

#1-Origin Uncle Sam; cover, chapter headings, & 2pgs. by Eisner (2 versions: dark cover, no price; light cover with price)			
	50.00	100.00	150.00
2-Cameos by The Ray, Black Condor, Quicksilver, The Red Bee, Alias The Spider, Hercules & Neon the Unknown. Eisner, Fine cover/story	27.50	55.00	82.50
3-Crandall story	15.00	30.00	45.00
4	12.00	24.00	36.00
5-8	7.00	14.00	21.00

NOTE: _Kotzky or Tuska stories-#4-8._

UNCLE SAM'S CHRISTMAS STORY
1958
Promotional Publ. Co. (Giveaway)

Reprints 1956 Christmas USA

	.35	.70	1.05

UNCLE SCROOGE (Walt Disney)
March, 1952 - Present
Dell Publishing Co./Gold Key #40 on

	Good	Fine	Mint
4-Color #386(#1)-in "Only a Poor Old Man" by Carl Barks-reprinted in Uncle Scrooge & D. Duck #1('65) & The Best of W.D. Comics ('74)	80.00	160.00	240.00
4-Color #456(#2)-in "Back to the Klondike" by Carl Barks-reprinted in Best of U.S. & D.D. #1('66)	40.00	80.00	120.00
4-Color #495(#3)-reprinted in Uncle Scrooge #105	20.00	40.00	60.00
#4	17.50	35.00	52.50
5-Reprinted in W.D. Digest #1	13.50	26.75	40.00
6-Reprinted in U.S. #106 & Best of U.S. & D.D. #1('66)	10.00	20.00	30.00
7-Reprinted in Best of D.D. & U.S. #2('67)	9.00	18.00	27.00
8-10: #9-Reprinted in U.S. #104. #10-Reprinted in U.S. #67	7.00	14.00	21.00
11-20	6.00	12.00	18.00
21-30	4.00	8.00	12.00
31-40	3.50	7.00	10.50
41-60	3.00	6.00	9.00
61-66,68-70: #70-Last Barks issue with original story	2.50	5.00	7.50
67,72,73-Barks reprints	1.00	2.00	3.00
71-Written by Barks only	1.00	2.00	3.00
74-1pg. Barks reprints	.65	1.35	2.00
75-81,83-Not by Barks	.65	1.35	2.00
82,84-Barks reprints begin	.65	1.35	2.00
85-100	.65	1.35	2.00
101-110	.40	.80	1.20
111-120	.25	.50	.75
121-141,143-147	.20	.40	.60
142-Reprints 4-Color #456 with cover	.25	.50	.75
Uncle Scrooge & Money(G.K.)-Barks reprint from WDC&S #130(3/67)	3.00	6.00	9.00
Uncle Scrooge Goes to Disneyland #1(1957-25¢) 20pgs. Barks	5.00	10.00	15.00

(See Dell Giants #33 & 55)

UNCLE SCROOGE & DONALD DUCK
June, 1965   (25¢) (Soft cover)
Gold Key

	Good	Fine	Mint
#1-Reprint of 4-Color #386(#1) & lead story from 4-Color #29	15.00	30.00	45.00

UNCLE WIGGILY (See 4-Color #179,221,276,320,
349,391,428,503,543, & March of Comics #19)

UNDERCOVER CRIME (Underground Crime #5)
1952
Fawcett Publications

	Good	Fine	Mint
#6	1.00	2.00	3.00

UNDERCOVER GIRL (Starr Flagg)
1952 - 1953
Magazine Enterprises

	Good	Fine	Mint
#5(#1)(A-1#62)	8.00	16.00	24.00
#6(A-1#98),#7(A-1#118)-All have Starr Flagg	6.00	12.00	18.00

UNDERDOG (TV)
July, 1970 - #10, Jan, 1972; 3/75 - Present
Charlton Comics/Gold Key

	Good	Fine	Mint
#1-10		.15	.30
#1-16(G.K.): #13-1st app. Shack of Solitude		.15	.30
Kite Fun Book('74, 5x7")-16pgs. Sou. Calif. Edison	.15	.30	.45

UNDERGROUND CRIME (Undercover Crime #6)
1952
Fawcett Publications

	Good	Fine	Mint
#5	1.00	2.00	3.00

UNDERSEA AGENT
Jan, 1966 - #6, Mar, 1967   (68 pgs.)
Tower Comics

	Good	Fine	Mint
#1-Davy Jones, Undersea Agent begins	.80	1.60	2.40
2-6: #2-Jones gains magnetic powers. #5-Origin & 1st app. of Merman. #6-Wood cover	.40	.80	1.20

NOTE: *Gil Kane* story-#3-6; covers-#4,5.

UNDERSEA FIGHTING COMMANDOS
May, 1952 - #3, Sept, 1952; 1964
Avon Periodicals

	Good	Fine	Mint
#1	1.50	3.00	4.50
2,3	1.00	2.00	3.00
IW Reprint #1,2('64)	.35	.70	1.05

UNDERWATER CITY, THE (See 4-Color #1324,1328)

UNDERWORLD (True Crime Stories)
Feb-Mar, 1948 - #9, June, 1949
D. S. Publishing Co.

	Good	Fine	Mint
#1-Sheldon Moldoff cover	1.75	3.35	5.00
2- " " "	1.20	2.40	3.60
3-9	1.00	2.00	3.00

UNDERWORLD CRIME
June, 1952 - #9, Oct, 1953
Fawcett Publications

Uncle Scrooge #28, © WDP

Uncle Scrooge #46, © WDP

Underworld #2, © DS

415

United Comics #1, © UFS

Unknown World #1, © Faw

Unknown Worlds #8, © ACG

	Good	Fine	Mint
(Underworld Crime cont'd)			
#1	1.75	3.35	5.00
2,4-9: #7-Bondage-torture cover			
	1.00	2.00	3.00
3-Kubert cover	1.50	3.00	4.50

UNDERWORLD STORY, THE
1950   (Movie)
Avon Periodicals

#1 (Scarce)	4.00	8.00	12.00

UNEARTHLY SPECTACULARS
Oct, 1965 - #3, Mar, 1967
Harvey Publications

#1-Tiger Boy	.65	1.35	2.00
2-Jack Q. Frost app.; Wood, Williamson, Adams, Kane art; reprints Thrill-O-Rama#2			
	1.50	3.00	4.50
3-Jack Q. Frost app.; Williamson/Crandall art; reprint from Alarming Adventures #1, 1962; 2pgs. Kirby art	1.35	2.75	4.00

UNEXPECTED, THE   (Formerly Tales of the --)
#105, Feb-Mar, 1968 - Present
National Periodical Publications/DC Comics

#105-115,117,118,120,122-127			
	.15	.30	.45
116,119,121,128-Wrightson stories			
	.65	1.35	2.00
129-132,134-136,139-156: #132-136, 52pgs.			
	.20	.40	.60
133,137,138-Wood stories	.20	.40	.60
157-162-(All 100pgs.)	.20	.40	.60
163-183		.20	.35

NOTE: *Adams covers-#110,112-118,121,124. Alcala stories-#140,144,150-153,156,157,168, 169. Anderson story-#122. Kirby stories-#127, 162. Wood inks-#122,137. Wrightson reprint- #161(2pgs.). Johnny Peril in #106-114,117.*

UNEXPECTED ANNUAL, THE (See DC Spec.Series #4)

UNITED COMICS
Aug, 1940 - #26, Jan-Feb, 1953
United Features Syndicate

#1-Fritzi Ritz & Phil Fumble			
	2.50	5.00	7.50
2-9-Fritzi Ritz, Abbie & Slats			
	1.00	2.00	3.00
10-26	.65	1.35	2.00

NOTE: *Abbie & Slats reprinted from Tip Top.*

UNITED NATIONS, THE   (See Classics Ill.
Special Ed.)

UNIVERSAL PRESENTS DRACULA (See Movie Classics)

UNITED STATES AIR FORCE PRESENTS: THE
HIDDEN CREW
1964   (36 pgs.)   (Full Color)
U.S. Air Force

	Good	Fine	Mint
Shaffenberger art	.65	1.35	2.00

UNKNOWN MAN, THE
1951   (Movie)
Avon Periodicals

No#-Kinstler cover	3.00	6.00	9.00

UNKNOWN SOLDIER (Formerly Star-Spangled War
#205, Apr-May, 1977 - Present   Stories)
National Periodical Publications/DC Comics

#205-211		.20	.35

UNKNOWN WORLD (Strange Stories From Another
June, 1952   World #2 on)
Fawcett Publications

#1-Painted cover by Norman Saunders			
	2.00	4.00	6.00

UNKNOWN WORLDS (See Journey Into --)

UNKNOWN WORLDS
Aug, 1960 - #57, Aug, 1967
American Comics Group/Best Synd. Features

#1	1.35	2.75	4.00
2-5	.75	1.50	2.25
6-19	.50	1.00	1.50
20-Herbie cameo	1.00	2.00	3.00
21-46	.30	.60	.90
47-Williamson story reprinted from Adventures Into the Unknown #96, 3pgs. + Craig story			
	.65	1.35	2.00
48-57: #49,54-Ditko art	.25	.50	.75

NOTE: *John Force, Magic Agent app.-#35,36,48, 50,52,54,56. Craig story-#36. Whitney story- #29.*

UNKNOWN WORLDS OF SCIENCE FICTION
12/74 - #6, 11/75; 12/76 (B&W Magazine)($1.00)
Marvel Comics Group

#1-Williamson/Wood reprint/Witzend #1, Neal Adams reprint/Phase 1; Brunner & Kaluta reprints	1.00	2.00	3.00
2-Brunner & Kaluta story	.60	1.20	1.80
3-6: #4,6-Brunner covers	.50	1.00	1.50
Special #1(12/76)-100pgs.-Newton cover			
	.50	1.00	1.50

(Unknown Worlds of Science Fiction cont'd)

NOTE: *Corben story-#4. Kaluta cover-#2.*
Morrow story-#3,5. Nino story-#3,6.

UNSANE
June, 1954
Star Publications

	Good	Fine	Mint
#15-Disbrow art	1.75	3.35	5.00

UNSEEN, THE
1952 - #15, July, 1954
Visual Editions/Standard Comics

#5,9,12,15-Toth art?	1.50	3.00	4.50
6-8,10,11,13,14: #6-1pg. Toth	.80	1.60	2.40

UNTAMED LOVE
January, 1950 - #5, Sept, 1950
Quality Comics Group (Comic Magazines)

#1-Ward cover, Gustavson art	4.00	8.00	12.00
2-5	2.00	4.00	6.00

UNTOUCHABLES, THE (TV)
1961 - #4, Oct, 1962
Dell Publishing Co.

4-Color #1237,1286	.65	1.35	2.00
#01879-207,#12-879-210(#01879-210 on inside)			
	.40	.80	1.20
Topps Bubblegum giveaway-2½x4½", 8pgs.(2 diff.)			
"The Organization","Jamaica Ginger"			
	1.00	2.00	3.00

UNUSUAL TALES (Blue Beetle & Shadow From Beyond #50 on)
Nov, 1955 - #49, Mar-Apr, 1965
Charlton Comics

#1	1.75	3.35	5.00
2-7,10	.75	1.50	2.25
8-Ditko story	1.00	2.00	3.00
9-20pgs. Ditko	1.25	2.50	3.75
11-68pgs.; 4 Ditko stys.	1.50	3.00	4.50
12,16-20	.40	.80	1.20
14,15-Ditko stories	.50	1.00	1.50
21,24,28-49	.30	.60	.90
22,23,25-27-Ditko stories	.40	.80	1.20

NOTE: *Ditko covers-#6,8,14,15,22.*

UP-TO-DATE COMICS
No date (1939?) (36pgs.)(B&W cover)(10¢)
King Features Syndicate

	Good	Fine	Mint
No#-Popeye & Henry cover; The Phantom, Jungle Jim by Raymond, The Katzenjammer Kids, Curley Harper	20.00	40.00	60.00

UP YOUR NOSE AND OUT YOUR EAR (Magazine)
April, 1972 - #2, June, 1972 (52pgs.)(Satire)
Klevart Enterprises

V1#1,2	.35	.70	1.05

USA COMICS (Hedy Devine #18 on?)
Aug, 1941 - #17, Fall, 1945
Timely Comics (USA)

#1-Origin Major Liberty, Rockman by Wolverton, & The Whizzer by Avison; The Defender with sidekick Rusty & Jack Frost begin; The Young Avenger only app.; S&K cover + one page	250.00	500.00	750.00
2-Origin Captain Terror & The Vagabond; last Wolverton Rockman	125.00	250.00	375.00
3-No Whizzer	100.00	200.00	300.00
4-Last Rockman, Major Liberty, Defender, Jack Frost & Capt. Terror; Corporal Dix app.	75.00	150.00	225.00
5-Origin American Avenger & Roko the Amazing; The Black Widow, The Blue Blade & Victory Boys, Gypo, the Gypsy Giant & Hills of Horror only app.; Sergeant Dix begins; no Whizzer	60.00	120.00	180.00
6-Captain America, The Destroyer, Jap Buster Johnson, Jeep Jones begin; Terror Squad only app.	60.00	120.00	180.00
7-Captain Daring, Disk-Eyes, the Detective by Wolverton app.; origin & only app. Marvel Boy; Secret Stamp begins; no Whizzer, Sergeant Dix	50.00	100.00	150.00
8-10: #9-Last Secret Stamp. #10-The Thunderbird only app.	30.00	60.00	90.00
11-17: #11-No Jeep Jones. #13-No Whizzer; Jeep Jones ends. #15-No Destroyer; Jap Buster Johnson ends	20.00	40.00	60.00

U.S. AGENT (See Jeff Jordan --)

U.S. AIR FORCE COMICS (Army Attack #38 on)
Oct, 1958 - #37, Mar-Apr, 1965
Charlton Comics

#1	.65	1.35	2.00
2-10	.35	.70	1.05
11-20	.20	.40	.60
21-37		.15	.30

NOTE: *Montes/Bache art-#33.*

USA IS READY
1941 (68 pgs.) (One Shot)

Untamed Love #1, © Qua

Unusual Tales #9, © CC

USA Comics #7, © MCG

U.S. Marines #4, © ME

Vacation In Disneyland (Dell) #1, © WDP

Valor #5, © WMG

(USA Is Ready cont'd)
Dell Publishing Co.

	Good	Fine	Mint
#1-War propaganda	4.00	8.00	12.00

U.S. BORDER PATROL COMICS (Sgt. Dick Carter of the --) (See Holyoke One Shot)

U.S. FIGHTING AIR FORCE
Sept, 1952 - #29, Oct, 1956
Superior Comics Ltd.

#1	1.35	2.75	4.00
2	.65	1.35	2.00
3-10	.50	1.00	1.50
11-29	.40	.80	1.20
IW Reprint #1,9(no date)	.25	.50	.75

U.S. FIGHTING MEN
1963 - 1964 (Reprints)
Super Comics

#10-Avon's-With the U.S. Paratroops			
	.50	1.00	1.50
11,12,15-18	.35	.70	1.05

U.S. JONES
Nov, 1941 - #2, Jan, 1942
Fox Features Syndicate

#1-U.S. Jones & The Topper begin			
	30.00	60.00	90.00
2	15.00	30.00	45.00

U.S. MARINES
1943 - #4, 1944; #5, 1952 - 1953
Magazine Enterprises/Toby Press

#1-Mart Bailey art	3.35	6.75	10.00
2-4	2.00	4.00	6.00
5(A-1#55)-Powell art, #6(A-1#60), #7(A-1#68),			
#8(A-1#72)	1.35	2.75	4.00
7-11(Toby)	.65	1.35	2.00

U.S. MARINES IN ACTION!, THE
1952
Avon Periodicals/Charlton Comics

#1-3: #3-Kinstler cover	1.50	3.00	4.50
1(Fall/1964-Charlton)		.20	.35

U.S. PARATROOPS (See With the --)

U.S. TANK COMMANDOS
July, 1952 - #4, March, 1953
Avon Periodicals

#1	1.50	3.00	4.50

	Good	Fine	Mint
2-4	.80	1.60	2.40
IW Reprint #1,8	.35	.70	1.05

NOTE: _Kinstler_ stories-#3,4,IW#1; covers-#1, 4,IW#1,8.

VACATION COMICS (See A-1 Comics #16)

VACATION IN DISNEYLAND
Aug, 1958 - Mar, 1965 (Walt Disney)
Dell Publ. Co./Gold Key(1965)

#1(1958-25c)	2.00	4.00	6.00
4-Color #1025-Barks art	4.00	8.00	12.00
#1(30024-508)(G.K.)-Reprints Dell Giant #30			
& cover to #1('58)	.50	1.00	1.50

VACATION PARADE (Picnic Party #6 on)
1950 - 1954 (116 pgs.) (25¢) (Walt Disney)
Dell Publishing Co.

#1-Donald Duck & Mickey Mouse; Carl Barks			
art, 55pgs.	50.00	100.00	150.00
2	6.00	12.00	18.00
3-5	3.00	6.00	9.00

VALLEY OF THE DINOSAURS (TV)(Hanna-Barbera)
April, 1975 - #11, Dec, 1976
Charlton Comics

#1-Howard inks	.20	.40	.60
2-11: #2-Howard inks	.15	.30	.45

VALLEY OF GWANGI (See Movie Classics)

VALOR
Mar-Apr, 1955 - #5, Nov-Dec, 1955
E.C. Comics

#1-Williamson/Torres story; Wood cover &			
story	12.00	24.00	36.00
2-Williamson cover & story; Wood story			
	8.00	16.00	24.00
3-Williamson & a Crandall story			
	7.00	14.00	21.00
4-Wood cover	7.00	14.00	21.00
5-Wood cover & story; Williamson/Evans			
story	5.00	10.00	15.00

NOTE: _Crandall_ stories-#3,4. _Ingels_ stories-#1,2,4,5. _Krigstein_ stories-#1-5. _Orlando_ stories-#3,4; cover-#3. _Wood_ stories-#1,2,5; covers-#1,4,5.

VAMPIRELLA (Magazine)
Sept, 1969 - Present
Warren Publishing Co.

#1-Intro. Vampirella	5.00	10.00	15.00

(Vampirella cont'd)	Good	Fine	Mint
2	3.50	7.00	10.50
3 (Scarce)	7.00	14.00	21.00
4-7	2.50	5.00	7.50

8-Vampi begins by Tom Sutton as serious
  strip (early issues-gag line)

	3.00	6.00	9.00
9-Smith art	3.50	7.00	10.50
10-No Vampi story	2.50	5.00	7.50

11-15: #11-Origin, 1st app. Pendragon. #12-
  Vampi by Gonzales begins, ends #34

	2.00	4.00	6.00
16-25	1.50	3.00	4.50

26-40: #28-Intro. Pantha. #31-Origin Luana,
  the Beast Girl. #32-Pantha ends

	1.20	2.40	3.60
41-45	.80	1.60	2.40
46-Origin	1.00	2.00	3.00
47-50: #50-Spirit cameo	.60	1.20	1.80
51-65	.50	1.00	1.50

Annual #1('72)-New origin Vampirella by
  Gonzales; reprints by Adams(#1), Wood(#9)

	6.00	12.00	18.00

NOTE: _Adams stories-#1,10,17,19,51. Bode'/_
Todd cover-#3. Bode'/Jones cover-#4. Brunner
story-#10. Corben stories-#30,31,33,54. Cran-
dall stories-#1,19, Frazetta covers-#1,5,7,
11,31. Jones stories-#5,9,12,27,32,33(w/
Wrightson),34,50,53,56. Ploog story-#14.
Barry Smith story-#9. Sutton story-#11. Wood
stories-#8-10,12,19,27; cover-#9. Wrightson
story-#33,63.

VAMPIRES & WEREWOLVES (Magazine)
1962 (One Shot)
Charlton Comics

#1	1.50	3.00	4.50

VAMPIRE TALES (Magazine)
Aug, 1973 - #11, June, 1975 (B&W) (75¢)
Marvel Comics Group

#1-Morbius, the Living Vampire begins by

Pablo Marcos	.65	1.35	2.00
2-Intro. Satana; Steranko reprint			
	.50	1.00	1.50
3-Satana app.	.40	.80	1.20
4-6,8-11	.40	.80	1.20
7-Kaluta art	.50	1.00	1.50
Annual #1(10/75)	.50	1.00	1.50

NOTE: _Alcala stories-#6,8,9. Everett story-_
#1. Heath story-#9. Infantino reprint-#3.

VARIETY COMICS
1944 - 1945; 1946
Rural Home Publications/Croyden Publ. Co.

	Good	Fine	Mint
#1-Origin Captain Valiant	3.00	6.00	9.00
2-Capt. Valiant	2.00	4.00	6.00
3(Croyden-1946)-Captain Valiant			
	1.75	3.35	5.00
4,5	1.35	2.75	4.00

VARIETY COMICS
1946; 1950 (132 pgs.)
Fox Features Syndicate (Hero Books)

#1(1946)-Blue Beetle & Jungle Jo			
	4.00	8.00	12.00

No#(1950)-See Fox Giants. Contents can vary
  and determines price.

VARSITY
1945
Parents' Magazine Institute

#1	.65	1.35	2.00

VAUDEVILLE AND OTHER THINGS
1900 (10½x13") (In Color) (18+pgs.)
Isaac H. Blandiard Co.

By Bunny	20.00	50.00	80.00

VAULT OF EVIL
Feb, 1973 - #23, Nov, 1975
Marvel Comics Group

#1(Reprints begin)	.15	.30	.45
2-10: #3,4-Brunner cover		.15	.30
11-23		.15	.30

NOTE: _Ditko reprints-#20-22. Drucker re-_
prints-#10(Mystic #52),13(Uncanny Tales#42).
Everett reprints-#11(Menace #2),13(Menace#4);
cover-#10. Krigstein reprint-#20(Uncanny
Tales #54).

VAULT OF HORROR (War Against Crime #1-11)
Apr-May, 1950 - #40, Dec-Jan, 1954-55
E.C. Comics

#12	75.00	150.00	225.00
13	37.50	75.00	112.50
14	30.00	60.00	90.00
15	25.00	50.00	75.00
16-19	17.50	35.00	52.50
20-25	15.00	30.00	45.00
26-36,38-40	10.00	20.00	30.00
37-Williamson story	12.00	24.00	36.00

NOTE: _Craig stories in all but #13 & 33; cov-_
ers-#12-40. Crandall stories-#33,34,39. Davis
stories-#17-38. Evans stories-#27,28,30,32,33.
Feldstein stories-#12-16. Ingels stories-#13-
20,22-40. Kamen stories-#15-22,25,29,35.

Variety #1('44), © RH

Vault Of Horror #21, © WMG

Vault Of Horror #40, © WMG

Venus #7, © MCG

Venus #18, © MCG

Vic Jordan #1, © Civil Service

(Vault of Horror cont'd)
Krigstein stories-#36,38-40. Kurtzman stories-#12,13. Orlando stories-#24,31,40. Wood stories-#12-14.

	Good	Fine	Mint
#1	2.00	4.00	6.00
2-5	1.50	3.00	4.50

V...-COMICS(Morse code for "V", 3 dots, 1 dash)
Jan, 1942 - #2, Mar-Apr, 1942
Fox Features Syndicate

	Good	Fine	Mint
#1-Origin V-Man & the Boys; The Banshee & The Black Fury, The Queen of Evil, & V-Agents begin	26.50	53.25	80.00
2	16.50	33.25	50.00

VENGEANCE SQUAD
July, 1975 - #6, May, 1976
Charlton Comics

#1	.20	.40	.60
2-6		.20	.35

VENUS
August, 1948 - #19, April, 1952
Marvel/Atlas Comics (LMC)

#1-Venus begins; Kurtzman's "Hey Look"	12.00	24.00	36.00
2,3,5	7.00	14.00	21.00
4-Kurtzman's "Hey Look"	8.00	16.00	24.00
6-9: #6-Loki app.	7.00	14.00	21.00
10-S/F end of the world	8.00	16.00	24.00
11,12	6.00	12.00	18.00
13-Everett cover only	7.00	14.00	21.00
14-19: Venus by Everett in all; #15-19-Everett covers	9.00	18.00	27.00

VERI BEST SURE FIRE COMICS
No date (Circa 1945) (Reprints Holyoke One-Holyoke Publ. Co.   Shots)

#1-Captain Aero, Alias X, Miss Victory, Commandos of the Devil Dogs, Red Cross, Hammerhead Hawley, Capt. Aero's Sky Scouts, Flagman app.	8.00	16.00	24.00

VERI BEST SURE SHOT COMICS
No date (Circa 1945)(Reprts.Holyoke One-Shots)
Holyoke Publ. Co.

#1-Capt. Aero, Miss Victory by Quinlan, Alias X, The Red Cross, Flagman, Commandos of the Devil Dogs, Hammerhead Hawley, Capt. Aero's Sky Scouts	10.00	20.00	30.00

VIC FLINT (Crime Buster --)
Aug, 1948 (Newspaper reprints)
St. John Publishing Co.

VIC FLINT
Feb, 1956 - #2, May, 1956 (Newspaper reprints)
Argo Publ.

#1,2	1.35	2.75	4.00

VIC JORDAN
April, 1945
Civil Service Publ.

#1-1944 daily newspaper reprints			
	1.50	3.00	4.50

VICKI (Humor)
Feb, 1975 - #4, July, 1975 (#1,2-68pgs.)
Atlas/Seaboard Publ.

#1-Reprints Tippy Teen	.15	.30	.45
2-4		.15	.30

VICKS COMICS
No date (Circa 1937-38) (64pgs. in color)
Eastern Color Printing Co.(Vicks Chemical Co.)

No#-Reprints from Famous Funnies (before #40). Contains 5pgs. Buck Rogers, 4pgs. from F.F. #15 & 1pg. from #16	75.00	150.00	225.00

VICKY
Oct, 1948 - #5, June, 1949
Ace Magazine

No#(10/48), #4(12/48)	1.00	2.00	3.00
No#(2/49), #5(6/49)	1.00	2.00	3.00

VICTORY COMICS
Aug, 1941 - #4, Dec, 1941
Hillman Periodicals

#1-The Conqueror by Bill Everett, The Crusader, & Bomber Burns begin; Conqueror's origin in text; Everett cover	40.00	80.00	120.00
2-Everett story	20.00	40.00	60.00
3,4	12.00	24.00	36.00

VIC TORRY & HIS FLYING SAUCER
1950 (One Shot)
Fawcett Publications

Powell art	5.00	10.00	15.00

VIC VERITY MAGAZINE
1945 - 1946 (A comic book)
Vic Verity Publications

(Vic Verity Mag. cont'd)	Good	Fine	Mint
#1-C.C. Beck art	2.00	4.00	6.00
2-7	1.35	2.75	4.00

VIGILANTE, THE (See 4-Color Comics #839)

VIKINGS, THE (See 4-Color Comics #910)

VIRGINIAN, THE (TV)
June, 1963
Gold Key

#10060-306	.20	.40	.60

VOODA (See Voodoo #21,22)

VOODOO (Vooda #21 on)
May, 1952 - 1955
Ajax-Farrell(Four Star Publ.)

#1	2.00	4.00	6.00
2-Rulah story reprt. + South Sea Girl from Seven Seas #2 by Baker (name changed from Alani to El'nee)	2.00	4.00	6.00
3-20: #20-Reprint/Seven Seas #4	1.50	3.00	4.50
21,22-Matt Baker art	1.75	3.35	5.00
Annual #1(1952)(25¢)	2.00	4.00	6.00

VOODOO (See Tales of --)

VOYAGE TO THE BOTTOM OF THE SEA (TV)
1961 - #16, April, 1970
Dell Publ. Co./Gold Key

4-Color #1230(Movie-'61)	1.20	2.40	3.60
#10133-412(G.K.-12/64)	.50	1.00	1.50
#2-5	.30	.60	.90
6-14	.25	.50	.75
15,16-Reprints	.15	.30	.45

VOYAGE TO THE DEEP
Sept-Nov, 1962 - #4, Nov-Jan, 1964
Dell Publishing Co.

#1	.65	1.35	2.00
2-4	.35	.70	1.05

WACKY ADVENTURES OF CRACKY (Also see Gold Key Spotlight)
Dec, 1972 - #12, Sept, 1975
Gold Key

#1	.15	.30	
2-12	.10	.20	

(See March of Comics #405)

WACKY DUCK (Formerly Dopey Duck?; Justice #3, Fall, 1946 - #6, Summer, 1947; #7 on)

Aug, 1948 - #2, Oct, 1948
Marvel Comics (NPP)

	Good	Fine	Mint
#3-6('46-47)	1.00	2.00	3.00
1,2(1948)	1.00	2.00	3.00
IW Reprint #1,2,7('58)	.20	.40	.60
Super Reprint #10(IW on cover, Super on in-side)	.20	.40	.60

WACKY QUACKY (See Wisco)

WACKY RACES (TV)
Feb, 1969 - #7, April, 1972 (Hanna-Barbera)
Gold Key

#1-7		.10	.20

WACKY WITCH (See March of Comics #374,398,410)
March, 1971 - #21, Jan, 1976
Gold Key

#1		.15	.30
2-21		.10	.20

WACKY WOODPECKER (See Two Bit --)
1958; 1963
I.W. Enterprises/Super Comics

IW Reprint #1,2,7(no date-reprints Two Bit--)			
	.20	.40	.60
Super Reprint #10('63)	.20	.40	.60

WAGON TRAIN (1st Series) (TV)
1958 - #13, July-Sept, 1962
Dell Publishing Co.

4-Color #895,971,1019	.80	1.60	2.40
#4(1-3/60)-#13(7-9/62)	.50	1.00	1.50

WAGON TRAIN (2nd Series)
Jan, 1964 - #4, Oct, 1964
Gold Key

#1	.25	.50	.75
2-4	.15	.30	.45

WALLY
Dec, 1962 - #4, Sept, 1963
Gold Key

#1-4	.15	.30	.45

WALT DISNEY COMICS DIGEST
June, 1968 - #57, Feb, 1976 (50¢ Digest Size)
Gold Key

#1-Reprints Uncle Scrooge #5			
	4.00	8.00	12.00

Voodoo #3, © Ajax

Voyage To The Deep #3, © Dell

Wacky Woodpecker #1, © I.W.

W.D. Comics Digest #1, © WDP

(Walt Disney Comics Digest cont'd)

	Good	Fine	Mint
2-4-Barks reprints	2.50	5.00	7.50
5-Daisy Duck by Barks(21pgs.)-last published story by Barks(art only)	2.50	5.00	7.50
6-13-All Barks reprints	1.75	3.35	5.00
14,15	1.00	2.00	3.00
16-Reprints Donald Duck #26 by Barks	2.00	4.00	6.00
17-20-Barks reprints	1.20	2.40	3.60
21-31,33,35-37-Barks reprints; #24-Toth Zorro	1.00	2.00	3.00
32	.65	1.35	2.00
34-Reprints 4-Color #318	2.00	4.00	6.00
38-Reprints Christmas in Disneyland #1	1.50	3.00	4.50
39-Two Barks reprts./WDC&S #272, 4-Color#1073 + Toth Zorro reprt.	1.20	2.40	3.60
40-Mickey Mouse reprints	.65	1.35	2.00
41,45,47-49	.40	.80	1.20
42,43-Barks reprints	.80	1.60	2.40
44-(Has Gold Key emblem, 50¢)-Reprints 1st story of 4-Color #29,256,275 & 282	3.00	6.00	9.00
44-Republished in 1976 by Whitman; not identical to original; slightly smaller, blank back cover, 69¢ cover price	1.00	2.00	3.00
46,50-Barks reprint	.80	1.60	2.40
51-Reprints 4-Color #71	1.00	2.00	3.00
52-Barks reprt/WDC&S#161,132	.80	1.60	2.40
53-Reprt/Dell Giant #30	.40	.80	1.20
54-Reprt. Donald Duck Beach Party #2	.40	.80	1.20
55-Reprt/Dell Giant #49	.40	.80	1.20
56-Reprt/Uncle Scrooge #32(Barks) + another Barks story	.80	1.60	2.40
57-Reprt/M.Mouse Almanac('57) & two Barks stories	.80	1.60	2.40

NOTE: #1-10, 196pgs.; #11-41, 164pgs.; #42 on, 132pgs. Old issues were being reprinted & distributed by Whitman in 1976.

WALT DISNEY CHRISTMAS SPECIAL
Winter, 1977   (228 pgs.)
Whitman Publishing Co.

#1-Almost all reprint material	.40	.80	1.20

WALT DISNEY PRESENTS
June-Aug, 1959 - #6, Dec-Feb, 1960-61
Dell Publishing Co.

4-Color #997	1.00	2.00	3.00
#2(12-2/59-60)-The Swamp Fox, El Fego Baca,			

	Good	Fine	Mint
Texas John Slaughter (Disney TV Show), 3-6	.75	1.50	2.25

WALT DISNEY SHOWCASE
Oct, 1970 - Present
Gold Key

	Good	Fine	Mint
#1-Boatniks (Movie)	.25	.50	.75
2-Moby Duck	.15	.30	.45
3-Bongo & Lumpjaw-reprts.	.15	.30	.45
4-Pluto-reprints	.15	.30	.45
5-$1,000,000 Duck(Movie)	.25	.50	.75
6-Bedknobs & Broomsticks (Movie)	.25	.50	.75
7-Pluto-reprints	.15	.30	.45
8-Daisy & Donald	.15	.30	.45
9-101 Dalmatians (Cartoon feature)-reprints 4-Color #1183	.20	.40	.60
10-Napoleon & Samantha (Movie)	.20	.40	.60
11-Moby Duck-reprints	.15	.30	.45
12-Dumbo-reprints 4-Color #668	.20	.40	.60
13-Pluto-reprints	.15	.30	.45
14-World's Greatest Athlete (Movie)	.20	.40	.60
15-3 Little Pigs-reprints	.15	.30	.45
16-Aristocats (Cartoon feature)-reprints Aristocats #1	.15	.30	.45
17-Mary Poppins-reprints M.P. #10136-501	.20	.40	.60
18-Gyro Gearloose (Barks reprints-4-Color #1047,1184)	.50	1.00	1.50
19-That Darn Cat-reprints T.D.C.#10171-602	.15	.30	.45
20-Pluto-reprints	.15	.30	.45
21-Li'l Bad Wolf & the Three Little Pigs	.15	.30	.45
22-Unbirthday Party with Alice in Wonderland-reprints 4-Color #341	.20	.40	.60
23-Pluto-reprints	.15	.30	.45
24-Herbie Rides Again (Movie)-sequel to "The Love Bug"	.20	.40	.60
25-Old Yeller (Movie)-reprints 4-Color #869	.20	.40	.60
26-Lt. Robin Crusoe USN (Movie)-reprints Lt. Robin Crusoe USN #10191-601	.20	.40	.60
27-Island at the Top of the World (Movie)	.20	.40	.60
28-Brer Rabbit, Bucky Bug reprints	.20	.40	.60
29-Escape to Witch Mountain (Movie)	.20	.40	.60
30-Magica De Spell-Barks reprints-Uncle Scrooge #36 & WDC&S #258	.25	.50	.75
31-Bambi (Cartoon feature)-reprints 4-Color #186	.20	.40	.60
32-Spin & Marty-reprint; Mickey Mouse Club	.15	.30	.45
33-Pluto	.15	.30	.45
34-Paul Revere's Ride with Johnny Tremain-4-Color #822 reprint	.15	.30	.45
35-Goofy	.15	.30	.45
36-Peter Pan-4-Color reprt.	.15	.30	.45
37-Tinker Bell & Jiminy Cricket-reprints 4-Color #982,989	.15	.30	.45
38-Mickey & the Sleuth, Part 1	.15	.30	.45
39-Mickey & the Sleuth, Part 2	.15	.30	.45
40-The Rescuers (Cartoon feature)	.15	.30	.45
41-Herbie Goes to Monte Carlo (Movie)-Sequel to "Herbie Rides Again"	.15	.30	.45
42-Mickey & the Sleuth	.15	.30	.45

WALT DISNEY'S COMICS & STORIES (Continuation
of Mickey Mouse Magazine) (#1-30 contain D.
Duck newspaper reprints)

Oct, 1940 - Present

Dell Publ. Co./Gold Key #264 on

	Good	Fine	Mint
#1-Donald Duck strip reprints by Al Taliaferro & Gottfredson's Mickey Mouse begin	500.00	1500.00	2500.00

(Prices vary widely on this book)

	Good	Fine	Mint
2	250.00	625.00	1000.00
3	150.00	300.00	450.00
4	110.00	220.00	330.00
5	90.00	180.00	270.00
6-10	75.00	150.00	225.00
11-14	60.00	120.00	180.00
15-17	40.00	80.00	120.00
18-21: #15-The 3 Little Kittens(17pgs.).#16- The 3 Little Pigs(29pgs.). #17-The Ugly Duckling(4pgs.)	33.00	66.50	100.00
22-30	25.00	50.00	75.00
31-1st Donald Duck by Carl Barks	175.00	350.00	525.00
32-Barks art	85.00	170.00	255.00
33-Barks art	70.00	140.00	210.00
34-Gremlins by Walt Kelly begin, end #41; Barks art	60.00	120.00	180.00
35,36-Barks art	50.00	100.00	150.00
37-Not by Barks	25.00	50.00	75.00
38-40-Barks art	35.00	70.00	105.00
41-50-Barks art	25.00	50.00	75.00
51-60-Barks art; #52-Li'l Bad Wolf begins, ends #203(not in #55)	20.00	40.00	60.00
61-70: Barks art. #61-Dumbo story. #63,64- Pinocchio stories. #65-Pluto story. #67, 68-M.Mouse art(Sunday reprints)by Bill Wright	15.00	30.00	45.00
71-80: Barks art. #75-77-Brer Rabbit stories, no Mickey Mouse .	12.00	24.00	36.00
81-87,89,90: #82-84-Bongo stories. #86-90- Goofy & Agnes app. #89-Chip 'n' Dale story	9.00	18.00	27.00
88-1st app. Gladstone Gander by Barks	10.00	20.00	30.00
91-97,99,100: Barks art. #96-No Mickey Mouse; Little Toot begins, ends #97	8.00	16.00	24.00
98-1st Uncle Scrooge app. in WDC&S	12.00	24.00	36.00
101-110-Barks art	7.00	14.00	21.00
111,114,117-All Barks	5.00	10.00	15.00
112-Drug(ether) issue (Donald Duck)	6.00	12.00	18.00
113,115,116,118,119,121-123: Not by Barks. #116-Dumbo x-over. #121-Grandma Duck be- gins, ends #168; not in #135,142,146,155	2.50	5.00	7.50
120-Barks pencils	3.00	6.00	9.00

	Good	Fine	Mint
124-130-All Barks	4.00	8.00	12.00
131,133-139-All Barks	3.50	7.00	10.50
132-Two Barks stories(D. Duck & Grandma Duck)	5.00	10.00	15.00
140-1st app. Gyro Gearloose by Barks	4.00	8.00	12.00
141-150-All Barks. #143-Little Hiawatha begins, ends #151,159	3.00	6.00	9.00
151-170-All Barks. #164-Has blank inside covers	2.00	4.00	6.00
171-200-All Barks	1.75	3.50	5.25
201-240: All Barks. #204-Chip 'n' Dale & Scamp begin	1.35	2.75	4.00
241-283: #241-Dumbo x-over. #249-Gyro Gear- loose begins, ends #274. #256-Ludwig Von Drake begins, ends #274	1.20	2.40	3.60
284,285,287,290,295,296,309-311-Not by Barks	.65	1.35	2.00
286,288,289,291-294,297,298,308-All Barks stories; #293(Grandma Duck's Farm Friends), 298(Daisy Duck's Diary-reprint)	1.00	2.00	3.00
299-307-All contain early Barks reprints (#43-117)	1.00	2.00	3.00
312-Last Barks issue with original story	1.00	2.00	3.00
313-327,329-334,336-341	.40	.80	1.20
328,335,342-351-Barks reprts.	.80	1.60	2.40
352-356-Barks reprints	.75	1.50	2.25
357-360-w/posters inside; Barks reprints	.75	1.50	2.25
361-400-Barks reprints	.65	1.35	2.00
401-429-Barks reprints	.40	.80	1.20
430,433,437,438,441,444,445-No Barks	.15	.30	.45
431,432,434-436,439,440,442,443-Barks reprts., 446,447(12/77-52pgs.)	.20	.40	.60

NOTE: Barks art in all issues No. 31 on, except where noted.
Kelly covers—(most) Nos. 34-94, 97-103, 105, 106, 110-123. The
whole number can always be found at bottom of title page in the
lower left-hand panel. Walt Disney's Comics & Stories featured
Mickey Mouse Serials which were in practically every issue from
No. 1 through No. 392. The titles of the serials, along with the
issues they are in, are listed in previous editions. Floyd Gottfred-
son Mickey Mouse Serials in issues No. 1-60, 63-66, 69-92 plus
"Mickey Mouse in a Warplant" (3 pgs.), and "Pluto Catches a Nazi
Spy" (4 pgs.) in No. 62; "Mythery Next Door," No. 93; "Sunken
Treasure," No. 94; "Aunt Marissa," No. 95; "Gangland," No. 98;
"Thanksgiving Dinner," No. 99; and "The Talking Dog," No. 100.
Mickey Mouse by Paul Murry No. 152 on. Al Taliaferro Silly Symphonies in No. 5—"Three Little Pigs;" No. 13—"Birds of a Feather;" No. 14—"The Boarding School Mystery;" No. 15—"Cookie-
land" and "Three Little Kittens;" No. 16—"Three Little Pigs;"
No. 17—"The Ugly Duckling," and "The Robber Kitten;" No.
19—"Penguin Isle;" and "Bucky Bug" in Nos. 20-23, 25, 26, 28
(one continuous story from 1932-34; first 2 pgs. not Taliaferro)

WALT DISNEY'S COMICS & STORIES
1943   (36pgs.)(Dept. store Xmas giveaway)
Walt Disney Productions

	Good	Fine	Mint
No#	70.00	140.00	210.00

Walt Disney's Comics & Stories #16, ©WDP

Walt Disney's Comics & Stories #33, ©WDP

Walt Disney's Comics & Stories #40, © WDP

Walt Disney's Comics & Stories #75, © WDP   Wambi #8(I.W.), © FH   War Adventures #6, © MCG

WALT DISNEY'S COMICS & STORIES
Mid 1940's ('45-48) (4 pgs. in color)
Dell Publishing Co.   (Slick paper)

	Good	Fine	Mint
Special Xmas offer-subscription form for			
WDC&S-(Reprints two different WDC&S covers			
with subscription forms printed on inside			
covers)	6.00	12.00	18.00

WALT DISNEY'S MAGAZINE (Formerly W.D. Mickey
Mouse Club Magazine) (50c) (Bi-mo.)
V2#4, June, 1957 - V4#6, Oct, 1959
Western Publishing Co.

V2#4-Stories & articles on the Mouseketeers,			
Zorro, Goofy & other Disney characters &			
people	1.35	2.75	4.00
V2#5,V2#6(10/57)	1.35	2.75	4.00
V3#1(12/57)-V3#6(10/58)	1.00	2.00	3.00
V4#1(12/58)-V4#6(10/59)	1.00	2.00	3.00

NOTE: V2#4-V3#6 were 11½x8½", 48pgs.;
V4#1 on were 10x8", 52pgs. (Peak circulation
of 400,000)

WALT DISNEY'S MERRY CHRISTMAS (See Dell
Giant #39)

WALT DISNEY'S MICKEY MOUSE CLUB MAGAZINE
(Becomes Walt Disney Mag.) (Quarterly)
Winter, 1956 - V2#3, 4/57 (11½x8½", 48pgs.)
Western Publishing Co.

V1#1	3.50	7.00	10.50
2-4	2.00	4.00	6.00
V2#1-3	1.50	3.00	4.50
Annual (1956)-Two diff.($1.50) Whitman, 120			
pgs., cardboard covers, 11-3/4"x8-3/4";			
reprints	5.00	10.00	15.00
Annual (1957)-Same as above			
	3.50	7.00	10.50

WALT DISNEY'S WHEATIES PREMIUMS
(See Wheaties)

WALT SCOTT'S XMAS STORIES (See 4-Color #959,
1062)

WAMBI, JUNGLE BOY
Spring, 1942 - #3, Spring, 1943; $4, Fall,
1948 - #18, Winter, 1952-53
Fiction House Magazines

#1-Wambi, the Jungle Boy begins			
	10.00	20.00	30.00
2,3(1943)	6.00	12.00	18.00
4-Origin in text('48)	2.00	4.00	6.00
5-10	1.75	3.35	5.00
11-18	1.35	2.75	4.00

	Good	Fine	Mint
IW Reprint #8('64)-reprints F.H. #12 with			
new cover	.65	1.35	2.00

WANTED COMICS
#9, Sept-Oct, 1947 - #53, April, 1953
Toytown Publications/Patches/Orbit Publ.

#9-11	1.00	2.00	3.00
12-Mentioned in Seduction of the Innocent,			
pg. 277	3.00	6.00	9.00
13-Cover/story on heroin racket			
	1.50	3.00	4.50
14-17	.90	1.80	2.70
18-Marijuana story	7.00	14.00	21.00
19-2pgs. on wanted dopepusher			
	1.50	3.00	4.50
20,22,23,25-53: #49-Buscema cover/story			
	.65	1.35	2.00
21,24-Krigstein story	1.50	3.00	4.50

WANTED: DEAD OR ALIVE (See 4-Color #1102,1164)

WANTED, THE WORLD'S MOST DANGEROUS VILLAINS
(See DC Special)
7-8/72 - #9, 8-9/73   (All reprints)
National Periodical Publications

#1-Reprints Batman, Green Lantern, & Green			
Arrow	.35	.70	1.05
2-Reprints Batman & The Flash			
	.25	.50	.75
3-Reprints Dr. Fate, Hawkman, & Vigilante			
	.25	.50	.75
4-Reprints origin Solomon Grundy from All-			
American #61	.25	.50	.75
5-Doll Man/Green Lantern	.25	.50	.75
6-Starman/Wildcat/Sargon	.25	.50	.75
7-Johnny Quick/Hawkman/Hourman; Baily, Mes-			
kin reprints	.25	.50	.75
8-Dr. Fate/Flash	.25	.50	.75
9-S&K Sandman/Superman	.25	.50	.75

NOTE: Infantino stories-#2,8. Kubert stories-
#3(inks),6,7.

WAR
July, 1975 - #9, Nov, 1976
Charlton Comics

#1		.15	.30
2-9		.10	.20

WAR ACTION
April, 1952 - #14, June, 1953
Atlas Comics (CPS)

#1	1.20	2.40	3.60
2-10,14	.75	1.50	2.25
11-13-Krigstein stories	1.50	3.00	4.50

WAR ADVENTURES
Jan, 1952 - #13, Mar, 1953
Atlas Comics (HPC)

	Good	Fine	Mint
#1	1.20	2.40	3.60
2-13: #3-Robinson story	.75	1.50	2.25

WAR ADVENTURES ON THE BATTLEFIELD
(See Battlefield)

WAR AGAINST CRIME! (Vault of Horror #12 on)
Spring, 1948 - #11, Feb-Mar, 1950
E.C. Comics

#1	20.00	40.00	60.00
2,3	15.00	30.00	45.00
4-9	13.50	26.75	40.00
10-1st Vault Keeper app.	45.00	90.00	135.00
11-2nd Vault Keeper app.	35.00	70.00	105.00

NOTE: *All have Craig covers.*

WAR AND ATTACK (Also see Special War Series#3)
Fall, 1964 - V2#63, Dec, 1967
Charlton Comics

#1-Wood art	.40	.80	1.20
V2#54(6/66)-#63		.20	.35

NOTE: *Montes/Bache art-#55,56,60,63.*

WAR AT SEA
#22, Nov, 1957 - #42, June, 1961
Charlton Comics

#22-42		.15	.30

WAR BATTLES
Feb, 1952 - #9, Dec, 1959
Harvey Publications

#1	1.20	2.40	3.60
2-9	.65	1.35	2.00

NOTE: *Powell art-#1-3.*

WAR BIRDS
1952
Fiction House Magazines

#1	1.75	3.35	5.00
2-7	1.00	2.00	3.00

WAR COMBAT (Combat Casey #6 on)
March, 1952 - #5, Nov, 1952
Atlas Comics (SAI)

#1	1.00	2.00	3.00
2-5	.60	1.20	1.80

WAR COMICS (See Key Ring Comics)

May, 1940 - #8, 1941
Dell Publishing Co.

	Good	Fine	Mint
#1-Sikandur the Robot Master, Sky Hawk, Scoop Mason, War Correspondent begin	7.00	14.00	21.00
2-Origin Greg Gilday	4.00	8.00	12.00
3-Joan becomes Greg Gilday's aide	4.00	8.00	12.00
4-Origin Night Devils	5.00	10.00	15.00
5-8	4.00	8.00	12.00

WAR COMICS
Dec, 1950 - #49, Sept, 1957
Marvel/Atlas (USA #1-41/JPI #42-49)

#1	1.75	3.35	5.00
2-7,9,10	1.00	2.00	3.00
8-Krigstein story	1.75	3.35	5.00
11-20	.75	1.50	2.25
21,23-37,39-42,44,45,47,48	.65	1.35	2.00
22-Krigstein story	1.50	3.00	4.50
38-Kubert/Moskowitz story	1.35	2.75	4.00
43,49-Torres stories	1.25	2.50	3.75
46-Crandall story	1.35	2.75	4.00

NOTE: *Drucker stories-#37,43,48. Everett story-#17. G. Kane story-#19. Orlando story-#42,48. Robinson story-#15.*

WAR DOGS OF THE U.S. ARMY
1952
Avon Periodicals

#1-Kinstler cover/story	2.00	4.00	6.00

WARFRONT
9/51 - #35, 1958; #36, 10/65; #37, 9/66 - #39, 2/67
Harvey Publications

#1	1.50	3.00	4.50
2-10: #4,5-Powell art	1.00	2.00	3.00
11-20	.65	1.35	2.00
21-35	.50	1.00	1.50
36-Dynamite Joe begins, ends #39	.25	.50	.75
37-39-Wood art, 2-3pgs.; Lone Tiger app.	.65	1.35	2.00

NOTE: *Kirby cover-#28,34. Nostrand stories-#4,6,15,25. Powell art-#20,28,34.*

WAR FURY
Sept, 1952 - #4, March, 1953
Comic Media/Harwell

#1	1.00	2.00	3.00
2-4	.65	1.35	2.00

War Against Crime #8, © WMG

War Birds #1, © FH

Warfront #1, © Harv

War Heroes #1, © Dell   Warlock #1, © MCC   Wartime Romances #6, © STJ

WAR GODS OF THE DEEP   (See Movie Classics)

WAR HEROES   (See Marine War Heroes)

WAR HEROES
1942 (no month); #2, 12/42 - #10, 10-12/42;
#11, 1944
Dell Publishing Co.

	Good	Fine	Mint
#1	3.50	7.00	10.50
2,3,5	2.00	4.00	6.00
4-Disney's Gremlins app.	3.50	7.00	10.50
6-11	1.50	3.00	4.50

NOTE: *#1 was to be released in July, but was delayed.*

WAR HEROES
1952 - #8, April, 1953
Ace Magazines

#1	1.00	2.00	3.00
2-8	.65	1.35	2.00

WAR HEROES
Feb, 1963 - #27, Nov, 1967
Charlton Comics

#1	.15	.30	.45
2-27: #27-1st Devils Brigade by Glanzman		.15	.30

NOTE: *Montes/Bache art-#3-7,21,25,27; covers-#3-7.*

WAR IS HELL
Jan, 1973 - #15, Oct, 1975
Marvel Comics Group

#1-Williamson reprint	.25	.50	.75
2-5	.20	.40	.60
6-15	.15	.30

NOTE: *Bolle reprint-#3. Powell, Woodbridge, story-#1. Sgt. Fury reprints-#7,8.*

WARLOCK   (The Power of --)
8/72 - #8, 10/73; #9, 10/75 - #15, 10/76
Marvel Comics Group

#1-Origin by Kane	1.20	2.40	3.60
2,3	.60	1.20	1.80
4-8: #4-Death of Eddie Roberts			
	.50	1.00	1.50
9-14-Starlin art in all	.60	1.20	1.80
15	.25	.50	.75

WARLORD, THE
1-2/76, #2, 3-4/76; #3, 10-11/76 - Present
National Periodical Publications/DC Comics

	Good	Fine	Mint
#1-Story cont'd. from 1st ish. Special #8			
	.35	.70	1.05
2-10	.20	.40	.60

WARPATH
Nov, 1954 - #3, April, 1955
Key Publications/Stanmor

#1	1.00	2.00	3.00
2,3	.50	1.00	1.50

WAR REPORT
Sept, 1952 - #5, May, 1953
Ajax/Farrell Publications (Excellent Publ.)

#1	1.00	2.00	3.00
2-5	.50	1.00	1.50

WARRIOR COMICS
1945   (1930's DC reprints)
H. C. Blackerby

#1-Wing Brady, The Iron Man, Mark Markon			
	1.75	3.35	5.00

WAR ROMANCES   (See True --)

WAR STORIES
1942 - #8, Feb-Apr, 1943
Dell Publishing Co.

#1	4.00	8.00	12.00
2-4	2.00	4.00	6.00
5-Origin The Whistler	2.50	5.00	7.50
6	2.00	4.00	6.00
7,8-Night Devils	3.00	6.00	9.00

WAR STORIES   (Korea)
Sept, 1952 - #5, May, 1953
Ajax/Farrell Publications (Excellent Publ.)

#1	1.00	2.00	3.00
2-5	.65	1.35	2.00

WAR STORIES   (See Star-Spangled --)

WART AND THE WIZARD
Feb, 1964   (Walt Disney)
Gold Key

#1(10102-402)	.40	.80	1.20

WARTIME ROMANCES
July, 1951 - #18, Nov, 1953
St. John Publishing Co.

#1	3.00	6.00	9.00

(Wartime Romances cont'd)	Good	Fine	Mint
2-5	2.00	4.00	6.00
6-18	1.35	2.75	5.00

NOTE: *Baker cover/art in all.*

WAR VICTORY ADVENTURES (#1-War Victory Comics)
Summer, 1942 - #3, Winter, 1943-44   (5¢)
U.W. Treasury Dept./War Victory/Harvey Publ.

#1-(Promtion of Savings Bonds)-Featuring America's greatest comic art by top synd- icated cartoonists; Blondie, Joe Palooka, Green Hornet, Dick Tracy, Superman, Gumps, etc.; (36 pgs.)	15.00	30.00	45.00
2	6.00	12.00	18.00
3-Capt. Red Cross(cover & text only); Powell art	4.00	8.00	12.00

WAR WAGON, THE (See Movie Classics)

WAR WINGS
October, 1968
Charlton Comics

#1		.15	.30

WASHABLE JONES & SHMOO
1953
Harvey Publications

#1	2.00	4.00	6.00

WASH TUBBS (See 4-Color Comics #11,28,53)

WATCH OUT FOR BIG TALK
1949
Giveaway

Dan Barry art (about crooked politicians)	1.00	2.00	3.00

WATER BIRDS AND THE OLYMPIC ELK (See 4-Color Comics #700)

WEATHER-BIRD (See Comics From --, & Free Comics to You--)   (Giveaway)
1958 - #15, 1962
International Shoe Co./Western Printing Co.

#1	.35	.70	1.05
2-15	.20	.40	.60

NOTE: *The numbers are located at the bottom of the bottom panel, pg. 1. All feature a character called Weather-Bird.*

WEATHER BIRD COMICS (See Comics From Weath-
1957   (Giveaway)   er Bird)
Weather Bird Shoes

No#-Contains a comic bound with new cover. Several combinations possible; contents determines price (30-50% of contents)

WEB OF EVIL
Nov, 1952 - #21, Dec, 1954
Comic Magazines/Quality Comics Group

	Good	Fine	Mint
#1-Jack Cole art	3.00	6.00	9.00
2-11-Jack Cole art	2.00	4.00	6.00
12,13,15-21	1.00	2.00	3.00
14-Crandall cover	1.50	3.00	4.50

WEB OF HORROR (Magazine)
Dec, 1969 - #3, Apr, 1970
Major Magazines

#1-Jones cover; Wrightson story	5.00	10.00	15.00
2-Jones cover; 2 Wrightson stories; Kaluta story	3.50	7.00	10.50
3-Wrightson cover; Brunner, Kaluta, Bruce Jones, Wrightson stys.	3.50	7.00	10.50

WEB OF MYSTERY
Feb, 1951 - #29, 1955
Ace Magazines (A.A Wyn)

#1-Lou Cameron art	1.50	3.00	4.50
2-10	1.00	2.00	3.00
11-29: #20 reprts./The Beyond #1	.75	1.50	2.25

NOTE: *This series was to appear as "Creepy Stories," but title was changed before publ. Cameron stories-#17,18-20,22,24,27; cover-#17.*

WEDDING BELLS
#2, April, 1954 - #19, 1956
Quality Comics Group

#2	.75	1.50	2.25
3-9	.60	1.20	1.80
10-Ward art, 9pgs.	1.50	3.00	4.50
11-19	.50	1.00	1.50

WEEKENDER, THE
1946   (52 pgs.)
Rucker Publ. Co.

V2#1-36pgs. comics, 16 in newspaper format with photos, 6pgs. on Disney filming of Pinocchio; Little Nemo story by Winsor McCay, Jr.	3.00	6.00	9.00

WEEKLY COMIC MAGAZINE
5/12/40   (16 pgs.) (Full Color)
Fox Publications

War Victory #1, © Harv

Web Of Evil #11, © Qua

Web Of Mystery #1, © Ace

Weekly Comic Mag. 5/12/40, © Fox   Weird Adventures #2, © Z-D   Weird Comics #9, © Fox

(Weekly Comic Magazine cont'd)

(1st Version)-8pg. Blue Beetle story, 7pg.
Patty O'Day story; 2 copies known to
exist.   Estimated value...... $100.00
(2nd Version)-7 two-pg. adventures of Blue
Beetle, Patty O'Day, Yarko, Dr. Fung,
Green Mask, Spark Stevens & Rex Dexter;
1 copy known to exist.
           Estimated value...... $90.00

Discovered with business papers, letters and exploitation material
promoting **Weekly Comic Magazine** for use by newspapers in the
same manner of **The Spirit** weeklies. Interesting note: these are
dated three weeks before the first **Spirit** comic. Letters indicate
that samples may have been sent to a few newspapers. These sections were actually 15½x22" pages which will fold down to an
approximate 8x10" comic booklet. Other various comic sections
were found with the above, but were more like the Sunday comic
sections in format.

WEIRD (Magazine)
1/66 - V8#6, 12/74; V9#2, 6/76 - Present
(V1-V8, 52pgs.; V9 on, 68pgs.) (No V9#1)
Eerie Publications

                         Good   Fine   Mint
V1#10(#1)-Intro. Morris the Caretaker of
  Weird(ends V2#10); Burgos art
                         .65   1.35   2.00
  11,12   .35   .70   1.05
V2#1-4(10/67) V3#1(1/68), V2#6(4/68)-V2#7,
  9,10(12/68), V3#1(2/69)-V3#4
                      .20   .40   .60
V2#8-Reprints Ditko's 1st story/Fantastic
  Fears #5   .25   .50   .75
  5(12/69)-Rulah reprint-"Rulah" changed to
  "Pulah"; LSD story-reprinted in Horror
  Tales V4#4, Tales From the Tomb V2#4, &
  Terror Tales V7#3   .25   .50   .75
V4#1-6('70), V5#1-6('71), V6#1-7('72), V7#1-6
  ('73), V8#1-6('74), V9#2-4('76)(no V9#1),
  V10#1-3('77)   .20   .40   .60

WEIRD ADVENTURES
May, 1950 - #10, July-Aug, 1951; 5-6/51
Ziff-Davis Publ./P.L. Publ. Co.

#1   1.50   3.00   4.50
2-10: #3-Bondage-torture cover
                      .75   1.50   2.25
#1(P.L.)(5-6/51)-Farrell reprints
                      .80   1.60   2.40

WEIRD CHILLS
July, 1954 - #3, Nov, 1954
Key Publications

#1-Wolverton story reprt./Weird Mysteries #4
                      7.00   14.00   21.00
2   1.00   2.00   3.00
3-Bondage cover   1.50   3.00   4.50

WEIRD COMICS

April, 1940 - #20, Jan, 1942
Fox Features Syndicate
                         Good   Fine   Mint
#1-The Birdman, Thor, God of Thunder(ends#5),
  The Sorceress of Zoom, Blast Bennett, Ty-
  phon, Voodoo Man, & Dr. Mortal begin;
  Fine cover   40.00   80.00 120.00
2   22.00   44.00   66.00
3,4   17.50   35.00   52.50
5-Intro. Dart & sidekick Ace(ends #20)
                     17.50   35.00   52.50
6,7-Dynamite Thor app. in each
                     15.00   30.00   45.00
8-Dynamo, The Eagle & sidekick Buddy &
  Marga, the Panther Woman begin
                     15.00   30.00   45.00
9   13.50   26.75   40.00
10-Navy Jones app.   13.50   26.75   40.00
11-16   12.00   24.00   36.00
17-Origin The Black Rider
18-20   10.00   20.00   30.00

Weird Fantasy #17/5, © WMG

WEIRD FANTASY (Formerly A Moon, A Girl, Romance; becomes Weird Science-Fantasy #23 on)
#13, May-June, 1950 - #22, Nov-Dec, 1953
E.C. Comics

#13(#1)(1950)   75.00 150.00 225.00
14   40.00   80.00 120.00
15,16   30.00   60.00   90.00
17(1951)   25.00   50.00   75.00
6-10   20.00   40.00   60.00
11-13(1952)   15.00   30.00   45.00
14-Frazetta/Williamson/Krenkel story, 7pgs.
                        30.00   60.00   90.00
15-Three Williamson/Evans stories 4,3,& 7pgs.
                        20.00   40.00   60.00
16-19-Williamson/Krenkel stories in all. #18-
  Williamson/Krenkel cover
                        17.50   35.00   52.50

Weird Fantasy #9, © WMG

Weird Fantasy #22, © WMG

Weird Horrors #7, © STJ

(Weird Fantasy cont'd)	Good	Fine	Mint
20-Frazetta/Williamson story, 7pgs.			
	25.00	50.00	75.00
21-Frazetta/Williamson cover & Williamson/			
Krenkel story	35.00	70.00	105.00
22	13.50	26.75	40.00

NOTE: *Crandall* story-#22. *Elder* story-#17.
Feldstein stories-#13(#1)-8; covers-#13(#1)-
18(#18 *w/Krenkel*),20. *Kamen* stories-#13(#1)-
16,18-22. *Krigstein* story-#22. *Kurtzman* stor-
ies-#13(#1)-17(#5),6. *Orlando* stories-#9-22
(2 stories in #16); covers-#19,22. *Severin/*
Elder stories-#18-21. *Wood* stories-#13(#1)-
14,17(2 stories ea. in #10-13). *Canadian re-*
prints exist; see Table of Contents.

WEIRD HORRORS (Nightmare #10 on)
Aug, 1952 - #9, Oct, 1953
St. John Publishing Co.

#1	1.75	3.35	5.00
2,5	1.00	2.00	3.00
3,4-Finesque art by Tuska			
	1.20	2.40	3.60
6-Ekgren cover	2.50	5.00	7.50
7-Ekgren cover; Kubert, Cameron stories			
	3.00	6.00	9.00
8,9-Kubert cvr/stories	2.50	5.00	7.50

WEIRD MYSTERIES
Oct, 1952 - #14, Jan, 1955
Gillmore Publications

#1-Partial Wolverton cover swiped from
splash page "Flight to the Future" in
Weird Tales of the Future #2

	5.00	10.00	15.00

2-"Robot Woman" by Wolverton; Bernard Bailey
cover-reprinted in Mister Mystery #18

	12.00	24.00	36.00

	Good	Fine	Mint
3,6,8-14: #8-Nostrand art			
	1.75	3.35	5.00

4-Swiped with editing from "The Man Who Never Smiled" by Wolverton; B. Bailey cover

	8.00	16.00	24.00
5-Wolverton story	8.00	16.00	24.00

7-Used in Seduction of the Innocent, pg. 5,
+ two illos. 4.00 8.00 12.00

WEIRD MYSTERIES (Magazine)
Mar-Apr, 1959   (68 pgs.)(35¢)(B&W)
Pastime Publications

#1-Torres art(?); E.C. swipe from TFTC #46
by Tuska-"The Ragman" 1.75 3.35 5.00

WEIRD MYSTERY TALES (See DC 100pg.Super Spec.)

WEIRD MYSTERY TALES
July-Aug, 1972 - #24, Nov, 1975
National Periodical Publications

#1-Kirby story	.40	.80	1.20
2,3-Kirby story	.25	.50	.75
4-8,10	.20	.40	.60
9-Redondo story	.20	.40	.60
11-20,22	.15	.30	.45
21-Wrightson cover	.20	.40	.60
23-Wood story	.20	.40	.60
24-Kaluta story	.20	.40	.60

NOTE: *Alcala* stories-#5,10,13,14. *Bolle* story-
#8. *Kaluta* cover-#1,2. *Nino* story-#6.

WEIRD SCIENCE (Formerly Saddle Romances)
(Becomes Weird Science-Fantasy #23 on)
#12, May-June, 1950 - #22, Nov-Dec, 1953
E.C. Comics

#12(#1)(1950)   85.00 170.00 255.00

Weird Science #13/2, © WMG

Weird Science #20, © WMG

Weird Science Fant. Annual #1, © WMG

Weird Science Fantasy #23, © WMG   Weird Tales Of The Future #3, © Aragon   Weird Tales Of The Future #4, © Aragon

(Weird Science cont'd)	Good	Fine	Mint
13	40.00	80.00	120.00
14,15(1950)	30.00	60.00	90.00
5-10	20.00	40.00	60.00
11-14(1952)	17.50	35.00	52.50
15-18-Williamson/Krenkel story in each			
	17.50	35.00	52.50
19,20-Williamson/Frazetta story, 7pgs. ea.			
#19-Used in Seduction of the Innocent			
	20.00	40.00	60.00
21-Williamson/Frazetta story, 6pgs.			
	20.00	40.00	60.00
22-Williamson/Frazetta/Krenkel story, 8pgs.			
	22.50	45.00	67.50

NOTE: _Elder stories-#14,19. Evans story-#22._
Feldstein stories-#12(#1)-8; covers-#12(#1)-
8,11. Ingels story-#15. Kamen stories-#12(#1)-
13,15-18,20,21. Kurtzman stories-#12(#1)-7.
Orlando stories-#10-22. Wood stories-#12(#1),
13(#2),5-22. (#9,10,12,13 all have 2 Wood
stories); covers-#9,10,12-22. Canadian re-
prints exist; see Table of Contents.

WEIRD SCIENCE-FANTASY(Formerly Weird Science
& Weird Fantasy; becomes Incredible S.F. #30)
#23, Mar, 1954 - #29, May-June, 1955
E.C. Comics

#23,24-Williamson & Wood stories in both			
	17.50	35.00	52.50
25-Williamson cover; Williamson/Torres/Kren-			
kel story + Wood sty.	20.00	40.00	60.00
26-Flying Saucer Report; Wood, Crandall,			
Orlando art	13.50	26.75	40.00
27	16.50	33.25	50.00
28-Williamson/Krenkel/Torres story; Wood			
story	20.00	40.00	60.00
29-Frazetta cover; Williamson/Krenkel &			
Wood story	40.00	80.00	120.00

NOTE: _Crandall stories-#26,27,29, Evans story-_
#26. Feldstein covers-#24,26,28. Kamen stories-
#27,28. Krigstein stories-#23-25. Orlando stor-
ies in all. Wood stories in all; covers-#23,27.

WEIRD SCIENCE-FANTASY ANNUAL
1952, 1953 (Sold thru the E.C. office & on
the stands in some major cities)
E.C. Comics

1952	120.00	240.00	360.00
1953	80.00	160.00	240.00

NOTE: _The 1952 annual contains stories from_
1951, and the 1953 annual from 1952. The
contents of each book will vary in same year.

WEIRD SUSPENSE STORIES (Canadian reprint of
Crime SuspenStories #2; see Table of Contents)

WEIRD SUSPENSE TALES
Feb, 1975 - #3, July, 1975
Atlas/Seaboard Publ.

	Good	Fine	Mint
#1-Tarantula begins	.20	.40	.60
2,3	.15	.30	.45

WEIRD TALES
1951 - 1952
Comic Media

#6-10	1.00	2.00	3.00
11-27	.65	1.35	2.00

WEIRD TALES OF THE FUTURE
March, 1952 - #8, July, 1953
S.P.M. Publ.#1/Aragon Publ./Stanmor Publ.

#1	5.00	10.00	15.00
2,3-Three Wolverton stories/covers in each.			
#3 has LSD-like story	15.00	30.00	45.00
4-"Jumpin Jupiter" satire by Wolverton;			
Wolverton cover	8.00	16.00	24.00
5-Two Wolverton stys/cover			
	15.00	30.00	45.00
6-Bernard Bailey cover	2.50	5.00	7.50
7-"The Mind Movers" swiped with editing from			
Wolverton's "The Brain Bats of Venus", Mr.			
Mystery #7; Bernard Bailey cover			
	8.00	16.00	24.00
8-Reprints Weird Mysteries #1(10/52) minus			
cover	1.50	3.00	4.50

WEIRD TALES OF THE MACABRE (Magazine)
Jan, 1975 - #2, Mar, 1975 (B&W) (75¢)
Atlas/Seaboard Publ.

#1-Jones cover	.50	1.00	1.50
2-Boris Valejo cover	.50	1.00	1.50

WEIRD TERROR (Also see Horrific)
Sept, 1952 - #13, Sept, 1954
Allen Hardy Associates (Comic Media)

#1	1.20	2.40	3.60
2-10	.80	1.60	2.40
11-13	.60	1.20	1.80

WEIRD THRILLERS
Sept-Oct, 1951 - #5, Oct-Nov, 1952
Ziff-Davis Publ. Co. (Approved Comics)

#1	1.50	3.00	4.50
2-Toth story	1.50	3.00	4.50
3-Kinstler + 2 Powell stories			
	1.35	2.75	4.00
4-Kubert story	1.50	3.00	4.50
5-Powell art	1.20	2.40	3.60

(Weird Thrillers cont'd)
NOTE: *Anderson stories-#1,2,3. Roussos story-*
#4. #2 & #3 reprinted in Nightmare #10 & 13;
#4,5 reprinted in Amazing Ghost Stories #? &
#15.

WEIRD WAR TALES
Sept-Oct, 1971 - Present
National Periodical Publications/DC Comics

	Good	Fine	Mint
#1-Kubert art	.50	1.00	1.50
2-Kubert(2pgs.) + Crandall reprint			
	.50	1.00	1.50
3,4-Kubert art	.35	.70	1.05
5,6,10-Toth art	.35	.70	1.05
7-Kubert art	.35	.70	1.05
8-Adams cvr/sty.(inks)	.80	1.60	2.40
9,11,12,14-16,18-20	.20	.40	.60
13-Redondo story	.25	.50	.75
17,22-Evans story	.25	.50	.75
21,23-34,37-40	.15	.30	.45
35-Evans story	.20	.40	.60
36-Crandall, Kubert reprt/#2			
	.20	.40	.60
41-45,47-50	.15	.30	.45
46-Evans story	.15	.30	.45
51-62		.20	.35

NOTE: *Alcala stories-#9,11,14-16,20,23,25-29,*
35,42-44,50,64. Baily story-#21. Chaykin sto-
ry-#40,61,62. Ditko story-#46,49. Drucker
stories-#2,3. Heath story-#59. Infantino re-
print-#5. Kaluta cover-#12. Maurer story-#5.
Meskin reprint-#4. Morrow cover-#54. Nino
story-#61.

WEIRD WESTERN TALES (Formerly All-Star West-
#12, 6-7/72 - Present (#12-52pgs.)   ern)
National Periodical Publications/DC Comics

#12-Bat Lash, Pow Wow Smith reprints; El Dia-			
blo by Adams/Wrightson	.75	1.50	2.25
13,15-Adams art + cvr.#15	.65	1.35	2.00
14-Toth art	.25	.50	.75
16-20: #19-Last El Diablo	.15	.30	.45
21-28,30-38	.15	.30	.45
29-Origin Jonah Hex	.20	.40	.60
39-Origin, 1st app. Scalphunter; Evans inks			
	.15	.30	.45
40,42-Evans inks	.15	.30	.45
41,43-45		.20	.35

NOTE: *Alcala stories-#16,17,19, Kubert cover-*
#12. Starlin cover-#44,45. Wildey story-#26.

WEIRD WONDER TALES
Dec, 1973 - #22, May, 1977
Marvel Comics Group

#1-Wolverton story reprint from Mystic #6

	Good	Fine	Mint
	.35	.70	1.05
2-5	.20	.40	.60
6-15	.15	.30	.45
16-18: Venus reprints by Everett/Venus #19,			
18 & 17	.15	.30	.45
19-Dr. Druid(Droom)reprts.		.20	.35
20-22		.20	.35

NOTE: *Ditko reprints-#4,5,11-13,19,20,21.*
Drucker reprint-#12. Everett reprints-#3
(Spellbound #16),#6(Astonishing #10),#9(Adv.
Into Mystery #5). Kirby reprints #6,11,13,18-
22; cover-#19,20. Krigstein reprint-#19.
Kubert reprint-#22. Torres reprint-#7. Wildey
reprint-#2.

WEIRD WORLDS (See Adventures Into --)

WEIRD WORLDS (Magazine)
V1#10(12/70),V2#1(2/71)-#3(6/71)   (52pgs.)
Eerie Publications

V1#10	.35	.70	1.05
V2#1-3	.25	.50	.75

WEIRD WORLDS
8-9/72 - #9, 1-2/74; #10, 10-11/74
National Periodical Publications

#1-Edgar Rice Burrough's John Carter of Mars			
& David Innes begin; Kubert cover			
	.65	1.35	2.00
2,3-Adams/Bunkers stories	.50	1.00	1.50
4-Kaluta story	.50	1.00	1.50
5-7-Last John Carter	.50	1.00	1.50
8-Iron Wolf begins by Chaykin			
	.35	.70	1.05
9,10-Chaykin art	.35	.70	1.05

NOTE: *John Carter by Anderson-#1-3. Kaluta*
covers-#5,6,10. Orlando story-#4.

WELCOME BACK, KOTTER (TV)
Nov, 1976 - #10, Mar-Apr, 1978
National Periodical Publications/DC Comics

#1	.20	.40	.60
2-10	.15	.30	.45

WELCOME SANTA (See March of Comics #63,183)

WELLS FARGO (See Tales of --)

WENDY PARKER COMICS
July, 1953 - #8, July, 1954
Atlas Comics (OMC)

#1	.80	1.60	2.40
2-8	.50	1.00	1.50

Weird Thrillers #1, © Z-D

Weird Worlds #1, © DC

Wendy Parker #1, © MCG

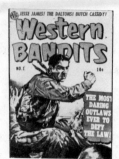
Western Bandits #1, © Avon

Western Bandit Trails #3, © STJ

Western Comics #25, © DC

WENDY, THE GOOD LITTLE WITCH
Aug, 1960 - Present
Harvey Publications

	Good	Fine	Mint
#1	2.00	4.00	6.00
2-10	1.00	2.00	3.00
11-20	.50	1.00	1.50
21-30	.20	.40	.60
31-95		.15	.30

(See Harvey Hits #7,16,21,23,27)

WENDY WITCH WORLD
1962 - Present
Harvey Publications

#1	1.00	2.00	3.00
2-10	.50	1.00	1.50
11-20	.20	.40	.60
21-53		.15	.30

WEREWOLF (Super Hero)
Dec, 1966 - #3, April, 1967
Dell Publishing Co.

#1		.35	.70	1.05
2,3		.20	.40	.60

WEREWOLF BY NIGHT (See Marvel Spotlight)
Sept, 1972 - #43, Mar, 1977
Marvel Comics Group

#1-Ploog art-cont'd./Marvel Spotlight #4			
	.65	1.35	2.00
2-7-Ploog art in all	.40	.80	1.20
8-10	.25	.50	.75
11,12,17-20	.20	.40	.60
13-16-Ploog art; #15-New origin Werewolf			
	.30	.60	.90
21-30	.20	.40	.60
31	.15	.30	.45
32-Origin & 1st app. Moon Knight			
	.15	.30	.45
33-Moon Knight concludes	.15	.30	.45
34,36-43		.20	.35
35-Starlin/Wrightson cvr.	.25	.50	.75

Giant-Size #2(10/74,68pgs.)(Formerly G-S Creatures)-Frankenstein app..35 .70 1.05
Giant-Size #3-5(7/75,68pgs.): #4-Morbius the Living Vampire app. .25 .50 .75
NOTE: *Ploog covers-#5-8,13-16. Ploog/Bolle story-#6. Sutton art-#9,11,16.*

WESTERN ACTION
1964
I.W. Enterprises

#7-Reprint		.35	.70	1.05

WESTERN ACTION
Feb, 1975
Atlas/Seaboard Publ.

	Good	Fine	Mint
#1-Kid Cody by Wildey & The Comanche Kid app.			
	.15	.30	.45

WESTERN ACTION THRILLERS
1937   (100 pgs.)

#1-Buffalo Bill & The Texas Kid			
	8.00	16.00	24.00

WESTERN ADVENTURES COMICS
Oct, 1948 - #6, Aug, 1949
Ace Magazines

No#(#1)-Sheriff Sal begins; Ingels cover			
	2.50	5.00	7.50
No#(#2)(12/48)	2.00	4.00	6.00
No#(#3,2/49)-#6	1.75	3.35	5.00

WESTERN BANDITS
1952
Avon Periodicals

#1-Butch Cassidy, The Daltons; Kinstler story			
	3.00	6.00	9.00

WESTERN BANDIT TRAILS
Jan, 1949 - #9, 1954
St. John Publishing Co.

#1-Tuska art; Baker cvr.	2.00	4.00	6.00
2-Baker cover	1.35	2.75	4.00
3-Baker cover/story, Tuska story			
	1.50	3.00	4.50
4-9	1.00	2.00	3.00

WESTERN COMICS (See Super DC Giant)
Jan-Feb, 1948 - #85, Jan-Feb, 1961
National Periodical Publications

#1-The Vigilante, Wyoming Kid begin			
	5.00	10.00	15.00
2-4-Last Vigilante	3.00	6.00	9.00
5-Nighthawk begins	2.50	5.00	7.50
6,7,9,10	2.00	4.00	6.00
8-Origin Wyoming Kid	2.00	4.00	6.00
11-20	1.75	3.35	5.00
21-40	1.35	2.75	4.00
41-60: #43-Pow Wow Smith begins, ends #85			
	1.00	2.00	3.00
61-85-Last Wyoming Kid; #77-Origin Matt Savage Trail Boss. #82-1st app. Fleetfoot, Pow Wow's girlfriend	.65	1.35	2.00

NOTE: *Gil Kane, Infantino art in most.*

432

TERN CRIME BUSTERS
0 - #10, Mar-Apr, 1952
jan Magazines

	Good	Fine	Mint
	3.50	5.00	10.50
-4	2.50	5.00	7.50
6-Wood stories	4.00	8.00	12.00
Six-Gun Smith begins by Wood,			
Wood story(S-G Smith)	4.00	8.00	12.00
Two Wood stories	5.00	10.00	15.00
Wood story	4.00	8.00	12.00

TERN CRIME CASES
, Dec, 1951
elty-Star Publications

White Rider & Super Horse			
	1.00	2.00	3.00

STERN DESPERADO COMICS (Formerly Slam Bang)
0 (Oct?)
cett Publications

	5.00	10.00	15.00

STERNER, THE (Wild Bill Pecos)
4, June, 1948 - #41, Dec, 1951
anted" Comic Group/Toytown/Patches

4	1.50	3.00	4.50
5-17	1.00	2.00	3.00
8,22-24,27-Krigstein stories			
	1.50	3.00	4.50
9-Meskin art	1.20	2.40	3.60
5(4/50)-Origin & 1st app. Calamity Kate,			
series ends #32; Quest app. #33. Krigstein			
art	1.75	3.50	5.25
8-41: #37-Lobo, the Wolf Boy begins			
	1.00	2.00	3.00

STERNER, THE
64
er Comics

er Reprint #15,16(Crack West.#65),17			
	.35	.70	1.05

STERN FIGHTERS
r-May, 1948 - V4#7, Mar-Apr, 1953
lman Periodicals/Star Publ.

#1-Simon & Kirby art	5.00	10.00	15.00
2,3	1.50	3.00	4.50
4,7-Krigstein stories	2.00	4.00	6.00
5,6,8-10,12	1.20	2.40	3.60
11-Williamson/Frazetta story			
	7.00	14.00	21.00
#1-Krigstein story	1.35	2.75	4.00

	Good	Fine	Mint
2-12	.80	1.60	2.40
V3#1-11	.65	1.35	2.00
12-Krigstein story	1.35	2.75	4.00
V4#1,4-6	.50	1.00	1.50
2,3-Krigstein story	1.20	2.40	3.60
7-Williamson/Frazetta story?			
	6.00	12.00	18.00
3-D#1(12/53)(Star Publ.)	4.00	8.00	12.00

NOTE: _Kinstler stories-V2#6,8,9,12; V3#2,5-7, 11,12._

WESTERN FRONTIER
1951
P.L. Publishers

#1	1.00	2.00	3.00
2-7	.65	1.35	2.00

WESTERN GUNFIGHTERS (1st Series)(Apache Kid
#20, 6/56 - #27, 8/57   #1-19)
Atlas Comics (CPS)

#20	.80	1.60	2.40
21,25-27	.80	1.60	2.40
22-Wood & Powell art	2.50	5.00	7.50
23-Williamson story	2.00	4.00	6.00
24-Toth story	1.35	2.75	4.00

WESTERN GUNFIGHTERS (2nd Series)
8/70 - #33, 11/75 (#1-6, 68pgs.; #7, 52pgs.)
Marvel Comics Group

#1-Ghost Rider, Fort Rango, Renegades & Gun-			
hawk app.	.35	.70	1.05
2-Williamson, Kubert reprt., 5pgs; Ghost			
Rider app.; Apache Kid reprints begin;			
origin Nightwind(Apache Kid's horse)			
	.25	.50	.75
3-Black Rider(Black Mask), Western Kid re-			
prints begin, end #6	.20	.40	.60
4-Smith art	.20	.40	.60
5-9: #6-Gunhawk, Wyatt Earp app; Ghost Rider			
dies. #7-Last Gunhawk, Ghost Rider(origin			
retold); death of Jamie Jacobs. #8-Outlaw			
Kid reprint	.20	.40	.60
10-Origin Black Rider by Kirby; Sequel to			
Matt Slade's origin	.20	.40	.60
11-17: #12-Matt Slade reprints begin(origin),			
end #15. #16-Kid Colt reprints begin			
	.15	.30	.45
18-Williamson reprint	.15	.30	.45
19-33		.15	.30

NOTE: _Everett inks-#6. Kirby stories-#1,11. Steranko cover-#14. Torres story-#26('57). Wildey reprints-#8,9. Woodbridge story-#27 ('57). Renegades in #4,5; Ghost Rider-#1-7._

Western Crime Busters #7. © Trojan

The Westerner #27. © Toytown

Western Fighters 3-D #1. © Hill

Western Hearts #1, © Std

Western Hero #77, © Faw

Western Love #2, © Prize

WESTERN HEARTS
Dec, 1949 - #10, Mar, 1952
Standard Comics

	Good	Fine	Mint
#1-Severin art, photo cvr.	2.50	5.00	7.50
2-Williamson/Frazetta story, 2pgs.			
	10.00	20.00	30.00
3	1.20	2.40	3.60
4-10-Severin & Elder, Al Carreno art			
	1.75	3.50	5.25

WESTERN HERO (Wow #1-69; Real Western Hero
May, 1949 - #112, Mar, 1952   #70-75)
Fawcett Publications

#76-79-Tom Mix, Hopalong Cassidy, & Gabby			
Hayes begin	3.50	7.00	10.50
80-112	2.00	4.00	6.00

WESTERN KID (1st Series)
Dec, 1954 - #17, Aug, 1957
Atlas Comics (CPC)

#1-Origin Western Kid	2.00	4.00	6.00
2-8	1.00	2.00	3.00
9,10-Williamson story in both, 4pgs. each			
	2.00	4.00	6.00
11-17	.75	1.50	2.25

WESTERN KID, THE (2nd Series)
Dec, 1971 - #5, Aug, 1972
Marvel Comics Group

#1-Reprints	.15	.30	.45
2,4,5: #4-Everett reprint		.15	.30
3-Williamson reprint	.15	.30	.45

WESTERN KILLERS
1948 - #64, May, 1949; #6, July, 1949
Fox Features Syndicate

#60-64, 6	1.50	3.00	4.50

WESTERN LIFE ROMANCES
Dec, 1949 - #2, Mar, 1950
Marvel Comics (IPP)

#1,2	1.20	2.40	3.60

WESTERN LOVE
July-Aug, 1949 - #5, Mar-Apr, 1950
Prize Publications

#1-S&K art	3.00	6.00	9.00
2,3,5-S&K art	2.50	5.00	7.50
4	1.50	3.00	4.50

NOTE: Meskin & Severin & Elder stories-#2,4,5.

WESTERN LOVE TRAILS
1949
Ace Magazines

	Good	Fine	Mi
#1	1.00	2.00	3.0

WESTERN MARSHAL (See Steve Donovan-- & Ern
Haycox's 4-Color #534,591,613,640(Based on
Haycox's "Trailtown"))

WESTERN OUTLAWS (My Secret Life #22 on)
1948 - #21, May, 1949
Fox Features Syndicate

#1	1.50	3.00	4.
2-21	1.00	2.00	3.

WESTERN OUTLAWS
Feb, 1954 - #21, Aug, 1957
Atlas Comics (ACI #1-14/WPI #15-21)

#1-Heath art	1.50	3.00	4.
2-10: #10-Everett story	1.00	2.00	3.
11,14-Williamson story in both, 6pgs. each			
	2.00	4.00	6.
12,13,16-18,20,21	.75	1.50	2.
15-Torres story	1.25	2.50	3.
19-Crandall story	1.35	2.75	4.

NOTE: Bolle story-#21. Powell story-#3.

WESTERN OUTLAWS & SHERIFFS(Formerly Best W
Dec, 1949 - #73, June, 1952
Marvel/Atlas Comics (IPC)

#60-65	1.35	2.75	4.
66-73: #68-Robinson sty.	1.00	2.00	3.

WESTERN PICTURE STORIES
Feb, 1937 - #4, 1937
Quality Comics Group

#1-Will Eisner art	16.50	33.25	50.
2-Will Eisner art	10.00	20.00	30.
3,4	9.00	18.00	27.

WESTERN PICTURE STORIES (See Giant Comics
Editions #6,11)

WESTERN ROMANCES (See Target --)

WESTERN ROUGH RIDERS
Nov, 1954 - #4, May, 1955
Gilmore Magazines #1/Stanmor Publications

#1	.80	1.60	2.
2-4	.50	1.00	1.

WESTERN ROUNDUP
June, 1952 - #25, Jan-Mar, 1959 (100 pgs.
Dell Publishing Co.

(Western Roundup cont'd)	Good	Fine	Mint
Gene Autry, Roy Rogers, Elliott, Brown,			
& Rex Allen begin	5.00	10.00	15.00
-5	3.00	6.00	9.00
-10	2.50	5.00	7.50
-13,16,17,19-24-Manning art	2.00	4.00	6.00
	1.75	3.35	5.00
,15,25	1.35	2.75	4.00
-Toth art	2.00	4.00	6.00

STERN TALES (Formerly Witches --)
1, Oct, 1955 - #33, July-Sept, 1956
rvey Publications

1,32-All S&K art; Davy Crockett app. in ea.	5.00	10.00	15.00
3-S&K art; Jim Bowie app.	5.00	10.00	15.00

STERN TALES OF BLACK RIDER (Formerly
ack Rider; Gunsmoke Western #32 on)
8, May, 1955 - #31, Nov, 1955
las Comics (CPS)

8-31	1.20	2.40	3.60

STERN TEAM-UP
vember, 1973
rvel Comics Group

-The Rawhide Kid & The Dakota Kid reprints;			
Gunsmoke Kid reprint by Jack Davis			
	.15	.30	.45

STERN THRILLERS (My Past Confessions #8 on)
g, 1948 - #7, Aug, 1949
x Features Syndicate

	2.00	4.00	6.00
-7	1.35	2.75	4.00
2-(Reprint, M.S.Dist.)1954? No date given			
(Becomes My Love Secret #53)			
	.65	1.35	2.00

ESTERN THRILLERS (Cowboy Action #5 on)
ov, 1954 - #4, Feb, 1955
tlas Comics (ACI)

1	1.75	3.35	5.00
2-4	1.00	2.00	3.00

ESTERN TRAILS
ay, 1957 - #2, July, 1957
tlas Comics (SAI)

1	1.00	2.00	3.00
2-Severin cover	.65	1.35	2.00

WESTERN TRUE CRIME (Becomes My Confessions)
1949 - #19, 1950
Fox Features Syndicate

	Good	Fine	Mint
#1	2.00	4.00	6.00
2,3,5-19	1.35	2.75	4.00
4-Craig story	2.00	4.00	6.00

WESTERN WINNERS (Formerly All-Western
Winners; Black Rider #8 on)
#5, Sept, 1949 - #7, Dec, 1949
Marvel Comics (CDS)

#5-7-Two-Gun Kid, Kid Colt, Black Rider; #6-			
Heath Kid Colt story	2.50	5.00	7.50

WEST OF THE PECOS (See 4-Color Comics #222)

WESTWARD HO, THE WAGONS (See 4-Color #738)

WHACK (Satire)
Oct, 1953 - #3, May, 1954
St. John Publishing Co.

#1-(3-D)-Kubert art	4.00	8.00	12.00
2,3-Kubert art in ea.	2.00	4.00	6.00

WHACKY (See Wacky)

WHAM (See Super Spy)
Nov, 1940 - #2, Dec, 1940
Centaur Publications

#1-The Sparkler, The Phantom Rider, Craig			
Carter and the Magic Ring, Detector,			
Copper Slug, & Speed Centaur begin	16.50	33.25	50.00
2-Origin Blue Fire & Solarman; The Buzzard			
app.	13.50	26.75	40.00

WHAM-O GIANT COMICS (98¢)
1967 (Newspaper size)(One Shot)(Full Color)
Wham-O Mfg. Co.

#1-Radian & Goody Bumpkin by Wally Wood;			
1pg. Stanley art	1.75	3.35	5.00

WHAT IF --?
Feb, 1977 - Present (52 pgs.)
Marvel Comics Group

#1	.50	1.00	1.50
2-6	.25	.50	.75

WHEATIES (Premiums) (32 titles)
1950 & 1951 (32 pgs.) (Pocket Size)
Walt Disney Productions

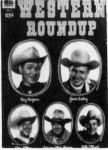

Western Roundup #2, © Dell

Western Thrillers #1, © Fox

Wham Comics #1, © Cen

Wheaties Premiums, © WDP

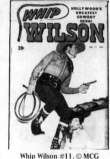

Whip Wilson #11, © MCG

Whirlwind Comics #1, © Nita Publ.

(Wheaties cont'd)

	Good	Fine	Mint
(Set A-1 to A-8, 1950)			
A-1 Mickey Mouse & the Disappearing Island			
A-2 Grandma Duck, Homespun Detective			
A-3 Donald Duck & the Haunted Jewels			
A-4 Donald Duck & the Giant Ape			
A-5 Mickey Mouse, Roving Reporter			
A-6 Li'l Bad Wolf, Forest Ranger			
A-7 Goofy, Tightrope Acrobat			
A-8 Pluto & the Bogus Money			
Per set......	15.00	30.00	45.00

(Set B-1 to B-8, 1950)
B-1 Mickey Mouse & the Pharoah's Curse
B-2 Pluto, Canine Cowpoke
B-3 Donald Duck & the Buccaneers
B-4 Mickey Mouse & the Mystery Sea Monster
B-5 Li'l Bad Wolf in the Hollow Tree Hideout
B-6 Donald Duck, Trail Blazer
B-7 Goofy & the Gangsters
B-8 Donald Duck, Klondike Kid
Per set...... 12.00 24.00 36.00

(Set C-1 to C-8, 1951)
C-1 Donald Duck & the Inca Idol
C-2 Mickey Mouse & the Magic Mountain
C-3 Li'l Bad Wolf, Fire Fighter
C-4 Gus & Jaq Save the Ship
C-5 Donald Duck in the Lost Lakes
C-6 Mickey Mouse & the Stagecoach Bandits
C-7 Goofy, Big Game Hunter
C-8 Donald Duck Deep-Sea Diver
Per set...... 12.00 24.00 36.00

(Set D-1 to D-8, 1951)
D-1 Donald Duck in Indian Country
D-2 Mickey Mouse and the Abandoned Mine
D-3 Pluto & the Mysterious Package
D-4 Bre'r Rabbit's Sunken Treasure
D-5 Donald Duck, Mighty Mystic
D-6 Mickey Mouse & the Medicine Man
D-7 Li'l Bad Wolf and the Secret of the Woods
D-8 Minnie Mouse, Girl Explorer
Per set...... 12.00 24.00 36.00

WHEELIE AND THE CHOPPER BUNCH
July, 1975 - #7, July, 1976 (Hanna-Barbera)
Charlton Comics

#1-7 .10 .20

WHEN KNIGHTHOOD WAS IN FLOWER (See 4-Color Comics #505,682)

WHEN SCHOOL IS OUT (See Wisco)

WHERE CREATURES ROAM
July, 1970 - #8, Sept, 1971
Marvel Comics Group

	Good	Fine	Min
#1-Kirby/Ditko reprints	.25	.50	.7
2-8-Kirby/Ditko reprints	.15	.30	.4

WHERE MONSTERS DWELL
Jan, 1970 - #38, Oct, 1975
Marvel Comics Group

#1-Kirby/Ditko reprints	.25	.50	.7
2-10: #4-Crandall reprt.	.20	.40	.6
11-37	.15	.30	.4
38-Williamson reprt./World of Suspense #3			
	.15	.30	.4

WHERE'S HUDDLES? (TV) (See Fun-In #9)
Jan, 1971 - #3, Dec, 1971 (Hanna-Barbera)
Gold Key

#1-3: #3 reprts. most #1 .10 .2

WHIP WILSON(Formerly Rex Hart; Gunhawk #12
#9, April, 1950 - #11, Sept, 1950
Marvel Comics

#9-11		2.50	5.00	7.5
IW Reprint #1('64)-Kinstler cover; reprints				
Marvel #11		1.00	2.00	3.0

WHIRLWIND COMICS
June, 1940 - #3, Sept, 1940
Nita Publication

#1-Cyclone begins(origin)	16.50	33.25	50.0
2,3	10.00	20.00	30.0

WHIRLYBIRDS (See 4-Color #1124,1216)

WHITE CHIEF-PAWNEE INDIANS
1951
Avon Periodicals

No#-Kit West app. 2.50 5.00 7.5

WHITE EAGLE INDIAN CHIEF (See Indian Chief

WHITE INDIAN
1953 - 1954
Magazine Enterprises

#11(A-1#94), 12(A-1#99), 13(A-1#104)-Frazet
reprints in all from Durango Kid
20.00 40.00 60.
14(A-1#117), 15(A-1#135)-Not Frazetta;
Torres art-#15 6.00 12.00 18.0
NOTE: #11 reprints from Durango Kid #1-4;
#12 from #5,9,10,11; #13 from #7,12,13,16.

WHITE PRINCESS OF THE JUNGLE (Also see Top
Jungle & Jungle Adventures)
July, 1951 - #5, Nov, 1952
Avon Periodicals

	Good	Fine	Mint
#1-Origin of White Princess & Capt'n Courage (reprt.); Kinstler cvr	7.00	14.00	21.00
2-Reprints origin of Malu, Slave Girl Princess from Avon's Slave Girl Princess #1 w/ Malu changed to Zora; Kinstler cover/story	5.00	10.00	15.00
3-Origin Blue Gorilla by Kinstler	5.00	10.00	15.00
4-Jack Barnum, White Hunter app.; reprint/ Sheena #9	3.00	6.00	9.00
5-Blue Gorilla by Kinstler	3.00	6.00	9.00

WHITE RIDER AND SUPER HORSE (Indian Warriors
1950 - 1951   #7 on)
Novelty-Star Publications/Accepted Publ.

#1-6	1.35	2.75	4.00
6-(Accepted reprint)	1.00	2.00	3.00

WHITE WILDERNESS (See 4-Color Comics #943)

WHITMAN COMIC BOOKS
1962   (136 pgs.) (B&W reprints)
(7-3/4"x5-3/4"; Hardcover)
Whitman Publishing Co.

#1-Yogi Bear
 2-Huckleberry Hound
 3-Mr. Jinks and Pixie and Dixie
 4-The Flintstones
 5-Augie Doggie & Loopy de Loop
 6-Snooper & Blabber Fearless Detectives/
   Quick Draw McGraw of the Wild West
 7-Bugs Bunny-reprints from #47,51,53,54 & 55
            each....   .50   1.00   1.50
 8-Donald Duck-reprints most of WDC&S #209-213.
   Includes 5 Barks stories, 1 complete Mickey
   Mouse serial & 1 Mickey Mouse serial missing the 1st episode   8.00 16.00 24.00
NOTE: Hanna-Barbera #1-6, original stories.
Dell reprints-#7 & 8.

WHIZ COMICS (See Thrill Comics)
#2, Feb, 1940 - #155, June, 1953
Fawcett Publications

#2(#1)-(No# on cover, #2 on inside)-Origin &
   1st app. Captain Marvel by C.C. Beck, Spy
   Smasher, Golden Arrow, Ibis the Invincible, Dan Dare, Scoop Smith & Lance O'Casey
   begin; #1 reprinted in Famous 1st Editions
                  1250.00 3125.00 5000.00

	Good	Fine	Mint
(Prices vary widely on this book)			
3(#2)-(No# on cover, #3 on inside)	500.00	1000.00	1500.00
3-(#3 on cover, #4 on inside)-Spy Smasher reveals I.D. to Eve	300.00	600.00	900.00
4-(#4 on cover, #5 on inside)	250.00	500.00	750.00
5-Captain Marvel wears button-down flap on splash page only	175.00	350.00	525.00
6-10: #7-Dr. Voodoo begins	120.00	240.00	360.00
11-14	70.00	140.00	210.00
15-18-Spy Smasher battles Captain Marvel in all; #15-origin Sivana; Dr. Voodoo by Raboy	90.00	180.00	270.00
19-Dr. Voodoo by Raboy begins, ends #24,			
20	45.00	90.00	135.00
21-Origin & 1st app. Lt. Marvels	50.00	100.00	150.00
22-24	35.00	70.00	105.00
25-Origin & 1st app. Captain Marvel Jr., x-over in Capt. Marvel; Capt. Nazi app.	80.00	160.00	240.00

Whiz Comics #2(#1). © Faw

26-30	25.00	50.00	75.00
31,32: #32-1st app. The Trolls	20.00	40.00	60.00
33-Spy Smasher, Captain Marvel x-over	25.00	50.00	75.00
34-40-The Trolls in #37	16.50	33.25	50.00
41-50: #47-1pg. origin recap; #43-Spy Smasher, Ibis, Golden Arrow x-over in Capt. Marvel	10.00	20.00	30.00
51-60: #52-Capt. Marvel x-over in Ibis. #57-Spy Smasher, Golden Arrow, Ibis cameo	7.00	14.00	21.00
61-70	6.00	12.00	18.00
71,74,77-80	5.00	10.00	15.00
72,73,75,76-Two Captain Marvel stories in each; #76-Spy Smasher becomes Crime Smasher	5.00	10.00	15.00

White Princess--#4, © Avon

Whiz Comics #34, © Faw

Whiz Comics #89, © Faw

Wilbur Comics #36, © AP

Wild Bill Elliott #2, © Dell

Wild Bill Hickok #4, © Avon

(Whiz Comics cont'd)	Good	Fine	Mint
81-100: #86-Captain Marvel battles Sivana			
Family	4.00	8.00	12.00
101,103-105	3.50	7.00	10.50
102-Commando Yank app.	3.50	7.00	10.50
106-Bulletman app.	3.50	7.00	10.50
107-152	3.00	6.00	9.00
153-155-(Scarce)	7.00	14.00	21.00
Wheaties Giveaway(1946)(Miniature)-6x8",			
32pgs.	5.00	10.00	15.00

NOTE: *Krigstein Golden Arrow-#75,78,91,95,96,
98,100. Wolverton ½ pg. "Culture Corner"-#65-
68,70-75,77-85,87-96,98-100,102-104,106,108,
109,115,125,126,128,129,133,134,136,143,146.*

WHODUNIT
Aug-Sept, 1948 - #3, Dec-Jan, 1948-49
D.S. Publishing Co.

#1-7pg. Baker story	1.75	3.50	5.25
2,3	1.00	2.00	3.00

WHO IS NEXT?
January, 1953
Standard Comics

#5-Toth story	2.50	5.00	7.50

WHO'S MINDING THE MINT? (See Movie Classics)

WILBUR COMICS
Summer, 1944 - #90, 10/65 (#1-46, 52pgs.)
MLJ Magazines/Archie Publ. #8 on

#1	8.00	16.00	24.00
2-4	4.00	8.00	12.00
5-1st app. Katy Keene	5.00	10.00	15.00
6-10	2.50	5.00	7.50
11-20	2.00	4.00	6.00
21-30(1949)	1.35	2.75	4.00
31-50	.80	1.60	2.40
51-90	.50	1.00	1.50

NOTE: *Katy Keene in #5-41,60 at least.*

WILD
Feb, 1954 - #5, Aug, 1954
Atlas Comics (IPC)

#1	2.50	5.00	7.50
2-5	1.75	3.35	5.00

WILD (This Magazine Is --) (Magazine)
Jan, 1968 - #3, 1968 (52pgs.) (Satire)
Dell Publishing Co.

#1-3	.35	.70	1.05

WILD BILL ELLIOTT

1950 - #17, Apr-June, 1955
Dell Publishing Co.

	Good	Fine	Mint
4-Color #278	3.00	6.00	9.00
#2-17	1.50	3.00	4.50
4-Color #472,520,643	1.50	3.00	4.50

WILD BILL HICKOK
Oct-Nov, 1949 - #28, May-June, 1956
Avon Periodicals

#1-Ingels cover	5.00	10.00	15.00
2-Painted cover	2.50	5.00	7.50
3,5-Painted covers	1.75	3.35	5.00
4-Painted cover by Gerald McCann; not			
Frazetta	1.75	3.35	5.00
6-10,12: #8-10-Painted covers			
	2.00	4.00	6.00
11,14-Kinstler cvr/story	2.50	5.00	7.50
13,15-18,20-24: #13,17,21,22-Kinstler cover.			
#17-Larsen, + Reinman art			
	1.25	2.50	3.75
19-Meskin story	1.75	3.50	5.25
25-27-Kinstler cover/story reprints			
	2.00	4.00	6.00
28-Kinstler cvr/story(new) + reprints/Last			
of the Comanches	2.00	4.00	6.00
IW Reprint #1-Kinstler cvr	.50	1.00	1.50
Super Reprint #10-12	.50	1.00	1.50

NOTE: *#25 contains numerous editing deletions
in both art & script due to code. Kinstler
covers-#6,11-14,18,20-22,24-28.*

WILD BILL HICKOK & JINGLES (Formerly
Cowboy Western) (See Blue Bird)
March, 1958 - 1960
Charlton Comics

#68,69-Williamson art	2.00	4.00	6.00
70-2pgs. Williamson art	1.00	2.00	3.00
71-76	.35	.70	1.05

WILD BILL PECOS (See The Westerner)

WILD BOY OF THE CONGO
#8, Oct-Nov, 1950 - #15, June, 1955
Ziff-Davis(Approved) #8-12,4,5('50-'51),
#3('54)/St. John #6-9,11 on

#8,9	1.35	2.75	4.00
10(2-3/51)-Origin	1.35	2.75	4.00
11(4-5/51),#12(8-9/51)	1.00	2.00	3.00
4(10-11/51),#5(Winter,'51)			
	1.00	2.00	3.00
6(Spring,'52)-#9(10/53)-St. John			
	1.00	2.00	3.00
3(4/54)-Ziff-Davis reprints #11('51),			
11-15(10/54-6/55)St. John; #14 reprints #12			

(Wild Boy of the Congo cont'd)

	Good	Fine	Mint
('51)	1.00	2.00	3.00

NOTE: *Baker covers on some issues.*

WILD FRONTIER (Cheyenne Kid #8 on)
Oct, 1955 - #7, April, 1957
Charlton Comics

	Good	Fine	Mint
#1-Davy Crockett	1.00	2.00	3.00
2-6-Davy Crockett in all	.40	.80	1.20
7-Origin Cheyenne Kid	.40	.80	1.20

WILD KINGDOM (TV)
1965   (Giveaway) (Regular size) (16 pgs.)
Western Printing Co.

Mutual of Omaha's --	.35	.70	1.05

WILD WEST (Wild Western #3 on)
Spring, 1948 - #2, July, 1948
Marvel Comics (WFP)

#1-Two-Gun Kid, Arizona Annie, Tex Taylor			
	4.00	8.00	12.00
2	2.50	5.00	7.50

WILD WEST (Black Fury #1-57)
#58, November, 1966
Charlton Comics

V2#58	.15	.30	.45

WILD WESTERN (Wild West #1,2)
#3, Sept, 1948 - #57, Sept, 1957
Marvel/Atlas Comics (WFP)

#3-Two-Gun Kid, Kid Colt, Blaze Carson			
	2.50	5.00	7.50
4-10	1.50	3.00	4.50
11-20: #15-Origin Red Larabee, Gunhawk			
	1.00	2.00	3.00
21-30	.90	1.80	2.70
31-40	.75	1.50	2.25
41-47,49-51,53,56,57	.65	1.35	2.00
48-Williamson/Torres story, 4pgs. + Mort			
Drucker story	2.00	4.00	6.00
52-Crandall art	1.35	2.75	4.00
54,55-Williamson story in both, 5 & 4 pgs.,			
#54 with Mayo	2.00	4.00	6.00

NOTE: *Annie Oakley* in #46,47. *Arrowhead* in
#35,36. *Black Rider* in #5,12,14,30,33,35,41.
Kid Colt in #27,30,33,35,36,41,46,47,52,54-
56. *Ringo Kid* in #29,39,41,46,47,52-56. *Two-
Gun Kid* in #30,33,35,36,41. *Wyatt Earp* in #47.

WILD WESTERN ACTION (Also see The Bravados)
March, 1971 - #3, June, 1971   (52 pgs.)

Skywald Publishing Corp.   (Reprints)

	Good	Fine	Mint
#1-Durango Kid, Straight Arrow; with all re-			
ferences to "Straight" in the story relett-			
ered to "Swift"; Bravados begin			
	.20	.40	.60
2-Billy Nevada, Durango Kid	.15	.30	
3-Red Mask, Durango Kid	.15	.30	

WILD WESTERN ROUNDUP
Oct, 1957; 1964
Red Top/Decker Publications/I.W. Enterprises

#1(1957)-Kid Cowboy reprt.	.65	1.35	2.00
IW Reprint #1('60-61)	.35	.70	1.05

WILD WEST RODEO
1953   (15¢)
Star Publications

#1-A comic book coloring book with regular			
full color cover & B&W inside			
	1.00	2.00	3.00

WILD WILD WEST, THE (TV)
June, 1966 - #7, Oct, 1969
Gold Key

#1,2-McWilliams art	.35	.70	1.05
3-7	.20	.40	.60

WILKIN BOY (See That --)

WILLIE COMICS (Formerly Ideal #1-4; Crime
#5, Fall, 1946 - #23, 3/50   Cases #24 on)
Marvel Comics (MgPC)

#5(#1)	.50	1.00	1.50
6,8,9,12,14-18,20-23	.40	.80	1.20
7,10,11,13,19-Kurtzman's "Hey Look"			
	1.50	3.00	4.50

WILLIE MAYS (See The Amazing --)

WILLIE THE PENGUIN (See Wisco)
April, 1951 - #6, April, 1952
Standard Comics

#1	.35	.70	1.05
2-6	.20	.40	.60

WILLIE THE WISE-GUY
Sept, 1957
Atlas Comics (NPP)

#1	.40	.80	1.20

Wild Frontier #1. © CC

Wild Western #45. © MCG

Willie Comics #15. © MCG

Wings Comics #24, © FH

Wings Comics #82, © FH

Winnie Winkle #6, © Chicago Tribune

WILLIE WESTINGHOUSE EDISON SMITH THE BOY INVENTOR
1906   (36 pgs.) (10x16") (in color)
William A. Stokes Co.

	Good	Fine	Mint
By Frank Crane	15.00	30.00	45.00

WILL ROGERS WESTERN (Also see Blazing Comics)
#2, Aug, 1950 - #5, 1951
Fox Features Syndicate

	Good	Fine	Mint
#2-5	1.50	3.00	4.50

WILL-YUM (See 4-Color Comics #676,765,902)

WIN A PRIZE COMICS
Feb, 1955 - #2, 1955
Charlton/Simon & Kirby

V1#1-S&K art	5.00	10.00	15.00
2-S&K art	4.00	8.00	12.00

WINDY & WILLY
1969
National Periodical Publications

#1-4-Reprints of Dobie Gillis with some art changes		.15	.30

WINGS COMICS
Sept, 1940 - #124, 1954
Fiction House Magazines

	Good	Fine	Mint
#1-Skull Squad, Clipper Kirk, Suicide Smith, Jane Martin, War Nurse, Phantom Falcons, Greasemonkey Griffin, Parachute Patrol, & Powder Burns begin	35.00	70.00	105.00
2	16.50	33.25	50.00
3-5	13.50	26.75	40.00
6-10	10.00	20.00	30.00
11-15	7.00	14.00	21.00
16-Origin Captain Wings	10.00	20.00	30.00
17-20	7.00	14.00	21.00
21-30	6.00	12.00	18.00
31-40	5.00	10.00	15.00
41-50	4.00	8.00	12.00
51-60: #60-Last Skull Squad	3.50	7.00	10.50
61-67: #67-Ghost Patrol begins (becomes Ghost Squadron #71)	3.00	6.00	9.00
68,69: #68-Clipper Kirk becomes The Phantom Falcon-origin, Part 1; Part 2-#69	2.50	5.00	7.50
70-72: #70-1st app. The Phantom Falcon in costume, origin-Part 3; Capt. Wings battles Col. Kamikaze in all	2.50	5.00	7.50
73-80	2.50	5.00	7.50

	Good	Fine	Mint
81-100	2.00	4.00	6.00
101-124: #111-Last Jane Martin	1.50	3.00	4.50

NOTE: *Bondage covers are common. Captain Wings battles Sky Hag #75,76; --Mr. Atlantis #85-92; --Mr. Pupin(Red Agent) #98-103. Bob Lubbers art on Capt. Wings-#70-103. Evans art-#85-103,108(Jane Martin). Jane Martin by Fran Hopper-#68-84; Suicide Smith by John Celardo-#76-103; Ghost Patrol by Maurice Whitman-#83-103; Skull Squad by M. Baker- #52-60; Clipper Kirk by Baker-#60,61.*

WINGS OF THE EAGLES, THE (See 4-Color #790)

WINKY DINK (Adventures of --)
#75, March, 1957   (One Shot)
Pines Comics

#75-Marv Levy cover/art	.35	.70	1.05

WINKY DINK (See 4-Color Comics #663)

WINNIE THE POOH
January, 1977 - Present   (Walt Disney)
Gold Key

#1	.15	.30	.45
2-4		.15	.30

WINNIE WINKLE
1930 - 1933 (48pgs)(B&W Daily strip reprints)
Cupples & Leon Co.

Book 1	6.00	12.00	18.00
Book 2-4	6.00	12.00	18.00

WINNIE WINKLE
1941 - 1949
Dell Publishing Co.

Large Feature Comic #2('41)	7.00	14.00	21.00
4-Color #94('45)	4.00	8.00	12.00
4-Color #174	2.50	5.00	7.50
#1(3-5/48)-Contains daily & Sunday newspaper reprints from 1939-41	3.00	6.00	9.00
2-7	1.75	3.35	5.00

WISCO/KLARER COMIC BOOK (Miniature)
1948 - 1953 (24pgs.; 3-1/2x6-3/4")
Given away by Wisco "99" Service Stations, Carnation Malted Milk, Klarer Health Wieners, Fleers Dubble Bubble Gum, & Rodeo All-Meat Wieners
Vital Publications/Fawcett Publications

	Good	Fine	Mint
Blackstone "Solves the Sealed Vault Mystery"			
	1.75	3.35	5.00
Blaze Carson in "The Sheriff Shoots It Out"			
(1950)	1.35	2.75	4.00
Captain Marvel & Billy's Big Game			
	20.00	40.00	60.00

(Prices vary widely on this book)

China Boy in "A Trip to the Zoo" #10			
	.65	1.35	2.00
Indoors-Outdoors Game Book	.65	1.35	2.00
Jim Solar Space Sheriff in "Battle for Mars,"			
"Between Two Worlds","Conquers Outer Space,"			
"The Creatures on the Comet","Defeats the			
Moon Missile Men","Encounter Creatures on			
Comet","Meet the Jupiter Jumpers","Meets			
the Man From Mars","On Traffic Duty","Out-			
laws of the Spaceways","Pirates of the			
Planet X","Protects Space Lanes","Raiders			
From the Sun","Ring Around Saturn","Robots			
of Rhea","The Sky Ruby","Spacettes of the			
Sky","Spidermen of Venus","Trouble on Mer-			
cury"	1.00	2.00	3.00
Johnny Starboard & the Underseas Pirates('48)			
	.65	1.35	2.00
Kid Colt in "He Lived by His Guns"(1950)			
	1.75	3.35	5.00
Little Aspirin as "Crook Catcher" #2(1950)			
	.65	1.35	2.00
Little Aspirin in "Naughty But Nice" #6(1950)			
	.65	1.35	2.00
Return of the Black Phantom			
	1.35	2.75	4.00
Secrets of Magic	1.00	2.00	3.00
Slim Morgan "Brings Justice to Mesa City" #3			
	1.00	2.00	3.00
Super Rabbit(1950)-Cuts Red Tape, Stops			
Crime Wave!	.65	1.35	2.00
Tex Farnum, Frontiersman(1948)			
	.65	1.35	2.00
Tex Taylor in "Draw or Die, Cowpoke!"(1950)			
	1.35	2.75	4.00
Tex Taylor in "An Exciting Adventure at the			
Gold Mine"('50)	1.00	2.00	3.00
Wacky Quacky in "All-Aboard"			
	.65	1.35	2.00
When School Is Out	.65	1.35	2.00
Willie in a "Comic-Comic Book Fall" #1			
	.65	1.35	2.00
Wonder Duck "An Adventure at the Rodeo of the			
Fearless Quack-er!"('50)	.65	1.35	2.00

WISE LITTLE HEN, THE
1934 (48pgs.); 1935; 1937   (Story book)
David McKay Publ.

1st book app. Donald Duck; Donald app. on cover with W.L. Hen & Practical Pig; Painted
cover; same artist as the B&W's from Silly
Symphony Cartoon, The Wise Little Hen(1934)

	25.00	50.00	75.00
1935 Edition with dust jacket; 40pgs. with			
color, 8-3/4"x9-3/4"	20.00	40.00	60.00
#888(1937)-9½x13", 12pgs. (Whitman) Donald			
Duck app.	15.00	30.00	45.00

WITCHCRAFT
Mar-Apr, 1952 - #6, Mar, 1953
Avon Periodicals

	Good	Fine	Mint
#1-Kubert art + 1pg.Check	5.00	10.00	15.00
2-Kubert & Check stories	4.00	8.00	12.00
3,4-Kinstler art, 1pg.	2.00	4.00	6.00
5-Kelly Freas cover	2.00	4.00	6.00
6	2.00	4.00	6.00

WITCHES TALES (Witches Western Tales #29,30)
Jan, 1951 - #27, Oct, 1954; #28, April, 1955
Witches Tales/Harvey Publications

#1	2.50	5.00	7.50
2-10	1.50	3.00	4.50
11-28: #27-Reprints #6 with diff. cover. #28-			
Reprints #8 with diff. cover			
	1.35	2.75	4.00

NOTE: *Nostrand stories-#18-26; 14,17(w/Powell).*
Powell stories-#3-7,11,19-25,27.

WITCHES TALES (Magazine)
V1#7, 7/69 - V7#1, 2/75 (52 pgs.) (B&W)
Eerie Publications

V1#7(7/69)-#9(11/69)	.35	.70	1.05
V2#1-6('70),V3#1-6('71)	.25	.50	.75
V4#1-6('72),V5#1-6('73),V6#1-6('74),V7#1			
	.20	.40	.60

NOTE: *Ajax/Farrell reprints in early issues.*

WITCHES' WESTERN TALES (Formerly Witches
Tales) (Western Tales #31 on)
#29, Feb, 1955 - #30, Apr, 1955
Harvey Publications

#29,30-S&K reprints from Boys' Ranch includ-			
ing cover	6.00	12.00	18.00

WITCHING HOUR, THE
Feb-Mar, 1969 - Present
National Periodical Publications/DC Comics

#1-Toth + Adams, 3pgs.	1.00	2.00	3.00
2,6,9,10	.25	.50	.75
3,5-Wrightson, Toth stys.	.90	1.80	2.70
4-Toth story	.75	1.50	2.25
7-Kaluta, Toth stories	.75	1.50	2.25

Witchcraft #1, © Avon

Witches Tales #15, © Harv

With The U.S. Paratroops #8, © I.W.

Women Outlaws #5, © Fox

Wonder Comics #1, © Fox

Wonder Comics #15, © BP

(Witching Hour cont'd)	Good	Fine	Mint
8-Adams story	.90	1.80	2.70
11,16-20	.20	.40	.60
12-Kane/Wood, Toth stys.	.80	1.60	2.40
13-Adams cover/story	.60	1.20	1.80
14-Williamson/Garzon, Jones stories; Adams			
cover	.75	1.50	2.25
15-Wood story	.30	.60	.90
21,22,24-33,35-37	.15	.30	.45
23,34-Redondo story	.20	.40	.60
38-(100pgs.); Toth reprint	.15	.30	.45
39-64		.20	.40
65-Two Redondo stories	.15	.30	.45
66-76		.20	.35

NOTE: _Adams_ covers-#7-11,13,14. _Alcala_ stories #24,27,33,41,43. _Anderson_ story-#38.
Morrow stories-#10,13,15,16.

WITH THE MARINES ON THE BATTLEFRONTS OF THE WORLD
1953 (no month) - #2, March, 1954
Toby Press

#1-John Wayne story	1.50	3.00	4.50
2-Monty Hall in #1,2	1.00	2.00	3.00

WITH THE U.S. PARATROOPS BEHIND ENEMY LINES
1951 - #6, Dec, 1952
Avon Periodicals

#1-Wood cvr & inside cvr.	3.00	6.00	9.00
2-6: #2-Kinstler art. #5-Kinstler cover/sty.			
#6-Kinstler art	1.50	3.00	4.50
IW Reprint #1(Wood cover), #8(Kinstler cvr)			
	.35	.70	1.05

WITNESS, THE
Sept, 1948
Marvel Comics (MMC)

#1-Everett cover (Rare)	8.00	16.00	24.00

WITTY COMICS
1945
Irwin H. Rubin Publ./Chicago Nite Life News#2

#1,2-The Pioneer, Junior Patrol			
	1.35	2.75	4.00
3-7-Skyhawk	1.00	2.00	3.00

WIZARD OF OZ
(See 4-Color #1308, Dell Jr. Treasury #5, Marvelous --, & Marvel Treasury of Oz)

WOLF GAL
(See Al Capp's --)

WOLFMAN, THE
(See Book & Record Set, Movie Classics)

WOMAN IN LOVE
(Feature Presentations #5)
Aug, 1949 - #4, Feb, 1950
Fox Features Synd./Hero Books

	Good	Fine	Mint
#1	2.00	4.00	6.00
2,3	1.50	3.00	4.50
4-Wood story	2.50	5.00	7.50

WOMAN OF THE PROMISE, THE
1950   (General Distr.)
Catechetical Guild

	1.50	3.00	4.50

WOMEN OUTLAWS
(My Love Memories #9 on)
July, 1948 - #8, Sept, 1949
Fox Features Syndicate

#1-Ill. in Seduction of the Innocent			
	8.00	16.00	24.00
2-8	3.00	6.00	9.00
3-Matt Baker art	4.00	8.00	12.00

WOMEN TO LOVE
No date (1953)
Realistic

No#	2.50	5.00	7.50

WONDER BOY
#16, 1955 - #18, July, 1955
Ajax/Farrell Publ.

#16,17	2.50	5.00	7.50
18-Phantom Lady app.	5.00	10.00	15.00

WONDER COMICS
(Wonderworld #3 on)
May, 1939 - #2, June, 1939
Fox Features Syndicate

#1-Wonder Man only app. by Will Eisner; Bob Kane art; Eisner cvr.	80.00	160.00	240.00
2-Yarko the Great, Master Magician by Eisner begins; Bob Kane art; Lou Fine cover			
	40.00	80.00	120.00

WONDER COMICS
May, 1944 - #20, Oct, 1948
Great/Nedor/Better Publications

#1-The Grim Reaper & Spectro, the Mind Reader begin	12.00	24.00	36.00
2-Origin The Grim Reaper; Super Sleuths begin, end #8,17	7.00	14.00	21.00
3-5	5.00	10.00	15.00
6-10: #8-Last Spectro. #9-Wonderman begins			
	4.00	8.00	12.00
11-14-Dick Devens, King of Futuria begins #11, ends #14	5.00	10.00	15.00

(Wonder Comics cont'd)   Good   Fine   Mint
15-Tara begins(origin), ends #20
                6.00 12.00 18.00
16,18: #16-Spectro app. 4.00   8.00 12.00
17,19,20: A few Frazetta panels each. #17-
   Last Grim Reaper. #19-The Silver Knight
   begins   5.00 10.00 15.00
NOTE: *Ingels covers-#11,12. Schomburg (Xela)*
covers (line)-#1-10; (painted)-#13-20.

WONDER DUCK (See Wisco)
1949 - #3, Mar, 1950
Marvel Comics (CDS)

#1-3   .65   1.35   2.00

WONDERFUL ADVENTURES OF PINOCCHIO, THE
(See Movie Comics)

WONDERFUL WORLD OF DUCKS (See Golden Picture
1975   Story Book)
Colgate Palmolive Co.

#1-Mostly reprints   .20   .40   .60

WONDERFUL WORLD OF THE BROTHERS GRIMM
(See Movie Comics)

WONDERLAND COMICS
Summer, 1945 - #9, Feb-Mar, 1947
Feature Publications/Prize

#1   1.50   3.00   4.50
2-9   1.00   2.00   3.00

WONDERS OF ALADDIN, THE (See 4-Color #1255)

WONDER WARTHOG MAGAZINE
Winter, 1967 - #2, Spring, 1967
Millar Publications

#1,2-Kurtzman + Gilbert Shelton art
             4.00   8.00 12.00

WONDER WOMAN (See All-Star Comics, Giant
Comics to Color, & Sensation Comics)

WONDER WOMAN
Summer, 1942 - Present
National Per. Publ./All-American Publ.

#1-Origin Wonder Woman retold (see All-Star
   #8); reprinted in Famous 1st Editions); H.G.
   Peter art begins 115.00 230.00 345.00
2   50.00 100.00 150.00
3   40.00 80.00 120.00
4,5   25.00 50.00 75.00
6-10   20.00 40.00 60.00

                     Good   Fine   Mint
11-20   13.50 26.75 40.00
21-30   10.00 20.00 30.00
31-40   8.00 16.00 24.00
41-44,46-50   5.00 10.00 15.00
45-Origin retold   8.00 16.00 24.00
51-70   4.00   8.00 12.00
71-90   2.50   5.00   7.50
91-100: #94-Robin Hood x-over. #98-Last H.G.
   Peter art   2.50   5.00   7.50
101-104,106-110: #107-1st app. Wonder Girl
               2.00   4.00   6.00
105-Wonder Woman's secret origin
               2.00   4.00   6.00
111-120   1.50   3.00   4.50
121-130   1.00   2.00   3.00
131-150   .75   1.50   2.25
151-170   .50   1.00   1.50
171-198   .35   .70   1.05
199,200-Jones covers .65   1.35   2.00
201-210: #202-Fafhrd & The Grey Mouser debut.
   #204-Return to old costume
                .20   .40   .60
211-217(All 100-68pgs.) .20   .40   .60
218-230: #224-Steve Trevor returns. #220-Adams
   assist   .15   .30   .45
231-240: #233-Morrow cover .20   .35
241-Starlin story   .15   .30   .45
Pizza Hut Giveaway(12/77)-Exact reprints of
   #60,62   .20   .40   .60
--Spectacular (12/77,$1.00)-Ditko, Heath art
                .35   .70   1.05

WONDERWORLD (Formerly Wonder Comics)
#3, July, 1939 - #33, Jan, 1942
Fox Features Syndicate

#3-The Flame begins; Wonder Man & Yarko the
   Great, Master Magician continues by
   Eisner   25.00 50.00 75.00
4   20.00 40.00 60.00
5-10   17.50 35.00 52.50
11-Origin The Flame 25.00 50.00 75.00
12-21   12.00 24.00 36.00
22-Origin The Black Lion & Cub
            12.50 25.00 37.50
23-27   10.00 20.00 30.00
28-Lu-Nar, the Moon Man begins; origin U.S.
   Jones   12.00 24.00 36.00
29,31-33   8.00 16.00 24.00
30-Origin Flame Girl 12.00 24.00 36.00
NOTE: *Yarko by Eisner-#3-10 (at least).*
Lou Fine covers/art-#4-11.

WOODSY OWL (See March of Comics #395)
Nov, 1973 - #10, Feb, 1976
Gold Key

Wonder Woman #16, © DC

Wonder Woman #30, © DC

Wonderworld #13, © Fox

Woody Woodpecker 4-Color #416, © W. Lantz

The World Around Us #6, © Gil

World Famous Heroes Mag #1, © Cen

(Woodsy Owl cont'd)	Good	Fine	Mint
#1		.15	.30
2-10		.10	.20

WOODY WOODPECKER (See Comic Album)
1947 - Present
Dell Publishing Co./Gold Key #73 on

	Good	Fine	Mint
4-Color #169,188	2.50	5.00	7.50
4-Color #202,232,249,264,288			
	2.00	4.00	6.00
4-Color #305,336,350	1.50	3.00	4.50
4-Color #364,374,390,405,416,431(1952)			
	1.00	2.00	3.00
#16-30('53-'55)	.50	1.00	1.50
31-72,76-80('55-'63)	.25	.50	.75
73-75(Giants, 84pgs.)	.40	.80	1.20
81-100	.20	.40	.60
101-120		.15	.30
121-162		.10	.20
Back to School #1(1952)	1.75	3.35	5.00
Back to School #2-4,6('53-'57)(No#5)(County Fair #5)	1.00	2.00	3.00
Christmas Parade #1(11/68-Giant)(G.K.)			
	.25	.50	.75
Clover Stamp-Newspaper Boy Contest('56)-9pg. story-Giveaway	.30	.60	.90
County Fair #5('56)-Formerly Back to School #2('58)	1.00	2.00	3.00
In Chevrolet Wonderland(1954-giveaway)-20pgs., full story line(Western Publ.)-Chilly Willy app.	1.75	3.35	5.00
Meets Scotty McTape(1953-Scotch Tape give-away, 16pgs, full size)1.35		2.75	4.00
Summer Fun #1(G.K.-'66,25¢).25		.50	.75

NOTE: 15¢ editions exist.

WOODY WOODPECKER (See Comic Album #5,9,13, Dell Giant #24,40,54, Golden Comics Digest #1,3,5,8,15,16,20,24,32,37,44, March of Comics #16,34,85,93,109,124,139,158,177,184,203, 222,239,249,261, & Super Book #12,24)

WOOLWORTH'S CHRISTMAS STORY BOOK (See Jolly Christmas Book & Happy Time Xmas Book)
1952 - 1954
Promotional Publ. Co.

No#	1.00	2.00	3.00

NOTE: 1952 issue-Marv Levy cover/art.

WORLD AROUND US, THE (Ill. Story of --)
Sept, 1958 - #36, Oct, 1961 (25¢)
Gilberton Publishers (Classics Illustrated)

#1-Dogs	2.00	4.00	6.00
2-Indians	1.00	2.00	3.00
3-Horses	1.00	2.00	3.00

	Good	Fine	Mint
4-Railroads	1.00	2.00	3.00
5-Space-Ingels art	2.00	4.00	6.00
6-F.B.I., The-Evans, Ingels art			
	2.00	4.00	6.00
7-Pirates-Ingels art	1.35	2.75	4.00
8-Flight-Evans, Ingels, Crandall art			
	2.00	4.00	6.00
9-Army-Ingels, Orlando art			
	2.00	4.00	6.00
10-Navy-Kinstler art	1.00	2.00	3.00
11-Marine Corps.	1.00	2.00	3.00
12-Coast Guard	1.00	2.00	3.00
13-Air Force	1.00	2.00	3.00
14-French Revolution-Crandall, Evans art			
	2.50	5.00	7.50
15-Prehistoric Animals-Al Williamson art, 6pgs. + Morrow art	3.50	7.00	10.50
16-Crusades	1.00	2.00	3.00
17-Festivals	1.00	2.00	3.00
18-Great Scientists-Crandall, Evans, Torres, Williamson, Morrow art 2.50		5.00	7.50
19-Jungle-Crandall, Williamson, Morrow art			
	2.50	5.00	7.50
20-Communications-Crandall, Evans art			
	2.50	5.00	7.50
21-Presidents	1.75	3.35	5.00
22-Boating-Morrow art	1.00	2.00	3.00
23-Great Explorers-Crandall, Evans art			
	1.75	3.35	5.00
24-Ghosts-Morrow, Evans	1.00	2.00	3.00
25-Magic-Evans,Morrow art	2.50	5.00	7.50
26-The Civil War	1.00	2.00	3.00
27-Mountains (High Advs.)-Evans, Morrow, Torres art	1.00	2.00	3.00
28-Whaling-Crandall, Evans, Morrow art			
	1.00	2.00	3.00
29-Vikings-Crandall, Evans, Torres, Morrow art	1.00	2.00	3.00
30-Undersea Adventure-Evans art			
	1.00	2.00	3.00
31-Hunting-Kirby art	1.00	2.00	3.00
32-For Gold & Glory-Morrow, Kirby, Crandall, Evans art	1.00	2.00	3.00
33-Famous Teens-Torres, Crandall, Evans art			
	1.00	2.00	3.00
34-Fishing-Evans art	1.00	2.00	3.00
35-Spies-Kirby, Evans, Morrow art			
	1.00	2.00	3.00
36-Fight for Life (Medicine)-Kirby art			
	1.00	2.00	3.00

(See Classics Ill. Special Edition)

WORLD FAMOUS HEROES MAGAZINE
Oct, 1941 - #4, Apr, 1942 (A comic book)
Comic Corp. of America (Centaur)

#1	7.00	14.00	21.00
2-4	3.50	7.00	10.50

WORLD FAMOUS STORIES
1945
Croyden Publishers

	Good	Fine	Mint
#1-Ali Baba, Hansel and Gretel, Rip Van Winkle, Mid-Summer Night's Dream	1.50	3.00	4.50

WORLD IS HIS PARISH, THE
1953   (15¢)
George A. Pflaum

The story of Pope Pius XII

	1.00	2.00	3.00

WORLD OF ADVENTURE (Walt Disney's--)
April, 1963 - Oct, 1963
Gold Key

#1-3-Disney TV characters; Savage Sam, Johnny Shiloh, Capt. Nemo, The Mooncussers	.35	.70	1.05

WORLD OF ARCHIE, THE (See Archie Giant Series Mag. #148,151,156,160,165,171,177,182, 188,193,200,208,213,225,232,237,244,249,456, 461)

WORLD OF FANTASY
May, 1956 - #19, Aug, 1959
Atlas Comics (CPC #1-15/ZPC #16-19)

#1	2.50	5.00	7.50
2-Williamson, 4pgs.	2.50	5.00	7.50
3-9	1.00	2.00	3.00
10,12-15	1.00	2.00	3.00
11-Torres story	1.25	2.50	3.75
16-Williamson, 4pgs.; Ditko, Kirby art	2.00	4.00	6.00
17-19-Ditko, Kirby art	1.50	3.00	4.50

NOTE: *Berg story-#8. Ditko story-#17,19. Everett covers-#4,5-7,9,13. Kirby covers-#15, 17-19. Krigstein story-#9. Morrow stories-#7, 8,14. Orlando stories-#8,13,14. Powell story-#8.*

WORLD OF GIANT COMICS, THE (See Archie All-Star Specials)

WORLD OF JUGHEAD, THE (See Archie Giant Series Mag. #9,14,19,24,30,136,143,149,152,157, 161,166,172,178,183,189,194,202,209,215,227, 233,239,245,251,457,463)

WORLD OF MYSTERY
June, 1956 - #7, June, 1957
Atlas Comics (GPI)

	Good	Fine	Mint
#1-Torres + Orlando story	2.00	4.00	6.00
2	1.00	2.00	3.00
3-Torres, Davis, Ditko stories,			
4-Davis story	2.00	4.00	6.00
5,7: #5-Orlando story	1.00	2.00	3.00
6-Williamson/Mayo story, 4pgs.	2.50	5.00	7.50

WORLD OF SUSPENSE
April, 1956 - #8, July, 1957
Atlas News Co.

#1-Orlando art	2.00	4.00	6.00
2,4-6,8	1.00	2.00	3.00
3,7-Williamson story in both, 4pgs. each;			
#7-with Mayo	2.00	4.00	6.00

NOTE: *Ditko story-#2. Everett story-#5; cover-#2,6. Orlando story-#5. Powell story-#8.*

WORLD OF WHEELS (Formerly Dragstrip Hotrodders)
Oct, 1967 - #32, June, 1970
Charlton Comics

#17-32-Features Ken King	.10	.20

WORLDS BEYOND (Worlds of Fear #2 on)
Nov, 1951
Fawcett Publications

#1-Powell art	1.75	3.35	5.00

WORLD'S FAIR COMICS (See N. Y. --)

WORLD'S FINEST COMICS (World's Best #1)
Spring, 1941 - Present (early issues-100pgs.)
National Periodical Publications/DC Comics

#1-The Batman, Superman, Crimson Avenger, Johnny Thunder, The King, Young Dr. Davis, Zatara, Lando, Man of Magic, & Red, White & Blue begin (inside covers blank)	180.00	360.00	540.00
2	90.00	180.00	270.00
3-The Sandman begins; last Johnny Thunder; origin & 1st app. The Scarecrow	70.00	140.00	210.00
4-Hop Harrigan app.; last Young Dr. Davis	40.00	80.00	120.00
5-Intro. & only app. TNT & Dan the Dyna-Mite; last King & Crimson Avenger	40.00	80.00	120.00
6-Star Spangled Kid begins; Aquaman app.; S&K Sandman with Sandy in new costume begins, ends #7	30.00	60.00	90.00
7-Green Arrow begins; last Lando, King & Red, White & Blue; S&K art	30.00	60.00	90.00

World Of Mystery #5, © MCG

World Of Suspense #4, © MCG

World's Finest Comics #15, © DC

World's Finest Comics #81, © DC   World's Greatest Songs #1, © MCG   Worlds Of Fear #5, © Faw

	Good	Fine	Mint
(World's Finest cont'd)			
8-Boy Commandos begin; last Red, White & Blue	30.00	60.00	90.00
9-Batman cameo in Star Spangled Kid;S&K art,			
10-S&K art	25.00	50.00	75.00
11-20: #18-Last Star Spangled Kid	16.50	33.25	50.00
21-30: #30-Johnny Peril app.	12.00	24.00	36.00
31-40: #33-35-Tomahawk app.	8.00	16.00	24.00
41-50: #41-Boy Commandos end. #42-Wyoming Kid begins, ends #63. #43-Full Steam Foley begins, ends #48. #49-Tom Sparks, Boy Inventor begins	6.00	12.00	18.00
51-60: #51-Zatara ends. #59-Manhunters Around the World begins, ends #62	5.00	10.00	15.00
61-70: #62(?)-Last ish. with square binding. #63-Capt. Compas app. #65-Tomahawk begins, ends #101	4.00	8.00	12.00
71-Batman & Superman begin as a team	7.00	14.00	21.00
72-80	3.00	6.00	9.00
81-90: #88-1st Joker/Luthor team-up	2.50	5.00	7.50
91-100: #94-Origin Superman/Batman team. #96-99-Kirby Green Arrow	2.00	4.00	6.00
101-120: #102-Tommy Tomorrow begins, ends#124. #105-2pgs. Kubert. #113-Intro. Miss Arrowette in Green Arrow; 1st Batmite/Mxyzptlk team-up	1.25	2.50	3.75
121-150: #125-Aquaman begins, ends #139. #140-last Green Arrow. #143-1st Mailbag. #148-Congorilla reprint	.80	1.60	2.40
151-174: #154-1st Supersons story. #161-25¢ Giant G-28. #170-25¢ Giant G-40	.60	1.20	1.80
(80pg. Giant G-28,G-40)	.80	1.60	2.40
175,176-Adams stories	1.00	2.00	3.00
177-200: #179-25¢ Giant G-52. #182-Silent Knight reprint/Brave & the Bold #6. #186-Johnny Quick reprint. #188-25¢ Giant G-64. #190-193-Robin reprints. #197-25¢ Giant G-76; Green Arrow app.	.30	.60	.90
(80pg. Giant G-52-G-76)	.50	1.00	1.50
201-Dr. Fate, Green Arrow app.	.25	.50	.75
202-204,206,207: #206-25¢ Giant G-88. #204, 205,207-212, 52pgs.	.25	.50	.75
(80pg. Giant G-88)	.40	.80	1.20
205-6pgs. Shining Knight by Frazetta/Adv.#153 & Tarantula reprints	.40	.80	1.20
208-Dr. Fate app.; Robotman & Ghost Patrol reprints	.25	.50	.75
209-Batman, Hawkman reprts.	.25	.50	.75
210-215: #210-Green Arrow app.; Black Pirate reprint. #211-Atom app.; G.A. Green Lant-			

	Good	Fine	Mint
ern reprt. #212-Jonn' Jonzz' app.; G.A. Air Wave & Grim Ghost reprint. #213-Robin app. #214-Vigilante app.; Two Face begins	.25	.50	.75
215-Intro. Batman Jr. & Superman Jr.	.30	.60	.90
216-222: #217-Metamorpho begins; Batman/Superman team-up begins	.20	.40	.60
223,226-Adams stories; 100pgs.; #226-S&K & Toth reprints	.40	.80	1.20
224,225,227-(100pgs.)	.25	.50	.75
228-Toth story; 100pgs.	.25	.50	.75
229,231-243		.20	.35
230-Adams story	.15	.30	.45
244-248,250: #244-$1.00 size begins	.40	.80	1.20
249-The Creeper begins by Ditko	.40	.80	1.20
251-Wonder Woman by Estrada/Wood	.40	.80	1.20

NOTE: _Adams covers-#174-176,178-180,182,183, 185,186,198-205,208-211,223,226(reprints), 244-246. Anderson stories-#121,122,204,245-247. Burnley cover-#7. Infantino story-#225. Kubert Zatara-#40-44. Morrow stories-#245-248. Orlando story-#224. Robinson Batman-#14,15; covers-#3,6._ (See 80 Pg. Giant #15)

WORLD'S GREATEST ATHLETE   (See Walt Disney Showcase #14)

WORLD'S GREATEST SONGS
Sept, 1954
Atlas Comics (Male)

	Good	Fine	Mint
#1-Heath & Harry Anderson art	1.00	2.00	3.00

WORLD'S GREATEST STORIES
Jan, 1949 - #2, May, 1949
Jubilee Publications

	Good	Fine	Mint
#1-Alice in Wonderland	2.00	4.00	6.00
2-Pinocchio	1.50	3.00	4.50

WORLDS OF FEAR (Worlds Beyond #1)
V1#2, 1952 - V2#10, June, 1953
Fawcett Publications

	Good	Fine	Mint
V1#2-6(9/52): #3-Evans art. #2,4,5-Powell art	1.35	2.75	4.00
V2#7-10: #10-Painted cvr.	.65	1.35	2.00

WORLDS UNKNOWN
May, 1973 - #8, Aug, 1974
Marvel Comics Group

(Worlds Unknown cont'd)   Good Fine Mint
#1-Reprint from Astonishing #54; Torres art
                                  .15   .30   .45
2-8   .15   .30
NOTE: _Adkins/Mooney art-#5. Kane art-#1,2;_
covers-#5,6,8. Sutton art-#2.

WORLD WAR STORIES
Apr-June, 1965 - #3, Dec, 1965
Dell Publishing Co.

#1   .25   .50   .75
2,3: #1-3-Glanzman art   .20   .40   .60

WORLD WAR II   (See Classics Special Ed.)

WORLD WAR III
Mar, 1952 - #2, 1952
Ace Periodicals

#1,2   2.50   5.00   7.50

WORST FROM MAD, THE   Annual)
1958 - #12, 1969 (Each annual cover is reprinted from the cover of the Mad issues
being reprinted)
E.C. Comics

No#(1958)-Bonus-Record labels & travel stickers; 1st Mad annual; reprints from Mad
   #29-34   5.00 10.00 15.00
#2(1959)-Bonus is small 33-1/3 rpm record
   entitled "Meet the Staff of Mad"; reprints/
   Mad #35-40   5.00 10.00 15.00
   3(1960)-20"x30" campaign poster "Alfred E.
   Newman for President;" reprint/Mad #41-46
                     3.50   7.00 10.50
   4(1961)-Sunday comics section; reprints/
   Mad #47-54   4.00   8.00 12.00
   5(1962)-Small 33-1/3 rpm record; reprints/
   Mad #55-62   3.50   7.00 10.50
   6(1963)-Small 33-1/3 rpm record; reprints/
   Mad #63-70   3.50   7.00 10.50
   7(1964)-Mad protest signs; reprints/Mad
   #71-76   2.00   4.00   6.00
   8(1965)-Build a Mad Zeppelin
                     2.50   5.00   7.50
   9(1966)-33-1/3 rpm record
                     2.50   5.00   7.50
10(1967)-Mad bumper sticker
                     2.00   4.00   6.00
11(1968)-Mad cover window stickers
                     2.00   4.00   6.00
12(1969)-Mad picture postcards
                     2.00   4.00   6.00
NOTE: _Covers: Bob Clarke-#8. Mingo-#7,9-12._

WOTALIFE COMICS

#3, 8-9/46 - #12, July, 1947; 1959
Fox Features Syndicate/Norlen Mag.
                        Good Fine Mint
#3-12-Cosmo Cat   .65 1.35 2.00
#1(1959-Norlen)-Atomic Rabbit, Atomic Mouse
                         .40   .80 1.20

WOTALIFE COMICS
1957 - #5, 1957
Green Publications

#1-5   .25   .50   .75

WOW COMICS
May, 1936 - #4, Nov, 1936
David McKay Publications/Henle Publ.

#1-Fu Manchu, Eisner story
                    40.00 80.00 120.00
   2-Ken Maynard, Fu Manchu, Popeye; Eisner
   art   30.00 60.00 90.00
   3-Eisner cover; Popeye, Fu Manchu
                   30.00 60.00 90.00
   4-Flash Gordon, Mandrake, Popeye; Eisner
   art   40.00 80.00 120.00

WOW COMICS   (Real Western Hero #70 on)
Spring, 1941 - #69, Fall, 1948
Fawcett Publications

No#(#1)-Origin Mr. Scarlet by S&K; Atom Blake,
   Roy Wizard begins; Diamond Jack, The White
   Rajah, Shipwreck Roberts only app.; the
   cover of this comic was printed on unstable paper stock and is rarely found in fine
   or mint condition. (Rare)
                 600.00 1500.00 2400.00
      (Prices vary widely on this book)
   2-The Hunchback begins 60.00 120.00 180.00
   3   30.00 60.00 90.00
   4-Origin Pinky   40.00 80.00 120.00
   5   30.00 60.00 90.00
   6-Origin The Phantom Eagle; Commando Yank
   begins   20.00 40.00 60.00
   7,8   20.00 40.00 60.00
   9-Capt. Marvel, Capt. Marvel Jr., Shazam
   app.; Scarlet & Pinky x-over
                          25.00 50.00 75.00
10-Mary Marvel begins   17.50 35.00 52.50
11-17,19,20   10.00 20.00 30.00
18-1st app. Uncle Marvel(10/43)
                          10.00 20.00 30.00
21-30: #28-Pinky x-over in Mary Marvel
                           6.00 12.00 18.00
31-40   4.00   8.00 12.00
41-50   3.00   6.00   9.00
51-60   2.50   5.00   7.50
61-69   2.00   4.00   6.00

Wow Comics #4, © DMP   Wow Comics #1, © Faw   Wow Comics #12, © Faw

Wyatt Earp #4, © Dell   X-Mas Comics #2, © Faw   X-Men #1, © MCG

<u>WRECK OF GROSVENOR</u> (See Superior Stories #3)

<u>WRINGLE WRANGLE</u> (See 4-Color Comics #821)

<u>WULF, THE BARBARIAN</u>
Feb, 1975 - #4, Sept, 1975
Atlas/Seaboard Publ.

	Good	Fine	Mint
#1-Origin	.25	.50	.75
2-Intro. Berithe the Swordswoman; Adams, Wood, Reese art	.20	.40	.60
3,4	.15	.30	.45

<u>WYATT EARP</u> (See Hugh O'Brian Famous Marshal--)

<u>WYATT EARP</u>
11/55 - #29, 6/60; #30, 10/72 - #34, 6/73
Atlas Comics/Marvel #23 on (IPC)

#1	1.35	2.75	4.00
2-Williamson story, 4pgs.	2.00	4.00	6.00
3-6,8-11	.75	1.50	2.25
7,12-Williamson stories, 4pgs. ea.; #12 with Mayo	2.00	4.00	6.00
13-20	.65	1.35	2.00
21,25-Davis story	1.25	2.50	3.75
22-24,26-29: #22-Ringo Kid app. #23-Kid From Texas app.	.60	1.20	1.80
30-Williamson reprt.('72)	.20	.40	.60
31,33,34-Reprints		.15	.30
32-Torres story reprint		.20	.40

NOTE: <u>*Kirby*</u> *cover-#25.* <u>*Maurer*</u> *story-#4.*
<u>*Wildey*</u> *stories-#24,28.*

<u>WYATT EARP FRONTIER MARSHAL</u> (See Blue Bird)
#12, Jan, 1956 - #72, Dec, 1967
Charlton Comics

#12-19	.30	.60	.90
20-Four Williamson stories-8,5,5 & 7 pgs.; 68pg. issue	2.50	5.00	7.50
21-30	.20	.40	.60
31-72		.20	.35

<u>X-MAS COMICS</u>
1941 - #2, 1942 (324 pgs.) (50¢)
#3, 1943 - #7, 1947 (132 pgs.)
Fawcett Publications

#1-Reprints Whiz #21, Capt. Marvel #3, Bulletman #2, Wow #3, & Master #18; Raboy back cover	120.00	240.00	360.00
2-Captain Marvel, Bulletman, Spy Smasher reprints	65.00	130.00	190.00
3-7-Funny animal	3.00	6.00	9.00

<u>X-MAS COMICS</u>
1949 - 1952   (196 pgs.)
Fawcett Publications

	Good	Fine	Mint
#4-7-Reprints from Whiz, Master, Tom Mix & Captain Marvel	12.00	24.00	36.00

<u>X-MEN, THE</u>
Sept, 1963 - Present
Marvel Comics Group

#1-Origin X-Men; 1st app. Magneto	20.00	40.00	60.00
2	10.00	20.00	30.00
3	6.00	12.00	18.00
4,5: #4-1st Quick Silver & Scarlet Witch	4.00	8.00	12.00
6-9	2.00	4.00	6.00
10-1st Silver-Age app. Ka-Zar	2.50	5.00	7.50
11,13-20: #11-1st app. The Stranger. #19-1st app. The Mimic	1.00	2.00	3.00
12-Origin Prof. X	1.00	2.00	3.00
21-30: #28-1st app. The Banshee	.75	1.50	2.25
31-37	.50	1.00	1.50
38-Origin The X-Men feature begins, ends #57	.50	1.00	1.50
39,40: #39-New costumes	.50	1.00	1.50
41-48: #42-Death of Prof. X (Changeling disguised as). #44-Red Raven app.(G.A.)	.40	.80	1.20
49-Steranko cover	.50	1.00	1.50
50,51-Steranko cover/stys.	.80	1.60	2.40
52	.25	.50	.75
53-Smith cover/story; 1st Smith comic book work	1.50	3.00	4.50
54,55-Smith cover	.75	1.50	2.25
56-63,65-Adams art. #65-Return of Prof. X	.75	1.50	2.25
64-1st Sunfire app.	.30	.60	.90
66	.25	.50	.75
67-80: #67-Reprints begin. #72-52pgs.	.20	.40	.60
81-93-Reprints end	.20	.40	.60
94-New X-Men begin	.20	.40	.60
95-100	.15	.30	.45
101-108		.20	.40
Giant-Size #1(Sum.'75,60¢)	.60	1.20	1.80
Giant-Size #2(11/75)-51pgs. Adams art reprint	.50	1.00	1.50
Special #1(12/70)-Kirby cover/art; origin The Stranger	.65	1.35	2.00
Special #2(11/71)	.50	1.00	1.50

NOTE: <u>*Adams*</u> *covers-#56-63,65.* <u>*Everett*</u> *cover-#73(w/Kane).* <u>*Kirby*</u> *stories-#1-17(#12-17-layouts); covers-#1-22,25,26,30,31,35.* <u>*Toth*</u> *story-#12.* <u>*Wood*</u> *inks-#14.*

<u>X, THE MAN WITH THE X-RAY EYES</u>
(See Movie Comics)

X-VENTURE
July, 1947 - #2, Nov, 1947   (Super heroes)
Victory Magazines Corp.

	Good	Fine	Mint
#1,2-Atom Wizard, Mystery Shadow, Lester			
Trumble	3.00	6.00	9.00

YAK YAK   (See 4-Color Comics #1186,1348)

YAKKY DOODLE & CHOPPER
Dec, 1962   (Hanna-Barbera)
Gold Key

#1		.15	.30

YANG   (See House of Yang)
Nov, 1973 - #13, May, 1976
Charlton Comics

#1-Origin	.20	.40	.60
2-5	.15	.30	.45
6-13		.15	.30

YANKEE COMICS   (#5,6-Small size)
Sept, 1941 - #6, June, 1942; #7, no date
Harry 'A' Chesler/William H. Wise #7

#1-Origin The Echo, The Enchanted Dagger,			
Yankee Doodle Jones, The Firebrand, & The			
Scarlet Sentry; Black Satan app.			
	17.50	35.00	52.50
2-Origin Johnny Rebel; Major Victory app.;			
Barry Kuda begins	12.00	24.00	36.00
3	10.00	20.00	30.00
4	8.00	16.00	24.00
5,6(Small size)	3.50	7.00	10.50
7(Wm. H. Wise)(Small size)no date; distr.			
thru Army PX's only	3.50	7.00	10.50

YANKS IN BATTLE
Sept, 1956 - #4, Dec, 1956
Quality Comics Group

#1	1.20	2.40	3.60
2-4	.75	1.50	2.25

YANKS IN BATTLE
1963
I.W. Enterprises

Reprint #3	.35	.70	1.05

YARDBIRDS, THE   (G.I. Joe's Sidekicks)
Summer, 1952
Ziff-Davis Publ. Co.

#1-By Bob Oskner	1.00	2.00	3.00

YARNS OF YELLOWSTONE
1972   (36 pgs.) (50¢)
World Color Press

	Good	Fine	Mint
Ill. by Bill Chapman	.25	.50	.75

YELLOW CLAW
Oct, 1956 - #4, April, 1957
Atlas Comics (MjMC)

#1-Origin by Joe Maneely	6.00	12.00	18.00
2-4-Kirby art in all; #2-Everett cover. #3-			
Severin/Kirby art	6.00	12.00	18.00

YELLOWJACKET   (Jack in the Box #11 on)
Sept, 1944 - #10, June, 1946
E. Levy/Frank Comunale

#1-Origin Yellowjacket; Diana, the Huntress			
begins	7.00	14.00	21.00
2-5	5.00	10.00	15.00
6-10	3.00	6.00	9.00

YELLOWSTONE KELLY   (See 4-Color Comics #1056)

YELLOW SUBMARINE   (See Movie Comics)

YOGI BEAR   (TV) (Hanna-Barbera)
Dec-Feb, 1959-60 - #42, Oct, 1970
Dell Publ. Co./Gold Key #10 on

4-Color #1067,1104,1162	.40	.80	1.20
#4(8-9/61)-#9(7-9/62)-Dell	.15	.30	.45
#10(10/62-G.K.),#11-titled "Y.B. Jellystone			
Jollies"-80pgs.	.20	.40	.60
12	.15	.30	.45
13(Surprise Party, 68pgs.)(7/63)			
	.20	.40	.60
14-42	.15	.30	.45
4-Color #1271,1349	.25	.50	.75
--Kite Fun Book('62,8pgs.)Soft cover; Pacific			
Gas & Electric giveaway; No#			
	2.00	4.00	6.00

YOGI BEAR   (See Dell Giant #41, March of Comics #253,265,279,291,309,319,337,344, Whitman Comic Books & Movie Comics under "Hey There It's --")

YOGI BEAR
Nov, 1970 - #35, Jan, 1976   (Hanna-Barbera)
Charlton Comics

#1-6,8-35		.15	.30
7-Summer Fun(Giant)52pgs.	.15	.30	.45

YOGI BEAR   (TV)
Nov, 1977 - Present

X-Venture #1. © Victory Mag.   Yanks In Battle #1. © I.W.

Yellow Claw #1, © MCG

Young Allies #11, © MCG   The Young Doctors #1, © CC   Young Love #5, © Prize

(Yogi Bear cont'd)
Marvel Comics Group

	Good	Fine	Mint
#1,2		.20	.35

YOGI BERRA (Baseball hero)
1951   (Yankee catcher)
Fawcett Publications

	Good	Fine	Mint
No#	4.00	8.00	12.00

YOSEMITE SAM (-- and Bugs Bunny)
Dec, 1970 - Present
Gold Key

	Good	Fine	Mint
#1	.15	.30	.45
2-10		.20	.35
11-49		.15	.25

(See March of Comics #363,380,392)

YOUNG ALLIES COMICS (All-Winners #21)
Summer, 1941 - #20, Oct, 1946
Timely Comics (Young Allies, Inc.)

#1-Origin The Young Allies; 1st meeting of
   Captain America & Human Torch; Red Skull
   app.; S&K cover & splash page
                   140.00 280.00 420.00
  2-Captain America & Human Torch app.; Simon
   & Kirby cover 65.00 130.00 195.00
  3-Fathertime, Captain America & Human Torch
   app.   47.50 95.00 142.50
  4-The Vagabond & Red Skull, Capt. America,
   Human Torch app. 35.00 70.00 105.00
  5-Capt. America & Human Torch app.
                  30.00 60.00 90.00
  6-10: #7-Origin Tommy Tyme & Clock of Ages;
   ends #19   17.50 35.00 52.50
  11-20   12.00 24.00 36.00

YOUNG BRIDES
Sept-Oct, 1952 - 1957
Feature/Prize Publications

V1#1-S&K art	3.00	6.00	9.00
2-4	1.75	3.35	5.00
V2#1-6-S&K art	2.00	4.00	6.00
V3#1-4	.65	1.35	2.00
#13-25,27,28-Kirby in some issues			
	.65	1.35	2.00
26-S&K art	.80	1.60	2.40
29-50	.50	1.00	1.50

YOUNG DR. MASTERS (See Advs. of Young Dr.
Masters)

YOUNG DOCTORS, THE
January, 1963 - #6, 1963
Charlton Comics

	Good	Fine	Mint
V1#1-6		.15	.30

YOUNG EAGLE
Dec, 1950 - #10, June, 1952; 1957
Fawcett Publications/Charlton

#1	2.50	5.00	7.50
2-9	1.50	3.00	4.50
10-Origin Thunder, Young Eagle's horse			
	1.50	3.00	4.50
4(1/57), 5(4/57)(CC)	.80	1.60	2.40

YOUNG HEARTS
Nov, 1949 - #2, Feb, 1950
Marvel Comics (SPC)

#1,2	.80	1.60	2.40

YOUNG HEARTS IN LOVE
1964
Super Comics

#17-Reprints Young Love V5#6, 4-5/62
                        .15   .30

YOUNG HEROES
#35, Feb-Mar, 1955 - #37, June-July, 1955
American Comics Group (Titan)

#35-37-Frontier Scout 1.00 2.00 3.00

YOUNG KING COLE (Becomes Criminals on the Run)
Fall, 1945 - V3#12, July, 1948
Premium Group/Novelty Press

#1	1.75	3.35	5.00
2-7	1.00	2.00	3.00
V2#1-7	.80	1.60	2.40
V3#1-12	.75	1.50	2.25

YOUNG LAWYERS, THE (TV)
Jan, 1971 - #2, April, 1971
Dell Publishing Co.

#1,2	.15	.30	.45

YOUNG LIFE (Teen Life #3 on)
Summer, 1945 - #2, Fall, 1945
New Age Publ./Quality Comics Group

#1,2	1.20	2.40	3.60

YOUNG LOVE
1949 - V6#1(#55), Mar, 1954
Prize(Feature) Publ. (Crestwood)

V1#1-S&K cover, 2 stories 3.50 7.00 10.50
  2-Photo covers begin, S&K story

(Young Love cont'd)	Good	Fine	Mint
	2.00	4.00	6.00
3,4,6-S&K art	2.00	4.00	6.00
5-No Kirby	1.00	2.00	3.00
V2#1-12-S&K art	1.75	3.35	5.00
V3#1-12-S&K art	1.35	2.75	4.00
V4#1-12,V5#1-6,V6#1-S&K art in most			
	1.20	2.40	3.60

NOTE: *Not all volumes had 12 issues; 55 issues total. Severin/Elder story-V2#3(#15).*

YOUNG LOVE
#42, 3-4/64 - #120, Winter, 1975-76;
#121, Oct, 1976 - Present
National Per. Publ.(Arleigh Publ. Corp.#49-
60)/DC Comics Inc.

#42-Diary of Mary Robin begins, ends #52			
	.20	.40	.60
43-63,65-67	.15	.30	.45
64-S&K art	.20	.40	.60
68-Life & Loves of Lisa St. Claire serial			
begins, ends #78; not in #69			
		.10	.20
69-(68pgs.)		.15	.30
70-72,74-77,81		.10	.20
73-Toth story	.20	.40	.60
78,79-"20 Miles to Heartbreak" by Toth &			
Coletta(Chapter 1 & 4, see Secret Hearts			
#141,142 for Chapter 2 & 3)			
	.20	.40	.60
80,82-Morrow art		.20	.40
83-120: #107-113-100pgs.		.15	.30
121,123-126		.15	.30
122-Toth art		.20	.40

YOUNG LOVER ROMANCES
#4, June, 1952 - #5, Aug, 1952
Toby Press

#4,5	.50	1.00	1.50

YOUNG LOVERS
#16, 1956 - #18, May, 1957
Charlton Comics

#16,17('56)	.40	.80	1.20
18-Elvis Presley photo cover, text story			
biography)	3.00	6.00	9.00

YOUNG MARRIAGE
June, 1950
Fawcett Publications

#1-Powell art	1.25	2.50	3.75

YOUNG MEN (--On the Battlefield #12-20(4/53))
#4, 6/50 - #11, 10/51: #12, 12/51 - #28, 6/54

Marvel/Atlas Comics (IPC)
	Good	Fine	Mint
#4	1.00	2.00	3.00
5-11	.80	1.60	2.40
12-23: #19-Everett story	.65	1.35	2.00
24-Origin Captain America, Human Torch, &			
Sub-Mariner which are revived thru #28			
	12.00	24.00	36.00
25-28	9.00	18.00	27.00

YOUNG REBELS, THE (TV)
January, 1971
Dell Publishing Co.

#1		.20	.35

YOUNG ROMANCE COMICS (The 1st romance comic)
Sept-Oct, 1947 - V16#4, June-July, 1963
Prize/Headline(Feature Publ.)

V1#1-Two S&K stories	5.00	10.00	15.00
2-5-S&K art	2.50	5.00	7.50
6-Two S&K stories, Robinson/Meskin story			
	2.50	5.00	7.50
V2#1(#7),V2#2(#8)-Three S&K stories each			
	2.50	5.00	7.50
3(#9)-S&K art	2.00	4.00	6.00
4(#10)-Two S&K stories	2.50	5.00	7.50
5(#11),6(#12)-One S&K story each			
	2.00	4.00	6.00
V3#1(#13)-photo covers begin; S&K art			
	1.50	3.00	4.50
2(#14),3(#15)-S&K art	1.50	3.00	4.50
4(#16)-Two S&K stories	2.00	4.00	6.00
5(#17)-One S&K story	1.50	3.00	4.50
6(#18)-S&K art	1.50	3.00	4.50
V4#1(#19)-5(#23)	1.50	3.00	4.50
6(#24)-One S&K story	1.50	3.00	4.50
V5-V12-S&K art in most	.80	1.60	2.40
V13-V15#1-3(4-5/62)	.25	.50	.75
V16#1-4(6-7/63)(Prize)	.20	.40	.60

NOTE: *Simon & Kirby art in most issues V1-V13.
Simon & Kirby covers-#1-12.*

YOUNG ROMANCE COMICS
#125, Aug-Sept, 1963 - #208, Nov-Dec, 1975
National Per. Publ.(Arleigh Publ. Corp.#127)

#125-153,155-162(Nat.Per.)	.15	.30	.45
154-Adams cover	.25	.50	.75
163,164-Toth art	.20	.40	.60
165-196: #170-Michell from Young Love ends,			
Lily Martin, the Swinger begins			
		.15	.30
197(100pgs.)-#208		.10	.20

YOUR DREAMS (See Strange World of --)

Young Men #24, © MCG

Young Romance #8, © Prize

Young Romance #24, © Prize

Zago #3, © Fox

Zegra #3, © Fox

Zip Comics #6, © MLJ

YOUR UNITED STATES
1946
Lloyd Jacquet Studios

	Good	Fine	Mint
Used in Seduction of the Innocent	3.50	7.00	10.50

YOUTHFUL HEARTS (Daring Confessions #4 on)
1952 - #3, 1952
Youthful Magazines

#1-Doug Wildey art	1.35	2.75	4.00
2,3	.80	1.60	2.40

YOUTHFUL LOVE (Truthful Love #2)
May, 1950
Youthful Magazines

#1	1.00	2.00	3.00

YOUTHFUL ROMANCES (Daring Love #15)
Aug-Sept, 1949 - #18, June, 1953
Pix-Parade/Ribage

#1-(titled Youthful Love)	1.00	2.00	3.00
2-7,9-18	.65	1.35	2.00
8-Wood cover	1.75	2.50	5.25

ZAGO, JUNGLE PRINCE (My Story #5 on)
Sept, 1948 - #4, March, 1949
Fox Features Syndicate

#1-Blue Beetle app.-partial reprint/Atomic #4	7.00	14.00	21.00
2,3-Kamen stories	5.00	10.00	15.00
4-Baker cover	5.00	10.00	15.00

ZANE GREY'S STORIES OF THE WEST
#27, Sept, 1955 - #39, Sept, 1958
Dell Publishing Co./Gold Key 11/64

4-Color #197('48),222,230,236('49)	2.50	5.00	7.50
4-Color #246,255,270,301,314,333,346	1.50	3.00	4.50
4-Color #357,372,395,412,433,449,467,484	1.35	2.75	4.00
4-Color #511-Kinstler art	1.50	3.00	4.50
4-Color #532,555,583,604,616,632,996('59)	1.25	2.50	3.75
#27-39	1.00	2.00	3.00
#1(10131-411)-(11/64-G.K.)-Nevada; reprints 4-Color #996	.65	1.35	2.00

ZANY (Magazine)(Satire)(See Ratfink & Frantic)
Sept, 1958 - #4, May, 1959
Candor Publ. Co.

	Good	Fine	Mint
#1-Bill Everett covers	1.00	2.00	3.00
2-4	.50	1.00	1.50

ZAZA, THE MYSTIC (This Magazine Is Haunted
April, 1956 - #11, Sept, 1956   V2#12 on)
Charlton Comics

#10,11	1.00	2.00	3.00

ZEGRA JUNGLE EMPRESS (My Love Life #6 on)
#2, 10/48 - #5, 4/49   (Formerly Tegra)
Fox Features Syndicate

#2	8.00	16.00	24.00
3-5	7.00	14.00	21.00

ZIGGY PIG AND SILLY SEAL
Fall, 1944 - #6, Fall, 1946
Timely Comics (CmPL)

#1-Vs. the Japs	2.00	4.00	6.00
2-6	1.25	2.50	3.75
IW Reprint #1('58)-Reprints/Krazy Komics	.35	.70	1.05
IW Reprint #2,7,8	.35	.70	1.05

ZIP COMICS
Feb, 1940 - #47, Summer, 1944
MLJ Magazines

#1-Origin Kalthar the Giant Man, The Scarlet Avenger & Steel Sterling; Mr. Satan, Nevada Jones & Zambini, the Miracle Man, War Eagle, Captain Valor begin	70.00	140.00	210.00
2	35.00	70.00	105.00
3	25.00	50.00	75.00
4,5	20.00	40.00	60.00
6-9: #9-Last Kalthar & Mr. Satan	17.50	35.00	52.50
10-Inferno, the Flame Breather begins, ends #13	17.50	35.00	52.50
11,12: #11-Inferno without costume	15.00	30.00	45.00
13-19: #17-Last Scarlet Avenger. #18-Wilbur begins	15.00	30.00	45.00
20-Origin Black Jack	20.00	40.00	60.00
21-26: #25-Last Nevada Jones. #26-Black Witch begins, last Capt. Valor	10.00	20.00	30.00
27-Intro. Web	12.00	24.00	36.00
28-Origin Web	12.00	24.00	36.00
29,30	8.00	16.00	24.00
31-38: #34-1st Applejack app. #35-Last Zambini, Black Jack. #38-Last Web issue	6.00	12.00	18.00
39-Origin Red Rube	6.00	12.00	18.00
40-47: #45-Wilbur ends	3.00	6.00	9.00

ZIP-JET (Hero)
Feb, 1953 - #2, Apr-May, 1953
Ziff-Davis Publ. Co.

	Good	Fine	Mint
#1,2-Rocketman reprints/Punch Comics	4.00	8.00	12.00

NOTE: *St. John issues also exist?*

ZIPPY THE CHIMP (CBS TV Presents --)
#50, March, 1957 - #51, Aug, 1957
Pines (Literary Ent.)

#50,51	.35	.70	1.05

ZODY, THE MOD ROB
July, 1970
Gold Key

#1		.15	.30

ZOO ANIMALS
#8, 1954 (36 pgs.) (15¢)
Star Publications

#8-(B&W-for coloring)	.40	.80	1.20

ZOO FUNNIES
1945 - #15, 1947
Charlton Comics/Children Comics Publ.

#101(#1)-1945	1.00	2.00	3.00
#2(9/45)-#5	.65	1.35	2.00
6-15: #8-Diana the Huntress app.			
	.65	1.35	2.00

ZOO FUNNIES (Nyoka #13 on)
July, 1953 - #12, July, 1955
Capitol Stories/Charlton Comics

#1	.65	1.35	2.00
2-7	.40	.80	1.20
8-12-Nyoka app.	1.50	3.00	4.50

ZOO PARADE (See 4-Color Comics #662)

ZOOM COMICS
Dec, 1945 (One Shot)
Carlton Publishing Co.

#1-Dr. Mercy, Satanas, from Red Band Comics;

	Good	Fine	Mint
Capt. Milksop origin retold	1.75	3.35	5.00

ZOOT (Rulah #17 on)
1946 - #16, July, 1948 (Two #13's & #14's)
Fox Features Syndicate

No#-Funny animal only	1.75	3.35	5.00
#2-Jaguar app.	5.00	10.00	15.00
3(Fall,'46)-#6-Funny animals			
	1.00	2.00	3.00
7-Rulah, Jungle Goddess begins(6/47)-			
origin	12.00	24.00	36.00
8-10	9.00	18.00	27.00
11-Kamen bondage cover	10.00	20.00	30.00
12	8.00	16.00	24.00
13(2/48),(4/48)	7.00	14.00	21.00
14(3/48),(5/48)	7.00	14.00	21.00
15,16	7.00	14.00	21.00

NOTE: *Kamen covers-#10-12; art-many issues.*

ZORRO (Walt Disney with #882)
May, 1949 - #15, Sept-Nov, 1961
Dell Publishing Co.

4-Color #228	4.00	8.00	12.00
4-Color #425,497	2.50	5.00	7.50
4-Color #538-Kinstler art	2.50	5.00	7.50
4-Color #574,617,732	2.00	4.00	6.00
4-Color #882,920,933,960,976-Toth art in all			
	2.00	4.00	6.00
4-Color #1003,1037('59)	1.35	2.75	4.00
#8(12-2/60)	1.00	2.00	3.00
9,12-Toth story	1.20	2.40	3.60
10,11,13-15	.80	1.60	2.40

ZORRO (Walt Disney)
Oct, 1965 - #9, March, 1968
Gold Key

#1-Toth art	1.00	2.00	3.00
2-4,6,8,9	.50	1.00	1.50
5,7-Toth art	.65	1.35	2.00

NOTE: *#1-9: reprints from Zorro 4-Color comics.*

Z-2 COMICS (Secret Agent --) (See Holyoke
One-Shot #7)

ZULU (See Movie Classics)

Zoot #8, © Fox

Zoot #14(3/48), © Fox

Zorro #1, © GK

OUR TENTH ANNIVERSARY YEAR   1/1978

1. ADULTS ONLY FOR UNDERGROUNDS (18 or over)
2. MINIMUM ORDER: $3.00 (we pay postage).
3. TAX: Calif.Residents add 6% of order.
4. FOREIGN ORDERS: Addt'l $1 per order.
5. DISCOUNT: 10% off on $25 or more!
6. INSURANCE:(U.S.Orders Only)(REQUIRED on orders over $25;Optional Under $25)-60¢
7. MAKE ALL CHECKS & MONEY ORDERS OUT TO: Comic Collector Shop(U.S.Currency Only)

* * * NEW RELEASES * * *
*BREAKDOWNS-$8.95(Art Spiegelman anthology 10x14;9 pgs.in color)
*ARIK KHAN #1-$1.00 (Frank Reyes)
*ONE #1-$1.00 (Garris,Phil & Steve)
*AREBA KOALA #1-75¢(John,Michelle Wozniak)
*BIZARRE SEX #6-$1.25 (Corben Cover)
*ZAP #9-$1.00
*SCARLETT PILGRIM-$1.00 (Trina)
*HOT STUF #5-$1.50(Corben,Arnold,Kirk)
*PHANTACEA #1-$1 (Dave Sim,Jim McPherson)
*WALLY WOOD'S WEIRD SEX FANTASIES-$1.00 (11 plates,12x16 portfolio;black & white)
*EISNER'S SPIRIT PORTFOLIO-$35.00(Color)
*BOOK OF DREAMS-$3.95(John Thompson;profusely illustrated date book/calendar for 1978 with space to record dreams,etc)
*FOG CITY COMICS #1-$1.00(Metzger,Holmes)
*RED RAIDER-$1.00(Continues WHITE COMANCHE)
*NO DUCKS-$1.00(Tim Boxell,Richard Larson)
*FRESCA ZIZIS-$1.00 (Melinda Gebbie)
*STAR*REACH #11-$1.25
*QUACK #6-$1.25

AIR PIRATES FUNNIES-$1.00(O'Neill Tabloid)
ALL ATOMIC-75¢ (Rifas)
ALL CANADIAN BEAVER-75¢ (Rand Holmes)
ALL DUCK-75¢ (Skursky,Sonntag,Ki...
ALL NEW UNDERGROUND COMIX:
 #1 ARMAGEDDON #1-$1.00(B...
 #2 HOT CRACKERS-75¢ (...
 #3 HIGH SCHOOL/MOUN...
 #4 BIG LEAGUE LA...
 #5 TWO FISTED...   ...n Bros.)
AMAZING ADU...
AMAZON-7...   ...son)
AMERI...   ...#1,2-75¢ea.(Welz)
AM...   ...2-$1.25ea.
 ...u (Boates Cover)
 ...(Corben,Kline,Strnad)
 ...#1-75¢ (Scott Shaw,etc.)
 ...7 - $1.50 ea.(Crumb,etc.)
 ...AGEDDON #1-$1,#2,3-$2ea.(B.Steel)
ARMAGEDDON #3 IS FOREVER-$3(Deluxe Ed.)
ARMORKINS-$1.00 (Larry Todd)
AN ARMY OF PRINCIPLES-75¢ (Rifas)
AUSTIN COMIX #1-75¢ (Joe Bates)
AUSTIN STONE #2-75¢ (Texas Artists)
AUTHENTIC VISIONARY-75¢ (Petertil)
BAKERSFIELD KOUNTRY KOMICS-75¢ (Welz)
BALLOON VENDOR-75¢ (Sheridan/Schrier)
BARBARIAN COMICS #1,2,3-$1 ea.,#4-$2.00
BARBARIAN WOMEN #1-$1,#2-$2(Full Color Story & Cover by S.C.Wilson in #2)
BARBARIAN KILLER FUNNIES-75¢ (Tom Bird)
*BAYCON'77 PROGRAM OF ART-$1.00
BENT-60¢ (S.Clay Wilson)
BERKELEY CON COMICS('74)-50¢
BICENTENNIAL GROSS OUTS-76¢ (Wm.Stout)
BIG APPLE COMIX #1-$1 (Adams,Wood,etc.)
BINKY BROWN MEETS VIRGIN MARY-75¢
*BIZARRE SEX #1,2,3,4,5-$1 ea.,#6-$1.25

*BODE'S BROADS-$5(Portfolio;19 sheets)
*DAS KAMPF-$2.50 ("Von" Bode)
BOOK OF INNER SPACE-35¢ (Omandu)
BRAIN FANTASY #1,2-75¢ ea.
BUM WAD-$1 (Dave Geiser--Full Color)
CALIFORNIA COMICS #1,2-$1 ea., #3-$2
 (#3--2 pg.Corben Nude;Ed Watson,etc.)
*CHECKERED DEMON-$1.00(S.Clay Wilson)
CHEECH WIZARD-75¢ (Bode)
CHEECH WIZARD/SCHIZOPHRENIA-75¢(Bode)
CLOUD #2-$1.00 (Cabarga,Kinney,etc.)
CLOWNS-75¢ (Dave Geiser)
COCAINE COMIX-75¢(Stout,DiCaprio,etc.)
COLLAGE #1-75¢(Tab.;O'Neill Interview)
COLOR-$1.25 (Moscoso--Full Color)
COMIX BOOK #1,2-$1.50ea.,#4,5-$1.00ea.
COMPLEAT FART-$1.00 (Lee Marrs)
COMPOST COMICS-75¢ (Metzger,Todd,etc.)
CONSUMER COMIX-75¢ (Kitchen,etc.)
COOCHY COOTY MEN'S COMIX-$1(Williams)
*CORPORATE CRIME-$1(Irons,Deitch,etc.)
*COVER-UP LOWDOWN-75¢(Kinney,Mavrides)
R.CRUMB'S COMICS & STORIES #1-50¢
ARTISTIC COMICS-$1.00
BIG ASS #1,2-75¢ ea.
BLACK & WHITE-75¢
CARLOAD O'COMICS PREVIEW ED.-$1(Color)
DESPAIR-75¢
HOMEGROWN-75¢
HYTONE #1-75¢
MELLOTOONS #2-$1.00
MR.NATURAL #1,2-75¢ ea.,#3-$1.00
MOTOR CITY #1,2-$1.00 ea.
PEOPLE'S COMICS-75¢
THE YUM YUM BOOK-$5.00 (ha...
*CRASH STREET KIDDS #1-7...
DAN O'NEILL #4,5-$1...
DEMENTED PERVERT...
DEVIANT SLICE...
DIRTY LAUND...   ...sky)
DITKO:AU...   ...,WHA-75¢ ea.
D.O...   ...ne Collection)
DO...   ...00 ea.(Richards)
 ...4-$1.00 ea.(Todd)
 ...MIX & STORIES #1,2-$1.25ea.
 ...(Dave Geiser)
 ...EAT #1-$1.00 (from Tante Leny)
 ...ATE DAMSELS-$1(Roberta Gregory)
 ...PERFECTO-75¢ (Crumb,etc.)
ENIGMA-75¢ (Larry Todd)
*ENGLISH COMIX (-$1.00 ea.):ROCK'N ROLL MADNESS #2;IT'S ONLY ROCK'N ROLL;ZIP; VIEW FM.THE VOID;ANIMAL WEIRDNESS; BRAIN STORM #3,4;STREET QUOMIX.
ETERNAL COMIX #1-75¢ (John Thompson)
*E.Z.WOLF-75¢ (Ted Richards)
*E.Z.WOLF'S ASTRAL OUTHOUSE-75¢(Richards)
FACTS O'LIFE SEX ED.FUNNIES-75¢
FANTAGOR #1-$1,#3(Color)-$1.25(Corben)
FAR OUT WEST-$1.00
*FAT FREDDY'S CAT #1,2,3-75¢ea.(Shelton)
*FAT FREDDY'S CAT Deluxe Pbk.-$3.95(#1-3)
*FEAR & LAUGHTER-$1(Todd,Stout,Shaw,etc)
FEDS'N HEADS #1-75¢ (Gilbert Shelton)
FEELGOOD FUNNIES-75¢ (F.Sturgeon)
FELCH-$1.00(Spain,Crumb,Williams)
*FIRST KINGDOM #1,2,3,4,5,6,7-$1.00 ea.
FLAMED OUT FUNNIES #1,2-75¢ea.(Murphy)
*SHARY FLENNIKEN'S SKETCHBOOK-$3.00
*DROUGHT CHIC-$2.50 (Shary Flenniken)
FORBIDDEN KNOWLEDGE-$1 (Jim Himes)
FOUR SKETCHBOOKS-75¢ (Spain,etc.)
*FREAK BROS. #1,2,3,4,5-75¢eac.(Shelton)
FREAK BROS.IN GERMAN-75¢(#1 Translated)
THE FUNNY BOOK #1-50¢,#2("The New")-$1
FUNNYBOOK #1-75¢ (Welz,Trina)
GAY HEARTHROBS #1-$1.00 (FulHorne)
GIRL FIGHT #1,2-60¢ ea.(Trina)
GIVE ME LIBERTY-75¢ (Shelton,etc.)
GIVE ME LIBERTY DELUXE ED.-$3.50
GIMME-75¢
GOD NOSE-75¢ (Jaxon)

SAMPLE PAGE
SEND 25¢ FOR CURRENT CATALOG OF FANZINES AND ALL UNDERGROUND COMIX

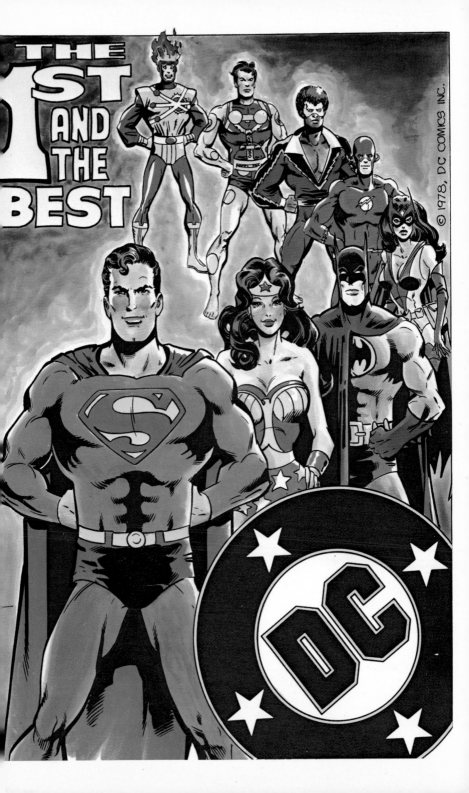

THE 1ST AND THE BEST

© 1978, DC COMICS INC.

DC

Amazing Adventures
COMICBOOK SHOP

WE ARE IN THE BUSINESS OF BUYING AND SELLING COMIC BOOKS
—Specialising in Marvels, Ducks & Timelys,
fine or better—

Whether you have one
book or thousands,
we want to buy.
Just send us a list
stating their condition.
We'll also work from
your want list;
just send it
to us with
an S.A.E.

AMAZING ADVENTURES — Sal Dichiera, Owner
3800 Noriega, San Francisco, CA 94122

(415) 661-1344 : 664-1849

Captain Midnight No. 2, 1942. © Faw

Captain Science No. 5, 1950
Wallace Wood cover art. © YM

Champ Comics No. 11, 1940
© Worth Publ. Co.

Classic Comics No. 29, 1946, © Gil

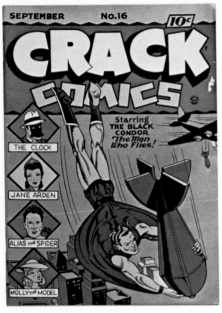

Crack Comics No. 16, 1941. © Qua

Detective No. 61, 1942. © DC

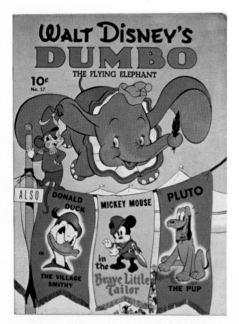

Four Color No. 17, 1941. © WDP

The Haunt Of Fear No. 10, 1951
Al Feldstein cover art
© WMG

The Hooded Menace, 1951
© Realistic Comics

The Incredible Hulk No. 1, 1962
© MCG

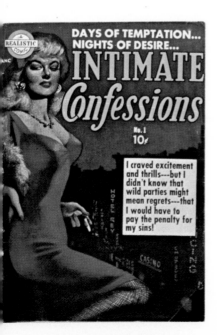

Intimate Confessions No. 1, 1951
© Realistic Comics

Joe Palooka Visits the Lost City, 1945
© Ham Fisher

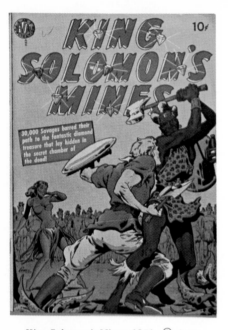

King Solomon's Mines, 1951. © Avon

Looney Tunes No. 17, 1943
© Leon Schlesinger

Marvel Mystery Comics No. 33, 1942
© MCG

4-Color No. 170, 1947. © WDP

Military No. 30, 1944
Bill Ward cover art. © DC(Qua)

Mister Mystery No. 12, 1953
Classic injury to the eye
© Aragon Mag.

More Fun Comics No. 62, 1940
© DC

National Comics No. 26, 1942
Reed Crandall cover art
© DC (Qua)

Our Gang No. 9, 1944
Walt Kelly cover art
© Loew's Inc.

Police Comics No. 25, 1941
Jack Cole Cover art.   ©   DC(Qua)

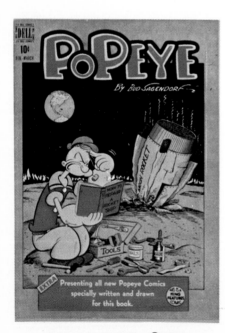

Popeye No. 5, 1949.   © King

Raggedy Ann & Andy No. 5, 1946
© Johnny Gruelle

4-Color No. 95, 1945. © Roy Rogers

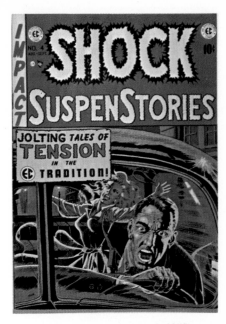

Shock SuspenStories No. 4, 1952
Wallace Wood cover art. © WMG

Silver Streak No. 13, 1941. © Lev

Slave Girl Comics No. 2, 1949. © Avon

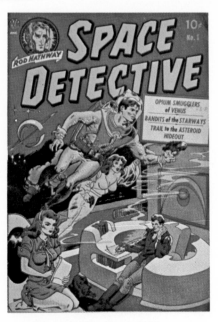

Space Detective No. 1, 1951
Wallace Wood cover art. © Avon

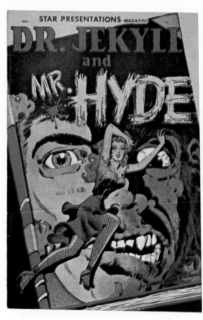

A Star Presentation No. 3, 1950
Wallace Wood cover art. © Fox

The Thing No. 14, 1954
Steve Ditko cover art. © CC

Sub-Mariner No. 10, 1943
Schomburg cover art. © MCG

Tarzan No. 1, 1948. © ERB

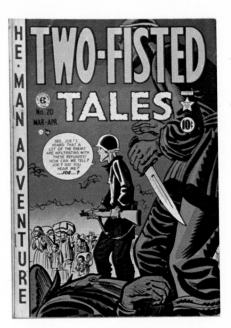

Two-Fisted Tales No. 20, 1951
Harvey Kurtzman cover art. © WMG

Weird Science No. 5, 1951
Al Feldstein cover art. © WMG

Weird Tales of the Future No. 2, 1952
Basil Wolverton cover art. © S.P.M. Publ.

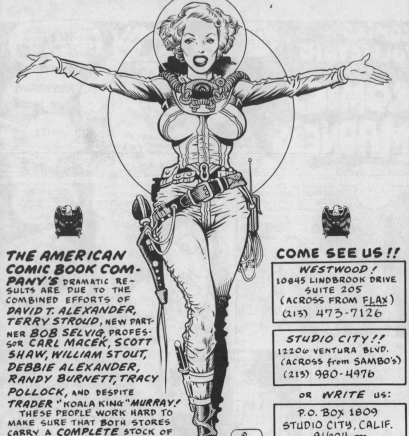

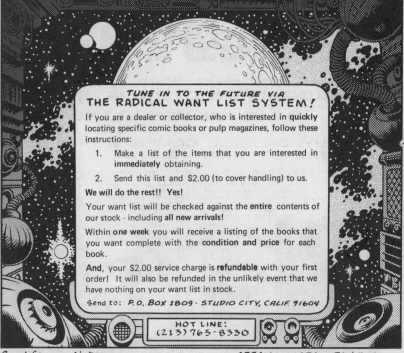

UH-OH!

KESEL 78 ©

Fantasy mail co.

NEW COMIC BOOK AND MAGAZINE SERVICE

Dear Collectors, Dealers, and Investors,

What do Superman, Detective Comics, Star Wars, Jack Kirby, and The Fantasy
Mail Company have in common? C'mon, guess! Yes, that's it - performance!
Each one is the longest running act in its field!

Admittedly, The Fantasy Mail Company's two year existance is small compared
to Superman's 40 year career, but in an area like comic books, where new
services appear and disappear overnight, our record is enviable indeed.

Sure, we've been in some tough spots. Like the time we never received our
Captain America and Iron Man Annuals (because of errors by the Publisher),
yet every customer who ordered received his copy.

That's what we're all about: performance. The ability to provide
consistently high service, at discount prices, to our customers throughout
the year, and in the years to come!

We are continually searching for related items of interest to round out
our monthly mailing list of new comic books and magazines. (NOTE: Editors,
publishers, and dealers, please send us a sample, house ad, and discount
rates if you have a product you'd like to have us carry.)

In addition to high quality fanzines, we are now supplying selected paper-
backs, hard bound books, art portfolios, calenders (in season), gum cards,
and posters.

And as usual, everything is sold for less than cover price!

NO. ITEMS/MONTH	1-49	50-99	100-299	300-499	500-
DISCOUNT	10%	20%	25%	30%	30%
POSTAGE & HANDLING FEES PER MONTH: U.S.					
WEEKLY SHIPMENTS	2.50	3.25	2¢	3¢	2¢
BIWEEKLY SHIPMENTS	1.25	2.00	1½¢	2¢	1½¢
MONTHLY SHIPMENTS	.75	1.75	1¢	1½¢	1¢
				(PER ITEM ORDERED)	

We know you want a service with good performance. Why not give us a try,
today! Send a long (business) self-addressed, stamped envelope for our
free current list. Canadian and Overseas customers are also welcome!

And mention the 1978 Comic Book Price Guide when writing!

Frank R. Johnson

BOX 7476
ROCHESTER, N.Y.
14615

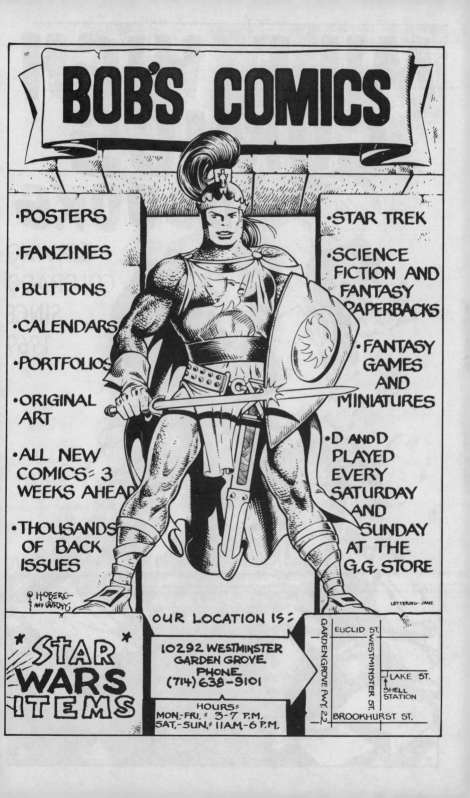

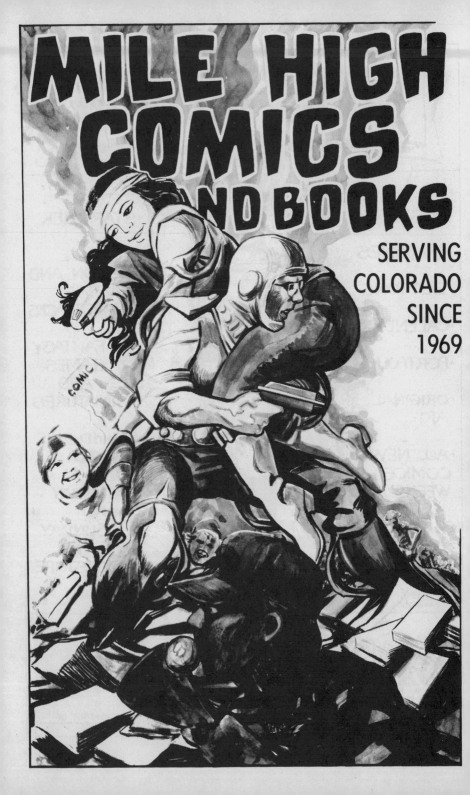

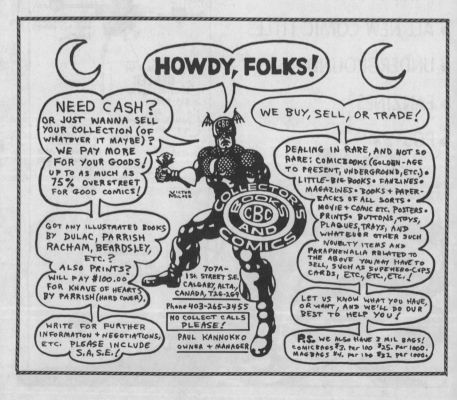

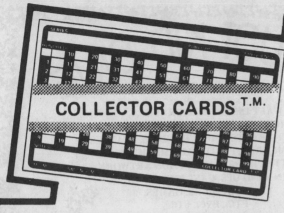

Copyright ©1977 Frank Brunner.

THE GRAPHIC FANTASY COMIC SHOP

3946 BROADWAY · OAKLAND, CALIFORNIA 94611 · (415) 658-7195 · OPEN 7 DAYS A WEEK

COLLECTORS' PRESS

Will Eisner's THE SPIRIT PORTFOLIO

This is the most beautiful Portfolio ever published. Will Eisner has lovingly created ten new paintings capturing the very essence of the adventures of THE SPIRIT. "The Hideaway", "The Scene of the Crime", "The Women", "The Duel", "Dead End", "The Convention", "The Rescue", "The Chase", "The Capture" and "The City" portray the various facets of THE SPIRIT and his myriad adversaries, allies and adventures. The finest color lithography and Strathmore textured art papers were blended to create ten Plates that capture the vibrant colors and textures of the original art. Two special Plates featuring an introduction to the Portfolio and preliminary pencil roughs of the finished paintings round out this extraordinary presentation. Twelve Plates (12" by 16") in all. To protect and display the Portfolio it is slipcased in a special hardbound gold embossed midnight blue cloth presentation case with special end papers reproducing Will Eisner's pencil originals. This is a Limited Edition of 1,500 Portfolios signed and numbered by Will Eisner. $35.00 per Portfolio.

Wally Wood's WEIRD SEX FANTASY PORTFOLIO

Sex and science fiction have always been Wally Wood's favorite subjects . . . in that order. In this Portfolio you will find the best elements of both. Wally Wood has created eleven brand new plates illustrated with the explosive force of Wood at his best. Learn the 426th. Position of the Lotus in "Freeball", be warned of alien sexual entrapment in "Venus Fly Trap", see what happens when the bugeyed monster rescues the hero from the evil princess in "Eternal Triangle", unchain your fantasies in the dungeon delights of "Tyrant", experience the second coming in "Messiah", plug in to the futuristic vibrator in "Perils of the Princess", soar to new heights of ecstasy in "Fantasy Flight", take a course in BEM Physiology in "Anatomy Lesson", conquer new territory in "Frontier", visit an extra terrestrial "Strip Poker" game and relive the classic Wally Wood hero, girl-in-distress and menacing Alien tableau in "Horizon" . . . and a special introduction by Wally Wood. Twelve Plates (12" by 16") in a gold embossed slipcase. This is a Limited Edition of 2,000 Portfolios signed and numbered by Wally Wood. Due to the sexual nature of this Portfolio you must state you are over 21 years old when ordering. $20.00 per Portfolio.

MAIL ORDER INFORMATION

Please pay by Money Order or Check only. Do not send cash. All orders are processed the day they are received, however, there is a two week delay for orders with personal checks to clear our bank.

All orders are SECURELY packed and mailed Parcel Post INSURED. Include additional postage for any other desired delivery. Please print your name and address CLEARLY when you order. Thank you.

BOX 1009 • CARMEL VALLEY, CALIFORNIA 93924 • (408) 659-3360

time travelers
HUGE SELECTION OF COMICS
OLD&NEW
SCIENCE FICTION
SPACE TOYS
DISNEY ITEMS
1511 2nd Ave
Seattle,Wa.
98101
624 7806
send 75¢ for sales list
I buy too!